T0361302

THE ROUTLEDGE COMPANION
TO TALENT MANAGEMENT

The field of Talent Management has grown and advanced exponentially over the past several years as organizations, large and small, public and private, global and domestic, have realized that to gain and sustain a global competitive advantage, they must manage their talents effectively. Talent Management has become a major theoretical and empirical topic of intellectual curiosity from various disciplinary perspectives, such as human resource management, arts and entertainment management, international management, etc. This Companion is an indispensable source that provides an authoritative, in-depth, and comprehensive examination of emerging Talent Management topics.

Divided into five thematic sections that provide a unique overarching structure to organize forty-one chapters written by leading and renowned international scholars, this Companion assesses essential knowledge, trends, debates, and avenues for future research in a single volume: Evolution and Conceptualization of Talent Management; The External Context of Talent Management; The Internal Context of Talent Management; Individuals, Workforce, and Processes of Talent Management; and Outcomes of Talent Management.

In this way, the Companion is essential reading for anyone involved in the scholarly study of Talent Management, including academic researchers, advanced postgraduate and graduate students, and management consultants. For further debate on Talent Management, readers might be interested in the supplementary volume *Contemporary Talent Management: A Research Companion*, sold separately.

Ibraiz Tarique, Ph.D., Chair, Department of Management and Management Science; and Professor of Human Resources and Talent Management at Lubin School of Business, Pace University, New York, New York, USA.

ROUTLEDGE COMPANIONS IN BUSINESS, MANAGEMENT AND MARKETING

Routledge Companions are prestige volumes which provide an overview of a research field or topic. Surveying the business disciplines, the books in this series incorporate both established and emerging research themes. Compiled and edited by an array of highly regarded scholars, these volumes also benefit from global teams of contributors reflecting disciplinary diversity.

Individually, *Routledge Companions in Business, Management and Marketing* provide impactful one-stop-shop publications. Collectively, they represent a comprehensive learning and research resource for researchers, postgraduate students and practitioners.

The Routledge Companion to International Hospitality Management
Edited by Marco A. Gardini, Michael C. Ottenbacher and Markus Schuckert

The Routledge Companion to Strategic Marketing
Edited by Bodo B. Schlegelmilch and Russell S. Winer

The Routledge Handbook of Financial Geography
Edited by Janelle Knox-Hayes and Dariusz Wójcik

The Routledge Companion to Asian Family Business
Governance, Succession, and Challenges in the Age of Digital Disruption
Edited by Ho-Don Yan and Fu-Lai Tony Yu

The Routledge Companion to Marketing Research
Edited by Len Tiu Wright, Luiz Moutinho, Merlin Stone and Richard P. Bagozzi

The Routledge Companion to Talent Management
Edited by Ibraiz Tarique

The Routledge Companion to Corporate Social Responsibility
Edited by Thomas Maak, Nicola M. Pless, Marc Orlitzky, and Sukhbir Sandhu

The Routledge Companion to Global Value Chains
Reinterpreting and Reimagining Megatrends in the World Economy
Edited by Renu Agarwal, Christopher Bajada, Roy Green and Katrina Skellern

For more information about this series, please visit: www.routledge.com/Routledge-Companions-in-Business-Management-and-Marketing/book-series/RCBUS

THE ROUTLEDGE COMPANION TO TALENT MANAGEMENT

Edited by
Ibraiz Tarique

Routledge
Taylor & Francis Group

NEW YORK AND LONDON

First published 2022
by Routledge
605 Third Avenue, New York, NY 10158

and by Routledge
2 Park Square, Milton Park, Abingdon, Oxon, OX14 4RN

Routledge is an imprint of the Taylor & Francis Group, an informa business

Library of Congress Cataloging-in-Publication Data
Names: Tarique, Ibraiz, editor.
Title: The Routledge companion to talent management / edited by Ibraiz
Tarique.
Description: 1 Edition. | New York : Routledge, 2021. | Series: Routledge
companions in business, management and marketing | Includes
bibliographical references and index.
Identifiers: LCCN 2021002520 (print) | LCCN 2021002521 (ebook) | ISBN
9781138202146 (hardback) | ISBN 9781315474687 (ebook)
Subjects: LCSH: Personnel management. | Employee selection. | International
business enterprises--Personnel management. | Organizational
effectiveness.
Classification: LCC HF5549 .R6388 2021 (print) | LCC HF5549 (ebook) | DDC
658.3--dc23
LC record available at https://lccn.loc.gov/2021002520
LC ebook record available at https://lccn.loc.gov/2021002521

ISBN: 978-1-138-20214-6 (hbk)
ISBN: 978-1-032-03828-5 (pbk)
ISBN: 978-1-315-47468-7 (ebk)

DOI: 10.4324/9781315474687

Typeset in Bembo
by KnowledgeWorks Global Ltd.

This book is dedicated to Zeryoon and Zaira whom I love very much.

CONTENTS

FIGURES

TABLES

FOREWORD

Talent management has emerged as one of the most significant topics in human resource management and international human resource management during the past twenty-five years. It has been widely embraced in both academia and in practice domestically and globally, both as talent management and as global talent management. Although already extensively written about, still much remains to be developed and researched. This book provides us an overview in one volume of our existing knowledge of a wide variety of topics, and then offers suggestions of what remains to be further developed and researched around the world at this time. As such, this book represents a huge undertaking – a community of more than one hundred outstanding scholars, researchers, and consultants, all with extensive knowledge and experience in talent management, from more than twenty countries.

In addition to a very useful introductory chapter, there are forty more chapters that are expertly organized by the editor into five coherent sections about talent management (TM) and written by the best scholars on those topics.

Section 1 focuses on *the evolution and conceptualization of talent management*. This section consists of five chapters that provide a historical analysis of talent management research, provide insights on where the field is today, and offer a way forward, both disciplinarily and methodologically, for further research.

Section 2 looks at the *external context of talent management*. Eleven chapters in this section examine TM from a macro or an external perspective. The goal of this section is to discuss research and findings related to the external context within which TM takes place and to suggest opportunities for further research.

Section 3 has seven chapters that focus on the *internal context of talent management*. More specifically, these chapters examine TM issues that are internal to an organization, such as how TM practices are designed and how talent is managed, viewed, and organized to support the goals within organizations. Ample suggestions for future research are provided.

Section 4 investigates *individuals, workforce, and processes of talent management*. Fourteen chapters in this section examine TM at the individual and group (workforce) levels, along with a focus on the organizational processes involved in effectively managing talent.

The final Section 5 examines *outcomes of talent management*. Three chapters cover topics related to assessment or the "effectiveness" of individuals, TM practices, and TM systems along with suggestions for further research.

Overall, each chapter attempts to offer a balanced overview of current knowledge in the specific topic of the chapter including important knowledge, issues, trends, and debates, and suggest many ideas and paths forward for further development and research in the future. It is a book that will prove to be invaluable for any researcher and practitioner focusing on talent management.

Randall S. Schuler
Distinguished Professor Emeritus
Rutgers University, U.S.A.
University of Lucerne, Switzerland

CONTRIBUTORS

Kathleen Bahr, Research Associate, Marriott School of Business, Brigham Young University, Utah, U.S.A.

Anneloes Bal, Data Scientist, Ministry of the Interior and Kingdom Relations, Netherlands

Cordula Barzantny, PhD. Associate Professor, Department of Human Resources Management and Business Law, TBS Business School, Toulouse, France

Allan Bird, PhD. Associate Vice President for International Affairs and Professor, Pacific University Oregon, Forest Grove, Oregon, U.S.A.

Jaime Bonache, PhD. Professor of Management, Carlos III University of Madrid, Madrid, Spain

Paul Boselie, PhD. Professor in Public Administration and Organization Science, Utrecht University, School of Governance, Utrecht, Netherlands

James A. Breaugh, PhD. Professor of Management, College of Business Administration, University of Missouri, St. Louis, Missouri, U.S.A.

Chris Brewster, PhD. Professor of International Human Resource Management, Henley Business School, University of Reading, Berkshire, United Kingdom

Brian Burgess, PhD. Candidate of Organizational Behavior, Broad College of Business, Michigan State University, Michigan, U.S.A.

Jean-Luc Cerdin, PhD. Professor of International Human Resource Management, ESSEC Business School, Cergy-Pontoise, France

Rachel Clapp-Smith, PhD. Professor of Leadership and Interim Associate Vice Chancellor for Academic Affairs, Purdue University Northwest, Indiana, U.S.A.

David G. Collings, PhD. Professor of Human Resource Management and Associate Dean for Research, Dublin City University Business School, Dublin, Ireland

Fang Lee Cooke, PhD. Associate Dean (Graduate Research) and Distinguished Professor (Human Resource Management and Asia Studies), Faculty of Business and Economics, Monash University, Melbourne, Australia

Dagmar Daubner-Siva, PhD. Senior Director HR Business Partnering, adidas International Trading AG, Lucerne, Switzerland

Nicky Dries, PhD. Associate Professor of Organizational Behavior (Research Professor – Senior BOFZAP), KU Leuven, Department of Work and Organisation Studies, Leuven, Belgium

Julia Eisenberg, PhD. Associate Professor, Management and Management Science Department, Lubin School of Business, Pace University, New York, U.S.A.

Paul Evans, PhD. Emeritus Professor of Organizational Behavior, The Shell Chair of Human Resources and Organisational Development, Emeritus, INSEAD, Fontainebleau, France

Marion Festing, PhD. Chair of Human Resource Management and Intercultural Leadership, ESCP Business School, Berlin, Germany

Kevin Groves, PhD. Professor of Organization Theory and Management, Graziadio Business School, Pepperdine University, California, U.S.A.

Julie Haddock-Millar, PhD. Associate Professor, Human Resource Management, Department of Management Leadership and Organizations, Middlesex University Business School, London, United Kingdom

Arno Haslberger, PhD. Senior Research Fellow, Middlesex University, London, United Kingdom

Len Karakowsky, PhD. Professor, Faculty of Liberal Arts and Professional Studies, York University, Toronto, Canada

Shaista E. Khilji, PhD. Professor of Human and Organizational Learning and International Affairs, George Washington University, Washington, DC, U.S.A.

Violetta Khoreva, PhD. Assistant Professor of Management and Organization, Department of Management and Organization, Hanken School of Economics, Finland

Karin A. King, PhD. Fellow, Department of Management, London School of Economics and Political Science, London, United Kingdom

Michael Koch, PhD. Lecturer in Human Resource Management and Organizational Behavior, University of Kent, Canterbury, United Kingdom

Igor Kotlyar, PhD. Associate Professor of Organizational Behavior and Human Resource Management, OntarioTech Business & IT, Ontario Tech University, Canada

Benjamin Krebs, PhD. Chair of International Business, Department of Management, Paderborn University, Paderborn, Germany

Miriam Lacey, PhD. Chair and Professor of Applied Behavioral Sciences, Graziadio Business School, Pepperdine University, California, U.S.A.

Bruno Lanvin, PhD. Executive Director, European Competitiveness Initiative (IECI), INSEAD, Fontainebleau, France

Jakob Lauring, PhD. Professor in the Department of Management, Aarhus University, Aarhus, Denmark

Alec Levenson, PhD. Senior Research Scientist, Center for Effective Organizations, Marshall School of Business, University of Southern California, California, U.S.A.

Heba Makram, PhD. Transformation Advisor, Future of Work Expert, Researcher, Dubai, United Arab Emirates,

Amina R. Malik, PhD. Associate Professor of Business, School of Business, Trent University, Durham, Canada

Elise Marescaux, PhD. Associate Professor of Human Resources Management and Head of the Department of People, IÉSEG School of Management, France

Anthony McDonnell, PhD. Full Professor of Human Resource Management and Head, Department of Management & Marketing, Cork University Business School, Ireland

Yvonne McNulty, PhD. Senior Lecturer, Management Discipline, School of Business and Law, Edith Cowan University, Australia

Mark E. Mendenhall, PhD. J. Burton Frierson Chair of Excellence in Business Leadership, Management Department, University of Tennessee at Chattanooga, Tennessee, U.S.A.

Maria Christina Meyers, PhD. Assistant Professor, Department of Human Resource Studies, Tilburg School of Social and Behavioral Sciences, Tilburg, Netherlands

Dana B. Minbaeva, PhD. Professor in Strategic and Global HRM, Vice President for International Affairs, Copenhagen Business School, Frederiksberg, Denmark

Joost Monster, Associate Consultant, Focus Orange, Netherlands

Shad Morris, PhD. William F. Edwards Distinguished Fellow and Associate Professor of Management, Marriott School of Business, Brigham Young University, Utah, U.S.A.

Margarita Nyfoudi, PhD. Assistant Professor of Human Resource Management and Organisational Behaviour, University of Birmingham, Birmingham, United Kingdom

James Oldroyd, PhD. Associate Professor of Strategy and Ford Motor/Richard Cook Research Fellow, Marriott School of Business, Brigham Young University, Utah, U.S.A.

Shaun Pichler, PhD. Professor of Management, Mihaylo College of Business and Economics, California State University, Fullerton, California, U.S.A.

Ramien Pierre, Ed.D. Adjunct Faculty Member, The George Washington University's Graduate School of Education and Human Development, Washington, DC, U.S.A.

Lovanirina Ramboarison-Lalao, PhD. Associate Professor, Management and Human Resources Management, EM Strasbourg Business School, Strasbourg, France

Eduardo Rodriguez-Montemayor, PhD. Senior Research Fellow, INSEAD's European Competitiveness Initiative, INSEAD, France

Chandana Sanyal, PhD. Senior Lecturer, Business School, Department of Leadership, Work and Organisations, Middlesex University, London, United Kingdom

Lynn Schäfer, PhD. Affiliated Researcher Talent Management Institute ESCP Business School, Head of People & Culture, Lition Energy Berlin, Germany.

Hugh Scullion, PhD. Professor in Organizational Behaviour and Human Resource Management, University of Hull, Hull, United Kingdom

Jan Selmer, PhD. Professor Emeritus, Department of Management, Aarhus University, Aarhus, Denmark

Kushal Sharma, PhD. Assistant Professor of Management, SolBridge International School of Business, Daejeon, South Korea

Parbudyal Singh, PhD. Professor of Human Resource Management, School of HRM, York University, Toronto, Canada

Agnieszka Skuza, PhD. Faculty of Management, Poznan University of Economics, Poland

Adam Smale, D.Sc. Dean, School of Management, Vaasan yliopisto, University of VAASA, Vaasa, Finland

Paul Sparrow, PhD. Emeritus Professor of International Human Resource Management, Lancaster Management School, Lancaster, United Kingdom

Jennie Sumelius, D.Sc. Assistant Professor of Human Resources Management, Hanken School of Economics, Helsinki, Finland

Stephen Swailes, PhD. Emeritus Professor, Huddersfield Business School, Huddersfield, United Kingdom

Konstantinos Tasoulis, PhD. Associate Professor in Human Resource Management, Department of Management and International Business, The American College of Greece, Greece

Marian Thunnissen, PhD. Professor of Dynamic Talent Interventions, Human Resources Management and Applied Psychology, Fontys University of Applied Sciences, Eindhoven, Netherlands

Jordi Trullen, PhD. Associate Professor in the Department of People Management and Organization, ESADE Business School, Barcelona, Spain

Vlad Vaiman, PhD. Associate Dean and Professor, Interim Program Director, EMBA/MBA/MSM, Lutheran University School of Management, California, U.S.A.

Pleun van Arensbergen, PhD. Lecturer at Hogeschool Van Hall Larenstein, VHL University of Applied Sciences, Leeuwarden, Netherlands

Marieke van den Brink, PhD. Full Professor of Gender and Diversity, Radbound University, Nijmegen, Netherlands

Anand van Zelderen, PhD. KU Leuven, Department of Work and Organisation Studies, Leuven, Belgium

Marius Wehner, PhD. Assistant Professor and Chair for Business Administration, Heinrich Heine University Duesseldorf, Germany

Sharna Wiblen, PhD. Assistant Professor, Faculty of Business and Law, Sydney Business School, University of Wollongong, Wollongong, Australia

1

TALENT MANAGEMENT

An Introduction

Ibraiz Tarique

Overview

There is considerable evidence that the field of talent management (TM) has grown exponentially over the last decade. Significant improvements have been made in understanding how the field has progressed, areas for improvement, and how the field needs to advance. A great deal of research has been conducted to assess a variety of topics across organizations, countries, and multiple levels of analyses (see Collings, 2014; Collings & Mellahi, 2009; Dries, 2013; Gallardo-Gallardo & Thunnissen, 2016; Gallardo-Gallardo, Thunnissen & Scullion, 2020; Khilji, Tarique & Schuler, 2015; Lewis & Heckman, 2006; Sparrow, Scullion, & Tarique, 2014; Tarique & Schuler, 2010; Thunnissen, Boselie, & Fruytier, 2013; Vaiman et al., 2021). Some studies have *focused on different types of employee groups* such as "stars" (e.g., Kang et al., 2018), high potential employees (e.g., Asplund, 2020; Jooss, McDonnell & Burbach, 2019), "A" players (e.g., Huselid, Beatty, & Becker, 2005), and expatriates (e.g., Collings, 2014).

A few studies have *described trends and cross-country differences* in Macro TM (e.g., Cooke, Saini, & Wang, 2014; Khilji, Tarique & Schuler, 2015; King & Vaiman, 2019; Lanvin & Monteiro, 2020) and issues related to *TM in global organizations* (e.g., Collings, Mellahi, & Cascio, 2019; Tarique & Schuler, 2018; Teagarden, 2020;). Others have analyzed a variety of topics such as *TM practices in organizations* (Latukha, 2018; Myers et al., 2020), *TM and employee commitment* (e.g., Luna-Arocas et al., 2020), *TM in the public sector* (e.g., Kravariti & Johnston, 2020), *burnout among talented employees* (Malik & Singh 2020), and *lack of rigorous empirical investigations in TM* (e.g., Thunnissen & Gallardo-Gallardo, 2019).

While interest in TM is growing, and recent research has provided valuable insight into various TM topics, there remain many opportunities for additional exploration and research; I highlight three:

- TM is multifaceted. There is a lack of consensus regarding TM's exact conceptualization illustrating the discipline's diverse nature with a multifaceted identity affected by many variables. *TM is defined from a variety of perspectives depending on the context, unit of analysis, and level of analysis;*
- TM is multidisciplinary. TM is continuously evolving across a variety of disciplines, including arts and entertainment, industrial/organizational psychology, military/armed forces, strategy, organizational behavior, human resource management, and cognitive psychology. The field is researched and studied by various professionals and researchers, such as management scholars, management consultants, organizational experts, labor economists, political scientists, and public administration specialists. *TM is a multidisciplinary effort that involves scholars and experts from different disciplines who cooperate and work together to improve our understanding of issues related to TM;*

DOI: 10.4324/9781315474687-1

- **TM is a bridge field.** The TM literature suggests that issues, problems, and ideas discussed by scholars are occasionally examined by HR/TM managers, professionals, and consultants. There is increased collaboration and transfer of knowledge between academics and practitioners, which has improved the quality of papers and findings and allowed managers and scholars to leverage each other's resources. *TM can be categorized as a "bridge field."*

Thus, I edited two books: this book (*Companion to Talent Management*) and its partner book (*Contemporary Talent Management: A Research Companion*, sold separately) that bring together 105 scholars and researchers from 21 countries in the context of the three opportunities (multifaceted, multidisciplinary, and bridge field) to provide academic researchers, advanced postgraduate and graduate students, and TM research consultants with an authoritative, in-depth, and comprehensive examination of critical scholarly topics related to TM that can encourage further research. More specifically, the aim is to provide an essential resource that will assist individuals and organizations that seek the convenience of two books that cover a spectrum of scholarly research on TM.

Organization of the Book[1]

This book is organized into five sections of varying lengths, each of which covers a separate agenda. Section I consists of five chapters that focus on *the evolution and conceptualization of talent management.* Section II consists of 11 chapters that look at TM's external context, that is, examine research and findings related to the external context within which TM takes place. Section III comprises 7 chapters that investigate the *internal context of TM.* More specifically, these chapters examine how TM practices are configured to support business goals and objectives. Section IV includes 13 chapters that examine *individuals, the workforce, and the processes of TM.* Section V brings this book to a close with three chapters that explore TM outcomes with a particular focus on assessment or the "effectiveness" of individuals, TM practices, and TM systems.

Chapter Topics

Section I

As mentioned earlier, chapters in section I focus on the evolution and conceptualization of talent management. Paul Sparrow (*Chapter 2*) provides a historical analysis of TM research, offers insights into where the field is today, and provides current and new researchers a way to move forward. David Collings and Dana Minbaeva in *Chapter 3* provide a mapping of conceptual boundaries using a micro-foundational approach as a diagnostic tool to help us identify some of the essential but under-researched issues that future research in this critical field must explore. *Chapter 4* by Karin King introduces the organizational TM system from the perspective of the employee's participation in the workforce. Kushal Sharma (*Chapter 5*) uses the resource-based theory to argue that if the field is to advance and become relevant to practice, it needs to adopt a dynamic capabilities view because of the limitations of the static view of talent. The final chapter in this section is by Heba Makram (*Chapter 6*), who lays out an updated broader framework of Value to describe how TM adds Value to earlier four value-driven processes.

Section II

Eleven chapters in section II examine TM from a macro or an external perspective and discuss research and findings related to the external context within which TM occurs. There are four chapters dedicated to the emerging topic of macro talent management.

Chapter 7 by Violetta Khoreva and Vlad Vaiman examines how macro and micro environments affect decision making at the organizational and individual levels. Shaista Khilji and Ramien Pierre, in

Chapter 8, further establish macro global talent management (MGTM) as an interdisciplinary concept and present five domains that directly impact TM systems within organizational, national, and international contexts. The notion of talent competitiveness at the country level is examined in *Chapter 9* by Paul Evans, Eduardo Rodriguez-Montemayor, and Bruno Lanvin. These authors take an interdisciplinary approach that jointly considers organizational practices and broader economic and social forces that shape talent development. Building on Chapter 9, Paul Evans, Eduardo Rodriguez-Montemayor, and Bruno Lanvin discuss their empirical model and database called the Global Talent Competitiveness Index (GTCI) in *Chapter 10* and show how GTCI can frame the complexities of country/city level TM in a logical way that stimulates both research and policy change. The next five chapters in this section focus on selected TM issues at the regional/country level of analysis. Fang Lee Cooke examines TM issues in Asia in *Chapter 11* and TM issues in Africa in *Chapter 12*. Jordi Trullen and Jaime Bonache in *Chapter 13* look at Latin America, while Agnieszka Skuza and Hugh Scullion focus on Europe in *Chapter 14*. The next chapter (*Chapter 15*) by Jean-Luc Cerdin, Chris Brewster, and Lovanirina Ramboarison-Lalao discusses how migrants are being, or are not being, integrated into Global Talent Management. Paul Boselie, Marian Thunnissen, and Joost Monster in *Chapter 16* focus on TM in public sector organizations and particularly on the current knowledge regarding the linkage between TM and performance in the public sector. The final chapter in this section, *Chapter 17* by Marian Thunnissen, Pleun van Arensbergen, and Marieke van den Brink, looks at how TM is organized in academic institutions.

Section III

Seven chapters in section III of this book focus on TM issues that are internal to an organization. Maria Christina Meyers and Anneloes Bal, in *Chapter 18*, visit the traditional topic of the nature versus nurture debate in TM. In the next chapter, Marion Festing and Lynn Schäfer (*Chapter 19*) focus on the interplay of heterogeneous workforces (especially concerning age and generational challenges) and TM. Dagmar Daubner-Siva, in the next chapter (*Chapter 20*), provides an understanding of the (dis-) connect between TM and diversity management in an attempt to dovetail the fields. *Chapter 21* by Nicky Dries, Elise Marescaux, and Anand van Zelderen compares and contrasts the TM versus the career management literature, highlighting areas of overlap and contradiction, and their implications for research and practice. In *Chapter 22*, Stephen Swailes examines TM within business ethics, focusing on the individual and evolutionary nature of talent to highlight ethical implications. Jennie Sumelius and Adam Smale, in *Chapter 23*, examine the issues relating to talent communication and strategic ambiguity in TM communication. In the final chapter (*Chapter 24*) of this section, Sharna Wiblen examines the strategic Value of talent and information technology (IT), focusing on the interrelationship between the two fields.

Section IV

As mentioned earlier, this section of the book includes 17 chapters that focus on the organizational processes involved in effectively managing talent. The first four chapters in this section focus on global topics. Allan Bird and Mark Mendenhall, in *Chapter 25*, share findings from the field of global leadership that can provide Value to both scholars and practitioners working in the field of TM. *Chapter 26* by Jan Selmer, Yvonne McNulty, and Jakob Lauring examines Adult Third Culture Kids (ATCKs) as high potential employees to provide an overview of essential issues that represent vital challenges when managing ATCKs as high potential employees. The next chapter (*Chapter 27*) by Cordula Barzantny and Rachel Clapp-Smith looks at the possible benefits and challenges of incorporating global mindsets into GTM strategies as an inclusive approach that can contribute to international success. Vlad Vaiman, Yvonne McNulty, and Arno Haslberger in *Chapter 28* explore expatriates' TM, focusing on two specific types of expatriates: assigned expatriates (AEs) and self-initiated expatriates (SIEs). The next two chapters focus on issues related to workforce differentiation. *Chapter 29* by Michael Koch and Elise Marescaux examines the link between workforce differentiation and TM. In contrast, Amina Malik and Parbudyal Singh in *Chapter 30* investigate B players' significance in the context of TM.

The next three chapter focuses on "Star" employees. Shad Morris, James Oldroyd, and Kathleen Bahr in *Chapter 31* provide an overview of important TM issues related to star employees. *Chapter 32* by Len Karakowsky and Igor Kotlyar examines how the receipt of status-based labels can influence the recipient's capacity to learn from experiences. Julia Eisenberg's chapter (*Chapter 33*) discusses research at the intersection of virtual teams and the management of stars to facilitate future research in this space.

The next three chapters focus on TM issues related to attracting talent. Anthony McDonnell and Agnieszka Skuza in *Chapter 34* illustrate the variety of tools organizations tend to use in identifying talent to articulate several future research avenues. James Breaugh, in *Chapter 35*, reviews research on talent acquisition to highlight issues meriting future investigation from a TM perspective.

The next four chapters in this section focus on TM issues related to talent development. *Chapter 36* by Miriam Lacey and Kevin Groves examines high potential employees' development, focusing on the complexity and interaction of the factors driving the unintended consequences of hipo programs and processes. Margarita Nyfoudi and Konstantinos Tasoulis provide a detailed review of the coaching literature from a TM perspective in *Chapter 37*. The next chapter, *Chapter 38*, by Chandana Sanyal and Julie Haddock-Millar provides an overview of the literature on leadership theories and how it has developed over the last 50 years.

Section V

The final section of the book includes three chapters that focus on TM outcomes and topics related to assessment or the "effectiveness" of TM. *Chapter 39* by Alec Levenson highlights critical aspects of talent analytics's current state and provides recommendations on areas for improvement. Brian Burgess and Shaun Pichler in *Chapter 40* integrate the TM and performance management literature to identify opportunities for utilizing TM and PM strategies to bolster HRM and delineate directions for future research in this area. In the final chapter of the book (*Chapter 41*), Benjamin Krebs and Marius Wehner aim to synthesize theoretical and empirical accounts on the relationship between TM and individual and organizational performance.

Overall, I hope that the chapters in this book provide several avenues for further research and encourage future researchers to investigate and improve our understanding of TM topics discussed in this book.

Acknowledgments

I am grateful to the authors for their interesting and thoughtful contributions, as well as for their willingness, patience, and constructiveness in handling the suggestions for improvement of their chapter drafts. The authors in this book bring a wealth of exceptional knowledge and enlightening perspectives on TM, and several authors have been seminal thinkers in TM. It has been an honor to have worked closely with such a distinguished group of authors.

I am also indebted to the publisher and editorial team of Brianna Ascher for playing a significant role in making this book possible. Ascher has been very supportive of the book and has been invaluable in providing the needed support and encouragement. Along with her team, including Naomi Round Cahalin, Ascher has helped make the process of completing this book an enjoyable one. I thank them for everything they have done.

I want to indicate my sincere appreciation and gratitude to my family for their endless support, constant encouragement, and motivation. I want to acknowledge the guidance and mentoring of Professor Randall Schuler over the last 15 years. Finally, I am thankful to my international HRM and TM friends, and my colleagues at Lubin School of Business, Pace University, for assistance and encouragement.

Author Bio

Dr. Ibraiz Tarique is a Full Professor and the Chair of the Department of Management and Management Science at Lubin School of Business, Pace University, New York City, New York. He earned his Ph.D. in Industrial Relations and Human Resource Management from Rutgers University (2005). His current academic research interest is in global talent management and international human resource management.

He has written extensively in academic and professional journals. His publications include articles in the *International Journal of Human Resource Management, Journal of World Business, Human Resource Management Review*, and *International Journal of Training and Development* and several scholarly book chapters. He has presented numerous papers at the Annual Academy of Management Meetings. He is the Associate Editor of the *International Journal of Human Resource Management*; Editor on *Focus Series on Global Talent Management*, Routledge, Taylor & Francis; Editor on *Companion to Talent Management*, Routledge, Taylor & Francis; Editor on *Contemporary Talent Management: A Research Companion*, Routledge, Taylor & Francis; and Fellow, Wilson Center for Social Entrepreneurship, New York, NY. He is also a member of several editorial boards of the international peer-reviewed journals, including *International Journal of Human Resource Management, Journal of Global Mobility, European Journal of International Management, Cross-Cultural Management: An International Journal, International Journal of Training and Development, Journal of Organizational Effectiveness, South Asian Journal of Global Business Research*, and *Advances in Global Leadership*.

Dr. Tarique has authored several books: *International Human Resource Management: Policies and Practices for Multinational Enterprises* 4th, 5th, & 6th editions (Routledge). *Seven Trends in Corporate Training and Development: Strategies to Align Goals with Employee Needs* (FT Press, Financial Times/Pearson), and *Strategic Talent Management: Contemporary Issues in International Context* (Cambridge University Press).

Dr. Tarique teaches Human Resource Management and Talent Management Courses at four levels: Executive MBA, Regular MBA, MSc in HRM, and Undergraduate Business Management.

Note

1 The opinions expressed in Chapters 2 to 41 are those of the chapter author(s) and do not necessarily reflect the opinions of the book editor

References

Asplund, K. 2020. When profession trumps potential: The moderating role of professional identification in employees' reactions to talent management. **International Journal of Human Resource Management,** 31(4): 539–561.

Collings, D. G. 2014. Integrating global mobility and global talent management: Exploring the challenges and strategic opportunities. ***Journal of World Business,*** 49(2): 253–261.

Collings, D. G., & Mellahi, K. 2009. Strategic talent management: A review and research agenda. ***Human Resource Management Review,*** 19(4): 304–313.

Collings, D. G., Mellahi, K., & Cascio, W. F. 2019. Global talent management and performance in multinational enterprises: A multilevel perspective. ***Journal of Management,*** 45(2): 540–566.

Cooke, F. L., Saini, D. S., & Wang, J. 2014. Talent management in China and India: A comparison of management perceptions and human resource practices. ***Journal of World Business,*** 49(2): 225–235.

Dries, N. 2013. The psychology of talent management: A review and research agenda. ***Human Resource Management Review,*** 23(4): 272–285.

Gallardo-Gallardo, E., & Thunnissen, M. 2016. Standing on the shoulders of giants? A critical review of empirical talent management research. ***Employee Relations,*** 38(1): 31–56.

Gallardo-Gallardo, E., Thunnissen, M., & Scullion, H. 2020. Talent management: Context matters. ***International Journal of Human Resource Management,*** 31(4): 457–473. doi: https://doi.org/10.1080/09585192.2019.1642645

Huselid, M. A., Beatty, R. W., & Becker, B. E. 2005. A players or A positions? ***Harvard Business Review,*** 83(12): 110–117.

Jooss, S., McDonnell, A., & Burbach, R. 2019. Talent designation in practice: An equation of high potential, performance and mobility. *The International Journal of Human Resource Management.* doi: https://doi.org/10.1080/09585192.2019.1686651

Kang, S., Oldroyd, J. B., Morris, S. S., & Kim, J. 2018. Reading the stars: Determining human capital's Value in the hiring process. *Human Resource Management,* 57(1): 55–64.

Khilji, S. E., Tarique, I., & Schuler, R. S. 2015. Incorporating the macro view in global talent management. *Human Resource Management Review,* 25(3): 236–248.

King, K. A., & Vaiman, V. 2019. Enabling effective talent management through a macro-contingent approach: A framework for research and practice. *Business Research Quarterly,* 22(3): 194–206.

Kravariti, F., & Johnston, K. 2020. Talent management: A critical literature review and research agenda for public sector human resource management. *Public Management Review,* 22(1): 75–95. doi: https://doi.org/10.1080/14719037.2019.1638439

Lanvin, B. & Monteiro, F. 2020. *The Global Talent Competitiveness Index.* 2020 Global talent in the age of artificial intelligence, *INSEAD, The Adecco Group,* and *Google.*

Latukha M. O. 2018. Talent development and its role in shaping absorptive capacity in emerging market firms: The case of Russia. *Advances in Developing Human Resources,* 20(4): 444–459.

Lewis, R. E., & Heckman, R. J. 2006. Talent management: A critical review. *Human Resource Management Review,* 16(2): 139–154.

Luna-Arocas, R., Danvila-Del Valle, I., & Lara, F. J. 2020. Talent management and organizational commitment: The partial mediating role of pay satisfaction. *Employee Relations,* 42(4): 863–881.

Malik, A. R., & Singh, P. 2020. The role of employee attributions in burnout of "talented" employees. *Personnel Review,* 49(1): 19–42. Retrieved from: doi: https://doi.org/10.1108/PR-02-2018-0064

Meyers, M. C., van Woerkom, M., Paauwe, J., & Dries, N. 2020. HR managers' talent philosophies: Prevalence and relationships with perceived talent management practices. *International Journal of Human Resource Management,* 31(4): 562–588.

Sparrow, P. R., Scullion, H., & Tarique, I. 2014. Strategic talent management: Future directions. In P. R. Sparrow, H. Scullion, & I. Tarique (Eds.), *Strategic Talent Management: Contemporary Issues in International Context* (pp. 278–302). Cambridge, UK: Cambridge University Press.

Tarique, I., & Schuler, R. S. 2010. Global talent management: Literature review, integrative framework, and suggestions for further research. *Journal of World Business,* 45(2): 122–133.

Tarique, I., & Schuler, R. 2018. A multi-level framework for understanding global talent management systems for high talent expatriates within and across subsidiaries of MNEs. *Journal of Global Mobility,* 6(1): 79–101.

Teagarden, M. B. 2020. Global talent management: The foundation of global competitiveness. *Thunderbird International Business Review,* 62(4): 327–328.

Thunnissen, M., Boselie, P., & Fruytier, B. 2013. A review of talent management: "Infancy or adolescence?" *The International Journal of Human Resource Management,* 24(9): 1744–1761.

Thunnissen, M. & Gallardo-Gallardo, E. 2019. Rigor and relevance in empirical TM research: Key issues and challenges. *BRQ Business Research Quarterly,* 22(3): 171–180.

Vaiman, V., Cascio, W. F., Collings, D. G., & Swider, B. W. 2021. The shifting boundaries of talent management. *Human Resource Management,* 60(2): 253–257.

SECTION I

Evolution and Conceptualization of Talent Management

2

THE HISTORY OF TALENT MANAGEMENT

Paul Sparrow

Introduction

This chapter shows how the language of "talent management" (TM), and the ways in which this language has subsequently been used to imply what should be involved in the field, has evolved over time. The label TM has brought with it many "fuzzy concepts", many implicit notions and assumptions, and indeed some overt ideologies. However, language is important, for it can be used to allow those who take us through the history of TM interested in a topic to "gain entry" to associated ideas, thereby changing their own practice and mindset.

The chapter is structured into seven sections. The first section takes us back to the period before the TM narrative began. It shows how there were six broadly parallel-in-time developments that helped "enable" the subsequent notion of TM: 1) the convergence and integration throughout the 1980s and 1990s of resourcing and career development into a single life-cycle perspective; 2) increasing individualization of organizations and the capturing of behavioral repertoires associated with organizational effectiveness by the competency movement; 3) developments in portfolio thinking and the use of frameworks to categorize managers across a performance-potential matrix; 4) the growth of the human resource planning movement in the 1980s and 1990s; 5) the argument that technical changes were leading to "informated" workplaces and that this was changing the power of talent; and finally 6) how this development came hand in hand with another intellectual shift that we had to move away from a pay-for-the-job approach in selection systems, towards a pay-for-the-person approach.

The second section then shows how it was only in the late 1990s and early 2000s, once these enabling concepts had gained ground, that we saw the use of TM as a label in its own right. By the early 2000s, a situation emerged that led to a significant shift in policy as organizations attempted to design competitive HR strategies. It introduces the most famous – perhaps now infamous – exposition of this position in the book *The War for Talent,* and examines how it reflected some of the six enabling concepts, but also how it introduced new ideas that were introduced into the field.

The third section shows how in parallel to this influential narrative, we saw important critiques of the "star talent" perspective, which argued that the new TM narrative was misdirecting the attention of those interested in the nature of organizational effectiveness. It shows how this led to attempts to develop a compromise between the two competing narratives by incorporating an organization design perspective into the TM narrative.

The fourth section shows how in the late 2000s, under the impetus of human capital management thinking, there were three significant developments in the study of TM. These led to the incorporation of decision science thinking and risk management thinking into the TM narrative, along with further refinement of the TM-organization design interface.

DOI: 10.4324/9781315474687-2

The fifth section shows how in the later 2000s the field arrived at another important juncture. There was by then a gap between the suggestions, observations, and exhortations coming from the academic community and the realities of organizational practice. It examines the narrative that came from practitioners at that time as they began to question their own practice.

The sixth section returns to the direction of academic study, and shows how at the very same time there was an adoption of a more global and comparative management perspective, notably as a result of attention by global talent management (GTM) and international HRM (IHRM) researchers moving into the field. This renewed the level of interest in the topic and brought with it the opportunity to strengthen our understanding and improve our practice.

The seventh section shows how not long after, a series of special issues emerged on the topic (a process continuing to this day). The chapter explains how these were intended to delineate the topical research issues, and build an extended community of academics, and lead to a progressive narrative on the challenges that remain.

Finally, the chapter concludes by identifying and examining four near-future areas of research and development for the field: the need to 1) re-theorize the topic; 2) put the strategy back into practice; 3) contextualize TM practice; and finally 4) conduct research that crosses levels of analysis.

The Intellectual Roots of Talent Management Thinking and its Enabling Concepts

In laying out the history of TM and the way in which the academic debates have developed throughout that time, this chapter develops a series of steps in the development of the field that we can use to help position the current stage of evolution in the field. The historical developments that are explained here will also serve as primers for, and introductions to, many of the other chapters in this volume. By teasing out some of the main strands of debate in this history, the chapter by definition has to cover a wide territory.

The intellectual roots of TM as an identifiable practitioner field can be traced back to a series of developments in HRM thinking that emerged in the 1980s and 1990s. As an academic field, it has only really been in the last decade that there has been broad coverage of the topic, built mainly around a series of journal special issues on the topic, interspersed by a growing number of stand-alone studies. However, many of the principles that have gone on to guide this more recent study, can of course be traced back to earlier academic debate and developments (Silzer & Dowell, 2010; Sparrow, Hird, & Balain, 2011). Sparrow, Scullion, and Tarique (2014) called these developments "enabling concepts". They argued that a number of intellectual developments helped to establish some of the base problems and assumptions that initially shaped and directed academic study, and later helped establish what has become a vibrant TM narrative. In historical terms, there were *six* broadly parallel developments (dealt with in this opening section) that have helped enable more recent study (see Table 2.1).

The first enabling concept was the convergence of resourcing and development functions. In the 1990s, roles emerged within the HR structures of larger organizations – typically called Heads of Resourcing – that focused on the general stewardship of a cadre of senior managers and directors. These roles brought together responsibilities for senior employee role rotation, development of the senior cadre, identifying members of the cadre with the highest potential for Board-level roles and, where considered necessary, the exiting of low performing members. It was this Head of Resourcing role that most often was later relabeled into that of Talent Director (Sparrow et al., 2011). The new portfolio of responsibilities of Talent Directors added critical role analysis, co-ordination of external search and recruitment relationships, executive strength benchmarking, and in some organizations, performance management and strategic workforce planning to the role mix. This bringing together of recruitment and career development responsibilities therefore led to the advocacy of a life cycle approach – managing employees across the total span of their tenure with the organization (Sparrow et al., 2014).

Table 2.1 Intellectual developments in the 1980s and 1990s that enabled the subsequent talent management narrative

Developments that enabled the subsequent talent management debate	Primary authors	Impact on the talent management debate
Convergence and integration of resourcing and career development into a single life-cycle perspective	Harvard Model of HRM (Beer, Spector, Lawrence, Mills & Walton, 1984)	General management role of stewardship of cadre of senior managers (management across total span of tenure) through critical role analysis, high potential identification, role rotation, and development
Increasing individualization of organizations and capturing of behavioral repertoires associated with organizational effectiveness	Competency movement (Boyatzis, 1982)	Behavioral event investigation (BEI) techniques used to inform design of assessment centers and career development workshops
Portfolio thinking and use of frameworks to categorize managers across a performance-potential matrix	Human resources portfolio (Odiorne, 1984)	Frameworks to facilitate the categorization of managerial employees and highlight "high potentials"
Growth of the human resource planning movement	Human capital and human resource accounting traditions (Boam and Sparrow, 1992; Gubman, 1998; Fitz-enz, 2000)	Focus on forecasting, planning and managing staffing in broader context of business needs. Augmenting short-term management development activity with long horizon activities
Technical changes leading to "informated" workplaces	Importance of intellective skills, and treating high-value, difficult-to-replace talent as a strategic asset (Zuboff, 1988)	Technological innovations and IT creating more fluid, social, distributed, and less hierarchical work arrangements, impacting the value and power of talent.
Move away from a pay-for-the-job approach in selection systems	Pay-for-the-person selection systems (Lawler, 1994)	To design HR systems around highly skilled people, especially those who possessed high levels of self-efficacy and who had what were called "job crafting" skills

Life cycle thinking can be seen in many of the practitioner definitions of TM that emerged in the 2000s. The American Productivity and Quality Center (2004) defined TM as involving cradle to grave processes to recruit, develop, and retain employees within an organization. The United Kingdom's Chartered Institute of Personnel and Development defined TM as the systematic attraction, identification, development, engagement/retention, and deployment of those individuals who through their potential have a positive immediate or long-term impact on organizational performance (CIPD, 2008). Avendon and Scholes (2010) defined TM as an integrated set of processes and procedures used in an organization to attract, get onboard, retain, develop, move, and exit talent to achieve strategic objectives.

The second enabling concept was the shift in thinking about management effectiveness, whereby it was seen as a series of behavioral competencies within the individual. Attention shifted to the codification of the ways in which skills, abilities, and motivations created these behavioral repertoires (Boyatzis, 1980). Being part of the observational school of management and leadership, this school of thought defined competencies as overt behavioral repertoires that were embedded within the person. Behavioral event investigation (BEI) techniques could be used to surface the most effective behaviors. Such behaviors were a proxy for underlying and covert mental functioning, and captured the previously under-stated interpersonal, informational, negotiating, and decision-making domains of management.

The behaviors in turn were rooted in skills, attitudes, values, personality traits, self-image, motivations, knowledge, or social roles, but what they had in common was an association with superior (excellent) performance.

The third enabling concept was the development of portfolio thinking about human assets, and the performance-potential matrix. Although still a sub-function of HRM, by the mid-1980s, newly labeled Talent Management functions began to emerge and develop their own identity. Having mastered the BEI techniques linked to the competency movement, they looked for frameworks that would facilitate the *categorization* of all their managerial employees, and identify and highlight so called "high potentials". For the majority of organizations, TM began to operate around a few core technologies and tools – notably systems that categorize people as talented based on evaluations of their performance and potential.

It is very hard to find the original ownership of what is known as the 9-Box model of performance-potential – a model that still dominates much thinking in TM today. The notion of human resource portfolios, categorized on the basis of performance and potential, began to be "cut and pasted" into consulting presentations and into designs for organization's TM systems (Sparrow et al., 2011). Consequently, a number of people lay claim to the notion, but Hird, Whelan, and Hammady (2010) traced the ideas back to a 1980s article by Odiorne (1984). Odiorne (1984) in turn borrowed his ideas from the Boston Consulting Group, which had developed the now famous product market portfolio, in which organizations managed a spectrum of businesses that were high or low in terms of the market share, and the growth of market. The high-high business units were "stars", the low-low ones "dogs", the high-low ones "cash cows", and low-high ones "problem children". Odiorne (1984) adopted this thinking to similarly categorize managers along a performance and a potential axis. "Cash cow" businesses became "work horse" managers, and "dog" businesses became "deadwood" managers! In the now ubiquitous 9-Box model, which has no ownership but intellectual routes in portfolio thinking, the language shifted again from being "deadwood" to "requires close scrutiny". However, the message was clear. HR was the function that categorizes people, and people represented a strategic portfolio that could be used to differentiate investments and focus them on the areas of most rapid, or most conse-quential, returns (Sparrow et al., 2011).

The fourth enabling concept was the human resource planning movement, with its focus on forecasting, planning, and managing staffing in the broader context of meeting business needs. By the 1990s it was argued that systems could be developed that built upon the competencies identified by "measuring" the effectiveness of the person, into a broader system of organization-level competencies. The identification of organization-level competencies required techniques of competency requirement forecasting (Boam & Sparrow, 1992) because the value of competencies (and therefore the value of the individual talent who possessed these competencies) waxed and waned over time. Some competencies emerged in value, others matured, some enabled specific short-term transitions but were then redun-dant, while others were core to performance regardless of strategic context. The portfolio of future com-petencies could be predicted by augmenting the individual-level BEI data with insight from strategic vision workshops, business process mapping, cultural analysis, business scenarios, and study of expert knowledge. This was not called TM as such, although it was in practice, but was instead described as a "total resource development system", used to coordinate and integrate the design of core HR processes, principally external recruitment, internal assessment and development, performance management, and business change, around an outcome of organizational effectiveness (Boam & Sparrow, 1992).

By the late 1990s, and growing out the human capital and human resource accounting traditions, claims were also being made that investment in talented employees resulted in significant financial benefit for organizations (Gubman, 1998). However, Fitz-enz (2000) argued that management teaching was either ignoring or avoiding the question of human value in business environments, or even worse, was throwing out gratuitous or simplistic platitudes about it. Fitz-enz (2000) argued that talent shortages were not solvable just by attending to productivity (which he saw as a by-product of good manage-ment). Rather, managers had to address fundamental issues around fulfillment at work, and this could only be based on knowledge of, and feedback on, achievement. Human capital planning required an integration of *five* core elements: planning, acquiring, maintaining, developing, and retaining human capital. In turn, in converting this human capital planning cycle into a TM system, the organization had to develop two (difficult to build) capabilities:

1. Measuring the impact that human capital (talent) had on the collective ability to execute an organization's business processes, evaluated and analyzed only against truly best practices, not simple and essentially copied processes.
2. The use of the forward-looking skills of trending, forecasting, and predicting.

This human capital perspective came to influence a number of later HR academics active in the TM field, with for example Cappelli (2008) defining TM as the process through which employers anticipate and meet their needs for human capital. It also had a considerable impact on the way that nascent TM functions were implored to think about their processes. It made it clear that any TM process had to be analyzed in terms of whether its impact helped reduce business performance, according to metrics such as operating costs, product or service costs, cycle time of important processes, error and defect rates, being able to do more with less, and customer or employee satisfaction. The original discussion of human capital planning was about the demonstration of lean, efficient, and effective performance through the efforts of talent, not the more lazy and fairytaled (his language) practice of bench-marking a portfolio of star managers.

Therefore TM functions needed to incorporate forward-looking skills of trending, forecasting, and predicting deemed necessary for the identification of relationships and patterns, fallacies in trends, finding meaning in variables and their predictable consequences, avoiding mixing up linkage and correlation with causation, and identifying data sensors (data that tip you off to the emergence of a problem or opportunity). Fitz-enz (2000) saw this requirement as a necessary yet dangerous art, but a manageable one.

The fifth enabling concept was the informating of workplaces and the power of individuals. This forced some uncomfortable realities to the surface of HR thinking – such as the nature of power. While organizations needed firm-wide systems of competency requirement forecasting and human resource development and HR planning processes, there were nonetheless a small number of people who, in the organizational world dating from the 1980s, could have an extraordinary impact on the organization. This observation was in fact embedded in the technical changes that were taking place at the time. Managers were for the first time being exposed to ideas about how information technology was transforming organizations. This development was captured by Zuboff (1988). She argued that technological innovations and IT, in creating more fluid, social, distributed, and less hierarchical work arrangements, were also impacting the value of talent. In an "informated" workplace, individuals and groups could create new meanings and new understandings through the information they used. As a consequence of these shifts, it was argued that a process of "upgrading" was taking place – and a need for people who had the power to understand business and social opportunities that now existed (this understanding was termed "intellective skills"). It was argued that such high-value, difficult-to-replace technical talent was best seen as a strategic asset.

Finally, the sixth enabling concept in the 1990s was the call to shift away from a pay-for-the-job approach in selection systems towards a pay-for-the-person approach (Lawler, 1994). The pay-for-the-job approach had always assumed that jobs could be designed, evaluated, and differentiated dependent on their size and complexity. Employees could therefore be fitted to the job (or fitted to the broader organization culture or values in which jobs sat) through the process of selection. However, the pay-for-the-person approach, following a similar logic to the "informated" workplace perspective, argued that jobs had become too flexible, uncertain, and unpredictable to be "sized" in any reliable or stable way. It was more appropriate to design HR systems around highly skilled people, especially those who possessed high levels of self-efficacy and who had what were called "job crafting" skills. The competent person, it was argued, had the capabilities to design their own jobs in appropriate ways, and sadly, not all people, despite our best intentions, either possessed or displayed these newly-important skills.

In reality, job evaluation and person-job matching, rather than person-organization matching, continued to dominate most HR practice for many years after this initial call. And in later years, Lawler (2008), reflecting his organization effectiveness and design perspective, made it clear that while his advocacy of pay-for-the-person thinking was motivated by the sense that "star" TM was *necessary*, such talent was never felt to be sufficient. He later argued that organizations had to seek a balance between sourcing great individual talent and melding individual talent into a collective organizational capability, and ensure that the knowledge of star talent was turned into performance. This requires equal attention to the processes that reliably create individual talent and a more collective capability.

There have been six historical themes in the development of talent management (see Table 2.2).

Table 2.2 Historical themes in the development of talent management

Talent management narrative Primary authors		Impact on thinking
War for talent narrative	Michaels, Handfield-Jones, & Axelrod (2001); Sears (2003)	Definition of talent extended to include an individual's social capital. HRM policy influenced by marketing thinking. Employee value propositions to manage attraction and retention behavior. Talent treated as consumers of the organization. Talent management seen as a leadership imperative and cultural mindset. Management of inter-person and intra-person competitions
Linking talent management and organization design	Huselid, Beatty & Becker (2005); Pfeffer (2001)	Critique of star talent perspective. Alternative categorization of job positions into A, B & C positions
Re-booting of human capital management and human resource accounting traditions to translate organizational capabilities into specifications for talent	Bhattacharya & Wright (2005); Boudreau, (2010); Boudreau & Jesuthasan (2011); Boudreau & Ramstad, (2005, 2006, 2007); Cappelli, (2008); Cascio & Boudreau (2010, 2012); Collings & Mellahi (2009); Ingham (2007); Nahapiet (2011); Sparrow, Hird, Hesketh, & Cooper (2010)	Evolution of workforce analytics into broader strategic workforce planning (SWP) activity. Governance of talent systems and incorporation of decision science and risk management thinking. Notions of clusters of talent and pivotal talent pools
Crisis of practitioner confidence	Avedon & Scholes (2010); Cheese, Thomas, & Craig (2008); Davies & Kourdi (2010); Gubman & Green, (2007); Schiemann (2009); Silzer & Dowell, (2010); Sparrow, Hird, & Balain (2011)	Debates over best bundles of differentiating practices. Linking of talent management to broader workforce engagement, and to knowledge management. Teasing out of alternative philosophies, providers, practices, and principles guiding practice
Globalization of the talent management agenda	Farndale, Scullion, & Sparrow (2010); Schuler, Jackson, & Tarique (2011); Scullion, Collings, & Caligiuri (2010); Sparrow (2007); Tarique & Schuler (2010)	Shift in employer competition from country level to regional labor markets. Increase in demand for expatriates and skills shortages. Globalization of some professional labor markets
Mobilization of more critical agendas	Al Ariss, Cascio, & Paauwe, (2014); Collings, Scullion, & Vaiman (2011); Collings, Scullion, & Vaiman (2015); Farndale, Morley, & Valverde (2019); McDonnell, Collings, & Burgess (2012); Scullion et al. (2010); Scullion, Vaiman, & Collings (2016); Vaiman & Collings (2013); Vaiman, Collings, & Scullion, (2017)	Awareness of cultural and institutional limitations. Delineation of talent management in different national contexts. Extension of conceptual and intellectual boundaries. Talent management moved to the intersection between HRM, strategy, and international business

The War for Talent Narrative

The developments that this chapter now goes on to document were all in fact iterations of this earlier groundwork. Although the six intellectual developments began to dominate much HRM thinking, it was however only really once we got to the late 1990s and early 2000s that we saw the use of TM as a label in its own right (Silzer & Dowell, 2010). What was new perhaps was the language of "talent management", and the ways in which this language has subsequently been used to imply what should be involved in the field. As is made clear throughout this chapter, this label brought with it many "fuzzy concepts", many implicit notions and assumptions, and indeed some overt ideologies. However, language is important, for it can be used to allow those interested in a topic to "gain entry" to associated ideas, thereby changing their own practice and mindset, whether for good or bad.

By the early 2000s, a situation emerged in which organizations were designing competitive HR strategies in their struggle as employers to "land" and "upskill" employees in what was presented as a cutthroat free-agent employment market (Sears, 2003). It was argued that businesses were at a moment of dramatic change – an inflexion point – and that this required a significant shift in policy. The most famous – perhaps now infamous – exposition of this position was the book *The War for Talent* by Michaels et al. (2001).

From a historical perspective it is important to note this book in turn was the product of a strand of earlier consulting research. It also reflected many of the six enabling concepts and assumptions discussed earlier:

- The definition of talent in the book reflected the earlier competency movement and notions of human capital, but extended effectiveness to also include an individual's social capital. Talent was defined as the sum of a person's abilities (gifts, skills, knowledge, experience, intelligence, judgement, attitude, character, and drive) and a sharp strategic mind, leadership ability, emotional maturity, communication skills, the ability to attract and inspire other talented people, entrepreneurial instincts, functional skills, and the ability to deliver results (Michaels et al., 2001).
- All the HR systems – but particularly performance appraisal, rewards and incentives, work or job design – were to be designed around a pay-for-the-person as opposed to pay-for-the-job philosophy.
- The argument that the whole HR system of an organization had to be aligned to a performance-led talent strategy reflected Odiorne's (1984) earlier notions about categorizing and differentiating employees into a portfolio. Rather than using a 9-Box performance-potential taxonomy, the differentiation of employees was infamously captured as A, B, and C players. This meant assessing the performance and potential of employees and pursuing an elite strategy, i.e., investing in the A players by giving them promotion, compensation, and development opportunities; affirming the potential of B players; and acting decisively (either quickly re-engaging or more likely removing) C players.

However, four new ideas were introduced into the TM narrative at this time through the book:

1. HRM policy was for the first time influenced by marketing thinking. First, TM was to rely on there being an employer brand, positioned to attract key people (the stars) and then to exceed their expectations. Second, it had to adopt the notion of employee value propositions (EVPs). In the same way that organizations asked why should you buy my product or service, they needed to ask why a highly talented person would want to work in their organization, then use the answer to convey a clear statement of some of the more explicit obligations that the organization would commit to for talent and develop a proposition that could drive attraction and retention behavior.
2. To the system of workforce segmentation and its identification and isolation of particularly critical workforce segments (which had prior antecedents in 9-Box thinking) was added another

marketing concept of "talent as consumers" and the dominance of their needs as consumers of the talent system – what did critical talent care about most? (O'Donnell, 2009; Watson Wyatt, 2009)? Talent management was therefore *not* about having sophisticated HR processes concerned with succession planning, recruitment, and compensation, it was argued, but rather having HR systems that differentiated and affirmed the status of talent, hiring assumed talented people and paying them more than they thought they were worth.

3. The notion of TM was considered to need a leadership imperative – a cultural *mindset*. The language of TM was used to signal the importance of the surrounding managerial culture to the success of any particular HR strategy. The book asked how organizations could develop, sustain, and manage "pools" of talent, how they could engrain a talent "mindset" into their culture, and how they could align their varied HR programs and processes more effectively towards the needs of the proposed small elite of talent. Corporate leaders needed to be obsessed with talent, and hold a deep-seated belief and mindset that having better talent at all levels enabled an organization to outperform its competitors.

4. The narrative stressed two such competitions: one between individual talent (an inter-personal TM focus), and one within the individual so that they could be of their best (an intra-personal talent perspective).

Incorporating the Talent Management-Organization Design Interface

The moment the War For Talent narrative began, it was (in academic circles, although not in the field of practice) immediately recognized as having strong ideological undertones. In the same year, Pfeffer (2001) produced a famous critique of the "star talent" perspective. Many years before the global financial crisis legitimized some of the discomfort, Pfeffer (2001) argued that a cultural mindset that emphasized a fight to source talented individuals was "hazardous" to the organization's broader health. The argument was that the new TM narrative was misdirecting the attention of those interested in the nature of organizational effectiveness. It assumed the wrong fulcrum for improving this effectiveness (i.e., focusing on people, or stars, at the expense of systems), and that given the way people behave in organizations, such a system would create a set of side effects that would nullify any human capital gains. His key objections were:

1. The Star approach emphasized individual performance at the expense of teamwork and would give rise to a system of disharmony between employees who in reality needed to work collaboratively. Market-led HR practices made it hard to share knowledge, ideas, and best practices.

2. Celebration of individual brilliance created an elitist and arrogant attitude, downplayed the importance of learning and wrongly assumed that those dubbed as "Stars" should have their way over otherwise perfectly good ideas coming from "B" or "C" players.

3. Organizations that adopted an "A" player approach to TM also relied heavily on monetary incentives to attract and retain these key individuals, making the approach expensive, non-strategic and easily imitable.

4. Labeling (especially as a C player) would lead to horn and halo effects (past performances biasing judgments about current performance and future potential), and a negative self-fulfilling prophecy. Lower expectations would lead to fewer resources being available to B and C players, demoralization, and thus poor performance, artificially inflating the contribution of A players.

5. The philosophy also suggested that individual ability was a fixed invariant trait, a dangerous assumption that was not supported by research on careers.

Huselid, Beatty, and Becker (2005) attempted a compromise between these two competing narratives, by incorporating more of an organization design perspective into the TM narrative. They co-opted the ABC language and applied it to positions:

- A positions are strategic by dint of having a disproportionate role in an organization's ability in executing some part of its strategy, yet there is wide variability in the quality of work displayed by employees in that position. The consequences of mistakes (in job design or in hiring the wrong employee) can have serious financial and performance repercussions.
- B positions are largely support roles that may be strategic for the company but the skills required to perform them are common and there may be little variability in the performance of employees in these positions.
- C Positions may be required for the company to function but are not strategic to its success and may easily be outsourced or even weeded out.

On the one hand, they wanted to ameliorate the ethical objections that some HR professionals had to classifying people as "A, B, or C", understanding that there might not be the same emotional reactivity to classifying positions – or segmenting jobs – within the organization. In a nod to the war for talent narrative, it was still argued that A position holders required autonomous decision making, enriched job design, and performance based compensation, but it called for a more targeted approach to the allocation of "star talent". Organizations did not need A players throughout their operations, only in A positions. However, by building an element of intrinsic reward in-built into these positions, and attracting those who seek job enrichment at their work place, the TM strategy could be less reliant on monetary rewards, thereby making the strategy more acceptable to the wider organization.

Returning the Debate to Human Capital Management and Human Resource Planning Traditions

A number of writers, coming from a human capital planning perspective helped refine Huselid et al.'s (2005) positions perspective (see for example Boudreau, 2010; Boudreau & Jesuthasan, 2011; Boudreau & Ramstad, 2005, 2006, 2007; Cappelli, 2008; Ingham, 2007). By the late 2000s, the early work on workforce analytics had evolved into the broader topic of strategic workforce planning (SWP). SWP was aimed at identifying the characteristics of human capital needed to achieve a strategic objective, and then scaling the activities needed to enable this. It used a combination of data and analytics to create insight into the relative value of specific talent to the execution of an important strategy, and the necessary investments and actions needed to avoid any loss of value. The workforce plan in essence became the talent component to the business strategy. This work was driven by developments in the field of human capital management (HCM) – notably human capital (or workforce) analytics and human capital accounting (HCA). Nahapiet (2011) later reminded us that the word capital reflects a concept from economics that denotes potentially valuable assets. This human capital management discourse had never gone away, but it had perhaps been somewhat subsumed by the war for talent narrative.

However, in the late 2000s, under the impetus of human capital management thinking, there were three significant developments in the study of TM and the research narrative:

1. The incorporation of decision science thinking.
2. The incorporation of risk management thinking.
3. Further refinement of the talent management organization design interface.

Boudreau and Ramstad (2006, 2007) helped incorporate decision science thinking into the TM narrative. They returned the TM field to the underlying question of how you can create value from your human capital and introduced two notions into the narrative:

1. The need for a "talentship decision science" with the goal of increasing "the success of the organization by improving decisions that depend on or impact talent resources" (2007, p. 25);
2. "Pivotal talent pools", which were groupings and clusters of talent (i.e., not just positions) in which differential human capital investments could make the biggest difference to strategic success, because the improvements in capabilities brought about by investment would have the most significant impact on competitiveness. Pivotal talent pools could exist in undervalued parts of the organization.

Their work also began to make some of the theoretical underpinnings of the TM field more explicit. It argued that TM research needed to be underwritten by both:

- human capital theory: to argue that the costs associated with the development and retention of talent should be viewed as investments on behalf of the firm;
- expectancy theory: to argue that people have choices about the investments they chose to make in themselves, and will make more investments if there are signals that they are in an area of special importance to the organization.

Reflecting their own intellectual inheritance, Boudreau and Ramstad (2006, 2007) returned our attention to one of the enabling concepts noted at the beginning of this chapter – the effective use of *metrics* and a more open form of strategic thinking needed to identify these pools. In terms of the evolving historical narrative, this early work made three additional contributions:

1. It highlighted the need to translate the organizational capabilities articulated in the strategy into specifications for talent.
2. It used a number of frameworks to segment the existing, or the target talent population, to urge practitioners to think about talent either on the basis of the centrality of the roles to the strategy,
3. It assessed the consequences or feasibility of the above, and helped organizations decide whether they should pursue "build" or "buy" talent strategies.

HR and business leaders were implored to broaden their traditional focus and develop frameworks to identify which decisions about human capital were most crucial, and then to connect these decisions logically to questions of organizational effectiveness.

The late 2000s also saw the incorporation of risk management thinking into the TM narrative. For example, Sparrow and Balain (2008) looked at organizations operating in environments where the business model was fluid and the successful technologies were as yet still to be demonstrated. They drew upon the work of Bhattacharya and Wright (2005) on options theory, to argue that as part of this management of risk, organizations in practice took out different "talent options" against the various projected developments of their business model. They attempted to "future-proof" their organization by attracting pools of talent associated with several alternative ways in which the organization might develop. The expense of having competing pools of talent was nothing compared to the cost of not having the winning pool. Therefore, in situations of continuous business model change, organizations needed to adopt a risk management approach, and this required the development of the capability to take out positions or options on key talent.

Cascio and Boudreau (2010, 2012) argued that talent strategies had to be risk aligned to balance the inherent risks in talent planning, with investments in talent for several future scenarios, according to their relative likelihood and risk. The answer to this problem was to use a risk optimization, management, and mitigation framework to look at human resource strategy and strategic workforce planning.

This application of risk management thinking into the TM narrative made three contributions to the debate of that time:

1. It raised questions about the governance of talent systems and their functional ownership (which might not be HR functions).
2. It made it clear that human capital strategies had to be built around the reduction of uncertainty, elimination of bad outcomes, and insurance against bad outcomes.
3. It cautioned against the illusion of predictability, but argued that increased precision in predictions about the future supply and demand for skills was still possible by the application of quality-control tools to TM, and could achieve the same "low-defect" rigour seen in engineering and operations processes.

The third development as a result of human capital management thinking was the further refinement of the TM-organization design interface. There was a further softening of the "star talent" approach and clarification of the links between TM and organization design. Collings and Mellahi (2009) were supportive of the notion that TM had to include activities and processes that systematically identified key positions that differentially contributed to the organization's sustainable competitive advantage, and the development of talent pools of high-potential and high-performance incumbents to fill these roles. However, they introduced three further refinements to the key positions philosophy that helped tie the TM narrative into the broader HRM narrative. They argued:

1. There must also be a human resource architecture (discussed later in the chapter) that facilitates the filling of these positions with competent incumbents and differentiates their management to ensure their continued commitment to the organization.
2. Building on the observations of Boudreau and Ramstad (2006, 2007), as TM was not just linked to top tier employees of the organization, and strategic positions did not just include those near the strategic core of the organization, TM should be seen as more contextual endeavor, and should become an organization-wide strategy.
3. Organizations should therefore de-link the TM strategy from leadership development and debates about star performers, though this aspect of TM was naturally still one part of a broad strategy.

This linkage between TM and organization design subsequently led to a series of further "refinements" to the position. The assessment of how "valuable" a role was a complex endeavour. Therefore it was argued that two additional capabilities were needed as part of any broader TM architecture:

- Business model analysis;
- Value analysis.

Identification of more or less strategic roles in the field of practice had always been used as part of a talent system, but by the 2010s, it had become of particular importance given the high levels of business model change then taking place. Changes in business model often meant that the relative contribution of important roles to the success of the organization also changed, and the success (or failure) of the business model could become crucially dependent on the job design of a small number of mission-critical jobs – key positions. Drawing upon Fitz-enz's (2000) arguments about the nature of human value in business environments, and Boudreau and Ramstad's (2006, 2007) ideas about the risks to that value being realized, Sparrow, Hird, Hesketh, and Cooper (2010) argued that the judgment of how important a role was, and the contribution that talent might make to that role, depended on three judgements about strategic value. How did a role, and the surrounding organization design, contribute to processes of value creation, value leverage, and value protection? Building on this further, Sparrow et al. (2011) then argued that in order to forge a workable link between TM and organization design, HR academics needed to co-opt business model analysis.

Self-Criticism from the World of Practice

At this point in the chapter, it is worth "drawing breath" and reflecting on the situation that the field seemed to have arrived at in the later 2000s. There was an increasingly yawning gap between the suggestions, observations, and exhortations coming from the academic community (and consulting community) and the realities of organizational practice. Some of the professional bodies for HR practitioners began to step into the debate, and practitioners began to question their own practice.

There was no agreement about the exact bundle of differentiating practices that should be involved in TM, but at least the thinking was similar to that seen in the high-performance work practices debates within the academic field of HRM. Organizations needed an additional or a strategically-integrated set of practices in order to be able to say that they were good at TM. Typically, these key activities, or components, revolved around the following (Gubman & Green, 2007; Silzer & Dowell, 2010):

- Identifying and recruiting talent (analysis of labor pools, benchmarking competitor strategies, decentralizing or centralizing recruitment strategies, coordinating preferred suppliers, establishing brand and reputation among key employee segments);
- Attracting talent to the organization (creation of employee value propositions, management of an employer brand);
- Minimizing attrition through engagement and retention (effective onboarding, aligning rewards and recognition structures, improving line management skills and engagement with talent, and retaining initiatives);
- Identifying key internal talent (systematic and effective approaches to affirm individuals with the status of talent, high-potential identification systems, identifying the roles that are most talent dependent, and using assessment instruments and frameworks);
- Managing talent flows (developing effective succession systems, creating flexibility in internal mobility, career management and planning systems, succession management);
- Developing employees (coaching and mentoring, flexible portfolios of development activities, learning opportunities and options for employees, team learning processes, strategic and operational leadership development programs, coaching);
- Delivering performance (organization talent review processes, linking data on organizational performance to the selection of talent, stretching the performance of talented individuals, managing under-performance).

These component practices had to be more than just a string of HR programs, practices and processes. They had to form part of a broader system that was driven by the business strategy and must be managed as a core business process (Gubman & Green, 2007; Silzer & Dowell, 2010).

Perhaps realizing that they were hard pressed to make sophisticated judgments about talent, organization design, and risk, and also well aware that their practices in reality fell far short of covering the above territory, practitioners themselves became more questioning of their achievements.

For example, Cheese, Thomas, and Craig (2008) from the United Kingdom argued that TM had to be managed hand in hand with broader workforce engagement, in order that the combined capacity and will of people to achieve an organization's goals was treated as a productive resource. Schiemann (2009), writing on behalf of the Society for Human Resource Management in the U.S.A., complained of unfocused activities, woefully inadequate measures in a nascent field, and a failure to accept that TM was not just a business issue, but a social issue. There was a need to change in the rules of the game and for TM to capture the issue of engagement (through what he called a need for people equity).

Davies and Kourdi (2010) feared that practitioners in the area had bought into the notion of star talent. They had worked with many people in doing this: with CEOs undertaking extensive talent reviews, with psychologists to assess people's capability, with technology specialists to introduce databases to capture skills across the workforce, with recruiters to scour the market for more talent, and with "the talent" themselves to act as coaches. Yet "the struggle [remained] systemic... in truth, we had meta-phorically put sticking plasters over the obvious issues without really getting to the root cause of the problem... it felt to us that organizations were operating in a talent 'doom loop'" (Davies & Kourdi, 2010: 3). Their critique of their own practice argued that TM needed to be about knowledge, innov-ation, and relationships that took place in their organizations today, rather than executive potential tomorrow – the vital many were as important as the special few. The idea that organizations could manage talent was an outdated conceit. And organizations needed to manage the social dimension in which talent was developed, rather than the capability and resources of individuals. They needed to manage how talent works – and that meant managing the whole ecology of an organization and its ability to create social capital.

There was a questioning of what was meant by the term "strategic" as a label for TM. Silzer and Dowell (2010) in the U.S.A. argued that the label "strategic" could only be earned if TM processes identified:

- Individuals who had individual competencies that enhanced or established competitive advan-tage and played a crucial role in identifying, developing, and protecting core organizational capabilities;
- Different talent for different business strategies – aligning talent profiles more specifically to both near-term and far-term organizational demands;
- Talent strategies that supported entering and surviving in other geographic markets.

Avedon and Scholes (2010), in a further rejection of the star talent philosophy, argued the label strategic TM required processes that enabled much more "contingent" talent pools. This meant managing four contingencies:

1. A flow of leadership talent with appropriate competencies through early career, mid-career, and late-career stages, building talent for strategic functions;
2. Talent for key functions of critical importance to the strategy at a given time, often technical specialists but also hybrid roles that become central to the effective delivery of a new business model, or in the pursuit of different strategic foci such as innovation, operational excellence, cus-tomer intimacy, or globalization;
3. Talent for strategic technologies, ensuring access to new educational disciplines and start-up activities;
4. Talent for strategic geographies, covering mature through to emerging markets.

Similarly, Sparrow et al. (2011) argued it was time for organizations "to question the tablets of stone". They teased out differences in the underlying philosophies, providers, practices, and principles of TM. They found immense variability of practice, the way that these practices were bundled together by organizations under the label or umbrella of TM, the underlying models of potential, leadership and human capability, career advancement and career derailment, and differences in the underlying *principles* – the fundamental rules that guided action and conduct within the TM system. After the global financial service crisis, a number of organizations had begun to re-stress the corporate values that talent managers were supposed to possess and display, re-specified the underlying leadership models by creating linkage between their TM and efforts to foster specific concepts or brands of lead-ership, such as authentic or sustainable leadership, and were attempting to re-stress the social purposes of their organizations.

It became evident that decisions around talent in practice were rarely optimal and there was often only a weak link to the previous academic narrative (Mäkela, Björkman, & Ehrnrooth, 2010; Vaiman, Scullion, & Collings, 2012). This was because:

- They were not based on the frameworks being promulgated by the human capital management academics, but were still driven by the informed preferences or intuitive instincts that senior managers had of the visible talent within their organization.
- Even when informed by data provided by HR functions, they lacked a synthesis, provision of usable metrics and analysis or any explanation of important nuances.
- They were also bounded by the natural cognitive limits of managers who had neither the time, capability, nor inclination to access data about all global talent – the inclination was to select those who were "good enough" based on previous experiences and beliefs about talent.

The Globalization of the Talent Management Agenda

Interestingly, the introduction of both more critical and more global academic debate came at exactly the same time as this period of practitioner self-critique. There was a sudden groundswell of interest and attention given to the topic. The first major development was the incorporation of international HRM traditions into the TM narrative.

Sparrow (2007) argued that the globalization of labor markets was leading to an interesting development, in which academics from a number of fields related to international management had started to come together, beginning around the late 2000s onwards, to address global TM issues. As a strange quirk of history, much of this work seemed to come to fruition in 2010 (Farndale, Scullion, & Sparrow, 2010; Schuler, Jackson, & Tarique, 2011; Scullion, Collings, & Caligiuri, 2010; Tarique & Schuler, 2010). A number of writers had begun to argue that global TM had become of increasing strategic importance to organizations Farndale et al. (2010) felt that a number of factors had led to this growth of interest of TM in a broader international context.

- An intensification of competition between MNEs, leading to an increased importance of innovation and learning across borders, in turn much dependent upon the quality of leadership talent;
- A shift in the competition between employers for talent from the country level to regional labor markets and different parts of a global network of talent;
- An increase in demand for expatriates with the capability to develop new markets, access to specialized talent to assist the execution of overseas projects and to develop emerging markets, managers with distinctive competencies and a desire to manage in culturally complex and geographically distant countries; and the need for highly mobile elites of management to perform boundary-spanning roles to help build social networks and facilitate the exchange of knowledge necessary to support globalization;
- Shortages of such capable leadership talent in many geographies and local labor markets, coupled with rapid shifts in demographic profiles that are impacting the supply of labor, the retention of key knowledge and capability, and the depth and breadth of future talent pipelines;
- The globalization of a number of professional labor markets (such as healthcare and information technology), the shift towards skills-related immigration systems, higher levels of international migration into domestic labor markets, and the growth of reverse migration patterns for returnee immigrants bringing skills and networks back to home markets;
- Growing demand for alternative forms of international assignments such as short-term assignments, commuter assignments, and the like.

For Scullion et al. (2010: 106) global TM included "all organizational activities for the purpose of attracting, selecting, developing and retaining the best employees in the most strategic roles... on a global scale". GTM had to take into account differences in the global strategic priorities of the organization and the differences in how talent should be managed across the national contexts in which they operated. Tarique and Schuler (2010) saw GTM as a subset of international HRM policies and practices that were focused on the attraction, retention, development, and mobilization of talent, in line with the strategic direction of a multinational enterprise.

The Mobilization of Critique Through Special Issues

This renewed interest, and adoption of a more global and comparative management perspective, brought with it the opportunity to strengthen our understanding and improve our practice. With the benefit of hindsight, it could be argued that this explosion of academic debate had the advantage of bringing the topic of TM to a wider academic audience, notably the global talent management (GTM) and international HRM (IHRM) researchers, but it also had the disadvantage that many of these researchers had not been HR strategy academics, and so were not automatically cognizant of some of the prior historical context. There was a period of a few years in which both communities "equalized" their insights, and slowly integrated each other's findings into their own narratives. This new group of GTM and IHRM researchers were, however, as outsiders moving into a field, quickly able to spot the many flaws and inconsistencies in the debates that seemed to have been taking place. They were also very well placed to understand the cultural and institutional limitations that seemed to surround what had previously been a very Anglo-Saxon HR led debate. These special issues therefore brought a wave of critical thinking into the field of TM. These criticisms were directed at practitioners (and the lack of attention by HR strategy and HCM researchers to the realities of practice); but also at the theoretical and contextual shortcomings in much of the prior narrative.

The new academic interest was evidenced by a number of special issues on the topic that were intended to delineate the topical research issues, and build an extended community of academics. The pursuit of GTM was covered in *Journal of World Business* (Scullion et al., 2010), European perspectives were covered in *European Journal of International Management* (Collings, Scullion, & Vaiman 2011), and Asia-Pacific perspectives in *Asia Pacific Journal of Human Resources* (McDonnell, Collings, & Burgess 2012). A general review of debate appeared in *International Journal of Human Resource Management* (Vaiman & Collings, 2013).

After this first bout of issues, later special issues focused on an analysis of current theories and future research directions in *Journal of World Business* (Al Ariss, Cascio, & Paauwe, 2014), general progress and prospects in *Human Resource Management Review* (Collings, Scullion, & Vaiman, 2015), the nature of strategic TM in *Employee Relations* (Scullion et al., 2016), the importance of a number of organization contextual factors in *Journal of Organizational Effectiveness: People and Performance* (Vaiman, Collings, & Scullion, 2017), and critical perspectives in *Business Research Quarterly* (Farndale, Morley, & Valverde, 2019).

The special issues from 2010–2013 raised two important questions:

- What did talent management look like in different national contexts?
- Was it a concept that had any resonance beyond its Anglo-Saxon origins?

It was argued that there was a geographical narrowness in our understanding of TM practice. Discussions around the practice had been dominated by both the study primarily of Anglo-Saxon organizations and by analysis of U.S. academics (Scullion & Collings, 2011). The effectiveness of and types of TM activities had yet to be fully understood in different national contexts (Stahl et al., 2012; Scullion & Collings, 2011). Indeed, once academics began to look at TM in relation to different stages of globalization and also across countries, it became apparent that there were many differences in the understanding of, definition of, meaning in, and goals of, TM (Collings et al., 2011; McDonnell et al., 2012).

Vaiman and Collings (2013) reflected on the first set of special issues by noting four challenges that remained:

1. Understanding the conceptual and intellectual boundaries of talent management;
2. The practice of talent management in different national contexts;
3. The practice of talent management in different types of organizations;
4. Understanding which elements of talent management are the most effective for organizational performance.

The earlier 2001 critique of an elite approach to TM by Pfeffer (2001) was picked up again in the early special issues in what might be called the elite versus egalitarian debate of the early 2010s. Many contrasts can be drawn in terms of TM philosophies, but one of the most obvious is whether the practices that come along with the philosophy are associated with a view that TM is best focused on the management of a small elite – those high-performance and high-potential individuals – or whether a more egalitarian, universal, and inclusive focus is also needed, one that looks at TM practices as it relates to the majority of all employees. The latter perspective of course found much favor in the early reviews of the field (Collings & Mellahi 2009; Schuler et al., 2011; Scullion & Collings, 2011). Sparrow et al. (2014) argued some of this criticism is directed at the assumption that individual talent is one of the most significant sources of competitive advantage. Some of the criticism reflected ideological discomfort with a differentiated approach to talent, or the balance between this approach and the other more collective and less hierarchical parts of a talent system. Some of it was a more ideological, or cultural, discomfort with some of the practices that seemed to have come hand in hand with the philosophy, especially the level of reward given to those differentiated by the system.

This academic debate also asked whether the field was still in a stage of infancy or had reached a stage of adolescence (Collings et al., 2011; Thunnissen, 2016; Thunnissen, Boselie, & Fruytier, 2013). There was still no precise definition of what was meant by TM and this was slowing down the development of the field (Collings & Mellahi, 2009; Garavan, Carbery, & Rock, 2012; Iles, Chuai, & Preece, 2010; Lewis & Heckman, 2006; Tarique & Schuler, 2010). Academics also argued (and have continued to argue) that there was still no consensus around the intellectual boundaries that would help us understand the topic (Collings et al., 2011).

In support of the charge of infancy, Thunnissen et al.'s (2013) search of the academic literature from 2001 to 2012 found that over 170,000 hits on Google Scholar could be boiled down to 62 documents on the subject, 43 of which were peer-reviewed articles in international journals, one-third of which presented some empirical evidence (mainly only since 2010), and talked primarily about the scope and scale of TM challenges faced by organizations (rather than actual practice), or reflected single case studies, or views from a particular geography. The other two-thirds were either conceptual or review-based (i.e., trying to define the field). Hence the conclusion was that even by 2013: "the majority of the academic literature is still conceptual, trying to respond to the question of what talent management is" (Thunnissen et al., 2013: 1749).

By 2016, however, the field was considered to have now reached a stage of what could be called adolescence, though it was still far from being mature (Thunnissen, 2016). There has been a tradition of using bibliometric and content analysis of publications in the field to try to capture the central issues being discussed, but also to critique the level of drift and self-referencing that has taken place (self in the context of a small group of researchers leading debates). A retrospective analysis of the recent empirical effort suggests that there remains a fragmented body of knowledge, that is scattered over a wide range of journals (Gallardo-Gallardo & Thunnissen, 2016), resulting in a lack of any stable theoretical foundation. Similarly, a systematic review of studies in leading journals (although only capturing studies until 2013) concluded that the field has evolved "at the intersection of HRM, strategy, international business and other related fields" (McDonnell, Collings, Mellahi, & Schule, 2017: 90).

Research has been conducted in two main contexts: the management of high-performers and high-potentials, and the identification of strategic positions and TM systems. On a positive note, most papers now draw, to some extent, on primary research. However, the authors argued there remains a need for greater clarity around the conceptual boundaries of TM, and more comprehensive and nuanced methodological approaches. Although 60% of studies have some empirical component, 56% of this is survey based, many studies still rely on convenience samples providing limited information on response rates, and 18% of studies are based on single case studies, drawn from widely different geographies. Less than 30% have any theoretical framing, and in many instances such framing is superficial. The latest content analysis by Thunnissen and Gallardo-Gallardo (2019) captures 174 peer-reviewed articles published between 2006 and 2017 that restate the charge that the quality of TM research is often worrisome and is hindering the progress of the academic field.

McDonnell et al. (2017: 117) also conclude that in order to move the field forward an overriding need is for "talent management [to be] concerned with understanding where value is added in organisations by human capital". Borrowing the architectural metaphor from the field of strategic human resource management, Sparrow and Makram (2015) have attempted to lay out how TM systems might be assumed to create value, to then capture this value, to leverage it around the organization, and finally to protect and preserve this value. They introduced the notion of TM architecture, which is the combination of systems, processes, and practices developed and implemented by an organization to ensure that the management of talent is carried out effectively. While on the surface these architectures might appear the same across organizations, in reality, they are underpinned by assumptions that are often unique to each organization, dependent on its business strategies, the insights of its organizational decision makers, and the talent philosophies inherent to each organization. They also argued that the field of TM is at an important juncture. Its development is being impeded by this rapid contextualization and the different values, assumptions, allegiances, and philosophies that are being surfaced. Sparrow and Makram (2015: 249) concluded that because of the "different values, assumptions, allegiances and philosophies [that] are being surfaced" in the evolving field of TM, "answering questions about value" is the core challenge that must now be addressed for the field to develop further.

Conclusions: Where Next for Talent Management Research?

Although the field is maturing as a result of significant debates about its breadth and focus (Sparrow & Makram, 2015), problems remain and the field remains disjointed. This chapter argues that there has been a process of developing arguments and counterarguments, and through this debate the field is becoming increasingly coherent rather than fragmenting. However, to avoid the danger of fragmentation, researchers need to maintain their focus by both developing strong theoretical arguments but also staying connected to the dynamics of practice.

Having finally reached a stage of adolescence, when we look now to the current and emerging debates within the field of TM, what do they suggest are likely to be the near-term directions that researchers will take? There seems to be four future developments:

1. re-theorizing the topic,
2. putting the strategy back into practice,
3. contextualizing talent management practice,
4. crossing levels of analysis.

The first near-term direction is the need to re-theorize TM. The burst of attention via special issues also opened up a debate around the need for better theorization in the area and a widening range of theoretical perspectives. Al Ariss et al. (2014) felt that despite this first burst of concerted attention, it was still consultant and practitioner research that had aggressively driven the discourse on TM, and there remained only a limited amount of peer-reviewed literature that showcased the gap between academic and practitioner interest in TM. There are grounds for optimism though in terms of the level of theoretical diversity, especially of late.

The early work, as noted, stemming from traditions as various as human capital management (Lepak & Snell, 1999, Wright & McMahan., 2011), strategic human resource management (SHRM) (Becker & Huselid, 2006; Lado & Wilson, 1994; Wright et al., 1994), the resource-based view (RBV) of the firm (Barney, 1991; Barney & Wright, 1998), marketing perspectives such as brand equity and signalling theory (Boudreau & Ramstad, 2005), and supply chain management (Cappelli, 2008). More recently, attention has been drawn to the contribution that might be made by social exchange theory (Wang-Cowham, 2011), resource dependency theory (Garavan, 2011), institutional theory (Iles et al., 2010), and learning theory (Oltra & Vivas-Lopez, 2013; Yoon & Lim, 2010), the theory of value (Bowman & Ambrosini, 2000; Sparrow & Makram, 2015), and strategy-as-practice theory (Makram, Sparrow, & Greasley, 2017).

At the time of writing, there is a period of reflection taking place among academics in the field. Farndale et al. (2019) argue that being built upon a wide range of academic and applied perspectives may be something which may over the course of time prove to be a strength, but is also potentially a weakness, depending on the capacity of researchers to coalesce dispersed theoretical insights and engage in robust evaluation studies. They believe there are now three sets of questions that need answering. First, there are ongoing debates around the conceptualization, theoretical development, and framing of the field. Does the construct of TM have some useful theoretical utility, and do these theories have useful explanatory power in understanding the mechanisms that govern different TM architectures? As we continue to forge links between TM and other useful fields and theories, is there any useful evidence regarding which boundaries are most useful? Second, do we have sufficiently exact contours around the practices involved in TM, and does any anatomy of practices help serve to advance previously generated insights from proximal fields such as strategic human resource planning and competency-based management? Third, what are the stakeholder perceptions and priorities related to the adoption of TM? As we begin to cross broader levels of analysis at the micro, meso, and macro levels, does study of TM help us understand under-researched issues in the contemporary employment relationship?

Indeed, there is a need to continue to integrate TM thinking with the traditions of human capital theory. For example, recent work on strategic human capital (Boon, Eckardt, Lepak, & Boselie, 2018) moving to the collective level of the total human capital resource argues that the management of the portfolio of talent, and in particular the range and dispersion of knowledge, skills, abilities, and other characteristics (KSAOs) raises important questions familiar to the field of education. Can one high-performer carry a group of average performers, or does a lower average reduce the potential of high-performers?

The second near-term direction therefore is the need to contextualize TM. This process began of course in the early special issues once they brought in a more international and comparative perspective. However, there is now a broader process of rapid contextualization taking place, understanding important variations in practice or philosophy. This process of contextualization (above and beyond understanding the different global perspectives on TM noted above) began with contributions that debated the assumptions and philosophies used to both define "talent" and "talent management", and to underpin its practice (Collings & Mellahi, 2009; Dries, 2013; Gallardo-Gallardo et al., 2013; Meyers et al., 2013).

The theme has also been picked up in another special issue. Vaiman et al. (2017) consider the importance of a number of organization context factors on the practice of TM: the role that organizational climate plays in supporting talent development and employee perceptions and interpretation of TM practices; the impact of diversity management within the TM debate, how key actors in organizations actually understand talent in the particular context of the organizations in which they work, and how the networks of scholars working in the TM area is influencing the evolving literature and the evolution of the field of research.

The third near-term direction is the need to put the strategy back into practice. The link between TM and performance, the assumed line of sight between the two systems, and the assumptions this rests upon, have all been discussed in the literature in recent years (Collings, 2014; Makram et al., 2017; Sparrow et al., 2014). Makram et al. (2017), in studying both the talent system designers and the talent system implementers from a strategy-as-practice perspective, had mixed conclusions in terms of the level of strategic thinking in practice. Harking back to Lewis and Heckman's (2006: 152), they lament that we needed to improve "the quality of talent conversations in organizations". They found that managers continue to view TM as a bundle, or set, of management ideologies manifested in all their HR-related practices, and that performance management was the cornerstone of their TM. There was little new thinking in the area. However, there was evidence that practitioners could engage with more critical thinking, principally in terms of four important dialogues: 1) the need to translate the corporate and business strategy into talent capabilities; 2) leveraging identified potential and capitalizing on it so they could get a return on their investment; 3) extending the capabilities of existing talent so that they could learn, acquire, and institutionalize new knowledge and skills; and 4) developing the right culture in the organization to nurture, develop, and grow its talent.

Reflecting on this link back to strategy, Sparrow et al. (2014) argued that there is a clear talent management/knowledge management link. Today's organizations need to be much more aware of the need to manage the collective wisdom of their talent. Effective TM is about getting talent to talk to each other. Organizations therefore need to focus less on just identifying and categorizing talent, and more on getting effective brokerage out of their talent's knowledge and insight (and indeed the talent that exists across the extended networks of organizations and institutions in which their organization operates). The field may therefore evolve into one that is less concerned about *talent management*, but more about *the management of talent*. HR functions need to proactively manage the talent that exists across what increasingly is a "distributed capability system".

Finally, as the last point makes clear, the fourth near-term direction is the need for our analysis to now cross – and create linkages between – important levels of analysis. The majority of TM research is still focused at the meso- (organizational) level, with only limited attention being paid to individual-level research. This short coming is now being addressed, and in the near future, we should expect to see some interesting research that brings the individual back into the frame (see for example King, 2015, 2016; Nijs, Gallardo-Gallardo, Dries, & Sels, 2014; Swailes & Blackburn, 2016).

In a similar vein, opportunities to expand the field from its meso (organizational) roots to micro (employee) and macro (societal) contexts abound. We are now seeing discussion of the rapidly evolving field of macro talent management (MTM). King and Vaiman (2019: 199) define a macro view of GTM as "the activities that are systematically developed by governmental and nongovernmental organizations expressly for the purpose of enhancing the quality and quantity of talent within and across countries and regions to facilitate innovation and competitiveness of their citizens and corporations". As MNEs build skills and capabilities around the world, researchers need to understand the role played by the associated activities such as global capability transfer, strategic workforce planning, and employer branding. As professional labor markets have themselves become highly globalized, MNEs are trying to harmonize their strategies across countries, markets and even cities. Reflecting such developments, a number of writers have recently begun to argue the links between this wider perspective on TM and the requisite strategies for MNEs, and have introduced the concept of "macro talent management" (Khilji, Tarique, & Schuler, 2015; Khilji & Schuler, 2016; Lanvin & Evans, 2014, 2015, 2017; Sparrow, Brewster, & Chung, 2017; Vaiman, Sparrow, Schuler, & Collings, 2018a, b). This emerging field incorporates the study of activities aimed at attracting, mobilizing, developing, and retaining top talent at the country-level. It examines country-level processes and their outcomes within organizations, including multi-national enterprises and nongovernmental organizations (NGOs), and individuals in order to ensure high-quality TM.

Again, we see a natural progression of thinking taking place within the field. Once researchers begin to lay out the core elements of TM systems or architectures, (Sparrow & Makram, 2015), then it becomes evident that we can think about these architectures across several levels of analysis. King and Vaiman (2019) have picked up on the notion of TM architectures to call for a similar investigation of the "architecture of external macro talent management systems". They note that as the available supply, composition, and flow of talent into and out of organizations is subjected to and shaped by complex political, institutional, technological, and cultural forces and systems. As researchers continue to contextualize TM and "nest" their analysis of TM architectures in their broader context, then they will continue to supplement the current and dominant firm-level orientation to TM with broader country-level system analyses. King and Vaiman (2019) believe this will see a continued move away from a primarily HR-centric orientation towards understanding TM in its organizational and business strategy context, and the broader cross-organization ways in which TM can operate.

In the final analysis, it is clear that the language of "talent management" has continued to evolve, as too have the paradigms that tell us what should be involved in the field. It is clearly true that the label TM continues to bring with as more new "fuzzy concepts" often before the field has answered some of the previous ones! However, this very same language has allowed us researchers to gain entry to a wide range of real-world phenomena and useful ideas that should be associated with these developments. We may yet be able to change our own practice and mindset.

References

Al Ariss, A., Cascio, W. F., & Paauwe, J. 2014. Talent management: Current theories and future research directions, *Journal of World Business,* 49(2): 173–179.

American Productivity and Quality Center. 2004. *Talent management: From competencies to organizational performance. Final report.* Houston, TX: American Productivity and Quality Center.

Avendon, M. J., & Scholes, G. 2010. Building competitive advantage through integrated talent management. In R. Silzer & B. E. Dowell (Eds.) *Strategy-driven talent management: A leadership imperative.* San Francisco, CA: Jossey-Bass-Society for Industrial and Organizational Psychology. pp. 73–122.

Barney, J. 1991. Firm resources and sustained competitive advantage. *Journal of Management,* 17(1): 99–120.

Barney, J., & Wright, P. M. 1998. On becoming a strategic partner: The role of human resources in gaining competitive advantage. *Human Resource Management,* 37(1): 31–46.

Becker, B. E., & Huselid, M. A. 1998. High performance work systems and firm performance: A synthesis of research and managerial applications. *Research in Personnel and Human Resources Management,* 16: 53–101.

Beer, M., Spector, B., Lawrence, P. R., Mills, Q. D., & Walton, R. E. 1984. *Managing human assets.* New York: Free Press.

Bhattacharya, M., & Wright, P. M. 2005. Managing human assets in an uncertain world: Applying real options theory to HRM. *International Journal of HRM,* 16(6): 929–948.

Boam, R., & Sparrow, P. R. (Eds.) 1992. *Designing and achieving competency: A competency based approach to developing people and organizations.* London: McGraw-Hill.

Boon, C., Eckardt, R., Lepak, D. P., & Boselie, P. 2018. Integrating strategic human capital and strategic human resource management. *The International Journal of Human Resource Management,* 29: 1, 34–67

Boudreau, J. W. 2010. *Retooling HR: Using proven business tools to make better decisions about talent.* Boston, MA: Harvard Business School Press.

Boudreau, J. W., & Jesuthasan, R. 2011. *Transformative HR: How great companies use evidence based change for sustainable advantage.* San Francisco, CA: Jossey-Bass.

Boudreau, J. W., & Ramstad. P. M. 2005. Talentship and the evolution of human resource management: from 'professional practices' to 'strategic talent decision science'. *Human Resource Planning,* 28(2): 17–26.

Boudreau, J. W., & Ramstad, P. M. 2006. Talentship and HR measurement and analysis: From ROI to strategic, human resource planning. *Human Resource Planning,* 29(1): 25–33.

Boudreau, J. W., & Ramstad, P. M. 2007. *Beyond HR: The new science of human capital.* Boston, MA: Harvard Business School Press.

Bowman, C., & Ambosini, V. 2000. Value creation versus value capture: Towards coherent definition of value in strategy. *British Journal of Management,* 11(1): 1–15.

Boyatzis, R. 1982. *The competent manager: A model for effective performance.* New York: John Wiley.

Cappelli, P. 2008. *Talent on demand: Managing talent in an age of uncertainty.* Boston, MA: Harvard Business School Press.

Cascio, W. F., & Boudreau, J. W. 2010. *Investing in people: Financial impact of human resource initiatives.* New York: Financial Times Press.

Cascio, W. F., & Boudreau, J. W. 2012. *A short introduction to strategic human resource management.* Cambridge: Cambridge University Press.

Cheese, P., Thomas, R. J., & Craig, E. 2008. *The talent powered organization: Strategies for globalization, talent management and high performance.* London: Kogan Page.

CIPD. 2008. Talent management: Design, implementation and evaluation. *CIPD Online Practical Tool.* London: CIPD.

Collings, D. G. 2014. The contribution of talent management to organisation success. In J. Passmore, K. Kraiger & N. Santos (Eds.) *The Wiley Blackwell handbook of the psychology of training, development and feedback.* London, Wiley Blackwell. pp. 247–260.

Collings, D. G., & Mellahi, K. 2009. Strategic talent management: A review and research agenda. *Human Resource Management Review,* 19(4): 304–313.

Collings, D. G., Scullion, H., & Vaiman, V. 2011. European perspectives on talent management. *European Journal of International Management,* 5(5): 453–62.

Collings, D. G., Scullion, H., & Vaiman, V. 2015. Talent management: Progress and prospects. *Human Resource Management Review,* 25(3): 233–35.

Davies, J., & Kourdi, J. 2010. *The truth about talent.* Chichester, UK: Wiley.

Dries, N. 2013. The psychology of talent management: A review and research agenda. *Human Resource Management Review,* 23(4): 272–285.

Farndale, E., Morley, M., & Valverde, M. 2019. Editorial. Talent management: Quo vadis? *Business Research Quarterly,* 22(3): 155–159.

Farndale, E., Scullion, H., & Sparrow, P. R. 2010. The role of the corporate human resource function in global talent management. *Journal of World Business,* 45(2): 161–168.

Fitz-enz, J. 2000. *The return on investment of human capital: Measuring the economic value of employee performance.* New York: American Management Association.

Gallardo-Gallardo, E., Dries, N., & González-Cruz, T. F. 2013. What is the meaning of 'talent' in the world of work? *Human Resource Management Review,* 23(4): 290–300.

Gallardo-Gallardo, E., & Thunnissen, M. 2016. Standing on the shoulders of giants? A critical review of empirical talent management research. *Employee Relations,* 38(1): 31–56.

Garavan, T. N. 2012. Global talent management in science-based firms: An exploratory investigation of the pharmaceutical industry during the global downturn. *The International Journal of Human Resource Management,* 23: 2428–2449.

Garavan, T. N., Carbery, R., & Rock, A. 2012. Managing talent development: Definition, scope and architecture. *European Journal of Training and Development,* 36(1): 5–24.

Gubman, E. L. 1998. *The talent solution: Aligning strategy and people to achieve extraordinary results.* New York: McGraw-Hill.

Gubman, E. L., & Green, S. 2007. *The four stages of talent management.* San Francisco, CA: Executive Networks.

Hird, M., Whelan, J., & Hammady, S. 2010. BAE: Using senior management assessment as part of a talent strategy. In P. R. Sparrow, M. Hird, & C. Cooper (Eds.) *Leading HR.* London: Palgrave MacMillan. pp.122–135.

Huselid, M. A., Beatty, R. W., & Becker, B. E. 2005. "A players" or "A positions?" The strategic logic of workforce management. *Harvard Business Review,* 83(12): 110–117.

Iles, P., Chuai, X., & Preece, D. 2010. Talent management and HRM in multinacional companies in Beijing: Definitions, differences and drivers. *Journal of World Business,* 45(2): 179–189.

Ingham, J. 2007. *Strategic human capital management: Creating value through people.* London: Butterworth-Heinemann.

Khilji, S. E., & Schuler, R. S. 2016. Talent management in the global context. In D. Collings, K. Mellahi, & W. Cascio (Eds.) *Oxford handbook of talent management,* Oxford, UK Oxford Press.

Khilji, S. E., Tarique, I., & Schuler, R. S. 2015. Incorporating the macro view in global talent management. *Human Resource Management Review,* 25(3): 236–248.

King, K. 2015. Global talent management: Introducing a strategic framework and multiple-actors model. *Journal of Global Mobility,* 3(3): 273–288.

King, K. 2016. The talent deal and journey: Understanding how employees respond to talent identification over time. *Employee Relations,* 38(1): 94–111.

King, K. A., & Vaiman, V. 2019. Enabling effective talent management through a macro-contingent approach: A framework for research and practice. *Business Research Quarterly,* 22(3): 194–206.

Lado, A. A., & Wilson, M. C. 1994. Human resource systems and sustained competitive advantage: A competency-based perspective. *The Academy of Management Review,* 19(4): 699–727.

Lanvin, B., & Evans, P. 2014. *The global talent competitiveness index 2013.* Human Capital Leadership Institute: INSEAD and Adecco Group.

Lanvin, B., & Evans, P. 2015. *The global talent competitiveness index 2015–16.* Human Capital Leadership Institute: INSEAD and Adecco Group, Switzerland.

Lanvin, B., & Evans, P. 2017. *The global talent competitiveness index 2016–17.* Human Capital Leadership Institute: INSEAD and Adecco Group, Switzerland.

Lawler, E. E. 1994. From job based to competency-based organizations. *Journal of Organizational Behavior,* 15, 3–15.

Lawler, E. E. 2008. *Talent: Making people your competitive advantage.* San Francisco, CA: Jossey-Bass.

Lepak, D. P., & Snell, S. A. 1999. The human resource architecture: Toward a theory of human capital allocation and development. *The Academy of Management Review,* 24(1): 31–48.

Lewis, R. E., & Heckman, R. J. 2006. Talent management: A critical review. *Human Resource Management Review,* 16, 139–154.

Mäkela, K., Björkman, I., & Ehrnrooth, M. 2010. How do MNCs establish their talent pools? Influences on individuals' likelihood of being labelled as talent. *Journal of World Business,* 45(2): 134–42.

Makram, H., Sparrow, P. R., & Greasley, K. 2017. How do strategic actors think about the value of talent management? Moving from talent practices to the practice of talent. *Journal of Organizational Effectiveness: People and Performance,* 4(4): 359–378.

McDonnell, A., Collings, D. G., & Burgess, J. 2012. Asia Pacific perspectives on talent management. *Asia Pacific Journal of Human Resources,* 50(4): 391–398.

McDonnell, A., Collings, D. G., Mellahi, K., & Schuler, R. 2017. Talent management: A systematic review and future prospects. *European Journal of International Management,* 11(1): 86–128.

Meyers, M.C., van Woerkom, M., & Dries, N. 2013. Talent – innate or acquired? Theoretical considerations and their implications for talent management. *Human Resource Management Review,* 23(4): 305–321.

Michaels, E., Handfield-Jones, H., & Axelrod, B. 2001. *The war for talent.* Boston, MA: Harvard Business School Press.

Nahapiet, J. 2011. A social perspective: Exploring the links between human capital and social capital. In A. Burton-Jones & J.-C. Spender (Eds.) *The Oxford handbook of human capital.* Oxford, UK: Oxford University Press. pp. 71–95.

Nijs, S., Gallardo-Gallardo, E., Dries, N., & Sels, L. 2014. A multidisciplinary review into the definition, operationalization, and measurement of talent. *Journal of World Business,* 49(2): 180–191.

Odiorne, G.S. 1984. *Human resources strategy: A portfolio approach.* San Francisco, CA: Jossey-Bass Inc.

O'Donnell, M. 2009. Talent management. *Deloitte HR Professionals Services.* http://www.deloitte.com/view/en_IE/ie/services/consulting/consulting-services/human-capital-advisory-services/987fa6c82b10e110Vgn VCM100000ba42f00aRCRD.htm

Oltra, V., & Vivas-Lopez, S. 2013. Boosting organizational learning through team-based talent management: What is the evidence from large Spanish firms? *The International Journal of Human Resource Management,* 24: 1853–1871.

Pfeffer, J. 2001. Fighting the war for talent is hazardous to your organization's health. *Organizational Dynamics,* 29(4): 248–259.

Schiemann, W. A. 2009. *Reinventing talent management: How to maximise performance in the new marketplace.* Hoboken, NJ: Wiley.

Schuler, R. S., Jackson, S. E., & Tarique, I. 2011. Global talent management and global talent challenges: Strategic opportunities for IHRM. *Journal of World Business,* 46, 506–16.

Scullion, H., & Collings, D. G. 2011. (Eds.) *Global talent management.* London: Routledge.

Scullion, H., Collings, D. G., & Caligiuri, P. 2010. Global talent management. *Journal of World Business,* 45(2): 105–108.

Sears, D. 2003. *Successful talent strategies: Achieving superior business results through market-focused staffing.* New York: American Management Association.

Silzer, R., & Dowell, B. E. 2010. Strategic talent management matters. In R. Silzer & B. E. Dowell (Eds.) *Strategy-driven talent management: A leadership imperative.* San Francisco, CA: Jossey-Bass Society for Industrial and Organizational Psychology. pp. 3–72.

Sparrow, P. R. 2007. Globalization of HR at function level: Four UK-based case studies of the international recruitment and selection process. *International Journal of Human Resource Management,* 18(5): 144–166.

Sparrow, P. R., & Balain, S. 2008. Talent proofing the organization. In C. L. Cooper and R. Burke (Eds.) *The peak performing organization.* London: Routledge, pp. 108–128.

Sparrow, P. R., Brewster, C., & Chung, C. 2017. *Globalizing human resource management.* London: Routledge

Sparrow, P. R., Hird, M., & Balain, S. 2011. *Talent management: Time to question the tablets of stone?* Centre for Performance-led HR White Paper 11/01. Lancaster University Management School.

Sparrow, P. R., Hird, M., Hesketh, A., & Cooper, C. L. 2010. *Leading HR.* London: Palgrave.

Sparrow, P. R., & Makram, H. 2015. What is the value of talent management? Building value-driven processes within a talent management architecture. *Human Resource Management Review,* 25(3): 249–263.

Sparrow, P. R., Scullion, H., & Tarique, I. 2014. *Strategic talent management: Contemporary issues in international context.* Cambridge: Cambridge University Press.

Stahl, G. K., Björkman, I., Farndale, E., Morris, S. S., Paauwe, J., Stiles, P., Trevor, J., & Wright, P. 2012. Six principles of effective global talent management. *MIT Sloan Management Review,* 53, 25–32.

Swailes, S., & Blackburn, M. 2016. Employee reactions to talent pool membership. *Employee Relations,* 38(1): 94–111.

Tarique, I., & Schuler, R. S. 2010. Global talent management: Literature review, integrative framework, and suggestions for further research. *Journal of World Business,* 45(2): 122–33.

Thunnissen, M. 2016. A review of talent management: 'Infancy or adolescence?' *Employee Relations,* 38(1): 57–72.

Thunnissen, M., Boselie, P., & Fruytier, B. 2013. A review of talent management: 'Infancy or adolescence?' *The International Journal of Human Resource Management,* 24(9): 1744–1761.

Thunnissen, M., & Gallardo-Gallardo, E. 2019. Rigor and relevance in empirical talent management research: Key issues and challenges. *Business Research Quarterly,* 22(3): 171–180.

Vaiman, V., & Collings, D. G. 2013. Talent management: Advancing the field. *The International Journal of Human Resource Management,* 24(9): 1737–1743.

Vaiman, V., Collings, D. G., & Scullion, H. 2017. Contextualising talent management. *Journal of Organizational Effectiveness: People and Performance,* 4(4): 294–297.

Vaiman, V., Scullion, H., & Collings, D. G. 2012. Talent management decision making. *Management Decision,* 50(5): 925–941.

Vaiman, V., Sparrow. P. R., Schuler, R., & Collings, D. 2018a. (Eds.) *Macro talent management: A global perspective on managing talent in developed markets.* London: Routledge.

Vaiman, V., Sparrow. P. R., Schuler, R., & Collings, D. 2018b. (Eds.) *Macro talent management in emerging and emergent markets: A global perspective.* London: Routledge.

Wang-Cowham, C. 2011. Developing talent with an integrated knowledge-sharing mechanism: An exploratory investigation from the Chinese human resource managers' perspective. *Human Resource Development,* 14: 391–407.

Watson Wyatt Worldwide. 2009. *5 rules for talent management in the new economy.* WatsonWyatt.com

Wright, P. M., & McMahan, G. C. 2011. Exploring human capital: Putting 'human' back into strategic human resource management. *Human Resource Management Journal,* 21(2): 93–104.

Wright, P. M., McMahan, G. C., & McWilliams, A. 1994. Human resources and sustained competitive advantage: A resource-based perspective. *The International Journal of Human Resource Management,* 5(2): 301–326.

Yoon, S. W., & Lim, D. H. 2010. Systemizing virtual learning and technologies by managing organizational competency and talents. *Advances in Developing Human Resources,* 12: 715–727.

Zuboff, S. 1988. *In the age of the smart machine: The future of work and power.* New York: Basic Books.

3
BUILDING MICRO-FOUNDATIONS FOR TALENT MANAGEMENT

David G. Collings

Dana B. Minbaeva

Introduction

Talent management (TM) has captured the attention of senior organizational leaders, human resource professionals, and academic scholars since entering the mainstream when McKinsey declared the *War for Talent* in the mid-1990s (Cappelli & Keller, 2017; Collings, Cascio, & Mellahi, 2017). While initial interest in the topic was largely restricted to a practitioner audience, since about 2009, we have seen a significant body of academic work on the topic emerge (Gallardo-Gallardo et al., 2013; Gallardo-Gallardo et al., 2020; McDonnell et al., 2017; Meyers et al., 2020). However, this literature is highly diverse, ranging from discussions of the conceptual boundaries of TM, to TM practices and the intended outcomes or effects of TM (Thunnissen et al., 2013: 1744). The literature has, however, failed to develop consensus around the meaning and definitions of TM (Cappelli & Keller, 2017; Collings & Mellahi, 2009). The link between TM and performance has also yet to be established (Collings et al., 2019), and indeed, there is little consensus on dominant TM practices. In many ways, the field is still operating with generic notions of "attract, develop, and retain" and lacks specificity.

Theoretically the foundations of the literature on TM are also diverse. For example, Gallardo-Gallardo et al. (2013) identified four dominant theoretical frameworks informing TM research – the resource-based view, international human resource management, employee assessment, and the institutional lens. They criticized the field for applying multiple frameworks in single projects, claiming that such combinations may create "an inconsistent 'story' and often also a severe mismatch between theory and data" (2013: 276). A more recent review by McDonnell et al. (2017) concluded that there are two primary streams of the literature that dominate TM research: "the management of high performers and high potentials, and the identification of strategic positions and TM systems" (2017: 86). The authors also lament the disjoined nature of the field and call for greater clarity around the conceptual boundaries of TM. Achieving such clarity is central to the exposition of the relevant underlying mechanisms of TM, which are currently only partially understood.

This chapter aims to begin to fill in this gap. We provide a mapping of conceptual boundaries using a micro-foundational approach (Felin & Foss, 2005). We then use this mapping as a diagnostic tool to help us identify some of the key but under-researched issues that future research in this important field must explore. We begin by defining TM and reviewing the basic logic behind the arguments of micro-foundations. Then we illustrate that the key state-of-the-art discussions in TM are currently happening at a number of different levels. We finally argue that these discussions will benefit from explicating underlying mechanisms at the individual level.

DOI: 10.4324/9781315474687-3

Defining Talent Management

Given the lack of agreement over defining talent management, it is important to be clear on how the construct is defined in the context of the current chapter. We adopt Collings and Mellahi's (2009) definition, which was identified by Gallardo-Gallardo et al. (2013) as the most cited definition of TM. They define TM as:

> … activities and processes that involve the systematic identification of key positions which differentially contribute to the organization's sustainable competitive advantage, the development of a talent pool of high potential and high performing incumbents to fill these roles, and the development of a differentiated human resource architecture to facilitate filling these positions with competent incumbents and to ensure their continued commitment to the organisation. (2009: 304)

This definition broadens the TM agenda beyond a sole focus on leadership talent and highlights the importance of key positions that have the potential to disproportionately contribute to competitive advantage. As we outline below, key positions thus become the locus of differentiation from a strategic perspective. They are defined by their centrality to organizational strategy and by the potential for significant difference in output between an average and top performer in the position (quality pivotal) or by the potential differential in output when the number of people in the role increase (quantity pivotal) (Becker & Huselid, 2006; Cascio & Boudreau, 2016; Collings & Mellahi, 2009; Minbaeva & Collings, 2013).

The focus on talent pools calls for a move from vacancy led recruitment toward "recruiting ahead of the curve" (Sparrow, 2007). This reflects an emphasis on "flow" or "process" notions of human capital, as opposed to the more traditional "static" or "stock" perspective on human capital (Burton-Jones & Spender, 2011; Collings et al., 2017). Peter Cappelli likens this approach to managing talent through a supply chain. This approach aims to minimize talent risk in the supply chain. Such risks can be qualitative, meaning the organization does not have the types of knowledge, skills, abilities, and other characteristics (KSAOs) required to deliver on its strategy, or quantitative, when the firm does not have the requisite number of people available to deliver on its strategy. The challenge for organizations is to systematically identify future business needs in terms of knowledge, skills, and capabilities that will be required in the future but are not currently available in house and recruit on this basis (Collings et al., 2019). Stahl et al.'s (2012) study of global TM confirmed that the high performing organizations they studied followed a talent pool strategy – recruiting the best people and then finding positions for them.

Finally, the differentiated HR architecture is intended to increase organizational performance through maximizing the work motivation, organizational commitment, and extra- role behavior of those in the talent pool (Collings & Mellahi, 2009). Extant research provides some support for this position. Marescaux et al. (2013) demonstrated that employees who perceived they had received more favorable treatment in the workplace displayed higher levels of affective commitment. Similarly, Gelens et al. (2014) found that being designated as "talent" was perceived as a signal of organizational support, which, in turn, triggered affective commitment. However, the evidence is not conclusive on the positive impact of differentiating HR, and there is ample opportunity for further study here (Collings, 2017; Meyers et al., 2017).

Micro-Foundations: A Brief Overview

Micro-foundations have been an important theme in management research and can be seen as an instance of "reductionism" (Foss, 2010). Advocates of the micro-foundations movement in management argue that micro-foundations must be provided as building management theories for three critical reasons:

1. Alternative explanations: There are likely to be many alternative lower-level explanations of macro-level phenomenon that cannot be rejected with macro-analysis alone. Even if a large sample can be constructed on the basis of macro units of analysis, a problem of alternative explanations may persist.

2. Managerial interventions/practices: The ultimate goal of managerial interventions is to modify individual behavior. However, not every organizational practice gets implemented as intended, and not everything that is implemented affects individual behaviors to a similar degree. The differences between intended and implemented managerial practices are caused by a range of organizational antecedents that would cause variations in the implementation across organizational units. There are also variations in individuals' reactions to the actual/implemented practices, which may explain differences in perceived practices. Hence, a single-level perspective can never be adequate for research on managerial interventions.

3. Fundamental causes and predictability: Fundamental to micro-foundations perspective is the recognition that micro-level phenomena are embedded in macro contexts and that "macro phenomena often emerge through the interaction and dynamics of lower-level elements" (Kozlowski & Klein, 2000).

All three arguments speak directly to the need for building micro-foundations in TM research. However, the fundamental question for TM research is "*where* this deep structure is located, as there may be several analytical levels below a given aggregate phenomenon" (Foss, 2010: 13; original italics). We argue that for TM, given its focus on KSAOs, individuals should be considered as ultimate "micro", and individual heterogeneity must be treated as a source of explanations for variance observed at organizational level.

Yet, until now, the TM field has taken a more collective level (aggregate) approach, reasoning in terms of "talent pools", "talent management systems", and "talent architecture", which are posited to somehow directly influence firm performance. However, the link between aggregate "talent" and performance at the organizational level is merely a correlation, and one that has yet to be verified empirically. Building a causal link between aggregate "talent" and performance will require acknowledgement of the fact that "the system's behavior is in fact *resultant* of the actions of its component parts" and hence "knowledge of how the actions of these parts combine to produce systematic behavior can be expected to give greater predictability than statistical relations of surface characteristics of the system (Coleman, 1990: 3). Because little attention has been paid to heterogeneity between individuals, nor indeed to heterogeneity within individual performance (Minbashian, 2017), it is reasonable to characterize the treatment of the linkages between TM practices and organizational performance as a black box. We argue that exposition of this black box is the most pressing challenge facing TM field. Finally, we know very little about the link between investments in TM and corporate performance (Collings, 2014; Collings et al., 2017). This is largely because we lack the understanding of the dynamic processes of aggregation from individual talent contribution to collective, organizational performance.

Overall, we argue that drilling for micro-foundations in TM will allow researchers to discover "novel aggregate consequences of explicitly micro-foundational assumptions" (Foss, 2010: 29). Because individuals are treated as a homogenous group, there are a number of questions that remain unanswered. "To fully explicate organizational analysing … one must fundamentally begin with and understand the individuals that compose the whole, specifically their underlying nature, choices, abilities, propensities, heterogeneity, purposes, expectations and motivation" (Felin & Foss, 2005: 441). This will also create a much more fine-grained understanding of how organizations are better able to cope with challenges associated with human-capital-based competitive advantage (Coff & Kryscynski, 2011).

Multiple Levels, Overlooked Individual Heterogeneity and Unanswered Questions

Currently, central discussions in TM are happening at a number of different levels. This may be a consequence of the diversity of theoretical frameworks applied in the area to date. Yet, in all of these discussions, heterogeneity of individuals is often assumed but not articulated.

We focus on two key ongoing conversations, which will benefit significantly from explicitly articulating micro-foundations:

1. Choosing the point of differentiation for TM
2. Building a differentiated architecture for organizational performance.

Choosing the Point of Differentiation: Strategic Positions or Stars

The notion of workforce differentiation is fundamental to TM. This focus emerged as a result of the squeeze on resources after the economic crisis of the 1970s when firms found it increasingly challenging to sustain an inclusive approach (Cappelli & Keller, 2017), combined with an increasing realization that investing equally in all employees led to unnecessarily high costs for firms (Becker & Huselid, 2006). Workforce differentiation has its roots in the strategy literature and emphasizes the importance of choices about where to invest in human capital (Collings, 2017). It recognizes that firms can create value through differences in the design and management of workforce strategy (Becker et al., 2009) and calls for a greater investment in employees expected to deliver greater value or return of investment for the firm (Collings, 2017; Gallardo-Gallardo et al., 2013; Huselid & Becker, 2011).

However, a key question for firms is choosing a point of differentiation for their TM systems. The individual star was identified as the nexus of differentiation in earlier approaches to TM (Collings, 2017). This work takes a bottom-up focus in theory development, and foregrounds the perspective that employees contribute to the firm's strategic objective simply because of their individual value and uniqueness (Becker & Huselid, 2006). This perspective was central to the McKinsey perspective emphasized in the War for Talent, and was given further credence by high profile advocates such as Jack Welch at General Electric. It recognizes a relatively small group of employees as generating the greatest value for the organization. Employees are thus classified into two broad groups: a small group of stars or A-players "with talent" and a larger group of B- and C-players who are considered average or below average performers (Meyers & von Woerkom, 2014).

This view is also reinforced by recent literature on stars that explains that star performance is better captured by a power distribution than a normal distribution, owing to the disproportionate out that these exceptional performers deliver (Aguinis & O'Boyle, 2014). A central notion to differentiating at the level of the individual employee is that talent is relatively stable and reflected in intelligence and other individual differences (DeLong & Vijayaraghavan, 2003; Meyers & von Woerkom, 2014; Pfeffer, 2001), or graduating from a top school (Gladwell, 2002). Hence, recruitment and selection are prioritized in the context of attracting top talent given the stable and innate view of talent underpinning the perspective (Vaiman et al., 2012). Performance management was also viewed as a key enabler of such differentiation as tools like forced distribution emerged as central in identifying talent and forcing managers to differentiate in identifying those employees (see Collings, 2017, for a more elaborate discussion).

More recently the locus of differentiation in TM has shifted to the job level and the importance of strategic or pivotal jobs as the driver of competitive advantage is central to this perspective (Boudreau & Ramstad, 2007; Becker et al., 2009; Collings & Mellahi, 2009). This shifts the focus to a top-down perspective in theorizing. As Becker and Huselid note "When employees are able to contribute to a firm's strategic objectives they have (strategic) value" and that "...not all strategic processes will be highly dependent on human capital" (2006: 904). In line with more recent shifts in the strategic HR literature, this reflects an increased focus on the practices that impact human capital rather than the human capital itself (Delery & Roumpi, 2017; Wright & McMahan, 1992). This approach recognizes that human capital is of little economic value unless it is deployed in the implementation of the organization's strategic intent (Becker & Huselid, 2006; Bowman & Hird, 2014) and that the organizational capabilities that harness this human capital are as central as the human capital itself in this context (Linden & Teece, 2014).

Theoretically dynamic capabilities are identified as the fulcrum of workforce differentiation (Collings, 2017; Collings et al., 2018). From this perspective, competitive advantage is found from the unique way in which a firm can execute business processes in implementing its strategy. Such capabilities are reflective of the unique history, assets, and capabilities that any firm possesses (Bowan & Hird, 2014) and generally built as opposed to bought (Rumelt, 1984). While the production and sale of a relatively defined and stable portfolio of goods and services can be achieved through stable capabilities or ordinary capabilities, in more fast-paced or evolving contexts more dynamic capabilities are called for (Linden & Teece, 2014). This is reflective of more recent theorizing on human capital that acknowledges the more dynamic business environment that firms are faced with and recognizes that static conceptualisations of human capital requirements are no longer effective (Cascio & Aguinis, 2008; Cappelli, 2008; Lepak et al., 2011). This perspective also considers the potential impact of the future value of human capital beyond its present value (Lepak et al., 2011).

Dynamic capabilities are reflective of the firm's capacity to integrate, build, and reconfigure internal and external resources in adapting and responding to the evolving business environment (Linden & Teece, 2014). Routines are identified as key in reconfiguring intangible assets, such as human and social capital, in ways that facilitate the renewability, augmentation, and creative responses to dynamic and unpredictable business conditions and have been applied to recent conceptualizations of TM (Collings, 2014; Collings et al., 2018; Teece et al., 1997). This reflects the value of organizational routines – repetitive, recognizable patterns of interdependent actions involving various actors through which work is accomplished in organizations – in creating stability and boosting efficiencies and guiding organizational activity (Feldman & Pentland, 2003).

In a recent example of this perspective, Collings et al. (2018) identify pivotal positions as the starting point in any consideration of TM (see also Cascio & Boudreau, 2016). Their approach very clearly reflects the job as the locus of differentiation, and they adopt a top-down approach to theorizing consistent with this logic.

The discussion around the point of differentiation could benefit greatly from strengthening the focus around individual heterogeneity. First, when arguing for the choice of critical/pivotal positions, the literature often fails to recognize the importance of the fit of the individual to the chosen strategic position, given the individual's KSAOs. O'Boyle and Kroska (2017) frame this question in the context of the great person theory, arguing that it is premised on the notion that some individuals innately display particular traits and abilities that make them destined for greatness regardless of context. Using the example of Julius Caesar, they question if he were born in 19th-century London, would he have risen to a similar level of prominence as he did in late-republican Rome two millennia previously? This view is reflective of earlier contributions to the TM literature were premised on loading the organization with star performers.

More recently this approach has been challenging. Recent research points to the potential benefits of stars to teams as boundary spanners providing early access to critical new knowledge (see Kehoe, Rosikiewicz, & Tzabbar, 2017) but equally the potentially destructive effect of star overload in firms (Groysberg, Polzer, & Elfenbein, 2011). For example, Aguinis, O'Boyle, Gonzalez-Mulé, and Joo (2016) point to the impact of environmental factors that can serve as conductors in enhancing emergence and star performance versus insulators that can minimize and impede stars (see also O'Boyle & Kroska, 2017). Yet, much of the literature continues to treat stars as a homogenous group and hence implying the additive effect overlooking issues of complementarity and possible synergies between stars.

Building a Differentiated Talent Architecture for organizational performance

As noted above, a central premise of differentiating the talent architecture is to increase organizational performance through maximizing the work motivation, organizational commitment, and extra-role behavior of those in the talent pool (Collings & Mellahi, 2009). The underlying objective is to invest disproportionately in positions that offer the potential for above average impact (Boudreau & Ramstad, 2007). This is consistent with recent strategic HRM literature that acknowledges that better management of the core workforce will likely have the greatest impact on value creation and sustainable competitive advantage (Delery & Shaw, 2001; Lepak & Snell, 1999; Schmidtt, Pohler, & Willness, 2017). This means that organizations should make informed decisions around the optimal level of talent required in key positions and other roles (Huselid & Becker, 2011) and the appropriate levels of investment in individuals in those roles (Collings, 2017).

A key tension that emerges in discussions of a differentiated HR architecture is that while heterogeneity in aspects of the employment experience has the potential to motivate those in the talent pool, it also raises the risk of perceptions of inequality or injustice for those outside the talent pool (De Boeck et al., 2018; Meyers et al., 2017). De Boeck et al.'s (2018) recent comprehensive review of the literature concerning how those who were and were not designated as talent reacted to the designation is a useful contribution in this regard. It is important to state that their findings should be considered with the caveat that there is little empirical research showing a direct relationship between workforce differentiation or strategic TM more broadly and organizational performance outcomes (Collings, 2017; Meyers et al., 2017). Indeed, the extant research has tended to focus on proxy measures of performance at the individual level, as opposed to organizational-level outcomes. A key example is affective commitment. Theoretically affective commitment has been proposed as a key bridge between TM and organizational performance (Collings & Mellahi, 2009; Gelens et al., 2014).

De Boeck et al.'s (2018) analysis showed that TM practices generally correlated with positive affective (job satisfaction and organizational commitment) and behavioral (task performance and reduced turnover intentions) outcomes, with smaller positive effects on cognitions (psychological contract fulfilment and beliefs in knowledge, skills, and abilities). An interesting finding from qualitative studies they reviewed was that talent status was simultaneously associated with more negative affective reactions such as stress and insecurity. However, when they compared the evidence on the differential impact between those designated as talent versus those not designated, the former was also correlated with higher reported levels of work effort and stronger intentions to remain with the organization.

The situation with regard to differences between the groups in terms of attitudinal and cognitive reactions was less clear. This was largely traced to imbalance between the perceived employer and employee obligations. Those designated as talent often expected to receive more from their employers than they were prepared to give in return and also reported higher levels of psychological contract breech. This suggests the designation of talent translates into a more demanding attitude towards their employer from the perspective of the talented employees (Meyers et al., 2017). However, we need far more research that considers both positive and negative impacts of bundles of TM practices and of the differentiated HR architecture has on these outcomes.

By bringing the individual level of analysis, we should be able to better understand how individual employees deliver performance outcomes that are linked to the strategic intent of the organization. Based on a micro-perspective, this literature positions individual knowledge, skills, abilities, and other characteristics (KSAOs) as positively related to performance regardless of context. Hence, the value is additive and a more-is-better approach is appropriate (c.f. Ployhart & Moliterno, 2011). Equally, as is evidenced through the human capital resources literature individual-level human capital is not necessarily isomorphic with firm-level human capital. This literature highlights that, while individual human capital may facilitate individual performance, this will not necessarily translate to firm-level performance (Ployhart & Molierno, 2011). This points to the value of micro-foundations in developing a multi-level understanding of TM to which we now turn.

Towards a Multi-Level Understanding of Talent Management

As we illustrate above, TM is discussed at multiple levels. We have also argued that regardless of the level, to advance the discussion, it must be rooted in the individual behaviors, since individuals are embedded in various contexts.

Figure 3.1 illustrates the causal relations of embeddedness and simplifies causal mechanisms underlying TM with "arrows" linking various "nodes" located at multiple levels of analysis. This visualization

Figure 3.1 Road map

should only be viewed as a map for future research, rather than a complete theoretical model. The model is further specified in the below guidelines for research and practice.

Guideline 1 (arrows 1, 2, and 3): *Future research and practice in talent management should be more explicit about the choice of the point of differentiation, its origins, and its consequences.*

Level: from macro (organizational) towards meso (working group), disaggregation.

Towards this, the starting point should be in business strategy and the guiding question is "What kind of organizational capabilities are needed to deliver our business strategy?" As a Chief Human Resource Officer (CHRO) explains: "Business strategy defines the capabilities needed to win. Those capabilities drive the definition of talent and the decisions about how it is deployed organizationally. All other processes support the deployment of talent to build capabilities" (Alziari, 2017: 379).

Depending on the point of differentiation, the differentiated talent architecture needs to be built. It should include TM practices aimed at developing individuals (e.g., stars or talents) and/or identifying critical/pivotal positions and ensuring they are resourced appropriately. A useful consideration is how core (HR practices that have equal value in all strategic business processes) and differentiated HR architectures (TM practices designed based on the point of differentiation) would interact in the organization. A central consideration is that employees perceived the system to be fair. For example, Bjorkman et al.'s (2013) research on perceptions of talent status and impacts on key individual level outcomes found that the perceptions of fairness of the system by which individuals were designated as talent were central in explaining their reaction to their designation. This is key, as individual employees may withhold effort if they perceive that the firm has not dealt fairly with them (Minbaeva, 2013; Wright & McMahan, 1992).

Guideline 2 (arrows 4 and 5): *Future research and practice in talent management should account for variance in individual perceptions of differentiated HR architecture, resulting in variance in AMO and subsequently individual behavioral responses to talent management.*

Level: micro-level, embedded individual.

To stimulate multi-level thinking in future studies, we suggest that TM practices included in the differentiated HR architecture could be further specified as intended, implemented, and perceived HR practices. Wright and Nishii (2007) define *intended* HR practices as those that are "tied directly to the business strategy or determined by some other extraneous influences" (p. 11), and distinguish such practices from *implemented* (those that "are actually implemented") and *perceived* (practices that are "perceived and interpreted subjectively by each employee") HR practices (Wright & Nishii, 2007: 11).

Fundamental to the understanding of the relationship between employee performance and organizational outcomes is the ability (individual KSAOs), motivation (drivers of individual behavior), and opportunity (conditions that enable or constrain task performance beyond an individual's direct control) (AMO) framework (Blumberg & Pringle, 1982). Generally expressed as Performance = $f(A \times M \times O)$, the factors interact in a multiplicative fashion. All three elements must be present for high performance; a low value on any dimension results in markedly lower performance outcomes (Blumberg & Pringle, 1982; Kim et al., 2015). Kim et al. (2015) liken this to a virtuous cycle, with each factor supporting the other two. If any of the three are weak, however, a vicious cycle may emerge, reducing value in the organization.

Guideline 3 (arrows 6 and 7): *Future research and practice in talent management should develop the measures for the effectiveness of talent management at the work-group level, which when aggregated could explain the variance in performance in between differentiated talent and core group. It should be possible to observe a disproportionate contribution of the differentiated talent to business performance.*

Level: aggregation from meso (working group) to macro (organizational).

With this guideline, we advocate a more nuanced understanding of how talent performance unfolds in the firm. We believe that a more expansive measure of "return on talent" should be developed at a working group level. The measure should capture a group-level shared response to the implemented differentiated HR architecture, treating some employees differently from others (based on the choice of the point for differentiation). Although individuals form the perceptions, a social information processing perspective suggests that such work-related perceptions are "filtered through the collective sense-making efforts of the group of employees with whom an individual most often works and interacts" (Kehoe & Wright, 2013: 370; see also Bowen & Ostroff, 2004).

Furthermore, when forming the judgments, employees who have no experience or cannot recall personal responses to differentiation are likely to rely on the experience of co-workers to whom they are socially close (Kehoe & Wright, 2013). To evaluate differentiation effectiveness, the analysis needs to be undertaken at the organizational level where the performance of the differentiated group needs to be compared to a non-differentiated one. For example, a growing body of literature on strategic TM calls for the consideration of pivotal *positions* as a key point of departure for building differentiated talent-management systems. After the pivotal positions are identified, the organization can investigate whether there is high variability in performance among the people who occupy them. This requires creating metrics able to capture performance variability. For example, Nathan Myhrvold, former Chief Technology Officer at Microsoft, says "the top software developers are more productive than average software developers not by a factor of 10X or 100X or even 1,000X but 10,000X" (Becker, Huselid, & Beatty, 2009: 61).

Equally, while this may be a relatively small proportion of overall employees (10–20% of employees), based on insights from the literature on "stars", we argue that these employees are likely to contribute disproportionately to unit performance. By definition, star employees display disproportionately high and prolonged performance relative to peers (Aguinis & O'Boyle, 2014; Call et al., 2015; O'Boyle & Kroska, 2017). The disproportionate impact of star employees is reflected in recent research that points to a power distribution in star performance where a smaller percentage of employees contribute a disproportionate amount of value, the so-called 80:20 rule (O'Boyle & Kroska, 2017). The value that stars generate is also considered to be multiplicative as opposed to additive in contributing to higher-level outcomes (O'Boyle & Kroska, 2017). The value of non-stars or so called "B-players" is of course recognized in enabling stars and in performing well in less pivotal roles (Groysberg & Lee, 2008). However, as noted above, individual capability and performance may not be fully isomorphic with firm-level outcomes, and the organizations TM system should be designed to maximize the contribution of star employees (Collings et al., 2018; Ployhart & Moliterno, 2011).

Implications

Implications for Research

Individual talent is simultaneously embedded in several contexts, such as the specific context of his/her team, organization, and the external business-network context. However, current research on TM often fails to recognize this multiple embeddedness of talent. Individual interactions with various contexts in which this individual is embedded may also be an important source for variance observed at supra-individual level (in addition to the variance created by individual heterogeneity). We argue that future research should recognize the nested nature of talent as it has implications for talent identification, talent mobility, and performance implications of TM programs.

Future research should also explicate the causal mechanisms behind the assumed aggregation from individual behavioral responses to the expected "return on talent" at the organizational level. Aggregation from "micro" to "macro" assumes complex interdependencies between action of individual and that of others in the same context. Explaining such interdependencies has proved to be a "main intellectual hurdle both for empirical research and for theory that treats macro-level relation via methodological individualism" (Coleman, 1986: 1323).

Theoretically, the HR process literature might represent a useful lens through which to explore these questions in the context of TM (Ehrnrooth & Björkman, 2012; Nishii, Lepak, & Schneider, 2008). This perspective can provide important insights into how individuals perceive TM practices and how this can impact on the effectiveness of these practices in achieving individual and unit level performance. An alternative theory which could significantly aid in exploring the micro-foundations perceptive is the human capital resources perspective (Ployhart & Moliterno, 2011; Ployhart, Nyberg, Reilly, & Maltarich, 2014; Weller, Hymer, Nyberg, & Ebert, 2018). Theoretically human capital resources provide a useful means of theorizing how individual human capital can be valuable for unit level outcomes.

Implications for Practice

A micro-foundations preceptive also has significant implications for practice. Key among those is a recognition that designing a TM system that appears to meet an organization's strategic requirements is a necessary but not sufficient condition to improve organizational effectiveness. This is because how that system and the practices underlying it are implemented will have a significant impact on their effectiveness. Equally significant is how these practices are perceived by the employees that are the target of the interventions. All three of these steps must be aligned for practices to have the desired effect. This brings the line managers as implementers of such practices to the fore as key stakeholders (Alfes, Truss, Soane, Rees, & Gatenby, 2013; Ehrnrooth & Björkman, 2012).

Conclusions

Despite over two decades of discussion of talent management, our understanding of the link between TM and organizational outcomes such as performance is very limited. In this chapter, we argue that this limited understanding is explained in part by the unclear conceptual and intellectual boundaries of the area. One key limitation in this regard is a poor understanding of the mechanisms by which TM links to organizational outcomes. Our argument is that a micro-foundations perspective provides a key building block in explicating the linkages between TM and these organizational outcomes. This is premised on our understanding of individuals as the key source of variance in organizational level outcomes. Our hope is that the chapter will motivate further research from this important prescriptive.

References

Aguinis, H., & O'Boyle, E. 2014. Star performers in 21st century organizations. *Personnel Psychology,* 67(2), 313–350.

Aguinis, H., O'Boyle Jr, E., Gonzalez-Mulé, E., & Joo, H., 2016. Cumulative advantage: Conductors and insulators of heavy-tailed productivity distributions and productivity stars. *Personnel Psychology,* 69(1), 3–66.

Alfes, K., Truss, C., Soane, E. C., Rees, C., & Gatenby, M., 2013. The relationship between line manager behavior, perceived HRM practices, and individual performance: Examining the mediating role of engagement. *Human Resource Management,* 52(6), 839–859.

Alziari, L. 2017. A chief HR officer's perspective on talent management. *Journal of Organizational Effectiveness: People and Performance,* 4(4): 379–383.

Becker, B., & Huselid, M. 2006. Strategic human resource management: Where do we go from here? *Journal of Management,* 32(6): 898–925.

Becker, B. E., Huselid, M. A. and Beatty, R. W. 2009. *The differentiated workforce: Translating talent into strategic impact.* Boston, MA: Harvard Business Press.

Blumberg, M. & Pringle, C. D. 1982. The missing opportunity in organizational research: Some implications for a theory of work performance. *Academy of Management Review,* 7(4): 560–569.

Boudreau, J. W., & Ramstad, P. M. 2007. *Beyond HR: The new science of human capital.* Boston, MA: Harvard Business Press.

Bowen, D. E., & Ostroff, C. 2004. Understanding HRM–firm performance linkages: The role of the "strength" of the HRM system. *Academy of Management Review,* 29, 203–221.

Bowman, C., & Hird, M. 2014. A resource-based view of talent management. In. P. Sparrow, H. Scullion & I. Tarique (Eds.), *Strategic talent management: Contemporary issues in international context:* 87–116. Cambridge, UK: Cambridge University Press.

Burton-Jones, A., & Spender, J. C. 2011. *The Oxford handbook of human capital.* Oxford, UK: Oxford University Press.

Call, M. L., Nyberg, A. J., & Thatcher, S. M. B. 2015. Stargazing: An integrative conceptual review, theoretical reconciliation, and extension for star employee research. *Journal of Applied Psychology,* 100: 623–640.

Cappelli, P. 2008. *Talent on demand: Managing talent in an uncertain age.* Boston, MA: Harvard Business School Press.

Cappelli, P., & Keller, J. R. 2017. The historical context of talent management. In D.G. Collings, K. M., & Cascio, W. F. (Eds.), *The Oxford handbook of talent management:* 23–42. Oxford, UK: Oxford University Press.

Cascio, W. F., & Aguinis, H. 2008. Research in industrial and organizational psychology from 1963 to 2007: Changes, choices, and trends. *Journal of Applied Psychology,* 93: 1062–1081.

Cascio, W. F., & Boudreau, J. W. 2016. The search for global competence: From international HR to talent management. *Journal of World Business,* 51: 103–114.

Coff, R. & Krycynski, D. 2011. Riling for micro-foundations of human capital based competitive advantages. *Journal of Management,* 37(5):1429–1443.

Coleman, J. S. 1986. Social theory, social research, and a theory of action. *American Journal of Sociology,* 91(5): 1309–1335.

Coleman, J. S. 1990. *Foundations of social theory.* Cambridge/London: The Belknap Press of Harvard University Press.

Collings, D. G. 2014. Integrating global mobility and global talent management: Exploring the challenges and strategic opportunities. *Journal of World Business,* 49: 253–261.

Collings, D. G. 2017. Workforce Differentiation. In D.G. Collings, K. Mellahi, & W. Cascio (Eds.), *The Oxford handbook of talent management.* Oxford, UK: Oxford University Press.

Collings, D. G., & Mellahi, K. 2009. Strategic talent management: A review and research agenda. *Human Resource Management Review,* 19: 304–313.

Collings, D. G, Mellahi, K., & Cascio, W. F. (Eds) 2017. *The Oxford handbook of talent management.* Oxford, UK: Oxford University Press.

Collings, D. G., Mellahi, K., & Cascio, W. F. 2019. Global talent management and performance in the MNE: Exploring its impact across multiple levels. *Journal of Management,* 45: 2, 540–566

De Boeck, G., Meyers, M. C., & Dries, N., 2018. Employee reactions to talent management: Assumptions versus evidence. *Journal of Organizational Behavior,* 39(2): 199–213.

Delery, J. E., & Roumpi, D. 2017. Strategic human resource management, human capital and competitive advantage: Is the field going in circles? *Human Resource Management Journal,* 27: 1–21.

Delery, J. E., & Shaw, J. 2001. The strategic management of people in work organizations: Review, synthesis, and extension. *Research in Personnel and Human Resource Management.* 20: 165–197. Bingley: Emerald Group Publishing.

Ehrnrooth, M., & Björkman, I., 2012. An integrative HRM process theorization: Beyond signalling effects and mutual gains. *Journal of Management Studies,* 49(6): 1109–1135.

Feldman, M. S., & Pentland, B. T., 2003. Reconceptualizing organizational routines as a source of flexibility and change. *Administrative Science Quarterly,* 48: 94–118.

Felin, T., & Foss, N. J. 2005. Strategic organization: A field in search of micro-foundations. *Strategic Organization,* 3, 441–455.

Foss, N. 2010. Micro-foundations for management research: What, why, and whither? *Cuadernos de Economía y Dirección de la Empresa,* 42: 011–034.

Gallardo-Gallardo, E., Dries, N., & González-Cruz, T. F., 2013. What is the meaning of "talent" in the world of work? *Human Resource Management Review,* 23(4): 290–300.

Gallardo-Gallardo, E., Thunnissen, M., & Scullion, H. 2020. Talent management: Context matters. *International Journal of Human Resource Management,* 31(4): 457–473.

Gelens, J., Hofmans, J., Dries, N., & Pepermans, R. 2014. Talent management and organisational justice: Employee reactions to high potential identification. *Human Resource Management Journal,* 24: 159–175.

Gladwell, M., 2002. The talent myth. *The New Yorker,* 22, 28–33.

Groysberg, B., & Lee, L. E. 2008. The effect of colleague quality on top performance: The case of security analysts. *Journal of Organizational Behavior,* 29: 1123–1144.

Groysberg, B., Polzer, J.T., & Elfenbein, H. A., 2011. Too many cooks spoil the broth: How high-status individuals decrease group effectiveness. *Organization Science,* 22: 722–737.

Huselid, M. A. & Becker, B. E. 2011. Bridging micro and macro domains: Workforce differentiation and strategic human resource management. *Journal of Management,* 37: 421–428.

Kehoe, R. R., Rosikiewicz, B. L., & Tzabbar, D. 2017. Talent and teams. In D.G. Collings, K. Mellahi, & W. Cascio (Eds.), *The Oxford handbook of talent management.* Oxford, UK: Oxford University Press.

Kehoe, R. R., & Wright, P. 2013. The impact of high-performance huan resource practices on employees' attitudes and behaviors. *Journal of Management,* 39, 366–391.

Kim, K. Y., Pathak, S., & Werner, S. 2015. When do international human capital enhancing practices benefit the bottom line? An ability, motivation, and opportunity perspective. *Journal of International Business Studies,* 46: 784–805.

Kozlowski, S. W. J., & Klein, K. J. 2000. A multilevel approach to theory and research in organizations. In S. W. J. Kozlowski, & K. J. Klein, (Eds.), *Multilevel theory, research, and methods in organizations: Foundations, extensions, and new directions:* 3–90. San Francisco: Jossey-Bass.

Lepak, D. P., & Snell, S. A. 1999. The human resource architecture: Toward a theory of human capital allocation and development. *Academy of Management Review,* 24: 31–48.

Lepak, D. P., Takeuchi, R., & Swart, J. 2011. Aligning human capital with organizational needs. In A. Burton-Jones, & J. C. Spender (Eds.), *The Oxford handbook of human capital.* Oxford, UK: Oxford University Press.

Linden, G., & Teece, D. 2014. Managing expert talent. In. P. Sparrow, H. Scullion, & I. Tarique (Eds.) *Strategic talent management: Contemporary issues in international context:* 87–116. Cambridge, UK: Cambridge University Press.

Marescaux, E., De Winne, S., & Sels, L., 2013. HR practices and affective organizational commitment: (When) does HR differentiation pay off? *Human Resource Management Journal,* 23(4): 329–345.

McDonnell, A., Collings, D.G., Mellahi, K., & Schuler, R., 2017. Talent management: A systematic review and future prospects. *European Journal of International Management,* 11(1): 86–128.

Meyers, M. C., De Boeck, G., & Dries, N. 2017. Talent or not: Employee reactions to talent designations. In D.G. Collings, K. Mellahi, & W. Cascio (Eds.), *The Oxford handbook of talent management.* Oxford, UK: Oxford University Press.

Meyers, M. C., & Van Woerkom, M. 2014. The influence of underlying philosophies on talent management: Theory, implications for practice, and research agenda. *Journal of World Business,* 49(2): 192–203.

Meyers, M. C., Van Woerkom, M., Paauwe, J., & Dries, N. 2020. HR managers' talent philosophies: Prevalence and relationships with perceived talent management practices. *The International Journal of Human Resource Management,* 31(4): 562–588.

Minbaeva, D. M. 2013. Strategic HRM in building micro-foundations of organizational knowledge-based performance. *Human Resource Management Review,* 23(4): 378–390.

Minbaeva, D. M., & Collings, D. 2013. Seven myths of global talent management. *International Journal of Human Resource Management,* 24(9): 1762–1776.

Minbashian A. 2017. Within-Person Variability in performance. In D.G. Collings, K. Mellahi, & W. Cascio (Eds.), *The Oxford handbook of talent management.* Oxford, UK: Oxford University Press.

Nishii, L. H., Lepak, D. P., & Schneider, B. 2008. Employee attributions of the "why" of HR practices: Their effects on employee attitudes and behaviors, and customer satisfaction. *Personnel Psychology,* 61(3): 503–545.

O'Boyle, E. H., & Kroska, S. 2017. Star Performers. In D. G. Collings, K. Mellahi, & W. Cascio (Eds.), *The Oxford handbook of talent management.* Oxford, UK: Oxford University Press.

Pfeffer, J. 2001. Fighting the war for talent is hazardous to your organization's health. *Organizational Dynamics.* Working Paper 1687.

Ployhart, R., & Moliterno, T. 2011. Emergence of the human capital resource: A multilevel model. *Academy of Management Review,* 36(1): 127–150.

Ployhart, R. E., Nyberg, A. J., Reilly, G., & Maltarich, M. A., 2014. Human capital is dead; long live human capital resources! *Journal of Management,* 40(2): 371–398.

Rumelt, R. P. 1984. Towards a strategic theory of the firm. In R. B. Lamb (Ed.), *Competitive strategic management:* 566–570. Engelwood Cliffs, NJ: Prentice-Hall.

Schmidt, J. A., Pohler, D., & Willness, C. R. 2017. Strategic HR system differentiation between jobs: Effects on firm performance and employee outcomes. *Human Resource Management.* doi:doi.10.1002/hrm.21836.

Sparrow, P. R., 2007. Globalization of HR at function level: Four UK-based case studies of the international recruitment and selection process. *The International Journal of Human Resource Management,* 18(5): 845–867.

Stahl, G., Björkman, I., Farndale, E., Morris, S.S., Paauwe, J., Stiles, P., Trevor, J., & Wright, P. 2012. Six principles of effective global talent management. *MIT Sloan Management Review,* 53(2): 25–42.

Teece, D. J., Pisano, G., & Shuen, A. 1997. Dynamic capabilities and strategic management. *Strategic Management Journal,* 18: 509–533.

Thunnissen, M., Boselie, P., & Fruytier, B. 2013. A review of talent management: 'Infancy or adolescence?'. *The International Journal of Human Resource Management,* 24(9): 1744–1761.

Vaiman, V., Scullion, H., & Collings, D. G. 2012. Talent management decision making. *Management Decision,* 50: 925–941.

Weller, I., Hymer, C., Nyberg, A. J., & Ebert, J. 2018. How matching creates value: Cogs and wheels for human capital resources research. *Academy of Management Annals,* 13(1). doi:https://doi.org/10.5465/annals.2016.0117

Wright, P., & McMahan, G. 1992. Theoretical perspectives for strategic human resource management. *Journal of Management,* 18(2): 295–320.

Wright, P., & Nishii, L. 2007. *Strategic HRM and organizational behavior: Integrating multiple levels of analysis.* Working Paper 07-05. CAHRS Working Paper Series, Cornell University.

4

THE EMPLOYEE AND TALENT MANAGEMENT

An Interaction Framed Through Three Lenses: Work, Team, and the Organization

Karin A. King

Introduction

Talent management has become an established priority for organizations today such that leaders commonly report "talent" as their top priority (PricewaterhouseCoopers, 2017), and the human capital that the talented employees are seen to possess are considered of crucial relevance to business performance advantage (G. S. Becker, 2008). Organizations manage their talent requirements through human resource (HR) processes that involve the attraction, development, and retention of human capital (Collings & Mellahi, 2009) as a central component of business value creation (Sparrow & Makram, 2015). Today, talent management (TM) has become of central relevance to business strategy and HR management (Al Ariss, Cascio, & Paauwe, 2014; Collings & Mellahi, 2009; Vaiman & Collings, 2013). The nature of today's global economy as increasingly dependent on knowledge workers further emphasizes the demand for people who have portable knowledge and skills (Cascio & Aguinis, 2008; Collings, Mellahi, & Cascio, 2019) and who may choose to contribute their individual human capital resources to their current employer or may choose to take their individual knowledge and experience outside of their current organization. However, in practice, TM as a strategic priority, is often reported to be challenging, one that eludes management's full control (PricewaterhouseCoopers, 2017) and presents a persistent constraint (Cappelli, 2009). Yet others have questioned whether "talent management" is simply another phrase for very good people management (Lewis & Heckman, 2006). Talent remains a top priority that leaders are increasingly concerned about (Cheese, 2010).

TM presents challenges to businesses that aim to employ TM to enable their organization's performance in service of its business objectives. Challenges range from claims of scarcity and shortage, which are not always well evidenced (Cappelli, 2008), to implementation issues (Mellahi & Collings, 2010), such as the difficulties achieving consistency in talent practices even when global and local HR practices are consistently defined (Morris et al., 2009). There are persisting challenges even in the scope and definition of TM (Collings & Mellahi, 2009). The challenges of implementing Society for Human Resource Management (SHRM) and TM strategy in practice may in part explain why the empirical SHRM literature has largely focused on process (Wright & McMahan, 2011). The process orientation, however, has resulted in limited consideration of the employee as a recipient of organizational SHRM practices (Wright & McMahan, 2011) and as a participant of organizational TM (King, 2015a, 2016b). In choosing to join an organization, individuals make decisions not only about their careers. In career decisions, employees also make choices regarding how and where they will contribute the individual human capital resources that they hold. As employees perceive and experience TM practices in their organizations, what "talent" means to them and "how" they experience TM in their organizations is

DOI: 10.4324/9781315474687-4

increasingly relevant to their employment experience, even as organizations continue to pursue effectiveness in TM.

While the structural and theoretical foundations of TM continue to evolve, the employee continues to be a central actor in the organizational TM system (King, 2015a) through whose performance the organization aims to achieve competitive performance advantage. TM is expected to create value for the organization (Sparrow & Makram, 2015) through the contribution of talented employees, but to do so requires the practice of TM to function effectively. Literature has argued that not enough is yet known about the implementation of HR practices (L. Nishii & Wright, 2008) including TM (Cappelli & Keller, 2014) or the employee response to organizational talent practices (Björkman, Ehrnrooth, Mäkelä, Smale, & Sumelius, 2013; Dries, 2013; King, 2016b). For example, being identified as talent by one's organization, which has only relatively recently been explored in the literature (Björkman et al., 2013) but is expected to be perceived as being of significance to the employee (Meyers, De Boeck, & Dries, 2017; Smale et al., 2015). As the scholarly TM literature continues to develop, it has become clear that a deeper understanding of the talent system and its consequences for the employee is necessary, given that the employee is a central participant in the organization's talent practices (King, 2015a). Lack of sufficient consideration of employee views of TM practices in their organizations to date has been called a "serious omission" (Björkman et al., 2013, p. 196). It is the employee as a central actor in the organizational talent system that is the topic of focus in this chapter.

In the literature, there are multiple definitions of talent and correspondingly, a range of approaches for TM. Philosophies of TM vary by organization and may include an inclusive or exclusive approach or a combination of both (Meyers & van Woerkom, 2014). Adopting a more inclusive approach, all employees in the organization may be viewed as the company's "talent" (Swailes & Blackburn, 2016). Adopting an exclusive approach, only a sub-set of the workforce is identified as talent, based on some criteria established by the organization, and this approach is often adopted in large global multi-nationals that manage talent on a global basis (Stahl et al., 2012). In practice, many organizations today adopt a blend of both approaches. That is, while they invite the contribution of all employees in the workforce to deliver high performance for the business-specific strategic purpose, they may additionally require close management of a differentially identified group of employees known as talent or high-potential employees. For the purposes of providing a broad introduction to the topic of TM from the employee's perspective, this chapter adopts a hybrid view of talent as referring to both the wider workforce of employees in an organization and including segments of the workforce that can be identified as talent pools, in which employees hold skills or experience that are of specific relevance to an organization's business strategy and competitive advantage. This hybrid view is also consistent with the scholarly literature that provides many examples of conceptual and empirical work from both perspectives.

This chapter aims to present an introduction to the organizational TM system from the perspective of the employee's participation in the workforce. To do so, the chapter is presented in four parts. The first section introduces the three-lens framework as a guide for the reader in this chapter and argues that to be effective in practice, TM must also be considered from the perspective of the employee. In the second section, a review of the literature is presented in three parts, corresponding to the three lenses of the framework: the individual, team and organizational lenses on TM. In the third section, limitations of the extant literature are discussed, followed by recommendations for future research. The final section presents recommendations for leaders and business managers today, following which the chapter is concluded.

This chapter presents three main learning points. First, TM is implemented as an organizational system and the employee is a central participant in TM (Dries, 2013; King, 2015a). Second, the implications of the use of TM in organizations can be described from the employee's perspective through at least three lenses: the employee's work and career, their team and manager, and their views of the organization. Third, managers in business and human resources in organizations today can support effective TM by considering how TM practices impact the experience of their employees in the organization. The following section introduces the framework to the reader.

Employees and Talent Management in their Organization:
A Three-Lens Framework

Talent management (TM), as presented in the chapters that appear previously in this volume, is concerned with how organizations use human resources <HR> strategy and practices to attract, develop, and retain individuals who possess the specific human capital of interest to their organization, for service of the strategic priorities of the business (Tarique & Schuler, 2010). The aim of TM is to systematically identify those employees who are high-performing and demonstrate high-potential for future performance in the roles that are most crucial to business performance (Collings & Mellahi, 2009). Through the implementation of a systematic approach, these employees are often managed as a pool, and developed to assume increasingly senior roles in the organization (Collings & Mellahi, 2009).

This is achieved through a differentiated HR structure of systems and processes designed to specifically manage the talent pool(s) (Collings & Mellahi, 2009) as priority segments of the workforce (Boudreau & Ramstad, 2005). Where the approach to TM is highly selective and only a limited proportion of the population are included in the talent pool, the approach is known as exclusive talent management, whereas when the approach to talent identification considers the wider workforce to be the organization's talent pool, this is known as inclusive talent management (Stahl et al., 2012). In exclusive TM systems, employees may be identified as top talent, high-potentials, or even as star employees (Huselid, Beatty, & Becker, 2005). An exclusive talent philosophy is also known as a form of workforce differentiation (B. E. Becker, Huselid, & Beatty, 2009).

Organizations generally implement TM practices as part of a wider strategic HR and employee engagement strategy. In order to design and implement TM strategies and practices that are effective in supporting the organization to attract, develop, and retain the talent that it requires to compete and grow over time, it is valuable to consider how such practices may fit with overall HR bundles and how these practices influence the workforce.

When we consider an organization's use of TM as one component of an integrated bundle of strategic HR management practices, it becomes evident that the use of TM practices must be considered in at least three levels at which we would reasonably expect there to be an interaction between the employee's employment experiences and the use of TM. The levels are: 1) the individual level interactions, which are concerned with the employee's individual work; 2) the team level interactions, which are concerned with the employee's line manager and team; and 3) the organizational level interactions, which are concerned with the employee's views and experience of their organization.

Figure 4.1 presents a simple three-lens framework that categorizes the potential range of interactions of organizational TM system from the central view of the employee.

In what follows, we will consider how TM may interact with the employee experience in the workplace, through each of the three lenses.

Individual Level Lens: The Employee's Work and Employment Relationship

Attributions

Research indicates that when HRM practices are implemented, employees make observations about these practices (L. H. Nishii, Lepak, & Schneider, 2008) and in doing so, employees perceive HRM practices as signals from their organization (Höglund, 2012). Employees then interpret these signals as indicators of the relative importance of specific work behaviors and learn to identify what is valued in the organization (Guest & Conway, 2002; Guzzo & Noonan, 1994; Höglund, 2012) and therefore what to prioritize in or to achieve performance and the status associated with a high-performer. As TM is often a highly visible practice and one that is intended to demonstrate the organization values its people, employees are very likely to observe TM practices to some degree. Based on Sense-making Theory (Weick, 1995), whereby employees seek to interpret and make sense of the signals they perceive in their day-to-day work within organizations, when employees observe HRM practices in the workplace,

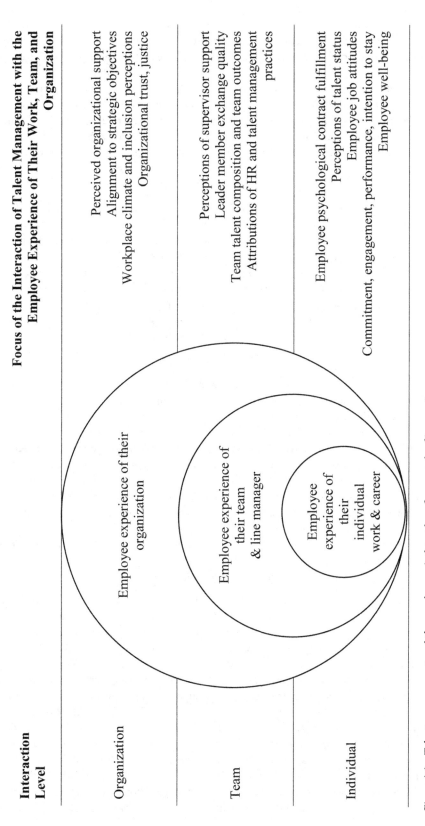

Focus of the Interaction of Talent Management with the Employee Experience of Their Work, Team, and Organization

Perceived organizational support
Alignment to strategic objectives
Workplace climate and inclusion perceptions
Organizational trust, justice

Perceptions of supervisor support
Leader member exchange quality
Team talent composition and team outcomes
Attributions of HR and talent management practices

Employee psychological contract fulfillment
Perceptions of talent status
Employee job attitudes
Commitment, engagement, performance, intention to stay
Employee well-being

Interaction Level

Organization

Employee experience of their organization

Team

Employee experience of their team & line manager

Individual

Employee experience of their individual work & career

Figure 4.1 Talent management and the employee: A three-lens framework of interaction

they infer the purpose of those practices and make what are known as attributions of "why" the organization undertakes these practices (L. H. Nishii et al., 2008). In the case of HR practices, research has shown that employees differentiate between at least two purposes for the use of HRM practices as either to control the employee or to support employees, or some combination of both (L. H. Nishii et al., 2008). In the case of TM, research that examines employee attributions of TM practices, that is, the "why" of TM has not yet been presented. However, given the nature of TM as an often-visible business strategic priority, researchers have argued that being included in one's organizational TM programs or identified as talent is likely to be associated with a promise of heightened exchange or investment in the employee's future career and development (King, 2016b).

Psychological Contract and Job Attitudes

The use of TM practices has been theorized to have consequences for the employee's individually-held psychological contract, that is, the views an employee develops regarding their obligations to their employer and their employer's obligations to them, within their overall employment relationship (Rousseau, 1989). These beliefs about obligations may be explicit or implicit (Rousseau, 1995) Specifically, as TM occurs within a context of social exchange in the workplace (Blau, 1964), the use of organizational TM practices is expected to be involved as one factor that shapes the employee's psychological contact, based on the premise that TM is a differentiated investment in specific employee's or pools of employees and therefore may signal increased exchanges between the employee and the organization. Psychological contracts have been shown to vary for specific groups of employees, such as high-potentials (Dries & De Gieter, 2014), which form part of the organization's talent pool, however, much more needs to be examined to closely understand the employee's psychological response to TM (Dries, 2013).

Research has shown that employees develop an awareness of their talent status (Meyers et al., 2017), and that talent status awareness is associated with positive employee attitudes (McDonnell, Collings, Mellahi, & Schuler, 2017). However, the literature argues that the relationship between employees identified as talented and their organizations, is not one of simple economic exchange (Thunnissen, Boselie, & Fruytier, 2013b), but that it involves expectations of enhanced exchange over time (King, 2016b). Research also theorizes that where information held by employees and the organization differs regarding the employee's status as talent or not, this asymmetry may create risk of psychological contract breach if perceived promises, for example of future career development, may be unfulfilled (Dries & De Gieter, 2014). Incongruence in talent status perception (whereby the assessment of the employee by the organization differs than the employee's self-assessment of talent status) mediates the relationship between the number of talent practices and contract fulfilment (Sonnenberg, van Zijderveld, & Brinks, 2014).

Perceived Talent Status

When an employee believes they have been identified by their organization as talent or included in a talent pool, this is known as perceived talent status (Dries & De Gieter, 2014). Employees who perceive talent status have been shown to hold several beneficial job attitudes moreso their peers who do not perceive talent status. Research has shown that TM practices do indeed influence job attitudes. For example, when an employee perceives they have been identified by their organization as "talent" or belong to their organization's talent pool, the employee is more likely to accept increasing performance demands, report increased commitment to building their competencies, support the strategic priorities of their employer in their daily work, and are less likely to leave their employment (Björkman et al., 2013).

Based on the signal of strategic value and differentiated identification of an employee as "talent", it has been theorized that talent status or perceived talent identification can be considered to be a crucial event in the employee organization relationship, defined as an event that can "suddenly and durably" change the nature of the employee-organization relationship (Ballinger & Rockmann, 2010, p. 373). Given the theorized influence of TM practices on the employee psychological contract, it is therefore not surprising that employees who perceive they have been identified by their organization as talented or identified as a member of the talent pool, are more likely to report they intend to stay with their organization than those who do not perceive they have been identified as talent. This opportunity for increased retention through using TM practices to identify and engage high-performing high-potential employees is an advantage for organizations that seek to retain their top talent for development and advancement to critical roles in future.

Talent Retention, Career Development, and Advancement Opportunities

Employees who perceive they have been identified by their organizations as talented, would reasonably expect to be provided with the additional resources and investment that status corresponds to in their specific organization (King, 2016b). While this investment, such as leadership development and mentoring, and developmental job assignments may vary by organization, some differentiated focus on the employee's development of their talent potential is a component of TM. Therefore, involvement in the talent pool is also a benefit to employees in their organization's investment in and focus on them and their career advancement.

Retention by the organization of its talent pool is a priority for most organizations today (Cappelli, 2008; Hausknecht, Rodda, & Howard, 2009) and research has shown that advancement opportunities is positively associated with retention of high-performers, and moreso than other employee groups (Hausknecht et al., 2009). While in practice, TM is linked with career progression, in empirical literature, more research is required to understand this increased exchange between the employee and their organization over time (King, 2015a, 2016b). Literature calls for a shift from the current focus of TM research primarily on talent retention (Thunnissen, Boselie, & Fruytier, 2013a) and on SHRM distal performance measures (Jiang, Lepak, Hu, & Baer, 2012) to more proximal outcomes (Boudreau & Ramstad, 2005; Boxall & Purcell, 2000). This focus on proximal outcomes may also help to shed light on possible unintended consequences of TM that have been highlighted in the literature. These include the exit of high-potential talent when in a dual-career couple (Petriglieri, 2018) and an increased sensitivity to employer investments when the employee is aware of their talent status compared to those who are not (Ehrnrooth et al., 2018). The second lens, the employee's view of their team and line manager, is considered in the next section.

Team Level Lens: The Employee's Team and Line Manager

At the team level, there are a number of interactions that are notable between the business's use of TM practices and the perceptions of employees within their teams and of their line managers. First, the supervisor is expected to play a significant role in TM given the supervisor's direct observation of performance daily (King, 2015a, 2016b). As line managers in today's organizations are increasingly responsible for HR practices that are increasingly devolved into the line rather than delivered directly by HR (Cappelli, 2013), the effectiveness of the line manager in performance of people management practices is increasingly important. Variation in line manager performance of people management activities has been shown to impact performance of the team (Mollick, 2012).

In the specific context of TM, line managers or supervisors are often the individual accountable for identification of talent and talent potential (King, 2016b), which is then discussed and reviewed by leadership in a two-step process of talent identification and assessment (Mäkelä, Björkman, & Ehrnrooth, 2010). Given the variability between planned HR practices and implemented HR practices (known as the "intended-actual gap") (L. Nishii & Wright, 2008), further research is needed to understand the influence of the line manager in motivating, engaging, and supporting talented employees and their teams.

Second, the nature of work in today's organizations is increasingly team-based and knowledge-based both of which have been shown to require considerable interaction with co-members of one's team in order to achieve high-performance. In the case of talent identified employees, little is known yet with regard to how team talent composition, that is, the presence and mix of talent identified and non-talent identified individuals within a given team affects the individual team member's motivation and performance or that of the overall team. What is clear is that the organization relies on employees voluntarily contributing their individual human capital resources in support of strategic priorities. As mentioned earlier, employees who believe they have been identified as talented by their organization are more likely to support their organization's strategic priorities and also more likely to stay (Björkman et al., 2013).

However it is not always clear to employees whether or not they have been identified as talent by their organization because organizations vary in their practice of disclosing talent status to employees or not. The often-vague approach to communication of talent status by organizations often appears opaque to employees and has been criticized as potentially detrimental to the employment relationship if TM practices are viewed as subjective, exclusive, or procedural unfair or unjust (Swailes, 2013b; Swailes & Blackburn, 2016; Swailes, Handley, & Rivers, 2016). Research indicates that only one-third of organizations today disclose talent assessments and ratings to their employees (Dries & De Gieter, 2014). Given the evidence that creating an inclusive culture in organizations contributes to performance and productivity as well as to the ability to attract talent (Nilsson & Per-Erik, 2012; L. H. Nishii, 2013), inadvertently creating a perceived exclusive culture through a non-transparent exclusive TM practice is a potential risk organizations must be aware of. Further, talent assessment practices or TM generally, may be perceived as being procedurally unjust (Swailes, 2013a, 2013b) if the criteria for inclusion in the talent pool are not well communicated, understood, or transparent.

The support of one's manager can also be seen as relevant to employees who experience TM or who are working in organizations that adopt TM practices. TM at its core involves the differentiation of individual employees and employee groups as "talent" or "talent pools" and is a dynamic process occurring over time rather than a single event (King, 2016b) and consequently, the line manager or supervisor is an important factor in TM (Asag-Gau & Dierendonck, 2011), whose support the employee may require to access resources for performance or development opportunities. In HRM, the direct supervisor has been argued to be the "missing link" as the central influence of the psychological contract as it develops and of PC fulfilment (McDermott, Conway, Rousseau, & Flood, 2013). Perceived supervisor support has been shown to moderate perceived organizational support and is positively associated with organizational commitment. Therefore, the extent to which talented employees perceive they are supported by their supervisors is also an important consideration. The third lens, the employee's view of their organization, is considered in the next section.

Organization Level Lens: The Employee's Organization

Development of Potential over Time

Organizations that use TM practices use various methods to assess the potential of employees (Dries & Pepermans, 2012) to develop skills and knowledge the organization will require in the future. This is the potential for the employee to advance to roles of increasing accountability (such as leadership positions) or roles of critical value to the business. Talent practices have been shown to mediate the skill-enhancing HRM practices that support overall human capital development for the firm (Höglund, 2012) and for its individual employees.

Performance and Organizational Value through Talent Management

Talent management is expected to create value for the organization as a differentiated management of specific segments or pools of the workforce identified as having potential for greater contribution to organizational performance (Collings & Mellahi, 2009) than other individual employees or workforce segments. The literature explains that there are four value-drivers of TM: value creation, value capture, value preservation, and value leverage (Sparrow & Makram, 2015). This is in part due to the expected enhanced alignment of talented employees to the business priorities and strategic goals, through the use of TM practices. Research has shown that indeed talent-identified employees do demonstrate greater support for the strategic priorities of their organizations (Björkman et al., 2013), however, further research is required to understand how this translates into the increased performance or value for the firm.

Perceived Organizational Support

In order to achieve competitive advantage through talent, organizations seek higher and competitive performance (Collings, 2014). To achieve this performance through the enhanced contribution of individual talented employees, the use of differentiated TM practices to provide additional support and management is warranted to achieve differentiated performance. From social exchange theory (Blau, 1964), we would expect that employees who perceive that heightened performance is expected of them may also reasonably expect additional support of their organization in exchange. We also know from psychological contract theory (Rousseau, 1989, 2011), that employees develop expectations about their implied contributions and rewards from their organizations. Talented employees may therefore expect to be provided with additional support by their organizations to deliver the heightened performance that they perceive is expected of them, however, the perceptions of employees as to their organizational support is not yet well examined.

A recent study has found that employees who have been designated as talent by their organizations, in an exclusive TM context, were significantly more likely to report that they feel supported by the organization (Gelens, Dries, Hofmans, & Pepermans, 2015). As being identified as talent by one's organization may be interpreted as a signal of support by the organization, other researchers call for consideration of potential unintended consequences of such signalling (Ehrnrooth et al., 2018). For example, there is some evidence that employees may struggle to manage with the challenges and demands of being identified talent (Petriglieri & Petriglieri, 2017). This highlights the need for greater examination of the role of organizational support in effective TM, to understand the influence of TM on employee well-being.

Organizational Climate

As mentioned earlier, organizations vary in their use of TM as an exclusive or inclusive practice (Stahl et al., 2012), such that only specifically identified individuals are seen as talent or alternatively, such that the whole workforce is understood to be the company's talent. Organizations have an opportunity to intentionally establish clear and consistent processes that support perceptions of procedural justice in TM and also to create an overall organizational climate that is supportive of talent, potential, development, and careers. Supportive climates have been shown to help both organizations and their employees to achieve high-performance and organizational commitment (L. H. Nishii, 2013; Ostroff, Kinicki, & Tamkins, 2003; Schneider, Ehrhart, & Macey, 2013) and improved customer service outcomes (Schulte, Ostroff, Shmulyian, & Kinicki, 2009). As a top stakeholder of TM, CEOs and their leadership teams are key actors in shaping TM (Boada-Cuerva, Trullen, & Valverde, 2019; King, 2015b) as a specific HR practice and can have a significant influence on how TM in undertaken in the firm and the climate that a strategic focus on talent may generate (King, 2016a).

In the previous sections of this chapter, organizational TM has been reviewed from the perspective of its interactions with the workforce and the perspective of the employee. A three-lens framework was introduced as a tool to structure the review of the range of interactions of organizational TM practices with the workforce. The following section, third in this chapter, presents a critical review of the TM literature from the perspective of the employee as a central actor. A summary overview of current knowledge and limitations is presented.

Limitations of the Current Literature and Opportunities for Future Research

As reviewed in the previous section, an organization's use of TM practices, as with any other HRM practice, inevitably has resulting implications for the workforce who experience the effects of the talent or HRM practices. The previous section has explored these interactions through a three-lens framework that represents the interaction of TM practices with the workforce at multiple levels. We have seen that the employee's experience of the overall climate of their workplace is impacted by HR practices, that an employee's experience of their work within a team and their perceived support of their line manager are also influenced by human resource practices. There is also evidence from research that perceived talent identification or perceived talent status also has influence on the employee's views of their individual careers and job attitudes.

As TM as a body of literature has only recently, albeit rapidly, emerged, there is much still to discover in theory development and in examining management practice. The TM literature requires further theoretical development and further empirical examination. As described, TM is positioned as a strategic endeavor of high importance to the organization and frequently (primarily in the exclusive model) involves a practice of differentiation of talent and potential for future career advancement. However, there is little yet known about how employees respond to talent identification processes or how perceived talent status influences the employee psychological contract or job attitudes. Lack of empirical insight as to the consequences of the organization's use of talent practices on their workforce and through the eyes of their employees presents a risk to organizations and may interfere with the organization's attempt to operationalise HR and TM practices effectively. Literature calls for increased individual level analysis of TM (Collings & Mellahi, 2009; Gelens, Dries, Hofmans, & Pepermans, 2013) to consider how TM responds to both organization and individual needs (Farndale, Pai, Sparrow, & Scullion, 2014) and as a relational construct (Al Ariss, Cascio, & Paauwe, 2014) beyond the primary process orientation currently.

The empirical examination of TM at each of these interaction levels as an organizational system is still emerging and requires further investigation. For example, the influence of team talent composition on team and individual level outcomes such as performance in support of innovative team work, has not been examined. Tensions continue to exist in the literature, such as how talent is defined and whether there is competitive value in adopting either exclusive or inclusive TM or some hybrid version of each. The current research is also limited in its consideration of cross-level interactions. For example, the influence of talent status awareness on the relationship between the employee and their leader and team and its influence on team-level work climate. Table 4.1 below, presents an overview of recommended future research themes, corresponding to each of the three lenses of interaction: the individual, the team, and the organization.

The following final section in this chapter briefly discusses how developing one's knowledge of TM and its influence on the workforce is important for business leaders and HR managers.

Talent Management and Today's Organizations

Both management practitioners and academic literature today recognize the potential value of talent and TM (Cappelli & Keller, 2014; INSEAD, Adecco, & HCLI, 2017; Stahl et al., 2012; Varma, 2005; Wright, Dunford, & Snell, 2001). TM by organizations today is expected to generate differentiated firm performance and competitive advantage outcomes through differentiated engagement and development of talented employees and their human capital. Consequently, understanding of the employee experience of TM through these three lenses is important. A critical understanding of the interaction of TM with the employee's experience of their work, their team and manager, and their views of the organization and future career opportunities is valuable if business leaders and HR practitioners are to effectively implement TM practices and systems to enable employee engagement. If effective, TM has the potential to foster engagement, to support an inclusive workplace, and to support employees to contribute actively as one of the central actors of the talent system.

This chapter has presented a three-lens framework that can be used by organizations to critically consider how their organizational TM strategy and practices can effectively support the attraction, engagement, development, and retention of talented employees who possess the human capital and potential required to create value and competitive advantage for the organization today and in the future. Opportunities exist to create and embed a climate supportive of talent and talent development through inclusive climate and while differentiating talent pools aligned with business strategic requirements for skills and workforce capability. Using the framework to examine how employees experience and respond to TM in their organizations, managers can further shape and design talent systems to best support employee experiences as active participants in TM.

Table 4.1 Future research opportunities in talent management

Level of study	Future research themes
Individual-level	• Talent status and employee job attitudes and behaviors • Employee psychological contract and the influence of talent management (TM) practices • Employee perceived talent status and its association with a range of job attitudes • Influence of TM practices on priority talent outcomes at the individual level (including innovation, performance, contribution of human capital) • TM as a relational construct and its influence on the employee-organization relationship • Employee attributions or beliefs as to why or for what purpose the organization undertakes TM and associated outcomes • Influence of talent organizational management practices on employee well-being
Team-level & line manager	• Role of line managers or supervisors in the day-to-day management of talent in the business • Influence of team talent composition on other individual team members and individual job attitudes (including engagement, commitment, work strain, inclusion, leader-member exchange) • Influence of team-based talent practices on employee perceptions of supervisor and organizational support
Organization or firm-level	• Influence of top management in TM effectiveness (including communication, decision making) • Influence of TM practices on organizational climate, including inclusion and diversity • Relationship between TM practices and firm-level outcomes (including workplace innovation, firm performance, corporate brand, employer brand, customer outcomes) • Investigation of the intended-actual gap in TM implementation (including estimations of cost, value, effectiveness, efficiency)
Cross level and multi-level	• Cross-level mechanisms by which TM creates competitive value through individual employee-level and team-level outcomes of priority interest (including contribution of human capital resources, proactive behaviors, problem solving, innovation, citizenship behaviors) • Cross-level investigation of the outcomes of TM practices at the individual, team, and firm level on a range of measures at each level (for example: individual human capital growth, team-based human capital development, firm level human capital growth) • Multi-level investigation of variance in TM outcomes relative to specified predictors of interest (such as the influence of line manager training in TM, use of exclusive versus inclusive talent philosophy, use of talent development programs)

Conclusion

This chapter has introduced talent management as an organizational system and has argued that the employee is a central actor in the talent system, whose perceptions of TM practices must be considered to conduct TM effectively in organizations today. A three-lens framework for considering the practice of TM and its interactions with the workforce is presented along with a review of the literature related to each of the three lenses: the individual, team, and organization. Adopting a hybrid view of TM, the chapter has considered how the implementation of TM practices in an organization may interact with the workforce and individual employee perceptions of their work today, their team and supervisor and their organization and future career. Finally, the chapter has argued that effective TM requires informed knowledge of the influence of TM on the employee and the wider workforce, and ongoing management of talent programs and practices by skilled HR managers and leaders in alignment with business requirements for talent.

TM continues to represent a promise of heightened organizational performance and competitive advantage through its people and their individual human capital resources. To resolve current implementation challenges and reach the expected value and advantage through talent, organizations are advised to examine how the use of TM practices fits with their overall HRM bundle of strategic people practices and to closely understand how their workforce and talented employees experience TM day to day in the organization in their work roles, teams, and interactions with their leaders, and over time in their developing careers.

References

Al Ariss, A., Cascio, W. F., & Paauwe, J. 2014. Talent management: Current theories and future research directions. *Journal of World Business,* 49(2): 173–179.

Asag-Gau, L., & Dierendonck, D. V. 2011. The impact of servant leadership on organizational commitment among the highly talented: The role of challenging work conditions and psychological empowerment. *European Journal of International Management,* 5(5): 463–483.

Ballinger, G. A., & Rockmann, K. W. 2010. Chutes versus ladders: Anchoring events and a punctuated-equilibrium perspective on social exchange relationships. *Academy of Management Review,* 35(3): 373–391.

Becker, B. E., Huselid, M. A., & Beatty, R. W. 2009. *The differentiated workforce: Transforming talent into strategic impact.* Cambridge, MA: Harvard Business Press.

Becker, G. S. 2008. Human capital. In E. David R. Henderson (Ed.), *The concise encyclopedia of economics.* Library of Economics and Liberty.

Björkman, I., Ehrnrooth, M., Mäkelä, K., Smale, A., & Sumelius, J. 2013. Talent or not? Employee reactions to talent identification. *Human Resource Management,* 52(2): 195–214.

Blau, P. M. 1964. *Exchange and power in social life.* New York, London: Wiley.

Boada-Cuerva, M., Trullen, J., & Valverde, M. 2019. Top management: The missing stakeholder in the HRM literature. *The International Journal of Human Resource Management,* 30(1): 63–95.

Boudreau, J. W., & Ramstad, P. M. 2005. Talentship, talent segmentation, and sustainability: A new HR decision science paradigm for a new strategy definition. *Human Resource Management,* 44(2): 129–136.

Boxall, P., & Purcell, J. 2000. Strategic human resource management: Where have we come from and where should we be going? *International Journal of Management Reviews,* 2(2): 183–203.

Cappelli, P. 2008. Talent management for the twenty-first century. *Harvard Business Review,* 86(3): 74–81.

Cappelli, P. 2009. A supply chain model for talent management. *People & Strategy,* 32(3): 4–7.

Cappelli, P. 2013. HR for neophytes. *Harvard Business Review,* 91(10): 25–27.

Cappelli, P., & Keller, J. 2014. Talent management: Conceptual approaches and practical challenges. *Annual Review of Organizational Psychology and Organizational Behavior,* 1(1): 305–331.

Cascio, W. F., & Aguinis, H. 2008. Staffing twenty-first-century organizations. *The Academy of Management Annals,* 2(1): 133–165.

Cheese, P. 2010. Talent management for a new era: What we have learned from the recession and what we need to focus on next. *Human Resource Management International Digest,* 18(3): 3–5.

Collings, D. G. 2014. The contribution of talent management to organization success, *The Wiley Blackwell handbook of the psychology of training, development, and performance improvement.* John Wiley & Sons, Ltd. pp. 247–260.

Collings, D. G., & Mellahi, K. 2009. Strategic talent management: A review and research agenda. *Human Resource Management Review,* 19(4): 304–313.

Collings, D. G., Mellahi, K., & Cascio, W. F. 2019. Global talent management and performance in multinational enterprises: A multilevel perspective. *Journal of Management,* 45(2): 540–566.

Dries, N. 2013. The psychology of talent management: A review and research agenda. *Human Resource Management Review,* 23(4): 272–285.

Dries, N., & De Gieter, S. 2014. Information asymmetry in high potential programs. *Personnel Review,* 43(1): 136–162.

Dries, N., & Pepermans, R. 2012. How to identify leadership potential: Development and testing of a consensus model. *Human Resource Management,* 51(3): 361–385.

Ehrnrooth, M., Björkman, I., Mäkelä, K., Smale, A., Sumelius, J., & Taimitarha, S. 2018. Talent responses to talent status awareness—Not a question of simple reciprocation. *Human Resource Management Journal,* 28(3): 443–461.

Farndale, E., Pai, A., Sparrow, P., & Scullion, H. 2014. Balancing individual and organizational goals in global talent management: A mutual-benefits perspective. *Journal of World Business,* 49(2): 204–214.

Gelens, J., Dries, N., Hofmans, J., & Pepermans, R. 2013. The role of perceived organizational justice in shaping the outcomes of talent management: A research agenda. *Human Resource Management Review,* 23(4): 341–353.

Gelens, J., Dries, N., Hofmans, J., & Pepermans, R. 2015. Affective commitment of employees designated as talent: Signalling perceived organizational support. *European Journal of International Management,* 9(1): 9–27.

Guest, D. E., & Conway, N. 2002. Communicating the psychological contract: An employer perspective. *Human Resource Management Journal,* 12(2): 22–38.

Guzzo, R. A., & Noonan, K. A. 1994. Human resource practices as communications and the psychological contract. *Human Resource Management,* 33(3): 447–462.

Hausknecht, J. P., Rodda, J., & Howard, M. J. 2009. Targeted employee retention: Performance-based and job-related differences in reported reasons for staying. *Human Resource Management,* 48(2): 269–288.

Höglund, M. 2012. Quid pro quo? Examining talent management through the lens of psychological contracts. *Personnel Review,* 41(2): 126–142.

Huselid, M. A., Beatty, R. W., & Becker, B. E. 2005. A players or A positions? *Harvard Business Review,* 83(12): 110–117.

INSEAD, Adecco, & HCLI. 2017. INSEAD Global Talent Competitiveness Index (GTCI) 2017: Talent and technology. In B. Lanvin, & P. Evans (Eds.): *INSEAD.*

Jiang, K., Lepak, D. P., Hu, J., & Baer, J. C. 2012. How does human resource management influence organizational outcomes? A meta-analytic investigation of mediating mechanisms. *Academy of Management Journal,* 55(6): 1264–1294.

King, K. A. 2015a. Global talent management: Introducing a strategic framework and multiple-actors model. *Journal of Global Mobility: The Home of Expatriate Management Research,* 3(3): 273–288.

King, K. A. 2015b. Sustained Value through Talent Management: A multi-stakeholder approach., *European Institute for Advanced Studies in Management (EIASM). 4th Workshop on Talent Management.* Valencia, Spain.

King, K. A. 2016a. The talent climate: Creating space for talent development through a strong talent system, *EIASM. European Institute for Advanced Studies in Management.* 5th workshop on talent management. Copenhagen, Denmark.

King, K. A. 2016b. The talent deal and journey: Understanding how employees respond to talent identification over time. *Employee Relations,* 38(1): 94–111.

Lewis, R. E., & Heckman, R. J. 2006. Talent management: A critical review. *Human Resource Management Review,* 16(2): 139–154.

Mäkelä, K., Björkman, I., & Ehrnrooth, M. 2010. How do MNCs establish their talent pools? Influences on individuals' likelihood of being labeled as talent. *Journal of World Business,* 45(2): 134–142.

McDermott, A. M., Conway, E., Rousseau, D. M., & Flood, P. C. 2013. Promoting effective psychological contracts through leadership: The missing link between HR strategy and performance. *Human Resource Management,* 52(2): 289–310.

McDonnell, A., Collings, D. G., Mellahi, K., & Schuler, R. 2017. Talent management: A systematic review and future prospects. *European Journal of International Management,* 11(1): 86–128.

Mellahi, K., & Collings, D. G. 2010. The barriers to effective global talent management: The example of corporate élites in MNEs. *Journal of World Business,* 45(2): 143–149.

Meyers, M. C., De Boeck, G., & Dries, N. 2017. Talent or not. In D. G. Collings, K. Mellahi, & W. F. Cascio (Eds.), *The Oxford handbook of talent management.* Oxford UK: Oxford University Press.

Meyers, M. C., & van Woerkom, M. 2014. The influence of underlying philosophies on talent management: Theory, implications for practice, and research agenda. *Journal of World Business,* 49(2): 192–203.

Mollick, E. 2012. People and process, suits and innovators: The role of individuals in firm performance. *Strategic Management Journal,* 33(9): 1001–1015.

Morris, S. S., Wright, P. M., Trevor, J., Stiles, P., Stahl, G. K., Snell, S., Paauwe, J., & Farndale, E. 2009. Global challenges to replicating HR: The role of people, processes, and systems. *Human Resource Management,* 48(6): 973–995.

Nilsson, S., & Per-Erik, E. 2012. Employability and talent management: Challenges for HRD practices. *European Journal of Training and Development,* 36(1): 26–45.

Nishii, L. H. 2013. The benefits of climate for inclusion for gender-diverse groups. *Academy of Management Journal,* 56(6): 1754–1774.

Nishii, L. H., Lepak, D. P., & Schneider, B. 2008. Employee attributions of the "why" of hr practices: Their effects on employee attitudes and behaviors, and customer satisfaction. *Personnel Psychology,* 61(3): 503–545.

Nishii, L. H., & Wright, P. M. 2008. Variability within organizations: Implications for strategic human resources management. In D. B. Smith (Ed.), *LEA's organization and management series. The people make the place: Dynamic linkages between individuals and organizations* (p. 225–248). Taylor & Francis Group/Lawrence Erlbaum Associate.

Ostroff, C., Kinicki, A. J., & Tamkins, M. M. 2003. Organizational culture and climate. *Handbook of Psychology.* John Wiley & Sons, Inc.

Petriglieri, J. 2018. Talent management and the dual-career couple. *Harvard Business Review,* 96(3): 106–113.

Petriglieri, J., & Petriglieri, G. 2017. The talent curse: Interaction. *Harvard Business Review,* 95(4): 19–19.

PricewaterhouseCoopers. 2017. *PricewaterhouseCoopers CEO survey.* PricewaterhouseCoopers, Inc.

Rousseau, D. M. 1989. Psychological and implied contracts in organizations. *Employee Responsibilities and Rights Journal,* 2(2): 121–139.

Rousseau, D. M. 1995. *Psychological contracts in organizations: Understanding written and unwritten agreements.* Thousand Oaks, CA: SAGE Publications.

Rousseau, D. M. 2011. The individual–organization relationship: The psychological contract. *APA handbook of industrial and organizational psychology, Vol 3: Maintaining, expanding, and contracting the organization,* pp. 191–220. Washington, DC: American Psychological Association.

Schneider, B., Ehrhart, M. G., & Macey, W. H. 2013. Organizational climate and culture. *Annual Review of Psychology,* 64(1): 361–388.

Schulte, M., Ostroff, C., Shmulyian, S., & Kinicki, A. 2009. Organizational climate configurations: Relationships to collective attitudes, customer satisfaction, and financial performance. *Journal of Applied Psychology,* 94(3): 618–634.

Smale, A., Ehrnrooth, M., Björkman, I., Mäkelä, K., Sumelius, J., & Taimitarha, S. 2015. Letting the chosen ones know: The psychological effects of talent status self-awareness. *Academy of Management Proceedings,* 2015(1): 16195.

Sonnenberg, M., van Zijderveld, V., & Brinks, M. 2014. The role of talent-perception incongruence in effective talent management. *Journal of World Business,* 49(2): 272–280.

Sparrow, P. R., & Makram, H. 2015. What is the value of talent management? Building value-driven processes within a talent management architecture. *Human Resource Management Review,* 25(3): 249–263.

Stahl, G. K., Björkman, I., Farndale, E., Morris, S. S., Paauwe, J., & Stiles, P. 2012. Six principles of effective global talent management. *MIT Sloan Management Review,* 53(2): 25–32.

Swailes, S. 2013a. The ethics of talent management. *Business Ethics: A European Review,* 22(1): 32–46.

Swailes, S. 2013b. Troubling some assumptions: A response to "The role of perceived organizational justice in shaping the outcomes of talent management: A research agenda". *Human Resource Management Review,* 23(4): 354–356.

Swailes, S., & Blackburn, M. 2016. Employee reactions to talent pool membership. *Employee Relations,* 38(1): 112–128.

Swailes, S., Handley, J., & Rivers, L. 2016. *Talent management: Critical perspectives.* Palgrave.

Tarique, I., & Schuler, R. S. 2010. Global talent management: Literature review, integrative framework, and suggestions for further research. *Journal of World Business,* 45(2): 122–133.

Thunnissen, M., Boselie, P., & Fruytier, B. 2013a. A review of talent management: 'Infancy or adolescence?'. *The International Journal of Human Resource Management,* 24(9): 1744–1761.

Thunnissen, M., Boselie, P., & Fruytier, B. 2013b. Talent management and the relevance of context: Towards a pluralistic approach. *Human Resource Management Review,* 23(4): 326–336.

Vaiman, V., & Collings, D. G. 2013. Talent management: Advancing the field. *The International Journal of Human Resource Management,* 24(9): 1737–1743.

Varma, A. 2005. Mark A. Huselid, Brian E. Becker, and Richard W. Beatty. The workforce scorecard: Managing human capital to execute strategy. *Human Resource Management,* 44(3): 359–361.

Weick, K. E. 1995. *Sensemaking in organizations (foundations for organizational science).* Thousands Oaks: Sage Publications Inc.

Wright, P. M., Dunford, B. B., & Snell, S. A. 2001. Human resources and the resource based view of the firm. *Journal of Management,* 27(6): 701–721.

Wright, P. M., & McMahan, G. C. 2011. Exploring human capital: Putting 'human' back into strategic human resource management. *Human Resource Management Journal,* 21(2): 93–104.

5

TALENT MANAGEMENT

From Resource-Based View to Dynamic Capabilities

Kushal Sharma

The Need for Talent Management

During the last decade, talent management (TM) has become a key management issue for business leaders (Collings, Mellahi, & Cascio, 2018; Gallardo-Gallardo et al., 2020; Groysberg & Connolly, 2015; King & Vaiman, 2019; Thunnissen, Boselie, & Fruytier, 2013). The interest in TM spiked after McKinsey consultants came up with the idea in the 1990s that organizations faced imminent shortage of talent, especially for filling positions of strategic importance (Mellahi & Collings, 2010; Minbaeva & Collings, 2013). The implication was that shortages emanating from multifarious reasons such as globalization, ageing workforce, and poaching (Preece, Iles, & Jones, 2013) pitted organizations against each other in a "war for talent" (Festing, Schäfer, & Scullion, 2013).

Underlying the perceived need to engage in this "war" is the assumption that possession of superior talent enables an organization to perform better than its competitors, i.e., achieve sustainable competitive advantage (SCA). Some implicit assumptions are that TM produces positive reactions among talented employees, such as higher engagement, retention, and other positive work attitudes (De Boeck, Meyers, & Dries, 2018). Some authors (e.g., Huselid, Beatty, & Becker, 2005; Morris, Snell, & Björkman, 2016) have suggested that firms should use *differentiated human resource architecture* to focus on those employees who can contribute more towards the success of an organization.

Existing Conceptualization of Talent and Talent Management

In an organizational context, the term *talent* refers to the quality of labor (Minbaeva & Collings, 2013) and *talent* is defined as "people who make valuable contributions to organizational objectives" (Morris et al., 2016: 724), the collection of those "exhibiting future leadership potential" (Mäkelä, Björkman, & Ehrnrooth, 2010: 134); "key individuals without whom the company would not operate so effectively" (Valverde, Scullion, & Ryan, 2013: 1842); and individuals who are a part of the "human capital in an organization that is both valuable and unique" (Vos & Dries, 2013: 1818). Others have defined talent as individuals who, in addition to being competent in terms of knowledge and skill, are "committed, motivated, loyal and closely involved with the company" (Valverde et al., 2013: 1843–1844); "individuals who can make a difference to organisational performance either through their immediate contribution or, in the longer-term, by demonstrating the highest levels of potential" (CIPD, 2014); and "those employees who are high performing and continuously improving within their current position...are mobile and have the potential and the willingness for further growth in other key positions" (Mäkelä et al., 2010: 137). Some authors claim that creativity (Tansley,

DOI: 10.4324/9781315474687-5

2011) and social capital – the ability to develop and maintain networks and relationships (McDonnell & Collings, 2011) – also are elements of talent.

From this short overview of how different scholars define talent, it is evident that definitions of talent are not fixed and that they may vary from organization to organization (Swailes, 2013). In short, there is no agreed upon definition of what constitutes talent. However, across all the definitions presented above, a common understanding appears to be that only a minority who differentially contribute to organizational success are talents (Tansley, 2011; Swailes, 2013). This minority is supposedly a "competitive weapon" (Mellahi & Collings, 2010: 143) or a source of competitive advantage (Oltra & Vivas-López, 2013). This idea that the focus on a selected few individuals produces the greatest benefits for an organization is the mainstream, exclusive view of talent.

Lewis and Heckman (2006) report that there are three distinct viewpoints of TM. The first perspective is simply a rebranding of traditional HR and involves the same activities such as recruitment and selection, development, and succession planning. The only differences between traditional HR management and TM from this perspective is that in TM, activities are carried out faster through the use of technology or outsourcing and that the scope of HR is expanded across the whole organization instead of being limited to a single unit. The second perspective is focused on the development of talent pools; emphasis is on finding internal talent rather than external. This perspective is closely linked with succession planning or HR planning. The third perspective has two variations: either consider that the goal of TM is to help every employee in the organization achieve high-performance, or manage highly talented employees selectively – this might sometimes involve hiring and differentially rewarding competent employees regardless of their roles or organization's requirements. Except that the last variation that is exclusive and elitist, all other perspectives summarized by Lewis and Heckman (2006) might be considered as variants of the inclusive school of thought identified by Festing et al. (2013).

To the three perspectives identified by Lewis and Heckman (2006), Collings and Mellahi (2009) add a fourth perspective that focuses on identifying key positions that can positively contribute towards SCA of the firm. This perspective is exclusive since it advocates that the focus of TM should be on a selected few positions and that the process of TM should start by identifying key positions rather than talented individuals. These authors note that the key positions are not strictly limited to the top positions and may vary between operating units. From their perspective, TM also involves the development of a "differentiated human resource architecture" so that the process of hiring competent candidates to key positions and obtaining commitment from such candidates faces is facilitated (Collings & Mellahi, 2009: 305). In their later work, Mellahi and Collings (2010) argue that TM systems that are grounded in identification of key positions should strive to assign "A performers" (Huselid et al., 2005) to such positions.

From the brief discussion of the literature on TM above, it is clear that regardless of whether scholars focus on strategic positions or on individuals who occupy those positions, advocates of TM conceptualize talent as a resource that can assist an organization to achieve SCA. Conceptualization of talent as a potential resource for generating SCA is largely influenced by Barney's (1991) seminal paper on resource-based view (RBV) of the firm and by subsequent ideas developed regarding RBV.

Resource-based View (RBV) of Talent

Rooted in the ideas of Penrose (1959) and Chandler (1977), RBV conceptualizes an organization as "a unique bundle of resources" and focuses on what kind of resources a firm should possess to acquire SCA (Santos & Eisenhardt, 2005) and consequently above-average financial performance (Becker & Huselid, 2006). By shifting the emphasis from external environmental factors to internal firm characteristics as sources of SCA, RBV legitimized the claim of HR practitioners that human resource has the potential to be a source of SCA (Wright, Dunford, & Snell, 2001). RBV is the most popular theory both for theory-building and empirical research in the field of Strategic Human

Resource Management (SHRM) (Wright et al., 2001). Since TM borrows many of its ideas from SHRM (Lewis & Heckman, 2006), it is of little surprise that TM should continue to be governed by the same ideas of RBV.

While laying down the main ideas of RBV, Barney (1991) notes that all aspects of a firm's resources are not strategically relevant. Researchers (e.g, Barney, 1991; Boxall, 1996; Kraaijenbrink, Spender, & Groen, 2010) add that to contribute towards achieving SCA, resources must be valuable, rare, inimitable, and nonsubstitutable (VRIN). Building on this idea, some researchers (e.g, Huselid et al., 2005) advocate for the idea of "differentiated human resource architecture" through which employees who contribute more towards a firm's success are rewarded more as compared to the employees who contribute less. The differentiated human resource architecture approach assumes that not all employees of an organization will be high-performers. Such an approach can be considered an exclusive form of TM. Huselid et al. (2005) recommend that organizations should fill important strategic positions with the best performers (A players) and support positions with "good" performers (B players). These authors further suggest that positions that do not add value should be eliminated along with the "non-performing" employees (C players) who occupy such positions. In practice, larger organizations tend to take a more exclusive view of talent than smaller organizations (Meyers et al., 2019).

In HR and TM literature, many scholars echo the idea that different resources (positions or employees) contribute differentially and thus should be treated differently. Kraaijenbrink et al. (2009) are of the opinion that typologies are needed to classify and differentiate between resources based on how they contribute to an organization's SCA. Popular typologies in HR and related literature often stem from Barney's (1991) work. For example, Lewis and Heckman (2006) categorize talent based on the interaction between nonsubstitutability and value, while Lepak and Snell (2002) classify employment modes on the basis of uniqueness (degree of rareness) and value.

Limitations of the Resource-based View

While typologies based on or inspired by Barney's (1991) VRIN resources – for example, Lepak and Snell's (2002) framework, Lewis and Heckman's (2006) talent typology, Kang and Snell's (2009) intellectual capital architecture – arepractically applicable tools for managing talent, they suffer from the following limitations:

- Treatment of talent devoid of larger context,
- RBV scholars (Barney, 1991; Barney, Ketchen, & Wright, 2011) divide a firm's resources into three categories: physical capital, human capital, and organizational capital. Of particular interest to human resource and talent scholars is the human capital resource, which comprises "training, experience, judgment, intelligence, relationships, and insight of *individual* managers and workers in a firm" (Barney, 1991: 101, italics original). RBV literature is criticized for overemphasizing the possession of individual resources and underemphasizing the important role of bundling resources and of human involvement in value creation (Kraaijenbrink et al., 2010). In the HR literature, there is an unwarranted tendency to view organizational performance as the simple aggregation of individual performance (Wright et al., 2001). Presented as a more focused approach than HRM, TM runs the risk of being too myopic a focus on individuals. In contemporary discussions on TM, the original emphasis by Barney (1991) on the term "individual" is pushed to such extreme that the mainstream view often understands talent as "nurtured by the competences of (especially relevant) single individuals" (Oltra & Vivas-López, 2013: 1857) and is discussed devoid of the larger context in which it exists. Such discussions are problematic because how employees perceive TM practices depends on their organizational context. For example, Asplund (2019) finds that TM might produce less favorable outcomes among employees in the education sector. Incompatibility between TM and the conceptualization of talent as a VRIN resource.

RBV has two foundational assumptions: 1) firms within an industry possess heterogeneous resources, and 2) those resources are not perfectly transferable across firms (Barney, 1991). Owing to this lack of mobility, it is assumed that heterogeneity can be sustained over time and thus can contribute towards SCA of a firm. However, unlike other resources, talent has agency of its own. Talent *has* mobility and cannot be *owned* by a firm in the material sense of ownership. So talent violates RBV's basic assumption of immobility as a precondition for SCA. To minimize the risk of losing top talent, firms might try to make their star contributors as unique as possible. The most obvious option is to convince talents to acquire firm-specific skills – such skills not only make talent unique and thus inimitable but also achieve the purpose of immobility. The anticipated result is that since firm-specific skills are not transferable across firms, competitors cannot derive significant benefits from acquiring such unique talents and thus talent is retained.

However, such a strategy might have a downside: although firms may be able to derive SCA, uniqueness and inimitability derived from firm-specific skills might result in opportunistic behavior from individuals who possess such skills (Schilling & Steensma, 2002). Accumulating firm-specific knowledge has its risks and the link between such knowledge and better financial performance is unclear (Wang et al., 2013). Firms "get stuck" with such individuals and they are unable to innovate or to adapt to changes in the environment. Such resources produce *core rigidities* – resources that were once valuable but have become obsolete and "inhibit development, generate inertia, and stifle innovation" (Ambrosini & Bowman, 2009: 32).

Moreover, there still is a possibility that firms might lose their talents despite the barriers they create. Although it is often argued that talent is not perfectly mobile owing to idiosyncratic skills, talent does not need to be perfectly mobile to be taken away from the focal firm. For example, even if competitors cannot make use of a talent's firm-specific skills, it would be worthwhile just to create a setback for the focal firm by luring away its key talent and depriving it of its most valuable resource (see Sturman, Walsh, & Cheramie, 2007). Or a talent might decide to leave the firm to start her own entrepreneurial venture. The point is that no matter how firm-specific the skills, a firm cannot be absolutely certain of retaining its talents. Hence, it is imperative that an effective TM system should account for such events and plan accordingly for the possibility that its key talents might leave. In other words, if it is to function smoothly, a TM system must not be bound by resource specificity. The first step is the acknowledgment that talent is mobile and that the attempt to retain top talent *at any cost* is an unjustified obsession.

Mobility of talent necessitates that firms prepare for the possibility that their top talent might leave. Such preparedness naturally involves finding a replacement in the event that a talent is lost so that the system continues to function smoothly. Such a scenario is incompatible with the assertion that talent is nonsubstitutable. It has been argued that "executive level human capital" – senior position holders in an organization – possess complex skills and hard-to-imitate, unique, and tacit knowledge often accumulated from learning in the course of a long career (Sturman et al., 2007). Executives possessing such knowledge and skills "while *replaceable*, cannot be duplicated" (292, italics added). The point here is that since it is replaceable, talent fails the test of nonsubstitutability. Even though the replacement talent might not have the exact, complex skills as the former talent, individuals need to be replaced if a firm is to operate efficiently.

In the context of organizations, all employees are required to perform a set of predefined activities depending upon their position in the organization. Such activities require some form of training – either formal or informal. As per Pfeffer (2001), individuals considered *talent* in performing such activities develop such skills not due to some kind of innate abilities but from training. This applies especially to managerial talent as managerial training is largely formalized and disseminated through structured education and training.

Finally, rare talents are no longer rare in the long run. Over time, skills considered rare get formalized and widely disseminated, especially if firms deem that they are useful and are willing to provide high compensation to talents with such skills. When other individuals observe that a certain individual (or a few individuals) possess some skills by virtue of which they command higher rents, they too become interested in developing such skills. Since skills are not uniquely and inherently attached to individuals, any reasonably competent person can copy such skills with proper training. In short, talent is definitely not inimitable and it is also not rare in the long run.

Misidentification of the Source of SCA

One of the accepted premises in TM is that talent is a potential source of SCA and debates are centered on pinpointing the exact source of SCA – the talents themselves, the positions they hold, or the skills they possess. Some argue that talents (individuals) produce SCA because competitors do not possess such talents. This argument is easily refuted since the focal firm's advantage is lost as soon as competitors are able to lure away the talent. Others argue that certain positions create SCA (e.g., Mellahi & Collings, 2010). However, SCA stems from the inability of competitors (both current and potential) to duplicate a focal firm's strategy (Barney, 1991). So the argument that positions create SCA is not very convincing as each position entails certain duties and responsibilities that competitors can easily replicate into their own structures when they identify such positions of advantage. Hence, as they are imitable, positions cannot be a source of SCA.

A less discussed third view could be that a certain set of unique skills create SCA. This assertion is also flawed because, as discussed earlier, individuals do not have inherent unique skills. Skills have to be developed through learning, engaging in training, experience, etc. So if one individual can develop a set of skills, another individual can more or less replicate such skills with proper training and development. Unless they are very idiosyncratic so as to be unusable by competitors, even skills cannot be a source of SCA. Especially in the case of managerial talent, highly idiosyncratic firm-specific skills appear unlikely.

RBV 2.0: Dynamic Capability Perspective as an Extension to RBV

The limitations of RBV pointed out in section 2 imply that talents, positions, and skills cannot be sources of SCA because RBV discusses talent without taking the broader context into account, because talent might be substituted, and because organizational positions as well as skills can be imitated. The counterargument to such an assertion is that talents, positions, and skills can be sources of SCA: talents can produce SCA if they continuously engage in training and development to gain new competencies; positions can produce SCA if new positions are continuously created; and skills can produce SCA if new skills are continuously invented and developed. The problem is that the current TM literature adopts a static RBV perspective. RBV explains how a firm can gain SCA only in equilibrium conditions and as such, it is ill-equipped to explain how the existing resource base of a firm can be refreshed in dynamic environments (Ambrosini & Bowman, 2009). RBV is inadequate in unpredictable environments characterized by emergence of new markets, new technologies, and drastic change in the value of resources (Kraaijenbrink et al., 2010). This limitation of RBV can be overcome by adopting a dynamic capabilities perspective.

Built upon Nelson & Winter's (1982) ideas of how routines shape and constrain firm-responses to changing environments (Ambrosini & Bowman, 2009), dynamic capabilities are defined as a firm's "ability to integrate, build, and reconfigure internal and external competences to address rapidly changing environments" (Teece, Pisano, & Shuen, 1997: 516). While both dynamic capabilities and RBV share similar assumptions, the major difference between the two is that while RBV is a static view, the dynamic capabilities view helps to explain how SCA is created through the evolution of a firm's resource base (Ambrosini & Bowman, 2009). Dynamic capabilities are "the organizational and strategic routines by which firms achieve new resource reconfigurations as markets emerge, collide, split, evolve, and die" (Eisenhardt & Martin, 2000: 1107). Rather than solely focus on the individual, dynamic capabilities perspective focuses on an organization's capability to utilize its human capital (Collings et al., 2018). This perspective has been adopted in studies of human capital development and TM in large and global organizations (e.g., Collings et al., 2018; Griffith & Harvey, 2001; Teece, 2007).

Impetus for the Push towards Dynamism

Criticism is directed towards TM primarily for being obsessed with a small closed group of elites and for ignoring the majority of employees. From an ethical and moral standpoint, acknowledgement that some individuals are more valuable than others might be controversial (Thunnissen et al., 2013). Critics of the approach of treating a selected few as talents argue that labeling a selected few as stars demotivates the majority, causing them to perform below their potential (e.g., Pfeffer, 2001). Another downside of differential treatment of a selected few employees is that those labeled "talent" might experience marginalization and resentment from co-workers who envy them for being "the brightest and the best" (Tansley, 2011: 270).

The above-mentioned problems arise largely because TM adopts a static view that understands talent as an enduring and unchanging quality of individuals. Not only is such conceptualization ethically unsound but it also misrepresents reality. Due to the static conceptualization of talent, extant TM literature assumes that *talents* will indefinitely be valuable and unique. However, this is not necessarily true. Over time, skills can become obsolete due to several reasons, e.g., change in technology. Or it is also possible that skills that were once rare are no longer rare because of change in workforce. Another possibility is that individuals not included in the talent pool can develop skills by themselves or with the help of their organizations to become talents.

Static view of talent might be one of the main reasons why exclusive TM is seen as being an unfair system and one that works at the peril of antagonizing the majority of employees. To gain acceptance as a legitimate process of managing talented employees, TM needs to be grounded on strong norms of fairness. This mindset – that there can and will be shifts in an organization's talent pool – might also serve the additional purpose of discouraging complacency from those labeled *talent* because they will have to continually upgrade their skills to remain a part of the talent pool.

Dynamic Capability and Its Applicability to TM

To address the issues of fairness discussed above and to meet the challenges of the changing business environment, organizations need to consider the following two types of dynamism:

Dynamism of Individuals

Communicating TM as a process that allows for movement of individuals in and out of talent pools is ethically justifiable and has better chances of acceptance by organizational members as it provides opportunities to those not initially included in the talent pool to join it later through hard work. As opposed to closed group of elites, talent pools can then be seen as accessible groups open to all individuals provided that they meet certain criteria. Hence it is likely that those not included in the talent pool will not only accept the system but also be willing to exert more effort to be a part of the talent pool. For this, talent needs to be defined not as inherent quality of individuals but as set of skills that can be developed through learning and refined through training and experience. Krishnan & Scullion (2017) propose, in the context of small and medium enterprises, that talent is dynamic and context-specific. This idea of dynamism equally applies to large and multinational organizations where the context plays an important role in determining organizational outcomes.

Dynamism of the Environment

Environment, the external context within which an organization operates, might be constantly changing with regards to governmental policies, political climate, and broader economic conditions. Dynamism of the external environment necessitates organizations to make changes to their existing human resource. However, changes of large magnitude are difficult to achieve mainly because organizations are incapacitated by their existing human resource architecture (Wright et al., 2001). This is precisely why a dynamic conceptualization of talent is needed as opposed to the static view that talent is constant. To achieve change, organizations might need to release some of their existing talent and acquire new talent (Wright et al., 2001). Research on boundaryless careers has revealed that a moderate levels of turnover is good for organizations pursuing exploratory knowledge because turnover allows inflow of new knowledge as well as diversity of knowledge and attitudes (Lazarova & Taylor, 2009). In support of this, some practitioners (see Aghina, De Jong, & Simon, 2011: 5) agree that releasing poor performers allows a firm to import "fresh talent and ideas".

Barriers to the Transition from RBV to Dynamic Capabilities

The preceding discussion points out some features of the dynamic capabilities and argues that it is a more rational and realistic representation of the environment within which an organization operates. Although it appears logical that TM should adopt a dynamic perspective, there are some barriers that contribute towards the perseverance of a static view of talent. In other words, some challenges prohibit a smooth transition from RBV to a dynamic capabilities perspective of TM. As discussed below, perhaps the most important one is the confusion regarding the concept of dynamic capability.

Confusion Surrounding Dynamic Capability

Barney (1991) argues that anything—whether it is an asset, a capability, or a process—that contributes towards increasing a firm's effectiveness and efficiency is a resource. In other words, RBV uses the terms resources and capabilities interchangeably to refer to a firm's tangible and intangible assets (Becker & Huselid, 2006). However, some scholars distinguish capability from resource and assert that capability serves as "intermediate goods" (Amit & Schoemaker, 1993: 35) that interacts with resources of a firm to make them more productive (Becker & Huselid, 2006). Penrose asserts that possession of resources does not create value; value creation depends on how those resources are deployed (Ambrosini & Bowman, 2009). Particularly regarding talents, firms need to have both talents (resource) as well the capability to manage them. Both are necessary; one without the other might not be sufficient to create SCA (Coff, 1999). This is the guiding principle behind conceptualization of capabilities as different from resources.

In line with Ambrosini & Bowman (2009: 33), this chapter defines dynamic capability as intentional organizational efforts to change its resource base. As defined here, dynamic capabilities are not resources but *repeatable processes* that interact with the existing resource base (Ambrosini & Bowman, 2009) to produce new resources. Such processes enable organizations to alter "their routines, services, products, and even markets over time" (Wright et al., 2001: 712). The term *dynamic* does not refer to capabilities that can change or evolve over time; rather, dynamic capabilities are quite stable (Ambrosini & Bowman, 2009).

Confusion Regarding the Source of Dynamism

Ambrosini and Bowman (2009: 30, 34) argue that the term *dynamic* refers to the environment, and "the dynamism does not consist in either the dynamic capability or the resource base". This chapter agrees with these authors that dynamic capabilities are stable processes but disagrees on the point about the static nature of the resource base. Ambrosini and Bowman (2009) might have considered only inanimate resources when they argued that the resource base is not dynamic. However, in the context of TM, human resources has agency and talents can upgrade their knowledge, skills, and competencies. Hence, this chapter conceptualizes talents not as passive receivers upon which organizational processes act to bring about changes but as a dynamic resource base that actively acts on itself as well as on organizational processes to produce change.

Confusion Regarding the Relationship between Dynamism and SCA

Although TM helps in producing SCA, it does not directly contribute to SCA. The idea of an indirect effect of the process on SCA is in line with Eisenhardt and Martin's (2000) assertion that the potential for SCA does not lie in dynamic capability itself but in the resource configurations it creates. Due to the general value-creating strategies to "acquire and shed resources, integrate them together, and recombine them" (Eisenhardt & Martin, 2000: 1107), this is a broad process that can be replicated in different organizations. Findings that multinational companies (MNCs) adopt more sophisticated and similar styles for managing talents (e.g., Mäkelä et al., 2010) further buttress the point that conceptualization of TM as a replicable process is a sensible approach.

The Practitioner-academic Divide

The gap between research and practice, especially in management science, is an ongoing issue, and TM as a field is not an exception. While one might expect that a field such as TM that traces its origins in the practitioner literature of the 1990s (e.g., Chambers, Foulton, Handfield-Jones, Hankin, & Michaels, 1998) would be closer to and reflect the workings of real organizations, the dearth of empirical studies has hindered its progress. This prevents academics from having a clear and accurate picture of the field. As an example, from a practical standpoint it appears likely that organizations would sometimes let go of poor performers even if they belong to talent pools, and at the same time include high-performers who were not initially included. If true, such practices would point towards the dynamism of the process. However, not a single empirical study on TM directly addresses this issue of movement within a talent pool. The result is that academic literature continues to build upon the extant, static view of talent while discounting the dynamic view, if not disregarding it altogether.

The main implication of the discussion in section 4 is that unless the confusion regarding dynamism and other barriers for the adoption of dynamic capabilities can be removed, TM will continue to be governed by the idea of stable and static nature of talent and thus misrepresent the TM issues surrounding organizations by disregarding the dynamism of the TM process.

Recommendations for Research

Adopting a dynamic capabilities view will help to develop coherent frameworks of TM that will be relevant to theory and practice alike for better conceptualizing talent and TM. This does not imply that we erase ideas based on RBV or forget the progress that the field has made so far. On the contrary, re-examining existing ideas from a dynamic capabilities lens will make research in this field richer and more relevant to practice. In this vein, some suggestions are made below about possible future avenues of TM research.

This chapter has argued that research has to account for the dynamism of the environment as well as the resource base. Thus, one possible area of research could be the impact of movement within a talent pool. In instances where organizations make new talent acquisitions, it might be interesting to study how a firm can successfully integrate the new resource by adjusting existing resources and/or transforming newly acquired resources (Kraaijenbrink et al., 2009).

Another area where research is needed is on the fairness aspect of exclusive TM. While it is argued in this chapter that a dynamic approach that provides opportunities for individuals to become part of talent pools or that penalizes under-performers within the pool by removing them might be perceived as fair by the stakeholders, such an assertion needs to be backed up by empirical data. It might also be interesting to revisit these TM issues from ethical and moral standpoints.

Perhaps most importantly, even when adopting a dynamic perspective, we need to compile existing knowledge in a coherent form so that we can draw upon prior research. In this regard, one of the frontiers in TM research is the establishment of linkages between different fields that study the same population of talented employees but name them differently as high-performing employees, high-potentials, stars, or talent. We need better integration and cross-linkages between the disparate fields that research high-performing employees.

From a research perspective, we also need to clearly delineate between traditional HRM research and TM research. If TM is not to be limited to merely being a management fad, it needs to carve out a niche and evolve as a separate discipline. All the research to date has slowly but surely clarified the boundaries between these two closely related disciplines; however, we need more theoretical grounding as well as empirical research to solidify TM's status as a separate discipline.

Conclusion

It its initial phases, TM might have been considered a management fad that would go away after a few years. That TM is still being discussed after more than 20 years since its emergence is a testimonial to the fact that it is here to stay. From infancy to adolescence (Thunnissen et al., 2013) to what we now might call early adulthood, the field has seen increasing growth and interest. It does not show any signs of going away; on the contrary, scholars have built upon the concept of TM and have applied it to the practices of multinational enterprises (MNEs). In MNEs, TM takes on an additional layer of complexity due to the global nature of MNEs' operations. TM practices of MNEs have thus been termed as global talent management (GTM), which is a sub-field of TM in its own right.

If the field is to advance and become relevant to practice, it needs to adopt a dynamic capabilities view because of the limitations of the static view of talent. Whereas TM has been built upon the resource-based idea that talent is a valuable, rare, inimitable, and nonsubstitutable (VRIN) resource, the notion that talent is a rare, inimitable, and nonsubstitutable static resource is incompatible with the idea of a dynamic TM system that seeks to provide a firm with the talent it needs to pursue SCA. The focus on dynamism is especially important as one of the main challenges for TM will be to establish itself as a legitimate effort to improve organizational efficiency in the face of accusations and criticisms that it focuses only on a minority and demotivates the majority. This is where a shift from a static to a dynamic view of talent will come in handy by increasing the perceived fairness and integrity of the system.

References

Aghina, W., De Jong, M., & Simon, D. 2011. How the best labs manage talent. *McKinsey Quarterly,* 1–6.

Ambrosini, V., & Bowman, C. 2009. What are dynamic capabilities and are they a useful construct in strategic management? *International Journal of Management Reviews,* 11(1): 29–49.

Amit, R., & Schoemaker, P. 1993. Strategic assets and organizational rent. *Strategic Management Journal,* 14(1): 33–46.

Asplund, K. 2019. When profession trumps potential: The moderating role of professional identification in employees' reactions to talent management. *The International Journal of Human Resource Management,* 1–23.

Barney, J. 1991. Firm resources and sustained competitive advantage. *Journal of Management,* 17(1): 99–120.

Barney, J. B., Ketchen, D. J., & Wright, M. 2011. The future of resource-based theory. In J. B. Barney, D. J. Ketchen & M. Wright (Eds.). *Journal of Management,* 37(5): 1299–1315.

Becker, B. E., & Huselid, M. A. 2006. Strategic human resources management: Where do we go from here? *Journal of Management,* 32(6): 898–925.

Boxall, P. 1996. The strategic HRM debate and the resource-based view of the firm. *Human Resource Management Journal,* 6(3): 59–75.

Chandler, A. D. 1977. *The visible hand: The managerial revolution in American business,* Vol. 52. Cambridge, MA: Harvard University Press.

CIPD. 2014. Talent management: An overview. *Chartered Institute of Personnel and Development.* http://www.cipd.co.uk/hr-resources/factsheets/talent-management-overview.aspx.

Coff, R. W. 1999. When competitive advantage doesn't lead to performance: The resource-based view and stakeholder bargaining power. *Organization Science,* 10(2): 119–133.

Collings, D. G., & Mellahi, K. 2009. Strategic talent management: A review and research agenda. *Human Resource Management Review,* 19(4): 304–313.

Collings, D. G., Mellahi, K., & Cascio, W. F. 2018. Global talent management and performance in multinational enterprises: A multilevel perspective. *Journal of Management,* 1–27.

De Boeck, G., Meyers, M. C., & Dries, N. (2018). Employee reactions to talent management: Assumptions versus evidence. *Journal of Organizational Behavior,* 39(2), 199–213.

De Vos, A., Dries, N., De Vos, A., & Dries, N. 2013. Applying a talent management lens to career management: The role of human capital composition and continuity. *The International Journal of Human Resource Management,* 24(9): 1816–1831.

Eisenhardt, K. M., & Martin, J. a. 2000. Dynamic capabilities: What are they? *Strategic Management Journal,* 21(10–11): 1105–1121.

Festing, M., Schäfer, L., & Scullion, H. 2013. Talent management in medium-sized German companies: An explorative study and agenda for future research. *The International Journal of Human Resource Management,* 24(9): 1872–1893.

Gallardo-Gallardo, E., Thunnissen, M., & Scullion, H. 2020. Talent management: Context matters. *International Journal of Human Resource Management,* 31(4), 457–473

Griffith, D. A., & Harvey, M. G. 2001. A resource perspective of global dynamic capabilities. *Journal of International Business Studies,* 32(3): 597–606.

Groysberg, B., & Connolly, K. 2015. The three things CEOs worry about the most. *Harvard Business Review Digital Articles,* 2–5.

Huselid, M. A., Beatty, R., & Becker, B. 2005. A players or a positions? The strategic logic of workforce management. *Harvard Business Review,* 83(12): 110–117.

Kang, S.-C., & Snell, S. A. 2009. Intellectual capital architectures and ambidextrous learning: A framework for human resource management. *Journal of Management Studies,* 46(1): 65–92.

King, K. A., & Vaiman, V. 2019. Enabling effective talent management through a macro-contingent approach: A framework for research and practice. *Business Research Quarterly,* 22(3), 194–206.

Kraaijenbrink, J., Spender, J.-C., & Groen, A. J. 2010. The resource-based view: A review and assessment of its critiques. *Journal of Management,* 36(1): 349–372.

Krishnan, T., & Scullion, H. 2017. Talent management and dynamic view of talent in small and medium enterprises. *Human Resource Management Review,* 27(3): 431–441.

Lazarova, M., & Taylor, S. 2009. Boundaryless careers, social capital, and knowledge management: Implications for organizational performance. *Journal of Organizational Behavior,* 30(1): 119–139.

Lepak, D. P., & Snell, S. A. 2002. Examining the human resource architecture: The relationships among human capital, employment, and human resource configurations. *Journal of Management,* 28(4): 517–543.

Lewis, R. E., & Heckman, R. J. 2006. Talent management: A critical review. *Human Resources Management Review,* 16(9): 139–154.

Mäkelä, K., Björkman, I., & Ehrnrooth, M. 2010. How do MNCs establish their talent pools? Influences on individuals' likelihood of being labeled as talent. *Journal of World Business,* 45(2): 134–142.

McDonnell, A., & Collings, D. G. 2011. The identification and evaluation of talent in MNEs. In D. G. Collings & H. Scullion (Eds.), *Global Talent Management.* New York and London: Routledge.

Mellahi, K., & Collings, D. G. 2010. The barriers to effective global talent management: The example of corporate élites in MNEs. *Journal of World Business,* 45(2): 143–149.

Meyers, M. C., van Woerkom, M., Paauwe, J., & Dries, N. (2019). HR managers' talent philosophies: Prevalence and relationships with perceived talent management practices. *The International Journal of Human Resource Management,* 31(4): 1–27.

Minbaeva, D., & Collings, D. G. 2013. Seven myths of global talent management. *The International Journal of Human Resource Management,* 24(9): 1762–1776.

Morris, S., Snell, S., & Björkman, I. 2016. An architectural framework for global talent management. *Journal of International Business Studies,* 47(6): 723–747.

Nelson, R., & Winter, S. 1982. *An evolutionary theory of economic change.* Cambridge, MA: Harvard University Press.

Oltra, V., & Vivas-López, S. 2013. Boosting organizational learning through team-based talent management: What is the evidence from large Spanish firms? *The International Journal of Human Resource Management,* 24(9): 1853–1871.

Penrose, E. 1959. *The theory of the growth of the firm.* Oxford, UK: Basil Blackwell.

Pfeffer, J. 2001. Fighting the war for talent is hazardous to your organization's health. *Organizational Dynamics,* 29(4): 248–259.

Preece, D., Iles, P., & Jones, R. 2013. MNE regional head offices and their affiliates: Talent management practices and challenges in the Asia Pacific. *The International Journal of Human Resource Management,* 24(18): 3457–3477.

Santos, F. M., & Eisenhardt, K. M. 2005. Organizational boundaries and theories of organization. *Organization Science,* 16(5): 491–508.

Schilling, M., & Steensma, H. 2002. Disentangling the theories of firm boundaries: A path model and empirical test. *Organization Science,* 13(4): 387–401.

Sturman, M. C., Walsh, K., & Cheramie, R. A. 2007. The value of human capital specificity versus transferability. *Journal of Management,* 34(2): 290–316.

Swailes, S. 2013. The ethics of talent management. *Business Ethics: A European Review,* 22(1): 32–46.

Tansley, C. 2011. What do we mean by the term "talent" in talent management? *Industrial and Commercial Training,* 43(5): 266–274.

Teece, D. J. 2007. Explicating dynamic capabilities: The nature and microfoundations of (sustainable) enterprise performance. *Strategic Management Journal,* 28(13): 1319–1350.

Teece, D. J., Pisano, G., & Shuen, A. 1997. Dynamic capabilities and strategic management. *Strategic Management Journal,* 18(7): 509–533.

Thunnissen, M., Boselie, P., & Fruytier, B. 2013. A review of talent management: "Infancy or adolescence?" *The International Journal of Human Resource Management,* 24(9): 1744–1761.

Valverde, M., Scullion, H., & Ryan, G. 2013. Talent management in Spanish medium-sized organisations. *The International Journal of Human Resource Management,* 24(9): 1832–1852.

Wang, H., Choi, J., Wan, G., & Dong, J. Q. 2013. Slack resources and the rent-generating potential of firm-specific knowledge. *Journal of Management,* (April). doi: https://doi.org/10.1177/0149206313484519.

Wright, P. M., Dunford, B. B., & Snell, S. A. 2001. Human resources and the resource based view of the firm. *Journal of Management,* 27(6): 701–721.

6

THE "VALUE" PERSPECTIVE TO TALENT MANAGEMENT

A Revised Perspective

Heba Makram

Introduction

Almost two decades have passed since the topic of talent management (TM) first emerged in recognition of the importance of an organization's precious talent. Since then, TM has gained mainstream interest, first from practitioners and then from academics, and has become a topic of considerable debate (McDonnell, Collings, Mellahi, & Schuler, 2017). The emergence of TM is mainly attributed to McKinsey et al. and the great concern they expressed about the increasingly competitive landscape for the attraction and retention of talent, resulting in a "war for talent" (Chambers, Foulton, Handfield-Jones, Hankin, & Michaels Ill, 1998).

Axelrod, Handfield-Jones, and Welsh (2001) and Dries (2013) argue that the popular war for talent notion is rooted in two assumptions: the first is to recognize talent as a source of competitive advantage that is critical to organizational success, the second is to recognize that the attraction and retention of talent have become increasingly difficult. Such assumptions emphasize the importance of TM to organizational success and bring its direct positive impact on bottom-line and competitive advantage to the forefront (Clake & Winkler, 2006; The Economist, 2006) (of course, such a statement is based on a belief rather than any demonstrated linkage).

This increased interest in TM was also triggered by a number of global challenges, such as: (a) changes in global demographics and economic trends associated with the decline in birth rates, (b) an increased number of retiring Baby Boomers, (c) the global mobility and diversity of workforce, (d) the globalization of business, and (e) the movement towards a knowledge-based economy (Beechler & Woodward, 2009; Schuler, Jackson, & Tarique, 2011). These challenges highlight the ability of organizations to attract, develop, and quickly deploy talented people with the requisite capital (be that human, social, intellectual, and political). Together these challenges led organizations to acknowledge the importance of TM to corporate success and the strategic role of high-potentials in creating economic value and enhancing organizational performance (Amit & Belcourt, 1999; Tymon, Stumpf, & Doh, 2010). It also created questions about the nature of talent, and the nature of the TM practices, processes, and systems developed and implemented to match this.

A substantial number of academic publications discussed TM over the last decade or two (Thunnissen, 2016), for example, in special issues such as the *International Journal of Contemporary Hospitality* (D'Annunzio-Green, 2008), the *Journal of World Business* (Al Ariss, Cascio, & Paauwe, 2014; Scullion, Collings, & Caligiuri, 2010), the *European Journal of International Management* (Collings, Scullion, & Vaiman., 2011), the *Asia Pacific Journal of Human Resource Management* (McDonnell, 2012), the *International Journal of Human Resource Management* (Vaiman & Collings, 2013), and the *Journal of Organizational Effectiveness:*

DOI: 10.4324/9781315474687-6

People and Performance (Vaiman, Collings, & Scullion, 2017) as well as a series of influential practitioner publications (Ashton & Morton, 2005; Creelman, 2004; Heinen & O'Neill, 2004; Michaels, Handfield-Jones, & Axelrod, 2001; Tucker, Kao, & Verma, 2005). Despite all these, the literature on TM is mainly characterized by a managerialist and unitarist orientation, and has a limited view of the human resource practices that might be involved (McDonnell et al., 2017; Thunnissen, Boselie, & Fruytier, 2013). It is also dominated by consultant and practitioner research (Al Ariss et al., 2014).

Some of the obvious limitations to the TM literature are the lack of consensus on the conceptual boundaries of the field (i.e., what TM is and what it is not) (McDonnell et al., 2017). There is also little knowledge about how TM systems are designed and implemented in organizations, with the main focus on understanding the broader context of TM rather than delving into the practices or processes that organizations use to effectively manage their talent (McDonnell et al., 2017). Thus, there remains a need for researchers to investigate the individual practices that are employed by organizations to manage talent and explain how these practices might (or might not) differ from other traditional HR practices.

The literature is also driven by narrow organizational views on the nature of TM. These views pay limited attention to the actual talent (i.e., individual human beings) and fail to examine their perspectives and their experience of TM (McDonnell et al., 2017; Thunnissen et al., 2013). Accordingly, there is a need for more empirical research that takes individual talent as its main unit of analysis and examines how talent perceives and experiences the practices of TM implemented by their organizations.

Despite such limitations, the field of TM is currently going through a critical stage of its development. It is at a turning point, and researchers have the opportunity to cross boundaries of the traditional and familiar HR literature landscape into other unaccustomed territories to draw on the theoretical developments in such fields. This chapter does exactly that. It recognizes the increased number of implicit value claims (Barney, 1991; Becker & Huselid, 1998; Collings & Mellahi, 2009; Lepak & Snell, 1999; Wright, Dunford, & Snell, 2001) that suggest that TM is a source of sustained competitive advantage and value creation.

The chapter provides a review of strategic management (Amit & Schoemaker, 1993; Gans & Ryall, 2017; Rumelt, 1984), value and value creation literature (Bowman & Ambrosini, 2000; Sirmon, Hitt, & Ireland, 2007; Skilton, 2014), and resource-based view (RBV) and dynamic capabilities literature (Barney & Clark, 2007; Helfat et al., 2007; Teece, Pisano, & Shuen, 1997). The objective is to revisit the previously proposed value model by Sparrow and Makram (2015) that suggests how TM may add value to organizations in relation to four value processes – value creation, value capture, value leverage, and value protection – and provide an updated theoretical perspective on how TM may generate value in relation to the proposed four value-driven processes.

Sparrow and Makram explain each of the four processes as follows:

> *Value creation* is the process through which the organization attracts, acquires and accumulates valuable and unique talent resources and exploits their potential to create value.
>
> *Value capture* is the process through which an organization then bundles its talent resources with other resources to increase their dependency on the organization context, and hence weaken their bargaining power.
>
> *Value leverage* is the process through which an organization develops and extends the captured capabilities of its talent resources to add new use value.
>
> *Value protection* is the process through which an organization develops isolating mechanisms to protect its talent resources from being lost to other competitors. (emphasis added; 2015: 250)

The chapter beings by first explaining how the notion of "value" is defined and understood in the literature. It then presents a critical review of the value literature, lays out the broader theory of value to describe how TM may add value in relation to the four value-driven processes, and provides an updated description of the initially proposed processes. It then concludes by providing direction of future research and implication to practice.

Value – What Does it Mean?

What is value? To understand what value is, we need to recognize that the nature of value is elusive, and the reason behind its elusiveness stems from the meanings of value that are strongly embedded in the foundations of economics and the study of market exchange (Vargo, Maglio, & Akaka, 2008). The nature of value has been widely debated and discussed in the literature. In his attempts to understand the meaning of value, Aristotle (1959) was one of the first to discuss the concepts of "exchange value" and "use value". To understand exchange value, he initially deliberated about whether "money" and "need" were conterminous (sharing common boundaries) with exchange value before rejecting both, explaining that money should not be a measure of value, and that a person's need lacked a unit of measurement. Aristotle was one of the first to consider these concepts, but they were subsequently picked up and elaborated on by other academics (e.g., Ambrosini & Bowman, 2000).

Despite being examined by many scholars in a special forum (Lepak, Smith, & Taylor, 2007), there seems to be a number of limitations in the value literature that hinders our understanding of what value is. For example, there is little consensus on the meaning of value (Pitelis, 2009). Lepak et al. (2007) suggest that this lack of consensus is perhaps the result of a number of factors. Firstly, they argue that the multi-disciplinary nature of the field of management introduces a plurality of perspectives related to the targets of value (i.e., who is value created for) and the potential sources of value (i.e., who creates value). This introduces a number of challenges, including developing a definition of value. Secondly, they argue that the difficulty of differentiating between the content of value and the process of value creation (i.e., what is value, who values what, and where does value reside) makes it difficult to understand value creation. Finally, they suggest that confusion about the processes of value creation and value capture has contributed to the existing disagreements and confusion surrounding the terms value and value creation.

A number of scholars have attempted to address this definitional problem. For example, Bowman and Ambrosini define two aspects of value:

- "perceived use value" – how customers perceive the quality and value of a service or a product in relation to their needs. Use value is "the specific qualities of the product perceived by customers in relation to their needs" (2000: 2);
- "exchange value" – the monetary amount customers are willing to pay in exchange for a desired good or service. Exchange value is "the monetary amount realized at a single point in time when the exchange of goods takes place" (2000: 3).

Both definitions suggest that value is subjective and is therefore predominantly dependent on the perceptions of customers and their willingness to exchange a monetary amount for the value received. Similarly, Pitelis (2009) defines value as the "perceived worthiness" of a product or service for a final target user. More recently, Bowman and Ambrosini (2010) argue that value has a different meaning for different stakeholder groups, and categorize a firm's key stakeholders as its customers, suppliers (of separable inputs and human inputs), and owners (Clarkson, 1995). In summary, then, value means different things to different stakeholders depending on their motivations and what they aim to optimize on (be it value for money, monetary amounts received in exchange for services and products, or efforts or return on investments).

Since judgments about value are subjective and dependent on perceptions, to understand the value of TM, there is a need to address two important questions: how is value created and how it is captured? The remainder of the chapter answers these questions and outlines the value of TM in relation to the four value-driven processes (initially introduced in Sparrow & Makram, 2015)

Value Creation and Talent Management

Creating value and the quest to achieve sustained competitive advantage are two critical concerns of researchers in strategic management and organization studies (Collis & Montgomery, 1995; Teece, 2007). Value is created when organizations exploit their internal resources and capabilities to implement strategies that enable them to respond to market opportunities (Andrews, 1971; Penrose, 1959). On the other hand, the literature on dynamic capabilities (Teece, 1982; Wernerfelt, 1984) suggests that value creation resides in the organization's ability to "integrate, build and reconfigure internal and external compiesetences" (Teece et al., 1997: 516) and in its capacity to "purposefully create, extend and modify its resource base" (Helfat, 2007: 4). Moreover, Sirmon et al. (2007) suggest that a firm's resource portfolio establishes an upper limit to the creation of value. Organizations should, therefore, structure their resource portfolio by acquiring a repertoire of resources (i.e., unique and valuable resources), accumulating resources (i.e., internally develop resources), and divesting resources (i.e., actively evaluate and divest less valuable resources) to be able to create value.

To conceptualize the process of value creation, there is a need to define the sources of value creation (i.e., who creates value). Lepak et al. (2007) suggest three sources of value creation: the individual (by developing unique tasks or services that are perceived to be valuable by target users), the organization (by inventing new ways of doing things to benefit target users), and society (by developing new programs and incentives intended to benefit its members). Relating this to TM, two sources of value creation can be identified: the individual talent, who create value when they develop their role and deliver novel and appropriate outcomes that appeal in the eyes of their employer (Lepak et al., 2007); and the organization, which creates value by inventing and devising the appropriate TM (i.e., practices, systems, and processes) that enable it to exploit the potential of their talent resource to work towards value creation (Wright & McMahan, 1992).

In the HRM literature, many scholars argue that employees are an important determinant of value creation due to their uniqueness, their ability to increase productivity by learning, the way they work together to help create the distinctive personality of the organization, and their ability to execute and deliver on organization strategies, as well as the HR systems and architectures implemented to link human resources with value creation in the organization (Garavan, Carbery, & Rock, 2012; Lepak & Snell, 2002; Peteraf, 2006; Pfeffer, 1994; Pitelis, 2007).

On the other hand, the SHRM literature describes the process of value creation in relation to how the HR systems (sets of processes, practices, and policies) implemented by the organization build employees' skills and motivate them to work towards achieving organizational goals and contribute to value creation (Wright & McMahan, 1992). It is argued that HR systems contribute to value creation when they elicit the desired behaviors that are critical to executing the strategies of value creation, and when they impact the skills and knowledge of valuable talent and their willingness to expend effort and express their talent in the workplace (Boxall, 2012; Huselid, 1995; Macduffie, 1995; Schuler & Jackson, 1987). Value creation is also described in terms of how HR systems foster and facilitate the generation, accumulation, and internalization of knowledge and spark the involvement and commitment of valuable talent (Lado & Wilson, 1994). The fundamental focus of these various explanations of value creation, both in the general management literature and the HRM literature, is the organization's "valuable talent" and their contribution to value creation.

Revised Perspective: Value is created when organizations implement the appropriate talent management systems and practices that enable them to attract, acquire, and accumulate valuable and unique talent resources and elicit the desired behaviors critical to value creation.

Value Capture and Talent Management

Much of the literature, for example, the RBV literature (Barney, 1991; Collis & Montgomery, 1995; Peteraf, 1993), focuses mostly on the concept of "value capture" rather than "value creation". Therefore, it is important to recognize that value capture and value creation are two distinct albeit related activities (Sparrow & Makram, 2015). In the strategic management literature, scholars have distinguished between these processes by recognizing that in some cases, firms that create value may be unable to capture this value if they need to share it with others such as customers, employees, or stakeholders (Makadok, 2001). This is referred to as "value slippage" (Lepak et al., 2007). On the other hand, in the coalitional game theory literature (Brandenburger & Nalebuff, 1995), it is suggested that value is captured through freedom of exchange, in which the value created by one partner is only captured when the resources and capabilities of the other partner are equal.

Others argue, that value capture (the realization of the exchange value) is determined by the bargaining relationship between parties. It is "a function of a bargaining process" (Bowman & Swart, 2007: 492) between the creators of value (i.e., customers, suppliers or employees) and the capturers of the value (i.e., firms), in which the economic basis of this bargaining relationship is a function of perceived dependence (Bowman & Ambrosini, 2000; Coff, 1999; Pfeffer, 1995). From this point of view, it is reasonable to say that the value created by a firm's resources becomes critical *only if the firm manages to capture that value*.

With respect to human capital as a source of value creation, it is argued that the bargaining power of employees is very much dependant on how they perceive themselves. For example, if they perceive their livelihood to be dependent on their organization, it is unlikely that they will exert strong bargaining power, but if they perceive that their role in the value-creation process is crucial, that the talent they possess is critical to their organization, and if they can take it elsewhere, then they will most likely exert strong bargaining power (Bowman & Swart, 2007).

The literature also suggests, that to capture the value that has been created, be it by human capital or other firm resources and capabilities, organizations need to create separate processes referred to as "isolating mechanisms" (Rumelt, 1984), which should enable them to capture any value they create. Isolating mechanisms can become strategies of value capture to obstruct the flow of knowledge thus increasing the uncertainty of imitation and preventing competitors from accessing and utilizing firm's resources, capabilities, and strategies (Lippman & Rumelt, 1982; Mahoney & Pandian, 1992). With the protection of isolating mechanisms, firms may enjoy capturing the value created by its resources and capabilities.

While talent can contribute to value creation, it is important to realize that this is mostly dependent on their willingness to share their knowledge, capabilities, and expertise with their organizations and willingness to engage in the process of value creation. In such a case, organizations need to develop the right systems that would enable them to capture the knowledge and expertise of their valuable talent, and stop the flow of such knowledge and expertise outside of the organization. This is important if an organization wishes to retain the value created by its talent resources.

Revised Perspective: Value is captured when organizations design and implement talent management systems and practices that enable them to extract the knowledge and expertise of their valuable and unique talent resources and thus weakening their bargaining power.

Value Leverage and Talent Management

Thinking about the role of TM in the creation and capture of value raises the question of whether there may be other ways in which TM may add value to organizations. A review of the literature brings to the surface two more value processes to which TM may contribute: value leverage and value protection.

Although value leverage was not widely discussed in the literature, we can detect several implicit debates to explain how TM may enable organizations to leverage the value being created by their talent resources. Bergmann Lichtenstein and Brush (2001) argue that owning resources and bundling them to develop capabilities is not enough to realize value creation; instead, firms need to leverage and extend their capabilities to ensure a continuous process of value creation.

Similarly, Miller et al. (2002) argue that a firm's resources and capabilities are of no value unless these can be extended to create more value and superior returns. To understand more how TM may enable organizations to leverage the value created by talent resources, we turn to the dynamic capabilities literature (Eisenhardt & Martin, 2000; Teece et al., 1997), which suggest that firms can leverage the value of their resources (be that tangible, intangible, or human resources) and capabilities by engaging in these activities that create, modify, and extend their resources base (i.e., acquisition, innovation, entrepreneurial, knowledge management) (Helfat, 2007).

On the other hand, from the RBV literature (Barney & Clark, 2007), we learn that value may be leveraged if a firm combines its resources and capabilities with its tacit knowledge in order to create novel and valuable outcomes (Sparrow & Makram, 2015). The process of value leveraging is therefore critical for the maintenance of value creation.

Perhaps the most relevant discussion to TM is one by Sirmon et al. (2007) in which they describe the process of value leverage in relation to a firm's ability to mobilize its idiosyncratic capabilities. The intent of mobilization is to identify the capabilities needed by the firm and design the capability configurations required to exploit such capabilities in a way that would enable the continued creation of value. Hamel and Prahalad (1994) argue that mobilizing firm capabilities requires an action of continuous adjustment to ensure that the appropriate capabilities are available for sustainable value creation. In addition, Sirmon et al. (2007) refer to the importance of capability coordination. Coordinating firm capabilities involves the effective and efficient integration of such capabilities to create the capability configurations required to implement leveraging strategies and thus result in sustainable value creation.

Moreover, debates in the TM literature make implicit reference to the process of value leverage, for example, Sparrow et al. (2010) argue that value leverage requires firms to invest in the appropriate TM practices to enable them to (a) build on their current talent capabilities, (b) manage the knowledge of their talent resources in ways that lead to executing strategic outcomes and (c) respond to talent shortage and recognize organizational capabilities that are central to the business model.

Similarly, Andreas et al. (2007) suggest that the process of value leverage includes those activities required to improve the efficiency and effectiveness of existing value creating resources such as: structuring talent resources, managing talent knowledge and transferring it across the organization to generate new ideas, and creating a collaborative and creative culture to effectively manage talent. Taking into consideration what has been suggested in the different lines of literatures, one can argue that in addition to enabling organizations to create and capture (acquire, accumulate, and exploit the potential of talent resources) value, TM may also enable organizations to continuously enjoy the process of value creation and value capture. This is perhaps possible when the processes, systems, and strategies of TM are designed to enable organizations to leverage the value of their talented rescores.

Revised Perspective: Value is leveraged when organizations design and implement talent management systems and practices that enable them to extend, mobilize (replicate), integrate, and deploy the capabilities of valuable and unique talent resources.

Value Protection and Talent Management

Although most of the scholarly discourse on the topic of value has focused mainly on understanding a firm's ability to create and capture value rather than understanding how it might protect the returns of value creation (Reitzig & Puranam, 2009), a number of discussions were detected to inform our thinking and understanding of value protection. For example, Rumelt (1984) suggests that organizations can only preserve value if they succeed in protecting their value-creating resources from being captured or duplicated by competitors. This involves deploying isolating mechanisms that prevent rivals from having access to value creating resources. Isolating mechanisms occur in situations, when the relationship between the firm's resources and the competitive advantage is not understood (i.e., causal ambiguity), when sources of competitive advantage are "socially complex" (i.e., embedded within the firm's relationships and social systems), and when decisions are "path-dependent" (i.e., on the firm's unique history).

On the other hand, Barney and Clark (2007) suggest that organizations can protect its valuable human resources from being imitated by other competitors if they succeed in developing a firm-specific skill base. This is accomplished by training and developing employees on processes and procedures that are specific to the organization (Hatch & Dyer, 2004), or by developing firm-specific knowledge and disseminating it throughout the organization (Senge, 2006). They also suggest the development of complex social systems that are not transferable across organizations and embedding talent resources within these systems can protect the value they create.

Strategic HRM scholars (i.e., Becker & Huselid, 2006; Huselid & Becker, 2011; Wright & McMahan., 2011) advocate that the development of an integrated HR system that provides a synergetic effect to manage valuable human resources rather than investing in independent practices contributes to value creation. Itami (1987) suggests that HR systems are considered "invisible assets" that can create value if they were deeply embedded in the organization operational system to enhance its capabilities. The interrelatedness and integration of the HR system components make it difficult if not impossible for competitors to imitate such system.

Scholars such as Barney (1991) and Collis and Montgomery (1995) suggest that causal ambiguity and path dependency are two key factors behind such difficulty of imitation. For example, without being able to understand how an HR system works and how its many elements and components interact and integrate, competitors cannot figure the precise practices and policies that generate value. Moreover, such practices and policies are usually developed over time, which precludes competitors from imme-diate imitation.

While there is no agreement on which HR practices constitute a high-performance work systems (HPWS), these systems play an important role in generating value to organizations and protecting their value creating resources (human capital) (Jackson, Schuler, & Jiang, 2014). A significant body of research suggests that there is a positive association between HPWS and employee retention (Gardner, Wright, & Moynihan, 2011; Huselid & Becker, 1997; Jensen, Patel, & Messersmith, 2013; Way, 2002).

From the social exchange theory (Stirpe & Zárraga-Oberty, 2017), we detect several arguments asserting how employees perceive such systems as signs of appreciation, recognition, and an employer attempt to build a long-term relationship with their employees. Such perceptions motivate employees to remain with their employer and equally invest in the relationship by performing and contributing to the organization success (Evans & Davis, 2005). Pioneers in the strategic HRM literature argued that HRM systems co-evolve along with business strategies where organizations develop their HR systems to implement specific business strategies to enable them to improve employees' commitment, involve-ment, and performance (Arthur, 1992; Camps & Luna-Arocas, 2009; Jackson et al., 2014).

Revised Perspective: Value is protected when organizations design and implement talent management systems and practices that are interrelated and integrated into ways that make it difficult for competitors to imi-tate these systems and thus enable them to introduce a number of isolating mechanisms to protect their valuable and unique talent resources.

Future Research Directions

First, while the theoretical development presented in this chapter attempts to address important questions about TM and value, there is an opportunity for future research to focus its efforts on examining the value of TM from both an organizational perspective and an individual talent perspective. The litera-ture could examine how the individual TM practices (that make up a TM system) are designed and implemented in organizations and whether the concepts of value are taken into consideration while these systems are being designed, or not. There is also an opportunity to examine how system designers think about and understand the value of TM, and how their perceived value (if it exists) might impact the design and the implementation of TM systems in organizations. Research could also benefit from examining how the value of TM is perceived by the individual talent themselves. This could sur-face interesting insights into whether there is a disconnect, or there is an alignment between system designers and individual talent views.

The proposed value model can also be used to generate several propositions for further empirical testing. Therefore, it may guide future research to examine the actual bundles of TM practices that might contribute to each of the proposed four value-driven processes and validate the above-proposed descriptions of each process.

Finally, researchers may want to use research methods that are designed to reveal the implicit assumptions and debates that shape an organization's practice and policy within the TM space. These methods will likely need to be qualitative, such as cognitive mapping techniques, if researchers wish to surface the working assumptions of talent strategists or techniques that reveal organizational narratives and sensemaking if researchers wish to understand the ways in which HRM functions put their strategy into practice.

Implications for Talent Management Professionals

This chapter has critically examined the use of the concepts of value in the TM discourse. It encourages talent professionals to step away from their traditional approach to TM and think more strategically about the design and implementation of TM systems. HR/TM professionals are encouraged to look at developments in other fields (i.e., strategic management) to understand how best TM systems may add value to organizations. The four value-driven processes (initially introduced by Sparrow & Makram, 2015, and revisited in this chapter) can be used as the blueprint to critique the TM practices implemented by organizations and decide whether these practices are adding value to the organization or not. These may also help HR/TM professionals view TM as a collective set of integrated practices rather than separate practices.

Conclusion

The critical review of the talent management literature should lead us to the following conclusions. First, despite the significant volume of publications and research in the TM field, there are still obvious gaps in the literature that require the attention of academics and researchers. One of these gaps is the dearth of empirical evidence to support the many implicit value claims (found in both academic and practitioner literature) that suggest that TM is a source of sustained competitive advantage and value creation (Barney, 1991; Becker & Huselid, 1998; Cascio & Boudreau, 2016; Lepak & Snell, 1999; Sparrow, Scullion, & Tarique, 2014; Wright et al., 2001).

This chapter sought to borrow and draw on the theoretical developments in other literature, such as strategic management, RBV, value and value creation, and dynamic capabilities, to explain the value of TM and how it may contribute to four value-driven processes (creation, capture, leverage, and protraction). This chapter has attempted to address an important question of TM and value. Its central argument suggests that the rational answer to the value question lies in the way in which the activities and practices of a TM system are designed and integrated to add value to organizations. It reinforces the idea that invigorating a better and broader way of thinking about TM and its practices (more specifically around its value) enables academics to develop a better understanding of how TM may add value to organizations, and how it may enable them to exploit the pote0ntial of their talent resources. Finally, it provides a revised perspective of the initially proposed value-driven process (Sparrow & Makram, 2015) in an attempt to further develop the value model to guide future research.

References

Al Ariss, A., Cascio, W. F., & Paauwe, J. 2014. Talent management: Current theories and future research directions. *Journal of World Business,* 49(2): 173–179.

Amit, R., & Belcourt, M. 1999. Human resources management processes: A value-creating source of competitive advantage. *European Management Journal,* 17(2): 174–181.

Amit, R., & Schoemaker, P. J. H. 1993. Strategic Assets and organisational rents. *Strategic Management Journal,* 14: 33–36.

Andreas, N. A., Annie, G., & Michael, S. 2007. A framework of intangible valuation areas and antecedents. *Journal of Intellectual Capital,* 8(1): 52–75.

Andrews, K. R. 1971. *The concept of corporate strategy.* Homewood, IL: Dow Jones-Irwin.

Aristotle. 1959. *Politics.* H. Rackham (trans.). London: Heinemann.

Arthur, J. B. 1992. The link between business strategy and industrial relations systems in American steel minimills. *Industrial and Labor Relations Review,* 45(3): 488–506.

Ashton, C., & Morton, L. 2005. Managing talent for competitive advantage: Taking a systemic approach to talent management. *Strategic HR Review,* 4(5): 28–31.

Axelrod, E. L., Handfield-Jones, H., & Welsh, T. A. 2001. War for talent, part two. *The McKinsey Quarterly:* 9.

Barney, J. 1991. Firm resources and sustained competitive advantage. *Journal of Management,* 17(1): 99–120.

Barney, J. B., & Clark, D. N. 2007. *Resource-based theory: Creating and sustaining competitive advantage.* Oxford, UK: Oxford University Press.

Becker, B. E., & Huselid, M. A. 1998. High performance work systems and firm performance: A synthesis of research and managerial applications. *Research in Personnel and Human Resources Management,* 16: 53–101.

Becker, B. E., & Huselid, M. A. 2006. Strategic human resources management: Where do we go from here? *Journal of Management,* 32(6): 898–925.

Beechler, S., & Woodward, I. C. 2009. The global "war for talent". *Journal of International Management,* 15(3): 273–285.

Bergmann Lichtenstein, B. M., & Brush, C. G. 2001. How do "resource bundles" develop and change in new ventures? A dynamic model and longitudinal exploration. *Entrepreneurship: Theory and Practice,* 25(3): 37.

Bowman, C., & Ambrosini, V. 2000. Value creation versus value capture: Towards a coherent definition of value in strategy. *British Journal of Management,* 11(1): 1–15.

Bowman, C., & Ambrosini, V. 2010. How value is created, captured and destroyed. *European Business Review,* 22(5): 479–495.

Bowman, C., & Swart, J. 2007. Whose human capital? The challenge of value capture when capital is embedded. *Journal of Management Studies,* 44(4): 488–505.

Boxall, P. 2012. High-performance work systems: What, why, how and for whom? *Asia Pacific Journal of Human Resources,* 50(2): 169–186.

Brandenburger, A., & Nalebuff, B. 1995. The right game: Use game theory to shape strategy. *Harvard Business Review,* 73(4): 57.

Camps, J., & Luna-Arocas, R. 2009. High involvement work practices and firm performance. *The International Journal of Human Resource Management,* 20(5): 1056–1077.

Cascio, W. F., & Boudreau, J. W. 2016. The search for global competence: From international HR to talent management. *Journal of World Business,* 51: 103–114.

Chambers, E. G., Foulton, M., Handfield-Jones, H., Hankin, S. M., & Michaels, E. G. 1998. The war for talent. *McKinsey Quarterly* (3): 44–57.

Clake, R., & Winkler, V. 2006. *Reflections on talent management.* London: CIPD.

Clarkson, M. B. E. 1995. A stakeholder framework for analyzing and evaluating corporate social performance. *The Academy of Management Review,* 20(1): 92–117.

Coff, R. W. 1999. When competitive advantage leads to performance: The resource-based view and stakeholder bargaining power. *Organization Science,* 10(2): 119–133.

Collings, D. G., & Mellahi, K. 2009. Strategic talent management: A review and research agenda. *Human Resource Management Review,* 19(4): 304–313.

Collings, D. G., Scullion, H., & Vaiman., V. 2011. European perspectives on talent management. *European Journal of International Management,* 5(5): 453–462.

Collis, D., & Montgomery, C. A. 1995. Competing on resources: Strategy in the 1990s. *Harvard Business Review,* 73(7–8): 118–128.

Creelman, D. 2004. *Return on investment in talent management: Measures you can put to work right now.* Washington, DC: Human Capital Institute.

D'Annunzio-Green, N., Maxwell, G., & Watson, S. 2008. Concluding commentary on the contemporary human resource issues for talent management in hospitality and tourism. *International Journal of Contemporary Hospitality Management,* 20: 831.

Dries, N. 2013. The psychology of talent management: A review and research agenda. *Human Resource Management Review,* 23(4): 272–285.

The Economist. 2006. *The CEO's role in talent management: How top executives from ten countries are nurturing the leaders of tomorrow.* London: The Economist.

Eisenhardt, K., & Martin, J. 2000. Dynamic capabilities: What are they? *Strategic Management Journal,* 21(Special): 1105–1122.

Evans, W. R., & Davis, W. D. 2005. High-performance work systems and organizational performance: The mediating role of internal social structure. *Journal of Management,* 31(5): 758.

Gans, J., & Ryall, M. D. 2017. Value capture theory: A strategic management review. *Strategic Management Journal,* 38(1): 17–41.

Garavan, T. N., Carbery, R., & Rock, A. 2012. Mapping talent development: Definition, scope and architecture. *European Journal of Training and Development,* 36(1): 5–24.

Gardner, T., Wright, P., & Moynihan, L. 2011. The impact of motivation, empowerment, and skill-enhancing practices on aggregate voluntary turnover: The mediating effect of collective affective commitment. *Personnel Psychology,* 64(2): 315.

Hamel, G., & Prahalad, C. 1994. Competing for the future. *Harvard Business Review,* 72(4): 122–130.

Hatch, N. W., & Dyer, J. H. 2004. Human capital and learning as a source of sustainable competitive advantage. *Strategic Management Journal,* 25(12): 1155–1178.

Heinen, J. S., & O'Neill, C. 2004. Managing talent to maximize performance. *Employment Relations Today,* 31: 67–82.

Helfat, C. E., Finkelstein, S., Mitchell, W., Peteraf, M. A., Singh, H., Teece, D. J., & Winter, S. F. 2007. *Dynamic capabilities: Understanding strategic change in organizations.* Malden, MA: Blackwell Pub.

Huselid, M. A. 1995. The impact of human resource management practices on turnover, productivity, and corporate financial performance. *Academy of Management Journal,* 38(3): 635.

Huselid, M. A., & Becker, B. E. 1997. The impact high performance work systems, implementation effectiveness, and alignment with strategy on shareholder wealth. *Academy of Management Best Papers Proceedings,* 8(1): 144–148.

Huselid, M. A., & Becker, B. E. 2011. Bridging micro and macro domains: Workforce differentiation and strategic human resource management. *Journal of Management,* 37(2): 421–428.

Itami, H. 1987. *Mobilizing invisible assets.* Cambridge, MA: Harvard University Press.

Jackson, S. E., Schuler, R. S., & Jiang, K. 2014. An aspirational framework for strategic human resource management. *The Academy of Management Annals:* 1–89.

Jensen, J. M., Patel, P. C., & Messersmith, J. G. 2013. High-performance work systems and job control. *Journal of Management,* 39(6): 1699–1724.

Lado, A. A., & Wilson, M. C. 1994. Human resource systems and sustained competitive advantage: A competency-based perspective. *The Academy of Management Review,* 19(4): 699–727.

Lepak, D. P., Smith, K. G., & Taylor, M. S. 2007. Value creation and value capture: A multilevel perspective. *Academy of Management Review,* 32(1): 180–194.

Lepak, D. P., & Snell, S. A. 1999. The human resource architecture: Toward a theory of human capital allocation and development. *The Academy of Management Review,* 24(1): 31–48.

Lepak, D. P., & Snell, S. A. 2002. Examining the human resource architecture: The relationships among human capital, employment, and human resource configurations. *Journal of Management,* 28(4): 517–543.

Lippman, S. A., & Rumelt, R. P. 1982. Uncertain imitability: An analysis of interfirm differences in efficiency under competition. *The Bell Journal of Economics,* 13(2): 418–438.

Macduffie, J. P. 1995. Human resource bundles and manufacturing performance: Organizational logic and flexible production systems in the world auto industry. *Industrial and Labor Relations Review,* 48(2): 197–221.

Mahoney, J. T., & Pandian, J. R. 1992. The resource-based view within the conversation of strategic management. *Strategic Management Journal,* 13: 363–380.

Makadok, R. 2001. Toward a synthesis of the resource-based and dynamic-capability views of rent creation. *Strategic Management Journal,* 22(5): 387–401.

McDonnell, A., Collings, D. G., & Burgess, J. 2012. Asia Pacific perspectives on talent management. *Asia Pacific Journal of Human Resources,* 50(4): 391–398.

McDonnell, A., Collings, D. G., Mellahi, K., & Schuler, R. 2017. Talent management: An integrative review and research agenda. *European Journal of International Management,* 11(1): 86–128.

Michaels, E., Handfield-Jones, H., & Axelrod, B. 2001. *The war for talent.* Boston, MA: Harvard Business Review Press.

Miller, D., Eisenstat, R., & Foote, N. 2002. Strategy from the inside out: Building capability-creating organizations. *California Management Review,* 44(3): 37–54.

Penrose, E. 1959. *The theory of the growth of the firm.* New York, NY: John Wiley.

Peteraf, M. A. 1993. The cornerstones of competitive advantage: A resource- based view. *Strategic Management Journal,* 14(3): 179–191.

Peteraf, M. A. 2006. *New domains and directions for research in organizational identity.* Presentation at the IIB Organizational Identity Workshop, Stockholm.

Pfeffer, J. 1994. *Competitive advantage through people: Unleashing the power of the workforce.* Boston, MA: Harvard Business School Press.

Pfeffer, J. 1995. Producing sustainable competitive advantage through the effective management of people. *Academy of Management Perspectives,* 9(1): 55–69.

Pitelis, C. N. 2007. A behavioral resource-based view of the firm: The synergy of Cyert and March (1963) and Penrose (1959). *Organization Science,* 18(3): 478–490.

Pitelis, C. N. 2009. The co-evolution of organizational value capture, value creation and sustainable advantage. *Organization Studies,* 30(10): 1115–1139.

Reitzig, M., & Puranam, P. 2009. Value appropriation as an organizational capability: The case of IP protection through patents. *Strategic Management Journal,* 30(7): 765–789.

Rumelt, R. 1984. Toward a strategic theory of the firm. In R. Lamb (Ed.). *Competitive strategic management:* 556–570. Englewood Cliffs, NJ: Prentice-Hall.

Schuler, R. S., & Jackson, S. E. 1987. Linking competitive strategies with human resource management practices. *The Academy of Management Executive,* 1(3): 207–219.

Schuler, R. S., Jackson, S. E., & Tarique, I. 2011. Global talent management and global talent challenges: Strategic opportunities for IHRM. *Journal of World Business,* 46(4): 506–516.

Scullion, H., Collings, D. G., & Caligiuri, P. 2010. Global talent management. *Journal of World Business,* 45: 105–108.

Senge, P. M. 2006. *The fifth discipline: The art and practice of the learning organization.* London: Random House Business.

Sirmon, D. G., Hitt, M. A., & Ireland, R. D. 2007. Managing firm resources in dynamic environments to create value: Looking inside the black box. *Academy of Management Review,* 32(1): 273–292.

Skilton, P. F. 2014. Value creation, value capture, and supply chain structure: Understanding resource–based advantage in a project–based industry. *Journal of Supply Chain Management,* 50(3): 74–93.

Sparrow, P. R., Hesketh, A., Hird, M., & Cooper, C. L. 2010. Performance-led HR. In P. R. Sparrow, M. Hird, A. Hesketh, & C. Cooper (Eds.). *Leading HR:* 1–22. London: Palgrave Macmillan.

Sparrow, P. R., & Makram, H. 2015. What is the value of talent management? Building value-driven processes within a talent management architecture. *Human Resource Management Review,* 25(3): 249–263.

Sparrow, P., Scullion, H., & Tarique, I. 2014. *Strategic talent management: Contemporary issues in international context.* Cambridge, MA: Cambridge University Press.

Stirpe, L., & Zárraga-Oberty, C. 2017. Are high-performance work systems always a valuable retention tool? The roles of workforce feminization and flexible work arrangements. *European Management Journal,* 35(1): 128–136.

Teece, D. J. 1982. Towards an economic theory of the multiproduct firm. *Journal of Economic Behavior and Organization,* 3(1): 39–63.

Teece, D. J. 2007. Explicating dynamic capabilities: The nature and microfoundations of (sustainable) enterprise performance. *Strategic Management Journal,* 28(13): 1319–1350.

Teece, D. J., Pisano, G., & Shuen, A. 1997. Dynamic capabilities and strategic management. *Strategic Management Journal,* 18(7): 509–533.

Thunnissen, M. 2016. Talent management. *Employee Relations,* 38(1): 57–72.

Thunnissen, M., Boselie, P., & Fruytier, B. 2013. A review of talent management: 'Infancy or adolescence?' *The International Journal of Human Resource Management,* 24(9): 1744–1761.

Tucker, E., Kao, T., & Verma, N. 2005. Next-generation talent management: Insights on how workforce trends are changing the face of talent management. *Business Credit,* 107(7–8): 20–27.

Tymon, W. G., Stumpf, S. A., & Doh, J. P. 2010. Exploring talent management in India: The neglected role of intrinsic rewards. *Journal of World Business,* 45(2): 109–121.

Vaiman, V., & Collings, D. 2013. Talent management: Advancing the field. *The International Journal of Human Resource Management,* 24(9): 1737–1743.

Vaiman, V., Collings, D. G., & Scullion, H. 2017. Contextualising talent management. *Journal of Organizational Effectiveness: People and Performance,* 4(4): 294–297.

Vargo, S. L., Maglio, P. P., & Akaka, M. A. 2008. On value and value co-creation: A service systems and service logic perspective. *European Management Journal,* 26(3): 145–152.

Way, S. A. 2002. High performance work systems and intermediate indicators of firm performance within the US small business sector. *Journal of Management,* 28(6): 765–785.

Wernerfelt, B. 1984. A resource-based view of the firm. *Strategic Management Journal,* 5: 171–180.

Wright, P. M., Dunford, B. B., & Snell, S. A. 2001. Human resources and the resource-based view of the firm. *Journal of Management,* 27(6).

Wright, P. M., & McMahan, G. C. 1992. Theoretical perspectives for strategic human-resource management. *Journal of Manage,* 18(2): 295–320.

Wright, P. M., & McMahan., G. C. 2011. Exploring human capital: Putting 'human' back into strategic human resource management. *Human Resource Management Journal,* 21(2): 93–104.

SECTION II

The External Context of Talent Management

7

TALENT MANAGEMENT

Decision Making in the Global Context

Violetta Khoreva

Vlad Vaiman

Introduction

The research field of talent management (TM) has received a remarkable degree of academic and practitioner interest in recent years (Cascio & Boudreau, 2016; Collings & Isichei, 2018; Collings, Scullion, & Vaiman, 2015; De Boeck, Meyers, & Dries, 2018; McDonnell, Collings, Mellahi, & Schuler, 2017; Morris, Snell, & Björkman, 2016; Jooss et al., 2019; Kravariti & Johnston, 2020; Beamond et al., 2020). Drawing upon ideas from human resource management (HRM), organizational behavior, the resource-based view, capability theories, and others, the field is now gradually maturing (Gallardo-Gallardo & Thunnissen, 2016; Krishnan & Scullion, 2017; Vaiman, Collings, & Scullion, 2017; Van den Broek, Boselie, & Paauwe 2018). Currently TM is a vital component of the world's most influential academic and practitioner-oriented conferences (e.g., Academy of Management Annual Meeting and EIASM Talent Management Workshop). Furthermore, during the period 2013–2018 the international *Journal of Human Resource Management*, the *Journal of World Business*, and the *Human Resource Management Review*, respectively, have published special issues on TM, all devoted to the conceptual and intellectual development of TM as an academic field.

Talent management also continues to be one of the priorities for companies worldwide (Cascio & Boudreau, 2016). As some say, "We bet on people, not on strategies" – unless the strategy is executed through people, there is little value in it. Indeed, companies are fully aware that they need to attract, develop, and retain talent in order to succeed in the current hyper-competitive and increasingly complex global economy.

Even though the field has been steadily developing, theoretical approaches to TM have rarely been integrated into empirical research, and a consensus on TM definitions and its principles has been rather difficult to find (Collings, Mellahi, & Cascio, 2017; Gallardo-Gallardo & Thunnissen, 2016; McDonnell et al., 2017; Thunnissen, 2016). For instance, Dries (2013: 274) articulated that "vague but appealing rhetoric" was the result of criticism questioning whether or not TM is not just another management fad.

Talent management in academia has been characterized by a variety of definitions and theoretical assumptions that have resulted in inconsistent "stories" (Gallardo-Gallardo & Thunnissen, 2016; Sonnenberg, van Zijderveld, & Brinks, 2014). Nonetheless, scholars agree that the main focus of TM is on the identification of key positions that add to the competitive advantage of companies, the human resource management architecture built to reinforce the process, and the impact of the process on a company's overall performance (Sparrow & Makram, 2015; Tatoglu, Glaister, & Demirbag, 2016).

DOI: 10.4324/9781315474687-7

The most cited definition of TM relates to the conceptual article by Collings and Mellahi (2009), according to which, talent management refers to:

> activities and processes that involve the systematic identification of key positions which differentially contribute to the organization's sustainable competitive advantage, the development of a talent pool of high potential and high performing incumbents to fill these roles, and the development of a differentiated human resource architecture to facilitate filling these positions with competent incumbents and to ensure their continued commitment to the organization. (2009: 304)

After reviewing 139 TM articles published between January 2001 and May 2014, Gallardo-Gallardo, Nijs, Dries, and Gallo (2015) specify four predominant theoretical frameworks in TM research. The central identified theoretical framework has been the resource-based view, which focuses on key positions that significantly contribute to organizational sustainable competitive advantage (Collings & Mellahi, 2009; Sparrow & Makram, 2015). The second identified framework has been international HRM, which is applied to improve the global success of firms through the adaptation of HRM practices to their internal and external contexts. The next identified framework has been employee assessment, which emphasizes the identification of leadership talent. Finally, institutionalism has been identified as a prevailing theoretical framework in TM; it investigates the cognitive and normative influence of institutions, and how these motivate actors (Gallardo-Gallardo et al., 2015).

The field of TM has been long criticized for focusing mostly on TM issues in a selected category of organizations, that is, U.S.-based organizations and multinational corporations (Ariss, Cascio, & Paauwe, 2014; Farndale, Pai, Sparrow, & Scullion, 2014; Gallardo-Gallardo & Thunnissen, 2016). Recently, academics have started to contextualize TM by investigating it in specific business sectors, such as small and medium-sized companies (Festing, Schäfer, & Scullion, 2013; Krishnan & Scullion, 2017) as well as in emerging markets (Vaiman, Sparrow, Schuler, & Collings, 2019; Tatoglu et al., 2016), demonstrating that "context is everything" (Sparrow & Makram, 2015: 249). For instance, academics state that TM continues to be a challenge for organizations operating in emerging economies (Tatoglu et al., 2016; Teagarden, 2018). In line with this conclusion, Beamond, Farndale, and Härtel (2016) have identified the following challenges related to TM in emerging economies: difficulties in replicating local tacit knowledge, skill shortages, strong competition between multinational corporations, and local players for available talent and retention of talent, lack of effective TM strategies, and the need to link TM strategies to managing gender and cultural diversity.

Our analysis of TM here would not be full, however, if we failed to mention the most current, theoretical framework in TM research that examines the phenomenon through a country-level lens, also known as macro talent management (Vaiman, Schuler, Sparrow, & Collings, 2018a; Vaiman, Schuler, Sparrow, & Collings, 2018b). More specifically, this approach expands the horizons of TM by departing from the company-level (micro-) context and exploring activities aimed at attracting, growing, developing, and retaining top talent, as well as studying the importance of talent flow, knowledge spillovers, and learning at a country (macro-) level (Vaiman et al., 2018a; 2018b). Unlike micro TM, the nascent field of macro TM is very multi-disciplinary, encompassing such fields as HRM, international business, economic geography, and political economy. In this chapter, we will concentrate on decision making in a micro- or company-level context.

Decision Making in Talent Management

The linkage between TM and management decision making in organizations has been studied in previous research (Boudreau and Ramstad, 2007; Vaiman, Collings, & Scullion, 2012). Boudreau & Ramstad (2007) define the goal of talentship decision science as "to increase the success of the organization by improving decisions that depend on or impact talent resources" (2007: 25) and argue that HR offers far greater potential when focusing on providing non-HR leaders, who ultimately make talent decisions, with the decision framework and data and analysis required to make key decisions around TM (Vaiman et al., 2012).

In general, TM decisions include those that optimize human capital within organizations: recruiting, performance management, succession planning, decision analytics, talent reviews, development planning, and support. Before making any sort of talent decision, however, it is essential to formulate the link between people and profit, and translate business goals into workforce needs and objectives. Once these needs and objectives are articulated, HR ought to cooperate with both organizational leaders and line managers to translate them into the competencies (skills, knowledge, and abilities) that will drive the business as well as TM decisions that will help a company to attract, develop, and retain the needed talent to accomplish business goals. For example, a business goal of gaining new customers may demand an investment in talent that can build relationships and effectively manage customer accounts. The organization would subsequently need to identify how much of that talent it already holds and how much it needs to recruit in order to achieve its goals.

Talent management decisions have usually been made without well-understood frameworks or consideration of the key relevant data (Boudreau, 2010). In coping with their limited ability to process such complex and incomplete data, managers often make decisions based on a subset of the information available, which may lead to biases in decision making (Vaiman et al., 2012). In a similar way, Boudreau and Jesuthasan (2011) and Mellahi and Collings (2010) argued that instincts, preferences, and biases of key stakeholders often impair TM decisions. Furthermore, Mäkela, Bjorkman, and Ehrnrooth (2010) applied the idea of bounded rationality to decision making in global TM. The framing of TM decisions in appropriate frameworks and maximizing the use of relevant data in the decision process have received increasing attention in recent years (Vaiman et al., 2012).

Academics have attempted to shift the nature of TM decisions beyond somewhat inaccurate and limited frameworks to decisions supported by scientific data and processes (Boudreau, 2010; Davenport, Harris, & Shapiro, 2010b). The aim was to advance decision makers' ability to make effective decisions around TM by means of sophisticated methods of analyzing employee data. The effective use of analytics and proven business tools in TM decision making has moved the field towards evidence-based management and has contributed to maximizing the effectiveness of the HR function to organizational decision making and performance (Boudreau & Jesuthasan, 2011; Davenport, Harris, & Morison, 2010a; Vaiman et al., 2012).

Shifting focus from activity-based HR metrics (such as number of training hours, number of hires against plan, etc.) to value metrics has been critical in communicating the success of effective TM decision making (Vaiman et al., 2012). Value metrics can include revenue per employee, cost per hire versus turnover, and return on investment. More complex financial models have been identified to measure succession planning and the effectiveness of development (Farley, 2005). Regardless of the metrics used, academics argued that HR metrics and TM decisions need to be closely related to business goals (Boudreau, 2010; Davenport et al., 2010b).

Several recommendations have been identified in previous research related to TM decision making. It has been advocated that TM decision making should be executed in partnership with line managers (Van den Broek et al., 2018). Indeed, HR needs to be an effective trainer, coach, and facilitator for line managers to ensure successful TM decision making. When leaders have a wealth of data on talent in the organization – who its employees are, what they can do, how well they do it now, what opportunities are available to encourage them to do it better – accurate TM decisions can be made (Farley, 2005). From a TM perspective, this is often facilitated by technology, and there is software that can assist in making right TM decisions. Furthermore, in order to make accurate TM decisions, critical talent data needs to be accessible from one location with the ability to reference that data to make decisions. For example, if demographic, performance, and skill/competence data are available in one location, identifying leadership potential can be accomplished much more quickly and reliably.

Several approaches that may provide a common language for line managers and HR professionals in TM decision making have been recognized (Pucik, Evans, Björkman, & Morris 2017). These approaches are a performance-based approach, a strategy-based approach, and a value-based approach. They are adopted from Briscoe and Hall's (1999) approaches to developing competency frameworks.

The *performance-based approach* entails focus on the characteristics of talents so that organizations can reproduce them (Chatman & Cha, 2003). This approach is pragmatic, and with appropriate cultural adjustment the results can easily be implemented in performance appraisal guides, selection criteria, and training programs. However, performance-based approach is oriented towards the past and the status quo rather than future-oriented (Pucik et al., 2017). This approach is appealing for slow-moving industries.

The *strategy-based approach* is a forward-looking method emphasizing translating strategy for the future into current TM decisions. It is a vital element of the scorecard approach to strategic management and execution (Fombrun, Tichy, & Devanna, 1984). This method aims to identify skills or competencies in talents that TM decisions makers need in order to execute the strategy, and to fill gaps in these skills and competencies through training, leadership development, performance management, and rewards (Pucik et al., 2017). It is future-oriented, and is often attractive for TM decision making in times of transformational change and to fast-moving competitive environments (Bartlett & McLean, 2006). One of the ways to implement the strategic approach to TM decision making is to obtain new strategic skills from outside, as it often happens in times of crisis (Pucik et al., 2017).

The *value-based approach* is strongly linked to normative integration. Following this tactic, TM decision makers value talent attitudes and beliefs relevant for building and maintaining a strong culture and an execution of organizational strategy. This approach is particularly suitable in knowledge-based organizations that cannot rely heavily on hierarchical mechanisms of control (Pucik et al., 2017).

The complexity of TM decision making is exacerbated by various macro and micro factors (Ariss et al., 2014). Macro (environmental) factors include profound demographic changes and increased diversity, intensified workforce mobility, rapid digitalization and technological innovations, and the growth of a multi-generational workforce. Micro (organization-level) factors include the development of small and medium-sized enterprises, rapid organizational transformations (mergers and acquisitions, strategic renewals, restructuring), and new workplace dynamics. Companies that regard talent as a key differentiator have no choice but to take into account the impact of these factors when engaging in TM decision making.

The Key Macro Factors Influencing Talent Management Decision Making in the Global Context

Profound Demographic Changes and Increased Diversity

The first macro factor, which has noteworthy consequences for the TM decision making, relates to *profound demographic changes and increased diversity*. The current world population of 7.7 billion (2019) is expected to reach 8.5 billion by 2030, 9.7 billion in 2050, and 10.9 billion in 2100 (UN DESA report, 2019). Compared to 2017, the number of persons aged 60 or above is expected to more than double by 2050 and more than triple by 2100, rising from 962 million in 2017 to 2.1 billion in 2050 and 3.1 billion in 2100 (UN DESA report, 2017). This trend is especially noticeable in the so-called developed world. In Europe, 25% of the population is already aged 60 years or over, and that proportion is projected to reach 35% in 2050 and 36% in 2100 (UN DESA report, 2017). Many organizations worldwide have already begun struggling with ways to control costs and find new ways to attract, retain, and prepare the youth labor force. In addition, continued democratic reforms, social equality tendencies, and refugee flows in many countries will result in the emerging availability of culturally diverse workforce with a growing number of female employees and minorities (Festing, Kornau, & Schäfer, 2015; Sidani & Ariss, 2014). For instance, in the U.S.A., women now make up a greater share of the workforce than ever before: 49%

of jobs were held by women in 2014, as opposed to 48% in 2001. This translates into 4.9 million more female workers since 2001, compared to 2.2 million additional male workers (Careerbuilder, 2016). The greater diversity of the labor force challenges employers to create TM practices that ensure they fully utilize the talents, skills, and values of all employees. Managing this diversity involves many different activities and decisions that touch upon many perspectives: staffing, work design, training perspective, compensation, etc.

Massive regional shifts are also expected: Africa's population is expected to double by 2050, while Europe's population is expected to condense (UN DESA report, 2017). The developing countries are expected to contribute 55% of the world's gross domestic product (GDP) by 2018 (UN report, 2018). These newer economies now have a large buying segment: the global middle class is expected to increase from 1.8 billion in 2009 to 3.2 billion in 2020, with Asia's middle class tripling in size to 1.7 billion by 2020 (BBC News, 2013). While both demographic changes and diversity bring risks to companies that fail to respond adequately, they also bring opportunities to organizations that are able to adapt rapidly (Ariss et al., 2014; Cooke, Saini, & Wang, 2014; Festing et al., 2015; Sidani & Ariss, 2014). Likewise, demographic changes and increased diversity generate substantial implications for TM decision making (Cooke et al., 2014; Festing & Schäfer, 2014; Festing et al., 2015; Sidani & Ariss, 2014). Companies may anticipate these changes by, for example, moving their business operations to emerging markets and new geographic locations where talent continues to develop (Beamond et al., 2016). At the same time, companies need to keep a nurturing eye on their already acquired talented employees, since competition for talent becomes more intense (Cooke et al., 2014).

Intensified Workforce Mobility

The second macro factor, which is a vital element of organization's approach to decision making in TM, concerns the *intensified workforce mobility*. Indeed, the number of people assigned by their employers to roles outside their home country has increased by 25% over the past decade, and it is expected to increase by 50% by 2020 (PricewaterhouseCoopers, 2018). Due to the increased workforce mobility, talented individuals now have more opportunities to go elsewhere, outside of their home locations (Collings, 2014). More and more such individuals are planning to relocate, and organizations have an opportunity to make their employment offers more appealing. Some companies recognize this factor and take steps to facilitate favorable conditions that allow talent movement, while others remain less active (Ariss et al., 2014).

As workforce mobility increases, the war for talent also becomes tougher (Collings, 2014; Vaiman, Haslberger, & Vance, 2015). Nowadays companies compete with their rivals that are located not only within their home region, but also with companies located all around the globe (Ariss et al., 2014; Khilji, Tarique, & Schuler, 2015). For effective TM decision making, organizations need to plan and implement customized efforts that can enable them to manage talent. They may need to cultivate rotation, coaching and training in order to reinforce their talent pool (Cooke et al., 2014). A strong company brand is another prerogative aimed at attracting and retaining talent. Organizations need, therefore, to invest heavily in company branding and create favorable conditions that allow talent relocation (Sidani & Ariss, 2014).

Rapid Digitalization and Technological Innovations

Rapid digitalization and technological innovations is the next factor impacting decision making in TM. More often people are online 24/7, being relentlessly flooded with information brought about by speedy advances in communication technologies. Rapid digitalization and technological innovations lead to global awareness and provide superior opportunities to people to access information. Rapid digitalization and technological innovations also allow project teams to work in remote locations across the world, easily accessing experts within and outside organizations. This macro factor modifies the skills employers need, replacing physical duties with knowledge-based ones. Companies begin to prioritize talent with technological skills, such as cloud computing, mobile technology, and data analytics (Ariss et al., 2014). This, in turn, transforms the process of recruitment, hiring, training, and development that companies employ to get and keep the best employees. For example, digital learning and networking tools become more accessible, and an increase in utilizing gamification and other fun learning techniques continues to emerge (Vesa, Hamari, & Warmelink, 2017), challenging the status quo.

In general, rapid digitalization and technological innovations lead to the formation of a workforce, which is well acquainted with advanced technologies. This technologically advanced workforce may expect high levels of autonomy and trust on the part of a potential employer. Furthermore, this workforce is not likely to follow strict directions at work, which is not expected of employees in highly structured companies that are usually characterized by low levels of independence and creativity. Organizations thus need to make sure that they can provide talent with the latest technologies as well as with a generous degree of empowerment (Ariss et al., 2014; Khilji et al., 2015; Kontoghiorghes, 2015). Companies also need to take a closer look at data security, as digitalization and technological advances lead to the rise of hackers and data theft (Khilji et al., 2015).

Multi-generational Workforce

Finally, the rise of a *multi-generational workforce* has a major impact on decision making in TM. As the world population grows, the Millennials (the generation born between roughly 1985 and 2000) enter the workforce in greater numbers. By 2020, the Millennials will make up over one-third of the global workforce (ManpowerGroup, 2016). While the Millennials are a major talent workforce, older employees remain to be valuable contributors. Interestingly, 75% of employees surveyed by Spherion believe that younger workers lack the business and life experience required for leadership positions, but 82% still believe that recruiting Millennials is critical to their organization's future success (Spherion, 2016). This multi-generational workforce of Baby Boomers, Gen X-ers (born between the mid-1960s and mid-1980s), and the Millennials generates a need for organizations to manage a highly diverse set of employees whose work habits vary widely. A generic approach to managing this new type of workforce is unlikely to function well, mostly due to markedly distinct needs and wants by each generation.

The Millennial generation, for instance, is substantially different from other generations (Festing & Schäfer, 2014; Vaiman et al., 2012). The majority of the Millennials look for jobs through social media. They value creativity, autonomy, continuous training, and development. They demand more opportunities for career advancement. They are not interested in having jobs for the rest of their lives. The Millennials expect a pleasant, flexible, and convenient work environment: if they are going to spend 8–10 hours a day in an office, it better be comfortable. The Millennials also require a more personalized community and thought-provoking communication in the work environment (Festing & Schäfer, 2014). At the same time, equipped with increased mobility, the Millennials are interested in remote work options, where work-life balance does not mean just a few extra days off or an extended parental leave (Khilji et al., 2015; Vaiman et al., 2015).

The Millennials are not solely looking for financial gains and rapid promotion. Conversely, they overwhelmingly value career development, which means that they are mindful about their career choices and select a new workplace cautiously. The Millennials expect a tailored approach from the recruitment process as well as from the job itself. Job flexibility is high on the agenda for the Millennials, which means that this generation is ready to work hard but on their own terms. For example in a survey, when Millennials were asked what attracts them to their current or future organization, 38% mentioned visibility and buy-in to the mission and vision of the organization, and 26% cited work-life balance (Futurestep [a division of KornFerry], 2016). Nearly all respondents emphasized flexibility in work hours and social component of the workplace as their top priorities (Futurestep, 2016).

The multi-generational workforce urges TM decision makers to customize their employee approaches. This new type of workforce reshapes the job market with a combination of relatively traditional job expectations of Baby Boomers and Gen X-ers, and radically new expectations of the Millennials. While companies are well aware of the values of "older" generations, the Millennials require distinctive conditions (Festing & Schäfer, 2014). Trying to keep up with the Millennial mindsets is an emerging challenge for TM decision makers (Ariss et al., 2014; Farndale et al., 2014). To keep up with this workforce, organizations need to deliver continuous training, developmental opportunities, and meaningful job tasks to its talent, which involve a high degree of creativity, independence, and inspiration (Cooke et al., 2014; Farndale et al., 2014). Companies are also counselled to provide the Millennials with accelerated career advancements opportunities, increased job flexibility, and self-reliance.

The Key Micro Factors Influencing Talent Management Decision Making in the Global Context

In line with macro factors influencing talent management, several micro factors are also worth discussing. Many of these micro (organization-level) factors are the outcomes of macro (or country-level, environmental) factors, since both are strongly interrelated (King & Vaiman, 2018).

Rise of Small and Medium-sized Enterprises

The first factor is related to the fact that TM is now gaining attention in small and medium-sized enterprises (SMEs). However, since SMEs usually have fewer resources, they tend to face particular limitations and risks when dealing with TM. While multinational corporations (MNCs) tend to have experts in specialized areas of TM, such as in assessment methodologies, diversity, or instructional design, SMEs may not have much specialized in-house expertise in the subject (Farndale et al., 2014; Sidani & Ariss, 2014). Furthermore, while MNCs can afford to invest in most reliable TM software, SMEs may not always have an opportunity to employ the kind of in-depth assessment of TM tools they would prefer (Farndale et al., 2014). Recruitment of the best talent in SMEs, therefore, becomes much more crucial, since their profit largely depends on the talent they recruit.

At the same time, SMEs may possess critical advantages over MNCs. SMEs can offer a highly customized approach towards their talented individuals, since they have fewer people in the organization in general, and hence, more knowledge about each of them. SMEs can also respond rapidly to individual needs and development preferences of talented employees. Since there tends to be much less hierarchy and bureaucracy in SMEs, as compared to MNCs, disseminating a talent mindset throughout the organization can take less time and effort. Finally, it may be easier to nurture a sense of belonging in talent in SMEs, where the contribution of each employee is usually more noticeable (Saini & Budhwar, 2008).

Companies where leaders take talent seriously may perform better on all aspects of TM than companies where talent is seen as a commodity (Saini & Budhwar, 2008). Therefore, in order for SMEs to reinforce TM decision making process, their organizational leaders need to possess the right mindset that would help them in nurturing and championing talent.

Rapid Organizational Transformations

Many organizations face challenges of reorganizing their business in the current hyper-competitive and increasingly complex global economy. Rapid organizational transformations (mergers and acquisitions, strategic renewals, restructuring) are thus more emerging factors impacting the complexity of decision making in TM.

Growing and emerging industries, such as game industry and nanotechnology, as well as those industries currently undergoing strategic renewal, such as the paper industry and pharmaceuticals, face rapid organizational transformations (Teece, Peteraf, & Leih, 2016). To adjust to the shrinking demands for their products and current economic slowdown, companies are forced to make difficult decisions like production capacity reduction, restructuring, and layoffs. Other real-world challenges faced by companies are global outsourcing, healthcare management, bribery, corruption, political risk, and poverty (Morris et al., 2016). Finally, prompt and ever-present competitors make sustainable competitive advantage a remote possibility, thus intensifying the role of chance and luck as its likely explanation (Beinhocker, 2006; Farjoun, 2007). In order to survive in current times, companies need to rely more on such tools as flexibility, experimentation, operational excellence, adaptive responses, and dynamic capabilities (Teece et al., 2016).

Given the increasing turbulence in the environments companies operate in, decision making in TM may look distinct in companies undergoing organizational transformations. Following the cutting-edge evolution of business strategy to echo more boundaryless and interconnected organization systems, the role of talent during organizational transformations is to act as self-initiated change agents, unlike in traditional global TM, which mainly positions talent as executors. This notion of a different role of talent during organizational transformations leads to a different understanding of the role of a company during the transformations as well. Whereas traditional TM sees the company as a facilitator in terms of "filling key positions with competent incumbents and ensuring their continued commitment" (Collings, & Mellahi, 2009: 304), the company should perform the role of a supporter during organizational transformations. In order to implement successful decision making in TM, companies should support the self-initiated change agents to ensure their continued efforts aimed at the organizational transformation.

New Workplace Dynamics

Driven by demographic changes, increased mobility, digitalization, and technological advances, as well as the entrance of the Millennials to the workforce, the workplace itself is undergoing a vast change (Collings, 2014; Farndale et al., 2014; Khilji et al., 2015; Kontoghiorghes, 2015). The days of loyalty, stability, and long-term retention are fading away. This leads to a formation of new workplace dynamics, another micro factor influencing decision making in TM. Nowadays, instead of having the policy of "pre-hire to retire", companies seek to build organizational culture, where the environment is forgiving, transparent, and developmental in nature (Fehr, Fulmer, Awtrey, & Miller, 2016). Instead of possessing "up or out" thinking, companies tend to follow "we can all succeed here" philosophy.

Since work can be completed by employees operating on the other side of the globe, companies rely less on permanent staff. Independent work or project-based work filling specific organizational needs becomes more prevalent (Cascio & Boudreau, 2016; Khilji et al., 2015). Therefore, some companies tend to possess only a small in-house staff accompanied by virtual networks of project employees and other independent workers (Cascio & Boudreau, 2016). Thus, talent might not work solely for one company, but rather offer their services to a number of organizations (Cerdin & Brewster, 2014).

New workplace dynamics obliges companies to provide a supportive, challenging, and self-motivated workplace to talented individuals, besides just a reasonable and attractive compensation package. That is why in highly competitive global markets, some organizations are not always able to amplify their compensation, and therefore need to go above and beyond. Thus, the trustworthy relationship between the company and the talent as well as a psychological contract fulfillment becomes a really strong bargaining tool for attracting, developing, and retaining talent (Ariss et al., 2014; Farndale et al., 2014; Festing & Schäfer, 2014; Sonnenberg et al., 2014). The willingness of companies to embrace flexibility in a way they manage talent is also becoming a new and essential differentiating factor (Cerdin & Brewster, 2014).

New workplace dynamics also change the nature of trust. Talented individuals have access to far more information than before (Ariss et al., 2014; Festing & Schäfer, 2014; Sonnenberg et al., 2014). They can compare compensation packages, developmental opportunities, and corporate culture against those of competitors at home and abroad, and they may share extensively their own experiences. As a result, organizations must ensure they fulfill the promises they communicate to their talent and make sure that everything, from culture to compensation packages, reinforces the intent to deliver on those promises (Ariss et al., 2014; Sonnenberg et al., 2014).

Low engagement among employees is an important and commonplace aspect of current workplace dynamics. Research has not produced a universal recipe for how to keep employees – especially, the talented ones – engaged, since they tend to attach more importance to establishing their own career path than to maintaining organizational loyalty, and may perceive their current companies merely as stepping stones to better jobs elsewhere (Cerdin & Brewster, 2014; Khoreva & van Zalk, 2016). Talented individuals do not "sell their skills" to employers, but rather volunteer their efforts at work (Ariss et al., 2014). They act more like a "consumer" choosing with whom they work, thereby challenging the traditional relationship with the employer and demanding a more tailored managerial approach.

Providing training and development opportunities is a tool that may increase work engagement and retention among talented employees (Cerdin & Brewster, 2014; Cooke et al., 2014; Khoreva & van Zalk, 2016; Kontoghiorghes, 2015; Vaiman et al., 2015). Organizations, therefore, may consider allocating more resources to training and development opportunities. Those companies that are able to satisfy these needs, may be one step ahead of their competitors in TM decision making (Cerdin & Brewster, 2014; Cooke et al., 2014). Furthermore, companies may need to redefine the way they set goals and evaluate performance, since the days of traditional appraisals and forced ranking are also ending. In order to be effective in TM decision making, companies should closely re-examine their performance processes, simplify their performance management systems, and focus more on coaching, mentoring, and continuous feedback (Khoreva & Vaiman, 2015).

COVID-19 Pandemic and Global Talent Management

COVID-19 has affected every sector across regions, countries, and industries (Caligiuri et al., 2020). The intersection of uncertainty, technology, and recession has changed the way talent is managed. For instance, the notion of a hybrid workforce of in-person and remote employees has gained more currency and traction in most industries such as education, banking, and healthcare. A recent study by Gartner found that 82% of respondents "will allow employees to work remotely some of the time" (Gartner, 2020). A similar study by PricewaterhouseCoopers found:

> PwC's June survey of executives and office workers shows that a permanent flexible workweek (and perhaps workday) has broad support. Most office workers (83%) want to work from home at least one day a week, and half of employers (55%) anticipate that most of their workers will do so long after COVID-19 is not a concern. (PricewaterhouseCoopers, 2020)

Theoretical and empirical research is needed to assess and measure the impact of this pandemic on international, national, and institutional levels, particularly in three important areas (Caligiuri et al., 2020): managing under uncertainty, facilitating international and global work, and redefining organizational performance.

Future Research Agenda

This chapter highlighted a number of key factors that are influencing decision making in TM now, as well as some emerging factors that will affect this decision making in the future. TM has now become even more central than before, as its careful planning and implementation may lead to sustainable growth and competitive advantage through the meaningful and timely investment in talent. Organizations need to respond quickly to these factors and develop innovative ways in order to attract and manage talent. More empirical studies are indeed needed to better monitor TM decision making in relation to the context in which it occurs. We thus suggest several avenues for future research.

First, future research is needed to examine how companies respond to macro and micro factors identified in the chapter. The current talent workforce is global, highly connected, technology-savvy, and demanding. It is also youthful, ambitious, filled with high expectations, and demanding more on-the-job learning opportunities, better or different compensation packages, work-life balance programs, as well as development opportunities. Future empirical studies may thus, for example, investigate how these features of current talent workforce influence TM decision making in the global context. It is important to keep in mind that macro and micro features identified in the chapter are embedded in multiple levels that need to be both analyzed and conceptualized at multiple levels. Advances in multi-level modeling will also help to amplify precision of quantitative research.

Next, future research that examines how global TM influences the choice for TM decision making could provide interesting insights. To this end, a first step would be to conduct discourse analyses that investigate current organizational TM decisions through examining official organizational policies or statements of decision makers, line managers, and HR professionals. In addition, comparative case analyses can be conducted to assess the implementation of TM decisions in different types of organizations.

Without a doubt, TM decision making may look differently in companies undergoing rapid organizational transformations (mergers and acquisitions, strategic renewals, restructuring) than in more stable MNCs (Tatoglu et al., 2016). Furthermore, SMEs may possess fewer resources and confront more limitations and risks when dealing with TM, in comparison to those of MNCs. TM decision making as well as TM strategies and policies may therefore have a different nature in these types of companies. In addition, qualitative methods can be used to gain insights into the relationships between global TM and TM decision making by investigating decision makers' attitudes to and experiences of dealing with global talent. As global TM is becoming increasingly important for organizations operating on a global scale, cross-cultural comparisons of the relationships between global TM and TM decision making might also be of interest (Farndale et al., 2014).

Finally, future research is suggested to focus on how companies balance the needs of short-term decision making of managing the companies with the long-term strategic decision making of global TM, which requires linking TM with corporate culture and business strategy (Vaiman et al., 2012). With the aim of advancing decision making in TM, more thorough frameworks are required to reveal the complex set of factors that shape TM in the international context (Gallardo-Gallardo et al., 2015; Tatoglu et al., 2016; Vaiman et al., 2012). For instance, the willingness of companies to adopt flexibility in a way they manage talent is becoming a differentiating factor. Future research may examine how this feature of current workforce dynamics influences TM decision making.

References

Ariss, A. A., Cascio, W. F., & Paauwe, J. 2014. Talent management: Current theories and future research directions. *Journal of World Business,* 49: 173–179.

Bartlett, C. A., & McLean, A. N. 2006. GE's talent machine: The making of a CEO. *Harvard Business School, Case 9-304-049.*

BBC News. 2013. Rise of the global middle class. *BBC News home page.* http://www.bbc.com/news/business-22956470, first accessed October 22, 2018.

Beamond, M., Farndale, E., & Härtel, C. 2016. MNE translation of corporate talent management strategies to subsidiaries in emerging economies. *Journal of World Business,* 51(4): 499–510.

Beamond, M. T., Farndale, E., & Härtel, C., E. J. 2020. Frames and actors: Translating talent management strategy to Latin America. *Management and Organization Review,* 16(2), 405–442.

Beinhocker, E. D. 2006. *The origin of wealth: Evolution, complexity and the radical remaking of economics.* Boston, MA: Harvard Business School Press.

Boudreau, J. W. 2010. *Retooling HR: Using proven business tools to make better decisions about talent.* Boston, MA: Harvard Business School Press.

Boudreau, J. W., & Jesuthasan, R. 2011. *Transformative HR: How great companies use evidence based change for sustainable advantage.* San Francisco, CA: Jossey-Bass.

Boudreau, J. W., & Ramstad, P. M. 2007. *Beyond HR: The new science of human capital.* Boston, MA: Harvard Business School Press.

Briscoe, J. P. & Hall, D. 1999. An alternative approach and new guidelines for practice. *Organizational Dynamics,* 28: 37–51.

Caligiuri, P., De, C. H., Dana, M., Verbeke, A., & Angelika, Z. 202). International HRM insights for navigating the COVID-19 pandemic: Implications for future research and practice. *Journal of International Business Studies,* 51(5), 697–713.

Careerbuilder. 2016. The changing face of today's workforce. *Business News Daily.* http://www.businessnewsdaily. com/7873-face-of-todays-workforce.html, first accessed October 22, 2018.

Cascio, W., & Boudreau, J. 2016. The search for global competence: From international HR to talent management. *Journal of World Business,* 51: 103–114.

Cerdin, J-L., & Brewster, C. 2014. Talent management and expatriation: Bridging two streams of research and practice. *Journal of World Business,* 49: 245–252.

Chatman, J., & Cha, S. E. 2003. Leading by leveraging culture. *California Management Review,* 45: 20–34.

Collings, D. G. 2014. Integrating global mobility and global talent management: Exploring the challenges and strategic opportunities. *Journal of World Business,* 49: 253–261.

Collings, D. G., & Isichei, M. 2018. The shifting boundaries of global staffing: Integrating global talent management, alternative forms of international assignments and non-employees into the discussion. *The International Journal of Human Resource Management,* 29: 165–187.

Collings, D. G., & Mellahi, K. 2009. Strategic talent management: A review and research agenda. *Human Resource Management Review,* 19: 304–313.

Collings, D. G., Mellahi, K., & Cascio, W. F. 2017. (Eds). *The Oxford handbook of talent management.* Oxford, UK: Oxford University Press.

Collings, D. G., Scullion, H., & Vaiman., V. 2015. Talent management: Progress and prospects. *Human Resource Management Review,* 25: 233–235.

Cooke, F. L., Saini, D. S., & Wang, J. 2014. Talent management in China and India: A comparison of management perceptions and human resource practices. *Journal of World Business,* 49: 225–235.

Davenport, T. H., Harris, J. G., & Morison, R. 2010a. *Analytics at work: Smarter decision, better results.* Harvard Business School Press, Boston, MA.

Davenport, T. H., Harris, J., & Shapiro, J. 2010b. Competing on talent analytics: What the best companies know about their people – and how they use that information to outperform rivals. *Harvard Business Review,* 88(10): 52–58.

De Boeck, G., Meyers, M.C., & Dries, N. 2018. Employee reactions to talent management: Assumptions versus evidence. *Journal of Organizational Behavior,* 39: 199–213.

Dries, N. 2013. The psychology of talent management: A review and research agenda. *Human Resource Management Review,* 23: 272–285.

Farjoun, M. 2007. The end of strategy? *Strategic Organization,* 5: 197–210.

Farley, C. 2005. HR's role in talent management and driving business results. *Employment Relations Today,* 32 (1): 55–61.

Farndale, E., Pai, A., Sparrow, P., & Scullion, H. 2014. Balancing individual and organizational goals in global talent management: A mutual-benefits perspective. *Journal of World Business,* 49: 204–214.

Fehr, R., Fulmer, A., Awtrey, E., & Miller, J. 2016. The grateful workplace: A multilevel model of gratitude in organizations. *Academy of Management Review,* 42(2): 361–381.

Festing, M., Kornau, A., & Schäfer, L. 2015. Think talent – think male? A comparative case study analysis of gender inclusion in talent management practices in the German media industry. *International Journal of Human Resource Management,* 26(6): 707–732.

Festing, M., & Schäfer, L. 2014. Generational challenges to talent management: A framework for talent retention based on the psychological-contract perspective. *Journal of World Business,* 49: 262–271.

Festing, M., Schäfer, L., & Scullion, H. 2013. Talent management in medium-sized German companies: An explorative study and agenda for future research. *International Journal of Human Resource Management,* 24: 1872–1893.

Fombrun, C., Tichy, N.M., & Devanna, M.A. 1984. *Strategic human resource management.* New York: Wiley.

Futurestep. 2016. *Millennials in the workplace.* http://www.futurestep.com, first accessed January 6, 2017.

Gallardo-Gallardo, E., Nijs, S., Dries, N., & Gallo, P. 2015. Towards an understanding of talent management as a phenomenon-driven field using bibliometric and content analysis. *Human Resource Management Review,* 25(3): 264–270.

Gallardo-Gallardo, E., & Thunnissen, M. 2016. Standing on the shoulders of giants? A critical review of empirical talent management research. *Employee Relations,* 38: 31–56.

Gartner, 2020. *Gartner survey reveals 82% of company leaders plan to allow employees to work remotely some of the time.* July 14, 2020. https://www.gartner.com/en/newsroom/press-releases/2020-07-14-gartner-survey-reveals-82-percent-of-company-leaders-plan-to-allow-employees-to-work-remotely-some-of-the-time.

Khilji, S. E., Tarique, I., & Schuler, R. S. 2015. Incorporating the macro view in global talent management. *Human Resource Management Review,* 25(3): 236–248.

Khoreva, V., & Vaiman, V. 2015. Intent vs. action: Talented employees and leadership development. *Personnel Review,* 44(2): 200–216.

Khoreva, V., & van Zalk, M. 2016. Antecedents of work engagement among high potential employees. *Career Development International,* 21(5): 459–476.

Jooss, S., McDonnell, A., Burbach, R., & Vaiman, V. 2019. Conceptualising talent in multinational hotel corporations. *International Journal of Contemporary Hospitality Management,* 31(10), 3879–3898.

King, K. A., & Vaiman, V. 2018. Macro talent management (MTM): What it is and why is it important to global talent management? In D. G. Collings, H. Scullion, & P. Caligiuri (Eds.), *Global Talent Management* (2nd ed.). London: Routledge.

Kontoghiorghes, C. 2015. Linking high performance organizational culture and talent management: Satisfaction/ motivation and organizational commitment as mediators. *The International Journal of Human Resource Management,* 27(16): 1833–1853.

Kravariti, F., & Johnston, K. 2020. Talent management: A critical literature review and research agenda for public sector human resource management. *Public Management Review,* 22(1), 75–95.

Krishnan, T. N., & Scullion, H. 2017. Talent management and dynamic view of talent in small and medium enterprises. *Human Resource Management Review,* 27(3), 431–441.

ManpowerGroup. 2016. *Millennial careers: 2020 Vision.* https://www.manpowergroup.com/wps/wcm/connect/ 660ebf65-144c-489e-975c-9f838294c237/MillennialsPaper1_2020Vision_lo.pdf?MOD=AJPERES, first accessed October 22, 2018.

Mäkela, K., Bjorkman, I., & Ehrnrooth, M. 2010. How do MNCs establish their talent pools? Influences on individuals' likelihood of being labelled as talent. *Journal of World Business,* 45 (2): 134–142.

McDonnell, A., Collings, D. G., Mellahi, K., & Schuler, R. 2017. Talent management: A systematic review and future perspectives. *European Journal of International Management,* 1: 86–128.

Mellahi, K., & Collings, D. G. 2010. The barriers to effective global talent management: The example of corporate elites in MNEs. *Journal of World Business,* 45: 143–149.

Morris, S., Snell, S., & Björkman, I. 2016. An architectural framework for global talent management. *Journal of International Business Studies,* 6: 723–747.

PricewaterhouseCoopers. 2018. *Workforce of the future: The competing forces shaping 2030.* https://www. pwc.com/gx/en/services/people-organisation/workforce-of-the-future/workforce-of-the-future-the-competing-forces-shaping-2030-pwc.pdf, first accessed October 22, 2018.

PricewaterhouseCoopers. 2020. *When everyone can work from home, what's the office for?* PwC's US remote work survey, June 25, 2020. https://www.pwc.com/us/en/library/covid-19/us-remote-work-survey.html.

Pucik, V., Evans, P., Björkman, I., & Morris, S. 2017. *The global challenge: International human resource management* (3rd ed.). Chicago: Chicago Business Press.

Saini, D. S., & Budhwar, P.S. 2008. Managing the human resource in Indian SMEs: The role of indigenous realities. *Journal of World Business,* 43: 417–434.

Sidani, Y., & Ariss, A. A. 2014. Institutional and corporate drivers of global talent management: Evidence from the Arab Gulf region. *Journal of World Business,* 49: 215–224.

Sonnenberg, M., van Zijderveld, V., & Brinks, M. 2014. The role of talent-perception incongruence in effective talent management. *Journal of World Business,* 49: 272–280.

Sparrow, P. R., & Makram, H. 2015. What is the value of talent management? Building value-driven processes within a talent management architecture. *Human Resource Management Review,* 25: 249–263.

Spherion. 2016. *Emerging workforce study survey findings.* https://www.spherion.com/workforce-insights/survey-findings/survey-findings-2016/, first accessed October 22, 2018.

Tatoglu, E., Glaister, A. J., & Demirbag, M. 2016. Talent management motives and practices in an emerging market: A comparison between MNEs and local firms. *Journal of World Business,* 51: 278–293.

Teagarden, M. B. 2018. Talent in emerging markets. *Thunderbird International Business Review,* 60(1): 3–4.

Teece, D., Peteraf, M., & Leih, S. 2016. Dynamic capabilities and organizational agility: Risk, uncertainty, and strategy in the innovation economy. *California Management Review,* 58(4): 13–35.

Thunnissen, M. 2016. Talent management: For what, how and how well? An empirical exploration of talent management in practice. *Employee Relations,* 38: 57–72.

UN DESA Report. 2017. *World population prospects: The 2017 revision.* United Nations Department of Economic and Social Affairs home page. first accessed October 22, 2018.

UN DESA Report. 2019. *World Population prospects 2019: Highlights.* https://population.un.org/wpp.

UN Report. 2018. *World economic situation and prospects 2018.* https://www.un.org/development/desa/dpad/ wp-content/uploads/sites/45/publication/WESP2018_Full_Web-1.pdf, first accessed October 22, 2018.

Vaiman, V., Collings, D. G., & Scullion, H. 2012. Talent management decision making. *Management Decision,* 50(5): 925–941.

Vaiman, V., Collings, D.G., & Scullion, H. 2017. Contextualising talent management. *Journal of Organizational Effectiveness: People and Performance,* 4(4): 294–297.

Vaiman, V., Haslberger, A., & Vance, C. M. 2015. Recognizing the important role of self-initiated expatriates in effective global talent management. *Human Resource Management Review,* 25: 280–286.

Vaiman, V., Schuler, R., Sparrow, P., & Collings, D. (eds.). 2018a. *Macro Talent Management: A Global Perspective on Managing Talent in Developed Markets,* New York City/London: Routledge.

Vaiman, V., Schuler, R., Sparrow, P., & Collings, D. (eds.). 2018b. *Macro Talent Management in Emerging and Emergent Markets: A Global Perspective,* New York City/London: Routledge.

Van den Broek, J., Boselie, P., & Paauwe, J. 2018. Cooperative innovation through a talent management pool: A qualitative study on coopetition in healthcare. *European Journal of Management,* 36(1): 135–144.

Vesa, M., Harviainen, J. T., & Warmelink, H. 2017. Computer Games and Organization Studies. *Organization Studies,* 38(2): 273–284.

8

GLOBAL MACRO TALENT MANAGEMENT

An Interdisciplinary Approach

Shaista E. Khilji

Ramien Pierre

Introduction

Today's organizations operate in a highly complex, global, and inter-dependent environment, where solutions of high-priority problems demand insights from multiple disciplines. Consider the issue of recruiting and developing talent globally. Research as well as practice indicate that management of global talent systems requires examination of macro environmental issues impacting both individuals and organizations, to include local government talent development policies (see for example, Cooke & Wang, 2019; Khilji & Keilson, 2014; King & Vaiman, 2019; Outila, Vaiman, & Holden, 2019; Vaiman et al., 2019): global labor market conditions/dynamics (see for example, Dickmann & Perry, 2019; Oettl & Agarawal, 2008; Ragazzi, 2014): global mobility (Collings, 2014; O'Sullivan & Collings, 2019): dias-pora strategies (Khilji & Keilson, 2014; Outila et al., 2019; Saxenian, 2005; Tung & Lazaraova, 2006): and multinational corporations' (MNC) organizational mechanisms that manage talent recruitment, selection, and development processes (Bjorkman et al., 2017; Collings, Mellahi, & Cascio, 2018; Ruel, Bondarouk, & Dresselhaus, 2014). The macro talent management (MTM) conceptual framework proposed by Khilji, Tarique, and Schuler (2015): and subsequent works (for example, Outila et al., 2019; Schuler & Khilji, 2017; Schuler, Tarique, & Khilji, 2018; Vaiman et al., 2019) adequately capture the multiplicity of the levels of analyses, from national/global to individual to organizational and back to the national/global, in terms of the many environmental factors, government policies, talent management (TM) functions, processes, and outcomes. Based on MTM frameworks, we argue that conceptual boundaries of global talent management (GTM) and MTM are not fixed and extend beyond a single discipline.

In this chapter, we aim to establish macro global talent management (MGTM) as an interdiscip-linary concept. We begin this chapter by highlighting the importance of inter-disciplinary research in international business research. Next, we present five domains that directly impact TM systems within organizational, national, and global contexts. We conclude with identifying questions that extend beyond a single discipline and could be used to further develop research that strengthens multi-level understanding of GTM. We use the term MGTM to highlight the integration of macro in the GTM field (Khilji et al., 2015; Schuler & Khilji, 2017; Schuler et al., 2018)

The Importance of an Interdisciplinary Approach

The calls for interdisciplinary research in the field of international business and human resource management are not new (Khilji, 2014; Sapinski, Ciupka, & Khlobystov, 2017). Several decades ago, Dunning, in his address as the outgoing president of the Academy of International Business, made a plea for more interdisciplinary research. He argued that in an ever increasingly complex world,

DOI: 10.4324/9781315474687-8

competitive advantage is dependent upon not one resource but rather combining interdependent capabilities "with each other and with complementary assets in different countries and cultures" (1989: 411). Other scholars from a variety of disciplines have also made a similar case for developing interdisciplinary research, basing their assertions upon the need to draw from knowledge, theory, and methods used in multiple disciplines to solve complex problems and/or develop a more holistic understanding of complex issues we face today (see for example, Aboelela et al., 2007; Cantwell & Brannen, 2011; Hasnas, Prentice, & Strudler, 2010; Judge et al., 2012; National Academy of Sciences, 2004; Sapinski et al., 2017). Aboellela et al. (2007): Judge et al. (2012): Wright (2011): and Zahra and Newey (2009) further establish the importance of interdisciplinary research by arguing that it is more influential in terms of its ability to fully answer critical questions, thus it has a greater impact than disciplinary research.

An examination of interdisciplinary research must begin with its definition. As expected, disparate definitions of interdisciplinary research abound in the literature. While it is true that the very concept of interdisciplinary research, with its complexity and multiplicity, defies one single coherent definition (Huutoniemi et al., 2010; Siedlok & Hibbert, 2014): it is nonetheless important to arrive at a common understanding to better support and undertake interdisciplinary research. In its simplest terms, inter-disciplinary research can be defined as a mode of research that transgresses traditional boundaries of a single discipline (Siedlok & Hibbert, 2014). However, based on a systematic literature review and interviews with researchers, Aboelela et al. present the definition of interdisciplinary research with more specificity. They state:

> Interdisciplinary research is any study or group of studies undertaken by scholars from two or more distinct scientific disciplines. The research is based upon a conceptual model that integrates theoretical frameworks from those disciplines, uses study design and methodology that is not limited to any one field, and requires the use of perspectives and skills of the involved disciplines throughout multiple phases of the research process (2007: 341).

As this definition implies, interdisciplinary research requires integration of perspectives and method-ologies, beyond composition of team members, through every phase of the research process. Here, interdisciplinary research is viewed as a *means* for building robust theory. In the same vein, National Academies of Press offer interdisciplinary research as that which

> integrates information, data, techniques, tools, perspectives, and/or theories from two of more disciplines or bodies of specialized knowledge to advance fundamental understanding or to solve problems whose solutions are beyond the scope of a single discipline or field of research practice (2005: 26).

This definition presents interdisciplinary research as an *output* to practically address problems of practice. In this chapter, we employ the latter definition, as it reminds us of not only inte-grating perspectives, but also helps us stay focused on the ultimate goal of advancing knowledge, understanding, and practice in GTM (beyond an organizational or individual level) to fully com-prehend the complexities of managing talent in today's globalized world, where organizations are not only competing with each other but where governments and their societies have also joined the race (Lanvin & Evans, 2014; Ragazzi, 2014; *The Economist*, 2011): thereby necessitating integration of multi-level perspectives and ideas (Khilji et al., 2015). In view of the growing evidence of national governments initiating efforts to upgrade their talent development systems for competitive advan-tage, *how do we develop an integrative understanding of MGTM beyond organizations to include the individual, national, and the global?* This serves as the focus of this chapter. We place an emphasis on delineating different research and practice domains and identifying broad questions that contribute to a more integrative understanding of MGTM.

Mgtm Research & Practice Domains

As mentioned previously, to help facilitate an interdisciplinary view, we use existing literature and frameworks (for example, Khilji et al., 2015; Schuler et al., 2018; Vaiman et al., 2019) that encapsulate environmental factors, processes, and outcomes related to MTM. We aim to highlight GTM as an inter-disciplinary phenomenon, and provide building blocks for future research in this area. Before we elaborate on different aspects of the model, it is important to mention that the MTM framework is non-linear, evolving, and complex (Khilji er al., 2015; Phene & Tallman, 2012; Schuler et al., 2018). Applying this understanding to MGTM, we can also view it as a system that requires interactions between different partners on a number of issues and levels, representing varying level of complexity.

In line with an expansive understanding of GTM, we adopt the following definition of MTM as proposed by Schuler & Khilji (2017: 2):

> Factors such as the demographics, the economic, educational, social and political conditions of countries and the policies, programs and activities that are systematically developed by governmental and non-governmental organizations expressly for the purpose of enhancing the quality and quantity of talent within and across countries and regions to facilitate productivity, innovation and competitiveness of their domestic and multinational enterprises for the benefit of their citizens, organizations, and societies for long-term advantage.

At this macro level, talent is defined to include a large majority of a country's population, similar to companies that pursue an *inclusive* approach in their TM activities. However, research has also shown that many countries (for example, Pakistan, Morocco, and Bangladesh) pursue an *exclusive* approach to target a small portion of the population, such as youth programs and assistance for high-performing citizens (Khilji & Keilson, 2014). Approaches to talent development may also be correlated with how "talent" is defined. For example, English, Russian, French, German, and Danish definitions of "talent" suggest it is "an innate giftedness that manifests itself in a particular field or endeavor and is linked to outstanding performance in some way" (Tansley, 2011: 268). Thus this understanding enhances intrinsic value of talent development. This differs from the Japanese definition of "talent" which emphasizes "talent as an accomplishment acquired and…the product of often years of striving to attain perfection" (Tansley, 2011: 269): thereby highlighting persistence of a long-term MTM agenda.

The MGTM Environment

Scholars have argued that globalization, intense competition (at the organizational and national levels): and population dynamics (in terms of an aging population in some developed countries and a substantially large young populations in emerging countries) as the most critical environment factors in the contemporary marketplace (Khilji et al., 2015; Schuler et al., 2018). Additionally, important environmental trends that have helped heighten the relevance of GTM at a macro level include: facilitating international migration to attract and retain global talent; a well-conceived and deliberate human development agenda to develop local talent; and the diaspora effect/brain circulation that has led to economic development through entrepreneurship, knowledge transfer, and experimentation (Khilji & Keilson, 2014; Oettl & Agrawal, 2008; Saxenian, 2005; Tung & Lazaraova, 2006).

Furthermore, we know that environment is dynamic and uncertain, and none of the identified factors are likely to remain stable or the same. Therefore, an understanding of MGTM needs to be continuously updated to refine existing theories, and/or develop new ones to keep pace with the evolving world and remain relevant (Cheng, Guo, & Skousen, 2011; Khilji, 2012a, 2012b). In sum, environment will always remain critical, and the trends and factors are likely to evolve and shift over time. This is important for developing a contextual understanding of MGTM.

MGTM Process and Outcome

In their seminal MTM work, Khilji et al. (2015) argue that talent produces knowledge flows, causes spillovers, and can be used for knowledge sharing as well as (organizational and national) learning. These aspects constitute GTM processes because they describe how talent relates to organizational and country level changes over time, identify patterns of activities and explain an observed relationship between talent and the desired outcomes of national competitiveness, innovation, and economic development (Liu et al., 2010; Oettl & Agrawal, 2008; Tung, 2008). By its very nature, process is diverse, evolving, and cannot be contained within a single paradigm (Van de Ven, 1992). This is also true of MGTM processes because a) these are likely to shift with the changes in environment, and as and how scholars/practitioners adopt new lenses to examine the old phenomena or continue to capture new phenomena, and b) these emanate from diverse disciplines and fields, including geography, economics, education, and international business, thus cannot be completely explained by a single paradigm. Hence a fuller understanding of the MGTM process (as proposed in their framework) would require multi-level analyses: individual, organizational, national, and even global.

The core functions of MGTM identified previously as talent planning, talent acquisition, talent development, and talent retention (Scullion, Collings & Caliguiri, 2010; Stahl et al., 2007; Tarique & Schuler, 2010) are part of the MGTM process, because these functions provide impetus for related MGTM activities. For example, even if we study the diaspora effect at the country level, we need to still discuss public policies and practices related to planning, attracting, and retaining talent nationally and globally. However, at the same time, our discussion indicates the importance of talent flow, knowledge spillovers, and learning in carrying out the basic core functions of MGTM. As global mobility has increased, and several governments have adopted an integrated human development agenda, it is equally important (if not more) to study talent flows and learning strategies/mechanisms to fully capture the essence of GTM at the macro level.

Finally, it is important to highlight the MGTM outcomes that predominantly relate to economic development, competitiveness, and innovation at the firm and national levels. We believe that when viewed from a macro perspective, MGTM requires an interdisciplinary approach because of a greater emphasis on achieving these outcomes in an intensely competitive and global environment. Incorporating a macro view advances MGTM to a policy and practice domain, and expands its scope to organizations, individuals, and countries. Using a multi-level lens reveals the richness of MGTM, draws our attention to the context in which it occurs, and illuminates its multiple consequences traversing levels of analysis (Hitt et al., 2007). It also captures the essence of complexities associated with managing talent globally, where organizations are not only competing with each other, but diasporas and national governments have also joined the race to acquire and retain talent globally.

This discussion highlights *at least* five domains applicable for integrated practice and research, including: 1) Policy Analysis, 2) Education, Learning, and Leadership Development, 4) Culture, Strategy, and Outcomes, 4) Organizations and HRM, and 5) Innovation. Below we describe the scope of each domain, as highlighted in the MGTM framework.

Policy Analysis

The human capital theory (HCT) links human capital to economic growth (Cornacchione, 2010; Lepak & Snell, 1999): and suggests that individuals and society derive economic benefits from investments in people (Becker, 1993; Sweetland, 1996). According to Becker (1993): investment in education and training are the most relevant types of investments in human capital. Thus as governments around the world focus upon spurring economic growth, by upgrading their local capabilities and building innovative capacities (Khilji & Keilson, 2014; Oettl & Agarawal, 2008; Ragazzi, 2014; Saxenian, 2005; Zweig, 2006): national talent has begun to take center stage in policy making. In addition, increased international talent mobility has led many countries to also compete to attract global talent and retain local talent (Beine, Docquier, & Rapport., 2008; Harvey, 2014; Vaiman, Scullion & Collings., 2012). As a result, countries have also become engaged in talent planning, including recruitment, development, and retention, in an effort to diversify their sources of talent and compete for talent globally (Lewin, Massini, & Peters, 2009; *The Economist*, 2006).

There is a trend to both develop their national talent (that countries own) as well as buy the already developed talent from elsewhere in the global market (through immigration and diaspora policies). For example, Harvey (2014) argues that as China transitioned from global labor-intensive manufacturing to knowledge economy, retaining and attracting talent has become an important component of its competitive strategy. In her review, Khilji (2012a) also shows that many governments (both developed and emerging economies, particularly Australia, Singapore, China, and Canada) have joined the hunt for global talent by developing merit-based immigrant and/or diaspora friendly policies (Ragazzi, 2014; *The Economist*, 2006). She argues that these efforts have been part of a government-led policy of strengthening the country through appropriate utilization, development, and acquisition of human talent.

Khilji and Keilson (2014) study the population-rich South Asian economies to outline various macro-level policies and programs that Bangladesh, Pakistan, and India have implemented to manage and develop national talent. They note that there is a greater emphasis on youth development programs in these countries because of their significantly large young population (up to 25%). Similarly other studies (see for example, Harvey, 2012; Harvey & Groutsis, 2012) demonstrate new policy initiatives in the Middle East, Hong Kong, United Kingdom, Canada, and Australia to manage a global talent pool. Collectively these studies highlight the importance of policy analysis in the study of MTM, and provide a glimpse into a wide array of national policies, including diaspora management, human development (education, leadership, and youth development): and immigration, that are considered central in attracting, retaining, and developing national talent.

Papademetriou and Sumption (2013: 35) argue that when governments "hunt for global talent" they are either expanding the pool of skilled persons that apply to their immigrant pool, designing policies to identify and select which applicants become immigrants, or some combination of both. Thus effective talent-management-informed immigration is not a two-way relationship between governments and potential immigrants. In fact, it is a three-way relationship among governments, potential immigrants, and employers. National immigration policies that were hostile to global talent circulation would dampen or derail local efforts to attract what Florida (2007) described as "transnational creative knowledge migrants".

At a much broader level, international organizations, such as the International Labor Organization, have been engaged in influencing and discussing migration and employment policy decisions at the global and national levels (see for example, Kuptsch & Eng Fong, 2006; Rihova & Streitska-Ilina, 2015; Wickramasekara, 2002). These studies collectively indicate that GTM is no longer an organizational effort. Rather it has become central in policy analysis and development. To facilitate this perspective, we need to pay particular attention to microeconomic migration policy (Harvey, 2014): macro-economic policies (Khilji & Keilson, 2014; Khilji & Khan, 2018) to focus on youth development, incentives for human development, diaspora policies, international talent mobility, and immigration policies.

Questions: From a policy perspective, a number of important questions emerge that demand attention as well as help to broaden the debate and incorporate multi-level analyses in the study of GTM. We begin with an overarching question: *What are national and global talent management agendas and programs?* Other questions include:

- *How do countries engage in adopting a national TM agenda?*
- *What challenges and opportunities are these faced with?*
- *How do market trends and environmental factors influence the adoption of different TM policies and strategies around the world?*
- *Do policy makers' intentions translate into effective adoption and implementation, and how do these impact organizations and individuals?*
- *How do organizations and individuals perceive, experience and benefit from a national TM agenda?*

Education, Learning, and Leadership Development

In the study of MGTM, the importance of human development has been highlighted (Khilji & Keilson, 2012; Khilji & Khan, 2018). As mentioned previously, whether it is developing talent in an organization or policy initiatives to develop youth within a broader national context, the ideas of education, training, and learning are central. GTM is intricately tied to developmental opportunities and possibilities for people to grow and further develop themselves (Borisova et al., 2017; Cutajar, 2013; Khilji, Schuler, & Tarique, 2015). Most often, these developmental efforts are aimed at enhancing skills, experiences, and competencies, particularly at the organizational level. It has also been argued that learning professionals play a key role in GTM by designing and delivering supportive learning activities within organizations. However, at the macro level, talent development oftentimes translates into policies that govern education, learning, and development of the workforce. This usually begins with strengthening educational (school) systems. Renzulli argues that "everyone has a stake in good schools because schools create and recreate a modern successful society" (2016: 80). Developing young talent begins as early as elementary school. This holistic approach is evidenced by educational reforms in a number of emerging economies and developed countries. For example, since 2000, higher educational institutions in Pakistan have undergone a deliberate rebirth as a result of the higher educational reforms that have aimed at improving access, quality, governance, and experience within higher education. These reforms are considered as a model for any emerging economy (The World Bank, 2018) and were introduced to change Pakistan from an agriculture based economy to a knowledge economy. Sanders (2018) offers examples from Singapore and Japan, where both countries have engaged in internationalization as a national policy to stay competitive in the 21st century. These have resulted in initiatives to promote world class universities and workforce development initiatives.

Building a competitive workforce requires a lifelong learning approach, that extends from educational institutions to workplaces or organizations (Illeris, 2018). It is, hence, also important to draw attention to workplace learning. Within an organization, learning must also be continuous and interactive. Managers must ensure that training and development systems are flexible and responsive to help individuals navigate today's rapidly changing industries and economies. In particular, the emphasis has been on leadership development, especially in view of an unprecedented flow of globalization in recent decades, significant growth of multinationals around the world, and the much-talked-about leadership shortages globally (Collings, Scullion and Caliguiri, 2018; Khilji, 2017). This point is further discussed below (refer to HRM and organizations). However, it is important to remember that effective partnerships between schools, businesses, and individuals can more effectively develop a globally competitive workforce (Hughes, Karp, & Orr, 2002).

Questions: An overarching question in this domain could be proposed as: *How do we provide learning and LD opportunities that strengthen organizational and national TM systems?*

Other questions that demand attention include:

- *What type of an organizational, industry, and country environments facilitates learning and leadership development?*
- *What types of socio-economic as well as organizational mechanisms enhance learning of the individuals and transfer of knowledge?*
- *How does educational leadership as well as corporate leadership/strategy relate to higher levels of MTM outcomes?*
- *How do educational partnerships between schools and workplaces evolve? How do these partnerships benefit individuals and group learning?*
- *How can we strengthen these partnerships?*
- *What programs and approaches are most conducive to effective leadership development and learning?*

Culture, Strategy, and Outcomes

As we start exploring macro TM globally, culture becomes an important consideration in terms of international comparative management and for studying its (i.e., organizational and national culture) influence on TM systems (Delong & Trutman, 2011; van Zyl, Mathafena, & Ras 2017). To fully optimize TM, organizations (and nations) have to create a "talent mindset" (Cutajar, 2013): i.e., instill a belief in the importance of developing and/or acquiring talent expressed through talent strategy and integrated activities. In their study, Musterd and Gritsai found that among the things that would attract transnational creative knowledge migrants to a particular region, cultural assets were the "icing on the cake" to jobs and other "classic factors" (2012: 351). National norms and values also have a strong impact on TM choices made by the managers and TM processes adopted by the organizations (Cutajar, 2013; Paauwe & Boslelie, 2003; Thunissen, 2015).

Research indicates that intended talent strategy and practices are also determined by the overall strategy of the organization, the internal and external environmental factors (Paauwe, 2014; Thunissen, 2015; Zyl et al., 2017). At the same time, all organizations go through certain organizational processes (see below) to manage and develop their talent. Hence those that adopt TM practices are aware of its positive impact on performance. From this description, strategy, culture (values, norms, and shared beliefs) and outcomes are interlinked. For example, Singapore, in adopting a national talent development agenda, is focused on enhancing its competitive advantage through development and retention of talent. Studies indicate that Singaporeans also have a "talent mindset" and shared belief in its positive outcomes (McNulty & Kaveri, 2019). Similarly, managers within organizations are aware of the positive outcomes of managing talent in terms of (for example) individual and team motivation, satisfaction, and profitability (Beechler & Woodward, 2009; Collings, 2014; Cutajar, 2013). They strengthen the positive outcomes by adopting an integrated TM approach, whereby organizational cultures and values support and inform their TM and business strategy (Paauwe, 2004; Wright & Nishii, 2013).

Questions: This is an interesting area of study, as it allows us to examine TM as an integrated system of strategies, values, and outcomes. An overarching question in this domain could be proposed as: *How do we create a talent mindset at the global, national and organizational levels that values both creativity and effort?* One could also explore the following questions that cut across levels of analysis to integrate the national with the global level efforts, organization, and the individual:

- *How do countries develop a "talent mindset" and influence adoption of TM practices at the national and organizational levels?*
- *How do organizations develop a "talent mindset" and influence adoption of national TM strategies? How does a "talent mindset" at the national level influence organizational approaches and individual experiences and outcomes related to GTM?*
- *How does a "talent mindset" at the organizational level influence individual perceptions, experiences, and outcomes related to GTM? How do GTM systems and practices relate to national and organizational outcomes?*
- *How do different countries engage in adoption and implementation of TM systems globally? How does GTM in one country influence another?*
- *How common is the perceived and actual integration of TM strategy, culture, and outcomes?*
- *What challenges, if any, are individuals, managers, and policy makers faced with in implementing an integrated view of TM?*

Organizations and HRM

This is probably the most researched and well-developed area in GTM research (Bjorkman et al., 2017). Within this stream of literature, the emphasis is on and organizational level analysis, whereby an organization's TM processes and functions are focused upon. TM functions, such as recruitment, selection, development, and performance management have received the most attention (Daubner-Siva et al., 2018). However, in some research, TM strategies have also been studied (see for example, Collings & Mellahi, 2009; Mellahi & Collings, 2010).

With a heavy emphasis on organizations and HRM, hence it is still the case that TM is most often defined as the creation and maintenance of human capital management systems designed to recruit, utilize, develop, and retain high-performing and high-potential employees to achieve organizational success (Kehinde, 2012; Scullion & Collings, 2010; Vladescu, 2012). In this stream of literature, managers and scholars have predominantly produced a competition-oriented approach (Bolander, Werr, & Asplund, 2017). Hence, TM has been widely viewed as the primary driver of organizational success in general (Barney, 1991a; Bartlett & Ghoshal, 1992; Kehinde, 2012; Sears, 2003; Vladescu, 2012) and a key component in maintaining competitive advantage in particular (Collings & Mellahi, 2009; Kehinde, 2012; Lewis & Heckman, 2006; Mellahi & Collings, 2010; Oehley & Theron, 2010). Effective TM is associated with numerous positive business outcomes, including improved processes, meeting current and future business needs, increased productivity, increased efficiency, and reduced risk and cost (Campeanu-Sonea et al., 2011; Kehinde, 2012; Mellahi & Collings, 2010).

An emphasis on functions has resulted in a narrower understanding of TM. First, some literature even considers TM synonymous with strategic human resource management, in that human capital management policies are linked to a company's overall strategic goals (Bhatnagar, 2007; Blackman & Kennedy, 2008; Creelman, 2004; McCauley & Wakefield, 2006; Schweyer, 2004). Second, researchers characterize TM as externally focused human capital strategies that organizations undertake to acquire sufficient numbers of highly skilled employees (Cappelli, 2008; Heinen & O'Neill, 2004; Michaels, Handfield-Jones, & Axelrod, 2001; Smart, 2005; Walker & LaRocco, 2002): thereby making TM an elitist approach, reserved for only the top talent. Finally, a third group of authors approach TM as an intra-organizationally focused activity that manages talented people by developing career pathways within the organization to ensure smooth leadership successions (Barlow, 2006; Berger, 2004; Blass, Knights, & Orbea, 2006; Boudreau & Ramstad, 2005; Groves, 2007; Jackson & Schuler, 1990; McCauley & Wakefield, 2006). Collings and Mellahi (2009) expand the Lewis and Heckman (2006) taxonomy of TM literature streams by identifying a fourth way TM is treated in the literature: TM as the focus of organizational positions that have or will have significant impact on organizational competitive advantage, as explained previously (Boudreau & Ramstad, 2005; Huselid, Beatty, & Becker, 2005).

Collectively these studies present TM as a narrow domain, that focuses on strategic goals, competitive advantage, a few dominant HR functions (retention, career, planning, and recruiting etc.): and leadership development (also mentioned previously). Most importantly, while there have been heated debates about the *inclusive* (involving all or many) and *exclusive* (involving only some) focus of TM activities within organizations (for example, refer to Ariss, Cascio, & Paauwe, 2014): a bulk of this discussion offers an elitist and *exclusive* understanding of TM, thereby further limiting its scope. In line with the previously stated definition of MTM, proposed by Schuler & Khilji (2017): an interdisciplinary understanding provides a broader and more inclusive definition of TM that impacts and incorporates many.

Bolander (2017) refers to a humanistic approach in TM where the emphasis is on inclusion. From a macro perspective, it is the humanistic approach that makes most sense in terms of developing the entire (global) workforce. As we have argued in this paper, it is important to address various levels of analyses in TM and by adopting an interdisciplinary lens, MTM allows us to extend the debate beyond competitive advantage to various domains, including policy, learning, education, development, innovation, and knowledge spillovers.

Questions: An overarching question could be proposed as: *How do we recruit, plan, develop, and retain talent at the organizational level using humanistic approaches?* Other questions include:

- *How do organizations facilitate the development of national and individual talent?*
- *How does national talent contribute to, and/or deter from organizational talent development?*
- *How do organizations cross fertilize opportunities for talent management systems within industries, nationally and globally?*
- *How does talent management add value to strategic competitive advantage beyond a single organization?*
- *What do organizations achieve by collaborating in the process of talent planning, development, and retention?*

Innovation

Scholars have argued that talent produces knowledge flows, causes spillovers, and can be used for knowledge sharing as well as (organizational and national) learning. As discussed previously, it is clear that macro institutional support, educational leadership, and corporate strategy and leadership can facilitate and/or hinder MTM in an environment. We present these aspects as MTM processes because they describe how talent relates to organizational and country level changes over time, identify patterns of activities, and explain an observed relationship between talent and the desired outcomes of (for example) national competitiveness, innovation, and economic development (Liu, et al., 2011; Oettl & Agrawal, 2008).

It is worth repeating that both governmental/NGO programs and organizational-level activities influence MTM processes. For example, greater global talent mobility stimulates international transmission of ideas (Agarwal et al., 2011; Kapur & McHale, 2005; Liu, et al., 2011): produces knowledge flows (Carr, Inkson, & Thorn, 2005; Di Maria & Lazarova, 2009): enhances learning (Furuya et al., 2009) and improves efficiency of the innovation process (Oettl & Agrawal, 2008). As people move and interact across organizations and societies, they provide greater access to knowledge and reduce the need to recreate knowledge that already exists elsewhere. They also gain diverse experiences and hence serve as a prime source of learning for organizations and societies (Di Maria & Lazarova, 2009).

Emerging evidence in international business literature indicates the importance of the impact of talent mobility on country-level innovation performance, well beyond the much-understood firm-level innovative capacities. For example, Oettl and Agrawal's (2008) study of cross-border movement of inventors (diaspora) presents an analysis of knowledge flow patterns as people move from one country (and firm) to another. Their analysis indicates that knowledge flows don't necessarily follow organizational boundaries as diaspora continue to develop and tap social relationships. They conclude that the receiving country (that diaspora returns to) learns and gains above and beyond the knowledge flow benefits enjoyed by the receiving firm. Based upon the findings, they emphasize the need for and the extensive role of national learning (from the diaspora) outside the traditional market mechanisms.

Liu et al.'s (2011) study of panel data, constituting technological characteristics of Chinese firms, and innovative performance also indicates that talent mobility is an important source of knowledge spillovers. They argue that returning diaspora's presence facilitates technology transfer to other firms in the receiving country, thereby leading to enhanced learning and economic growth. Both of these studies are pioneers in examining the value of talent mobility to the global economy. These provide evidence of the complexity of MTM as a phenomenon in the global marketplace, the role of corporate strategy and leadership, as well as good insights for broadening the scope of TM to include discussions relating to knowledge flows, innovation, learning, and competitiveness, which have not been sufficiently addressed in core TM literature.

Questions: Much like other domains, one could propose many questions that cut across levels and domains. An overarching question could include: *How does talent and TM systems strengthen innovation nationally and globally?* Other questions could include:

- *How does talent mobility expand international knowledge and learning mechanisms, and lead to enhanced levels of global competitiveness?*
- *How do national talent policies limit and/or expand opportunities of innovation and knowledge flows?*
- *What role does talent management directly play in strengthening innovation within organization, nationally and globally?*

Conclusions

In this chapter, we have highlighted (at least) five domains that can be used to adopt an interdisciplinary perspective to the study and practice of GTM. These domains, along with the broader question that each domain represents, are captured in Figure 8.1.

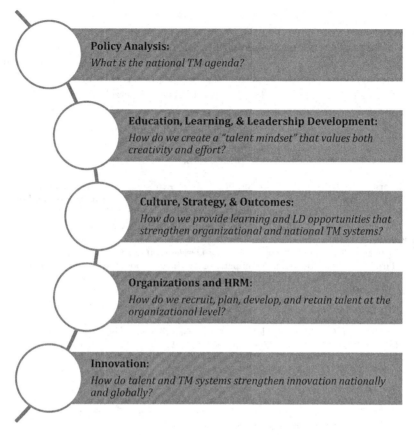

Figure 8.1 The macro global talent management domains

It is important for researchers to recognize the broader and inter-disciplinary scope of MGTM, as has been discussed in this chapter. We encourage practitioners and researchers to use the conceptual framework (Figure 1) and proposed questions to further engage in research, practice, and policy that cut across disciplines. The study of MGTM is related to not only TM at the country and cross-country level but also at the individual and organizational levels. Our intention is to engage scholars in integrative interdisciplinary analyses thereby improving understanding of TM theory, policy, and practice. We would also like to mention that aforementioned MGTM domains don't necessarily capture an exhaustive list of disciplines, i.e., trends, outcomes, and processes. As scholars continue to explore the multiple aspects of MGTM as a phenomenon, they are likely to unravel and add other issues to this framework. Hence, we admit we have merely scratched the surface based upon our current understanding of the global environment. We hope other researchers continue to critique and build upon it.

At this stage, it is important to delineate how MGTM benefits from an interdisciplinary view. First, by broadening its focus, an interdisciplinary view allows us to see intricacies of relationships across a variety of TM domains, such as policy impacting TM planning efforts within organizations, or talent mindset impacting the development of leaders within an organization. Second, an interdisciplinary view truly offers an *inclusive* focus on national (and even global) population thus providing larger populations greater access to TM systems. Scholars have argued that TM is not an elite function reserved for the few (Swailes, Downs, & Orr, 2014). An interdisciplinary view broadens scope and implications for developing effective global, national, and organizational TM systems. Third, MGTM helps us develop cohesive and coherent TM efforts at the organizational, national, and global levels, that are better able to withstand the test of time and context. Finally, an interdisciplinary view is likely to improve synergies across policies, processes, functions, and outcomes thus strengthening the national and global TM systems.

MGTM calls for governments around the world to rethink their role in society (Khilji et al., 2015). They will have to become more active in the TM activities necessary for companies and individuals to thrive and be productive. They will need to enhance the attractiveness of their countries, although the processes for doing so will require real long-term thinking (Woetzel, 2015). And the ways to completely capture the essence of the practice and policy of MGTM would require an inter-disciplinary research agenda. This has served as the main premise of this chapter.

References

Aboelela, S. W., Larson, E., Bakken, S., Carrasquillo, O., Formicola, A., Glied, S. A., Haas, J., & Gebbie, K. M. 2007. Defining interdisciplinary research: Conclusions from a critical review of the literature. *Health Services Research,* 42(1): 329–346. doi: https://doi.org/10.1111/j.1475-6773.2006.00621.x.

Ariss, A., Cascio, W. F., & Paauwe, J. 2014. Talent management: Current theories and future direction. *Journal of World Business,* 49(2): 173–179.

Barlow, L. 2006. Talent development: The new imperative? *Development and Learning in Organizations,* 20(3): 6–9.

Barney, J. 1991a. Firm resources and sustained competitive advantage. *Journal of Management,* 17(1): 99.

Bartlett, C. A., & Ghoshal, S. 1992. Building competitive advantage through people. *MIT Sloan Management Review,* 43(2): 34–41.

Becker, G. (1993). *Human capital: A theoretical and empirical analysis, with special reference to education.* Chicago: The University of Chicago Press.

Beechler, S., & Woodward, I. C. 2009. The global "ward for talent". *Journal of International Management,* 15(3): 273–285. doi:https://doi.org/10.1016/j.intman.2009.01.002.

Beine, M., Docquier, F., & Rapoport, H. 2008. Brain drain and human capital formation in developing countries: Winners and losers. *The Economic Journal,* 118(528): 631–652. doi:https://doi.org/10.1111/j.1468-0297.2008.02135.x.

Berger, L. 2004. Creating a talent management system for organization excellence: Connecting the dots. In L. A. Berger & D. R. Berger (Eds.): *The talent management handbook: Creating organizational excellence by identifying, developing, and promoting your best people:* New York: McGraw-Hill. pp. 3–21.

Bhatnagar, J. 2007. Talent management strategy of employee engagement in Indian ITES employees: Key to retention. *Employee Relations,* 29(6): 640–663.

Björkman, I., Ehrnrooth, M., & Mäkelä, K., Smale, A., & Sumelius, J. 2014. Talent management in multinational corporations. In D. G. Collings, K. Mellahi & W. F. Cascio (Eds). *The Oxford handbook of talent management.* Oxford, UK: Oxford University Press.

Blackman, D., & Kennedy, M. 2008. Talent management: Developing or preventing knowledge and capability? *Paper presented at the meeting of International Research into Public Sector Management,* Brisbane, Australia.

Blass, E., Knights, A., & Orbea, A. 2006. Developing future leaders: The contribution of talent management. *Paper presented at the meeting of Ashridge Business School Fifth International Annual Conference on Leadership,* Ashridge, UK.

Bolander, P., Werr, A., Asplund, K. 2017. The practice of talent management: A framework and typology. *Personnel Review,* 46(8): 1523–1551. doi: https://doi.org/10.1108/PR-02-2016-0037.

Borisova, O. N., Silayeva, A. A., Saburova, L. N., Belokhvostova, N. V., & Sokolova, A. P. 2017. Talent management as an essential element in a corporate personnel development strategy. *Academy of Strategic Management Journal,* 16(1): 31–46.

Boudreau, J. W., & Ramstad, P. M. 2005. Talentship and the evolution of human resource management: From "professional practices" to "strategic talent decision Science". *Human Resource Planning,* 28(2): 17–26.

Cantwell, J., & Brannen, M. Y. 2011. Positioning JIBS as an interdisciplinary journal. *Journal of International Business Studies,* 42(1): 1–9. doi: https://doi.org/10.1057/jibs.2010.50.

Campeanu-Sonea, E., Sonea, A., Gabor-Supuran, R., & Muresan, A. 2011. Organizational competence: A developmental framework. *Management & Marketing,* 6(2): 301–318.

Cappelli, P. 2008. *Talent on demand: Managing talent in an age of uncertainty.* Boston: Harvard Business School Press.

Cheng, J. L. C., Guo, W., & Skousen, B. 2011. Advancing new theory development in the field of international management. *Management International Review,* 51(6): 787–802. doi:https://doi.org/10.1007/s11575-011-0105-0.

Collings, D. G. 2014. Integrating global mobility and global talent management: Exploring the challenges and strategic opportunities. *Journal of World Business,* 49(2): 253–261. doi:https://doi.org/10.1016/j.jwb.2013.11.009.

Collings, D. G., & Mellahi, K. 2009. Strategic talent management: A review and research agenda. *Human Resource Management Review,* 19(4): 304–313.

Collings, D., Mellahi, K., & Cascio, (2018). Global talent management and performance in multinational enterprises: A multilevel perspective. *Journal of Management,* 45(2): 540–566.

Collings, D., Scullion, H., & Caliguiri, P. (2018). *Global talent management.* New York: Routledge.

Creelman, D. 2004. *Talent management: The special challenge of small and medium-sized enterprises* (White Paper). White River Junction, VT: Human Capital Institute.

Cooke, F. L., & Wang, M. (2019). Macro talent management in China. In V. Vaiman, P. Sparrow, R. Schuler, & D. Collings (Eds.), *Macro talent management in emerging and emergent markets: a global perspective.* Oxford, UK: Routledge.

Cornacchione, E. B., Jr (2010). Investing in human capital: Integrating intellectual capital architecture and utility theory. *The Journal of Human Resource and Adult Learning,* 6(1): 29–40.

Cutajar, B. 2013. *The impact of organizational culture on the management of employee's talent.* A dissertation submitted to The University of Leicester, UK for fulfillment of Doctor of Social Sciences.

Daubner-Siva, D., Ybema, S., Vinkenburg, C. J., & Beech, N. 2018. The talent paradox: Talent management as a mixed blessing. *Journal of Organizational Ethnography,* 7(1): 74–86, doi:https://doi.org/10.1108/JOE-01-2017-0002.

Delong, D., & Trutman, S. 2011. *The executive guide to high impact talent management.* Chicago: McGraw Hill.

Dickmann, M., & Perry, E. (2019). Migration: Managing macro talent management at the city and country level. In V. Vaiman, P. Sparrow, R. Schuler, & D. Collings (Eds.), *Macro talent management in emerging and emergent markets: a global perspective.* Oxford, UK: Routledge.

Dunning, J. H. 1989. The study of international business: A plea for a more interdisciplinary approach. *Journal of International Business Studies,* 20(3): 411–436. doi:https://doi.org/10.1057/palgrave.jibs.8490371.

Findlay, A., & Cranston, S. 2015. What's in a research agenda? An evaluation of research developments in the arena of skilled international migration. *International Development Planning Review,* 37(1): 17–31.

Groves, K. S. 2007. Integrating leadership development and succession planning best practices. *Journal of Management Development,* 26(3): 239–260.

Harvey, W. S. 2014. Winning the global talent war: A policy perspective. *Journal of Chinese Human Resource Management,* 5(1): 62–74.

Harvey, W., & Groutsis, D. 2012. Skilled migrants in the Middle East: Definitions, mobility and integration. *International Journal of Business and Globalisation,* 8(4). doi:https://doi.org/10.1504/IJBG.2012.047080.

Hasnas, J., Prentice, R., & Strudler, A. 2010. New directions in legal scholarship: Implications for business ethics research, theory, and practice. *Business Ethics Quarterly,* 20(3): 503–531. doi:https://doi.org/10.5840/beq201020332.

Heinen, J. S., & O'Neill, C. 2004. Managing talent to maximize performance. *Employment Relations Today,* 31(2): 67–82.

Hitt, M. A., Beamish, P. W., Jackson, S. E., & Mathieu, J. E. 2007. Building theoretical and empirical bridges across levels: Multilevel research in management. *Academy of Management Journal,* 50(6): 1385–1399. doi:https://doi.org/10.5465/amj.2007.28166219.

Hughes, K., Karp M.M., & Orr. M.T. 2002. Business partnerships for American education. *Journal of Vocational Education and Training,* 54(3): 365–368.

Huselid, M., Beatty, R., & Becker, B. 2005. A players or A positions? The strategic logic of workforce management. *Harvard Business Review,* 83(12): 110–117.

Huutoniemi, K., Klein, J. T., Bruun, H., & Hukkinen, J. 2010. Analyzing interdisciplinarity: Typology and indicators. *Research Policy,* 39(1): 79–88. doi:https://doi.org/10.1016/j.respol.2009.09.011.

Illeris, K. (2018). *Contemporary theories of learning: learning theorists in their own words.* Oxford, UK: Routledge.

Jackson, S. E., & Schuler, R. S. 1990. Human resource planning: Challenges for industrial/organizational psychologists. *American Psychologist,* 45(2): 223–239.

Judge, W., Weber, T., & Muller-Kahle, M. 2012. What are the corelates of interdisciplinary research: The case of corporate governance. *Academy of Management Education & Learning,* 11(1): 82–94.

Kehinde, J. S. 2012. Talent management: Effect on organizational performance. *Journal of Management Research,* 4(2): 178–186.

Khilji, S. E. 2012a. Does south Asia matter? Rethinking south Asia as relevant in international business research. *South Asian Journal of Global Business Research,* 1(1): 8–21.

Khilji, S. E. 2012b. An ambicultural Asian model: Management and culture in Pakistan. In M. Warner (Ed.): *Managing across diverse cultures in East Asia: Issues and challenges in a changing world:* London: Routledge.

Khilji, S. E. 2014. Human aspect of interdisciplinary research. *South Asian Journal of Global Business Research,* 3(1): 2–10.

Khilji, S. E., & Keilson, B. 2014. In search of global talent: Is south Asia ready? *South Asian Journal of Global Business Research,* 3(2): 114–134.

Khilji, S. E., & Khan, M. S. 2018. One chance to make a global impact through local development: A review of Pakistan's national talent development policies. In F. M. Nafukho, K. Dirani, & B. Irby (Eds). *Talent development and the global economy: Perspectives from around the world.* IAG Publishing.

Khilji, S. E., Tarique, I. & Schuler, R. S. 2015. Incorporating the macro view in global talent management. *Human Resource Management Review,* 25(3): 236–248.

King, K. A., & Vaiman, V. (2019). Enabling effective talent management through a macro-contingent approach: A framework for research and practice. *Business Research Quarterly,* 22(3): 194–206.

Kuptsch, C. & Eng Fong, P. 2006. *Competing for global talent.* International Labour Office Geneva. http://www.oit.org/wcmsp5/groups/public/—dgreports/—dcomm/—publ/documents/publication/wcms_publ_9290147768_en.pdf.

Lanvin, B. & Evans, P. 2014. *The Global Talent Competitiveness Index 2014.* Human Capital Leadership Institute (INSEAD and Adecco Group).

Lepak, D. P., & Snell, S. A. 1999. The human resource architecture: Toward a theory of human capital allocation and development. *Academy of Management Review,* 24(1): 31–48. doi:https://doi.org/10.5465/amr.1999.1580439.

Lewin, A. Y., Massini, S., & Peeters, C. 2009. Why are companies offshoring innovation? The emerging global race for talent. *Journal of International Business Studies,* 40(6): 901–925. doi:https://doi.org/10.1057/jibs.2008.92.

Lewis, R. E., & Heckman, R. J. 2006. Talent management: A critical review. *Human Resource Management Review,* 16(2): 139–154.

Liu, X., Lu, J., Filatotchev, I., Buck, T., & Wright, M. 2010. Returnee entrepreneurs, knowledge spillovers and innovation in high-tech firms in emerging economies. *Journal of International Business Studies,* 41(7): 1183–1197. doi:https://doi.org/10.1057/jibs.2009.50.

McCauley, C., & Wakefield, M. 2006. Talent management in the 21st century: Help your company find, develop, and keep its strongest workers. *Journal for Quality and Participation,* 29(4): 4–7.

McNulty, Y., & Kaveri, G. 2019. Macro talent management in Singapore: An analysis based on local media. In V. Vaiman, P. Sparrow, R. Schuler, & D. Collings (Eds.), *Macro talent management in emerging and emergent markets: A Global perspective.* Oxford, UK: Routledge.

Mellahi, K. & Collings, D. G. 2010. The barriers to effective global talent management: The example of corporate elites in MNEs. *Journal of World Business,* 45(2): 143–149.

Michaels, E., Handfield-Jones, H., & Axelrod, B. 2001. *The war for talent.* Cambridge, MA: Harvard University Press.

Musterd, S., & Gritsai, O. 2013. The creative knowledge city in Europe: Structural conditions and urban policy strategies for competitive cities. *European Urban and Regional Studies,* 20(3): 343–359.

National Academies Press. 2005. Facilitating interdisciplinary research. https://www.nap.edu/catalog/11153/facilitating-interdisciplinary-research.

Oehley, A. M. & Theron, C. C. 2010. The development and evaluation of a partial talent management structural model. *Management Dynamics,* 19(3): 2–28.

Oettl, A., & Agrawal, A. 2008. International labor mobility and knowledge flow externalities. *Journal of International Business Studies,* 39(8): 1242–1260. doi:https://doi.org/10.1057/palgrave.jibs.8400358.

O'Sullivan, Collings, D. (2019). Clusters and talent development: Optimizing the potential of skilled mobility within spatial agglomeration. In V. Vaiman, P. Sparrow, R. Schuler, & D. Collings (Eds.), *Macro talent management in emerging and emergent markets: a global perspective.* Oxford, UK: Routledge.

Outila, V., Vaiman, V., & Holden, N. (2019). Macro talent management in Russia. Addressing entangled challenges in managing talent on the country level. In V. Vaiman, P. Sparrow, R. Schuler, & D. Collings (Eds.), *Macro talent management in emerging and emergent markets: A global perspective.* Oxford, UK: Routledge.

Paauwe, J. 2004. *HRM and performance: Achieving long-term viability.* Oxford, UK: Oxford University Press.

Paauwe, J., & Boslelie, P. 2003. Challenging "strategic HRM" and the relevance of the institutional setting. *Human Resource Management Journal,* 13(3): 56–70. doi:https://doi.org/10.1111/j.1748-8583.2003.tb00098.x.

Papademetriou, D. G., & Sumption, M. 2013. *Attracting and selecting from the global talent pool–policy challenges.* Washington, DC: Migration Policy Institute.

Phene, A., & Tallman, S. 2012. Complexity, context and governance in biotechnology alliances. *Journal of International Business Studies,* 43(1): 61–83. doi:https://doi.org/10.1057/jibs.2011.53.

Ragazzi, F. 2014. A comparative analysis of diaspora policies. *Political Geography,* 41: 74–89.

Renzulli, J. S. 2016. Applying gifted education pedagogy to total talent development of all students. *Theory into Practice,* 44(2): 80–89.

Rihova, H., & Strietska-Ilina, O. 2015. *Guidelines for inclusion of skills aspects into employment-related analyses and policy formulation.* International Labour Office, Skills and Employability Branch, Employment Policy Department, Geneva. http://www.ilo.org/wcmsp5/groups/public/—ed_emp/—ifp_skills/documents/publication/wcms_534308.pdf.

Ruël, H., Bondarouk, T., & Dresselhaus, D. 2014. Global talent management in multinational corporations and the role of social networks. *Social media in strategic management* (Advanced Series in Management, Volume 11) Emerald Group Publishing Limited, pp. 217–243.

Sanders, J. 2018. International partnership strategies and practices at four case study global universities in Singapore and Japan. *Conference on Higher Education Research.* October 2018.

Sapinsky, A., Ciupka, S., & Khlobystov. L 2017. *Introduction.* Human resource management: an interdisciplinary perspective. https://www.researchgate.net/profile/Aleksander_Sapinski/publication/322764689_Human_resources_management-interdisciplinary_perspective/links/5a6f20130f7e9bd4ca6dabdd/Human-resources-management-interdisciplinary-perspective.pdf.

Saxenian, A. 2005. From brain drain to brain circulation: Transnational communities and regional upgrading in India and China. *Studies in Comparative International Development,* 40(2): 35–61. doi:https://doi.org/10.1007/BF02686293.

Schuler, R., & Khilji, S. E. (2017). Global talent management. In. D. Collings, K. Mellahi, and W. Cascio (Eds.) *Oxford handbook of talent management,* Oxford, UK: Oxford Press.

Schuler, R., Tarique, I., & Khilji, S.E. (2018). Macro talent management in the United States: Frameworks, contexts, processes and outcomes. In V. Vaiman, P. Sparrow, R. Schuler, & D. Collings (Eds.), *Macro talent management: A global perspective in managing talent in developed countries.* London: Taylor & Francis.

Schweyer, A. 2004. *Talent management systems: Best practices in technology solutions for recruitment, retention and workforce planning.* Toronto, Ontario: John Wiley & Sons.

Scullion, H., Collings, D., & Caliguiri, P. 2010. Global talent management. *Journal of World Business,* 45(2): 105–108.

Sears, D. 2003. *Successful talent strategies: Achieving superior business results through market-focused staffing.* New York: Amacom.

Siedlok, F., & Hibbert, P. 2014. The organization of interdisciplinary research: Modes, drivers and barriers. *International Journal of Management Reviews,* 16(2): 194–210, doi:https://doi.org/10.1111/ijmr.12016.

Smart, B., 2005. *Topgrading: How leading companies win by hiring, coaching, and keeping the best people.* New York: Penguin Group.

Stahl, G., Bjorkman, I., Farndale, E., Morris, S., Paauwe, J., Stiles, P., Trevor, J., & Wright, P., 2007. *Global talent management: How leading multinationals build and sustain their talent pipeline.* INSEAD Working Paper Series.

Swailes, S., Downs, Y., & Orr, K. 2014. Conceptualizing inclusive talent management: Potential, possibilities and practicalities. *Human Resource Development International,* 17 (5): 529–535.

Sweetland, S. R. 1996. Human capital theory: Foundations of a field of inquiry. *Review of Educational Research,* 66(3): 341–359. doi:https://doi.org/10.3102/00346543066003341.

Tansley, C. 2011. What do we mean by the term "talent" in talent management? *Industrial and Commercial Training,* 43(5): 266–274.

Tarique, I., & Schuler, R. S. 2010. Global talent management: Literature review, integrative framework, and suggestions for further research. *Journal of World Business,* 45(2): 122–133. doi:https://doi.org/10.1016/j.jwb.2009.09.019.

The Economist, 2006. *The world is our oyster.* Oct. 5, 2006. Accessed Nov. 18, 2018. Available at https://www.economist.com/special-report/2006/10/05/the-world-is-our-oyster.

The Economist. 2011. *The magic of diasporas.* Nov.19. Accessed Nov. 18, 2018. Available at https://www.economist.com/leaders/2011/11/19/the-magic-of-diasporas.

Thunnissen, M. 2016. Talent management: For what how and how well? An empirical investigation of talent management practices. *Employee Relations,* 38(1): 57–72.

Tung, R. L. (2008). Brain circulation, diaspora, and international competitiveness. *European Management Journal,* 26(5): 298–304.

Tung, R. L., & Lazarova, M. 2006. Brain drain versus brain gain: An exploratory study of ex-host country nationals in Central and East Europe. *The International Journal of Human Resource Management,* 17(11): 1853–1872. doi:https://doi.org/10.1080/09585190600999992.

Vaiman, V., Scullion, H., Collings, D. 2012. Talent management decision making. *Management Decision,* 50(5): 925–941. doi:https://doi.org/10.1108/00251741211227663.

Vaiman, V., Sparrow, P., Schuler, R., & Collings, D. (2019). *Macro talent management in emerging and emergent markets: a global perspective.* Oxford, UK: Routledge.

Van de Ven, A. H. 1992. Suggestions for studying strategy process: A research note. *Strategic Management Journal,* 13(51): 169–188. doi:https://doi.org/10.1002/smj.4250131013.

van Zyl, E., Mathafena, R., & Ras, J. 2017. The development of talent management framework for the private sector. *SA Journal of Human Resource Management,* 15, 1–19.

Vladescu, A. 2012. The possibility of implementing talent management in the public sector. *Management & Marketing,* 7(2): 351–362.

Walker, J. W., & LaRocco, J. M. 2002. Talent pools: The best and the rest. *Human Resource Planning,* 25(3): 12–14.

Wickramasekara, P. 2002. *Asian labor migration: Issues and challenges in an era of globalization.* International Migration Papers, International Migration Programme, International Migration Office, Geneva. Retrieved on November 5, 2018 from http://www.waseda.jp/gsaps/eaui/educational_program/PDF_WS2015/ Lecture5_Reading1_Honda.pdf.

Woetzel, J. 2015. *How Asia can boost productivity and economic growth.* McKinsey and Company.

World Bank (2018). *Country summary of higher education.* Accessed from http://siteresources.worldbank.org/ EDUCATION/Resources/278200-1121703274255/1439264-1193249163062/Pakistan_countrySummary. pdf.

Wright, B. E. (2011). Public administration as an interdisciplinary field: Assessing its relationship with the fields of law, management, and political science. *Public Administration Review,* 71(1): 96–101.

Wright, P., & Nishii, L. H. 2013. Strategic HRM and organization behavior: Integrating multiple levels of analysis. In J. Paauwe, D. E. Guest, & P. M. Wright (Eds.), *HRM and performance: Achievements and challenges.* London: Wiley, pp. 97–110.

Zahra, S. A., Newey, L. R. 2009. Maximizing the impact of organization science: Theory-building at the intersection of disciplines and/or fields. *Journal of Management Studies,* 46(6): 1059–1075. doi:https://doi. org/10.1111/j.1467-6486.2009.00848.x.

Zweig, D. 2006. Competing for talent: China's strategies to reverse the brain drain. *International Labour Review,* 145(1–2): 65–90. doi:https://doi.org/10.1111/j.1564-913X.2006.tb00010.x.

Zyl, E., Mathafena, R., & Ras, J. 2017. The development of talent management framework for the private sector. *SA Journal of Human Resource Management,* 15(2): 1–15.

9

TALENT COMPETITIVENESS

A Framework for Macro Talent Management

Paul Evans

Eduardo Rodriguez-Montemayor

Bruno Lanvin

Introduction

The dominant focus of the field of talent management (TM) that has emerged since the late 1990s, initially among practitioners and later among academic scholars, is at the organizational and individual level of analysis. TM has been defined as the process whereby organizations anticipate and meet their needs for talent in strategic jobs (Cappelli & Keller, 2017). But there have been a growing number of calls to pay more attention to macro talent management (MTM) at the level of nations and cities, hitherto largely left to the field of economics (Ariss, Cascio, & Paauwe, 2014; Björkman & Welch, 2015; Khilji, Tarique, & Schuler, 2015; King & Vaiman, 2019; Kryscynski & Ulrich, 2015; Tung, 2016).

The need to focus more research attention on MTM is understandable since organizational TM is strongly embedded in the national context. Organizations develop their TM systems and individuals make career choices in the complex socioeconomic environment of nations, with their different labor market norms, educational systems, and cultural traditions (see Khilji et al., 2015). Employers in developed countries tend to fill vacant positions more through recruitment rather than internal development, becoming dependent on the national or city labor markets (Cappelli, 2008; Cappelli & Keller, 2017). Yet, the presence in many developed nations of large skills gaps and skill mismatches (with many people ill-qualified for their jobs) points to dysfunctions in MTM.

In Europe, for example, unemployment rose from 7% in 2008 to 10.8% in 2013, while there were around two million vacancies available in the European Union (OECD, 2015); four in 10 businesses in the EU reported difficulties in finding staff with the right skills (CEDEFOP, 2015). A study of OECD countries suggests that one-quarter of workers report a mismatch between their existing skills and those required for their job (McGowan & Andrews, 2015). And a database for European countries on skills points to a shortage of people with high-level skills intersecting across different knowledge areas along with a growing surplus of routine and physical skills (OECD, 2017). Emerging countries also face serious talent bottlenecks aggravated by the large informal sector of the economy and the misallocation of talent that this conveys (Cooke, 2017).

Furthermore, we are witnessing wide socioeconomic transformational changes that affect TM. For example, "the grand challenges of our times" outlined by George, Howard-Grenville, Joshi, and Tihanyi (2016) urgently require interdisciplinary research to guide policy at the national and city level. Technology, globalization, and demographic change all affect the adequacy of the pool of skills that nations have access to, while also transforming educational, employment, and social protection systems (Evans & Rodriguez-Montemayor, 2017).

With this context and with such transformational challenges in mind, the aim of this and the next chapter is to provide a rigorous conceptualization of MTM that facilitates systematic understanding of

DOI: 10.4324/9781315474687-9

how talent is managed at the country or city level. This chapter establishes the theoretical foundations for that endeavor, built around a concept that we call the talent competitiveness (TC) of nations and cities. We draw on the TM field but also on the literature and debates in economics and labor economics, organizational psychology, and cultural anthropology, so as to take a step to providing a framework that jointly takes into account organizational practices and wider economic and social forces that shape talent development.

Existing frameworks such as that provided by Khilji and Schuler (2017) represent a useful step toward structuring this field so as to connect micro, meso, and macro phenomena. They view MTM as "the activities that are systematically developed by governmental and nongovernmental organizations expressly for the purpose of enhancing the quality and quantity of talent within and across countries and regions to facilitate innovation and competitiveness of their citizens and corporations."

Building on this, we believe that more analytic clarity is needed to permit comparisons, learning, and facilitating research. The TC framework is based on an input-output reasoning. A focus on activities or processes (what we will call "levers" or policy domains) is desirable to guide policy action, reflecting an HRM perspective. This is the input side of the TC framework. The output side is a conceptualization of the stock of human capital of nations and the economic value it produces. In developing our framework, we attempt to integrate HRM perspectives on the input side and the human capital perspectives from economics on the output side (Boon, Eckardt, Lepak, & Bosselie, 2017).

The functions and processes of MTM identified in this chapter need to be formulated in ways that make them measurable. The next chapter presents an empirical model that makes use of the TC framework, called the Global Talent Competitiveness Index (GTCI). The objective of the framework and model is to facilitate comparison and benchmarking for researchers as well as policy makers in governments, cities, and corporations, as well as identifying emerging trends and challenges in the macro talent arena. Although Chapter 9 and Chapter 10 (next chapter) are self-contained, they offer a better perspective of the concept of TC if read back-to-back.

Section 1 of this chapter provides a definition of talent competitiveness and outlines the context in which it emerged. Sections 2 and 3 focus on the output side, where the issue is how to capture the stock of human capital of a nation. Section 2 explains how talent is conceptualized at the country level in terms of two types of skills that are reflected in educational systems and organizations: technical and generalist. Section 3 addresses the impact of these two types of talent on economic performance. Section 4 focuses on the input side by offering the rationale behind what we call the four pillars or policy/practice levers of TC, namely *attracting, developing, retaining,* and building or adjusting the *enabling context.* Section 5 briefly discusses how the overall concept of TC fits with the ultimate objective of achieving the *prosperity* of nations. Section 6 concludes with some remarks about how the concept of TC contributes to the emerging literature of MTM and how it can inform national debates about talent development.

Defining Talent Competitiveness

We formally define talent competitiveness (TC) as *the set of policies and practices, as well as the enabling context, that allow a country or a city to attract, develop, and retain the human capital that contributes to its prosperity.* As mentioned earlier, this definition fits well with other definitions of MTM, though it should be noted that the notion of "competitiveness", signifying the quality of being as good or better than others of a comparable nature, emphasizes comparison between countries and cities on key talent factors. Such comparisons in the shape of research data or benchmarking facilitate learning and improvement.

The idea of thinking of talent in terms of competitiveness can be linked to the philosophy of the Global Competitiveness Index, produced annually since 2004 by the World Economic Forum. Its objective is to assess "the ability of countries to provide high levels of prosperity to their citizens by measuring the set of institutions, policies, and macro/micro economic factors that influence current and medium-term prosperity" (World Economic Forum, 2017). Authoritative empirical assessments like this provide measures of effectiveness that governments around the world take seriously; other examples are the Global Innovation Index (2017), initially developed by INSEAD and now published annually by INSEAD; Cornell and the World Intellectual Property Organization; and the World Bank's Ease of Doing Business Index. The talent component of national competitiveness is now becoming fundamental as nations transition deeper into the knowledge economy (Powell & Snellman, 2004).

The concept of "talent competitiveness" and the idea of developing a talent competitiveness index crystalized in discussions between Bruno Lanvin (then at INSEAD) and the government of Singapore, a country that focuses its successful national development strategy on managing talent, taking the nation in fifty years from third world status to a higher level of economic prosperity in per capita terms than the U.S.A. and most of Europe (see Osman-Gani & Tan, 1998).

Conceptualizing Talent at the Country Level

How should one conceptualize "talent" in such a way that it is potentially measurable at the country and city level, providing meaningful comparisons across the world?

The concept of talent is often loosely used (Gallardo-Gallardo, Dries, & Gonzalez-Cruz, 2013), leading to confusion that is incompatible with the measurement requirements of empirical cross-country analyses. Our focus is on talent as the characteristics of people – their skills, abilities, and competences. Unskilled labor that is easily found and substitutable is outside the talent arena; in our definition, secondary school education is an indicator of the minimum qualification for an occupation requiring the degree of skill associated with talent.

This is consistent with the concept of human capital as first defined in the seminal paper by Schultz (1961), and then the subsequent elaboration by Gary Becker and the Chicago school that formalized the concept of human capital as the knowledge, skills, and similar attributes that enable productive work, largely the product of investments in education. Our view of talent at the level of countries is hence closely related to this concept of human capital. Adam Smith had already in the 18th century looked upon human beings as "productive" capital. The combination of the abilities of all the inhabitants of a country created its aggregate capital and this has long been found to be a driver of economic growth and development (e.g., Becker, 1964; Lucas 1988; Schultz, 1961). Human capital as a productive factor of the economy becomes more important as we move further into a post-industrial knowledge society where it is information, knowledge, and intellectual skills that drive economic growth (Benkler, 2006; Powell & Snellman, 2004) rather than physical inputs such as machinery.

Organizations segment their workforce based on employees' competences or the nature of roles performed, to reflect different differential potential to generate value (Collings, 2017). There are two main tracks. One is based on expertise, leading to promotion and development up vertical functional or professional paths. The other track is based on leadership, involving job rotation and broadening experiences to avoid the myopic trap of excessive focus on competence rather than necessary vision, external networking, and setting organizational direction (see research on leadership transitions by Ibarra (2015), summarized by Pucik, Evans, Björkman, & Morris, 2017).

At the country level, two similar broad tracks are found in national educational systems: a specialist track associated with vocational, technical, and professional training (what we call vocational-technical (VT) skills), and a generalist track involving broader, interdisciplinary knowledge and networks with a global perspective (what we call generalist-adaptive (GA) skills)[1]. Countries need plumbers and welders, software programmers and accountants, nurses, and technicians to function effectively. But they also need to innovate and grow, steering themselves through an increasingly complex, ambiguous, and uncertain future. Both countries and organizations need, in addition to expertise, the adaptive work of leadership that is associated with innovation and change (Heifetz, 1994). Excessively narrow specialization handicaps innovation and leadership, which in today's interdependent world requires a global network and mindset (Hanushek, Schwerdt, Woessmann, & Zhang, 2011; Keep, Mayhew, & Payne, 2006).

Conceptually, this differentiation is between *expertise-based skill* that is technical or vocational in nature, and *broad generalist skill* that characterizes the matric, baccalauréat, abitur, or high school leaving exam in most countries. It is important to note two points in passing. First, generalist education puts off the time when a specialist area of expertise that is typically the basis for career entry must be chosen. National systems vary greatly in how and when they stream people into expertise.

In the U.S.A., university students typically begin to specialize in their last two senior years of college study, often pursuing that area of expertise through postgraduate study. Switzerland in sharp contrast has a dual school system starting from age 12. Students are asked to reflect on their vocation, fostered by carefully designed visits to banks, robotics factories, hospitals, and the like, with a choice at age 15 between a vocational oriented education and the generalist "maturité" or high school leaving exam that leads to university (Lanvin, Evans, & Rasheed, 2014).

Europe has a tradition of requiring students to specialize at their time of university choice, although different countries take different routes. In France, the baccalauréat has lost its value as a streaming mechanism, allowing students to enter university only to be screened out after one or two years of study. The rapid pace of societal and technological change argues for so-called T-shaped skills (European Commission, 2016; Hansen & Oetinger, 2001) combining specialized expertise with broad-based generalist understanding.

In summary, we define talent at the country or city level as skilled labor for which workers have a training or skill set, typically associated with at least a completed secondary education. We distinguish between two types of skills: those that are expertise based (technical or vocational) and those that, in addition to technical expertise, involve broader generalist or adaptive skills associated with leadership, entrepreneurship, and innovation. The latter adaptive skills are typically associated with tertiary education. Education thus serves as a proximate indicator of talent.

The Economic Impact of Talent

The idea of competitiveness emphasizes that skills and competences of labor must produce economic value for a nation or city, as they must do for an enterprise. Building on the differentiation between expertise (VT skills) and generalist/adaptive skills, how can one conceptualize the economic value of skills in ways that are measurable?

An individual who has many years of education in a particular area of expertise, but who cannot find or create a job, has no economic impact. Indeed the impact is negative since the cost of education to society has no corresponding benefit and the person becomes a burden on the social protection system of that country. What this means is that *employability* is an important outcome variable of talent in many contexts, particularly for VT skills. It refers to the extent to which secondary and tertiary education systems respectively equip students with the skills needed by businesses, and it is attracting attention as an important topic for HRM research (van Harten et al., 2017).

The field of economics has documented the presence of many types of skills mismatches in different economies that affect the employability prospects of people, and the productivity of firms (Quintini (2011) presents a comprehensive review of the literature. Such mismatches include skill gaps or shortages created by an under-skilled workforce, as well as field-of-study mismatches, both of which make it difficult for firms to find the skills they need to be competitive. Other people are over-qualified for their current jobs, which means that country-level resources are being wasted in human capital investments. Recent empirical work by the OECD has contributed to a better understanding of such mismatches by going beyond qualifications and educational credentials with direct measurement of skills of adult people in the workforce (OECD, 2015).

NEET statistics on the percentage of youth "Not in Education, Employment or Training" suggest that employability has not been a guiding criterion behind policies regarding secondary and higher education in many countries. Across the 27 EU countries, the NEET percentage of youth was 15.4% in 2012; it reached a peak of 31.3% in the Middle East and North Africa (ILO, 2015). A high percentage of university graduates in countries like Botswana, South Korea, and South Africa cannot find jobs (to take some countries with above average expenditure on education) because their education has not equipped them with skills that have any value in the labor marketplace (Economist, 2017; Meyer, 2016).

In contrast, Danish flexicurity policies provide generous social protection to unemployed people under the condition that they retrain so as to make themselves employable. Indeed, employability is a variable that is most relevant at the national level since companies have little interest in investing in the employability of any but their low performing staff.

Employability depends on the specific economic structure of each country. The supply of specific qualifications does not always create its own demand (Keep et al., 2006). It is not enough to follow the mantra of "educating more for getting better jobs" as employability is a relative concept that depends on supply and demand within the labor market (Moreau & Leathwood, 2006). For example, many Arab countries have invested much in education in their quest to transit into a knowledge economy. The entire region, from the resource-rich countries of the Gulf to Algeria and Morocco at the other end of the MENA region, shares an unfortunate common denominator – that of high youth unemployment. In these countries the demand side has failed, notably because of the lack of development of the private sector (Lanvin & Rodriguez-Montemayor, 2017). The jobs that young people vie for are in the now bloat public sector.

In MENA, un-employability is to a great extent a structural problem with decades of history, part of what our TC framework calls "the enabling context" where, for example, private sector clusters are so important. The planning of skills supply and demand, involving close collaboration between government, business, education, and other social partners, becomes vital for employability (see UKCES, 2017, and Reddy, Bhorat, Powell, Visser, and Arends, 2016, for UK and South African examples).

Employability should not only be seen in the context of salaried employment. Since 30% of the adult population of the U.S.A. and Europe work today not as salaried personnel but as freelance agents (Evans & Rodriguez-Montemayor, 2017), often facilitated by the emerging platform economy, employability extends to entrepreneurship and starting one's own freelance enterprise. To build on the Danish flexicurity example above, these are among the state-facilitated options for unemployed people.

Ensuring employability ranks high in the policy agenda of many countries, and it requires setting the right policies and coordination with the private sector. For these policies to have an effect, historical and cultural aspects also matter. In many countries such as South Korea, the generalist track is viewed as being the path to success, and the expertise-based vocational track is of far lower status. The result is that some 30% of high school and university graduates cannot find jobs. In contrast, unemployment is remarkably low in Switzerland, where 70% of all secondary school children follow the vocational track.

What is the talent impact of generalist skills? Why do we care about generalist skill development? The answer lies in the economics and psychology of *innovation and growth*. The day-by-day functioning of society relies on bakers and electricians, robotics technicians, legal assistants, nurses, and heart surgeons, on the skills of people with expertise. But growth and innovation stem from the interfaces between disciplines and fields. Innovators like Thomas Edison, to take an often-cited example, were not super-creative experts but people who could tap into expertise in different fields, gathering the support of key stakeholders so as to create something new. To use the language of network theory, they bridged structural holes of knowledge and experience (Balkundi & Kilduff, 2006; Burt, 1992).

Although generic education and competences have been linked in the literature to adaptability, cross-field work, and collaboration (Hanushek et al., 2011; Heijke et al., 2003), the generalist skills underlying innovation, creativity in design, entrepreneurship, and leadership are different from VT expertise in the sense than they cannot be entirely "taught" through formal education. VT skills can be acquired through education, or better still through a combination of school learning and practice, as in apprenticeships.

Much remains to be done to map out the skills underlying innovation. Skills for innovation involve broad cross-functional or cross-discipline learning. Universities such as Finland's Aalto are trying to reinvent this aspect of university education by bringing together schools of science, design and architecture, engineering and business-economics. But they also involve project skills, problem-solving skills, and social-collaborative skills that are perhaps learned more through the way in which subject matters are taught than through the curriculum and content of education, as well as through challenging experience. Aoun (2017), the president of Northeastern University in Boston, Massachusetts, U.S.A., with its good track record for university innovation and graduate employment, argues that experiential learning internships and projects foster the creative skills that are needed in a world where machines are rapidly taking over routine tasks.

Indeed, talent competitiveness is not only about people and the skills they have acquired but also about the systems in which they operate – organizations, industries, and the institutional structure of the nation. The functioning of a nation enables ordinary people to do extraordinary things, as put by Drucker (2012). These are part of the enabling context, and this leads us on to explore the input side of the TC equation.

The Four Pillars of Talent Competitiveness

We turn now to the conceptualization of the levers of TC, the policy and practice domains (or what we call pillars, to use a modeling term) through which a country or city can build and nurture the skilled human capital that we call talent, be it expertise-based or generalist, or increasingly a combination of both. Transposing the Attract-Grow-Retain paradigm of HRM to the level of economies, these four pillars are built around the processes of *attracting*, *developing*, and *retaining* talent that take place in an *enabling context*. They are briefly outlined below, together with their rationale. Some key issues are discussed in passing where they raise important issues of particular relevance to MTM, such as the structure of growing talent.

The Enabling Context

Skills, no matter how important, do not drive entirely the productivity or, ultimately, the wealth of nations (Buchanan, Anderson, & Power, 2017; Keep & Mayhew, 1999). Albeit crucial for talent competitiveness, the pool of skills in a country is but one element driving productivity and prosperity. Evidence on the productivity differences between the UK, France, Germany, and the U.S.A. in the 1980s–1990s suggests that skills accounted for between one-fifth and one-eighth of the relative productivity gaps between them (O'Mahoney & de Boer, 2002).

The enabling context within which talent development, attraction, and retention takes place can be viewed in terms of four interrelated landscapes: the regulatory, market, labor, and management landscapes. Our discussion below is reflected in the GTCI model that we outline in the next chapter; concepts that are measured in this model are indicated in bold text, with the first letter capitalized.

The Regulatory Landscape

When one thinks of the context that enables or handicaps TC, it is government policy and regulations that springs foremost to mind. Government policies and regulations reflect different political ideologies and value systems that are beyond the bounds of the TC arena. What is important for TC is whether government policy is seen as coherent and effectively put into practice. So the conception of the regulatory environment should include assessments of government effectiveness and of the quality of regulation.

Sound dialogue between the stakeholder communities that constitute a society is important. While government policies can directly target objectives of "national human resource development" (Wang & Swanson, 2008), government intervention is usually needed to coordinate the efforts of various stakeholders (and shoulder the "big push") towards such developmental objectives, so the quality of business-government relations is of particular importance.

While governments often are in a better position than private actors to inform long-term strategic investment in human capital via the educational system, particularly with respect to the objective of employability, the so-called "triple helix" of government-industry-education relations fuels the dynamics of innovation (Etzkowitz & Leydesdorff, 2000). Some economists argue for a more entrepreneurial role of government, suggesting that government initiatives historically were vital to the development of technologies such as those incorporated in the Apple iPhone (Mazzucato, 2016).

Among the factors that get in the way of effective government, considered globally, the most damaging, is perhaps the absence of the rule of law, including corruption, red tape, and cronyism as well as excessive central planning. If government serves the personal interests of a particular individual, clique, or ethnic or tribal group in a non-transparent way rather than the interests of the wider community, as in the case of many lower income countries, this will handicap the talent competitiveness of the nation. Equally damaging will be political instability, since business and citizens need predictability.

The Market Landscape

There are many elements to the market landscape of an economy, and a parsimonious model needs to focus on those that are most important and related to talent. Central elements of a market economy are competition and the ease of doing business, which stimulate efficiency and innovation and in turn talent development. Countries tend to have a concentration of firms in sectors or clusters where they have developed comparative advantages (Ferner, Edwards, & Tempel, 2012), and thus have different requirements for skills. The literature on skills ecosystems has indicated how nations and regions tend to develop a "high-skill equilibrium" supported by these clusters of firms (Keep & Mayhew, 1999). Such high-skilled clusters of firms develop in places that invest in R&D and technology. The vital backbone of a networked and increasingly digitalized culture is its ICT infrastructure.

The Labor Landscape

The labor landscape and its regulation are particularly important for talent competitiveness. In the labor economics field, there has been much research and debate over how to reconcile competing interests in workforce regulation. Botero et al. (2004) show that heavier regulation of labor is associated with lower labor force participation and higher unemployment, especially of the young. France until recently has been a topical case in point.

Business wants flexibility. The freedom to hire and fire, to set employment terms, and to be free of constraining regulations allows employers to adjust rapidly to changing markets and circumstances. As discussed in the next chapter, this freedom is particularly important for enterprises as they adjust to societal transformations, notably the way in which technology is changing the talent scene. But employees desire security and social protection. Hence, social protection measures are included in the GTCI model (as a part of sustainability in its retention pillar).

Economists pay attention to a third leg in the labor landscape, based empirically on the effectiveness of Danish reforms that were introduced thirty years ago – the so-called flexicurity system that has become an EU reference, currently being introduced in France. Denmark is one of the countries in the world where it is easiest to hire and fire, but it also has strong trade unions and a deep attachment to social protection. However, such protection is linked to what economists call active labor market policies, measures such as training, start-up incentives, supported employment, and rehabilitation that facilitate skill reconversion and employment reintegration in the event of a job loss. Such policies may work better for employment than employment protection regulations (Mortensen & Pissarides, 1999).

Specifically, a Danish engineer who loses their job because of technology or market changes will receive up to 90% of pay, but for a two-year period. The unemployed person has an obligation to retrain, explore a start-up, or consider a move to another part of the country or a lower paid class of work. Failure to assume the individual obligations that will lead to reemployment within two years results in progressive loss of benefits. Research shows that today few Danes lose their jobs because they are fired; most take the initiative to leave and retrain or reskill themselves, taking advantage of these active labor market policies (Kristensen, 2016).

A final element of the labor market to single out is the quality of labor-employer cooperation. In many countries, talent competitiveness is handicapped by a legacy of adversarial relationships for historical or ideological reasons. In countries as diverse as South Korea, South Africa, Argentina, or France, necessary policy changes that would facilitate talent development and prosperity have been handicapped and delayed by such adversarial relations.

The Management Landscape

As flagged before, how workers are managed is often more important for productivity than the skills they possess (see Keep, Mayhew, & Payne, 2006). Enhanced economic performance depends on how skills are employed and managed. Even companies with access to talent and technology can succumb to mismanagement. High performance work practices that support employees to develop the full range and their potential skills and value are a vital part of the TC context, through its business landscape (Hall & Lansbury, 2006).

Research in an emerging sub-field of economics has consistently shown that management practices that are rooted in meritocracy and professionalism – paying close attention to the recruitment of the right people, the setting of goals, the development of people to achieve those goals, and to the measurement and reward of performance – have the potential to achieve substantially higher levels of productivity (and growth and survival) of firms for a given level of human capital. Management practices, or what we call professional management, account for roughly a quarter of the 30% productivity gap between the United States and Europe, and an even bigger proportion of the productivity gap with emerging countries (Bloom et al., 2012; Bloom & Van Reenen, 2010).[2] It is well known that innovative workplace practices can increase performance through the use of systems of related practices that enhance worker participation, make work design less rigid, and decentralize managerial tasks (Ichniowski, Kochan, Levine, & Strauss, 1996).

Management practices and business culture also play a significant role in attracting experienced foreign talent and returnees and ensuring the transfer of their knowledge and experience, as empirical results based on GTCI research show (Evans & Rodriguez-Montemayor, 2016). In some societies, getting ahead relies more on family connections, status and age, and guanxi-type relationships rather than on professional merit.

Despite the benefits identified in diverse contexts, the reality is that there is substantial variation in management practices across organizations in every country and every sector, mirroring the wide spread of productivity and profitability within industries (Bloom et al., 2012). The management landscape in the TC framework could benefit from careful elaboration on institutional and cultures differences, guided by empirical research and measurement availability. For example, there is evidence that government and founder-owned firms are often poorly managed, while multinational, dispersed shareholder, and private-equity-owned firms are typically well managed. Family-owned firms are badly managed if run by family members compared with similar family-owned firms run by external CEOs (Bloom & Van Reenen, 2010).

The enabling context does just that; it provides the context. In contrast, growing, attracting, and retaining talent have a direct impact on skills. We turn now to discuss these three levers of TC.

Growing Talent

Growing or developing talent is the policy/practice lever that is most central to TC; as noted earlier, education and training are the most important investments in human capital (Schultz, 1961). Taking income as a measure of the value of skills, high school and college education in the United States greatly raise a person's income, even after netting out the direct and indirect costs of schooling and adjusting for family background. Similar evidence at many points in time from over a hundred countries with different cultures and economic systems points to the same conclusion, although the relative gains are generally larger in less-developed countries where there are fewer people with a higher education (Becker, 1994; Economist, 2018).

Growing talent is usually regarded as a task for the formal educational system. This is the focus that still predominates in disciplines such as economics, in part driven by the type of data available at the level of countries. While the best comparative metrics focus on formal education, this should not blind us to the fact that growing talent (or skill formation as it is called in some disciplines) is not limited to the years of formal schooling. Schultz (1961) had recognized that in addition to formal education, on-the-job training, and even life experiences (such as migrating from rural to urban areas) are contributors to human capital accumulation. Indeed, our conceptualization of developing talent includes three components.

The first is *formal education*, which is typically viewed in terms of level or years of education – from primary school through secondary to higher or tertiary education. However, the state of formal education is rarely assessed in terms of orientation, specialist versus generalist, even at secondary and tertiary levels where this distinction is important, as discussed earlier. So available comparative educational metrics do not capture the fact that 70% of the pupils in Swiss secondary schools pursue a vocationally-oriented apprenticeship education in contrast with 18% of secondary students in South Korea, for example. The GTCI model captures formal education through enrollment measures (vocational and tertiary enrollment), complemented by national measures of the quality of education: expenditure on tertiary education, ability in reading, math and science (using the OECD's PISA scores from its world-wide program for student assessment), and the ranking of its universities.

The second component is *lifelong learning* or continuous education, which is becoming more salient as innovation speeds up the process of change and people live longer. Fifty years ago, some people could hold the same job for an entire career, whereas as today's Millennials are expected to transition between multiple careers (Evans & Rodriguez-Montemayor, 2017; Gratton, 2011). Who will offer access to the corresponding learning opportunities? Organizations used to assume a responsibility for their employees' development, but they increasingly restrict such investments to those with the potential to occupy key roles (Cappelli, 2008). Today, systematic skill formation requires strong cooperation between social partners (employers, unions, and municipalities or governments) at the firm, sector, industry, or national levels (see Hall & Lansbury, 2006).

The influence of national workforce development, dating back to Harrison, Weiss, and Gant (1995), has led to institutional innovations such as the widespread creation of sectorial learning and skills councils that advise on skill priorities for their respective industries, including for vocational training. Governments increasingly intervene in lifelong learning or skill formation, either through encouraging ecosystem partnerships or by providing a menu of training programs to people who lose jobs (active labor market policies mentioned above) or more widely to its citizens, as in Singapore's SkillsFuture or France's Compte Personnel d'Activité.

We need research that clearly conceptualizes lifelong learning. The proxy indicators that are used in the GTCI model (see Chapter 10) are the prevalence of training in national firms, the attention paid by companies to employee development, and the quality of local management schools.

We think of the third component of developing talent as *access to growth opportunities*. One can argue that much, perhaps most, of development happens not through education or training but via individual experiences. Our research on managers convinced us that perhaps 80% of adult development happens through challenging experiences: a new job, an opportunity that presents itself, a difficult situation, moving to a new location (Evans, Pucik, & Björkman, 2011: 311–320). Indeed, a commonly used corporate formula guiding people development is 70-20-10: 70% of development happens on-the-job, 20% is facilitated by informal or formal coaching and support, while 10% is provided by training.

There are widespread cultural differences between nations on the degree of access to such challenging growth opportunities. In Nordic cultures, for example, young students are expected to take initiative in schools where learning is project-oriented, and there is a high degree of delegation and empowerment in the enterprises. By contrast, schools in South Korea, however sophisticated, are regimented, oriented to passing standardized tests; enterprises are more hierarchic so that employees are expected simply to follow the orders and instructions of their bosses. Additionally networks have always facilitated individual growth, as network theory emphasizes (Burt, 1992), allowing individuals to tap into the knowledge, experience, and views of others. This is emphasized today by the rise and prominence of social media tools such as LinkedIn.

In the TC framework, we distinguish between two aspects of growth opportunities. The first component is *empowerment*, reflecting the extent to which a person is expected to learn through experience and challenge rather than following orders. Delegation of authority provides a good proxy indicator of this. The other element is voice, being able to express views, opinions, and rights are a vital part of learning and growth (Kwon, Farndale, & Park, 2016).

The second component is *collaboration*, including the availability of social and professional networks that facilitate learning and development. Research shows clearly the importance of cognitive diversity for innovation and high performance. Teams of diverse individuals outperform talented individuals on complex and challenging tasks, though only if they have strong collaborative skills (see Evans & Rodriguez-Montemayor, 2017, and Lanvin, Evans, & Rodriguez-Montemayor, 2017, for a review of research and practical developments over the last two decades).

The GTCI model includes two measures of such collaborative diversity at the national level: the extent of collaboration within organizations and collaboration between organizations. It should be added that collaboration is so important for sustainable innovation and inclusion that the OECD is extending its PISA criteria for the assessment of student performance to include collaborative problem-solving skills (OECD, 2018).

Attracting Talent

There are two potential talent pools for a nation or a city: its local population and the wider talent pool outside its borders. In the context of the demographic changes mentioned in the introduction, many countries are seeking to attract skilled and specialized talent from abroad. So, talent attraction can be divided into two concepts that we call internal openness and external openness.

Starting with *internal openness*, to what extent are there barriers that restrict the talent supply, limiting access to the talent pool to those of a particular gender, race, or ethnic group, of a certain religious affiliation, or those coming from certain cliques or social classes? To what extent is the concept of talent "inclusive" in a particular country?

Gender is to a greater or lesser extent a barrier in most regions of the world, reflected in the gender earnings gap. If one is born female, access to university may sometimes be limited, with few female graduates. And in many countries, leadership opportunities for women is an important indicator of national inclusiveness. Minorities in some countries are denied access to educational and high-status work opportunities in overt or subtle ways, and so measures of the tolerance of minorities and of immigrants should be included in the TC framework.

Additionally, the concept of social mobility captures the fact that the socio-economic status of parents may strongly influence the opportunities of their children to improve their economic situation. All the forms of exclusion mentioned above undermine the discourse of employability. There is strong evidence that social background, gender, ethnicity, and age all have an impact on the opportunities available (Brown & Heskith, 2004; Moreau & Leathwood, 2006; Putman, 2015).

Turning to *external openness*, migration has played a major role in the development of many developed nations, including Singapore (43% of its adults were born abroad), but also Switzerland (with 27%), the United States, Canada, New Zealand, Australia, and Ireland, to name a few.

Economists agree that the immigration of high-skilled people such as scientists and engineers, but also top managers and business executives, enhances economic growth (Boeri et al., 2012; Haque & Kim, 1994). Moreover, few small or medium-sized countries can expect to develop within their own borders all the specialized expertise they need in the face of accelerating change, and so the Nordic nations are taking talent attraction from abroad seriously (Andersson, King-Grubert, & Lubanski, 2016). Developing countries try to attract back their talented diaspora to exploit local opportunities as well as the possibilities that Internet and technology start-ups offer for development (see Agrawal, Cockburn, & McHale, 2006; Kerr, 2008).

Aging societies increasingly need young talent. There has been a growing reliance in developed nations on recruiting foreign students, especially in expertise-based science and engineering fields, notably from Asia (Teitelbaum, 2014). In the United States, foreigners have accounted for more than half of the net increase in the labor force of scientists and engineers since 1995 (Kerr & Lincoln, 2010). Skilled people born abroad are more likely to be entrepreneurs and innovators. They are twice as likely to start a business (including high-growth start-ups), and they patent at double the native rate (Hunt & Gauthier-Loiselle, 2010).

Overall, skilled migrants fill skill gaps in the local economy and are significant tax contributors. In short, they create jobs and wealth rather than taking jobs from nationals. Indeed, some influential academics go further. Richard Florida argues cogently that lasting competitive advantage stems from attracting, as well as developing and retaining, what he calls the "creative class" rather than competing for goods, services, or capital in an age when growth can only come from innovation (Florida 2002, 2005).

Differentials in economic growth remain a key driver of talent migration since they largely explain differences in the quality and quantity of talent migration. Indian engineers trained locally by national institutes of technology (NITs) would often pursue graduate studies in the U.S.A. and then profit from the opportunities in Silicon Valley. But as India opened up its economy during the last decade and started to grow at rates of more than 5%, they came back to work for successful Indian multinationals such as InfoSys, Tata, or Mittal, as well as developing local businesses.

Mobility is becoming an intrinsic element of the talent development process at the individual level, reinforced by mobility of students under the Erasmus program. Talent is increasingly mobile, and mobility is becoming part of talent development. If brain drain was the 20th-century concern, "brain circulation" in the interests of innovation is a 21st-century leitmotiv (Lanvin, Evans, & Rodriguez-Montemayor, 2016; Tung, 2016; see Boeri et al., 2012 for a review of research on high skilled talent mobility). Indeed, mobility may be a significant contributor to the development of adaptive and innovative skills. A high percentage of entrepreneurs and innovators have origins abroad, as mentioned above, and there is solid evidence that people with deep international experience have more creative problem-solving ability (Godart, Maddux, Shipilov & Galinsky, 2015; Maddux & Galinsky, 2009).

External openness is assessed on two dimensions in the GTCI model that is outlined in the next chapter. The first is *attracting business* (foreign direct investment, technology transfer, and the prevalence of foreign ownership). The second component is *attracting people*, with measures of the migrant stock of countries and of international students. These are complemented by survey measures of brain gain, the extent to which countries can attract talent from abroad.

Retaining Talent

One of the laws of human capital theory is that people with skills that are not specific to the firm will always have opportunities elsewhere. Extending this to nations, people who do not have a deep attachment to their nations and cultures may be tempted to seek work abroad. The higher the value of people, the more they will have attractive opportunities on the other side of the proverbial road.

Indeed, attracting and retaining talent are two sides of the same coin. Attracting a skilled immigrant technician from Poland to fill a skills gap in Luxembourg is a skill gain for Luxembourg but a potential talent loss for Poland. The reason why someone leaves a location is a push factor (low salary, absence of opportunity, polluted living environment), while the reason why someone moves to a particular new location is a balance with pull factors (better job, lower taxation and higher take-home pay, better schooling for children, versus obstacles such as learning a new language and culture, and having less connectedness with the community) (Andersson, King-Grubert & Lubanski, 2016).

Having acknowledged that attraction and retention are interrelated, we conceptualize retention with two elements that we call sustainability and lifestyle. Growing talent is not sustainable unless the forces of attraction and retention balance out favorably for a country. To take an illustrative example, India and China could not afford the costs of providing a world-class education for their top STEM (science, technology, engineering, math) students, so the very best undergraduates were encouraged to pursue graduate studies abroad, notably at the top universities in the United States or Europe. But those students received highly paid and challenging opportunities there, which meant that both countries found it difficult to attract back what China calls its "sea turtles". Similarly, an informal study of innovative Danish business leaders found that most of them felt a pull abroad, partly because of high taxation of their income at home, but more because egalitarian Danish values meant that they had to hide from public eyes the lifestyle they could afford. Some resolved this by maintaining foreign residencies (Evans & Engsbye, 2002).

Building on this Danish example, the experience of various European cities that have invested in talent attraction and retention suggest that while it is above all the jobs that attract people, lifestyle counts, particularly when it comes to retention (Andersson et al., 2016). In the same way as much organizational research on retention can be summarized by the aphorism that "people don't quit companies, they quit bosses", so there appears to be some truth in the saying that talent does not quit cities and countries, they quit lifestyle problems and obstacles, such as poor integration into the local culture (absence of friendship networks), difficulties in schooling children, absence of medical care, violence, and instability that leads to a permanent sense of insecurity. Indeed, we acknowledge that the retention pillar of TC is conceptually less tight because of this close relationship between push and pull factors of attraction and retention, which might argue for collapsing talent attraction and retention into a single pillar.[3]

Having reviewed the four pillars or levers of TC, analogous for countries to the processes that corporations employ, we turn now to a brief discussion of the ultimate aim of TC or if one prefers, its dependent variable for countries. For corporations, the assumption behind HRM is that effective processes lead to corporate performance. In our TC definition, we linked policies and practices (the four talent pillars) to human capital (two types of talent with different economic impacts) and in turn to prosperity. But what does prosperity imply?

Talent and Prosperity: Some Underlying Assumptions

Talent competitiveness is not an "end" in itself; it is a "means" for achieving national goals of prosperity, along with other factors such as the industrial policy, diversification, the infrastructure behind innovation, and productivity. As suggested by Peter Drucker, what is decisive in the performance of human capital "is not how much capital is being invested…it is the productivity of that capital" (Drucker, 2002). For this reason, the TC concept considers not only the differentiated shape of talent (expertise and generalist) but also the different outcomes of these two types of talent, as well as their anchoring in different institutional structures such as educational systems.

While the construct of talent competitiveness is framed in the context of today's global capitalist system, one should not ignore current debates that argue for rethinking capitalism on the grounds that it is not sustainable or inclusive (Jacobs & Mazzucato, 2016). Vital perspectives go beyond economic prosperity; broader perceptions of progress include well-being, trust, longer term externalities, tradeoffs, and preferences (Rangan, 2015). To take the example of higher education, this was historically linked to religious and political community building rather than economic aims. Today, we may critique universities in some countries since students cannot find jobs, but tertiary education may serve broader aims such as building collective meaning across worldwide elites (Shofer, Ramirez, & Meyer, 2016).

Other macro studies in the area of human resource development have focused on the broader concept of "human development". Lynham and Cunningham maintained that: "when nations are the targeted performance system, the purpose of human resource development becomes to develop and unleash human expertise for national economic performance, political and social development, growth, and well-being" (2006: 119). The UN Human Development Index (UNDP, 2016), for instance, has adopted a multidimensional construct that measures human well-being in domains such as health, access to education, or political freedoms. Michael Porter has piloted a Social Progress Index of nations (Porter & Stern, 2017), in which social progress is defined as the capacity of a society to meet the basic needs of its citizens, and to create building blocks that allow them to sustain quality of life and reach their full potential.

While human development is a worthy objective, it is reasonable to focus the concept of talent competitiveness on national economic performance, while acknowledging broader ends such as the importance of inclusion and sustainability. More economic output eventually leads to improvements in "human development" outcomes. The broader concept of human development has its foundations in the seminal work of Lewis who delineated the wide benefits of economic growth:

> the advantage of economic growth is not that wealth increases but it increases the range of human choice—the case for economic growth is that it gives man greater control over his environment, and thereby increases his freedom— economic growth also gives us freedom to choose greater leisure. (Lewis, 1955: 420–421)

Conclusion and Avenues for Further Research

The concept of TC that we have outlined, along with its accompanying framework, aims at bringing analytic rigor to the emerging domain of country/city level MTM. With its input-output framework, it bridges HRM/TM and human capital perspectives. The HRM/TM orientation, with its focus on processes, is reflected in the four input-side levers of enabling, attracting, developing, and retaining talent. The human capital perspective is seen in the output side focus on country-level stock of knowledge and skills, distinguishing between two types of human capital or talent: VT (expertise-based) and adaptive-generalist (associated with leadership, entrepreneurship, and innovation). This distinction between types of human capital is rooted in the structure of educational systems and organizations, and each type is associated with different economic outcomes.

Important avenues for research are raised by the multidimensional TC framework. On the human capital output side, research is needed to investigate what makes young people "employable" in the context of the different labor demand structures that we noted, also considering the growing importance of freelance rather than salaried employment. Research is needed to map out more clearly the generalist/adaptive skills underlying innovation, leadership, and entrepreneurship. And as discussed in the next chapter, how can employability and adaptability be combined to meet the needs of a fast-changing economic environment?

Turning to the HRM/TM input parameters or TC levers, since economic prosperity involves far more than skills, the enabling lever captures the significant elements of the "environment" in which TM takes place – the ecosystem created by regulations and market dynamics, as well as by labor market policies and management practices. Mapping out the management landscape is particularly fertile territory for TM scholars since it is under-investigated (see the important work of economists Bloom & Van Reenen mentioned earlier).

As for the developing lever, attention to macro talent development requires broadening the predominant focus on formal education to the conceptualization and empirical exploration of both lifelong learning and to the role of growth opportunities, notably challenging experiences including experiential learning internships. What are the roles of individuals, firms, and governments in providing this? What are the implications for universities, where continuing education is often only an appendix to core studies? Furthermore, the factors underlying talent attraction and retention are closely related at this macro level – the dynamics of attraction and retention need conceptual and empirical unpacking.

It is difficult to isolate the impact of any single initiative or action in the talent space since the success of one policy depends upon the presence of the others. For instance, research about how inclusive practices interact with better collaboration might help explain innovation (as a talent outcome) in different countries and cities. A complete theory of talent competitiveness will only be complete when a theory of change maps out the complexity of linkages in the system.

The intention behind the TC framework was to build an empirical model, incorporating the best available data from different sources, a model that could inform policy makers and provide benchmarking lessons. That model would also inform researchers, providing them with comparable data within a clear analytic framework. The GTCI (Global Talent Competitiveness Index) is outlined in the next chapter, leading to a discussion of some of challenges for research.

Notes

1 In the empirical model that is outlined in the next chapter, these Generalist-Adaptive skills are also called global knowledge skills.
2 One of the interesting aspects of this research initiative is that management practices can be aggregated and compared at the country level. There is a substantial variation in management practices across organizations in every country and every sector, mirroring the wide spread of productivity and profitability within industries.
3 Pay and taxation rates are important factors for retention (as well as attraction) but they are not measured in GTCI because of lack of available, reliable data that is comparable across countries and cities.

References

Agrawal, A., Cockburn, I., & McHale, J. 2006. Gone but not forgotten: Knowledge flows, labor mobility and enduring social relationships. *Journal of Economic Geography,* 6: 571–591.

Andersson, M., King-Grubert, M., & Lubanski, N. 2016. *Innovating talent attraction: A practitioner's guide for cities, regions and countries.* Copenhagen: U Press.

Ariss, A. A., Cascio, W. F., & Paauwe, J. 2014. Talent management: Current theories and future research directions. *Journal of World Business,* 49: 173–179.

Autor, D. 2015. Why are there still so many jobs? The history and future of workplace automation. *Journal of Economic Perspectives,* 29(3): 3–30.

Balkundi, P., & Kilduff, M. 2006. The ties that lead: A social network approach to leadership. *The Leadership Quarterly,* 17(4): 419–439.

Becker, G. 1994. *Human capital: A theoretical and empirical analysis, with special reference to education* (3rd ed.). University of Chicago Press Books.

Björkman, I., & Welch, D. 2015. Framing the field of international human resource management research. *International Journal of Human Resource Management,* 26(2): 136–150.

Bloom, N., Genakos, C., Sadun, R., & Van Reenen, J. 2012. Management practices across firms and countries. *Academy of Management Perspectives,* 26(1): 12–33.

Bloom, N., Sadun, R., & Van Reenen, J. 2010. Does product market competition lead firms to decentralize? *American Economic Review,* 100: 434–438.

Bloom, N., & Van Reenen, J. 2010. Why do management practices differ across firms and countries? *Journal of Economic Perspectives,* 24(1): 203–224.

Boeri, T., Brucker, H., Docquier, F., & Rapoport, H. 2012. *Brain drain and brain gain: The global competition to attract high-skilled migrants.* Oxford University Press.

Boon, C., Eckardt, R., Lepak, D. P., & Bosselie, P. 2017. Integrating strategic human capital and strategic human resource management. *International Journal of Human Resource Management,* 29(1): 34–67.

Botero, J. C., Djankov, S., La Porta, R., Lopez-de-Silanes, F., & Schliefer, A. 2004. The regulation of labor. *Quarterly Journal of Economics,* 119(4): 1339–1382.

Brown, P., & Hesketh, A. 2004. *The mismanagement of talent: Employability and jobs in the knowledge economy.* New York: Oxford University Press.

Brynjolfsson, E., & McAffee, A. 2014. *The second machine age: Work, progress, and prosperity in a time of brilliant technologies.* New York: W.W. Norton.

Buchanan, J., Anderson, P., & Power, G. 2017. Skill ecosystems. In D. Finegold, K. Mayhew, & C. Warhurst (Eds.), *The Oxford handbook of skills and training.* Oxford, UK: Oxford University Press.

Burt, R. S. 1992. *Structural holes: The social structure of competition.* Cambridge, MA: Harvard University Press.

Cappelli, P. 2008. *Managing talent in an age of uncertainty.* Boston, MA: Harvard Business School Press.

Cappelli, P., & Keller, J. R. 2017. The historical context of talent management. In D. G. Collings, K. Mellahi, & W. F. Cascio (Eds.), *The Oxford handbook of talent management.* Oxford, UK: Oxford University Press.

Cedefop. 2015. *Skill shortages and gaps in European enterprises: Striking a balance between vocational education and training and the labour market.* Cedefop reference series, No 102. Luxembourg: Publications Office. Available at doi: http://dx.doi.org/10.2801/042499

Collings, D. G. 2017. Workforce differentiation. In D. G. Collings, K. Mellahi, & W. F. Cascio (Eds.), *The Oxford handbook of talent management.* Oxford, UK: Oxford University Press.

Collings, D. G., & Mellahi, K. 2009. Strategic talent management: A review and research agenda. *Human Resource Management Review,* 19: 304–313.

Cooke, F. L. 2017. Talent management in emerging economies. In D. G. Collings, K. Mellahi, & W. F. Cascio (Eds.), *The Oxford handbook of talent management.* Oxford, UK: Oxford University Press.

Deming, D. J. 2015. The growing importance of social skills. NBER Working Paper No. 21473, August, National Bureau of Economic Research.

Drucker, P. 2002. They're not employees, they're people. *Harvard Business Review,* February; 80(2): 70-7,128.

Drucker, P. 2012. *Management.* New York: Routledge.

Economist. 2017. *South Africa has one of the world's worst education systems.* 7 January.

Economist. 2018. *Going to university is more important than ever for young people—but the financial returns are falling.* 3 February.

Edvinsson, L., & Malone, M. 1997. *Intellectual capital.* New York: Harper Business.

Etzkowitz, H., & Leydesdorff, L. 2000. The dynamics of innovation: From National Systems and 'Mode 2' to a triple helix of university-industry-government relations. *Research Policy,* 29: 109–123.

European Commission. 2016. The future of work: Skills and resilience for a world of change. Europe Political Strategy Centre. *Strategic Notes,* (13).

Evans, P. 2000. The dualistic leader: Thriving on paradox. In S. Chowdhury (Ed.), *Management 21C,* New York: Prentice Hall-Financial Times.

Evans, P., & Engsbye, M. 2002. 'Danmark og danskerne foran den globale udfordring'. In P. Evans, V. Pucik, J-L. Barsoux, & M. Engsbye, *Den globale udfordring: Danmark og Danskerne og det Internationale Perspektiv.* Copenhagen: JP Boger.

Evans, P., Pucik, V., & Björkman, I. 2011. *The global challenge: International human resource management.* New York: McGraw-Hill.

Evans, P., & Rodriguez-Montemayor, E. 2016. International mobility and talent attraction: a research commentary. In B. Lanvin & P. Evans (Eds.), *Global Talent Competitiveness Index 2015-16.* INSEAD, Fontainebleau, France. https://www.insead.edu/global-indices/gtci

Evans, P., & Rodriguez-Montemayor, E. 2017. Are we prepared for the talent overhaul induced by technology? A GTCI research commentary. In B. Lanvin & P. Evans (Eds.), *Global Talent Competitiveness Index 2017.* INSEAD, Fontainebleau, France. https://www.insead.edu/global-indices/gtci

Evans, P., & Rodriguez-Montemayor, E. 2018. Organising to leverage diversity: A GTCI research commentary. In B. Lanvin & P. Evans (Eds.), *The Global Talent Competitiveness Index, 2018.* INSEAD, Fontainebleau, France. www.insead.edu/global-indices/gtci

Ferner, A. M., Edwards, T., & Tempel, A. 2012. Power, institutions and the cross-national transfer of employment practices in multinationals. *Human Relations,* 65: 163–187.

Frey, C. B., & Osborne, M. A. 2017. The future of employment: How susceptible are jobs to computerization? *Technological Forecasting & Social Change,* 114: 254–280.

Frey, C. B., Osborne, M. A., & Holmes, C. 2016. *Technology at work: The future is not what it used to be.* Oxford Martins School, Oxford University. www.oxfordmartin.ox.ac.uk/downloads/reports/Citi_GPS_Technology_Work_2.pdf

Florida, R. L. 2002. *The rise of the creative class.* New York: Basic Books.

Gallardo-Gallardo, E., Dries, N., & Gonzalez-Cruz, T. F. 2013. What is the meaning of 'talent' in the world of work? *Human Resource Management Review,* 23(4): 290–300.

George, G., Howard-Grenville, J., Joshi, A., & Tihanyi, L. 2016. Understanding and tackling societal grand challenges through management research. *Academy of Management Journal,* 59(6): 1880–1895.

Global Information Technology Report. 2016. *Innovating in the digital economy.* In S. Baller, S. Dutta, & B. Lanvin (Eds.). INSEAD, Cornell University & the World Economic Forum. http://www3.weforum.org/docs/GITR2016/WEF_GITR_Full_Report.pdf

Global Innovation Index 2017. INSEAD, Cornell University, and the World Intellectual Property Organization. www.globalinnovationindex.org

Godart, F. C., Maddux, W., Shipilov, A. V., & Galinsky, A. D. 2015. Fashion with a flair: Professional experience abroad facilitate creative innovations of organizations. *Academy of Management Journal,* 58(1): 195–220.

Hall, R., & Lansbury, R. D. 2006. Skills in Australia: Towards workforce development and sustainable skill ecosystems. *Journal of Industrial Relations,* 48(5): 575–592.

Hanushek, E., Schwerdt, G., Woessmann, L., & Zhang, L. 2011. General education, vocational education, and labor-market outcomes over the life-cycle. *The Journal of Human Resources,* 51(1): 48–87.

Haque, N., & Kim, S. A. 1994. *Human capital flight: Impact of migration on income and growth.* IMF Working Paper, 94/155.

Harbison, F., & Myers, C. A. 1964. *Education, manpower, and economic growth: Strategies of human resource development.* New York: McGraw-Hill.

Harrison, B., Weiss, M., & Gant, J. 1995. *Building bridges: Community development corporations and the world of employment training.* New York: Ford Foundation.

Heifetz, R. A. 1994. *Leadership without easy answers.* Cambridge, MA: Belknap Press of Harvard University Press.

Heijke, H., Meng, C., & Ris, C. 2003. Fitting to the job: The role of generic and vocational competencies in adjustment and performance. *Labour Economics,* 10: 215–229.

Hunt, J., & Gauthier-Loiselle, M. 2010. How much does immigration boost innovation? *American Economic Journal: Macroeconomics,* 2(2): 31–56.

Ibarra, H. 2015. *Act like a leader, think like a leader.* Boston, MA: Harvard Business School Press.

Ichniowski, C., Kochan, T. A., Levine, D., Olson, C., & Strauss, G. 1996. What works at work: Overview and assessment. *Industrial Relations,* 35(3): 299–333.

ILO. 2015. What does NEETs mean and why is the concept so easily misinterpreted? ILO Technical Brief No. 1. Geneva. http://www.ilo.org/wcmsp5/groups/public/@dgreports/@dcomm/documents/publication/wcms_343153.pdf.

Jacobs, M., & Mazzucato, M. 2016. Rethinking capitalism: An introduction. In M. Jacobs & M. Mazzucato (Eds.), *Rethinking capitalism: Economics and policy for sustainable and inclusive growth.* Chichester UK: Wiley-Blackwell.

Keep, E., & Mayhew, K. 1999. The Assessment: Knowledge, skills and competitiveness. *Oxford Review of Economic Policy,* 15(1): 1–15.

Keep, E., Mayhew, K., & Payne, J. 2006. From skills revolution to productivity miracle—not as easy as it sounds? *Oxford Review of Economic Policy,* 22(4), 539–559.

Kerr, W. R. 2008. Ethnic scientific communities and international technology diffusion. *Review of Economics and Statistics,* 90(3): 518–537.

Kerr, W. R., & Lincoln, W. F. 2010. The supply side of innovation: H-1B visa reforms and U.S. ethnic invention. *Journal of Labor Economics,* 28(3): 473–508.

Khilji, S. E., & Schuler, R. S. 2017. Talent management in the global context. In D. G. Collings, K. Mellahi, & W. F. Cascio (Eds.), *The Oxford handbook of talent management.* Oxford, UK: Oxford University Press.

Khilji, S. E., Tarique, I., & Schuler, R. S. 2015. Incorporating the macro view in global talent management. *Human Resource Management Review,* 25: 236–248.

King, K. A., & Vaiman, V. 2019. Enabling effective talent management through a macro-contingent approach: A framework for research and practice. *Business Research Quarterly,* 22(3), 194–206.

Kristensen, P. H. 2016. Constructing chains of enablers for alternative economic futures: Denmark as an example. *Academy of Management Perspectives,* 30(2): 153–166.

Kryscynski, D., & Ulrich, D. 2015. Making strategic human capital relevant: A time-sensitive opportunity. *Academy of Management Perspectives,* 29(3): 357–369.

Kwan, C. W., & Siow, R. 2013. Business ecosystems; Developing employable talent to meet Asia's needs. In B. Lanvin & P. Evans (Eds.), *The Global Talent Competitiveness Index 2013.* INSEAD Report, Singapore. https://www.insead.edu/global-indices/gtci

Kwon, B., Farndale, E., & Park, J. G. 2016. Employee voice and work engagement: Macro, meso and micro-drivers of convergence? *Human Resource Management Review,* 26: 327–337.

Lanvin, B. 2017. Benchmarking cities as key players on the global talent scene. In B. Lanvin & P. Evans (Eds.), *The Global Talent Competitiveness Index 2017: Talent and technology.* INSEAD, Fontainebleau France. https://www.insead.edu/global-indices/gtci

Lanvin, B., & Evans, P. 2013. *The Global Talent Competitiveness Index 2013.* INSEAD, Singapore. https://www.insead.edu/global-indices/gtci

Lanvin, B., & Evans, P. 2017. *The Global Talent Competitiveness Index 2017: Talent and technology.* INSEAD, Fontainebleau. https://www.insead.edu/global-indices/gtci

Lanvin, B., & Evans, P. 2018. *The Global Talent Competitiveness Index 2018: Diversity for Competitiveness.* INSEAD, Fontainebleau, France. https://www.insead.edu/global-indices/gtci

Lanvin, B., Evans, P., & Rasheed, N. 2014. Growing talent for today and tomorrow. In B. Lanvin & P. Evans (Eds.), *The Global Talent Competitiveness Index, 2014.* INSEAD, Singapore. https://www.insead.edu/global-indices/gtci

Lanvin, B., Evans, P., & Rodriguez-Montemayor, E. 2016. Attracting and mobilising talent globally and locally. In B. Lanvin & P. Evans (Eds.), *The Global Talent Competitiveness Index, 2015-16.* INSEAD, Fontainebleau, France. https://www.insead.edu/global-indices/gtci

Lanvin, B., Evans, P., & Rodriguez-Montemayor, E. 2017. Shifting gears: How to combine technology and talent to shape the future of work. In B. Lanvin & P. Evans (Eds.), *The Global Talent Competitiveness Index, 2017.* INSEAD, Fontainebleau, France. https://www.insead.edu/global-indices/gtci

Lanvin, B., Evans, P., & Rodriguez-Montemayor, E. 2018. Diversity as a lever for talent competitiveness. In B. Lanvin & P. Evans (Eds.), *The Global Talent Competitiveness Index, 2018.* INSEAD, Fontainebleau, France. https://www.insead.edu/global-indices/gtci

Lanvin, B., & Rodriguez-Montemayor, E. 2017. *The MENA Talent Competitiveness Index.* INSEAD, Centre for Economic Growth, & Google. www.insead.edu/sites/default/files/assets/dept/centres/ceg/docs/mtci-report-2017.pdf

Lewin, A. Y., Massini, S., & Peeters, C. 2009. Why are companies offshoring innovation? The emerging global race for talent. *Journal of International Business,* 40: 901–925.

Lewis, W. A. 1955. *The theory of economic growth.* Homewood, IL: Irwin.

Lynham, S. A., & Cunningham, P. W. 2006. National human resource development in transitioning societies in the developing world: Concepts and challenges. *Advances in Developing Human Resources,* 8(1): 116–135.

Maddux, W., & Galinsky, A.D. 2009. Cultural borders and mental barriers: The relationship between living abroad and creativity. *Personality & Social Psychology,* 96(5): 1047–1061.

Mahoney, J. T., & Kor, Y. Y. 2015. Advancing the human capital perspective on value creation by joining capabilities and governance approaches. *Academy of Management Perspectives,* 29(3): 296–308.

Mazzucato, M. 2016. Innovation, the state and patient capital. In M. Jacobs & M. Mazzucato (Eds.), *Rethinking capitalism: Economics and policy for sustainable and inclusive growth.* Chichester UK: Wiley-Blackwell.

McGowan, M. A., & Andrews, D. 2015. *Skill mismatch and public policy in OECD countries.* Economics Department Working Papers No. 1210, ECO/WKP(2015)28. Paris, OECD.

Meyer, T. (Ed.). 2016. *Shaping Africa's talent.* Randburg, South Africa: KR Publishing.

Moreau, M. P., & Leathwood, C. 2006. Graduates' employment and the discourse of employability: A critical analysis. *Journal of Education and Work,* 19(4): 305–324.

Mortensen, D.T., & Pissarides, C. 1999. Unemployment responses to 'skill-biased' technology shocks: The role of labour market policy. *Economic Journal,* 109(455), 242–265.

OECD. 2015. *Getting skills right: Assessing and responding to changing skill needs.* Directorate For Employment, Labour and Social Affairs, DELSA/ELSA(2015). OECD Publishing, Paris.

OECD. 2017. *Getting skills right: Skills for jobs indicators.* OECD Publishing, Paris. doi: http://dx.doi.org/10.1787/9789264277878-en

OECD. 2018. *Preparing our youth for an inclusive and sustainable world: The OECD PISA global competence framework.* Paris, OECD. www.oecd.org/education/Global-competency-for-an-inclusive-world.pdf.

O'Mahoney, M., & de Boer, W. 2002. *Britain's relative productivity performance: Updates to 1999.* National Institute for Economic and Social Research, London.

Osman-Gani, A. M., & Tan, W. L. 1998. Human resource development: The key to sustainable growth and competitiveness of Singapore. *Human Resource Development International,* 1(4): 417–432.

Porter, M. E., & Stern, S. 2017. *Social progress index 2017.* Social Progress Imperative, Washington, DC. www.socialprogressindex.com

Powell, W., & Snellman, K. 2004. The knowledge economy. *Annual Review of Sociology,* 30: 199–220.

Pucik, V., Evans, P., Björkman, I., & Morris, S. 2017. *The global challenge: International human resource management* (3rd ed).Chicago: Chicago Business Press.

Putman, R. D. 2015. *Our kids: The American dream in crisis.* New York: Simon & Schuster.

Quintini, G. 2011. *Over-qualified or under-skilled: A review of existing literature.* OECD Social, Employment and Migration Working Papers, No. 121. OECD Publishing, Paris.

Rangan, S. 2015. *Performance and progress: Essays on capitalism, business, and society.* Oxford, UK: Oxford University Press.

Ready, V., Bhorat, H., Powell, M., Visser, M., & Arends, F. 2016. *Skills supply and demand in South Africa.* Labour Market Intelligence Publication, Human Sciences Research Council, Pretoria. http://www.lmip.org.za/sites/default/files/documentfiles/LMIP_SkillsSupplyandDemand_Sept2016_Author_0.pdf

Saisana, M., Dominiguez-Torreiro, M., & Becker, W. 2018. JRC statistical audit of the Global Talent Competitiveness Index 2018. In B. Lanvin & P. Evans (Eds.), *The Global Talent Competitiveness Index, 2018*. INSEAD, Fontainebleau, France. https://www.insead.edu/global-indices/gtci

Saxenian, A. 2002. Silicon Valley's new immigrant high-growth entrepreneurs. *Economic Development Quarterly,* 16: 20–31.

Schofer, E., Ramirez, F. O., & Meyer, J. W. 2016. *The societal effects of higher education: Cross-national analyses, 1960-2012*. University of California Irvine, Working Paper.

Schultz, T. W. 1961. Investment in human capital. *American Economic Review,* 51(1): 1–17.

Susskind, R., & Susskind, D. 2015. *The future of the professions: How technology will transform the work of human experts*. Oxford, UK: Oxford University Press.

Teitelbaum, M. S. 2014. *Falling behind? Boom, bust, and the global race for scientific talent*. Princeton University Press.

Tung, R. L. 2016. New perspectives on human resource management in a global context. *Journal of World Business,* 51(1): 142–152.

UKCES. 2010. *Skills for jobs: Today and tomorrow*. UK Commission for Employment and Skills. https://www.gov.uk/government/uploads/system/uploads/attachment_data/file/339954/national-strategic-skills-audit-for-england-2010-volume-1-key-findings.pdf

UNDP. 2017. *Human development reports*. http://hdr.undp.org/en/global-reports.

Van Harten, J., De Cuyper, N., Guest, D., Fugate, M., Knies, E., & Forrier, A. 2017. Special issue of international human resource management: An international perspective. *International Journal of Human Resource Management,* 28: 2831–2835.

Wang, G., & Swanson, H. 2008. The idea of national HRD: An analysis based on economics and theory development methodology. *Human Resource Development Review,* 7: 79–106.

Williamson, P. J, & De Meyer, A. 2012. Ecosystem advantage: How to successfully harness the power of partnerships. *California Management Review,* 55: 24–46.

World Bank. 2017. *Doing business 2017: Equal Opportunity for All*. Washington, DC: World Bank. doi:10.1596/978-1-4648-0948-4

World Economic Forum. 2017. *The global competitiveness report*. www.weforum.org/reports/the-global-competitiveness-report-2017-2018.

10

THE GLOBAL TALENT COMPETITIVENESS INDEX

An Empirical Assessment and Lessons for Macro Talent Management

Paul Evans

Eduardo Rodriguez-Montemayor

Bruno Lanvin

Introduction

Organizations develop and access the talent that they need in the context of a complex and changing socioeconomic environment. To guide research on macro talent management (MTM) at the country and city level, a rigorous analytic framework is needed. The previous Chapter 8 provides such a framework, built around the concept of talent competitiveness (TC), defined as *the set of policies and practices, as well as the enabling context, that allow a country or a city to attract, develop, and retain the human capital that contributes to its prosperity.* The stock of human capital in a country is assessed in terms of two different skill-knowledge sets—expertise-based (vocational-technical), and adaptive-generalist skills associated with leadership, entrepreneurship, and innovation.

The different elements of this conceptual framework need to be formulated in ways that make them measurable. This chapter introduces an empirical model and database called the Global Talent Competitiveness Index (GTCI), based on the TC framework. Compiled and released annually with updated data covering 119 countries, the fifth annual GTCI report was published in January 2018 (Lanvin & Evans, 2018). The aim of this empirical framework is to facilitate comparison and benchmarking for researchers as well as policy makers in governments, cities and corporations. GTCI draws on the best, most recent, and most authoritative data collected by international organizations such as the World Economic Forum, the Organisation for Economic Co-operation and Development (OECD), International Labour Organization (ILO), the World Bank, and the United Nations. Governments have ready access to such data, but their challenge is to interpret the figures through analytically sound comparisons, with access to the interpretations and lessons of other countries, which should also be the aim of such a framework. As for scholars, they need to have easy access to reliable data, within a clear analytic framework that guides debate, discussion, and focused research.

The operationalization of TC into an empirical framework such as GTCI enables organizations and national policy makers to identify talent trends and challenges, assessing systematically how to adapt to "the grand challenges of our times". Such challenges are technological, demographic, and economic (George, Howard-Grenville, Joshi, & Tihanyi, 2016). First, technological changes involving digitalization, automation, algorithms, and artificial intelligence require deep reforms in our educational systems to meet new competence/skill requirements, as well as a rethinking of our employment

DOI: 10.4324/9781315474687-10

policies (Brynjolfsson & McAfee, 2014; Evans & Rodriguez-Montemayor, 2017). Second, demographic changes due to low birth rates and higher life expectancy in high-income countries raise many policy challenges, notably concerning immigration and international mobility of high skills (see Boeri, Brucker, Docquier, & Rapoport, 2012). Third, the challenge of rising inequalities across the world (Milanovic, 2016) needs to be factored into the talent equation (Bapuji, 2015).

It is fair to say that, over the last few decades, the field of organization talent management (TM) has tended to focus on the exclusive at the expense of the inclusive, and very much on strategically important talent for the corporation (Collings & Mellahi, 2009; Collings, 2017). Yet, managing talent at the level of society implies tackling problems of lack of inclusion, inequality of opportunity, and limited social mobility. Together with challenges of low employability of university graduates, high youth unemployment, and inadequate facilitation of lifelong learning as technologies and markets change, these inequalities may be contributing to social fractures and populism across the world. The political uncertainty that this creates may create obstacles to adopting appropriate responses.

This chapter is organized as follows. Section 1 describes the rationale and data of the GTCI and shows some selected results. Based on the findings of five years of GTCI research, section 2 discusses the transformational challenges confronting MTM. Section 3 explores directions for future research. The concluding section summarizes the contribution of the GTCI to policy and practice.

Global Talent Competitiveness Index: The Empirical Approach

The previous chapter framed the concept of TC, with its six pillars of enabling, attracting, growing, and retaining both the specialized vocational/technical skills that are essential to the functioning of an economy and the adaptive/generalist skills that allow an economy to grow, innovate, and change. The aim of this model is to provide an empirical assessment of TC, with its component elements, so as to guide research, benchmarking, and learning. It is undertaken through the computation of a composite model called the Global Talent Competitiveness Index. A brief introduction to composite models may help the reader before turning to the GTCI overview.

The Use of Composite Indicators

The parallel progress of the field of development economics with Simon Kuznets and Gunnar Myrdal, on the one hand, and on the other hand, the field of human capital (pioneered by Schultz, 1961) that gave rise to some of the first cross-country empirical comparisons of economic progress. A study by Harbison-Myers combined these advances in a composite index, exploring the economic development realities of 75 countries (Harbison & Myers, 1964). The Harbison-Myers Composite Index of Economic Development had a prominent position in the subsequent economics literature, and it became a forerunner of the UN Human Development Index. Many such composite models have been developed since then, such as the Global Competitiveness Index and the Global Innovation Index mentioned in the previous chapter. Other models exist in the human capital arena, but most built around key talent factors, without the analytic traction provided by focusing on the relationship between input levers and output consequences for human capital, and sometimes without any explicit analytic model.[1]

The virtue of such composite models is that they capture the multifaceted nature of complex phenomena, showing interdependencies and conveying data in a potent way. In developing the GTCI, INSEAD drew on fifteen years of experience with two other composite models: the Networked Readiness Index, created in 2001, (see the Global Information Technology Report, 2016) and the Global Innovation Index, initiated in 2007 (see Global Innovation Index, 2017, 2018, 2019).

Composite indices combine reliable data from various sources into a model, based on a conceptual framework, and they provide indicative measures in some form of ranking that facilitates comparisons. Since the GTCI was to be audited annually, it was built to be both conceptually and empirically solid. The value of the GTCI lies in its ability to summarize different aspects of talent competitiveness in a more efficient and parsimonious manner than is possible if the variables and dimensions were taken separately. Empirically, the variables tap into the most reliable and authoritative sources that have worldwide coverage, and they are tested statistically to ensure that the data matches as closely as possible to the conceptualization. The data and sources used by GTCI are listed in the Appendix to this chapter.

To be useful for benchmarking and subsequent learning, such an index should cover a wide number of countries in developed and emerging economies. However, lack of solid comparable data across a large number of countries constraints such models. For example, pay, taxation and lifestyle factors are important for the attraction and retention of talent, yet there is no reliable comparative data on such factors for a sufficiently wide array of economies; and similarly for apprenticeship schemes associated with expertise-based vocational training and education. In contrast, the measurement of employability relating to vocational-technical (VT) skills became possible recently when reliable data on the ability of nations to match skills to jobs became available.

Faced with lack of worldwide data, global composite indices traditionally rely on proxies. For example, educational attainment can be seen as a proxy for expertise talent and generalist talent (secondary school typically means an orientation to VT skills, while tertiary education means more generalist skills). To take another example discussed in the previous chapter, delegation of authority can be used as a proxy for the growth opportunity that experience provides.

The insights that such a model provides are only as good as the reasoning behind the model and the quality of its data. The quality of that reasoning can, however, be assessed by a statistical audit that verifies coherence, the reliability of the components of the model and its multilevel structure, its parsimoniousness, and its sensitivity or robustness. The creators of the GTCI model decided that it should undergo such an audit each year, performed by the Joint Research Centre (the statistical office of the EU) and published as a chapter in the GTCI annual report. According to this audit, GTCI has proved since the outset to be remarkably robust and statistically reliable (Saisana, Dominiquez-Torreiro, & Becker, 2018).

The GTCI Model

Since its first release in 2013, the GTCI has undergone some incremental changes but without significant modification of the conceptual structure that was outlined in the previous chapter. An adapted generalized version of the GTCI model is shown in Figure 10.1. The empirical results can be found in the annual GTCI Reports (available at www.insead.edu/global-indices/gtci).

GTCI is a composite index relying on more than sixty variables from reliable sources, distributed across six pillars, and covering a variety of countries (GTCI Report, 2018, 2019, 2020). The various variables and countries have increased over time. The 2018 GTCI Index relied on 68 variables covering 119 countries, and the variables have increased to 72 with the 2020 GTCI Index, now with 132 countries.

The GTCI Index is designed as an "Input-Output model", in the sense that it combines an assessment of, on the one hand, what countries do to enable, develop, attract, and retain talent (the four input pillars or levers of TC) and, on the other hand, the stock of human capital and economic outcomes derived from this pool of talent – the two output pillars of VT and generalist-adaptive (GA) skills with their economic impact. In the GTCI reports, GA skills are referred to as global knowledge skills.

Each pillar consists of two or three sub-pillars, reflecting the conceptualization outlined in the previous chapter. For instance, consistent with that discussion, the two output pillars of VT skills and GA skills are each evaluated using sub-pillars that measure the strength of the pool of skills and the economic impact of those skills – employability measures such as the absence of skill gaps for VT skills, and talent impact measures of innovation and entrepreneurship for GA skills.

Each sub-pillar is typically populated by three to seven variables. Computation involves normalizing each individual variable and then aggregating the data into a single score by assigning weights to each pillar. Each sub-pillar score is derived as the simple arithmetic average of the individual variables that it includes. The GTCI Index score is the arithmetic average of the scores obtained by a particular country on each of these six pillars.

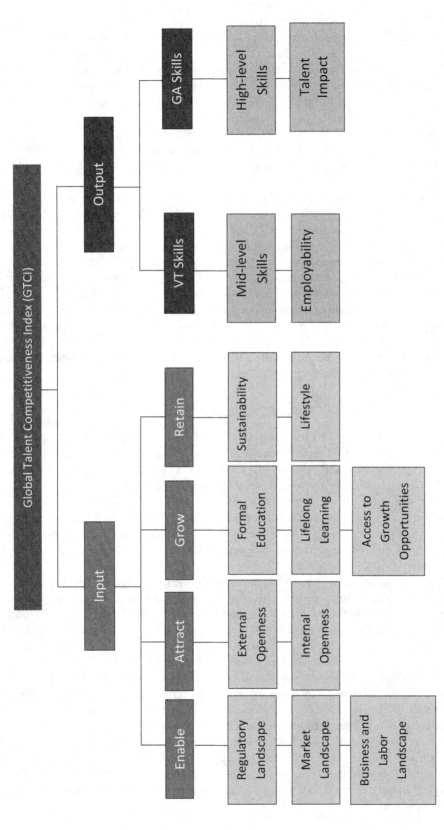

Figure 10.1 The Global Talent Competitiveness Index framework

Adapted from GTCI Report (2018)
VT Skills = vocational and technical skills; GA Skills = generalist–adaptive or global knowledge skills

Table 10.1 The GTCI rankings in 2018, 2019, 2020*

Ranking 2018	Ranking 2019	Ranking 2020
Switzerland	Switzerland	Switzerland
Singapore	Singapore	United States
United States	United States	Singapore
Norway	Norway	Sweden
Sweden	Denmark	Denmark
Finland	Finland	Netherlands
Denmark	Sweden	Finland
United Kingdom	Netherlands	Luxembourg
Netherlands	United Kingdom	Norway
Luxembourg	Luxembourg	Australia

*Based on data from GTCI 2018, 2019, 2020 reports

Table 10.1 provides the ranking in 2018, 2019, and 2020 for the top ten countries, based on the average of the six pillars.

Transformational Challenges Confronting MTM

The GTCI model and index tries to encompass the essential elements of TC at the country level. This breadth is complemented each year by focusing on a specific theme, widening the data through further research and interviews with prominent scholars and authorities on that theme. MTM is at the heart of some transformational "grand challenges", as mentioned in the Introduction, and the GTCI themes have tended to focus on these.

An underlying trend that was clear from the outset of GTCI is the way in which technology is changing the global talent scene. This was the theme of the Report in 2017, complemented with a focus in the 2020 Report on the talent impact of artificial intelligence. Additionally, it became apparent that a critical factor in responding to such transformational challenges is ecosystems for TM—close collaboration between government, cities, business, and the representatives of labor. So in this section, we focus on this transformational "What" and "How" at the level of nations.

Other themes that have been explored are growing talent for today and tomorrow (2014), highlighting the need for a renaissance of vocational and technical education (as discussed in the previous chapter); talent attraction and international mobility (2015–16) that emphasizes the importance of steering "brain circulation" (Saxenian, 2002) rather than brain drain/gain; and diversity for competitiveness (2018), with a particular emphasis on the importance of cognitive diversity in teams for innovation and high performance, and the corresponding necessity for collaborative skills and entrepreneurial talent (2019).

How Technology Is Changing the Work and Talent Scene

Research at the Massachusetts Institute of Technology (Autor, 2015; Brynjolfsson & McAffee, 2014), Harvard University (Deming, 2015), and Oxford University (Frey, Osborne, & Holmes, 2016; Frey & Osborne, 2017; Susskind & Susskind, 2015) have alerted opinion and decision makers to the hitherto invisible but deep ways in which digitalization, algorithms, robotics, and artificial intelligence are changing the world of work. Put simply, any routine task can and in all probability will be performed by machines. This has already resulted in a hollowing out of the economies of developed nations. It is not just factory jobs that get done better by robots, it is also work in professions like law, accountancy, journalism, and consulting that are increasingly relying on algorithms. In many kinds of surgery, the precision of robots exceeds that of humans, and fundamental research in genetics and other fields now needs intensive usage of artificial intelligence. So technology is changing radically the way we look at labor and employment.

Our conclusion is that it is hence important to think beyond automation, understanding the way in which organizations and work practices are changing with new business models enabled by the digital economy and platforms. The 20th-century tradition of salaried work, often with a single employer over one's lifetime, is giving way to freelance employment. More than 30% of the population in the Western World today earn all or part of their income as freelancers, in a world where getting a mortgage, car loan, or unemployment benefits is typically dependent on being a salaried employee (see Evans & Rodriguez-Montemayor,2017). Work will not disappear, contrary to some dire forecasts that robots are taking over. But work and employment will be different. While certain less skilled jobs will remain (the hairdresser is the prototypical example), countries have to help their populations to understand that their children will have three, four, five, or more different careers during their lives.

Educational systems must be reformed to facilitate massive and continuous upskilling. Children need the ability to "learn how to learn", which Finnish research suggests is molded at play school (Sahlberg, 2015), essential to acquire new skills continuously and to take advantage of new work opportunities as they arise. The traditional Program for International Student Assessment (PISA)-basics of literacy, math, and science at primary school remain vital, together with knowledge/skills that make people employable acquired at secondary and university education. In addition collaborative problem solving, project, and interpersonal skills are required for collaborative innovation and entrepreneurship. We hear many debates on the respective virtues of a broad liberal education versus a specialized education that makes people employable (GA versus VT in our GTCI terms). But the paradigm in the globalized technology-driven 21st-century world is not either/or but both/and duality (Evans, 2000). People need both the technical expertise that makes them employable *and* the broad project and social skills that allow them to contribute to a world of innovation and entrepreneurship.

These are immense challenges for our educational systems. The head of state digitalization for Denmark, Europe's most digitally prepared state according to EU rankings (EurActiv, 2015), told us that after 15 years of creating a digital infrastructure, the new focus should be on the competences that a digital society needs, and the key pillar will be educational and teaching reform (Evans & Rodriguez-Montemayor, 2017). The government of Denmark launched a Disruption Council of experts to help steer the nation through such reforms. In contrast, South Korea has one of the most sophisticated IT infrastructures in the world and excels on PISA scores, but it lags behind in TC because of a regimented educational system focused on standardized tests. There is a parallel challenge involving change in our employment systems so that they reflect the realities of a world when many people are free agents and most will spend part of their lives in such roles; and where countries learn how to facilitate the necessary transitions, job/career changes, and mobility of people through what economists call "active labor market policies", such as those exemplified by the Danish flexicurity system.

In 2017, the GTCI assessed empirically the readiness of 118 countries for this technology-driven change, based on criteria from our analysis and appropriate empirical measures. Only 10 are reasonably well positioned. In order of their GTCI ranking, these ten countries are Switzerland, Singapore, the United Kingdom, Denmark, the Netherlands, Ireland, Canada, New Zealand, the United Arab Emirates, and Bahrain. Among the criteria for readiness for change was the importance of collaboration between social partners, which emerged as a key factor in managing transformational change at the outset of the GTCI.

Managing Transformational Change: The Importance of Eco-system Partnerships

Actions to deal with national challenges such as the impact of technology on society, the reform of educational systems, and the development of new skills for different work and employment opportunities require close exchange and collaboration between and within government, municipalities, business and labor representatives, and educational institutions. The imperative of collaboration within such ecosystems surfaced in our first GTCI 2013 Report, which featured examples of skills development to meet new needs and opportunities in India and Singapore (Kwan & Siow, 2013; see also Williamson & De Meyer, 2012; Etzkowitz & Leydesdorff, 2000; Mahoney & Kor, 2015).

Among the many examples of the importance of partnership for national governance is the vocational educational system of Switzerland that contributes to its performance as the world's leading country on TC and on innovation. Philippe Gnaegi, former Swiss minister of education and chairman of the Swiss Federal Institute for Vocational Education and Training, told us that the foundation of a system that also facilitates high employment in that country (only 3.6% youth unemployment, contrasting with a European area average of 20% in 2016) is the close partnerships between Swiss cantons (regional governments), the Federal government, business firms, and technical training institutions. The system is constantly evolving and changing, rooted in nearly a hundred years of collaboration dating back to 1921.

Thus, when we undertake a country assessment, one of the first GTCI figures that we look at is collaboration among stakeholders. That collaboration exists in many rapidly growing developing countries, such as Malaysia, Rwanda, Kazakhstan, and Panama, though it is sometimes associated with authoritarian rule or rule by elitist cliques that "impose" collaboration. It does not exist in countries that have failed so far to deliver on their potential, notably some of the BRICS (Brazil, Russia, India, China, South Africa), except in the form of corruption at the government-business boundary. South Africa is one of the worst performing countries on virtually all indicators of ecosystem partnership, and Brazil is not much further ahead.

Because of the fundamental importance of ecosystem collaboration, at the outset of GTCI in 2013, we agreed with Richard Florida (2002) that cities and regions will become the focal arena for talent competitiveness in the future. To return to the United States, the country is so big, diverse, and complex that it is difficult in this type of democratic society to build across-the-board collaboration; one cannot compare the U.S. or China with a city-state such as Singapore. However, if one were to take cities as ecosystems, there is no doubt that San Francisco (California) and the Bay area would rank among the most talent competitive regions of the world. Similarly, it is misleading to assess China as a state, with its gulf between rural and urban regions. Instead, one should look at Hong Kong, Shanghai, and the emerging metropolises such as Guiyung, that few people in the West have heard about.

For this reason, GTCI launched in 2017 a pilot version of a global city index, based on a comparable but different model, initially covering 46 cities across six continents – the Global City Talent Competitiveness Index (GCTCI) (Lanvin, 2017). One of the initial insights coming from this beta analysis is that smaller "smart cities" with good infrastructure, well connected to the world by broadband and international airports but offering lifestyle advantages, may have significant advantages over mega-metropolises in attracting and organizing talent. Smaller cities, including off-the-map places in North America and Europe, may be the talent leaders of the future.

Directions for MTM Research

In the emerging sub-field of macro talent management, the assumption is that comparisons between countries shed light on important questions for research. What are some of the important challenges that merit research attention? It is important to note that such research must draw on interdisciplinary knowledge.

How to Combine Employability with Adaptability?

Employability, which the TC framework links to specialized and practical VT expertise, is certainly an important and undervalued element of MTM around the world, as seen in debates over the school/ university-to-work transition, skills gaps, and youth unemployment. While employability needs more research attention, many have argued that rapid societal change and workforce adaptability requires a broad-based general education (e.g., Streeck, 1989; Keep et al., 2006). Is there a tradeoff between these perspectives, or can talent development systems combine both in some form of T-shaped concept, as EU policy recommendations suggest (EU Commission, 2016)? Comparative research may help shed light on this complex set of issues. German research suggests that with rapid technological change, gains in youth employment from vocational education with apprenticeships may be offset by less adaptability and thus diminished employment later in life (Hanushek et al., 2011).

This does not appear to happen in Switzerland, a country with a different dual education system that is also a world-leader on innovation. Swiss vocational education emphasizes innovation skills for changing industry needs as well as practical skills for an immediate job (Federal Department of Foreign Affairs,

2016). Adaptability argues for some degree of generalist education, but can this also be fostered by learning skills, which the Finns believe is instilled above all at play school age (Sahlberg, 2017)? Research bridging different levels of analysis is needed as parents and policy makers around the world struggle with such questions. With the acceleration of technological change, such questions for research become urgent.

What Is the Impact of Lifelong Learning on Talent Development?

A related set of research questions stems from viewing talent development as a lifelong process, encompassing experience and adult learning as well as formal education. As lifelong learning becomes institutionalized in nations around the world, spurred by accelerating change, how does this impact our concept of education? Should the dualistic apprenticeship model be extended from secondary education to life-long learning? What is the impact on universities, where continuing education is often only an appendix to core undergraduate and graduate activities? Building on Danish Flexicurity experiences outlined in the previous chapter, how can active labor market practices foster greater flexibility in making necessary career transitions? One should bear in mind that nearly a third of adults in western economies today work in free-lance roles, outside any organizational umbrella, and that salaried employees may soon become a minority.

How Can TM Assist in Building a More Inclusive Society?

The field of talent management with its focus on organizations has generally adopted an exclusive paradigm focused on talent that is strategically important for the firm (Collings & Mellahi, 2009). While there are debates around this, fueled by the importance for organizations of diversity (Baker & Kelan, 2017), the challenge of how to build a more inclusive society is emerging as a major theme for economists (Summers & Ball, 2015; Jacobs & Mazzucato, 2016) and for political and business leaders (this was the focus of the World Economic Forum in Davos, January 2018).

People may accept that skills, opportunities and wealth are not equally distributed in society, and that economic progress means that some will be favored by globalization, innovation, and digitalization, while others fall by the wayside. But when falling by the wayside means moving without dignity to the poverty line, when social and racial origins imply a low probability that one's children will lead a better life, when worsening Gini-coefficients suggest that already striking income inequalities are increasing even more across the world, then the path to future prosperity may be washed away by the landslide of negative votes and a rising tide of populism.

Research on how MTM processes can build inclusive prosperity is thus highly opportune. At the level of countries, the educational sector plays a critical role in inclusiveness (or internal openness as called in the GTCI). Primary and secondary education are normally regarded as the means to provide all young students with equal opportunities regardless of socio-economic background. More research is needed to understand how to reform educational systems in order to leverage diversity and inclusion. This requires addressing the question of how to transition from historically standardized educational systems to a system that taps into differences, as OECD research suggests (Burns & Van Damme, 2018). But it also requires paying attention to the competences that need to be developed to allow individuals to collaborate effectively in a multi-cultural, inter-connected world. As mentioned in the previous chapter, the OECD is broadening its PISA assessment of student competences to include collaborative problem solving, necessary to capitalize on diversity (OECD, 2018). An overarching question is how should nations differentiate their workforce development so that people with different talents perform optimally?

Given the Importance of Mobility, How Can Countries Compete in the Global War for Talent?

Talented people tend to be mobile. As discussed earlier, there has been more and more attention to the growing international mobility of talent. But maybe the causality is also the other way around? Maybe it is mobility – or diverse and multifaceted educational and work experiences – that helps develop creative talent? Economists have tended to focus on the role of formal education and training in developing talent, neglecting factors that are more difficult to measure – such as mobility. Management researchers know that there is much more to talent development than formal education. What is the role of mobility in developing talent? This is another complex area in which evidence and understanding often remain anecdotal.

We need a better understanding of **what makes nations and cities attractive to talent**. The answers will surely be contingent on demographic differences such as life stage, culture, and other factors cutting across different levels of analysis. It is important to understand why a location is attractive since there is some evidence that the local presence of talent is one of the most important reasons why companies chose a location for their operations. Organizations have moved R&D and other innovation functions to Asia for talent reasons (Lewin, Massini, & Peeters, 2009). Developed economies need to understand better how educational and growth opportunities, led by the regulatory, market, and business contexts, are conducive to attracting foreign talent. For emerging markets, how can they ensure the education of their best talent abroad while maintaining diaspora links that can lead to a step jump on the path to prosperity rather than feeding a brain drain?

The questions may be different for countries at different stages of development, so **what are the key dimensions of MTM that differentiate developed from emerging nations**? Building on the pioneering research in economics discussed in the previous chapter (Bloom & Van Reenen, 2012), an important question to explore is the extent to which management practices differentiate between developed and emerging nations (management practices are perhaps more measurable and tangible than cultural differences). While many emerging countries have based their developmental strategies on the growth of manufacturing and labor-intensive industries, cheap labor today is less and less an advantage. The new question is whether digital technology can assist emerging countries to leapfrog the otherwise slow process of developing a talent infrastructure. One area of research is to identify the skills required at different development stages of different countries (Wang & Swanson, 2008). For that, policies for improving talent competitiveness in emerging markets must also take into account changes in their developmental objectives. Indeed, supporting a high-skill ecosystem seems indispensable in developing countries, and so the question is what would be the industries that should lead the way, or more broadly: How is Industry 4.0 going to change the parameters of global talent competition?

Conclusion

The Global Talent Competitiveness Index (GTCI), and its underlying conceptual framework outlined in chapter 9, are intended to frame the complexities of country/city level talent management in an analytic way that stimulates both research and policy change. A complete picture of macro TM is achieved by looking at inputs and outputs, and by linking micro, meso, and macro forces. Researchers will find in this model both conceptual reasoning as well as the most sound available data.

As an action tool, assessment models such as GTCI facilitate the systematic identification of policy priorities as well as comparative lessons, particularly important in the context of technological, demographic, and economic transformations facing societies. Work and talent are undergoing fundamental change. Such tools and analytic data can help inform the debates that need to take place between governments (both at the country and city level), business, the educational system, and citizens about how the future of work can be better anticipated and shaped, especially with the perspective of reducing inequalities and nurturing higher levels of inclusion worldwide.

Note

1 Other models at that macro or national level that can be highlighted include IMD's World Talent Report, built around the three factors of investment, appeal, and readiness; the World Economic Forum's Human Capital Index, focused on four human capital outputs (capacity, deployment, development, and know how); and the

Intellectual Capital model encapsulating the "hidden value of individuals, enterprises, institutions, communities, and regions that are current and potential sources of wealth creation" (Edvinson & Malone, 1997). Additionally, consulting companies produce talent indices, though often with irregular periodicity. The Hays Global Skills Index in partnership with Oxford Economics is in its sixth edition, built around seen factors such as educational flexibility, labor market flexibility, and wage pressures.

References

Autor, D. 2015. Why are there still so many jobs? The history and future of workplace automation. *Journal of Economic Perspectives,* 29: 3–30.

Baker, D. T., & Kelan, E. K. 2017. Integrating talent and diversity management. In D. G. Collings, K. Mellahi, & W. F. Cascio (Eds.), *The Oxford handbook of talent management.* Oxford, UK: Oxford University Press.

Bapuji, H. 2015. Individuals, interactions and institutions: How economic inequality affects organizations. *Human Relations,* 68(7): 1059–1083.

Bloom, N., & Van Reenen, J. 2010. Why do management practices differ across firms and countries? *Journal of Economic Perspectives,* 24: 203–224.

Boeri, T., Brucker, H., Docquier, F., & Rapoport, H. 2012. *Brain drain and brain gain: The global competition to attract high-skilled migrants.* Oxford, UK: Oxford University Press.

Brynjolfsson, E., & McAffee, A. 2014. *The second machine Age: Work, progress, and prosperity in a time of brilliant technologies.* New York: W.W. Norton.

Burns, T., & Van Damme, D. 2018. Education and diversity: Challenges and opportunities. In B. Lanvin & P. Evans, (Eds.), *The Global Talent Competitiveness Index, 2018.* INSEAD, Fontainebleau, France. http://www.insead.edu/global-indices/gtci.

Collings, D. G. 2017. Workforce differentiation. In D. G. Collings, K. Mellahi, & W. F. Cascio (Eds.), *The Oxford handbook of talent management.* Oxford, UK: Oxford University Press.

Collings, D. G., & Mellahi, K. 2009. Strategic talent management: A review and research agenda. *Human Resource Management Review,* 19: 304–313.

Deming, D. J. 2015. *The growing importance of social skills.* NBER Working Paper No. 21473, August, National Bureau of Economic Research.

Etzkowitz, H., & Leydesdorff, L. 2000. The dynamics of innovation: From national systems and 'mode 2' to a triple helix of university-industry-government relations. *Research Policy,* 29:109–123.

EurActiv. 2016. EU countries issue mea culpas for poor marks on internet connectivity. *EurActiv.com,* February 26. http://www.euractiv.com/section/digital/news/eu-countries-issue-mea-culpas-for-poor-marks-on-internet-connectivity.

Evans, P., & Rodriguez-Montemayor, E. 2017. Are we prepared for the talent overhaul induced by technology? A GTCI research commentary. In B. Lanvin & P. Evans (Eds.), *Global Talent Competitiveness Index 2017.* INSEAD, Fontainebleau, France. http://www.insead.edu/global-indices/gtci.

Evans, P., & Rodriguez-Montemayor, E. 2018. Organising to leverage diversity: A GTCI research commentary. In B. Lanvin & P. Evans (Eds.), *The Global Talent Competitiveness Index, 2018.* INSEAD, Fontainebleau, France. http://www.insead.edu/global-indices/gtci.

Federal Department of Foreign Affairs, Switzerland. 2016. *Switzerland's vocational educational and training system: A model for apprenticeships in the United States.* Washington, DC: Embassy of Switzerland in the United States. http://www.swissemb.org/apprenticeships.

Florida, R. L. 2002. *The rise of the creative class.* New York: Basic Books.

Frey, C. B., & Osborne, M. A. 2017. The future of employment: How susceptible are jobs to computerization? *Technological Forecasting & Social Change,* 114: 254–280.

Frey, C. B., Osborne, M. A., & Holmes, C. 2016. *Technology at work: The future is not what it used to be.* Oxford Martins School, Oxford University. http://www.oxfordmartin.ox.ac.uk/downloads/reports/Citi_GPS_Technology_Work_2.pdf.

George, G., Howard-Grenville, J., Joshi, A., & Tihanyi, L. 2016. Understanding and tackling societal grand challenges through management research. *Academy of Management Journal,* 59: 1880–1895.

Global Information Technology Report. 2016. *Innovating in the digital economy.* INSEAD, Cornell University & World Economic Forum. http://www3.weforum.org/docs/GITR2016/WEF_GITR_Full_Report.pdf.

Global Innovation Index. 2017. INSEAD, Cornell University, and the World Intellectual Property Organization. https://www.globalinnovationindex.org.

Global Innovation Index. 2018. INSEAD, Cornell University, and the World Intellectual Property Organization. https://www.wipo.int/edocs/pubdocs/en/wipo_pub_gii_2018.pdf.

Global Innovation Index. 2019. INSEAD, Cornell University, and the World Intellectual Property Organization. https://www.wipo.int/edocs/pubdocs/en/wipo_pub_gii_2019.pdf.

Global Talent Competitiveness Index (GTCI) Reports. 2013–2020. INSEAD, Fontainebleau, France. https://www.insead.edu/global-indices/gtci.

Hanushek, E., Schwerdt, G., Woessmann, L., & Zhang, L. 2011. General education, vocational education, and labor-market outcomes over the life-cycle. *Journal of Human Resources,* 51: 48–87.

Harbison, F., & Myers, C. A. 1964. *Education, manpower, and economic growth: Strategies of human resource development.* New York: McGraw-Hill.

Jacobs, M., & Mazzucato, M. 2016. Rethinking capitalism: An introduction. In M. Jacobs & M. Mazzucato (Eds.), *Rethinking capitalism: Economics and policy for sustainable and inclusive growth.* Chichester UK: Wiley-Blackwell.

Keep, E., Mayhew, K., & Payne, J. 2006. From skills revolution to productivity miracle—not as easy as it sounds? *Oxford Review of Economic Policy,* 22(4).

Kwan, C.W., & Siow, R. 2013. Business ecosystems: Developing employable talent to meet Asia's needs. In B. Lanvin & P. Evans (Eds.), *The Global Talent Competitiveness Index 2013.* INSEAD, Singapore. https://www.insead.edu/global-indices/gtci.

Lanvin, B. 2017. Benchmarking cities as key players on the global talent scene. In B. Lanvin & P. Evans (Eds.), *The Global Talent Competitiveness Index 2017: Talent and technology.* INSEAD, Fontainebleau France. https://www.insead.edu/global-indices/gtci.

Lanvin, B., & P. Evans. 2018. *The Global Talent Competitiveness Index 2018: Diversity for Competitiveness.* INSEAD, Fontainebleau, France. https://www.insead.edu/global-indices/gtci.

Lanvin, B., Evans, P., & Rodriguez-Montemayor, E. 2018. Diversity as a lever for talent competitiveness. In B. Lanvin & P. Evans (Eds.), *The Global Talent Competitiveness Index, 2018.* INSEAD, Fontainebleau, France. https://www.insead.edu/global-indices/gtci.

Lewin, A. Y., Massini, S., & Peeters, C. 2009. Why are companies offshoring innovation? The emerging global race for talent. *Journal of International Business,* 40: 901–25.

Mahoney, J. T., & Kor, Y. Y. 2015. Advancing the human capital perspective on value creation by joining capabilities and governance approaches. *Academy of Management Perspectives,* 29(3): 296–308.

Milanovic, B. 2016. *Global inequality: A new approach for the age of globalization.* Cambridge, MA: Harvard University Press.

OECD. 2018. *Preparing our youth for an inclusive and sustainable world: The OECD PISA global competence framework.* Paris, OECD. https://www.oecd.org/education/Global-competency-for-an-inclusive-world.pdf.

Sahlberg, P. 2015. *Finnish lessons 2.0: What can the world learn from educational change in Finland?* New York: Teachers College Press.

Saisana, M., Dominiguez-Torreiro, M., & Becker, W. 2018. JRC statistical audit of the Global Talent Competitiveness Index 2018. In B. Lanvin & P. Evans (Eds.), *The Global Talent Competitiveness Index, 2018.* INSEAD, Fontainebleau, France. https://www.insead.edu/global-indices/gtci.

Saxenian, A. 2002. Silicon Valley's new immigrant high-growth entrepreneurs. *Economic Development Quarterly,* 16: 20–31.

Schultz, T. W. 1961. Investment in human capital. *American Economic Review,* 51: 1–17.

Streek, W. 1989. Skills and the limits of neo-liberalism. *Work, Employment and Society,* 3: 89–105.

Summers, L. H., & Ball, E. 2015. *Report of the Commission on Inclusive Prosperity.* Center for American Progress. https://www.americanprogress.org/issues/economy/reports/2015/01/15/104266/report-of-the-commission-on-inclusive-prosperity.

Susskind, R., & Susskind, D. 2015. *The future of the professions: How technology will transform the work of human experts.* Oxford, UK: Oxford University Press.

United Nations. 2017. *International migration stock.* United Nations Department of Economic and Social Affairs. http://www.un.org/en/development/desa/population/migration/data/estimates2/estimatestotal.shtml.

Wang, G., & Swanson, H. 2008. The idea of national HRD: An analysis based on economics and theory development methodology. *Human Resource Development Review,* 7: 79–106.

Williamson, P. J., & De Meyer, A. 2012. Ecosystem advantage: How to successfully harness the power of partnerships. *California Management Review,* 55: 24–46.

11
TALENT MANAGEMENT IN ASIA

Fang Lee Cooke

Introduction

The important political and economic role of Asia in the global politico-economy is well recognized, not least because of its rapidly rising education levels and economic growth (e.g., Asian Development Bank, 2011; Australian Government, 2012; Cooke, Schuler, & Varma, 2020; Huiyao, 2019; Lagarde, 2016). It is believed that Asian countries, including developing countries such as China and India, are leading the world in digitalization, innovation, and connectivity (Deloitte Insights, 2017). But what are some of the human resource challenges that may be holding these countries back in their development?

This chapter reviews the status quo of research on talent management (TM) in the world's most populated, culturally diverse, and economically vibrant continent – Asia. It examines how societal factors, including institutional, human capital, and cultural factors, shape the national TM contexts and practices. It highlights a number of major challenges confronting this continent and some of the initiatives adopted by nation states to combat the bottleneck in their economic development caused by talent shortage. The chapter notes that Asian countries may face different sets of challenges derived from their institutional conditions and cultural traditions. These include, for example: population ageing in Japan, South Korea, and China; relatively high turnover of the young workforce in China, India, Malaysia, and Vietnam; and heavy dependence in Singapore and Middle East countries on international migrants from the region and outside it for their skill supply.

Drawing on extant research, the chapter reveals a number of human resource management (HRM) practices that have been found effective in TM in different countries and industrial sectors. It highlights implications of TM for multinational corporations (MNCs) operating in and from Asia. The chapter concludes with a set of research agendas for future studies. It is important to note at the outset that Asia is a vast continent and represents a constellation of civilizations with a diverse range of political systems, different stages of economic development, cultural traditions and religious values. Thus, what is presented in this chapter is inevitably over-simplified and incomplete.

Societal Characteristics of Talent Management

The examination of TM issues in Asia necessitates a broad survey of the macro conditions for talent development before focusing on the organizational level to assess HRM practices and management challenges. In this section, we outline a number of macro-level features of TM, including educational systems, talent mindsets, talent shortages, and state policy interventions.

DOI: 10.4324/9781315474687-11

Elitist Approach to Talent Selection for Development

Despite various degrees of influence of democratic ideology, Asian countries are largely hierarchical societies that respect seniority and authority, and are tolerant of inequality stemming from social classes, albeit increasingly challenging it (e.g. Cooke & Kim, 2018). In many countries, an elitist approach is adopted for TM, which is deeply embedded in national education systems informed by traditional culture, such as that found in East Asia. The East Asian societies (e.g., China, Japan, and South Korea) have a strong belief in Confucian values, which treat education as the highest form of activity that will raise one above the crowds (e.g., Cooke, Saini, & Wang, 2014; Meng et al., 2016). In China, only the academically best performing school students are selected to enter higher education each year; this offers them an improved chance for getting a good job and embarking on a good career (Cooke & Wang, 2018).

In South Korea, developing students' creative potential through education is deemed critical for the nation to maintain a competitive advantage (Lee, 2016). According to Lee (2016: 40), invention-gifted education "is one approach that can both foster creativity and develop inventive talent", and South Korea is "distinctive in its systematic approach to talent identification and talent development across the elementary and middle grades". It is believed that invention education brings benefits to the individuals and the society not least because it can "promote dynamically the development of high-level performance in invention" (Lee, 2016: 47) and enables individuals "to contribute something of social value" (Lee, 2016: 48).

As education levels are rising across Asian countries, individuals are competing not only for a place in the university, but for a place in the best university they can reach to better their life chances. Such a differentiated or exclusive approach to identifying, selecting, and developing talent from a young age means that potential opportunities for individuals are set early in their life, making it more difficult for late-developed talents to enter the formal system and flourish. Such an approach is functionalist and utilitarian, which can be explained from a resource perspective, since educational and other social resources are scarce and cannot be equally distributed if nation states wish to catch up and compete in the global economy.

Inadequacy of the Education System

Research has commonly revealed the inadequacy of the education system in many developing Asian states; it is believed that this undermines the development of young talents prior to their employment (e.g., Azman, Sirat, & Pang, 2016). For example, Azman et al. (2016: 316) examined the role of Malaysian higher education institutions in raising the human capital stock needed for the nation to compete as a high-income country in the future. They revealed a number of inadequacies in the system that undermine the country's efforts in talent development, including: the relatively poor quality of research activities of academics, poor resourcing, the emphasis on quantity rather than quality of the university graduates following the expansion of the higher education sector in 1997, and a narrow and low skill-base of the Malaysian workforce compared with that of Organisation for Economic Co-operation and Development (OECD) countries. Aziz, Afthanorhan, and Awang's (2016) study also observed the problems of mismatch between university curriculum and market demands. These inadequacies are believed to be a consequence of the transitional nature of the country's reforms and "incomplete structural changes occurring in the national system" (Azman et al., 2016: 316).

Problems observed in the Malaysian higher education system are also commonly reported in other Asian countries such as China and India (c.f. Cooke et al., 2014). A direct consequence of the inadequacy of the higher education system in talent development is the mismatch between what has been produced in higher education institutions and what is most needed by employers (e.g. World Bank, 2007). A significant knock-on effect of this mismatch is the war for talent that has developed in these countries, a problem that is often exacerbated by brain drain through the emigration of top talents (see below).

Labor Market (De)regulation and the Growth of Informal Employment

Effective TM in the 21st century requires an efficient labor market environment. Many Asian countries have been through labor market regulation reforms in recent decades, for different reasons. For example, in Japan and South Korea, labor market deregulation was a key feature in the nations' economic recovery strategy following the economic crisis in 1992 (for Japan) and 1997 (for Japan and South Korea) (c.f. Cooke & Brown, 2015). The erosion of the life-time employment system in these two countries has disrupted the internal career structure in many corporations. Many talented (young) workers ended up in contingent employment, with limited prospects of upgrading into the formal segment of the labor market where they can obtain high quality jobs and utilize their talents more fully. Similar situations are found in the Chinese context, where the government has been promoting graduate entrepreneurship (self-employment) to transfer the employment pressure from the state to university graduates and their families. Employers are also increasingly offering contingent employment to contain costs (Cooke, 2018).

By contrast, according to the World Bank India Country Overview published in 2008, India's labor regulations are "among the most restrictive and complex in the world" (cited in Bagga, 2013: 4). A major negative consequence of this regulatory environment is that approximately 90% of the workforce ended up in informal employment with poor job quality, as employers bypass the regulations by hiring contingent workers and through agency employment. Even in the high-tech sector, where many of the young graduate IT talents are employed, as India becomes a popular destination country for business process outsourcing (BPO), job quality is poor, characterized by low pay, unsociable working hours, and the absence of job security and career progress opportunities (e.g., D'Cruz & Noronha, 2012; Remesh, 2014). As Remesh's (2014) study shows, a significant proportion of those working in the Indian IT BPO sector are employed as non-regular workers and are largely unprotected by the labor laws.

Similarly, Beerepoot and Hendriks's (2013) study of employees working in the Baguio BPO sector in the Philippines reveals that these graduate employees tend to be employed below their level of competence and education. However, they are motivated to work in this sector for short-term financial gain, and more importantly, to enhance their human capital (e.g., language proficiency and work experience) to emigrate to developed countries to advance their career opportunities and financial well-being (see discussion of brain drain below).

A negative consequence of the excessive use of contingent employment is the breakdown of employee commitment to the employing organization, and the dismantling of any career structure that is essential to nurturing and utilizing talents for mutual benefits. It also raises additional HR challenges of attracting, motivating, and retaining talents at the organizational level (see below). More broadly, the growth of gig economies, sharing economies, and platform economies in Asia, facilitated by the development of IT, is raising various HR issues related to legal coverage, talent attraction and flow, flexibility policy, and losses and gains among stakeholders in a transnational context (e.g. Tam, 2017). It raises fundamental questions about how the talent market should/could be regulated in Asia (and beyond) to ensure equitable growth opportunities for all.

Societal Culture

Societal cultural values, traditional and newly developed, have been found influential in shaping the talent mindsets and TM practices (also see below for further discussion on TM practices at the organizational level). For example, Latukha and Selivanovskikh's (2016) comparative study of IT firms in Russia, China, and India revealed a number of social factors that influence TM practices. Specifically, the caste system, the colonial administration legacy, individualism, the family-inclusive management framework, long-standing work relationships, and supervisor-subordinate relationships grounded on trust, are found in India; whereas growth pace, acceptance of Western-inspired practices, Confucianism and *guanxi*, respect for seniority, avoidance of conflicts, and the primacy of courteous work relationships, are found to be characteristic in China (Latukha & Selivanovskikh, 2016).

Similarly, Gibb and Zhang's (2017: 79) study of three real estate companies in China showed that *guanxi* influence "is clearly present in the experience of TM, though this is not the sole or always dominant influence on choices, considerations, challenges, and consequences." Nevertheless, *guanxi* plays an influential role, both positive and negative, "in defining, attracting, developing, and retaining talent in the Chinese context" (Gibb & Zhang, 2017: 79).

At a broader level, a key challenge to TM in contemporary workplaces in Asia is to develop a mindset of independent and creative thinking. Given the hierarchical culture characterized by obeying authority and following procedures, turning talents from "followers" into "leaders" will require considerable effort. It may also encounter resistance from the older generation of the workforce who are less well educated and less innovative in their thinking, and are more used to gaining promotion through seniority (tenure) rather than merit (e.g., Azman et al., 2016; Cooke & Saini, 2010).

Talent Shortages

Talent shortage is a shared feature in many developing Asian countries and has become a bottleneck for economic growth, despite the rising level of education. For example, Aziz et al.'s (2016) study of Malaysian Islamic banking institutions (IBIs) showed that the sector requires a workforce of approximately 200,000 by 2020; however, the sector only had 11% of that required figure. Despite the relatively large number of graduates being produced by Islamic banking education and who are available in the job market, IBIs are still facing "a critical shortage of talent" and have to develop their own because of the mismatch of demand and supply (Aziz et al., 2016: 1), as noted earlier. According to Aziz et al. (2016: 2), the global Islamic banking assets witnessed a compounded annual growth rate of around 17% from 2009 to 2013. Moreover, Islamic banking assets in six core markets—Qatar, Malaysia, Indonesia, Saudi Arabia, UAE, and Turkey—are on course to touch US$1.8 trillion by 2019.

Extant research suggests that in addition to academic knowledge developed at the university, talents should be equipped with other competencies required at workplaces, including the ability to cope with organizational change and associated challenges, and other practical skills (e.g. Aziz et al., 2016). The limitations of university curricula, which tend to be too academic and theoretical and not sufficiently practical to meet employers' demands, have been observed in other countries, like China, India, and Fiji, where the author has conducted research. As higher education institutions in these countries are trying to raise their international ranking by becoming more research-led and channeling resources into these activities, further disconnection with the needs of employers and the need for practical skills in the workplace may be inevitable in the foreseeable future.

Migration and Brain Drain

The talent shortage problem is exacerbated by the emigration of the most talented professionals and students from less developed countries to more developed ones within and outside the continent, notably in the Asia Pacific region (e.g., Australia and New Zealand) and further away continents like Europe and North America. Some of the migrations are associated with skilled migration programs launched by developed economies to fill their skill gaps. So much so that it has led to brain drains in many developing Asian countries (e.g., Gaillard, Gaillard, & Krishna, 2015). According to the United Nations (2016: 1–2):

> Globally, there were 244 million international migrants in 2015. Of these, nearly 58 per cent lived in the developed regions, while the developing regions hosted 42 per cent of the world's total. Of the 140 million international migrants living in the global North in 2015, 85 million, or 61 per cent, originated from a developing country, while 55 million, or 39 per cent, were

born in the North. Meanwhile, 90 million, or 87 per cent, of the 103 million international migrants residing in the global South in 2015 originated from other parts of the developing world, while 13 million, or 13 per cent, were born in the North.… Europe and Asia combined hosted nearly two-thirds of all international migrants worldwide in 2015, with 76 million international migrants living in Europe and 75 million in Asia. Northern America hosted the third largest number of international migrants in 2013 (54 million).

The United Nations (2016: 3) further reported that in 2015:

Asia-to-Asia was the largest regional migration corridor in the world, with some 59 million international migrants born in that region residing in another country of Asia. From 2000 to 2010, the Asia-to-Asia corridor grew by an average of 1.5 million international migrants per year, a figure that increased to 1.6 million between 2010 and 2015.

While statistics are not available to capture precisely the talent inflows and outflows in each Asian country, it is reasonable to conclude that the talent flows have been mainly from less developed to more developed regions within the continent and across continents. This is in spite of the fact that migrated talents from less developed countries may be filling jobs of relatively low grade and below their human capital level in the destination countries (e.g., Cooke, Zhang, & Wang, 2013). Hyun (2005) coined the term "bamboo ceiling" to describe the barriers to their career progression (e.g., Diversity Council Australia, 2014). As Crowley-Henry and Ariss (2018) pointed out, skilled migrants are under-recognized by their employers, and more effective HRM practices need to be put in place to utilize their talents more effectively.

It is important to note that talent emigration is not only taking place in developing Asian countries, but also occurring in the more developed nations such as South Korea. For example, Song and Song (2015: 349) revealed that in South Korea, almost two-thirds of doctoral students intended to seek opportunities in the U.S.A. post-degree, which is a considerable rise compared with around 40% of doctoral students wanting to do so in the 1990s. While talent flow into Asian countries is also taking place, for example, through repatriation of nationals of Asian countries or self-expatriation of non-Asian nationals, mostly for temporary employment, these talent inflows do not offset talent outflows in many developing Asian countries. According to a report produced by the IMD world Competitiveness Centre (2017), Asia is a main talent exporting continent, whereas North America and Australia are among the main talent importers.

State Policy Intervention and Reverse Brain Gain

To combat talent shortages and to reverse the trend of brain drain (Saxenian, 2005), many Asian countries have implemented two-prong policy initiatives to update the skill level of their nationals on the one hand, and to attract expatriates (e.g., Singapore and Arabic countries) and repatriate talents from their own countries (e.g., China, India, Malaysia) on the other. While studies have shown that these policy initiatives have had some effects in raising the workforce's skill level and attracting overseas talents and returnees (e.g., Lu & Zhang, 2015; Singh & Krishna, 2015, on India), nation states continue to encounter the problem of losing their best trained talents to better-off countries.

For example, Khilji and Keilson's (2014) study provided a detailed account of state policy interventions, including education reforms, youth programs, citizenship policies for its diaspora, and more, in the last three decades in three southern Asia states – Bangladesh, India, and Pakistan – where the population is relatively young with limited access to formal education. Their study highlights the "prevalence of the paradox of development and retention particularly in Bangladesh and Pakistan, where youth is also being trained to emigrate" (Khilji & Keilson, 2014: 114).

It is also important to note that some of the development programs aimed at raising the competence level of nationals are politically driven. As Khilji and Keilson (2014: 120) reported:

> Leadership and empowerment have emerged as important catchwords for many youth initiatives in Pakistan, and a number of NGOs have been established to focus upon youth development, leadership and empowerment, including Youth Parliament, Pakistan Youth Alliance, School of Leadership, Youth Advocacy, Youth for Peace, etc.

In Malaysia, Azman et al. (2016: 316) observed that although "the issue of human capital development has taken centre stage in numerous reform agendas of Malaysia… a change in mindset is the first necessary step towards nurturing and developing" a talent pool. In particular, they question if the current "policy that emphasises the tapping of potential of overseas diasporas for home country development needs to be reviewed because many talented Malaysians abroad continue to adopt an outdated view of the socio-political situation" (Azman et al., 2016: 320). Instead, the authors argued, Malaysian policy should aim to source overseas talent globally in general to attract those "who view Malaysia as a land of opportunity" and overseas Malaysian diaspora can contribute to the country's development from a distance (Azman et al., 2016: 320).

In China, a series of reverse brain drain or brain circulation programs have been introduced since the late 1980s (c.f. Lu & Zhang, 2015; Zweig & Wang, 2013 for an overview). The main purpose of these programs is to attract highly trained and accomplished overseas Chinese scientists, engineers, academics, and entrepreneurs to return to China through developing favorable conditions at home. However, turning these programs into successful outcomes remains a key challenge for various reasons, not least due to insufficient institutional and organizational support for the repatriates (e.g. Cooke & Wang, 2018; Lu & Zhang, 2015; Zweig & Zhang, 2013).

Talent Management at the Organizational Level

At the organizational level, research evidence overwhelmingly points to talent attraction and retention problems, which is not surprising, given the severe talent shortages that many countries and firms are facing in Asia. Although evidence that having a well-developed talent management system will be beneficial to organizational performance (e.g. Latukha & Veselova, 2019), many firms have yet to acquire their competence in talent management. Research evidence also found that certain HRM practices appear to be effective for different aspects of TM, to some degree. We discuss these practices in this section.

Effective HR Practices for Talent Management – Research Evidence

Sparrow and Makram (2015) proposed four value-driven processes in TM architectures, which are largely resource-oriented and thus build strategic capability and focus on exploitation (see Table 1). Existing research evidence in Asian countries reveals emerging TM practices related to these processes across different industrial sectors and ownership forms, as indicated in Table 11.1. There are, undoubtedly, other TM practices that may be effective but not yet uncovered by research.

For talent attraction, Sharma and Jyotsna Bhatnagar's (2009: 118) study of TM strategy in an Indian pharmaceutical firm showed that adopting a talent mindset and building a TM strategy based on competency profiling has helped the organization "recruit the best talent from the best pharmaceutical organizations." This indicates that firms may be more inclined to poach rather than grow their talent internally, given the fierce competition and fast-paced development of the industry (e.g., Sovanjeet, 2014). In countries where there is a shortage of workforce due to population ageing, an organized approach may be in place for recruiting temporary immigrants into the country. For example, Conrad and Meyer-Ohle's (2017a) study suggests that brokers play a particular important role in attracting immigrant talents into Japan, aided by the Japanese employment system.

Table 11.1 Talent management: Processes and practices in Asia

Four value-driven processes*	Research evidence of effective TM practices
TM and value creation (recruiting valuable talents and creating processes for talents to create values through TM architectures)	Building a talent mindset, knowledge sharing, employer branding, alignment of beliefs and values
TM and value capture (crafting know-how, capturing and exploiting these new capabilities)	Investment in current talent, training and development
TM and value amplification (leveraging combined individual and organizational resources to achieve novel and valuable outcomes through TM architectures)	Knowledge sharing, knowledge transfer, global mindset
TM and value protection (retention and preservation)	TM practices focusing on competencies, learning, job enrichment, knowledge transfer, leadership style, job satisfaction, commitment, engagement, informal recruitment methods

Based on Sparrow and Makram's (2015: 254–259) Four Value Driven Processes.

Employer branding, an area that has attracted emerging research, albeit one that many firms in Asia have yet to become more sophisticated in (e.g., Meyer & Xin, 2018), appears to be quite effective in talent acquisition amid a war for talent across different industrial sectors (e.g., Amelia & Nasution, 2016; Srivastava & Bhatnagar, 2010). For example, Amelia and Nasution's (2016: 226) study of the Indonesian mining industry, which is a main contributor to the country's economy, found that few universities in Indonesia offer mining related programs, and that the limited number of potential mining talents singled out job security, financial stability, company's image, work-life balance, safe working environments and facilities, and training and development, as the most attractive aspects of the company they would choose to work for.

Aligning the beliefs and values of the job candidate and the organization has also been found beneficial to enhancing talents' organizational engagement and commitment, which in turn lead to organizational success, as one of Meng et al.'s (2016: 141) interviewees disclosed:

> We highly value the talent who has rich experience in the fields of construction and marketing, and pay much attention to understand their experience of project type, size, and charged work in details. Taking the applicant of construction management as an example, if someone has experienced more than five complete medium-sized or large projects, and being through each crucial part of projects, it means that this person not only has solid professional knowledge, and has strong potential of resource integration. Also, we pay equal attention to career aspirations. The applicant who treats building a house like the production of himself or belonging to a team, is more welcome in our company. Conversely, we don't tend to hire people who only value money or power. Actually, few applicants meet our requirements. We have to cherish intra-organization employees and pay more expectations and support to them.

In terms of creating processes for talents to create values, Chai, Kim, and Kim's (2018) study of a work and learning dual system (WLDS) model for talent development in South Korea revealed that WLDS plays an important role in talent development at workplaces through public-private partnerships. Wang-Cowham's (2011: 391) study of 20 Chinese HR practitioners found that "incorporating a knowledge-sharing socialization mechanism with talent development programs has a nurturing and supporting effect on learning and development", and that the "mechanism can be used to facilitate organization-wide knowledge sharing and support both organization-led and self-managed talent development programs." Similarly, Zheng's (2009: 482) survey of 281 service MNCs in six Asian countries – Indonesia, Malaysia,

Philippines, Singapore, Taiwan, and Thailand – found that "skill training and development programs are seen to be significantly associated with capacity to deliver quality service and on firm growth as perceived by managers surveyed". Raman, Chadee, Roxas, and Michailova's (2013) study found that global mindset, TM, and partnership quality significantly contribute to the performance of offshore service providers from the Indian IT BPO sector.

Ulrich and Allen's (2014: 1) study of 570 small-and-medium sized enterprises (SMEs) in Singapore, China and India, which assesses the impact of these SMEs' 13 TM processes on "business performance as moderated by the strategy and growth patterns of the firm", revealed that "investments in managing current talent have more impact on business performance than hiring new talent or retaining existing talent" in general. This suggests that firms might as well accept that talent turnover is inevitable and that they should spend resources to get the most out of the current talent instead of spending resources in vain trying to retain those who intend to leave.

For talent retention to preserve organizational values/assets, Rana, Goel, and Rastogi's (2013) study of Indian public sector (engineering) companies shows that TM practices that focus on competencies, knowledge, learning, job enrichment through broad-based group work, and technological knowledge transfer are effective in retaining their best talents. Bhatnagar's (2007: 640) study suggested that "a good level of engagement may lead to high retention, but only for a limited time" in the Indian IT sector. Zheng's (2009: 482) study of TM practices of MNCs in the six Asian countries mentioned above also found that "[n]ot all formalised HR practices lead to talent retention"; instead, some informal recruitment methods used by Asian-bred firms "have contributed to better retention rates".

Leadership appears to play a critical role in talent retention. For example, Khalid, Pahi, & Ahmed's (2016: 608) study of the Pakistan commercial banking sector found that there is "a strong and positive relationship between leadership style and employee retention" and that job satisfaction and organization commitment mediate the relationship between leadership style and employee retention. Zhang et al.'s (2015: 1021) study of "the effect of leadership styles on talent retention strategies" and on the effectiveness of post-merger and acquisition (M&A) integration in the Chinese context showed that "an authoritative, coaching, task-focused and relationship-focused approach has a positive influence on talent retention and effective post-M&A integration." The same study also found "autocratic, empowering, democratic and pacesetting leadership styles...to be unsuitable during post-merger integration" (Zhang et al., 2015: 1045). Park and Kim's (2018: 1) study also found that "the leaders' vision of talent indirectly affected their organizational commitment via HR functions" in the Korean context.

In short, given the severe skill shortage and the war for talent in many developing Asian countries, investment in TM is a high-risk strategy, and firms certainly need to be more savvy in identifying what TM practices would be most effective and channel resources into developing them.

Challenges Ahead

Given the legacy of the education systems and labor market environments of Asian countries, many of which are in a process of political, economic, and social transition and transformation, firms in and from Asia are likely to face a number of challenges. These challenges are further compounded by the relatively weak strategic HR/TM capacity of Asian firms, as evidenced below (see also Cooke & Kim, 2018; Meyer & Xin, 2018; Wang & Sun, 2018).

Talent Management for MNCs

As Asia has been a major foreign direct investment (FDI) recipient in the last few decades, and with a growing amount of outward FDI from the leading economies in the continent such as Japan, South Korea, China, and India (c.f. United Nations Conference on Trade and Development, 2016), the TM situation in Asia is likely to pose additional challenges to MNCs operating in the continent, as well as Asian MNCs operating globally (see also Meyer & Xin, 2018). For example, Shi and Handfield's (2012:

163) study of recruitment and retention of Chinese university graduate employees in global logistics companies revealed that the scarcity of well qualified university graduates specializing in global supply chain management has created "a gap between the expectations of Chinese employees and the perceived reality of foreign managers relative to what constitutes competitive salary, benefits, and job satisfaction conditions". This indicates a need to review and adjust what is offered by the firm in light of the local market conditions to attract and retain university graduate talents (Shi & Handfield, 2012).

Preece, Iles, & Jones's (2013: 3474) study identified key HR and TM challenges to setting up a regional headquarters in Asia Pacific by a Japanese-owned auto company. In particular, the firm faced "problems in translating leadership capability at one level in the region to capable accomplishment at the next level, and this had implications for leadership and senior manager development" (Preece et al., 2013: 3474). Reasons associated with this "middle management vacuum" were the focus on senior leadership development at the early stage of setting up the regional headquarters, and that "junior managers and supervisors in the region tended to focus upon following or implementing rules and regulations, and received at best only limited mentoring in more strategic matters from their seniors" (Preece et al., 2013: 3471). Junior national managers and supervisors in the region not being part of the intra-region or inter-region networks contributed to the problems. The same study also revealed that while the MNC wanted "regional entrepreneurs" to lead, it did not have a clear idea of what this means and how it might differ from "national entrepreneurs" (Preece et al., 2013: 3474).

The rigidity of staffing practices of Japanese firms and the emphasis on developing (managerial) talent through an internal labor market has been well documented (e.g., Cooke & Kim, 2018). This tradition is deeply embedded and creates additional challenges for Japanese MNCs. For instance, Conrad and Meyer-Ohle's (2017b: 1) study of the hiring practices of Japanese MNCs found that these firms are making slow attempts to internationalize themselves through "internal internationalization" by hiring foreign fresh university graduates and developing them internally as "global talent". Conrad and Meyer-Ohle (2017b: 1) argued that these TM practices are necessarily an institutional response "to the particularities of Japan's employment system. Aiming at internationalizing headquarters from within, it contributes to resolving the internationalization conundrum of Japanese MNEs, but rather than overcoming the existing ethnocentric HR model it accommodates this orientation". The same study also showed that while Japanese MNCs "have started to introduce inpatriation programs for foreign subsidiary staff, these initiatives remain small in size and scale and appear not to be very ambitious in developing such staff" (Conrad & Meyer-Ohle, 2017b: 12). Nevertheless, Japanese MNCs adopting this "attenuated ethnocentric model" may face acculturation and retention issues of these inpatriates when/ if they find the Japanese employment system alien and fail to meet their career expectations (Conrad & Meyer-Ohle, 2017b: 14).

Similarly, Yang's (2015: 1076) study showed that while "enjoying success in their home territory" in terms of HRM and employee commitment, Korean MNCs "seem to struggle in their overseas subsidiaries to replicate this success in attracting/retaining talent". In particular, Korean MNCs' clan control and prevalent collectivist cultural values may be incompatible with western employees' perception of fairness and individualistic culture. Key features of clan control include, for example: "a paternalistic management style" which "compensates for some of the organization design weaknesses of Korean companies"; close monitoring of overseas subsidiaries by using Korean expatriates for top management positions who are sent for overseas assignments as part of a continuous test of their loyalty to the organization; and putting new recruits through several weeks' training and testing "on the founding family's history and values (Korean MNCs are invariably chaebols founded and controlled by one or two families)" (Yang, 2015: 1082).

Even when operating in countries with broadly similar cultural heritages within the region, MNCs may encounter mismatch of perceptions between expatriates and host country employees regarding their TM practices, which undermines the MNCs' efforts in global TM. For instance, Vance, Chow, Paika, and Shin's (2013: 985) survey study of 67 Korean expatriates and 202 Chinese host employees of Korean MNCs in China revealed "a significant difference between the Korean expatriates and"

Chinese workers "on a majority of the survey measures, particularly those related to training relevance, feedback, supportive climate and transfer of training". This suggests "a gap in perceptions and expectations regarding effective employee training between Korean expatriates and the Chinese labor force", which compromises the MNC's efforts in raising productivity through development of the competence of the Chinese employees as part of the MNC's overall TM policy and practice (Vance et al., 2013: 997). Vance et al. (2013: 999) further argue that "these gaps should be considered as possible obstacles to optimal knowledge transfer in ongoing efforts to improve global talent management".

Emerging market MNCs (EMNCs) from this region may face, not only liability of foreignness, but also liability of emergingness, in their attempt to attract talent for their overseas subsidiaries, especially in developed economies (see Meyer & Xin, 2018 for an analysis of obstacles to and strategy for TM for EMNCs). For instance, Held and Bader (2018: 510) applied the image and signaling theory to study the organizational attractiveness of MNCs to German business students, and found that these research targets preferred U.S. "over Chinese and Russian companies as future employers, confirming the existence of the liability of emergingness". The same study also found that females are more put off than their male counterparts by an EMNC with a poor corporate image. These findings suggest that EMNCs not only need to develop a better corporate image through corporate/employer branding, but also, and more importantly, need to develop a global understanding of and competence in ethical standards and practices relevant to specific societal contexts in order to attract and retain talents. More broadly, Meyer and Xin (2013: 11) observed that local talents tend to pay attention to "not only financial rewards but also … career prospects, personal autonomy of work, and corporate social responsibility"; yet, few EMNCs prioritize these aspects.

Adopting an Inclusive Approach to Talent Management

As discussed earlier, Asian societies and firms largely adopt an elitist approach to classifying talent, and channel resources to attract, develop, utilize, and retain them. This relatively narrow approach to TM means that many talents may not have been given the opportunity to fulfil their potential for the benefit of the nation, the company and themselves. Existing research and practical evidence in the Asian context suggest that there is a need to adopt a more inclusive approach to TM by key stakeholders. This involves at least three dimensions: 1) adopting a more inclusive approach to home talents from diverse politico-socio-economic and personal backgrounds; 2) raising the labor standards and work-related well-being of knowledge workers who work in the offshore BPO sector in developing Asian countries like India, the Philippines, and Thailand; and 3) developing tailored HRM practices to manage repatriated nationals and foreign expatriates/skilled immigrants.

For instance, Kulkarni and Scullion's (2015: 1169) study of "training and placement agencies in India aimed at employment of persons with a disability" revealed "the preference of agencies to engage in non-traditional and ad hoc approaches to build and showcase underutilized talent of those with a disability". They concluded that "persons with a disability are an underutilized human resource and that utilizing their abilities should be a key part of an inclusive approach to talent management" (Kulkarni & Scullion, 2015: 1169). Sovanjeet's (2014) study of HRM issues and challenges in pharmaceutical firms in India suggests that there is a high level of gender inequality that needs to be addressed to attract talent.

On a broader scale, Remesh's (2014) study reveals equality and diversity issues that are intersected with gender, ethnicity, religiosity, and social class in India. In particular, firms providing offshore BPO services tend to cream off skilled workers and offer relatively better quality jobs ("higher end") than the domestic BPO businesses ("lower end"). IT software engineers are more likely to come from highly educated families and from better-off segments of the social hierarchy. Therefore, employment in the IT BPO sector tends to entrench pre-existing social inequalities in Indian society, "through disproportionately favouring higher caste and class groups" (Remesh, 2014: 45). Furthermore, there is a clear gender divide – "compared to their male counterparts, women are increasingly pushed to low-end and low paying jobs… with bleak career prospects and upward mobility" (Remesh, 2014: 45). It is quite likely that similar equality and diversity issues may be found in the BPO sector in other Asian economies that share broadly similar historic, cultural, and economic development trajectories, and where there are persistent labor market inequalities, intersecting gender, religion, race, ethnicity, social class, and migration status.

Studies have also shed light on TM issues related to managing repatriates and skill immigrants. For example, Kunasegaran et al.'s (2016: 370) study of repatriates in the Malaysian context revealed that while returned managerial talents are "very much in demand", organizational support is essential to the successful adaptation of the returnees to their repatriated life and work. Similarly, Ismail, Umar Baki, Kamaruddin, and Malik (2016) argued that while political factors in the host country (push factors) and social support of the home country (pull factor) have influenced, among other factors, repatriates' career aspirations and decision to return to their home country, Malaysia, well-designed HR policies and practices need to be put in place at the organization level to facilitate the adaptation of the expatriates. These may include, for example, childcare support, reverse cultural adaptation training, knowledge-transfer mechanisms, and learning and personal growth opportunities.

Crowley-Henry and Ariss (2018: 2066) argue that firms tend to overlook skilled migrants as "potential global talents for their business operations" and that this valuable cohort "could play key roles in areas such as global leadership, cross-cultural management, and strategic internationalization of their companies, among others." They further argue that by "adopting a more inclusive approach to TM and purposefully including skilled migrants within the potential talent pools of high-performers in the organization... organizations should... be able to reap the rewards of having an international workforce."

It is important to note that adopting an inclusive approach to TM, as illustrated above, should not just be seen from a utilitarian perspective; more importantly, it is an ethical stance of the employing organization to demonstrate their corporate social responsibility through an ethical HRM strategy that is free from discriminatory practices or any social groupings.

Talent Management in Smaller Firms

Much of the existing research on TM in the Asian context has focused on larger domestic firms and MNCs. There is limited knowledge of the TM practices adopted in small-and-medium-sized enterprises (SMEs) and what challenges they are grappling with (e.g., Kaliannan, Abraham, & Ponnusamy, 2016; Stokes et al., 2016). This is a significant research gap, given that SMEs make a significant contribution to the economy and employment, and that they are often disadvantaged in terms of talent attraction and retention vis-à-vis the competition from larger domestic firms and MNCs. A couple of studies provide insights into the TM situations in SMEs.

For example, Cui, Khan, and Tarba (2016: 1) explored "how strategic talent management (STM) is defined and understood" by Chinese SMEs in the service sector and TM strategies in Chinese SMEs. The study revealed that "managers have different views about talent: according to some, STM means simply having a right candidate in the right job category" and that "work environment, career advancement opportunities, and a good compensation package are acknowledged as a best strategy for attracting talent" (Cui et al., 2016: 1). This study further suggests that SMEs studied adopt "both a universalist and a selective performance-oriented approach" to TM (Cui et al., 2016: 1).

Similarly, Kaliannan et al.'s (2016: 393) study of TM practices "that influence job satisfaction and organizational commitment among employees in Malaysian SMEs" found that there is "a gap between employees and employers in terms of expectations" of TM practices. While employees "are looking for better training opportunities and some form of remuneration and recognition that demonstrates full potential at work", "Generation X managers find it difficult to manage their generation Y subordinates due to differences in value and attitude towards work" (Kaliannan et al., 2016: 393). It may be that these problems also occur in larger firms, as the country is in transition from a seniority- to a merit-based performance and reward system, an issue that has also been observed in the Indian context (Cooke & Saini, 2010).

Conclusions

Talent management remains under-developed in the Asian context, both in research and practice. This chapter provides a glimpse of the broader TM environment and challenges at the macro and micro level, as well as TM practices and preferences of employers and individuals. Talent has often been associated with human capital in extant research into TM. However, it is clear that talent required by firms in different societal and business contexts includes a more extensive range of capital, such as social capital and cultural capital. Equally, a narrow definition tends to be adopted in defining talent, whereas a more inclusive approach to talent and corresponding TM strategy will enable Asian nations to aid their (accelerated) economic and social development efforts.

Extant research of TM in the Asian context has provided useful insights on the characteristics of, and challenges to, TM derived from different cultural values and institutional systems. This cautions against the adoption of a universalist approach to TM, with strong implications for MNCs (e.g., Vance et al., 2013). Moreover, although mainstream TM literature has argued for more strategic and codified TM architectures and practices for effective TM, in the Asian business context, informal TM practices may continue to have their values and may be more effective than some of the formal ones, not least in smaller and private firms that continue to rely heavily on family and community networks and informal ties. Research on TM in specific countries, therefore, needs to consider their broader national context, industrial position in the global value chain, and so forth. This necessitates the mobilization of a broader set of theoretical perspectives than the current preoccupations, such as human capital theory, a resource-based view, social identity theory, agency theory, cross-cultural theory, regulatory theory, political economy theories, sociological theories, and so forth. TM practice will also benefit from a broader approach that is informed by research evidence.

Finally, characteristics, challenges, and problems associated with TM revealed in this chapter have several management implications. One is that firms in Asia need to identify their talent requirements and where they can source the talent needed. Another is that firms need to develop their TM capability by designing appropriate TM policies and practices that are in line with their business strategy and labor market conditions. In particular, being able to map out talent flows, both internally and externally, and design suitable talent utilization packages, rather than being fixated on an internal labor market may be a practical choice for fast growing firms. Such a multi-pronged approach may indicate a departure from the mainstream strategic HRM prescription.

References

Amelia, N., & Nasution, R. A. 2016. Employer branding for talent attraction in the Indonesian mining industry. *International Journal of Business,* 21(3): 226–242.

Asian Development Bank. 2011. *Asia 2050: Realizing the Asian century.* https://www.adb.org/publications/asia-2050-realizing-asian-century, first accessed on 12th August 2017.

Australian Government. 2012. *Australia in the Asian century white paper.* http://www.defence.gov.au/whitepaper/2013/docs/australia_in_the_asian_century_white_paper.pdf, first accessed on 12th August 2017.

Aziz, M. I., Afthanorhan, A., & Awang, Z. 2016. Talent development model for a career in Islamic banking institutions: A SEM approach. *Cogent Business & Management,* 3(1): 1–11.

Azman, N., Sirat, M., & Pang, V. 2016. Managing and mobilising talent in Malaysia: Issues, challenges and policy implications for Malaysian universities. *Journal of Higher Education Policy & Management,* 38(3): 316–332.

Bagga, G. 2013. Why Indian talent is going to waste. *Human Resource Management International Digest,* 21(2): 3–4.

Beerepoot, N., & Hendriks, M. 2013. Employability of offshore service sector workers in the Philippines: Opportunities for upward labour mobility or dead-end jobs?. *Work, Employment and Society,* 27(5): 823–841.

Bhatnagar, J. 2007. Talent management strategy of employee engagement in Indian ITES employees: Key to retention. *Employee Relations,* 29(6): 640–663.

Chai, D. S., Kim, S., & Kim, M. 2018. A work and learning dual system model for talent development in South Korea: A multiple stakeholder view. *Advances in Developing Human Resources,* 20(4): 410–427.

Conrad, H., & Meyer-Ohle, H. 2017a. Brokers and the organization of recruitment of "global talent" by Japanese firms—A migration perspective. *Social Science Japan Journal,* 21(1): 67–88.

Conrad, H., & Meyer-Ohle, H. 2017b. Overcoming the ethnocentric firm? – Foreign fresh university graduate employment in Japan as a new international human resource development method. *International Journal of Human Resource Management.* doi:10.1080/09585192.2017.1330275.

Cooke, F. L. 2018. Talent management in emerging economies. In D. Collings, K. Mellahi, & W. Cascio (Eds.), *The Oxford handbook of talent management.* Oxford, UK: Oxford University Press.

Cooke, F. L., & Brown, R. 2015. *The regulation of non-standard forms of work in China, Japan and Republic of Korea.* International Labour Organization Working Paper, Conditions or Work and Employment Series, No. 64, Geneva, Switzerland.

Cooke, F. L., & Kim, S. H. (Eds.). 2018. *Human resource management in Asia.* London: Routledge.

Cooke, F. L., & Saini, D. S. 2010. How does the HR strategy support an innovation-oriented business strategy? An investigation of institutional context and organizational practices in Indian firm. *Human Resource Management,* 49(3): 377–400.

Cooke, F. L., Saini, D., & Wang, J. 2014. Talent management in China and India: A comparison of management perceptions and human resource practices. *Journal of World Business,* 49(2): 225–235.

Cooke, F. L., Schuler, R., & Varma, A 2020. Human resource management research and practice in Asia: Past, present and future. *Human Resource Management Review,* 30(4): doi: https://doi.org/10.1016/j.hrmr.2020.100778.

Cooke, F. L., & Wang, M. 2018. Macro-level talent management in China. In V. Vaiman, R. Schuler, P. Sparrow, & D. Collings (Eds.), *Macro talent management.* London: Routledge.

Cooke, F. L., Zhang, J. Y., & Wang, J. 2013. Chinese professional immigrants in Australia: A gendered pattern in (re)building their careers. *International Journal of Human Resource Management,* 24(13–14): 2628–2645.

Crowley-Henry, M., & Ariss, A. A. 2018. Talent management of skilled migrants: Propositions and an agenda for future research. *International Journal of Human Resource Management,* 29(13): 2054–2079.

Cui, W., Khan, Z., & Tarba, S. Y. 2016. Strategic talent management in service SMEs of China. *Thunderbird International Business Review:* 1–12.

D'Cruz, P., & Noronha, E. 2012. Cornered by conning: Agents' experiences of closure of a call centre in India. *The International Journal of Human Resource Management,* 23(5): 1019–1039.

Deloitte Insights 2017. *Economic growth and development in Asia: What is the role of digital? Voice of Asia.* https://www2.deloitte.com/insights/us/en/economy/voice-of-asia/may-2017/digital-role-economic-growth.html, first accessed on 12 March 2018.

Diversity Council Australia. 2014. *Cracking the cultural ceiling: Future proofing your business in the Asian century.* Sydney: Author.

Gaillard, J., Gaillard, A. M., & Krishna, V. V. 2015. Return from migration and circulation of highly educated people: The never-ending brain drain. *Science Technology & Society,* 20(3): 269–278.

Gibb, S., & Zhang, S. 2017. Guanxi influence and talent management in Chinese organisations; evidence from the real estate sector. *Human Resource Development International,* 20(1): 79–98.

Held, K., & Bader, B. 2018. The influence of images on organizational attractiveness: Comparing Chinese, Russian and US companies in Germany. *The International Journal of Human Resource Management,* 29(3): 510–548.

Huiyao, W. 2019. In 2020, Asian economies will become larger than the rest of the world combined - here's how. *World Economic Forum.* https://www.weforum.org/agenda/2019/07/the-dawn-of-the-asian-century/.

Hyun, J. 2005. *Breaking the bamboo ceiling: Career strategies for Asians.* New York, NY: Harper Collins.

IMD World Competitiveness Centre 2017. *IMD World Talent Rankings 2017: Talent Flow.* https://www.imd.org/wcc/world-competitiveness-center-publications/talent-ranking–talent-flow/, first accessed on 12 March 2018.

Ismail, M., Umar Baki, N., Kamaruddin, N. A. Y., & Malik, A. 2016. Reverse brain drain: Career aspirations of Malaysian repatriates. *Global Business and Management Research: An International Journal,* 8(4), 1–18.

Kaliannan, M., Abraham, M., & Ponnusamy, V. 2016. Effective talent management in Malaysian SMEs: A proposed framework. *Journal of Developing Areas,* 50(5), 393–401.

Khalid, N., Pahi, M. H., & Ahmed, U. 2016. Losing your best talent: Can leadership retain employees? The dilemma of the banking sector of Hyderabad Sindh, Pakistan: A mediation investigation. *International Review of Management & Marketing,* 6(3): 608–616.

Khilji, S. E., & Keilson, B. 2014. In search of global talent: Is south Asia ready? *South Asian Journal of Global Business Research,* 3(2), 114–134.

Kulkarni, M., & Scullion, H. 2015. Talent management activities of disability training and placement agencies in India. *International Journal of Human Resource Management,* 26(9): 1169–1181.

Kunasegaran, M., Ismail, M., Rasdi, R. M., Ismail, I. A., & Ramayah, T. 2016. Talent development environment and workplace adaptation: The mediating effects of organisational support. *European Journal of Training & Development,* 40(6): 370–389.

Lagarde, C. 2016. *Asia's advancing role in the global economy.* International Monetary Fund. https://www.imf. org/en/News/Articles/2015/09/28/04/53/sp031216, first accessed on 10 March 2018.

Latukha, M., & Selivanovskikh, L. 2016. Talent management practices in IT companies from emerging markets: A comparative analysis of Russia, India, and China. *Journal of East-West Business,* 22(3): 168–197.

Latukha, M., & Veselova, A. 2019. Talent management, absorptive capacity, and firm performance: Does it work in China and Russia? *Human Resource Management.* doi:10.1002/hrm.21930.

Lee, S. 2016. Identifying and developing inventive talent in the Republic of Korea. *Gifted Child Today,* 1: 40–50.

Lu, X., & Zhang, W. 2015. The reversed brain drain: A mixed-method study of the reversed migration of Chinese overseas scientists. *Science Technology & Society,* 20(3): 279–299.

Meng, F. X., Wang, X. M., Chen, H. J., Zhang, J., Yang, W., Wang, J., & Zheng, Q. Q. 2016. The influence of organizational culture on talent management: A case study of a real estate company. *Journal of Chinese Human Resource Management,* 7(2): 129–146.

Meyer, K. E., & Xin, K. R. 2018. Managing talent in emerging economy multinationals: Integrating strategic management and human resource management. *The International Journal of Human Resource Management,* 29(11): 1827–1855.

Park, S., & Kim, E.-J. 2018. Organizational culture, leaders' vision of talent, and HR functions on career changers' commitment: The moderating effect of training in South Korea. *Asia Pacific Journal of Human Resources,* 1–24. doi:10.1111/1744-7941.12192.

Preece, D., Iles, P., & Jones, R. 2013. MNE regional head offices and their affiliates: Talent management practices and challenges in the Asia Pacific. *The International Journal of Human Resource Management,* 24(18): 3457–3477.

Raman, R., Chadee, D., Roxas, B., Michailova, S. 2013. Effects of partnership quality, talent management, and global mindset on performance of offshore IT service providers in India. *Journal of International Management,* 19: 333–346.

Rana, G., Goel, A. K., & Rastogi, R. 2013. Talent management: A paradigm shift in Indian public sector. *Strategic HR Review,* 12(4): 197–202.

Remesh, B. 2014. Interrogating employment in IT and ITES/BPO sector: Quantity, quality and disparities. In B. Paul (Ed.), *Jobs and livelihoods: Mapping the landscape:* 40–47. Mumbai: IRIS Knowledge Foundation.

Saxenian, A. 2005. From brain drain to brain circulation: Transnational communities and regional upgrading in India and China. *Studies in Comparative International Development,* 40: 35–61.

Sharma, R., & Bhatnagar, J. 2009. Talent management – competency development: Key to global leadership. *Industrial and Commercial Training,* 41(3): 118–132.

Shi, Y., & Handfield, R. 2012. Talent management issues for multinational logistics companies in China: observations from the field. *International Journal of Logistics Research and Applications: A Leading Journal of Supply Chain Management,* 15(3): 163–179.

Singh, J., & Krishna, V. V. 2015. Trends in brain drain, gain and circulation: Indian experience of knowledge workers. *Science Technology & Society,* 20(3): 300–321.

Song, H. Z., & Song, E. 2015. Why do South Korea's scientists and engineers delay returning home? Renewed brain drain in the new millennium. *Science Technology & Society,* 20(3): 349–368.

Sovanjeet, M. 2014. HR issues and challenges in pharmaceuticals with special reference to India. *Review of International Comparative Management,* 15(4): 423–430.

Sparrow, P. R., & Makram, H. 2015. What is the value of talent management? Building value-driven processes within a talent management architecture. *Human Resource Management Review,* 25: 249–263.

Srivastava, P., & Bhatnagar, J. 2010. Employer brand for talent acquisition: An exploration towards its measurement. *Vision the Journal of Business Perspective,* 14(14): 25–34.

Stokes, P., Liu, Y., Smith, S., Leidner, S., Moore, N., & Rowland, C. 2016. Managing talent across advanced and emerging economies: HR issues and challenges in a Sino-German strategic collaboration. *International Journal of Human Resource Management,* 27(20): 2310–2338.

Tam, S. 2017. *Asia's rising 'gig' economy is creating a challenge for HR,* CIPD Asia Ltd. https://www.cipd. asia/news/hr-news/asia-gig-economy-challenge-hr?utm_medium=email&utm_source=cipd&utm_ campaign=PMAsia_weekly&utm_term=84892&utm_content=PMAsia_weekly_170817-10780-48204- 20170817010718-Asia%27s%20rising%20%E2%80%98gig%E2%80%99%20economy%20is%20creating%20 a%20challenge%20for%20HR, first accessed on 17 Aug 2017.

Ulrich, D., & Allen, J. 2014. Talent accelerator: Understanding how talent delivers performance for Asian firms. *South Asian Journal of Human Resources Management,* 1(1): 1–23.

UNCTAD (United Nations Conference on Trade and Development). 2016. *World investment report 2016: Investor nationality-policy challenges.* http://unctad.org/en/pages/PublicationWebflyer.aspx?publicationid=1555.

United Nations, Department of Economic and Social Affairs, Population Division 2016. *International migration report 2015* (ST/ESA/SER.A/384).

Vance, C. M., Chow, I. H. S., Paika, Y., & Shin, K. Y. 2013. Analysis of Korean expatriate congruence with Chinese labor perceptions on training method importance: Implications for global talent management. *The International Journal of Human Resource Management,* 24(5): 985–1005.

Wang, J., & Sun, J. M. 2018. Talent development in China: Current practices and challenges ahead. *Advances in Development Human Resources,* 20(4): 389–409.

Wang-Cowham, C. 2011. Developing talent with an integrated knowledge-sharing mechanism: An exploratory investigation from the Chinese human resource managers' perspective. *Human Resource Development International,* 14(4): 391–407.

World Bank. 2007. *Malaysia and the knowledge economy: Building a world-class higher education system.* Washington: Author.

Yang, I. 2015. Cross-cultural perceptions of clan control in Korean multinational companies: A conceptual investigation of employees' fairness monitoring based on cultural values. *International Journal of Human Resource Management,* 26(8): 1076–1097.

Zhang, J., Ahammad, M. F., Tarba, S. Y., Cooper, C. L., Glaister, K. W., & Wang, J. 2015. The effect of leadership style on talent retention during merger and acquisition integration: Evidence from China. *The International Journal of Human Resource Management,* 26: 1021–1050.

Zheng, C. 2009. Keeping talents for advancing service firms in Asia. *Journal of Service Management,* 20(5): 482–502.

Zweig, D, & Wang. H. 2013. Can China bring back the best? The Communist Party organizes China's search for talent. *The China Quarterly,* 215: 590–615.

12

TALENT MANAGEMENT IN AFRICA

Challenges, Opportunities, and Prospects

Fang Lee Cooke

Introduction

The deepening pace and level of economic and technological globalization in the last two decades or so and the improving conditions for investment have increasingly made Africa an attractive location for business. This has not only opened up new opportunities for foreign director investment (FDI) and multinational companies (MNCs), but also increased the demand for talent (e.g., Deloitte, 2014; Ernst & Young, 2014). African countries face several sets of intertwined challenges in strategic human resource management (HRM) and talent management (TM) (e.g., Cooke, Wood, & Horwitz, 2015; Mwila & Turay, 2018; Tarique, Briscoe, & Schuler, 2016). For the purpose of this chapter, we define talent management as the management of skilled and professional employees. We hold the view that TM is an integral part of human resource management and human capital development.

In this chapter, we examine opportunities for and challenges to TM in the African context, focusing on both expatriates and indigenous talent. Given the limited research on TM in the African context (see also Anlesinya, Amponsah-Tawiah, & Dartey-Baah, 2019 for review), we draw on literature on HRM, human capital, and migration studies. Our analysis is cast at the macro level and, where appropriate, from a historical perspective. The intention is to develop a more comprehensive understanding of the challenges that confront many African countries in their development endeavors, and what future research may do to facilitate policy decisions and management practices conducive to improving TM and human resource development more broadly. It is important to note that Africa is a vast continent with diverse historical, socio-cultural, and institutional characteristics and in different stages of economic development across countries. A level of over-generalization is therefore inevitable.

This chapter consists of three main sections in addition to this Introduction and a Conclusion. The first main section summarizes key challenges to TM and major HRM interventions, spanning international talent mobility at the more macro level and challenges related to TM at the industry and firm level. The second and third sections provide directions for future research and managerial implications, respectively. The chapter concludes by urging for a more nuanced and inclusive approach to investigating TM issues in the contemporary African context, taking into account its rich historical and cultural traditions as well as institutional diversity and economic trajectory.

Challenges to Talent Management and HRM Interventions

Extant research on HRM and TM in the African context has revealed several major challenges at various levels. In this section, we first discuss macro-level challenges, focusing mainly on the deployment of foreign expatriates on the one hand, and the loss of home talents though migration

DOI: 10.4324/9781315474687-12

on the other. We then discuss issues related to TM in the public sector, which will have an important knock-on effect on TM down-stream, due to deficiencies in policy decision-making. We also examine the prospect of affirmative action policies to address workplace inequality and create a level playing field for talented individuals to rise and shine. Challenges to HRM and TM at the industry and firm level are then discussed. This is followed by further discussion of HRM and TM practices in MNCs and their implications. Some of these issues are overlapped and intertwined, reflecting the persistent historical, institutional, and culture characteristics, as well as more recent developments as African states experience their economic and institutional transition/transformation.

Global Talent Mobility: The Deployment of Expatriates

Africa has a long tradition of foreign firms extensively deploying expatriate workers, largely due to the widespread skill shortages on the continent. Despite the rising level of education of the African population, the deployment of expatriates has not diminished, due to its economic expansion, brain drain (Brumfield & White, 2016), and the tendency for firms to keep the managerial positions for their home country nationals to maintain control (Akorsu & Cooke, 2011). According to Brumfield and White (2016: 15), "it is estimated that, collectively, African countries employ more than 250,000 expatriates at a cost of approximately $20 billion per year".

Expatriates working in Africa may be broadly categorized into two groups. One involves those who migrate across the continent, often from poorer to richer countries in search of better opportunities. They are mostly young and relatively well-educated or skilled individuals. This growing talent flow has been fuelled by a continent-wide trend to deregulation, encompassing labor market reforms, a reduced emphasis on active industrial policy, and the opening of markets to international competition (Cooke et al., 2015a). The other group are expatriates from outside Africa who are professionals and/or managerial-level executives. These are two broad and distinct groups of expatriates enjoying markedly different employment terms and conditions. The former often suffer inferior status in the host country, whereas the latter may be privileged by coming from developed countries or being professional/managerial elites from emerging economies. Wood, Mazouz, Yin, and Cheah (2014) argued that many MNCs tend to adopt a default mode of employing expatriates wherever it is possible; at the same time, such policies may open up divides between foreign firms and local communities.

The deployment of expatriates is not confined to western firms operating in Africa, nor to the professional and technical category of staffing only. As FDI and MNCs from emerging economies, such as China, grows in Africa, they also bring their own expatriates as well as hiring third country nationals to fill key positions. For instance, Cooke et al.'s (2015b) study of four mining firms in Africa found that these firms adopt a resource-intensive HR strategy to attract and retain professional and technical mining employees from China, as fewer and fewer people are prepared to work as expatriates in Africa and endure hardship and separation from their family.

As an example, one Chinese mining firm operating in Zimbabwe as a joint venture rented good quality apartments, provided designated vehicles and local drivers, and provided a cook and cookbook from the region where the Chinese expatriates came from to provide homely meals for the Chinese expatriates (Cooke et al., 2015b). The separation of the expatriates, who were seen to enjoy much better living conditions and were in a higher organizational hierarchy than the local staff, inevitably created barriers between the two cohorts of the workforce, adding further challenges to the management of the mining operations. As resentment of Chinese businesses emerges and intensifies in various parts of Africa, such privileges that the Chinese expatriate employees enjoy may attract further criticism (e.g., Alden, 2007; Cooke, 2014; Jansson et al., 2009). We will discuss further TM in MNCs later in the chapter.

Global Talent Mobility: The Loss of Talent through Brain Drain

Global mobility of human capital has long been a feature in African migration history, which has had negative consequences for the development of Africa. Adopting a historical perspective and drawing on data from various sources, Brumfield and White's (2016: 1) study identified "five options for talent development (stealing, buying, borrowing, developing, and retaining talent) that have impacted [Africa's] past and present access to talent" and suggested that these options "can be redirected towards the continent's future advancement." According to Brumfield and White (2016: 4), "Africa's potential talent continues to be diverted" out of Africa. In particular, the exodus of skilled labor has been driven by the talent acquisition programs of other countries to fill their skill gaps. These international migrations have taken place across regions and continental borders. It was reported that some 30 million Africans (approximately 3% of the population) have migrated internationally, many of whom are talented individuals (Ratha et al., 2011, cited in Brumfield & White, 2016: 5).

According to the International Organization for Migration (IOM) database, 436,000 Nigerians migrated to the United Kingdom and the United States in 2013. This figure was close to all Nigerians who were reported to have migrated to other countries in Africa (IOM 2013, cited in Brumfield & White, 2016). Similarly, the IOM statistics indicated that 62,431 Ethiopians migrated to Sudan, over 195,000 landed in the U.S., and 150,000 made their way to Saudi Arabia (IOM, 2013, cited in Brumfield & White, 2016). It was estimated that, globally, migrants of Sub-Saharan African origins made up about 40% of all migrating skilled workers, and some 80,000 managers and 23,000 academic professionals from those regions took positions abroad each year in the period from 1990 to 1995 (Banya & Zajda, 2015, cited in Brumfield & White, 2016).

A notable sector in which Africa has lost its talent to developed nations is healthcare. It was estimated that 20% of African physicians and 10% qualified nurses went abroad to pursue their careers (Clemens & Pettersson, 2008). Poppe et al.'s (2014) study shows that African medical professionals chose to migrate to Austria and Belgium for three main reasons: education, political instability or insecurity in their home country, and family reunion.

More broadly, well educated professionals are enticed to migrate *en masse* to more developed countries. Those who go abroad for training may stay in the host country or cross over to other developed countries to pursue further education and training, better career prospects, and a more affluent life style. A direct consequence of this global human mobility is the deprivation of African societies "of the innovative capacity of some of its best and brightest members" (Brumfield & White, 2016: 4). The phenomenon of "brain drain" from less developed to developed countries has been widespread in the last few decades, fuelled by the rising level of education standards in less developed countries, economic globalization, the aging workforce in developed countries, and the relaxation of many nation states' immigration policies to facilitate international skilled immigration (e.g., Bach, 2010; Cooke & Bartram, 2015). While "buying" talent from less developed nations may not bring "exclusive nor permanent privileges" to the immigrating country (Brumfield & White, 2016: 11), it can be argued that Africa has taken its toll more than other less developed regions, and such a human capital outflow has deprived the continent of its most needed resources for development.

Many migrants from Africa see job seeking in the developed world as a temporary measure. There is a large pool of highly skilled Africans in the developed world with an interest in returning at some stage to the continent (Black & King, 2004). Such individuals are likely to have richer local knowledge and face fewer adjustment problems than expatriates, making them an attractive target for firms seeking to enhance their talent base. While such reverse brain drain (or brain circulation) is a welcome resource to Africa in general and firms in Africa more specifically, such global talent mobility may at the same time be a source of widening social inequality, as local talented individuals who do not have international education and experience will lose out to the overseas returnees.

Talent Shortage in the Public Sector and Its Broader Impact

(Re)building African nations, communities, and organizations requires, among other things, strategic vision and competence from the public sector. However, one key challenge in the public sector is "retaining talented leaders and aspiring leaders" (Davies & Frolova, 2016: 67). Davies and Frolova (2016: 67) identified a number of "internal and external barriers such as low prioritization of talent management, corruption, lack of funding and a skilled labor shortage". Sub-optimal public leadership (which itself, in many settings, represents a partial outcome of shortfalls in education and training) undermines the prospect of addressing the talent shortage problem in African nations in several ways (Davies & Frolova, 2016). One is the capacity to formulate human resource development programs at the national and industry level through informed education and training policies. Another is the lack of resources to devote to education and training, particularly if limited revenues are channelled through to the privileged cohort.

The deficiency of leadership development is not confined to the public sector, but across sectors. As Modisane's (2018) study revealed, there is limited attention to leadership development in both research and practice in Africa. Without a well-resourced public sector and a well-educated workforce, the development of African countries and the further development and deployment of talent in other sectors remain a severe challenge. That said, increasing the supply of talent does not necessarily lead to increased demand without adequate HRM policies and practices at the industry and firm level.

Inequality and Affirmative Action

Inequality, in particular gender and ethnic inequality, remains an on-going political and social problem in many African countries (e.g., Lee, 2014), and is reflected in workplaces. Inequality starts with imbalances in educational opportunities, which prevents talented individuals from developing their human capital and being well-prepared for their career. Such disadvantages in one's early stage of life cannot be adequately remedied through affirmative action later. In addition, in many developing countries, extended informal networks provide vital social support in the absence of effective institutions. At the same time, this may lead to pressures to hire and promote individuals based on their position in such networks, rather than on their talent and skill sets (Parboteeah, Seriki, & Hoegl, 2014). As a result, nepotism persists in these societies, which undermines the adoption of a strategic approach to human resource development and TM that is merit-based and fairness-oriented.

Like many other developing societies, gender inequality persists in Africa due to the prevailing patriarchal norm. For example, Adisa, Cooke, and Iwowo's (2019: 146) study in the Nigerian context found that "patriarchy shapes women's behaviour in ways that undermine their performance and organizational citizenship behaviour." The study further reveals that patriarchal attitudes, often practiced at home, are frequently brought to the workplace. "This transference affects women's workplace behaviour and maintains men's (self-perceived) superior status quo, whereby women are dominated, discriminated against, and permanently placed in inferior positions" (Adisa et al., 2019: 146). This means that many talented women are deprived of opportunities for career development and advancement in the organization (Adisa et al., 2019).

In many nation states, affirmative action policies have been introduced to address gender discrimination issues, but their effects have been limited. For example, Mathur-Helm's (2005: 56) study revealed that companies in South Africa are still not ready "to accept women as professional equals, resulting in government legislation and policies working against women's growth and advancement instead of working in their favour." Similarly, in evaluating affirmative action policies in Africa, Okedele (2020) found that, while the adoption of affirmative action policies has led to significant gains for women in politics, much more progress needs to be made on substantive representation in order to improve the status and lives of women beyond the quota system. Until then, many talented female employees will remain disadvantaged and under-utilized in their workplaces.

Affirmative action policies address not only gender discrimination issues, but also racial issues. While these policies may not have yielded universal effects for those in disadvantaged races, existing research evidence suggests that affirmative action has led to a reversed form of discrimination and therefore created new casualties (e.g., Archibong & Adejumo, 2013). For example, de Beer, Rothmann, and Pienaar's (2016) study found that non-designated (white male) employees experience more job insecurity than their designated (black male) counterparts, though this is not necessarily associated with a higher level of turnover intentions. This reverse discrimination would lead to sub-optimal development and utilization of talented individuals.

It is clear that affirmative action in Africa and South Africa, where there has been more research evidence, has yielded mixed results, an outcome that is not conducive to talent utilization on an equal footing across race, gender, and abilities.

Talent Management Challenges at the Industry and Firm Level

A number of studies of TM issues at the organizational level have exemplified challenges to talent attraction and retention, reflecting the failures of the labor market and other institutions (also see Horwitz, 2013; Kamoche, Chizema, Mellahi, & Newenham-Kahindi, 2012). This is hardly surprising, given the broader TM context that we have discussed so far. For example, Amankwah-Amoah and Debrah's (2011) study of TM in the aviation industry of Africa showed that the shortage of human capital in this area is to a large extent a result of the labor market failings, inadequate human capital development function, and heightened demands for talent due to industry expansion, a situation that has been exacerbated by brain drain to other continents, which has kept pace with economic globalization. Increased competition between firms has led to intensified rivalry between firms for scarce talent. This tendency, noted by Amankwah-Amoah and Debrah (2011) in the case of the African airline industry, is clearly relevant to many other sectors as well.

Ayentimi, Burgess, and Dayaram (2019: 143) studied macro-institutional conditions in Ghana and the challenges to HRM program development and implementation. They point to six dimensions that may undermine firms' HRM advancement: "the regulatory system, education and training arrangement, labor market conditions, cultural barriers, political actors' intrusion, and economic uncertainty". This finding points to the immense challenges attending talent development and utilization. Without major reforms in the human capital formation system, which requires an overhaul of the education, training, and health systems, it is unlikely that a sufficient stock of skilled workers will be produced in the foreseeable future (e.g., Jackson, 2012; Pillay, 2006), even if there were suitable jobs available. In the meantime, a direct consequence of scarcities for highly skilled workers is the war for talent among employers and the resultant job hopping and wage hypes (e.g., Horwitz, 2012; Wood et al., 2014).

In line with the trends of HRM research globally, research on TM in the African context has also revealed that certain HRM practices are effective in attracting, motivating, and retaining talented employees. For example, Hlanganipai and Musara's (2016: 164) study found that there are "significant effects of the frequency of training needs assessment on career and TM effectiveness"; in particular, significant effects of "induction, career-focused job rotation practices, provision of mentors on career and talent development effectiveness are also shown".

Mensah, Bawole, and Wedchayanon's (2016) study of TM in the Ghanaian context found that TM practices are positively associated with employee performance, moderated by employee satisfaction and commitment. Van Zyl, Mathafena, and Ras' (2017: 1) study of TM in the private sector in a number of African countries mapped out key dimensions essential to TM, including talent "attraction, sourcing and recruitment, deployment and transitioning, growth and development, performance management, talent reviews, rewarding and recognising, engagement and retention".

Wang and Cuervo-Cazurra (2017) further suggested that African firms can overcome their human capital void, or lessen its negative impact, and improve firm's performance by developing joint venture with MNCs as a means of organizational upgrading. However, as the country-level human capital stock increases and the indigenous firms become less dependent on their foreign partners for learning, this strategy may become less critical. Moreover, forming joint ventures with foreign MNCs may carry its own drawbacks, such as a reliance on expatriates, as discussed earlier, thus reducing the anticipated solution of talent shortage.

Talent Management in MNCs

The rise of foreign director investment (FDI) in Africa in the last two decades has attracted not only further investment from established MNCs from developed economies, but also the growing presence of MNCs from emerging markets both within and beyond the continent (Cooke et al., 2015a). Such MNCs will have very different approaches to TM, which differ significantly from the skilled expatriate model favored by many longer-established MNCs operating in the continent.

For example, Oppong, and Gold (2016: 345-347) observed that HRM practices adopted by MNCs from developed economies in the gold mining industry in Ghana as a TM framework were not indigenous-friendly. In particular, "neo-colonisation and hegemonic dynamics form the social order in the industry…in the form of non-development of local managers" (Oppong & Gold, 2016: 345). In addition, to "perpetuate the control and dominance[,] attempts are made to sustain the social order…to prevent the TMD process that can transfer power to local managers" (Oppong & Gold, 2016: 345). "The social order, and attempts to sustain it…become established in which local managers find themselves as a dominated group" (Oppong & Gold, 2016: 345). The continuous imposition of headquarter ideas and values resulted in the dominance of home country work values and HRM policies and practices at the expense of Ghanaian cultural values and practices. This was not conducive to encouraging the Ghanaian workforce to unleash their full potential, as they felt ill-fitted to the organizational culture and were unfamiliar with the business (Oppong & Gold, 2016).

Azungah's (2017) study of strategic HRM practices of Western MNCs in Africa found that parent country nationals tend to favor importing the parent country's strategic HRM practices embedded in western values (i.e., standardization), whereas host country nationals prefer to adopt localized practices that are in line with the African cultural and institutional characteristics (i.e., localization). This means that the deployment of managerial staff in foreign MNCs in African subsidiaries will have strong implications for TM.

Emerging market (e.g., China, India, and South Africa) MNCs may be less concerned with "reforming" local ways of doing things. However, they may introduce new practices that challenge local conventions in different ways. For example, many Chinese MNCs have adopted the model of employing expatriates even in semi-skilled positions, as alluded to earlier in the chapter. The ease of internal communication and cultural similarity (in the case of hiring despatched workers from the home country) may facilitate the intention to bypass host country labor regulations, thus achieving better control of the workforce and driving costs down (in the case of hiring undocumented migrants), or even, in some instances, expressing outright prejudice (Cooke et al., 2015b; Cooke et al., 2018; Lee, 2009). However, such practices also tend to worsen external relations, and are not conducive to facilitating human capital development and talent utilization in the host countries.

It should be noted that, although Chinese MNCs have been heavily criticized for relying significantly on the large-scale import of labor from China into Africa to fill a wide range of job roles, they do engage in quite significant training interventions (Cooke, 2014; Cooke et al., 2018). The latter focus not only on existing and potential staff, but also on providing training to host country government officials on engaging with Chinese business (Cooke et al., 2015b).

Future Research Directions

This chapter has a number of implications for future research. Firstly, research on TM in Africa is only emerging (Anlesinya et al., 2019), and extant literature on or relevant to understanding talent in Africa focuses heavily on South Africa. The situation, role of various stakeholders, and prospect of TM in other regions in Africa is much less explored. Given the vast complexity and diversity of African countries, future research should adopt a more nuanced and holistic approach to exploring in greater depth a range of issues that confront nation states and sub-national regions in their human capital development and TM endeavor. These may include: the examination of their education and training system, equal opportunity policy and practice, the level of presence and influence of MNCs, the pace and direction of economic development, and the parallel reform of institutional systems.

In addition, the role of language needs to be explored, as non-Anglo-lingual countries and nationals may be disadvantaged in the MNC setting. The role of language in international HRM has gained research attention in recent years. It has been argued that language plays an important social function in that it shapes people's social perceptions, personal identity, intergroup relations, and ability to engage in knowledge transfer in workplaces, and subsequently, individuals' career mobility (Itani, Järlström, & Piekkari, 2015; Karhunen, Kankaanranta, Louhiala-Salminen, & Piekkari, 2018; Peltokorpi, 2015). This would mean that multilingual host country nationals may hold added competitive advantages (i.e., more social capital) than those with less language proficiencies.

Secondly, TM in Africa, and indeed HRM more generally, is very under-theorized. Adeleye (2011) cautioned against a cultural relativist approach to theorizing HRM in the diverse African contexts. This is because cross-cultural accounts may discount the role of institutions and the impact of the strategic choices of key actors. Future research may extend Adeleye's argument by adopting a more comprehensive approach to studying TM, that takes into account the diverse and evolving culture, market, and institutions of African states, and the embeddedness of organizations in these societal settings. As Horwitz (2015: 2786) pointed out, based on his review of HRM in MNCs in Africa, multiple theories, such as "comparative political economy and institutional theory, labour market and HRM modes of analysis, cultural paradigms of indigenous management thought", may offer complementary explanatory power to interpret HRM phenomena so as to advance our understanding of clusters of HRM practices, and by extension here, TM practices.

Thirdly, future research may adopt a qualitative or mixed-method approach to capture the nuances of TM in organizations. As O'Neil and Koekemoer (2016) observed, there has been a decline in qualitative research in the last two decades in the organizational psychology and HRM field in the South African context, in spite of the recognized value of this approach and on-going calls for its adoption globally.

Finally, there is much room to broaden TM research as part of HRM, incorporating migration studies. Given the high level of labor/talent mobility across Africa and between African and other continents, studies of TM need to examine the conditions of home and destination countries, and how patterns of global talent mobility may mirror closely changes in national immigration policy in a given period of time, often targeting particular skill groups to address specific industry/sectoral needs.

Implications for Policy and Practice

There has been growing emphasis in the scholarly literature on the need and urgency for developing indigenous talent (Kamoche, Siebers, Mamman, & Newenham-Kahindi, 2015). For instance, Abbott, Goosen, and Coetzee (2013) observed that apartheid has left behind a legacy of chronic human underdevelopment in South Africa. This has implications for policy at the macro level and TM practice at the organizational level.

In policy terms, it is clear that the education and training system remains inadequate in producing home grown talents, largely due to its historical legacy. Similarly, despite statutory requirements for affirmative action, entrenched political and social inequality means that the majority of women and other disadvantaged groups have not been granted equal access to career development (e.g., Lee, 2014). As a result, good jobs often go to those privileged with personal networks and social status. Tighter monitoring and implementation scrutiny are necessary if a greater level of effectiveness of the affirmative action policies is to be achieved (Okedele, 2020).

Moreover, despite the rapid growth of FDI in the continent, African states may not hold the upper hand to facilitate the development of innovation policy tailored to their country's needs rather than that of the foreign investors. For instance, Walwyn and Naidoo's (2020: 33) study found that South Africa's innovation policy for its manufacturing industry "is dominated by supply-side measures" with "limited assistance for market development." The authors argue that rebalancing "the innovation policy mix towards the use of more demand-side instruments, combined with generic rather than population targeted policies, could address these deficiencies and improve the prospects for the sector" (Walwyn & Naidoo, 2020: 33). Autonomy in the development and implementation of innovation policy is essential to the conception of a talent development and deployment policy in the nation states.

In terms of TM policy and practice at the organizational level, managers cannot rely on the external labor market to provide highly talented and skilled labor. Shortfalls in national training systems in many national contexts mean not only that there is intense competition for talent, but also that many individuals with high potential may not be able to realize their abilities in the workplace (Gellman, 2015). A further problem is that identifying talent may be difficult, given the inconsistencies in formal educational qualifications in some countries. As such, firms may have to rely on promoting high commitment HRM practices as a solution, allowing firms more time to get to know engaged workforces, as a basis for informal talent spotting, as well as the development of more advanced human resource development (HRD) strategies and systems.

Firms also need to establish a strategic HRD system that covers all levels of career opportunities. In examining the case of Mauritius, Dusoye, and Oogarah (2016) found that there is little usage of strategic HRD on the islands, and the primary focus is on the operational level. This means that highly talented individuals may not have any opportunity to realize their potential by progressing to senior management position in the organizations. Firms may need to consider what the most effective ways are to develop talent. For example, Mallaby, Price, and Hofmeyr (2017) explored the challenges in developing talented functional specialists into general managers in South Africa. They concluded that the managed exposure of talented individuals to the challenges of general managerial roles is often more effective than training. In developing talent from within, attention also needs to be given to experiential learning and informal and unrecorded knowledge bases (Parboteeah et al., 2014). Mwila et al. (2018) argue for an increased role for psychometric testing to spot and secure talent. On the one hand, shortfalls in national education systems require firms to identify measures of talent not based on qualifications. On the other hand, psychometric testing may incorporate cultural biases, bringing with it problems of implementation in a multi-cultural environment (Meiring et al., 2005).

More fundamentally, although talents are motivated to migrate overseas for many reasons, an important reason is material conditions (Poppe et al., 2014). For example, in looking at the academic labor market, Theron et al. (2014) found that poor pay was the principal cause behind a brain drain to more conducive climates. Employing organizations in Africa therefore need to provide competitive terms and conditions (e.g., attractive salary packages, training and development opportunities, and clear career progression paths) in the face of global competition for their talents. They also need to exert pressure on their government agencies to continue to improve the macro environment so that talent will stay.

The existence of talent is meaningless unless it is used effectively. For instance, Makhubela and Ngoepe (2018) investigated knowledge retention in a mining company in South Africa and found that, although a knowledge retention policy was in place, not all employees were aware of it, and the management was not fully supportive of the knowledge retention initiatives. On a more positive note, Wood and Bischoff's (2020: 32) study of the South African clothing and textile industry revealed that intensive international competition and a high level of unemployment have created an interdependent relationship between the employer and the employees and enabled firms to find innovative ways of managing tacit knowledge, which have helped these firms to survive and thrive.

For MNCs, the deployment of expatriates as a default mode proves increasingly unsustainable, not only owing to pushback from host country authorities, communities, and other institutional actors such as the trade unions, but also because it can make engagement with local stakeholders and clients more challenging. There is now evidence, at least from the Chinese firms, of localization of the majority of their staff to demonstrate their commitment to a long-term stay in Africa.

Conclusion

This chapter examined key challenges to TM in the African context. It highlights a number of trends and issues of relevance to TM policy and practice in African countries. Like other developing parts of the world, African states face serious talent shortages, but are constrained by serious drawbacks in their education and training system, employment system, and HRM at the organizational level. The African context is a rapidly changing one, albeit with enduring political and cultural diversity and economic disparity. We therefore urge a more nuanced and inclusive approach to investigating TM issues in the contemporary African context, taking into account its rich historical and cultural traditions as well as institutional diversities and economic trajectories.

Acknowledgement

The author would like to thank Geoffrey Wood for his insights in an earlier version of this chapter.

References

Abbott, P., Goosen, X., & Coetzee, J. 2013. The human resource function contribution to human development in South Africa. *SA Journal of Human Resource Management,* 11(1): 1–14.

Adeleye, I. 2011. Theorising human resource management in Africa: Beyond cultural relativism. *African Journal of Business Management,* 5(6): 2028–2039.

Adisa, T., Cooke, F. L., & Iwowo, V. 2019. Mind your attitude: The impact of patriarchy on women's workplace behaviour. *Career Development International,* 25(2): 146–164.

Akorsu, A., & Cooke, F. L. 2011. Labour standard application among Chinese and Indian firms in Ghana: Typical or atypical? *The International Journal of Human Resource Management,* 22(13): 2730–2748.

Amankwah-Amoah, J., & Debrah, Y, A. 2011. Competing for scarce talent in a liberalised environment: Evidence from the aviation industry in Africa. *The International Journal of Human Resource Management,* 22(17): 3565–3581.

Anlesinya, A., Amponsah-Tawiah, K. and Dartey-Baah, K. 2019. Talent management research in Africa: Towards multilevel model and research agenda. *African Journal of Economic and Management Studies,* 10(4), 440–457.

Archibong, U. & Adejumo, O., 2013. Affirmative action in South Africa: Are we creating new casualties? *Journal of Psychological Issues in Organizational Culture,* 3(S1): 14–27.

Ayentimi, D., Burgess, J., & Dayaram, K. 2019. Macro-institutional conditions in Ghana and the challenges to HRM program development and implementation. *Thunderbird International Business Review,* 61(2): 143–156.

Azungah, T. 2017. Strategic human resource management practices of Western MNEs in Africa: Standardization, localization or both? *Journal of Business Studies,* 4(1): 17–36.

Bach, S. 2010. Managed migration? Nurse recruitment and the consequences of state policy. *Industrial Relations Journal,* 41(3): 249–266.

Banya, K., & Zajda, J. 2015. Globalisation, the brain drain, and poverty reduction in Sub-Saharan Africa. In J. Zajda (Ed.), *Second international handbook on globalisation, education and policy research.* Netherlands: Springer. doi: http://doi.org/10.1007/978-94-017-9493-0.

Black, R., & King, R. 2004. Editorial introduction: Migration, return and development in West Africa. *Population, Space and Place,* 10(2): 75–83.

Brumfield, K. J., & White, H. L. 2016. A multilateral approach for optimizing Africa's access to strategic human talent. *African Social Science Review,* 8(1): 1–22.

Clemens, M. A., & Pettersson, G. 2008. New data on African health professionals abroad. *Human Resources for Health,* 6(1). doi: http://doi.org/10.1186/1478-4491-6-1.

Cooke, F. L. 2014. Chinese multinational firms in Asia and Africa: Relationships with institutional actors and patterns of employment practices. *Human Resource Management,* 53(6): 877–896.

Cooke, F. L., & Bartram, T. 2015. Human resource management in healthcare and aged care: Current challenges and towards a research agenda. *Human Resource Management,* 54(5): 711–735.

Cooke, F. L., Wang, D., & Wang, J. 2018. State capitalism in construction: Staffing practices and labor relations in Chinese construction firms in Africa. *Journal of Industrial Relations,* 60(1): 77–100.

Cooke, F. L., Wang, J., Yao, X. Xiong, L., Zhang, J. Y., & Li, A. 2015b. Mining with a high-end strategy: A study of Chinese mining firms in Africa and human resources implications. *The International Journal of Human Resource Management,* 26(21): 2744–2762.

Cooke, F. L., Wood, G., & Horwitz, F. 2015a. Multinational firms from emerging economies in Africa: Implications for research and practice in human resource management. *The International Journal of Human Resource Management,* 26(21): 2653–2675.

Davies, P., & Frolova, Y. 2016. Retaining leadership talent in the African public sector: An assessment of the HR challenge. *Journal of Leadership, Accountability and Ethics,* 13(3): 67–78.

de Beer, L. T., Rothmann, S. & Pienaar, J. 2016. Job insecurity, career opportunities, discrimination and turnover intention in post-apartheid South Africa: Examples of informative hypothesis testing. *The International Journal of Human Resource Management,* 27(4): 427–439.

Deloitte 2014. **Africa human capital trends 2014: Engaging the 21st-century workforce.** https://www2.deloitte.com/content/dam/Deloitte/global/Documents/HumanCapital/dttl-human-capital-trends-africa.pdf, first accessed on 15 March 2018.

Dusoye, I. C., & Oogarah, K. 2016. Is Mauritius ready to become the HRD leader in Africa? *European Journal of Training and Development,* 40(4): 215–231.

Ernst and Young 2014. *Realising potential: EY 2014 Sub-Saharan Africa talent trends and practices survey.* http://www.ey.com/Publication/vwLUAssets/EY-2014-SSA-Talent-Trends-Survey-Report/$FILE/EY-2014-SSA-Talent-Trends-Survey-Report.pdf, first accessed on 10 March 2018.

Gellman, L. 2015, Dec 09. Careers: Nurturing talent is hard in Africa: Local business leaders are scarce amid lack of top schools, lower pay than in other regions. *Wall Street Journal.* https://search.proquest.com/docview/1746797992?accountid=13044.

Hlanganipai, N., & Musara, M. 2016. Training and development for career management and talent development in wholesale and retail industry in South Africa. *Journal of Psychology in Africa,* 26(2): 164–166.

Horwitz, F. M. 2012. Evolving human resource management in Southern African multinational firms: Towards and Afro-Asian nexus. *The International Journal of Human Resource Management,* 23: 2938–2958.

Horwitz, F. M. 2013. An analysis of skills development in a transitional economy: The case of the South African labour market. *The International Journal of Human Resource Management,* 24(12): 2435–2451.

Horwitz, F. M. 2015. Human resources management in multinational companies in Africa: A systematic literature review. *The International Journal of Human Resource Management,* 26(21): 2786–2809.

International Organization for Migration. 2013. *World Migration Report 2013.* https://publications.iom.int/books/world-migration-report-2013

Itani, S., Järlström, M., & Piekkari, R. 2015. The meaning of language skills for career mobility in the new career landscape. *Journal of World Business,* 50(2): 368–378.

Jackson, T. 2012. Reframing human resource management in Africa: A cross-cultural perspective. *International Journal of Human Resource Management,* 13: 998–1018.

Kamoche, K., Chizema, A., Mellahi, K., & Newenham-Kahindi, A. 2012. New directions in the management of human resources in Africa. *The International Journal of Human Resource Management,* 23: 2825–2834.

Kamoche, K., Siebers, L. Q., Mamman, A., & Newenham-Kahindi, A. 2015. The dynamics of managing people in the diverse cultural and institutional context of Africa. *Personnel Review,* 44(3): 330–345.

Karhunen, P., Kankaanranta, A., Louhiala-Salminen, L., & Piekkari, R. (018. Let's talk about language: A review of language-sensitive research in international management. *Journal of Management Studies,* 55(6): 980–1013.

Lee, C. K. 2009. Raw encounters: Chinese managers, African workers and the politics of casualisation in Africa's Chinese enclaves. *The China Quarterly,* 199: 647–666.

Lee, H. A., 2014. Affirmative action regime formation in Malaysia and South Africa. *Journal of Asian and African Studies,* 51(5): 511–527.

Mallaby, S. J., Price, G., & Hofmeyr, K. 2017. The transition to general management in South Africa. *SA Journal of Human Resource Management.* (Online) 2071-078X, (Print) 1683-7584.

Makhubela, S., & Ngoepe, M., 2018. Knowledge retention in a platinum mine in the North West Province of South Africa. *South African Journal of Information Management,* 20(1): 1–8. doi: https://doi.org/10.4102/sajim.v20i1.905.

Mathur-Helm, B. 2005. Equal opportunity and affirmative action for South African women: A benefit or barrier? *Women in Management Review,* 20(1): 56–71.

Mensah, J. K., Bawole, J. N., & Wedchayanon, N. 2016. Unlocking the "black box" in the talent management employee performance relationship: Evidence from Ghana. *Management Research Review,* 39(12): 1546–1566.

Modisane, K. T. 2018. Finding the niche to reposition leadership in Africa's developing economies for the global highway: Review of literature on leadership development programmes – methods and techniques. *Human Resource Development International,* 21(1): 12–23.

Mwila, N. K., & Turay, M. I. S. 2018. Augmenting talent management for sustainable development in Africa. *World Journal of Entrepreneurship, Management and Sustainable Development,* 14(1): 41–49.

Okedele A. 2020. Women, quotas, and affirmative action policies in Africa. In: O. Yacob-Haliso & T. Falola (Eds.), *The Palgrave handbook of African women's studies.* Cham: Palgrave Macmillan. doi: https://doi.org/10.1007/978-3-319-77030-7_80-1.

O'Neil, S., & Koekemoer, E. 2016. Two decades of qualitative research in psychology, industrial and organisational psychology and human resource management within South Africa: A critical review. *SA Journal of Industrial Psychology,* 42(1): 1–16.

Oppong, N. Y., & Gold, J. 2016. Developing local managers in the Ghanaian mining industry: An indigenous talent mode. *Journal of Management Development,* 35(3): 341–359.

Parboteeah, K. P., Seriki, H. T., & Hoegl, M. 2014. Ethnic diversity, corruption and ethical climates in sub-Saharan Africa: Recognizing the significance of human resource management. *The International Journal of Human Resource Management,* 25(7): 979–1001.

Peltokorpi, V. 2015. Corporate language proficiency and reverse knowledge transfer in multinational corporations: Interactive effects of communication media richness and commitment to headquarters. *Journal of International Management,* 21(1): 49–62.

Pillay, P. 2006. Human resource development and growth: Improving access to and equity in the provision of education and health services in South Africa. *Development Southern Africa,* 23: 63–83.

Poppe, A., Jirovsky, E., Blacklock, C., Laxmikanth, P., Moosa, S., De Maeseneer, J., Kutalek, R., & Peersman, W. 2014. Why sub-Saharan African health workers migrate to European countries that do not actively recruit: A qualitative study post-migration. *Global Health Action,* 7, 24071. doi: https://doi.org/10.3402/gha.v7.24071.

Tarique, I., Briscoe, D., & Schuler, R. 2016. *International human resource management: policies and practices for multinational enterprises* (5th ed). New York: Routledge.

Theron, M., Barkhuizen, N., & du Plessis, Y. 2014. Managing the academic talent void: Investigating factors in academic turnover and retention in South Africa. *SA Journal of Industrial Psychology,* 40(1): 1–14.

Van Zyl, E. S., Mathafena, R. B., & Ras, J. 2017. The development of a talent management framework for the private sector. *SA Journal of Human Resource Management,* 15(0): 1–19.

Walwyn, D., & Naidoo, S. 2020. Policy mixes and overcoming challenges to innovation in developing countries: Insights from a mixed methods study of South Africa's manufacturing sector. *African Journal of Science, Technology, Innovation and Development,* 12(1): 33–46.

Wang, S., & Cuervo-Cazurra, A. 2017. Overcoming human capital voids in underdeveloped countries. *Global Strategy Journal,* 7(1): 36–57.

Wood, G., & Bischoff, C. 2020. Challenges and progress in integrating knowledge: Cases from clothing and textiles in South Africa. *Journal of Knowledge Management,* 24(1): 32–55.

Wood, G., Mazouz, K., Yin, S. X., & Cheah, J. 2014. Foreign direct investment from emerging markets to Africa: The HRM context. *Human Resource Management,* 53: 179–201.

13

TAKING STOCK OF HRM RESEARCH IN LATIN AMERICA

Implications for Talent Management

Jordi Trullen

Jaime Bonache

Introduction

The concept of talent management (TM), understood as the identification of key positions within the firm, the development of a talent pool to fill these roles, and the design of differentiated HR architectures to facilitate individuals' access to these positions (Collings & Mellahi, 2009) is recognized as a key priority in today's economy (e.g., Economist Intelligence Unit, 2006; Hill, 2016; Gallardo-Gallardo, Thunnissen, & Scullion, 2020). This is especially true in the emerging BRICS economies (Brazil, Russia, India, China, and South Africa), where there continues to be a shortage of qualified candidates for technical and leadership positions (Beamond, Farndale, & Härtel, 2016). Nevertheless, only a handful of TM studies come from emerging economies (Gallardo-Gallardo, Nijs, Dries, & Gallo, 2015; Gallardo-Gallardo, Thunnissen, & Scullion, 2017), or consider the role of macro contextual factors in the adoption of TM policies (King & Vaiman, 2019; Sidani & Al Ariss, 2014; Sun, Peng, Lee, & Tan, 2015).

This is also true in the case of Latin America (LATAM). While attracting and retaining talent remains the foremost priority of many firms in the region that compete internationally (Exame, 2013; Melguizo & Pages-Serra, 2017), and a major concern for foreign multinational corporations (MNCs) operating there (Beamond, Farndale, & Härtel, 2020), research on TM in Latin America is very scarce and published only locally (e.g., Freitag, Ohtsuki, Ferreira, Fischer, & Almeida, 2014).

This is surprising for several reasons. First, Latin American economic growth in the first decade of this century, with a surge in multilatinas (i.e., LATAM multinationals), has substantially increased management scholars' interest in the region (Aguilera, Ciravegna, Cuervo-Cazurra, & Gonzalez-Perez, 2017; Aguinis et al., 2020; Hermans et al., 2017; Husted & de Sousa-Filho, 2019; Mingo, Junkunc, & Morales, 2018; Nicholls-Nixon, Davila Castilla, Sanchez Garcia, & Rivera Pesquera, 2011; Vassolo, De Castro, & Gómez-Mejía, 2011). Second, TM and retention are especially crucial in this area because of local talent shortages coupled with significant foreign direct investment (Beamond, Farndale, & Härtel, 2016), and its countries are still not competitive enough when attracting and retaining talent (Herranz Acebuche, 2017). Finally, the transfer of TM policies and practices from the US to LATAM needs to consider local institutional and contextual factors, which so far remain under-researched (Gallardo-Gallardo et al., 2017).

Despite this dearth of research, there is, however, a considerable amount of work in the broader HRM literature that is contextualized in LATAM (Davila & Elvira 2008). The goal here will be to review this selected HR literature to identify practices and policies related to TM in three areas: attracting, developing, and retaining talent. An additional goal will be to reflect on how LATAM cultural traits

DOI: 10.4324/9781315474687-13

may affect the adoption of these practices and policies. The first section here describes the LATAM context, paying particular attention to its cultural dimension and how it may affect this adoption. The second section reviews selected LATAM-related HR literature and links it to the different TM areas. We conclude with a section describing significant areas for future research, which seems crucial given the paucity of research.

The Latin American Context

LATAM is generally understood to be the entire continent of South America, along with Mexico, Central America, and the Caribbean. This comprises 33 countries, with a population close to 644 million in 2018 and a GDP of US$5,787 trillion (World Bank, 2018a). In only 15 years, GDP in LATAM nearly tripled, rising from US$2,287 trillion in 2000 to a maximum of US$6,405 trillion in 2014. Between 2003 and 2016, the share of the population living in extreme poverty in the region fell from 24.5% to 9.9%. In a period of about 20 years, LATAM moved from having highly unstable closed economies ruled by authoritarian regimes, to economies that were more stable and open to investment and trade, as well as more democratic (Santiso, 2007), attracting more than 12% of world total foreign direct investment by 2011 (UNCTAD, 2018).

All of these factors, as well as the role played by regional multinationals (Aguilera et al., 2017), led the region to acquire and retain more talent than ever before (Israel, 2012). However, the region has not fulfilled its true potential in terms of TM, partly due to the economic crisis and the end of a period of continuous growth in commodity prices in the 2010s (INSEAD, 2018). Only Chile and Costa Rica appear among the top 40 countries in the Global Talent Competitiveness Index (INSEAD, 2018), while the four biggest economies – Brazil, Mexico, Argentina, and Colombia – ranked 73rd, 71st, 49th, and 67th, respectively. Future economic growth that is sustainable will depend on the capacity of these countries to reduce inequality in ways that allow the poor to both benefit from and contribute to such growth (World Bank, 2018b). TM policies will play a key role in that respect, reaching out to silent stakeholders, such as the local youth and indigenous communities (Davila & Elvira, 2018).

Although LATAM countries differ in several aspects, such as size, demographics, cultural values, and level of economic development, they still share many common features that justify examining them as a distinctive region (Hartmann & Davila, 2014). In terms of per capita GDP in U.S. dollars, LATAM countries still lag significantly behind high-income OECD economies (World Bank, 2018a). They also share a fairly similarly ranking on the Gini index of inequality (a measure of statistical dispersion intended to represent the wealth distribution of a nation's residents), with Uruguay having the least inequality (41.6) and Colombia the most (53.5), compared to the EU recorded 2015 average of 31.0, and Canada 31.3 in 2014. LATAM is characterized by major wage inequality, with a small number of high quality jobs for skilled professionals and myriad employees earning the minimum wage (Pérez Arrau, Eades, & Wilson, 2012). Other commonly cited aspects that may influence the effectiveness of TM policies and practices include workplace discrimination (Pérez Arrau et al., 2012) and the major role played by trade unions (Davila & Elvira, 2005; Senén, Gomes, & Medwid, 2018).

From a cultural perspective and despite differences across LATAM (Lenartowicz & Johnson, 2003), both the World Values Survey (Inglehart & Carballo, 1997) and the GLOBE study (Javidan, Dorfman, Sully de Luque, & House, 2006) place the region's countries in a single group. In particular, the GLOBE study ranks LATAM societies with relatively high scores for cultural dimensions, such as In-Group Collectivism and Power Distance, and with low ones for Performance Orientation. High in-group collectivism suggests that, on average, individuals in these countries tend to feel proud and loyal towards their organizations, as well as towards their families. High power distance scores imply that Latin Americans do not expect power to be distributed evenly, accepting authority, power differentials, status differences, and inequality. Respect for authority and the importance of in-group social relationships also inform a typical LATAM cultural trait, namely, paternalism (Davila & Elvira, 2015). This involves a manager's or owner's moral obligation to treat their subordinates or employees as if they were extended family in exchange for their personal support (Hartmann & Davila, 2014, Rodriguez & Rios, 2009; Rodriguez & Stewart, 2017). This implies a greater degree of tolerance of low performers in exchange for their loyalty (Rodriguez & Rios, 2009).

Talent Management in the Latin American Context

The context briefly described above may influence the adoption of TM policies and practices in LATAM firms. While TM's underlying principles, such as emphasis on meritocracy and work-force segmentation, may benefit both companies and employees, their introduction in LATAM may prove more difficult than in the English-speaking countries where they originated. For example, in LATAM countries, with high levels of collectivism, employees may feel uncomfortable being singled out as "talent" (Diaz-Saenz & Witherspoon, 2000). Similarly, supervisors in paternalistic cultures may also be more reluctant to make clear distinctions among their subordinates for fear of losing face. The meritocratic principles underlying TM policies may also encounter more difficulties when adopted by LATAM firms. Prioritizing potential and performance as the only basis for decisions may put managers in an awkward position, especially when they have emotional bonds with their employees. Latin American managers may feel that other aspects, such as employees' tenure or loyalty towards the group, should also be taken into account when making top talent decisions (Davila & Elvira, 2012).

The previous arguments suggest that the adoption of TM practices and policies focusing on work-force differentiation may be difficult in LATAM, and this precept finds some support in the little empirical evidence we have thus far (Abreu, Menergon, & Miyazaki, 2003; Ferrazza, Burtet, & Scheffer, 2015; Piedras, 2015). For example, when discussing TM in a recent KPMG report on this issue in Mexico, Piedras (2015) adopts an inclusive approach (i.e., all employees are considered talent) rather than an exclusive one (i.e., talent refers to a small group of employees labeled as high-potentials).

The unease with exclusive or elitist TM approaches is also evident in the academic literature, which has been published mostly in Brazil. For example, Abreu et al. (2003) adopt a critical view of TM's focus on workforce differentiation, which they consider responsible for the increasing marginalization of those employees within organizations that are not labeled as "talent". More recently, Ferrazza et al. (2015) have explored the TM programs of three large organizations in Porto Alegre (Brazil) in different industries (software development, telecommunications, and higher education), finding that only one of the organizations is adopting an exclusive approach. In addition, several studies highlight the confusion in Brazilian firms over the definition of TM (Ferrazza et al., 2015; Freitag & Fischer, 2013; Walker & Ferreira, 2012), with many managers simply confusing TM with strategic human resource management (HRM).

Despite the difficulties mentioned in transferring TM systems to LATAM, there are several reasons why managers should not be discouraged. First, evidence from the introduction of other systems, such as high-performance work systems, shows that LATAM firms can also benefit from them (Bonache, Trullen, & Sanchez, 2012). Second, there is a long tradition in LATAM firms of importing systems that differ greatly from the local modus operandi (Mellahi, Frynas, & Collings, 2016). Finally, LATAM managers and employees might well align their values with those of their organizations if they perceive them to be more competent and successful. Indeed, there is evidence that LATAM employees want their employers to create more meritocratic work environments (Mercer, 2017).

We shall now review selected HR literature with a focus on LATAM to identify practices and policies related to TM. In so doing, we shall also illustrate how practices may be adapted to the local context, while maintaining their potential for attracting, developing, and retaining talent. At the same time, we shall show how local practices sometimes need to be replaced with new ones to avoid losing talent.

Talent Management in Latin America: Main Trends and Themes

While there is a lack of research that directly addresses TM policies and practices in LATAM, there are several studies addressing HRM more generally (Davila & Elvira 2008; Elvira & Davila, 2005). A selected review of these studies is useful for identifying TM practices and policies by focusing on three large TM areas: 1) attraction and selection, 2) development, and 3) retention.

Talent Acquisition and Selection

LATAM has been described as a kinship society, where HR practices are highly influenced by strong ties among individuals, either in the form of family relationships or close friendships (Davila & Elvira, 2015). It follows that the use of internal networks through employee referrals can benefit firms operating in the region when attracting talent (Greer & Stephens, 1996), being more likely to reproduce a "family-like" feeling inside the organization, hence increasing social capital (Gomez & Sanchez, 2005). For example, in a study on common HR practices in Peru, Sully de Luque and Arbazia (2005) argue that while 70% of recruitment decisions were based on the right qualifications for the position, another 30% were commonly based on background information, including schooling, family, and friends. The authors emphasize that social contacts through family and academic connections were key. Huo, Huang, and Napier (2002) have studied recruitment and selection practices in different countries including Mexico, where they find that having the right connections (e.g. school, family, friends, etc.) was considered by respondents as a top three hiring criterion. As a result of these strong networks, employee referrals (especially for family members and close friends) are widely used as a talent attraction practice in LATAM (Davila & Elvira, 2015).

While attracting talent through internal networks may make sense, selecting talent exclusively on that basis may have negative consequences. Dense networks can favor in-group members over out-group members in ways that are discriminatory, decreasing the much needed diversity that improves firm performance. Several authors concur, and provide a critical view of existing policies. For example, Rodriguez (2010) has criticized the importance of a candidate's pedigree in selection decisions. By pedigree she means who these candidates knew, with whom they were associated, who recommended them, and that person's degree of influence. Age (Rego et al., 2018) and gender (Stobbe, 2005) discrimination are also present in LATAM, especially in connection with executive positions (Stobbe, 2005; Flabbi, Piras, & Abrahams, 2017), where women are clearly under-represented, despite gender parity in the general working population.

In sum, while there are accrued benefits to using strong networks in the attraction of talent in LATAM, there are also risks associated with selection decisions made on that basis. Despite the present economic recession, LATAM firms continue to struggle to attract talent (Melguizo & Pages-Serra, 2017; Towers Watson, 2015). Hence, employers with a reputation for equal opportunity and non-discrimination as regards career advancement are likely to attract better candidates (Ready, Hill, & Conger, 2008). Newburry, Gardberg, & Sanchez (2014), using a large sample of more than 76,000 individuals in 80 firms within five LATAM countries, have found that members of marginalized groups (e.g., gender, education, and income) were more attracted to foreign-based and international firms, which they thought were more likely to break with established cultural patterns, such as interpersonal relationships prevailing over organizational procedures. This gives these companies a first-mover advantage in both attracting and selecting highly committed talent that may be untapped by competitors.

Talent Development

We shall discuss here research that has addressed three main areas for talent development in Latin America: training, workplace participation, and performance management. First, it has been noted that LATAM firms' greater internationalization and participation in global markets increases their need for a highly trained workforce (Hartmann & Davila, 2014), as well as the continuous need to upgrade basic skills in labor intensive industries. As many as 50% of LATAM firms cannot find candidates with the necessary skills, compared to 36% of firms in OECD countries (ManpowerGroup, 2015), and this short-fall is particularly acute in sectors that are more beneficial for development and industrial upgrading (Melguizo & Pages-Serra, 2017).

Any attempt at talent development needs to take the local context into account. For example, while MNCs in developed economies rely extensively on national educational systems, recruiting the graduates they need from technical universities, this is often not possible in LATAM, where the vast majority of people fail to complete secondary education (Friel, 2011). In Brazil, large MNCs such as Vale or Petrobras have moved fast to deal with their own talent shortages by creating strong corporate education programs (Sparkman, 2015). In addition, a combination of public and private initiatives has developed both in Brazil and Argentina to provide the local workforce with industry-specific competencies. In the case of Brazil, the National Service for Industrial Learning (Serviço Nacional de Aprendizagem Industrial [SENAI]) has established a vast network of professional colleges, with 809 centers across the country teaching certificate programs in oil and gas, civil construction, metal-lurgy, and many other industries (Sparkman, 2015). Herranz Acebuche (2017) likewise calls for apprenticeships that combine classroom and workplace training as a good way to develop young talent in LATAM.

Needless to say, training programs have to be seen as opportunities for career advancement, avoiding discriminatory practices. This does not always seem to be the case in LATAM firms. Respondents in the study by Rodriguez (2010) on Chilean firms declared that training programs were unilaterally decided by line managers without any input from employees. Aycan (2005) argues that in cultures with a low performance orientation and high levels of collectivism and power distance, training is more likely to be decided based on criteria of in-group favoritism, regardless of strategic needs.

In addition to training, HRM scholars have also studied employees' participation in work-related decision-making as a path towards talent development in LATAM. While more participative decision-making processes and greater employee autonomy are likely to contribute to talent development, cultural traits typical of LATAM countries, such as power distance and uncertainty avoidance, may constrain firms' ability to adopt such practices (Aycan, 2005; Elvira & Davila, 2005; Thomas, 2015). As a result, innovative HRM practices, such as the use of self-managing teams, may be hard to implement. Delegation is also likely to be constrained by the paternalistic and authoritarian values held by local managers, who assume that employees need to be told what to do because they lack the necessary abil-ities to make their own decisions (Parnell, 2010; Perez Arrau et al., 2012; Rodriguez, 2010; Rodriguez & Rios, 2009; Rodriguez & Stewart, 2017; Sposato, 2019).

Notwithstanding cultural barriers, some authors provide examples of the successful introduction of participative practices (Gomez, 2004; Nakata, Gomes da Silva, Freitag, & Ferrari Cálcena, 2011). For example, in a series of very interesting studies on the introduction of "learning organization" work practices, such as constant communication, employee involvement, a team structure, and horizontal organization in a Mexican subsidiary of a U.S. MNC, Gomez (2004) shows how managers successfully introduced the imported practices by making some very slight adjustments and slowing down the pace of change. It thus seems that well-orchestrated and consistent management actions can moderate the impact of national value differences on the transferability of participative management practices.

Finally, talent can also be developed by adopting sound performance management systems. LATAM organizations seem to be converging in the adoption of such systems. For example, Davila and Elvira (2007) have studied the adoption of such systems by three Mexican MNCs that included elements common to the systems in other foreign MNCs, such as managing-by-objectives with quarterly adjust-ment periods, bi-annual performance appraisals with feedback interviews, use of multi-source feed-back, and a combination of business objectives and competencies as appraisal criteria. Performance management policies are often modeled on the basis of foreign MNCs, which influence local firms through industry meetings where "best practices" are shared (Osland & Osland, 2005).

In a recent study, Mellahi et al. (2016) report how three large Brazilian MNCs standardized their performance management policies and practices in all their subsidiaries, regardless of whether these were located in developing or developed countries. More interestingly, they show that these performance management systems do not reflect local Brazilian values, but instead are heavily influenced by the global best practices also used by foreign MNCs. In another study on performance management in a large Brazilian MNC, Geary and Aguzzoli (2016) arrive at a similar conclusion, showing how the Brazilian firm exports the same system (based on U.S. best practice standards) to its subsidiaries in four developed countries (Canada, United Kingdom, Switzerland, and Norway).

There is also some evidence, nonetheless, that implementing these performance management systems is easier said than done (Towers Watson, 2015). For example, DeVoe and Iyengar (2004) have shown that Latin American managers tended to assign better performance ratings to subordinates who fulfilled their expectations about proper employee behavior, regardless of their actual performance. Rodriguez (2010) shows that performance appraisals in the Chilean organizations surveyed lacked credibility, and managers' "perceptions of loyalty and good behavior equaled good performance" (436). Similarly, Davila and Elvira (2007) in the study mentioned above show that appraisals reproduced paternalistic relationships between managers and subordinates, whereby employees expected their supervisors to tell them what to do in order to obtain a good evaluation.

In sum, while the adoption of performance management systems seems to be spreading in LATAM countries, some studies also show that intended and actual performance management practices often differ. While feedback needs to be provided in ways that respect the local culture and prevent losing face (Gomez & Sanchez, 2005), prioritizing loyalty over performance undermines the meritocratic principles that lead to higher talent development.

Talent Retention

Some of the lack of meritocracy described in LATAM firms is also evident when talking about reward policies. There is evidence that compensation is often not linked to performance (Towers Watson, 2015), but to seniority (Rodriguez, 2010; Von Glinow, Drost, & Teagarden, 2002), and in some cases to other criteria, such as having good relationships with one's supervisor or having a strong educational background (Davila & Elvira, 2007).

There is also some evidence supporting the idea that individual incentives seem to be less effective in LATAM. For example, Cristiani and Peiró (2019) recently found that calculative HRM practices (which included the use of individual incentives for different types of employees) were unrelated to employee turnover in Uruguay. In another study, Miller, Hom, and Gomez-Mejia (2001) analyzed the compensation systems of 155 U.S.-owned plants in Mexico (i.e., maquiladoras), and found that productivity-based individual incentives increased (rather than decreased) turnover, as local employees preferred more collectivistic forms of recognition, such as profit-sharing schemes.

While team-based incentives may be preferred in collectivistic cultures, this does not detract from the value of performance-based pay for LATAM firms (Bonache et al., 2012). In fact, Lowe, Milliman, De Cieri, and Dowling (2002) report that when Latin American managers were asked about their desired compensation practices (rather than existing ones), they were positively inclined towards the use of pay incentives linked to an employee's job performance; and there is some evidence that rewarding performance can also be effective in LATAM. For example, Sully de Luque and Arbazia (2005) report that pay-for-performance schemes are increasingly common in Peru, especially in sales positions. Andonova and Zuleta (2007) describe the successful introduction of incentive pay systems in Hacienda Gavilanes, a sugarcane farm in Colombia.

Whether more meritocratic forms of pay can indeed be successfully adopted in LATAM remains an empirical question. It is possible, as suggested by Bonache et al. (2012), that the level of performance orientation in each country's own culture moderates the extent to which pay-for-performance is more or less effective.

Finally, it is worth noting that in addition to financial rewards, other benefits, such as those associated with healthcare, children's scholarships, mortgage credits, or membership of recreational clubs for employees and their families, are extremely relevant in LATAM (Elvira & Davila, 2005). The importance of community and family values in these societies makes employees especially appreciative of these symbolic rewards of an employer's gratitude (Gomez & Sanchez, 2005). Foreign MNCs also understand this, and adapt their reward systems to better address their employees' needs (Rodriguez & Rios, 2007), even if they still try to link such rewards to better performance levels.

Towards a Research Agenda for Latin American Talent Management

Our review of selected HR literature identifying practices and policies related to TM has helped us identify some of the opportunities and challenges associated with their adoption. While there are a variety of topics and issues that may well deserve further attention, we select four key areas that we believe are crucial for practitioners and academics alike when addressing TM in Latin America.

The Role of Cultural Barriers

Our review of LATAM HRM-related studies on different TM areas calls for the need to take the local context into consideration when adopting these systems, but it also shows that some local practices are contradictory, with basic TM tenets such as workforce differentiation and meritocracy. Hence, suggesting that TM systems should adapt to the local culture seems only partially appropriate when seen through the lenses of LATAM HRM research.

Our review has shown that some local adaptations of TM policies are advisable, while others are clearly counterproductive. It is simply untrue that more cultural adaptation leads to more TM efficiency. There are adjustments to imported "best practices" that seem to make sense and improve their effectiveness. For example, in the area of talent development, research singles out innovative ways in which LATAM firms may overcome local constraints to provide their employees with the best possible training.

In other domains, however, such adaptation seems to hinder rather than enhance firms' ability to attract, develop, and retain talent. For example, in the area of performance management, there is some evidence pointing to the use of biased proxies for assessing performance, such as perceived similarity, educational background, or employee loyalty to the supervisor. Additionally, even when TM policies seem to contradict core aspects of LATAM culture, such as power distance or risk avoidance, they can still be effectively implemented if other factors (e.g., use of pilot projects, management commitment, and training) are considered.

Future research should perhaps be more focused and specifically analyze the central and peripheral aspects of TM systems and the extent to which local adaptations remain faithful to core principles. What adaptations seem to work better? Which practices departing from "the local way of doing things" seem to be working particularly well? How do MNCs differ from local companies in TM? If there are differences, which ones obtain better results? What are the ones preferred by employees? Are MNCs really less discriminatory? In sum, how can TM programs be adapted to the LATAM context without losing their strategic intent?

Talent Development

Talent development in LATAM may be the one area that should receive more attention in the short term, not only at the organizational level, but also at the national level. Talent development is key because it also positively impacts on talent attraction and retention. First, high-potential jobseekers are more attracted to organizations with a reputation for investing in their careers (Ready et al., 2008). Second, talent development also increases retention to the extent that such investments are linked to well-established career paths. Research shows that talent initiatives are likely to increase organizations' internal social capital and organizational commitment (Gomez & Sanchez, 2005; Sully de Luque & Arbazia, 2005). Given the low salaries and scant possibilities for job mobility in developing countries, training often leads to career advancement (Drost, Frayne, Lowe, & Geringer, 2002), being perceived as a reward, and not only as a tool for developing work-related skills. As a result, employees are more likely to value the firm's investment in them, and reciprocate with higher levels of loyalty.

There are several signs of the need for more research on innovative ways to develop talent in the region. While LATAM overall has a huge working age population (Salazar-Xirinachs, 2016), approximately two out of every five young people are unemployed and/or not in education (Melguizo & Pages-Serra, 2017). About half of those who do work do so in the informal economy (Herranz Acebuche, 2017). The 2018 edition of the Global Talent Competitiveness Index (INSEAD, 2018) shows that LATAM has an overall skills shortage that is particularly acute in vocational and technical skills. According to Herranz Acebuche (2017), this is because many young people do not finish their education (only one out of three Latin Americans aged 25–29 have college or higher technical school education), and there is a disconnection between the training offered in technical schools and the needs of the companies hiring their graduates.

While there are no readymade solutions, organizations need to invest in the upskilling of their staff and provide young people with work-based opportunities (Adecco, 2017). One particularly promising avenue for further exploration is the use of apprenticeships (Herranz Acebuche, 2017; Melguizo & Pages-Serra, 2017). There is a pressing need for more research on companies' best practices in this area, and how such programs may be adopted in LATAM countries, given their particular institutional contexts (Friel, 2011).

Leadership Development

One particular area within talent development that requires particular attention involves senior management, both in local firms and in foreign firms operating in the region. The topic of leadership development is a constant in the research on global TM, as firms continue to struggle to find individuals with the right skills to operate in multi-cultural environments (Vaiman, Scullion, & Collings, 2012). In the case of LATAM, Behrens (2010) contends that the leadership styles of foreign-appointed heads of subsidiaries tend to be inadequate, arguing that these leaders are often perceived as "technocrats" that stifle creativity and lack the charisma that Latin American employees expect of senior managers. Behrens also argues that successful leaders in LATAM necessarily need to be associated with these societies' paternalistic values, hence projecting an image of calm and protection, which shows employees that they are valued beyond the narrow confines of a commercial or purely exchange-based relationship. Similarly, Davila and Elvira (2012) advocate a new type of leadership in LATAM, which they label as "humanistic". According to these authors, a humanistic orientation emphasizes leaders' relational and community-oriented traits, in contrast to economistic views that emphasize transactional aspects, such as goal-setting and accountability.

There is a need for more research that tests some of the assumptions in these studies. As shown when reviewing the HRM literature, managers' paternalistic values are not without risks, as they may counteract such practices as performance feedback (Davila & Elvira, 2007) or work delegation (Perez Arrau et al., 2012), which are crucial for talent development. Paternalistic leadership styles can also contribute to a lack of workforce differentiation in rewards, hence damaging workforce retention. Thus, while it seems wrong to ignore the paternalistic nature of LATAM societies, more research is needed on how to develop leaders capable of adopting TM initiatives in ways that are locally effective.

Female Managers

One area that also deserves further attention is the inclusion of women in the labor market, and more specifically, in leadership positions. While women's participation in the labor market has already risen to 53% in LATAM, it is still significantly below the average of 65% for OECD countries (Bosch, 2017).

Similarly, while the lack of female corporate leadership is a worldwide phenomenon, it is more acute in LATAM countries (Flabbi et al., 2017). For example, the number of women in middle management in Mexico is barely 23%, in Chile it is 24%, and in Peru 29% (Davidson & Burke, 2017). These figures drop to 13–14% when taking into account top management positions in Mexico or Peru, and to 8% in Chile. It is estimated that 433 of the top 500 LATAM companies had no women executives in top management positions (Flabbi et al., 2017; Zabludovsky, 2017), although the figures available date back to 2012. Not only that, but as pointed out by Zabludovsky (2017), segregation is also horizontal, as women managers seem to be overwhelmingly concentrated in a restricted number of fields, such as marketing, communication, and HRM. "Machismo" and in-group collectivism may limit women's advancement prospects in LATAM firms (Newburry et al., 2014).

While social role theory (Eagly, Wood, & Diekman, 2000) may partly explain these differences on the basis of different socialization processes between men and women in these countries, the fact is that corporate cultures also play a significant role. In particular, foreign companies seem to have taken the lead in LATAM on this issue, and the presence of women in management positions in foreign-owned firms in LATAM is significantly higher than in locally owned ones (Zabludovsky, 2017). This may be the reason Latin American women tend to be more attracted to foreign or more international firms (Newburry et al., 2014).

In sum, the data seem to point to a shortage of women in management positions in LATAM. More research is needed on this particular employee group, and on how TM initiatives can address the causes of this problem, both in foreign companies operating in the region and, maybe more importantly, in local ones.

Conclusion

Our review of the LATAM HRM literature in connection with the different TM areas has shown that several LATAM firms are already adopting policies and practices that are consistent with the underlying tenets of TM systems, such as workplace differentiation and meritocracy. It has also shown that the adoption of some of these practices may be difficult due to cultural barriers, and that hybrid solutions combining aspects of both local and foreign practices may sometimes be a good solution (Davila & Elvira, 2005). Finally, we have provided our own view of crucial areas deserving further research because of their practical relevance for LATAM firms. As our knowledge of TM in Latin America is very limited, more research is needed on almost all fronts. We trust this chapter both helps and encourages those interested in pursuing research in this area, as well as those practitioners adopting TM initiatives in their own firms.

References

Abreu, Y. I. F., Menergon, L. F., & Miyazaki, M. O. 2003. *Comprometimento e seu uso como instrumento de controle e retenção de talentos: Uma leitura crítica.* Paper presented at the annual meeting of ANPAD.

Aguilera, R. V., Ciravegna, L., Cuervo-Cazurra, A., & Gonzalez-Perez, M. A. 2017. Multilatinas and the internationalization of Latin American firms. *Journal of World Business,* 52(4): 447–460.

Aguinis, H., Villamor, I., Lazzarini, S. G., Vassolo, R. S., Amorós, J. E., & Allen, D. G. 2020. Conducting management research in Latin America: Why and what's in it for you? *Journal of Management,* 46(5): 615–636.

Andonova, V., & Zuleta, H. 2007. The effect of enforcement on human resources practices: A case study in rural Colombia. *International Journal of Manpower,* 28: 344–353.

Aycan, Z. 2005. The interplay between cultural and institutional/structural contingencies in human resource management. *International Journal of Human Resource Management,* 16: 1083–120.

Beamond, M. T., Farndale, E., & Härtel, C. E. 2016. MNE translation of corporate talent management strategies to subsidiaries in emerging economies. *Journal of World Business,* 51: 499–510.

Beamond, M. T., Farndale, E., & Härtel, C. E. 2020. Frames and actors: Translating talent management strategy to Latin America. *Management and Organization Review,* 16(2): 405–442.

Behrens, A. 2010. Charisma, paternalism, and business leadership in Latin America. *Thunderbird International Business Review,* 52 (1): 21–29.

Bonache, J., Trullen, J., & Sanchez, J. I. 2012. Managing cross-cultural differences: Testing human resource models in Latin America. *Journal of Business Research,* 65: 1773–1781.

Bosch, M. J. 2017. Women in management in Chile. In M. J. Davidson & R. J. Burke (Eds.), *Women in management worldwide: Signs of progress* (3rd ed.): 249–267. New York: Routledge.

Collings, D., & Mellahi, K. 2009. Strategic talent management: A review and research agenda. *Human Resource Management Review,* 19: 304–313.

Cristiani, A., & Peiró, J. 2019. Calculative and collaborative HRM practices, turnover and performance. *International Journal of Manpower,* 40: 616–642.

Davidson, M. J., & Burke, R. J. (Eds.) (3rd ed.) 2017. *Women in management worldwide: Signs of progress.* New York: Routledge.

Davila, A., & Elvira, M. (Eds.) 2008. *Best human resource management practices in Latin America.* New York: Routledge.

Davila, A., & Elvira, M. 2012. Humanistic leadership: Lessons from Latin America. *Journal of World Business,* 47: 548–554.

Davila, A., Elvira, M. 2015. Human resource management in a kinship society: The case of Latin America. In F. Horwitz, & P. Budhwar (Eds.), *Handbook of human resource management in emerging markets:* 372–392. UK: Edward Elgar Publishing.

Davila, A., & Elvira, M. 2018. Revisiting the Latin American HRM model. In C. Brewster, W. Mayrhofer, & E. Farndale (Eds.), *Handbook of research in comparative human resource management* (2nd ed.). Cheltenham: Edward Elgar Publishing.

DeVoe, S. E., & Iyengar, S. S. 2004. Managers' theories of subordinates: A cross-cultural examination of manager perceptions of motivation and appraisal of performance. *Organizational Behavior and Human Decision Processes,* 93: 47–61.

Diaz-Saenz, H. R., & Witherspoon, P. D. 2000. Psychological contracts in Mexico: Historical, familial, and contemporary influences on work relationships. In D. M. Rousseau, & R. Schalk (Eds.), *Psychological contracts in employment: Cross-national perspectives:* 158–175. Thousand Oaks, CA: Sage.

Drost, E. A., Frayne, C.A., Lowe, K. B., & Geringer, J. M. 2002. Benchmarking training and development practices: A multi-country comparative analysis. *Human Resource Management,* 41: 67–86.

Eagly, A. H., Wood, W., & Diekman, A. H. 2000. Social role theory of sex differences and similarities: A current appraisal. In T. Eckes & H. M. Trautner (Eds.), *The developmental social psychology of gender:* 123–174. Mahwah, NJ: Erlbaum.

Economist Intelligence Unit. 2006. *The CEO's role in talent management: How top executives from ten countries are nurturing the leaders of tomorrow.* London: The Economist.

Encyclopaedia Britannica. 2017. *List of countries in Latin America.* https://www.britannica.com/topic/list-of-countries-in-Latin-America-2061416, first accessed September 2017.

Elvira, M., & Davila, A. (Eds.). 2005. *Managing human resources in Latin America: An agenda for international leaders.* New York: Routledge.

Exame. 2013. *Como ganhar a guerra pelos talentos.* http://www.bv.fapesp.br/namidia/noticia/85480/ganhar-guerra-talentos/, first accessed May 2017.

Ferrazza, D. S., Burtet, C. G., & Scheffer, A. B. B. 2015. O que as organizações entendem por gestão de talentos? *Revista Eletrônica de Administração,* 801: 222–247.

Flabbi, L., Piras, C., & Abrahams, S. 2017. Female corporate leadership in Latin America and the Caribbean region: Representation and firm-level outcomes. *International Journal of Manpower,* 38 (6): 790–818.

Freitag, B. B., & Fischer, A. L. 2013. Talentos em gestão e gestão de talentos: Análise da literatura acadêmica e de práticas corporativas. *Seminarios em Administração,* 8: 1–15.

Freitag, B. B., Ohtsuki, C. H., Ferreira, M. A. M., Fischer, A. L., & Almeida, K. N. T. 2014. A gestão de talentos no campo da gestão de pessoas: tema emergente? *Revista de Administração da UFSM,* 7(4): 629–643.

Friel, D. 2011. Forging a comparative institutional advantage in Argentina: Implications for theory and praxis. *Human Relations,* 64: 553–572.

Gallardo-Gallardo, E., Nijs, S., Dries, N., & Gallo, P. 2015. Towards an understanding of talent management as a phenomenon-driven field using bibliometric and content analysis. *Human Resource Management Review,* 25: 264–279.

Gallardo-Gallardo, E., Thunnissen, M., & Scullion, H. (2017): Special issue of *International Journal of Human Resource Management.* A contextualized approach to talent management: Advancing the field. *International Journal of Human Resource Management,* doi: 10.1080/09585192.2016.1275292.

Gallardo-Gallardo, E., Thunnissen, M., & Scullion, H. (2020). Talent management: Context matters. *The International Journal of Human Resource Management,* 31(4), 457–473.

Geary, J., & Aguzzoli, R.J. 2016. Miners, politics and institutional caryatids: Accounting for the transfer of HRM practices in the Brazilian multinational enterprise. *Journal of International Business Studies,* 47: 968–996.

Gomez, C. 2004. The influence of environmental, organizational, and HRM factors on employee behaviors in subsidiaries: A Mexican case study of organizational learning. *Journal of World Business,* 39: 1–11.

Gomez, C., & Sanchez, J. 2005. HR's strategic role within MNCs: Helping build social capital in Latin America. *International Journal of Human Resource Management,* 16: 2189–2200.

Greer, C.R., & Stephens, G. K. 1998. Employee relations issues for U.S. companies in Mexico. *California Management Review,* 38: 121–146.

Hartmann, A.M., & Davila, A. R. 2014. Ideologies and practices of management in Latin America. In B. Christiansen (Ed.), *Handbook of research on economic growth and technological change in Latin America:* 20–46. Hershey, PA: IGI Global.

Hermans, M., Newburry, W., Alvarado-Vargas, M.J., Baldo, C. M., Borda, A., Durán-Zurita, E. G., & Olivas-Lujan, M. R. (2017), Attitudes towards women's career advancement in Latin America: The moderating impact of perceived company international proactiveness. *Journal of International Business Studies,* 48(1): 90–112.

Herranz Acebuche, D. 2017. *Latin Americas has the world's biggest skills gap. Apprenticeships could close it.* World Economic Forum. https://www.weforum.org/agenda/2017/03/latin-america-has-the-world-s-biggest-skills-gap-apprenticeships-could-close-it/.

Hill, A. 2016. Changing face of advisers' war for talent. *Financial Times.* https://www.ft.com/content/dbd794f6-990d-11e6-8f9b-70e3cabccfae, first accessed September 2017.

Huo, Y., Huang, H., & Napier, N. K. 2002. Divergence or convergence: A cross national comparison of personnel selection practices. *Human Resource Management,* 41: 31–44.

Husted, B. W., & de Sousa-Filho, J. M. 2019. Board structure and environmental, social, and governance disclosure in Latin America. *Journal of Business Research,* 102: 220–227.

Inglehart, R., & Carballo, M. 1997. Does Latin America exist? (And is there a Confucian culture?): A global analysis of cross-cultural differences. *Political Science & Politics,* 30: 34–46.

INSEAD. 2018. *The Global Talent Competitiveness Index 2018.* Fontainebleau, France.

Israel, E. (2012). Now hiring: Brazil wants more professionals. *Reuters.* Available at https://www.reuters.com/article/uk-brazil-immigration/now-hiring-brazil-wants-more-foreign-professionals-idUSLNE87N02920120824, first accessed December 17, 2018.

Javidan, M., Dorfman, P., Sully de Luque, M., & House, R. J. 2006. In the eye of the beholder: Cross cultural lessons in leadership from project GLOBE. *Academy of Management Perspectives,* 20: 67–90.

King, K. A., & Vaiman, Vlad. 2019. Enabling effective talent management through a macro-contingent approach: A framework for research and practice. *Business Research Quarterly,* 22: 194–206.

Lenartowicz, T., & Johnson, J.P. 2003. A cross-national assessment of the values of Latin America managers: Contrasting hues or shades of gray. *Journal of International Business Studies,* 34: 266–284.

Lowe, K., Milliman, J., De Cieri, H., & Dowling, P. 2002. International compensation practices: A ten country comparative analysis. *Human Resource Management,* 41: 45–66.

ManpowerGroup. 2015. *2015 Talent shortage survey.* http://www.manpowergroup.com/wps/wcm/connect/db23c560-08b6-485f-9bf6-f5f38a43c76a/2015_Talent_Shortage_Survey_US-lo_res.pdf?MOD=AJPERES, first accessed September 2017.

Melguizo, A., & Pages-Serra, C. 2017. *In Latin America, companies still can't find the skilled workers they need.* World Economic Forum. https://www.weforum.org/agenda/2017/03/in-latin-america-companies-still-can-t-find-the-skilled-workers-they-need/, first accessed September 2017.

Mellahi, K., Frynas, J. G., & Collings, D. G. 2016. Performance management practices within emerging market multinational enterprises: The case of Brazilian multinationals. *International Journal of Human Resource Management,* 27: 876–905.

Mercer. 2017. *Mercer global talent trends study 2017.* https://www.mercer.com/content/dam/mercer/attachments/global/Talent/talent-trends/gl-2017-mercer-global-talent-trends-infographic-latam.pdf, first accessed September 2017.

Miller, J. S., Hom, P. W., & Gomez-Mejia, L. R. 2001. The high cost of low wages: Does maquiladora compensation reduce turnover? *Journal of International Business Studies,* 32: 585–595.

Mingo, S., Junkunc, M., & Morales, F. 2018. The interplay between home and host country institutions in an emerging market context: Private equity in Latin America. *Journal of World Business,* 53: 653–667.

Nakata, L. E., Gomes da Silva, M. T., Freitag, B. B., & Ferrari Cálcena, E. J. 2011. Cultura como alma do negócio: o caso da Promon. *Revista de Carreiras e Pessoas (ReCaPe),* 1(1): 63–89.

Newburry, W., Gardberg, N. A., & Sanchez, J. I. 2014. Employer attractiveness in Latin America: The association among foreignness, internationalization and talent recruitment. *Journal of International Management,* 20: 327–344.

Nicholls-Nixon, C. L., Davila Castilla, J., Sanchez Garcia, J., & Rivera Pesquera, M. 2011. Latin America management research: Review, synthesis, and extension. *Journal of Management,* 37: 1178–1227.

Osland, A., Osland, J. S. 2005. Contextualization and strategic international human resource management approaches: The case of Central America and Panama. *International Journal of Human Resource Management,* 16: 2218–2236.

Parnell, J.A. 2010. Propensity for participative decision making in Latin America: Mexico and Peru. *International Journal of Human Resource Management,* 21: 2323–2338.

Perez Arrau, G., Eades, E., & Wilson, J. 2012. Managing human resources in the Latin American context: The case of Chile. *International Journal of Human Resource Management,* 23: 3133–3150.

Piedras, A. 2015. *La nueva guerra por el talento: hora de cambiar.* Mexico: KPMG.

Ready, D. A., Hill, L. A., & Conger, J. A. 2008. Willing the race for talent in emerging markets. *Harvard Business Review,* December: 1–10.

Rego, A., Vitória, A., Tupinambá, A., Júnior, D., Reis, D., Cunha, M., & Lourenço-Gil, R. 2018. Brazilian managers' ageism: A multiplex perspective. *International Journal of Manpower,* 39: 414–433.

Rodriguez, D., & Rios, R. 2007. Latent premises of labor contracts: paternalism and productivity. *International Journal of Manpower,* 28 (5): 354–368.

Rodriguez, D., & Rios, R. 2009. Paternalism at a crossroads: Labour relations in Chile in transition. *Employee Relations,* 31(3): 322–333.

Rodriguez, J. K. 2010. Employment relations in Chile: Evidence of HRM practices. *Relations Industrielles/ Industrial Relations,* 65: 424–446.

Rodriguez, J. K., & Stewart, P. 2017. HRM and work practices in Chile: The regulatory power of organisational culture. *Employee Relations,* 39: 378–390.

Salazar-Xirinachs, J. M. 2016. The future of work, employment and skills in Latin America and the Caribbean. *Pensamiento Iberoamericano,* 2/3a época.

Santiso, J. (2007). *Latin America's political economy of the possible: Beyond good revolutionaries and free-marketeers.* Cambridge, MA: MIT Press.

Senén, C., Gomis, R., & Medwid, B. 2018. Human resource management and sector analysis in emerging countries: A comparative study of automotive subsidiaries operating in Latin America. *E-Journal of International and Comparative Labour Studies,* 7 (3): 73–94.

Sidani, Y., & Al Ariss, A. 2014. Institutional and corporate drivers of global talent management: Evidence from the Arab Gulf region. *Journal of World Business,* 49: 215–224.

Sparkman, T. E. 2015. The factors and conditions for national human resource development in Brazil. *European Journal of Training and Development,* 39: 666–680.

Sposato, M. 2019. Understanding paternalistic leadership: A guide for managers considering foreign assignments. *Strategy & Leadership,* 47(5): 47–52.

Stobbe, L. 2005. Doing machismo: Legitimating speech acts as a selection discourse. *Gender, Work & Organization,* 12: 105–123.

Sully de Luque, M. F., & Arbazia, L.A. 2005. The complexity of managing human resources in Peru. *International Journal of Human Resource Management,* 16: 2237–2253.

Sun, S.L., Peng, M. W., Lee, R. P., & Tan, W. 2015. Institutional open access at home and outward internationalization. *Journal of World Business,* 50: 234–246.

Thomas, D. 2015. *The moderating effects of power distance and collectivism on empowering leadership and psychological empowerment and self-leadership in international development organizations.* Unpublished doctoral dissertation, Regent University, Virginia.

Towers Watson. 2015. *Towers Watson talent management and rewards pulse survey.* https://www.towerswatson.com/en/Insights/IC-Types/Ad-hoc-Point-of-View/2015/07/employee-surveys-insights-2015, first accessed September 2017.

UNCTAD. 2018. *World investment report.* United Nations Conference on Trade and Development, Geneva, Switzerland.

Vaiman, V., Scullion, H., & Collings, D. 2012. Talent management decision making. *Management Decision,* 50(5): 925–941.

Vassolo, R. S., De Castro, J. O., & Gomez-Mejia, L. R. 2011. Managing in Latin America: Common issues and a research agenda. *Academy of Management Perspectives,* 25: 22–36.

Von Glinow, M. A., Drost, E. A., & Teagarden, M. B. 2002. Converging on IHRM best practices: Lessons learned from a globally distributed consortium on theory and practice. *Human Resource Management,* 41: 23–140.

Walker, E. C., & Ferreira, M. A. A. 2012. Contribuições dos motivadores de rh na gestão e retenção de talentos: um estudo sobre jovens engenheiros na alcoa. *Revista de Carreiras e Pessoas (ReCaPe),* 2(1): 40–71.

World Bank (2018a). *Data center.* https://data.worldbank.org/region/latin-america-and-caribbean, first acessed December 17, 2018.

World Bank (2018b). *Latin American and Caribbean overview.* http://www.worldbank.org/en/region/lac/overview, first accessed December 17, 2018.

Zabludovsky, G. 2017. Women in management in Mexico. In M. J. Davidson & R. J. Burke (Eds.), *Women in management worldwide: Signs of progress* (3rd ed.): 141–155. New York: Routledge.

14

TALENT MANAGEMENT IN EUROPEAN ORGANIZATIONS

Agnieszka Skuza

Hugh Scullion

Introduction

Over the last two decades, there has been a substantial growth in the number of practitioner reports stating that talent management (TM) has emerged as the top priority and that it will remain a key challenge companies will face in the near future (CIPD, 2017; Ernst & Young, 2018; Human Capital Institute, 2019; Manpower Group, 2018; PricewaterhouseCoopers, 2019). TM's growing significance is based on the assumption that TM is a key source of competitive advantage and that for organizations to succeed, they need talented employees who are in abundance. The imperative of the "war for talent" that dominates the TM rhetoric is based on the premise that tightening labor market conditions make attracting and retaining talented employees more and more difficult. The supply concerns come from the changing nature of demographics characterized by an ageing workforce and declining birth rates. This couples with the rapid process of globalization and increasing internationalization (competition for talent has shifted from the country level to regional and global levels) and also with the growth of knowledge-based economies, which results in the rising need to hire high value workers in more complex roles.

In spite of the importance of TM for organizational practice, academic contributions to the literature on talent management were until recently quite limited. In their recent TM literature review, McDonnell et al. (2017) shows that the majority of academic publications on talent management were published after 2008 with a more steady growth trajectory noted after 2010.

Until 2010, the advances in the field of TM were also mainly based on the practitioner U.S.-based view, with North American thinking and research dominating the TM debates. However, the growing interest in the topic and the need to depart from the U.S. narrative have led many researchers to study TM in other domains. McDonnell et al.'s (2017) review shows that European-based research highly dominates current empirical efforts in this field. In this chapter, we introduce the European context of talent management, and we consider some evidence of the nature of talent management in European organizations.

The European Context of Talent Management

The context in which talent management takes place in Europe differs significantly from that of the U.S.A. (Brewster, 2004; Collings, Scullion, & Vaiman, 2011). For example, research (Bayireddi, 2019; Meyers, Woerkom, & Dries, 2019; Paauwe, 2004; Sparrow & Hiltrop, 1997; Thurley & Wirdenius, 1991) has demonstrated that within Europe, some characteristics of TM and HRM generally are quite

DOI: 10.4324/9781315474687-14

distinct from U.S. patterns. The differences include organization structure and management control systems and processes, with European companies putting stronger emphasis on socialization and American firms concentrating more on formalization and centralization (Brewster, 2007; Haddock-Millar, Sanyal, & Muller-Camen, 2016; Scullion & Brewster, 2001).

European companies have a longer history of moving people across the boarders due to the small size of their local markets, which helped them to observe the impact of cultural and societal diversity on organizational behavior. This contributed to a much larger degree of autonomy that is typical in European overseas subsidiaries. It also resulted in more successful oversight of their managers. There is evidence that European expatriate "failure rates" are much lower than North Americans', and Europeans are better prepared for their expatriate talent roles.

More recently, EU integration has added much more dynamic talent movement across borders. Substantial legal and administrative regulations within the EU helps to freely move talent across Europe, which substantially increases experience in how the interchange between specific social and institutional contexts of each country influences organizational and individual (managerial) effectiveness and performance. Such experiences are then translated into management models. The National Research Mentoring Network (NRMN) research report (2015) shows that values and culture fit are among the three most important determinants of high potential and that they are much more important in European high-potential models than in those of North American companies.

Nikandrou et al. (2006) stress the importance of the contextual paradigm in Europe, in contrast to the American universalist approach. The contextual paradigm emphasizes the need to focus on understanding and explaining differences in HRM systems in different contexts (cultural values, norms, societal structure, language, etc.). The universalist approach to HRM has often been criticized by European researches for its narrowness of perspectives and objectives, and a vast majority of European research calls for applying the contextual approach to analyzing TM in Europe. Such an approach seems obvious since the European model of HRM is located in different contexts in which both cultural and institutional regulations of each European country differently influence the corporate strategy and approach to HRM. Unlike in the U.S.A., HRM in Europe is highly dependent on legislation in the employment area, which is quite unique worldwide. High state involvement includes, for example, regulations with regard to recruitment, dismissal, and pay policies; government involvement in training and development (e.g., through state subsidy); or the influential power of trade unions. One of the consequences of such an approach is that multiple stakeholders are involved in HRM issues (Brewster, 2007), and this is often apparent in European publications on HRM, and recently also in European research on TM.

Applying cultural or institutional perspectives to analyze differences between HRM in different European countries is common in TM research in Europe. The cultural approach sees the cultural distinctiveness of each country or region and analyzes the influence of the workplace values on organizational or individual behaviors and assumptions that determine TM logic (see for example Skuza, Scullion, & McDonnell, 2013; Valverde et al., 2013). The institutional approach sees institutions of a country influencing social arrangements in that country. This may concern general or vocational education, the legal system, or industrial relations systems and their influence on TM (see for example Bousseba & Morgan, 2008; Dries & Pepermans, 2008; Festing et al., 2013). As such, the majority of European TM research focuses on career management issues (see for example DeVos & Dries, 2013; Stahl & Cerdin, 2004; Tansley & Tietze, 2013), which is driven by various government and labor regulations that obligate companies to put in place career and training plans for every employee (Bersin, 2010).

It may also influence a more advanced and systematic approach to TM and career management noted in European organizations when compared to U.S. firms. U.S. companies use the more "pinball" approach to TM (hiring people and moving them around to different jobs) and are more interested in addressing underperformance by replacing staff than by fostering staff development, which is common within Europe (more in Bersin, 2010; Hillmann, 2014). As a result, European employees tend to stay longer in the same company and talent identification from within is a much more used option than talent acquisition, attracting particular attention of researchers and practitioners to career development issues.

European research on TM also goes beyond the focus on big multinational enterprises (MNEs), which traditionally was a central focus of U.S. TM empirical works. A growing number of authors are giving consideration to the small and medium-sized enterprise (SME) sector (Festing et al., 2013; Valverde et al., 2013). The European context closely tied with the idea of European integration (Collings et al., 2011) points to the national and supranational arrangements with this regard. The active support of the national and European institutions (with regard to legislative and financial assistance) helped SMEs to internationalize across Europe and increased substantially the need to challenge the current assumptions on TM strongly embedded in the context of MNEs. Giving the magnitude of this emerging field of research, in this chapter, we will discuss in detail the empirical achievements of European authors, and we claim that building a comparative understanding of TM practices among SMEs will provide an important contribution in developing our knowledge on TM. We will now turn to the analysis of the key research themes among European contributors.

Key Research Themes in Europe

Reviewing European research, we distinguish among a few dominant themes of research. First, we observed substantial focus on the effect that TM might have on individuals. In contrast to the short-term shareholder approach that dominates U.S. studies (focused on improving organizational performance), European research investigates the perspective of various stakeholders and their reactions to TM practices, providing a more pluralist understanding of TM. Second, authors analyze talent career development issues testing and challenging some assumptions of the career management literature (especially with regard to boundaryless career concept). In addition, some of them study career management in the context of TM from the macro-level perspective, and therefore, we also present an example of such studies. Third, contributors examine the challenges that organizations face in Europe in various institutional and cultural contexts. Fourth, they increasingly investigate TM in other organizational settings, focusing their empirical works on the so far highly neglected context of SMEs. This last research theme will be presented in the next section.

Effect of Talent Management on Individuals

The first important theme in recent European studies concerns the influence of TM on individuals. Authors examine whether the talent status may have positive or negative consequences for attitudinal effects and performance outcomes of various organizational stakeholders. The majority of empirical works draw on social exchange theory with the focus on the psychological contract perspective, which suggests that when corporations invest in their employees, the employees are likely to reciprocate in a positive way.

For example, in the study of 17 Finnish, Swedish, and Norwegian multinationals, followed by a study among 126 respondents from various organizations in Finland, Hoglund (2012) examined both the direct and indirect effects of HRM practices on human capital from a talent management perspective, adding talent inducement as a mediating variable. He applied the psychological contract perspective to assess employee perceptions on the extent to which organizations induce talent (mainly with regard to career and promotion opportunities) and the effect of such perceptions on the obligation to develop skills. The results of Hoglund's study confirmed that "differential treatment of employees based on criteria constituting talent can have positive effects on employee motivation and felt obligations to develop skills and apply these in service of the organization" (Hoglund, 2012, 136). While the direct effect of skill-enhancing HRM practices on human capital turned out to be insignificant, the total indirect effect of skill-enhancing HRM practices on human capital through talent inducements turned out to be significant, which shows the positive consequences that TM may have on employees' attitudes and psychological contract obligations.

The psychological contract perspective on TM was also adopted by Bjorkman et al. (2013). Building on the social-exchange perspective, the authors argue that inclusion in the talent pool is perceived as an indication of employer commitment toward the individual and an important signal that the employer fulfills its contract obligations. The study based on 11 Nordic MNEs prove that individuals who know their talent status reciprocate through positive attitudes and behaviors (e.g., commitment to building competencies, commitment to increasing performance demands, identification with the unit), actively support of the organizational strategic priorities, and are less likely to have turnover intentions (Bjorkman et al., 2013). Their findings show significant differences between those who know they have been identified as "talent", those who have not, and those who don't know. Bjorkman et al. (2013) conclude that informing talented individuals of their status has a motivational effect that is consistent with the predictions of social exchange theory and that such results confirm the logic of TM. At the same time, they prove that informing individuals that they are not talents has little negative effect and that the reaction of those employees to their talent status might be mediated by the transparency and fairness of the identification process.

Similar results were achieved by Swailes and Blackburn (2016) in their qualitative study conducted in Northern Europe (they do not indicate the exact country). Swailes and Blackburn examined the attitudes of employees in talent pools and those not in talent pools, confirming that inclusion in the talent pool is a signal that the organization values talents' contribution and that it fulfills the psychological contract by investing in the talents' future careers. However, contrary to Bjorkman et al. (2013), Swailes and Blackburn (2016) noticed that those not included in the talent pool expressed less support from their line managers, more concerns that access to pools was unfair, less positive feelings about their development opportunities, and lower motivation towards career development. Moreover, the researchers point out the risk of possible talent disenchantment if talent programs do not live-up to expectations. They even suggest that possible threats in elite talent programs may be less than that of a disaffected majority of employees not included, and more than that of a disenchanted critical minority (high-potentials and/or high-performers) whose expectations are unsatisfied (during or after the program). These might have disproportionate negative outcomes for the organization.

The dynamics between TM and individuals was also studied by Sonnenberg et al. (2014) in their study of 21 European MNCs. Drawing on the psychological contract perspective, the authors examined the effect of perceived TM practices, talent-differentiation strategies, and incongruent talent perceptions on psychological-contract fulfillment. Sonnenberg et al. emphasize that TM practices will not automatically profit from the increased psychological contract fulfillment unless they ensure that those practices are perceived appropriately and utilized by the targeted employees. Achieving this will substantially increase the signalling value of TM. The authors point out that greater attention to TM leads to better understanding of who is viewed as talent by the organization, leading to a higher perception that the organization fulfills its promises. Lack of clear communication leaves space for misinterpretations of who is perceived as talent, which in turn leads to false expectations and a number of undesired consequences, such as higher turnover intentions and lower motivation. An important observation of the research was that in the studied companies, exclusive talent differentiation strategies were dominant in spite of the common declaration of the use of inclusive approaches. The authors also found that an exclusive approach is much more effective in minimizing talent-perception incongruence (more practices are perceived as intended), which in turn leads to higher effectiveness of talent management efforts (Sonnenberg et al., 2014).

The dominance of the exclusive approach to Sonnenberg et al. (2014) is also proved in McDonnell et al. (2010), which highlights the importance of a non-managerial group of TM stakeholders. Based on 260 MNCs operating in Ireland, the authors investigated whether MNCs identify talent pools other than the management group. While in empirical works, considerable focus has been placed on managers and leaders as indicative of "talent", much less is known on the identification and management of talent beyond mangers or leaders. McDonnell et al. point out that while managers as enablers of organizational strategies are more likely to have a strategic contribution, other employees can have a substantial impact on competitive advantage through technical, product, process, and/or customer knowledge (see Thompson & Heron, 2005). McDonnell et al. (2010) confirmed that MNCs indeed identify a key group of non-managerial employees based on the knowledge and skills critical to the achievement of the organization's competitive strategy. They also found that MNCs introduce differentiated HR practices for the different employee categories, and that non-talent employees were much less likely to be offered financial participation schemes, variable pay schemes, and a policy of paying in the top or second quartile. As such, the study highlights that not all employees possess the knowledge and skills that are strategically important, which supports an exclusive approach to TM. McDonnell et al. (2010) also inform the future research of the need to include more stakeholders (other than managers) in the TM analysis and to explore the impact of differentiated approaches on productivity and performance of those employees.

Career Development Issues

The second stream of research on TM in Europe focuses on career management issues. De Vos and Dries (2013) investigated how organizations' human capital composition (in terms of both uniqueness and strategic value) affects the way they design and implement their career management policies. Their findings based on 306 companies located in Belgium confirmed that human capital composition (measured by a relative number of high value, high-uniqueness employees) predicts the degree to which organizations attach importance to continuity as a career management goal. This confirms that human capital composition influence the organization's approach to career management (the preference for intra-organizational "bounded" careers). Organizations with a high-value and high-uniqueness workforce focus more than those with low-value and low-uniqueness employees on individual outcomes and accountability. They also provide more opportunities for intra-organizational mobility and a higher number of formalized career management practices (De Vos & Dries, 2013). The authors challenge the assumption that the organizational career is dead and that it is dominated by self-directedness and personal agency. They point to the need to acknowledge that career management is still an organizational concern of a strategic value and that its importance will increase especially with the growth of the "war for talents" dynamics. De Vos and Dries (2013) conclude that there is a need for more empirical research on contemporary careers in light of the human capital trends described in the TM literature (which advocates a renewed attention for continuity) and that findings should be cross validated in different cultural and labor market characteristics, which might highly influence career management approaches.

The boundaryless career concept was also challenged by Dries and Pepermans's (2008) qualitative study of high-potentials and HR managers or consultants involved in high-potential management in Belgium. The authors found that such a career model is out of kilter in the expectations of high-potentials, who continue to expect more traditional career options demonstrated in high upward mobility and low inter-organizational mobility. The study advances our understanding of how workforce segmentation might affect organizational career structures – from the boundaryless orientation of non-core employees whose employability is key to progress with inter-organizational career paths, to non-boundaryless career opportunities for high-potentials and experts (who are difficult to replace and possess organization-specific professional knowledge and skills) who move within the organization. Establishing stimulating career tracks for high-potentials and key experts is a key challenge that organizations face. Although talents like to manage their own careers, at the same time, they expect long-term career perspectives and upward advancement within the organization.

An earlier study conducted by Stahl and Cerdin (2004) also questions the universality of the boundaryless career model to some degree. They examined repatriation issues among French and German expatriates and found that nationality may be an important factor in the applicability of such a career model. Despite dissatisfaction in both groups with regard to repatriation plans, German expatriates had a much more positive attitude towards their international assignments than their French counterparts. This finding can be explained by the fact that the German expatriates were more willing to leave their companies upon return than their French counterparts, showing strong evidence of a "boundaryless career" orientation. While for both German and French expatriates international assignment was a competitive asset that makes them more valuable to the external labor market, the French were more concerned about their future career advancement within their companies. Stahl and Cerdin (2004) point out that in France, the potential development rests on political tournament with political process outweighing achievement.

The importance of networks and political manoeuvring (Fesser & Pellissier-Tanon, 2007) might be an important factor that makes the French perceive an international assignment as more risky – it may put them at an informational and networking disadvantage. The German approach to management development follows the model that promotes functional career paths and expertise-based competition, and as such they perceive expatriation as more instrumental to promotion, and they are more confident that there is a high demand for their international expertise on the labor market. Stahl and Cerdin (2004) conclude that companies that do not take an integrated approach to international assignments and fail to have effective international career development and repatriation systems, are more likely to have dissatisfied managers who may be willing to leave their companies upon repatriation. However, the actual scale of talent voluntary turnover depends on their nationality, which determines the preferred career model.

Further research on career management in TM context was conducted by Maxwell and MacLean (2008) in the hospitality and tourism sector in Scotland. Contrary to the above mentioned studies, Maxwell and MacLean focus on the industry perspective, taking a macro-level approach to TM and career management. The authors draw our attention to TM potential to contribute to improving standards of management and career development and, subsequently, perceptions of the industry as an employer and a service provider. The hospitality and tourism industry in Scotland, in spite of its importance for the economy, suffers from "the highest profile of poor treatment of employees" (Maxwell & MacLean, 2008: 826), making it difficult to attract and retain talented employees. The notion of poor management, poor development, and lack of investments in talents in the sector was common among study participants. As the industry relies in large measure on a younger workforce that has a clear perception of their career development expectations, TM becomes of a particular interest within the industry. Identifying and growing talents within the organizations helps to offer alluring career opportunities and attracts more talented employees, which according to respondents, is in abundance within the sector. Maxwell and MacLean (2008) conclude that TM has the potential to improve the quality of the workforce in the hospitality and tourism sector in Scotland, which will in turn enhance business offerings.

Institutional and Cultural Context

A third key research theme on talent management in Europe focuses on the institutional and cultural context for deployment of TM practices. Below we present examples of two studies with this respect. The first study presented by Boussebaa and Morgan (2008) highlights the conflicts and tensions involved in implementing TM systems uniformly across borders. The authors explore how differences between the British and French national institutional contexts manifest themselves in different approaches to TM and different TM practices. Their findings point to the tensions that emerge in the utilization of a framework of TM developed in the United Kingdom and France, which resulted in the complete failure of implementation of common high-potential identification and development processes.

The British logic underscoring the TM framework assumed egalitarianism (equal opportunities for all managers) and meritocracy, meaning that talent identification and career progress are depended on assessment of differential individual performance and potential, which should be measured by internally administered tests and developed by coaching, mentoring, or training. In France, however, talent was not assessed internally, but externally through the *grandes écoles* system that is the top tier of the higher education system. Potential in France is identified at the point of entry, where the diploma from *grandes ecoles* already proves potential, and career progress is then subsequently based on seniority, international mobility, and political tasks of activating the networks from the *grandes écoles*.

Boussebaa and Morgan (2008) also showed deep divergence in talent development practice that created various conflicts and misunderstandings between the two managerial groups. For example, the British preference for pragmatism and eagerness of putting things into practice conflicted with the French inclination towards intellectualism and abstract reflection; this had a serious impact on French *cadres* who felt that their ideas were not allowed to be fully developed and reported a high level of dissatisfaction and frustration. Overall, Boussebaa and Morgan (2008) emphasize that the failure of the UK-instituted integrative effort within TM was the result of the lack of understanding of the institutional context that varies in both countries, leading eventually to UK HQ switching away from the idea of developing a transnational managerial cadre. Boussebaa and Morgan conclude that as the nature of management as a system of authority varies markedly across European societies, MNCs must consider those differences very carefully in their efforts to develop globally capable managerial talents, which are at the heart of each MNC's competitive advantages.

Another study that helps us to understand the influence of institutional and cultural context on talent management in Europe was conducted by Skuza et al. (2013) within multinationals in Poland. In spite of the increasing significance of the region in the European economy, empirical research on TM in this region is practically non-existent (Vaiman & Holden, 2011). Advanced economic transition in the Central Eastern Europe (CEE) region often leads to the assumption of a high level of convergence of Western and Eastern models, while insufficient knowledge about management practices and work relationships in post-communist countries may result in misinterpretations and misunderstandings between local subsidiaries and their foreign headquarters (see Dobosz-Bourne & Jankowicz, 2006; Piske, 2002).

Skuza et al. (2013) identified several key challenges to TM deployment particular to the CEE region. First, they highlighted that competencies and skills that are typically regarded as key in identifying high-potentials in Western organizations appear not to be used in organizations in Poland, where technical abilities dominate over leadership or personal skills. They also found that managers are very cautious in identifying high-potentials for fear of losing their own positions, and that promotions are based on personal networks rather than on more objective measures used in TM frameworks. The importance of informal relationships and private networks that limit objective and fair identification and promotion of high-potentials has previously been noted as a common practice in post-communist countries (Kiriazov et al., 2000).

Another factor typical to the region was a lack of recognition of individual successes, which often resulted in discouragement to undertake a talent role and the creation of a negative atmosphere around TM. In addition, cultural factors led to an unwillingness to include employees in the decision-making process, a low level of innovativeness and willingness to learn, and short-termism and lack of transparency in the evaluation process. All those challenges were identified as major obstacles to TM effectiveness. Skuza et al. (2013) conclude that understanding the mental models of employees and managers will be the key aspect in undertaking effective TM through CEE countries, and that the cultural processes influencing managerial practices in the region are still in a period of change, resulting in management models not quite converging yet with Western models (Vaiman & Holden, 2011).

The institutional and cultural perspective is also used among researchers studying TM in SMEs. We will now move to distinctive TM issues experienced in SMEs, and we will review the emerging research on TM in European SMEs.

Talent Management in European SMEs

As discussed above, the bulk of research on TM focuses on the large multinational enterprises, and research highlights the dominance of exclusive approaches. However, research highlights that the majority of companies worldwide are small- and-medium sized enterprises (SMEs) and that these organizations play a key role in the global economy. A recent study by the OECD highlighted that over 99% of companies in OECD and G20 countries are SMEs. There is considerable debate and lack of consensus over the definition of SMEs (for a review, see Krishnan & Scullion, 2017): however, it is widely recognized that SMEs play a strategic role in most regions of the world.

Despite the importance of SMEs in the global economy, there is a dearth of research on TM in the SME context. Recently, however, some empirical research has emerged on TM in the European context (Festing et al., 2013; Festing et al., 2016; Viverde et al., 2013). This research highlights major differences between MNEs and SMEs in their approach to TM, which reflects important differences more generally between SMEs and large firms in relation to their overall approach to HRM (Rabi & Gilman, 2012).

Several authors have identified the key features of SMEs as having a personalized management style, together with a centralized authority, informal and dynamic strategies, flat and flexible structures, and a strong emphasis on innovation and resource scarcity (Ates et al., 2013; Festing et al., 2017). These features impact on approaches to HRM and TM, and SMEs are seen to adopt distinctive approaches to HR (Heneman et al., 2000; Rabi & Gilman, 2012; Storey et al., 2010).

Valverde, Scullion, and Ryan (2013) identify some particular features of HRM in SMEs. They highlight the high degree of informality as an important characteristic of HRM in SMEs and the informal organizational culture in SMEs. They also note the role of owner managers and the lack of specialized HR functions (Bacon et al., 1996; Dundon & Wilkinson, 2009; Storey et al., 2010).

SMEs operate in an increasingly competitive global environment, and the growing competition for talent across many sectors means that strategies to attract, retain, and develop managerial and technical talent are a major challenge for many SMEs (Festing, 2007; Krishnan & Scullion, 2017). The limited knowledge of the brands of SMEs and the lack of resources and professional expertise make talent attraction more difficult in SMEs

Festing et al. (2017) highlight the TM challenges for SMEs in terms of talent attraction and talent retention. A recent study highlighted that the main HR problem faced by SMEs was attracting employees for key posts (Krishnan & Scullion, 2017). There is very little research on talent retention in SMEs, but the positive working atmosphere in SMEs is seen as a strong positive factor, while lessor opportunities for career development and training and development is seen as negative (Ates et al., 2013; Festing, 2007).

The quantitative study by Festing, Schafer, and Scullion (2013) makes a contribution to the conceptual and empirical understanding of TM in German SMEs. A key finding of the study was the preference of most German SMEs to choose a more inclusive approach to TM and to target all or most employees as talent. This was in contrast with the research on large MNEs where a more exclusive or elitist approach is favored. This highlights that TM practices vary in different types of organizations. The study highlighted that the retention-based TM approaches of German SMEs reflects the long-term development orientation in the German national business system. A further important finding of the Festing et al. (2013) study was the high levels of cooperation used by German SMEs in terms of cooperation and networks with other institutions in response to shortages of talent in the context of full employment in Germany.

Viverde, Scullion, and Ryan's qualitative research (2013) examined TM in Spanish medium-sized companies. A major finding of the study was that although the companies did not operate with formal TM policies, TM practices (albeit informal) were effectively pursued. Despite the lack of formal TM policies, talent identification worked effectively and the firms could define talent in the specific SME context. In the particular context of medium-sized Spanish SMEs, loyalty, commitment, flexibility, collegiality, etc. were seen as important for talent identification. The study showed that the absence of formal TM policies had little impact on the firms' ability to attract and retain talent (Viverde, Scullion, & Ryan, 2013), a finding that challenged previous research.

In addition, it has been argued that SMEs prefer to adopt an informal approach to TM due to the preference for a personalized management style and the more egalitarian culture in SME management (Krishnan & Scullion, 2017). An interesting and important finding of the study was that both exclusive and inclusive approaches to TM were present, which challenged the view that exclusive or inclusive approaches must prevail. In the former case, the more favored treatment enjoyed by the talents was resented by those not in the talent pool.

Overall these studies highlight the differences in TM in European SMEs and large MNEs and provided some insights into talent issues in the context of European SMEs. The studies shed light on the issue of what does talent mean in the European SME context and also what type of employees European SMEs are looking for. These studies suggest that SMEs seek to hire staff with more generalist than specialist knowledge due to the wider range of tasks required of staff in SMEs (Festing et al., 2013; Viverde et al., 2013).

The study of TM in SMEs in European is still very limited and in the earliest stages of development. More empirical research is required on the meaning of talent in the SME context, and there is a need for further empirical research comparing formal TM policies versus informal practices in the European SME context. Also, more research is required into talent issues in the large variety of SME types. There is a serious research gap relating to TM in global SMEs, particularly in the emerging markets as SMEs account for the bulk of employment in these markets, and we need to know more about the distinctive challenges faced by SMEs in these markets. There is also a lack of theory and conceptual work in this area, which is partly addressed by recent work that contributes to our understanding of why approaches to TM in SMEs differ from that in large organizations and how TM issues in SMEs vary with the evolution of the firm (Krishnan & Scullion, 2017).

Conclusion and Areas of Future Research

Our chapter has examined a number of key themes that influence talent management at the organizational level and the individual level in European organizations. Early studies of TM were mainly focused on North American organizations, but the last decade has seen a rapid growth of research on TM in Europe (Sparrow et al., 2014). Some key debates in TM have been critically reviewed in the European context, including the exclusive versus inclusive approach to the TM debate, the link with TM, the psychological contract in the European context, and the link between TM and career management in the European context.

Future research on TM in European organizations should examine the need to balance organizational and individual perspectives, and to understand the perceptions of different talents in different contexts. There is a need for more research on the issues surrounding the attraction, development, and retention of female talent in European organizations, and the factors that influence female participation in the talent pool. Surprisingly, given the continuing shortages of leadership talent, this remains an under-researched area. Further research is also required on TM in SMEs in Europe, an area that is conceptually and empirically underdeveloped. Finally, further research on TM in Europe is required in under-researched contexts, particularly in the public sector and in voluntary organizations where organizational culture has a strong influence on approaches to TM.

References

Ates, A., Garengo, P., Cocca, P., & Bititci, U. 2013. The development of SME managerial practice for effective performance management. *Journal of Small Business and Enterprise Development,* 20(1): 28–54.

Bacon, N., Ackers, P. Storey, J., & Coates, D. 1996. It's a small world: Managing human resources in small businesses. *International Journal of Human Resource Management,* 7(1): 82–100.

Bayireddi, M. 2019. *Recruiting in Europe? How talent acquisition differs overseas.* ERE Recruiting Intelligence.

Bersin J. 2010. *Learning and talent management in Europe.* https://joshbersin.com/2010/01/learning-and-talent-management-in-europe/.

Bjorkman, I., Ehrnrooth, M., Mäkelä, K., Smale, A., & Sumelius, J. 2013. Talent or not? Employee reactions to talent identification. **Human Resource Management,** 52: 195–214.

Boussebaa, M., & Morgan, G. 2008. Managing talent across national borders: The challenges faced by an international retail group. **Critical Perspectives on International Business,** 4(1): 25–41.

Brewster, C. 2004. European perspectives on human resource management. **Human Resource Management Review,** 14, 365–382.

Brewster, C. 2007. European perspectives on human resource management. **European Journal of International Management,** 1(3), 239–259.

Chartered Institute of Personnel Development. 2015. **Resourcing and talent planning 2017.** Annual Survey Report, CIPD.

Collings, D. G., Scullion, H., & Vaiman, V. 2011. European perspectives on talent management. **European Journal of International Management,** 5(5): 453–462.

De Vos, A., & Dries, N. 2013. Applying a talent management lens to career management: The role of human capital composition and continuity. **The International Journal of Human Resource Management,** 24: 1816–1831.

Dries, N., & Pepermans, R. 2008. Real high potential careers: An empirical study into the perspectives of organisations and high potentials. **Personnel Review,** 37(1): 85–108.

Dundon, T., & Wilkinson, A. 2009. HRM in small and medium sized enterprises. In D. G. Collings & G. Wood (Eds.), **Human resource management: A critical approach.** London: Routledge.

Ernst & Young. 2018. **Global leadership forecast.** The Conference Board, Australia.

Festing, M. 2007. Globalisation of SMEs and implications for international human resource management research and practice. **International Journal of Globalisation and Small Business,** 2(1): 5–18.

Festing, M., Harsch, K., Schafer, L., & Scullion, H. 2017. Talent management in small and medium sized enterprises. In D. G Collings, W. Cascio, & K Melahi (Eds.), **Oxford handbook of talent management.** Oxford, UK: Oxford University Press.

Festing, M., Schafer, L., & Scullion, H. 2013. Talent management in medium sized German companies: An explorative study and research agenda. **International Journal of Human Resource Management,** 24(9): 1872–1893.

Haddock-Millar J., Sanyal C., & Müller-Camen M. 2016. Green human resource management: A comparative qualitative case study of a United States multinational corporation. **The International Journal of Human Resource Management,** 27(2): 192–211.

Heneman, R. L., Tansky, J. W., & Camp, S. M. 2000. Human resource management practices in small and medium-sized enterprises: unanswered questions and future and future research perspectives. **Entrepreneurship Theory and Practice,** 25(1): 11–26.

Hillmann, V. 2014. **Hire & fire vs. corporate training: HR practices in the U.S. and Europe.** http://www.humanresourcesiq.com/hr-talent-management/articles/human-resource-management-practice-in-the-u-s-and.

Hoglund, M. 2012. Quid pro quo? Examining talent management through the lens of psychological contracts. **Personnel Review,** 41(2): 126–142.

Human Capital Institute. 2019. **Talent pulse 5.2: Bridging the skills gap with workforce development strategies.** https://nationalfund.org/wp-content/uploads/2018/06/TP5-2-Bridge-Skills-Gap-NationalFund-1.pdf

Krishnan, T. N., & Scullion, H. 2017. Talent management and dynamic view of talent in small and medium enterprises. **Human Resource Management Review,** 27(3): 431–441.

ManpowerGroup. 2018. Solving the talent shortage. Build, buy, and bridge. **Talent Shortage Survey 2018.**

Maxwell, G. A., & MacLean S. 2008. Talent management in hospitality and tourism in Scotland. Operational implications and strategic actions. **International Journal of Contemporary Hospitality Management,** 20(7): 820–830.

McDonnell, A., Collings D. G., Mellahi K., & Schuler R. 2017. Talent management: A systematic review and future prospects. **European Journal International Management,** 11(1): 86–128.

McDonnell, A., Lamare, R., Gunnigle, P., & Lavelle, J. 2010. Developing tomorrow's leaders – evidence of global talent management in multinational enterprises. **Journal of World Business,** 45: 150–160.

Meyers, M. C., Woerkom M., Paauwe J., &Dries N. 2019. HR managers' talent philosophies: Prevalence and relationships with perceived talent management practices. **The International Journal of Human Resource Management,** 31(4): 562–588.

Nikandrou, I., Campos, E., Cunha, R., & Papalexandris, N. 2006. HRM and organisational performance: Universal and contextual evidence. In H. H. Larsen, & W. Mayrhofer (Eds.), **Managing human resource in Europe:** 177–96. London: Routledge.

NTMN. Potential. Who's doing what to identify their best? **Talent Strategy Group.** New York.

Paauwe, J. 2004. **HRM and performance: Achieving long-term viability.** New York: Oxford University Press Inc.

PricewaterhouseCoopers. 2019. **CEO curbed confidence spells caution.** 22nd Annual Global CEO Survey: The Talent Challenge.

Rabi, S. O., & Gilman, M. W. 2012. Human resource management in small to medium-sized enterprises. In R. Kramar & J. Syeds (Eds.), *Human resource management in global context: A critical approach.* Basingstoke: Palgrave Macmillan.

Scullion, H., & Brewster, C. 2001. Managing expatriates: Message from Europe. *Journal of World Business,* 36: 346–365.

Skuza, A., Scullion H., & McDonnell, A. 2013. An analysis of the talent management challenges in a post-communist country: The case of Poland. *The International Journal of Human Resource Management,* 24: 453–470.

Sonnenberg, M., van Zijderveld, V., & Brinks, M. 2014. The role of talent-perception incongruence in effective talent management. *Journal of World Business,* 49(2): 272–280.

Sparrow, P., & Hiltrop, J. M. 1997. Redefining the field of European human resource management: a battle between national mindsets and forces of business transition. *Human Resource Management,* 36(2): 201–219.

Stahl, G. K., & Cerdin, J. L. 2004. Global careers in French and German multinational corporations. *Journal of Management Development,* 23(9): 885–902.

Storey, D.J., Saridakis, G., Sen-Gupta, S., & Edwards, P. K. (2010). Linking HR formality with employee job quality: The role of firm and workplace size. *Human Resource Management,* 49(2): 305–329.

Swailes S., & Blackburn M., (2016). Employee reactions to talent pool membership. *Employee Relations,* 38(1): 112–128.

Thurley, K., & Wirdenius, H. 1991. Will management become "European"? Strategic choice for organisations. *European Management Journal,* 9(2): 127–134.

Valverde, M., Scullion, H., & Ryan, G. 2013. Talent management in Spanish medium sized organisations. *International Journal of Human Resource Management,* 24 (9): 1832–1852.

15

TALENT MANAGEMENT AND MIGRATION

Jean-Luc Cerdin

Chris Brewster

Lovanirina Ramboarison-Lalao

Introduction

Increasingly, multinational enterprises (MNEs) and even indigenous organizations are beginning to take a wider view of their potential workforce: human resource management (HRM) and talent management (TM) are becoming more international and more global (Vaiman, Sparrow, Schuler, & Collings, 2019a, b). We can see this in the way that, for example, hospitals in the richer countries recruit medical staff from around the world (Tsugawa, Jena, Orav, & Jha, 2017). We can see it in the way that businesses transfer work to countries where there are appropriate skills, or where the labor force and related/unregulated labor markets offer cheap human resources (Álvarez-Galván, 2012; OECD, 2013). We can also see opportunities for such international thinking in the movement of workers across international borders: migration.

This chapter focuses on the way that such migrants are being, or are not being, integrated into what has been referred to as global talent management (GTM) (Schuler, Jackson, & Tarique, 2010; Scullion & Collings, 2011). There is a debate in the TM literature (Reis, 2016; Schuler & Tarique, 2012) about whether it is an inclusive subject, covering all possible talents within and beyond the organization, or whether it is an exclusive subject covering only an elite. We do not have space here to enter this debate, but this chapter is founded on the assumption that TM is an inclusive subject.

The chapter has the following format. We explore the concept and extent of migration and examine the sub-categories of migration, arguing that migrants can be classified into a three by three matrix. Some of these categories have been integrated into the TM strategies of organizations and some of them remain outside. We build a case for organizations to include all categories of migrants into their TM thinking.

Understanding Migration

The latest estimates in 2019 were that there are around 272 million migrant workers around the world (United Nations, 2019). Problems of definition and measurement bedevil the area, but it seems that migration has been increasing significantly over recent years (International Organization for Migration, 2018; World Bank, 2017). The many factors pushing workers to leave their home country to seek work and security in other countries include war, climate change, income inequality, the changing availability of and attraction of work in other countries, increasing knowledge, and increasing ease of communication. Migrants are either forced out of their home country (in which case they are usually referred to as refugees) or attracted to the new country (Cerdin, Abdeljalil Diné, & Brewster, 2014) in an attempt to better their situation.

DOI: 10.4324/9781315474687-15

Migration is controversial. It has been close to the center of major political discussions in many of the developed countries in the last few years. It was one of the key issues in the decision of the United Kingdom to leave its major trading partner, the European Union (Burrell et al., 2019). Historically, countries used to be less well delineated than they are now (they were mostly the lands of the rulers). One hundred years ago, with the end of the First World War, passports, and then residency permits and work permits, were introduced, so that the state had more control over who lived within its borders. Migration became political. In the last few years, the increasing amount of migration has led, particularly in the developed countries, to vociferous and often virulent debates.

For receiving societies, migration has obvious advantages and disadvantages. On the plus side, migrants help to redress the demographic balance of these countries, providing younger and more active workers to increasingly aging and sclerotic societies. They boost economies, bring in skills that the receiving society has not had to invest in to develop, and are often available to do the work that the indigenous population does not want to do, and at rates that the indigenous population will not accept (Rodriguez & Mearns, 2012). Migrants are significantly more entrepreneurial than indigenous populations (Vandor & Franke, 2016).

The societies that they leave may also benefit significantly from remittances that the migrants send back home (Singh, 2013; World Bank-Knomad, 2016). Remittances constitute a substantial element to international trade. The World Bank Group (2016, p. xii) estimated that worldwide remittance flows exceeded US$600 billion, though unrecorded flow will add considerably to that. Two-thirds of this money goes to developing countries – well over three times the amount of aid they receive (World Bank Group, 2019).

On the negative side, in the receiving countries migrants put pressure on local communities, requiring social services, health systems, housing, and employment, and perhaps driving down local wages. For the societies that they leave, the better qualified emigrants will be a crucial loss of rare skills.

There is a unique issue in the European Union, where citizens from any of 27 (after the UK left) member countries, and from three or four associated countries, are free to move to, work in, buy property in, and enjoy the social benefits and healthcare system of any of the other countries. This puts Europe in a different position in terms of migration to any other region of the world. Europe as a whole still, of course, has significant migration in from non-European countries, of the kind that would be recognized in any other part of the globe, but intra-EU mobility adds an extra dimension.

Most migrants work. They are human resources, but they are rarely considered in discussions of TM. The lack of serious TM for immigrants is evident. There is a drastic underutilization of the skills of qualified migrants and lesser qualified migrants are often badly exploited (Rodrigue & Mearns, 2012). There are question-marks over the capacity of migration systems to strategically support the skill needs of employers (see for example Dench, Hurstfield, Hill, & Akroyd 2006; Sparrow, 2008). Organizations appear readier to exploit incoming migrants to undercut the local workforce than to access the potential benefits of closing skills gaps and increasing productivity.

There are rich pickings here for political controversy. There are complex challenges inherent in the migration process that are related to governance, workers' rights and security, and the linkages between migration, and development and international co-operation. In this chapter, our primary focus is on the under-recognized and hence under-researched connection between migration and international human resource management.

Defining Who Is a Migrant

International organizations such as the United Nations (UN; 1998), the International Labor Organization (ILO; 2014), and the Organization for Economic Co-operation and Development (OECD; 2003) generally define a long-term migrant as a person who moves to a country other than that of their usual residence for a period of at least a year (12 months), whereby the country of destination becomes their new country of normal residence. The person will be a long-term emigrant from the perspective of the country of departure, and a long-term immigrant from that of the country of arrival. A short-term migrant is a person who moves to a country other than that of their usual residence for a period of at least three months but less than 12 months except in cases where the movement to that country is for purposes of recreation, holiday, visits to friends or relatives, business, medical treatment, or religious pilgrimage (United Nations, 1998).

These definitions have not been widely adopted by academic scholars and have proved difficult to apply. For example, and relevant to our case discussing business and management issues, these definitions offer no clear distinction between migrants and expatriates (particularly the now widely-used, self-initiated expatriate; Andresen, Al-Ariss, & Walther, 2012; Cerdin & Selmer, 2014; Suutari & Brewster, 2000) and short-term migrants, and many of the issues and consequences are similar (Al Ariss, 2010). A short-term migrant may well expect to work in the host country and go back to their own country within a limited timescale, but so do short-term expatriates (or, in the UN definition, migrants on business). Furthermore, the categories may not be consistent over time: a migrant may have every intention and expectation of staying in the host (their new home) country, and the self-initiated expatriate may have every intention and expectation of going home within a short period. In some cases, the former will go home within a few months or years, and in other cases the latter may stay on for the rest of their lives.

The difficulty of defining the concept of migration rests partly on the fact that migration is a multi-disciplinary topic (covered by, for example, economists, applied geographers, anthropologists, IHRM academics). Academics generally tend to consider migration within the wider process of international "movement", covering all forms of human mobility. It has generally been neglected by management scholars and even by IHRM scholars. Addressing the topic from the IHRM and GTM perspectives adds value as it allows consideration of the mobilization and utilization of another element in the international talent pool. Given the discussion of talent shortages and large numbers of migrants that there are, ignoring this source makes little sense. Thus, discussion of migration in the business and management literature can help organizations to attain their strategic business purposes while better recognizing the work-life experiences and needs of migrants. These perspectives offer avenues to studying the choices organizations make about resourcing strategies for international migrants, new forms of international working, and knowledge transfer that might offer flexible employment forms.

Key Figures and Facts about Migration

For analysis purposes, the UN divides the world into the poor and economically struggling countries of the South and the rich, developed countries of the North (even though some of the former are geographically much further north than some of the latter). According to UN estimates, South-South migration is as common as South-North migration (United Nations, 2013). In 2013, approximately 82.3 million international migrants who were born in the South were residing in other Southern countries. This is roughly the same number of international migrants who have left the South and are now living in the North (81.9 million). Figures for international migrants from the North and residing in the North were estimated at 53.7 million, whereas a much smaller number of 13.7 million international migrants from the Northern countries lived in the South.

Countries vary markedly in the numbers of migrants and levels of foreigners. The exact definition of these terms is crucial in making international comparisons. The most commonly applied criteria used in defining a "migrant" are nationality and place of birth. Any person who has ever moved from their country of birth to their current country of residence falls within the category of "migrant" or "foreign-born population". So, the migrant category includes persons who still have the nationality of their country of origin but may also include persons with strong family ties to the host country. The foreign-born population includes persons born abroad and will include in that nationals of their current country of residence (Thite, Srinivasan, Harvey, & Valk, 2009).

The definitions vary by country. Differing legislation governing the acquisition of nationality in each country has an influence on the reported size of the foreign-born and the total foreign population. In some countries, children automatically acquire citizenship if born there (*jus soli,* the right of soil), whereas in others they keep the nationality of their parents at birth (*jus sanguinis,* the right of blood). Some countries allow them to keep the nationality of their parents at birth and grant citizenship of the host country when they reach their majority. Thus, residency requirements vary from as few as three years in Canada to as many as ten in other countries. In Australia, Canada, and New Zealand, rates of naturalization are high, as they are also in some European countries such as Belgium, Sweden, and the Netherlands.

Reasons for trends vary and are usually linked to a complexity of different explanations (Castles, de Haas, & Miller, 2014). Obviously, the size and wealth of a country are great attractors, as are perceived safety and security, and perceived welfare support. The (mainly European) countries that have a history of international expansion and empire tend to have larger numbers of migrants. The foreign-born populations include persons born abroad as nationals of their current country of residence. The prevalence of such persons among the foreign-born can be significant in some countries, especially in those such as France and Portugal, which granted citizenship to their colonies and now receive large inflows of home-country repatriates from those former colonies.

The intrinsic meaning of migration will be different in different contexts. In a large country like Japan, with a homogeneous population, migrants may be seen as exotic and strange. This may also apply to emigrants; for such a large country, Japan has a very limited diaspora. By contrast, in Australia, another Pacific rim country, almost all the population consists of migrants or the family of relatively recent migrants. In the United Arab Emirates, the overwhelming majority of the population (more than eight out of every ten people) consists of migrants or expatriates (Mohyeldin & Suliman, 2006).

It is important to make the point that wherever there is immigration, there is almost certainly always illegal immigration – migrants who are not known to the authorities in that country, or are known to the authorities but have not been repatriated by them. Almost by definition, we have much less information on this group, but they will often be working in the host society and are a largely un-researched aspect of the labor market (see for example Bloch, Sigona, & Zetter, 2011).

Despite the extensive work carried out by the ILO and other international bodies, there remains a real need to take stock of what has been achieved so far with a view to identifying clearly what remains to be done to address the multiple aspects of the issues of migration and emigration from an HRM perspective (ILO, 2014).

Typologies of Migration and the Consequences for GTM

Migrants are by no means a coherent group. In fact, there are many types of migrants, and the overall category can be analyzed in a variety of ways. There is, for example growing interest in numerous aspects of migration: a) the movement of highly-qualified migrants and knowledge workers; b) the development of a more globalized labor market for craft skilled employees, for example, the influx of Polish immigrants into the UK operating as self-employed businesses; c) the growth of "global care chains", where the lifestyle of relatively wealthy individuals and households in developed countries is made possible by people without qualifications from the second or third world, and involves the transfer of services associated with childcare, homecare, and personal care such as nannies and maids; and d) the gravitation of productivity towards, and hence development of, global cities, such as London, Paris, and New York.

With our focus here on the connection of such migrants to international HRM, we apply an analytical frame that examines migrants in terms of their employment options, looking at their individual characteristics and their organizational relevance. In this section, we adopt a multilevel perspective in order to better understand migration (Al Ariss & Crowley-Henry, 2013; Al Ariss & Syed, 2011). We apply a three-level framework, following work on expatriation (Haak-Saheem & Brewster, 2017) to

Table 15.1 A typology of migration

Characteristics	Senior management	Middle and lower management	Low status
Gender	Majority males	Mixed, mostly male	Mixed
Age	Generally 35–60	Different age groups	Different age groups
Compensation package	Attractive packages, including housing, education, etc.	Salary, sometimes expenses	Salary (sometimes proportion "held-back")
Time	Typically, 3 years	Varies, aiming to stay as long as possible	Short to mid-range stay
Family	In host country	Varies	In home country
Motivation	High income, good experience in an emerging market	Good income, safe country	Income, remittances home to support family
Resign and return to home country	Yes, at any time	It depends, in most cases after completing the contract period	No, only after completing the contract period
Impact of nationality	Westerners have an advantage. Skin color and nationality indicate how people and colleagues deal with each other	Yes, obvious discrimination based on skin color and nationality	Usually no, because only certain nationalities would work in these jobs

Source: adapted from Haak-Saheem & Brewster, 2017: 431.

divide migrants into high, medium, and low-paid, and we consider individual, organizational, and societal implications (see Table 15.1).

Our argument is that in order to have a nuanced understanding of migration, it is important to recognize individual, organizational, and macro-social factors, which are all relevant influences. For example, at the individual level, factors that matter include: the type of migration (high skilled/medium skilled/low skilled migrants; legal/illegal migration); the country of origin, ethnicity, and gender of migrants; and the various forms of social capital that migrants have. At the organizational level, issues that matter include: the role of national origin sector/size of the company, which might influence how and which migrants they recruit; and the history and experience of the company in terms of recruiting migrants. Finally, at the macro-social level, issues such as legislation and the role and attitudes of professional bodies as well as the extent of migration (common or rare) and the country's history of migrant communities (positive or negative) and changes over time all influence migration. These three levels should be seen as interacting with each other rather than being separate.

Given space limitations, our discussion below does not aim to be exhaustive but rather attempts to tackle some key relevant topics on migration of relevance to HRM at each of the three levels mentioned.

Understanding The Micro-Individual Level of Migration

A major distinction between migrants lies in their levels of qualification and hence, generally, in their level of reward. Highly qualified migrants (QIs) have recently been the focus of a strand of the management literature. These are migrants who hold at least a bachelor's degree when they migrate (Zikic, Bonache, & Cerdin, 2010). The management literature has generally not studied lesser qualified migrants, such as those with lower level accountancy, nursing, information technology (IT) qualifications, or specific manual skills. Nor has it studied migrants with few or no qualifications, although they have been examined by disciplines such as economics, sociology, economic geography, or political science, and in journals dedicated to migration issues.

Many of these unqualified migrants may be highly skilled, with years of experience and considerable knowledge and capabilities as plumbers, woodworkers, IT specialists, and so on, and often find work readily and contribute significantly to the talent base of the country. Qualified migrants are more easily related to the issue of TM as they bring their qualifications to their employers (Cerdin et al., 2014). Mulholland and Ryan (2014), studying intra-EU migration, see highly skilled migration as a key issue for the global talent pool of the host economy. Highly, medium, and low qualified migrants confront different challenges in their host country. We detail these below.

Highly Qualified Migrants

Even highly qualified migrants may face employment difficulties. They often earn below the equivalent level of qualifications and skill for nationals and are frequently under-utilized (Almeida, Fernando, & Sheridan, 2012; Ramboarison-Lalao, Al Ariss, & Barth, 2012). There is often a lack of qualification recognition by employers during the hiring process, because of a lack of knowledge of, or lack of trust in, the immigrant's home-based qualification-awarding system, ignorance of their overseas-based work experience (Almeida et al., 2012), and, in addition, discrimination and prejudice (Almeida et al., 2012; Evans & Kelley, 1991).

Qualified immigrants (QI) are not themselves a homogenous group. On the contrary, they present considerable diversity in many aspects, such as their motivation to migrate, their career orientations, and their integration in the host country. For instance, Zikic et al. (2010: 667) find three career orientations among QIs in France, Spain, and Canada, namely "embracing, adaptive and resisting orientations – with each portraying distinct patterns of motivation, identity and coping". The embracing career orientation corresponds to migrants who are highly motivated to overcome barriers they perceive as natural. They are ready to acquire the skills to face their new reality as migrants. Migrants with the adaptive career orientation are motivated by the prospect of success, with a particular focus on family success. Survival jobs may be part of their strategy to adjust to their host country. They are quite positive, although less so than those with an embracing career orientation, despite career difficulties and obstacles they must overcome when they arrive in the host country. Finally, the resisting career orientation describes migrants stuck with the former professional identity they had before migrating. As they cannot find new motivations to cope with their new situation, they become discouraged by all barriers, both personal and professional. As a result, they see their migration as a career failure.

Cerdin et al. (2014) developed a 2 by 2 matrix that focuses on motivations and identifies four orientations (see Cerdin et al., 2014 for more details), with some similarities to the Zikic et al. (2010) categories: Dream, Felicitous, Chance, and Desperate migrants. Dream migrants are those who have long wanted to settle in their host country, attracted by stories about it. Felicitous migrants are pushed from their home country, but are also attracted to their new host country. Chance migrants are also forced out of their home country, but in this case "find themselves" in the host country without having had any real previous attraction to it. Desperate migrants are the ones pushed from their home country and actively not wanting to be in their new one.

Organizations need to take into account these different types of migrants in order to put into place adequate support policies. For instance, selecting migrants would require assessing and acknowledging "the unique combination of risks, gains and losses that varies for each QI" (Cerdin et al., 2014: 165). Motivation to migrate has an impact on a migrant's integration in the host country. Understanding the stories behind QI's migration matters for the organization, since future job performance is at stake. Organizational integration policies, such as support from the HRM department with residency and work permits or language training, can have a positive impact on immigrants' motivation and integration. However, the efficacy of integration policies depends on the type of qualified immigrant. These policies have a greater impact on Felicitous and Desperate migrants than on Dream and Chance migrants (Cerdin et al., 2014).

Medium Qualified Migrants

There is no research on medium qualified migrants, but it seems that generally they manage to integrate themselves into the host society. Their skills are needed, and they are often more visible than those of high or low qualified migrants. There is an overlapping group between those with medium qualifications and no qualifications, which are people with medium, few, or no educational qualification, but through experience and learning-by-doing have become highly skilled. Thus, health or accountancy skills may come from either category and are attractive to employers, as are manual skills such as those of carpenters or metalworkers. In many cases such migrants are entrepreneurial and set up in business in their own right, sometimes struggling and sometimes being very successful.

Migrants with Few or No Qualifications

Poorly educated migrants generally get low earnings, often because of their inability to speak the local language. As a result, they may live in a "language minority enclave" with few opportunities for training and employment (Chiswick, 1991). Illegal immigration is much more likely among poorly educated rather than qualified immigrants. Low skilled migrants face specific obstacles in the process of integration. Beyond the challenge of obtaining a legal work permit (Barron et al., 2016), one of the major obstacles they face is the lack of "language capital", i.e., speaking, reading, and writing skills in the host language (e.g., Chiswick, 1991).

Natives generally have less favorable attitudes towards poorly educated migrants in comparison with medium or high qualified migrants, not for material self-interest reasons, but rather as a result of cultural and ideological factors (Hainmueller & Hiscox, 2010). Poorly educated migrants may face these negative attitudes toward them in their work environment, and, as a result, their integration both inside and outside the organization may be more difficult than the integration of qualified immigrants. They are even more likely to have to confront discrimination and racialism (Bloch et al., 2011), pay gaps (Siebers & Van Gastel, 2015), and precarious and vulnerable work conditions (Ahmad, 2008; Potter & Hamilton, 2014). They are also more likely to end up working unlawfully in the black or shadow economy (Bloch, 2013).

Educational levels may determine what integration policies could be implemented to help migrants to perform well in organizations. While the policy of "selective immigration" operated in France or Australia, for example, is clearly biased in favor of QIs compared to lower-qualified staff, HR managers who employ migrants still have to be aware of the complexity and often harsh conditions of lower-status occupations. The HRM problems of motivation, integration, the psycho-social risk of burn-out, acculturation of foreign staff, etc., must be addressed by HR managers, in order to maximize the value of these often "neglected talents". Such organizational issues, depending on the social responsibility of managers, are legitimate not only for QI, but also for most migrants.

Understanding The Meso-Organizational Level of Migration

As other chapters in this book show, organizations play an important role in managing and benefiting from the talents of their workforce, and this includes their migrant workforce. Foley and Kerr (2013) examined the impact of the ethnic origin of scientists and engineering innovators on the international activity of the U.S. companies that employ them. Their work addressed three particular questions: 1) How far do such innovators enable multinational expansion into countries associated with their own ethnicity? 2) In what way do these innovators affect how the multinational's research and development (R&D) and patenting activities are distributed throughout the world? 3) Do multinationals that employ ethnic innovators have less need for joint venture partners in developing affiliates in countries associated with the ethnicity of these employees?

Analyses were made of official data on innovators in conjunction with that on the operations of international affiliates of U.S. multinationals. For the former, extensive data were consulted from the U.S. Patent and Trademark Office on all patents granted in the period from 1975 to 2008, inferring the ethnicity of the innovators on the basis of their names by means of commercial databases of ethnic name origins. For the latter, data were drawn from the U.S. Direct Investment Abroad surveys conducted by the Bureau of Economic Analysis (BEA) for the years 1982, 1989, 1994, 1999, and 2004, which cover details such as the measures of assets, sales, employment, and employment compensation, as well as where R&D takes place and structures of ownership for the affiliate in question.

Results show that the percentage of U.S. domestic patents awarded to Indian and Chinese ethnicities, for example, doubled and tripled, respectively. From the analyses, it is apparent that there is indeed a link between greater percentages of innovation on the part of company employees of a given ethnicity and greater activity on the part of their employer company in affiliates in countries related to that same ethnicity. This is naturally more so among multinationals that are initiating activities abroad and therefore have reason to value the knowledge and connections of ethnic innovators. The findings also indicate that these ethnic innovators are enabling a change in how and where innovation takes place, facilitating the conducting of R&D as well as the generation of patents in foreign countries, and allowing multinationals greater ownership of foreign affiliates thanks to the insights provided into foreign markets. U.S. multinational firms are also, as suggested by the results, less and less dependent on local joint venture partners for their affiliates abroad.

The "reverse" phenomenon, the impact of the organization on migrants, is often negative. For example, Rodriguez and Mearns (2012) discuss issues, at the meso-organizational level, that influence migrants' employment. Such issues include: restrictions on migrants' physical mobility, poor work conditions and abuse by employers, and culture-related stereotypes leading to discrimination.

The case of migrant nurses in the health sector is of interest here for its explanatory power. Newton, Pillay, and Higginbottom (2012) reviewed recent literature covering migration and experiences of transition of internationally educated nurses (IENs). The authors conducted a database search of CINAHL (Cumulative Index to Nursing and Allied Health Literature), Medline, Scopus, and Web of Science, followed by a hand-search of certain prominent nursing journals, resulting in 21 articles to comprise quantitative and qualitative sources. The searches admitted only articles published in English between January 2004 and June 2009.

Findings showed that while a principal reason for migration is the expectation of improved income and/or career advancement, it seems such hopes are generally disappointed when it comes to the nurses' employment experiences. Some of the challenges which emerged were: 1) long, expensive, and complex processes of migration with little help provided by employers; 2) barriers of language and communication both personal and professional, feeling an outsider, and dissimilarity of nursing education and practice; 3) obtaining recognition of credentials such as licenses and registration from the home country was difficult, and it was hard to achieve them in the destination country; and 4) experience of discrimination, stereotyping, marginalization, limited support from peers or managers, skills and qualification unacknowledged/rejected by patients and colleagues, and unfair treatment – migrant nurses being given the most difficult assignments or unsocial shifts, or being overlooked for promotion.

In sum, companies such as multinationals can play a key role in mobilizing their migrants' human resources to meet their business strategies and knowledge diffusion. Qualified migrants in particular are a significant part of the global talent pool. They could be of considerable value in operating abroad and they have the potential to improve a multinational's competitive advantage in foreign locations.

Understanding The Macro-Social Level of Migration

While individual migrants might be seen now to have greater agency in choosing where in the world to work, there are, in reality, borders and restrictions on migration control international mobility, making migration accessible to some individuals and not to others, and restricting the countries to which migrants can move (Rodriguez & Mearns, 2012). One of the most important determinants of which/when/how migrants enter a country is migration policies. Migration policies are constituted by legislation and administrative rules that determine the way labor immigrants enter the country as well as their access to employment. They also regulate diversity actions practiced in the organizations and sanctions against discrimination. Migration policies result from the interaction of political, management, financial, and administrative mechanisms that guide a host country (or a group of countries in the case of the European Union) governments' actions in reaching goals that may be in the public interest or for other interests such as the governing party's advantage (Windsor, 2002).

The case of the European Union (EU) is useful to illustrate the complexity of migration at the macro-social level. The free movement of labor between member states is a fundamental feature of the EU. The immigration of non-EU nationals is by intergovernmental agreements in the hands of nation-states, with EU policies accepted only when these are compatible with national interests (Lettner, 1997). The outcome is that immigration flows within the EU cannot be readily constrained by nation states, though they can use administrative devices to limit it somewhat, but they continue to have a legitimate choice in relation to extra-EU immigration. The nation-states often have contrasting visions of the utility of an international workforce, especially as unemployment rates of nationals in the EU vary greatly from one country to another.

Lettner (1997) explains that immigration policies that are developed by EU countries have two important dimensions. First is geographic admission that determines access to residence and work within the national territory, governed by asylum and policies of labor immigration. Second is granting access to citizenship rights: civil, political, and social rights, governed by naturalization policies. Civil rights include freedom of movement and work; political rights include such matters as voting; and social rights refer here to eligibility for welfare state programs, such as public education, healthcare, and family allowances, as well as unemployment and retirement benefits.

The policies of naturalization in European countries restrict access to citizenship by imposing a list of conditions before a foreigner can become naturalized. Such a model of migration, based on the two dimensions discussed above, is expected to serve mostly the national interests of EU countries, such as the economic well-being of existing citizens and the preservation of a national culture and identity (Bauböck & Faist, 2010).

Al Ariss (2009) explains that in the latter part of the 1980s, with the rise of anti-foreigner right-wing extremism in Western European countries, most national governments tightened their migration policies for non-EU nationals. Thus, increased migration pressures from outside the EU territory generated increased activity to coordinate their migration policies. This was facilitated by a compromise, namely that none of the EU member countries would be declared migration states.

The decision-making power with respect to immigration matters remains unbalanced between the EU institutions and the governments of the EU countries. Historically, the European Parliament has been in favor of the eventual granting of equal rights for legally resident non-EU nationals, such as in terms of their movement and work in member states. However, the decision-making process remains primarily in the hands of public officials of member states, most of whom prefer migration policies that are restrictive. By analyzing the making of migration policies in the EU, Guiraudon (2003) concludes that the failure of EU countries to coordinate their policies of immigration and integration is expected to reinforce the emergence in the future of policies that are anti-immigrant and anti-EU unification.

Differences in the rights accorded to legal resident non-EU nationals compared to EU nationals are manifest in EU immigration policies. For example, citizens of member states automatically become EU citizens as a sort of secondary citizenship. EU citizens have the right to travel and live freely in the member states, as well as the right to vote and to become candidates in municipal and European Parliament elections in their country of residence. Such rights do not apply to non-EU citizens.

Relevance of This Typology to TM Policies/Practices

A limitation of much of the literature on international HRM and GTM has been that it has paid attention to only a restricted part of an MNE's human resources, sometimes just the assigned expatriates, sometimes both expatriates and local employees. A comprehensive definition of IHRM, and a broad, non-elitist view of GTM, though, would cover all the human resources of the organization around the world, though necessarily perhaps with special attention to expatriates (Cerdin & Brewster, 2014; Mäkelä & Brewster, 2009) and the organizational benefits of developing a global mindset (Levy, Beechler, Taylor, & Boyacigiller, 2007) among its employees. But the people on a company's expatriate roster are not the only people they have with international experience. Self-initiated expatriates (SIEs) are much cheaper for the organization and share many of the benefits of assigned expatriates for the organization (Andresen, Al Ariss, & Walther, 2012; Suutari & Brewster, 2000). So are bi-cultural employees (Furusawa & Brewster, 2015), and so are migrants.

To get the best value out of the migrants, an organization needs to know what kind of migrants they are dealing with, in what situation, and how best to manage them. The theoretical typology given here indicates the type of migrants that will participate in the labor force. Clearly, managing Dream migrants, who will generally be positive about their location and their employment, but may be less willing to share their understanding of their previous country, for example, will be different from managing Chance migrants, who may be ready to leave, or Desperate migrants, who have limited commitment to the organization and the country. There will also be a time dimension: recently arrived migrants will have better connections to their home country than migrants who have been in the country twenty years but may compensate by being better able to interpret between the two cultures. Different strategies will be appropriate for different kinds of migrant.

In broad terms, organizations that operate internationally would gain from utilizing all the internationally experienced employees within their staff. That includes not just expatriates but also others with knowledge of different environments, cultures, and languages. To do that, organizations first need to monitor the international nature of their whole workforce and ensure that records are kept of international experience, language skills, and cultural knowledge. Organizations should create an environment that welcomes diversity; should enable and encourage professional mentorships of migrants; should prepare co-workers and managers to positively receive and integrate them; should ensure that managers understand the recruitment and integration of those with international experience and knowledge; and should perceive and monitor the payback of assigning migrants to relevant positions within their area of expertise.

Specific HRM Practices for Migrants

Even though migrants may require specific TM policies, those policies need to be fully integrated in the overall GTM of the organizations. These policies could aim to help migrants overcome the barriers they face. As there is diversity among migrants, the first step for an organization would be to identify those barriers according to the type of expatriates in order to implement relevant HRM policies. Policies could be aimed at increasing efforts to adjust and finally to integrate in terms of life satisfaction, job satisfaction, and career success (Cerdin et al., 2014). In the end, the organizations have to make sure the migrants, like all employees, perform well.

As the theory of motivation to integrate (Cerdin et al., 2014) suggests, the decision to migrate itself can be the source of some barriers. Thus, organizations should understand the motivations to migrate when managing migrants. The motivation to migrate is especially complex for qualified immigrants. The impact of integration policies varies according to the type of QI (Cerdin et al., 2014) and, therefore, these policies need to be appropriately tailored. For instance, support from the organization in the form of mentoring would work better for Dream and Felicitous immigrants, while the impact would be smaller for Chance and Desperate immigrants (Cerdin et al., 2014). In terms of career orientations, the adaptive and the resisting QIs would need more support for their career than the embracing QIs for whom crafting a new career path may be easier (Zikic et al., 2010).

Organizations may want to assess the cultural intelligence of their managers who are dealing with migrants to help them develop their management skills towards individuals coming not only from a different culture but also from a different background. The story behind a migration might be distressing. Dealing with these stories, such as fleeing a war, could require specific skills from the management team. Management training may be necessary for organizations recruiting migrants. Organizations that regularly recruit migrants may have a strong interest in investing in this type of training for their managers and GTM staff. This would facilitate migrants' recruitment and integration. Migrants would also benefit from specific coaching and counselling, depending on their story related to their migration and the efforts they are ready to make once in their host country.

Management could be a challenge, particularly when migrants have not yet mastered the local language, which may be more of an issue for medium and lower qualified migrants than skilled ones. Technical skills may also be an issue. For skilled migrants, establishing the equivalence of academic degrees may be tricky, in particular in some strictly regulated professions such as law or medicine. Unqualified migrants, almost by definition, lack certain technical skills, which are not always easy to acquire, particularly when there are language issues. This is why little development can occur before the issue of language is resolved.

Lowly qualified migrants may be more sensitive than the QIs to the issues of compensation. By no means all countries have established national minimum wages and, even where there are, levels vary considerably. In some countries, migrants may be attractive to employers precisely because they are prepared to work for lower pay. In some cases, they may accept work doing jobs locals would turn down. Career issues would also be very different between migrants with different levels of qualification. Organizations could help QIs to re-establish themselves in their earlier careers or grow into a new career path in the host countries. For other migrants, career management may not be a priority.

Clearly, HRM policies address migrants who entered the host country legally. When organizations recruit migrants prior to their arrival in the country, they need to ensure the legality of the migration. Managing migrants requires some administrative expertise. The level of administrative complexity depends on the countries involved in the migration process. The experience of the host country, and specifically of the host organizations, will play an important role and may be complicated by a lack of stability in the migration policies of a country. For instance, in France, the *circulaire Géant* in 2011 tightened the criteria for the issuance of residence permits to non-EU graduates. Some organizations, for instance in the IT sector, were unable to recruit skilled migrants to cope with labor shortage. Organizations may be constrained to recruit migrants from specific locations, narrowing their talent pool.

Conclusion

Bringing together the two usually distinct scholarly fields of migration studies and global talent management (GTM) requires overcoming two main challenges. The first concerns distinguishing the population of migrants from other forms of international mobility. The distinction between assigned expatriates, self-initiated expatriates, and migrants remains uncertain. Individuals can move from one category to another one. Within the category of migrants, there is also a great diversity. This second challenge related to the diversity of migrants leads to the implementation of specific GTM policies tailored to the particular characteristics of each category. Even within one category, such as qualified immigrants, GTM policies also need to take into account a diverse population. Lesser qualified migrants pose a significant challenge as they have been ignored in the management literature and are not part of most GTM policies. Yet, training could be a way to enhance these migrants' performance. Human resource management policies are crucial to make all types of migrants contribute to organizational performance.

Overall, we support the point made by Thunnissen, Boselie, and Fruytier (2013) that in talent management context matters. Migration is an important context, and policies need to acknowledge it.

Key Learning Points

- The academic distinctions between assigned expatriates, self-initiated expatriates, and migrants are in reality blurry-edged and fluid. People move from one category to another.
- Migrants are a significant element of the international workforce with knowledge and skills that can aid the internationalization of the organization. Monitoring and record-keeping beyond the standard expatriate/local distinction would pay dividends. Migrants can be a cost-effective option for internationalization.
- Different kinds of migrants will have different motivations and will need different forms of management to be of most value to the organization. The four types of qualified migrants – Dream, Felicitous, Chance, and Desperate, with their particularities –need to be addressed by GTM policies. In all cases, integration policies help migrants to integrate. However, in general, integration policies have a greater impact on Felicitous and Desperate migrants than on Dream and Chance migrants.

References

Ahmad, A. 2008. 'Dead men working: Time and space in London's (illegal) migrant economy', *Work Employment & Society,* 22: 301–318.

Al Ariss, A. 2009. *Careers of skilled immigrants: A study of the capital accumulation and deployment experiences of the Lebanese in France.* PhD thesis.

Al Ariss, A. 2010. Modes of engagement: Migration, self-initiated expatriation, and career development. *Career Development International,* 15(4): 338–358.

Al Ariss, A., & Crowley-Henry, M. 2013. Self-initiated expatriation and migration in the management literature: Present theorizations and future research directions. *Career Development International,* 18(1): 78–96.

Al Ariss, A., & Syed, J. 2011. Capital mobilization of skilled migrants: A relational perspective. *British Journal of Management,* 22(2): 286–304.

Almeida, S., Fernando, M., & Sheridan, A. 2012. Revealing the screening: Organisational factors influencing the recruitment of immigrant professionals. *The International Journal of Human Resource Management,* 23(9): 1950–1965.

Álvarez-Galván, JL. 2012.*Outsourcing and service work in the new economy: The case of call centres in Mexico.* Newcastle: Cambridge Scholars Publishing.

Andresen, M., Al Ariss, A., & Walther, M. 2012. *Self-initiated expatriation: Mastering the dynamics.* New York: Routledge.

Barron, P., Bory, A., Chauvin, S., Jounin, N., & Tourette, L. 2016. State categories and labour protest: Migrant workers and the fight for legal status in France. *Work Employment & Society,* 30: 631–648.

Bauböck, R., & Faist, T. 2010. *Diaspora and transnationalism: Concepts, theories and methods.* Amsterdam: Amsterdam University Press.

Bloch, A. 2013. The labour market experiences and strategies of young undocumented migrants. *Work Employment & Society,* 27: 272–287.

Bloch, A., Sigona, N., & Zetter, R. 2011. Migration routes and strategies of young undocumented migrants in England: A qualitative perspective. *Ethnic and Racial Studies,* 34(8): 1286–1302.

Burrell, K., Hopkins, P., Isakjee, A., Lorne, C., Nagel, C., Finlay, R., Nayak, A., Benwell, M. C., Pande, R., & Richardson, M. 2019. Brexit, race and migration. *Environment and Planning C: Politics and Space,* 37(1): 3–40.

Castles, S., de Haas, H., & Miller, M. J. 2014. *The age of migration: International population movements in the modern world.* Basingstoke, Palgrave Macmillan.

Cerdin, J-L., Abdeljalil Diné, M., & Brewster, C. 2014. Qualified immigrants' success: Exploring the motivation to migrate and to integrate. *Journal of International Business Studies,* 45(2): 151–168.

Cerdin, J-L., & Brewster, C. 2014. Talent management and expatriation: Bridging two streams of research and practice. *Journal of World Business,* 49(2): 245–252.

Cerdin, J-L., & Selmer, J. 2014. Who is a self-initiated expatriate? Towards conceptual clarity of a common notion. *The International Journal of Human Resource Management,* 25(9): 1281–1301.

Chiswick, B. R. 1991. Speaking, reading, and earnings among low-skilled immigrants. *Journal of Labor Economics,* 9(2): 149–170.

Dench, S., Hurstfield, J., Hill, D., & Akroyd, K. 2006. *Employers use of migrant labour: Main Report.* London.

Evans, M. D. R., & Kelley, J. 1991. Prejudice, discrimination, and the labor market: Attainments of immigrants in Australia. *American Journal of Sociology,* 97: 721–759.

Foley, F., & Kerr, W. R. 2013. Ethnic innovation and U.S. multinational firm activity. *Management Science,* 59(7): 1529–1544.

Furusawa, M., & Brewster, C. 2015. The bi-cultural option for international human resource management: The Japanese/Brazilian *Nikkeijin* example. *Journal of World Business,* 50(1): 133–143.

Guiraudon, V. 2003. The constitution of a European immigration policy domain: A political sociological approach. *Journal of European Public Policy,* 10(2): 263–282.

Haak-Saheem, W., & Brewster, C. 2017. Hidden' expatriates: International mobility in the United Arab Emirates as a challenge to current understanding of expatriation. *Human Resource Management,* 27(3): 423–439.

Hainmueller, J., & Hiscox, M. J. 2010. Attitudes toward highly skilled and low-skilled immigration: Evidence from a survey experiment. *American Political Science Review,* 104(01): 61–84.

International Labour Organization (ILO). 2014. *Fair migration: Setting an ILO agenda. Report of the ILO Director General to the International Labour Conference.* Geneva, International Labour Office.

International Organization for Migration (IOM). 2018. *World migration report 2018.* Geneva, UN Migration Agency.

Lettner, H. 1997. Reconfiguring the spatiality of power: The construction of a supranational migration framework for the European Union. *Political Geography,* 16(2): 123–143.

Levy, O., Beechler, S., Taylor, S., & Boyacigiller, N. A. 2007. What we talk about when we talk about 'global mindset': Managerial cognition in multinational corporations. *Journal of International Business Studies,* 38: 231–258.

Mäkelä, K., & Brewster, C. 2009. Inter-unit interaction contexts, interpersonal social capital and the differing levels of knowledge sharing. *Human Resource Management,* 48(4): 591–613.

Mohyeldin, A., & Suliman, T. 2006. Human Resource management in the United Arab Emirates'. In P. Budhwar & K. Mellahi, *Managing human resources in the Middle East.* London, Routledge.

Mulholland, J., & Ryan, L. 2014. Doing the business: Variegation, opportunity and intercultural experience among intra-EU highly-skilled migrants. *International Migration,* 52(3): 55–68.

Newton, S., Pillay, J., & Higginbottom, G. 2012. The migration and transitioning experiences of internationally educated nurses: A global perspective. *Journal of Nursing Management,* 20, 534–550.

Organisation for Economic Co-operation and Development (OECD). 2003. *Glossary of statistical terms.* http://stats.oecd.org/glossary/detail.asp?ID=1284.

Organisation for Economic Co-operation and Development (OECD). 2013. *OECD factbook 2013. Economic, environmental and social statistics.* Paris: OECD Publications.

Potter, M., & Hamilton, J. 2014. Picking on vulnerable migrants: Precarity and the mushroom industry in Northern Ireland. *Work Employment & Society,* 28: 390–406.

Ramboarison-Lalao, L., Al Ariss, A., & Barth, I. 2012. Careers of qualified migrants: Understanding the experiences of Malagasy physicians in France. *Journal of Management Development,* 31: 116–129.

Reis, C. 2016. *Careers and talent management: A critical perspective.* New York: Routledge.

Rodriguez, J. K., & Mearns, L. 2012. Problematising the interplay between employment relations, migration and mobility. *Employee Relations,* 34(6): 580–593.

Schuler, R. A., Jackson, S.E. Tarique, I. 2010. Global talent management and global talent challenges: Strategic opportunities for IHRM. *Journal of World Business,* 46(4): 506–516.

Schuler, R. A., & Tarique, I. 2012. Global talent management: Theoretical perspectives, systems, and challenges, *Handbook of research in international human resource management:* 205–219. Cheltenham: Elgar.

Scullion, D., & Collings G. 2011. *Global talent management.* New York: Routledge.

Siebers, H., & Van Gastel, J. 2015. Why migrants earn less: In search of the factors producing the ethno-migrant pay gap in a Dutch public organization. *Work Employment & Society,* 29(3): 371–391.

Singh, S. 2013. *Globalization and money: A global south perspective.* New York: Rowman & Littlefield.

Sparrow, P. R. 2008. *International recruitment, skills supply and migration.* Sector Skills Development Agency (SSDA) Catalyst Report, Issue No. 4: 1–20.

Suutari, V., & Brewster, C. 2000. Making their own way: International experience through self-initiated assignments. *Journal of World Business,* 35(4): 417–436.

Thite, M., Srinivasan, V., Harvey, M., & Valk, R. 2009. Expatriates of host-country origin: Coming home to test the waters. *International Journal of Human Resource Management,* 20(2): 269–285.

Thunnissen, M., Boselie, P., & Fruytier, B. 2013. Talent management and the relevance of context: Towards a pluralistic approach. *Human Resource Management Review,* 23(4): 326–336.

Tsugawa, Y., Jena, A. B, Orav E. J., & Jha, A. K. 2017. Quality of care delivered by general internists in US hospitals who graduated from foreign versus US medical schools: Observational study. *BMJ,* 356: j273. https://www.bmj.com/content/356/bmj.j273

United Nations. 1998. *Recommendations on statistics of international migration. Revision 1.* Statistical Papers. Series M, No. 58, Glossary. New York: United Nations.

United Nations. 2013. *Population facts.* Department of Economic and Social Affairs, Population Division September (2013/3). New York: United Nations.

United Nations. 2019. *International migration report 2019.* New York: United Nations.

Vaiman, V., Sparrow, P., Schuler, R., & Collings, D. C. (Eds.) 2019a. *Macro talent management: A global perspective on managing talent in developed markets.* New York and London: Routledge.

Vaiman, V., Sparrow, P., Schuler, R., & Collings, D. C. (Eds.) 2019b. *Macro talent management: A global perspective on managing talent in developed markets.* New York and London: Routledge.

Vandor, P., & Franke, N. 2016. See Paris and… found a business? The impact of cross-cultural experience on opportunity recognition capabilities. *Journal of Business Venturing,* 31(4): 388–407.

Windsor, D. 2002. Public affairs, issues management, and political strategy: Opportunities, obstacles, and caveats. *Journal of Public Affairs,* 1(4): 382–415.

World Bank Group-KNOMAD. 2016. *Migration and remittances: Recent developments and outlook.* Washington, DC: World Bank.

World Bank Group. 2017. *Migration and development.* http://pubdocs.worldbank.org/en/992371492706371662/ Migration and Development Brief 27.pdf.

World Bank Group. 2019. *Migration and remittances: Recent developments and outlook.* International Bank for Reconstruction and Development, The World Bank, https://www.knomad.org/sites/default/files/2019-04/Migrationanddevelopmentbrief31.pdf, first accessed on June 17, 2019.

Zikic, J., Bonache, J., & Cerdin, J-L. 2010. Crossing national boundaries: A typology of qualified immigrants' career orientations. *Journal of Organizational Behavior,* 31(5): 667–686.

16

TALENT MANAGEMENT AND PERFORMANCE IN THE PUBLIC SECTOR

Paul Boselie

Marian Thunnissen

Joost Monster

Introduction

Talent management (TM) is one of the most popular themes in contemporary human resource management (HRM). TM is often defined as the systematic attraction, identification, development, engagement/retention, and deployment of talents (e.g., CIPD, 2006; Scullion, Collings, & Caligiuri, 2010). In practice, TM has gained popularity, mainly because of a growing awareness that human resources (employees) can be seen as the source of competitive advantage of an organization in the current knowledge intensive economy (Boxall & Purcell, 2016). Several societal developments such as globalization, technological developments (e.g., automation and robotization), and demographic developments (an aging population) have an effect on the demand for and availability of talent on the labor market.

Often the TM issues of information technology or high-tech companies are used as examples to set the scene. However, TM is not just a private sector hype. Public sector organizations are also confronted with HR challenges such as labor market scarcity and the unpopularity of certain public sector jobs. For example, in the Netherlands, health care (mainly medical doctors, nurses, and managers) and education (primarily teachers in primary and secondary education) suffer significantly from the chronic shortages of talent in the labor market (for more information see www.arbeidsmarktcijfers.nl). In many countries (e.g., Belgium, the Netherlands, and Germany), the public sector covers a significant part of the total labor market, with the government as one of the biggest employers in the country. Issues regarding the attraction, development, and deployment of talent can affect the performance of these organizations and, subsequently, the fulfillment of their public task. For example, Dutch newspapers frequently report the waiting lists for patients in mental health care due to a lack of staff, and schools in primary education are sometimes forced to increase the number of children in a classroom due to shortages in staff.

Despite these issues in practice, current research on TM is primarily focused on private sector organizations, in particular on the TM issues of large organizations operating on a global scale (Collings, Scullion, & Vaiman, 2011; Thunnissen & Gallardo-Gallardo, 2017). However, since the circumstances and characteristics of private sector organizations differ from those in public or non-profit sector organizations (Christensen, Laegrid, Roness, & Rovik, 2007), the current concepts and assumptions in the TM literature related to the context of private and multinational organizations are likely less than adequate to describe and study TM in organizations in other contexts.

Little attention is paid to specific TM issues in public sector organizations, how they define talent, and how successful they are in their battle for talent (Thunnissen, Boselie, & Fruytier, 2013). A review of empirical TM research by Thunnissen and Gallardo-Gallardo (2017) shows that just a minority of

DOI: 10.4324/9781315474687-16

publications are focused on TM issues in public sector organizations, such as health care institutes (e.g., Powell et al., 2012), higher education institutes (e.g., Thunnissen & Van Arensbergen, 2015), or local or central government organizations (e.g., Barkhuizen, 2014).

In addition, many scholars in the field argue that TM should be aimed at supporting organizations in reaching their goals, as well as in gaining competitive advantage by achieving organizational excellence (Thunnissen et al., 2013). Up until now, most of the conceptual TM literature points at the potential value of TM for the organization – in terms of efficiency, organizational flexibility, profit, and competitive advantage (e.g., Cappelli, 2008; Collings & Mellahi, 2009) – in line with the resource based view notions (De Boeck, Meyers, & Dries, 2018). Whether TM actually contributes to these outcomes is not clear, because up until now empirical research regarding the effects of TM is scarce; few empirical research studies investigate the outcomes of TM, and if they do, they investigate prevalent effects employee level outcomes (De Boeck et al., 2018; Thunnissen & Gallardo-Gallardo, 2017).

The value of TM for society as a whole is only mentioned in some conceptual TM papers (e.g., Boudreau & Ramstad, 2005), but is not investigated in empirical TM research. The conceptual focus on organizational level outcomes on the one hand, and the empirical focus on employee level outcomes on the other hand, can, however, be the result of the complexity of measuring TM effects in combination with the maturity of the TM discipline.

For public sector organizations, it is even more difficult to define organizational performance. A public sector organization has to deal with multiple stakeholders inside and outside the organization. It has serve to several "masters", and therefore should satisfy multiple goals. Claiming that TM primarily contributes to organizational well-being in terms of efficiency and flexibility ignores the specific context of public sector organizations have to address. Therefore it is important to increase our understanding of TM in the public sector, and in particular on the assumed relationship between TM and performance.

In sum, for TM we can identify multiple gaps in current TM literature and research:

1. The lack of empirical research on TM in the public sector, for example, in terms of what is actually applied in public sector organizations (Boselie & Thunnissen, 2017);
2. The lack of empirical research on the impact of TM on different types of outcomes, such as societal, organizational, and/or employee outcomes, in line with the Harvard Model for HRM (Beer, Boselie, & Brewster, 2015);
3. Little conceptual and empirical knowledge on the linkage between TM and performance in the public sector (Thunnissen & Gallardo-Gallardo, 2017).

This chapter aims to address these gaps, as it focuses on TM in public sector organizations and in particular on the current knowledge regarding the linkage between TM and performance in the public sector. The central research question of this chapter is: What do we know about the impact of talent management on organizational outcomes, employee well-being, and societal well-being in public sector organizations?

To answer this question we conducted an exploratory literature review that provides an overview of the insights from a select number of empirical publications on TM in public sector organizations. The overall objective of the chapter is to encourage dialogue among all TM scholars about the outcomes of TM, and in particular in the public sector, and to encourage further research in this area.

This chapter is organized into four sections. First, we will explore the academic debate regarding the linkage between HRM and performance, and in particular to the extent to which this discussion suits the specific public sector context. Three models will be presented to introduce the reader into the relationship between TM and performance in public sector organizations: 1) the multidimensional performance approach of the Harvard HRM-model (Beer et al., 2015); 2) the HR-process model (Wright & Nishii, 2013); and 3) the HRM-value chain in public sector organizations (Vandenabeele, Leisink, & Knies, 2013). These three models are used to build a TM value chain for public sector organizations.

In the second section of the chapter, the methodology for our review study is presented. A total of 29 articles on empirical research on TM in the public sector are included in this exploratory review. In the third section, the findings of the review study are put central. First we will discuss what is studied in general in empirical TM in the public sector, and subsequently we zoom in on the research regarding outcomes of TM. The chapter ends with a discussion of the findings and suggestions for further research on TM in the public sector.

Talent Management and Performance in the Public Sector: A Conceptual Framework

For a better understanding of the relationship between TM and performance in the public sector, the existing and long-lasting general HRM and performance debate can be a guideline. The HRM and performance debate started with ground-breaking studies by Arthur (1994) and Huselid (1995) that had an impact on further empirical research on the added value of HRM. The early HRM and performance studies focused mainly on the effects of HRM practices on organizational outcomes such as productivity, profits, sales, and market value (Boselie et al., 2015). The majority of these outcomes are irrelevant for the public sector context, although public sector organizations are also challenged by defining public sector performance and the way to affect it with the right people management (Knies et al., 2018).

In the early 2000s, the general HRM and performance debate not only focused on organizational outcomes, but also on employee outcomes such as job satisfaction, motivation, turnover, absence due to illness, and commitment. It reflects the problem of defining and measuring performance beyond simple financial indicators. In a reaction to the 1990s, HRM and performance research Guest (1997) pointed out the need for new models and theory on what is performance and how to measure it. He made a plea for more theory and models on: 1) What is HRM?; 2) What is performance and how can we measure it?; and 3) What is the relationship between the two?

More than two decades later. it is generally acknowledged that HRM can have a positive impact on certain outcomes (Paauwe & Farndale, 2017), yet for the public sector it often seems difficult to measure performance and to determine the effects of HRM on performance (see for example, the special issue on strategic HRM and public sector performance, guest edited by Knies, Boselie, Vandenabeele, & Gould-Williams, 2018).

To understand the added value of TM in the public sector context – TM and performance – three popular HRM models will be presented in line with Guest's (1997) plea for theories and models on what is HRM, what is performance, and what is the relationship between the two. These models are:

1. the Harvard HRM-model, which identifies different (possible) outcomes of TM in terms of individual well-being, organizational effectiveness, and societal well-being, also known as a multidimensional performance approach by Beer, Boselie, & Brewster (2015);
2. the HR-process model of Wright and Nishii (2013), disentangling the "route" from intended HR practices to actual outcomes in separate stages;
3. the HRM-value chain made specific for the public sector by Vandenabeele et al. (2013).

What Is Performance in the Public Sector?

Academics involved in the public sector performance debate state that in the measurement of performance, context specific characteristics have to be taken into account. Private companies define organizational performance in terms of productivity, service quality, sales, profits, market share, and market value. However, the public sector context is much more complex because of the significant impact of institutional mechanisms, such as the presence and influence of multiple stakeholders inside and outside public sector organizations, the role of the government (including the authorizing environment), the relevance of politics, and the impact of public values linked to institutions and culture (Christensen, Laegrid Roness, & Rovik, 2007; Leisink, Boselie, Hosking, & Van Bottenburg, 2013).

In many public sector contexts, organizational performance is affected by political choices, professional norms and values determined by professional bodies and professional associations, and regulatory, authorities that check safety, quality, and integrity of public sector organizations (Vandenabeele et al., 2013). The organizational performance in public sector organizations is therefore more heterogeneous, context specific, and highly dependent on regulations, political decisions, and external stakeholders.

The Harvard Model (Beer et al., 1984; Beer et al., 2015) is the oldest model to explain HRM outcomes and the relevance of context. The model heavily builds on multiple stakeholder theory and situational factors known from strategic contingency approaches of the 1970s and 1980s. Overall, the Harvard Model incorporates multiple stakeholders such as managers, shareholders, trade unions, employees, and government in combination with acknowledging contextual factors that are assumed to affect the shaping of HRM and its impact on performance. Performance is defined as a multidimensional construct acknowledging 1) organizational effectiveness, 2) employee well-being, and 3) societal well-being as equally important long-term consequences in the value chain of an organization.

In addition, the authors of the model assume possible tensions between the three performance dimensions. This is exactly the type of "What is performance?" (Guest, 1997) that fits the nature of performance debates – measurement and impact – in public sector contexts. The lessons from the Harvard Model for TM and performance in the public sector, therefore, are mainly focused on acknowledging multiple stakeholders, context, and a multidimensional performance framework.

The Link between HRM and Performance

A few years ago, Wright and Nishii (2013') developed the HR Process Model that addresses Guest's (1997) question "What is HRM?" Their model was groundbreaking because of the differentiation between intended HRM practices, actual HRM practices, and perceived HRM practices. The intended HRM practices represent the policies and the decision making with respect to HRM. The actual HRM practices refer to the implementation of HRM, often by line managers at different levels of the organization. Finally, the perceived HRM practices refer to the way HRM is internalized and experienced by employees.

In a perfect situation, there is full alignment of intended, actual, and perceived HRM practices. In practice, there are often significant differences between the stages of the HRM chain in the HR Process Model causing variance. Wright and Nishii (2013) put a heavy emphasis on the relevance of a consistent and coherent approach, and to communication and information to all the actors involved (line of sight), and line managers as HRM enactors, to prevent variety in the HR-process.

The Complex Relationship between HRM and Performance in the Public Sector

For a further contextualization of HRM and performance, the model by Vandenabeele et al. (2013) is insightful. They developed an HRM value chain including the HR Process Model by Wright and Nishii (2013), the AMO model (abilities, motivation, and opportunity to participate), public service performance and public administration on public values and public value. In this specific public sector context, Vandenabeele and colleagues (2013) make a distinction between the authorizing environment and public values. The authorizing environment consists of politician and stakeholder influences. The stakeholders can be situated outside and inside the organization, i.e., governmental policy makers, political parties and unions, audit offices, and governmental advisory bodies, as well as managers and public service workers within the organization.

Public values refer to the public sectors' contribution to society (e.g., service to society as a whole, social cohesion, and sustainability), and how public sector organizations and their employees should behave in relation to their environment, such as politicians and citizens, referring to values such as loyalty, responsiveness, accountability, honesty, and integrity (Jørgensen & Bozeman, 2007). The public values are determined by the existing institutional and cultural framework. The shaping of HRM and the effects of HRM in a public sector context are complicated and often fuzzy. The Vandenabeele et al. (2013) model can be a guideline for understanding the value chain in public sector contexts.

TM Value Chain for Public Sector Organizations

Guest's (1997) three questions can also be applied to TM and performance in the public sector context. The Harvard Model (Beer et al., 1984; Beer et al., 2015), the HR Process Model (Wright & Nishii, 2013), and the Vandenabeele et al. (2013) model provide HRM and public sector specific frameworks for putting TM and performance into perspective:

- For the "What is the value of TM in terms of performance and outcomes?" question, the Harvard Model with its multiple stakeholder perspective, situational factors, and multidimensional performance construct is helpful;
- For the "What is TM?" question, we can use the HR Process Model with its distinction between intended, actual, and perceived HRM practices;
- The "What is the relationship between TM and performance?" in the public sector question is addressed by the Vandenabeele et al. (2013) model with its public sector specificity.

First, in line with Boselie and Thunnissen (2017), we expect that this general HRM value chain designed for the public sector context is also applicable to a TM value chain for public sector organizations (see also the integrated and dynamic TM model of Thunnissen & Gallardo-Gallardo, 2017). When we apply the HR Process Model by Wright and Nishhi (2013) to TM, we assume that a TM strategy reflects the management intentions towards talents (intended TM strategy), the TM implementation is related to management actions (actual TM practices), and the TM perceptions represent the way TM is perceived by its receivers (the employees) who are confronted with the TM strategy and interventions (perceived TM practices).

Second, TM interventions and perceptions are assumed to result in employee reactions (abilities, motivation, and opportunities) and, subsequently, in TM outcomes. The TM outcomes will be defined by the Harvard Model (Beer et al., 2015) in terms of organizational well-being (public service performance), employee well-being (for example, in terms of employee health and job satisfaction), and societal well-being (for example, client and citizen satisfaction). The concept of societal well-being is closely related to the Public Administration concept of public value (Moore, 1995). Public organizations do not aim for maximizing sales, profits, or market value. Instead public organizations often have an alternative goal labeled public value, for example, in terms of high-quality education in schools and safe health care in hospitals.

The contextualization and conceptualization of TM in relationship to multiple outcomes (individual, organizational, and societal) was also picked up by Thunnissen, Boselie, and Fruytier (2013) in a multi-level and multidimensional TM approach. The authors argue that too little attention is paid to the societal relevance of TM in combination with the macro implications of TM. The latter is now highlighted and stressed in what has become known as Macro TM, or the human capital potential and development within different regions and countries (Thunnissen, Schippers, & Boselie, 2018; Vaiman, Sparrow, Schuler, & Collings, 2018).

Finally, HRM in the public sector implies a contextualization of the whole value chain, including the input (HRM choices), the mediators and moderators (the interventions and perceptions), and results (multidimensional performance indicators). In line with the Vandenabeele et al. model (2013), we assume that the external context will continuously affect the complete TM value chain, from the development of the intended TM strategy, through the actual implementation of TM and the outcomes of TM (see Figure 16.1).

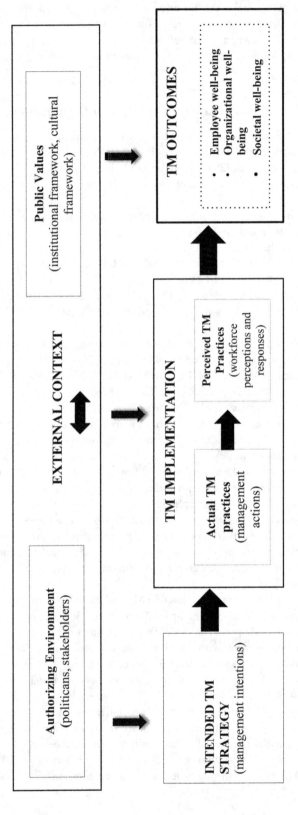

Figure 16.1 TM value chain for the public sector

Methodology

To gain insight in TM in the public sector, in particular in what is already known about the relationship between TM and performance in the public sector, we conducted an exploratory literature review. The selection of studies for the analysis was based on multiple criteria. First, we focused on publications discussing empirical research on TM in the public sector, thus conceptual papers were excluded. Second, only studies published in international academic journals were included. Working papers, dissertations, book chapters, and reports are not included in the overview. Third, we only included articles written in English and published in peer-reviewed journals that are acknowledged in Web of Science or Scopus as a quality standard for the articles used for further analysis. Fourth, many TM research studies investigate TM in multiple sectors, including the public sector as one of the sectors (see Thunnissen & Gallardo-Gallardo, 2017).

Since it is not possible to extract the specific information about the public sector in those papers, we decided to only include studies in which the data were collected in the public sector exclusively. We utilized Web of Science and Scopus databases for article identification and retrieval. The terms "talent" and "talent management" as search strings in title, key words, and abstract of the article. Often the terms talent or talent management are used superficially to attract the attention of the reader to a hot topic, while in the end the paper is on another subject (see Thunnissen & Gallardo-Gallardo, 2017).

To be included in the review the article had to be on TM or on a clearly related theme (for example, graduate development programs in the study of Clarke, 2017), big performers in public sector organizations (as in the study of Van de Wal, 2017), and attracting international postdoctoral students in university contexts (as in the study by Brosi & Welpe, 2015). We did not set a timeframe for the selection. All empirical publications published up until mid-2018 were included. In the end, a total of 29 empirical articles on TM in the public sector context were identified. All publications are marked with a *in the References list.

The publications were analyzed in a number of ways. First, we identified some bibliometric data of the publications, in terms of journals, authors, and years of publication. Second, we focused on the context (the country and subsector of data collection) and the methodology (methods and respondents included in the study). Third, we recorded how the talent and TM were operationalized. Finally, the focus was put on the TM process and the outcomes of TM: Is there attention in the publication for outcomes of TM, and in what way? In the next section, the results of this analysis will be presented.

Results

Journals, Year of Publication and Authors

The selection process resulted in a total of 29 articles presenting findings of empirical research on TM in the public sector. Previous reviews (e.g., Gallardo-Gallardo, Nijs, Dries, & Gallo, 2015) show that 2006 was the starting point of the academic attention for TM, and that after some calls for more empirical research by renowned TM scholars (Collings & Mellahi, 2009; Lewis & Heckman, 2006), empirical research increased significantly since 2010 (see Thunnissen & Gallardo-Gallardo, 2017).

One of the earliest empirical publications on TM in the public sector we found was published in 2008 on TM by Kock and Burke (2008). This country-level case study, based on secondary analysis of policy documents and reports, describes the rise and implementation of TM in the South Africa public service. The majority of papers (15 articles), however, are from a more recent date and are published in 2016, 2017, and 2018. This is more than six years later than the "publication explosion" since 2010 identified by Thunnissen and Gallardo-Gallardo (2017).

Only a quarter of all articles were published in the regular HRM journals, with two articles published in *Personnel Review* and three articles in *Employee Relations*. The majority of the papers in the overview stem from a wide range of journals that are management journals in general (e.g., *European Management Journal, Journal of World Business*), or specifically focused on management and policy making in the public sector (e.g., *Public Personnel Management, Public Money & Management*) or sector specific (e.g., *Studies in Higher Education, Journal of Health Organization and Management*).

Nearly 40 scholars were involved writing the empirical papers. Some authors appear in multiple journal articles, in particular Thunnissen (four articles; focus on higher education), the group of scholars Macfarlane, Powell, and Duberley (two articles; focus on health care), and Clarke (two articles; focus on graduate development programs in public sector), which probably reflects the research focus and expertise of these TM scholars or the richness of their dataset.

The Research Context

We see that the data are gathered in a variety of national contexts, although the data from four countries prevail. Six articles were based on UK data, for example, Harris and Foster's study (2010) on TM, equality and diversity in two British public sector organizations. Five articles include data from the Netherlands, for example, the article by Thunnissen and Van Arensbergen (2015) on TM in Dutch academia. Three articles are based on data from South Africa including a study by Barkhuizen (2014) on TM in South African local government institutions, and also three articles are grounded in Australian research, for example, Liang, Howard, Leggat, and Bartram's study (2018) on health service management competencies in health care contexts.

The other articles are based on data from different countries, for example, from other African and Asian countries. There are also seven articles in which TM approaches in multiple countries are compared, e.g., the study on public sector TM schemes in Thailand, Malaysia, and Singapore by Poocharoen and Lee (2013).

Education and health care seem to attract the most academic interest. Nearly half of the articles on TM were focused on higher education (seven articles) (e.g., Erasmus, Naidoo, & Joubert, 2017; Paisey & Paisey, 2016) or on health care organizations such as hospitals (seven articles) (e.g., Day et al., 2014; Groves, 2011). Both universities and hospitals employ professionals (scientists and medical specialists) that can be considered as core employees or talents that play a strategic role in the organization's success. This might be an explanation for the popularity of TM in these two public sector contexts. Other public sectors include public services, primary and secondary schools, local governments, and public electricity utilities (e.g., Barkhuizen, 2014; Rhodes & Brundrett, 2012).

Research Methods

Half of the articles (14) articles apply qualitative research methods using semi-structured interviews, unstructured interviews, focus groups, documents, and secondary data. Four papers are purely based on the analysis of secondary data, on a sector level. Only two articles apply a pure quantitative research method using survey questionnaires. In five articles, we have identified a mixed methods technique combing, for example, interviews and survey data. This dominance of qualitative research could be expected in the relatively young academic field of TM, but is, however, in contrast to the general development of the TM field, in which quantitative research methods are more often used (Thunnissen & Gallardo-Gallardo, 2017).

Note that we only found two articles that use some kind of longitudinal method (e.g., Thunnissen, 2016). From a TM and performance perspective, only longitudinal data can lead to the determination of causal relationships between TM and outcome.

Research Population

The review shows that empirical TM research is mainly focused on the organizational perspective. Half of the articles in our database present the data from a multi-level study in which managers, selection committee members, HRM, and/or employees are included as respondents and share their experiences with the implementation of TM in the organization (e.g., Mtshali, Proches, & Green, 2018). In additions, a quarter of the articles exclusively reflect management's perceptions and experiences with the implementation of a TM system in the organization (e.g., Paisey & Paisey, 2016). Approximately a quarter of the articles have employees as core respondents groups, presenting their perceptions and reactions to TM (e.g., Clarke, 2017; Swailes & Blackburn, 2016).

Defining Talent Management

One of the core debates in TM is related to the inclusive (the talents or abilities of all employees) or the exclusive approach to TM (aimed at attracting and retaining a select group of employees) (Gallardo-Gallardo, Dries, & Gonzalez- Cruz, 2013). Inclusive TM builds on the notion that every employee has talents that can be developed and used in an organization. The inclusive TM approach is also closely related to "the good employer notions" in combination with "equality" fundaments that are charac-teristic for many public sector contexts (Boselie & Thunnissen, 2017). Many public sector contexts have a rich history in aiming for "the good employer" for its workforce, all workers being equal. Research shows that public sector organizations apply both exclusive and inclusive TM approaches (e.g., Thunnissen & Buttiens, 2017).

The studies on TM in the public sector emphasize the exclusive talent approach, and investigate the attraction and retention of an elite group of employees. This starts with the definition for TM used in the articles. Most articles refer in their own words to the TM definition of the Chartered Institute of Personnel and Development (CIPD). The CIPD describes TM as the systematic attraction, identifica-tion, development, engagement/retention, and deployment of talents.

Suk Kim and Kotchegura (2017), for example, define TM as the systematic attraction, identification, development, engagement/retention, and deployment of those individuals who are of particular value to an organization, either due to their high potential for the future or because they are in business/ operationally-critical roles. Groves (2011) sees TM as an integrated set of processes, programs, and cul-tural norms in an organization designed and implemented to attract, develop, deploy, and retain talent to achieve strategic objectives and meet future business needs. Heilmann (2010) describes TM as a set of HRM practices, such as recruiting, selection, compensation, performance management, development, career succession planning, and retention practices.

The CIPD definition of TM can be seen as a micro HRM bundles that consists of multiple single HR practices that are aligned together according to strategic HRM notions (Boselie, 2014). Moreover, this definition highlights organizational well-being and does not refer to employee or societal well-being, which we, in line with Beer et al. (2015), also mentioned as potential outcomes of TM.

Some papers refer to vague talent definitions such as "highly skilled workers", "individuals who are critical in achieving organizational goals", or "public sector "superheroes" (Day et al., 2014). Other studies explicitly discus the attraction and retention of leadership talent (e.g., Macfarlane et al., 2012; Mtshali, Proches, & Green, 2018). Some studies focus on an inclusive talent approach (e.g., Erasmus, Naidoo, & Loubert, 2017) or compare the perceptions of talents selected for a talent pool versus the employees not selected (Swailes & Blackburn, 2016)

The TM Process

Nearly 40% of the studies (11 articles) are focused on the implementation of TM (i.e., the actual practices in the terms of Wright and Nishii, 2013). Examples are the study of Van den Brink et al. (2013) on the actual selection process of academic talents in Dutch universities, or the paper by Powel et al. (2016) on the implementation of TM in the British health care system. Many of these studies are qualitative studies investigating the experiences and perceptions of actors involved in TM, including employees, which makes it difficult to separate perceptions from the actions in the TM process.

Just a handful of papers are focused on either the intended TM strategy (four articles; e.g., Glenn, 2012) or the employee perceptions and reactions (four articles; e.g., Clarcke & Scurry, 2017; Mensah & Bawole, 2017). Investigating the whole TM process, from intended practices to outcomes, is scarce, although the studies by Swailes and Blackburn (2016) and Thunnissen (2016) offer interesting insights in this matter. The concept of societal well-being receives no attention.

The Vandenabeele et al. (2013) model shows the continuing impact of contextual factors on the HRM process in public sector organizations. In most papers exploring the influence of factors and actors in the context on TM is not the core quest in the study, although they do mention some issues that hinder effective implementation, such as unclear definitions, different perceptions of talent, or the ambiguous role of the line manager (Mtshali et al., 2018; Powell et al., 2016). Interesting are the studies focusing on the implementation of TM schemes in the public sector of a specific country (e.g., Kock & Burke, 2008; Poocharoen & Lee, 2013; Van der Wal, 2017), because they, in line with the upcoming stream of research on MTM, mainly focus on the institutional and market developments and impact factors organizations have to deal with when implementing TM.

The Added Value of TM in Public Sector Contexts

Consistent with previous reviews (Gallardo-Gallardo et al., 2015; Thunnissen & Gallardo-Gallardo, 2017), our exploratory review shows that the effectiveness of TM is underexplored in research on TM in the public sector. In 18 articles, effects on performance were not the subject of study. The articles investigate, for example, the operationalization of talent, the competencies of leadership talent, or actual TM practices such as the implementation of a TM practice, such as the recruitment or selection of talent (e.g., Erasmus et al., 2017; Rhodes & Brundrett, 2012; Saddozai et al., 2017; Thunnissen & Buttiens, 2017; Thunnissen & Van Arensbergen, 2015; Van den Broek et al., 2017).

Some publications, however, hint to a possible relation between TM and outcomes, but cannot build these arguments on empirical evidence because they did not gather empirical data on this matter. In the research by Glenn (2012), for example, the effects of TM on getting the right people in the right place are still to be evaluated. Other articles are very speculative and assume effects, although they did not investigate these effects themselves. Groves (2011), for instance, argues that when all the phases are implemented, sustainable competitive advantage can be achieved. Clarke and Scurry (2017) claim that TM with good implementation, including psychological contract attention, has the potential to be beneficial. Nonetheless, we also notice that other studies are very careful with claims regarding the relationship between TM and performance. For example, Suk Kim and Kotchegura (2017) write that the results have been modest because none of the countries has managed to implement a comprehensive strategy to attract and retain talent.

The other 11 articles included in this review provided empirical data concerning the effects of TM inducements (e.g. Madichie & Nyakang'o, 2016; Paisey & Paisey, 2016), although in some studies these effects were found accidently or indirectly. For example, Day et al. (2014) did not intentionally investigate TM effects, but their study on talents of health care leaders found that if health care leaders have certain talents and abilities, this results in better health care and a more healthy population, although the causality is not straightforward. In other words, a reversed causality cannot be excluded.

Studies that mention organizational performance find diverse results regarding the relation between TM and this performance. Macfarlane et al. (2012), for instance, conclude that there is empirical evidence for the impact of a "hard" TM policy on the performance of the British National Health System. Yet, this evidence is limited, partly due to the difficulty of defining performance. Additionally, Mtshali et al. (2018) find that despite the rigorous TM process, there was no increase in organizational performance, because of multiple factors, but mainly because of failures in implementation.

Studies investigating TM effects are dominated by a focus on employee level outcomes: individual employee performance. Swailes and Blackburn (2016) find that performance of individuals in talent pools is increased because of exclusive TM rather than inclusive policies and practices. However, the question of reversed causality could be asked here, too, because Powell et al. (2013) conclude that performance is important in the selection of talents and that there is limited robust evidence for the effectiveness of TM.

However, the study by Van der Wal (2017) found that the nationwide introduction of private sector practices in the public sector, such as employer branding and recruitment efforts, seem to enhance the performance of a country. These successful countries managed to speak out to intelligent individuals whose key motivations correspond with the intellectual challenges and complexities public sector jobs in dynamic contexts have to offer. This is partly underlined by Brosi and Welpe (2015) who claim that good employer branding (mostly the quality of the relation with the mentor) positively influences performance.

Besides the positive effects, some studies address the "dark side" of TM in public sector organizations. Poocharoen and Lee (2013), for example, found that TM can help to increase individual performance, however, the performance related pay and appraisal should be transparent in order to cause no harm to the rest of the organization, in particular related to jealousy that can negatively affect performance. Moreover, Barkhuizen (2014) found that poor TM practices increase employee working hours, which in turn can lead to poor individual and organizational performance, showing an undesired risk of (bad) TM.

What worries us is that there is little clarity about the outcome indicators used in the articles. There is a tendency of focusing on attitudinal and behavioral outcome measurement (at the employee level) linked to TM interventions, but given the research methods (mainly qualitative), it is not straightforward what is exactly being measured. Poocharoen and Lee (2013), for example, focus on motivation of talents and non-talents. Rhodes and Brundrett (2012) look at an enhanced commitment of talented staff, an improved pipeline of high-quality leaders and more support for school improvement. Organizational performance as a final outcome is problematic, probably as a direct result of the public sector context in which public service performance is ambiguous and contested (Knies et al., 2018).

Overall the empirical studies in our review reveal that the effects of TM on performance are fuzzy or absent. There is no convincing empirical evidence for a positive effect of TM on performance on the basis of the 29 empirical articles selected in this study. Only a few articles in our analysis find an effect of TM, yet the number of articles is too low to draw conclusions. This is partly caused by the wide focus of empirical studies in the area of public sector TM, some of which are not aimed at the added value of TM as such. Almost every study assumes a link between TM and organizational performance, but it is often not the real focus of the study. And there is almost no quantitative work about TM in the public sector.

Conclusion and Areas of Further Research

The central research question of this chapter is: What do we know about the impact of talent management on organizational outcomes, employee well-being, and societal well-being in public sector organizations? We started off with the ambition of presenting a review of findings that could contribute to the further development of TM research, for example, through the development of new propositions and hypotheses, and practical implications for public sector organizations who apply TM in their organization. Although there are many publications discussing empirical TM research, we could only identify 29 empirical articles on TM in the public sector. Of those 29 articles, more than half of the articles in reality did not present empirical findings on the impact of TM. The empirical TM research in the public sector goes in multiple directions.

Those studies that focus on outcomes or performance show a tendency towards the measurement of performance according to private sector standards, i.e., a focus on organizational well-being or on employee well-being in the light of the importance for organizational performance. There is a risk of neglecting the (public) contexts in these approaches. We conclude that while TM as a discipline has reached a stage of adolescence (see also Thunnissen et al., 2013, and the Oxford University Press Handbook of Talent Management, 2017), the empirical research on TM in the public sector in general; on the link between TM and public sector in specific, the research is still in its infancy.

This research area could benefit from the developments related to the HRM and performance debate that emerged in the mid-90s. In that ongoing debate, we observe (a) an increase in the number of empirical studies; (b) the inclusion of employee related outcomes (for example, employee well-being in terms of employee health, vitality, and burnout risks); (c) theoretical expansion using theories from different scientific fields (for example, the resource-based view from strategic management and the social exchange theory from applied psychology); (d) increased methodological rigor using both sophisticated research designs and advanced research methods (for example, multilevel analysis); (e) the inclusion of multiple internal and external stakeholders; and (f) first attempts to expand the concept of performance (organizational effectiveness and employee well-being) with societal well-being or what is known as public value creation in Public Administration.

The TM community has to be careful not to reinvent the HRM and performance wheel through linking empirical TM research to the general HRM and performance debate using insights from both HRM and organizational behavior.

Knies et al. (2018) show that public sector performance is difficult and challenging from a practitioner and academic point of view. That, however, does not mean that organizational effectiveness, employee well-being and societal well-being (or public value) are irrelevant. On the contrary, some degree of employee differentiation in terms of TM within a public sector context is most likely to affect the multi-dimensional performance construct suggested in the Harvard Model (Beer et al., 2015).

More research is required to open that public sector "black box" of TM effects. It is therefore too early to formulate propositions or hypotheses. Context specific models, such as the one by Vandenabeele et al. (2013), are required to put the theories, research designs, and research methods into perspective. Context matters (Paauwe & Farndale, 2017) and public sector characteristics affect the shaping of HRM, TM, performance, and the possible linkages (Boselie & Thunnissen, 2017).

Overall, we think it is important to do more empirical research on talent management in public sector organizations. This suggests the inclusion of public sector sensitive theories, such as public service motivation theory (Vandenabeele et al., 2013) and more recent theoretical insights from what is becoming known as behavioral public administration theory, focused on affecting attitudes and behaviors of public sector workers. The public sector context is very different from the private sector on which the majority of HRM and TM models are based. The intrinsic motivation of public sector workers is often linked to their occupation (for example, nurses, police officers, firefighters, and teachers) in combination with certain deeper drivers for working in that specific organizational environment, wanting to cure people, help and rescue citizens, or contribute to the development of children.

In addition, the often highly institutionalized public sector contexts, in terms of both normative and coercive mechanisms, require public administration and institutional theories to fully understand the different mechanisms that affect managerial choices, underlying processes, and outcome choices. The above potentially requires a multidisciplinary approach using theoretical insights from the fields of HRM, organizational behavior (psychology), public administration and organization studies.

We suggest the application of both quantitative and qualitative research methods. Quantitative research through large (longitudinal) surveys or field experiments on TM and performance could benefit from multilevel research designs taking into account both TM input and TM outcomes at individual employee, team, and organization level. Qualitative research through case study designs could also be applied to TM and performance research in the public sector to better understand the whole TM value chain and the underlying TM processes from input to final output. The use of mixed methods (both qualitative and quantitative research) is quite common in contemporary mainstream HRM research.

The 29 empirical articles on TM and performance in the public sector that we identified and analyzed in this chapter were published in a variety of journals, with only a quarter of the articles published in regular academic HRM journals. We suggest focusing TM and performance papers in the public sector targeting the HRM journals with their HRM audience and community given the fact that the public sector is a significant area in practice in combination with the mainstream HRM focus on large private sector organizations.

References

⋆articles with an asterisk are included in the literature review

Arthur, J. B. 1994. Effects of human resource systems on manufacturing performance harrheilm and turnover. *Academy of Management Journal,* 37(3): 670–687.

⋆Barkhuizen, N. 2014. How Relevant Is Talent Management in South African Local Government Institutions? *Mediterranean Journal of Social Sciences,* 5(20): 2223.

Beer, M., Boselie, P., & Brewster, C. 2015. Back to the future: Implications for the field of HRM of the multistakeholder perspective proposed 30 years ago. *Human Resource Management,* 54(3): 427–438.

Boselie, P. 2014. *Strategic human resource management: A balanced approach* (2nd ed.). New York: McGraw Hill.

Boselie, P., Dietz, G., & Boon, C. 2005. Commonalities and contradictions in HRM and performance research. *Human Resource Management Journal,* 15(3): 67–94.

Boselie, P., & Thunnissen, M. 2017. Talent management in the public sector. In D. G. Collings, K. Mellahi, & W. F. Cascio (Eds.), *The Oxford handbook of talent management.* Oxford, UK: Oxford University Press.

Boxall, P., & Purcell, J. 2016. *Strategy and human resource management* (4th ed.). Palgrave Macmillan.

⋆Brosi, P., & Welpe, I. M. 2015. Employer branding for universities: What attracts international postdocs?. *Journal of Business Economics,* 85(7), 817–850.

Christensen, T., Lægreid, P., Roness, P. G., & Røvik, K. A. 2007. *Organization theory and the public sector: Instrument, culture and myth.* Routledge.

CIPD. 2006. *Talent management: Understanding the dimensions.* London: CIPD.

⋆Clarke, M. 2017. Building employability through graduate development programmes: A case study in an Australian public sector organisation. *Personnel Review,* 46(4): 792–808.

⋆Clarke, M., & Scurry, T. 2017. The role of the psychological contract in shaping graduate experiences: A study of public sector talent management programmes in the UK and Australia. *The International Journal of Human Resource Management:* 1–27.

⋆Day, M., Shickle, D., Smith, K., Zakariasen, K., Moskol, J., & Oliver, T. 2014. Training public health superheroes: five talents for public health leadership. *Journal of Public Health,* 36(4): 552–56.

De Boeck, G., Meyers, M. C., & Dries, N. 2018. Employee reactions to talent management: Assumptions versus evidence. *Journal of Organizational Behavior,* 39(2): 199–213.

⋆Erasmus, B., Naidoo, L., & Joubert, P. 2017. Talent management implementation at an open distance e-learning higher educational institution: The views of senior line managers. *The International Review of Research in Open and Distributed Learning,* 18(3).

Gallardo-Gallardo, E., Dries, N., and González- Cruz, T. 2013. What is the meaning of talent in the world of work? *Human Resource Management Review,* 23(4): 290–300.

Gallardo-Gallardo, E., & Thunnissen, M. 2016. Standing on the shoulders of giants? A critical review of empirical talent management research. *Employee Relations,* 38(1): 31–56.

⋆Glenn, T. 2012. The state of talent management in Canada's public sector. *Canadian Public Administration,* 55(1): 25–51.

⋆Groves, K. S. 2011. Talent management best practices: How exemplary health care organizations create value in a down economy. *Health Care Management Review,* 36(3): 227–240.

⋆Harrisr, L. & Foster, C. 2010. Aligning talent management with approaches to equality and diversity. *Equality, Diversity and Inclusion: An International Journal,* 29(5): 422–435.

⋆Heilmann, P. 2010. To have and to hold: Personnel shortage in a Finnish healthcare organisation. *Scandinavian Journal of Public Health,* 38(5): 518–523.

Huselid, M. A. 1995. The impact of human resource management practices on turnover, productivity, and corporate financial performance. *Academy of Management Journal,* 38(3): 635–672.

Jørgensen, T. B., & Bozeman, B. 2007. Public values: An inventory. *Administration and Society,* 39(3): 354–381.

Knies, E., Boselie, P., Gould-Williams, J. & Vandenabeele, W. 2018. Strategic human resource management and public sector performance: context matters. *The International Journal of Human Resource Management,* 29(1): 1–13

⋆Kock, R., & Burke, M. 2008. Managing talent in the South African public service. *Public Personnel Management,* 37(4): 457–470.

⋆Liang, Z., Howard, P. F., Leggat, S., & Bartram, T. 2018. Development and validation of health service management competencies. *Journal of Health Organization and Management,* 32(2): 157–175.

⋆Macfarlane, F., Duberley, J., Fewtrell, C., & Powell, M. 2012. Talent management for NHS managers: Human resources or resourceful humans? *Public Money & Management,* 32(6): 445–452.

⋆Madichie, N. O., & Nyakang'o, M. 2016. An exploratory insight into the workplace demographic challenges in the public sector: A Kenyan perspective. *Employee Relations,* 38(6): 859–885.

⋆Mensah, J. K., & Bawole, J. N. 2017. Person–job fit matters in parastatal institutions: Testing the mediating effect of person–job fit in the relationship between talent management and employee outcomes. *International Review of Administrative Sciences,* 86(3): 479–495.

Moore, M. 1995. *Creating public value: Strategic management in government.* Cambridge, MA: Harvard University Press.

★Mtshali, Z., Proches, C. N. G., & Green, P. 2018. Challenges that hinder effective implementation of a talent management system: A case of a public electricity utility company in Africa. *International Journal of Applied Engineering Research,* 13(2): 1286–1293.

★Paisey, C., & Paisey, N. J. 2016. Talent management in academia: The effect of discipline and context on recruitment. *Studies in Higher Education,* 1–19.

Paauwe, J., & Farndale, E. 2017. *Strategy, HRM, and Performance: A Contextual Approach.* Oxford University Press.

★Poocharoen, O., & Lee, C. 2013. Talent management in the public sector: A comparative study of Singapore, Malaysia, and Thailand. *Public Management Review,* 15(8): 1185–1207.

★Powell, M., Duberley, J., Exworthy, M., Macfarlane, F., & Moss, P. 2013. Has the British National Health Service (NHS) got talent? A process evaluation of the NHS talent management strategy?. *Policy Studies,* 34(3): 291–309.

★Rhodes, C., & Brundrett, M. 2012. Retaining leadership talent in schools. *International Studies in Educational Administration,* Commonwealth Council for Educational Administration & Management (CCEAM), 40(1).

★Saddozai, S. K., Hui, P., Akram, U., Khan, M. S., & Memon, S. 2017. Investigation of talent, talent management, its policies and its impact on working environment. *Chinese Management Studies,* 11(3): 538–554.

Scullion, H., Collings, D. G., & Caligiuri, P. 2010. Global talent management. *Journal of World Business,* 45(2): 105–8.

Sparrow, P., Schuler, R., & Collings, D. 2018. *Macro talent management: A global perspective on managing talent in developed markets.* Routledge Publishers.

★Suk Kim, P., & Kotchegura, A. 2017. Talent management in government in times of economic instability: selected cases from the BRICS countries. *Public Money & Management,* 37(1): 7–14.

★Swailes, S., & Blackburn, M. 2016. Employee reactions to talent pool membership. *Employee Relations,* 38(1): 112–128.

★Thunnissen, M. 2016. Talent management: For what, how and how well? An empirical exploration of talent management in practice. *Employee Relations,* 38(1): 57–72.

Thunnissen, M., Boselie, P., & Fruytier, B. 2013. Talent management and the relevance of context: Towards a pluralistic approach. *Human Resource Management Review,* 23(4): 326–336.

★Thunnissen, M., & Buttiens, D. 2017. Talent management in public sector organizations: a study on the impact of contextual factors on the TM approach in Flemish and Dutch public sector organizations. *Public Personnel Management,* 46(4): 391–418.

Thunnissen, M. & Gallardo-Gallardo, E. 2017. *Talent management in practice: An integrated and dynamic approach.* Bringley: Emerald Publishing.

Thunnissen, M., Schippers, J., & Boselie, P. 2018. *Macro talent management in the Netherlands: A critical analysis of growing and retaining talent in the Netherlands.* Routledge.

★Thunnissen, M., & Van Arensbergen, P. 2015. A multi-dimensional approach to talent: An empirical analysis of the definition of talent in Dutch academia. *Personnel Review,* 44(2): 182–199.

Vandenabeele, W. V., Leisink, P. L. M., & Knies, E. 2013. Public value creation and strategic human resource management: Public service motivation as a linking mechanism. In P. L. M. Leisink, P. Boselie, M. van Bottenburg, & D. M. Hosking (Eds.). *Managing social issues: A public values perspective:* 37–54. Cheltenham: Edward Elgar.

★Van den Brink, M., Fruytier, B., & Thunnissen, M. 2013. Talent management in academia: Performance systems and HRM policies. *Human Resource Management Journal,* 23(2): 180–195.

★Van den Broek, J., Boselie, P., & Paauwe, J. 2017. Cooperative innovation through a talent management pool: A qualitative study on coopetition in healthcare. *European Management Journal,* 36(1): 135–144.

★Van der Wal, Z. 2017. Small countries, big performers: In search of shared strategic public sector HRM practices in successful small countries. *International Journal of Public Administration,* 40(5): 443–458.

Van De Voorde, K., Paauwe, J., & Van Veldhoven, M. 2012. Employee well-being and the HRM–organizational performance relationship: A review of quantitative studies. *International Journal of Management Reviews,* 14(4): 391–407.

Wright, P. M., & Boswell, W. R. 2002. Desegregating HRM: A review and synthesis of micro and macro human resource management research. *Journal of Management,* 28(3): 247–276.

Wright, P. M., & Nishii, L. H. 2013. Strategic HRM and organizational behaviour: Integrating multiple levels of analysis. In J. Paauwe, D. Guest, & P. Wright (Eds.). *HRM & performance: Achievements & challenges:* 97–110. Chichester: Wiley.

17

TALENT MANAGEMENT IN ACADEMIA

Marian Thunnissen

Pleun van Arensbergen

Marieke van den Brink

Introduction

For universities, the "human resources", in particular the scientific staff, are the most valuable asset for the success of the organization (Van Balen & Van den Besselaar, 2007). The presence of highly quali-fied academic staff is not only extremely important for the quality of education programs, university research, and the universities' reputation, but also for the knowledge condition in a region (Baldini, Fini, & Grimaldi, 2015; Enders et al., 2011; Lanvin & Monteiro, 2019; Lilles & Rõigas, 2017). In par-ticular during the course of the last decade, higher education (HE) institutes in Europe were ascribed an important role in the strengthening of the European position in the global knowledge economy (Enders et al., 2011). Contributing to the knowledge economy the European HE system had to become more competitive, and for these investments in quality and excellence were deemed necessary, along with increased transparency, accountability, and efficiency (Enders et al., 2011).

At the same time, many European universities are facing an ageing workforce and need to replace the retiring "baby boom professors" with a new generation of academics (Pilichowski, Arnould, & Turkisch, 2008). Some academic disciplines, such as humanities, have to deal with a surplus of potential academics due to the poor career prospects inside and outside academia. Meanwhile, other disciplines, for example in the fields of nature and science, suffer chronic shortages of talented academic staff (e.g., Gilliot, Overlaet, & Verdin, 2002).

For all universities, finding the most talented people is a key strategic issue (Van den Brink, Fruytier, & Thunnissen, 2013), but the competition for highly educated and academic talents is fierce because other organizations are also involved in this "war for talent" (Holley et al., 2018; Stahl et al., 2012). The question arises if, and how, universities attract, retain, and deploy their human resources to win this battle for talent. In this chapter on talent management (TM) in academia, we aim to answer that question.

TM is often described as the systematic attraction, identification, development, engagement/reten-tion, and deployment of talents (Gallardo-Gallardo, Thunnissen, & Scullion, 2019; Scullion, Collings, & Caligiuri, 2010). Within their TM definitions, authors define talent in different ways. The var-iety of terms used to define talent reflects one of the most central debates in TM – whether TM is an inclusive or an exclusive approach (Gallardo-Gallardo, Dries, & Gonzalez-Cruz, 2013). The exclusive approach – often adopted by academics in the field of management (including human resource man-agement [HRM]) – focuses on an elite group of employees whose skills, abilities, and performance are unique and very valuable for the organization, and/or occupy strategically important positions within the organization (e.g., Collings & Mellahi, 2009). The inclusive view on talent – dominant in the

DOI: 10.4324/9781315474687-17

field of positive psychology and Human Resources Development – is aimed at the identification and mobilization of the strengths of all employees, and assures that all employees work in a context and organizational climate that enables them to use and develop their talents (Meyers & Van Woerkom, 2014; Swailes, Downs, & Orr, 2014). In practice, both the inclusive and the exclusive approach (and also hybrid forms) occur (Stahl et al., 2012).

This chapter explores in more detail the TM approach adopted by academic organizations. The chapter is organized into three sections. We start with mapping the broader organizational and institutional context, and present the most important reforms in the universities' external environment, in the academic organization, academic work, and the academic staff. This chapter focuses on the context of European universities in general, and, predominantly based on our research, on the context of Dutch public universities specifically.

We then move to the second section of the chapter where we describe how universities manage and mobilize their talents, and how their TM approach is affected by the aforementioned reforms. The Netherlands has fourteen public universities providing bachelor, master, and doctoral education, and only one private university. Many universities have separate HR policies for their academic and support staff. This chapter is about the specific TM approaches for the academic staff. In the final section of the chapter, the discussion, we present dilemmas and tensions in managing talent in academia and present some recommendations for future research.

Mapping the Context: Academia in Transition

A Short History Lesson

There are not many organizations as old as the universities in Europe. The history of European universities goes back to the Middle Ages, with the first Western European university founded in 1088 in Bologna, Italy (Sanz & Bergan, 2006). Since the late 18th century, the European universities were organized analogous to the classic Humboldt University in Berlin, emphasizing the importance of freedom, autonomy, and creativity in finding new knowledge and deepening the understanding of ourselves and the world around us (Waaijer, 2015). A collegial governance system was dominant, and interference by the outside world was regarded as unacceptable because it collided with the autonomy, professionalism, and expertise of the independent scientist.

This classic ideal continued to exist for almost two centuries, until a series of fundamental reforms urged the Dutch universities to dismantle this classic organizational model (Zomer & Benneworth, 2011). First, the enormous increase in students from all layers of society in the 1960s, the baby boom generation born after the second world war caused a transition from elite to mass education and led to growing investments in HE and a rise in the number of academic staff (Vincent-Lancrin, 2006). Two decades later, the economic stagnation in the 1980s forced the HE to be more cost effective. To secure the standards and quality of HE, the Bologna process led in the 1999s to the harmonization of the architecture of the European Higher Education system, opening the doors for students from abroad (Teelken, 2019).

Second, the role of the government has changed. The direct interference and state control have decreased since the 1980s, and Dutch HE institutes have obtained greater institutional autonomy to promote efficiency, cost-effectiveness, flexibility, and an entrepreneurial spirit. In exchange for institutional autonomy the national government demanded quality and accountability (in measurable objectives) in return (Enders et al., 2011).

Third, the European funding landscape changed considerably, with a shift from block funding towards project funding (Lepori et al., 2007). To an increasing extent, universities are encouraged to compete for external funding from industry, national, and European research councils. The Dutch government lowered direct and structural research funding of institutes, and increased the provision of individual research budgets via the Netherlands Organization for Scientific Research (NWO) (Castelló,

Pyhältö & McAlpine, 2018; Heiligers & Van Steen, 2008; Lepori et al., 2007). The competition to get a grant is fierce, and only academics with the best track record are eligible to get a grant (Herschberg, Benschop, & Van den Brink, 2018; Van Arensbergen & Van den Besselaar, 2012; Van Arensbergen, Van der Weijden, & Van den Besselaar, 2014a).

Finally, the number of external stakeholders involved in and affecting HE institutes has increased significantly (VSNU, 2018), which has led to a multiplicity of norms and expectations to meet (Zanoni, et al., 2016). The competition and greater institutional (financial) autonomy was meant to stimulate European HE institutions to become more sensitive to the varied consumers' demands for relevance, and the production of *useful* knowledge and *relevant* teaching necessary to solve societal and economic issues has been emphasized (Enders et al., 2011; Zomer & Benneworth, 2011).

The Changing Academic Organization and Its Staff

Due to these developments, the liberalization of the academic institutes took place and the entrepreneurial university arose (e.g., Meyer et al., 2005; Zomer & Benneworth, 2011). External economic and managerial pressures demanding efficiency, effectiveness, accountability, and flexibility were adopted by internal actors whose power base has grown during the past decades (i.e., [professional] managers and support staff), and they implemented regulations, measurable standards, and performance management systems to coordinate and control academic performance (Thunnissen & Buttiens, 2017). As a result, academics became more dependent on managerial and administrative staff controlling these systems (e.g., De Jong et al., 2011; De Weert, 2001). While organizational units became more interrelated, the core activities of the university (research and education) became more loosely coupled (De Weert, 2001). This resulted in a differentiation and specialization in work activities and skills (e.g., Musselin, 2007), in which research has greater value and status than teaching.

Furthermore, there is a change in the academic employment position. In the 1980s, a two-tier structure in education was introduced, making a clear cut between the education in general scientific skills in the first phase (available for all people), and the training in research skills in the second phase (restricted to a group of excellent students) (Hazue & Sprangenberg, 1991; Hulshof, Verrijt, & Kruijthoff., 1996). From that moment doctoral candidates in the second phase were hired as employees with a fixed-term contract, because the employee status would make it easier to control the recruitment and development of candidates (Hulshof *et al.,* 1996).

Many people perceived the PhD-phase as the first step in an academic career. However, the possibilities to pursue an academic career were limited because the majority of the existing academic staff – all employed in the 1960s and 1970s to provide education to the massive "baby-boom" student population then entering – did not show any tendency to leave the academic organization (Auriol, Felix, & Schaaper, 2010; Einaudi, Heuer, & Green, 2013; Hulshof et al., 1996). In order to increase organizational flexibility, new recruited academic staff was hired on a fixed-term or part-time contract (e.g., Bryson, 2004; De Weert, 2001; Herschberg et al., 2018; Musselin, 2007).

Currently two-third of the academics in the Netherlands are employed on a temporary basis, most of them are academics in the lower academic positions (VSNU, 2018). Moreover, research shows most of them will never get a permanent position in a university. Less than 30% of the PhDs and postdoc researchers in the Netherlands get a permanent job as a lecturer or researcher at a Dutch university (De Goede, Belder, & De Jonge, 2013). This job insecurity, combined with a lack of career possibilities and obscure promotion criteria, are major sources of dissatisfaction for young academics in the Netherlands (e.g., Thunnissen, 2015; Teelken & Van der Weijden, 2018; Van Balen, 2010; Waaijer et al., 2017).

The academic self is also changing. An increasing number of scholars come from abroad (Holley et al., 2018). Recent research shows that the amount of foreign academics working in Dutch universities increased from 20% in 2005 to 33% in 2015; in the field of nature and science a whopping 45% of the academics are from abroad (Scholten, Koier, & Horlings, 2017). Moreover, Parker and Jay (1995) point at the rise of the "new academic". Besides the traditional scientific skills, new skills have become important features of excellent academics: cooperation, networking skills, leadership, and especially entrepreneurship (Thunnissen & Van Arensbergen, 2015; Van Arensbergen et al., 2014a; Van den Brink & Benschop, 2012; Verbree, Van der Weijden, & Van den Besselaar, 2012;).

Talent Management in Academia

Up until the 1990s, the Ministry of Education, Cultural Affairs and Science was responsible for the direct governance and control of the Dutch public universities, including personnel management. In the late 1990s, the Ministry acknowledged that personnel management could only be shaped inside the academic organization, and delegated this responsibility to the individual HE institutes (Heiligers & Van der Steen, 2008). Within the university, the management responsibilities were further delegated to the university departments and research group, so personnel management became a line management responsibility.

In 2000, Van Vught Thijssen concluded that academic personnel management indeed had come to bloom. Personnel policies and practices at universities shifted from administration, basic job descriptions, performance appraisals, and carrying out collective agreements, towards a pro-active and strategic aligned HRM system. Yet, despite the advancements made, Van Vught Thijssen (2000) also warned that the universities were not ready and able to respond adequately to the massive outflow of retiring academics in the near future, and this would be a risk for the international competitive position of Dutch universities. Her study was a wakeup call for many universities, as they were strongly unaware of this worrying scenario that would lead to serious problems when nothing would change. In order to attract and retain excellent academics TM became a strategic priority for many universities.

Several studies investigated how (and how well) Dutch universities manage their talented academic staff. Van den Brink (2010) conducted an extensive (mixed-method) study on the process of recruitment and selection for professorial appointments within Dutch universities. Van Arensbergen (2014) also investigated talent selection, but in the context of grant allocation by funding organization NWO. Thunnissen (2015, 2016) investigated the intended and actual TM approach of five university departments, and how this was perceived by the academic staff. In this section, these studies (supported with other empirical publications) are used to present how universities 1) identify and select talent, 2) develop and retain talent, 3) manage the outflow of talent, and 4) how successful they are in doing so (in terms of perceived value).

Talent identification and selection

What is academic talent and how is it selected? Studies by Thunnissen and Van Arensbergen show that academic talent has both traditional (critical, analytical, top-level knowledge, and skills, etc.) and the academic skills (e.g., creative, innovative, entrepreneurial), social capital (communication, cooperation, and networking skills), and is strongly driven and able to prove this potential in excellent performance (Heuritsch, Waaijer, & Van der Weijden, 2016; Thunnissen & Van Arensbergen, 2015).

Academic excellence is clearly related to excellent performance in research (and often not in teaching), in terms of publications in top journals and obtaining research funds (Hammerfelt, 2017; Thunnissen & Van Arensbergen, 2015; Van Arensbergen & Van den Besselaar, 2012; Van Balen, 2010; Van den Brink & Benschop, 2012). However, research also suggest that the precise operationalization of talent is highly subjective. In fact, who is considered as talent is a social construction by key actors in the identification and selection process (Van Arensbergen et al, 2014a; O'Connor & O'Hagan, 2016). In Dutch academia, this selection process takes place inside and outside the university. Both processes, and their subjectivity, are discussed below.

We start with the selection process *outside* the university. In the previous section we already mentioned the growing importance of grants. Although grants were introduced to stimulate and reward excellence in research and education, at least at the individual level, they resulted in an intensified competition in academic careers because the ability to acquire funding became an essential enabler for career advancements (e.g., Van Balen & Van Besselaar, 2007; Van den Besselaar & Sandström, 2015; Waaijer, Teelken, Wouters, & Van der Weijden; 2018). More and more universities offer a position to academics with a grant, for the duration of the grant.

The study by Van Arensbergen (2014) on the talent selection process by NWO shows that when spotting talent at the university level, the interviewed grant panel members (who are academics themselves) indicate that the right mixture of abilities, personal characteristics, and performance discriminates talents from their peers. Specifically, strong motivation and social skills are emphasized. However, in their role as grant panel members, they have a much narrower interpretation of talent and mainly focus on traditional academic abilities in combination with performance. In the first selection round they predominantly look for the best track record, mainly based on a résumé. Only in the second round of the selection process (in which applicants are invited for a panel interview) do intrapersonal characteristics become more important. Some applicants with a "good but not excellent" track record and grant proposal move up in the final ranking after showing their strong motivation, enthusiasm, and communication skills during the interview or vice versa.

This narrow interpretation of talent in the grant selection process is often adopted in the formal selection criteria and procedures *within* the university (Van Arensbergen et al., 2014a). Traditionally the identification of academic excellence is done by the academic community, making use of intersubjective evaluations instead of objective criteria (Van Balen, 2010; O'Connor & O'Hagan, 2016). To stimulate open procedures in which every applicant gets a fair chance, the HRM department developed and implemented regulations and protocols regarding the recruitment and selection process (Thunnissen, 2015, 2016; Van Balen, 2010; Van den Brink et al., 2010). Nonetheless, research shows a gap between the intended policy by the HR staff and the actual implementation by the academic managers in practice. The role of the HRM staff is mainly administrative and their impact is limited, because in the actual selection process, the influence of the academic community still is dominant (e.g., Thunnissen, 2016; Thunnissen & Buttiens, 2017).

The study by Van den Brink (2010) was one of the first studies that explicitly investigated the recruitment and selection of professors within Dutch universities. Her research revealed that despite the regulations and protocols, the recruitment and selection process was highly informal and not transparent. She detected a gender bias in the selection of professors due to closed procedures (which are not open to competition), scouting via the informal, male academic networks, the limited number of females in the selection committees, and a lack of transparency in selection procedures and practice.

Other studies also show that talent selection within the Dutch academic system is an informal and micro-political process (Herschberg, Benschop, & Van den Brink, 2018; Thunnissen, 2015; Van Arensbergen et al., 2014a; Van Balen, 2010;), in which the academic managers (deans, research directors, heads of research groups, etc.) play a crucial role (Holley et al., 2018). In most departments the selection of academics at the beginning of their career is the responsibility of full professors using their own often subjective selection method, often based on a mixture of proven performance (reflected in grades, papers, etc.) and, most of all, the professors' personal impression of the potential of the young academic. For the medium and senior academic positions, a formalized, open selection procedure by a selection committee is gaining acceptance, but they are also often neglected when a brilliant top talent can be recruited (Thunnissen, 2016; Van den Brink et al., 2010).

Van den Brink and Benschop (2014) call the academic managers gatekeepers, because they determine who may enter the academic community. This gatekeeping process is cut up in different stages, and in each stage, excellence is re-assessed. Since, especially in academia, the effectiveness and quality of the creative, academic work is rather unpredictable, the organization aims to keep the employment relationship as flexible as possible, and with every continuation of the contract the university has a new moment to decide who can stay or have to leave the system (Van Balen, 2010; Van Balen & Van den Besselaar, 2007). Because of the scarcity of positions, only the best academics are selected for an academic position, or even better, an academic career. This results in an "up-or-out" system that is characteristic for consultancy agents and law firms (Thunnissen, 2016).

Talent Development and Retention

Like in the classic Humboldt University, the identification and selection of talents is still the core activity in academic TM. Less formal attention is paid to the development and retention of talents. Thunnissen's (2015, 2016) study on academic TM shows that the TM approach of the university departments is one-dimensional and fragmented. First, the departments used different approaches for the academics at the beginning of their career and the more experienced academics. In the PhD phase, university departments use an inclusive and developmental approach to TM: PhD development programs are often standard policy, and are provided to all PhD's in the department.

The TM policies for the more senior academic positions are exclusive and performance oriented, in which the "tenure track system" plays and important role. This is a top talent program available for the most excellent performing academics, which ensures them a career path towards professor but only when they meet the predetermined performance criteria. In the performance appraisal, the focus is put on research activities, and to a lesser degree to the teaching activities. There is little attention for the development of academics with a fixed-term contract, such as postdoc researchers and lecturers, and they run the risk of being deprived of career and development opportunities and, eventually, of dropping out (Herschberg *et al.,* 2018; Holley et al., 2018; Thunnissen, 2016).

Second, in their TM approach, the university departments address a limited set of talent components. The focus is put on either developing the classic academic, intellectual abilities (i.e. scientific understanding and academic expertise) for the junior positions, or on academic performance and leadership skills for the senior positions. The development of the "new" academic abilities (such as creativity and entrepreneurship) and the intrapersonal characteristics (such as motivation and drive), which are all also mentioned as important talent features, get no special attention in formal TM policy.

Third, like in the selection of talents, empirical research also points to a discrepancy between the intended and actual TM practices regarding the development and retention of talent. Managing professors take the liberty to deviate from the formal regulations and agreements to achieve the outcomes they find essential. Some managing professors even think that after the talent selection, a formal TM approach is not necessary because they believe in a "self-propelling" academic (Thunnissen, 2016; Van Balen, 2010). The employees detect a great deal of variation in the implementation by the supervising professors, and this causes talents (at all levels) to criticize whether the treatment has been just and fair (Holley et al., 2018; Thunnissen, 2015).

Turnover and Exit of Talent

Hardly any attention is paid to a controlled turnover and exit of talent (Thunnissen, 2105). Some university departments encourage young scholars to (temporarily) leave the department to acquire some international work experience (Van Balen, 2010). This is often supported by the international academic network of either the supervisor or the employee his- or herself. Even though 70% of the young academics end up having a job outside academia (De Goede *et al.,* 2013), this transition to a career outside academia is besides occasional job interview training that is often not supported (Van der Schoot, Yerkes, & Sonneveld, 2010). Supervisors and HR hardly provide any labor market information (especially about the possibilities outside the academia), nor information about employment trajectories of previous PhDs and career advice. PhD candidates make little use of career centers, and mainly use the Internet and their networking to obtain a new job (Van der Schoot et al., 2010).

Leaving the academic community is regarded as a taboo within academia and is often considered a failure. Therefore, early career researchers hardly dare to openly explore and ask for advice about career opportunities outside academia. However, more and more HR policy advisors are gaining awareness of their role, adding value in this process, and offering activities to young academics to get them in contact with employers and jobs in non-academic settings (Van der Weijden et al., 2017).

The Value of TM

The studies by Thunnissen (2015, 2016) investigated the value of TM in academia, and showed that there is a large discrepancy between the perceptions of the organization and the employees in this matter. Both stakeholders have a biased, one-dimensional view. For the organization, TM mainly has economic value: increased flexibility and efficiency in managing the workforce is the dominant objective for many universities. To achieve this aim, an exclusive TM approach was implemented, with its accent on the attraction, identification, and deployment of excellent performing academics. From an organizational perspective, the TM system was regarded as effective and valuable.

The talented employees, on the other hand, mostly have non-economic goals they want to see fulfilled via TM: a meaningful and challenging work environment and opportunities for professional growth, becoming manifest in actual upward career advancement (Thunnissen, 2016). The academic selves show the preference for an inclusive, strength-based TM approach that enhances their personal and professional development. The economically oriented needs of the organization collide with the non-economic interests of the talents, and, as could be expected, the employees are, generally speaking, not satisfied with the inducements made by the organization. Yet, most academics interviewed in Thunnissen's research retained and even made some career progress. In the employee's perspective, the academic advancements and successes are the result of their own effort and ambition, and not so much the inducements by the organization.

Discussion

In this chapter, we described how universities have managed and mobilized their human capital in the changing institutional context. Several studies indicate that the Dutch universities shifted from a collegial system to manage the recruitment and employment of personnel, to a more managerial model for TM. Yet, in the actual implementation, the traditional collegial system of personnel management is still dominant. This lack of congruence leads to tensions and dilemmas. In this section, we address the most dominant tensions and dilemmas in managing academic talent, and present some recommendations for future research.

Tensions and Dilemmas

Who Is in the Lead?

This chapter illustrates that TM consists of multiple underlying processes, in which several actors participate. The interests and talent philosophies of multiple actors have a significant impact on the implementation and effectiveness of TM (Meyers & Van Woerkom, 2014; Thunnissen & Buttiens, 2017). Despite the formal TM policy, the actors involved in the implementation process (specifically academic management) can act in a different and unforeseen way. Many studies show that TM in academia is most of all the responsibility of the scientific community. The impact of the HR department is marginal, although this may be changing due to the increasing impact of performance management systems and regulations. The managing full professors and the dean take the crucial decisions on labelling and enabling talents. This gives them the opportunity to adjust the talent definition to their department's needs and preferences.

The tension between the role of HR and line management is not unique for the academic context. What is unique for the context of academia is the involvement of external stakeholders in talent identification and selection. As we have pointed out before, the external stakeholder NWO has a significant and increasing impact as well, since personal research grants are seen as a crucial criterion in selection procedures and performance appraisals (Van Arensbergen *et al.,* 2014a). Heiligers and Van der Steen (2008) already posed in 2008 that the funding programs for individual academics were effective, but also could reduce the institutes own responsibility to develop a career policy. This warning seems to be justified. So, even though the universities are (as an employer) responsible for the attraction and retention of their talented academics, the actual identification and selection of talent is often not in the hands of the academic organization but of an external organization such as NWO (Van Arensbergen, 2014; Van Balen & Van den Besselaar, 2007).

Homogeneity versus Diversity?

The elite academics involved in the recruitment and selection of new staff not only have the power to decide who is excellent, but also to make explicit claims about their own definition of excellence and knowledge of the talent pool (Herschberg et al., 2018; Van den Brink & Benschop, 2012). Any talent not seen or recognized by them is therefore not considered excellent. These judgments concerning excellence are made by academics who are already eminent, and those at the top of the various informal scientific hierarchies exercise considerable power over the standards that govern their fields.

Candidates who wish to advance their careers and produce results accepted as significant contributions to knowledge must comply with the standards set by these leaders (Gregory, 2009; Holgersson, 2013). Elite academics often select candidates congruent with their own personal and scientific preferences (Van Arensbergen et al, 2014a; Van den Brink & Benschop, 2012). The wish to "clone" (Essed, 2004) oneself is understandable, and has some merit, but risks the exclusion of dissimilar people, often women and ethnic minorities. This might not serve the long-term interests of science as diverse perspectives can add value to the scientific endeavor. The person selected is not necessarily the best or creative academic, but rather the most suitable or the one most similar to the recruiters. It seems questionable whether "more of the same" advances creative and innovative science.

How to Differentiate between Similar Talents?

Within the university departments, academic managers struggle with the question of how to take care of the talents in the "gray area". They can easily identify the top talents and the absolute non-talents, both relatively small groups, but what about the group in the middle? They might have qualities that do not directly qualify them individually as talent, but which are valuable for a research group. Is it therefore worth investing in the employees in the gray-area, who may not excel on the traditional criteria? The question arises whether a differentiated approach towards talent is required, such as an inclusive, strength-based approach for optimal development of academics within this gray-area to enable them to enhance their specific strengths so they can differentiate themselves from other academics, and an exclusive approach for retaining and developing the positive outliers.

The grant panel members also struggle with the dilemma of the gray area, comprising the majority of the applicants of about equal average quality. These applicants may vary on which aspects they excel in and to what extent, resulting in minimal differences in their average quality around the cutoff point (the point above which the candidates will be given grants and under which they are rejected). Therefore, the review panels spend most of their time discussing the applicants around the cutoff point (Van Arensbergen et al., 2014a). Panel members are very aware of the potential consequences of their decisions, because a rejection can mean the end of the applicant's scientific career. At the same time, they indicate that they are aware of the subjectivity of their decisions, inherent to any process of group decision making (Van Arensbergen, Van der Weijden, & Van den Besselaar, 2014b).

Transparency Versus Autonomy?

This dilemma involves the desire to control and objectify recruitment and development versus the strong desire for academic freedom. The section on TM in Dutch academia reveals that academic TM (in particular recruitment, selection, and promotion) is realized in a rather amateur and ad hoc manner. HRM managers have formulated protocols and rules for academic recruitment and selection that provide steps and guidelines for the decision makers and committee members involved. However, the implementation of these protocols seems to be a different matter (Van den Brink et al., 2010). At all stages of the selection process (and with every time a decision is made about continuing a contract) there are actions that go against the regulations for transparency. The various academics in the process have their own agendas, which interfere with the goal of increasing the openness and formalization of procedures.

We detect a difference between HR managers who stress the importance of a more professionalized approach, and the academics who are critical or even cynical about the policies concerning transparency and performance indicators and tend to dismiss them as time-consuming bureaucracy and a violation of their academic freedom (Van den Brink, et al., 2010). They maintain that these HRM policies curtail their professional expertise and that the need for more "accountability" restricts their freedom to select the best candidates on an academic basis.

Conclusion and Recommendations

With their focus on excellence, the university is a breeding ground for talent. However, with the rise of the entrepreneurial university, the universities have adopted a "hard" approach to managing and mobilizing their academic staff, in which they accentuate individual performance and production. With this exclusive TM approach, the organization's interests are well served, but the well-being of the talents is undermined. Although the representatives of the organization think their TM approach policy is effective, the question still remains whether their TM approach is indeed effective, but most of all, desirable and ethical.

The studies in this chapter showed the institutes' TM system shows little care for the intrinsic motives of the academics to excel in their work. The universities attempt to motivate their employees in an extrinsic way. The possibility of pursuing an academic career after obtaining tenure is used as a "carrot" to reward academics, while performance agreements are used to pressure academics to be productive (the "stick"). The ones who do not meet the performance agreements do not get tenure, or are reprimanded in another way, (e.g., by reducing their research time). This approach is incompatible with the self-propelling power that is so characteristic for most academics. Many Dutch academics and students have protested against these developments and wonder whether the efficiency and flexibility lead to decreasing quality in research and education (e.g., De Jonge Akademie, 2011).

According to these stakeholders the current academic approach creates productive but non-committed scholars and leaves little room for diversity, which can be a risk for the academic organization in the long run. Recently, Dutch universities acknowledge these issues and a change towards more appreciation for education and societal impact has started (VSNU, 2018).

The data discussed in this chapter are based on research conducted in the Netherlands, but other studies on HRM, TM, and academic careers in HE in, for example, France, the United Kingdom, or Japan, show similar results. A comparative study by Buchholz et al. (2009) indicates that way American universities manage and employ their academic staff (with its tenure track system and its emphasis on individual excellence and performance) is copied as a good example by many universities in other countries, including the Netherlands. Nonetheless, we recommend more in-depth empirical research on academic TM in other countries, in which the specific institutional context of that country (cf. Deem, 2001) is taken into account.

The present study showed that the success of a TM policy is probably more dependent on the actors involved in the implementation of TM than on the (consistent and strategically linked) TM policy. Within Dutch academia, this particularly refers to the full professors who manage their own team of researchers and teachers. Most research on the role of the managing professor is conducted from the perspective of his or her subordinates (e.g., Van Balen, 2010). The perspective of the academic manager themselves needs further exploration in empirical research.

Finally, the hard, exclusive approach to TM probably does not harmonize with the corporate social responsibilities and tasks of the Dutch public university. It is remarkable that the Dutch universities do so little to invest in the development of the largest portion of their workforce (i.e., their temporary staff). To increase their chances in the external labor market, they should develop more skills and competencies than the purely academic skills. We argue that, as a public sector organization, a university needs to apply a TM policy that looks beyond the boundaries of the organization. It is necessary to focus explicitly on the outflow of talented young academics who are not permanently appointed. Although there is a lot of research on careers inside academia, there is limited information about the career possibilities for academics outside academia. This needs further empirical exploration.

References

Auriol, L., Felix, B., & Schaaper, M. 2010. Mapping careers and mobility of doctorate holders: Draft guidelines, model questionnaire and indicators. *OECD Science, Technology and Industry Working Papers*, (1): 1.

Baldini, N., Fini, R., & Grimaldi, R. 2015. The transition towards entrepreneurial universities: An assessment of academic entrepreneurship in Italy. In A. N. Link, D. S. Siegel, & M. Wright (Eds.), *Chicago handbook of university technology transfer and academic entrepreneurship:* 218–244. Chicago, IL: University of Chicago Press.

Benschop, Y., & Van den Brink, M. 2014. Power and resistance in gender equality strategies: comparing quotas and small wins. *The Oxford handbook of gender in organizations:* 332–352.

Bryson, C. 2004. What about the workers? The expansion of higher education and the transformation of academic work. *Industrial Relations Journal*, 35(1): 38–57.

Buchholz, K., Gülker, S., Knie, A., & Simon, D. 2009. *Attraktivität von arbeitsbedingungen in der wissenschaft im internationalen vergleich. Wie Erfolgreich Sind Die Eingeleiteten Wissenschaftspolitischen Initiativen Und Programme*, Berlin: EFI 2008, 192S.

Castelló, M. Pyhältö, K., & McAlpine, L. 2018. European cross-national mixed-method study on early career researcher experience:, In A. Jaeger, & A. Dinin (Eds.), *The postdoc landscape: The invisible Scholars:* 143–174. London: Elsevier Academic Press.

Collings, D. G., & Mellahi, K. 2009. Strategic talent management: A review and research agenda, *Human Resource Management Review*, 19(4): 304–313.

Deem, R. 2001. Globalisation, new managerialism, academic capitalism and entrepreneurialism in universities: Is the local dimension still important? *Comparative Education*, 37(1): 7–20.

De Goede, M., Belder, B., & De Jonge, J. 2013. *Feiten en cijfers: Academische carrières en loopbaanbeleid.* The Hague: Rathenau Institute.

De Jong, S. P. L., Van Arensbergen, P., Daemen, F., Van der Meulen, B., & Van den Besselaar, P. 2011. Evaluation of research in context: An approach and two cases. *Research Evaluation*, 20(2): 61–72.

De Jonge Akademie. 2010. *Rendement van Talent, aanbevelingen voor een motiverend en stimulerend loopbaanbeleid.* Amsterdam.

De Weert, E. 2001. Pressures and prospects facing the academic profession in the Netherlands. *Higher Education*, 41(1): 77–101.

Einaudi, P., Heuer, R., & Green, P. 2013. Counts of postdoctoral appointees in science, engineering, and health rise with reporting improvements. *National Science Foundation, National Center for Science and Engineering Statistics.* (NSF 13-334) Arlington, VA.

Enders, J., De Boer, H. F., File, J., Jongbloed, B., & Westerheijden, D. F. 2011. Reform of higher education in Europe. In J. Enders, H. F. De Boer, & D. F. Westerheijden (Eds.), *Reform of higher education in Europe:* 1–10. Rotterdam: Sense Publishers.

Essed, P. 2004. Cloning amongst professors: normativities and imagined homogeneities, *NORA*, 12: 113–122.

Gallardo-Gallardo, E., Dries, N., & González-Cruz, T. 2013. What is the meaning of talent in the world of work?. *Human Resource Management Review*, 23(4): 290–300.

Gallardo-Gallardo, E., Thunnissen, M., & Scullion, H. 2019. *Talent management: context matters.* doi: https://doi.org/10.1080/09585192.2019.1642645.

Gilliot, D., Overlaet, B., & Verdin, P. 2002. Managing academic personnel flow at universities. *Tertiary Education and Management,* 8(4): 277–295.

Gregory, M. 2009. Inside the locker room: Male homosociability in the advertising industry. *Gender, Work & Organization,* 16: 323–347.

Hammarfelt, B. 2017. Recognition and reward in the academy: Valuing publication oeuvres in biomedicine, economics and history. *Aslib Journal of Information Management,* 69(5): 607–623.

Hazue, C. & Sprangenberg J. 1991. *University research performance: Measurement, management and optimization.* The Hague: Ministerie van Onderwijs en Wetenschappen.

Heiligers, D., & Van Steen, J. 2008. *Beleidsdoorlichting "Versterking van de aantrekkingskracht op en de loopbaanmogelijkheden van jonge en talentvolle onderzoekers".* The Hague: Ministerie van OCW.

Herschberg, C., Benschop, Y., & Van den Brink, M. 2018. Selecting early career researchers in times of precarity: The influence of discourses of internationalisation and excellence on formal and applied selection criteria in academia, *Higher Education,* 76(2): 807–825.

Holgersson, C. 2013. Recruiting managing directors: Doing homosociality. *Gender, Work & Organization,* 20: 454–466.

Holley, K., Kuzhabekova, A., Osbaldiston, N., Cannizzo, F., Mauri, C., Simmonds, S., Teelken, T., & Van der Weijden, I. 2018, Global Perspectives on the postdoctoral scholar experience. In. A. Jaeger, & A. Dinin. (Eds.), *The postdoc landscape. The invisible Scholars:* 203–226. London: Elsevier Academic Press,

Hulshof, M., Verrijt, A., & Kruijthoff, A. 1996. *Promoveren En De Arbeidsmarkt: Ervaringen Van De 'Lost Generation'.* Zoetermeer: Ministerie van OC&W.

Lanvin, B., & Monteiro, F. 2019. *The Global Talent Competitiveness Index, 2019: Entrepreneurial talent and competitiveness.* INSEAD Business School, Adecco Group and Human Capital Leadership Institute.

Lepori, B., Van den Besselaar, P., Dinges, M., Potì, B., Reale, E., Slipersæter, S., Theves, J. & Van der Meulen, B. 2007. Comparing the evolution of national research policies: What patterns of change? *Science and Public Policy,* 34(6): 372–388.

Lilles, A., & Rõigas, K. 201. How higher education institutions contribute to the growth in regions of Europe. *Studies in Higher Education,* 42(1): 65–78.

Meyer, J., Ramirez, F., Frank D., & Schofer, E. 2005. Higher education as an Institution. In P. Gumport. *Sociology of higher education, contributions and their contexts.* Baltimore: John Hopkins University Press.

Meyers, M., & Van Woerkom, M. 2014. The influence of underlying philosophies on talent management: Theory, implications for practice, and research agenda. *Journal of World Business,* 49(2): 192–203.

Musselin. C. 2007. *Transformations of academic work: Facts and analysis.* Berkeley, CA: Center for Studies in Higher Education.

O'Connor, P., & O'Hagan, C. 2016. Excellence in university academic staff evaluation: a problematic reality? *Studies in Higher Education,* 41(11): 1943–1957.

Pilichowski, E., Arnould, E., & Turkisch, É. 2008. Ageing and the Public Sector. *OECD Journal on Budgeting,* 7(4): 1–40.

Sanz, N. & Bergan, S. 2006. *The heritage of European universities,* 2nd ed.). *Higher Education Series,* No. 7, Council of Europe.

Scholten, W., Koier, E., & Horlings, E. 2017. *Grensverleggers: Internationale mobiliteit van onderzoekers en de Nederlandse positie in de mondiale strijd om talent.* The Hague: Rathenau Instituut.

Scullion, H., Collings, D. G., & Caligiuri, P. 2010. Global talent management. *Journal of World Business,* 45(2): 105–108.

Stahl, G., Björkman, I., Farndale, E., Morris, S., Paauwe, J., Stiles, P., Trevor, J., & Wright, P. 2012. Six principles of effective global talent management. *MIT Sloan Management Review,* 53(2): 24–32.

Swailes, S., Downs, Y., & Orr, K. 2014. Conceptualising inclusive talent management: potential, possibilities and practicalities. *Human Resource Development International,* 17(5): 529–544.

Teelken, C. 2019. The higher education system in the Netherlands: Overview and analysis of changes induced by the Bologna Process. In B. Broucker, K. De Wit, J. Verhoeven, & L. Leišytė. *Higher Education System Reform an International Comparison after Twenty Years of Bologna.* https://doi.org/10.1163/9789004400115_004.

Teelken, C., & Van der Weijden, I. 2018. The employment situations and career prospects of postdoctoral researchers. *Employee Relations,* 40(2): 396–411.

Thunnissen, M. 2015. *Talent management in Academia: An exploratory study in Dutch universities using a multinational approach.* PhD-thesis, Utrecht University.

Thunnissen, M. 2016. Talent management: For what, how and how well? An empirical exploration of talent management in practice. *Employee Relations,* 38(1): 57–72.

Thunnissen, M., & Buttiens, D. 2017. Talent management in public sector organizations: A study on the impact of contextual factors on the TM approach in Flemish and Dutch public sector organizations. *Public Personnel Management,* 46(4): 391–418.

Thunnissen, M., & Van Arensbergen, P. 2015. A multi-dimensional approach to talent: an empirical analysis of the definition of talent in Dutch academia. *Personnel Review,* 44(2): 182–199

Van Arensbergen, P. 2014. *Talent proof. Selection processes in research funding and careers.* The Hague: Rathenau Instituut.

Van Arensbergen, P. & Van den Besselaar, P. 2012. The selection of scientific talent in the allocation of research grants. *Higher Education Policy,* 25, 381–405.

Van Arensbergen, P., Van der Weijden, I. & Van den Besselaar, P. 2014a. Different views on scholarly talent: What are the talents we are looking for in science? *Research Evaluation,* 23(4): 273–284.

Van Arensbergen, P., Van der Weijden, I., & Van den Besselaar, P. 2014b. The selection of talent as a group process: a literature review on the social dynamics of decision making in grant panels. *Research Evaluation,* 23(4): 298–311.

Van Balen, B. 2010. *Op het juiste moment op de juiste plaats. Waarom wetenschappelijk talent een wetenschappelijke carrière volgt.* The Hague: Rathenau Institute.

Van Balen, B., & Van den Besselaar, P. 2007. *Universitaire loopbanen. Een verkenning van problemen en oplossingen.* The Hague: Rathenau Instituut.

Van den Besselaar, P., & Sandström, U. 2015. Early career grants, performance, and careers: A study on predictive validity of grant decisions. *Journal of Infometrics,* 9(4): 826–838.

Van den Brink, M. 2010. *Behind the scenes of science: Gender practices in the recruitment and selection of professors in the Netherlands.* Amsterdam: Pallas Publications.

Van den Brink, M., & Benschop, Y. 2012. Gender practices in the construction of academic excellence: Sheep with five legs. *Organization,* 19(4): 507–524.

Van den Brink, M., Fruytier, B., & Thunnissen, M. 2013. Talent management in academia: Performance systems and HRM policies. *Human Resource Management Journal,* 23(2): 180–195.

Van de Schoot, R., Yerkes, M. A., & Sonneveld, H. 2012. The employment status of doctoral recipients: An exploratory study in the Netherlands. *International Journal of Doctoral Studies,* 7: 331–348.

Van Vucht Tijssen 2000. *Talent voor de toekomst, Toekomst voor Talent.* Utrecht.

Verbree, M., Van der Weijden, I., & Van den Besselaar, P. 2012. Academic leadership of high-performing research groups. In S. Hemlin, C. Martin Allwood, B. Martin, M. D. Mumford (Eds.), *Creativity and Leadership in Science, Technology, and Innovation* (pp. 113–148).

Vincent-Lancrin, S. 2006. What is changing in academic research? Trends and futures scenarios. *European Journal of Education,* 41(2): 169–202.

VSNU. 2018. *Ruimte voor investeringen en talent. Inzicht in de ambities en knelpunten van de Nederlandse universiteiten en mogelijke financiële oplossingen.* VSNU.

Waaijer, C. J. F. 2015. The coming of age of the academic career: differentiation and professionalization of German academic positions from the 19th century to the present. *Minerva,* 53(1): 43–67.

Waaijer, C. J. F., Belder, R., Sonneveld, H., Van Bochove, C.A., & Van der Weijden, I. C. M. 2017. Temporary contracts: Effects on job satisfaction and personal lives of recent PhD graduates. *Higher Education,* 74(2): 321–339.

Waaijer, C. J., Teelken, C., Wouters, P. F., & van der Weijden, I. C. 2018. Competition in science: Links between publication pressure, grant pressure and the academic job market. *Higher education policy,* 31(2): 225–243.

Zanoni, P., de Coster, M., Van den Brink, M., & Berger, L. 2016. Kwetsbare superhelden: Academici onder neoliberale governance. *Thema,* 2: 36–41.

Zomer, A., & Benneworth, P. 2011. The rise of the university's third mission. In J. Enders, H. F. De Boer, & D. F. Westerheijden (Eds.), *Reform of higher education in Europe:* 81–102. Rotterdam: Sense Publishers.

SECTION III

The Internal Context of Talent Management

18

HARD WORK OR HARD-WIRED?

The Nature-Nurture Debate on Talent

Maria Christina Meyers

Anneloes Bal

Introduction

When thinking about the extraordinary achievements of successful athletes, musicians, or businesspeople, consider for example: Serena Williams, Usain Bolt, Adele, the Beatles, Coco Chanel, and Bill Gates. All of us sometimes wonder whether we could have ever become equally successful if only we had worked a little harder. Or would hard work never have been enough because we simply did not *have it in us*? These questions about the origins of success relate to the ongoing nature-nurture debate on talent, which is a "topic of enduring fascination to scientists and non-scientists alike" (Hambrick et al., 2016: 45). Is talent determined by our genetic make-up (innate) or is it the result of hard work (acquired)? Case studies of excellent performers highlight the difficulty in answering this question by pointing to both genetic factors as well as hard work as determinants of success.

Consider, for instance, the Ukrainian-born ballet dancer Sergei Polunin, who, at the age of 20, became the youngest ever male principal dancer of the British Royal Ballet. In Steven Cantor's documentary on the life and career of Polunin ("Dancer", 2016), Polunin's family and friends attest to both nature (e.g., extreme joint flexibility witnessed in Polunin as a baby) and nurture (e.g., dedication and support by his entire family; longer training hours than his peers) as sources of his success.

In the business context, a similar picture emerges. On the one hand, successful entrepreneurs and executives are often notorious for their innate intellectual abilities or personality characteristics. For example, Steve Jobs (co-founder and CEO of Apple) displayed mental abilities that were far superior to peers his age when he was a child (Isaacson, 2011). On the other hand, the childhood tales of successful businesspeople typically also refer to the exceptionally stimulating environments in which they were raised. PepsiCo's CEO Indra Nooyi, for instance, reports that her mother asked her and her sister every day to write a short speech about what they would do if they became president (Feloni, 2015).

The question "Is talent innate or acquired?" is particularly relevant for the practical field of organizational talent management (TM) (cf., Gallardo-Gallardo, Dries, & González-Cruz, 2013; Meyers, van Woerkom, & Dries, 2013; Nijs et al., 2014). Broadly speaking, TM concerns the identification, selection, motivation, development, and retention of those employees who are considered to be talented (Gallardo-Gallardo & Thunnissen, 2016; Schuler, Jackson, & Tarique 2011). Arguably, the way in which talent is defined will influence the design of TM (Gallardo-Gallardo, Dries, & González-Cruz, 2013; Meyers & van Woerkom, 2014). If talent is defined as innate, TM will focus primarily on attracting and retaining employees who possess this innate talent (e.g., Bonet & Hamori, 2017). If talent is defined as acquired, by contrast, TM will focus much more on the development of talent in employees who promise to become excellent performers in the future (e.g., Day & O'Connor, 2017). This is related

DOI: 10.4324/9781315474687-18

to the discussion as to whether organizations should make or buy (or rent) talented employees (Cappelli, 2008; Lengnick-Hall & & Andrade 2008). Furthermore, the nature-nurture debate on talent bears important implications for talent identification (Mäkelä, Björkman, & Ehrnrooth 2010; McDonnell, Collings, & Carbery, 2019; Silzer & Church, 2009). The notion of innate talent implies that talent is a stable construct that can be assessed with established instruments such as intelligence and personality tests. The notion of acquired talent, by contrast, implies that talent is a dynamic construct that develops over time and that is therefore more difficult to assess.

A quick scan of the scientific literature reveals that the nature-nurture debate on talent is far from being resolved. On the one hand, the argument that employee talent is innate is supported by research indicating that the largely heritable factor intelligence is one of the strongest predictors of job performance (e.g., Schmidt & Hunter, 1998). On the other hand, the argument that talent is acquired is supported by research on expert performance demonstrating that the world's best performers in a variety of domains have dedicated significantly more time to systematic, supervised practice than average performers (Ericsson, Krampe, & Tesch-Römer, 1993; Ericsson & Pool, 2016).

This chapter addresses the nature-nurture debate on talent in the recent TM literature and explores which view on talent is predominant among TM scholars. This chapter also identifies and reviews influential theoretical publications in the area of TM. Definitions of talent and talent management will be extracted from the identified publications to explore whether the definitions point to an innate or acquired view on talent. As the TM literature so far does not offer a thorough discussion of the nature-nurture debate, this chapter will also address literature on expert performance that comprises an extensive body of theoretical and empirical work that can shed light on the question of whether talent is innate or acquired. Finally, building on TM, as well as expert performance literature, implications for TM practice and avenues for future research will be derived.

Literature Review

To determine whether the scientific TM literature takes a clear stance in the nature-nurture debate on talent, we conducted a literature search to identify articles with the term "talent management" in the title, abstract, or keywords. To guarantee a minimum quality of selected articles, we restricted the search to four scientific, peer-reviewed, English-language journals that are forerunners in the area of TM research and have published special issues on the topic in the past: *Employee Relations, Human Resource Management Review, International Journal of Human Resource Management,* and *Journal of World Business.* To limit the scope of our search, we only included conceptual or review papers in this analysis. Empirical papers and case studies were excluded. The search resulted in 51 publications that met our search criteria. All identified articles were published between 2006 and 2020 (we considered all articles published before August 2020).

We extracted the definitions of both "talent" and "talent management" from all identified articles. This allowed us to code the definitions based on the perspective on talent that was presented (talent as *innate* versus *acquired*). Thirty-nine articles ($k = 39$) included a definition of TM that could be coded. The remaining articles could not be coded because $k = 9$ articles did not include a TM definition, and $k = 3$ articles included a range of different definitions. Similarly, $k = 27$ articles included a codable definition of talent. The remaining articles either did not include a definition of talent ($k = 17$) or referred to a range of different definitions ($k = 7$), and thus could not be coded.

Building on work by Meyers et al. (2013), TM and talent definitions with reference to the terms *"developing", "training",* and *"making talent"* were coded as definitions that suggested acquired talent. Definitions with reference to the terms *"identifying", "selecting", "attracting", "recruiting",* and *"buying talent"* were coded as suggesting innate talent. In addition, definitions of talent were also coded as suggesting acquired talent if they referred to *"knowledge", "skill", "commitment",* or *"experience"* (which can be changed or acquired), and as suggesting innate talent if they referred to *"personality characteristic", "character", "(personality) trait", "disposition", "intelligence", "natural",* or *"stable".*

Definitions that referred to *"high-performance"* were coded as ambiguous because performance can potentially result from an innate predisposition as well as learning. Similarly, definitions referring to the term *"high-potential"* were also coded as ambiguous given that the term "potential" implies some form of latent, presumably innate feature that will only result in excellent performance if nourished and developed (Silzer & Church, 2009). Note that there are potentially other terms that might hint at either innate or acquired talent (e.g., intellect, general cognitive ability), but we did not come across those terms in the identified definitions.

Results

Definitions of Talent Management

Coding the definitions of talent management revealed that there was not a single definition that reflected an outspoken position in the nature-nurture debate on talent. According to Al Ariss, Cascio, and Paauwe (2014), early publications on TM placed a strong emphasis on attracting and selecting employees with innate talent for senior leadership roles. However, the present review revealed that this is not the case anymore. The definition of TM that was most commonly referred to ($k = 17$) by the articles that were included in this review was the following definition by Collings and Mellahi (2009, 304):

> We define strategic talent management as activities and processes that involve the systematic identification of key positions which differentially contribute to the organisation's sustainable competitive advantage, the development of a talent pool of high potential and high performing incumbents to fill these roles, and the development of a differentiated human resource architecture to facilitate filling these positions with competent incumbents and to ensure their continued commitment to the organisation.

This definition reflects one that cannot be clearly coded as either suggesting innate or acquired talent because it a) builds on a position's approach to TM (cf., Huselid, Beatty, & Becker, 2005) proposing that the identification of high-impact organizational positions is even more central than the identification of talent; b) refers to the "development of a talent pool" that can be achieved by either acquiring talented employees externally or developing them internally; and c) addresses high-potential employees, who are assumed to possess innate features that, if developed, allow them to become highly successful (Silzer & Church, 2009).

Most other definitions ($k = 14$) imply that TM is a specific subset of human resource (HR) practices used to attract, identify, select, develop, motivate, and retain talented employees (e.g., Gallardo-Gallardo, Thunnissen, & Scullion, 2020; Meyers & van Woerkom, 2014; Schuler, Jackson, & Tarique, 2011) containing elements that are indicative of the nature perspective (e.g., attract), as well as of the nurture perspective (e.g., develop). In line with this, some articles explicitly discuss that TM combines internal development of talent ("making it") and external recruitment ("buying it") (e.g., Al Ariss, Cascio, & Paauwe, 2014; Vaiman & Collings, 2013). In summary, the analysis of TM definitions thus indicates that TM scholars do not take an outspoken position in the nature-nurture debate on talent. They seem to recognize both nature and nurture as predictors of talent.

Definitions of Talent

A similar picture emerges when analyzing the 27 identified definitions of talent. Twenty-three ($k = 23$) of the definitions were coded as ambiguous. Most often, this was due to defining talent as a person's (high) potential, which alludes to influences of both nature and nurture ($k = 14$). As an example, consider King's (2016: 94) definition proposing that "talented employees are high-performing employees recognised as having high potential for future performance". Another group of definitions ($k = 4$) refers to lists of features of talented employees that include both mainly innate (e.g., personality and intelligence) and acquired components (e.g., knowledge, skills, and abilities). Festing and Schäfer (2014: 263), for instance, propose that talents "can be characterized through a variety of characteristics, such as competencies, skills, abilities, experience, knowledge, intelligence, character, and drive, or the ability to learn and grow within an organization". Other definitions, such as Nijs, Gallardo-Gallardo, Dries, and Sels' (2014: 182) definition of talent as "systematically developed innate abilities of individuals that are deployed in activities they like, find important, and in which they want to invest energy", explicitly address the combination of both innate and acquired components ($k = 5$).

Only a minority ($k = 3$) of definitions equated talent with lists of features that mainly covered acquired, changeable components. For instance, Vaiman, Haslberger, and Vance (2015: 281) propose that employees' talents are "measured by their knowledge, skills, and abilities", while Schiemann (2014: 282) sees talent "as the collective knowledge, skills, abilities, experiences, values, habits and behaviors of all labor that is brought to bear on the organization's mission". One remaining article ($k = 1$) defines talent as an individual's human as well as social capital (Crane & Hartwell, 2019). Whereas human capital refers to both innate (e.g., intelligence) and acquired (e.g., skills) components, social capital refers to a structure that is developed in interactions with others. In conclusion, however, the definitions of talent do not point to a clear predominance of one perspective, similar to the definitions of TM.

Perspectives on Talent in other Disciplines

Given that the TM literature does not address the nature-nurture debate on talent in much detail (for an exception, see for instance Meyers, van Woerkom, & Dries, 2013), we will draw on literature on expert performance to uncover relevant scientific insights that might contribute to the debate. Over the years, research on expert performance has resulted in an extensive, and refined body of scientific evidence concerning the question of whether talent is innate or acquired (e.g., Ericsson, 2014; Hambrick & Tucker-Drob, 2015; Macnamara, Moreau, & Hambrick, 2016). Similar to literature on TM that deals with exceptionally good performers in organizations, literature on expert performance deals with individuals who are exceptionally good in a certain domain. However, in contrast to literature on TM, literature on expert performance is not limited to the organizational domain, but also includes performance domains such as music, sports, and arts. Therefore, many of the examples that will be given in the following section will also refer to these domains.

The scientific study of expert performance has been strongly influenced by Anders Ericsson's work on deliberate practice, defined as "individualized practice with training tasks [...] with a clear performance goal and immediate informative feedback" (Ericsson, 2016: 351). The work of Ericsson and colleagues builds on earlier work by behaviorist Watson (1930) who suggested that success can best be explained by intense training, as well as by Simon and Chase (1973) who studied chess players and concluded that it was impossible to reach the level of chess grandmaster without a decade worth of training (i.e., 10,000–50,000 hours), later popularized as the *10,000-hour Rule* (Gladwell, 2008).

In line with this, Ericsson, Krampe, and Tesch-Römer (1993) proposed that superior accomplishment in any domain can best be explained by the hours of deliberate practice an individual is capable of accumulating. As a strong advocate of the nurture perspective, Ericsson (2014) claimed that there is currently no scientific evidence for innate factors other than height and body size as predictors of expert performance. The scientific evidence regarding the predictive value of deliberate practice, by contrast, is supposedly abundant (e.g., Ericsson, Krampe, & Tesch-Römer, 1993; Law, Côté, & Ericsson, 2007).

Contrary to this claim, meta-analyses have found that deliberate practice accounted for only 12% of variance in performance averaged across diverse domains (games, music, sports, education, and professions) (Macnamara, Hambrick, & Oswald, 2014), for 18% of variance in sports performance (Macnamara, Moreau, & Hambrick, 2016), and for 36% of variance in music performance (Platz et al., 2014). This led to the conclusion that "deliberate practice appears to be an important piece of the expertise puzzle but not the only piece and not necessarily the largest piece" (Macnamara, Moreau, &

Hambrick, 2016: 334). A relevant finding in the light of organizational TM is that deliberate practice accounted for only 1% of variance of performance in professions, which can potentially be explained by the fact that it is difficult to define and design deliberate practice in the work context. Furthermore, deliberate practice seems less efficient in predicting performance in complex contexts that can change in unforeseen ways, such as the business context (Macnamara, Hambrick, & Oswald, 2014).

In light of this evidence, researchers have concluded that it is necessary to recognize that expert performance is a construct that is determined by a variety of factors, including both nature and nurture (Hambrick et al., 2016; Ackerman, 2014; Macnamara, Moreau, & Hambrick, 2016). Extreme positions in the nature-nurture debate on expert performance have even been criticized as "fundamentally silly" (Ackerman, 2014). Theoretical models such as Gagné's (2015) Comprehensive Model of Talent Development (CMTD) and Ullén, Hambrick, and Mosing's (2016) Multifactorial Gene–Environment Interaction Model (MGIM) try to capture the resulting complexity of expert performance (termed "talent" by Gagné). Gagné's model comprises two developmental processes – from genotypic foundations to physical and mental natural abilities, and from natural abilities to competencies or talents in diverse fields of expertise. Those two processes are "catalyzed", that is, activated and sustained, by both environmental and intrapersonal factors (Gagné, 2015). Ullén, Hambrick, and Mosing (2016) suggest that psychological traits (e.g., ability and motivation) are related to the engagement in deliberate practice. Deliberate practice, in turn, predicts changes in physiology and neurology which, ultimately, explain expertise. Both genetic and environmental factors can have direct, joint, or interactive effects on these relations and processes (Ullén, Hambrick, & Mosing, 2016).

To disentangle these rather complex models, we will provide a brief summary of six commonly mentioned influential factors that are assumed to contribute to expert performance next to deliberate practice (for more extensive reviews, see Hambrick et al., 2016; Ullén, Hambrick, & Mosing, 2016).

Genetic Factors

Genetic factors have been repeatedly shown to play a role in expertise, most notably in large-scale twin studies (e.g., Mosing et al., 2014; Plomin et al., 2014; Wesseldijk, Mosing, & Ullén, 2019). Nowadays, genetic factors are most commonly understood as genotypic foundations that strongly, but not perfectly, influence the development of natural, basic abilities in the mental (e.g., cognitive ability) and physical domain (e.g., hand morphology) (Ackerman, 2014; Gagné, 2015; Hambrick et al., 2016; Ullén, Hambrick, & Mosing, 2016).

As an example, consider competitive swimmer Michael Phelps (U.S.) who won a record-breaking number of 23 Olympic gold medals. It is said that Phelps' tall and lean physique and, in particular, his natural body proportions of a long torso and relatively shorter legs have given him a "natural" competitive advantage (Brooks, 2011) that has largely been determined by genetic factors. Interestingly, a twin study among more than 10,000 Swedish twins has also uncovered genetic effects on engagement in (music) training and practice (Mosing et al., 2014), indicating that our genes may influence later expertise via effects on investment in practice. Young Bill Gates' inherent interest in computers and his incessant efforts to receive more computer time at school (Becraft, 2014) might be an example of the influence of genes on practice.

Environmental or Opportunity Factors

Scholars mention that environmental or opportunity factors contribute to expertise. These include a supportive family, the access to specific (national) campaigns and resources that foster the development of abilities, as well as the absence of influential parasitic or infectious diseases (Gagné, 2015; Hambrick et al., 2016). Take Germany as an example, on the one hand, dropping medal counts at both Olympic summer and winter games are partly ascribed to a lack of infrastructure and incentives to develop young, talented athletes in many of the Olympic disciplines. On the other hand, the country has a well-functioning infrastructure to foster and promote soccer talent potentially contributing to the success of the German national soccer team in international competitions (Siemes, 2014).

Developmental Factors

Developmental factors play a role including the age at which a person started training in the target domain. This determines whether an individual gains experiences in the domain's critical periods. Research in the domain of music has for instance shown that musicians who are native speakers of a non-tonal language, such as English, can only acquire perfect pitch before the age of 7 (Hernandez & Li, 2007). A second relevant developmental factor is the domain's peak age, which is determined by the human ageing process and resulting increases or decreases in abilities (Ackerman, 2014; Hambrick et al., 2016). In intellectual domains such as academia, the peak age is estimated to be in the mid-thirties to early-forties (Hambrick et al., 2016).

Practice Factors

Practice factors other than deliberate practice represent a fourth component of expertise. Expertise is not only determined by the narrowly defined deliberate practice (Ericsson, Krampe, & Tesch-Römer, 1993), but also by gaining experience through playing, working, doing chores, and through what Gagné (2015) termed spontaneous learning (Macnamara, Moreau, & Hambrick, 2016). As an example, consider fashion designer Coco Chanel who initially started to design hats as an enjoyable pastime.

Ability Factors and Personality Factors

The final two factors, ability factors and personality factors, are interesting in that they appear to result from a combination of genetic and respectively environmental or developmental factors (Gagné, 2015). It has been estimated that about 50% of the variance in cognitive abilities is accounted for by genetic factors, and about 30 to 50% of the variance in personality (Plomin et al., 2016). Ability factors include mental components such as a person's working memory capacity and general mental ability (IQ) (Hambrick et al., 2016; Ullén, Hambrick, & Mosing, 2016), as well as physical components such as the mass, strength, and anaerobic power of muscles (Gagné, 2015; Tucker & Collins, 2012). Personality factors that determine expertise comprise a person's level of confidence, grit ("the rage to master"), openness, motivation, and the disposition to experience performance anxiety, among others (Gagné, 2015; Macnamara, Moreau, & Hambrick, 2016; Ullén, Hambrick, & Mosing, 2016).

When considering expertise in organizational practice, the most commonly discussed topic is whether leadership expertise is innate or acquired. The question *"Are leaders made or born?"* (e.g., Johnson et al., 2012; Silzer & Borman, 2017) has preoccupied organizations for decades. While some researchers propose that the emergence of leadership abilities depends mostly on adequate leadership development opportunities (Day & O'Connor, 2017; Ruvolo, Peterson, & LeBoeuf, 2004), others claim that leadership appears fairly hard-wired and does not change much across a person's career (Sorcher & Brant, 2002).

Parallel to research on other forms of expertise, scholars have conducted twin studies to explore the heritability of leadership. These studies have shown that genetic factors account for about 30% of the variance in the number and seniority of leadership positions that an individual is holding (Arvey et al., 2006; Arvey et al., 2014). This means that leadership expertise is at least partly determined by genes (similar to personality traits), but that environmental influences play an even larger role. In particular, developmental experiences at work have been found to be important (Arvey et al., 2007). Based on available research evidence, Silzer and Borman (2017) propose that leadership potential is likely to be the result of complex interactions between rather stable, innate factors, such as a person's level of dominance and extraversion; slightly less stable, trait-like characteristics, such as self-efficacy; and the developmental contexts in which individuals find themselves.

In summary, research evidence clearly demonstrates the complexity of the development of expert performance or manifested talent. Consequently, the scientific field seems to move beyond the nature versus nurture debate towards a discussion of how nature and nurture relate to and interact with one another to produce outstanding individual performance (Ackerman, 2014; Gagné, 2015; Hambrick et al., 2016). In the most basic terms, we can conclude the following: Individuals must considerably invest in training and practice if they aim to become outstanding in a certain activity. However, even the most rigorous practice cannot entirely compensate for genetic disadvantages, limited (early) opportunities, or unfavorable timing.

Implications for Practice

Literature on expert performance points to the conclusion that manifested talent originates in complex processes involving both nature and nurture. In line with this, common definitions of talent and TM seem to circumnavigate the nature-nurture debate and regard talent as "an object or an outcome irrespective of its origins" (Krishnan & Scullion, 2016: 9). It is therefore unsurprising that current organizational TM approaches take the different potential origins of talent into account and strive for a balance between acquiring talent externally and developing it internally (Al Ariss, Cascio, & Paauwe, 2014; Vaiman & Collings, 2013). In light of the available evidence, this strategy seems most functional in ensuring that key organizational positions can be filled with talented individuals.

Even though the available research evidence regarding the nature-nurture debate does not point to a single, most important predictor of talent, it has some important practical implications, in particular, with regard to talent identification. As both nature and nurture seem to affect talent, talent identification procedures should also cover both aspects. This means that the common organizational practice to assess talent solely based on ratings of past performance (Mäkelä, Björkman, & Ehrnrooth, 2010) might fall short of identifying the most competent candidates.

Silzer and Church (2009) advocate the identification of potential based on the combined assessment of rather stable personality traits and mental abilities (foundational dimension), almost equally stable, but partly context-dependent features that predict an individual's ability to learn and grow, such as adaptability and motivation (growth dimension), as well as career-path specific skills that can, at least to some extent, be developed, such as leadership or technical skills (career dimension).

The suggested assessment is well-aligned with available research evidence pointing out that general mental abilities and personality traits (e.g., conscientiousness) are strong predictors of performance in work-related contexts (Hambrick, Burgoyne, & Oswald, 2019a; Judge et al., 2007; Schmidt & Hunter, 1998, 2004). Moreover, it is feasible in the light of twin studies that uncovered a genetic influence on an individual's engagement in learning and practice (Mosing et al., 2014), which, in turn, predicts one's level of accomplishment (Hambrick & Tucker-Drob, 2015).

These findings highlight that there are underlying, stable factors that determine a person's motivation and drive to learn in a specific area (cf. literature on vocational interests, Hambrick, Burgoyne, & Oswald, 2019b; Van Iddekinge et al., 2011), which should not be disregarded when assessing organizational talent or potential. Finding the areas in which individuals are inherently most motivated to learn and grow, as advocated in literature on strengths-based approaches to TM (Meyers & van Woerkom, 2014) and on person-job fit in TM (Krishnan &Scullion, 2016), should therefore be a priority in talent management.

Strengths-based approaches to TM view employee talents as "employee attitudes and behaviors that come naturally to them; that drive, motivate and energize them; that they value and like; and that make them feel authentic and true to themselves" (Meyers & van Woerkom, 2014: 197). These approaches build on the assumption that the greatest progress and (performance) gains can be realized when investing in the areas of an employee's strengths (Buckingham & Clifton, 2001). While strengths-based approaches are inherently inclusive, that is, they subscribe to the idea that all employees are talented, the underlying idea of identifying strengths (cf. definition of talent given before) and finding organizational positions that allow for the maximum amount of strength use can also be applied to more exclusive approaches.

Furthermore, emphasizing person-job fit in TM implies that the context, for instance, the position that needs to be filled, determines which employees will and will not be identified as talents (Krishnan & Scullion, 2016). This highlights the relevance of the question "potential for what?" in talent identification (McDonnell, Collings, & Carbery, 2019; Silzer & Church, 2009) and calls into question the validity of widely-used talent identification approaches such as the so-called 9-Grid that rates employees on their generic, (context-free) performance and potential.

Taking literature on strengths and person-job fit into account might be particularly beneficial for organizations who follow the common position-based approach to TM (Collings & Mellahi, 2009; Huselid, Beatty, & Becker, 2005), where the identification of key strategic positions is a first step in TM decision making. While we do not aim to question the necessity of this first step, we think that the challenge in the subsequent steps will be to not lose sight of the individual employees and their specific strengths, drives, and ambitions when trying to find the "right person" for a specific key position.

Limitations of the Literature Review and Directions for Future Research

The present review of the TM literature is subject to the limitation of a rather restricted scope. Its focus on conceptual work in four dedicated, high-quality journals implies that relevant scientific work in other outlets as well as relevant work that is empirical in nature may have been excluded. While an all-encompassing review of the TM literature may have resulted in different outcomes, we reason that the picture that emerges from the present review is fairly representative of the current state of the TM literature for the following three reasons. First, conceptual work usually serves as the basis for empirical work. Second, focusing on four peer-reviewed journals that are well-known outlets for TM research helps to guarantee the scientific quality of the reviewed articles. Third, we are confident that our review includes representative work of the most renowned TM scholars (cf. social network analysis by Gallardo-Gallardo, Arroyo Moliner, & Gallo, 2017) who drive the development of the scientific field.

An additional limitation is that the present review looks at definitions of talent and TM without taking the role of context into account. Recent theoretical work suggests that both definitions may be context-dependent (Gallardo-Gallardo, Thunnissen, & Scullion, 2020; Krishnan & Scullion, 2017). This implies that we may find a stronger emphasis on innate talent in some contexts, and a stronger emphasis on acquired talent in others. It also implies that we need to develop a more dynamic view of talent (Krishnan & Scullion, 2017). The meaning of talent may change, whenever the context changes. To explore the dynamic, context-dependent nature of talent, we would need more conceptual and empirical work on talent and TM in different contexts (Gallardo-Gallardo, Thunnissen, & Scullion, 2020).

A related suggestion for future research would be to conduct more systematic empirical research on the development of talent over time. So far, longitudinal studies on TM are lacking (De Boeck, Meyers, & Dries, 2018), but they would be required to explore trajectories of talent in the professional domain. More specifically, tracking employees over the course of several years will allow researchers to investigate how, under which circumstances, and in which contexts, talent emerges. Building on models of expertise development (e.g., Gagné, 2015), longitudinal studies can help pinpoint the catalysts in the work environment or in the employees themselves that determine whether outstanding natural abilities become manifest in outstanding performance. The fact that prior research has shown that performance levels of talented employees can drop when transferred to different work contexts (Groysberg, 2010; Huckman & Pisano, 2006), calls for more research exploring organizational-, group-, or individual-level factors that allow talented employees to maintain their performance levels across contexts and situations (Collings & Mellahi, 2013).

A related important avenue for future research is the sustainable management of talent, that is, TM systems and practices that enable the continued maintenance of very high-performance levels while safeguarding the health and well-being of talented employees (van der Klink et al., 2016). This avenue for future research builds on the finding that every performance domain has a peak age (e.g., approximately between ages 35 and 45 in intellectual domains) (Hambrick et al., 2016). In the wider HRM literature, age-related changes in social, mental, and physical abilities are a widely discussed topic (e.g., Kooij et al., 2010), and we suggest that TM scholars build on this body of literature to explore how organizations can best support talented employees across the wide span of their working lives.

Research on sustainable, organizational TM is also relevant because research on expert performance acknowledges that too much pressure on talented individuals – in particular in domains where they lack genetic predispositions – can cause physical and mental harm (Ackerman, 2014; Baker, 2003). Similarly, qualitative studies in the area of organizational TM have started to uncover potential negative effects of being part of a talent pool on employee health and well-being (De Boeck, Meyers, & Dries, 2018). Talent pool members have indicated feeling insecure, stressed, and alienated from their true selves due to increasing but often ambiguous organizational expectations and demands (e.g., Dries & De Gieter, 2014; Tansley & Tietze, 2013). Even though these negative reactions among talents can jeopardize the overall effectiveness of TM, the topic has not received much research attention yet.

A final point for future TM research relates to the finding that deliberate practice fails to account for much variance in performance in contexts that are difficult to predict such as organizational contexts (Macnamara, Hambrick, & Oswald, 2014). Organizations are thus facing the challenge of developing a pool of agile and flexible, talented employees who are well-equipped to respond to ever-changing environments. Research that explores both individual (e.g., learning agility) (Dries, Vantilborgh, & Pepermans, 2012) and organizational factors (e.g., leader support as an antecedent of adaptive performance) (Jundt, Shoss, & Huang, 2015) that allow individuals to perform excellently in low-predictability contexts are thus direly needed.

References

Ackerman, P. L. 2014. Nonsense, common sense, and science of expert performance: Talent and individual differences. *Intelligence,* 45: 6–17. doi: https://doi.org/10.1016/j.intell.2013.04.009.

Al Ariss, A., Wayne F. C., & Jaap, P. 2014. Talent management: Current theories and future research directions. *Journal of World Business,* 49(2): 173–179. doi: http://dx.doi.org/10.1016/j.jwb.2013.11.001.

Arvey, R. D, Nan Wang, Z. S., & Wendong, L. 2014. The biology of leadership. In D. V. Day (Ed.), *The Oxford handbook of leadership and organizations:* 73–90. Oxford, UK: Oxford University Press.

Arvey, R. D., Rotundo, M. Johnson, W., Zhen Zhang, B. J. A., & McGue, M. 2006. The determinants of leadership role occupancy: Genetic and personality factors. *The Leadership Quarterly,* 17(1): 1–20. doi:10.1016/j.leaqua.2005.10.009.

Arvey, R. D., Zhen Zhang, B. J. A., & Krueger, R. F. 2007. Developmental and genetic determinants of leadership role occupancy among women. *Journal of Applied Psychology,* 92(3): 693–706.

Baker, J. 2003. Early specialization in youth sport: A requirement for adult expertise? *High Ability Studies,* 14(1): 85–94.

Becraft, M. B. 2014. *Bill Gates: A biography.* Santa Barbara, CA: Greenwood Biographies.

Bonet, R., & Hamori, M. 2017. Talent Intermediaries in talent acquisition. In D. G. Collings, K. Mellahi, & W. F. Cascio (Eds.), *The Oxford handbook of talent management:* 249–267. Oxford, UK: Oxford University Press.

Brooks, M. 2011. *Developing swimmers.* Champaign, IL: Human Kinetics.

Buckingham, M. & D. O. Clifton. 2001. *Now, discover your strengths.* New York: Free Press.

Cappelli, P. 2008. Talent management for the twenty-first century. *Harvard Business Review,* 3: 74–81.

Collings, D. G., & Mellahi, K. 2009. Strategic talent management: A review and research agenda. *Human Resource Management Review,* 19: 304–313. doi: https://doi.org/10.1016/j.hrmr.2009.04.001.

Collings, D. G., & Mellahi, K. 2013. Commentary on "Talent—innate or acquired? Theoretical considerations and their implications for talent management". *Human Resource Management Review,* 23(4): 322–325. doi: http://dx.doi.org/10.1016/j.hrmr.2013.08.003.

Côté, J. K., Ericsson, A., & Madelyn P. L. 2005. Tracing the development of athletes using retrospective interview methods: A proposed interview and validation procedure for reported information. *Journal of Applied Sport Psychology,* 17(1): 1–19. doi:10.1080/10413200590907531.

Crane, B. & Hartwell, C. J. 2019. Global talent management: A life cycle view of the interaction between human and social capital. *Journal of World Business,* 54(2): 82–92. doi: https://doi.org/10.1016/j.jwb.2018.11.002.

Day, D. D., & O'Connor, P. M. G. 2017. Talent development: Building organizational capability. In D. G. Collings, K. Mellahi, & W. F. Cascio (Eds.), *The Oxford handbook of talent management:* 343–360. Oxford, UK: Oxford University Press.

De Boeck, G., Meyers, M. C., & Dries, N. 2018. Employee reactions to talent management: Assumptions versus evidence. *Journal of Organizational Behavior,* 39(2): 199–213. doi:10.1002/job.2254.

Dries, N., & De Gieter, S. 2014. Information asymmetry in high potential programs: A potential risk for psychological contract breach. *Personnel Review,* 43(1): 136–162. doi: https://doi.org/10.1108/PR-11-2011-0174.

Dries, N., Vantilborgh, T., & Pepermans, R. 2012. The role of learning agility and career variety in the identification and development of high potential employees. *Personnel Review,* 41(3): 340–358. doi:10.1108/00483481211212977.

Ericsson, K. A. 2014. Why expert performance is special and cannot be extrapolated from studies of performance in the general population: A response to criticisms. *Intelligence,* 45: 81–103. doi: https://doi.org/10.1016/j.intell.2013.12.001.

Ericsson, K. A. 2016. Summing up hours of any type of practice versus identifying optimal practice activities. *Perspectives on Psychological Science,* 11(3): 351–354. doi:10.1177/1745691616635600.

Ericsson, K. A., Krampe, R. T., & Tesch-Römer, C. 1993. The role of deliberate practice in the acquisition of expert performance. *Psychological Review,* 100(3): 363–406. doi:10.1037/0033-295x.100.3.363.

Ericsson, K. A., & Pool, R. 2016. *Peak: Secrets from the new science of expertise.* Boston, MA: Houghton Mifflin Harcourt.

Feloni, R. 2015. Pepsi CEO Indra Nooyi explains how an unusual daily ritual her mom made her practice as a child changed her life. *Business Insider,* 9.

Festing, M., & Schäfer, L. 2014. Generational challenges to talent management: A framework for talent retention based on the psychological-contract perspective. *Journal of World Business,* 49(2): 262–271. doi: http://dx.doi.org/10.1016/j.jwb.2013.11.010.

Gagné, F. 2015. From genes to talent: The DMGT/CMTD perspective. *Revista de Educacion,* 368: 12–39. doi: http://dx.doi.org/10.4438/1988-592X-RE-2015-368-289.

Gallardo-Gallardo, E., Dries, N., & González-Cruz, T. F. 2013. What is the meaning of 'talent' in the world of work? *Human Resource Management Review,* 23(4): 290–300. doi: http://dx.doi.org/10.1016/j.hrmr.2013.05.002.

Gallardo-Gallardo, E., Moliner, L. A., & Gallo, P. 2017. Mapping collaboration networks in talent management research. *Journal of Organizational Effectiveness: People and Performance,* 4(4): 332–358. doi:10.1108/JOEPP-03-2017-0026.

Gallardo-Gallardo, E., & Thunnissen, M. 2016. Standing on the shoulders of giants? A critical review of empirical talent management research. *Employee Relations,* 38(1): 31–56.

Gallardo-Gallardo, E., Thunnissen, M., & Hugh Scullion. 2020. Talent management: Context matters. *The International Journal of Human Resource Management,* 31(4): 457–473. doi:10.1080/09585192.2019.1642645.

Gladwell, M. 2008. *Outliers: The story of success.* London, UK: Penguin Books.

Groysberg, B. 2010. *Chasing stars: The myth of talent and the portability of performance.* Princeton, NJ: Princeton University Press.

Hambrick, D. Z., Burgoyne, A. P., & Oswald, F. L. 2019a. Domain-general models of expertise: The role of cognitive ability. In P. Ward, J. M. Schraagen, J. Gore, & E. Roth (Eds.), *The Oxford handbook of expertise.* Oxford, UK: Oxford University Press.

Hambrick, D. Z, Burgoyne, A. P., & Oswald, F. L. 2019b. The role of interests in the development of expertise: A multifactorial perspective. In C. D. Nye & J. Rounds (Eds.), *Vocational interests in the workplace: Rethinking behavior at work:* 280–300. New York: Routledge.

Hambrick, D. Z., Macnamara, B. N., Campitelli, G., Ullén, F., & Mosing, A. M. 2016. Beyond born versus made: A new look at expertise. In H. B. Ross (Ed.), *Psychology of Learning and Motivation:* 1–55. Academic Press.

Hambrick, D. Z., & Tucker-Drob, E. M. 2015. The genetics of music accomplishment: Evidence for gene–environment correlation and interaction. *Psychonomic Bulletin & Review,* 22(1): 112–120. doi:10.3758/s13423-014-0671-9.

Hernandez, A. E., & Ping, L. 2007. Age of acquisition: Its neural and computational mechanisms. *Psychological Bulletin,* 133(4): 638-650. doi:10.1037/0033-2909.133.4.638.

Huckman, R. S., & Pisano, G. P. 2006. The firm specificity of individual performance: Evidence from cardiac surgery. *Management Science,* 52(4): 473–488. doi:10.1287/mnsc.1050.0464.

Huselid, M. A., Beatty, R. W., & Becker, B. E. 2005. A players or A positions? The strategic logic of workforce management. *Harvard Business Review,* 83(12): 110–117.

Isaacson, W. 2011. *Steve Jobs.* New York: Simon & Schuster.

Johnson, A. M.,. Vernon, P. A., McCarthy, J. M., Molson, M.,. Harris, J. A., & Jang, K. L. 2012. Nature vs. nurture: Are leaders born or made? A behavior genetic investigation of leadership style. *Twin Research,* 1(4): 216–223. doi:10.1375/twin.1.4.216.

Judge, T. A., Jackson, C. L., Shaw, J. C., Scott, B. A., & Rich, B. L. 2007. Self-efficacy and work-related performance: The integral role of individual differences. *Journal of Applied Psychology,* 92(1): 107–127. doi:10.1037/0021-9010.92.1.107.

Jundt, D. K., Shoss, M. K., & Huang, J. L. 2015. Individual adaptive performance in organizations: A review. *Journal of Organizational Behavior,* 36(S1): S53–S71. doi:10.1002/job.1955.

King, K. A. 2016. The talent deal and journey: Understanding the employee response to talent identification over time. *Employee Relations,* 38(1): 94–111. doi: https://doi.org/10.1108/ER-07-2015-0155.

Kooij, D. T. A. M., Jansen, P. G., Dikkers, J. S., & De Lange, A. H. 2010. The influence of age on the associations between HR practices and both affective commitment and job satisfaction: A meta-analysis. *Journal of Organizational Behavior,* 31(8): 1111–1136. doi:10.1002/job.666.

Krishnan, T. N., & Scullion, H. 2017. Talent management and dynamic view of talent in small and medium enterprises. *Human Resource Management Review,* 27(3): 431–441. doi: https://doi.org/10.1016/j.hrmr. 2016.10.003.

Law, M. P., Côté, J., & Ericsson, K. A. 2007. Characteristics of expert development in rhythmic gymnastics: A retrospective study. *International Journal of Sport and Exercise Psychology,* 5(1): 82–103. doi:10.1080/1612 197X.2008.9671814.

Lengnick-Hall, M. L., & Andrade, L. A. 2008. Talent staffing systems for effective knowledge management. In V. Vaiman & C. Vance (Eds.), *Smart Talent Management-Building Knowledge Assets for Competitive Advantage:* 33-65. Cheltenham, UK: Edward Elgar.

Macnamara, B. N., Hambrick, D. Z., & Oswald, F. L. 2014. Deliberate practice and performance in music, games, sports, education, and professions. *Psychological Science,* 25(8): 1608–1618. doi:10.1177/0956797614535810.

Macnamara, B. N., Moreau, D., & Hambrick, D. Z. 2016. The relationship between deliberate practice and performance in sports. *Perspectives on Psychological Science,* 11(3): 333–350. doi:10.1177/1745691616635591.

Mäkelä, K. B. I., & Ehrnrooth, M. 2010. How do MNCs establish their talent pools? Influences on individuals' likelihood of being labeled as talent. *Journal of World Business,* 45(2): 134–142. doi: https://doi. org/10.1016/j.jwb.2009.09.020.

McDonnell, A., Collings, D. G., & Carbery, R. 2019. The identification and evaluation of talent in multinational enterprises. In D. G. Collings, H. Scullion, & P. M. Caligiuri (Eds.), *Global Talent Management:* 74–89. New York: Routledge.

McDonnell, A., Collings, D. G., Kamel M., & Schuler, R. 2017. Talent management: A systematic review and future prospects. *European Journal of International Management,* 11(1): 86–128.

Meyers, M. C., & van Woerkom, M. 2014. The influence of underlying philosophies on talent management: Theory, implications for practice, and research agenda. *Journal of World Business,* 49(2): 192–203. doi: http://dx.doi.org/10.1016/j.jwb.2013.11.003.

Meyers, M. C., van Woerkom, M., & Nicky Dries. 2013. Talent — Innate or acquired? Theoretical considerations and their implications for talent management. *Human Resource Management Review,* 23(4): 305–321. doi: http://dx.doi.org/10.1016/j.hrmr.2013.05.003.

Mosing, M. A., Madison, G., Pedersen, N. L., Kuja-Halkola, R., & Fredrik Ullén. 2014. Practice does not make perfect: No causal effect of music practice on music ability. *Psychological Science,* 25(9): 1795–1803. doi:10.1177/0956797614541990.

Nijs, S., Gallardo-Gallardo, E., Dries, N., & Sels, L. 2014. A multidisciplinary review into the definition, operationalization, and measurement of talent. *Journal of World Business,* 49(2): 180–191. doi: http://dx.doi. org/10.1016/j.jwb.2013.11.002.

Platz, F., Kopiez, R., Lehmann, A. C., & Wolf, A. 2014. The influence of deliberate practice on musical achievement: A meta-analysis. *Frontiers in Psychology* 5, 6.

Plomin, R., John C. D., Knopik, V. C., & Neiderhiser, J. M. 2016. Top 10 replicated findings from behavioral genetics. *Perspectives on Psychological Science,* 11(1): 3–23. doi:10.1177/1745691615617439.

Plomin, R., Shakeshaft, N. G., McMillan, A., & Trzaskowski, M. 2014. Nature, nurture, & expertise. *Intelligence,* 45: 46–59. doi: https://doi.org/10.1016/j.intell.2013.06.008.

Ruvolo, C. M., Peterson, S. A., & LeBoeuf, J. N. G. 2004. Leaders are made, not born: The critical role of a developmental framework to facilitate an organizational culture of development. *Consulting Psychology Journal: Practice and Research,* 56(1): 10–19. doi:10.1037/1061-4087.56.1.10.

Schiemann, W. A. 2014. From talent management to talent optimization. *Journal of World Business,* 49(2): 281–288. doi: http://doi.org/10.1016/j.jwb.2013.11.012.

Schmidt, F. L., & Hunter, J. E. 1998. The validity and utility of selection methods in personnel psychology: Practical and theoretical implications of 85 years of research findings. *Psychological Bulletin,* 124(2): 262–274. doi:10.1037/0033-2909.124.2.262.

Schmidt, F. L., & Hunter, J. E. 2004. General mental ability in the world of work: Occupational attainment and job performance. *Journal of Personality and Social Psychology,* 86(1): 162–173. doi:10.1037/0022-3514.86.1.162.

Schuler, R. S., Jackson, S. E., & Tarique, I. 2011. Global talent management and global talent challenges: Strategic opportunities for IHRM. *Journal of World Business,* 46(4): 506–516. doi: http://dx.doi.org/10.1016/j.jwb.2010.10.011.

Siemes, C. 2014. Olympia Bilanz: Der deutsche Sport hat ein Problem [Taking stock of the Olympic games: German sport in trouble]. *Zeit Online.*

Silzer, R. F. & Borman, W. C. 2017. The potential for leadership. In D. G. Collings, K. Mellahi, & W. F. Cascio (Eds.), *The Oxford handbook of talent management:* 87–114. Oxford, UK: Oxford University Press.

Silzer, R., & Church, A. H. 2009. The pearls and perils of identifying potential. *Industrial and Organizational Psychology: Perspectives on Science and Practice,* 2(4): 377–412. doi: https://doi.org/10.1111/j.1754-9434.2009.01163.x.

Simon, H. A., & William, G. C. 1973. Skill in chess. *American Scientist,* 61(4): 394–403.

Sorcher, M., & James B. 2002. Are you picking the right leaders? *Harvard Business Review,* (2): 80–87.

Tansley, C., & Tietze, S. 2013. Rites of passage through talent management progression stages: An identity work perspective. *The International Journal of Human Resource Management,* 24(9): 1799–1815. doi: https://doi.org/10.1080/09585192.2013.777542.

Tucker, R., & Collins, M. 2012. What makes champions? A review of the relative contribution of genes and training to sporting success. *British Journal of Sports Medicine.* doi:10.1136/bjsports-2011-090548.

Ullén, F., Hambrick, D. Z., & Mosing, M. A. 2016. Rethinking expertise: A multifactorial gene–environment interaction model of expert performance. *Psychological Bulletin,* 142(4): 427–446. doi:10.1037/bul0000033

Vaiman, V., & Collings, D. G. 2013. Talent management: Advancing the field. *The International Journal of Human Resource Management,* 24(9): 1737–1743. doi:10.1080/09585192.2013.777544.

Vaiman, V. Haslberger, A., & Vance, C. M. 2015. Recognizing the important role of self-initiated expatriates in effective global talent management. *Human Resource Management Review,* 25(3): 280–286. doi: http://doi.org/10.1016/j.hrmr.2015.04.004.

van der Klink, J. J., Ute Bültmann, A. B., Wilmar B., Schaufeli, F., Zijlstra, R. H., Abma, F. I., Brouwer, S., & van der Wilt, G. J. 2016. Sustainable employability – definition, conceptualization, and implications: A perspective based on the capability approach. *Scandinavian Journal of Work, Environment & Health* (1): 71–79. doi:10.5271/sjweh.3531.

Van Iddekinge, C. H., Roth, P., Putka, D., & Lanivich, S. 2011. Are you interested? A meta-analysis of relations between vocational interests and employee performance and turnover. *Journal of Applied Psychology,* 96(6): 1167–1194. doi:10.1037/a0024343.

Watson, J. B. 1930. *Behaviorism.* New York: W. W. Norton.

Wesseldijk, L. W., Mosing, M. A., & Ullén, F. 2019. Gene–environment interaction in expertise: The importance of childhood environment for musical achievement. *Developmental Psychology,* 55(7): 1473–1479. doi: http://dx.doi.org.tilburguniversity.idm.oclc.org/10.1037/dev0000726.

19

TALENT MANAGEMENT AND GENERATIONAL DIFFERENCES

Marion Festing

Lynn Schäfer

Introduction

These are times of significant demographic challenges in many industrialized countries characterized by an aging workforce, declining birth rates, the reduced availability of younger employees, and various generations at work. At this time, understanding and managing age-related and generational differences in talent management (TM) is of major importance for academics and practitioners alike (Becker, 2011; Collings, Mellahi, & Cascio, 2019; D'Amato & Herzfeldt, 2008; Gallardo-Gallardo, Thunnissen, & Scullion, 2020; Jenkins, 2008; Schuler, Jackson, & Tarique, 2011; Tarique & Schuler, 2018)

In many companies, large and small, talent is often conceptualized in terms of early career or young high-potential employees characterized by high future leadership potential (Festing, Kornau, & Schäfer, 2014b; Mäkelä, Björkman, & Ehrnrooth, 2010). At the same time, the skills, competences, experiences, and talent of older workers are often ignored and not included in strategic development plans. While there is, of course, no common understanding of when a worker is "old", there are some indications, for example, given by the German statistical office, that defines employees over 45 as "old employees" (Becker, 2011: 44). Bearing in mind the demographic situation, heterogeneous workforces – not only with respect to age – will increasingly be a reality. Therefore, a homogeneous approach to managing talent must be questioned.

This chapter focuses on this research question, addressing the interplay of heterogeneous workforces (especially with respect to age and generational challenges) and TM. As a result, we consider the specific age-related preferences, needs, and expectations of talents and go beyond the research stream that focuses on individuals as subjects that need to be managed (Tansley, 2011; Thunnissen, Boselie, & Fruytier, 2013).

First, we provide a review of the admittedly scarce literature concerning this important aspect of TM research, following which we discuss various theoretical perspectives explaining the relationship between generations and TM, such as social identity, social-exchange theory perspectives, and unconscious bias. This acts as the basis for deriving avenues for future research as well as practical implications.

Talent Management and Generational Diversity

Managing Human Resources and Talent

In this chapter, we adopt the broad definition of TM suggested by Stahl et al. (2007), namely an organization's ability to attract, select, develop, and retain key employees (in a global context). The broad field of human resource management (HRM) is defined as all "policies, practices, and

DOI: 10.4324/9781315474687-19

systems that influence employees' behavior, attitudes, and performance" (Noe, Hollenbeck, Gerhart, & Wright, 2010). Acknowledging that TM is part of HRM, the differentiation is concerned with the notion of highly talented individuals who are supposed to be of "pivotal" strategic importance (Collings & Mellahi, 2009; Schuler & Tarique, 2012) and who play a crucial role in achieving corporate performance (Collings & Mellahi, 2009; Tansley et al., 2007). In addition, research shows that TM, especially those activities directed at talent development and retention, has a positive impact not only on organizational performance, but also on employee motivation, commitment, contribution, and intention to stay in the organization (Bethke-Langenegger, Mahler, & Staffelbach, 2011; Björkman, Ehrnrooth, Mäkelä, Smale, & Sumelius, 2013; Chami Malaeb, 2012; Dries, Forrier, De Vos, & Pepermans, 2014).

Another finding of a study by Björkman et al. (2013) concluded that it was especially important to "inform talented individuals of their status," by communicating that they belong to a designated target group, to attain these positive attitudinal outcomes. Therefore, in the discussion of the following theoretical perspectives on TM, an individual (subject) talent perspective with differentiated investments in those being officially communicated and labeled as "talent" is pursued.

The intensively discussed "war for talent" means that talents are scarce, but due to the demographic developments described above, TM also needs to cope with an increasingly more diversified workforce (Bhalla, Dyrchs, & Strack, 2017). In this context, the aging population, accompanied by a higher share of older employees, who can be observed particularly in Japan, the U.S.A., and Germany (Lanvin & Evans, 2016; World Economic Forum, 2011), must be considered in addition to the various younger generations present in the workplace. Consequently, managing a diverse workforce, not only with respect to gender, sexual orientation, nationality, religion, race, or disabilities, but especially considering age, and understanding and managing generational differences in TM have been cited as major challenges in TM research (Benson & Brown, 2011; D'Amato & Herzfeldt, 2008; Festing & Schäfer, 2014; Jenkins, 2008; Schuler et al., 2011; Tarique & Schuler, 2010). The next section discusses this challenge.

Generations and Generational Differences

Generations, generational units, or cohorts are defined as individuals who share the same "inborn way of experiencing life and the world" (as cited in Ng, Lyons, & Schweitzer, 2012: 283). This means that groups of people born around the same time share the same common events (e.g., war) and experiences (e.g., media, culture, and parents) during childhood and adolescence, thereby leading to similar values and attitudes within each cohort (Arsenault, 2004; Chaney, Touzani, & Ben Slimane, 2017; Ng et al., 2012; Twenge, Campbell, Hoffman, & Lance, 2010). Labels and birth-years of generations vary slightly (see Crampton & Hodge, 2007 for alternative categorization); however, the most commonly known classifications of the four generations at work, according to Twenge et al. (2010), are the Silent Generation (1925–1945), the Baby Boomers (1946–1964), Generation X (1965–1981), and Generation Y (1982–1999), the latter also referred to as Millennials. More recently, discussions have emerged on whether there is a new generation, born in the mid-to-late 1990s after the Millennials, referred to as Generation Z (Seemiller & Grace, 2016; Scholz, 2014).

The term Baby Boomers refers to the generation born after World War II, who experienced a rise in economic prosperity, which in turn made them optimistic, which heavily influenced their way of thinking, such as believing in lifetime employment with a company and loyalty to an employer. Research has found that Baby Boomers are generally more satisfied with their job and valued job security, and they are less likely to change employers, compared to Generation X (Benson & Brown, 2011; Burke, 2004; Crampton & Hodge, 2007).

Generation X, which is supposed to be less loyal to a company and more open to changing jobs than the Baby Boomers, value work-life balance, autonomy, and independence more. This generation has grown up with the Internet, television, and mobile devices and is technological-savvy (Benson &

Brown, 2011; Burke, 2004; Jenkins, 2008; Lub, Bal, Blomme, & Schalk, 2016; Smola & Sutton, 2002; Twenge et al., 2010).

Generation Y is known for placing even more emphasis on work-life-balance, development opportunities, training, meaningful work, and social responsibility (Anderson, Baur, Griffith, & Buckley, 2017; Cennamo & Gardner, 2008; DelCampo, Haggerty, Haney, & Knippel, 2011; Vaiman, Scullion, & Collings, 2012). Members of this cohort are reported to be even less loyal and more individualistic, compared to previous generations. So, when looking for an employer, they will choose the one that treats their employees as individuals and really cares about their workforce (Terjesen & Frey, 2008).

Generation Z has grown up with 24/7 access to the Internet, mobile devices, social media (e.g., YouTube, Facebook) and is about to enter the workplace in the near future. A great deal has been said and written about this *truly global generation* in daily press, blogs, and newspapers (Seemiller & Grace, 2016; Scholz, 2014); however, research on distinct work values is scarce (Iorgulescu, 2016: 48). What is definitely true for these *digital natives* (Prensky, 2012) is that they are largely dependent on their devices, are used to accessing big amounts of information and data, and are always on. This influences their expectations regarding potential workplaces and employers with respect to learning possibilities as well as availability of information.

A study by Universum (2015) surveyed close to 50,000 high school graduates worldwide (born between 1996 and 2000), asking them about their future careers, work, and life. Interestingly, when asked about their greatest fears regarding work life, the majority mentioned foremost not finding a job that matched their personality, followed by the fear of having no development opportunities. Further, more than 55% responded that they were interested in starting their own company, and in some regions, like the Middle East and Central and Eastern Europe, this number was close to 75% (Universum, 2015: 11). Choosing to start their own business rather than pursuing a more conventional corporate career demonstrates Generation Z's entrepreneurial aspirations and initiatives and the wish to make an impact (Iorgulescu, 2016). Therefore, to attract and retain talent from Generation Z, a sense of purpose, development opportunities, flexible working conditions, and work-life balance seem to be of major importance.

Generations are a popular topic in the media and daily press, and they are commonly used in consumer market segmentation or branding (Chaney et al., 2017; Williams & Page, 2011); nonetheless, academic studies have reported mixed results, and so researchers call for caution in this regard. Whereas some researchers use biological age for age diversity research, to study work-related outcomes or organizational tenure (seniority, job experience), other studies (see Smola & Sutton, 2002) find that differences in work values (e.g., job satisfaction, organizational commitment, company loyalty, lifetime employment, and work-life balance) are influenced more by generational experiences than by career stages, maturity, or the biological age of employees (Anderson et al., 2017; Benson & Brown, 2011; Crampton & Hodge, 2007; Dries, Pepermans, & de Kerpel, 2008; Jenkins, 2008; Smola & Sutton, 2002; Twenge et al., 2010).

Similar to other conceptual classifications, critiques on the subject address the lack of mutual exclusiveness between generations, arguing that there are people born in between two generations or at the beginning and at the end of a generational cohort who might share experiences with their own generational cohort as well as with the previous or the next generation (Arsenault, 2004; Benson & Brown, 2011). These are sometimes referred to as "tweeners" (Arsenault, 2004: 125), acknowledging that there might be crossover effects (e.g., significant events affecting every generation).

Another question that is often raised is whether the differences between generations are similar in different regions of the world, because the common concept of generations that develops within sociohistoric locations contradicts a global generational categorization. Although peer-reviewed academic articles and longitudinal insights investigating generational differences in work values and attitudes are scarce (Benson & Brown, 2011; De Meuse & Mlodzik, 2010; Lyons & Kuron, 2014; Parry & Urwin, 2011; Twenge et al., 2010; Twenge & Campbell, 2008), since the rise of modern communication technology and the global reach of historical and formative events, there has been widespread agreement on the existence of "global generations", albeit at least spanning Western cultures, where most of the research on generations and empirical insights has been conducted (Lub et al., 2016; Van der Smissen, Schalk, & Freese, 2013).

Explaining Generational Challenges in Talent Management

The Need for Generational Talent Management

The change in global workforce demographics, associated with increased diversity, is affecting organizations, HRM, and TM alike (Collings, Mellahi, & Cascio, 2019; Farndale, Biron, Briscoe, & Raghuram, 2015; Schuler et al., 2011). However, only a few diversity dimensions, such as gender (Festing et al., 2014b) or disability (Fujimoto, Rentschler, Le, Edwards, & Härtel, 2014), have been investigated in the context of TM, and there is a lack of research considering different generations or age groups in this domain. Based on the assumption that generations vary with respect to work values (Benson & Brown, 2011; Burke, 2004; Crampton & Hodge, 2007; Jenkins, 2008), as shown above, it is likely that talent from different generational cohorts will respond differently to TM practices. In the following, several theoretical perspectives are discussed through a generational lens, and connections with and implications for TM are outlined.

Social Identity, Generations, and Talent Management

A theoretical perspective that might explain the group dynamics emerging from diversity, including generational differences, is social identity theory (see for example Ashforth, Harrison, & Corley, 2008; Björkman et al., 2013; Tajfel & Turner, 1979; Turner, 1975; Turner, Brown, & Tajfel, 1979). This theoretical perspective postulates that individuals belonging to a specific group share similar beliefs and attitudes (Allen & Wilder, 1975), which in turn leads to increased intragroup cohesiveness and cooperation, and favors discrimination between an in-group and an out-group. The phenomenon of in-group favoritism may occur, since resources such as prestige or power can be unequally distributed between the two groups, albeit favoring the in-group (Tajfel & Turner, 1979; Turner et al., 1979).

Following in-group favoritism, this cohort can also be defined as elite, i.e. a superior group—an impression that is perceived inside and outside the group (Alvesson & Robertson, 2006). In this case, identity construction occurs through reflection and mirroring (Hatch & Schultz, 2002), and can be strengthened by using labels that secure the in-groups' identities' legitimacy (Glynn & Abzug, 2002).

Relating insights from social identity theory to the various generations active in the workforce can help in understanding how a single personal attribute, such as generational belonging, which is often associated with a certain age group, might account for friction in organizations. For example, generations such as Gen Y or Gen Z might label themselves as such, to stress common features and develop and display strengths as an in-group while at the same time excluding out-groups such as older employees. For example, if Gen Y represents scarce young talents, and therefore the in-group in the organization is characterized as valuing work-life balance, training, development opportunities, and looking for mobility in their early careers (Cennamo & Gardner, 2008; DelCampo, 2007; DelCampo et al., 2011; Vaiman et al., 2012), then this group might have a stronger probability than older generations being treated with HR measures that correspond to their individual values and preferences, because in the latter group priorities were different.

If several generations are at work in one organization, this may create conflicts, because differing priorities and treatments – as well as possibly different rewards – between groups become obvious. Therefore, different solutions must be found while at the same time guaranteeing fairness and organizational justice for all generations active in the organization, i.e., between in-group and out-group employees.

Although with this short social-identity based reasoning, we only consider one single personal characteristic (belonging to a specific generation) as the basis for creating a distinct group within the organization, without a clearly defined boundary, and while neglecting intersectionality including multiple social identities (Hornsey & Hogg, 2000; Ramarajan, 2014), this perspective nevertheless helps to illustrate some key issues to be considered from a TM perspective.

Social Exchange Theory, Generations, and Talent Management

Another theoretical perspective from which to look at TM and generational challenges is the social exchange perspective, or to be more precise, the psychological contract theory (Rousseau, 1990). According to this approach, "psychological contracts are individual beliefs in reciprocal obligations between employees and employers," whereby "two parties to a relationship, such as employee and employer, may each hold different beliefs regarding the existence and terms of a psychological contract" (Rousseau, 1990: 391).The psychological contract can be used as a framework to study aspects of the employment relationship between highly talented individuals, focusing particularly on the exchange of perceived promises, commitments, and obligations with respect to TM practices and activities (Guest & Conway, 2002; Herriot & Pemberton, 1997; Höglund, 2012; Rousseau, 1989; Schein, 1980; Sonnenberg, Koene, & Paauwe, 2011).

Festing and Schäfer (2014) argue that TM, which is about offering talented individuals inclusion in talent pools, differential treatment, investments in the development of one's talent, participation in talent development programs, etc., is perceived as a *signal*, an indication that "his or her contribution is valued" (Festing et al., 2014b: 266). By offering encompassing, highly engaged, and long-term-oriented TM activities (compared to, for example, short-term and only limited to current job training), the organization sends a clear signal that the talent is appreciated and valued, and that it is attempting to meet the expectations of its employees, which creates higher emotional involvement and interdependency (Bethke-Langenegger et al., 2011; Höglund, 2012; Lub et al., 2016; Rousseau, 1995; Sonnenberg, 2011).

Depending on how well an employer manages to keep promises and match talents' beliefs and expectations, the contract can be fulfilled (meeting the expectation), breached (a perception that the organization has failed to deliver its obligation), or even violated (failure to fulfill promised obligations and to comply with the terms of a contract, e.g., no opportunities for talent development) (Morrison & Robinson, 1997; Rousseau, 1995; Rousseau & Tijoriwala, 1998).

The differing states of the psychological contract (fulfilled, breached, violated) can either positively or negatively influence talents' attitudes and behavior concerning, for instance, job satisfaction and organizational commitment (Benson, Brown, Glennie, O'Donnel & O'Keefe, 2018; Conway & Briner, 2005; Freese, 2007). For example, contract violation as the most extreme form can cause adverse, negative reactions resulting in attitudinal and behavioral outcomes such as decreased loyalty, less job performance and commitment, and the intention to quit (Morrison & Robinson, 1997; Rousseau, 1995; Sonnenberg, 2011).

Moreover, the employment relationship has changed over time. Flexible contracts, boundaryless and protean careers, a changing environment, globalization, and rapid technological advancements all combine to affect the values and expectations and demands of generations, thereby influencing the fulfillment and content of the psychological contract, sometimes also referred to as "new deals" (Benson & Brown, 2011; D'Amato & Herzfeldt, 2008; Jenkins, 2008; Smola & Sutton, 2002; Van der Smissen et al., 2013: 312).

However, it is still difficult to examine and study specific terms with respect to the psychological contract of the talented individual, as it can comprise various aspects and items with deviating priorities for each individual. For instance, nowadays, the focus is more on employability, training and development opportunities, and flexible work structures than on job security in former times (Freese & Schalk, 2008).

In the context of generational challenges, it is therefore argued that people of different ages react differently to TM practices. Hence, a TM approach that emphasizes development, coaching, employability, and career opportunities, as well as work-life balance, highly reflects the priorities of Generations Y and Z and will lead to a higher psychological contract fulfillment for these younger talents than for older workers (e.g. Baby Boomers) (Accenture, 2010; Festing & Schäfer, 2014; Van der Smissen et al., 2013).

This is confirmed by a recent study by Lub et al. (2016), who investigated whether generations respond differently to psychological contract fulfillment. They found that Baby Boomers and Generation X are more motivated by social atmosphere, while Generation Y is more motivated by job content (e.g., challenging and varied job) and career development (e.g., self-development). Overall, generational differences moderate the relationship between psychological contract fulfillment and organizational outcomes, such as affective commitment and turnover intention (Lub et al., 2016).

Accordingly, to influence talented individuals' intention to stay, the psychological contract might be a useful perspective from which to understand changes in the employment relationship, and so organizations should differentiate their TM practices to best address the needs and preferences of each generation to fulfill their expectations.

Unconscious Bias, Generations, and Talent Management

In another avenue of investigation, research demonstrates that there is gender bias in, for example, selection and evaluation processes (Smith, Paul, & Paul, 2007), performance management (Festing, Knappert, & Kornau, 2014a), and TM based on the philosophy "think talent – think male" (Festing et al., 2014b). Further illustrations include female talent, disadvantaged based on gender bias and sex discrimination against entering top TM programs (Festing et al., 2014b), or migrants, who are disadvantaged in talent selection and development processes due to their national and/or cultural background.

With respect to age and generations, in many organizations stereotypes prevail, which include negative features associated with older workers. One such case is the age-deficit model, postulating that mental capacity decreases over time. However, findings from gerontological research indicate that this is only the case from about 80 years onward, at which point a decline in intelligence, reduced learning ability, and capacity (productivity) can be expected (Becker, 2011: 41). These findings question the assumption that older workers have a lesser ability to learn, and that investments in training and development do not generate a positive return on investment, due to shorter tenure and retirement. Other stereotypes include the poor performance stereotype (assuming older workers are less productive and motivated) or a higher resistance to change (older workers are less flexible and adaptable).

While above we speak about stereotypes that bear some uncertainties, it is probably true, however, that older workers, in societies where seniority is valued, are more costly (due to higher wages, using more benefits) (Posthuma & Campion, 2009). Posthuma & Champion (2009) confirmed in their research that there is an age bias in recruiting, promotion, evaluation, and appraisal, and a "general preference for younger workers" (2009: 171) that results in fewer training opportunities for older workers and their under-representation in TM programs.

The prevalence of rather negative stereotypes associated with age is discriminatory against older workers and bears the risk of an unconscious or conscious age bias in TM, or more precisely in talent reviews, performance evaluations, and appraisals of talents. Therefore, belonging to a specific generation could increase or decrease the likelihood of being identified as a talent and receive development opportunities within an organization. For example, if IT skills are ascribed to the young rather than to the older generations, and although older employees may possess these skills as well, there is a risk of an unconscious bias leading automatically to the selection of employees belonging to younger generations as talents. In this context, it is interesting to note that, according to a study of the Entertainment Software Association (ESA, 2013), nearly half of the population in the United States older than 50 years old play video games—an unexpected fact that confirms the risk of ascribing certain skills and behaviors to one generation only.

Another study on age diversity management in Germany found that competencies, such as strategic thinking and coping with stress, will improve over time, whereas divergent thinking and performance motivation are at least the same for younger and older workers (Becker, 2011). Thus, it does not confirm the negative stereotypes often related to age or to belonging to a certain generation.

In conclusion, to avoid an unconscious bias and aim for inclusion according to the definition by Roberson (2006: 215) as "a person's ability to contribute fully and effectively to an organization", TM should investigate some rules and recommendations regarding all elements thereof. This will be elaborated in the implications for future research.

Conclusion

Future Research Areas

As already indicated in the context of social identity, future research should investigate the effectiveness of all TM elements. The definition of talents should be reconsidered very consciously; for example, can only young people representing a specific generation be talents, or is there room for a talent definition that is more encompassing? Concerning the TM approach, it has to be decided whether different career paths and multiple careers for talents can be defined that fill the need of one group valuing fast and steep career progression and possibly even freelance careers, while at the same time keeping more traditional intra-organizational career patterns (e.g., Lanvin & Evans, 2016). Especially given the changing circumstances and increasing flexibility demands in many organizations, future TM research should investigate whether there are differences with respect to freelancers, contingent workers, or permanent staff (Bhalla et al., 2017; Vaiman, 2010).

Trying to incorporate and integrate new perspectives through which TM and generational challenges can be analyzed, in this book chapter, social identity, social exchange theory – namely psychological contract theory – and unconscious bias were introduced, attempting to enrich the research domain and establish valuable links between TM and psychological or socio-psychological concepts. However, further research is needed in all three theoretical areas to understand better the linkages and relationships between generations, TM, and the respective theories.

Trying to enrich the research field of TM even more, further research avenues could adopt other theoretical perspectives as well. For example, using resource dependence theory (Pfeffer & Salancik, 2003), those resources that are of critical importance to the company could be identified as core features in the talent definition and design of TM. This should lead to a focus on critical competencies and skills of the talents rather than on age-related criteria. It would be interesting to see whether and how such an argumentation would be related to the exclusive view of talents and to what extent inclusive approaches can be considered following this perspective.

When analyzing the interplay between generations and talent from a resource-based view (Barney, 2001; Peteraf, 1993; Wernerfelt, 1984), it could be investigated to what extent the integration of various generations within the talent pool or the workforce can create a unique resource able to contribute to the competitive advantage of the organization. Using this approach, it would be interesting to compare the success of defining age-homogenous groups as compared to age-heterogeneous groups as talents. It could be that a homogenous consideration of young talents is too limited, especially when firms have to respond to the challenges of creativity and innovation, where diversity is much needed (Eagly, 2013).

Another promising theoretical perspective for analyzing this topic could be the consideration of organizational justice, including equity arguments. Pursuing this research avenue, various input and output relations could be considered without reflecting one specific generational perspective to avoid respective bias (Adams, 1963; Greenberg, 1987). These ideas for future research are, of course, not exhaustive but underline that the need for further exploration is enormous.

Further studies could also start by questioning the approach to studying generational diversity as one single aspect of diversity. This means that future research should not only focus on generation-related research, but also address all diversity aspects such as gender, nationality, religion, race, and disabilities, to allow for a theoretical inclusion of everyone (Roberson, 2006). In this case, we could speak about social identity complexity (Roccas & Brewer, 2002), taking into account multiple social identities through various in-group memberships. Miller, Brewer, and Arbuckle observed:

> The idea behind the complexity construct is that it is not only how many social groups an individual identifies with that matters but, more importantly, how those different identities are subjectively combined to determine the overall inclusiveness of the individual's ingroup memberships. (2009: 79)

Possibly a TM approach considering intersectionality could help blur generation-related in- and out-groups and reduce potential conflicts. Previous research results indicate that social identity complexity reflecting intersectionality helps create more tolerance of other groups (Miller et al., 2009) and is negatively related to in-group favoritism (Brewer & Pierce, 2005). Therefore, research beyond age covariates, examining the effects of other forms of discrimination and diversity aspects with generations and age and intersectionality, could also represent a fruitful avenue for future research (Hornsey & Hogg, 2000; Posthuma & Campion, 2009; Ramarajan, 2014).

Research aiming at the development of an inclusion index for TM reflecting this complexity, allowing the potential disclosure of deeply rooted and embedded conceptual bias (Festing & Schäfer, 2015; Lanvin & Evans, 2016), could also help introduce a more informed and balanced perspective. So far, a global talent competitiveness index for cities and regions exists, evaluating enablers such as infra-structure, living conditions, and aspects such as education, health, and safety issues (Lanvin & Evans, 2016). For TM from an organizational perspective, such an inclusion index could include elements such as talent definition, selection, and evaluation criteria, the selected TM approach, underlying career orientation (vertical versus horizontal), and an evaluation of each element, in connection with whether and to what extent bias or discrimination exists. This diagnosis could help in creating a more inclusive environment, and by providing talent from each generation, gender, religion, and national background with the same chances to be considered as talent (Festing & Schäfer, 2015).

Eventually, further research could also consider different types of organizations, such as start-ups or large, old-economy multinational corporations. While in this book chapter, the discussions were purely conceptual, when designing research projects based on these ideas, further contextual and situational factors such as the company setting and the local and national environment should be considered, especially in empirical investigations. The way in which a national culture influences age stereotypes or other diversity parameters, and comparative research insights into TM and generations, would also be necessary to generate new insights (Lyons & Kuron, 2014; Parry & Urwin, 2011). Lastly, with respect to methodological challenges, additional empirical longitudinal insights would be desirable to shed more light on this topic.

To conclude, this book chapter on TM and generational challenges has shown that the field of TM is still lacking theoretical foundations, and although many papers have been published in this emerging research domain, the field still offers numerous avenues for future research. Outlining potential conceptual interdependencies, relationships, and discussing theoretical outcomes of TM and social identity, social exchange, and unconscious bias are meant to enrich the discussion on context-oriented, inclusive TM practices (Thunnissen et al., 2013).

Practical Implications

As depicted in this chapter, each generation has its own work-related values and attitudes (Crampton & Hodge, 2007; Jenkins, 2008), and there is the potential to learn from these generational differences to create a more effective and tailored way to attract, select, develop, motivate, and retain talent in organizations (D'Amato & Herzfeldt, 2008). Thus, implementing a talent strategy or TM measures that do not reflect these generational differences (or potentially even other diversity aspects such as gender, nationality, etc.), and treating everyone the same, is truly questionable. Also, it can be said that age stereotypes and unconscious bias should be avoided and different target groups addressed to include talent of all ages in TM.

One option could be analyzing the workforce according to age and generations, becoming aware of how fast a company is aging, and adopting a lifecycle approach to TM (Armutat, 2009; Becker, 2011), including generation-specific incentives (compensation, motivation), development possibilities, and career prospects according to the varying needs of the generations. Making people aware of age and generational differences, for example, in sensitizing workshops and awareness training, could also be another means of reducing the negative effects of age stereotyping. Former research has shown that this approach has the potential to mitigate race, gender discrimination, and sexual harassment (Posthuma & Campion, 2009).

In times of digitalization, transformation, constant change, and demographic turmoil, one major requirement for organizations will be to address connectedness, collaboration, and co-creation in TM practices, as well as train employees of all ages in lifelong learning (Lanvin & Evans, 2016). Consequently, while bearing in mind different generations and offering generation-specific activities, the focus should be on encouraging autonomy and collaboration over authority and hierarchy, focusing on cross-generational mentoring, networking, intergenerational learning, and knowledge exchange to avoid the loss of critical organizational knowledge from experienced employees (Becker, 2011; De Meuse & Mlodzik, 2010; Iorgulescu, 2016). In this respect, mentoring tandems, part-time retirement, project oriented career paths, work-life balance, temporary work, senior advisor careers, reverse mentoring (e.g., Millennials or digital natives teaching Baby Boomers the use of technical skills), cross-generational trainings or talent development, and rewarding team-based outcomes and work instead of individual performance can also foster generational collaboration. These are often cited as tools to bridge the generational gap and foster intra-generational knowledge exchange (Becker, 2011; Kaplan, Sanchez, & Hoffman, 2017; Marcinkus Murphy, 2012).

On a higher level, creating age-appropriate jobs, age-inclusive employment practices, reforming labor markets to make it easier for older workers to change jobs, and adapting housing and infrastructure to the needs of an aging society are important societal aspects to prepare for an aging population (Billett, Dymock, Johnson, & Martin, 2011; Lanvin & Evans, 2016). While these practices have been discussed often and hold a high level of plausibility, more research is needed to prove their effectiveness further.

References

Accenture. 2010. *How effective are talent management practices: Talent management research.* Accenture Talent & Organization Performance.

Adams, J. S. 1963. Towards an understanding of inequity. *The Journal of Abnormal and Social Psychology,* 67(5): 422.

Allen, V. L., & Wilder, D. A. 1975. Categorization, belief similarity, and intergroup discrimination. *Journal of Personality and Social Psychology,* 32(6): 971.

Alvesson, M., & Robertson, M. 2006. The best and the brightest: The construction, significance and effects of elite identities in consulting firms. *Organization,* 13(2): 195–224.

Anderson, H. J., Baur, J. E., Griffith, J. A., & Buckley, M. R. 2017. What works for you may not work for (Gen) Me: Limitations of present leadership theories for the new generation. *The Leadership Quarterly,* 28(1): 245–260.

Armutat, S. 2009. *Lebensereignisorientiertes Personalmanagement. Eine Antwort auf die demografische Herausforderung.* Bielefeld, G: Bertelsmann Verlag.

Arsenault, P. M. 2004. Validating generational differences: A legitimate diversity and leadership issue. *Leadership and Organization Development Journal,* 25(2): 124–141.

Ashforth, B. E., Harrison, S. H., & Corley, K. G. 2008. Identification in organizations: An examination of four fundamental questions. *Journal of management,* 34(3): 325–374.

Barney, J. B. 2001. Is the resource-based "view" a useful perspective for strategic management research? Yes. *Academy of Management Review,* 26(1): 41–56.

Becker, M. 2011. Optimistisch altern!, *Talent Management:* 39–56: Springer.

Benson, J., & Brown, M. 2011. Generations at work: Are there differences and do they matter? *International Journal of Human Resource Management,* 22(9): 1843–1865.

Benson, J., Brown, M., Glennie, M., O'Donnell, M., & O'Keefe, P. (2018). The generational "exchange" rate: How generations convert career development satisfaction into organisational commitment or neglect of work. *Human Resource Management Journal,* 28(4): 524–539.

Bethke-Langenegger, P., Mahler, P., & Staffelbach, B. 2011. Effectiveness of talent management strategies. *European Journal of International Management,* 5: 524–539.

Bhalla, V., Dyrchs, S., & Strack, R. 2017. *Twelve forces that will radically change how organizations work.* The Boston Consulting Group.

Billett, S., Dymock, D., Johnson, G., & Martin, G. 2011. Overcoming the paradox of employers' views about older workers. *The International Journal of Human Resource Management,* 22(06): 1248–1261.

Björkman, I., Ehrnrooth, M., Mäkelä, K., Smale, A., & Sumelius, J. 2013. Talent or Not? Employee reactions to talent identification. *Human Resource Management,* 52(2): 195–214.

Brewer, M. B., & Pierce, K. P. 2005. Social identity complexity and outgroup tolerance. *Personality and Social Psychology Bulletin,* 31(3): 428–437.

Burke, M. E. 2004. *Generational differences. Survey report.* Alexandria: Society for Human Resource Management (SHRM).

Cennamo, L., & Gardner, D. 2008. Generational differences in work values, outcomes and person-organisation values fit. *Journal of Managerial Psychology,* 23(8): 891–906.

Chami Malaeb, R. 2012. Talent management as a key driver to employee performance. In B. Chapelet, & M. LeBerre (Eds.), *Producing new knowledge on innovation management:* 209–222. Grenoble, France: PUG.

Chaney, D., Touzani, M., & Ben Slimane, K. 2017. *Marketing to the (new) generations: Summary and perspectives.* London: Taylor & Francis.

Collings, D. G., & Mellahi, K. 2009. Strategic talent management: A review and research agenda. *Human Resource Management Review,* 19(4): 304–313.

Collings, D. G., Mellahi, K., & Cascio, W. F. (2019). Global talent management and performance in multinational enterprises: A multilevel perspective. *Journal of Management,* 45(2): 540–566.

Conway, N., & Briner, R. B. 2005. *Understanding psychological contracts at work.* New York: Oxford University Press.

Crampton, S. M., & Hodge, J. W. 2007. Generations in the workplace: Understanding age diversity. *The Business Review,* 9(1): 16–22.

D'Amato, A., & Herzfeldt, R. 2008. Learning orientation, organizational commitment and talent retention across generations: A study of European managers. *Journal of Managerial Psychology,* 23(8): 929–953.

De Meuse, K. P., & Mlodzik, K. J. 2010. A second look at generational differences in the workforce: Implications for HR and talent management. *People & Strategy,* 33(2): 50–58.

DelCampo, R. G. 2007. Understanding the psychological contract: A direction for the future. *Management Research News,* 30(6): 432–440.

DelCampo, R. G., Haggerty, L. A., Haney, M. J., & Knippel, L. A. 2011. *Managing the multi-generational workforce.* Surrey, UK & Burlington, VT: Gower.

Dries, N., Forrier, A., De Vos, A., & Pepermans, R. 2014. Self-perceived employability, organization-rated potential, and the psychological contract. *Journal of Managerial Psychology,* 29(5): 565–581.

Dries, N., Pepermans, R., & de Kerpel, E. 2008. Exploring four generations' beliefs about career. Is "satisfied" the new "successful"? *Journal of Managerial Psychology,* 23(8): 907–928.

Eagly, A. H. 2013. Women as leaders: Leadership style versus leaders' values and attitudes In R. J. Ely, & A. J. C. Cuddy (Eds.), *Gender and work: Challenging conventional wisdom.* Boston, MA: Harvard Business School Press.

Entertainment Software Association. 2013. *Nearly half of Americans older than 50 play video games.* May 20, 2017. http://www.theesa.com/article/nearly-half-americans-older-50-play-video-games/.

Farndale, E., Biron, M., Briscoe, D. R., & Raghuram, S. 2015. A global perspective on diversity and inclusion in work organisations. *The International Journal of Human Resource Management,* 26(6): 677–687.

Festing, M., Knappert, L., & Kornau, A. 2014a. Gender-specific preferences in global performance management: An empirical study of male and female managers in a multinational context. *Human Resource Management,* 54(1): 55–79.

Festing, M., Kornau, A., & Schäfer, L. 2014b. Think talent – think male? A comparative case study analysis of gender inclusion in talent management practices in the German media industry. *International Journal of Human Resource Management,* 26(6): 707–732.

Festing, M., & Schäfer, L. 2014. Generational challenges to talent management: A framework for talent retention based on the psychological-contract perspective. *Journal of World Business,* 49(2): 262–271.

Festing, M., & Schäfer, L. 2015. Conceptual bias in HRM - Gender inclusion and implications for other diversity dimensions, *Opening Organizations: Managing Diversity and Inclusion through HRM, 75th Annual Meeting of the Academy of Management.* Vancouver, Canada.

Freese, C. 2007. *Organizational change and the dynamics of psychological contracts: A longitudinal study.* Ridderkerk, NL: Ridderprint.

Freese, C., & Schalk, R. 2008. How to measure the psychological contract? A critical criteria-based review of measures. *South African Journal of Psychology,* 38(2): 269–286.

Fujimoto, Y., Rentschler, R., Le, H., Edwards, D., & Härtel, C. E. 2014. Lessons learned from community organizations: Inclusion of people with disabilities and others. *British Journal of Management,* 25(3): 518–537.

Glynn, M. A., & Abzug, R. 2002. Institutionalizing identity: Symbolic isomorphism and organizational names. *Academy of Management Journal,* 45(1): 267–280.

Greenberg, J. 1987. A taxonomy of organizational justice theories. *Academy of Management Review,* 12(1): 9–22.

Guest, D., & Conway, N. 2002. Communicating the psychological contract: an employer perspective. *Human Resource Management Journal,* 12(2): 22–38.

Hatch, M. J., & Schultz, M. 2002. The dynamics of organizational identity. *Human Relations,* 55(8): 989–1018.

Herriot, P., & Pemberton, C. 1997. Facilitating new deals. *Human Resource Management Journal,* 7(1): 45–56.

Höglund, M. 2012. Quid pro quo? Examining talent management through the lens of psychological contracts. *Personnel Review,* 41(2): 126–142.

Hornsey, M. J., & Hogg, M. A. 2000. Assimilation and diversity: An integrative model of subgroup relations. *Personality and Social Psychology Review,* 4(2): 143–156.

Iorgulescu, M.-C. 2016. Generation Z and its perception of work. *Cross-Cultural Management Journal,* 18(1): 9.

Jenkins, J. 2008. Strategies for managing talent in a multi-generational workforce. *Employment Relations Today,* 34(4): 19–26.

Kaplan, M., Sanchez, M., & Hoffman, J. 2017. Intergenerational strategies for establishing sustainable work environments, *Intergenerational Pathways to a Sustainable Society:* 141–162. Cham, Switzerland: Springer.

Lanvin, B., & Evans, P. 2016. *The Global Talent Competitiveness Index, 2015:* Talent attraction and international mobility; growing talent for today and tomorrow: INSEAD, Adecco, HCLI.

Lub, X. D., Bal, P. M., Blomme, R. J., & Schalk, R. 2016. One job, one deal… or not: Do generations respond differently to psychological contract fulfillment? *The International Journal of Human Resource Management,* 27(6): 653–680.

Lyons, S., & Kuron, L. 2014. Generational differences in the workplace: A review of the evidence and directions for future research. *Journal of Organizational Behavior,* 35(S1).

Mäkelä, K., Björkman, I., & Ehrnrooth, M. 2010. How do MNCs establish their talent pools? Influences on individuals' likelihood of being labeled as talent. *Journal of World Business,* 45(2): 134–142.

Marcinkus Murphy, W. 2012. Reverse mentoring at work: Fostering cross-generational learning and developing millennial leaders. *Human Resource Management,* 51(4): 549–573.

Miller, K. P., Brewer, M. B., & Arbuckle, N. L. 2009. Social identity complexity: Its correlates and antecedents. *Group Processes and Intergroup Relations,* 12(1): 79–94.

Morrison, E. W., & Robinson, S. L. 1997. When employees feel betrayed: A model of how psychological contract violation develops. *The Academy of Management Review,* 22(1): 226–256.

Ng, E. S., Lyons, S., & Schweitzer, L. 2012. *Managing the new workforce: International perspectives on the millennial generation.* Cheltenham, UK & Northhampton, MA: Edward Elgar.

Noe, R. A., Hollenbeck, J. R., Gerhart, B., & Wright, P. M. 2010. *Human resource management: Gaining a competetive advantage* (7. intern. student ed.). New York: McGraw-Hill.

Parry, E., & Urwin, P. 2011. Generational differences in work values: A review of theory and evidence. *International Journal of Management Reviews,* 13(1): 79–96.

Peteraf, M. A. 1993. The cornerstones of competitive advantage: A resource-based view. *Strategic Management Journal,* 14(3): 179–191.

Pfeffer, J., & Salancik, G. R. 2003. *The external control of organizations: A resource dependence perspective.* Stanford, CA: Stanford University Press.

Posthuma, R. A., & Campion, M. A. 2009. Age stereotypes in the workplace: Common stereotypes, moderators, and future research directions. *Journal of Management,* 35(1): 158–188.

Prensky, M. R. 2012. *From digital natives to digital wisdom: Hopeful essays for 21st century learning.* Thousand Oaks, CA: Corwin Press.

Ramarajan, L. 2014. Past, present and future research on multiple identities: Toward an intrapersonal network approach. *Academy of Management Annals,* 8(1): 589–659.

Roberson, Q. M. 2006. Disentangling the meanings of diversity and inclusion in organizations. *Group & Organization Management,* 31(2): 212–236.

Roccas, S., & Brewer, M. B. 2002. Social identity complexity. *Personality and Social Psychology Review,* 6(2): 88–106.

Rousseau, D. M. 1989. Psychological and implied contracts in organizations. *Employee Responsibilities and Rights Journal,* 2: 121–139.

Rousseau, D. M. 1990. New hire perceptions of their own and their employer's obligations: A study of psychological contracts. *Journal of Organizational Behavior,* 11(5): 389–400.

Rousseau, D. M. 1995. *Psychological contracts in organizations: Written and unwritten agreements.* Thousand Oaks, CA: Sage.

Rousseau, D. M., & Tijoriwala, S. A. 1998. Assessing psychological contracts: Issues, alternatives and measures. *Journal of Organizational Behavior,* 19: 679–695.

Schein, E. H. 1980. *Organizational psychology.* Englewood Cliffs, NJ: Prentice-Hall.

Scholz, C. 2014. *Generation Z: Wie sie tickt, was sie verändert und warum sie uns alle ansteckt.* Weinheim: John Wiley & Sons.

Schuler, R. S., Jackson, S. E., & Tarique, I. 2011. Global talent management and global talent challenges: Strategic opportunities for IHRM. *Journal of World Business,* 46(4): 506–516.

Schuler, R. S., & Tarique, I. 2012. Global talent management: Theoretical perspectives, systems, and challenges. In G. K. Stahl, I. Björkman, & S. Morris (Eds.), *Handbook of research in international human resource management:* 205–219. Cheltenham, UK: Edward Elgar.

Seemiller, C., & Grace, M. 2016. *Generation Z goes to college:* John Wiley & Sons.

Smith, J. L., Paul, D., & Paul, R. 2007. No place for a woman: Evidence for gender bias in evaluations of presidential candidates. *Basic and Applied Social Psychology,* 29(3): 225–233.

Smola, K., & Sutton, C. 2002. Generational differences: Revisiting generational work values for the new millennium. *Journal of Organizational Behaviour,* 23(4): 363–382.

Sonnenberg, M. 2011. Talent – Key ingredients, *Accenture Talent & Organization Performance.* Amsterdam.

Sonnenberg, M., Koene, B., & Paauwe, J. 2011. Balancing HRM: The psychological contract of employees. *Personnel Review,* 40(6): 664–683.

Stahl, G. K., Björkman, I., Farndale, E., Morris, S. S., Paauwe, J., Stiles, P., Trevor, J., & Wright, P. M. 2007. Global talent management: How leading multinationals build and sustain their talent pipeline, *INSEAD Working Papers Collection:* 1–36: INSEAD.

Tajfel, H., & Turner, J. C. 1979. An integrative theory of intergroup conflict. In W. G. Austin, & S. Worchel (Eds.), *The social psychology of intergroup relations:* 33–47. CA: Brooks/Cole.

Tansley, C. 2011. What do we mean by the term 'talent' in talent management? *Industrial & Commercial Training,* 43(5): 266–274.

Tansley, C., Turner, P. A., Foster, C., Harris, L. M., Stewart, J., Sempik, A., & et al. 2007. *Talent: Strategy, management, measurement.* Plymouth, UK: Chartered Institute of Personal & Development.

Tarique, I., & Schuler, R. S. 2010. Global talent management: Literature review, integrative framework, and suggestions for further research. *Journal of World Business,* 45(2): 122–133.

Terjesen, S., & Frey, R.-V. 2008. Attracting and retaining Generation Y knowledge worker talent. In V. Vaiman, & C. M. Vance (Eds.), *Smart talent management:* 66–89. Cheltenham, UK: Edward Elgar.

Thunnissen, M., Boselie, P., & Fruytier, B. 2013. Talent management and the relevance of context: Towards a pluralistic approach. *Human Resource Management Review,* 23(4): 326–336.

Turner, J. C. 1975. Social comparison and social identity: Some prospects for intergroup behaviour. *European Journal of Social Psychology,* 5(1): 1–34.

Turner, J. C., Brown, R. J., & Tajfel, H. 1979. Social comparison and group interest in ingroup favouritism. *European Journal of Social Psychology,* 9(2): 187–204.

Twenge, J. M., & Campbell, S. M. 2008. Generational differences in psychological traits and their impact on the workplace. *Journal of Managerial Psychology,* 23(8): 862–877.

Twenge, J. M., Campbell, S. M., Hoffman, B. J., & Lance, C. E. 2010. Generational differences in work values: Leisure and extrinsic values increasing, social and intrinsic values decreasing. *Journal of Management:* 1–26.

Universum. 2015. *Generation Z grows up.* May 20, 2017. http://universumglobal.com/insights/generation-z-grows/.

Vaiman, V. 2010. *Talent management of knowledge workers: Embracing the non-traditional workforce.* Basingstoke, UK: Palgrave Macmillan.

Vaiman, V., Scullion, H., & Collings, D. 2012. Talent management decision making. *Management Decision,* 50(5): 925–941.

Van der Smissen, S., Schalk, R., & Freese, C. 2013. Contemporary psychological contracts: How both employer and employee are changing the employment relationship. *Management Revue,* 24(4): 309–327.

Wernerfelt, B. 1984. A resource-based view of the firm. *Strategic Management Journal,* 5(2): 171–180.

Williams, K. C., & Page, R. A. 2011. Marketing to the generations. *Journal of Behavioral Studies in Business,* 3: 1.

World Economic Forum. 2011. *Global talent risk: Seven responses.* Geneva: World Economic Forum.

20

IT'S NOT EITHER/OR, IT'S BOTH-AND

The Paradox Between Exclusive Talent Management and Inclusive Diversity Management

Dagmar Daubner-Siva

Introduction

Talent management (TM) and diversity management have been high on the agenda of both HR theory (Collings, Scullion, & Vaiman, 2015; Dries, 2013; Gallardo-Gallardo, Thunnissen & Scullion, 2020; Özbilgin, Tatli, & Jonsen, 2015) and practice (e.g., Bhalla, Caye, Lovich, & Tollman, 2018; CIPD, 2017; Meyers et al., 2020). At first glance, diversity management and TM seem to build on overlapping or complementing aims and principles. Diversity management is broadly defined as organizational activities to reduce intergroup inequalities with the aim to enable equal development and career progression for all employees (Holck, Muhr, & Villesèche, 2016; Linnehan & Konrad, 1999; Oswick & Noon, 2014; Tatli & Özbilgin, 2012). Diversity management is concerned with the promotion of an organizational culture that leverages the overall diversity within the entire organization (Özbilgin et al., 2015). In other words, diversity management aims to foster work environments in which every employee – irrelevant of their personal attributes such as gender, race, or educational background – can realize their potential in order to add value to the organization. In a similar vein, TM is concerned with the development and implementation of a human resource architecture to fill key positions with high-potential and high-performing (i.e., talented) employees, to sustain the organization's competitive advancement (cf. Collings & Mellahi, 2009). Together, diversity management builds on the underlying assumption that *all* employees count and have something valuable to offer for their organization, while TM aims to identify and develop the *few* "best" employees to ensure the organization's future success. Thus, the more inclusive the TM processes are, the more likely an organization will create a strong talent pipeline that meets the future demands of an organization. From this perspective, TM and diversity management together secure that an organization benefits from the qualities of all potential talents within its entire staff.

However, despite the apparent connection between TM and diversity management, there seems to be a misalignment between diversity and TM. The literature on diversity management and TM mirrors this gap. The diversity management literature acknowledges the tension between talent shortages and underutilization of diverse talent and calls for integrating diversity management with TM research (e.g., Al Ariss & Sidani, 2016; Singh & Point, 2004; Tatli, Vassilopoulou, & Özbilgin, 2013; Thomas, 2010). The TM literature remains largely silent about the connection to diversity management. Sheehan and Anderson (2015) even suggest there might be negative effects of TM for the diversity and inclusion of employees, and highlight avenues for future research that could uncover "the shadow side" of TM. So, perhaps, TM and diversity management do not sit well together after all?

DOI: 10.4324/9781315474687-20

Relevance of Paradox Lens for Talent Management and Diversity Management

The clash between the underlying aims and benefits of talent management and diversity management queues up within other tensions that have previously been described and discussed in the human resource management (HRM) literature (Al Ariss & Sidani, 2016; Aust, Brandl, Keegan, & Lensges, 2017; Boselie, Brewster, & Paauwe, 2009; Boxall & Purcell, 2011; Evans, 1999; Francis & Keegan, 2006). Examples of management tensions in the HRM field include the conflicting poles of human relations and efficiency improvement, tensions between employee advocacy and top management agency, the temporal tradeoff between short- and long-term orientation, or coping with tensions in performance appraisal systems (Evans, 1999; Kozica & Brandl, 2015).

Boselie et al. (2009) provide a literature review of HRM studies that evolved over the last 30 years and derive a list of dualities that should receive further attention in HRM research. One of the highlighted dualities is the friction between pluralist approaches versus unitarist approaches in HRM research. While the unitarist approach builds on the assumption that HRM practices are equally relevant and beneficial for both the employee and the employer, the pluralist approach promotes considering potential different interests and perceptions of organizational actors, such as employees, line managers, HR professionals, or top managers (Boselie et al., 2009; Janssens & Steyaert, 2009). Thus, the pluralist approach recognizes the existence of tensions and the benefits of pro-actively addressing them (Aust et al., 2017).

Resulting insights from addressing and proactively dealing with tensions in HRM literature are two-fold. First, they point to the potential negative effects of HRM practices for individual employees, such as traditionally marginalized groups like women or older workers (Janssens & Steyaert, 2009). Second, dealing with tensions in HRM literature provides insights into the active role of HR actors and thus emphasizes the positive effects of engaging with unavoidable tensions (Aust, Brandl, & Keegan, 2015; Ehnert, 2009; Evans, 1999). Rather than considering tensions as something negative that has to be suppressed, these contributions suggest frictions in theory and practice to be positive, as they provide sources for change and innovation (Aust et al., 2015).

Going beyond the description of two opposing poles, paradox theory has recently been advocated in HRM research to systematically analyze HRM tensions (Aust et al., 2015; Ehnert, 2009). Adopting a paradox lens means to consider conflicting demands or opposing perspectives, with the awareness that in practice, the simultaneous existence of tensions cannot be avoided and persists over time (Eisenhardt, 2000; Lewis, 2000; Raisch, Hargrave, & van de Ven, 2018). Thus, *living* with tensions is an inevitable part of work life. This implies that the move from conceptual thinking to practice (living) is key, although *thinking* dualities or tensions are only recently proposed in HRM research, whereas *living* dualities are happening every day. For that reason, adopting a paradox perspective facilitates effective responses to everyday tensions. Rather than looking at either/or options with the aim to give priority to one pole of a tension and not to the other, adopting a paradox lens implies embracing a both-and approach, in which all contradicting poles of the tension are considered to a more equal extent. In doing so, adopting a paradox lens acts as an analytical tool (Ehnert, 2009) that allows for new perspectives, for rethinking existing contradictions, and for recognizing more complex relationships that enable organizational learning (Lewis, 2000; Raisch et al., 2018).

In sum, building on the relevance of TM, diversity management and paradox theory in the HRM literature, the general contribution of this chapter lies in systematically explaining the emergence and meaning of dovetailing, that is interweaving and aligning TM and diversity management in both in theory and practice. The purpose of this chapter is to increase the understanding of the (dis-)connect between TM and diversity management in an attempt to dovetail the fields.

The remainder of this chapter is organized in four sections. Following this introduction, I outline the history and definition of diversity management. Next, I summarize seminal gender studies that connect diversity research with paradox theory. Third, I elaborate the exclusion-inclusion paradox by interweaving the fields of TM and diversity management through the paradox lens. Fourth, I discuss implications of the exclusion-inclusion paradox on the individual and organizational level, before concluding by promoting the value of multiple perspectives in TM research and practice.

Brief History and Definition of Diversity Management

The evolution of diversity management stems from legal affirmative action (AA) and equal opportunity (EO) regulations, and dates back to the 1970s in the U.S.A. (Kelly & Dobbin, 1998). In the 1990s, there was a movement from externally initiated legal compliance activities towards a more internally initiated business-needs driven approach that emerged as a voluntary corporate initiative directed at the systematic recruitment and retainment of diverse employees (Prasad, Pringle, & Konrad, 2006; Pringle & Strachan, 2015). While diversity management has its origins in the U.S.A., diversity initiatives have gained importance in other parts of the world, such as Europe, Asia, and the Middle East (Prasad et al., 2006).

Compositional Approach

Before moving towards defining diversity management, I will briefly explain the concept of workplace diversity. In general, there are two perspectives that can be distinguished when defining workplace diversity. The first perspective, often referred to as *compositional approach*, focuses on individual differences that distinguish members of a group (or unit) from each other. Within the compositional approach, one can distinguish between a narrow or broad definition (Morrison, Lumby, & Sood, 2006). Narrow definitions of diversity date back to early equal opportunities legislation and address observable characteristics such as gender, age, or ethnicity (Morrison et al., 2006; Oswick & Noon, 2014). Broader definitions of diversity additionally include non-observable characteristics, such as organizational tenure, personality, or sexual orientation, and can further be distinguished between demographic or psychological attributes (Jonsen, Maznevski, & Schneider, 2011; Morrison et al., 2006). Critics of the compositional approach to diversity argue that this perspective does not account for systematic inequalities between certain (historically marginalized) groups within a unit (Guillaume, Brodbeck, & Riketta, 2012; Linnehan & Konrad, 1999; Prasad et al., 2006).

Relational Approach

In contrast to the compositional approach to diversity stands the second perspective on diversity, referred to as *relational approach*. This diversity perspective focuses on "the relationship between an individual's characteristics (e.g., in respect to a demographic or personality attribute) and the distribution of these characteristics in the individual's unit" (Guillaume et al., 2012: 81). Thus, in the relational perspective, diversity describes the extent to which an individual's characteristics are similar or dissimilar to other individuals in the same unit (Guillaume et al., 2012). Accordingly, the degree to which individuals are impacted is depended on their (dis-)similarity to other members in the same unit. Therefore, rather than focusing on individual differences independent of the context, the relational approach considers that intergroup interaction within a unit is inclusive of power differences, which may lead to systematic inequalities in opportunities and consequences between members of varying social groups (Prasad et al., 2006; Tatli & Özbilgin, 2012). Konrad (2003) connects the relational approach to group identity by arguing: "sets of individuals find themselves sharing a common fate as organizations systematically treat them to various routines and standard operating procedures" (p. 8).

In this chapter, I define workplace diversity in line with the relational approach to diversity, in the attempt to address systematic inequalities of historically disadvantaged groups, in particular, women in the workforce. By doing so, I acknowledge the structural component of diversity plus an asymmetric distribution of power (Prasad et al., 2006; Tatli & Özbilgin, 2012).

Against the background of globalization processes, there are many drivers for multinational organizations to invest in diversity management, in the attempt of increasing inclusion of a diverse workforce. In this context, the meaning of inclusion extends beyond the representation of individuals' characteristics as it simultaneously embraces respecting and valuing differences (Prasad et al., 2006). Thus, as organizations attempt to "manage" the diversity of their employee population, they implicitly acknowledge the structural inequalities for various employee groups in the attempt to change the situation for the historically disadvantaged groups. In line with this understanding, I integrate Özbilgin et al.'s (2015) description who define global diversity management as:

> Planning, coordination and implementation of a set of management strategies, policies, initiatives and training and development activities that seek to accommodate diverse sets of social and individual backgrounds, interests, beliefs, values and ways of work in organizations with international, multinational, global and transnational workforces and operations. (2015: 10)

Building on this definition of global diversity management, the next section highlights seminal studies that applied the paradox perspective in order to contribute to the understanding of prevalent gendered practices leading to systematic exclusion in the private sector.

Connecting Diversity Research with Paradox Theory

Acknowledging the structural component of diversity, gender studies that explore systematic inequalities highlight the contradictory and ambiguous nature of how gender is done in organizations. Focusing on the private sector, I will summarize four relevant studies that illustrate how applying a paradox lens to gender inequality facilitates the sensemaking process of the dynamic and complex nature of gender practices in organizations (Van den Brink & Stobbe, 2009). Along the continuum of upward mobility, the visibility paradox (Faulkner, 2009a, 2009b), the ambition paradox (Sools, Van Engen, & Baerveldt, 2007), and the boardroom paradox (Pesonen, Tienari, & Vanhala, 2009) exemplify that women face tensions and double bind situations throughout their career trajectory (Daubner-Siva, Vinkenburg, & Jansen, 2017). The fourth paradox, the meritocracy paradox (Castilla & Benard, 2010) may occur at different career stages and is therefore relevant across organizational hierarchies.

Visibility Paradox

The *visibility paradox* was researched in engineering workplaces but might also occur in other workplace situations with unbalanced gender rations. This paradox highlights that female engineers face the double bind of being simultaneously visible (as women) and invisible (as subject matter experts) (Faulkner, 2009a, 2009b). The impact of this double bind situation creates issues for women engineers, which their male colleagues rarely face. Being invisible as subject matter expert means that women have to work harder to establish their professional credentials and exposure in order to be taken seriously. This continuously required effort might impact women's confidence over time. Simultaneously, their constant visibility as women brings contradictory pressures to feel a part of the male dominated culture while maintaining their femininity. The visibility paradox is key to understand how women engineers experience workplace cultures and may serve as a key factor in explaining challenges to retain and progress women engineers (Faulkner, 2009b).

Ambition Paradox

The *ambition paradox* describes that both men and women are expected to show ambition without being overly overt about it, or, as Sools et al. (2007: 424) formulate the paradox: "Show that you want to gain promotion without showing you want to." Women, however, face a heightened dilemma of showing ambition in the "right" way, especially in combination with the general expectation that young women are bound to have children and as a consequence will lose all interest, and thus ambition, for advancing their career (Sools et al., 2007).

Boardroom Paradox

The *boardroom paradox* (Pesonen et al., 2009) highlights opposing elements in the discourses of female boardroom members about accessing and succeeding in corporate boards. While the discourse of competence considers boardroom access and success as gender-neutral practice, the discourse of gender builds on essential differences. Pesonen et al. (2009: 340) summarize this paradox as follows: "gender simultaneously matters and is irrelevant".

Meritocracy Paradox

The *meritocracy paradox* exemplifies the role of organizational culture in maintaining prevailing inequalities. Castilla and Benard (2010) highlight in a series of three experimental studies that as an organizational culture advocates meritocracy, managers are more likely to promote and reward men in comparison to women. These results stand in contrast to the general acceptance of meritocratic systems as a fair organizational practice, where "everyone has an equal chance to advance and obtain rewards based on their individual merits and efforts" (Castilla & Benard, 2010: 543). Thus, in the attempt to create fair and transparent treatment for all employees, unfair treatment is reproduced. Similar to the findings from Castilla and Benard's (2010) study, Kumra's (2014) review of meritocracy points out that the seemingly objective and fair character of the construct can be supplemented with a rather subjective notion and unfairness.

In summary, the outlined seminal gender studies highlight that women are exposed to paradoxical situations throughout their career as visibility, ambition, and competence might serve as indicators for identifying employee potential and meritocratic systems are utilized for analyzing employee performance. Acknowledging the persistent contradicting factors on the individual as well as organizational level is particularly relevant for TM, as the identification and development of high-potential and high-performing employees depicts the core of TM activities.

The Exclusion-Inclusion Paradox

In comparison to diversity management, the paradox lens has been applied to a lesser extent to the HRM sub-domain of TM (Daubner-Siva et al., 2017). While the current TM literature does not provide one consistent TM definition, I consider TM in line with Collings and Mellahi's (2009) definition as basis for this chapter:

> Activities and processes that involve the systematic identification of key positions which differentially contribute to the organization's sustainable competitive advantage, the development of a talent pool of high potential and high performing incumbents to fill these roles, and the development of a differentiated human resource architecture to facilitate filling these positions with competent incumbents and to ensure their continued commitment to the organization (Collings & Mellahi, 2009: 305).

The above definition provides clarity on *what* TM contains by emphasizing the need for heightened consideration of critical roles within an organization in the attempt to fill those with the most talented employees to ensure sustainable performance. This definition is thus in line with the dominance of the exclusive approach in recent TM literature (Swailes, 2013). Yet, it does not provide insights or recommendations on *how* the identification and development of a talent pool should be managed.

Therefore, the TM definition is seemingly disjointed to organizational activities aiming at decreasing systematic inequalities between social groups within an organization. In order to further depict the potential tensions that may result from this disconnection, consider a fictitious case organization that I will call "Midanu". Showcasing Midanu represents a typical situation that I encountered during the course of my dissertation trajectory in various organizations:

> Midanu exemplifies an international operating organization where the management cadre emphasizes the relevance of diversity management – as well as talent management as relevant pillars to drive and implement strategic priorities. The vision of representing a diverse and inclusive work environment is translated to recruiting initiatives. In specific, the goal is to attract and hire more women into Midanu, and recent initiatives have increased the percentage of recruited women at all levels.
>
> At the same time, a consistent talent management process is defined and implemented across Midanu. Similar to other large organizations, the talent process in Midanu includes "global performance standards, supported by global leadership competency profiles and standardized performance appraisal tools and processes" (Stahl et al., 2012: 30). Talents are identified according to an agreed upon set of talent identification criteria and developed through specifically tailored training programs in order to successfully meet future demands.
>
> Despite these well-intended initiatives, Midanu does not hone a diverse leadership pipeline, meaning that women do not seem to make it in and/or through the talent program. So, while Midanu seemingly adheres to diversity as well as talent management practices, the success of both initiatives is not satisfying. In terms of diversity objectives, no significant changes are observable with regards to increasing the percentage of women leaders throughout the hierarchy; in terms of talent management, those talents "who make it", are male, and rather similar to the existing top management squad. Transformational change seems difficult to realize as the existing power structure is reproduced.
>
> In sum, despite the attempts to recruit diverse set of employees, Midanu's talent pipeline is filled with a homogeneous group, i.e., the diversity is not automatically transferred to this employee population. While the scenario described in Midanu might remain unrecognized for a period of time, the tension becomes salient in times when legal regulations are changed towards a quota that represents an increased number of women in the leadership pipeline or in times when financial success stagnates.

Midanu's case illustrates that neglecting the connection between TM and diversity management, organizations may risk reproducing existing power inequalities as they design and embed differentiated human resource architecture to fill key positions with identified talents. Daubner-Siva et al. (2017) explored the conceptual tensions that exist between diversity management and TM and linked the paradox perspective to the relatively young research field of TM. By doing so, the authors coined the exclusion-inclusion paradox, described as "the quest for organizations to establish an exclusive TM architecture for high-potential employees, while simultaneously embracing inclusive diversity management principles that allow all employees to unfold their talents" (Daubner-Siva et al., 2017: 327). Following Lüscher and Lewis' (2008) approach to sensemaking, the authors utilized the three steps of formulating a problem, unpacking a dilemma and ultimately expressing the oscillating poles of the exclusion-inclusion paradox (Daubner-Siva et al., 2017).

Transferring these process steps to the fictitious company Midanu, the described tensions can be summarized as the following problem: *If Midanu's talent identification and talent development processes are purposefully exclusive, how can Midanu achieve diversity and inclusion at all levels?* Focusing on criteria, such as a standardized performance appraisal approach to identify high-performers or assessing behavioral aspects by considering leadership competencies, might create unintended disadvantages for female employees that are not being addressed prior to the explicit problem statement. Expressing this problem is the first step to bringing the seemingly disconnected aspects of TM and diversity management together and thus might facilitate to work through the tensions (Lüscher & Lewis, 2008).

Unpacking a dilemma as a second step further uncovers the contradicting poles by articulating either/or choices (Daubner-Siva et al., 2017; Lüscher & Lewis, 2008). Transferred to Midanu, the dilemma can be phrased as follows: *Should Midanu primarily either focus on establishing an exclusive talent management architecture, or on embedding inclusive talent management practices?* Focusing on two contradicting poles, a dilemma implies that a choice needs to be made between the alternatives (Ehnert, 2009). In Midanu's case, it seems that in the past, the choice has primarily been made for the exclusive TM architecture while neglecting the inclusive TM practices. The results of this choice can be observed in the homogeneous talent pipeline and the fact that the diversity ambitions are not fulfilled in the midterm. Daubner-Siva et al. (2017) refer to the TM and diversity management literature and argue that based on the scant evidence of aligning the two fields, this dilemma is currently passively addressed in the form of repression by not actively dealing with it. Defensive, or passive, reactions offer temporal solutions to overcome tensions, without providing longer-term relief and thus do not acknowledge the persistent co-existence of contradicting poles (Jarzabkowski, Lê, & Van de Ven, 2013; Smith & Lewis, 2011).

The third step, expressing the paradox, requires to consistently oscillate between conflicting poles because opposing solutions are interwoven and no choice can resolve the tension (Lüscher & Lewis, 2008). Translating the exclusion-inclusion paradox articulates as follows for Midanu: *Establishing an exclusive talent management architecture at Midanu for developing those deemed as high-potentials while simultaneously embracing inclusive diversity management principles that allow every employee to uncover and evolve their particular talents to thrive in Midanu towards their highest performance and potential.*

Actively addressing the exclusion-inclusion paradox thus means to consider contradicting tensions to a more equal extent and to embrace a both-and mindset (Smith & Lewis, 2011). Acknowledging the dynamic, persistent, and interdependent nature of exclusive TM and inclusive diversity management enables thus new perspectives and creativity, while resisting the urge to reach resolution (Daubner-Siva et al., 2017). Thus, dealing actively with the exclusion-inclusion paradox implies to foster a plurality of perspectives by engaging both TM and diversity management principles simultaneously. For Midanu, this active response might translate into establishing inclusive talent identification process while focusing on exclusive talent development.

In summary, I have illustrated the exclusion-inclusion paradox through the example of a fictitious organization called Midanu by following a three-step approach. First, I formulated the problem in order to bring the disconnected aspects between co-existing and seemingly unrelated diversity management and TM activities to the fore. Second, I further unpacked the contradictions by framing either/or choices and highlighted that these do not offer long-term relief to the tensions between exclusive TM and inclusive diversity management. Third, I applied the exclusion-inclusion paradox to Midanu. Expressing the paradox is the fist step towards enabling a both-and mindset in order to actively address the tensions by consistently alternating between the conflicting poles of exclusive TM and inclusive diversity management. Next, I will discuss implications of the exclusive-inclusive paradox for organizations, TM and diversity management professionals, as well as for employees.

Discussion and Areas of Further Research

The identification and development of high-potential and high-performing employees depicts the core of TM. Yet, existing TM definitions do not seem to provide insights on *how* the identification and development of a talent pool should be managed. Based on the previous sections, I propose to dovetail TM and diversity management by applying the paradox perspective. While the paradox lens has not yet been widely related to the TM field, I argue that applying the paradox perspective brings the inherent tensions to the fore that exist between TM and diversity management. Expressing these tensions is the first step towards actively working through the outlined exclusion-inclusion paradox. Actively responding to the exclusion-inclusion paradox thus provides insights on *how* the identification and development of a talent pool should be managed, namely by creating greater alignment between the fields of TM and diversity management. Adopting a paradox perspective for TM thus enhances Collings and Mellahi's (2009) definition. Furthermore, linking TM to diversity management contributes to overcoming systematic inequalities between women and men at work. For organizations like Midanu this might entail analyzing the extent women are exposed to paradoxical situations throughout their career when performance, visibility, ambition, and competence serve as indicators for identifying employee potential (cf. Castilla & Benard, 2010; Faulkner, 2009a; Pesonen et al., 2009; Sools et al., 2007).

Taking the previously described seminal studies on paradoxes in diversity management into account, activities such as educating TM professionals and line managers about the potential negative impact for female employees or co-creating processes that minimize gender biases together with diversity management professionals might serve as concrete interventions to dovetail diversity management and TM activities. This implies acknowledging the systematic impact of biased actions for certain groups of employees and might contribute to growing confidence in women and men to support organizational system and structure change. Doing so is shifting the focus away from approaches to focus on women's perceived behaviors in organizations towards initiatives with broader organizational impact, addressing the interplay of practices and processes that result in continuing inequalities in organizations (Acker, 2006). A recent study with male and female young professionals highlights that when asked to speak about perceived gender inequalities, female young professionals seem to believe in their own agency rather than changing systems and structures (Kelan, 2014). Actively responding and working through the exclusion-inclusion paradox thus bears practical implications on individual as well as organizational levels.

On an individual level, openly sharing and discussing the exclusion-inclusion paradox might enable individuals to recognize the shaping forces of inequality and contribute to cultural change (Daubner-Siva et al., 2017; Kelan, 2014). This might be realized by encouraging reflection moments for practitioners, line managers, and talents to create awareness of the exclusion-inclusion paradox. Acknowledging that an inherent characteristic of paradoxes is the fact that they cannot be avoided, such reflection moments might create the space to actively approach the exclusion-inclusion paradox and to encourage organizational actors to work through it (Beech, Burns, de Caestecker, MacIntosh, & MacLean, 2004; Jarzabkowski et al., 2013).

Another aspect that might contribute to the active exploration of the exclusion-inclusion paradox is the mindset that individuals inhibit towards paradoxes. Recent studies on the microfoundations of organizational paradox uncovered individuals' varied approaches to paradox and introduced the concept of a paradox mindset (Miron-Spektor, Ingram, Keller, Smith, & Lewis, 2018). The authors define a paradox mindset as "the extent to which one is accepting of and energized by tensions" (26). Studies show that individuals with a higher paradox mindset tend to be more energized and motivated by paradoxes, whereas those with a lower paradox mindset tend to suffer from reduced performance, innovation, and satisfaction (Miron-Spektor et al., 2018).

Adopting a paradox mindset towards the tensions between exclusive TM and inclusive diversity management implies considering the competing demands between TM and diversity management as contradictory as well as interdependent. By approaching these tensions with a both-and mindset, organizational actors have the opportunity to find new solutions that integrate the alternative demands or they frequently shift attention and resources between the demands. As a result, individuals are aware of and approach the tensions between TM and diversity management as opportunities to learn and grow rather than showing defensive behaviors (Miron-Spektor et al., 2018). Adopting a paradox mindset might also encourage those employees who are labeled as talents in an organization to consider the opportunities as well as risks associated to their talent status (Daubner-Siva, Ybema, Vinkenburg, & Beech, 2018).

From an organizational perspective, understanding and expressing the exclusion-inclusion paradox enables leaders of talent departments to make an informed choice on how to prioritize their resources. Organizational actors have the choice to respond in a defensive manner, which however inhibits the exploration of new, creative ways to work (Jarzabkowski et al., 2013). Alternative reactions include more active responses to the exclusion-inclusion paradox. This implies ensuring simultaneous attention to both exclusion and inclusion principles over time by purposefully oscillating between alternatives (Aust et al., 2015; Daubner-Siva et al., 2017; Jarzabkowski et al., 2013). Doing so enables TM and diversity management practitioners to further their collaboration towards integrating diversity considerations in the design and implementation of TM activities.

Baker and Kelan (2017) argue that organizations should aim to develop all leaders in an organization to recognize and reflect on inequalities and propose inclusive leadership trainings, implicit bias awareness training, or increased awareness on personal privileges to further integrate TM and diversity management. Vinkenburg (2017) develops and describes design specifications for systemic diversity interventions that address the paradox of meritocracy. Stohlmeyer Russel and Moskowitz Leper (2017) portray how they overcame similar challenges as described for the case organization Midanu. To address retention challenges at Boston Consulting Group (BCG), the authors successfully supported the design and implementation of a leadership development program that supported female leaders to work through double binds situations at work (Stohlmeyer Russell & Moskowitz Lepler, 2017).

In addition to these avenues for practical implication on individual and organizational levels, further research in the area would contribute to sustainably dovetail TM and diversity management. Qualitative methodologies such as (auto-)ethnographic research or action research might shed light whether and to what extent gender differences are at play for male and female talents in organizations and how they perceive the benefits and risks of being identified as talents. A recent autoethnographic study uncovering the "talent paradox" provides an example of this form of research (Daubner-Siva et al., 2018). Further ethnographic accounts would advance TM research by offering a more nuanced and contextualized understanding on the interplay between TM and diversity management. A relevant subset of employees might be dual career couples, as they are exposed to challenges around ambition, flexibility, and mobility in case organizational talent architectures do not embrace an inclusive mindset towards talent development (Petriglieri, 2018). Furthermore, longitudinal studies would enable drawing conclusions on the effects of dovetailing TM and diversity management.

Conclusion

Considering the connection (or lack thereof) between talent management and diversity management through the prism of paradox contributes to the ongoing maturation process of the TM literature as it sheds light on potential exclusion effects of existing TM practices. While recent publications have acknowledged the gap between diversity management and TM (cf. Al Ariss, Cascio, & Paauwe, 2014; Baker & Kelan, 2017; Festing, Kornau, & Schäfer, 2015; Sheehan & Anderson, 2015) dovetailing TM and diversity management does not have a long record (Daubner-Siva et al., 2017).

In this chapter, I have outlined the history and definition of diversity management. I connected diversity research with paradox theory by outlining seminal gender studies that exemplify that women are exposed to paradoxical situations throughout their career. Next, I elaborated on the exclusion-inclusion paradox through a fictitious case organization. In essence, the exclusion-inclusion paradox articulates the continuous quest for organizations to establish an exclusive TM architecture while simultaneously embracing inclusive diversity management principles. Expressing this paradox enables an active response by dovetailing TM and diversity management activities. I then moved on to discuss implications of the exclusion-inclusion paradox on individual and organizational levels.

Taken together, I promote the value of multiple perspectives in TM research and practice. By inviting pluralism, open dialogue, and criticism, TM scholars as well as practitioners have the opportunity to engage in real-life issues in organization towards the promotion of intellectual inclusivity and flexibility (Morrell & Learmonth, 2015) when considering both diversity management and talent management simultaneously.

References

Acker, J. 2006. Inequality regimes: Gender, class, and race in organizations. *Gender & Society,* 20(4): 441-464. doi:10.1177/0891243206289499

Al Ariss, A., Cascio, W. F., & Paauwe, J. 2014. Talent management: Current theories and future research directions. *Journal of World Business,* 49(2): 173-179.

Al Ariss, A., & Sidani, Y. 2016. Comparative international human resource management: Future research directions. *Human Resource Management Review,* 26(4): 352-358. doi:https://doi.org/10.1016/j.hrmr.2016.04.007.

Aust, I., Brandl, J., & Keegan, A. 2015. State-of-the-art and future directions for HRM from a paradox perspective: Introduction to the special issue. *Zeitschrift für Personalforschung,* 29(3-4): 194-213.

Aust, I., Brandl, J., Keegan, A. E., & Lensges, M. 2017. Tensions in managing human resources: Introducing a paradox framework and research agenda. In W. K. Smith, M. L. Lewis, P. Jarzabkowski, & A. Langley Eds.), *Oxford handbook of organizational paradox.* Oxford, UK: Oxford University Press.

Baker, D. T., & Kelan, E. K. 2017. Integrating talent and diversity management. In D. G. Collings, K. Mellahi, & W. F. Cascio (Eds.), *The Oxford handbook of talent management:* 521-536. Oxford, UK: Oxford University Press.

Beech, N., Burns, H., de Caestecker, L., MacIntosh, R., & MacLean, D. 2004. Paradox as invitation to act in problematic change situations. *Human Relations,* 57(10): 1313-1332. doi:10.1177/0018726704048357.

Bhalla, V., Caye, J. M., Lovich, D., & Tollman, P. 2018. *A CEO's guide to talent management today* https://www.bcg.com/publications/2018/ceo-guide-talent-management-today.aspx.

Boselie, P., Brewster, C., & Paauwe, J. 2009. In search of balance – managing the dualities of HRM: An overview of the issues. *Personnel Review,* 38(5): 461-471. doi: 10.1108/00483480910977992.

Boxall, P., & Purcell, J. 2011. *Strategy and human resource management.* New York: Palgrave Macmillan.

Castilla, E. J., & Benard, S. 2010. The paradox of meritocracy in organizations. *Administrative Science Quarterly,* 55(4): 543-676.

CIPD. 2017. *Resourcing and talent planning* https://www.cipd.co.uk/knowledge/strategy/resourcing/surveys?utm_medium=vanity&utm_source=various&utm_campaign=res_resourcingsurvey.

Collings, D. G., & Mellahi, K. 2009. Strategic talent management: A review and research agenda. *Human Resource Management Review,* 19(4): 304-313.

Collings, D. G., Scullion, H., & Vaiman, V. 2015. Talent management: Progress and prospects. *Human Resource Management Review,* 25(3): 233-235. doi:http://dx.doi.org/10.1016/j.hrmr.2015.04.005.

Daubner-Siva, D., Vinkenburg, C. J., & Jansen, P. G. W. 2017. Dovetailing talent management and diversity management: The exclusion-inclusion paradox. *Journal of Organizational Effectiveness: People and Performance,* 4(4): 315-331. doi:10.1108/JOEPP-02-2017-0019.

Daubner-Siva, D., Ybema, S., Vinkenburg, C. J., & Beech, N. 2018. The talent paradox: Talent management as a mixed blessing. *Journal of Organizational Ethnography,* 7(1): 74-86. doi:https://doi.org/10.1108/JOE-01-2017-0002.

Dries, N. 2013. Talent management, from phenomenon to theory: Introduction to the Special Issue. *Human Resource Management Review,* 23(4): 267-271. doi:http://dx.doi.org/10.1016/j.hrmr.2013.08.006.

Ehnert, I. 2009. *Sustainable human resource management: A conceptual and exploratory analysis from a paradox perspective.* Heidelberg: Physica-Verlag.

Eisenhardt, K. M. 2000. Paradox, spirals, ambivalence: The new language of change and pluralism. *Academy of Management Review,* 25(4): 703-705. doi:10.5465/amr.2000.3707694.

Evans, P. A. 1999. HRM on the edge: A duality perspective. *Organization,* 6(2): 325-338.

Faulkner, W. 2009a. Doing gender in engineering workplace cultures. I. Observations from the field. *Engineering Studies,* 1(1): 3-18.

Faulkner, W. 2009b. Doing gender in engineering workplace cultures. II. Gender in/authenticity and the in/visibility paradox. *Engineering Studies,* 1(3): 169-189.

Festing, M., Kornau, A., & Schäfer, L. 2015. Think talent–think male? A comparative case study analysis of gender inclusion in talent management practices in the German media industry. *The International Journal of Human Resource Management,* 26(6): 707-732.

Francis, H., & Keegan, A. 2006. The changing face of HRM: In search of balance. *Human Resource Management Journal,* 16(3): 231-249. doi:10.1111/j.1748-8583.2006.00016.x.

Gallardo-Gallardo, E., Thunnissen, M., & Scullion, H. 2020. Talent management: Context matters. *The International Journal of Human Resource Management,* 31(4): 457-473.

Guillaume, Y. R. F., Brodbeck, F. C., & Riketta, M. 2012. Surface- and deep-level dissimilarity effects on social integration and individual effectiveness related outcomes in work groups: A meta-analytic integration. *Journal of Occupational and Organizational Psychology,* 85(1): 80-115. doi:10.1111/j.2044-8325.2010.02005.x.

Holck, L., Muhr, S. L., & Villesèche, F. 2016. Identity, diversity and diversity management: On theoretical connections, assumptions and implications for practice. *Equality, Diversity and Inclusion: An International Journal,* 35(1): 48-64. doi:10.1108/EDI-08-2014-0061.

Jarzabkowski, P., Lê, J., & Van de Ven, A. H. 2013. Responding to competing strategic demands: How organizing, belonging, and performing paradoxes coevolve. *Strategic Organization,* 11(3): 245-280.

Jonsen, K., Maznevski, M. L., & Schneider, S. C. 2011. Diversity and its not so diverse literature: An international perspective. *International Journal of Cross Cultural Management,* 11(1): 35-62.

Kelan, E. 2014. From biological clocks to unspeakable inequalities: The intersectional positioning of young professionals. *British Journal of Management,* 25, 790–804. doi:10.1111/1467-8551.12062.

Kelly, E., & Dobbin, F. 1998. How affirmative action became diversity management: Employer response to antidiscrimination law, 1961 to 1996. *American Behavioural Scientist,* 41(7): 960-984.

Konrad, A. M. 2003. Special issue introduction: Defining the domain of workplace diversity scholarship. *Group & Organization Management,* 28(1): 4-17. doi:10.1177/1059601102250013.

Kozica, A., & Brandl, J. 2015. Handling paradoxical tensions through conventions: The case of performance appraisal. *German Journal of Human Resource Management,* 29(1): 49-68. doi:10.1177/239700221502900103.

Kumra, S. 2014. Gendered constructions of merit and impression management within professional service firms. In S. Kumra, R. Simpson, & R. J. Burke (Eds.), *The Oxford handbook of gender in organizations:* 269–290. Oxford, UK: Oxford University Press.

Lewis, M. W. 2000. Exploring paradox: Toward a more comprehensive guide. *Academy of Management Review,* 25(4): 760-776. doi:10.5465/amr.2000.3707712.

Linnehan, F., & Konrad, A. M. 1999. Diluting diversity: Implications for intergroup inequality in organizations. *Journal of Management Inquiry,* 8(4): 399-414. doi:10.1177/105649269984009.

Lüscher, L. S., & Lewis, M. W. 2008. Organizational change and managerial sensemaking: Working through paradox. *Academy of Management Journal,* 51(2): 221-240.

Meyers, M. C., van Woerkom, M., Paauwe, J., & Dries, N. 2020. HR managers' talent philosophies: Prevalence and relationships with perceived talent management practices. *The International Journal of Human Resource Management,* 31(4): 562–588.

Miron-Spektor, E., Ingram, A., Keller, J., Smith, W. K., & Lewis, M. W. 2018. Microfoundations of organizational paradox: The problem is how we think about the problem. *Academy of Management Journal,* 61(1): 26-45. doi:10.5465/amj.2016.0594.

Morrell, K., & Learmonth, M. 2015. Against evidence-based management, for management learning. *Academy of Management Learning & Education,* 14(4): 520-533. doi:10.5465/amle.2014.0346.

Morrison, M., Lumby, J., & Sood, K. 2006. Diversity and diversity management:messages from recent research. *Educational Management Administration & Leadership,* 34(3): 277-295. doi:10.1177/1741143206065264.

Oswick, C., & Noon, M. 2014. Discourses of diversity, equality and inclusion: Trenchant formulations or transient fashions? *British Journal of Management,* 25(1): 23-39. doi:10.1111/j.1467-8551.2012.00830.x.

Özbilgin, M., Tatli, A., & Jonsen, K. 2015. *Global diversity management. An evidence based approach 2nd ed.).* New York: Palgrave Macmillan.

Pesonen, S., Tienari, J., & Vanhala, S. 2009. The boardroom gender paradox. *Gender in Management: An International Journal,* 24(5): 327-345.

Petriglieri, J. 2018. Talent management and the dual-career couple. *Harvard Business Review,* 2.

Prasad, P., Pringle, J. K., & Konrad, A. M. 2006. Examining the contours of workplace diversity: Concepts, contexts, and challenges. In A. M. Konrad, P. Prasad, & J. K. Pringle (Eds.), *Handbook of workplace diversity:* 1-24. London Sage.

Pringle, J. K., & Strachan, G. 2015. Duelling dualisms. In R. Bendl, I. Bleijenbergh, E. Henttonen, & A. J. Mills (Eds.), *The Oxford handbook of diversity in organizations:* 39-61. Oxford, UK: Oxford University Press.

Raisch, S., Hargrave, T. J., & van de Ven, A. H. 2018. The learning spiral: A process perspective on paradox. *Journal of Management Studies,* 55(8): 1507-1526. doi:10.1111/joms.12397.

Sheehan, M., & Anderson, V. 2015. Talent management and organizational diversity: A call for research. *Human Resource Development Quarterly,* 26(4): 349–358. doi:10.1002/hrdq.21247.

Singh, V., & Point, S. 2004. Strategic responses by European companies to the diversity challenge: An online comparison. *Long Range Planning,* 37, 295-318.

Smith, W. K., & Lewis, M. W. 2011. Toward a theory of paradox: A dynamic equilibrium model of organizing. *Academy of Management Review,* 36(2): 381-403.

Sools, A. M., Van Engen, M. L., & Baerveldt, C. 2007. Gendered career-making practices: On doing ambition or how managers discursively position themselves in a multinational corporation. *Journal of Occupational and Organizational Psychology,* 80(3): 413-435.

Stahl, G. K., Björkman, I., Farndale, E., Morris, S. S., Paauwe, J., Stiles, P., & Wright, P. 2012. Six principles of effective global talent management, *MIT Sloan Management Review,* 53(2): 24-32.

Stohlmeyer Russell, M., & Moskowitz Lepler, L. 2017. How we closed the gap between men's and women's retention rates. *Harvard Business Review.* https://hbr.org/2017/05/how-we-closed-the-gap-between-mens-and-womens-retention-rates, first accessed July 12, 2017.

Swailes, S. 2013. Troubling some assumptions: A response to "The role of perceived organizational justice in shaping the outcomes of talent management: A research agenda". *Human Resource Management Review,* 23(4): 354-356. doi:http://dx.doi.org/10.1016/j.hrmr.2013.08.005.

Tatli, A., & Özbilgin, M. 2012. An emic approach to intersectional study of diversity at work: A Bourdieuan framing. *International Journal of Management Reviews,* 14(2): 180-200. doi:10.1111/j.1468-2370.2011.00326.x.

Tatli, A., Vassilopoulou, J., & Özbilgin, M. 2013. An unrequited affinity between talent shortages and untapped female potential: The relevance of gender quotas for talent management in high growth potential economies of the Asia Pacific region. *International Business Review,* 22(3): 539-553. doi:http://dx.doi.org/10.1016/j.ibusrev.2012.07.005.

Thomas, R. R. 2010. World class diversity management. *A strategic approach.* San Fransisco: Berrett-Koehler Publishers Inc.

Van den Brink, M., & Stobbe, L. 2009. Doing gender in academic education: The paradox of visibility. *Gender, Work & Organization,* 16(4): 451-470. doi:10.1111/j.1468-0432.2008.00428.x.

Vinkenburg, C. J. 2017. Engaging gatekeepers, optimizing decision making, and mitigating bias: Design specifications for systemic diversity interventions. *The Journal of Applied Behavioral Science,* 53(2): 212-234. doi:10.1177/0021886317703292.

21

TALENT MANAGEMENT AND CAREER MANAGEMENT

Nicky Dries

Elise Marescaux

Anand van Zelderen

Introduction

Studies estimate that around 65% of organizations worldwide have talent management programs in place (Church, Rotolo, Ginther, & Levine, 2015; Collings, Mellahi, & Cascio, 2019; Dries & De Gieter, 2014). Talent management (TM) typically revolves around the identification of a "talent pool", referring to the 1–10% of the most high-performing, high-potential employees in the organization (Finkelstein, Costanza, & Goodwin, 2017). Inspired by a "war for talent" discourse (Michaels, Handfield-Jones, & Axelrod, 2001), companies have become convinced that they should groom their most talented employees (i.e., their "A players") for positions of strategic importance, while directing their "B players" towards support positions, and their "C players" towards the exit (Huselid, Beatty, & Becker, 2005).

The notion of the war for talent is rooted in two main assumptions (Beechler & Woodward, 2009). First, in a knowledge economy context, traditional sources of competitive advantage are losing their edge, whereas human talent is a renewable resource not easily replaceable or recruited away from a competitor. Second, attracting and retaining high-potential employees is becoming increasingly difficult as a result of specific demographic and psychological contract trends. Organizations worry that a consumerist attitude has taken hold of their employees, in which the organization is considered a resource to the individual just as much as the other way around (Dries, Forrier, De Vos, & Pepermans, 2014). TM programs have been defined as:

> activities and processes that involve the systematic identification of key positions which differentially contribute to the organization's sustainable competitive advantage, the development of a talent pool of high potential and high performing incumbents to fill these roles, and the development of a differentiated human resource architecture to facilitate filling these positions with competent incumbents and to ensure their continued commitment to the organization. (Collings & Mellahi, 2009: 305)

A typical target for such TM programs is to increase the commitment, engagement, and loyalty of those employees the organization can least afford to lose (Church et al., 2015).

Somewhat paradoxically, considering its focus on achieving retention and commitment through differentiation, the typical mode of communication about TM seems to be strategic ambiguity, meaning that openness and clarity are deliberately avoided (Dries, Schleicher, Tierens, Hofmans, Gelens, & Pepermans, 2017) thus creating information asymmetries in which one party (i.e., the organization) has

DOI: 10.4324/9781315474687-21

more or better information than the other (i.e., the employee). At the heart of the TM secrecy phenomenon (Dries & De Gieter, 2014) lies the assumption that although those who attain the highly coveted talent status are likely to react positively to TM, negative reactions among those not assigned such a status by their organizations (who are by definition in the majority) are likely to cancel out these positive reactions when considering the net effect of TM on the organization as a whole (Marescaux, De Winne, & Sels, 2013). As a result, organizational decision makers are increasingly calling into question the legitimacy of their existing TM programs, often leading to (quick or temporary) solutions where talent status is kept secret from employees, even from employees identified as "talents" (Sonnenberg, van Zijderveld, & Brinks, 2014).

These observations beg the question: Why do organizations insist on differentiating between employees on a matter they themselves deem so sensitive that they feel they cannot possibly communicate it transparently? What are important ethical issues here, since talent status is an important predictor of internal career advancement opportunities – that is, a lack of clarity about one's talent status can interfere with an employee's career decision-making process (Gelens, Dries, Hofmans, & Pepermans, 2013)? In addition, what are the implications for TM practices if the secrecy phenomenon implies that the status of "talented" versus "less talented" employees cannot be *visibly* different?

The above paradox becomes even more apparent when comparing the strategic human resource management literature to the careers literature. The management literature identifies TM as "strategic imperative" (Ashton & Morton, 2005: 28), whereas the careers literature refers to TM as "at best an anachronism, and at worst a false promise used to keep valuable employees in organizations" (Baruch & Peiperl, 1997: 356; De Vos & Dries, 2013). So where does the truth lie? Should TM be buried alongside the traditional view of the organizational career, which, according to some voices in the careers literature is "dead" (Hall, 1996)? Or can TM (still) offer added value to organizations and individual career actors alike, even in today's "postmodern" career context?

The goal of this chapter is to compare and contrast the assumptions about TM held in the TM versus the career management literature, highlighting areas of overlap and contradiction, and their implications for research and practice. The chapter is organized as follows. First, we discuss the history of careers and how present-day theories of career create a possible paradox with prevailing assumptions about careers in the TM literature. Second, we discuss three features of TM that distinguish the phenomenon from career management more generally (i.e., TM creates status differences, TM creates labeling effects, and TM creates highly specific social exchange dynamics). We conclude with some specific suggestions for further research based on all of the above.

Is The Traditional Organizational Career Path "Dead"? Implications For Talent Management

"The career is dead, long live the career!" is the title of Douglas (Tim) Hall's seminal 1996 book on postmodern careers. Indeed, the careers literature more generally appears to actively sponsor the idea that the notion of the traditional-organizational career has been replaced by more "boundaryless" forms of career – broadly defined as a range of possible career forms that defy traditional employment assumptions, such as working for one employer, in one location, following a linear career path, for most of one's life (Arthur & Rousseau, 1996: 6).

A Brief History of Careers

The historical evolution of the global economy, from being centered mostly around agriculture to the postmodern information era, has strongly shaped the framework and the boundaries within which individual careers can be enacted today. Around the onset of the 19th century, the industrial revolution marked the end of the agricultural economy, in which the dominant social institution was the family and young people simply inherited their parents' occupations (Savickas, 2000).

The dawning of the industrial economy was characterized by the appearance of large, bureaucratically structured organizations providing careers for life. Job security was all but guaranteed to employees, who reciprocated by offering their employers their loyalty and dedication. Since the typical organizational structure was hierarchical, "career" implied vertical movement, and career success was defined by upward advancement on the corporate ladder (Savickas, 2000; Spurk, Hirschi, & Dries, 2019; Van Esbroeck, 2008). Even today (and problematically so), the notion of hierarchical advancement within an organization remains associated with career success, although the organizational structures at the origin of this association have changed considerably (Arnold & Cohen, 2008; Spurk et al., 2019; Sullivan, 1999).

In the second half of the 20th century, society was transformed through globalization, and many organizations grew into multinational corporations. Scientific and technical evolutions brought societies worldwide into the information era. The postindustrial economy, characterized by the declining importance of manufacturing relative to information technology and knowledge management, was a fact (Van Esbroeck, 2008). As a result, organizational and societal structures changed dramatically. Economic globalization and the restructuring of organizations (through downsizing, delayering, outsourcing, and offshoring) have fundamentally altered the structure and nature of jobs and careers (Maranda & Comeau, 2000).

As many organizations have been flattening their hierarchical structures, the traditional premises upon which careers relied appear to be fading. Organizations can no longer promise a career for life, as they could before when the economy was more stable and predictable (Savickas, 2000). Careers in today's postmodern society are thus believed to no longer be "logical, stable, depictable and predictable" (Van Esbroeck, Tibos, & Zaman, 2005: 6). Instead, they have become a more or less unpredictable series of small steps made by individuals who are continuously negotiating work and non-work aspects of life throughout their lifespan. As careers are no longer "owned" by organizations, the responsibility for career management is now placed primarily in the hands of the individual employee, who must develop transferable skills and adaptive strengths to cope in an environment without definite securities (Savickas, 2000; Spurk et al., 2019). Instead of being depicted as a ladder (the typical metaphor for steady upward movement), careers can now be described as a "lattice", enabling multiple career paths and possibilities for lateral job enrichment, rather than upward movement alone (Iles, 1997).

Based on these historical evolutions, the recent careers literature strongly advocates the belief that more and more employees – especially those who are most high-performing and high-potential – are acting like "free agents" (Tulgan, 2001). Moreover, this is a *favorable* evolution, liberating employees from the paternalistic practice of having an organization manage their careers (Van Buren, 2003). Consequently, several authors have called into question the sustainability of the concept of TM (e.g., Baruch & Peiperl, 1997; Kuznia, 2004; Pannell & Mendez, 2019; Tulgan, 2001).

A Talent Management Paradox?

Contrasting the literature on TM with the postmodern careers literature, a talent management paradox seems to emerge, in that TM is simultaneously depicted as utterly outdated (in the careers literature; e.g., Baruch & Peiperl, 1997; Crowley-Henry, Benson, & Al Ariss, 2018), and as more pivotal than ever for the competitive advantage of organizations (in the management literature; e.g., Buckingham & Vosburgh, 2001; Pannell & Mendez, 2019).

Specifically, the careers literature advocates that organizations facing the economic pressures of the 21st century world of work can no longer promise long-term employment to their employees, let alone a rapid progression along the organizational ladder (Arthur & Rousseau, 1996), leading some authors to conclude that "there is no future for hipos [high-potentials], at least not as we have known the phenomenon.... There are quite a few hipos, and very few places at the top" (Baruch & Peiperl, 1997: 354). As such, the premise underlying TM programs – that hard work and the display of exceptional talent will be rewarded by a steady progression in the organizational hierarchy – is seemingly undermined (Baruch

& Peiperl, 1997; Crowley-Henry et al., 2018). The TM literature, on the other hand, refers to the "war for talent" as the number-one people management challenge of the early 21st century (Michaels et al., 2001; Pannell & Mendez, 2019).

A first possible way to interpret the TM paradox is by assuming that TM practice is (hopelessly) lagging behind the realities of current-day careers (Baruch & Peiperl, 1997; Pannell & Mendez, 2019). However, despite the fact that both TM and the organizational career have been declared dead repeatedly over the last few decades, a volume of research indicates that claims about the speed and inevitability of the shift from organizational-traditional to more boundaryless career types have to be put into perspective (e.g., Forrier, Sels, & Verbruggen, 2005; Granrose & Baccili, 2006; Sullivan, 1999; Walton & Mallon, 2004).

Guest and Mackenzie Davey (1996) wrote: "It is never quite clear whether those writing [about "new careers"] are describing current developments, identifying outliers as illustrations of inevitable trends or prescribing the shape of things to come which any organization that wishes to survive should heed" (22). European studies, especially, have found that to date only a small percentage of employees are actually in a boundaryless career (in which employees change employers and long for change and flexibility) whereas over half of employees still report being in "bounded" careers (in which employees stay with their employer and aspire stability; see Forrier et al., 2005; Rodrigues & Guest, 2010; Rodrigues, Guest, & Budjanovcanin, 2016).

Moreover, the postmodern careers literature seems to assume that organizational-traditional career types are no longer *wanted* by employees (Tulgan, 2001). Recent empirical work has come to the conclusion, however, that the majority of employees continue to desire more traditional career types (Rodrigues & Guest, 2010). Forrier et al.'s (2005) study, for instance, found that although respondents set career goals relating to career self-management, continuous learning and autonomy, they still regarded these aspects of careers mostly as a means to achieving objective career outcomes such as promotions. Walton and Mallon (2004), in their study of boundaryless careers, concluded that "although the boundaries of career have shifted, they have not melted into thin air" (77). These and other authors have questioned the portability of the boundaryless career concept to other than U.S. settings, the value people place on job security and the unionization of organizations (two cultural and institutional elements that tend to reinforce the "old" psychological contract) being at the heart of the discussion (Dries, 2011).

A second take on the TM paradox involves assuming that traditional-organizational careers can, in fact, still exist, but only for "privileged" groups such as employees identified as talents. In fact, it is quite likely that exactly *those* employees who are still in a position to receive internal career benefits such as job security and upward advancement opportunities are *also* those who are most likely to thrive in the postmodern career landscape—because they have the highest levels of employability and the best transferable skills (Dyer & Humphries, 2002; Tulgan, 2001). Indeed, studies of organizational career management practices targeted specifically at talents have found that there are many practices that are reserved for talents only (e.g., Dries & Pepermans, 2008). Organizations want to know who their talents are (identification practices), grow and advance them strategically (development practices), and prepare them for upward job moves (succession planning practices). As career investments in this group of employees are higher than average, more resources are allocated to preventing them from making inter-organizational moves (e.g., retention management practices) (see Dries & Pepermans, 2008, for more information on career management practices targeted specifically at high-potential employees).

In sum, "talents" are still eligible for traditional-organizational careers if they want them, simply because organizations prefer to engage internal successors for top management positions, and are willing to invest heavily in those that demonstrate the talent and the drive to progress within the organization. The need for a stable core of talented employees who genuinely know the organization and its background is probably far from evanescent. It seems talents are still getting "the old deal" as they are promised long-term career perspectives and upward advancement. One could wonder about all other employees, who are less likely to receive promotions and be targeted for retention, but apparently also less likely to get proper training. Are they getting neither the old career deal nor the new (Dries et al., 2014)?

Distinguishing Talent Management from Career Management

With its focus on individual career outcomes (e.g., Sullivan & Baruch, 2009), personal accountability for career management (see the literature on the "protean" career; e.g., Hall, 2004), inter-organizational mobility (see the literature on the "boundaryless" career; e.g., Arthur & Rousseau, 1996), and its decreased interest in formalized organizational career management practices (De Vos, Dewettinck, & Buyens, 2009), the recent careers literature, at least at first glance, seems to be grounded in a number of assumptions that run diametrically opposite to those in the TM literature (see De Vos & Dries, 2013 for more information on the conflicting assumptions in the career and talent management literature).

While most authors position TM as part of the broader set of career management practices in an organization, some have stated that TM is a "mindset" and thus, an all-encompassing characteristic of an organization much like organizational culture (e.g., Chuai, Preece, & Iles, 2008). In fact, many organizations seem unwilling to explicitly define what TM does and does not cover, calling it a mindset because they like to use the term "talent" as a euphemism for "people" in light of their employer branding (Dries, 2013). The operationalization of TM as a mindset is generally advised against, however, as it is difficult to translate into workable practices (Lewis & Heckman, 2006).

The tendency of the TM literature to slide off into vague but appealing rhetoric is causing commentators to question whether TM is not just a management fashion. Management fashions are characterized by conceptual ambiguity, combined with an underlying sense of urgency created by fashion setters (e.g., consultants, business schools, management gurus), which is yet to be legitimized by sound evidence and robust theory (Iles et al., 2010). As the characteristics of a management fashion seem to apply to TM, at least at first glance, in recent years several groups of authors have examined whether TM is just "old wine in new bottles" (e.g., Chuai et al., 2008; Huang & Tansley, 2012; Iles et al., 2010; Tansley, 2011). Unequivocally, however, they concluded that TM does in fact add value over career management practices more generally.

TM differs from career management in that it is believed to be less egalitarian and more elitist by definition (Collings & Mellahi, 2009). Some have said that TM is to career management what gifted education is to education (see Gagné, 2004), implying that the needs of talented employees are notably different from those of the "average" employee (Ledford & Kochanski, 2004). More inclusive approaches to TM are found in the literature as well (e.g., Swailes, Downs, & Orr, 2014; Warren, 2006); several authors have stated, however, that workforce differentiation is the key differentiating principle between TM and career management more generally (Boudreau & Ramstad, 2005; Collings & Mellahi, 2009).

More often than not, the practice of leaving room for interpretative flexibility about TM (Iles, Preece, & Chuai, 2010) results in discrepancies between organizational discourse and practice (Gill, 2002). In a study involving eight in-depth case studies, Truss, Gratton, Hope-Hailey, McGovern, and Stiles (1997) found that although organizations prefer to adopt a soft, humanist TM discourse (focusing on the "H" in HRM), their actual *practices* are typically more reflective of a hard, instrumental approach (focusing on the "R" in HRM), aimed at improving the bottom-line performance of the organization with the interests of the organization prevailing over those of individual employees. Gill (2002) argues that this type of observable discrepancies between discourse and practice pose a serious threat to the reputation of TM practitioners as legitimate business partners; and that although a hard discourse is generally less attractive, it is certainly to be preferred over a TM credibility debate.

In what follows, we discuss three core features of TM that distinguish it from career management more generally: TM is status-organizing, TM creates labeling effects, and TM creates highly specific social exchange dynamics.

Talent Management Creates Status Differences

One way of looking at TM as a unique phenomenon is to reframe our understanding of what it means to be identified as a "talent" as a specific form of status. Status can be defined as an individual's consensually acknowledged social worth relative to other individuals, as manifested in the differential deference individuals enjoy in the eyes of others (Piazza & Castelluci, 2014). Status issues permeate organizational life, as the attainment of status is a fundamental motive for organizational actors, and determines the resources they can marshal in aid of a favored cause (Chen, Peterson, Phillips, Podolny, & Ridgeway, 2012).

Four core features of status distinguish this construct from related constructs such as reputation (which is about being known) and power (which is about being in control) (Piazza & Castellucci, 2014). First, status is differentiating, in that it leads to the unequal distribution of privileges such as deference and resources. Second, status is hierarchical, in that it orders actors according to their social worth, based on their characteristics or abilities. Third, status is socially constructed, in that it is based on subjective judgments. And fourth, status is consensual, in that it is based on socially agreed-upon judgments (Chen et al., 2013; Deephouse & Suchman, 2008). Status-organizing processes, then, are defined as "any process in which evaluations of and beliefs about the characteristics of actors become the basis of observable inequalities in face-to-face social interaction" (Berger, Rosenholtz, & Zelditch, 1980: 479).

Three basic principles central to TM – workforce differentiation, artificial resource restriction, and interpersonal excellence (defined below) – bridge the constructs of talent and status theoretically (Nijs, Gallardo-Gallardo, Dries, & Sels, 2014). First, the principle of workforce differentiation (i.e., "the investment of a disproportionate amount of resources in employee groups for which disproportionate returns are expected"; Becker, Huselid, & Beatty, 2009: 3) refers to how, according to the TM literature, organizational resources should be distributed among employees.

This practice results in "heterogeneity in aspects of the employment experience, through, for example, differential investment in development, rewards or career opportunity, within and between workgroups" (Becker et al., 2009; Collings, 2017), a segmentation of the workforce, into more and less talented individuals, based on the strategic value a given employee is expected to contribute (Huselid & Becker, 2011). Talent identification, indeed, is formally defined as the identification of a talent pool comprised of high-potential, high-performing incumbents capable of contributing to their organization's sustainable competitive advantage (Collings & Mellahi, 2009). Legitimized by its (assumed) disproportionate contributions to team and organizational performance, this elite group enjoys increased deference and resources (Aguinis & O'Boyle, 2014).

Second, it is important to note that the unequal allocation of resources in TM is not due to resource scarcity necessarily, but that the size of the talent pool (typically between 1 and 10% of an organization's employees), in itself, is arbitrarily and artificially restricted. There is no specific reason why organizations would be unable to identify 25, 50, or even 90% of their employees as talents, especially considering the fact that many organizations do not offer career guarantees, or even a formal development program, for their talents (Dries & Pepermans, 2008).

Artificial resource restriction is defined as:

> [organizations artificially restricting] the distribution of a certain benefit to employees (even when the scarcity of a resource is not caused by physical limitations to the amount of benefits available), for instance accounting or law firms that limit the number of associates who make partner. (Ho, 2005: 121)

Again, this principle corresponds perfectly to the status construct, which entails the granting of membership to a group with distinctive characteristics or abilities that enjoys positional advantages (Deephouse & Suchman, 2008).

Third, the principle of interpersonal excellence dictates that talent should be operationalized as:

> the outstanding mastery of systematically developed abilities and knowledge in at least one field of human activity to a degree that places an individual at least among the top ten percent of age peers who have attempted to master the specific skills of that field or fields as well, and who have learned and practiced for approximately the same amount of time. (Gagné, 2004: 120)

Status, as well, captures hierarchical relations among individuals, with status differences being rooted in relative assessments of individuals compared to referent others (Piazza & Castellucci, 2014). In work organizations, talent is typically evaluated by giving performance ratings to people on a set of predefined domains (Silzer & Church, 2009), which are then forced-ranked to identify top-tier employees (Nijs et al., 2014).

Organizations are typically afraid that the status differences caused by TM will result in arrogance in those selected for the program, and jealousy in those not selected (De Boeck, Meyers, & Dries, 2018). Consequently, studies estimate that 70 to 80% of organizations do not communicate openly about their TM policies and decisions to employees (Church et al., 2015), although 83% of organizations report a desire to increase TM transparency in the future (Bravery et al., 2017). This secrecy inherent to TM programs sets in motion a highly unique and interesting phenomenon whereby a new form of status – highly sensitive due to the "talent" label – is first created, and subsequently concealed from employees using strategic ambiguity tactics (Dries et al., 2017).

Therefore – and highly uniquely so – talent status is both liminal and ambiguous. It is liminal since, rather than implying a status with immediate tangible benefits, being labeled talent is a promise for status attainment in the future (Beech, 2011). It is ambiguous since, more often than not, organizations adopt an approach of strategic ambiguity (Dries et al., 2017), secrecy (Costas & Grey, 2014), or rhetorical obfuscation (Huang & Tansley, 2012) in communicating about their TM practices and decisions to employees.

This not only creates a very unique type of status (i.e., liminal and ambiguous) but also a very unique type of organizational secrecy. First, although there is some literature on status non-disclosure (Phillips, Rothbard, & Dumas, 2009), status ambivalence and ambiguity (Zielyk, 1966), and prototype ambiguity (Bartel & Wiesenfeld, 2013), to our knowledge there has hardly been any research on the effects of forms of status where the focal person is not aware *of their own status*. Second, although quite a lot is known about the effects of secrecy on high- and low-status employees from the pay secrecy literature, its theoretical assumptions cannot be directly applied to TM secrecy for one simple reason: under conditions of pay secrecy, even when employees are not aware of their coworkers' salaries, they are at least still aware *of their own* (Colella, Paetzold, Zardkoohi, & Wesson, 2007).

Talent Management Creates Labeling Effects

In the U.S. literature, much more so than in the European literature, the TM phenomenon is typically equated to performance management, in particular the management of "star performers" (Aguinis & O'Boyle, 2014) or "A-players" (Becker et al., 2009). Although it is true that there are clear linkages between TM and performance management – since the identification of employees as "talents" is commonly based on performance and potential scores given by supervisors (Collings & Mellahi, 2009) – one very specific feature of TM sets it apart from other, related phenomena: the use of the "talent" label itself. Labeling theory states that the identity and behavior of individuals is determined or influenced by the terms used to socially categorize them (Ashforth & Humphrey, 1995).

First of all, the identification and labeling of people as talented is believed to produce Pygmalion effects, in that the positive affirmation of being assigned the "talent" label, through heightened self-confidence and role commitment, might lead to increases in performance (Eden, 1984). As a consequence, the criterion used to evaluate the predictive validity of the identification of a person as talented (i.e., his or her performance at a later point in time) is, at least partly, an artifact of self-fulfilling prophecy (Larsen, London, Weinstein, & Raghuram, 1998). It is conceivable, for instance, that talents who are aware of their status achieve a higher performance level as a result of the positive feedback encapsulated in the label itself.

Research on the Pygmalion effect has repeatedly demonstrated that high expectations conveyed by a credible, authoritative source motivate employees to do even better in the future. This effect is expected to be self-perpetuating. Once set upon a high-performance track by the positive leadership of a supervisor with high expectations, subordinates have been found to sustain high-performance on their own (Eden, 1984; Kierein & Gold, 2000). We thus expect that differences in performance between talents and non-talents will be more pronounced when they are aware of their respective status. If this is true (and there has been a lot of experimental research implying that it is; see Eden, 1984), one implication *might* be that organizations should expand their talent pools to include as many employees as possible rather than engaging in exclusive selection procedures (Buckingham & Vosburgh, 2001).

A second type of self-fulfilling prophecy is the occurrence of "success syndrome" (McCall, 1998), a phenomenon whereby early career sponsorship of employees identified as talented leads to exceptional success for that cohort, without being able to separate whether the success is attributable to the employees' talent, or the additional organizational support they have received because of their talent label (see also the literature on sponsored career mobility (e.g., Ishida, Su, & Spilerman, 2002; Larsen et al., 1998; Vinkenburg, Jansen, Dries, & Pepermans, 2014).

In stark contrast to the literature on the Pygmalion effect is the (equally widespread) assumption of talent identification resulting in "crown prince syndrome" (Dries, 2013). The crown prince syndrome describes the phenomenon whereby people who believe they are assured a spot in their organizations' senior management (much like crown princes) lose their motivation to work for it (Dries & Pepermans, 2008). Among HR practitioners, this type of assumption has led to the belief that it is better to hide from people whether or not they are seen as talented (Roussillon & Bournois, 2002). Although there is much more empirical support for Pygmalion-type effects than for crown prince effects, beliefs of the talent label leading to arrogance and complacency are widespread among organizational decision makers (Larsen et al., 1998). In the academic world, as well, some department heads are known to be hesitant to award tenure to young professors as they believe it will lead to a decrease in achievement motivation and productivity (e.g., Yining, Gupta, & Hoshower, 2006).

Talent Management Creates Highly Specific Social Exchange Dynamics

To date, the TM literature has not yet offered any real theory of what the experience of being identified as a talent by one's organization feels like, although empirical studies *have* been done on the topic, often adopting a relatively shallow social exchange framework. Being granted talent status by one's organization is "good" and can be expected to lead to "positive" reactions in return (De Boeck et al., 2018). Social exchange implies that one party provides a service to another party and, in doing so, obligates the latter to reciprocate by providing an unspecified but valued service to the former (Blau, 1964). According to Cropanzano & Mitchell (2005), the generally agreed upon essence of social exchange theory is that "social exchange comprises actions contingent on the rewarding reactions of others, which over time provide for mutually and rewarding transactions and relationships" (890).

Thunnissen, Boselie, and Fruytier (2013); Björkman, Ehrnrooth, Mäkelä, Smale, and Sumelius (2013); and Tiwari and Lenka (2015), among others, propose that organizations that invest in their employees will reap the benefits of that investment because employees are likely to return the favorable treatment. A similar, social exchange-inspired assumption is found in empirical studies claiming that organizational investments in the employment relationship (e.g., by selecting an employee into a talent pool) induce talented employees to reciprocate (Björkman et al., 2013; Du Plessis, Barkhuizen, Stanz, & Schutte, 2015; Gelens et al., 2014; Khoreva & Vaiman, 2015). In sum, TM scholars tend to assume that the exchange relationship between employers and their talented employees can be almost entirely understood through the norm of reciprocity (e.g., Gelens, Dries, Hofmans, & Pepermans, 2015). Some important elements of social exchange theory have so far been largely neglected in the TM literature (i.e., uncertainty, social identity, social comparison, and power) (De Boeck et al., 2018).

First of all, the TM literature so far has largely neglected the fact that status liminality and ambiguity create a large amount of uncertainty in the exchange relationship between talents and their organizations (De Boeck et al., 2018). Outside of the TM literature, however, there has been some discussion of the role of uncertainty in social exchange. According to social exchange theory, the main difference between social and economic exchanges is that the resources exchanged in the former are unspecified and subjective (Cook & Rice, 2003). Such uncertainties about the basis of the exchange relationship can furthermore be expected to intensify employees' emotional responses (Cook & Rice, 2003). Consequently, the ambiguous communication about TM practices by organizations towards their employees may create negative affective reactions in their talents, as well as increase the risk of psychological contract breach (Dries & De Gieter, 2014). Several (experimental) studies have also found that high uncertainty can lead to *higher* levels of commitment among exchange partners, which they explain through the theoretical assumption that increases in commitment might serve as compensation mechanisms with a view of mitigating risk in the exchange relationship (Savage & Bergstrand, 2013).

Second, several qualitative studies in which employees identified as talents were interviewed uncovered identity struggles in this group (Dubouloy, 2004; Tansley & Tietze, 2013). In general, the TM literature would greatly benefit from a deeper discussion of the relationship between social identity and talent status (De Boeck et al., 2018). Social identity theory was in part developed to counter the perceived focus on purely instrumental considerations in social exchange theory (Restubog, Hornsey, Bordia, & Esposo, 2008). Specifically, the theory proposes that employees do not only react to how their organization treats them objectively, but that their reactions are also determined by identity-relevant information communicated by this treatment (e.g., whether they are valued in-group members or marginalized out-group members). In that sense, TM practices are not just practices, but also symbolic carriers of meaning (see also signaling theory, Dries et al., 2014; King, 2016).

Feeling excluded (as might be the case for non-talents) (Swailes & Blackburn, 2016) is predicted to lead to psychological withdrawal from the organization. Employees who feel valued by their organization, on the other hand, over time integrate more and more of its perceived attributes into their self-concept, which explains Tansley and Tietze's (2013) observations of experienced conformity pressures in talents. De Boeck et al. (2018) proposed that the literature on employee reactions to TM would benefit from a closer examination of the optimal balance between organizational identification and authenticity (for talents) and of the effects of feeling excluded on social identity (for non-talents).

Third, in addition to social identity, the related process of social comparison is likely crucial in understanding group-level reactions to TM. Social comparison theory refers to the natural tendency of people to compare themselves to close others ("targets") in figuring out who they are themselves, based on both upward comparison to targets who are perceived as better, and downward comparison to targets who are perceived as less well off than themselves. Interestingly, social comparison theory states that potential threats to a person's self-image as a result of upward comparison can be buffered by attributing the difference (for instance, in performance) to exceptional qualities on the side of the target, thereby increasing the distance between the focal person and the target, and making comparison less meaningful (Alicke, LoSchiavo, Zerbst, & Zhang, 1997).

The implication of this latter theoretical assumption for TM is that extremely exclusive TM practices may in fact evoke less negative reactions in non-talents than moderately exclusive TM practices (Swailes et al., 2014). Put in very simple terms, what would *you* find the less favorable scenario: not belonging to a talent pool that comprises 1% of your organization's population (meaning that you are among the 99% not identified as talents), or not belonging to a talent pool comprising 30% of the population? Interestingly, this directly contradicts the implications of self-fulfilling prophecy research as to the optimal "exclusiveness" of TM (see earlier in this chapter; e.g., Larsen et al., 1998; van Zelderen, Dries, & Marescaux, 2019).

Power, finally, refers to the inequalities resulting from ongoing relations of social exchange, as some actors control more highly valued resources than do others (Cook & Rice, 2003). In the context of TM, such inequalities can be found at two different levels: the inequality between management and employees (e.g., in access to information), and the inequality created between talents and non-talents (e.g., in access to career investments). Interestingly, power is also a function of the dependence of one actor on another (Cook & Rice, 2003). As the core tenet of the TM literature is that organizations rely on their talented employees to create value (Thunnissen et al., 2013), we can assume that talented employees to some extent hold power over their organizations; their organization's performance "depends" on their discretionary effort.

Although the topics of power and inequality are implicitly discussed in the TM literature, especially in the more recent stream on more inclusive forms of TM (Swailes et al., 2014), a more deliberate examination of these concepts and their potential role in TM research is probably needed to fully understand the unique effects of TM on employees.

Conclusion and Suggestions for Further Research

Although "careers for life" are admittedly a reality from a distant past (Sullivan & Baruch, 2009), the organizational career is far from dead. In its enthusiasm to advocate self-directedness and personal agency (Arnold & Cohen, 2008; Dries, 2011) the recent careers literature may have lost sight of the fact that careers still serve strategic purposes for organizations, especially now that "war for talent" dynamics are becoming more pressing (Guest & Mackenzie Davey, 1996; Michaels et al., 2001). In fact, current economic conditions may warrant a renaissance of (research into) organizational careers and organizational career management practices, as the careers of many people are still enacted more often than not within the context of an organization (Hall & Las Heras, 2009). It appears that the careers literature and the TM literature are complementary, at least in some respects (see De Vos & Dries, 2013, for more information).

The careers literature might take lessons from the TM literature by acknowledging careers as an organizational concern that relates to its broader strategic human resource management practices (De Vos & Dries, 2013). The TM literature, on the other hand, might do well to acknowledge career actors' free agency. As Inkson (2008) pointed out, humans do not act as rationally and predictably as other resources. Therefore, studying TM from a resource-based view (RBV) perspective alone may not advisable. Insights from the careers literature, for example, from the work on subjective career success (e.g. Dries, Pepermans, & Carlier, 2008) and career orientations (e.g. Gerber, Wittekind, Grote, & Staffelbach, 2009), might help TM researchers formulate recommendations on how organizations might achieve continuity as a result of their career management practices (see Dries, 2013, for more information).

Dries (2013) offers a concrete roadmap for future research on TM. For example, some topics for further research include the identification of significant constructs and theories, the retroactive examination of the processes through which talents make sense of their careers, and the longitudinal examination of the effects of TM on employees' careers (see Dries & Pepermans, 2008, for more topics).

Methodologically, there are three main limitations in existing research that need to be addressed in future research. First, the limitation of not being able to demonstrate *causality*. If we want to study the effects of TM on employees' careers, we need to be able to exclude the reverse causality hypothesis that the projected outcomes of TM (e.g., increased performance motivation of "talents") are actually predictors of talent status. To date only cross-sectional studies on TM exist, at least on the quantitative end. There have, however, been two qualitative studies that have followed talents over time (Dubouloy, 2004; Thunnissen, 2016).

Another issue related to causality is that some quantitative studies claiming to study the effects of talent status lack control groups of non-talents (De Boeck et al., 2018). Pretest-posttest intervention studies, longitudinal field studies, and lab experiments are all potential designs that would help rule out reverse causality explanations for our review findings, and distinguish between short- and long-term effects of TM on employees' careers.

The second limitation is that of existing research adopting a single *measurement level*. To date, quantitative research on TM has either used employees as respondents, or HR managers (although some qualitative studies have interviewed both employees and HR managers) ((e.g., Dries & Pepermans, 2008). If we want to understand how TM practices are shaped by industry and organizational culture, for instance, and how these trickle down into perceived HR practices and individual employee outcomes, finally amounting into group-level and organizational-level effects in terms of morale and performance, we need multilevel studies.

Future research could look into the effects of organizational size, sector, structure, and culture on TM programs and their links to internal career opportunity structures (Dries & Pepermans, 2008). Also, future studies should go beyond predicting outcomes of TM at the individual level (such as career satisfaction), and take a multilevel approach, also including outcomes at the team and organizational level, such as team and organizational morale, climate, and performance (Boudreau & Ramstad, 2005; Silzer & Dowell, 2010).

The third limitation is *fragmentation* in terms of operationalizations and measures of TM and talent status that hinder accumulation of knowledge across studies (De Boeck et al., 2018). Clearly, TM covers a much broader range of management practices than the mere assignment of employees to talent categories (Dries et al., 2008; Silzer & Dowell, 2010). In addition, in existing studies it is quite difficult to disentangle the effects of TM practices and talent status on employee outcomes, so that we cannot conclude with certainty which of them is causing the effects (Gelens et al., 2013). Qualitative approaches may be better suited than survey studies for studying TM in all its breadth.

One specific avenue for further research on the relationship between TM and careers would be to dig deeper into what people with a more "boundaryless" career orientation actually want from their careers. Several authors have suggested that organizational careers can potentially also accommodate the needs of boundaryless career actors, on the condition that they are characterized by sufficient internal career transition opportunities and gradual job enrichment (De Cuyper & De Witte, 2011). Furthermore, in order to study "truly boundaryless" careers, it might be interesting to look specifically into the careers of self-employed people, project workers, and entrepreneurs (Sullivan & Arthur, 2006).

References

Aguinis, H., & O'Boyle, E. 2014. Star performers in twenty-first century organizations. *Personnel Psychology,* 67(2): 313-350.

Alicke, M. D., LoSchiavo, F. M., Zerbst, J., & Zhang, S. 1997. The person who outperforms me is a genius: Maintaining perceived competence in upward social comparison. *Journal of Personality and Social Psychology,* 73(4): 781-789.

Arnold, J., & Cohen, L. 2008. The psychology of careers in industrial and organizational settings: A critical but appreciative analysis. In G. P. Hodgkinson & J. K. Ford (Eds.), *International review of industrial and organizational psychology:* 1-44). London, UK: Wiley.

Arthur, M. B., & Rousseau, D. M. 1996. *The boundaryless career: A new employment principle for new organizational era.* New York: Oxford University Press.

Ashforth, B. E., & Humphrey, R. H. 1995. Labeling processes in the organization. *Research in Organizational Behavior,* 17: 413-461.

Ashton, C., & Morton, L. 2005. Managing talent for competitive advantage. *Strategic HR Review,* 4(5): 28-31.

Bartel, C. A., & Wiesenfeld, B. M. 2013. The social negotiation of group prototype ambiguity in dynamic organizational contexts. *Academy of Management Review,* 38(4): 503-524.

Baruch, Y., & Peiperl, M. 1997. High-flyers: Glorious past, gloomy present, any future? *Career Development International,* 2(7): 354-358.

Becker, B., Huselid, M., & Beatty, D. 2009. *The differentiated workforce.* Boston, MA: Harvard Business Press.

Beech, N. 2011. Liminality and the practices of identity reconstruction. *Human Relations,* 64(2): 285-302.

Beechler, S., & Woodward, I. C. (2009). The global "war for talent". *Journal of International Management,* 15(3): 273-285.

Berger, J., Rosenholtz, S. J., & Zelditch, M. 1980. Status organizing processes. *Annual Review of Sociology,* 6: 479-508.

Björkman, I., Ehrnrooth, M., Mäkelä, K., Smale, A., & Sumelius, J. 2013. Talent or not? Employee reactions to talent identification. *Human Resource Management,* 52(2): 195-214.

Blau, P. M. 1964. *Exchange and power in social life.* Transaction Publishers.

Boudreau, J. W., & Ramstad, P. M. 2005. Where's your pivotal talent? *Harvard Business Review,* 83(4): 23-24.

Bravery, K. et al. 2017. *Global talent trends study 2017: Empowerment in a disrupted world.* Hong Kong: Mercer.

Buckingham, M., & Vosburgh, R. M. 2001. *The 21st century human resources function: It's the talent, stupid! Human Resource Planning,* 24(4): 17-23.

Chen, Y., Gupta, A., & Hoshower, L. 2006. Factors that motivate business faculty to conduct research: An expectancy theory analysis. *Journal of Education for Business,* 81(4): 179-189.

Chen, Y., Peterson, R. S., Phillips, D. J., Podolny, J. M., & Ridgeway, C. L. 2012. Introduction to the special issue: Bringing status to the table—attaining, maintaining, and experiencing status in organizations and markets. *Organization Science,* 23: 299-307.

Chuai, X., Preece, D., & Iles, P. 2008. Is talent management just 'old wine in new bottles'? The case of multinational companies in Beijing. *Management Research News,* 31(12): 901-911.

Church, A. H., Rotolo, C. T., Ginther, N. M., & Levine, R. 2015. How are top companies designing and managing their high-potential programs? A follow-up talent management benchmark study. *Consulting Psychology Journal: Practice and Research,* 67(1): 17.

Colella, A., Paetzold, R. L., Zardkoohi, A., & Wesson, M. J. 2007. Exposing pay secrecy. *Academy of Management Review,* 32(1): 55-71.

Collings, D. G. 2017. Workforce differentiation. In D. G. Collings, K. Mellahi, & W. F. Cascio (Eds.), *Oxford handbook of talent management.* Oxford, UK: Oxford University Press.

Collings, D. G., & Mellahi, K. 2009. Strategic talent management: A review and research agenda. *Human Resource Management Review,* 19(4): 304-313.

Collings, D. G., Mellahi, K., & Cascio, W. F. 2019. Global talent management and performance in multinational enterprises: A multilevel perspective. *Journal of Management,* 45(2): 540-566.

Cook, K. S., & Rice, E. 2003. Social exchange theory. In J. Delamater (Ed.), *The handbook of social psychology:* 53-76. New York: Kluwer Academic/Plenum.

Costas, J., & Grey, C. 2014. Bringing secrecy into the open: Towards a theorization of the social processes of organizational secrecy. *Organization Studies,* 35(10): 1423–1447.

Cropanzano, R., & Mitchell, M. S. 2005. Social exchange theory: An interdisciplinary review. *Journal of Management,* 31(6): 874-900.

Crowley-Henry, M., Benson, E. T., & Al Ariss, A. 2018. Linking talent management to traditional and boundaryless career orientations: Research propositions and future directions. *European Management Review,* early online.

De Boeck, G., Meyers, M. C. & Dries, N. 2018. Employee reactions to talent management: Assumptions versus evidence. *Journal of Organizational Behavior* (IRIOP Annual Review Issue), 39(2): 199-213.

De Cuyper, N., & De Witte, H. 2011. The management paradox: Self-rated employability and organizational commitment and performance. *Personnel Review,* 40(2): 152-172.

De Vos, A., Dewettinck, K., & Buyens, D. 2009. The professional career on the right track: A study on the interaction between career self-management and organizational career management in explaining employee outcomes. *European Journal of Work and Organizational Psychology,* 18(1): 55-80.

De Vos, A., & Dries, N. 2013. Applying a talent management lens to career management: The role of human capital composition and continuity. *International Journal of Human Resource Management,* 24(9): 1816-1831.

Deephouse, D., & Suchman, M. 2008. Legitimacy in organizational institutionalism. In R. Greenwood, C. Oliver, K. Sahlin, & R. Suddaby (Eds.), *The Sage handbook of organizational institutionalism:* 49–77. London: Sage.

Dries, N. 2011. The meaning of career success: Avoiding reification through a closer inspection of historical, cultural and ideological contexts. *Career Development International,* 16(4): 364-384.

Dries, N. 2013. The psychology of talent management: A review and research agenda. *Human Resource Management Review,* 23(4): 272-285.

Dries, N., & De Gieter, S. 2014. Information asymmetry in high potential programs. *Personnel Review,* 43(1): 136–162.

Dries, N., Forrier, A., de Vos, A., & Pepermans, R. 2014. Self-perceived employability, organization-rated potential, and the psychological contract. *Journal of Managerial Psychology,* 29: 565-581.

Dries, N., & Pepermans, R. 2008. "Real" high-potential careers: An empirical study into the perspectives of organisations and high potentials. *Personnel Review,* 37: 85-108.

Dries, N., Pepermans, R., & Carlier, O. 2008. Career success: Constructing a multidimensional model. *Journal of Vocational Behavior,* 73(2): 254-267.

Dries, N., Schleicher, D., Tierens, H., Hofmans, J., Gelens, J., & Pepermans, R. 2017. *Secrecy, status ambiguity, and power in organizational talent management programs.* Presented at the 33rd Colloquium of the European Group for Organization Studies in Copenhagen, Denmark on July 7th.

Dries, N., Van Acker, F., & Verbruggen, M. 2012. How 'boundaryless' are the careers of high potentials, key experts and average performers? *Journal of Vocational Behavior,* 81(2): 271-279.

Dubouloy, M. 2004. The transitional space and self-recovery: A psychoanalytical approach to high-potential managers' training. *Human Relations,* 57: 467-496.

Du Plessis, L., Barkhuizen, N., Stanz, K., & Schutte, N. 2015. The management side of talent: Causal implications for the retention of generation Y employees. *Journal of Applied Business Research,* 31: 1767.

Dyer, S., & Humphries, M. 2002. Normalising work-place change through contemporary career discourse. In L. Morrow, I. Verins, & E. Wills (Eds.), *Mental health and work: Issues and perspectives.* Australia: Common Wealth of Australia.

Eden, D. 1984. Self-fulfilling prophecy as a management tool: Harnessing Pygmalion. *Academy of Management Review,* 9: 64–73.

Finkelstein, L. M., Costanza, D. P., & Goodwin, G. F. 2018. Do your high potentials have potential? The impact of individual differences and designation on leader success. *Personnel Psychology,* 71(1): 3-22.

Forrier, A., Sels, L. and Verbruggen, M. 2005. *Career counseling in the new career era: A study about the influence of career types, career satisfaction and career management on the need for career counseling.* KU Leuven Research Report.

Gagné, F. 2004. Transforming gifts into talents: The DMGT as a developmental theory. *High Ability Studies,* 15: 119–147.

Gelens, J., Dries, N., Hofmans, J., & Pepermans, R. 2013. The role of perceived organizational justice in shaping the outcomes of talent management: A research agenda. *Human Resource Management Review,* 23(4): 341-353.

Gelens, J., Dries, N., Hofmans, J., & Pepermans, R. 2015. Affective commitment of employees designated as talent: Signalling perceived organisational support. *European Journal of International Management,* 9: 9-27.

Gerber, M., Wittekind, A., Grote, G., & Staffelbach, B. 2009. Exploring types of career orientation: A latent class analysis approach. *Journal of Vocational Behavior,* 75(3): 303-318.

Gill, C. 2002. Two-dimensional HRM: Limitations of the soft and hard dichotomy in explaining the phenomenon of HRM. *RMIT working paper,* 4.

Granrose, C. S., & Baccili, P. A. 2006. Do psychological contracts include boundaryless or protean careers? *Career Development International,* 11(2): 163-182.

Guest, D., & MacKenzie Davey, K. 1996. Don't write off the traditional career. *People Management,* 2: 22-23.

Hall, D. T. 1996. *The career is dead, long live the career: A relational approach to careers.* San Francisco, CA: Jossey-Bass.

Hall, D. T., & Las Heras, M. 2009. Long live the organisational career. In A. Collin, & W. Patton (Eds.), *Vocational psychological and organisational perspectives on career: Towards a multidisciplinary dialogue:* 181–196. Rotterdam, The Netherlands: Sense Publishers.

Ho, V. T. 2005. Social influence on evaluations of psychological contract fulfillment. *Academy of Management Review,* 30(1): 113-128.

Huang, J., & Tansley, C. 2012. Sneaking through the minefield of talent management: The notion of rhetorical obfuscation. *The International Journal of Human Resource Management,* 23(17): 3673-3691.

Hughes, J. C., & Rog, E. 2008. Talent management: A strategy for improving employee recruitment, retention and engagement within hospitality organizations. *International Journal of Contemporary Hospitality Management,* 20, 743-757.

Huselid, M. A., Beatty, R. W., & Becker, B. E. 2005. 'A players' or 'A positions'? *Harvard Business Review,* 83(12): 110-117.

Iles, P. 1997. Sustainable high potential career development: A resource-based view. *Career Development International,* 2(7): 347-353.

Iles, P., Preece, D., & Chuai, X. 2010. Talent management as a management fashion in HRD: Towards a research agenda. *Human Resource Development International,* 13(2): 125-145.

Inkson, K. 2008. Are humans resources? *Career Development International,* 13(3): 270-279.

Ishida, H., Su, K., & Spilerman, S. 2002. Models of career advancement in organizations. *European Sociological Review,* 18(2): 179-198.

Khoreva, V., & Vaiman, V. 2015. Intent vs. action: Talented employees and leadership development. *Personnel Review,* 44: 200-216.

Kierein, N. M., & Gold, M. A. 2000. Pygmalion in work organizations: A meta-analysis. *Journal of Organizational Behavior,* 21: 913-928.

King, K. A. 2016. The talent deal and journey: understanding the employee response to talent identification over time. *Employee Relations,* 38: 94-111.

Kuznia, K. 2004. *The rhetoric and reality of fast track management development programs.* Mid-West Academy Proceedings.

Larsen, H. H., London, M., Weinstein, M., & Raghuram, S. 1998. High-flyer management-development programs: Organizational rhetoric or self-fulfilling prophecy? *International Studies of Management & Organization,* 28(1): 64-90.

Ledford, G. & Kochanski, J. 2004. Allocation training and development resources based on contribution. In L. Berger & D. Berger (Eds.), *The talent management handbook: Creating organizational excellence by identifying, developing and promoting your best people:* 218-229. New York, NY: McGraw-Hill.

Lewis, R. E., & Heckman, R. J. 2006. Talent management: A critical review. *Human Resources Management Review,* 16(2): 139-154.

Marescaux, E., De Winne, S., & Sels, L. 2013. HR practices and affective organisational commitment: (When) does HR differentiation pay off? *Human Resource Management Journal,* 23(4): 329-345.

McCall, M. W. 1998. *High flyers: Developing the next generation of leaders.* Boston, MA: Harvard Business School Press.

Michaels, E., Handfield-Jones, H., & Axelrod, B. 2001. *The war for talent.* Boston, MA: Harvard Business School Press.

Nijs, S., Gallardo-Gallardo, E., Dries, N., & Sels, L. 2014. A multidisciplinary review into the definition, operationalization, and measurement of talent. *Journal of World Business,* 49(2): 180-191.

Pannell, M., & Mendez, A. 2019. Reimagining talent management. *HR Future,* 1: 24-25.

Phillips, K. W., Rothbard, N. P., & Dumas, T. L. 2009. To disclose or not to disclose? Status distance and self-disclosure in diverse environments. *Academy of Management Review,* 34(4): 710-732.

Piazza, A., & Castellucci, F. 2014. Status in organization and management theory. *Journal of Management,* 40(1): 287-315.

Restubog, S. L. D., Hornsey, M. J., Bordia, P., & Esposo, S. R. 2008. Effects of psychological contract breach on organizational citizenship behaviour: Insights from the group value model. *Journal of Management Studies,* 45(8): 1377-1400.

Rodrigues, R. A., & Guest, D. 2010. Have careers become boundaryless? *Human Relations,* 63(8): 1157-1175.

Rodrigues, R., Guest, D., & Budjanovcanin, A. 2016. Bounded or boundaryless? An empirical investigation of career boundaries and boundary crossing. *Work, Employment and Society,* 30(4): 669-686.

Roussillon, S., & Bournois, F. 2002. Identifying and developing future leaders in France. In C. B. Derr, S. Roussillon, & F. Bournois (Eds.), *Cross-cultural approaches to leadership development:* 51-60. Westport, CT: Quorum Books.

Savage, S. V., & Bergstrand, K. 2013. Negotiating the unknown: The role of uncertainty in social exchange. *Sociology Compass,* 7(4): 315-327.

Savickas, M. L. 2000. Renovating the psychology of careers for the twenty-first century. In A. Collin & R. Young (Eds.), *The future of career:* 53-68. New York: Cambridge University Press.

Silzer, R., & Church, A. H. 2009. The pearls and perils of identifying potential. *Industrial and Organizational Psychology: Perspectives on Science and Practice,* 2: 377-412.

Silzer, R., & Dowell, B. E. 2010. *Strategy-driven talent management: A leadership imperative.* San Francisco, CA: Jossey-Bass.

Sonnenberg, M., van Zijderveld, V., & Brinks, M. 2014. The role of talent-perception incongruence in effective talent management. *Journal of World Business,* 49(2): 272-280.

Sullivan, S. E. 1999. The changing nature of careers: A review and research agenda. *Journal of Management,* 25(3): 457-484.

Sullivan, S. E., & Arthur, M. B. 2006. The evolution of the boundaryless career concept: Examining physical and psychological mobility. *Journal of Vocational Behavior,* 69(1): 19-29.

Sullivan, S. E., & Baruch, Y. 2009. Advances in career theory and research: A critical review and agenda for future exploration. *Journal of Management,* 35(6): 1542-1571.

Swailes, S., & Blackburn, M. 2016. Employee reactions to talent pool membership. *Employee Relations,* 38(1): 112-128.

Swailes, S., Downs, Y., & Orr, K. 2014. Conceptualising inclusive talent management: potential, possibilities and practicalities. *Human Resource Development International,* 17(5): 529-544.

Tansley, C. 2011. What do we mean by the term 'talent' in talent management? *Industrial and Commercial Training,* 43(5): 266-274.

Tansley, C., & Tietze, S. 2013. Rites of passage through talent management progression stages: An identity work perspective. *The International Journal of Human Resource Management,* 24: 1799-1815.

Thunnissen, M. 2016. Talent management: For what, how and how well? An empirical exploration of talent management in practice. *Employee Relations,* 38(1): 57-72.

Thunnissen, M., Boselie, P., & Fruytier, B. 2013. Talent management and the relevance of context: Towards a pluralistic approach. *Human Resource Management Review,* 23(4): 326-336.

Tiwari, B., & Lenka, U. 2015. Building and branding talent hub: an outlook. *Industrial and Commercial Training,* 47: 208-213.

Truss, C., Gratton, L., Hope-Hailey, V., McGovern, P., & Stiles, P. 1997. Soft and hard models of human resource management: A reappraisal. *Journal of Management Studies,* 34(1): 53-73.

Tulgan, B. 2001. Winning the talent wars. *Employment Relations Today,* 23(1-2): 37-51.

Van Buren, H. J. 2003. Boundaryless careers and employability obligations. *Business Ethics Quarterly,* 13(2): 131-149.

Van Esbroeck, R. 2008. Career guidance in a global world. In J. A. Athanasou & R. Van Esbroeck (Eds.), *International handbook of career guidance:* 23-44. London: Springer.

Van Esbroeck, R., Tibos, K., & Zaman, M. 2005. A dynamic model of career choice development. *International Journal for Educational and Vocational Guidance,* 5: 5-18.

van Zelderen, A., Dries, N., & Marescaux, E. 2019. Using social comparison theory to explain why a manager should remain secret about talent status. Presented at the 34th Annual SIOP Conference in National Harbor, Maryland.

Vinkenburg, C. J., Jansen, P. G., Dries, N., & Pepermans, R. 2014. Arena: A critical conceptual framework of top management selection. *Group & Organization Management,* 39(1): 33-68.

Walton, S., & Mallon, M. 2004. Redefining the boundaries? Making sense of career in contemporary New Zealand. *Asia Pacific Journal of Human Resources,* 42(1): 75-95.

Warren, C. 2006. Curtain call: Talent management. *People management,* 3: 24-29.

Zielyk, I. V. 1966. On ambiguity and ambivalence. *The Pacific Sociological Review,* 9(1): 57-64.

22

EXCLUSIVE TALENT MANAGEMENT

Examining Ethical Concerns and Boundaries

Stephen Swailes

Introduction

Understanding the contribution of talented individuals to society and to organizations has a long history. The specific use of the term "talent management" (TM) has captured attention for over 20 years, but neither the extensive literature on the ethics of human resource management (HRM) (see Alzola, 2018; Deckop, 2006; Greenwood, 2013; Provis, 2010) nor the burgeoning literature on TM have given it much ethical scrutiny (Painter-Morland, Kirk, Deslandes, & Tansley, 2019). This is surprising given that by its very nature it seems vulnerable to selection bias, exploitation of participants, and abuse of power by senior managers.

Two reasons might account for the lack of ethical treatment. First, TM as a relatively recent label, although long established as an interest (Cappelli, & Keller, 2017; Swailes, 2016), post-dates much of the initial ground-clearing interest in the ethics of HRM. Second, there are definitional problems given the ambiguous nature of TM that plays-out in many ways. Since TM often focuses on small groups of employees in large organizations (exclusive TM), any ethical treatment of it must connect to some extent with previous ethical analysis of HRM. As such, and for scholars and practitioners interested in managing talent in business organizations, this chapter surfaces areas of concern with exclusive TM and the ethical questions they raise.

The chapter first outlines frameworks commonly used in business ethics before defining TM for the purposes of the analysis that follows. The individual and evolutionary nature of talent is then considered to highlight ethical implications. The headline outcomes from applying commonly used ethical frameworks are revealed before considering ethical concerns with becoming and staying talented.

Ethics in HRM

In a groundbreaking article, Legge (1998) asked if HRM is ethical and whether it can be ethical. A basic problem for her was that HRM practice had become wedded to the rhetoric of capitalism, individualism, and competitive advantage. While not rejecting the idea of ethical capitalism, she felt it was hard to imagine how managing people could be ethical if the prevailing economic order was not ethical. Related concerns are the "ethical tensions" that arise from the commodification of labor (Jack, Greenwood, & Schapper, 2012) since the treatment of humans as resources, assets, and capital runs the risk of denying their innate humanism. As such, HRM, and by implication TM, are ethically problematic from the start.

Traditional HRM fields include recruitment and selection, performance management, reward management, training, management development, and employee relations. More recently, strategic HRM

DOI: 10.4324/9781315474687-22

grapples with linking an organization's HRM architecture to its business performance. All these fields, although not so much employee relations, are touched by TM albeit on a smaller scale given its traditional focus on small sets of people deemed to possess high potential. Each field gives rise to ethical concerns: executive pay (Moriarty, 2009), reward (Moriarty, 2012), hiring (Bruton, 2015), appraisal (Jacobs, Belscak, & Hartog, 2014) and strategic HRM (Van Buren, Greenwood, & Sheehan, 2011).

These issues along with many other business practices are examined using a range of ethical frameworks: in particular, consequentialism, duty ethics and virtue ethics. Consequentialism focuses on the probable outcomes (consequences) of alternative courses of action. Often the probable outcomes can only be estimated and the course that yields the greatest expected utility (often interpreted as the greatest good for the greatest number) or the least harm would be favored. For consequentialists, if an HRM practice is judged to have a good chance of boosting organizational performance, which in turn boosts job security, then it would be deemed a right action in relation to not implementing the same practice.

However, it is often impossible to know all the future consequences of an action, and sometimes an action that many would think is bad is carried out in order to achieve a greater good. Few people, for instance, would welcome compulsory redundancy, but if making some people redundant improves the job security of others, then it becomes acceptable to consequentialists. However, a problem with consequentialism is that it can cut across issues of justice and values in determining courses of action.

In contrast, duty ethics determines courses of action by using principles (or rules) that help to judge whether an action is acceptable. Principles are designed to sort good actions from bad ones. If making someone redundant is deemed morally wrong, then in duty ethics, no one should be made redundant even though the viability of a larger workforce may be reduced. Duty ethics therefore can become absolutist in saying what should or should not happen, and some duties can be contradictory.

With roots in ancient Greek philosophy, virtue ethics is concerned with the virtues and moral character of the person(s) carrying out an act rather than with its consequences or with rules. Traditional virtues include honesty, justice, and courage, and by possessing these and other virtues a person can live morally well. In virtue ethics, actions are examined in terms of whether a virtuous person would do them. Although virtue ethics tells us how to make good decisions, it is less clear than duty ethics or consequentialism when it comes to choosing between difficult decisions.

These three meta-theories are all useful but they are abstract. Organizational justice is a more applied approach that is being increasingly used in HRM situations, including recruitment, wage differentials, and grievance handling (Provis, 2010). Justice concerns the fairness that employees perceive in the ways that decisions are made, the ways that the outcomes of those decisions are distributed, the communications processes used, and the ways in which they are treated as individuals. In essence, the more employees perceive fairness in organizational practices the more favorable their reactions will be.

Organizational justice is an important theoretical mediator between TM practices and employee reactions (Gelens, Dries, Hofmans, & Pepermans, 2013; O'Connor & Crowley-Henry, 2019). Another recent approach, care ethics, perhaps speaks to the roots of HRM by focusing on interpersonal relationships and seeing care as a virtue. It is a less masculine and more feminine approach that focuses on individuals and puts care at the center rather than on applying principles or weighing outcomes.

However, although individual ethical frameworks are informative in their own ways, they often lead to conflicting conclusions over whether something is right or wrong, ethical or unethical. Nevertheless, they are used later to reveal what they say about TM and to bring out a range of ethical issues and questions for scholars and TM practitioners. This approach is intended to keep debates and research surrounding TM in touch with contemporary societal concerns.

Conceptualizing Exclusive Talent Management

"Talent" is sometimes used as a general term for labor or to describe an entire workforce but not so here. Nor is TM treated as a euphemism for HRM. Although such labeling is commonplace, especially in the practitioner literature, if TM is not conceptualized in terms of a focus on a minority of high-potential people, there seems little to set it apart from broader organizational approaches to human resource development and the ethical issues therein. Unless otherwise stated, and consistent with the mainstream definition (Collings, Cascio, & Mellahi, 2017: 5), exclusive TM is taken here to mean the differential treatment of a small percentage of employees, usually managers or professionals, who have somehow been identified as showing high potential for advancement in an organization.

In essence, exclusive TM assumes that the knowledge, skills, and abilities of the talented are worth differential treatment compared to an undifferentiated, homogeneous approach to employee development. Although TM is operationalized in different ways to suit different organizational contexts, variations of the exclusive approach actively look for present and future employees with high potential for adding value, provide them with a different development experience to that enjoyed by the rest of the workforce, and align them with key positions that are thought to contribute disproportionately to sustaining the organization's competitive advantage (Collings & Mellahi, 2009).

Exclusive approaches offer a different HR architecture (Becker & Huselid, 2006) to the talented, and seem to be the most common perhaps because through their focus on small numbers, they are relatively simple for senior managers and HR departments to conceptualize and put into practice. An organization may run several talent pools at the same time spanning management levels or professional fields with each pool deserving a different investment approach to access the particular skills that it brings together (Morris & Snell, 2010). The focus of the chapter is on exclusive TM because it is the dominant approach and because its assumptions and practices provide ample scope for ethical scrutiny.

The Nature of Talent and Ethical Considerations

The ethics of HRM usually examine particular approaches to managing people. Talent management can be treated in this way, but TM has an added dimension since it is dealing with talent as a property of individuals and an appreciation of the nature of talent, what causes it, and how it changes is helpful in surfacing ethical issues. Indeed, a consideration of talent *per se* provides a good reason to justify why organizations should keep looking for it.

Models of talent development agree that talent in a wide range of domains is a combination of genetic endowment, individual factors, factors pertaining to childhood, environmental factors, as well as education, training, and practice (Kaufman, 2013). Excellent achievement is the outcome of complex interactions between individual traits (cognitive and non-cognitive abilities, high motivation, and commitment towards particular tasks, emotional stability, and personality variables) and environmental factors, such as family conditions, support, and education. While much of the variation in outstanding achievement is unexplained, intelligence and other cognitive abilities (e.g., social skills) are the most important single predictors (Trost, 2000: 323).

Gagne's (2005, 2015) model of talent development sees an individual's natural abilities (partly genetic in origin) shaped by interpersonal catalysts (such as temperament), environmental catalysts (family, incidents during life), and chance. These four components positively or negatively influence the systematic informal and formal development processes that the individual undertakes and through which talent in a particular domain is developed. In simpler terms, talent development can be seen as "a feature of person development fuelled by the dynamic interaction between a changing individual and a changing context" (Schoon, 2000: 222). At points in time, these dynamic interactions produce displays of talent that may only be short-lived.

Simonton's theory of emergenesis is also useful here. Simonton (1999: 436) defines talent as, "any innate capacity that enables an individual to display exceptionally high-performance in a domain that requires special skills and training". This definition has some traction in management situations. Talent requires practice to achieve high standards and assumes that the innate characteristics, such as cognitive abilities, personality traits, and interests, are present that are required to "have what it takes" to stand-out in a particular domain. An individual's "endowed capacity" usually consists of "physical, physiological, cognitive and dispositional traits that facilitate the manifestation of superior expertise in a talent domain" (Simonton, 2001: 39).

In relation to genetic bases, the display of a talent requires the display of a set of traits in combination with each other, and that the traits are not simply additive but multiplicative. This means that if any trait is absent or present in a small quantity, then the talent cannot manifest itself. In a given domain, a particular weighting of underlying talent traits is needed for that talent to be optimized. Furthermore, different domains that rely on the same traits may require them in different degrees. In the field of genetic inheritance, this pattern is called emergenic.

The talent of an individual can thus be seen as the product of a set of weighted contributing components (varying in number and type from domain to domain). Good looks for example, are known to contribute to career success, possibly operating through better education, greater self-confidence, and/or greater employer perceptions of abilities (Hamermesh, 2011). Personal attractiveness may be important in some work domains, such as modeling, although the weighting for good looks is probably small in most workplaces. The "untalented" are those who lack one or more essential components necessary for a particular domain. For example, a person with no inclination for interpersonal cooperation will not be considered talented in a domain where this component is necessary.

Implications of the Multidimensional and Multiplicative View

The multidimensional and multiplicative view of talent has good explanatory power when used to interpret work situations and explains why people who, while good at many aspects of their job, do not make it onto talent lists because they lack a particular trait, such as the ability to create useful networks, such that they cannot fulfill the organization's vision of talent that has been shaped by its strategic intent. In another organization, which requires the same traits but in different weightings, the same person's networking trait, while still modest, may be sufficiently well developed for them to make the talent pool because networking is not such a big part of the organization's construction of talent.

The multidimensional multiplicative model means that talent does not fit a normal curve (Simonton, 2005: 315). In contrast, in a given domain at a point in time, most people will not have the combination of traits necessary to display talent. As such, talent is confined to a small number of people producing highly skewed distributions of talent, and this helps to justify exclusive approaches to finding and developing talent. The more complex the talent domain is, the more highly skewed the distribution becomes. There is empirical support for this since, although job performance distributions can be normally distributed (Beck, Beatty, & Sackett, 2014), the distributions of stars are not (O'Boyle & Kroska, 2017).

Other implications are that the different traits required for a particular talent will develop across different times so that people will arrive at their talents at different ages and only when the last component of talent has matured. But as the components possessed by an individual continue to change over time, then the optimum configuration of traits so highly prized in one place and time will also change (Simonton, 1999). This suggests that talents have a lifecycle and, depending on what they are, may flourish only briefly. This explanation of talent development takes us beyond the familiar managerial rhetoric of talent shortages as the justification for finding talent.

Organizations need to keep assessing their talent base because the various components of a talent develop throughout life. Each component is a function of time and will start developing at time 1 and stop developing at time 2. Talents develop incrementally in people and may only exist for short time. Coupled with changing social constructions of talent by organizations, the shifting nature of individual talents of use to organizations provides a sound basis for their continued evaluation. With this in mind, the chapter now turns to look at ethical concerns with exclusive TM.

An Ethical Overview of Talent Management

Sector Effects

An organization's approach to TM has to be legitimate, i.e., consistent with the norms and expectations that function within a sector. However, norms and expectations differ between sectors, for example, public and private (Boyne, 2002; Buelens & Van den Broeck, 2007). The legal and political status of an organization can also be expected to have some influence (van Krieken, 2006). Although organizations are expected to comply with the ethical codes of the societies in which they operate, limited liability in particular offers executives a level of protection against various forms of unethical conduct. Where TM is implemented, then it serves the legal personality of an organization, which is given character and form by the interests of senior managers. In combination with organizational culture and sector traditions that inform political and managerial practices (Orr & Vince, 2009), the legal personality creates an "ethical space which generates its own patterns of conduct and organizational action" (van Krieken, 2006: 84) and thus determines the legitimacy of certain actions within that space.

Appreciating sector traditions provides a useful background to ethical analysis. In market economies, the market for talent follows supply and demand. Against a background narrative of talent shortages, which may be self-serving (Swailes, 2013a), profit-seeking firms will offer compensation and psychological rewards equivalent to the market worth of the talent they need. Psychological attractors may include the promise of learning and development experiences that enhance future employability. So long as firms do not reward talent beyond its market worth (its marginal product) and what talent could obtain elsewhere, then the provision of TM appears just (Boatright, 2010). But determining the appropriate level of talent development and thus the design of talent programs is difficult and requires much guesswork. It is difficult, for example, for the people running talent programs to know how much of a person's subjective performance, good or bad, is due to the individual or due to factors that they had no influence over.

The supply of talented individuals, present and future, is a function of a firm's ability to identify genuinely talented people, and this assumes they know where to look. Institutional forces (Boxenbaum & Jonsson, 2006) that push firms in the same and similar fields to mimic each other's approaches to managing people may be sources of inefficiency. Johnson (2012) put forward three moral hazards of market economies that seem relevant to TM:

- The commoditization of people such that their "humanness" is overlooked.
- Exploitation in the form of abusing employee goodwill, using people when convenient, and discarding them when their usefulness is over.
- Defining people in economic terms such that, for example, promotion, more rewarding work, or development are only offered to employees when management sees an investment return.

Exclusive TM might also be problematized if it exists largely for the benefit of shareholders (not for the benefit of participants) and if it follows a masculine philosophy that preserves power relations (Bierema, 2009).

High-Potentials as Stakeholders

Employees have a stake in the organization they work for because they are affected by its decisions and hold some level of risk in it (Greenwood & Freeman, 2011). It is worthwhile considering, therefore, whether a small group of employees deemed to have above average ability should be treated as a distinctive stakeholder sub-group. At the heart of exclusive TM is the differential treatment of employees and ethical problems may arise depending upon how differentiation occurs.

On one hand, TM extends beyond the narrow focus on economic performance and treats a corporate stakeholder group in accord with its needs for accelerated development. On the other hand, if the corporate reason for differentiating and running TM programs is motivated by improved economic performance, then we are back to the narrow profit-focused view of managers' obligations to shareholders that cuts across duty ethics (Bowie, 1999).

The Consequences of Talent Management

One difficulty with an ethical analysis of TM is that of determining with any accuracy its consequences, which surely vary from place to place. Overall, the evidence that TM contributes much to organizational performance is lacking (Collings, 2015; Collings, Mellahi, & Cascio, 2019). However, exclusive TM may unmask good future leaders and resolve some current organizational problems. It may also provide protection to senior managers who create the "rules of engagement". It is of course impossible to quantify these possibilities so they are reduced to guesswork, and there is an unknown time lag over which such effects might occur. At the organizational level, it should be possible to isolate the consequences of individual talent strategies such as negative reactions among employees who are excluded from exclusive programs (De Boeck, Meyers, & Dries, 2018; Marescaux, DeWinne, & Sels, 2013; Swailes & Blackburn, 2016), enhanced contributions by employees in talent pools (Ehrnrooth et al., 2018), and political behavior among the talented (Peteriglieri & Peteriglieri, 2017). Yet rigorous within-organization evaluation of talent programs, if it occurs, has not attracted much research attention.

It should be possible for organizations to evaluate the consequences of their talent strategies (Swailes, 2013b) particularly at the individual level, to reach decisions about the utility that is created by them and react accordingly. If, for example, an evaluation found that talent was being identified fairly, that the talented were experiencing more enriching work while simultaneously enhancing their employability and the working lives of those who work with them, then utilitarian ethics would judge the talent strategy favorably even though people excluded from the programs were disadvantaged (harmed) by not having access to the same opportunities.

Duty ethics gives greater traction to the principles used in running a particular talent strategy, for example, the principle that employees have a right to be treated equally and a right not to be harmed by the preferential treatment given to a small group deemed to be talented. If senior managers have an obligation to help employees to flourish, then running talent programs should help more employees to flourish than would otherwise occur.

A problem, however, is the binary nature of being in or out of a talent pool such that they would have to run over sufficient time to give all talented employees a chance of participating. This might involve running different talent pools for different employee groups. The idea that senior managers should act in ways that enable most of their employees to reach their potential seems fairly universal. It is hard to justify why this should not be so. But exclusive TM does not, by definition, address most employees, so it falls down on universality.

Under duty ethics, therefore, concerns about the ways that people are treated including justice take center stage, which in relation to TM would scrutinize how resources (such as learning, development budgets, and senior management attention) are distributed across a workforce (distributive justice), the processes, and management activities that lie behind a senior management decision to distribute resources in a particular way (procedural justice), and the extent and quality of the communications between employees and senior management in reaching decisions about the nature and content of a talent program (interactional justice).

Virtue ethics (Hartman, 2008; Kuchinke, 2017) with its focus on the individual and how they behave also informs an understanding of TM. Core concerns for virtue ethics are the moral character of the people running talent programs and to what extent virtues, such as integrity, honesty, and justice, are integrated into the learning and development opportunities provided such that talent pool members develop themselves on these and other dimensions. The poorer a talent program is at developing virtues relevant to the organization, the more problems virtue ethics would have with the program. There are also questions around what virtues a particular talent program should be targeting and by what processes are these identified.

Care ethics (Armitage, 2018; Schuman, 2001) focuses, in this context, on the care obligations that employers have towards their employees. It involves caring about others, taking care of them, and ensuring that the care needs of others are met. In exclusive talent programs, it could be argued that organizations are extending an ethics of care approach to what they see as a particularly valuable set of employees. However, if participation in a talent pool causes stress and derailment, then these outcomes would be troubling for care ethics.

Perhaps of greater concern would be that, in exclusive approaches, the majority workforce is not receiving any enhanced level of care. It is only when we approach something like a truly inclusive talent strategy (Swailes, Downs, & Orr, 2014) in which each employee's development needs and potential are targeted, would TM become unproblematic for care ethics. Fully inclusive talent programs are quite rare, and by definition cannot treat every employee as having high potential if talent is something that is measured in relation to others. Instead, they would be more concerned with an individual's absolute talents and not how they compare to others. Inclusive talent programs, such as they exist, would accept that some employees have low development potential and/or ambitions, but the point is that each and every employee is supported such that they have the ability to function as they would wish to, even if that means helping them to move to other roles outside the organization where their talents would be put to more rewarding use.

Talent Recognition

The subjectivity of being recognized as talented has been appreciated for some time. Mills's (1956) damning critique of what happens when executives look for next generation leaders is summarized here as it usefully sets the scene for a consideration of the ethics of talent recognition. His chapter on chief executives in *The Power Elite* tells us much about how the talented in corporate America were recognized:

> If it is to count in the corporate world, talent, no matter how defined, must be discovered by one's talented superiors. It is in the nature of the morality of corporate accomplishment that those at the top do not and cannot admire that which they do not and cannot understand. (Mills, 1956: 141)

His advice to employees with aspirations for the top is crystal clear. Only the "broadened man" will rise because specialists are not sufficiently "alerted to profit". The closer to the top one gets, the more important access to the cliques holding power and political influence becomes. To make their organizations self-perpetuating, "chief executives feel that they must perpetuate themselves or men like themselves" (139). What they look for is, of course, intangible, and they talk about sound judgement, the broadened view, and even how a person looks or would look as an executive. These attributes are far more important than technical knowledge and skills. Mills was sceptical that anything like managerial ability actually existed other than observing that, to the extent that it does exist, it consists of usefulness to those above and of knowing one's inabilities. It is about fitting in with those in power, "in personal manner and political view, in social ways and business style" and being like those who have already made it. What matters is being sound to the point of personifying the "standards of soundness" (142).

Mills would have little sympathy with the idea that talent is something that can be managed, at least not in business organizations. For sure, executives look for it and contenders are tried and tested. But for Mills what matters at the top is how one talks and what one says, spinning the decisions already made or about to be made to emphasize one's wise judgement, filling others with hope and always being what others expect you to be (see also Lever & Swailes, 2018; Peteriglieri & Peteriglieri, 2017 on this point).

If this is an accurate description of what is really happening, then how far can such social processes be managed? If it is accurate, then "talent markets" or "talent fairs" seem better tags than TM.

Performance Appraisal

Given its political overlay, it is hard to see how exclusive TM can function effectively without some form of robust evaluation of an individual's past performance and future potential. Evaluating performance and potential, however, is perhaps the most ethically problematic field in HRM. At the heart of the matter is a tension between organizations treating employees as resources and looking for ways of developing their capabilities while simultaneously surveilling (Townley, 2005), evaluating, comparing, and classifying them based on their perceived worth to the organization (Winstanley, 2000).

There is substantial evidence that performance appraisal is often flawed. Specific problems include appraiser bias (Lefkowitz, 2000), rating inflation (Fried, Levi, Ben-David, & Tiegs, 1999), impression management (Brown & Lim, 2010), and demoralization of appraisees (Belschak & Den Hartog, 2009). Furthermore, there is little evidence that appraisal has overall positive effects on individuals or organizations. Some companies are replacing traditional ratings-based appraisal with faster and more regular feedback (Simms, 2017).

Traditional appraisal also tends to focus on overcoming a person's weaknesses rather than recognizing and playing to their strengths. An employee's apparent weaknesses, however, may be relative to the particular job they are doing, so an ethical concern arises about pushing people harder in jobs they have come to struggle with. A more humanistic approach calls for greater willingness to look for ways of redeploying people to better suit their strengths, although there are of course practical constraints on how far organizations can do this, and it is much easier to seek "better" methods of appraisal.

Talent Management as a Civilizing Process

Central to exclusive TM is comparison of employees against an organization's social construction of talent, for example, being decisive, persuasive, and results-focused. These various ideals embed "conditions of worth" (Winstanley, 2000: 201). Appraisal feedback for many is fuelled by comparison to conditions of worth with positive feedback being set against and contingent upon how much a person is deemed to match the several conditions. When positive feedback only comes from conformance to conditions, which for many employees might not be a shared model of what is right and good, the person's emotions and true feelings can be suppressed (Winstanley, 2000). This danger is more acute for ambitious employees who want to compete for recognition in the talent pool (Peteriglieri & Peteriglieri, 2017). In exclusive strategies therefore, these tensions seem inevitable. Organizations are in effect saying, "we want you to develop your knowledge, skills and abilities but only against criteria that we think are important today".

If elevation to a talent pool is seen as a form of reward for above average contributions to an organization then, so long as contributions are truly greater than those of others who are excluded, then inclusion can be seen as fair and just, and consistent with distributive justice. Again, however, we are reminded of the absolute requirement for reliable assessment of individual contributions if fairness and justice are to be present. Complicating this requirement in performance appraisal is "the profoundly symbolic nature of organizational life" (van Krieken, 2006: 87). An employee's worth is largely a matter of how they are perceived by senior managers, and this is proportional to their ability to manage their own image.

This view of evaluation mirrors Eliasian accounts of seventeenth century court society (Elias, 1983), where the most prized skill was the ability to control one's emotions in order to enhance one's position. There is a parallel with exclusive TM (see Lever & Swailes, 2018), since to compete in talent pools and compete for the scarce attention of senior managers, employees have to engage in self-discipline. To be successful, the talented have to display the "correct" behavior (etiquette) and discipline themselves in the face of antipathy, disagreement, and perhaps hostility to what others are advocating. Here, TM requires the separation of one's authenticity in order to act out organizational scripts, although such behavior is not solely confined to employees in talent programs.

TM creates sets of social interdependencies as personal networks expand and the arena in which talent is displayed requires participants to regulate their conduct and coordinate their actions with the actions of others. Failure to do so compounds the uncertainty about organizational actions that talent programs help to reduce. Exclusive talent programs can be expected to exert a civilizing process (Elias, 2000; Lever & Swailes, 2018) among organizational elites brought about by the increasing social interdependence and self-constraint necessary if employees are to coordinate their actions to gain advantages. The ethical question arising here thus concerns the suppression of authenticity (Winstanley, 2000) necessary to maintain the required etiquette and to prosper in the talent pool.

Talent Program Design and Operation

A further ethical concern arises in relation to the transparency of how talent schemes are operated. At extremes, some organizations identify talented employees but do not inform them that they are on a talent list (Dries & De Gieter, 2014; Ehrnrooth et al., 2018). This seems perverse, and the reliability and fairness of the processes that lead to listing in such situations must attract suspicion, as would the fairness and distribution of resources such as senior management time and enhanced access to development opportunities. This situation suggests that the more a talent scheme is hidden from plain sight, the more ethical concerns it will produce.

Knowing that talent schemes can be associated with, although may not cause, a diminished sense of value and worth among the excluded (Swailes & Blackburn, 2016) raises important questions about how organizations should design and communicate their talent schemes to avoid harmful fallout. To minimize ethical concerns, organizations should involve employees in program design from the outset to the point of reaching some democratic agreement about what superior performance and high potential mean in the particular organizational context (Swailes, 2013b). This democratic process would take into account the purpose of the business, its corporate strategy, competitor behavior, institutional forces, and the organization's unique disposition towards the idea of differentiating among employees. With an agreed set of talent criteria in place, equality of opportunity to access development programs is critical, although given that some jobs contribute more to organizational success than others (O'Boyle & Aguinis, 2014), the nature of a person's job will be a limiting factor. Positive action to increase participation by groups that are traditionally underrepresented in talent schemes may be necessary.

Equality of opportunity and equality of outcome are different things. A worthwhile consideration applicable to selection and promotion situations (Noon, Healy, Forson, & Oikelome, 2013) is that so long as the processes of distributing talent recognition are fair, then the outcome must also be just. Manipulating a fair process to gain greater representation from a previously underrepresented group creates injustice and could disadvantage others who better match the selection criteria. A utilitarian argument in such situations would be that injustice done to some employees could be offset by gains to underrepresented groups, but both procedural and distributive justice would be compromised causing resentment among some of those who are excluded. In practice, organizations should ensure the fairness of systems while being alert to the outcomes their systems produce.

It is also important to consider the long-term effects of talent status on the talented and Daubner-Siva's (2016) detailed autoethnographic account of life in a talent pool highlights dangers for the chosen ones. In her case, the initial elation at being deemed talented was later tempered by risk of job loss due to structural changes brought about by new management priorities. Kotlyar (2013) also noted that elevation to a talent pool can be later offset by the effects of negative feedback on performance and future potential. Knowing more about becoming and staying talented is a promising area for further research.

Conclusions and Further Research

From an ethical viewpoint, there are no strong indicators that exclusive TM is unethical even though it may harm some of the individuals that it touches. Indeed, given that individual talents take time to mature, it is right that organizations should periodically look for talent over and above and regardless of the often expressed instrumental and managerial needs to link talent to competitive advantage. However, it is clear that certain approaches to TM would generate ethical concerns and most likely concerns for practice. Particular dangers that organizations must overcome include unfair and unreliable talent identification, fallout from excluded employees, and disproportionate allocation of organizational resources to the talented.

A key question is what is the nature and form of the approach to TM that is being evaluated? TM can vary widely on the percentage of employees that is included, their seniority, duration in a talent pool, the extent of development, the visibility of the talent program to others, and even the extent to which the talented know they are labeled as such. To help ensure that a particular talent strategy passes ethical scrutiny, it is necessary to evaluate its design, operation and outcomes.

This is an area ripe for greater understanding. In particular, more knowledge is needed on how organizations design and evaluate their talent strategies and on the effects of talent status awareness. It is important for future research to isolate the contrasting influences on program design (Adebola, 2018) to help unravel the true motives behind them, as this leads to a better appreciation of their virtues. From virtue ethics, if senior managers run talent programs to create conditions in which the talented can fulfill their potential and help others do the same, then the ethical possibilities are high. However, the development of others has to be a deliberate intention from the outset. If development is by chance then even if people in talent pools all realize their potential questions would still remain about the managerial motives behind the scheme and their attitudes to those who are overlooked.

Better TM evaluation therefore promises to reveal the values that underpin talent programs, for example, to identify what senior managers are really looking for, which is important if only for further ethical analysis. Also important is the legitimacy of the organization's talent strategy and how the strategy connects to competitive advantage (Bowen & Ostroff, 2004). A critical issue is whether internal and external markets for talent are efficient. If discourses of talent shortages are false and self-serving, and if talent identification processes are unreliable, then talent management in some organizations has fundamental flaws.

As well as identifying ethical concerns with the ways that TM can be approached, it is worth noting its potential to create better organizational ethics. Hatcher (2006), for instance, suggests that HRD, of which TM is a component, has more potential than other areas to promote ethical behavior since HRD specifically targets behavioral change. Mature and socially aware talent programs should expose participants to ethical dilemmas and analysis as a way of improving the ethical performance of organizations (Cardy & Selvarjan, 2006). Despite the considerable pitfalls in designing ethical TM programs, there is nothing that cannot be fixed by responsive and reflective management. Better still, good management should spot substantive ethical issues in the first place and manage them away.

Acknowledgement

I am grateful to Christopher Cowton and to Dean K. Simonton for their helpful comments during the production of this chapter.

References

Adebola, S. 2018. Why do organizations run talent programmes? Insights from UK organizations. In B. Adamsen & S. Swailes (Eds.), *Managing talent: Understanding critical perspectives:* 187-213. London: Palgrave Macmillan.

Alzola, M. 2018. Decent work: The moral status of labor in human resource management. *Journal of Business Ethics,* 147: 835–853.

Armitage, A. 2018. Is HRD in need of an ethics of care? *Human Resource Development International, 21*: 212-231.

Beck, J. W., Beatty, A. S., & Sackett, P. R. 2014. On the distribution of job performance: The role of measurement characteristics in observed departures from normality. *Personnel Psychology, 67*: 531-566.

Becker, B. E., & Huselid, M. A. 2006. Strategic human resources management: Where do we go from here? *Journal of Management, 32*: 898-925.

Belschak, F. D., & Den Hartog, D. N. 2009. Consequences of positive and negative feedback: The impact of emotions on extra-role behaviours. *Applied Psychology: An International Review, 58*: 274-303.

Bierema, L. L. 2009. Critiquing human resource development's dominant masculine rationality and evaluating its impact. *Human Resource Development Review, 8*: 68-96.

Boatright, J. R. 2010. Executive compensation: Unjust or just right. In G. G. Brenkert, & T. L. Beauchamp (Eds.), *The Oxford handbook of business ethics:* 161-201. Oxford, UK: Oxford University Press.

Bowen, D. E., & Ostroff, C. 2004. Understanding HRM-firm performance linkages: The role of the 'strength' of the HRM system, *Academy of Management Review, 29*: 203-221.

Bowie, N. 1999. *Business ethics. A Kantian perspective.* Oxford, UK: Blackwell.

Boxenbaum, E., & Jonsson, S. 2006. Isomorphism, diffusion and decoupling. In R. Greenwood, C. Oliver, K. Sahlin, & R. Suddaby (Eds.), *The SAGE handbook of organizational institutionalism:* 78-98, London: SAGE.

Boyne, G. A. 2002. Public and private management: What's the difference? *Journal of Management Studies, 39*: 97-122.

Brown, M., & Lim, V. S. (2010). Understanding performance management and appraisal: Supervisory and employee perspectives. In A. Wilkinson, N. Bacon, T. Redman, & S. Snell (Eds.), *The SAGE handbook of human resource management:* 191-209, London: SAGE.

Bruton, S. 2015. Looks-based hiring and wrongful discrimination. *Business & Society Review, 120*: 607-635.

Buelens, M., & Van den Broeck, H. 2007. An analysis of differences in work motivation between public and private sector organizations. *Public Administration Review, 67*: 65-74.

Cappelli, P., & Keller, J. R. 2017. The historical context of talent management. In D. G. Collings, K. Mellahi, & W. F. Cascio (Eds.), *The Oxford handbook of talent management:* 23-40, Oxford, UK: Oxford University Press.

Cardy, R. L., & Selvarjan, T. T. 2006. Beyond rhetoric and bureaucracy: Using HRM to add ethical value. In J. R. Deckop (Ed.), *Human resource management ethics:* 71-85. Greenwich, CT: IAP.

Collings, D. G. 2015 The contribution of talent management to organizational success. In K. Kraiger, J. Passmore, N. Rebelo dos Santos, & S. Malvezzi (Eds.), *The psychology of training, development, and performance improvement:* 247-260, Chichester: Wiley Blackwell.

Collings, D. G., Cascio, W. F., & Mellahi, K. 2017. Introduction. In D. G. Collings, K. Mellahi, & W. F. Cascio (Eds.), *The Oxford handbook of talent management:* 3-22, Oxford, UK: Oxford University Press.

Collings, D. G., & Mellahi, K. 2009. Strategic talent management: A review and research agenda. *Human Resource Management Review, 19*: 304-313.

Collings, D. G., Mellahi, K., Cascio, W. F. 2019. Global talent management and performance in multinational enterprises: A multilevel perspective. *Journal of Management, 45*: 540-566.

Daubner-Siva, D. 2016. *Dealing with dualities: A paradox perspective on the relationship between talent management and diversity management.* Amsterdam: Amsterdam Business Research Institute.

De Boeck, G., Meyers, M., & Dries, N. 2018. Employee reactions to talent management: Assumptions versus evidence. *Journal of Organizational Behavior, 39*: 199-213.

Deckop, J. R. 2006. *Human resource management ethics.* Greenwich, CT: IAP.

Dries, N., & De Gieter, S. 2014. Information asymmetry in high potential programmes: A potential risk for psychological contract breach. *Personnel Review, 43*: 136-162.

Ehrnrooth, M., Bjorkman, I., Makela, K., Smale, A., Sumelius, J., & Taimitarha, S. 2018. Talent responses to talent status awareness: Not a question of simple reciprocation. *Human Resource Management Journal, 28*: 443-461.

Elias, N. 1983. *The court society,* Oxford, UK: Basil Blackwell.

Elias, N. 2000. *The civilising process: Sociogenetic and psychogenetic investigations.* Oxford, UK: Blackwell.

Fried, Y., Levi, A., Ben-David, H., & Teigs, R. 1999. Inflation of subordinates' performance ratings: Main and interactive effects of rater negative affectivity, documentation of work behaviour and appraisal visibility. *Journal of Organizational Behavior, 20*: 431-444.

Gagne, F. 2005. From gifts to talents. The DMGT as a development model. In R. J. Sternberg, & J. E. Davidson (Eds.), *Conceptions of giftedness* (2nd ed.): 98-119, Cambridge, UK: Cambridge University Press.

Gagne, F. 2015. From genes to talent: the DMGT/CMTD perspective, *Revista de Educacion, 368*(4-6): 12-37.

Greenwood, M. 2013. Ethical analysis of HRM: A review and research agenda. *Journal of Business Ethics, 114*: 355-366.

Gelens, J., Dries, N., Hofmans, J., & Pepermans, R. 2013. The role of perceived organizational justice in shaping the outcomes of talent management: A research agenda. *Human Resource Management Review, 23*: 341-353.

Greenwood, M., & Freeman, R. E. 2011. Ethics and HRM: The contribution of stakeholder theory. *Business, & Professional Ethics,* 30: 269-292.

Hamermesh, D. S. 2011. *Beauty pays: Why attractive people are more successful.* Princeton, NJ: Princeton University Press.

Hartman, E. M. 2008. Reconciliation in business ethics: Some advice from Aristotle. *Business Ethics Quarterly,* 18: 253-265.

Hatcher, T. 2006. An examination of the potential of human resource development (HRD) to improve organizational ethics. In J. R. Deckop, *Human resource management ethics:* 87-110. Greenwich, CT: IAP.

Jack, G., Greenwood, M., & Schapper, J. 2012. Frontiers, intersections and engagements of ethics and HRM. *Journal of Business Ethics, 111:* 1-12.

Jacobs, G., Belscak, F., & Hartog, D. 2014. (Un)Ethical behaviour and performance appraisal: The role of affect, support and organizational justice. *Journal of Business Ethics,* 121: 63-76.

Johnson, C. E. 2012. *Organizational ethics: A practical approach* (2nd ed.). London: SAGE.

Kaufman, S. B. (Ed.) 2013. The complexity of greatness. *Beyond talent or practice.* Oxford, UK: Oxford University Press.

Kotlyar, I. (2013). The double edge sword of 'high potential' expectations. *Europe's Journal of Psychology,* 9: 581-596.

Kuckinke, K. P. 2017. The ethics of HRD practice. *Human Resource Development International,* 20: 361-370.

Lefkowitz, J. 2000. The role of interpersonal affective regard in supervisory performance ratings: A literature review and proposed causal model. *Journal of Occupational and Organizational Psychology,* 73: 67-85.

Legge, K. 1998. Is HRM ethical? Can HRM be ethical? In M. Parker (Ed.) *Ethics & organizations:* 150-172, London: Sage.

Lever, J., & Swailes, S. 2018. Paralysing rebellion: Figurations, celebrity and power in elite talent management. In B. Adamsen, & S. Swailes (Eds.), *Managing talent: Understanding critical perspectives:* 35-51, London: Palgrave Macmillan.

Marescaux, E., DeWinne, S., & Sels, L. 2013. HR practices and affective organizational commitment: (When) does HR differentiation pay off? *Human Resource Management Journal,* 23: 329-345.

Mills, C.W. 1956 [2000]. *The Power Elite.* Oxford, UK: Oxford University Press.

Moriarty, J. 2009. How much compensation can CEOs permissibly accept? *Business Ethics Quarterly, 19:* 235-250.

Moriarty, J. 2012. Justice in compensation: A defense. *Business Ethics: A European Review,* 21: 64-76.

Morris, S. S., & Snell, S. A. 2010. The evolution of HR strategy: Adaptations of increasing global complexity. In A. Wilkinson, N. Bacon, T. Redman, & S. Snell (Eds), *The SAGE handbook of human resource management:* 84-99, London: SAGE.

Noon, M., Healy, G., Forson, C., & Oikelome, F. 2013. The equality effects of the 'hyper-formalization' of selection. *British Journal of Management, 24:* 333-346.

O'Boyle, E., & Aguinis, H. 2012. The best and the rest: Revisiting the norm of normality of individual performance. *Personnel Psychology,* 65: 79-119.

O'Boyle, E., & Kroska, S. 2017. Star performers. In D. G. Collings, K. Mellahi, & W.F. Cascio (Eds.), *The Oxford handbook of talent management:* 43-65, Oxford: Oxford University Press.

O'Connor, E., & Crowley-Henry, M. 2019. Exploring the relationship between exclusive talent management, perceived organizational justice and employee engagement: Bridging the literature. *Journal of Business Ethics,* 156: 903-917.

Orr, K., & Vince, R. 2009. Traditions of local government. *Public Administration,* 87: 655-677.

Painter-Morland, M., Kirk, S., Deslandes, G., & Tansley, C. 2019. Talent management: The good, the bad and the possible. *European Management Review,* 16: 135-146.

Peteriglieri, J., & Peteriglieri, G. 2017. The talent curse. *Harvard Business Review,* 95(3), 88-94.

Provis, C. 2010. Ethics and HRM. In A. Wilkinson, N. Bacon, T. Redman, & S. Snell (Eds.), *The SAGE handbook of human resource management:* 475-489, London: SAGE.

Schoon, I. 2000. A life span approach to talent development. In K. A. Heller, F. J. Moncks, R. J. Sternberg, & R. F. Sabotnik (Eds.), *International handbook of giftedness and talent* (2nd ed.): 213-225. Oxford, UK: Elsevier.

Schumann, P. L. 2001. A moral principles framework for human resource management ethics. *Human Resource Management Review,* 11: 93-112.

Simms, J. 2017. Appraisal...12 months, *People Management,* 6: 44-48.

Simonton D. K. 1999. Talent and its development: An emergenic and epigenetic model. *Psychological Review,* 106: 435-457.

Simonton, D. K. 2001. Talent development as a multidimensional, multiplicative, and dynamic process. *Current Directions in Psychological Science,* 10: 39-43.

Simonton, D. K. 2005. Genetics of giftedness: The implications of an Emergenic-Epigenetic model. In R. J. Sternberg, & J. E. Davidson (Eds.), *Conceptions of giftedness* (2nd ed.): 312-326. Cambridge, UK: Cambridge University Press.

Swailes, S. 2013a. Troubling some assumptions: A response to "The perceived role of organizational justice in shaping the outcomes of talent management: A research agenda." *Human Resource Management Review,* 23: 354-356.

Swailes, S. 2013b. The ethics of talent management. *Business Ethics: A European Review,* 22: 32-46.

Swailes, S. 2016. The cultural evolution of talent management: A memetic analysis. *Human Resource Development Review, 15:* 340-358.

Swailes, S., & Blackburn, M. 2016. Employee reactions to talent pool membership. *Employee Relations,* 38: 112-128.

Swailes, S., Downs, Y., & Orr, K. 2014. Inclusive talent management: Potential, possibilities and practicalities. *Human Resource Development International,* 17: 529-544.

Townley, B. 2005. Performance appraisal and the emergence of management. In C. Grey, & H. Willmott (Eds.), *Critical management studies: A reader:* 304-323, Oxford, UK: Oxford University Press.

Trost, G. (2000). Prediction of excellence in school, higher education and work. In K. A. Heller, F. J. Moncks, R. J. Sternberg, & R. F. Sabotnik (Eds.), *International handbook of giftedness and talent* (2nd ed): 317-327. Oxford, UK: Elsevier.

Van Buren, H., Greenwood, M., & Sheehan, C. 2011. Strategic human resource management and the decline of the employee focus. *Human Resource Management Review,* 21: 209-219.

Van Krieken, R. 2006. The ethics of corporate legal personality. In S. R. Clegg, & C. Rhodes (Eds.), *Management ethics: Contemporary contexts:* 77-96, London: Routledge.

Winstanley, D. 2000. Conditions of worth and the performance management paradox. In D. Winstanley, & J. Woodall (Eds.), *Ethical issues in contemporary human resource management:* 189-207. Basingstoke: Macmillan.

23

TALENT MANAGEMENT AND THE COMMUNICATION OF TALENT STATUS

Jennie Sumelius

Adam Smale

Introduction

An important goal of "exclusive" talent management (TM) is to commit and retain a key group of employees by acknowledging them as being essential to the future performance of the organization (Iles, Chuai, & Preece, 2010). However, communicating talent status to employees can be a sensitive and complicated matter, which, if not carried out effectively, can have unintended consequences (Dries & De Gieter, 2014; Silzer & Church, 2009). This is evident in the existing TM literature that has identified both positive (e.g., Björkman, Ehrnrooth, Mäkelä, Smale, & Sumelius, 2013) and negative (e.g., Gelens, Dries, Hofmans, & Pepermans, 2013; Ehrnrooth, Björkman, Mäkelä, Smale, Sumelius, & Taimitarha, 2018) effects of employee awareness of their talent status. Thus, talent communication can be said to play a key role in TM strategy implementation.

While some organizations pride themselves on the openness and transparency of their communication about talent, other organizations are described as adopting a "strategic ambiguity" in their approach to communication, characterized by vagueness and secrecy (Dries et al., 2014). One explanation for the latter approach is that since an exclusive approach to talent management requires the differential treatment of employees (Gelens et al., 2013), organizations are concerned that transparency in communication will result in negative attitudes and behaviors both among those who have been identified as talent and those who have not. For employees who are not identified as high-potentials ("B" players[1]) this might include feelings of envy, decreased commitment, and turnover intentions, whereas for the "talent", the fear is that they become complacent, self-satisfied, and develop unrealistic expectations about their future (Dries & De Gieter, 2014).

In this chapter, we review selected literature on talent status communication from the individual employee perspective, which is a small but rapidly emerging area within TM research (McDonnell et al., 2017). Communication about talent status has not been problematized in the TM literature, but research suggests that it can be a sensitive and complex issue capable of influencing the reactions of those identified and not identified as talent. To structure the review, we discuss issues relating to talent communication in connection with two broad approaches: 1) open TM communication, which follows the philosophy that no promotion is permanent and employees must keep competing with others to maintain their status (for more on this see Pucik, Evans, Björkman, & Morris, 2017, chapter 7); and 2) strategic ambiguity in TM communication, whereby firms for strategic reasons maintain a certain level of ambiguity in their communication about talent status to employees (Dries & Pepermans, 2008; Gelens et al., 2013). The underlying assumption behind this intentional ambiguity is that the costs and benefits of not communicating talent status outweigh those of open

DOI: 10.4324/9781315474687-23

communication. This is because it allows for the existence of multiple interpretations by employees as to who possesses talent status (Dries & De Gieter, 2014). The chapter concludes with a suggested agenda for future research that sits at the intersection between communication, talent status, and employee reactions.

Approaches to Talent Communication

Corporate TM tends to be either inclusive, in that all employees are considered talent, or exclusive, in which only a certain small group of employees (e.g., the top 5%) are viewed as talent (Gallardo-Gallardo, Dries, & Cruz, 2013). While the rationale for inclusive TM tends to be that people are the key resource in expert, knowledge-intensive, white-collar work, the question this poses is how TM then differs from human resource management (HRM) (Lewis & Heckman, 2006). It has been widely argued in previous TM literature that the main difference between HRM and TM is precisely the concept of workforce differentiation (Chuai, Preece, & Iles, 2008; Iles et al., 2010), and the exclusive approach to TM is by many considered the most common in organizations (Collings & Mellahi, 2009).

In this chapter, we adopt the following definition of TM: "the differential management of employees according to their relative potential to contribute to an organization's competitive advantage" (Gelens et al., 2013: 342). The central purpose of exclusive TM is to retain, motivate, and increase commitment levels among key employees by providing them with enhanced and differentiated development opportunities within the organization. From a communication point of view, exclusive TM is also where the majority of interesting questions lie.

In practice, organizations are faced with essentially three options of communication, each with its own advantages and disadvantages: inform all employees (talent and non-talent); inform only those identified as talent; or inform neither. In addition to this, difficult questions organizations must face include: How to approach the management of meaning around the term "talent" or "high-potential" across the organization? What are the intended messages (now and looking forward)? How to communicate the desired balance between exclusivity and inclusivity? How to raise expectations of talented employees about their future without making them complacent or creating false promises? We discuss some of these issues and review the extant research in connection with two commonly adopted approaches to talent communication.

Open TM Communication

One approach available to organizations is to communicate openly about talent status throughout the organization to all employees. This kind of approach has been popularized by the likes of General Electric and its "Session C" (Bartlett & McClean, 2006) – an annual people review in which managers' performance and career development opportunities are openly discussed and evaluated. Appliance manufacturer Haier is another example that adopts a so-called "racetrack" model based around transparency and fairness (Pucik et al., 2017). In essence, this means that employees have the possibility to demonstrate their capabilities in ongoing, internal races in which they all continuously need to prove their own capabilities in order to maintain rewards and earn promotions. This then triggers new races that need to be won, since no position or reward is guaranteed to last if performance levels drop.

One advantage with this approach of explicitly communicating talent status is the positive, motivational message it sends to employees identified as talent. Some empirical TM research testifies to this effect, showing that employees who believe they have been identified as talent are more likely to exhibit a range of positive behavioral and attitudinal outcomes, such as increased work motivation and commitment (Collings & Mellahi, 2009), more positive views about their future prospects (Swailes & Blackburn, 2016), affective commitment (Gelens, Dries, Hofmans, & Pepermans, 2015), increased willingness to take on demanding work and build valuable competencies, support company strategic priorities, identify with the organization, and reduced intentions to quit (Björkman et al., 2013).

Based on tournament logic (e.g., Claussen et al., 2014; Rosenbaum, 1979), another advantage of an open, racetrack approach is that while it is competitive and exclusive, individuals may perceive a merit-based system as fair. This resonates with previous research on organizational justice and TM, which posits that employees, both talent and B players, are likely to be more accepting of less positive outcomes if they believe that the decision-making process has been fair (Gelens et al., 2013; Slan-Jerusalim & Hausdorf, 2007). Furthermore, B players are more likely to believe that they too can become talent in the future if they perceive there to be a fair talent system in place. This motivates them to continue working towards that goal by exhibiting positive rather than negative attitudes and behaviors. Support for this can be found in work that shows the positive effects of transparent organizational communication on employee perceptions of organizational reputation (Men, 2014), employee trust (Rawlins, 2008), and engagement (Men & Hung-Baesecke, 2015).

Communication Challenges

The main communication challenges of open TM systems relate to the consistent clarification of the "rules of the race" on the one hand, and the effective management of key tensions on the other. In terms of the "rules", transparency requires the organization to send strong and consistent signals about the meaning of talent so that employees are able to develop shared interpretations. Particularly important are shared interpretations about fairness since the vast majority of employees targeted in this communication will not be part of the organization's talent pool. At the very least this will require effective communication about the criteria for talent pool inclusion and how decisions about talent pool inclusion are made – both talent and B players need to understand what is expected of them.

Much of this communication will rest on effective implementation, and especially the ability of individual line managers across the organization to apply the rules consistently, and justify their decisions in line with intended corporate goals and cultural values (Stahl et al., 2012). This may be difficult to achieve in practice, especially in large multinationals where employees' have diverse views on the quality of their performance appraisals (e.g., Sumelius et al., 2014) that commonly constitute the main source of input into talent decisions. Open TM communication not only shines the spotlight on talent, but also on other actors involved in the talent processes, line managers in particular (Dries & De Gieter, 2014).

In terms of key tensions, it is important to strike the right balance between exclusivity and inclusivity in open TM systems. While this can be said of any exclusive TM system, it is especially important in open TM systems since the distinction is an integral part of the system's purpose and design. The communication challenge rests in how to bestow exclusive, motivation-enhancing talent status on those identified as talent so that they feel like members of a valued in-group, while simultaneously communicating messages of inclusivity to the B players who comprise the backbone of the organization (Malik & Singh, 2014; Marescaux, De Winne, & Sels, 2013). Some organizations like Haier try to achieve this by communicating the tenets of the racetrack model whereby exclusivity today (talent pool exclusion) may turn into inclusivity tomorrow (talent pool inclusion) should the employee's performance level increase sufficiently. Being told that talent can also "fall out" of talent pools is designed to communicate to B players that exclusion may only be short term and future talent pool inclusion is still partly in their own hands.

A related tension is how to manage communication about what talent pool members can expect in terms of exclusive treatment such as "talent only" training and development opportunities. For the motivating effects of open talent identification to work, talent pool membership needs to come across as enticing (worth achieving as well as defending). Part of this feeling derives from "selling" the value of this higher status. However, there are likely to be limits, strategically and legally, to how openly organizations should articulate these differences – feelings of inclusivity will be a lot harder to sustain if the perceived gap between the talent and non-talent grow too large.

From a psychological contract perspective (Rousseau, 1995), organizations and line managers also need to avoid communicating in ways that raise talents' expectations beyond what they are committed and able to deliver. The role of communication is central for making explicit the terms of exchange, and allow both talent and B players to make sense of what King (2016) refers to as the "talent deal". This is by no means straightforward, especially since talent identification can be construed as more of a curse (e.g., being in the spotlight) than a blessing (Petriglieri & Petriglieri, 2017), depending on what it entails for talent in terms of work effort versus perceived benefits.

Strategic Ambiguity in TM Communication

Defined as deliberate attempts to maintain a degree of information asymmetry between insiders who possess useful information and those who do not (Eisenberg, 1984), strategic ambiguity in communication about talent status from an organizational point of view may be advantageous since it allows for multiple interpretations of messages. This may allow unconfirmed assumptions to persist.

For talent, strategic ambiguity can come in the form of being labeled talent, but receiving little or no communication about the implications of possessing this status in terms of development opportunities and workload. This allows the organization to avoid making unrealistic promises, and may help to address fears that talents' expectations become too high. Or, this could include not communicating openly about talent pool criteria and who else has been identified. This might allow the organization to escape the kind of scrutiny that befalls open and transparent TM systems, which may help to maintain an appearance of fairness and a merit-based focus. For non-talent, strategic ambiguity might create conditions in which employees believe that they are talent even though they might in fact not be. This may result in a situation where both the organization and individual enjoy the benefits that come with this false perception in terms of work motivation and commitment (Collings & Mellahi, 2009).

Exclusive TM systems that adopt an effective open communication approach are likely to struggle to avoid generating negative feelings among those not identified as talent. Among this group of B players, research attests to the likely existence of disappointment, resentment, disengagement (Silzer & Church, 2009), decreased motivation and performance (Gelens et al., 2013; Nijs, Gallardo-Gallardo, Dries, & Sels, 2014), and jealousy and frustration (Dries & De Gieter, 2014, Malik & Singh, 2014). From an organizational point of view, this raises the question of whether only communicating about talent status to those identified as talent would in fact be the best approach.

The answer to this question is not straightforward, evidenced by empirical findings (Dries & De Gieter, 2014; Ehrnrooth et al., 2018; Sumelius, Smale, & Yamao, 2019) that indicate that those *identified as talent* can react adversely to finding out about their talent status. For instance, studies have found that talents' self-awareness about their special status can lead to feelings of complacency, self-satisfaction, arrogance, and increased expectations towards the organization in terms of development opportunities (Dries & De Gieter, 2014; Malik & Singh, 2014). This, coupled with the potentially negative reactions and behaviors of the larger group of B players, might reasonably lead organizations not to communicate about talent status to either talent or B players.

The above mentioned considerations have led some companies – more than many might think, in our view – to adopt an approach to talent status communication characterized by strategic ambiguity. For example, many Finnish multinationals, such as engineering company KONE, have formal TM systems but do not formally communicate about talent status to anyone (Smale, Björkman, & Saarinen, 2015). However, considering that the central tenet of exclusive TM is to signal to key employees that their work effort is valued and that they are important for the future success of the organization, some form of communication to key employees seems essential in order to reap the benefits of TM. Otherwise, one could question the decision to implement an exclusive approach to TM in the organization in the first place. If an organization identifies talent but does not communicate this to the talent in question, we would argue that the organization is more accurately described as engaging in succession planning rather than TM.

Communication Challenges

The communication challenges in organizations that employ a strategic ambiguity approach to their communication about talent are different from the challenges associated with the open approach. The challenges with strategic ambiguity mostly revolve around determining the optimal degree of information asymmetry for each element of the TM system, and then managing communication to preserve this asymmetry in ways that help the organization to achieve its TM goals. This also involves addressing certain tensions, but the tensions are again different in nature.

As discussed above, ambiguity can be introduced into a variety of different elements of an organization's TM system: withholding information about who and who else has been identified, what the exact talent pool criteria are, how long talent status lasts, what forms of differential treatment one can expect, among others. Each element requires the organization to think about the advantages and disadvantages (for both talent and non-talent) of introducing ambiguity in communication. As the empirical research we have reviewed suggests (see Table 23.1), forecasting employee reactions to talent communication is already likely to be difficult, let alone under conditions of purposeful ambiguity.

In terms of tensions, a communication approach that builds on strategic ambiguity relies on managers being able to comply with a corporate policy of vagueness and secrecy while at the same time providing signals, or "answers", about how individuals should interpret and react to the lack of full information (Björkman et al., 2013). This will require a delicate balance between verbal and non-verbal cues, but especially the non-verbal, which may include performance appraisal ratings, invitations to "special" programs or selection for assignments. This might extend to the more controversial area of non-communication that includes a range of communication tactics ranging from keeping quiet and claiming ignorance (see e.g., Connelly et al., 2012 regarding knowledge hiding), to misinformation and white lies.

Another tension lies in how much attention organizations and managers should direct towards formal versus informal communication. In the absence of formal communication, employees will naturally turn to more informal channels of communication in the search for answers to important questions. In light of the political nature of organizations, this information search is likely to occur via internal "grapevine activity" (Dries & De Gieter, 2014; Sumelius et al., 2019) and to be fueled by rumors. While the outcomes of these informal information seeking processes might be positive and support a strategic ambiguity approach, they may also be harmful to both employee and organization. For example, a rumor that an employee has been identified as talent based purely on being a personal friend of the boss – whether truthful or not – is unlikely to benefit either party, neither in terms of the conclusions others may draw about them as individuals, nor the TM system as a whole.

Table 23.1 Summary of selected empirical studies on employee reactions to talent identification

Study	Method & Sample	Attitudes & Behaviors of Talent	Attitudes & Behaviors of B Players
Dries & Pepermans (2007) *"Real" high-potential careers: An empirical study into the perspectives of organisations and high-potentials*	• 14 high-potentials in six organizations (plus data from 20 organizational representatives, in seven additional organizations) in Belgium • Talent aware of their status • Qualitative interview study	• Expected upward career moves • Intended to remain in the organization • Viewed their own assertiveness as key for their success • Unclarity/ambiguity about organization's intention with TM: Talent development opportunities a way to "monitor for failure" and test employees in disguise	Not included in study
Slan-Jerusalim & Hausdorf (2007) *Managers' justice perceptions of high-potential identification practices*	• 123 employees in 76 companies in Canada, both talent and 'B' players • Talent aware of their status • Quantitative study	• Manager input, open communication, and formal program evaluation contributed to higher perceptions of procedural justice (for both talent and B players) • Having been identified as talent did not result in higher perceived distributive justice	
Björkman et al. (2013) *Talent or not? Employee reactions to talent identification*	• 767 employees in nine Nordic MNCs • Self-perceptions of talent status (yes, no, don't know) • Quantitative study	• Self-perceived talent are more likely than others to commit to increasing performance demands, developing skills valuable to the company, supporting strategic firm priorities, identifying with their subsidiary • Employees who think they are talent have lower turnover intentions than those who think they are not talent/do not know	• No significant differences between self-perceived B players and employees who did not know their talent status • Employees who did not know their status equally likely to leave the company as those who know they have been identified as talent
Dries & De Gieter (2014) *Information asymmetry in high-potential programs: A potential risk for psychological contract breach*	• 20 talent from nine organizations in Belgium (also 11 HR directors) • Talent all aware of their special status • Qualitative interview study	• Expect special organizational support in achieving career goals and guidance, development opportunities, special projects, and adequate rewards • Intend to remain in the organization provided their expectations are met • Ambiguity about implications of talent status	Not included in study
Sonnenberg et al. (2014) *The role of talent-perception incongruence in effective talent management*	• 2660 employees (88% Dutch) in 21 European organizations • Talent and B players • Quantitative survey	• If talent are unaware that they have a special status, they may not participate in the talent activities intended for them	• If B players perceive themselves to be talent, they may mistakenly interpret TM practices as being intended for them, which may result in disappointment and resentment

Reference	Data / Methodology	Findings	
Gelens et al. (2015) *Affective commitment of employees designated as talent: Signalling perceived organisational support*	• Study 1: 203 employees in one company in Belgium, both talent and B players • Study 2: 195 employees, in one company in Belgium: some management trainees, some not • Archival data: Everyone aware of their (non) status • Quantitative studies	• Talent (and management trainees) felt greater perceived organizational support compared to B players, which in turn triggered affective commitment • Affective commitment of talent (but not trainees) higher than that of B players • No significant direct relationship between talent/designation as trainee and affective commitment	
Swailes & Blackburn (2016) *Employee reactions to talent pool membership*	• Matched samples of employees (talent and B players) in one case company operating in Northern Europe • 17 interviews with talent and 17 with B players • Quantitative and qualitative data (open-ended questions and questions answered on a Likert scale)	Talent more positive regarding: • Quality of support from line managers • Access to talent pools (bias free and well balanced) • Overall development opportunities • Access to work-based skill development • Knowledge and skill development during the past year • Company commitment to their future career • Career development in the company	• B players perceived lower support from the organization, stronger feelings of unfairness, lower expectations of interest in them from the organization
Ehrnrooth, Björkman, Mäkelä, Smale, Sumelius, & Taimitarha (2018) *Talent responses to talent status awareness- not a question of simple reciprocation*	• Quantitative survey data • 321 employees in eight Finnish organizations • Talents (formally identified), some aware of their status and others not	• Awareness of one's status as talent makes individuals more sensitive regarding what they are offered by the company • Self-aware talents respond more strongly to psychological contract fulfilment and leadership development practices; target setting and evaluative feedback are less effective as a management tool	• Not included in study
Sumelius, Smale, & Yamao (2019) *Mixed signals: Employee reactions to talent status communication amidst strategic ambiguity*	• Qualitative interview data • 24 interviews with talents and B players • Aware of their talent status (self-reported)	Immediate reactions: • Pride and happiness • Increased self-esteem • Sense of achievement Long-term sense-making: • Increased motivation and commitment • Pressure and stress	Immediate reactions: • Disappointment and resentment • Indifference Long-term sense-making: • Dis-identification • Cognitive dissonance

Towards A Future Research Agenda

TM research examining the experiences and reactions of individual employees is emerging yet scarce (McDonnell et al., 2017). One of the explanations provided for the mixed findings we have reviewed regarding employee reactions (talent and non-talent) concerns the role of communication. However, there remains fairly little empirical work that explicitly investigates TM from a communication perspective and how this might help us understand employee interpretations and responses to messages they receive from various kinds of TM systems. In this section, we map out an agenda for future research that illustrates how a communication perspective can help to shed more light on how and why individual employees – both talent and B players – react in different ways.

Communication and the TM Process

In terms of theory, one obvious starting point would be to draw on TM's parent field of HRM and recent developments in HRM process theorization. Building on signaling theory (Guzzo & Noonan, 1994; Suazo, Martínez, & Sandoval, 2009), the HRM process approach assigns a central role to how organizations and managers communicate about HRM, which sends signals to employees about what is expected, valued, and rewarded (Bowen & Ostroff, 2004). Malik and Singh's (2014) conceptual framework extends the HRM process meta-features (visibility, understandability, legitimacy of authority, relevance, instrumentality, validity, consistency, consensus, and fairness) to outline ways in which individuals' perceptions may differ about high-potential programs.

Based on HR attribution theory (Nishii, Lepak, & Schneider, 2008), the framework goes on to argue that talent and B player perceptions of these features will influence the kinds of attributions they make about the programs, which will in turn affect their commitment and organizational citizenship behaviors. While the issue of fairness has already attracted some empirical attention (Slan-Jerusalim & Hausdorf, 2007), most of the other features in Malik and Singh's (2014) framework remain unexamined. From a communication perspective, we would suggest that employee perceptions of *visibility* (explicit and implicit information sharing about workforce segmentation), *consistency* (talent being managed through a consistent and differentiated HR architecture), and *consensus* (agreement among senior level management about the significance of top talent) are among the most interesting for future study.

Communication Actors and the "Talent Deal"

Perhaps the most common theoretical approach to studying individual reactions to TM is social exchange theory and the psychological contract perspective (e.g., Björkman et al., 2013; Festing & Schäfer, 2014; King, 2016). One way to extend this is to build on the idea that line managers – as the key link between TM strategy and employee reactions – are the main psychological contract brokers (McDermott et al., 2014). Future research could thus examine the role line managers play in communication about talent and how this influences employee views about their own obligations and those of their employer/manager.

As outlined in our review above, managers are likely to face complex and quite different challenges depending on the kind of communication approach adopted by the organization (e.g., how to achieve a balance between exclusivity and inclusivity in their communication with subordinates, how to use verbal and non-verbal cues in the context of strategic ambiguity). How managers perceive and handle these challenges merits further research, since the way in which news is communicated to employees is likely to weigh heavily on their perceptions of for instance fairness, especially in cases where the outcome is unfavorable for them (Patient & Skarlicki, 2010).

In line with the multi-actor model by King (2015), this could extend to different "communication actors" including top management and HR managers. For instance, we know a lot more about manager-employee communication and psychological reactions of employees within the context of the performance appraisal, but we know very little about the communication that takes place concerning talent status (Ehrnrooth et al., 2015). Our review of the literature also reveals that we know little about the talent communication processes that take place among top management, for example where the CEO, senior managers, and corporate HR in corporate talent review sessions present and jointly assess potential talent pool candidates.

Communicating Talent Status across Cultures

While open, candid, and transparent TM communication is evident in organizations from a range of different countries, there remains a clear cultural, Anglo-Saxon bias in this approach to communication and to TM research overall (Thunnissen, Boselie, & Fruytier, 2013; Gallardo-Gallardo & Thunnissen, 2016). Empirical TM research now covers an ever-growing number of developed and developing country contexts (Cooke, Saini, & Wang, 2014; Iles, Chuai, & Preece, 2010; Tymon, Stumpf, & Doh, 2010), but the individual employee perspective and issues concerning cross-cultural TM communication within these different contexts remains largely ignored (Dries, 2013).

We believe that there are interesting questions around the topic of communication, some of which require a greater problematization of communication than has thus far been the case. For instance, while there are many meanings behind the term "talent" (Gallardo-Gallardo et al., 2013; Tansley, 2011), do terms such as "talent" and "high-potential" possess a high level of cross-cultural equivalence? Do the meanings change when translated into the local language? How effective are open and strategic ambiguity approaches to TM communication in cultures that utilize high-context versus low-context communication, or in egalitarian versus non-egalitarian societies? While cases such as Haier suggest that open and transparent TM communication has succeeded despite the Chinese cultural tendency to save face (Pucik et al., 2017), these are often anecdotal accounts. How well this works in practice from the managers and employees view, and how easy it is to transfer a TM communication strategy from one country context to another remains unexplored.

Legal and Ethical Perspectives on Talent Status Communication

Communication about talent status also raises interesting legal and ethical issues. From a legal perspective, the laws (e.g., Data Protection and Data Privacy) regulating what kinds of information organizations can hold about employees, who this can be shared with and how, and the rights that employees have to access this information varies from country to country. The general tightening of this legislation, for instance in Europe, may lead to situations where employees have the right to see whether they have been included in a talent pool and the evaluation this was based on. In organizations employing strategic ambiguity, this may force them to "come clean" or to simply hold less information to preserve asymmetry. Whether such legal developments result in more or less transparency, and how this influences TM communication differentially in different legal settings will be an interesting future line of enquiry.

From an ethical standpoint, Swailes (2013) highlights some of the ethical concerns that are associated with the creation and treatment of a managerial elite. Some of the resulting ethics-related questions for organizations he presents as an ethical guide are essentially questions that need to be resolved via effective communication: Why is an elitist talent program needed and how is this articulated to all? To what extent do the organization's views of talent embody virtue and eliminate gender bias? How will employees not in the program feel about being excluded?

In terms of strategic ambiguity, keeping employees in the dark about talent pool criteria and their talent status, their future career could also be seen as unethical (Pucik et al., 2017), especially if, to enforce this managers are required to ignore, mislead, or lie to employees. How organizations and managers deal with such ethical dilemmas in communication, and how employees in different country and organizational contexts view the ethical dimension of exclusive TM, may also help to shed light on the reactions of employees.

Talent Status Communication: Event or Process?

Much of the conceptual and empirical work on employee reactions to talent status is silent on how employees came to find out about their status, what their views of themselves were before they found out, and how the effects of knowing unfolded over time. An important overarching question in this regard is whether organizational communication and self-awareness of being a talent or not should be conceptualized as an event or a journey (King, 2016).

In terms of how employees find out, one can imagine that whether one receives this information from the CEO in their office, via a standardized email from HR, or via a rumor from a colleague, it very likely will make a difference to how one reacts – at least in the short term. Situational factors surrounding how an employee finds out (e.g., the credibility of the source, whether you perceive to be the first or last to know, whether there is a personal touch or the opportunity to ask questions), are likely to send signals about the value of talent status in addition to the status itself.

A related question that is particularly pertinent for strategic ambiguity is whether the differences in reactions between talent and non-talent are partly driven by them finding out about talent status in different ways. It may be the case, for example, that talent are informed directly about their status, but non-talent have to work this out for themselves via inference and arduous information seeking activities. We suggest that this kind of information be included in future studies, and that particular emphasis is placed on the under-researched experiences of B players (Delong & Vijayaraghavan, 2003; Malik & Singh, 2014).

Without knowing how talent or B players viewed themselves, their employer, and their psychological contract before becoming aware of their talent status, it is problematic to talk about reactions or to draw conclusions about how status has affected one individual or group compared to another. Some Finnish HR directors we have spoken to about strategic ambiguity during our own research (Björkman et al., 2013) are quick to point out that talent "already know", alluding to the fact that in some instances (e.g., sales positions), high-performance can be self-evident and reinforced by praise and positive performance evaluations. For these individuals, talent identification might be more confirmation than revelation. Psychologically, however, this is likely to have a far smaller impact on their attitudes and behaviors compared to those for whom talent status comes as a positive or negative surprise.

When studying the effects of talent status communication, future research might also benefit from making a distinction between short-term reactions where communication is viewed as an event, and longer-term sensemaking where communication is part of a continuous process of self and other evaluation and re-evaluation. Many existing studies in TM suffer from cross-sectional designs and/or a lack of information about when individuals came to be aware of their status. Few studies track the movements of talent and non-talent to ask about the extent to which TM and its communication was a significant factor in why they left their previous organization.

We know quite little about how individuals make sense of their status over time, the kinds of cognitive and psychological processes they experience (e.g., cognitive dissonance, social identification) (see e.g., Dries, 2013), and the kinds of long-term outcomes that result (stress, anxiety, career success, voluntary turnover, promotion). Longitudinal research designs that follow the intertwined processes of discovering, reacting to, and making sense of talent communication are thus sorely needed. Some of the work on the dynamics of star status gain and loss may be useful in this regard (Bothner, Kim, & Smith, 2012).

Note

1 In line with Malik and Singh (2014) we use the term 'B' players when referring to employees not included in the talent pool and avoid using terms such as non-talent or non-high-potential employees because of their potential negative connotations.

References

Bartlett, C. A. & McLean, A. N. 2006. *GE's talent machine: The making of a CEO,* (Harvard Business School Case no. 9-304-049). Boston, MA: Harvard Business School Publishing.

Björkman, I., Ehrnrooth, M., Mäkelä, K., Smale, A. & Sumelius, J. 2013. Talent or not? Employee reactions to talent identification. *Human Resource Management,* 52: 195–214.

Bothner, M. S., Kim, Y-K. & Smith, E. B. 2012. How does status affect performance? Status as an asset vs. status as a liability in the PGA and NASCAR. *Organization Science,* 23: 2, 416–433.

Bowen, D., & Ostroff, C. 2004. Understanding HRM-firm performance linkages: The role of the "strength" of the HRM system. *Academy of Management Review,* 29: 204–221.

Chuai, X., Preece, D., & Iles, P. 2008. Is talent management just "old wine in new bottles"? The case of multinational companies in Beijing. *Management Research News,* 31(12): 901–911.

Claussen, J., Grohsjean, T., Luger, J., & Probst, G. 2014. Talent management and career development: What it takes to get promoted. *Journal of World Business,* 49(2): 236–244.

Collings, D. G., & Mellahi, K. 2009. Strategic talent management: A review and research agenda. *Human Resource Management Review,* 19(4): 304–313.

Connelly, C. E., Zweig, D., Webster, J., & Trougakos, J. P. 2012. Knowledge hiding in organizations. *Journal of Organizational Behavior,* 33(1): 64–88.

Cooke, F. L., Saini, D. S., & Wang, J. 2014. Talent management in China and India: A comparison of management perceptions and human resource practices. *Journal of World Business,* 49(2): 225–235.

Delong, T. J., & Vijayaraghavan, V. 2003. Let's hear it for B players. *Harvard Business Review,* 81(6): 96–103.

Dries, N. 2013. The psychology of talent management: A review and research agenda. *Human Resource Management Review,* 23(4): 272–285.

Dries, N. & De Gieter, S. 2014. Information asymmetry in high potential programs: A potential risk for psychological contract breach. *Personnel Review,* 43:1, 136–162.

Dries, N., Forrier, A., De Vos, A., & Pepermans, R. 2014. Self-perceived employability, organization-rated potential, and the psychological contract. *Journal of Managerial Psychology,* 29(5): 565–581.

Ehrnrooth, M., Björkman, I., Mäkelä, K., Smale, A., Sumelius, J., & Taimitarha, S. 2018. Talent responses to talent status awareness—Not a question of simple reciprocation. *Human Resource Management Journal,* 28(3): 443–461.

Eisenberg, E. M. 1984. Ambiguity as strategy in organizational communication. *Communication Monographs,* 51(3): 227–242.

Festing, M., & Schäfer, L. 2014. Generational challenges to talent management: A framework for talent retention based on the psychological-contract perspective. *Journal of World Business,* 49(2): 262–271.

Gallardo-Gallardo, E., Dries, N., & González-Cruz, T. F. 2013. What is the meaning of 'talent' in the world of work? *Human Resource Management Review,* 23(4): 290–300.

Gallardo-Gallardo, E., & Thunnissen, M. 2016. Standing on the shoulders of giants? A critical review of empirical talent management research. *Employee Relations,* 38: 31–56.

Gelens, J., Dries, N., Hofmans, J., & Pepermans, R. 2013. The role of perceived organizational justice in shaping the outcomes of talent management: A research agenda. *Human Resource Management Review,* 23(4): 341–353.

Gelens, J., Dries, N., Hofmans, J., & Pepermans, R. 2015. Affective commitment of employees designated as talent: Signalling perceived organisational support. *European Journal of International Management,* 9(1): 9–27.

Guzzo, R. A., & Noonan, K. A. 1994. Human resource practices as communications and the psychological contract. *Human Resource Management,* 33(3): 447–462.

Iles, P., Chuai, X., & Preece, D. 2010. Talent management and HRM in multinational companies in Beijing: Definitions, differences and drivers. *Journal of World Business,* 45(2): 179–189.

King, K. A. 2015. Global talent management: Introducing a strategic framework and multiple-actors model. *Journal of Global Mobility,* 3(3): 273–288.

King, K. A. 2016. The talent deal and journey: Understanding how employees respond to talent identification over time. *Employee Relations,* 38(1): 94–111.

Lewis, R. E., & Heckman, R. J. 2006. Talent management: A critical review. *Human Resource Management Review,* 16(2): 139–154.

Malik, A. R. & Singh, P. 2014. 'High potential' programs: Let's hear it for 'B' players.' *Human Resource Management Review,* 24: 330–346.

Marescaux, E., De Winne, S., & Sels, L. 2013. HR practices and affective organisational commitment: (When) does HR differentiation pay off?. *Human Resource Management Journal,* 23(4): 329–345.

McDermott, A. M., Conway, E., Rousseau, D. M., & Flood, P. C. 2013. Promoting effective psychological contracts through leadership: The missing link between HR strategy and performance. *Human Resource Management,* 52(2): 289–310.

McDonnell, A., Collings, D. G., Mellahi, K., & Schuler, R. 2017. Talent management: A systematic review and future prospects. *European Journal of International Management,* 11(1): 86–128.

Men, L. R. 2014. Internal reputation management: The impact of authentic leadership and transparent communication. *Corporate Reputation Review,* 17(4): 254–272.

Men, L. R., & Hung-Baesecke, C. J. F. 2015. Engaging employees in China: The impact of communication channels, organizational transparency, and authenticity. *Corporate Communications: An International Journal,* 20(4): 448–467.

Nijs, S., Gallardo-Gallardo, E., Dries, N., & Sels, L. 2014. A multidisciplinary review into the definition, operationalization, and measurement of talent. *Journal of World Business,* 49(2): 180–191.

Nishii, L. H., Lepak, D. P., & Schneider, B. 2008. Employee attributions of the "why" of HR practices: Their effects on employee attitudes and behaviors, and customer satisfaction. *Personnel Psychology,* 61(3): 503–545.

Patient, D. L., & Skarlicki, D. P. 2010. Increasing interpersonal and informational justice when communicating negative news: The role of the manager's empathic concern and moral development. *Journal of Management,* 36(2): 555–578.

Petriglieri, J. & Petriglieri, G. 2017. The talent curse. *Harvard Business Review,* 5-6: 88–94.

Pucik, V., Evans, P., Björkman, I. & Morris, S. 2017. *The global challenge: International human resource management* (3rd ed.). Chicago, IL: Chicago Business Press.

Rawlins, B. 2008. Measuring the relationship between organizational transparency and employee trust. *Public Relations Journal,* 2(2): 1–21.

Rosenbaum, J. E. 1979. Tournament mobility: Career patterns in a corporation. *Administrative Science Quarterly,* 24(2): 220–241.

Rousseau, D. M. 1995. *Psychological contracts in organizations: Understanding written and unwritten agreements.* Thousand Oaks: Sage.

Silzer, R., & Church, A. H. 2009. The pearls and perils of identifying potential. *Industrial and Organizational Psychology,* 2(4): 377–412.

Slan-Jerusalim, R., & Hausdorf, P. A. 2007. Managers' justice perceptions of high potential identification practices. *Journal of Management Development,* 26(10): 933–950.

Smale, A., Björkman, I. & Saarinen, J. 2015. *Pushing the right buttons: Global talent management at KONE Corporation.* Teaching case (no. 415-111-1), Case Centre.

Smale, A., Ehrnrooth, M., Björkman, I., Mäkelä, K., Sumelius, J., & Taimitarha, S. 2015. Letting the chosen ones know: The psychological effects of talent status self-awareness. *Academy of Management Proceedings* (1): 16195.

Sonnenberg, M., van Zijderveld, V., & Brinks, M. 2014. The role of talent-perception incongruence in effective talent management. *Journal of World Business,* 49(2): 272–280.

Stahl, G., Björkman, I., Farndale, E., Morris, S. S., Paauwe, J., Stiles, P., … & Wright, P. 2012. Six principles of effective global talent management. *Sloan Management Review,* 53(2): 25–42.

Suazo, M. M., Martínez, P. G., & Sandoval, R. 2009. Creating psychological and legal contracts through human resource practices: A signaling theory perspective. *Human Resource Management Review,* 19(2): 154–166.

Sumelius, J., Björkman, I., Ehrnrooth, M., Mäkelä, K., & Smale, A. 2014. What determines employee perceptions of HRM process features? The case of performance appraisal in MNC subsidiaries. *Human Resource Management,* 53(4): 569–592.

Sumelius, J., Smale, A., & Yamao, S. 2019. Mixed signals: Employee reactions to talent status communication amidst strategic ambiguity. *International Journal of Human Resource Management,* 1–28.

Swailes, S. 2013. The ethics of talent management. *Business Ethics: A European Review,* 22(1): 32–46.

Swailes, S., & Blackburn, M. 2016. Employee reactions to talent pool membership. *Employee Relations,* 38(1): 112–128.

Tansley, C. 2011. What do we mean by the term "talent" in talent management? *Industrial and Commercial Training,* 43(5): 266–274.

Thunnissen, M., Boselie, P., & Fruytier, B. 2013. Talent management and the relevance of context: Towards a pluralistic approach. *Human Resource Management Review,* 23(4): 326–336.

Tymon, W. G., Stumpf, S. A., & Doh, J. P. 2010. Exploring talent management in India: The neglected role of intrinsic rewards. *Journal of World Business,* 45(2): 109–121.

24

E-TALENT

Connecting Information Technology and Talent Management

Sharna Wiblen

Introduction

Discourses about the importance of talent management (TM) assert that the caliber of people employed by an organization, as well as the practice of effectively managing those people, will lead to significant beneficial organizational and financial outcomes. This talk about talent facilitates the positioning of TM as one of the most important issues for senior executives and organizations worldwide with industry and practitioner surveys continuingly positioning TM as imperative for organizations' operations and vital for competitive positioning in this disrupted and interconnected context (see for example, PricewaterhouseCoopers, 2018, 2019, 2020).

The requirement for countries to source and retain quality talent continues to dominate macro conversations because how nations, not just organizations, develop their human capital assets "can be a more important determinant of their long-term success than virtually any other factor" (World Economic Forum, 2017: vii). The synthesis of these broader macro discourses contributes to the salient and compelling normative assumption that the deliberate and intentional management of talent prevails notwithstanding nation, an organization's size, ownership structure, location, or industry.

Operating in parallel to the discussion around TM is the assertion that information technologies (IT) are beneficial for organizing processes. Given that IT pervades personal and professional domains, it is of little surprise that countless industry, professional, and vendor providers advocate for its use in TM. Indeed, attesting to the appeal of functionality, flexibility, cost-effectiveness, and workforce differentiation, the use of IT in TM is big business. Notably, the global talent management software market is projected to grow from US$5.3 billion in 2014 to US$11.4 billion by 2019. North America is expected to be the largest market for spending and adoption of TMS (MarketsandMarkets, 2017). There is also evidence of organizations moving away from proprietary or on-premises technologies and migrating towards cloud-based software. Gartner reports that more than US$1 trillion in IT spending will result from the shift to the "cloud" (Gartner Inc., 2016), with cloud-based HR software to account for 50% or more of total HR technology spending in 2017 (Gartner Inc, 2014).

Given all the talk about TM and technology, it is of little surprise that issues relating to these are front of mind for CEOs. The 20th CEO Survey, published by PricewaterhouseCoopers, and based on the insights of 1,379 CEOs in 79 countries, reported within the context of the one report that CEO\s frame the speed of technological change simultaneously as both a major threat and avenue of opportunity with strengthening investments in digital and technological capabilities and human capital required to capitalize on new innovations (PricewaterhouseCoopers, 2017: 12). Similarly, the 2019 PricewaterhouseCoopers report found that the speed of technological change was a major concern among CEOs (PricewaterhouseCoopers, 2019: 3).

DOI: 10.4324/9781315474687-24

Given the strategic value of talent and IT, the rest of this chapter examines the interrelationship between IT and TM. The chapter's first two sections highlight the complexity encasing the conceptualization of "technology" and introduces three theoretical perspectives researchers can adopt to examine the role of IT within organizational contexts. The rest of the chapter focuses on e-talent[1], a term used to refer to the interrelationship between IT and TM, and illustrates two primary ways that IT benefits TM. A future research agenda highlights the imperative need for studies of TM to acknowledge and critically reflect on the role and influence of a salient and potentially powerful actor that is largely omitted from the current talk about talent.

Types of Information Technologies

The meaning, structure, and form of IT are constantly evolving. As the landscape changes, so too does our understanding of what is meant when referring to "technology". Defining and measuring IT, in the general sense, is fraught with challenges because technology has both a physical and a procedural dimension (Orlikowski & Scott, 2008). The physical components include the hardware, software, and communication network infrastructures. While these are separate from individuals, the physical aspect is nothing without individuals using it in organizational tasks (Marler & Parry, 2016). Therefore, when we think about the use of IT in TM, we need to consider aspects of the computer (the desktop, laptop, monitor, keyboard, mouse, network connections, operating system, software, add-ons, etc.) as well as the individuals who use the technology. IT, while able to assist with the implementation of strategic decisions, can only complement the decision-making process. IT is only a tool. Human actors are essential in the design, implementation, and appropriation of any technologically enabled software, platform, or system.

Organizations can select from various IT platforms and vendors to support both traditional human resource management (HRM) processes, such as recruiting and onboarding, performance management, succession planning, learning, and development, as well as exclusive and strategic TM processes, such as talent acquisition, identification, development, and retention. The advent of personal computers, laptops, tablets, and smartphones has added to this.

Fueling the growth of the surge in the use of innovative IT platforms in HRM and TM is the advancement of sophisticated enterprise resource planning (ERP) software (Marler & Parry, 2016). ERPs are business software packages that impose standardized procedures on the input, use, and dissemination of data across an organization, and integrate business process and associated workflows (Dery, Grant, Harley, & Wright, 2006a). ERPs are typically used in large organizations to carry out the most common business functions, including human resources (HR), finance and accounting, sales and distribution, manufacturing, and logistics (Davenport, Harris, & Shapiro, 2010; Dery, Hall, & Wailes, 2006).

Packaged ERP software systems offer organizations cutting-edge "best practices", a set of proven or exemplary business scenarios preconfigured into the software (Yeow & Sia, 2008). Notably, these so-called best practices are created by vendors and then built into the "material properties" of the software, which then dictate aspects of HRM and TM processes. Technology vendors determine the number and order of events in any given organizational process.

Particularly pertinent to TM is the creation of processes for "ranking" individuals according to their talent "scores". TM "algorithms" are core to the concept of e-talent because algorithms determine the criteria and processes of workforce differentiation. According to Orlikowski and Scott:

> algorithms are a set of step-by-step instructions to achieve the desired result in a finite number of moves… they form the basic ingredient of all computer programs, telling the computer what specific steps to perform and in what specific order with what priority or weighting so as to accomplish a specific task. (2015: 210)

Vendors have benefitted from an expanding HR technology market driven by the growth and availability of cloud-based IT. Cloud computing, commonly promoted and marketed as Software as a Service

(SaaS), allows organizations to acquire and deploy vendor-designed technologies at a significantly lower cost. This is because organizations can transition away from expensive proprietary (designed and owned by an organization) or on-premises technology, towards a model of ubiquitous, convenient, and a shared pool of configurable resources available on-demand (Mell & Grance, 2011). Organizations can out-source the software design, configuration, and management to vendors in exchange for a licensing fee. Improvements and innovations, such as amendments to codes, algorithms, and workflow processes, are updated and upgraded automatically by the vendor. In most situations, however, ownership and control of the IT remain with the vendor, not the organization.

While there is a wide body of knowledge around the use of IT in organizations, the literature is separated into the study of electronic human resource management (eHRM) and human resource information systems (HRIS). Although there are competing definitions of HRIS, it is generally agreed that an HRIS is a system used to acquire, store, manipulate, analyse, retrieve, and distribute informa-tion regarding an organizations human resources to support HRM and managerial decision-making (Bondarouk & Ruël, 2008; Dery, Hall, Wailes, & Wiblen, 2013; Johnson, Lukaszewski, & Stone, 2016; Kavanagh & Johnson, 2015) and includes the hardware, software, people, policies, processes, and data. An HRIS is an information system largely associated with the HR function, with the users of this system and its information largely residing in HR (Dery et al., 2013; Wiblen, Grant, & Dery, 2010).

E-HRM, in contrast, "...is the technical unlocking of HRIS for all employees of an organization" (Ruël, Bondarouk, & Looise, 2004: 17). Again, while there are numerous definitions of eHRM within this chapter the term refers to the "configurations of computer hardware, software, and electronic networking resources that enable intended or actual HRM activities (e.g., policies, practices, and ser-vices) through individual and group-level interactions within and across organizational boundaries" (Marler & Fisher, 2013: 21). E-HRM involves the implementation and delivery of HR functionality enabled by a HRIS that connects an internal (employees and managers) and external (job applicants) and the decisions that various stakeholders (mainly HR) make (Johnson et al., 2016). Notwithstanding conceptual distinctions, both HRIS and e-HRM have greatly improved many operational, transac-tional, and strategic aspects of HRM.

Regardless of the specific terms used to refer to the "technology", organizations need to decide the extent to which the chosen IT aligns with existing and future operational processes and business strategies. In other words, organizations need to determine whether to adopt a technology or business-driven IT strategy. When electing to select and implement vendor designed (such as those offered by SAP SuccessFactors, Workday, Oracle, etc.) technology, the technology will influence the direction of the corporation (Apigian, Ragu-Nathan, Ragu-Nathan, & Kunnathur, 2005). This is because the newly selected IT comes with an array of pre-configured practices that are embedded into the technology.

The provision of practices and processes for "how" internal stakeholders requires decisions about the extent to which the organization will customize the technology. Specifically, Wiblen et al. (2010) note that organizations will need to determine whether they will amend their existing processes to fit with the processes pre-configured into the vendor technology. Tailoring existing process to conform to the technology is a "vanilla" or configured implementation. This type of implementation affords an opportunity to consider and/or engage in process reengineering because "the implementation of any new information system represents an immense change from the way processes and decisions were previously made" (Bedell & Canniff, 2014: 82). Organizations, during the process mapping stage of an implementation (whereby existing and future processes are compared), can elect to establish new practices that mirror the promoted "best practices" embedded into the newly selected technology.

The alternative business-driven approach, known as a customized implementation, requires vendors to change the functionality and material properties of their software to fit with the organization's existing processes. This is significant cost and limits the ability to deploy vendor designed upgrades and innovations automatically. These factors help account for why most organizations are encouraged to select, implement, and maintain a "vanilla" (basic and standard version) of the chosen ERP, eHRM, or HRIS. Regardless of the approach, the implications of this decision for organizations are typically complex (Dery, Grant, & Wiblen, 2009; Grant, Dery, Hall, Wailes, & Wiblen, 2009; Wiblen et al., 2010). There are also implications for TM. The decision can directly influence the meaning of talent, what skills and capabilities are required to be housed in IT and HR functions, and the practice of TM within organizations (Wiblen et al., 2010).

Newer technological innovations including social media and applications (apps) offer organizations new, smart, and digital processes and content. While these have far-reaching implications for how organizations attract talent and potentially for how organizations practice TM, scholarly discussion of these innovations will not be undertaken in this chapter, as the discussion of e-talent focuses primarily on the role of IT in identifying and managing talented individuals within organizations.

Theoretical Approaches to the Study of Information Technology

Three broad sets of theoretical perspectives have advanced our understanding of IT: technological determinism, social constructionism, and sociomateriality. Each of these perspectives holds some assumptions about what kinds of knowledge are possible and the potential impact of IT within organizational contexts.

Technological Determinism

Technological determinism is associated with the positivist epistemological paradigm of social research and knowledge creation. A positivist (or what some refer to as an objectivist) epistemology is founded on the assumption that there is an objective reality that is discoverable. A positivist perspective holds that meaning, and therefore meaningful reality, exists apart from any consciousness. Therefore understandings of the world and reality (and of IT) and an objective "truth" is discoverable (Crotty, 1998).

With relation to the study of IT, the positivist and technological determinist theoretical perspective positions IT as a distinct independent measurable variable that has predictable consequences for organizations (Marler & Fisher, 2013; Orlikowski & Scott, 2008). More specifically, technology is a "distinct entity that interacts with various aspects of the organization" (Orlikowski & Scott, 2008: 439). That is, the implementation and use of IT is a causal factor that is expected to create predictable, theoretically-determined consequences (Marler & Fisher, 2013) examinable at the individual, group, enterprise, and inter-organizational level.

Although this approach has been employed in previous studies (see for example Farndale, Paauwe, & Hoeksema, 2009; Marler & Dulebohn, 2005; Marler, Fisher, & Ke, 2009), no study to date has applied technological determinism to the study of TM. A key weakness of this theoretical perspective, however, is its inability to acknowledge that social factors and context play a role in the use of IT because it asserts that the impact of IT is a given.

Social Constructionism

Social constructionist approaches emerged as a response to the above-noted determinist research and reject the view that there is an "objective" truth waiting to be discovered. Truth or meaning, rather, comes into existence in and out of how individuals engage with the realities of our world. Knowledge is established in the mind and therefore meaning is constructed (not objective) (Crotty, 1998).

From a social constructionist perspective, the study of IT involves recognizing that the meaning and perceived value of technologically-enabled processes are open to debate and contestation (Pinch & Bijker, 1984), whereby individuals within organizations collectively interact with IT to co-construct the trajectory of a particular technology (Anteby, Chan, & DiBenigno, 2016). Rather than proclaiming that the role of IT in TM is predetermined, this perspective treats technology as an emergent concept that evolves over time (Orlikowski & Scott, 2008) with users required to interact with the facilities and material properties of the technology.

Social constructionists are cognizant of the norms and protocols and "interpretative schemes" (such as the skills, knowledge, and the assumptions about the technology that the user brings to bear) (Dery et al., 2006; Wiblen et al., 2010) associated with using any given technology. IT is not an independent variable, but rather part of a complex system of organizing. The logic here, Orlikowski and Scott (2016) argue, is that technology is not valuable, meaningful, or consequential by itself; it only becomes so when people engage with it in their everyday work.

Studies that employ constructionist approaches argue that IT itself does not solely determine what constitutes talent or how talent is managed, but rather that the meanings of talent, the practice of TM, and the use of e-talent are constructed through an iterative and interpretative process (Wiblen et al., 2010). Based on a single site case study, for example, Wiblen et al. (2010) showed how the transition from a proprietary to a vendor designed system reshaped the understanding of the talent requirements in both the HR and IT departments, in their case organization. This was because the technologically-enabled change influenced the skills and capabilities required of HR and IT employees, and their "talent" pre- and post-implementation. Therefore e-talent technologies can be used in multiple ways, both between and within organizations. This is because social factors, context, and previous experiences can influence and shape the use of IT within organizational boundaries.

Sociomateriality

Sociomateriality, a third theoretical perspective, emerged in light of perceived limitations of both positivist (technological determinist) and constructionist approaches to adequately explain the selection and use (or non-use) of IT within organizing processes. Sociomateriality is a theory that acknowledges the intersection between technology, work, and organization.

In contrast to technological determinism that prioritizes the material properties technology, and social constructionism that prioritizes the social relations encompassing the use of technology, "sociomateriality stands out as a symbol for the interest in the social and the technical, and in particular, the subtleties of their contingent intertwining" (Cecez-Kecmanovic, Galliers, Henfridsson, Newell, & Vidgen, 2014:809). From this perspective, it is impossible for individuals, and therefore researchers, to see actors acting separately from the e-talent technology and the objects that constitute their practice. That is when a manager undertakes TM and they are only able to do this through, and with, an array of technologies. The relationship between the social and the technical are not fixed or static. Rather the relationship between IT and TM are emergent and variable.

While much can be said about the co-evolution of the study of IT from positivist (the meaning and impact of IT are objective and pre-given), to social constructionism (the meaning and impact of IT is influenced by individuals and contextual factors), to sociomateriality, whereby the meaning of IT is influenced simultaneously by both material (the pre-configured processes and algorithms embedded within IT) and the social (individual perspectives and contextual factors), the differing views of IT referred to here are not to be viewed as agreed upon compartmentalizations. Rather, this section aimed to highlight how epistemology and the three theoretical perspectives illustrated hold numerous assumptions about the creation of knowledge and meaning and that these differing assumptions influence whether scholars and practitioners acknowledge and critically reflect on the role of IT in TM.

The Benefits of E-Talent: Employing it in Talent Management

While there is much talk about the benefits of IT for more traditional HRM processes that apply to entire workforces (for an extensive review, see Marler & Fisher, 2013), consideration of e-talent – the use of IT in TM processes – is largely absent with only a handful of studies acknowledging IT as a specific TM actor (see for example Wiblen, 2016; Wiblen, Dery, & Grant, 2012). This is perplexing given our technology-enabled and interconnected world and the inability to "practice" TM without employing IT. Notwithstanding, with this need to enhance our detailed understanding of e-talent through empirical analysis, broader discourses propose (implied or explicitly) that IT benefits TM in two significant ways: facilitation of a TM "system", and the provision of a technologically-enabled mechanism to capture and generate data and analytics about an organization's "talent".

Talent Management Systems

As a core benefit of e-talent, the use of IT in TM is the facilitation of a TM system that enables organizations to transition from "individualistic" to "systems" approaches to the proactive management of the internal talent pool. Extant talk about the first internal TM practice (talent identification) presents an array of normative and prescriptive assumptions about the processes through which certain individuals should be evaluated to identify high-performing and high-potential employees. The vast majority of vendors, consultants, and academic publications advocate for strategic and/or systematic approaches to TM, and more specifically talent identification with strategic TM underpinned by the assertion that systematic, integrated, and proactive processes are the most effective. While it would be vehemently debated whether any organization would elect to enact policies and practices not informed by or aligned to strategic ambitions, numerous academic and vendor publications actively campaign for advancement beyond individualistic, intuitive, and gut-feel approaches to identifying "talent". This has given rise to conversations about the value of wider macro and system-level perspective of TM.

The perceived need for the creation of a TM system is frequently expressed as a core component within prevailing definitions of TM and global TM (GTM) with many publications including Beamond, Farndale, and Härtel (2016) and drawing on Collings and Mellahi to present the concept of TM as:

> ...activities and processes that involve the *systematic identification* of key positions that differentially contribute to the organisation's sustainable competitive advantage, the development of a talent pool of high-potential and high-performing incumbents to fill these roles, and the development of a differentiated human resource architecture to facilitate fulfilling these component incumbents and to ensure their continued commitment to the organisation. (2009: 304)

Others, including Tarique and Schuler (2010) and Khilji, Tarique, and Schuler (2015: 237) similarly require a TM system by when defining GTM as "*systematically* utilsing IHRM activities... to attract, develop and retain individuals with high levels of human capital (e.g. competency, personality, motivation) consistent with the strategic directions of the multinational enterprise..." (Tarique and Schuler, 2010: 124).

Implicit within definitions that conceptualize TM as a system-level activity is the implementation and appropriation of IT. That is, IT is the mechanism to create and administer the TM "system". As stated previously, the emergence of increasingly sophisticated vendor designed and packaged software creates an environment where organizations can now purchase, rather than internally devise, a set of practices, sometimes heralded as "best practices" to be implemented and enacted across the organization. The transition towards cloud computing and software-as-a-service has enhanced the ability to acquire "best of breed" software or intentionally select, implement, and appropriated various technologies based on specific TM needs and functionality.

Technology vendors and consultants, such as Korn Ferry, Oracle, and ELMO, promote IT as a core enabling mechanism to enact an integrated (rather than systematic) TM system and software suite that facilitates processes for differentiating talent and ensuring alignment between business strategy and talent strategy. The acquisition of packaged e-talent software enables organizations to streamline numerous TM processes including talent acquisition, development, engagement, rewards, and succession. The use of technologically-enabled TM processes also encourages consistency in the "how" of TM because the components of the "system" are defined and configured into the material properties of the software.

IT, in addition to the provision of processes, also guides organizations in how to define the concept of talent. In many circumstances, IT vendors provide organizations with a pre-defined list of skills and capabilities that they can utilize to guide the criteria for evaluating an individual's performance and potential. In other words, IT provides structured dialogue, language, and common definitions of the skills and capabilities required of individuals to be identified as "talent". By creating "high-performer", "high-potential", and "success" profiles, organizations articulate factors such as the competencies and behaviors, personal attributes, technical and professional knowledge, and experience required for individuals to be classified as "talent". Assertions about systematic approaches prescribe that employees should be subjected to the same set of policies and processes that give authority and mandates for action, with IT able to imply conditions for control and performance imperatives whereby they dictate whom, how, and where of TM practices (Wiblen, Grant, & Dery, 2015).

While establishing systematic and consistent processes for talent identification are widely heralded as the most effective and core to a strategic approach to TM, there exists a paradoxical relationship between the theoretical and practical ideals of TM and the use of IT in talent identification. Although numerous stakeholders theoretically advocate for a one-size-fits-all and systematic understanding of the skills and capabilities required of talent subjects, the realization of these ideals "in practice" may arbitrarily create externally defined boundaries around the "who", "what", and "how" of TM.

Operating in parallel to arguments that assert that all employees should be subjected to the same TM processes (Iles, Chuai, & Preece, 2010; Stainton, 2005) are also concerns that a systematic approach can result in the identification of "talent clones" (McDonnell, 2011). Enacting TM on a well-defined or systematic understanding of the talent concept could, in practice, be indicative of a rigid approach that prioritizes homophily at the expense of the ability to recognize idiosyncratic characteristics and attribute value to difference and diversity (Highhouse, 2008; Mäkelä, Björkman, & Ehrnrooth, 2010). A more nuanced understanding of talent and the enactment of processes that possess dexterity and fluidity, Wiblen et al. (2015) argue, may enable organizations to respond to, and capitalize on, changes in macro factors such as broader business models and digital disruption. Daubner-Siva, Vinkenburg, and Jansen (2017) also hint to the practical challenges associated with realizing the touted benefits of systems approaches as organizations grapple with simultaneously balancing the paradoxical relationship between diversity (difference) and talent (different degrees of similarity) agendas. Therefore, IT and its ability to facilitate a technologically-enabled TM system can, in practice, both enable and constrain TM.

Talent Data and Talent Analytics

Advocates of e-talent posit that advances in IT will increase capabilities to select, retain, and manage talent assets more effectively through the provision of dynamic, real-time data, metrics, and analytics (Levenson, 2014). This proclaimed benefit focuses on producing technically enabled talent-based data to improve decision-making processes with an emphasis on evidence-based management (Rousseau & Barends, 2011).

Many have professed that there is a relationship between people-based resources, including talent and firm performance (Collings, 2014; McDonnell, Collings, Mellahi, & Schuler, 2017; Thunnissen, Boselie, & Fruytier, 2013a, b). This includes the established adage that is frequently appropriated within a corporate discourse that "our people are our greatest asset" (Boudreau, Ramstad, & Dowling, 2002:4). This rhetoric, combined with arguments that talent has the potential to increase an organization's competitive advantage provide organizations with a compelling business case to generate data about the impact of TM policies and processes. Each of these sentiments, by design and word selection, implying that the "talent" and hence the value of an individual, and the financial impact and outcomes of TM, are quantifiable, therefore allocating data and analytics a prominent role.

The generation of metrics and data, via technologically-mediated capabilities, enable organizations to make decisions about talent through the conscientious, explicit, and judicious use of the best available evidence, incorporating the evidence into the decision-making process and then evaluating the outcome of the decision taken (Barends, Rousseau, & Briner, 2014; Marler & Boudreau, 2017).

More specifically, conversations that proclaim a relationship between talent, TM, and firm performance state that organizations should implement and appropriate TM through technologies because technology provides stakeholders, other than just HR professionals, with access to data (Schalk, Timmerman, & den Heuvel, 2013; Stone & Dulebohn, 2013; Williams, 2009) as technology vendors are embedding applications with functionality that promise to move beyond traditional reporting capabilities to providing the ground work for the above mentioned data and evidence-based decision making (Jones, 2014).

Data are representative of the "facts" of transactions that occur in organizations on a daily basis. The data, when interpreted, becomes information, which given meaning, becomes knowledge. Knowledge, therefore, consists of the procedures one follows to use data and information to make decisions and conduct business (Marler & Floyd, 2014: 36). Notably, both TM and human capital scholars agree that organizations should use the best available scientific evidence upon which to base decisions about human resources, human capital, or talent. It is here that discourses about the importance of talent "metrics", "data", and "analytics" become prominent.

Not surprisingly there is an array of, and at times competing perspectives of what, if any, are the differences between metrics, analytics, and data. Davenport, Harris, and Shapiro (2010) coined the term "talent analytics" to draw on the principles of scientific decision making to advocate for the removal of subjectivity in TM. In their seminal piece *Competing on Talent Analytics*, the authors argue that enterprise systems (such as ERPs, eHRM, and HRIS modules) should be utilized to gather, analyze, and distribute talent metrics throughout an organization. Davenport et al. assert that e-talent is critical for effective TM and summarize the capabilities required via the acronym Delta: "access to high quality data, enterprise orientation, analytical leadership, strategic targets, and analysts" (2010: 57). After a systematic review of "HR Analytics", Marler and Boudreau (2017), recognized the inherent relationship between IT and people-based practices and concluded that HR (and talent) analytics is: "A HR practice enabled by IT that uses descriptive, visual, and statistical analyses of data related to HR processes, human capital, organisational performance, and external economic benchmarks to establish business impact and enable data-driven decision-making" (2017: 15).

The intent of IT vendors and consultants to provide practices and services that encourage organizations to base decisions on data, rather than intuition, affords IT this second and equally beneficial role in TM. Although Davenport and Harris note that in principal, analytics can be performed using paper, pencil, and a slide rule, "...any sane person using analytics today would employ IT... [including] the reporting and analytical modules of major enterprise systems (SAP and Oracle)" (2007: 7).

As highlighted previously, e-talent (including SAP and Oracle) provides organizations with access to "best practices" via licensing arrangements. This includes the processes and algorithms utilized to evaluate and identify talent. These algorithms (which include coding, sorting, filtering, and ranking) are designed and configured by vendors and then embedded into the software. In addition to standardizing HR and TM workflow procedures, e-talent via embedded algorithms is the mechanism to conduct workforce differentiation (a core component of TM).

Implicit in references to analytics is the normative assumption that the "value" of an individual is calculable and quantifiable, and therefore, frames "talent" as a measurable construct. Generations of people and talent-based measurements facilitate the ranking of all, or a specific cohort, of employees according to their allocated performance (Brady, Bolchover, & Sturgess, 2008) and potential scores. Organizations can rank individuals according to their talent status and make talent pool determinations based on these scores. Such talent pool decisions, therefore, are primarily founded on the data generated via the preconfigured algorithms embedded within e-talent.

Despite apparent acceptance that e-talent capabilities can measure an individual's performance, there are reservations around whether an individual's "potential" can be effectively evaluated (see for example Mellahi & Collings, 2010). These sentiments have significant practical implications for TM because it can be argued that talent is so complex and includes all the subtleties of life and organizations, and therefore, is unable to be condensed to a single talent measure, score, or analytic.

Data and the resulting talent analytics are largely pre-determined by the e-talent vendor rather than the organization. There is evidence that the move towards the cloud and licensed-based e-talent technologies has implicitly transferred responsibility for updating and innovating TM practices to external technology vendors. Rather than maintain talent coding and software design capabilities internally, many organizations are looking to e-talent vendors to provide innovations in processes and criteria. It is important to note, however, that e-talent vendors have a stake in promoting their technologies, their product, or their service.

Caution should be exercised, however, in the use and application of technological-enabled talent algorithms. Algorithms present a particular ontology. In other words, the algorithms embedded in e-talent present a particular view of the world and a certain understanding of the skills and capabilities valued within talent subjects. The processes of individual evaluations, the criteria of evaluation and the formulae for calculating talent scores and rankings, do not exist as discoverable concepts. Rather they are designed by e-talent vendors.

Algorithms and talent analytics are an extension of human consciousness and subjective experience (for example individuals may hold different ideas of the definition of talent and how talent should be effectively managed), however, the views of one set of stakeholders is called upon to underpin the definitions and processes embedded into the technology. Studies and discussions of the use of e-talent, therefore, need to acknowledge the inability of algorithms and talent analytics to present an objective approach to TM.

Even early on in their journey of advocating for an enhanced role of analytics and data-decision making, Davenport and Harris acknowledged that "…any quantitative analysis relies upon a series of assumptions. When conditions behind the assumptions no longer apply, the analyses should no longer be employed" (2007: 14). This significant limitation still applies today and into the future regardless of technology innovations. It is, therefore, important to recognize that there is no such thing as a neutral algorithm and the proclaimed perception that e-talent can facilitate objective TM is a fallacy. All analytics represent a particular definition and understanding of talent, and we need to be mindful of what or whose singular perception of talent and view of the world is prioritized.

Despite the rhetoric regarding the positive relationship between TM and IT, the reality appears to depict a less positive picture. In contrast to the assertions that stakeholders, and in particular, HRM can use the material properties of e-talent to play a greater role in talent identification and management, Wiblen (2016) and Wiblen et al. (2012) present qualitative evidence that contradicts this theorized relationship. These two studies challenge the extent to which e-talent data is used to inform talent decisions (McDonnell et al., 2017). They show that e-talent data and analytics, may not be afforded a primary role in TM, despite availability. Similarly, Marler and Boudreau (2017), in their evidence-based review, concluded that "despite evidence linking the adoption of HR analytics to organizational performance that adoption of HR analytics is very low and academic research, and therefore, evidence on this topic is sparse" (Marler & Boudreau, 2017:3).

The above section outlined two core benefits of e-talent: the ability to implement TM systems through the standardization of workflow processes and the capability to capture and generate talent data and analytics. A remaining key question concerns the extent to which the standardization of language around the definitions of talent is, in practice, beneficial. While capturing and enacting a standardized definition of talent through e-talent may be framed as robust, it may result in bounded and constrained approaches to managing an organization's most important resource – its talent.

A Future Research Agenda for E-Talent

Although TM is currently separated into distinct fields of analysis and enquiry, there exists an inherent intersection between TM and IT. This chapter argues that TM, although contextually and organizationally-specific, affords a prominent role implicitly for IT as the acquisition, identification, development, and retention of talent through proactive, intentional, and strategically aligned practices are technologically-medicated practices. Organizations, senior executives, line managers, and employees are inherently required to engage with various forms and types of IT while undertaking TM practices. Future empirical examinations of TM concepts (definitions and ideas), objects (policies and practices), and subjects (the individuals privy to TM) therefore, should critically reflect on the role of technology and highlight views and interests of this currently hidden and obstructed actor.

To develop a contemporary research agenda for both TM and IT studies, we must be mindful of the ever changing discourses pertaining to the importance of talent and the reality that nearly all forms of work today entail the digital and generally involve some form of computing device or digital phenomena (Orlikowski & Scott, 2016). Given that technology permeates nearly all aspects of our personal and professional lives, it is imperative that we adopt a critical approach to the design and use of e-talent in organizing processes and within organizational boundaries. To do so, future research could usefully extend our understanding through an examination of e-talent in organizational contexts.

Conceptualizations of "Talent"

To enhance our understanding of e-talent, we need a better understanding of the processes through which "talent" is attributed meaning (for more information, see Wiblen & McDonnell, 2020). Much debate surrounds the question of how to effectively conceptualize "talent". The literature suggests that organizations, via a process of negotiation, can decide whether "talent" is indicative of certain individual employees (Blass, 2007; Jones, Whitaker, Seet, & Parkin, 2012; Whelen & Carcary, 2011), valuable skills and capabilities (McDonnell, Lamare, Gunnigle, & Lavelle, 2010; Wiblen et al., 2012; Wiblen et al., 2010), pivotal roles and positions (Boudreau, 2003; Collings & Mellahi, 2009; Mellahi & Collings, 2010), or its entire workforce (Thunnissen et al., 2013a). Despite these advances, we still know little about how talent is defined and how these conceptualizations come to be materialized in organizations.

A deeper and more explicit consideration of language can illuminate the processes through which the concept of talent is attributed meaning. Such studies can also identify how those meanings are brought into being and enacted through TM practices. Specific examination of whose meaning (is it a particular individual, group of individuals, or the e-talent vendors) of talent is brought into being and prioritized within organizational boundaries could illuminate some of the practical tensions experienced within organizations. Examining the non-neutral relationships within organizations has the potential for far-reaching implications for society as well as social responsibility and diversity issues that influence processes of organizing.

Explicit Acknowledgement of the "Technology"

A major outstanding question concerns the nature and form of e-talent and the associated "technology". Technologies and technological artifacts should receive significant attention in studies of TM. Given the notable absence of studies employing a socialmaterial approach to the study of e-talent, this area of knowledge might benefit from greater consideration of the insightful studies of the use of information systems in organizing practices other than human resources and TM. The undoubted connection between organizations and technology suggests that consideration of both the material components of the software, the physical presence of the technological artifact, as well as the social processes into which technology is implemented and appropriated, is central to the study of TM.

Creation of Algorithms

The specific materializations of work and TM include digital platforms other than e-talent technologies. Orlikowski and Scott (2016), when proposing a research agenda for digital work, stated that the world of work today is operated by complex algorithms and continual streams of data that have the potential to profoundly transform how work is done. An algorithm erects boundaries around "if-then" code that uses inputs to execute a defined set of steps and by consequence dictates the processes of TM. What has changed, however, is that these algorithms are embedded at multiple layers of the organization and can profoundly influence the "who", "what", and "how" of TM.

Given the proliferation of e-talent and the associated talent algorithms, it is imperative that we undertake research that critically examines the creation and appropriation of these technologically mediated capabilities. More specifically, it would be useful to delve into the processes of algorithm creation in e-talent to ask how algorithms are created and how do formulae come to be configured in the material properties of the software; to determine what individuals are involved in, and responsible for, the processes of creation and design; and to ask how these algorithms come to be materialized within organizing processes. Further critical reflections on the role of e-talent are essential, as neither technology nor algorithms are neutral.

Extent of Managerial Agency

While e-talent vendors build physical affordances and constraints into the material properties of their software that seek to encourage certain patterns of use and behavior, users recognized by Leonardi and Barley (2010) are able to appropriate these features in ways that are either consistent or inconsistent with the vendor's intentions. A further research agenda, therefore, could explicitly examine the role of actors within technology use, founded upon the assertion that e-talent is subjected to the managerial agency. Recognizing the co-constitution between the social and the technical requires shifting the primary unit of analysis from the technology or processes of use towards an appreciation of how various social constructions of IT come into play and entwine with the material properties pre-configured and embedded into the e-talent software.

Studies from these perspectives could also usefully acknowledge that the use of e-talent is influenced by existing social and power structures. Whether actors frame e-talent as enabling or, alternatively, constraining TM, will have implications for its acceptance and use in organizations, as all information technologies are subjected to individual and managerial agency.

Implications for HRM and HR Skills

Given the ubiquitous proliferation of IT and its inherent connection to TM, it is perplexing that we do not know more about the implications of e-talent for HRM and HR skills. Greater discussion about how innovations in e-talent are changing or disrupting the HR profession would be useful. Of particular interest is the influence of broader corporate discourses about the value of "Big Data" on HR managers and more specifically, whether these discussions alter or reframe the skills and capabilities deemed valuable within HRM.

We can ask how the shift towards e-talent and the perceived salience of "metrics", "data", and "analytics" shapes how HRM functions and HR professionals undertake TM; have innovations in technological capabilities enhanced the perceived need for, and acquisition of, coding and/or mathematical skills; and whether organizations seek to attain these skills externally via consultants or house them internally.

In conclusion, while there continues to be much talk about the importance of TM and IT, we still have much to learn about how organizations employ technological capabilities in TM. A key point on which to conclude is that while the proclaimed benefits of e-talent are vast and auspicious, it is important to acknowledge that e-talent is only a tool, and while it can enable and improve evidence-based decision-making, it requires human interaction, management, and supportive organizational policies and processes to do so effectively.

Note

1 I am grateful to Dr. Kristine Dery for her contribution to establishing the concept of e-talent.

References

Anteby, M., Chan, C. K., & DiBenigno, J. 2016. Three lenses on occupations and professions in organizations: Becoming, doing, and relating. *Academy of Management Annals,* 10(1): 183–244.

Apigian, C. H., Ragu-Nathan, B. S., Ragu-Nathan, T. S., & Kunnathur, A. 2005. Internet technology: The strategic imperative *Journal of Electronic Commerce Research,* 6(2): 123.

Barends, E., Rousseau, D., & Briner, R. 2014. *Evidence-based management: The basic principles.* Amsterdam: Centre for Evidence-based Management.

Beamond, M. T., Farndale, E., & Härtel, C. E. J. 2016. MNE translation of corporate talent management strategies to subsidiaries in emerging economies. *Journal of World Business,* 51(4): 499–510.

Bedell, M. D., & Canniff, M. L. 2014. Systems considerations in the design of a human resource information system: Planning for implementation. In M. J. Kavanagh, M. Thite, & R. D. Johnson (Eds.), *Human resource information systems: Basics, applications, and future directions* (3rd ed.): 57–81. Thousand Oaks, CA: SAGE Publications Inc.

Blass, E. 2007. *Talent management: Maximising talent for business performance.* Executive Summary: 1–12. London: Chartered Management Institute & Ashbridge Consulting.

Bondarouk, T. V., & Ruël, H. 2008. HRM systems for successful information technology implementation: Evidence from three case studies. *European Management Journal,* 26(3): 153–165.

Boudreau, J. W., Ramstad, P. M., & Dowling, P. J. 2002. *Global talentship: Towards a decision science connecting talent to global strategic success* (CAHRS Working Paper 02-21). Ithaca: New York Cornell University, School of Industrial and Labor Relations, Center for Advanced Human Resource Studies.

Brady, C., Bolchover, D., & Sturgess, B. 2008. Managing in the talent economy: The football model for business. *California Management Review,* 50(4): 54–73.

Cecez-Kecmanovic, D., Galliers, R. D., Henfridsson, O., Newell, S., & Vidgen, R. 2014. The sociomateriality of information systems: current status, future directions. *MIS Quarterly,* 38(3): 809–830.

Collings, D. G. 2014. The contribution of talent management to organization success. In K. Kraiger, J. Passmore, N. R. Dos Santos, & S. Malvezzi (Eds.), *The Wiley-Blackwell handbook of the psychology of training, development, and performance improvement:* 247–260. Online John Wiley & Sons, Ltd.

Collings, D. G., & Mellahi, K. 2009. Strategic talent management: A review and research agenda. *Human Resource Management Review,* 19(4): 304–313.

Crotty, M. 1998. *The foundations of social research: Meaning and perspective in the research process.* Crows Nest: Allen & Unwin.

Daubner-Siva, D., Vinkenburg, C. J., & Jansen, P. G. W. 2017. Dovetailing talent management and diversity management: The exclusion-inclusion paradox. *Journal of Organizational Effectiveness: People and Performance,* 4(4): 315–331.

Davenport, T. H., & Harris, J. G. 2007. *Competing on Analytics: The new science of winning.* Boston, MA: Harvard Business School Press.

Davenport, T., Harris, J., & Shapiro, J. 2010. Competing on talent analytics. *Harvard Business Review,* 88(10): 53–58.

Dery, K., Grant, D., Harley, B., & Wright, C. 2006a. Work, organisation and enterprise resource planning systems: An alternative research agenda. *New Technology, Work and Employment,* 21(3): 199–214.

Dery, K., Grant, D., & Wiblen, S. 2009. *Human resource information systems: Replacing or enhancing HRM.* Paper presented at the 15th World Congress of the International Industrial Relations Association IIRA 2009, The New World of Work, Organisations and Employment, Sydney, Australia.

Dery, K., Hall, R., & Wailes, N. 2006. ERPs as 'technologies-in-practice': social construction, materiality and the role of organisational factors. *New Technology, Work and Employment,* 21(3): 229–241.

Dery, K., Hall, R., Wailes, N., & Wiblen, S. 2013. Lost in translation? An actor-network approach to HRIS implementation. *The Journal of Strategic Information Systems,* 22(3): 225–237.

Farndale, E., Paauwe, J., & Hoeksema, L. 2009. In-sourcing HR: Shared service centres in the Netherlands. *International Journal of Human Resource Management,* 20(3): 544–561.

Gartner Inc. 2014. *Market guide for human capital management suite applications.* In G. Inc. (Ed.). https://www.gartner.com/doc/2950821/market-guide-human-capital-management

Gartner Inc. 2016. Gartner says by 2020 "cloud shift" will affect more than $1 trillion in IT spending. Garner Inc. http://www.gartner.com/newsroom/id/3384720

Grant, D., Dery, K., Hall, R., Wailes, N., & Wiblen, S. 2009. Human resource information systems (HRIS): An unrealised potential Annual CIPD Centres' Conference. Nottingham, United Kingdom.

Highhouse, S. 2008. Stubborn reliance on intuition and subjectivity in employee selection. *Industrial and Organizational Psychology,* 1(3): 333–342.

Iles, P., Chuai, X., & Preece, D. 2010. Talent management and HRM in multinational companies in Beijing: Definitions, differences and drivers. *Journal of World Business,* 45(2): 179–189.

Johnson, R., Lukaszewski, K. M., & Stone, D. L. 2016. The evolution of the field of human resource information systems: Co-evolution of technology and HR processes. *Communications of the Association for Information Systems,* 38(28): 533–553.

Jones, J. T., Whitaker, M., Seet, P.-S., & Parkin, J. 2012. Talent management in practice in Australia: individualistic or strategic? An exploratory study. *Asia Pacific Journal of Human Resources,* 50(4): 399–420.

Jones, K. 2014. Conquering HR analytics: Do you need a rocket scientist or a crystal ball? *Workforce Solutions Review,* 5: 43–44.

Kavanagh, M. J., & Johnson, R. D. 2015. Evolution of human resource management and human resource information systems. In M. J. Kavanagh, M. Thite, & R. D. Johnson (Eds.), *Human resource information systems: Basics, applications and future directions* (3rd ed.). Thousand Oaks, CA: SAGE Publications Inc.

Khilji, S. E., Tarique, I., & Schuler, R. S. 2015. Incorporating the macro view in global talent management. *Human Resource Management Review,* 25(3): 236–248.

Leonardi, P. M., & Barley, S. R. 2010. What's under construction here? Social action, materiality, and power in constructivist studies of technology and organizing. *The Academy of Management Annals,* 4(1): 1–51.

Levenson, A. 2014. The promise of big data for HR. *People & Strategy,* 36(4): 22–26.

Mäkelä, K., Björkman, I., & Ehrnrooth, M. 2010. How do MNCs establish their talent pools? Influences on individuals' likelihood of being labeled as talent. *Journal of World Business,* 45(2): 134–142.

MarketsandMarkets. 2017. *Talent management software market worth $11,367.0 million by 2019.* Marketsandmarkets. http://www.marketsandmarkets.com/PressReleases/talent-management-software.asp

Marler, J. H., & Boudreau, J. W. 2017. An evidence-based review of HR Analytics. *The International Journal of Human Resource Management,* 28(1): 3–26.

Marler, J. H., & Dulebohn, J. H. 2005. *A model of employee self-service technology acceptance,* Vol. 24: 137–180. Emerald Group Publishing Limited.

Marler, J. H., & Fisher, S. L. 2013. An evidence-based review of e-HRM and strategic human resource management. *Human Resource Management Review,* 23(1): 18–36.

Marler, J. H., Fisher, S. L., & Ke, W. 2009. Employee self-service technology acceptance: A comparison of pre-implementation and post-implementation relationships. *Personnel Psychology,* 62(2): 327–358.

Marler, J. H., & Floyd, B. D. 2014. Database concepts and applications in human resource information systems. In M. J. Kavanagh, M. Thite, & R. D. Johnson (Eds.), *Human resource information systems: Basics, applications, and future directions* (3rd ed.): 34–56. Thousand Oaks, CA: SAGE Publications, Inc.

Marler, J. H., & Parry, E. 2016. Human resource management, strategic involvement and e-HRM technology. *International Journal of Human Resource Management,* 27(19): 2233.

McDonnell, A. 2011. Still fighting the war for talent? Bridging the science versus practice gap. *Journal of Business and Psychology,* 26(2): 169–173.

McDonnell, A., Collings, D. G., Mellahi, K., & Schuler, R. 2017. Talent management: A systematic review and future prospects. *European Journal of International Management,* 11(1): 86–128.

McDonnell, A., Lamare, R., Gunnigle, P., & Lavelle, J. 2010. Developing tomorrow's leaders: Evidence of global talent management in multinational companies. *Journal of World Business,* 45(2): 150–160.

Mell, P., & Grance, T. 2011. The NIST definition of cloud computing. Recommendations of the National Institute of Standards and Technology. In NIST (Ed.), *Special Publication 800-145.* Gaithersburg, MD.

Mellahi, K., & Collings, D. G. 2010. The barriers to effective global talent management: The example of corporate élites in MNEs. *Journal of World Business,* 45(2): 143–149.

Orlikowski, W. J., & Scott, S. V. 2008. Sociomateriality: Challenging the separation of technology, work and organization. *The Academy of Management Annals,* 2: 433–474.

Orlikowski, W. J., & Scott, S. V. 2015. The algorithm and the crowd: Considering the materiality of service innovation. *MIS Quarterly,* 39(1): 201–216.

Orlikowski, W. J., & Scott, S. V. 2016. Digital work: A research agenda. In B. Czarniawska (Ed.), *A research agenda for management and organizational studies:* 88–96. Northampton, MA: Edward Elgar Publishing.

Pinch, T. J., & Bijker, W. E. 1984. The social construction of facts and artefacts: Or how the sociology of science and the sociology of technology might benefit each other. *Social Studies of Science (Sage),* 14(3): 399–441.

PricewaterhouseCoopers. 2018. *21st CEO survey: The anxious optimist in the corner office.* https://www.pwc.com/gx/en/ceo-survey/2018/pwc-ceo-survey-report-2018.pdf

PricewaterhouseCoopers. 2019. *22nd CEO survey: CEOs' curbed confidence spells caution.* https://www.pwc.com/gx/en/ceo-survey/2019/report/pwc-22nd-annual-global-ceo-survey.pdf

PricewaterhouseCoopers. 2020. *23rd CEO survey: Navigating the rising tide of uncertainty.* https://www.pwc.com/gx/en/ceo-agenda/ceosurvey/2020.html

Rousseau, D. M., & Barends, E. G. R. 2011. Becoming an evidence-based HR practitioner. **Human Resource Management Journal,** 21(3): 221–235.

Ruël, H., Bondarouk, T., & Looise, J. K. 2004. **E-HRM: Innovation or irritation? An exploration of web-based human resource management in large companies.** Utrecht: Lemma Publishers.

Schalk, R., Timmerman, V., & den Heuvel, S. V. 2013. How strategic considerations influence decision making on e-HRM applications. **Human Resource Management Review,** 23(1): 84–92.

Stainton, A. 2005. Talent management: Latest buzzword or refocusing existing processes? **Competency and Emotional Intelligence,** 12(1): 39–43.

Stone, D. L., & Dulebohn, J. H. 2013. Emerging issues in theory and research on electronic human resource management (eHRM). **Human Resource Management Review,** 23(1): 1–5.

Tarique, I., & Schuler, R. S. 2010. Global talent management: Literature review, integrative framework, and suggestions for further research. **Journal of World Business,** 45(2): 122–133.

Thunnissen, M., Boselie, P., & Fruytier, B. 2013a. A review of talent management: 'infancy or adolescence?' **The International Journal of Human Resource Management,** 24(9): 1744–1761.

Thunnissen, M., Boselie, P., & Fruytier, B. 2013b. Talent management and the relevance of context: Towards a pluralistic approach. **Human Resource Management Review,** 23(4): 326–336.

Whelen, E., & Carcary, M. 2011. Integrating talent and knowledge management: Where are the benefits? **Journal of Knowledge Management,** 15(4): 675–687.

Wiblen, S. 2016. Framing the usefulness of eHRM in talent management: A case study of talent identification in a professional services firm. **Canadian Journal of Administrative Sciences,** 33(2): 95–107.

Wiblen, S., Dery, K., & Grant, D. 2012. Do you see what I see? The role of technology in talent identification. **Asia Pacific Journal of Human Resources,** 50(4): 421–438.

Wiblen, S., Grant, D., & Dery, K. 2010. Transitioning to a new HRIS: The reshaping of human resources and information technology talent. **Journal of Electronic Commerce Research,** 11(4): 251–267.

Wiblen, S., Grant, D., & Dery, K. 2015. Questioning the value of a consistent approach to talent management: When one best way is not enough. Paper presented at the Academy of Management Conference, Vancouver, Canada.

Wiblen, S., & McDonnell, A. (2020). Connecting 'talent' meanings and multi-level context: A discursive approach. **The International Journal of Human Resource Management,** 31(4), 474–510.

Williams, H. 2009. Job analysis and HR planning. In M. Thite, & M. J. Kavanagh (Eds.), **Human resource information systems: Basics, applications, and future directions:** 251–276. California: SAGE Publications Inc.

World Economic Forum. 2017. **The global human capital report 2017. Preparing people for the future of work.** World Economic Forum.

Yeow, A., & Sia, S. K. 2008. Negotiating "best practices" in package software implementation. **Information and Organization,** 18(1): 1–28.

SECTION IV

Individuals, Workforce, and Processes of Talent Management

25

A VIEW FROM ACROSS THE WAY

Perspectives on Talent Management from the Field of Global Leadership

Allan Bird

Mark E. Mendenhall

Beginning a Conversation

The nascent fields of talent management (TM) and global leadership (GL) share a common origin. Both emerged in the late 1990s, as management scholars responded to industry concerns about the global supply of human talent due to complex demographic shifts, rapid technological advances, and globalization (Bird & Mendenhall, 2016; McDonnell, Collings, Mellahi, & Schuler, 2017). This research almost immediately bifurcated into separate sub-fields based on different levels of analysis in research foci. TM research concentrated mostly on macro-level, organizational systems and processes associated with talent attraction, recruitment, remuneration, performance appraisal, and retention. Meanwhile, GL researchers tended to focus on examining the micro, individual-specific components of global human talent: global leaders. At the risk of oversimplification, TM research has generally focused on *how* organizations should and do structure processes to manage human talent while GL research has generally focused on *what* constitutes talent in individual global leaders and how that talent can be developed in individuals (McDonnell et al., 2017; Oddou & Mendenhall, 2018).

Our aim in this chapter is to share findings from the field of GL that we argue can provide value to both scholars and practitioners working in the field of TM. To do so, we will be focusing our integrative efforts specifically on the area of global talent management (GTM). A recent review of the TM literature found that one-third of the research in the field "focused on the management of talent within MNCs, labelled as GTM" (McDonnell et al., 2017: 109), thus it is arguable that there is a definitive difference between TM and GTM, especially given that the domain of human talent in the 21st century is global versus local in nature for medium and large firms. The crux of the challenge for such companies in the current global marketplace is hiring and retaining individuals who are capable of leading and working across global boundaries at all levels of employment.

While scholars in both camps have been generally aware of each other's work, there has been little integration or cross-fertilization between the two fields of GTM and GL, with only a few exceptions (see for example Deters, 2017). Our purpose is to initiate this conversation and our recommendations are less critiques than they are simply sharing what GTM looks like from our vantage point in the GL field. Accordingly, we heartily invite GTM scholars to share their observations of the GL field from their standpoint as well, so that GL scholars can benefit from their views. Our chapter ensues as follows: first, we will provide a summary overview of the GL field, and then we will derive from it new areas of consideration for GTM scholars and practitioners to contemplate undertaking in their work.

DOI: 10.4324/9781315474687-25

Global Leadership: An Overview

A review of the field of global leadership is beyond the scope of this chapter (for comprehensive reviews of the field see: Bird & Mendenhall, 2016; Jokinen, 2005; Mendenhall, Li, & Osland, 2016; Mendenhall, Osland, Bird, Oddou, Stevens, Maznevski, & Stahl, 2018). When first introduced to the GL field, a commonly asked question usually takes the form of something like this: "Why insert the term 'global' in front of 'leadership?' Isn't all leadership just leadership?" With the explosion of globalization in the late 1990s, the context in which leaders found themselves having to function dramatically shifted in nature, intensity, and complexity.

According to Bird and Mendenhall (2016: 118):

> Leaders of organizations found themselves crossing borders across all dimensions of business and government more rapidly, more constantly, and more frequently than they had in previous decades. Global supply chains became the norm. Global markets became the norm. Immediate, real-time global communication with all stakeholders became the norm. Global knowledge sharing became the norm. Global finance systems became the norm. Global competitors became more ubiquitous and dangerous. Global careers became increasingly important.... Something was changing – the world of business seemed less "international" in nature and more, somehow, "global" in nature...in other words, the world seemed less linear and more nonlinear in nature.

The global context produced challenges for leaders that seemed to require different types of competencies than what were necessary for domestic contexts or traditional leadership milieus. This led to the increasing awareness that having a country-specific or area specialty as a business person was no longer adequate for international business, rather leaders now had to be able to work across and span multiple national, cultural, technological, political, and economic borders (and the constituents in each) simultaneously in real time.

Early efforts to conceptualize what global leadership actually entailed relied on the analysis of expert global leaders and drawing from findings of studies of phenomena thought to be similar in nature to GL (global mobility, personality, intercultural communication, transformation, comparative leadership, and global management) to inform theorizing and research direction (Bird & Mendenhall, 2016). This process eventually led scholars to propose and refine various construct definitions of global leadership. While this is an ongoing effort, much progress has been made in delineating the boundary conditions of GL (Reiche, Bird, Mendenhall, & Osland, 2017).

One of the primary research areas in the GL field has been the study of competencies necessary for GL effectiveness (Bird, 2018; Bird, Mendenhall, Stevens, & Oddou, 2010; Cumberland, Herd, Alagaraja, & Kerrick, 2016; Jokinen, 2005; Osland, Bird, Mendenhall, & Osland, 2006), which has proven to be efficacious in understanding the GL phenomenon and in guiding practice. As the content domain of global leadership competencies became more firmly established and circumscribed, many scholars and practitioners turned their attention to the consideration of how the competencies associated with GL effectiveness can be developed in managers. Empirical studies (e.g., Björkman & Mäkelä, 2013; Caligiuri, 2006; Caligiuri & Tarique, 2014; Dragoni et al., 2014; Huesing & Ludema, 2017) and GL developmental models derived from the fields of expatriate adjustment, adult education, cognitive-behavior therapy, and systems theory (Oddou & Mendenhall, 2018) provide robust direction for organizations that desire to address head-on the challenge of developing global leaders. In addition to the study of competencies and their development, scholars have also investigated other dimensions of GL, such as assessment and measurement (Bird & Stevens, 2018), leading global teams (Maznevski & Chui, 2018), role types (Reiche et al., 2017), knowledge creation and transfer (Bird & Oddou, 2018), leading global change (Osland, 2018b), ethical responsibility (Stahl, Pless, Maak, & Miska, 2018). The vast majority of work in each of these areas has been done from a micro-level perspective, with implications derived for practice being focused on individual leaders and managers. It is from this corpus of research that we will propose potentially fruitful topics for GTM scholars to consider integrating into their theorizing and empirical research efforts.

For the purposes of this chapter, when we speak of global leadership we will operate from the most recent operationalization of the construct (for a review of the various construct definitions of global leadership, please see Mendenhall, Reiche, Bird, & Osland, 2012) proposed after a review of GL literature and the development of a GL role typology (Reiche et al., 2017: 556): "The processes and actions through which an individual influences a range of internal and external constituents from multiple national cultures and jurisdictions in a context characterized by significant levels of task and relationship complexity."

Three Topics of Conversation

While a variety of observations could be shared for possible integrative areas between the GL and GTM fields, we will focus on three that we believe hold the most promise and are of primary importance to the effectiveness of GTM systems. We would like to have conversations around the following topics: 1) what constitutes global talent? 2) how do you know what type of global talent you need? and 3) how do you enhance existing global talent or develop it where it is lacking?

What Constitutes Global Talent?

In their comprehensive review of the TM field, McDonnell et al. (2017: 86) concluded that their "review also demonstrates that there has been limited attention placed on individual talents as the unit of analysis" and they go on to note that:

> Moreover, there is the issue of how talent is identified by organisations. In particular, what do organisations look for in individuals when determining whether they are key talent or not? It is likely that achieving a high level of performance will be important but does this equate to talent or are there additional factors/characteristics that one needs to display.... The review demonstrated much use of the term "high potential" but we are typically left wondering when it comes to understanding what is viewed as potential. (2017: 117)

Extensive research in the GL field clearly shows that an individual's past technical/job performance is a necessary but insufficient criterion for assessing current or potential GL talent. In 2002, the first review of GL research that investigated antecedents of GL effectiveness was conducted, revealing 56 competencies associated with GL (Mendenhall & Osland, 2002). Since that time, reviewers have found even more, but despite this seeming "competency cornucopia" social scientists have been unable to delineate the predominant competencies associated with GL effectiveness (for a review of the GL competency domain, see Bird, 2018) and various GL competency models have been constructed that share strong conceptual overlaps in their framing of the critical competencies necessary for GL (for a review of these models, see Osland, 2018a). For the purposes of this chapter, we have chosen the most recently published GL competency framework for our conversation (Mendenhall et al., 2017) and it is illustrated in Figure 25.1

As Figure 25.1 illustrates, competencies associated with business and organizational acumen are critical to GL. However, two other dimensions of competencies (and these or similar dimensions appear in virtually all existing GL competency models) are critical as well: 1) competencies associated with effectively interacting with people who differ culturally from the individual leader; and 2) competencies associated with managing one's self. Regarding the latter dimension, Bird (2018: 92) notes that the extant literature clearly shows that "leading in a global context is personally challenging and requires a special mix of capabilities for managing oneself."

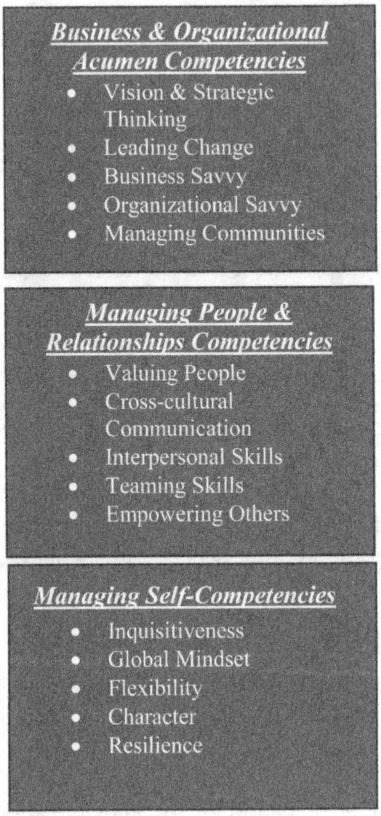

Figure 25.1 A framework of nested global leadership competencies

Adapted from Mendenhall, M. E., Osland, J., Bird, A., Oddou, G. R., Stevens, M. J., Maznevski, M. L., & Stahl, G. K. (Eds.). (2017). *Global leadership: Research, practice, and development:* 139. Routledge.

On first glance, the fifteen competencies illustrated in Figure 25.1 may seem to be too broad or vague in nature to be practicable for HR executives to work with. Nevertheless, scholars working in the field of GL have developed robust assessment instruments that either measure these competencies directly or the sub-competencies that constitute them (for a review of these assessment instruments, see Bird & Stevens, 2018). Thus, conceptual and practical assistance is available for both scholars and practitioners working in the GTM area to address McDonnell et al.'s (2017) concern for the need to better understand the additional factors/characteristics that are associated with identifying potential and current global talent beyond job performance.

Frankly, those of us working in GL have been somewhat amazed at the lack of conceptual nuance that exists both in models of TM/GTM and actual organizational TM/GTM processes. Without an understanding of the underlying dimensions of individual global talent, how can it be effectively managed? Many of us consult with organizations in addition to conducting research on GL, and the identification processes for finding external and internal talent that we have seen in firms usually seems unnecessarily simplistic, atheoretical, and regrettably incomplete in design. Our observations parallel that of McDonnell and his colleagues that identification is based not so much on the competencies that an individual must possess but rather on such criteria as past work performance, reputation of the institution from which the person graduated, superficial assumptions (e.g., she is from Hong Kong so she meets the qualification of being globally astute), perceptions of a candidate's intellectual brilliance (which can be a dangerous mix in combination with a paucity of commensurate cross-cultural communication skills in numerous cultures around the world), and false generalizations ("he was outstanding on his expatriate assignment in London so he will be a great regional manager over Asia-Pacific"). Without an empirically-based framework to identify and assess global talent, from a GL perspective, it seems that no matter how elegant the design of the TM/GTM system, it won't produce the hoped for global talent – or, at best, it will effectively manage pseudo-global talent (individuals who were thought to possess GL potential but who in reality did not).

Superstitious policies and programs are called such because they are not based on theory or empirical evidence, but instead invoke ambiguous or fuzzy perceptions of what are thought to be causal relationships, such as when an athlete associates successful performance with wearing "lucky socks." A common superstitious practice in global leadership development is that of sending a manager on an international assignment with the expectation that the assignment will help the manager develop competencies that will aid in leading globally. However, few firms have systematically addressed the use of international assignments as developmental mechanisms by examining what specific elements of an international assignment facilitate the development of specific global leader capabilities. As a consequence, firms hope that managers develop, but are unclear as to how that development actually occurs.

The development of TM approaches and practices themselves may be mired in pre-global frameworks and perspectives, failing to fully comprehend or acknowledge the unique challenges presented by the global context (Osland, Bird, & Oddou, 2012). Elsewhere (Mendenhall et al., 2012), we have noted the tendency of many leadership scholars to approach the study of global leadership as a little "g", big "L" phenomenon, focusing their attention on established leadership theory and viewing the global context as a straightforward extension beyond a single country setting. We sense a similar strain in the talent management literature.

Even when firms acknowledge that the global talent management may require focusing on a distinctive set of GL competencies, there is scant evidence that firms are actually assessing their talent on these competencies. In a survey of major global firms, Stahl et al. (2007) found that, although firms purport to value competency assessment, a substantially smaller number actually do it. Nor does much seem to have changed over the last decade. Lee and Douiyssi (2017) found that just 14% of 124 global firms they surveyed were engaged in assessment. It seems reasonable to conclude that firms may be managing their global talent but not in ways that establish baselines and chart development.

What Type of Global Talent Do You Need?

A second conversation long overdue between the global leadership and talent management camps zeroes in on the type of global talent that is needed. Looking at the global talent management literature from the outside, the emphasis appears to be primarily on technical or business "brilliance." Individuals who set themselves apart through their drive, ingenuity, innovativeness and ability to perform at a high level. No doubt there is more to talent than those general and idealized characteristics. There are likely myriad characteristics and competencies that distinguish talent that should also be considered.

What seems lacking, however, is an explicit acknowledgment that different work contexts and circumstances may call for different qualities, and that the competencies that lead to high-performance in one position may not be appropriate for another. This seems to be widely overlooked at both the strategic, assessment, and practice/program level in TM systems. In fact, Black, Morrison, and Gregersen (1999) conclude that some intercultural competencies associated with GL are actually the "glue" that holds organizational/administrative and business acumen-related competencies together and serve as their catalysts.

This issue is not unique to TM, however, as scholars in the GL field have also wrestled with this issue for the past several decades. For GL research, one way forward was to focus on the context of GL roles and the competencies associated with those roles. Recently, Reiche, Bird, Mendenhall, and Osland (2017) developed a typology of GL roles that explicates the relationship between context, position, and role requirements. In doing so, they surface important differences in GL roles that appear to have direct application to a conversation about what types of global talent are needed.

Reiche et al. (2017) contend that GL roles vary along two dimensions of complexity – task and relationship – and that specific role requirements are a function of this variation. Each of these dimensions encompasses distinctive qualities that shape the GL role.

Task complexity is characterized by variety and flux. Variety in the task context is reflected in such things as diversity of business models and organizational forms, as well as in competitive approaches and governance behaviors. It encompasses essential elements of the task environment such as regulatory jurisdictions, languages, sociocultural milieu, customers and markets, and the degree of variation found within each of these. Flux addresses the destabilizing change as it relates to three facets of change: frequency, intensity, and unpredictability. Taken all together, variety and flux across the elements of the task context influences the range and quantity as well as the ambiguity of tasks a global leader may confront in any given role.

The two constructs constituting the complexity of the relationship context are boundaries and interdependence. Boundaries characterize a given configuration of social structure. Global leader roles entail a host of relationships that cross myriad boundaries, including ones that are organizational, political, cultural, and linguistic, to name a few. These boundaries differ in terms of variety and number. Interdependence focuses on the degree to which the relationships a global leader attends are interconnected and how closely. For example, it's not uncommon for a global firm's research and development activities to be distributed across multiple locations and yet require intense collaboration.

Developing a 2x2 of task and relationship complexity (see Figure 25.2), Reiche et al. (2017) propose a typology of four GL profiles: incremental global leadership, operational global leadership, connective global leadership, and integrative global leadership. Each type requires distinctive role behaviors that, in turn, entail particular competencies (for more details, see Reiche et al., 2017).

Incremental global leadership is characterized by low task and relationship complexity. The context is likely to be stable, predictable, and relatively bounded. A leader occupying a position as an export director in a global firm that operates primarily through licensing would be one example of this type of GL role. In that role, the leader might engage in incremental change efforts, focus on technical innovation, use routinized and standardized forms of communication, and create a vision that is narrow in scope.

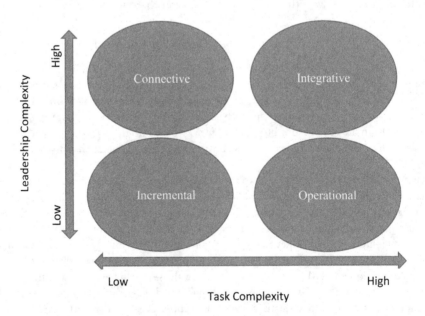

Figure 25.2 A typology of global leadership roles

Adapted from Reiche, B. S., Bird, A., Mendenhall, M. E., & Osland, J. (2017). *Contextualizing global leadership: A typology of global leadership roles*. **Journal of International Business Studies**, 48: 560.

Operational global leadership involves high task complexity and low relationship complexity. The context entails high cognitive demands responding to task conditions that are quite complex due to high levels of environmental variety, likely stemming from varying regulatory regimes, many customers, and wide variance in customer needs. A leader of product development in a firm that provides financial services to global customers is an example of operational global leadership. Role requirements might entail the need to locally adapt task prioritization, allocation of resources, and problem-solving processes. Additionally, scanning, attending, processing, and continuously analyzing disparate operational information would be essential. Finally, there would also be a need to lead varying operational changes at the local level.

Connective global leadership, in contrast to operational global leadership, is characterized by low task complexity and high relationship complexity. In this context, leaders function in roles where the tasks are specialized and bounded, but where there is a high demand for social flexibility, probably because constituents are diverse and geographically dispersed. Moreover, interdependencies among the different constituents are likely to be extensive. A good example of this type of leadership position would be someone who heads a global distributed team responsible for managing a firm's back office. Their role would require them to learn the nuances of distinct interaction contexts, continuously adapt and respond to different partners' behaviors, build interaction frequency and intensity through frequent travel and virtual communication, and leverage social friction in order to solve problems.

Lastly, the *integrative global leadership* role involves high task and high relationship complexity. The demands of this context are a consequence of myriad, dynamic task conditions, while simultaneously managing relationships that span a wide range of interconnected constituents. The interaction between the high task and high relationship complexities further increases the demands of this context. Integrative global leadership roles are often found in senior executive positions of global multi-unit firms. Leaders in those roles find it necessary to recognize and handle trade-offs and paradoxes across both task and relationship domains, often seeking synergistic solutions. They engage in regular coordination and integration activities across tasks and constituent groups. Contextualizing change initiatives and implementation processes, often through distributed leadership processes is also common.

Reflecting on the GL role typology and attendant behaviors, it is evident that effective TM will require careful, strategic attention to the impact of role types on the assessment of selection and development needs. One place where TM scholars might start is to identify the specific competencies that are associated with specific role behaviors for each of the types. This, in turn, could provide direction as to what competencies to select for, as well as a determination as to what can be reasonably developed.

A related area of potential progress is performance appraisal. Conventional practice is to evaluate individuals on the performance in their current position. Often it is these appraisals that are used in determining who should be promoted or assigned to other positions. However, if there are differing GL roles, then organizations run a significant risk of placing a high-performer in one role into a position where they may not have the capabilities to succeed. TM scholars and practitioners need to consider whether their performance appraisal systems adequately evaluate performance in future positions or in higher levels of the organization. This is yet another area where dialogue between GL and TM scholars could be particularly fruitful.

How Do You Enhance and Develop Global Talent?

Developing global leaders, particularly through a focus on GL competencies, has received increasing attention (Caligiuri & De Santo, 2001; Caligiuri, 2006; Debrah & Rees, 2011; Gregersen, Morrison, & Black, 1998; Osland & Bird, 2018). TM scholars have demonstrated a similar interest in competency development (Deters, 2017; Sharma & Bhatnagar, 2009; Stahl et al., 2007). Our impression, however, is that despite the obvious relevance to TM, GL scholars have devoted significantly more attention to the development question. Though the majority of theorizing in this area is tied to static competency models, from early on there has also been a focus on process models of GL competency development (Osland & Bird, 2018). McCall and Hollenbeck (2002) and the Chattanooga Model (Osland & Bird, 2018) provide two examples.

Across the various models, several conclusions have emerged that appear to diverge from programs and processes commonly deployed by TM approaches. First, there is a much stronger emphasis on experiential mechanisms rather than "training programs". Examples of this include the use of international assignments (Johnston, 2014) and international volunteerism projects (Caligiuri & Thoroughgood, 2015; Maak, Pless, & Borecká, 2014). A second assumption is that effective development must be individualized – the equifinality of effective global leadership compels a personalized development focus that addresses an individual's current competency configuration. Third, corporations that do GL development right experience increased organizational commitment and heightened talent retention (Caligiuri, Mencin, & Jiang, 2013; Pless, Maak, & Stahl, 2011; White & Rosamilia, 2010).

The first two conclusions – the experiential mechanism and the individualization requirement – would seem to present a substantive challenge for corporate TM systems. At the same time, this also frames the question in terms that TM systems are likely to find easy to comprehend. Global leadership talent becomes a "make or buy" decision. If the decision is to make, then what is the cost? What resources of money, manpower, and time will be required? What level of developmental outcome can be achieved, and at what level of probability/certainty? We believe a conversation between the GL and TM camps holds great potential for mutual benefit.

Areas of Further Research

Our conversation has elicited a variety of avenues for future research by GTM scholars in regard to GL. They can be summarized as follows.

Extend Identification Models

Draw upon findings in the GL competency literature to more fully capture the scope of criteria that should be used in the global talent identification process. The GL research literature clearly shows that other competencies in addition to job performance, educational pedigree, and IQ are important for success in the global context. Talent is more than technical/business brilliance; the GL literature delineates additional criteria that GTM scholars might fruitfully take into consideration in extending their models.

Focus on Understanding the Nature of GL Types

A primary purpose of GTM – to find and retain talent – is to fill future organizational roles in the global context; however, the GTM literature tends not to focus on delineating the specific skills needed to master the roles that talent is being selected to fill. Thus, there is a "competency–role match" gap within GTM models. Models in global leadership, such as the typology framework described above, can provide guidance in filling this gap in both GTM research and practice.

Integrate GL Development Models into GTM Processes

GL scholars have focused heavily on studying how managers develop into GLs, and their findings have clear implications for GTM research and practice in terms of privileging experiential processes and individualized development schemes in GTM models. Interestingly, these two foci have been found to produce talent retention in firms that deploy them as part of their leadership development programs (Caligiuri et al., 2013; Pless et al., 2011; White & Rosamilia, 2010).

A Conclusion, but Only to the Beginning of a Longer Conversation

We began this chapter by noting that the fields of talent management and global leadership share a common origin and yet, like twins separated at birth, had spent little time exploring what they had in common. Our intent in this chapter was to identify several areas where we see opportunities for further conversations, areas of intersection and common interest where each might have something to contribute to and receive from the other. Acknowledging that we are not intimately familiar with the TM literature, we chose instead look to areas of our own field where we saw something that might contribute to TM.

Scholars in the TM field might respond in several ways. It's possible that we are mistaken and that our perceptions are but a mirage, that TM and GL have few areas of mutual overlap. If so, then we welcome a conversation of where we got things wrong. Another possibility is that there are opportunities for joint gains for sharing from our respective fields. If so, then we welcome the opportunity to carry this conversation further. We're particularly interested in the insights of scholars who see contributions that TM research might make to the GL field. Our hope is that this is not the end, but rather the beginning of a longer and broader conversation.

References

Bird, A. 2018. Mapping the content domain of global leadership competencies. In M. E. Mendenhall, J. S. Osland, A. Bird, G. R. Oddou, M. L. Maznevski, M. J. Stevens, & G. K. Stahl (Eds.), *Global leadership: Research, practice, and development:* 119–142. London: Routledge.

Bird, A., & Mendenhall, M. E. 2016. From cross-cultural management to global leadership: Evolution and adaptation. *Journal of World Business,* 51: 115–126.

Bird, A., Mendenhall, M. E., Stevens, M. J., & Oddou, G. R. 2010. Defining the content domain of intercultural competence for global leaders. *Journal of Managerial Psychology,* 25(8): 810–828.

Bird, A., & Oddou, G. R. 2018. Global leadership knowledge creation and transfer. In M. E. Mendenhall, J. S. Osland, A. Bird, G. R. Oddou, M. L. Maznevski, M. J. Stevens, & G. K. Stahl (Eds.), *Global leadership: Research, practice, and development:* 302–324. London: Routledge.

Bird, A., & Stevens, M. J. 2018. Assessing global leadership competencies. In M. E. Mendenhall, J. S. Osland, A. Bird, G. R. Oddou, M. L. Maznevski, M. J. Stevens, & G. K. Stahl (Eds.), *Global leadership: Research, practice, and development:* 143–175. London: Routledge.

Björkman, I., & Mäkelä, K. 2013. Are you willing to do what it takes to become a senior global leader? Explaining the willingness to undertake challenging leadership development activities. *European Journal of International Management,* 7(5): 570–586.

Black, J. S., Morrison, A., & Gregersen, H. 1999. *Global explorers: The next generation of leaders.* New York: Routledge.

Caligiuri, P. M. 2006. Developing global leaders. *Human Resource Management Review,* 16: 219–228.

Caligiuri, P., & De Santo, V. 2001. Global competence: What is it and can it be developed through global assignments? *Human Resource Planning,* 24(3): 37–35.

Caligiuri, P., Mencin, A., & Jiang, K. 2013. Win-win-win: The influence of company-sponsored volunteerism programs on employees, NGOs, and business units. *Personnel Psychology,* 66: 825–860.

Caligiuri, P., & Tarique, I. 2014. Individual-level accelerators of global leadership development. In J. S. Osland, M. Li, & Y. Wang (Eds.), *Advances in global leadership* (Volume 8): 251–267. Bingley, UK: Emerald Group Publishing Limited.

Caligiuri, P., & Thoroughgood, C. 2015. Developing responsible global leaders through corporate-sponsored international volunteerism programs. *Organizational Dynamics,* 44: 138–145.

Cumberland, D. M., Herd, A., Alagaraja, M., & Kerrick, S. A. 2016. Assessment and development of global leadership competencies in the workplace. *Advances in Developing Human Resources,* 18(3): 301–317.

Debrah, Y. A., & Rees, C. J. 2011. The development of global leaders and expatriates. In A. W. K. Harzing, & A. Pinnington (Eds.), *International Human Resource Management* (3rd ed.): 377–408. London: Sage Publications.

Deters, J. 2017. *Global leadership talent management: Successful selection of global leadership talents as an integrated process.* Bingley, UK: Emerald Publishing Limited.

Development Dimensions International, Inc. 2009. *Global leadership forecast 2008/2009: Overcoming the shortfalls in developing leaders.* http://www.ddiworld.com.

Dragoni, L., Oh, I. S., Tesluk, P. E., Moore, O. A., VanKatwyk, P., & Hazucha, J. 2014. Developing leaders' strategic thinking through global work experience: The moderating role of cultural distance. *Journal of Applied Psychology,* 99(5): 867–882.

Gregersen, H. B., Morrison, A. J., and Black, J. S. 1998. Developing leaders for the global frontier. *Sloan Management Review,* 40: 21–32.

Huesing, T., & Ludema, J. D. 2017. The nature of global leaders' work. In J. S. Osland, M. Li, & M. E. Mendenhall (Eds.), *Advances in global leadership* (Volume 10): 3–40. Bingley, UK: Emerald Publishing Limited.

Johnston, A.G. 2014. Short-term business travel and development of executive leader global mindset. *Advances in Global Leadership,* 8: 293–316.

Jokinen, T. 2005. Global leadership competencies: A review and discussion. *Journal of European Industrial Training,* 29(2–3): 199–216.

Lee, J., & Douiyssi, D. 2017. BGRS 2017 talent mobility trends survey: Changing the conversation – Transforming mobility for the future. *BGRS.com.*

Maak, T., Pless, N. M., & Borecká, M. 2014. Developing responsible global leaders. *Advances in Global Leadership,* 8: 339–364.

McCall, M. W. Jr, & Hollenbeck, G. P. 2002. *Developing global executives: The lessons of international experience.* Boston, MA: Harvard Business School Press.

McDonnell, A., Collings, D. G., Mellahi, K, & Schuler, R. 2017. Talent management: A systematic review and future prospects. *European Journal of International Management,* 11(1): 86–128.

Mendenhall, M. E., Li, M., & Osland, J. S. 2016. Five years of global leadership research, 2010–2014: Patterns, themes, and future directions. In J. S. Osland, M. Li, & M. E. Mendenhall (Eds.), *Advances in global leadership* (Volume 9): 401–426. Bingley, UK: Emerald Publishing Limited.

Mendenhall, M. E., & Osland, J. S. 2002. *An overview of the extant global leadership research.* Symposium presentation at the Academy of International Business, Puerto Rico. June, 2002.

Mendenhall, M. E., Osland, J. S., Bird, A., Oddou, G. R., Maznevski, M. L., Stevens, M. J., & Stahl, G. K. 2018. *Global leadership: Research, practice, and development* (3rd ed.). London: Routledge.

Mendenhall, M. E., Reiche, B. S., Bird. A., & Osland, J. S. 2012. Defining the 'global' in global leadership. *Journal of World Business,* 47: 493–503.

Mendenhall, M. E., Weber, T. J., Arnardottir, A., & Oddou, G. R. 2017. Developing global leadership competencies: A process model. *Advances in global leadership:* 117–146. Bingley, UK: Emerald Publishing Limited.

Oddou, G. R., & Mendenhall, M. E. 2018. Global leadership development: Processes and practices. In M. E. Mendenhall, J. S. Osland, A. Bird, G. R. Oddou, M. L. Maznevski, M. J. Stevens, & G. K. Stahl (Eds.), *Global leadership: Research, practice, and development:* 229–270. London: Routledge.

Osland, J. S. 2018a. An overview of the global leadership literature. In M. E. Mendenhall, J. S. Osland, A. Bird, G. R. Oddou, M. L. Maznevski, M. J. Stevens, & G. K. Stahl (Eds.), *Global leadership: Research, practice, and development:* 57–116. London: Routledge.

Osland, J. S. 2018b. Leading global change. In M. E. Mendenhall, J. S. Osland, A. Bird, G. R. Oddou, M. L. Maznevski, M. J. Stevens, & G. K. Stahl (Eds.), *Global leadership: Research, practice, and development:* 325–362. London: Routledge.

Osland, J. S. & Bird, A. 2018. Process models of global leadership development. In M. E. Mendenhall, J. S. Osland, A. Bird, G. R. Oddou, M. L. Maznevski, M. J. Stevens, & G. K. Stahl (Eds.), *Global leadership: Research, practice, and development:* 179–199. London: Routledge.

Osland, J. S., Bird, A., Mendenhall, M. E., & Osland, A. 2006. Developing global leadership capabilities and global mindset: A review. In G. K. Stahl & I. Björkman (Eds.), *Handbook of research in international human resource management:* 197–222. Northampton, MA: Edward Elgar Publishing.

Osland, J. S., Bird, A., & Oddou, G. 2012. The context of expert global leadership. *Advances in global leadership:* 107–124. Bingley, UK: Emerald Group Publishing Limited.

Pless, N. M., Maak, T., & Stahl, G. K. 2011. Developing responsible global leaders through International Service Learning Programs: The Ulysses experience. *Academy of Management Learning and Education,* 10(2): 237–260.

Reiche, B. S., Bird, A., Mendenhall, M. E., & Osland, J. S. 2017. Contextualizing leadership: A typology global leadership roles. *Journal of International Business Studies,* 48: 552–572.

Sharma, R., & Bhatnagar, J. 2009. Talent management–competency development: Key to global leadership. *Industrial and Commercial training,* 41(3), 118–132.

Stahl, G. K., Björkman, I., Farndale, E., Morris, S. S., Paauwe, J., Stiles, P., & Wright, P. M. 2007. Global talent management: How leading multinationals build and sustain their talent pipeline. *INSEAD Faculty and Research Working Papers,* 24.

Stahl, G. K., Pless, N. M., Maak, T., & Miska, C. 2018. Responsible global leadership. In M. E. Mendenhall, J. S. Osland, A. Bird, G. R. Oddou, M. L. Maznevski, M. J. Stevens, & G. K. Stahl (Eds.), *Global leadership: Research, practice, and development:* 363–388. London: Routledge.

White, K., & Rosamilia, T. 2010. Developing global leadership: How IBM engages the workforce of a globally integrated enterprise. White paper. IBM Global Business Services.

26

THIRD CULTURE KIDS

Early Talent Potential for Global Work?

Jan Selmer

Yvonne McNulty

Jakob Lauring

Introduction

Recent decades have seen rapid growth in the globalized economy. To remain successful in the international business arena, multinational corporations (MNCs) have realized the importance of global human resource management (HRM) strategies, because having the right people has been recognized as the key to sustaining a global competitive edge (Beechler & Woodward, 2009; Collings, 2014a). One popular strategy is that of expatriate employment to enable organizations to manage their labor force internationally (Doherty & Dickmann, 2013; Kraimer, Bolino, & Mead, 2016; McNulty & Brewster, 2017). Thus, an increasing number of foreign subsidiaries are staffed with expatriates. Vance, Sibeck, McNulty, and Hogenauer (2011) suggest that over the past decade, the demand for expatriates has increased given that:

> global competence among managers and professionals translates into increased cross-cultural sensitivity and relationship-building capability, more effective problem solving, and greater creativity. Other benefits include more effective self-management and adjustment to foreign surroundings, greater ability to build multinational teams, improved ability to deal with rapid change and uncertainty, and enhanced savvy in adjusting and responding to differing competitive and political environments (2011: 31).

Not surprisingly, the acquisition and development of international talent has become important for MNCs (Farndale, Pai, Sparrow, & Scullion, 2014; Farndale, Scullion, & Sparrow, 2010). Scullion and Collings (2006) noted that international companies face severe challenges in attracting, retaining, and developing the necessary managerial talent for their global operations (see also Collings, 2014b). But academic research on talent management (TM) is still in its infancy, depending mostly on disjointed primary research (e.g., De Vos & Dries, 2013; Furusawa & Brewster, 2014; King, 2015), while more comprehensive methodological approaches are needed (McDonnell, Collings, Mellahi, & Schuler, 2017).

Generally, the management of talent can be said to be a strategic human resource plan to improve organizations' abilities to reach their goals. This idea departs from the anticipation of required human capital for an organization and the planning to meet those needs. As such, TM can be described as the systems and processes that enable a company to attract, develop, and retain highly qualified

DOI: 10.4324/9781315474687-26

employees (Huang & Tansley, 2012; McKinsey, 2008). More precisely, Collings and Mellahi (2009) define TM as:

> activities and processes that involve the systematic identification of key positions that differentially contribute to the organization's sustainable competitive advantage, the development of a talent pool of high-potential and high-performing incumbents to fill these roles, and the development of a differentiated human resource architecture to facilitate filling these positions with competent incumbents, and to ensure their continued commitment to the organization. (304)

The main focus of TM is to identify and support talented people in order to use their skills and competencies. However, cultivating social skills and integrating individuals in the organization to retain them could be equally important (Stahl et al., 2012). This is especially true when dealing with global organizations (e.g., Hartman, Feisel, & Schober, 2010; Iles, Chuai, & Preece, 2010).

With the internationalization of businesses a global dimension of TM has emerged (Al Ariss, Cascio, & Paauwe, 2014). Global TM includes organizational procedures to attract, select, develop, and keep the best employees in the most important roles worldwide (Vaiman, Scullion, & Collings, 2012). The importance of global TM to the performance of MNCs has become widely acknowledged in recent years (Bethke-Langenegger, Mahler, & Staffelbach, 2011; Makela, Bjorkman, & Ehrnrooth, 2010; Tarique & Schuler, 2010). This is backed up by research findings emphasizing the centrality of international employee mobility as a key element of international companies' global talent strategies (Collings, 2014a; McNulty & De Cieri, 2016).

While attempts to address global talent shortages has seen modest success (Minbaeva & Collings, 2013; Vaiman & Collings, 2013), an emerging body of research suggests that international and/or mobility experiences early in life can be helpful for developing global competencies that promote organizational effectiveness and individual career success in adulthood (Vance, 2005; Vance & Paik, 2006). Some of these early mobility experiences occur during undergraduate and graduate education coursework and include international internships, study abroad, cross-cultural virtual teamwork, short-term experiential learning within a specific global industry context (e.g., international cruise industry, travel agency operational design), and short travel study tours (McKenzie et al., 2010; Metcalf, 2010; Vance et al., 2011). These approaches provide not only the opportunity to learn about international business environments, but also allow the practical application of many domestic business concepts and skills in an intercultural context. Indeed, the expatriate training literature recommends various forms of intense experiential learning in order to be successful in the foreign working environment (Bird et al., 1999; Black et al., 1992).

A separate set of studies in line with the above has explored the suitability of Adult Third Culture Kids (ATCKs) as expatriates, suggesting that their international experiences as children represents a distinct and unique form of intense intercultural experiential learning that can be leveraged in adulthood. ATCKs are individuals with at least six months international experience during adolescence (Melles & Schwartz, 2013; Selmer & Lauring, 2014; Tarique & Weisbord, 2013; Useem, Useem, & Donoghue, 1963). They are often individuals who accompanied their parents to live and work in another country when they were children (Greenholtz & Kim, 2009; Lyttle, Barker, & Cornwell, 2011).

It has been speculated that international organizations could focus their global TM initiatives on such individuals with early intercultural experiences as they may be more culturally sensitive than monocultural adults who, as children, have been born and raised in only one cultural location (Bonebright, 2010; Lam & Selmer, 2004a; Selmer & Lam, 2004). For this reason, Ward (1989: 57) has described ATCKs as "the prototype [citizens] of the future." However, it is still a standing question whether MNCs are able to utilize this high-potential resource.

In this regard, Becker, Beatty, and Huselid (2009) argue that many companies fall into the trap of spending too much time and money on low performers, while high-performers do not receive the necessary resources, development opportunities, or rewards. We argue that in relation to global TM, ATCKs may be worth paying special attention to. This could be in line with the argument of Becker et al. (2009) that there is a need for developing a differentiated workforce that is difficult for competitors to copy. Workforce differentiation as a strategy should be perceived as a diversified HR promoting those employees that are most important to key global business objectives. In order to achieve this, HR functions should differentiate employees according to their contribution to the execution of global strategy and develop differentiated human resource activities based on this classification.

The most important individuals are those employees who address vital international business challenges and who are critical for achieving a competitive global advantage (Huselid, Beatty, & Becker, 2005). In relation to global TM, they should possess superior capabilities and competencies valued according to how they fit to the requirements of the specific international business strategy.

In a global light, ATCKs could be those who truly create organizational value that can make or break a global strategy, that have the most valuable international skills, and that are generally the hardest to replace. Hence, ATCKs could be perceived as an investment to be managed differently compared to monocultural peers. They need to be identified, then developed and nurtured differently, and they should receive the necessary resources, development opportunities, and rewards to be successful. In other words, they could have high potential but need special attention to be placed in critical positions so that they will stay with the organization and eventually emerge as key expatriates or global leaders.

The goal of the current chapter is first, to view ATCKs as high-potential employees, and second, to provide an overview of important issues that represent key challenges when managing ATCKs as high-potential employees.

The remainder of the chapter is divided into five sections. The first section describes central concepts in the understanding of ATCKs as talented workers in a global labor market. In the second section, the advantages of using ATCKs as high-potential employees are described, while the disadvantages are outlined in the third section. The fourth section discusses important questions for future research to answer. Finally, the last section is a short conclusion of the chapter.

Overview: Key Concepts in the ATCK Literature

The larger frame of reference here rests on the construct of cultural identity, referring to a person's subjective sense of belonging to a cultural group (Benet-Martínez & Haritatos, 2005; Cheng, Lee, Benet-Martínez, & Huynh, 2014; Lauring, 2008; Nguyen & Benet-Martínez, 2007, 2010). Being exposed to a culture does not necessarily mean identifying with that culture. For example, according to Berry (1990), immigrants may have dual cultural experiences depending on the degree of identification with their home and host cultures: 1) marginalization (not identifying with either culture); 2) separation (identifying with the home culture only); 3) assimilation (identifying with the host culture only); and 4) integration (identifying with both cultures).

The latter type of identification in two cultures constitutes *biculturalism.* As opposed to monoculturals who only identifying with one culture, biculturals have internalized and feel attached to two different cultures (Benet-Martínez & Haritatos, 2005; Hong et al., 2000). This can be seen as a subset of a larger group of *multiculturals* who have internalized and identify with more than one culture (Brannen & Thomas, 2010; Fitzsimmons, Liao & Thomas, 2017; Lücke, Kostova, & Roth, 2014). The cultural identities of individuals may exist on a continuum called *identity plurality* that ranges from monocultural to multicultural. Together with *identity integration*, referring to what extent individuals integrate their cultural identities as opposed to keeping them separate, these two dimensions create a map of *identity patterns* (Fitzsimmons, 2013; Fitzsimmons, Liao, & Thomas, 2017).

Identification with two cultures can create a third, hybrid, or hyphenated culture (Benet-Martínez & Haritatos, 2005; Kwon, 2019; LaFramboise et al., 1993), being the discrepancy between the two cultures of the *place of departure* and the *place of settlement* (Benjamin & Dervin, 2015). The feeling of belonging to a third culture has been associated with growing up internationally as a "third culture kid"

(TCK) (Dewaele & van Oudenhoven, 2009; Fail, Thompson, & Walker, 2004; Peterson & Plamondon, 2009; Useem, Donoghue, & Useem, 1963; Walters & Auton-Cuff, 2009). Pollock and Van Reken (2009) define a TCK as:

> [A] person who has spent a significant part of his or her developmental years outside the parents' culture. The TCK frequently builds relationships to all of the cultures, while not having full ownership in any. Although elements from each culture may be assimilated into the TCK's life experience, the sense of belonging is in relationship to others of similar background. (13)

Thus, the "third culture" does not represent an actual geographical space (i.e., a specific country or nationality) as much as it represents a sub-culture of belonging among those sharing the same experience of repetitive mobility involving geographical and social detachment, relocation, and resettlement (Benjamin & Dervin, 2015; Cranstone, 2017). The third culture is thus not a physical place but a virtual space in which no clear cut characteristics about permanency or national culture exist. Rather, the third culture is nation-less and fluid, with inhabitants who are in equal measure "cultural chameleons" while also being "culturally homeless" (Hoersting & Jenkins, 2011). In contrast, the second culture is a permanent physical place in the host country that provides a rooted cultural and sociological backdrop and framework for the grind of TCKs' daily life.

Parents of TCKs have mostly been conceptualized as having a higher social and economic status as privileged expatriates (e.g., as diplomats, military personnel, missionaries, teachers, or other expatriates working in international business) (Peterson & Plamondon, 2009). Despite the risk of conceptual dilution, a debate has ensued suggesting to extend the concept of TCKs to groups of children who are, for example, refugees or immigrants, international adoptees, or the children of multicultural parents (Le Bigre, 2015; Tanu, 2015; Van Reken & Bethel, 2005). To do so would nonetheless cause a problem for the TCK construct (see Cottrell, 2011), given that the defining characteristic of the TCK "insider" sub-culture is the "experience of a cross-cultural lifestyle, high mobility (theirs or others') and expected repatriation"; repatriation, of course, being what distinguishes TCKs from migrants and monocultural children (Tanu, 2015: 17).

For this reason, children that sit on the fringe of the TCK construct have been conceptualized more broadly as *cross-cultural kids*[1] (CCKs) (Van Reken & Bethel, 2005) and *global nomads* (Langford, 1998; McCaig, 2002; McLachlan, 2007), which encapsulates a wider group and is not dependent on geography alone. Included in the CCK cohort are children from international marriages (e.g., born to an "expatriate" father and a "local" mother) as well as middle- and upper-class local children attending international schools (as is the case, for example, in China) (Tanu, 2015). Although much of the early literature has been about American TCKs (Useem & Useem, 1967), subsequent research has found similarities in other geographical locations such as British TCKs in Hong Kong (Lam & Selmer, 2004b), Central-Eastern European TCKs (Trabka, 2015), and TCKs in Germany (Meyer, 2015).

Adult TCKs (ATCKs) are those with one or more TCK experiences during their childhood who have attained the age of 18 (Bonebright, 2010; Selmer & Lam, 2004; Tarique & Weisbord, 2013). ATCK characteristics include growing up in families with origins in different countries, possibly holding more than one passport, and speaking several languages.[2]

There is no general consensus on the minimum period of a stay in another country to qualify as a TCK (and consequently be considered an ATCK). Useem (2001) used a minimum period of one year while other studies suggest a minimum of two (Hoersting & Jenkins, 2011) or three years (e.g., Lyttle et al., 2011; Moore & Barker, 2012). A minimum period of six months has also been applied (e.g. Melles & Schwartz, 2013; Selmer & Lauring, 2014). Moreover, the age span defining adolescence has varied across studies (Melles & Schwartz, 2013; Moore & Barker, 2012; Selmer & Lauring, 2014).

Since TCKs gain their multicultural experiences in their formative years (i.e., when they are highly impressionable), they have been argued to be capable of adapting and changing their skills very quickly (Sheard, 2008). For this reason, TCKs may be able to develop their third-cultureness even after a short period of multicultural exposure, as it may be the individual experiences rather than the length of stay that constitutes the critical requirement for a child to acquire a third culture (Lam & Selmer, 2004b).

ATCKs as High Potential Employees: Advantages

Adolescence has been argued to be the most important developmental period of life and thus a time of critical learning (Schwartz et al., 2005; Selmer & Lam, 2004). Hence, children who have been exposed to early intense experiential learning in international contexts may possess a heightened understanding and perception of how to handle people from different cultures. These early international experiences would make them open-minded, flexible in their mindset, and more tolerant towards people's differences in terms of behavior and thinking (Lyttle et al., 2011). Accordingly, researchers generally agree that ATCKs can be characterized as diplomatic, multicultural, multilinguistic, and functional in a variety of business and social settings. Spending their developmental years in a foreign culture triggers TCKs' identification with the "third culture" (e.g., Fail, Thompson, & Walker, 2004), which differs from the single-cultural identities of mono-culturals (Selmer & Lam, 2004).

McNulty and Carter (2014) argue that ATCKs' life experiences come from being raised in a truly cross-cultural and a highly mobile world where the surroundings regularly change in chronic cycles of separation and loss. In experiencing a new culture, adolescents may be influenced in significant ways by their alien surroundings, triggering a lifelong lasting effect that endows them as being able to fit in and feel "at home" wherever they go. Notably, some scholars have found that patterns of identity vary among ATCK individuals, where some ATKCs may not even acknowledge a specific third culture identification (Hanek, 2017; Moore & Barker, 2012) despite that in theory it is shown to exist.

Nonetheless, the early adoption of cross-cultural skills creates in TCKs a suitability for handling change, relating to other cultures, and communicating across differences (Bonebright, 2010; Lam & Selmer, 2004a; Selmer & Lam, 2004). Notwithstanding an ongoing debate that there are both positive and negative outcomes resulting from ATCKs' early intercultural experiences (Bonebright, 2010; Westropp, Cathro, & Everett, 2016)[3], in the context of international business, ATCKs represent a potentially valuable commodity in the TM landscape.

Cultural Sensitivity

Cultural sensitivity can be described as an individual's ability to develop a positive emotion towards understanding and appreciating cultural differences that promotes appropriate and effective behavior in intercultural communication (Søderberg, Krishna, & Bjørn, 2013). In the ATCK context, it could be argued that cultural sensitivity facilitates an understanding of host country nationals (Mol, Born, Willemsen, & Van Der Molen, 2005) and/or third country nationals more broadly, due to ATCKs being more open-minded towards out-group members (Dewaele & van Oudenhoven, 2009), having less authoritarian attitudes (Peterson & Plamondon, 2009), and being less prejudiced (Melles & Schwartz, 2013). ATCKs, as a result of their intense childhood international experiences, may also show higher levels of creativity (Hanek, 2017).

The potential for ATCKs to harness a high level of global work effectiveness rests largely in their cultural sensitivity being rooted in behaviors and skills that are acquired early in life (during childhood) and which become deeply rooted in the individual during their formative years (Tarique & Weisbord, 2013). Cultural sensitivity is thus a somewhat natural state of being for ATCKs, making them ideal global work candidates.

Propensity for Global Careers

In situations of choice and decision making, individuals holding a third cultural identity would be expected to choose options representing their global identity (Zhang & Khare, 2009), including career options. Due to their interest in international careers (Gerner & Perry, 2000), many ATCKs select college majors that help them to develop an "internationalism" career anchor (Lazarova et al., 2014), thus leading to work abroad as, for example, international policy diplomats, English as a second language teachers, and doctors and nurses (Cottrell, 2002).

Indeed, based on their research findings, Tarique and Weisbord (2013) advise recruiters to contact foreign schools and universities to locate and identify ATCKs coming from diverse or multicultural families, who have lived in several countries, speak multiple languages, and have personality traits of openness to experience. Since not all of these personal characteristics can be easily generated by cross-cultural training prior to deployment on an international assignment, recruiting ATCKs already possessing such traits could be important.

Although ATCKs participate in higher education to a very large extent, they tend to have unconventional educational paths. For obvious reasons of mobility, many do not receive a degree from the first college they attend, and studying at three or more colleges is common. Dropping out is common and many finish their degree only in their twenties (Bonebright, 2010). Nonetheless, research provides some empirical support for the contention that the multicultural abilities acquired at adolescence by the TCKs may be long-lasting, if not permanent (Selmer & Lauring, 2014). Consequently, there may be some good reasons to recruit ATCKs as expatriates.

As ATCKs tend to maintain global dimensions throughout their lives (e.g., relationships and networks) (Cottrell & Useem, 1994), they are likely to engage in some forms of professional work that supports their cross-cultural identity. This does not suggest that ATCKs will automatically gravitate towards global work and/or global careers because of their high-mobility childhood. Rather, it implies that they may be open to, and more accepting of, the "potential of mobility" because their high mobility childhood has normalized the global career as one of many choices available to them (Trabka, 2015: 199). Moreover, a global career for ATCKs may not always involve geographical mobility (see Tharenou, 2005). International work in domestic jobs that require global work responsibilities could just as easily leverage an ATCK's unique skillset as much as physically relocating abroad might do.

Adjustment to Global Work

Cross-cultural adjustment has for a long time been shown as a key characteristic relative to expatriates' performance and success when working abroad (see Takeuchi, 2010). Correspondingly, a lack of adjustment is frequently proposed to be a major cause of expatriate failure (Bhaskar-Shrinivas et al., 2005), including a lack of adjustment among accompanying family members (Black & Stephens, 1989; de Leon & McPartlin, 1995). Expatriate adjustment is defined as "the degree of fit or psychological comfort and familiarity that individuals feel with different aspects of foreign culture" (Takeuchi, 2010: 1041).

Adjustment has been conceptualized as pertaining to the psychological comfort related to differences in general adjustment (weather, food, and living conditions), work adjustment (work values, expectations, and standards), and interactional adjustment (communication styles, interpersonal communication) (Bhaskar-Shrinivas et al., 2005; Hechanova et al., 2003). Cockburn (2002) reported that ATKCs are more likely to adjust when living abroad as their high-mobility childhoods have taught them to be flexible and adaptive. Based on a quantitative study of TCKs in Hong Kong, Lam and Selmer (2004b) found them to possess distinct personal characteristics in terms of flexibility, international awareness, and experience. Such characteristics could be useful to increase ATKCs' general, work, and interaction adjustment, relative to non-ATCKs, in terms of the job requirements of global work and the ensuing responsibilities they will take on in international positions.[4]

Walters and Auton-Cuff (2009) argue that due to disruption of their identity development during adolescence, ATCKs become used to adjusting and readjusting to new environments (also see Nathanson & Marcenko, 1995) which can further assist their work adjustment in global environments. Indeed, in a sample of ATCKs from 13 countries, Tarique and Weisbord (2013) found empirical evidence supporting the proposal by Bonebright (2010), Lam and Selmer (2004a), and Selmer and Lam (2004) that ATCKs have a propensity to become successful expatriates.

Among the important personal characteristics that we suggest could be related to ATCKs adjustment to global work are the variety of early international experience, cultural novelty of early international experience, language diversity, family diversity, and openness to experience (e.g., Abe, 2018; Lauring, Guttormsen, & McNulty, 2019; Waal & Born, 2020). Furthermore, among the positive aspects found in empirical studies, ATCKs have been shown to demonstrate higher social sensitivity than their monocultural counterparts (Lyttle, Barker, & Cornwell, 2011), and Sheard (2008) reported that TCKs in China express more tolerant views. Lam and Selmer (2004b) found similar results with regard to tolerance. Earlier findings by Gerner, Perry, Modelle, and Archbold (1992) showed that internationally mobile adolescents rated themselves as more culturally accepting and as demonstrating more flexibility in interacting with different cultural groups compared to their monocultural peers.

They also found TCKs to be more open towards different language usages and possessing greater linguistic abilities. In line with this, Moore and Barker (2012) found ATCKs to be better intercultural communicators. In part, this may be explained by Moore and Barker's (2012) findings of ATCKs being more likely to have multiple cross-cultural behaviors, interests, and values. Other research has found TCKs to relate well to individuals of different races, ethnicities, religions, and nationalities in various contexts (Eidse & Sichel, 2004; Useem & Downie, 1976). Additionally, it has been proposed that TCKs are apt to show a general concern for their surroundings and people not part of their own social circle (Lam & Selmer, 2004). Finally, Dewaele, and Oudenhoven's (2009) found ATCKs to possess higher cultural empathy.

ATCKs as High Potential Employees: Disadvantages

Loss and Grief

TCKs' continuous mobility resulting in multiple cultural identities for them as ATCKs does not result only in benefits. Indeed, the advantages of "third-cultureness" often comes at a cost. Some studies stress the negative effects of a cross-cultural upbringing (Long, 2020; Nathanson & Marcenko, 1995; Weeks et al., 2010).

A lifestyle of chronic change and mobility may result in feelings of being restless and culturally marginalized (Pollock & van Reken, 2009). This may be linked to what Greenholtz and Kim (2009) describe as the paradox of global nomadism, that cultural hybrids may seem at home in any cultural context, but could feel at home only among others with a similar third-culture background. Such individuals can find change to be an "ironic constant", due to constant moves by their own family and others around them (Bushong, 2013; Hervey, 2009). Therefore, they seldom experience full ownership of any culture and, as ATCKs, may be prone to high levels of mobility across the various boundaries that constitute their lives: home, family, intimate relationships, and career. Because they have experienced cultural shocks early in life before they have had the opportunity to gain a sense of who they are and where they belong (see Schwartz, Cote, & Arnett, 2005), they may experience trouble in acquiring a sense of belonging and a sense of identity (Fail, Thompson, & Walker, 2004; Hoersting & Jenkins, 2011).

It has been reported that the mobile lifestyle of a TCK may result in a clouded or confused sense of identity as they reach adulthood (Grimshaw & Sears, 2008; Hervey, 2009; Murphy, 2003), which often arises from a misunderstanding that the international part of their story is a "dynamic which has shaped them profoundly" as opposed to being simply a "matter of geography" (Bushong, 2013: 56). This, in line with belongingness theory (Baumeister & Leary, 1995), may lead to unresolved grief issues (Gilbert, 2008) that, if not addressed, subsequently impacts on their life and career choices as ATCKs, which we discuss next.

Rootlessness

Another common side-effect reported in the TCK literature is that of rootlessness (Bushong, 1988; Wertsch, 1991). Fail et al. (2004) found that most TCKs either feel like they belong in multiple places, or that they belong nowhere. Dewaele and van Oudenhoven (2009) found statistical evidence for TCKs being significantly less emotionally stable than mono-cultural kids. Bushong (2013), in her counseling practice, finds that ATCKs are frequently delayed in their emotional development into adulthood compared to their monocultural peers, due to a lack of time during childhood to process the grief arising from a chronic state of constant mobility. Manifesting as repressed and unresolved feelings of grief, loss, rootlessness, and a confused sense of belonging, these issues typically begin to be addressed only at the point when they stop being mobile (i.e., "take a breath"). This is commonly at about the age of 30, when they are expected to have settled down and "are now in the emotional space where they can focus on their history" (56).

Westropp et al. (2016) found that although ATCKs were open minded, were internationally motivated, and had an enhanced cultural understanding, they were also "rootless chameleons". Hoersting and Jenkins (2011) studied adults that had a geographically mobile childhood and described them as "culturally homeless". Such "lostness" in ATCKs arises from "changing cultural environments at critical stages in life, which interrupt traditional processes for learning cultural balance and belonging" (Bushong, 2013: 56). It has been found to lead to anxiety and depression (Bushong, 2013), and lower self-esteem (Hoersting and Jenkins, (2011).

Given that the result of cultural exposure may sometimes be negative, individuals who have lived in a foreign culture are sometimes less open to other cultural values (Cheng, Clerkin, Lee, & Dries, 2011), becoming more prejudiced as a result (Pollock & Van Reken, 2009). The paradox of global nomadism, then, is that while TCKs could seem at home in any cultural context, they may feel at home only among others with a similar cultural background (Greenholtz & Kim, 2009). The search for others is a likely reason why various ATCK networking and social support organizations have been created (e.g., www.denizenmag.com; www.figt.org, www.tckid.com) as a means to cater to this unique type of commonality (Bonebright, 2010).

The downside of childhood mobility is that not all ATCKs respond to their early international experiences in the same way; whereas some embrace their cross-cultural experiences and learn to leverage its benefits, others see their internationally mobile upbringing as having trapped them in a life over which they had no control (i.e., they view their childhood as an unfortunate circumstance forced upon them as a result of their parents' career choice) (Tanu, 2015).

Early rootlessness during childhood often results in one of two outcomes for ATCKs as they enter adulthood: 1) an unspoken permission to continue to participate in many cultures as an almost automatic extension, and embracing, of their high mobility childhood (where the real challenge is to stay in one place); or conversely, (2) a deliberate rejection of a high-mobility lifestyle in favor of remaining in one geographical location for the rest of their lives. Some ATCKs who come to loathe the impermanent nature of their childhood may opt for a rooted and permanent adult life (to "settle down") in which career and family mobility is deliberately avoided for a stable relationship and for the well-being of their partner and children.

These ATCKs voluntarily remove themselves from the opportunities presented by global work. Indeed, Trabka (2015) found in her comparative study of Polish and American TCKs that mobility is not a priority in ATCKs' professional life, where being independent and adopting a freelancing career model were more important objectives and mobility would be undertaken only when the right opportunities arose. Our point is that, despite the rare skillset of social and cultural capital they acquire at a young age, not all ATCKs are willing to leverage these skills by engaging in global work (Bushong, 2013), with consequent implications for the sourcing of global talent.

Future Research Agenda

Since the academic research on ATCKs is relatively undeveloped, there are a number of new avenues that we propose could be taken. As our focus is on business expatriation, ATCKs may be suitable as expatriates (Selmer & Lam, 2004; Lam & Selmer, 2004a) and part of a global TM effort (Al Ariss, Cascio, & Paauwe, 2014). This includes both corporate and non-corporate assigned expatriates (AEs)[5] as well as self-initiated expatriates (SIEs),[6] with the latter likely to constitute a higher proportion of ATCKs given their preference for independence and a free-agent career model (Trabka, 2015). In the case of self-initiated mobility, the preference for expatriation may become even more pronounced since the ATCK will be required to obtain their global work opportunity without home country organizational support, something they are undoubtedly used to arising from an early life of necessary adaptability.

There are a number of issues that may impact on the suitability of ATCKs as an important element of a global TM strategy. One such issue is the effect of rootlessness and identity confusion felt by many. Potential downsides of the ATCK global worker needs further exploration in relation to how valuable ATCKs are as global talent and for which types of assignments they should be engaged. For example, if ATCKs are rootless nomads, they may not necessarily be relied on to stay in the organization for a long time. Thus, short-term assignments or work involving frequent international business travel may be preferable to expensive long-term strategic assignments where expatriate attrition can impact on organizational performance. Research questions include:

RQ1: Are ATCKs more, or less, likely to engage in assigned versus self-initiated expatriation?
RQ2: Which forms of global talent management are better suited to ATCKs in relation to 1) leveraging their social and cultural capital; 2) their attrition; and 3) obtaining a satisfactory expatriate ROI?

Further research is needed to explore whether ATCK expatriates may have an advantage over TCAs (their mono-cultural counterparts) in terms of interaction and work adjustment. Although Selmer and Lauring (2014) did not find any such advantage for ATCK self-initiated expatriate academics in Hong Kong, it may still exist under other circumstances. It would be important to vary the location and type of expatriates to test if their early findings are robust in different situations. Similarly, since the inter-group differences in their study were somewhat weak, it would be necessary to test for various mediators and moderators. For example, gender, age, and level of education may have an influence on the advantage of ATCK expatriates over TCAs (mono-culturals).

Recently, Fitzsimmons, Liao, and Thomas (2017) also found that individuals who integrated their cultural identities experienced higher levels of personal well-being than those who kept them separate. It would be relevant and interesting to test if that also holds for ATCKs in terms of their general adjust-ment, for whom they have created their third, hybrid, or hyphenated cultural identity by a process of integration (Benet-Martínez & Haritatos, 2005; LaFramboise et al., 1993). Research questions include:

RQ3: In the context of (a) self-initiated expatriation and (b) assigned expatriation, are ATCKs likely to (i) adjust and (ii) perform better than TCAs (monoculturals)?
RQ4: To what extent is (a) expatriate interaction adjustment and (b) expatriate work adjustment impacted by ATCKs' (i) age, (ii) gender, and (iii) level of education?
RQ5: To what degree does cultural identity integration for ATCKs impact on their general adjustment?

A further line of research concerns theoretically developing the TCK construct in relation to its boundary conditions as well as theoretical foundation. An ongoing debate has centred around the continued relevance of the TCK term to adequately describe the people it intends. Trabka (2015: 187) suggests that, aside from Americans and those in South-East Asia, the term is "approached rather sus-piciously by researchers all over the world." A key issue is to identify what is meant by "culture" in the TCK label wherein people who identify with a particular culture often do not do so homogenously but instead choose "components of the cultural tool kit to construct their actions and identities" (p. 188). Thus, the TCK identity is not necessarily a shared cultural identity as much as it is an amalgam of *shared experiences* representing a "transnational youth" (Tanu, 2015: 14).

In the context of expatriation for ATCKs, further research is needed to determine which sets of shared experiences are more likely to result in ATCKs attraction to global work and which characteristics of their shared experiences can enhance expatriate performance. Similarly, the distinction between TCKs, CCKs, and TCAs is an important one (see Bushong, 2013), because the point at which the individual experiences mobility for the first time (childhood versus adulthood) is likely to impact on their propensity to engage in expatriate job changes as well as the types of global work experiences they are likely to pursue. An understanding of ATCKs motives for global work can therefore benefit in the TM process.

Takeuchi (2010: 1044) suggests that expatriate adjustment can be better studied through the lens of person-situation interaction (see Pervin, 1989) because it "explains individual behaviors by emphasizing the continuous and multitudinous interactions between person characteristics and situational characteristics". For ATCKs, this is a particularly appropriate context in which to examine how a personal life history of early chronic mobility interacts with the host-country environment in which they are undertaking global work to impact on their adjustment, performance, propensity to undertake further mobility (willingness to go), and tendency to engage in job changes (retention). One's life history may also impact on how the ATCK handles personal crises while working abroad (McNulty, Lauring, Jonasson, & Selmer, 2019).

Bushong (2013) argues that it is not the geography of the ATCK experience but the dynamic and complex interplay of international experiences that explains individuals' behavior. In the context of expatriation, then, interactions between an ATCK's person and situational characteristics is likely to be a better explanation for their expatriation choices than simply relying on their prior international exposure. Research questions include:

RQ6: Does the term "TCK" adequately describe the people it intends?

RQ7: Which sets of shared experiences are more or less likely to result in ATCKs attraction to global work?

RQ8: Which characteristics of ATCKs' shared experiences enhance expatriate performance?

RQ9: Do differences among TCK sub-types (e.g., CCAs, TCAs) explain outcomes related to expatriates' (a) propensity to engage in expatriate job changes, and (b) the types of global work experiences they pursue?

Conclusion

In this chapter, we have defined the main concepts associated with TCKs life experience, ranging from the constructs of cultural identity and biculturalism, to the specific concept of TCKs and ATCKs. Indicating their cultural sensitivity, we have discussed ATCKs as high-potential global talent. While pointing out their advantages, there are also disadvantages arising from the TCK experience, making the suitability of ATCKs as a talent potential for global work questionable. A future research agenda has been outlined to further explore this under-researched field of investigation. That said and done, we must admit that the main proposition – whether ATCKs have a talent potential for global work – remains in large part unanswered. Although our review appears promising in that ATCKs seem to be good candidates for expatriation, much more empirical and theoretical work is needed before we can respond to this proposition with confidence.

Notes

1 Defined as a person who is living or has lived in – or meaningfully interacted with – two or more cultural environments for a significant period of time during childhood (Pollock & Van Reken, 2009: 31).

2 ATCKs should not be confused with third culture adults (TCAs) on the basis that the latter make their first cross-cultural move as adults, not as children (Bushong, 2013). International university students are a good example of TCAs.

3 Notably, the positive view has been generally represented in expatriate research (e.g., Selmer & Lam, 2004; Tarique & Weisbord, 2013) whereas the negative view has featured strongly in psychologically oriented literature (e.g., Peterson & Plamondon, 2009; Walters & Auton-Cuff, 2009).

4 This is, of course, our educated assumption based on a broad overview of the literature, notwithstanding findings by Selmer and Lauring (2014) showing that ATCKs (among self-initiated expatriate academics) in Hong Kong adjusted better than their mono-cultural peers but only in relation to general adjustment.

5 Defined as "people whose careers often unfold within one organization which seek to help them improve their career advancement within the company through multiple long-term assignments" (McNulty & Brewster, 2017: 32).

6 SIEs are "individuals who initiate and usually finance their own expatriation and are not transferred by organizations. They relocate to a country of their choice to pursue cultural, personal, and career development experiences, often with no definite time frame in mind' (Shaffer et al., 2012: 1286).

References

Abe, J. A. A. 2018. Personality, well-being, and cognitive-affective styles: A cross-sectional study of adult third culture kids. *Journal of Cross-Cultural Psychology,* 49(5): 811–830.

Al Ariss, A., Cascio, W. F., & Paauwe, J. 2014. Talent management: Current theories and future research directions. *Journal of World Business,* 49(2): 173–179.

Baumeister, R., & Leary, M. R. 1995. The need to belong: Desire for interpersonal attachments as a fundamental human motivation. *Psychological Bulletin,* 117: 497–529.

Becker, B. E., Huselid, M. A., & Beatty, R. W. 2009. *The differentiated workforce: Transforming talent into strategic impact.* Boston, MA: Harvard Business School Press.

Beechler, S. & Woodward, I. 2009. The global "war for talent". *Journal of International Management,* 15(3): 273–285.

Benet-Martínez, V., & Haritatos, J. 2005. Bicultural identity integration (BII): Components and psychosocial antecedents. *Journal of Personality,* 73(4): 1015–1050.

Benjamin, S., & Dervin, F. 2015. *Migration, diversity, and education: Beyond third culture kids.* London, UK: Palgrave Macmillan.

Bethke-Langenegger, P., Mahler, P., & Staffelbach, B. 2011. Effectiveness of talent management strategies. *European Journal of International Management,* 5(5): 524–539.

Bhaskar-Shrinivas, P., Harrison, D. A., Shaffer, M. A., & Luk, D. M. 2005. Input-based and time-based models of international adjustment: Meta-analytic evidence and theoretical extensions. *Academy of Management Journal,* 48: 259–281.

Bird, A., Mendenhall, M., Osland, J. & Schneider, S. 1999. Adapting and adjusting to other cultures: What we know but don't always tell. *Journal of Management Inquiry,* 8(2): 152–165.

Black, J. S., Gregersen, H. B., & Mendenhall, M. E. 1992. *Global assignments: Successfully expatriating and repatriating international managers.* San Francisco, CA: Jossey-Bass.

Black, J. S., & Stephens, G. 1989. The influence of the spouse on American expatriate adjustment and intent to stay in Pacific Rim overseas assignments. *Journal of Management,* 15: 529–544.

Bonebright, D. A. 2010. Adult third culture kids: HRD challenges and opportunities. *Human Resource Development International,* 13(3): 351–359.

Bushong, B. 1988. Where do I sleep tonight? MKs and mobility. *Evangelical Missions Quarterly:* 352–356.

Bushong, L. 2013. *Belonging everywhere and nowhere: Insights into counseling the globally mobile.* Indianapolis, IN: Mango Tree Intercultural Services.

Cheng, C.-Y., Clerkin, C., Lee, F. & Dries, E. 2011. *Traveling abroad and creative performance: A mediation model.* Unpublished manuscript. Singapore Management University.

Cockburn, L. 2002. Children and young people living in changing worlds: The process of assessing and understanding the 'third culture kid'. *School Psychology International,* 23: 475–484.

Collings, D. G. 2014a. Integrating global mobility and global talent management: Exploring the challenges and strategic opportunities. *Journal of World Business,* 49(2): 253–261.

Collings, D. G. 2014b. Toward mature talent management: Beyond shareholder value. *Human Resource Development Quarterly,* 25(3): 301–319.

Collings, D. G., & Mellahi, K. 2009. Strategic talent management: A review and research agenda. *Human Resource Management Review,* 19: 304–313.

Cottrell, A. 2011. Explaining differences: TCKs and other CCKs, American and Japanese TCKs. In G. Bell-Villada & N. Sichel (Eds.), *Writing out of limbo: International childhoods, global nomads and third culture kids:* 57–77. Newcastle upon Tyne, UK: Cambridge Scholars Publishing.

Cottrell, A., & Useem, R. 1994. ATCKs maintain global dimensions throughout their lives. *Newslinks: The newspaper of international schools services,* XIII(4).

Cranston, S. 2017. Self-help and the surfacing of identity: Producing the third culture kid. *Emotion, Space and Society,* 24: 27–33.

de Leon, C. & McPartlin, D. 1995. Adjustment of expatriate children. In J. Selmer (Ed.), *Expatriate management: New ideas for international business:* 197-214. Westport, CT: Quorum Books.

De Vos, A. & Dries, N. 2013. Applying a talent management lens to career management: The role of human capital composition and continuity. *The International Journal of Human Resource Management,* 24(9): 1816-1831.

Dewaele, J., & J.P. van Oudenhoven 2009. The effect of multilingualism/multiculturalism on personality: No gain without pain for third culture kids? *International Journal of Multilingualism,* 6(4): 443–459.

Doherty, N., & Dickmann, M. 2013. Self-initiated and assigned expatriates: Talent management and career considerations. In V. Vaiman & A. Haslberger (Eds.), *Managing talent of self- initiated expatriates: A neglected source of the global talent flow:* 234–255. London: Palgrave McMillan.

Eidse, F., & Sichel, N. 2004, *Unrooted childhoods: Memoirs of growing up global.* Yarmouth, ME: Intercultural Press.

Fail, H., Thompson, J., & Walker, G. 2004. Belonging, identity and third culture kids: Life histories of former international school students. *Journal of Research in International Education,* 3(3): 319–338.

Farndale, E., Pai, A., Sparrow, P., & Scullion, H. 2014. Balancing individual and organizational goals in global talent management: A mutual-benefits perspective. *Journal of World Business,* 49(2): 204–214.

Farndale, E., Scullion, H., & Sparrow, P. 2010. The role of the corporate HR function in global talent management. *Journal of World Business,* 45(2): 161–168.

Fitzsimmons, S., Liao, Y., & Thomas, D. 2017. From crossing cultures to straddling them: An empirical examination of outcomes for multicultural employees. *Journal of International Business Studies,* 48(1): 63–89.

Furusawa, M. & C. Brewster 2014. The bi-cultural option for global talent management: The Japanese/Brazilian Nikkeijin example. *Journal of World Business,* 50(1): 133–143.

Gerner, M. E., & Perry, F. L. Jr. 2002. Gender differences in cultural acceptance and career orientation among internationally mobile and non-internationally mobile adolescents. In M. G. Ender (Ed.), *Military brats and other global nomads: Growing up in organization families:* 165–191. Westport, CT: Praeger.

Gerner, M. E., Perry, F. L. Jr., Modelle, M. A., & Archbold, M. 1992. Characteristics of internationally mobile adolescents. *Journal School of Psychology,* 30(2): 197–214.

Greenholtz, J., & Kim, J. 2009. The cultural hybridity of Lena: A multi-method case study of a third culture kid. *International Journal of Intercultural Relations,* 33(5): 391–398.

Hanek, K. J. 2017. Biculturals, monoculturals, and adult third culture kids: Individual differences in identities and outcomes. In Y. McNulty & J. Selmer (Eds.), *Research handbook of expatriates:* 451–467. London: Edward Elgar.

Hartman, E., Feisel, E., & Schober, H. 2010. Talent management of western MNCs in China: Balancing global integration and local responsiveness. *Journal of World Business,* 45(2): 169–178.

Hechanova, R., Beehr, T. A., & Christiansen, N. D. 2003. Antecedents and consequences of employees' adjustment to overseas assignment: A meta analytic review. *Applied Psychology: An International Review,* 52: 213–236.

Hervey, E. 2009. Cultural transitions during childhood and adjustments to college. *Journal of Psychology and Christianity,* 28(1): 3–12.

Hoersting, R. C., & Jenkins, S. R. 2011. No place to call home: Cultural homelessness, self-esteem and cross-cultural identities. *International Journal of Intercultural Relations,* 35(1): 17–30.

Huang, J., & C. Tansley 2012. Sneaking through the minefield of talent management: The notion of rhetorical obfuscation. *International Journal of Human Resource Management,* 23(17): 3673–3691.

Huselid, M. A., Beatty, R. W., & Becker, B. E. 2005. "A players" or "A positions?" The strategic logic of workforce management. *Harvard Business Review,* 12: 110–117.

Iles, P., Chuai, X., & Preece, D. 2010. Talent management and HRM in multinational companies in Beijing: Definitions, differences and drivers. *Journal of World Business,* 45(2): 179–189.

King, K. 2015. Global talent management: Introducing a strategic framework and multiple-actors model. *Journal of Global Mobility,* 3(3): 273–288.

Kraimer, M., Bolino, M., & Mead, B. 2016. Themes in expatriate and repatriate research over four decades: What do we know and what do we still need to learn? *Annual Review of Organizational Psychology and Organizational Behavior,* 3: 83–109.

Kwon, J. 2019. Third culture kids: Growing up with mobility and cross-cultural transitions. *Diaspora, Indigenous, and Minority Education,* 13(2): 113–122.

LaFromboise, T., Coleman, H., & Gerton, J. 1993. Psychological impact of biculturalism: Evidence and theory. *Psychological Bulletin,* 114(3): 395–412.

Lam, H., & Selmer, J. 2004a. Are former "third culture kids" the ideal business expatriates? *Career Development International,* 9(3): 109–122.

Lam, H., & Selmer, J. 2004b. Perceptions of being international: Differences between British adolescents living abroad and those at home. *International Education Journal,* 5(3): 360–373.

Langford, M. 1998. Global nomads, third culture kids, and international schools. In M. Hayden & J. Thompson (Eds.), *International education: Principles and practice:* 28–43. Sterling, VA: Stylus Publishing.

Lauring, J. 2008. Rethinking social identity theory in international encounters: Language use as a negotiated object for identity making. *International Journal of Cross Cultural Management,* 8(3): 343–361.

Lauring, J., Guttormsen, D. S., & McNulty, Y. M. 2019. Adult third culture kids: Adjustment and personal development. *Cross Cultural & Strategic Management,* 26(3), 387–400.

Lazarova, M., Cerdin, J., & Liao, Y. 2014. The internationalism career anchor: A validation study. *International Studies of Management and Organization,* 44(2): 9–33.

Le Bigre, N. 2015. Talking about 'home': Immigrant narratives as context for TCKs. In S. Benjamin & F. Dervin (Eds.), *Migration, diversity, and education - beyond third culture kids:* 121–142. London: Palgrave Macmillan.

Long, K. 2020. Fractured stories: Self-experiences of third culture kids. *Journal of Infant, Child, and Adolescent Psychotherapy,* 19(2): 134–147.

Lyttle, A. D., Barker, D. G., & Cornwell, T. L. 2011. Adept through adaptation: Third culture individuals' interpersonal sensitivity. *International Journal of Intercultural Relations,* 35(5): 686–694.

Mäkela, K., Björkman, I., & Ehrnrooth, M. 2010. How do MNCs establish their talent pools? Influences on individuals' likelihood of being labeled as talent. *Journal of World Business,* 45(2): 134–142.

McCaig, N. 2002. Raised in the margin of the mosaic: Global nomads balance worlds within. *International Educator* (Spring): 10–17

McDonnell, A., Collings, D. G., Mellahi, K., & Schuler, R. S. 2017. Talent management: A systematic review and future prospects. *European Journal of International Management,* (forthcoming).

McKenzie, R., Lopez, T., & Bowes, D. 2010. Providing international opportunities for business students: a guide to planning a short-term study abroad program at regional and small universities. *American Journal of Business Education,* 3(8): 59–65.

McKinsey2008. *Why multinationals struggle to manage talent.* London: McKinsey & Company.

McLachlan, D. 2007. Global nomads in an international school: Families in transition. *Journal of Research in International Education,* 6(2): 233–249.

McNulty, Y. & Brewster, C. 2017. The concept of business expatriates. In Y. McNulty & J. Selmer (Eds.), *Research handbook of expatriates:* 8–31. London: Edward Elgar.

McNulty, Y., & De Cieri, H. 2016. Linking global mobility and global talent management: The role of ROI. *Employee Relations,* 38(1): 8–30.

McNulty, Y., Lauring, J., Jonasson, C., & Selmer, J. 2019. Highway to hell? Managing expatriates in crisis. *Journal of Global Mobility,* 9(2): 157–180.

Metcalf, L. 2010. Creating international community service learning experiences in a capstone marketing-projects course. *Journal of Marketing Education,* 32(2): 155.

Melles, E. A., & Schwartz, J. 2013. Does the third culture kid experience predict levels of prejudice? *International Journal of Intercultural Relations,* 27(2): 260–267.

Meyer, H. 2015. Boundaries and the restriction of mobility within international school communities: A case study from Germany. In S. Benjamin & F. Dervin (Eds.), *Migration, diversity, and education - beyond third culture kids:* 59–84. London: Palgrave Macmillan.

Minbaeva, D., & Collings D. 2013. Seven myths of global talent management. *International Journal of Human Resource Management,* 24(9): 1762–1776.

Mol, S. T., Born, M., Willemsen, M. E., & Van Der Molen, H. T. 2005. Predicting expatriate job performance for selection purposes: A quantitative review. *Journal of Cross-Cultural Psychology,* 36(5): 590–620.

Moore, A. M., & Barker, G. G. 2012. Confused or multicultural: Third culture individuals' cultural identity. *International Journal of Intercultural Relations,* 36(4): 553–562.

Nathanson, J. Z., & Marcenko, M. 1995. Young adolescents' adjustment to the experience of relocating overseas. *International Journal of Intercultural Relations,* 19(3): 413–424.

Pervin, L. A. 1989. Persons, situations, interactions: The history of a controversy and a discussion of theoretical models. *Academy of Management Review,* 14: 350–360.

Pollock, D. C., & van Reken, R. 2009. *Third culture kids: The experience of growing up among worlds* (Rev. ed.). Boston, MA: Nicholas Brealey.

Schwartz, S. J., Côté, J. E., & Arnett, J. J. 2005. Identity and agency in emerging adulthood. *Youth & Society* 37(2): 201–229.

Scullion, H., & Collings, D. G. 2006. *Global staffing.* London: Routledge.

Selmer, J., & Lam, H. 2004, 'Third-culture kids': Future business expatriates? *Personnel Review,* 33(4): 430–445.

Selmer, J., & Lauring, J. 2014. Self-initiated expatriates: An exploratory study of adjustment of adult third-culture kids vs. adult mono-culture kids. *Cross Cultural Management,* 21(4): 422–436.

Shaffer, M., Kraimer, M. L., Chen, Y-P., & Bolino, M. C. 2012. Choices, challenges, and career consequences of global work experiences: A review and future agenda. *Journal of Management,* 38(4): 1282–1327.

Sheard, W. 2008. Lessons from our kissing cousins: Third culture kids and gifted children. *Roeper Review,* 30(1): 31–38.

Stahl, G., Björkman, I., Farndale, E., Morris, S. S., Paauwe, J., Stiles, P., Trevor, J. & Wright, P. 2012. Six principles of effective global talent management. *Sloan Management Review,* 53(2): 25–42.

Søderberg, A.-M., Krishna, S., & Bjørn, P. 2013. Global software development: Commitment, trust and cultural sensitivity in strategic partnerships. *Journal of International Management,* 19(4): 347–361.

Takeuchi, R. 2010. A critical review of expatriate adjustment research: Progress, emerging trends, and prospects. *Journal of Management,* 36: 1040–1064.

Tanu, D. 2015. Toward an interdisciplinary analysis of the diversity of 'third culture kids. In S. Benjamin & F. Dervin (Eds.), *Migration, diversity, and education - beyond third culture kids:* 13–35. London: Palgrave Macmillan.

Tarique, I., & Schuler, R. S. 2010. Global talent management: Literature review, integrative framework, and suggestions for further research. *Journal of World Business,* 45(2): 122–133.

Tarique, I., & Weisbord, E. 2013. Antecedents of dynamic cross-cultural competence in adult third culture kids (ATCKs). *Journal of Global Mobility,* 1(2): 139–160.

Tharenou, P. 2005. International work in domestic jobs: An individual explanation. *International Journal of Human Resource Management,* 16(4): 475–496.

Trabka, A. 2015. Experiences of Polish and American third culture kids in a comparative perspective. In S. Benjamin & F. Dervin (Eds.), *Migration, diversity, and education - beyond third culture kids:* 187–208. London: Palgrave Macmillan.

Useem, J., Useem, R. H., & Donoghue, J. 1963. Men in the middle of the third culture: The roles of American and non-Western people in cross-cultural administration. *Human Organization,* 22(3): 169–179.

Useem, R. H., & Downie, R. D. 1976. Third-culture kids. *Today's Education,* 65(3): 103–105.

Useem, R. & J. Useem 1967. The interfaces of a binational third culture: A study of the American community in India. *Journal of Social Issues,* 22(1): 130–143.

Vaiman, V., & Collings, D. 2013. Talent management: Advancing the field. *International Journal of Human Resource Management,* 24(9): 1737–1743.

Vaiman, V., Scullion, H., & Collings, D. 2012. Talent management decision making. *Management Decision,* 50(5): 925–941.

Vance, C. 2005. The personal quest for building global competence: A taxonomy of self-initiating career path strategies for gaining business experience abroad. *Journal of World Business,* 40(3): 374–385.

Vance, C. 2006. AmCham-based international internships: A cost-effective distance field learning model for improving MBA international business education. In C. Wankel, & R. DeFillippi (Eds.), *New visions of graduate management education: research in management education and development:* 283–305. Greenwich, CT: Information Age Publishing.

Vance, C., & Paik, Y. 2006. *Managing a global workforce: Challenges and opportunities in international human resource management.* New York: M.E. Sharpe.

Vance, C., Sibeck, G., McNulty, Y., Hogenauer, A. M., & Paik, Y. 2011. Building global competencies through experiential coursework in international travel and tourism. *Journal of International Education in Business,* 4(1): 30–41.

Van Reken, R., & Bethel, P. 2005. Third culture kids: Prototypes for understanding other cross-cultural kids. *Intercultural Management Quarterly,* Fall: 3, 8–9.

Waal, M. F. D., & Born, M. P. 2020. Growing up among cultures: intercultural competences, personality, and leadership styles of third culture kids. *European Journal of International Management,* 14(2): 327–356.

Walters, K. A., & Auton-Cuff, F. P. 2009. A story to tell: The identity development of women growing up as third culture kids. *Mental Health, Religion and Culture,* 12(7): 755–772.

Ward, T. 1989. The MK's advantage: Three cultural contexts. In P. Echerd & A. Arathoon (Eds.), *Understanding and nurturing the missionary family:* 49–61. Pasadena, CA: William Carey Library.

Weeks, K. P., Weeks, M., & Willis-Muller, K. 2010. The adjustment of expatriate teenagers. *Personnel Review,* 39(1): 24–43.

Wertsch, M. E. 1991. *Military brats.* New York: Harmony Books.

Westropp, S., Cathro, V., & Everett, A. M. 2016. Adult third culture kids' suitability as expatriates. *Review of International Business and Strategy,* 26(3): 1–18.

Zhang, Y., & A. Khare 2009. The impact of accessible identities on the evaluation of global versus local products. *Journal of Consumer Research,* 36(3): 524–537.

27

THE BENEFITS AND CHALLENGES OF INCORPORATING GLOBAL MINDSET INTO GLOBAL TALENT MANAGEMENT STRATEGIES

Cordula Barzantny

Rachel Clapp-Smith

Introduction

A persistent concern among multinational enterprises (MNEs) is how to develop the global talent within their ranks to remain competitive in an increasingly complicated global environment. Despite this concern, the reality of how well MNEs do in this regard is underwhelming. Levy et al. (2015) indicate that employees from MNEs' parent country perceive more leadership opportunities than employees from subsidiary countries. This troubling reality indicates that MNEs have yet to truly maximize their "global" talent pool. Rather, they seem to focus on developing the cross-cultural competence of headquarter talent, signaling little opportunity for advancement to nationals across the MNE beyond the parent country (Caligiuri & Bonache, 2016; for empirical examples see Khoreva, Vaiman, & Van Zalk, 2017; McDonnell, Hickey, & Gunnigle, 2011; Stahl et al., 2012;).

There has been considerable interest in the topic of the importance of a "global mindset" over the last few years among both academics and practitioners (e.g., Connell, 2020; Goxe & Belhoste, 2019; Nonis et al., 2020). This chapter argues that there are possible benefits and challenges of incorporating global mindset (e.g., Andresen & Bergdolt, 2017, 2019) into talent management (TM) strategies, offering a truly inclusive approach to have all organizational actors contribute to MNE value creation, capture, leverage, and protection (McDonnell et al., 2017; Sparrow & Makram, 2015).

Bringing global talent management (GTM) and global mindset together as different areas of research offers useful and significant implications for research and management practice in the international context. We take a multiple actors perspective (King, 2015) to uncover the impact of global mindset on GTM systems. We provide suggestions for optimal global mindset development techniques for the various actors within the TM system and provide propositions for research and practice considerations.

Talent management has been defined in many ways in the academic literature (for recent reviews, see Cascio & Boudreau, 2016; Collings, McDonnell & McMackin, 2017; Gallardo-Gallardo & Thunnissen, 2016; Thunnissen, Boselie, & Fruytier, 2013a) since there is a fundamental lack of coherent acceptance as to the meaning of "talent" in the world of work (Gallardo-Gallardo, Dries, & González-Cruz., 2013; Lewis & Heckman, 2006; Schiemann, 2014; Tansley, 2011) and global TM similarly has little consensus (Al Ariss, 2014; Dries, 2013; Meyers & van Woerkom, 2014; Tarique & Schuler, 2010; see also the extensive, systematic review by McDonell et al., 2017).

DOI: 10.4324/9781315474687-27

Because our propositions address the management of a global workforce, we adopt the definition of GTM put forth by Tarique and Schuler:

> global talent management is about systematically utilizing IHRM activities (complementary HRM policies and practices) to attract, develop, and retain individuals with high levels of human capital (e.g., competency, personality, motivation) consistent with the strategic directions of the multinational enterprise in a dynamic, highly competitive, and global environment. (2010: 124)

Global mindset is a cognitive process that helps individuals mediate the tensions between local demands and global efficiencies (Bartlett & Ghoshal, 1998; Levy, Beechler, Taylor, & Boyacigiller, 2007) that are inevitable in an MNE strategy. Global mindset consists of two dimensions: cosmopolitanism and cognitive complexity (Levy et al., 2007). Although a recent systematic review of the global mindset literature yielded 25 unique definitions of global mindset (Andresen & Bergdolt, 2017), we borrow the most rigorously derived definition: "a highly complex cognitive structure characterized by an openness to and articulation of multiple cultural and strategic realities on both global and local levels, and the cognitive ability to mediate and integrate across this multiplicity" (Levy et al., 2007: 244).

In times of international and global competitiveness, MNEs must be committed to building and enhancing employees' global mindset, which could be done through global mobility and talent development. This stipulates the need to develop both the cosmopolitanism and cognitive complexity dimensions of global mindset among multiple actors within MNEs and, hence, how to foster them becomes a central element in a GTM system.

We adopt King's (2015) multiple actors-model of GTM, which is built on a systems theory perspective. King suggests using a systems-view to understand how all the actors (leaders and top management, HR and TM managers, supervisors and managers, and the talent pool of employees) within MNEs contribute to the strategic effectiveness of GTM. We consider how developmental resources can be applied effectively across the GTM system. In doing so, we propose that global mindset serves as an important and, at times, critical attribute for building an inclusive GTM system.

In the following sections we first explain the primary challenges MNEs face in GTM. We then provide an overview of King's (2015) multiple actors model, followed by a more in-depth description of global mindset and how it can be developed. We then apply global mindset development to the multiple-actors model of GTM and suggest four propositions about how to apply global mindset development to the four main actors in the GTM system. We conclude with the limitations and future opportunities for research without forgetting about managerial practice considerations.

Global Talent Shortages and Global Talent Management

Within MNEs "shortages of international management talent have been shown to be a significant constraint on the successful implementation of global strategies" (Farndale, Scullion, & Sparrow, 2010: 161). Offering some possible clues to this shortage of global talent on the one hand and lack of apparent opportunity for advancement among global talent outside of the parent country on the other, Mäkelä, Björkman, and Ehrnrooth (2010) found evidence for what influences how top and divisional managers together with relevant HR managers make decisions about including employees in the corporate talent pool.

Most organizations have rigorous performance appraisal systems that provide the semblance that selection, promotion, and training are conducted in systematic ways. Some authors have detected imperfections in the TM identification of MNEs (McDonnell 2011; McDonnell, Lamare, Gunnigle, & Lavelle, 2010; Mellahi & Collings, 2010). As a result, what is often overlooked is the way in which unconscious biases filter into the process. Most notable of these biases, as Mäkelä et al. (2010) found, are the cultural and institutional distance between the locations of a potential member of the talent pool and the decision makers; homophily between the individual and the decision makers; and the network position of the candidate.

In short, MNEs struggle to reach their corporate goals because, as research indicates (Cerdin & Brewster, 2014; Collings, 2014a; Collings & Isichei, 2018; Farndale, Pai, Sparrow, & Scullion, 2014; Mellahi & Collings, 2010), their GTM strategies appear to be exclusive to the parent country nationals, rather than inclusive of their entire talent pool across all subsidiary country locations. This seems to ignore an important global resource of talent in the wider international subsidiaries' network and worldwide context of corporate operations. Furthermore, the literature underlines the importance of the selection of individuals with predispositions and antecedents of global mindset (Clapp-Smith et al., 2007; Story et al., 2014)

To address this misalignment between a corporate strategy and a GTM strategy, we suggest that fostering a global mindset within human resources management practices will affect GTM strategies to be inclusive of all potential talent across subsidiary country locations, not merely by virtue of employee nationality or location (HQ home country versus subsidiary). The relevance of a global mindset to GTM is to help GTM professionals and managers recognize how and when local talent can address global strategic objectives and when global talent can contribute to local needs.

Selecting and promoting local talent to global roles ultimately allows an MNE to have a much clearer understanding of the markets it serves and the opportunities that exist on the local and global level. With such a truly cross-fertilizing "global network" approach, inclusive GTM offers equal opportunities and more attractive considerations of job and development challenges to emerged and emerging locations for local high-potentials wherever they are in the world (Dewhurst, Pettigrew, Srinivasan, & Choudhary, 2012).

An inclusive approach to TM can also prevent global talent "shortages" since a possible talent pool is larger and better prepared and developed with a consciousness of strategic HRD and a possible stakeholder approach (see Collings, 2014b). Furthermore, such a GTM strategy, when it is well communicated and implemented, sets positive signals also to subsidiary human resources at the internal (job satisfaction, commitment, etc.) but also external (employer brand) level.

Overview of Global Talent Management and its Multiple Actors

The mere size of an MNE requires GTM strategies and planning across various sites, business units, countries, and regions to support and improve business value at the local and global levels. GTM strategies should make it possible for MNEs to reach their goals at various levels of their international operations (Al Ariss, 2014; Scullion & Collings, 2010; Scullion, Collings, & Caligiuri, 2010; Schuler, Jackson, & Tarique, 2011). Every GTM activity to recruit, motivate, retain, develop, reward, and help people perform is part of a corporate GTM system that is most effective when linked to strategic workforce building, training, and planning. Overall, a GTM system relates to development of an appropriate HR architecture to identify, recruit, and support the globally mobile population (Collings, 2014a) while enhancing performance of the international organization.

By taking this systems perspective on GTM and applying the multiple-actors model (King, 2015), which considers how all actors across the MNE contribute to the effectiveness of GTM, we consider four employee groups (or actors) within the MNE who will benefit from initiatives to develop a global mindset as a means to understand how "value is created and managed through the activity of the actors" (2015: 280). The four actors' categories are leadership and top management teams (TMT) of the MNE, front-line managers and supervisors, human resources and talent managers, and finally, the talent pool of current and potential employees, across the entire MNE. King (2015) outlines the role these actors play in the GTM system, and we argue that a global mindset among these actors allows them to more effectively fulfill their roles, i.e., whether they are at TMT level, frontline supervisors, HR and GT managers, or employees with individual contributors' roles.

The multiple-actors model suggests that the leadership and top management play the role of setting a MNEs GTM strategy, championing initiatives that generate, leverage, protect value, and create a climate (King, 2017) that allows the link between a GTM strategy and performance to emerge. To deliver the GTM strategy, human resources and talent managers are then responsible for designing the GTM system that enables all functions of the organization to maximize their value generation by attracting, developing, deploying, and retaining talent for the MNE (Becker, Huselid, & Beatty, 2009; Boudreau, 2010; Collings, Scullion, & Vaiman, 2011).

The HR actor is uniquely positioned, "as guardian of the employee relationship for the organization" (King, 2015: 282), to influence the value generation among the other actors by supporting top management, coaching front-line supervisors, and facilitating engagement of the employee talent pool in TM initiatives. The managers or front-line supervisors are responsible for the GTM practices, i.e., enacting and putting into daily practice the processes that emerge from the GTM strategy (see also Ulrich, 2015, 2016).

Finally, the pool of employee talent, King's (2015) term for the broad spectrum of all other employees whose talent ultimately need development, experiences the system as the focal point and creates "short-term value through in-role performance and long-term value through their ongoing development and deployment in the talent system" (2015: 282).

In understanding who the actors are and how they create value within the GTM system, we now define the construct of a global mindset in more detail and explain how its dimensions can be developed. Then, we map the development of these dimensions on to the four actors discussed above to suggest how they can more effectively carry out their roles in the GTM system.

Defining Global Mindset

More recent definitions of global mindset crystallize many different definitions in the literature. A short review trying to identify the various foci among the most recent studies lead to five main perspectives according to different authors and schools of thought (see Table 27.1). Although a recent systematic review of the global mindset literature yielded 25 unique definitions of global mindset (Andresen & Bergdolt, 2017), we borrow the most rigorously derived definition: "a highly complex cognitive structure characterized by an openness to and articulation of multiple cultural and strategic realities on both global and local levels, and the cognitive ability to mediate and integrate across this multiplicity" (Levy et al., 2007: 244). In deriving this definition, Levy and colleagues uncovered that previous research has viewed global mindset from two different lenses, addressing either cultural (Perlmutter, 1969) or strategic (Bartlett & Goshal, 1987) challenges in an MNE. Levy et al. suggested that global mindset be defined as a multi-dimensional construct, namely, consisting of cosmopolitanism to address cultural challenges and cognitive complexity to address strategic challenges (Levy, Beechler et al., 2015).

Cognitive complexity involves the ability to differentiate many stimuli and cues and to find a means to organize, reconcile, or integrate these stimuli. In short, individuals with a cognitively complex structure can see the world through many shades of gray. As such, cultural stimuli are not organized into simplistic either/or, good/bad, right/wrong, weird/normal categories. Rather, they see multiple categories and can accept the connections among them.

For instance, cognitive complexity helps individuals see past stereotypes, to recognize the complexity of cultural norms, and to understand that cultural norms have as many unifying characteristics as they do differences. An oft cited example might be the cognitively simplistic view that the French are arrogant and rude, whereas the cognitively complex perspective might be that the French who live in Paris have similar cultural norms to other large urban centers, whereas the cultural norms in other regions of France involve warmth, openness, and a hospitality that one might experience in other less urban environments around the world.

Whereas cognitive complexity is associated with the mental models used for sensemaking about the strategic perspective, cosmopolitanism describes the curiosity and learning that accompanies the

Table 27.1 Selected literature on global mindset

Areas of global mindset (GM) with different perspectives (foci) in the literature	*Selected research*
1 The definition aspect: papers are mostly focused on delineating the similarities and dissimilarities between two constructs, like global mindset and cultural intelligence, global mindset at different levels	Andreesen & Berdolt, 2017; Lovvorn & Chen, 2011; Ramsey et al., 2016; Story & Barbuto, 2011; VanderPal, 2014
2 Antecedents and outcomes of global mindset	Hruby et al., 2016; Kedia & Mukherji, 1999; Story et al, 2014
3 The relationship between global mindset and leadership	Clapp-Smith & Vogelgesang, 2014; Cseh et al., 2013; Osland, 2013; VanderPal, 2014
4 Instilling global mindset among students at the international *education* level and mostly among business students	Chan et al., 2018; Chan, Fung, & Yau, 2018; Cseh & Croco, 2020; Mikhaylov, 2014; Nonis et al., 2020
5 Internationalization of firms through global mindset (organizational level)	Nadkarni et al., 2011; Paul, 2000; Vătămănescu et al., 2020

cultural challenges. **Cosmopolitanism** is characterized by an openness to experiencing novel cultural stimuli and an ability to mediate the local and global dynamics of the stimuli. For instance, whereas one local norm might be associated with attitudes (and thus policies) towards maternity and paternity leave, a cosmopolitan perspective might be an openness to this norm and an articulation of what it could mean for global strategic implementation.

Recently, some MNEs (Safronova, 2016) have adopted the practice of providing certain minimum parental-leave policies to respond to local regulations *and* to set a globally integrated policy above and beyond other local regulations. This *glocal* standard and globally harmonized employee benefit can be part of an inclusive HRM policy that facilitates global mobility across countries, subsidiaries, and business units. It furthermore sets incentives to attract globally mobile talent and fosters talent retention.

Given the need to develop both the cosmopolitanism and cognitive complexity dimensions of global mindset for various actors within MNEs, how to develop and enhance them becomes a central element in a GTM system (for a critical perspective see Goxe & Belhoste, 2019). Scholars suggest that because cognitive complexity is inherently the cognitive structures of individuals, its development must be considered over a long-time horizon and that it is far from linear.

Indeed, the development of cognitive complexity has been described as a series of S-curves (Gupta & Govindarajan, 2002), cognitive shifts (Murtha, Lenway, & Bagozzi, 1998), a process of unframing and reframing (Bartunek, 1988), and a process requiring meta-awareness (Clapp-Smith, 2009). In each case, these shifts in cognitive schema are often in response to experiences that trigger an awareness that current mental models are no longer sufficient for making sense of the situation (Clapp-Smith & Hughes, 2007). This process, then, requires first a broadening of differentiation (i.e., adopting more categories to understand events), followed by integration (i.e., recognizing how the expanded categories are related). This complex process requires time to unravel and experiences that are sufficiently novel to trigger a need for development.

We suggest, then, that exposure to a variety of challenging situations as well as travel accompanied by coaching and/or journaling that guides reflection provide a means to foster the cognitive shift necessary to develop cognitive complexity. As such, a GTM system with a global mobility component can be a beneficial tool for developing the cognitive complexity dimension as long as it also embeds methods to prompt reflection and learning objectives.

Whereas cognitive complexity helps individuals recognize multiple strategic dynamics, cosmopolitanism contributes to recognizing multiple cultural dynamics involved in the success of the MNE (Levy et al., 2007). Once again, multiple contextual and cultural experiences can contribute to the development of cosmopolitanism, but MNEs would be well served to foster curiosity and openness about cultural differences by encouraging "Questions Thinking" (Adams, Schiller, & Cooperrider, 2004). "Because questions are fundamentally related to action and reflection, they spark and direct attention, energy, and effort" (2004: 107).

More specifically, we argue that ethnocentrism is a default response for most human beings and that exposure to other cultures can trigger an automatic cognitive process of assessing differences as "weird, unnatural, strange, and not normal," using the home culture for the standard of "normal." Such thinking creates immense problems for an MNE, not the least of which is signaling to all host country locations that their way of conducting business is not "normal." Therefore, development activities require teaching tactics to suspend such automatic judgment and find ways to challenge cultural assumptions.

We believe that teaching and embedding Questions Thinking into the organizational climate is a practical way for organizations to develop cosmopolitanism in the multiple actors of the GTM system (King, 2017). In short, it helps the multiple actors understand the cultural dynamics at local levels, so that they can more effectively mediate what these dynamics mean for the global strategy of the MNE.

At the center of Questions Thinking is the Learner-Judger Mindset Model, which holds that when individuals try to make sense of a situation, cue, or context, in essence they are searching for answers. But the conclusions that individuals reach depend heavily on the questions they ask, often unconsciously. When the questions are judger questions, such as "What is wrong with this situation?" the only response can be an ethnocentric judgement about the other or the self. But when the question is a learner question, such as "What can I learn from this situation?" then a curiosity is sparked and cross-cultural interactions become opportunities to learn, rather than nuisances to overcome. Coupling a standard of Questions Thinking with international exposure creates a means by which MNEs can develop cosmopolitanism in multiple actors.

Therefore, MNEs must be committed to vary the challenging situations and contexts while sending employees, supervisors, and HR and talent managers to multiple country locations. Such experiences can entail expatriate packages (designed for developmental purposes as opposed to preaching doctrine of parent country values), brief international business trips linked to tasks and management challenges, with a developmental goal embedded in the trip, or exchange programs, in which employees visit other host country locations (for a review on the various forms of global work experiences, see Shaffer et al., 2012). Such exchanges do not need to be unidirectional, i.e., parent country nationals (PCNs) visiting host country locations. Rather, to truly build a GTM system, the global mindset development must involve all employees (host country nationals [HCN] & third-country nationals [TCN]) visiting the parent and other host locations.

Developing Global Mindset for the Four Actors

In considering how global mindset must develop among the multiple actors of the GTM system, we map the multiple actors (King, 2015) onto the two dimensions of global mindset, cognitive complexity, and cosmopolitanism to consider when certain dimensions are important and when they are absolutely

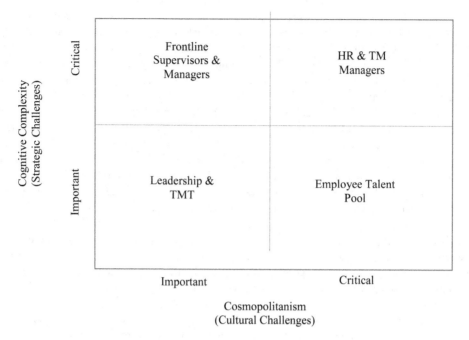

Figure 27.1 Developmental focus of global mindset for the Multiple GTM Actors

critical in achieving a GTM strategy. Considering high versus low levels of each dimension is irrelevant as, in our view, high levels of global mindset are important to all actors in the system. However, from the perspective of how MNEs could maximize their developmental activities, we do suggest which dimension becomes *critical* to performing certain roles within the GTM system versus when high levels of each dimension are merely *important* (see Figure 27.1).

The actors that have the most critical need for both cognitive complexity (strategic challenges) and cosmopolitanism (cultural challenges) are the human resources and talent managers. These actors hold the key to the success of the GTM system. They are responsible for mapping the strategic direction of the MNE onto the GTM strategy and building a TM architecture that creates, captures, leverages, and protects value for the organization (King, 2015; Sparrow & Makram, 2015). Therefore, we suggest that developmental activities that build both cognitive complexity and cosmopolitanism are critical for human resources and talent managers. Particularly as the facilitators of the system, HR managers must be the champions of Questions Thinking, the designers of global mobility programs that not only move people around internationally, but also take advantage of both, brief business trips, and long-term stays as opportunities for developing talent and thus, providing structured learning around each travel and mobility experience.

Alternatively, at the upper echelons of an MNE, or the executive leadership and top management team, we suggest that having high levels of global mindset is important in the GTM system. This may seem counter-intuitive that we do not recommend global mindset as critical for these actors. Because they are responsible for setting strategic direction for the MNE, their role in the GTM system is similarly strategic. In many respects, these leaders set the "tone" for the talent climate of the organization, the signal that Levy, Taylor et al. (2015) found lacking in their study, i.e., whether the talent pool perceives a "global" TM system or TM geared towards parent country nationals (PCNs). From this regard, global mindset of the MNE leadership is important in achieving a truly GTM system.

Copious research has addressed the importance of global mindset in establishing a transnational strategy, i.e., achieving the delicate balance of global and local imperatives (Bartlett & Goshal, 1998; Kedia & Mukherji, 1999) or an internationalization strategy (Nadkarni, Hermann, & Perez, 2011). These perspectives must be similarly applied to strategic TM as they are to operational strategy. Therefore, it is important that global mindset is primed (Clapp-Smith & Vogelgesang, 2014) for senior leadership with respect to TM in the same manner it would be for operational strategy. Senior leaders must consider how their TM strategy aligns with their operational strategy, including, how global talent is defined, where it is found, and, most importantly, how the TMT will champion TM strategy across all host country locations (and not merely as a parent country initiative). While we suggest that the leadership of an MNE must have sufficient levels of both dimensions of global mindset to effectively execute on the strategic objectives, we also make an assumption about how globally minded executives might already be, i.e., that their rise to an executive position within an MNE is only possible with some level of global mindset already formed.

Furthermore, we assume that most MNE executives have sufficient work related international and travel experiences during their career to have had at least created opportunities for development. In terms of applying developmental resources to senior leadership, we suggest that primes and "boosters" to their existing levels of global mindset be regularly applied, but that intense interventions may be best applied to other actors in the system. Although, many senior leaders have already acquired some or significant international business travel, this does not automatically mean that they have maximized the learning that can result from these events. Thus, for senior leadership, coaching that focuses on retrospective reflection of international work experiences can foster a deeper and accelerated cognitive shift.

The frontline supervisors and managers play a critical role in executing the strategy, in short, by how they approach the day-to-day operations of the organization. As a result, it is critical that global mindset development associated with these actors is concentrated on developing cognitive complexity. When managers and supervisors can recognize the complexity involved with the global strategy of the MNE, they can more effectively utilize TM practices embedded in the system to make the day-to-day realities translate into achieving strategic objectives.

High levels of cognitive complexity afford managers the ability to integrate many, seemingly competing, realities into functional activities and practices. Thus, the TM system must create developmental opportunities for both cognitive complexity and cosmopolitanism, but strategic interventions are best served in the realm of cognitive complexity. Not only do such interventions facilitate managers performing in their current positions, but they also help develop capacity for eventual mobility into more senior positions. Despite suggesting that cognitive complexity is critical and cosmopolitanism important for these actors, we also assume that prior experiences as employees in the talent pool will have had development opportunities focused on cosmopolitanism. This leads us, then, to our final group of actors in the GTM system.

The talent pool of employees ultimately experience the talent strategy, talent architecture, and talent practices as performers of the day-to-day operations and as potential talent for management. While having the cognitive schema to interpret and understand the complexity of global strategy is important, as members of an MNE who may not yet have strategic voice but inevitably are affected by contextual and cultural dynamics, development activities around cosmopolitanism is critical.

If an MNE is to incorporate a climate of Questions Thinking, an ideal target for fostering this type of learning is the employee talent pool. Interventions around learning Questions Thinking can be beneficial in many attributes associated with job performance. However, we suggest that learning that comes from challenging situations, programs, and through managers have a distinctly cross-cultural component to it. As such, an organizational climate that seeks to learn about and appreciate the nuances of cultural diversity will ultimately be well placed to capture and leverage value from the TM system. Job performance involving cross-cultural interactions will be successful in the shorter term, and the talent will be well groomed for promotion within the organization in the long term. To set up a successful GTM with a global mindset, we suggest the following propositions:

Proposition 1: For HR and TM managers, it is *critical* that development activities address both the cosmopolitanism and cognitive complexity dimensions of global mindset.

Proposition 2: For MNE leadership/TMT, it is *important* that development activities address both the cosmopolitanism and cognitive complexity dimensions of global mindset.

Proposition 3: For frontline supervisors and managers, it is *critical* that development activities focus on the cognitive complexity dimension of global mindset, while it is important to foster cosmopolitanism.

Proposition 4: For the employee talent pool, it is *critical* that development activities focus on the cosmopolitanism dimension of global mindset, while important to foster cognitive complexity.

Unlike Andresen and Bergdolt (2017), we think that organizational TM systems need individuals with a global mindset at every level of actors, and also at the operational one. Since individuals with a global mindset see business practices as an integrated part of a larger business system and not as isolated elements in a specific context only, a GTM system has an overarching need for globally minded individuals at all levels. Any actor can add value to the organizations through TM awareness and understanding of a systematic IHRM *consistent with the strategic directions of the MNE in a dynamic, highly competitive,* local and *global environment* (adapted from Tarique & Schuler, 2010).

An efficient, sustainable GTM system shall focus on value generation for stakeholders beyond shareholders (see Collings, 2014b). Furthermore, it has to integrate multiple perspectives, with inspirations from various country and organizational contexts, while observing interdependencies and interdisciplinarity with a possible macro-level viewpoint (Khilji, Tarique, & Schuler, 2015).

Limitations and Areas for Further Research

We have painted a rosy picture of how MNEs may fully maximize their global talent pool by building a GTM system with global mindset development as the bedrock for achieving value creation, capture, leverage, and protection. As lovely as this picturesque system may seem, when "fantasy meets reality" (Sveningsson & Larsson, 2006), all managers must face the inevitable obstacles and barriers to creating such a system. In short, humans are limited and fallible, and many elements of human behavior and cognition can create these barriers. Namely, automatic cognitive processes, and thus, biases and stereotypes, can be steadfast for the simple reason that they can go unnoticed. Furthermore, development is a lovely prospect, but often works best when targets of development have some level of openness to learn and "developmental readiness" (Hannah & Avolio, 2010).

A further limitation hinges on the developmental resources available to MNEs, which will always be constrained to some extent and therefore, require some cost/benefit analysis to determine optimal distribution. Furthermore, there may also be institutional exclusion and limited, filtered access to talent pools (Goxe & Belhoste, 2019, Mäkelä et al., 2010). More empirical research is needed to increase the knowledge about various tools and possible elements of GTM like the management of compensation and benefits or the overall management of global mobility. McNulty and De Cieri (2016) inquire with an innovative approach of return on investment by expatriates how global mobility is linked to GTM. Our aim has been to suggest a framework to assist in determining those trade-offs, but we recognize that reality often poses far more limitations than optimal solutions would suggest.

One of these limitations involves a persistent question among global mindset scholars, namely, who needs a global mindset? The debate became openly discussed in 2010 at a conference (Barzantny, 2010) in which the fictitious character, Joe the Plumber from Memphis, Tennessee, who does not have a passport, became the archetype of the person who may not need a global mindset. At the center of the debate is the question of whether individuals with truly domestic roles within an organization need to have a global mindset.

For those who argue that Joe the Plumber from Memphis does not, the argument hinges on two aspects: the amount of contact that Joe has with people from other cultures in the course of his daily routine and the strategic importance for Joe of understanding global market trends and connections for his business. Instead, the individual embedded in a multinational enterprise (MNE) with some degree of global responsibility (see Reiche et al., 2016 for a description of degree of global leadership roles) most certainly needs a global mindset and developmental efforts, and therefore should focus on this person with greater global leader potential.

The other side of the argument, in which the need for a global mindset is more inclusive, i.e., that Joe the Plumber could indeed benefit from developing a more global outlook, hinges on migration and demographic trends over the decades that have made local populations more culturally diverse. There are more multicultural individuals in the work force (Fitzsimmons, 2013), more self-initiated expatriates (Andresen, Al Ariss, & Walther, 2013), and more mobility in general that causes cultures to mix and mingle more frequently (for typologies see Andresen, Dickmann, & Suutari, 2018; Baruch, Dickmann, Altman, & Bournois, 2013; McNulty & DeCieri, 2015).

In short, national boundaries no longer confine cultural norms and values to be location-specific, neither do they constrain the mobility of people. Rather, culture is embedded in the individual (Chao & Moon, 2005). As such, Joe's plumbing clients and employees in Memphis could very well operate from a different cultural paradigm, and having an openness to these could contribute to the growth of Joe's business.

Our stance on this debate is that all talent benefits from developing a global mindset. A more globally minded workforce, regardless of the degree of international or hierarchical responsibility within their role, can mediate their local responsibilities with the global strategy. Furthermore, employees displaying a global mindset may be considered as potential global talent and benefit from more internationally developed, global careers (Bücker & Poutsma, 2010; King, 2017; Ng, Van Dyne, & Ang, 2009; Ulrich, 2015). Given that we are supportive of the latter side of the debate, i.e., a more inclusive application of global mindset, we quite ironically have focused our chapter on the former side of the debate, namely, how to incorporate global mindset into the MNE TM strategy. Given this limitation, we suggest that further research focus on the latter, more inclusive perspective of global mindset.

Conclusion

The foundations for global mindset and its practical application for performance in the business world need continuous contextualization (Thunnissen, Boselie, & Fruytier, 2013b), since local conditions may differ and evolve despite an ongoing global convergence. Employees with an established level of global mindset will supposedly be more flexible and adaptable to these environmental conditions and develop greater capabilities for global leadership in the future. This is where TM comes into play in the most inclusive understanding.

The present paper offers a review of the three major ways in which global mindset and TM overlap. We argue first that global mindset integrated into any TM architecture shall foster the development of high-potential employees with global leadership skills for competitive advantage in globalizing markets. Second, when taking an inclusive approach for managing a multi-cultural workforce, this allows efficient intra-employee and employee/leader functioning inside and outside the organization for sustained corporate value creation. Third, the global mindset paired with a GTM system can help strategic leadership and HR professionals to understand high-potential talent in a more inclusive and differentiated way at various levels of the organization enriching global but also local perspectives.

Following this review of possible overlap, or even cross-fertilization, we consider how HR might develop a global mindset among the many potential constituents it serves with a proposed basic model. Our model offers conceptualizations for future empirical studies, which should address the possible challenges and perceived benefits of global mindset for global (and *glocal*) TM strategies. We recognize that there is certainly no one best way for integrating global mindset with TM, but rather a best fit with strategic objectives of the organization, its culture, and HR policies and practices (Boudreau & Ramstad, 2005; Garrow & Hirsch, 2008).

References

Adams, M. G., Schiller, M., & Cooperrider, D. L. (2004). With our questions we make the world. In D. L. Cooperrider, & M. Avital, (Eds.). *Constructive discourse and human organization (Advances in appreciative inquiry),* Volume 1: 105–124.) Emerald Group Publishing Limited.

Al Ariss, A. (2014). *Global talent management. Challenges, strategies, and opportunities.* London: Springer.

Andresen, M., Al Ariss, A., & Walther, M. (2013). *Self-initiated expatriation. Individual, organizational, and national perspectives.* London: Routledge.

Andresen, M., & Bergdolt, F. (2017). A systematic literature review on the definitions of global mindset and cultural intelligence – merging two different research streams. *International Journal of Human Resource Management,* 28(1): 170–195. doi: https://doi.org/10.1080/09585192.2016.1243568

Andresen, M., & Bergdolt, F. (2019). Individual and job-related antecedents of a global mindset: An analysis of international business travelers' characteristics and experiences abroad. *The International Journal of Human Resource Management.* doi: https://doi.org/10.1080/09585192.2019.1588349

Andresen, M., Dickmann, M., & Suutari, V. (2018). Typologies of internationally mobile employees. In M. Dickmann, V. Suutari, & O. Wurtz (Eds.), *The management of global careers: Exploring the rise of international work:* 33–62. London: Palgrave Macmillan.

Bartlett, C. A., & Ghoshal, S. (1987). Managing across borders: New strategic requirements. *Sloan Management Review,* 28 (4): 7–17.

Bartlett, C. A., & Ghoshal, S. (1998). *Managing across borders: The transnational solution* (2nd ed.). Boston, MA: Harvard Business School Press.

Bartunek, J. (1988). The dynamics of personal and organizational reframing. In R. E. Quinn & K. S. Cameron (Eds.). *Paradox and transformation: Toward a theory of change in organization and management:* 137–162. Cambridge, MA: Ballinger.

Baruch, Y., Dickmann, M., Altman, Y., & Bournois, F. (2013). Exploring international work: Types and dimensions of global careers. *The International Journal of Human Resource Management,* 24(12): 2369–2393. doi: https://doi.org/10.1080/09585192.2013.781435

Barzantny, C. (2010). Cultural intelligence (CQ) and Global mindset (GloMi)– Can we get some light in the international jungle. Professional Development Workshop convened at the Annual Meeting of the Academy of Management, Montréal, Canada, August 7, 2010.

Becker, B. E., Huselid, M. A., & Beatty, R. W. (2009). *The differentiated workforce: Transforming talent into strategic impact.* Boston, MA: Harvard Business Press.

Boudreau, J. W. (2010). *Retooling HR: Using proven business tools to make better decisions about talent.* Boston, MA: Harvard Business Review Press.

Boudreau, J. W., & Ramstad, P. (2005). Talentship and the evolution of human resource management: From professional practices to strategic talent decision science. *Human Resource Planning Journal,* 28(2): 17–26.

Bücker, J., & Poutsma, E. (2010). Global management competencies: A theoretical foundation. *Journal of Managerial Psychology,* 25(8): 829–844.

Caligiuri, P., & Bonache, J. (2016). Evolving and enduring challenges in global mobility. *Journal of World Business,* 51(1): 127–141.

Cascio, W. F., & Boudreau, J. W. (2016). The search for global competence: From international HR to talent management. *Journal of World Business,* 51(1): 103–114. doi: http://doi:10.1016/j.jwb.2015.10.002

Chan, K. C., Fung, H.-G., & Yau, J. (2018). Advancing learning in international business related to a global mindset: An introduction. *Journal of Teaching in International Business,* 29(1), 1–3.

Chan, K. C., Fung, A., Fung, H.-G., & Yau, J. (2018). A conceptual framework for instilling a global mindset in business students. *Journal of Teaching in International Business,* 29(1), 4–19.

Chao, G. T., & Moon, H. (2005). The cultural mosaic: A metatheory for understanding the complexity of culture. *Journal of Applied Psychology,* 90(6), 1128–1140.

Cerdin, J.-L., & Brewster, C. (2014). Talent management and expatriation: Bridging two streams of research and practice. *Journal of World Business,* 49(2), 245–252. doi: https://doi.org/10.1016/j.jwb.2013.11.008

Clapp-Smith, R. (2009). *Global mindset development during cultural transitions.* PhD thesis, University of Nebraska, Organizational Behavior and Leadership.

Clapp-Smith, R., & Hughes, L. (2007). Unearthing a global mindset: The process of international adjustment. *Journal of Business & Leadership: Research, Practice, and Teaching,* 3(1): 99–107.

Clapp-Smith, R., Luthans, F., & Avolio, B. J. (2007). The role of psychological capital in global mindset development. In M. Javidan, R. M. Steers, & M. A. Hitt (Eds.). *The global mindset (Advances in international management)* Volume 19: 105–130. Emerald Group Publishing Ltd.

Clapp-Smith, R., & Vogelgesang, G. (2014). Defining the "mindset" in global mindset: Reconciling disparate paradigms. In J. S. Osland, M. Li, & L. Wang (Eds.), *Advances in global leadership,* Volume 8: 205–228. Bingley, UK: Emerald.

Collings, D. G. (2014a). Integrating global mobility and global talent management: Exploring the challenges and strategic opportunities. *Journal of World Business,* 49(2): 253–261. doi: https://doi.org/10.1016/j.jwb.2013.11.009

Collings, D. G. (2014b). Toward mature talent management: Beyond shareholder value. *Human Resource Development Quarterly,* 25(3): 301–319. doi: https://doi.org/10.1002/hrdq.21198

Collings, D. G., & Isichei, M. (2018). The shifting boundaries of global staffing: Integrating global talent management, alternative forms of international assignments and non-employees into the discussion. *International Journal of Human Resource Management,* 29(1): 165–187. doi: https://doi.org/10.1080/09585192.2017.1380064

Collings, D. G., McDonnell, A., & McMackin, J. (2017). Talent management. In P. Sparrow, & C. Cooper (Eds.), *A research agenda for human resource management – HR strategy, structure, and architecture:* 29–54. Cheltenham, UK: Edward Elgar.

Collings, D. G., Scullion, H., & Vaiman, V. (2011). European perspectives on talent management. *European Journal of International Management,* 5(5): 453–62. doi: https://doi.org/10.1504/EJIM.2011.042173

Connell, L. (2020). Facing a digital future with a global mindset. *People & Strategy,* 43(1), 63–54.

Cseh, M., & Crocco, O. S. (2020). Globalizing HRD academic practice: Developing a global mindset for teaching and research. *Advances in Developing Human Resources,* 22(1), 57–71. doi: https://doi.org/10.1177/1523422319886288

Cseh, M., Davis, E. B., & Khilji, S. E. (2013). Developing a global mindset: Learning of global leaders. *European Journal of Training & Development,* 37(5): 489–499. doi: https://doi-org.hub.tbs-education.fr/10.1108/03090591311327303

Dewhurst, M., Pettigrew, M., Srinivasan, R., & Choudhary, V. (2012). How multinationals can attract the talent they need? *McKinsey Quarterly,* 3: 92–99.

Dries, N. (2013). The psychology of talent management: A review and research agenda. *Human Resource Management Review,* 23(4): 272–285. doi: https://doi.org/10.1016/j.hrmr.2013.05.001

Farndale, E., Pai, A., Sparrow, P., & Scullion, H. (2014). Balancing individual and organizational goals in global talent management: A mutual-benefits perspective. *Journal of World Business,* 49(2): 204–214. doi: https://doi.org/10.1016/j.jwb.2013.11.004

Farndale, E., Scullion, H., & Sparrow, P. (2010). The role of the corporate human resource function in global talent management. *Journal of World Business,* 45(2): 161–168. doi: https://doi.org/10.1016/j.jwb.2009.09.012

Fitzsimmons, S. R. (2013). Multicultural employees: A framework for understanding how they contribute to organizations. *Academy of Management Review,* 38(4): 525–549. doi: https://psycnet.apa.org/doi/10.5465/amr.2011.0234

Gallardo-Gallardo, E., Dries, N., & González-Cruz, T.F. (2013). What is the meaning of 'talent' in the world of work? *Human Resource Management Review,* 23(4): 290–300. doi: https://psycnet.apa.org/doi/10.1016/j.hrmr.2013.05.002

Gallardo-Gallardo, E., & Thunnissen, M. (2016). Standing on the shoulders of giants? A critical review of empirical talent management research, *Employee Relations,* 38(1): 31–56. doi: https://doi.org/10.1108/ER-10-2015-0194

Garrow, V., & Hirsch, W. (2008). Talent management: Issues of focus and fit. *Public Personnel Management,* 37(4): 389–402. doi: https://doi.org/10.1177%2F009102600803700402

Goxe, F., & Belhoste, N. (2019). Be global or be gone: Global mindset as a source of division in an international business community. *European Management Review,* 16(3), 617–632. doi: https://doi.org/10.1111/emre.12300

Gupta, A. K., & Govindarajan, V. (2002). Cultivating a global mindset. *Academy of Management Executive,* 16(1): 116–126. http://www.jstor.org/stable/4165818

Hannah, S. T., & Avolio, B. J. (2010). Ready or not: How do we accelerate the developmental readiness of leaders? *Journal of Organizational Behavior,* 31(8): 1181–1187. doi: https://doi.org/10.1002/job.675

Hruby, J., Watkins-Mathys, L., & Hanke, T. (2016). Antecedents and outcomes of a global mindset: A thematic analysis of research from 1994 to 2013 and future research agenda. In J. S. Osland, M. Li, & M. E. Mendenhall (Eds.), *Advances in Global Leadership,* Volume 9: 213–280. Bingley, UK: Emerald.

Kedia, B. L., & Mukherji, A. (1999). Global managers: Developing a mindset for global competitiveness. *Journal of World Business,* 34(3): 230–251. doi: https://doi.org/10.1016/S1090-9516(99)00017-6

Khilji, S. E., Tarique, I., & Schuler, R. S. (2015). Incorporating the macro view in global talent management. *Human Resource Management Review,* 25(3): 236–248. doi: https://doi.org/10.1016/j.hrmr.2015.04.001

Khoreva, V., Vaiman, V., & Van Zalk, M. (2017). Talent management practice effectiveness: Investigating employee perspective. *Employee Relations,* 39(1): 19–33. doi: https://doi.org/10.1108/ER-01-2016-0005

King, K. A. (2015). Global talent management: Introducing a strategic framework and multiple-actors model, *Journal of Global Mobility,* 3(3): 273–288. doi: https://doi.org/10.1108/JGM-02-2015-0002

King, K. A. (2017) The talent climate: Creating an organisational context supportive of sustainable talent development through implementation of a strong talent system, *Journal of Organizational Effectiveness: People and Performance,* 4(4): 298–314. doi: https://doi.org/10.1108/JOEPP-03-2017-0023

Levy, O., Beechler, S., Taylor, S., & Boyacigiller, N. A. (2007). What we talk about when we talk about 'global mindset': Managerial cognition in multinational corporations. *Journal of International Business Studies,* 38(2): 231–258. doi: https://doi.org/10.1057/palgrave.jibs.8400265

Levy, O., Beechler, S., Taylor, S., & Boyacigiller, N. A. (2015). Global mindset. In *Wiley encyclopedia of management,* Volume 6, International Management. doi: http://doi.org/10.1002/9781118785317.weom060094

Levy, O., Taylor, S., Boyacigiller, N. A., Bodner, T. E., Peiperl, M. A., & Beechler, S. (2015). Perceived senior leadership opportunities in MNCs: The effect of social hierarchy and capital. *Journal of International Business Studies,* 46(3): 285–307. doi: https://doi.org/10.1057/jibs.2014.53

Lewis, R. E., & Heckman, R. J. (2006). Talent management: A critical review. *Human Resource Management Review,* 16(2): 139–154. doi: https://doi.org/10.1016/j.hrmr.2006.03.001

Lovvorn, A.S., & Chen, J.J. (2011). Developing a global mindset: The relationship between an international assignment and cultural intelligence. *International Journal of Business and Social Science,* 2(9): 275–283.

Mäkelä, K., Björkman, I., & Ehrnrooth, M. (2010) How do MNCs establish their talent pools? Influences on individuals' likelihood of being labeled as talent. *Journal of World Business,* 45(2): 134–142. doi: https://doi.org/10.1016/j.jwb.2009.09.020

McDonnell, A. (2011). Still fighting the 'war for talent'? Bridging the science versus practice gap. *Journal of Business and Psychology,* 26(2): 169–173. doi: https://psycnet.apa.org/doi/10.1007/s10869-011-9220-y

McDonnell, A., Collings, D. G., Mellahi, K. & Schuler, R. (2017). Talent management: A systematic review and future prospects. *European Journal of International Management,* 11(1): 86–128. doi: https://doi.org/10.1504/EJIM.2017.081253

McDonnell, A., Hickey, C., & Gunnigle, P. (2011). Global talent management: exploring talent identification in the multinational enterprise. *European Journal of International Management,* 5(2): 174–193. doi: https://doi.org/10.1504/EJIM.2011.038816

McDonnell, A., Lamare, R., Gunnigle, P., & Lavelle, J. (2010). Developing tomorrow's leaders – evidence of global talent management in multinational companies. *Journal of World Business,* 45(1): 150–160. doi: https://doi.org/10.1016/j.jwb.2009.09.015

McNulty, Y., & De Cieri, H. (2016). Linking global mobility and global talent management: the role of ROI. *Employee Relations,* 38(1): 8–30. doi: https://doi.org/10.1108/ER-08-2015-0157

Mellahi, K., & Collings, D. G. (2010). The barriers to effective global talent management: The example of corporate élites in MNEs. *Journal of World Business,* 45(2): 143–149. doi: https://doi.org/10.1016/j.jwb.2009.09.018

Meyers, M. C., & van Woerkom, M. (2014). The influence of underlying philosophies on talent management: Theory, implications for practice, and research agenda. *Journal of World Business,* 49(2): 192–203. doi: https://doi.org/10.1016/j.jwb.2013.11.003

Mikhaylov, N. S. (2014). Towards cosmopolitan outlook: Development of global mindset in international management education. *Advances in Business-Related Scientific Research Journal,* 5(2): 171–182.

Murtha, T. P., Lenway, S. A., & Bagozzi, R. P. (1998). Global mind-sets and cognitive shift in a complex multinational corporation. *Strategic Management Journal,* 19(1): 97–114. doi: https://doi.org/10.1002/(SICI)1097-0266(199802)19:2<97::AID-SMJ943>3.0.CO;2-2

Nadkarni, S., Hermann, P., & Perez, P. D. (2011). Domestic mindsets and early international performance: The moderating effect of global industry conditions. *Strategic Management Journal,* 32(5): 510–531. doi: https://doi.org/10.1002/smj.888

Ng, K.-Y., Van Dyne, L. & Ang, S. (2009). Developing global leaders: The role of international experience and cultural intelligence. In W. H. Mobley, (Ed.). *Advances in Global Leadership,* Volume 5: 225–250. Bingley, UK: Emerald Group Publishing Limited.

Nonis, S. A., Relyea, C., & Hunt, C. S. (2020). Developing students global mindset: An event-based approach. *Journal of Teaching in International Business,* 31(2), 130–153. doi: https://doi.org/10.1080/08975930.2020.1796894

Osland, J. S. (2013). An overview of the global leadership literature. In M. Mendenhall, J. Osland, A. Bird, G. Oddou, M. Maznevski, M. Stevens, & G. Stahl (Eds.), *Global leadership: Research, practice, and development* (2nd ed.): 40–79. London: Routledge.

Paul, H. (2000). Creating a global mindset. *Thunderbird International Business Review,* 42(2): 187–200. doi: https://doi.org/10.1002/1520-6874(200003/04)42:2<187::AID-TIE4>3.0.CO;2-7

Perlmuter, H. V. (1969). The tortuous evolution of the multinational corporation. *Columbia Journal of World Business,* 4(1): 9–18.

Ramsey, J.R., Abi Aad, A., Jiang, C., Barakat, L., & Drummond, V. (2016) Emergence of cultural intelligence and global mindset capital: A multilevel model. *Multinational Business Review,* 24(2): 106–122. doi: https://doi.org/10.1108/MBR-12-2015-0062

Reiche, B. S., Bird, A., Mendenhall, M. E., & Osland, J. (2017). Contextualizing leadership: A typology of global leadership roles. *Journal of International Business Studies,* 48(5): 552–572. doi: https://doi.org/10.1057/s41267-016-0030-3

Safronova, V. (2016, Dec 19). Kering's latest luxury: A generous parental leave policy. *The New York Times.* https://search-proquest-com.pnw.idm.oclc.org/docview/1850909935?accountid=13361

Schiemann, W. A. (2014). From talent management to talent optimization. *Journal of World Business,* 49(2): 281–288. doi: https://doi.org/10.1016/j.jwb.2013.11.012

Schuler, R. S., Jackson, S. E., & Tarique, I. (2011). Global talent management and global talent challenges: Strategic opportunities for IHRM. *Journal of World Business,* 46(4): 506–516. doi: https://doi.org/10.1016/j.jwb.2010.10.011

Scullion, H., & Collings, D. G. 2010. (Eds.). *Global Talent Management.* London: Routledge.

Scullion, H., Collings, D. G., & Caligiuri, P. (2010). Global talent management. *Journal of World Business,* 45(2): 105–108. doi: https://doi.org/10.1016/j.jwb.2009.09.011

Shaffer, M. A., Kraimer, M. L., Chen, Y., & Bolino, M. C. (2012). Choices, challenges, and career consequences of global work experiences: A review and future agenda. *Journal of Management,* 38(4): 1282–1327. doi: https://doi.org/10.1177%2F0149206312441834

Sparrow, P. R., & Makram, H. (2015). What is the value of talent management? Building value-driven processes within a talent management architecture. *Human Resource Management Review,* 25(3): 249–263. doi: https://doi.org/10.1016/j.hrmr.2015.04.002

Stahl, G. K., Björkman, I., Farndale, E., Morris, S. S., Paauwe, J., Stiles, P., Trevor, J., & Wright, P. (2012). Six principles of effective global talent management. *MIT Sloan Management Review,* 53(2): 25–32.

Story, J. S. P., & Barbuto, J. E. (2011). Global mindset: A construct clarification and framework. *Journal of Leadership & Organizational Studies,* 18(3): 377–384. doi: https://doi.org/10.1177/1548051811404421

Story, J. S. T., Barbuto, J. E., Luthans, F., & Bovaird, J. A. (2014). Meeting the challenges of effective international HRM: Analysis of the antecedents of global mindset. *Human Resource Management,* 53, 131–155. doi: https://doi:10.1002/hrm.21568

Sveningsson, S., & Larsson, M. (2006). Fantasies of leadership: Identity work. *Leadership,* 2(2): 203–224. doi: https://doi.org/10.1177/1742715006062935

Tansley, C. (2011). What do we mean by the term "talent" in talent management?, *Industrial and Commercial Training,* 43(5): 266–274. doi: https://doi.org/10.1108/00197851111145853

Tarique, I., & Schuler, R. S. (2010). Global talent management: Literature review, integrative framework, and suggestions for further research. *Journal of World Business,* 45(2): 122–133. doi: https://doi.org/10.1016/j.jwb.2009.09.019

Thunnissen, M., Boselie, P., & Fruytier, B. (2013a). A review of talent management: 'Infancy or adolescence?' *International Journal of Human Resource Management,* 24(9), 1744–1761. doi: https://doi:10.1080/0958519 2.2013.777543

Thunnissen, M., Boselie, P., & Fruytier, B. (2013b). Talent management and the relevance of context: Towards a pluralistic approach. *Human Resource Management Review,* 23(4): 326–336. doi: https://doi.org/10.1016/j.hrmr.2013.05.004

Ulrich, D. (2015). From war for talent to victory through organization. *Strategic HR Review,* 14(1/2): 8–12.

Ulrich, D. (2016). HR at the crossroads. *Asia Pacific Journal of Human Resources,* 54(2): 148-164. doi: https://doi.org/10.1111/1744-7941.12104

VanderPal, G. (2014). Global leadership, IQ and global quotient. *Journal of Management Policy & Practice,* 15(5): 120–134.

Vătămănescu, E., Alexandru, V., Mitan, A., & Dabija, D. (2020). From the deliberate managerial strategy towards international business performance: A psychic distance vs. global mindset approach. *Systems Research and Behavioral Science,* 37(2), 374–387. doi: https://doi.org/10.1002/sres.2658

Vogelgesang L. G., Virick, M., & Clapp-Smith, R. (2016). Harnessing global mindset to positively impact advances in global leadership through international human resource management practices. In J. S. Osland, M. Li, & M. E. Mendenhall (Eds.), *Advances in Global Leadership,* Volume 9: 325–349. Bingley, UK: Emerald.

28

HERDING CATS

Expatriate Talent Acquisition and Development

Vlad Vaiman

Yvonne McNulty

Arno Haslberger

Introduction

International mobility for work in today's employment landscape is increasing. About 3% of the world's total population live and work abroad (OECD, 2017), more than at any time in history (see OECD, 2018, 2019). Most are of working age (20–59 years) and about half are women (UNPD, 2018). The focus of this chapter is the talent management (TM) of a particular type of internationally mobile individual – expatriates. Expatriation involves a physical relocation to another country, with or without accompanying family members as appropriate, for work and with the intention of staying there for a limited time (McNulty & Brewster, 2017a; Shaffer, Kraimer, Chen, & Bolino, 2012).

Expatriates are high-skilled individuals working in important positions in companies with international operations who consequently enjoy generous and "highly paid" terms and conditions of employment (McNulty & Brewster, 2019). They are predominantly used by many multinational enterprises (MNEs) for governance, control, and leadership functions either as senior executives running a major subsidiary or acting as knowledge experts (Harzing, 2001; Torbiörn, 1997). Recent scholarship has referred to these individuals as "high-status", as distinct from lower-status expatriates, such as low-wage domestic workers, security guards, cleaners, beauticians, construction, and agricultural workers (Özçelik, Haak-Saheem, Brewster, & McNulty, 2019).

International work has for a long time been studied in the context of high-status expatriates (Takeuchi, Tesluk, Yun, & Lepak, 2005). Some of these people are assigned expatriates (AEs), sent by their organization (Shaffer et al., 2012). Others make their own way to a country as self-initiated expatriates (SIEs) to take up a job they have applied for or to find employment when they get there (Suutari & Brewster, 2000). Whether assigned or self-initiated, they cost MNEs a considerable amount of money in salary and benefits, insurance, taxes, and HRM administration, which is why their "talent management" is a crucial aspect of the benefits companies hope to derive from employing (and deploying) them.

The TM of expatriates is important to MNEs. Many expatriates hold key positions and possess desirable knowledge, skills, and abilities (e.g., leadership capabilities) that create competitive advantages for the organization (Caligiuri & Bonache, 2016; Collings & Isichei, 2018; Vaiman & Collings, 2014), thus requiring a very specialized type of attention that is typically termed "global talent management" (GTM) (Tarique & Schuler, 2010).

This chapter is dedicated to the TM of expatriates, who represent an important segment of a modern workforce. We begin by discussing TM in different national contexts. We then examine how "expatriate talent" is defined with a specific focus on AEs and SIEs. Next, we discuss two aspects of TM activities – attraction and development – that are related to the various types of expatriates organizations employ,

DOI: 10.4324/9781315474687-28

with a focus on value creation, return on investment (ROI), and retention. We conclude by outlining key areas for future research.[1]

Talent Management

As the academic field of TM is maturing, it is important to include approaches pertinent to different national contexts (Vaiman & Collings, 2012). TM challenges remain some of the most salient and urgent issues for organizations all over the world, from developing countries to emerging economies to highly developed nations. In addition to national perspectives, regional and international perspectives are gaining in importance. The influence of globalization adds emphasis to the importance of TM in the supranational context. In recognition of this, the following definition of global talent management (GTM) has been introduced by Tarique and Schuler:

> A subset of IHRM activities (systematically linked IHRM policies and practices) to attract, develop, retain, and mobilize individuals with high levels of current and potential human capital consistent with the strategic directions of the multinational enterprise to serve the objectives of multiple stakeholders. (2010: 123)

For them and other authors, the main idea behind the concept of GTM is that organizations face increasing competition for talent on a global scale and encounter major challenges in attracting, developing, and retaining their key employees (King, 2015; Tarique & Schuler, 2010; Vaiman & Collings, 2014). GTM considers the differences in global strategic priorities of organizations (e.g., globalization versus local adaptation) and the variations across national or regional contexts when deciding how talent is managed in different countries (Vaiman, Scullion, & Collings, 2012).

GTM includes the basic concept of TM, blended with a greater number of variables, complex relationships, and interdependencies (Farndale, Pai, Sparrow, & Scullion, 2014; Minbaeva & Collings, 2013). Combining the descriptions offered by Vaiman, Haslberger, and Vance (2015) and Tarique and Schuler (2012), GTM is a set of strategic initiatives that orbit around the following TM activities:

- Attracting talent from both the internal and external labor markets.
- Developing employees, emphasizing those who either possess or are in the process of acquiring skills critical to organizational success, and those that have high potential to succeed in the organization.
- Managing talent flows, including mobilizing employees and facilitating their movement across regional or national boundaries.
- Ensuring the retention of talented employees.

GTM is the program by which many companies aim to achieve their globalization agenda through people. GTM is also the platform through which many individuals hope to realize their international career aspirations and goals (McNulty & De Cieri, 2016). Thus, GTM at the individual, organizational, and country level are inter-related. The objective of determining how GTM (and the return on investment it produces) can strategically support broader TM initiatives is essential (see Minbaeva & Collings, 2013 and Collings, 2014 for commentaries). First, however, we must consider some of the people through whom GTM is to be realized, in this case, expatriates.

What is Expatriate Talent?

The New Oxford American Dictionary defines an expatriate as "a person who lives outside their native country" (New Oxford American Dictionary). As such, expatriation is as old as human history or at least as long as there have been recognizable native countries. Scholarly work about expatriate talent has been around for at least six decades (McNulty & Selmer, 2017), with the bulk of research focused on business expatriates in employment (McNulty & Brewster, 2017b). A common observation about much of the research on expatriates is that little attention has been paid to the definition of the term. McNulty and Brewster (2017a) found that all but two of the 25 most cited articles on expatriates or expatriation failed to offer a definition of their core construct (expatriate). At the same time, they found that there is a proliferation of more than 100 terms related to expatriates and expatriation.

The study of expatriates is currently at a crossroads in terms of its definitional meaning. Who is an expatriate (*noun*), and what does it mean to expatriate (*verb*)? There are many recent examples to illustrate that expatriation is an unsettled field, where multiple terms are used to mean the same thing, thus creating confusion. Even those concerned with systematic classification, with clarity and parsimony as major goals, do not always succeed. Frequently, these studies tend to overstate their contribution without clarifying similarities between their "new" term and terms that already exist. Consider the following:

- The 2004 edition of a standard textbook on international HRM lists some 22 types of "international employees" (Briscoe & Schuler, 2004), including expatriates. This was before the introduction of self-initiated expatriates (SIEs) (Suutari & Brewster, 2000), which has since led to further proliferation (see McNulty & Brewster, 2017a).
- Baruch, Dickman, Altman, and Bournois (2013) offer a systematic classification of global career patterns that focuses on a core group of 20 types and dimensions of global careers, resulting in a (rather unwieldly) theoretically-possible 128 categories. It is based on seven dichotomies derived from a complex approach including a review of prior literature.
- Mayerhofer, Hartmann, Michelitsch-Riedl, and Kollinger (2004) developed a new name for frequent flyers (those who go on frequent business trips abroad) as a means of avoiding confusion with airline loyalty programs. Their creative new term "flexpatriate" attempted to replace the older, more descriptive "international business traveler", but has only added to the confusion (see Mäkelä, Sarenpaa, & McNulty, 2017).
- Shaffer, Kraimer, Chen, and Bolino (2012) distinguish between expatriates (corporate and SIEs) and global travelers. In the latter category, they separate further into short-term assignees, flexpatriates, and international business travelers. Since the term "flexpatriate" entered as a synonym for those who go on frequent business trips, their novel use of the term constitutes a drift in meaning and may add to construct confusion.
- The most common distinction among expatriates currently is organization-assigned expatriates (AEs) versus SIEs (Alshahrani & Morley, 2015; Tharenou, 2013). Some authors add a third category – skilled migrants (Tharenou, 2015). Additionally, Tharenou (2015) distinguishes between short-term assignees, global managers whose careers involve multiple international moves over a long time span, inpatriates moving from abroad to the headquarters location, and corporate SIEs.
- Collings, Scullion, and Morley (2007) differentiate between traditional expatriates (AEs) and "alternative forms" of expatriation and types of expatriates (SIEs/skilled migrants/others). This has resulted in the term "global work arrangements" to capture all types of international workers across a range of short- and long-term assignments, and flexible versus fixed contract roles. Mayrhofer and Reiche (2014) applied this approach, for example, to a special issue on "diverse global work arrangements" in the *Journal of Global Mobility*.
- Adding confusion to the SIE literature is Doherty, Richardson, and Thorn's (2013) liberal approach in defining SIEs where, in their special issue in *Career Development International,* they accepted a broad spectrum of definitions of SIEs offered by the contributing authors.
- In an attempt to address this disarray, Cerdin and Selmer (2014) developed four SIE "conditions" for defining those who engaged in self-initiated *work* abroad. While the conditions differ from those offered by Doherty et al. (2013), the authors nonetheless retain the same label (SIE), thus adding further confusion. McNulty and Brewster (2017b), acknowledging both definitions, attempted to bring order into this by referring to "employed SIEs" versus the more general "SIEs".

- Adding to the expansion of SIE types, Arp, Hutchings, and Smith (2013: 313) focus on a sub-category of SIEs, namely foreign executives in local organizations (FELOs). These are "foreign individuals at executive level who hold local managerial positions supervising host country nationals in local organizations where they have their headquarters".

We note there have been several attempts to provide a systematic classification and definition of expatriate types (Andresen, Bergdolt, Margenfeld, & Dickmann, 2014; Baruch et al., 2013; Cerdin & Selmer, 2014; McNulty & Brewster, 2017a; Meyskens, Von Glinow, Werther, & Clarke, 2009; Shaffer et al., 2012). While the different forms of expatriation and expatriate types are potentially interesting and informative, their proliferation leads to construct conflation that makes comparison of results from different studies difficult, if not impossible (McNulty & Brewster, 2017a).

Cerdin and Selmer's (2014) study about SIEs represents one of two promising attempts to clarify who expatriates are. While the classification of SIEs they offer covers only part of what we are interested in here, their approach nonetheless represents a step forward. McNulty and Brewster offer the most recent attempt to overcome the "jangle fallacy, i.e. the use of many different terms to imply the same meaning" facing this field (2017a: 36).

McNulty and Brewster (2017a) use prototype theory to define the term "business expatriate". They start with the premise that the term "cannot be defined by means of a single set of criteria", that it consists of "a clustered and overlapping set of categories" where "not every member is equally representative in the category at every point in time," and that the "concept is blurred at the edges" (2017a: 42). The authors suggest the following attributes that, taken together, describe the prototypical business expatriate: 1) they are "organizationally employed"; 2) their stay abroad has a "planned temporary nature" (2017a: 43); 3) their employment is based on being a non-citizen of the host country, even if they hold dual nationality; and 4) their employment must be legal in principle and requires compliance with local laws for the employment of non-citizens. This definitional approach allows for a reasonably clear, yet fuzzy definition of the term – in line with messy reality.

Based on these considerations and conditions, McNulty and Brewster define a business expatriate as "legally working individuals who reside temporarily in a country of which they are not a citizen in order to accomplish a career-related goal, being relocated abroad either by an organization, by self-initiation or directly employed within the host-country" (2017a: 46). It includes all of what has been termed "traditional expatriates", most SIEs, and small minorities of international business travelers and commuters, as well as some international migrants.

We adopt McNulty and Brewster's (2017a) definition of business expatriates as representative of the majority of expatriate talent. We focus the remainder of our discussion on the categories of assigned and self-initiated expatriates they list:

- Organization-assigned expatriates (AEs): parent country nationals (PCNs), third country nationals (TCNs), inpatriates, short-term assignees (STAs), and expatriates of host country origin (EHCOs);
- Self-initiated expatriates (SIEs): localized expatriates (LOPATs), permanent transferees (PTs), and foreign executives in local organizations (FELOs).

AEs are people whose careers often unfold within one organization, which seeks to help them improve their career advancement within the company through multiple long-term assignments. AEs may, during their career, move from one organization to another – a familiar occurrence around repatriation time. AEs have been simultaneously referred to as company-assigned expatriates (or CAEs), corporate expatriates, or company-backed expatriates. AEs usually relocate abroad for periods of time of between two and five years, which is in line with them being provided traditional career management that is controlled and directed by the organization to facilitate a match between organizational and individual needs in pursuit of its continued competitive advantage. AEs typically repatriate to the home-country as deemed necessary. The crucial part of the definition is that their employer sends them. Examples of

AEs are parent-country nationals (PCNs), third country nationals (TCNs), expatriates of host country origin (EHCOs), short-term assignees, and inpatriates.

In contrast to AEs, SIEs are individuals who initiate and usually finance their own expatriation, are not transferred by organizations, and relocate often with no definite time frame in mind (Suutari & Brewster, 2000). About half of SIEs work for multinational corporations and global companies (Tharenou, 2013). Many organizations try to hire them to overcome some of the staffing difficulties related to AEs. Unlike many AEs, SIEs are less inhibited by organizational and occupational constraints, and are more prepared to take charge of their careers instead of waiting for an organization to arrange career opportunities involving international experience. SIEs have high agency and are usually externally recruited. Usually, they take control of their careers independent of a particular organization, abandoning corporate security in favor of autonomy and flexibility. Unlike migrants, SIEs do not intend to stay abroad permanently even if their stays exceed the duration of a typical AE assignment of three to five years. Examples of SIEs include foreign executives in local organizations (FELOs), localized expatriates (LOPATs), and permanent transferees (PTs).[2]

Talent Management of Expatriates

Business expatriates are the focus of this chapter because they represent the bulk of non-domestic human capital that falls within the remit of an organization's TM. They are frequently the most educated and experienced segment of the international workforce, often holding powerful – and expensive – positions. While their numbers may be less than other groups of non-domestic employees, such as working holiday makers, seasonal workers, and non-managerial international employees (Haslberger & Vaiman, 2013), they typically represent the most value to organizations in terms of prior and current investment in their knowledge, skills, and abilities. For this reason, they garner the most attention from a TM perspective so as to 1) optimize the value created by them, 2) capture and leverage this value as a measure of an acceptable return on investment (ROI) from international working arrangements, and 3) retain and preserve their value creation potential (Sparrow & Makram, 2015).

In the following sections, we discuss two aspects of TM activities – attraction and development – related to the different types of business expatriates, with a focus on value creation, ROI, and retention.

Attracting Expatriates

The potential talent pool of business expatriates has never been larger, particularly since there is greater awareness that business expatriates engage in many types of international work arrangements beyond only organization-assigned expatriation. Expatriates engaged in self-initiated mobility (as FELOs, LOPATs, and PTs), for example, can benefit organizations as a source of less-expensive talent than AEs, thereby helping them to address problems of international talent shortages. Their employment can also help companies meet cost-cutting targets. The focus on SIE-talent opens venues for young opportunists and localized expatriate professionals (LOPATs) who may have previously been hidden from the TM agenda. Despite the obvious benefits of a larger talent pool, many companies still complain that "finding talent" remains one of their most challenging problems. For instance, the Boston Consulting Group (2007, 2008, 2009) found that TM is one of five key challenges facing companies, one that executives feel least prepared to manage.

The problems associated with "attracting expatriate talent" may fade away if we expand what we mean by, and where we look for, said talent. McNulty and Brewster (2017b) list seven sub-types of expatriates, across two types of expatriation (assigned and self-initiated). These seven types describe many of the employees active in the international labor market, where expatriate talent is most likely to be found. Attracting expatriate talent is aided by understanding the types of international work arrangements these international workers seek, and the types of expatriation they typically engage in, such as parent country nationals, third country nationals, short-term assignees, inpatriates (reverse expatriates), expatriates of host country origin/returnees, permanent transferees, localized expatriates, and foreign executives in local organizations (McNulty & Vance, 2017).

There are many factors that attract employees to the international labor market, including professional aspirations, family and personal life, demand for one's occupation, politics, financial goals, and even personality. For most expatriates, whether AE or SIE, the value gained by their participation in the international labor market is undeniable. International experience acquired through global mobility can be a critical asset. Those with sought-after human capital willing to move internationally know that they are in high demand. Increasing numbers of expatriates are rejecting the "one assignment" concept of expatriation, instead stringing together self-directed (re)assignments across multiple companies to meet their long-term personal and professional aspirations and building career capital. Career capital is important to expatriates. It includes the energy, values, skills, and networks built up over a working life, as well as competencies that can be used within and across companies (Dickmann & Doherty, 2008).

An important question is whether each sub-type of expatriate is likely to undertake assigned or self-initiated expatriation. Prior research has viewed AEs as a form of talent that is easier to attract and retain than SIEs, who are considered less loyal because of their "free agent" attitude and self-directed lifestyle. This fixed view of "orientation" as AE or SIE has recently been debunked. Career orientation in expatriates, as a pattern of work-related preferences, may or may not remain stable through one's working life (Gubler et al., 2014).

McNulty and Vance (2017) suggest that, although most studies of expatriates have explored careers as unfolding in a mostly linear fashion within either the assigned or self-initiated context, there is evidence that expatriates shift between these contexts in either direction. Individual expatriates are not exclusively sub-types of either AEs governed by complete company control over their careers, or of SIEs retaining complete individual control of their careers. Instead, they change their orientations and become a different AE or SIE sub-type depending on international career opportunities and choices that arise. For example, while a global career may unfold entirely as a PCN (AE orientation) or as a PT or LOPAT (SIE orientation), the orientation can also change, often opportunistically, to fit the individual's salient professional needs and personal circumstances (Baruch, 2004; Mendenhall & Macomber, 1997).

Changes in expatriates' career orientation present several challenges to companies wishing to attract expatriate talent. First, the question arises, what sub-type of expatriate is required (for what purpose are they needed)? Then, where is this type of expatriate likely to be found and recruited from? If an AE is required, they are likely to be found in the home country, but there dual-career and family issues are likely to interfere with a willingness to go abroad (Harvey et al., 2009). If an SIE is required, the person may be found living abroad already or wanting to live abroad, which avoids most traditional barriers to mobility. However, SIEs may be less loyal and pursuing their own individual ROI, in form of career capital, to benefit themselves more than their organizations (McNulty & De Cieri, 2016).

The link between SIEs and individual ROI is important. McNulty & De Cieri (2016) posit that the overall expatriate ROI[3] that employers expect from expatriates is a combination of corporate and individual costs and benefits. Corporate ROI is focussed on net benefits that accrue to companies arising from expatriation, whereas individual ROI is defined as "the perceived benefits that accrue to expatriates arising from international assignment experience in relation to professional and personal gains" (McNulty & Inkson, 2013: 35).

Expatriate ROI is relevant for GTM because of the inter-relatedness of corporate and individual ROI. Psychological contract fulfillment, for example, influences strongly perceived individual ROI gains and losses, which in turn impacts on expatriates' behavior related to ROI outcomes (McNulty & De Cieri, 2016; McNulty, De Cieri, & Hutchings, 2013). The content of, changes to, and breaches of the psychological contract influence expatriates' engagement, loyalty, and quit intentions abroad. The missing link between what organizations hope to gain and what matters to expatriate employees suggests a critical misalignment. The outcomes expected from GTM initiatives and the contribution expatriates are willing to make to ensure GTM success are at odds. This, in turn, can have implications for expatriate retention.

The evaluation of how critical the expatriate's role is and of the likelihood that he or she will remain long enough to produce the ROI required constitutes a second challenge. In other words, will their performance justify sending them abroad or employing them and how predictable is this? These challenges illustrate that the value of sophisticated GTM stems not only from advantages in attracting and recruiting "typical" talent (i.e., PCNs) but in gaining an understanding of how to effectively use the various sub-types of expatriates and of the possible changes in career orientation (AE versus SIE).

Developing Expatriates

Expatriates usually are expensive to deploy and manage (Nowak & Linder, 2016), which is why expatriates should be part of the global talent pool so that they can become high-performing employees producing an adequate ROI. However, not all expatriates are managed as talent. Some companies deploy expatriates out of convenience to perform tactical roles that could be performed by local hires rather than in a fashion that warrants the expense (McNulty, De Cieri, & Hutchings, 2009). These companies struggle to connect the dots between expatriation and GTM, thus the identification of "talent" remains weak. Many companies continue to use expatriates without ever linking them to strategic goals such as the development of future global leaders (Minbaeva & Collings, 2013; McNulty & De Cieri, 2016).

One useful way to develop and manage the flow of expatriate talent is to understand that expatriates are not a one-size-fits-all human capital solution. As discussed, expatriates generally fall into two streams according to the type of expatriation they engage in: organization-assigned expatriation and self-initiated expatriation. The distinction between AEs and SIEs is important. The development of international business skills and gaining foreign work experience are increasingly viewed as an essential part of career progression for employees in global companies, and are viewed as prerequisites for senior management positions (Suutari, Brewster, Dickmann, Mäkelä, Tanskenan, & Tornikoski, 2017). The traditional route through which this has been achieved – assigned expatriation – is a very expensive undertaking.

SIEs represent an attractive alternative expatriation model in the contemporary landscape of GTM because, while still often costlier than members of the local population, they are cheaper to employ than AEs (McNulty & Brewster, 2019). Self-initiated expatriation, though, brings with it additional challenges typically not faced when managing AEs, or at least less frequently. SIEs' reasons for working internationally and their career aspirations and orientations may be at odds with organizational interests, and there are additional retention issues (i.e., higher organizational mobility) (Biemann & Andresen, 2010).

For example, PCNs and TCNs are, at times, sent abroad by their company as a reward for their performance in the parent country of the organization. In the absence of a clear business reason, this would constitute a failure of GTM (McNulty & De Cieri, 2016). If there is a good reason to use expatriates, companies view PCNs and TCNs, although expensive, as less risky to deploy, given their deep organizational knowledge and strong loyalty, than localized expatriates (LOPATs) already at the host location (McNulty & Brewster, 2019). LOPATs initially do not have organizational knowledge, being recruited directly from the host-country labor market. While LOPATS are usually less expensive than PCNs and TCNs, they are riskier candidates from a retention standpoint, given their short tenure with the company and their SIE status (i.e., having comparatively low organizational commitment and low aversion to job changes).

Not all expatriates deployed today are necessarily recognized and treated as "talent". To reiterate, given the expensiveness of employing expatriates this is a mistake, except for occasional special circumstances when urgent business needs override the strategic GTM mindset. Those who have been recognized as talent (and those with high potential to become part of the talent pool) usually get more attention from their organizations (e.g., developmental opportunities to enhance their competencies including leadership skills). A contemporary TM approach needs to focus on developing most expatriates as talent.

Development efforts aimed at expatriates vary in their specificity. Programs fall into two categories: general programs to increase the pool of expatriate candidates and specific ones tied to particular international assignments (Collings, Scullion, & Morley, 2007). **General programs** focus on assignment independent personal development. They are fully transferable from one assignment to the next. They transmit process knowledge and competences relevant for expatriation and allow the participants to grow and learn without a specific target. This may include the enhancement of some aspects of cultural intelligence (CQ) such as metacognitive CQ, which includes "planning, monitoring and revising mental models of cultural norms for countries or groups of people" and motivational CQ related to "the capability to direct attention and energy toward learning about and functioning in situations characterized by cultural differences" (Ang et al., 2007: 338).

Other areas for general development are knowledge about the process of adjustment to a new environment and culture; stress reactions when moving abroad and how to find relief; dealing with home sickness; maintaining contacts to friends and family; and awareness of one's substitution capacity and how to enhance it (Shaffer, Harrison, Gregersen, Black, & Ferzandi, 2006). General programs may range from cross-cultural events at work on the most universal end to short-term business trips, international project work, and commuter assignments in the cross-over area between general and specific development.

An increasingly important component of personal development for expatriates is to enhance their leadership capabilities (Boudreau & Ramstad, 2003; Holt & Seki, 2012). The experience of working in another country with different ways of doing business and coping with the reality of different cultures and institutions is one the most effective leadership development tools that organizations have (Mäkelä et al., 2016). Because expatriation is a "mind-stretching" experience for high-potential employees, it provides for organizations an opportunity to assess whether an individual has the necessary leadership abilities and character to work in situations with a lot of "unknowns" (Reiche, Bird, Mendenhall, & Osland, 2017; Yeung, 1995).

Specific programs provide assignment-dependent content that is of limited transferability. They transmit factual knowledge about the assignment location. They develop cognitive CQ such as "knowledge of the norms, practices and conventions in different cultures… This includes knowledge of the economic, legal and social systems of different cultures and subcultures…and knowledge of basic frameworks of cultural values" and assignment-specific behavioral CQ such as "the capability to exhibit appropriate verbal and non- verbal actions when interacting with people" (Ang et al., 2007: 338). Learning the host country language also falls into this category.

There is another aspect of expatriate development that is not focused on the individual expatriates but on the expatriate management system. Comprehensive GTM requires expertise in the acquisition and management of SIE talent (Vaiman & Collings, 2014). Therefore, HR departments must develop their recruitment and selection competencies in the global and all relevant local labor markets.

The development and deployment of expatriates are expensive. Unless they create the superior results that strategically aligned TM programs produce (Collings, Scullion, & Vaiman, 2011; Ernst & Young, 2010), the related expense is hard to justify.

Key Areas for Further Research

Although there has been a lot published about GTM, its link to expatriation is under-developed. We propose a number of new avenues for research to address this gap. As the focus of most talent programs is on high-status expatriation, a large part of an MNE's GTM effort will be directed towards AEs. However, SIEs are likely to constitute a higher proportion of the expatriate population because they are less expensive to employ and manage (McNulty & Brewster, 2019). Nonetheless, without home country organizational support, their career development may fall through the cracks, leading to turnover and the potential loss of key talent for the MNE – something it would want to avoid (Mäkelä et al., 2016). While SIEs may not be relied on to stay in the organization for a long time, their "short-term expatriate ROI" (McNulty

& De Cieri, 2016) may still provide the MNE with an important competitive advantage. Thus, GTM focused on SIEs can impact on organizational performance. Research questions include:

RQ1: To what extent is GTM focused on SIEs compared to AEs? What accounts for differences (if they exist)?

RQ2: Which forms of global talent management are better suited to SIEs as compared to AEs in relation to (a) leveraging their social and cultural capital; (b) their attrition; and (c) obtaining short- versus long-term expatriate ROI?

RQ3: To what extent, and how, does the global talent management of SIEs increase their retention in MNEs?

RQ4: What are the benefits and costs of global talent management for SIEs and MNEs?

A further line of research concerns theoretically developing what is meant by GTM in the context of expatriation. The GTM construct is often viewed as a form of employee talent development that spans more than one MNE location and which includes international locations. In other words, if GTM is offered to local employees in every location where the company employs them, including in any international offices it may have, then the company beliefs that it offers TM on a "global" scale (i.e., global talent management).

This is very different, however, from the purpose of GTM being able to move employees *across* international borders, which is our focus here. The distinction is key, as it determines for whom and why GTM is important from the MNEs perspective, including how much it will invest in GTM and for what purposes. A key issue, then, is to re-examine GTM for expatriates and to identify what it means for organizations in their day-to-day practice. This area of research will make clearer what GTM involves and for whose benefit. Research questions include:

RQ5: Does the term "global talent management" adequately describe the construct intended when it is linked to expatriation?

RQ6: How do MNEs define global talent management?

RQ7: How is global talent management operationalized in MNEs?

A third area of research is to examine the impact of GTM on expatriates and their employing organizations. In other words, does GTM deliver on its promise and is it a worthwhile endeavor that reaps its intended benefits? Much of the research about GTM explains and justifies (almost *ad nauseum*) why GTM is necessary and what it should deliver. But does it? GTM can be an expensive undertaking when expatriation is used as a key tool for high-potential talent and leadership development. Yet, we know very little about the actual benefits it brings to the organizations funding it and the employees who relocate abroad to take advantage of it. This leads to our final set of research questions:

RQ8: For what purpose do MNEs use global talent management? Are the purposes formally articulated as part of a business case for GTM initiatives?

RQ9: Who funds GTM initiatives that are linked to expatriation – the sending or receiving organization? Is funding a barrier to or an opportunity for investing in expatriation?

RQ10: How are GTM outcomes measured?

Conclusion

Expatriates represent both problems and solutions for companies. AEs are "known quantities" that have the trust of the parent company, but they are expensive compared to local hires and they may lack local savvy. SIEs generally are less expensive than AEs and often have more local expertise, but they have no roots in the parent company and are open to job changes and may be inherently less loyal to their employers. Thus, they can be hard to retain. The pool of SIE talent in the international labor market can help organizations solve some pressing global staffing problems. These include: 1) shortages of suitable internal candidates; 2) controlling the costs of global mobility; and 3) the need to foster strong local ties quickly.

Smart companies can address global staffing challenges by employing different types of expatriates that are best suited to the situation, for example, EHCOs or FELOs when skilled talent is not available locally (problem 1), local foreign hires when cost considerations are important (problem 2 above), and LOPATs when local ties are paramount (problem 3). There will be implications for expatriate talent attraction and development arising from differences in the types of expatriates used. A sophisticated GTM approach depends on appropriate competencies of the HRM function to successfully "herd the *expatriate* cats". The extent to which companies understand who they are employing, how, and why, will determine the success of their GTM efforts.

Notes

1 There are, of course, exceptions. Sometimes an urgent business need requires sending an expatriate, who is not considered part of the talent pool. But these exceptions should be kept to a minimum.
2 It is important to mention that the management of expatriate talent must include non-traditional business expatriates not only by type of assignment and international work experience, but also by family situation as described by McNulty, Y. and Hutchings, K. 2016. Looking for global talent in all the right places: A critical literature review of non-traditional expatriates. *International Journal of Human Resource Management*, 27(7): 699-728.
3 Expatriate ROI is defined as "a calculation in which the financial and non-financial benefits to the firm are compared with the financial and non-financial costs of the international assignment, as appropriate to the assignment's purpose" (McNulty & Tharenou, 2004: 73).

References

Alshahrani, S. T., & Morley, M. J. 2015. Accounting for variations in the patterns of mobility among conventional and self-initiated expatriates. *International Journal of Human Resource Management,* 26(15): 1936–1954.

Andresen, M., Bergdolt, F., Margenfeld, J., & Dickmann, M. 2014. Addressing international mobility confusion: Developing definitions and differentiations for self-initiated & assigned expatriates as well as migrants. *International Journal of Human Resource Management,* 25(16): 2295–2318.

Ang, S., Van Dyne, L., Koh, C., Ng, K. Y., Templer, K. J., Tay, C., & Chandrasekar, N. A. 2007. Cultural intelligence: Its measurement and effects on cultural judgment and decision making, cultural adaptation and task performance. *Management and Organization Review,* 3(3): 335–371.

Arp, F. 2014. Emerging giants, aspiring multinationals and foreign executives: Leapfrogging, capability building, and competing with developed country multinationals. *Human Resource Management,* 53(6): 851–876.

Arp, F., Hutchings, K., & Smith, W. A. 2013. Foreign executives in local organisations: An exploration of differences to other types of expatriates. *Journal of Global Mobility,* 1(3): 312–335.

Axelrod, B., Handfield-Jones, H., & Michaels, E. 2002, A new game plan for C players. *Harvard Business Review,* 126(1): 80–88.

Baruch, Y. 2004. Transforming careers: From linear to multidirectional career paths – organizational and individual perspectives. *Career Development International,* 9(1): 58–73.

Baruch, Y., Dickmann, M., Altman, Y., & Bournois, F. 2013. Exploring international work: Types and dimensions of global careers. *International Journal of Human Resource Management,* 24(12): 2369–2393.

Biemann, T., & Andresen, M. 2010. Self-initiated foreign expatriates versus assigned expatriates: Two distinct types of international careers? *Journal of Managerial Psychology,* 25(4): 430–448.

Boston Consulting Group. 2007. *The future of HR: Key challenges through 2015.* Dusseldorf, Boston Consulting Group.

Boston Consulting Group. 2008. *Creating people advantage: How to address HR challenges worldwide through 2015,* Boston, MA: Boston Consulting Group.

Boston Consulting Group. 2009. *Creating people advantage: How to address HR challenges during the crisis and beyond,* Boston, MA: Boston Consulting Group.

Boudreau, J., & Ramstad, P. 2003. Strategic HRM measurement in the 21st century: From justifying HR to strategic talent leadership. In M. Goldsmith, R. Gandossy, & M. Efron (Eds.), *HRM in the 21st century:* 79–90. New York: Wiley.

Briscoe, D. R., & Schuler, R. S. 2004. *International Human Resource Management* (2nd ed.). London: Routledge.

Caligiuri, P., & Bonache, J. 2016. Evolving and enduring challenges in global mobility. *Journal of World Business,* 51(1), 127–141

Cerdin, J.-L., & Selmer, J. 2014. Who is a self-initiated expatriate? Towards conceptual clarity of a common notion. *International Journal of Human Resource Management,* 25(9): 1281–1301.

Collings, D. G., & Isichei, M. 2018. The shifting boundaries of global staffing: Integrating global talent management, alternative forms of international assignments and non-employees into the discussion. *International Journal of Human Resource Management,* 29(1), 165–187.

Collings, D. G., & Mellahi, K. 2009. Strategic talent management: A review and research agenda. *Human Resource Management Review,* 19(4): 304–13.

Collings, D. G., Scullion, H., & Morley, M. J. 2007. Changing patterns of global staffing in the multinational enterprise: Challenges to the conventional expatriate assignment and emerging alternatives. *Journal of World Business,* 42(2): 198–213.

Collings, D. G., Scullion, H., & Vaiman, V. 2011. European perspectives on talent management. *European Journal of International Management,* 5(5): 453–462.

Dickmann, M., & Doherty, N. 2008. Exploring the career capital impact of international assignments within distinct organizational contexts. *British Journal of Management,* 19(2): 145–161.

Doherty, N., & Dickmann, M. 2013. Self-initiated and assigned expatriate: A review and directions for future research. In V. Vaiman, & A. Haslberger (Eds.), *Managing talent of self-initiated expatriates: A neglected sources of the global talent flow:* 234–255. London: Palgrave MacMillan.

Doherty, N., Richardson, J., & Thorn, K. 2013. Self-initiated expatriation: Career experiences, processes and outcomes. *Career Development International,* 18(1): 6–11.

Dowling. P., Festing, M., & Engle, A. 2013. *International Human Resource Management* (6th ed.). Cengage.

Edström, A., & J. Galbraith 1977. Transfer of managers as a coordination and control strategy in multinational organisations. *Administrative Science Quarterly,* 22(2): 248–263.

Ernst & Young. 2010. *Managing today's global workforce: Evaluating talent management to improve business.* London, Ernst & Young.

Farndale, E., Pai, A., Sparrow, P., & Scullion, H. 2014. Balancing individual and organizational goals in global talent management: A mutual-benefits perspective. *Journal of World Business,* 49(2), 204–214.

Gubler, M., Arnold, J. & Coombs, C. 2014. Organizational boundaries and beyond: A new look at the components of a boundaryless career orientation. *Career Development International,* 19(6): 641–667.

Harvey, M., Novicevic, M., & Breland, J. W. 2009. Global dual-career exploration and the role of hope and curiosity during the process. *Journal of Managerial Psychology,* 24(2): 178–197.

Harzing, A.-W. 2001. Of bears, bumble-bees, and spiders: The role of expatriates in controlling foreign subsidiaries. *Journal of World Business,* 36(4), 366–379.

Haslberger, A., & Vaiman, V. 2013. Self-initiated expatriates: A neglected source of the global talent flow. In V. Vaiman & A. Haslberger (Eds.), *Managing talent of self-initiated expatriates: A neglected source of the global talent flow:* 1–15. London: Palgrave MacMillan.

Holt, K., & Seki, K. 2012. Global leadership: A developmental shift for everyone. *Industrial and Organizational Psychology,* 5: 196–215.

Huselid, M. A., Beatty, R. W., & Becker, B. E. 2005, A players or A positions? The strategic logic of workforce management. *Harvard Business Review,* 129(12): 110–117.

Khilji, S. E., Tarique, I., & Schuler, R. S. 2015. Incorporating the macro view in global talent management. *Human Resource Management Review,* 25(3), 236–248.

King, K. A. 2015. Global talent management Introducing a strategic framework and multiple actors model. *Journal of Global Mobility,* 3(3): 273–288.

Lewis, R. E., & Heckman, R. J. 2006. Talent management: A critical review. *Human Resource Management Review,* 16: 139–154.

Makela, L., Sarenpaa, K., & McNulty, Y. 2017. International business travelers, short-term assignees and international commuters. In Y. McNulty & J. Selmer. *The Research Handbook of Expatriates:* 276–294. London, Edward Elgar.

Mayerhofer, H., Hartmann, L. C., Michelitsch-Riedl, G., & Kollinger, I. 2004. Flexpatriate assignments: A neglected issue in global staffing. *International Journal of Human Resource Management,* 15(8): 1371–1389.

Mayrhofer, W., & Reiche, B. S. 2014. Guest editorial: Context and global mobility: Diverse global work arrangements. *Journal of Global Mobility,* 2(2).

McNulty, Y. 2013. Are self-initiated expatriates born or made? Exploring the relationship between SIE orientation and individual ROI. In V. Vaiman & A. Haslberger (Eds.). *Talent management of self-initiated expatriates: A neglected source of global talent:* 30–58. UK, Palgrave-McMillan.

McNulty, Y. 2016. Why expatriate compensation will change how we think about global talent management. In Y. Guo, P. Dowling, & R. Hussain (Eds.). *Global talent management and staffing in MNEs:* 123–148. Bingley, UK: Emerald.

McNulty, Y., & Brewster, C. 2017a. Theorizing the meaning(s) of 'expatriate': Establishing boundary conditions for business expatriates. *The International Journal of Human Resource Management,* 28(1), 27–61.

McNulty, Y., & Brewster, C. 2017b. The concept of business expatriates. In Y. McNulty & J. Selmer. *Research handbook of expatriates:* 21–60. London, Edward Elgar.

McNulty, Y., & Brewster, C. 2019. *Working internationally: Expatriation, migration and other global work.* Cheltenham, UK: Edward Elgar.

McNulty, Y., & De Cieri, H. 2016. Linking global mobility and global talent management: The role of ROI. *Employee Relations,* 38(1), 8–30.

McNulty, Y., De Cieri, H., & Hutchings, K. 2009. Do global firms measure expatriate return on investment? An empirical examination of measures, barriers and variables influencing global staffing practices. *International Journal of Human Resource Management,* 20(6): 1309–1326.

McNulty, Y., De Cieri, H., & Hutchings, K. 2013. Expatriate return on investment in Asia Pacific: An empirical study of individual ROI versus corporate ROI. *Journal of World Business,* 48(2): 209–221.

McNulty, Y., & Hutchings, K. 2016. Looking for global talent in all the right places: A critical literature review of non-traditional expatriates. *International Journal of Human Resource Management,* 27(7): 699–728.

McNulty, Y., & Selmer, J. 2017. Overview of early expatriate studies, 1952 to 1979. In Y.McNulty & J.Selmer. *Research handbook of expatriates:* 3–20. London, Edward Elgar.

McNulty, Y., & Vance, C. 2017. Dynamic global careers: A new conceptualization of expatriate career paths. *Personnel Review,* 46(2), 205–221.

Mendenhall, M., & J. Macomber 1997. Rethinking the strategic management of expatriates from a non-linear dynamics perspective. In D. Saunders & Z. Aycan (Eds.). *New approaches to employee management:* 41–61. Greenwich, CT, JAI Press.

Meyskens, M., Von Glinow, M. A., Werther, J. W. B., & Clarke, L. 2009. The paradox of international talent: Alternative forms of international assignments. *International Journal of Human Resource Management,* 20(6): 1439–1450.

Minbaeva, D., & Collings, D. G. 2013. Seven myths of global talent management. *The International Journal of Human Resource Management,* 24(9), 1762–1776.

Moeller, M. & B. S. Reiche 2017. Inpatriates: Two decades of research - review, synthesis and outlook. In Y. McNulty & J. Selmer. *Research handbook of expatriates:* 218–240. London, Edward Elgar.

New Oxford American Dictionary. n.d. Supplied with Apple OS X Version 10.12.3.

Nowak, C., & Linder, C. 2016. Do you know how much your expatriate costs? An activity-based cost analysis of expatriation. *Journal of Global Mobility,* 4(1): 88–107.

OECD. 2017. *G20 Global displacement and migration trends report.* Paris: OECD.

OECD. 2018. *2018 International migration and displacement trends and policies report to the G20.* OECD.

OECD. 2019. *2019 International migration and displacement trends and policies report to the G20.* OECD.

ORC Worldwide 2004. *Survey of localization policies and practices.* New York.

Özçelik, G., Haak-Saheem, W., Brewster, C., & McNulty, Y. 2019. An international perspective: Hidden expatriates. In S. Nachmias, & V. Caven (Eds.), *Hidden inequality in modern organizations: volume 2, employment practices.* Hampshire, UK: Palgrave/Springer.

Reiche, B., Bird, A., Mendenhall, M., & Osland, J. 2017. Contextualizing leadership: A typology of global leadership roles. *Journal of International Business Studies,* 48: 552–572.

Reiche, B. S., Kraimer M., & Harzing, A.-W. 2009. Inpatriates as agents of cross-unit knowledge flows in multinational corporations. In P. Sparrow (Ed.). *Handbook of international human resource management: Integrating people, process and context:* 151–170. Chichester, Wiley.

Scullion, H., & Collings, D. 2006. *Global staffing.* London, Routledge.

Shaffer, M., Harrison, D., Gregersen, H., Black, J., & Ferzandi, L. 2006. You can take it with you: Individual differences and expatriate effectiveness. *Journal of Applied Psychology,* 91(1): 109–125.

Shaffer, M. A., Kraimer, M. L., Chen, Y.-P., & Bolino, M. C. 2012. Choices, challenges, and career consequences of global work experiences: A review and future agenda. *Journal of Management,* 38(4): 1282–1327.

Sparrow, P. R., & Makram, H. 2015. What is the value of talent management? Building value-driven processes within a talent management architecture. *Human Resource Management Review,* 25(3): 249–263.

Suutari, V., & Brewster, C. 2000. Making their own way: International experience through self-initiated foreign assignment. *Journal of World Business,* 35(4): 417–436.

Suutari, V., Brewster, C., Dickmann, M., Mäkelä, L., Tanskenan, J., & Tornikoski, C. 2017. The effect of international work experience on the career success of expatriates: A comparison of assigned and self-initiated expatriates. *Human Resource Management,* 57(1): 37–54.

Tait, E., De Cieri, H., & McNulty, Y. 2014. The opportunity cost of saving money: An exploratory study of permanent transfers and localization of expatriates in Singapore. *International Studies of Management & Organization,* 44(3): 79–94.

Takeuchi, R., Tesluk, P., Yun, S., & Lepak, D. 2005. An integrative view of international experience. *Academy of Management Journal,* 48(1): 85–100.

Tarique, I., & Schuler, R. S. 2010. Global talent management: Literature review, integrative framework, and suggestions for future research. *Journal of World Business,* 45: 2, 122–133.

Tarique, I., & Schuler, R. 2012. Global talent management literature review: A special report for SHRM Foundation. *SHRM,* October 2012.

Tharenou, P. 2013. Self-initiated expatriates: an alternative to company-assigned expatriates? *Journal of Global Mobility,* 1(3): 336–356.

Tharenou, P. 2015. Researching expatriate types: The quest for rigorous methodological approaches. *Human Resource Management Journal,* 25(2): 149–165.

Thite, M., Srinivasan, V., Harvey, M., & Valk, R. 2009. Expatriates of host-country origin: Coming home to test the waters. *The International Journal of Human Resource Management,* 20(2): 269–285.

Torbiörn, I. 1997. Staffing for international operations. *Human Resource Management Journal,* 7(3): 42–52.

United Nations Population Division (UNDP). 2018. *Sustainable cities, human mobility and international migration.* New York, NY: UNDP.

Vaiman, V., & Collings, D. 2014. Global talent management. *Routledge companion to human resource management.* London: Routledge.

Vaiman, V., Haslberger, A., & Vance, C. M. 2015. Recognizing the important role of self-initiated expatriates in effective global talent management. *Human Resource Management Review,* 25: 280–286.

Vaiman, V., Scullion, H., & Collings, D. G. 2012. Talent management decision making. *Management Decision,* 50(5): 925–941.

Vance, C. M., & Vaiman, V. 2008. Smart talent management: On the powerful amalgamation of talent management and knowledge management. In V. Vaiman, & C. Vance (Eds.), *Smart talent management: Building knowledge assets for competitive advantage:* 1–15. Northampton, MA: Edward Elgar.

Yeung, A. 1995. Developing leadership capabilities of global corporations: A comparative study in eight nations. *Human Resource Management,* 34(4): 529–548.

29

TALENT MANAGEMENT AND WORKFORCE DIFFERENTIATION

Michael Koch

Elise Marescaux

Introduction

During the last decades, employment relationships have undergone substantial changes. For instance, market influences have led to a decline in average worker tenure, increased restructuring through layoffs and growing use of contingent workers, outsourcing, and variable incentive pay (Bidwell, Briscoe, Fernandez-Mateo, & Sterling, 2013; Dencker & Fang, 2016). This development, in turn, is associated with an increased inequality in the distribution of rewards, which are more and more based on the ability and performance of individuals and their contribution to firm success (ibid).

In this context, many business organizations have changed their approach to managing people. Instead of a one-size-fits-all approach, they have begun to customize, or differentiate, the way they attract, develop, and retain talent. Workforce differentiation refers to the disproportional investment of resources in those positions or employees in the company where one expects dispro-portionate returns (Becker, Huselid, & Beatty, 2009). These employees are often labeled "stars", "high-performers", "high-potentials", or simply "talents" (all terms are used interchangeably in the following). In a quote reminiscent of Orwell's *Animal Farm*, Ulrich estimated that "The harsh reality of managing people is that differentiation must occur, with some employees more equal than others" (Ulrich, 2005: 11).

Indeed, a growing number of companies have implemented different forms of workforce differentiation programs. GlaxoSmithKline, for instance, has stated that "it is essential that we have key talent in critical positions and that the careers of these individuals are managed centrally" (Huselid, Beatty, & Becker, 2005: 114). Likewise, firms such as IBM, General Electric, and Microsoft also have implemented differentiation programs. It is estimated that in the UK alone, three-fifths of employers have a formal talent management (TM) strategy in place, which usually focuses on select key employees (CIPD, 2015).

Workforce differentiation is closely related to TM (cf., Meyers et al., 2020). Although there is no uni-versally agreed-upon definition of TM, a recent and influential definition refers to:

> activities and processes that involve the systematic identification of key positions which differ-entially contribute to the organization's sustainable competitive advantage, the development of a talent pool of high potential and high performing incumbents to fill these roles, and the development of a differentiated human resource architecture to facilitate filling these positions with competent incumbents and to ensure their continued commitment to the organization. (Collings & Mellahi, 2009: 304)

DOI: 10.4324/9781315474687-29

This definition includes a particular emphasis on differentiation, illustrating the link between TM and workforce differentiation (Gelens, Dries, Hofmans, & Pepermans, 2013). Moreover, focusing on "talents" implies that talent differentiation is as vital to firms as customer segmentation; this was hailed as a "paradigm shift" in human resource management (Boudreau & Ramstad, 2005).

Several questions have emerged in the context of managing talent. One of them relates to the exclusivity of what constitutes talent and which types of employees should receive investments from companies. The view championed by Collings and Mellahi (2009) or Huselid et al. (2005), which associates TM with strategically important jobs or employees, implies an exclusive definition of what talent is. Workforce differentiation practices, such as the identification and promotion of "high-potentials", match with this exclusive view. In contrast to that, there have been attempts to develop an inclusive definition of talent, which holds that TM and company investments should apply to all workers. This view assumes that "all (or at least most) employees are or could be talented at something, given sufficient training and opportunity" (Swailes, Downs, & Orr, 2014: 4).

Another, related debate considers whether talent is innate or acquired. Workforce differentiation schemes recognize that there are very few exceptional performers and that even with identical amounts of training, some employees will always outperform others (Meyers, van Woerkom, & Dries, 2013). In that regard, workforce differentiation practices are closer to the view that regards talent as innate.

Considering the apparent link between workforce differentiation and TM, the aim of this chapter is to explore the concept of workforce differentiation by reviewing both past theoretical and empirical insights and connecting it with TM to show its added value to this field. Specifically, we start off with an overview of the antecedents of workforce differentiation. Secondly, we review existing theoretical and empirical research on the consequences of workforce differentiation, both positive and negative. Finally, we conclude this chapter with a set of recommendations for future research, which could advance both insights into workforce differentiation as well as TM.

Antecedents of Workforce Differentiation

An important debate within workforce differentiation is whether it should focus on jobs or people (Cappelli & Keller, 2014). One stream of (mostly prescriptive) literature calls for a focus on strategic jobs, and not people. This literature argues that, to prevent "putting the cart before the horse", strategic jobs should be the basis for differentiation, independent of the respective employee staffed on a strategic job (Huselid et al., 2005), resulting in the exhortation "Put Strategy, Not People, First" (Becker et al., 2009: 1). Once these strategic jobs (or "pivotal positions") are identified, an organization should be concerned with building talent pools of individuals who can fill the roles which differentially contribute to an organization's sustained competitive advantage (Collings & Mellahi, 2009). This position assumes that workforce differentiation is a top-down process that should start with the strategy of the firm. It furthermore assumes that once the strategy is established, suitable employees to fill strategic roles can be easily identified and recruited.

On the opposite side of the spectrum, another strand of research has focused on so-called "stars" (i.e., high-status and high-performing individuals) (e.g., Groysberg, 2010). Based on novel research that shows that performance follows a power law distribution instead of a normal distribution (O'Boyle & Aguinis, 2012), it is assumed that "the majority of overall productivity is due to a small group of elite workers" (Aguinis & O'Boyle, 2014: 315). Human resource management, then, "may need to accommodate the rise of stars and change focus from the necessary many to the elite few" (Aguinis & O'Boyle, 2014: 341). The idea of a "law of the few" has also been discussed in the popular science literature. For instance, referring to the Pareto principle, Malcolm Gladwell asserts that "in any situation roughly 80 percent of the 'work' will be done by 20 percent of the participants" (Gladwell, 2000: 19). This again implies that not all employees are equally talented and productive and, hence, the largest HR investments should be targeted towards the "stars".

The question regarding which employees should be the focus of scarce investment resources has been called "an evergreen question" (Cappelli & Keller, 2014: 10). There is a considerable body of research that examines this question from a strategic, resource-based angle. In the resource-based view, employees are regarded as resources that can be sources of sustained competitive advantage if they are valuable, rare, inimitable, and non-substitutable (Molloy & Barney, 2015).

In their seminal contribution, Lepak and Snell (1999) provided a framework for differentiation grounded in the resource-based view that has had a large influence on the subsequent literature on strategic HRM. Lepak and Snell distinguished between four different employment modes: 1) internal development, 2) acquisition, 3) contracting, and 4) alliance, with the former two being internal and the latter two being external modes (note that Lepak and Snell's architecture considers the external as well as the internal labor market).

In Lepak and Snell's human resource architecture, employment modes are associated with different HR configurations (i.e., particular ways of managing people). Here, HR configurations are subject to a differentiation of the strategic importance of employees across two dimensions: uniqueness of human capital and value of human capital. Assuming that each dimension can take either a "high" or a "low" state, four different HR configurations emerge (e.g., 2 X 2 matrix): collaborative HR, commitment-based HR, compliance-based HR, and market-based HR (Lepak & Snell, 1999). Most notably, employees in the upper-right quadrant (e.g., commitment-based HR) can be regarded as core employees since they possess skills that are both valuable and unique. This makes them a potential source of competitive advantage and therefore, firms have an interest in building a commitment based, long-term relationship with these employees through extensive HR investments.

Empirical research has indeed found that many organizations employ HR systems that differentiate between core and support employees. In particular, non-manufacturing industries, in which employees play an important role in the realization of firm objectives, have been found to differentiate more strongly between core and support employees (Lepak, Taylor, Tekleab, Marrone, & Cohen, 2007). Moreover, in line with Lepak and Snell's (1999) HR architecture model, empirical research found that organizations invest differentially in their employees depending on their value and uniqueness (Krausert, 2017; Lepak & Snell, 2002; Melián-González & Verano-Tacorante, 2004).

A number of studies focus on the specific criteria or competencies that firms use or should be using to identify "high-potentials" or "talents". This work is congruent with recent trends towards using competency profiles to identify valuable employees (McDonnell, 2011). For example, competencies such as teamwork, vision, performance motivation (Pepermans, Vloeberghs, & Perkisas, 2003), or learning agility (Dries, Vantilborgh, & Pepermans, 2012) have been suggested as antecedents of workforce differentiation. Further notable influences are an individual's career orientation (Dries, 2009; Dries & Pepermans, 2007), above-average job performance (e.g., Mäkelä, Björkman, & Ehrnrooth, 2010), relationship quality (Golik, Blanco, & Czikk, 2017), or social competence (Finkelstein, Costanza, & Goodwin, 2017).

A stream of publications in books and practitioner outlets (e.g., Becker et al., 2009; Cantrell & Smith, 2010) also provide "how-to" advice on differentiating either strategically important people or positions. This literature on workforce differentiation is to be seen in the wider context of prescriptive frameworks for HR strategy that dominate a large part of the practitioner literature on HRM. The philosophy undergirding this literature is that there is small elite of employees whose skills are rare, hard to find, and difficult to replace and who add disproportionate amounts of value (Sparrow & Makram, 2015). Workforce differentiation should establish ways of identifying these employees or positions, and the ultimate objective is to promote and develop these high-performance and high-potential employees, and exit the less valuable ones (e.g., Krausert, 2017).

Apart from the focus on jobs or people as well as the criteria used for differentiation, other antecedents are also likely. At the macro-level, workforce differentiation might not be equally embedded in every national culture. Some countries have a strong cultural tradition towards equality rooted in a system of collective bargaining (e.g., Belgium; Marescaux, De Winne, & Sels, 2013; Sels, Janssens, Van den Brande, & Overlaet, 2000). This reduces the room for workforce differentiation substantially as opposed to countries in which the culture is predominantly individualistic and predisposed towards differentiation (e.g., the U.S.A.; Rousseau, 2005). Hence, the national culture might strongly influence an organization's ability and room to differentiate between jobs and/or people in the organization.

At the organizational level, the general TM strategy of a company will matter. A fundamental distinction exists between exclusive and inclusive TM (Meyers & Van Woerkom, 2014). The former focuses on identifying, developing, and motivating a small subset of talents or high-potentials. In that sense, the organization differentiates between those employees considered talented and those who are not by allocating more resources (e.g., developmental opportunities) to the former group (Dries, 2013). Inclusive TM, on the other hand, focuses on identifying every employee's talent and nurturing it (Swailes et al., 2014). This implies that all employees can be involved in TM and are allocated resources, yet in a differentiated manner as not all employees have the same talent.

Finally, even at the team level, there might be potential antecedents to workforce differentiation. Line managers could for example be a major source of workforce differentiation. The essence of leader-member exchange theory is that managers invest more resources and time into those employees they consider most valuable and share a close relationship with (Liden, Sparrowe, & Wayne, 1997). This results in differential treatment within teams (Rosen, Slater, Chang, & Johnson, 2013). To sum it up, the above highlights that antecedents to workforce differentiation might exist at different levels of analysis.

Consequences of Workforce Differentiation

Workforce differentiation is assumed to create value for the organization in terms of productivity, innovation, profitability, etc. The initial logic behind it builds on organizational theory (Lepak & Snell, 1999). For example, as mentioned above, Lepak and Snell (1999) argue that organizations can achieve a higher return on investment by targeting their resources (e.g., investments in terms of performance management, training, compensation, etc.) towards positions that require highly unique and valuable skills, knowledge, and abilities and/or towards employees who possess such SKA's (the so-called stars, high-performers, or high-potentials in the organization).

Among other things, the resource-based view of the firm is used to support this claim, stressing that such targeted investments strongly contribute to the creation of valuable, rare, inimitable and nontransferable human and social capital, hence giving the firm a competitive edge (Lepak & Snell, 1999; Sparrow & Makram, 2015). Similarly, others refer to Pareto's "law of the vital few" mentioned earlier, arguing that only a subset of employees in the organization add disproportional value to the organization through superior human and social capital (Aguinis & O'Boyle, 2014; O'Boyle & Aguinis, 2012).

Hence, from a strategic point of view, investing resources disproportionally in that small group of employees should pay off tremendously for an organization, especially when those employees occupy positions that are close to the organization's strategic core competences (Aguinis & O'Boyle, 2014). By investing in their performance management, development, compensation, etc., the organization ensures the continued motivation, engagement, commitment, and performance of their most valuable employees (Collings & Mellahi, 2009; Collings, Mellahi, & Cascio, 2019), thus contributing to firm performance. Yet, despite the theoretical and intuitive appeal of targeting HRM investments towards employees that generate the highest value for the organization (e.g., high-potentials), empirical research depicts a more complicated picture. We provide an overview of selected research below outlining the benefits as well as downsides. To do so, we make use of different research streams that study workforce differentiation in particular domains (e.g., research on contingent labor, pay dispersion, and i-deals, etc.) as well as from a TM point of view.

The Benefits of Workforce Differentiation

Firstly, the TM literature suggests that hiring stars and investing more resources into their development, motivation, and retention enhances a firm's potential to innovate by drawing on their superior human and social capital (Dokko & Rosenkopf, 2010; Dries, 2013). Moreover, stars have the potential to influence those around them positively, for example serving as a motivational role model for other co-workers and contributing to co-workers' performance through collaboration (Call, Nyberg, & Thatcher, 2015; Lockwood & Kunda, 1997).

Secondly, research on pay dispersion showed the benefits of differentiating between employees in terms of financial rewards since this increased both individual and group effectiveness (for a systematic overview, see Downes & Choi, 2014). Similarly, yet going beyond just pay, Marescaux et al. (2013) showed that employees who receive more favorable HR practice outcomes (e.g., more developmental opportunities, benefits, autonomy, flexibility, etc.) display higher affective organizational commitment. A final example concerns the strong indications that organizations can benefit from allocating specific, individualized resources or arrangements to single individuals through negotiation (i.e., so-called i-deals) (Rousseau, 2005). More specifically, employees who receive favorable treatment through i-deals are found to exhibit higher commitment, engagement, pro-active behavior, job satisfaction, etc. (for a meta-analytic overview, see Liao, Wayne, & Rousseau, 2016).

These benefits in terms of employee attitudes, behavior, and performance are typically explained in different ways. Firstly, tying resource allocations to employees' performance or skills, knowledge, and abilities can motivate employees to develop themselves and perform at a higher level, thus benefiting the organization. This resonates with a fundamental theory of fairness, i.e., equity theory (Adams, 1965). Equity theory argues that employees judge the fairness or equity of outcome differences (e.g., pay differences). Outcome differences are only considered fair or equitable in so far as they are proportional to differences in inputs, such as performance, skills, knowledge, etc. (Morand & Merriman, 2012)). When considered fair, employees are motivated by outcome differences and will potentially put in more effort to achieve more desirable outcomes (Walster, Hatfield, Walster, & Berscheid, 1978).

Secondly, social exchange theory (Blau, 1964) argues that employees who perceive their organization to invest in their development, well-being, and a long-term relationship with them, will maintain a social exchange relationship with their employer characterized by reciprocation (Gould-Williams, 2007). Specifically, in return for this favorable treatment, they will show more favorable attitudes and behaviors towards the organization (Marescaux et al., 2013). Finally, being on the receiving end of more favorable treatment by the organization can also strongly boost one's self-esteem, which subsequently generates more favorable attitudes and behaviors towards the organization (Liu, Lee, Hu, Kwan, & Wu, 2013).

The Disadvantages of Workforce Differentiation

Yet, we also find many indications that the competitive edge generated by workforce differentiation may be overestimated. Firstly, Stirpe, Bonache, and Revilla (2014) showed the downside of mixing both standard contract workers (e.g., full-time, permanent contract employees who receive a great deal of HR investments) with contingent workers (e.g., temporary contract workers who are typically managed through low HR investments). Specifically, they found HR investments to be counterproductive (in terms of sales and value added) when a high degree of contingent workers were present in the organization. The authors speculate that this differential treatment undermines cooperation and the creation of shared mental models and languages among employees.

Secondly, in the field of TM, Call et al. (2015) mention the risk of overvaluing a firm's stars, engaging in highly excessive investments to attract and retain them into the firm, which can eventually destroy value rather than create it. Research by Groysberg, Lee, and Nanda (2008) attested to this by showing that organizations that poach star analysists from other companies recorded lower performance for these stars as opposed to their previous work environment, which lasted up to five years after being hired. The authors found that this results from an underestimation of the importance of firm-specific resources, systems, processes, and social support in explaining star performance. Specifically, the drop in performance was especially salient when the stars moved to a company with more limited capabilities than their previous employer and when they moved solo without bringing along their former team. Moreover, this study also observed negative stock-market reactions for firms hiring a star, which could be attributed to investors' belief that hiring stars is value-destroying as they have a lower threshold to leave the organization, are more likely to be pulled away by competitors and, hence, are not worth the excessive investment (Call et al., 2015; Groysberg et al., 2008).

Thirdly, negative cross-over effects are possible on co-workers who are not considered as valuable for the organization and, hence, are not allocated as many favorable resources as others. This implies complex individual social-psychological consequences of workforce differentiation. Specifically, due to the inequality created by workforce differentiation, issues of jealousy, envy, and interpersonal conflicts may arise (Marescaux, De Winne, & Rofcanin, 2019).

Social comparison theory as well as equity theory can be used to explain this. Social comparison theory argues that employees have the inherent tendency to compare themselves with co-workers (Greenberg, Ashton-James, & Ashkanasy, 2007; Wood, 1996). This theory is especially relevant to the context of workforce differentiation as this implies treating employees differently by allocating more resources to those employees the organization considers more valuable. As mentioned above, building on social comparison theory, Marescaux et al. (2013) showed that employees who are believed to be targeted with high investments from their organization (e.g., in terms of training, bonuses, benefits, feedback, flexibility, etc.) compared to their co-workers exhibited higher affective organizational commitment. Yet, this benefit was more than outweighed by the negative reaction among those perceiving to draw the short straw, putting into question whether it truly pays off (in terms of organizational commitment at least) to invest differently in employees.

Related to this, several studies have found that high-performers are often the target of victimization (i.e., harmful interpersonal behavior) by co-workers (e.g., Kim & Glomb, 2014; Lam, Van der Vegt, Walter, & Huang, 2011). Because high-performers are often granted more social and financial resources, a social comparison process with co-workers triggers envy and subsequent harmful behavior towards these stars (Kim & Glomb, 2014). As a result of this victimization, high-performers have a higher chance of suffering from reduced well-being and exhibit a higher intention of leaving the organization as well as reduced productivity. Hence, Kim and Glomb (2014) conclude that the victimization of these stars can undermine the investments made by the organization in ensuring their continued commitment and performance.

Equity theory builds further on this (cf. above) arguing that employees react particularly negatively when they perceive outcome differences to be unfair. For example, in the field of pay dispersion, Trevor and Wazeter (2006) showed that employees with low relative pay compared to others perceived lower pay equity as a function of pay dispersion. Moreover, showing the implications beyond just equity perceptions, Wang, Zhao, and Thornhill (2015) found that pay dispersion increases employees' voluntary turnover. Similarly, Marescaux, De Winne, and Sels (2017) showed that employees have a strong tendency to consider co-workers' i-deals (e.g., financial bonuses and flexible work hours) to be unfair, which subsequently triggers negative behavioral reactions. Finally, and importantly, in the realm of TM, Gelens et al. (2013) rightly warn against the justice implications of allocating more resources to high-potentials in the organization, as this can potentially backfire among those employees not considered talented.

Discussion and Suggestions for Future Research

The aim of this chapter was to explore the concept of workforce differentiation in relation to TM by reviewing both past selected theoretical and empirical insights. We focused on outlining the antecedents and consequences of workforce differentiation, connecting it explicitly with findings from the TM literature.

Research regarding the antecedents of workforce differentiation has provided some valuable insights, but important questions remain to be answered. In a recent review of the literature on stars, Call et al. (2015: 627) noted that "although star employees capture the attention of both scholars and practitioners, the review finds that most research takes an *ex post* view by accepting stars' existence and seeking to understand the consequences, rather than focusing on understanding how stars emerge". Similarly, the antecedents of an employee belonging to a "pivotal" or preferred workforce category remain largely unexplored.

Although employee performance and potential (Lewis & Heckman, 2006) as well as strategic importance of individuals or jobs (Lepak & Snell, 1999; Becker et al., 2009) are often cited as differentiation criteria that companies should employ, little is known about the actual characteristics that are exhibited by individuals labeled as "talent", "high-potential", or "core employee". Generally speaking, there is too much focus on what *should be*, and little research on *what are*, the antecedents of workforce differentiation. The literature reviewed above is mostly concerned with what competencies "high-potentials" or "talents" *should* possess, not what competencies they actually exhibit.

A theoretically more fertile perspective would not be to look at competencies that are deemed to be important in particular contexts, but to examine general individual-level behavioral and relational antecedents of workforce differentiation. For instance, future research could examine how the quality of the relationship between an employee and their manager impacts workforce differentiation decisions.

A major conclusion concerning the consequences of workforce differentiation is that this practice does not straightforwardly benefit the organization, despite its theoretically intuitive appeal. Apart from empirical support for its benefits, we identified many examples of research showing the potential pitfalls of workforce differentiation. Resolving these conflicting findings might be a question of looking at moderators, explaining under which circumstances an organization can derive benefits from workforce differentiation or not.

Some clues as to which moderators matter can be found in existing research, yet we develop some more ideas for future research as well. Firstly, the work context may matter. For example, Shaw, Gupta, and Delery (2002) showed that pay dispersion harms firm performance more strongly when employees need to work closely together. Similarly, Marescaux et al. (2017) showed that in highly interdependent environments, employees are more likely to consider a co-worker's i-deal to be unfair as opposed to an environment in which employees work independently from one another. In an interdependent environment, social comparison is much more likely due to a high amount of interaction (Ang, Van Dyne, & Begley, 2003). Moreover, it is typically more difficult to justify and defend treating one or more employees more favorably than others, considering that individual contributions to the team are difficult to identify (Kirkman & Shapiro, 2000; Marescaux et al., 2017).

Secondly, legitimizing differential outcome allocations may circumvent many of the downsides mentioned above. For example, pay dispersion research suggests that pay dispersion benefits the organization only when differences in pay are based on explained and legitimate differences in performance or contributions (Kepes, Delery, & Gupta, 2009; Shaw & Gupta, 2007; Trevor, Reilly, & Gerhart, 2012). In this case, differences in pay are considered fair and can motivate employees to perform better to achieve a more desirable outcome. Similarly, employees are found to react more positively to co-workers' i-deals when they perceive the i-deal to be allocated in response to exceptional performance or a specific individual need and when they perceive a high chance of obtaining a similar arrangement in the future if they meet the same criteria (Lai, Rousseau, & Chang, 2009; Marescaux & De Winne, 2015).

A final example is drawn from justice research, which has frequently shown that people can deal with an unfavorable outcome, as long as the procedures that were followed to decide that outcome are considered fair (i.e., the so-called "fair process effect") (Brockner, 2002; Krehbiel & Cropanzano, 2000). Hence, the policies and procedures behind the allocation of differential outcomes need to follow a set of rules typically associated with procedural fairness: decisions need to be made consistently, free of bias, ethically, etc. (Leventhal, 1980). Accordingly, Shaw and Gupta (2007) showed the importance of communicating the rules and procedures that determine pay (differences) to employees to derive a benefit from pay dispersion.

Yet, paradoxically, organizations might find it easier to not communicate about differential treatments in the workplace nor the procedures behind it. This secrecy might help avoid or reduce negative reactions and conflicts in the workplace as employees are kept in the dark and negative social comparisons are avoided (Colella Paetzold, Zardkoohi, & Wesson, 2007). Moreover, it safeguards employees' sense of privacy (Sundstrom, Burt, & Kamp, 1980). Hence, an interesting path for future research is to discern the merits and costs of both strategies (i.e., communication versus secrecy).

Beyond these examples, which are connected to the work context or how organizations implement and communicate differentiation to its employees, future research could also focus on more individual and team-related variables. On an individual level, employees' social comparison orientation could be relevant. Social comparison is one of the most fundamental processes of self-evaluation that occurs when people receive feedback about their performance (Festinger, 1954).

In a social comparison, people compare their own task and social feedback with that of other relevant peers (Alicke, Zell, & Guenther, 2013). Two directions of comparison occur: downward comparisons, wherein individuals compare themselves with peers who perform worse; or upward comparisons, wherein they compare themselves with better-performing peers. Both types of comparison trigger affective reactions. Although there are exceptions (Collins, 1996), people engaging in downward comparisons typically feel better about themselves than people who engage in upward comparisons (Strickhouser & Zell, 2015).

As argued above, workforce differentiation schemes spark social comparison processes and competitiveness in the employees they affect. An employee with a high rating from a workforce differentiation outperforms peers and engages in downward comparison, which in turn should elicit positive affective reactions. Employees with low ratings perform less well than their peers, leading to upward comparisons and possibly negative affective reactions. Some people have a stronger tendency than others to engage in social comparisons and are more sensitive to the outcomes of comparison processes (Buunk & Gibbons, 2007). The construct of social comparison orientation captures this individual tendency. An individual's social comparison orientation is bound to exacerbate or buffer reactions to workforce differentiation schemes. For instance, employees with a low social comparison orientation might be less likely to react strongly to favorable or unfavorable differentiation outcomes. Future research should examine to which extent this is indeed the case.

Concerning the team, group identification might be relevant to consider in the context of workforce differentiation. Group identification refers to the degree to which group members "merge their sense of self with the group" (Ashmore, Deaux, & McLaughlin-Volpe, 2004; Kim & Glomb, 2014: 621). Experimental identity research suggests that when employees identify strongly with their group, their focus shifts from individual to group performance and success (Brewer & Weber, 1994). Hence, Kim, and Glomb (2014) showed that strong group identification shields employees from feeling envy towards more successful group members and the negative consequences of this envy. The authors speculate that this is because high-performing and successful team members strongly contribute to group performance, which is important for employees with a strong sense of group identification. As a result, they do not feel harmed or threatened by the superior team member. Likewise, in the context of workforce differentiation, identifying strongly with the group might prevent negative reactions from employees who are unfavorably treated as opposed to other team members.

Finally, the concept of workforce differentiation as well as most of its research is relatively U.S.-centric with a few exceptions (e.g., Piasecki, 2019). There might be a strong cultural component to it. As mentioned above, some countries have a strong cultural tradition towards equality (e.g., Belgium; Marescaux et al., 2013; Sels et al., 2000), while others are predominantly individualistic and predisposed towards differentiation (e.g., the U.S.A.; Rousseau, 2005). Apart from influencing the room for workforce differentiation, this cultural element might also affect employees' tolerance for it, as differentiation might be more tolerated – and perhaps thus be more beneficial for organizations – in a culture that is predisposed towards it (Marescaux et al., 2013). As such, we would encourage future research to also consider this cultural component, investigating whether U.S.-based theories on workforce differentiation also hold in other cultural contexts or – alternatively – need to be fine-tuned to fit with such a cultural dimension.

References

Adams, J. S. 1965. Inequity in social exchange. In L. Berkowitz (Ed.), *Advances in Experimental Social Psychology:* 267–299. New York: Academic Press.

Aguinis, H., & O'Boyle, E. 2014. Star performers in twenty-first century organizations. *Personnel Psychology,* 67(2): 313–350.

Alicke, M. D., Zell, E., & Guenther, C. L. 2013. Social self-analysis. *Advances in Experimental Social Psychology,* 48: 173–234.

Ang, S., Van Dyne, L., & Begley, T. M. 2003. The employment relationships of foreign workers versus local employees: A field study of organizational justice, job satisfaction, performance, and OCB. *Journal of Organizational Behavior,* 24(5): 561–583.

Ashmore, R. D., Deaux, K., & McLaughlin-Volpe T. 2004. An organization framework for collective identity: Articulation and significance of multidimensionality. *Psychological Bulletin,* 130(1): 80–114.

Axelrod, B., Handfield-Jones, H., & Michaels, E. 2002. A new game plan for C players. *Harvard Business Review,* 80(1): 80–90.

Becker, B. E., Huselid, M. A., & Beatty, R. W. 2009. *The differentiated workforce,* Cambridge, MA: Harvard Business Press.

Bidwell, M., Briscoe, F., Fernandez-Mateo, I., & Sterling, A. 2013. The employment relationship and inequality: How and why changes in employment practices are reshaping rewards in organizations. *The Academy of Management Annals,* 7(1): 61–121.

Blau, P. 1964. *Exchange and power in social life.* New York, NY: Wiley.

Boudreau, J. W., & Ramstad, P. M. 2005. Talentship, talent segmentation, and sustainability: A new HR decision science paradigm for a new strategy definition. *Human Resource Management,* 44(2): 129–136.

Brewer, M. B., & Weber, J. G. 1994. Self-evaluation effects of interpersonal versus intergroup social comparison. *Journal of Personality and Social Psychology,* 66(2): 268–275.

Brockner, J. 2002. Making sense of procedural fairness: How high procedural fairness can reduce or heighten the influence of outcome favorability. *The Academy of Management Review,* 27(1): 58–76.

Buunk, A. P., & Gibbons, F. X. 2007. Social comparison: The end of a theory and the emergence of a field. *Organizational Behavior and Human Decision Processes,* 102(1): 3–21.

Call, M. L., Nyberg, A. J., & Thatcher, S. 2015. Stargazing: An integrative conceptual review, theoretical reconciliation, and extension for star employee research. *Journal of Applied Psychology,* 100(3): 623–640.

Cantrell, S., & Smith,. D. 2010. *Workforce of one: Revolutionizing talent management through customization.* Cambridge, MA: Harvard Business Press.

Cappelli, P., & Keller, J. 2014. Talent management: Conceptual approaches and practical challenges. *Annual Review of Organizational Psychology and Organizational Behavior,* 1(1): 305–331.

Carrell, M. R., & Dittrich, J. E. 1978. Equity theory: The recent literature, methodological considerations and new directions. *Academy of Management Review,* 3(2): 202–210.

CIPD. 2015. *Learning and development 2015 – Annual survey report.* https://www.cipd.co.uk/Images/learning-development_2015_tcm18-11298.pdf

Colella, A., Paetzold, R. L., Zardkoohi, A., & Wesson, M. J. 2007. Exposing pay secrecy. *Academy of Management Review,* 32(1): 55–71.

Collings, D. G., & Mellahi, K. 2009. Strategic talent management: A review and research agenda. *Human Resource Management Review,* 19: 304–313.

Collings, D. G., Mellahi, K., & Cascio, W. F. 2019. Global talent management and performance in multinational enterprises: A multilevel perspective. *Journal of Management,* 45(2): 540–566.

Collins, R. L. 1996. For better or worse: The impact of upward social comparison on self-evaluations. *Psychological Bulletin,* 119(1): 51–69.

Dencker, J. C., & Fang, C. 2016. Rent seeking and the transformation of employment relationships: The effect of corporate restructuring on wage patterns, determinants, and inequality. *American Sociological Review,* 81(3): 467–487.

Dokko, G., & Rosenkopf, L. 2010. Social capital for hire? Mobility of technical professionals and firm influence in wireless standards committees. *Organization Science,* 21(3): 677–695.

Downes, P. E., & Choi, D. 2014. Employee reactions to pay dispersion: A typology of existing research. *Human Resource Management Review,* 24(1): 53–66.

Dries, N. 2009. Antecedents and outcomes in careers of high potentials, key experts and average performers. *Proceedings of the Academy of Management Meeting,* (1). doi:10.5465/AMBPP.2009.44246737

Dries, N. 2013. The psychology of talent management: A review and research agenda. *Human Resource Management Review,* 23(4): 272–285.

Dries, N., & Pepermans, R. 2007. "Real" high-potential careers: An empirical study into the perspectives of organisations and high potentials. *Personnel Review,* 37(1): 85–108.

Dries, N., Vantilborgh, T., & Pepermans, R. 2012. The role of learning agility and career variety in the identification and development of high potential employees. *Personnel Review,* 41(3): 340–358.

Festinger, L. 1954. A theory of social comparison processes. *Human Relations,* 7(2): 117–140.

Finkelstein, L. M., Costanza, D. P., & Goodwin, G. F. 2017. Do your high potentials have potential? The impact of individual differences and designation on leader success. *Personnel Psychology.* https://doi.org/10.1111/peps.12225.

Gelens, J., Dries, N., Hofmans, J., & Pepermans, R. 2013. The role of perceived organizational justice in shaping the outcomes of talent management: A research agenda. *Human Resource Management Review,* 23(4): 341–353.

Gelens, J., Dries, N., Hofmans, J., & Pepermans, R. 2015. Affective commitment of employees designated as talent: Signalling perceived organisational support. *European Journal of International Management,* 9(1): 9–27.

Gladwell, M. 2000. *The tipping point: How little things can make a big difference.* Boston: Little, Brown.

Golik, M. N., Blanco, M. R., & Czikk, R. 2017. On the trail of line managers as talent spotters. *Human Resource Development International,* 21(5): 1–22. doi:10.1080/13678868.2017.1385195.

Gould-Williams, J. 2007. HR practices, organizational climate and employee outcomes: evaluating social exchange relationships in local government. *The International Journal of Human Resource Management,* 18(9): 1627–1647.

Greenberg J., Ashton-James, C. E., & Ashkanasy, N. M. 2007. Social comparison processes in organizations. *Organizational Behavior and Human Decision Processes,* 102: 22–41.

Groysberg, B. 2010. *Chasing stars: The myth of talent and the portability of performance.* Princeton University Press.

Groysberg, B., Lee, L. E., & Nanda, A. 2008. Can they take it with them? The portability of star knowledge workers' performance. *Management Science,* 54(7): 1213–1230.

Huselid, M. A., Beatty, R. W., & Becker, B. E. 2005. 'A players' or 'A positions'? The strategic logic of workforce management: *Harvard Business Review:* 110–117.

Kepes, S., Delery, J., & Gupta, N. 2009. Contingencies in the effects of pay range on organizational effectiveness. *Personnel Psychology,* 62(3): 497–531.

Kim, E., & Glomb, T. M. 2014. Victimization of high performers: The roles of envy and work group identification. *Journal of Applied Psychology,* 99(4): 619.

Kirkman, B. L., & Shapiro, D. L. 2000. Understanding why team members won't share: An examination of factors related to employee receptivity to team-based rewards. *Small Group Research,* 31(2): 175–209.

Krausert, A. 2017. HR differentiation between professional and managerial employees: Broadening and integrating theoretical perspectives. *Human Resource Management Review,* 27(3): 442–457.

Krehbiel, P. J., & Cropanzano, R. 2000. Procedural justice, outcome favorability and emotion. *Social Justice Research,* 13(4): 339–360.

Lai, L., Rousseau, D. M., & Chang, K. T. T. 2009. Idiosyncratic deals: Coworkers as interested third parties. *Journal of Applied Psychology,* 94(2): 547–556.

Lam, C. K., Van der Vegt, G. S., Walter, F., & Huang, X. 2011. Harming high performers: A social comparison perspective on interpersonal harming in work teams. *Journal of Applied Psychology,* 96(3): 588.

Lepak, D. P., & Snell, S. A. 1999. The human resource architecture: Toward a theory of human capital allocation and development. *Academy of Management Review,* 24(1): 31–48.

Lepak, D. P., & Snell, S. A. 2002. Examining the human resource architecture: The relationships among human capital, employment, and human resource configurations. *Journal of Management,* 28(4): 517–543.

Lepak, D. P., Taylor, M. S., Tekleab, A. G., Marrone, J. A., & Cohen, D. J. 2007. An examination of the use of high-investment human resource systems for core and support employees. *Human Resource Management,* 46(2): 223–246.

Leventhal, G. S. 1980. What should be done with equity theory? New approaches to the study of fairness in social relationships. In K. J. Gergen, M. S. Greenberg, & R. H. Willis (Eds.). *Social exchange: Advances in theory and research:* 27–55. New York: Plenum.

Lewis, R. E., & Heckman, R. J. (2006). Talent management: A critical review. *Human Resource Management Review,* 16(2): 139–154.

Liao, C., Wayne, S. J., & Rousseau, D. M. 2016. Idiosyncratic deals in contemporary organizations: A qualitative and meta-analytical review. *Journal of Organizational Behavior,* 37(1): 9–29.

Liden, R. C., Sparrowe, R. T., & Wayne, S. J. 1997. Leader–member exchange theory: The past and potential for the future. *Research in Personnel and Human Resources Management,* 15: 47–120.

Liu, J., Lee, C., Hui, C., Kwan, H. K., & Wu, L. Z. 2013. Idiosyncratic deals and employee outcomes: The mediating roles of social exchange and self-enhancement and the moderating role of individualism. *Journal of Applied Psychology,* 98(5): 832.

Lockwood, P., & Kunda, Z. 1997. Superstars and me: Predicting the impact of role models on the self. *Journal of Personality and Social Psychology,* 73(1): 91.

Mäkelä, K., Björkman, I., & Ehrnrooth, M. 2010. How do MNCs establish their talent pools? Influences on individuals' likelihood of being labeled as talent. *Journal of World Business,* 45(2): 134–142.

Marescaux, E., & De Winne, S. 2015. Equity versus need: How do co-workers judge the distributive fairness of i-deals? In M. Bal & D. Rousseau (Eds.), *Idiosyncratic deals between employees and organizations: Conceptual issues, applications and the role of co-workers.* London: Routledge.

Marescaux, E., De Winne, S., & Rofcanin, Y. 2019. Co-worker reactions to i-deals through the lens of social comparison: The role of fairness and emotions. *Human Relations,* early view online.

Marescaux, E., De Winne, S., & Sels, L. 2013. HR practices and affective organisational commitment: (When) does HR differentiation pay off? *Human Resource Management Journal,* 23(4): 329–345.

Marescaux, E., De Winne S., & Sels, L. 2017. Idiosyncratic deals from a distributive justice perspective: Examining co-workers' voice behavior, *Journal of Business Ethics,* early view online.

McDonnell, A. 2011. Still fighting the "war for talent"? Bridging the science versus practice gap. *Journal of Business and Psychology,* 26(2): 169–173.

Melián-González, S., & Verano-Tacorante, D. 2004. A new approach to the best practices debate: Are best practices applied to all employees in the same way? *The International Journal of Human Resource Management,* 15(1): 56–75.

Meyers, M. C., & van Woerkom, M. 2014. The influence of underlying philosophies on talent management: Theory, implications for practice, and research agenda. *Journal of World Business,* 49(2): 192–203.

Meyers, M. C., van Woerkom, M., & Dries, N. 2013. Talent — innate or acquired? Theoretical considerations and their implications for talent management. *Human Resource Management Review,* 23(4): 305–321.

Meyers, M. C., van Woerkom, M., Paauwe, J., & Dries, N. (2020). HR managers' talent philosophies: Prevalence and relationships with perceived talent management practices. *The International Journal of Human Resource Management,* 31(4): 562–588.

Molloy, J. C., & Barney, J. B. 2015. Who captures the value created with human capital? A market-based view. *Academy of Management Perspectives,* 29(3): 309–325.

Morand, D. A., & Merriman, K. K. 2012. "Equality theory" as a counterbalance to equity theory in human resource management. *Journal of Business Ethics,* 111(1): 133–144.

O'Boyle Jr., E., & Aguinis, H. 2012. The best and the rest: Revisiting the norm of normality of individual performance. *Personnel Psychology,* 65(1): 79–119.

Pepermans, R., Vloeberghs, D., & Perkisas, B. 2003. High potential identification policies: an empirical study among Belgian companies. *Journal of Management Development,* 22(8): 660–678.

Piasecki, P. (2019). Dimensions of HR differentiation. *Baltic Journal of Management,* 14(1): 21–41.

Rosen, C. C., Slater, D. J., Chang, C. H., & Johnson, R. E. 2013. Let's make a deal: Development and validation of the ex post i-deals scale. *Journal of Management,* 39(3): 709–742.

Rousseau, D. M. 2005. *I-deals, idiosyncratic deals employees bargain for themselves.* ME Sharpe.

Sels, L., Janssens, M., Van den Brande, I., & Overlaet, B. 2000. Belgium, a culture of compromise. In D. M. Rousseau & R. Schalk (Eds.), *Psychological contracts in employment: Cross-national perspective.* Thousand Oaks, CA: Sage Publications, Inc.

Shaw, J. D., & Gupta, N. 2007. Pay system characteristics and quit patterns of good, average, and poor performers. *Personnel Psychology,* 60(4): 903–928.

Shaw, J. D., Gupta, N., & Delery, J. E. 2002. Pay dispersion and workforce performance: Moderating effects of incentives and interdependence. *Strategic Management Journal,* 23(6): 491–512.

Sparrow, P.R., & Makram, H. 2015. What is the value of talent management? Building value-driven processes within a talent management architecture. *Human Resource Management Review,* 25(3): 249–263.

Stirpe, L., Bonache, J., & Revilla, A. 2014. Differentiating the workforce: The performance effects of using contingent labor in a context of high-performance work systems. *Journal of Business Research,* 67(7): 1334–1341.

Strickhouser, J. E., & Zell, E. 2015. Self-evaluative effects of dimensional and social comparison. *Journal of Experimental Social Psychology,* 59(0): 60–66.

Sundstrom, E., Burt, R. E., & Kamp, D. 1980. Privacy at work: Architectural correlates of job satisfaction and job performance. *Academy of Management Journal,* 23: 101–117.

Swailes, S., Downs, Y., & Orr, K. 2014. Conceptualising inclusive talent management: potential, possibilities and practicalities. *Human Resource Development International,* 17(5): 529–544.

Trevor, C. O., Reilly, G., & Gerhart, B. 2012. Reconsidering pay dispersion's effect on the performance of interdependent work: Reconciling sorting and pay inequality. *Academy of Management Journal,* 55(3): 585–610.

Trevor, C. O., & Wazeter, D. L. 2006. A contingent view of reactions to objective pay conditions: Interdependence among pay structure characteristics and pay relative to internal and external referents. *Journal of Applied Psychology,* 91(6): 1260.

Ulrich, D. 2005. 'Foreword'. In M. A. Huselid, B. E. Becker, & R. W. Beatty (Eds.), *The workforce scorecard. managing human capital to execute strategy,* Boston, MA: Harvard Business School Publishing.

Walster, E. H., Hatfield, E., Walster, G. W., & Berscheid, E. 1978. *Equity: Theory and research.* Boston, MA: Allyn and Bacon, Inc.

Wang, T., Zhao, B., & Thornhill, S. 2015. Pay dispersion and organizational innovation: The mediation effects of employee participation and voluntary turnover. *Human Relations,* 68(7): 1155–1181.

Wood, J. V. 1996. What is social comparison and how should we study it? *Personality and Social Psychology Bulletin,* 22: 520–537.

30

TALENT MANAGEMENT

A Focus on the Supporting Cast of "B" Players

Amina R. Malik

Parbudyal Singh

Introduction

Talent management (TM) has been a topical issue among practitioners since 1997 when McKinsey and Company (Michaels, Handfield-Jones, & Axelrod, 2001) warned companies about the upcoming labor shortages and highlighted the significance of attracting, developing, and retaining high-performers in the company's success (McDonnell, Collings, Mellahi, & Schuler, 2017). Corresponding with this increased prominence, TM has received considerable attention within the academic community over the past two decades, resulting in a relatively large body of literature (Amankwah, 2020; De Boeck, Meyers, & Dries, 2018; McDonnell et al., 2017; Meyers et al., 2020).

TM has become so important among academics that special issues in academic journals are being dedicated to it; for example, *Human Resource Management Review* had two special issues on TM in 2013 (Dries, 2013) and in 2015 (Collings, Scullion, & Vaiman, 2015); *The International Journal of Human Resource Management* had a special issue in 2013 (Vaiman & Collings, 2013); *Journal of World Business* had one in 2010 (Scullion, Collings, & Caliguiri, 2010); and *Employee Relations* had another special issue in 2016 (Scullion, Vaiman, & Collings, 2016). More so, *The International Journal of Human Resource Management* invited papers for another special issue on TM in 2018 that aimed to further improve our understanding of how contextual factors impact the conceptualization, implementation, and effectiveness of TM (Gallardo-Gallardo, Thunnissen, & Scullion, 2017). More recently, *Human Resource Management* had a special issue on the "shifting boundaries of talent management" (Vaiman et al., 2021).

This growing significance is based on the premise that superior TM can lead to a sustainable competitive advantage for organizations locally as well as globally (Collings & Isichei, 2018; Morris, Snell, & Björkman, 2016); however, empirical evidence to support this assertion is lacking (Collings, 2014b; Son, Park, Bae, & Ok, 2018). Surprisingly, none of the research articles in the above-mentioned special issues addressed the needs of employees who are excluded from TM programs (i.e., "B" players).

An organization's workforce is comprised of different groups of employees. "A" players or "star" employees, also known as value creators, are top performers and constitute about the top 20% of the organizational workforce; B players are known as "value sustainers" and are defined as those employees who are average performers, who mostly meet (rather than exceed) their work expectations, and constitute about 70% of organizational employees; and "C" players, also known an value destroyers, are poor performers and form the bottom 10% of the organizational workforce (Cappelli & Keller 2017; Malik & Singh, 2014).

A players are dedicated, exceptional performers who have the ability to drive performance of their teams and organization; however, teams comprised of all A players often do not work well due to

DOI: 10.4324/9781315474687-30

internal competition, leading to a toxic, counterproductive work environment (Mankins, Bird, & Root, 2013). B players are the heart and soul of every organization, and they tend to stay longer with their current organizations (Lucas, 2017). Their jobs have significant implications for the achievement of organizational strategic objectives as they provide crucial support to employees in strategic positions (Malik & Singh, 2014).

The characteristics of B players are different from the characteristics of A and C players (see Becker, Huselid, & Beatty, 2009 for details). Given that B players form the majority of the organizational workforce, the lack of attention to this group is a significant omission in the TM literature. Since organizations tend to be secretive about their "talent" list, as they do not want to create friction among different groups of employees (Silzer & Church, 2010), this tendency presents significant challenges to researchers in terms of investigating B players' work experiences (Gelens, Hofmans, Dries, & Pepermans, 2014). In this chapter, we focus on B players in the context of TM.

This chapter is organized as follows. First, we define TM and explain the significance of B players in the context of TM. Then, we provide an overview of the existing research on the impact of talent identification on employee outcomes; this section is based on the assumption that A players are identified as "talent" while B players are not. We conclude with a discussion on future research directions.

Talent Management: Definitions

In the first review article on TM, Lewis and Heckman (2006) lamented that there was no consistent definition of TM. Today, a decade and a half later, and despite a number of review articles on conceptualizations of TM, a review article by McDonnell et al. (2017) mentioned that the field is still hampered by the lack of an agreed definition of TM.

In the literature, TM has been conceptualized in a number of ways: re-labeling of human resource management (i.e., practices that select, attract, develop, and retain the best employees in the organization) (Al Ariss, Cascio, & Paauwe, 2014; Farndale, Scullion, & Sparrow, 2010); human resource planning (i.e., succession planning) (Al Ariss et al., 2014; Collings & Mellahi, 2009); human resource development (i.e., developing employees' human capital for specific strategic requirements) (Collings, 2014a; Iles, Chuai, & Preece, 2010); exclusive versus inclusive approaches (i.e., who is it that possesses talent?) (Gallardo-Gallardo, Dries, & González-Cruz, 2013; Meyers & van Woerkom, 2014; Thunnissen, Boselie, & Fruytier, 2013a); and as a broader phenomenon (i.e., integrating individuals, organizations, and society embracing equality and diversity in societies) (Thunnissen, Boselie, & Fruytier, 2013b).

In conceptualizing TM, emphasis has been placed on the inclusive and exclusive approaches of TM that treat employees differently (De Boeck et al., 2018). In the inclusive approach to TM, all employees are perceived to possess talent, and it is the employer's responsibility to provide all employees with opportunities and resources to develop themselves so they can reach their potential (Iles et al., 2010; Meyers & van Woerkom, 2014). However, in the exclusive approach to TM, only employees who are perceived to possess unique skills and capabilities and whose skillsets are difficult to replace are considered as talent receive differential resource investment from their organization (Gallardo-Gallardo et al., 2013; Thunnissen et al., 2013a). The assumption is that organizations would incur huge costs if they invest equally in employees since they differ in terms of their knowledge, skills, and abilities (Lepak & Snell, 2002). The empirical research on TM suggests a combination of different organizational approaches to manage employees; however, the exclusive approach to TM is more common and relatively fewer organizations rely on the inclusive approach (Garavan, Carbery, & Rock, 2012; Iles et al., 2010; McDonnell et al., 2017). In line with this research, this chapter focuses on the exclusive approach to TM.

It has been argued that the exclusive approach to TM follows Pareto's "law of the vital few", which suggests that there are only a few employees in the organization who contribute to the majority of its success (Iles et al., 2010; Swailes, 2013). Following this law, the basic premise of TM is workforce differentiation (Malik, Singh, & Chan, 2017); that is, organizations differentiate their workforces in terms of their value and contributions to the organization, resulting in more resource investment for employees whose skills and contributions are identified as highly valuable and unique compared to employees whose skills are not that valuable and whose competencies can be easily replaced (Crowley-Henry & Al Ariss, 2018).

In other words, exclusive TM policies and practices are specifically targeted towards A players while excluding B players. One example of such exclusive approach to TM is "high-potential" programs that organizations implement to systematically develop, socialize, and advance A players, who demonstrate great potential to contribute to their success (Silzer & Church, 2010). Employees are identified as A players by their senior management through a nomination process (Karakowsky & Kotlyar, 2012; Silzer & Church, 2010) or through a formal performance appraisal system (Cappelli & Keller, 2014). Consequently, this small group of employees receives more resource investment from the organization in terms of mentoring, the provision of accelerated developmental programs, and more promotional opportunities (Campbell & Smith, 2010).

B Players in the Context of Talent Management

The success of any organization not only depends on the performance of a few top A players, but also on the contribution of all other employees. As Delong and Vijayaraghavan argued, "our understandable fascination with star performers can lure us into the dangerous trap of underestimating the vital importance of the supporting actors" (2003: 96). They contend that companies' long-term performance is very much dependent on the commitment and the contribution of B players (i.e., average performers). Other researchers also acknowledge the contributions of the supporting cast of employees in an organization's success and stress their efforts should not be ignored (Beechler & Woodward, 2009; Guthridge, Komm, & Lawson, 2008). Delong and Vijayaraghavan (2003) emphasized these employees are the best "supporting actors" of the organization because of their crucial support to top performers in strategic positions that create value for the organizations (Becker et al., 2009; Huselid, Beatty, & Becker, 2005).

Organizations must rely on B players to fill non-strategic roles and provide support to A players. Exclusive TM programs, where the focal employees are A players, and B players are excluded, may create psychological tension among employees and even exacerbate perceptions of inequity and unfairness among employees who are excluded from these programs (McDonnell et al., 2017). Swailes (2013) raised concerns that signaling to some employees that they are inferior could lead to negative emotions and feelings among employees, who may consider their exclusion as suppressing opportunities to flourish and develop themselves. If B players in supportive and non-strategic positions are not managed properly, they may be very costly to organizations (Huselid et al., 2005; Lucas, 2017).

Scholars and practitioners contend that this special focus of TM policies and practices on A players results in the creation of a segmented workforce (Dries, Van Acker, & Verbruggen, 2012; Iles et al., 2010). Aguinis and colleagues mentioned that "the workforce differentiation construct is clearly an employer focused-model, which is likely to have positive impacts on high performers in strategic roles" (2011: 426).

Employees who do not fall under the category of star employees may be adversely affected; as Lepak et al. mentioned, "groups that receive less investment…, may experience inequity and display less than desired attitudes and behaviors as a result" (2006: 46). They highlighted the significance of non-core employees, arguing that these employees are even more important for the firm's overall effectiveness. However, organizations often fail to value their contributions and, consequently, their long-term performance suffers (Delong & Vijayaraghavan, 2003). Since workforce differentiation is the main premise of exclusive TM policies (Gelens et al., 2014), we use TM, workforce differentiation, and HR differentiation interchangeably in this chapter.

Current Research on Talent Management and Employee Outcomes: Effects of Talent Identification on A and B Players

There is a general belief among scholars and practitioners that TM is imperative for improved organization performance (Glaister, Karacay, Demirbag, & Tatoglu, 2018). A few studies have looked at the outcome of TM at the macro level (Bethke-Langenegger, Mahler, & Staffelbach, 2011). However, scholars highlight the need to examine the value of TM at the individual level (Thunnissen et al., 2013b). For example, Luna-Arocas and Morley stated that "the impact of TM has mainly focused on outcomes at the macro level yet TM practices not only affect macro-level outcomes, but also more proximal ones, such as employee attitudes and behaviours" (2015: 31). Scholars argue that this process has rarely been examined at the individual level (Thunnissen et al., 2013b), thus resulting in calls for more research on the "humanistic" element of workforce differentiation (De Boeck et al., 2018; Garavan et al., 2012).

Perhaps as a result of these calls, since 2012, research has shown progress on how workforce differentiation could impact individual level outcomes (i.e., employees' reactions, attitudes and behaviors). The dominant theoretical frameworks in this stream of research use social exchange (Blau, 1964), psychological contract (Robinson & Rousseau, 1994), and justice theories (Adams, 1963). Some studies have solely looked at the talent pool (Dries & De Gieter, 2014; Khoreva et al., 2017), while others have examined the differences between the talent and non-talent pools.

For example, Marescaux, De Winne, and Sels (2013) collected survey data from 13,639 employees in Belgium and examined the impact of HR differentiation on employee outcomes. While drawing on social exchange theory (Blau, 1964), they argued that employees consider HR practices as a signal of appreciation; consequently, employees feel obligated to reciprocate with positive attitudes. Additionally, they argued that since HR practices result in goal attainment, the perceived favorability of HR practices results in positive emotions, thus enhancing their affective commitment. Their study found that positive perceived favorability of HR practices resulted in favorable employee outcomes (i.e., affective commitment); however, the relationship was curvilinear and attenuated at positive levels. Their study also showed that perceived unfavorability of HR practices resulted in negative employee outcomes. They argued that HR differentiation is a double-edge sword, such that the losses among employees feeling disadvantaged may even outweigh the benefits/gains among those feeling privileged.

Moreover, Björkman, Ehrnrooth, Mäkelä, Smale, and Sumelius (2013) collected self-reported data from 769 managers and professionals in nine Nordic multinational corporations and examined the direct effect of talent identification on employee attitudes. Using insights from social exchange theory (Blau, 1964) and psychological contract theory (Rousseau, 1989), their study found that employees who were formally identified as "talent" were more likely to possess organizationally-beneficial attitudes (such as commitment to increasing performance demands, to building competencies that are valuable for their employers, and to actively support its strategic priorities; identification with the focal unit; and lower turnover intent) compared to those employees who either perceived they were not identified as talent or did not know whether they were identified as talent.

Drawing on social exchange (Blau, 1964) and justice (Greenberg, 1990) theories, Gelens et al. (2014) collected data from 203 high-potential (hipo) and non-hipo employees in a large company in Belgium. Using archival data for hipo identification, they found that hipo employees had higher levels of job satisfaction and exerted more work effort as compared to non-hipo employees. They also examined the role of justice perceptions and demonstrated that hipo employees had higher perceptions of distributive justice, and that distributive justice mediated the relationships between hipo identification and employee outcomes (job satisfaction and work effort).

The mediating relationship between hipo identification and work effort through distributive justice was further moderated by employees' perceptions of procedural justice such that the mediating effect appeared at higher and lower levels of procedural justice. The moderating effect of procedural justice on the mediating path for job satisfaction was non-significant. In other words, their study found that employees exerted more work effort when they perceived that workforce differentiation procedures were fair, and less effort when they perceived the procedures to be unfair.

More recently, Gelens, Dries, Hofmans, and Pepermans (2015) conducted two different studies that examined the role of perceived organizational support in the relationship between talent identification and affective commitment. They drew on signalling theory (Spence, 1973) and argued that talent identification serves as a signal of organizational support, which affects employees' affective commitment. For the first study, data were collected from 128 hipo and 75 non-hipo employees in a large company in the financial sector in Belgium, and for the second study, the data were gathered from 120 trainees and 100 non-trainees from another company in the financial sector in Belgium. Both studies found that employees who were designated as talent had higher perceptions of organizational support and affective commitment, and also that perceived organizational support mediated the relationship between talent designation and affective commitment.

Sonnenberg, van Zijderveld, and Brinks (2014) examined the effects of TM practices and incongruent talent perceptions on the fulfillment of psychological contract for 2,660 respondents within 21 organizations. Their study found that the greater use of TM practices resulted in higher perceptions of psychological contract fulfillment; however, this positive relationship was weakened by incongruent talent perceptions by the organizational representatives and also by the employees. They concluded that TM practices must be perceived and utilized by the targeted employees; otherwise it would lead to talent-perception incongruence, resulting in misperceptions and false expectations from employees.

More recently, Swailes and Blackburn (2016) examined employees' reactions to talent pool membership in a public-sector organization and found that employees included in talent pools were more confident about their career progression than employees not included in talent pools; the latter group reported feelings of less support from their line managers and reduced perceptions of organization's commitment towards their development. Additionally, Malik, Singh, and Chan's (2017) empirical study demonstrate that employees' perceptions of organizational trust play an important role in influencing the relationship between high-potential employees' talent identification, and their attributions about such programs.

Overall, almost all empirical studies demonstrate the positive impact of talent identification on A players or employees identified as high potential, and negative or at least less favorable impact on employees who are not identified as talent (in other words, B players). Even though TM practices and workforce differentiation impact all employees, little attention has been paid to unintended consequences of TM to employees who are excluded from these programs.

In their critical review, Lacey and Groves (2014) stated that although many companies have proudly developed and implemented TM systems and are undertaking various corporate social responsibility (CSR) initiatives towards customers, communities, shareholders, and other stakeholders, there may be an inherent incompatibility between these two approaches. They contend that excluding the majority of employees from various developmental programs and privileges of hipo programs contradicts the true spirit of CSR. They suggested that organizations implementing TM programs as well as pursuing CSR initiatives must deal with several fundamental issues including "expanding access to hipo programs, enhancing the hipo employee selection processes via greater emphasis on lead indicators of hipo, and improving rater reliability across assessment tools" (Lacey & Groves, 2014: 399).

Consistent with this view, Swailes (2013) mentioned that many organizations justify singling out a few employees as hipos; however, HR managers and professionals need to address several ethical issues (such as talent identification, feelings of exclusion, feelings of inequity, and care and concern for all employees, to name a few) resulting from the implementation of TM programs. Despite all the above mentioned positive outcomes, these unintended consequences could be the reason why most of the TM programs end up in failure (Groysberg, 2010; Karakowsky & Kotlyar, 2012; Martin & Schmidt, 2010).

Talent Management Policies and Practices

HR practitioners and consultants need to consider the fairness of the talent identification process. If B players perceive the process to be unjust, they would elicit more unfavorable attitudes and behaviors (Gelens at al., 2015). To increase employees' fairness perceptions, competency modeling may be used by organizations to evaluate employees' current performance and highlight areas where improvement is needed (Campion, Fink, Ruggeberg, Carr, Phillips, & Odman, 2011). Organizations should also build trustworthy relationships with employees and provide a supportive culture where all employees feel valued and supported (Malik, Singh, & Chan, 2017).

When it is not possible for organizations to invest equally in employees, other HR practices such as flexible work options or telecommuting, open communication, increased participation in decision making, and work-life balance, to name a few, should be provided to B players. It is important that managers value the contributions of B players, irrespective of their motivation to become A players, as some employees deliberately choose not to become top performers (Delong & Vijayaraghavan, 2003). Helping B players see the big picture and how their roles add value (or ensure against decreasing value) can help organizations manage them effectively.

Future Research Directions

TM has a managerialist orientation (Thunnissen et al., 2013a), and the employee voice is missing from the existing TM literature (McDonnell et al., 2017). Although researchers have explored the experiences of A players when they are identified as talent and provided with more organizational resources (Dries & De Gieter, 2014), we suggest the voices of B players also need to be heard.

Current research on TM uses both quantitative and qualitative research (McDonnell et al., 2017), with quantitative research increasing significantly since 2011. We acknowledge the merits of quantitative research; however, we suggest scholars use qualitative research tools to provide a richer understanding of B players' experiences of exclusion from these programs. Doing so may be daunting and researchers may face resistance from the employers due to the fear of negative consequences for B players (Church, Rotolo, Ginther, & Levine, 2015). The good news is, for qualitative research, researchers do not need large sample sizes, and in-depth interviews with selected B players would suffice. Inquiries, such as these, would have the potential to assess the true impact of these programs on employees who are in the majority but are excluded from these programs; this may also help to explore the "darker" side of TM.

This research avenue would help us to investigate fundamental questions, such as whether B players are contented with where they are at the organizational level and choose not to be a part of A players group due to extra responsibilities and challenging work (Delong & Vijayaraghavan, 2003). This type of research can also offer insights into whether they are trapped in the "Golem effect" (Babad, Inbar, & Rosenthal, 1982), a situation wherein employees perceive their supervisors have lower expectations from them and then these expectations lead to employee behaviors that impair their performance levels. In other words, this effect suggests that excluded employees lower their self-expectations, and consequently their performance level declines.

Pfeffer stated that the war for talent results in:

> the creation of a self-fulfilling prophecy where those labeled as less able become less able because they are asked to do less, given fewer resources, training, and mentoring, and become discouraged—in the process ensuring that the organization has way too many people who are in the process of dropping out of the competitive fray. (2001: 249)

To address this gap, in-depth interviews could be conducted with employees in organizations having TM programs but who are excluded from these programs; their work-related attitudes could be compared with those employees in organizations having inclusive TM programs where no special treatment is given to any group and no group is "degraded". If the difference is attributed to their exclusion, then having an exclusive TM program may highlight the risk of demoralizing the majority by excluding them.

Another important research avenue is to study the role of line managers in the development and retention of B players. Research suggests line managers' interaction with their employees will influence how they feel regarding their value and contributions, and these feelings are instrumental in shaping their work-related attitudes (Purcell & Hutchinson, 2007). However, evidence shows that employees not included in the programs (such as B players) perceive little support from their line managers or others in the organization (Swailes & Blackburn, 2016). It is quite possible that the lack of managerial support and less availability of resources and investment for B players do not allow them to perform at an exceptional level, and the lack of developmental opportunities hinders their career progression. However, if they are surrounded by supportive management who care about their well-being as well as development, they might be able to create positive outcomes for themselves by accessing information, resources and career opportunities that might not be available to them otherwise (Gelens et al., 2013; Liao, Toya, Lepak, & Hong, 2009).

Greenwood (2002) emphasized that managers have an ethical obligation to attend to the needs of all those who have a stake in the organization, which suggests that the skills, abilities, and competencies of *all* employees need to be developed. Additionally, research consistently suggests that B players have lower perceptions of equity as compared to employees included in the TM programs (Gelens et al., 2014; Swailes & Blackburn, 2016). Questions remain on what role line managers can do to ameliorate these perceptions of inequity to get the most out of organization's TM programs without adversely affecting B players, and how can they achieve these position outcomes.

We also have a limited understanding about the characteristics of B players. Since B players have never been the focus of any TM empirical studies, we cannot comment directly on their demographics and characteristics; however, we can draw inferences based on a few studies that have looked at the characteristics of employees who were identified as talent. In Sonnenberg's et al. (2014) study, the majority of the employees identified as talent were male and highly educated. Since females comprise almost half of the working population but are still rare in managerial positions (Commission, 2012), does this mean that the majority of the female employees in the organizations are characterized as B players?

Leadership potential is considered as an important ingredient in talent searches (Swailes, 2013); however, leadership theory had traditionally been described in masculine terms (Billing & Alvesson, 2000), highlighting the characteristics such as being tough, aggressive, competitive, and unemotional – characteristics that are often more displayed by men. Additionally, full-time, permanent positions, long working hours, full dedication to work domain, etc., are also other ingredients in talent searches, which many women lack since a higher proportion of part-time jobs are held by women (Swailes, 2013).

Since no past study has specifically looked at the non-talent pool, researchers need to examine the composition of this group. If findings reveal a majority of women in a non-talent pool, suggestions should be made to practitioners and organizations to identify biases in their talent selection processes. Many societies are still struggling with gender inequities in terms of pay, career progression, etc. (Lips, 2013). TM has the potential not only to produce outcomes at the individual and organizational levels, but also at the societal level (Thunnissen et al., 2013b). Scholars need to investigate to what extent existing TM practices are gender-inclusive or gender-biased to determine the effectiveness of TM practices at the societal level.

Although some scholars advocate the best practice approach to TM (Garrow & Hirsh, 2008) and others stress the contextual relevance of TM (Beechler & Woodward, 2009; Thunnissen et al., 2013b), the current TM literature does not fully examine contextual variables to explain the related processes (Gallardo-Gallardo et al., 2017). Scholars need to pay attention to internal as well as external factors to examine how TM processes are conceptualized and implemented in organizations. To illustrate, organizations having a benevolent climate may help in reducing B players' negative emotions and feelings about their exclusion due to the belief that the organization has a sincere interest in their well-being, compared to organizations where self-interest prevails (Sanders, Dorenbosch, & de Reuver, 2008).

Scholars may also look at organizational TM programs through the lens of Bowen and Ostroff's framework of the strength of HRM system (Bowen & Ostroff, 2004). This approach would allow scholars to focus on the processes related to the implementation of TM by paying attention to the different meta-features of TM programs (such as visibility, relevance, understandability, and fairness of TM) (Malik & Singh, 2014).

In addition to internal factors, there is also a need to examine external factors. To do this, an explicit comparison of differences in TM practices in different contexts would be useful (Swailes, 2013). For example, Festing, Kornau, and Schäfer (2015) suggested that the more male-dominated industries are likely to have more gender-biased TM practices where talent is identified more in terms of stereo-typical masculine characteristics (such as assertiveness and competitiveness). Tatli, Vassilopoulou, and Özbilgin (2013) found gender inequality in TM programs in five countries in the Asia-Pacific region and suggested gender quotas to be included in TM strategies.

Exclusive global TM practices that result in many employees being classified as B players may not be suitable for organizations and their subsidiaries in collectivist national cultures (Swailes, 2013) as these would contradict their cultural values and beliefs. Moreover, some countries are more culturally diverse and have open skilled immigration policies than others. Skilled immigrants may have the relevant experiences and can add a lot of value to firms by bringing their diverse skillsets. However, the reality is immigrants' skills are underutilized and they earn considerably less compared to host country nationals (Quintini, 2011; Reitz, 2007).

It may not be a stretch to assume that immigrants are often not included proportionately in the list of A players. Recently, Crowley-Henry and Al Ariss (2016) paid attention to the talent management of skilled immigrants and theorized on how including skilled immigrants in TM practices can result in sustainable competitive advantage for firms. However, much more empirical work (preferably ethno-graphic studies) is needed to explore the lived experiences of skilled immigrants with their respective employers' TM processes (Crowley-Henry & Al Ariss, 2018). Furthermore, studying intersectionality, such as combining migrant status with gender, would offer interesting insights to existing studies (Crowley-Henry & Al Ariss, 2018), since both demographics may be important determinants of employee non-talent status as B players.

In addition to the consideration of different external contexts, comparative case studies of different companies using different approaches to manage employees in the same external context (i.e., same country, same sector, same industry) should also be conducted. While keeping the context constant, researchers may be able to identify the effectiveness of different approaches to TM (inclusive versus exclusive) in the same context.

Concerns have been raised that when organizations create a segregated workforce by excluding many employees from TM programs, teamwork would suffer (Pfeffer, 2001; Swailes, 2013); however, these relationships have not been examined as yet. As such, there is a need to examine the effectiveness of different approaches to TM in terms of their effects on teamwork. If creating an elitist culture (as in the case of the exclusive TM) impedes teamwork, encourages internal competition and promotes a zero-sum game (Pfeffer, 2001; Swailes, 2013), positive outcomes in terms of improved organizational performance may not be achieved. Under such circumstances, employees who feel they are left behind would most likely leave the organization, resulting in high employee turnover and diminishing organizational performance.

From the existing research, we know that the attitudes and behaviors of B players (i.e., non-hipo employees) are less favorable, compared with employees who are identified as A players. Researchers need to identify conditions under which these negative consequences would be diminished. One of the factors could be employees' level of trust in their employer. Many past empirical studies have drawn on social exchange theory to assess the impact of talent identification on employee attitudes and behaviors.

Blau's (1964) framework of social exchange also highlighted the role of trust in social exchange relationships; however, there is a dearth of research examining the role of trust in explaining the social exchange basis of employee work-related outcomes in the TM literature (King, 2016). Exploring the role of organizational trust while examining these relationships is important because TM has changed the way organizations manage their workforce (Malik et al., 2017); consequently, the employment relationships between employers and their employees have changed as well (Al Ariss et al., 2014; King, 2016; Sonnenberg et al., 2014).

There is a compelling need to examine another important, but neglected, phenomenon: talent derailment, an employee's failure or under performance at the next level, which is a major concern in TM (Martin & Schmidt, 2010). Several individual and organizational factors may contribute to the talent derailment, such as, the lack of ability to establish good relationships with others, the lack of emotional intelligence, the lack of organizational support to build superior competencies required at the higher level (Ross, 2013; Sweis, Al Sharef, Jandali, Obeidat, & Andrawes, 2018). Research on identifying factors that result in talent derailment in organizations is lacking.

Additionally, we have little understanding on what happens when employees are being told they are no longer in the TM program. Researchers need to focus on the experiences of employees (B players) who are being dropped from TM programs and re-join the "non-talent" pool. How do they feel and cope? Do organizations provide them support to go through this transitioning phase or are they mostly left on their own? How is their "expulsion" perceived by other employees in the organization? These are important questions that future research still needs to focus on.

Conclusion

Although TM policies and practices are important for an organization's competitive success, ignoring B players may risk demoralizing and unsettling the majority of the organizational workforce, resulting in reduced organizational performance. If this is true, this would defeat the whole purpose of TM programs. Without considering TM more broadly and examining its cross-over effects on excluded employees, we cannot ascertain the effectiveness of these programs. It is our hope that this chapter will encourage scholars to pay specific attention to B players who have been under-studied in the TM literature.

References

Adams, J. 1965. Inequity in social exchange. In L. Berkowitz (Ed.), *Advances in experimental social psychology,* Vol. 2: 267–299. New York: Academic Press.

Aguinis, H., Boyd, B. K., Pierce, C. A., Short, J. C., Huselid, M. A., & Becker, B. E. 2011. Bridging micro and macro domains: Workforce differentiation and strategic human resource management. *Journal of Management,* 37(2): 421–428.

Al Ariss, A., Cascio, W., & Paauwe, J. 2014. Talent management: Current theories and future research directions. *Journal of World Business,* 49(2): 173–179.

Amankwah, A. J. (2020). Talent management and global competition for top talent: A co-opetition-based perspective. *Thunderbird International Business Review,* 62(4), 343–352.

Babad, E., Inbar, J., & Rosenthal, R. 1982. Pygmalion, Galatea, and the Golem: Investigations of biased and unbiased teachers. *Journal of Educational Psychology,* 74(4): 459.

Becker, B., Huselid, M., & Beatty, R. 2009. *The differentiated workforce: Translating talent into strategic impact.* Boston, MA: Harvard Business Press.

Beechler, S., & Woodward, I. C. 2009. The global "war for talent". *Journal of International Management,* 15(3): 273–285.

Bethke-Langenegger, P., Mahler, P., & Staffelbach, B. 2011. Effectiveness of talent management strategies. *European Journal of International Management,* 5(5): 524–539.

Billing, Y., & Alvesson, M. 2000. Questioning the notion of feminine leadership: A critical perspective on the gender labelling of leadership. *Gender, Work & Organization,* 7(3): 144–157.

Björkman, I., Ehrnrooth, M., Mäkelä, K., Smale, A., & Sumelius, J. 2013. Talent or not? Employee reactions to talent identification. *Human Resource Management,* 52(2): 195–214.

Blau, P. 1964. *Exchange and power in social life.* New York: John Wiley & Sons.

Bowen, D., & Ostroff, C. 2004. Understanding HRM-firm performance linkages: The role of the "strength" of the HRM system. *Academy of Management Review,* 29(2): 203–221.

Campbell, M., & Smith, R. 2010. *High-potential talent: A view from the leadership pipeline.* Greensboro, NC: Centre for Creative Leadership. http://insights.ccl.org/wp-content/uploads/2015/04/highPotentialTalent.pdf

Campion, M., Fink, A., Ruggeberg, B., Carr, L., Phillips, G., & Odman, R. 2011. Doing competencies well: Best practices in competency modeling. *Personnel Psychology,* 64(1): 225–262.

Cappelli, P., & Keller, J. 2014. Talent management: Conceptual approaches and practical challenges. *Annual Review of Organizational Psychology and Organizational Behavior,* 1(1): 305–331.

Cappelli, P., & Keller, J. 2017. The historical context of talent management. In D. Collings, K. Mellahi, & W. Cascio (Eds.), *The Oxford handbook of talent management:* 23–42. Oxford, UK: Oxford University Press.

Church, A., Rotolo, C., Ginther, N., & Levine, R. 2015. How are top companies designing and managing their high-potential programs? A follow-up talent management benchmark study. *Consulting Psychology Journal: Practice and Research,* 67(1): 17–47.

Collings, D. 2014a. Integrating global mobility and global talent management: Exploring the challenges and strategic opportunities. *Journal of World Business,* 49(2): 253–261.

Collings, D. 2014b. Toward mature talent management: Beyond shareholder value. *Human Resource Development Quarterly,* 25(3): 301–319.

Collings, D., & Isichei, M. 2018. The shifting boundaries of global staffing: Integrating global talent management, alternative forms of international assignments and non-employees into the discussion. *The International Journal of Human Resource Management:* 21(9), 165–187.

Collings, D., & Mellahi, K. 2009. Strategic talent management: A review and research agenda. *Human Resource Management Review,* 19(4): 304–313.

Collings, D., Scullion, H., & Vaiman, V. 2015. Talent management: Progress and prospects. *Human Resource Management Review,* 25(3): 233–235.

Commission, E. 2012. *Women in economic decision-making in the EU: Progress report. A Europe 2020 initiative.* Luxembourg: Publication Office of the European Union.

Crowley-Henry, M., & Al Ariss, A. 2018. Talent management of skilled migrants: Propositions and an agenda for future research. *The International Journal of Human Resource Management:* 29(13), 2054–2079.

De Boeck, G., Meyers, M. C., & Dries, N. 2018. Employee reactions to talent management: Assumptions versus evidence. *Journal of Organizational Behavior,* 39(2): 199–213.

Delong, T., & Vijayaraghavan, V. 2003. Let's hear it for B players. *Harvard Business Review,* 81(6): 96–103.

Dries, N. 2013. Talent management, from phenomenon to theory: Introduction to the Special Issue. *Human Resource Management Review,* 23(4): 267–271.

Dries, N., & De Gieter, S. 2014. Information asymmetry in high potential programs a potential risk for psychological contract breach. *Personnel Review,* 43(1): 136–162.

Dries, N., Van Acker, F., & Verbruggen, M. 2012. How 'boundaryless' are the careers of high potentials, key experts and average performers? *Journal of Vocational Behavior,* 81(2), 271–279.

Farndale, E., Scullion, H., & Sparrow, P. 2010. The role of the corporate HR function in global talent management. *Journal of World Business,* 45(2): 161–168.

Festing, M., Kornau, A., & Schäfer, L. 2015. Think talent–think male? A comparative case study analysis of gender inclusion in talent management practices in the German media industry. *The International Journal of Human Resource Management,* 26(6): 707–732.

Gallardo-Gallardo, E., Dries, N., & González-Cruz, T. 2013. What is the meaning of 'talent' in the world of work? *Human Resource Management Review,* 23(4): 290–300.

Gallardo-Gallardo, E., Thunnissen, M., & Scullion, H. 2017. Special issue of *International Journal of Human Resource Management:* A contextualized approach to talent management: advancing the field. *International Journal of Human Resource Management,* 1–4.

Garavan, T., Carbery, R., & Rock, A. 2012. Mapping talent development: Definition, scope and architecture. *European Journal of Training and Development,* 36(1): 5–24.

Garrow, V., & Hirsh, W. 2008. Talent management: Issues of focus and fit. *Public Personnel Management,* 37(4): 389–402.

Gelens, J., Dries, N., Hofmans, J., & Pepermans, R. 2015. Affective commitment of employees designated as talent: Signalling perceived organisational support. *European Journal of International Management,* 9(1): 9–27.

Gelens, J., Hofmans, J., Dries, N., & Pepermans, R. 2014. Talent management and organisational justice: Employee reactions to high potential identification. *Human Resource Management Journal,* 24(2): 159–175.

Glaister, A., Karacay, G., Demirbag, M., & Tatoglu, E. 2018. HRM and performance—The role of talent management as a transmission mechanism in an emerging market context. *Human Resource Management Journal,* 28 (1): 148–166.

Greenberg, J. 1990. Organizational justice: Yesterday, today, and tomorrow. *Journal of Management,* 16(2): 399–432.

Greenwood, M. 2002. Ethics and HRM: A review and conceptual analysis. *Journal of Business Ethics,* 36(3): 261–278.

Groysberg, B. 2010. *Chasing stars: The myths of talent and the probability of performance.* Princeton, NJ: Princeton University Press.

Guthridge, M., Komm, A., & Lawson, E. 2008. Making talent a strategic priority. *McKinsey Quarterly,* 1(1): 48–59.

Huselid, M., Beatty, R., & Becker, B. 2005. 'A players' or 'A positions'? *Harvard Business Review,* 83(12): 110–117.

Iles, P., Chuai, X., & Preece, D. 2010. Talent management and HRM in multinational companies in Beijing: Definitions, differences and drivers. *Journal of World Business,* 45(2): 179–189.

Karakowsky, L., & Kotlyar, I. 2012. Do 'high-potential' leadership programs really work? *The Globe and Mail.* http://www.theglobeandmail.com/report-on-business/careers/management/do-high-potential-leadership-programs-really-work/article4248330/

Khoreva, V., Vaiman, V., & Van Zalk, M. 2017. Talent management practice effectiveness: Investigating employee perspective. *Employee Relations,* 39(1): 19–33.

King, K. 2016. The talent deal and journey: Understanding how employees respond to talent identification over time. *Employee Relations,* 38(1): 94–111.

Lacey, M., & Groves, K. 2014. Talent management collides with corporate social responsibility: creation of inadvertent hypocrisy. *Journal of Management Development,* 33(4): 399–409.

Lepak, D., & Snell, S. 2002. Examining the human resource architecture: The relationships among human capital, employment, and human resource configurations. *Journal of Management,* 28(4): 517–543.

Lepak, D., Takeuchi, R., Erhardt, N., & Colakoglu, S. 2006. Emerging perspectives on the relationship between HRM and performance. In R. Burke, & C. Cooper (Eds.), *The human resources revolution: Why putting people first matters:* 31–54. Oxford, UK: Elsevier.

Lewis, R., & Heckman, R. 2006. Talent management: A critical review. *Human Resource Management Review,* 16(2): 139–154.

Liao, H., Toya, K., Lepak, D., & Hong, Y. 2009. Do they see eye to eye? Management and employee perspectives of high-performance work systems and influence processes on service quality. *Journal of Applied Psychology,* 94(2): 371–391.

Lips, H. 2013. The gender pay gap: Challenging the rationalizations. Perceived equity, discrimination, and the limits of human capital models. *Sex Roles,* 68(3-4): 169–185.

Lucas, S. 2017. Who's on your bench? Why you should focus on the B team: *Business.com.* https://www.business.com/articles/why-you-should-focus-on-the-b-players/

Luna–Arocas, R., & Morley, M. 2015. Talent management, talent mindset competency and job performance: The mediating role of job satisfaction. *European Journal of International Management,* 9(1): 28–51.

Malik, A., & Singh, P. 2014. 'High potential' programs: Let's hear it for 'B' players. *Human Resource Management Review,* 24(4): 330–346.

Malik, A., Singh, P., & Chan, C. 2017. High potential programs and employee outcomes: The roles of organizational trust and employee attributions. *Career Development International,* 22(7): 772–796.

Mankins, M., Bird, A., & Root, J. 2013. Making star teams out of star players. *Harvard Business Review,* 91(1-2): 74–78, 144.

Marescaux, E., De Winne, S., & Sels, L. 2013. HR practices and affective organisational commitment: (When) does HR differentiation pay off? *Human Resource Management Journal,* 23(4): 329–345.

Martin, J., & Schmidt, C. 2010. How to keep your top talent. *Harvard Business Review,* 88(5): 54–61.

McDonnell, A., Collings, D., Mellahi, K., & Schuler, R. 2017. Talent management: A systematic review and future prospects. *European Journal of International Management,* 11(1): 86–128.

Meyers, M., & van Woerkom, M. 2014. The influence of underlying philosophies on talent management: Theory, implications for practice, and research agenda. *Journal of World Business,* 49(2): 192–203.

Meyers, M. C., van Woerkom, M., Paauwe, J., & Dries, N. (2020). HR managers' talent philosophies: Prevalence and relationships with perceived talent management practices. *International Journal of Human Resource Management,* 31(4), 562–588.

Michaels, E., Handfield-Jones, H., & Axelrod, B. 2001. *The war for talent.* Boston: MA: Harvard Business Press.

Morris, S., Snell, S., & Björkman, I. 2016. An architectural framework for global talent management. *Journal of International Business Studies,* 47(6): 723–747.

Pfeffer, J. 2001. Fighting the war for talent is hazardous to your organization's health. *Organizational Dynamics,* 29(4): 248–259.

Purcell, J., & Hutchinson, S. 2007. Front-line managers as agents in the HRM-performance causal chain: Theory, analysis and evidence. *Human Resource Management Journal,* 17(1): 3–20.

Quintini, G. 2011. Over-qualified or under-skilled: A review of existing literature. **OECD Social, Employment, and Migration Working Papers,** No. 121, OECD Publishing.

Reitz, J. 2007. Immigrant employment success in Canada, part II: Understanding the decline. **Journal of International Migration and Integratio,** 8(1): 37–62.

Robinson, S., & Rousseau, D.1994. Violating the psychological contract: Not the exception but the norm. **Journal of Organizational Behavior,** 15(3): 245–259.

Ross, S. 2013. Talent derailment: A multi-dimensional perspective for understanding talent. **Industrial and Commercial Training,** 45(1): 12–17.

Rousseau, D. 1989. Psychological and implied contracts in organizations. **Employee Responsibilities and Rights Journal,** 2(2): 121–139.

Sanders, K., Dorenbosch, L., & de Reuver, R. 2008. The impact of individual and shared employee perceptions of HRM on affective commitment: considering climate strength. **Personnel Review,** 37(4): 412–425.

Scullion, H., Collings, D., & Caliguiri, P. 2010. Global talent management. **Journal of World Business,** 45(2): 105–108.

Scullion, H., Vaiman, V., & Collings, D. 2016. Strategic talent management: Introduction to special issue. **Employee Relations,** 38(1): 1–1.

Silzer, R., & Church, A. 2010. Identifying and assessing high-potential talent. In R. Silzer, & B. Dowell (Eds.), **Strategy-driven talent management: A leadership imperative,** Vol. 28: 213–280. San Francisco, CA: Jossey-Bass.

Son, J., Park, O., Bae, J., & Ok, C. 2018. Double-edged effect of talent management on organizational performance: The moderating role of HRM investments. **The International Journal of Human Resource Management:** 1–29. doi: https://doi.org/10.1080/09585192.2018.1443955

Sonnenberg, M., van Zijderveld, V., & Brinks, M. 2014. The role of talent-perception incongruence in effective talent management. **Journal of World Business,** 49(2): 272–280.

Spence, M. 1973. Job market signaling. **The Quarterly Journal of Economics,** 87(3), 355–374.

Swailes, S. 2013. The ethics of talent management. **Business Ethics: A European Review,** 22(1): 32–46.

Swailes, S., & Blackburn, M. 2016. Employee reactions to talent pool membership. **Employee Relations,** 38(1): 112–128.

Sweis, R. J., Al Sharef, R., Jandali, D., Obeidat, B. Y., & Andrawes, N. 2018. The relationship between project team members' effectiveness and acknowledgment of talent: Team members' perspective. **International Journal of Construction Education and Research,** 14(2): 141–160.

Tatli, A., Vassilopoulou, J., & Özbilgin, M. 2013. An unrequited affinity between talent shortages and untapped female potential: The relevance of gender quotas for talent management in high growth potential economies of the Asia Pacific region. **International Business Review,** 22(3): 539–553.

Thunnissen, M., Boselie, P., & Fruytier, B. 2013a. A review of talent management: 'Infancy or adolescence?'. **The International Journal of Human Resource Management,** 24(9): 1744–1761.

Thunnissen, M., Boselie, P., & Fruytier, B. 2013b. Talent management and the relevance of context: Towards a pluralistic approach. **Human Resource Management Review,** 24(3): 326–336.

Vaiman, V., Cascio, W. F., Collings, D. G., & Swider, B. W. 2021. The shifting boundaries of talent management. **Human Resource Management,** 60(2): 253–257.

Vaiman, V., & Collings, D. 2013. Talent management: Advancing the field. **The International Journal of Human Resource Management,** 24(9): 1737–1743.

31

IT'S CROWDED AT THE TOP

How to Retain and Reward Star Employees

Shad Morris

James Oldroyd

Kathleen Bahr

Introduction

Star employees represent a small group of select employees able to perform well above the norm (Aguinis & O'Boyle, 2014; Call, Nyberg, & Thatcher, 2015; O'Boyle, 2017; Ready, Conger, & Hill, 2010; Tsabbar & Kehoe, 2014). In a sense, stars represent a mutation of the normal employee, able to perform super-human feats for the organization. But if Marvel Comics and writer Stan Lee have taught us anything, it's that stars have weaknesses and sometimes that which makes them valuable to the organization can end up hurting them and the organizations they work for. In other words, while few actually make it to the top in terms of performance, once they get there, star performers become crowded with myriad help requests and they can become overloaded with work, thereby experience decreased performance and increased turnover (Oldroyd & Morris, 2012).

This chapter demonstrates many points related to star employees. First, it demonstrates how organizations can proactively manage stars to ensure that the inevitable crowding of their workload is effectively controlled and coordinated to ensure they stay on top... and stay in the organization. We highlight talent management practices targeted at star employees to help them with these work overload burdens. In particular, we examine how talent practices can increase individual competencies to take on more role behaviors of helping other employees. We also explore organizational processes geared specifically to help ensure stars have the right tools and appropriate motives for efficiently helping others with work that could benefit from star expertise. We also examine network structures that can ease star burdens and help them to focus on their strengths.

We next examine the movement of star employees between firms. We examine the difference of movement between stars and their non-star peers, and also the difference of movement within the group of stars themselves. We highlight the idea that not all stars have equal value, and that the tenure of the star and the status of the organization can affect the value of the star. We also examine the human capital of stars – both specific and generic – and the advantage of human capital for the stars and the company. We propose a framework of renegotiation, wherein decision rights are slowly given to the emerging star. This renegotiation process can help stars with high human capital stay within the organization as they continue to progress. We conclude by outlining a future research agenda for managing and understanding star talent, value, and human capital.

The Pros and Cons of Stars

Star employees are people who perform substantially better than the average worker (Groysberg, Lee, & Nanda, 2008; Oldroyd & Morris, 2012). On one hand, star employees are vital for organizational

DOI: 10.4324/9781315474687-31

survival as they often produce a large percentage of the outputs for an organization. For example, 80% of company sales are often attributable to 20% of their employees (Aoyama et al., 2010). A study across multiple industries points out the top quartile of employees are responsible for over 50% of company production (Aguinis, 2012). In professional service industries, an organization's top performers both generate the bulk of that organization's business and constitute its core knowledge assets (Eccles & Crane, 1988).

Studies of scientists and academic researchers have consistently found that employees at the top of the performance distribution are many times more valuable than their lower-performing colleagues (e.g., Cole & Cole, 1973; Ernst, Leptein, & Vitt, 2000; Narin & Breitzman, 1995). Moreover, when employees perform well in one area, they are also likely to perform well in other areas, as they have greater access to resources and autonomy (Aguinis, O'Boyle, Gonzalez-Mule, & Joo, 2016). Finally, some stars, known as "relational stars", are particularly good at making others around them more productive as well (Grigoriou & Rothaermel, 2014).

On the other hand, star employees are some of the most volatile groups of employees within an organization. For example, Kang, Oldroyd, Morris, and Kim (2017) found that not only are stars more likely to leave the organization than non-stars, but stars are also much less loyal to firms that do not have sufficient status. In other words, they tend to go where the money and status are, exhibiting less loyalty than their lower performing peers. In fact, while many star employees do stay in their firms, even among them it is the brightest stars who leave the most often (Ganco, Ziedonis, & Agarwal, 2015). Moreover, Chen and Garg (2018) found that stars who leave an organization and come back do the firm a favor. Their absence helps the organization overcome its reliance on the star employee and build capabilities in other members of the firm.

Part of the reason that stars may be more likely to leave is that they are also more likely to burn out and become overloaded with work than their non-star peers (Oldroyd & Morris, 2012). Because of the high levels of burnout and overwork, their high visibility makes these employees more widely recruited than their less visible peers (Groysberg et al., 2008). In fact, unlike traditional theories of turnover where employees must engage in job search behaviors, stars often do not need to contact employers (Aguinis & O'Boyle, 2014). Because of their high visibility, companies actively recruit stars (Gardner, 2005; Insead & Chatain, 2008).

This paradox of receiving exponentially high levels of performance from stars while at the same time receiving extra high levels of burnout and turnover from them leads to employers' love/hate relationship with their star employees. To help ease this tension between stars and their employers, we suggest some talent management practices managers can adopt to help improve the retention and continued performance of stars.

Managing the Work Overload of Stars

Reducing the Number of Ties and Volume

The simplest way to help stars manage overload is to limit the amount of information they receive (Oldroyd & Morris, 2012). Limiting the volume can readily be accomplished by selectively reducing the number of contacts in a broker's network. Removing redundant nodes in a network decreases the volume while not affecting access to novel information flow. Interestingly, selectively managing the number of ties individuals have may not only reduce volume but also eliminate redundancy and create structural holes in the network space surrounding them as others have advocated (Burt, 1997).

While reducing the number of ties may have a profound effect on both network and information processing constraint, the reduction of network ties is not a trivial effort. Peet and Watts (2004) demonstrated that social networks are affiliatory in nature. New ties added to a network are all likely to connect to the same nodes. While a vast number of ties are likely to increase the status and the reputation of individuals, they are also likely to paralyze the information flow surrounding them. They will become bottlenecks (Cross & Parker, 2004), they will eventually be bypassed, or they will absorb uncertainty via the dumbing-down or vast simplification of the information they receive (Simon, 1958).

Two studies provide some empirical evidence that smaller more focused networks provide more value to individuals (Aral & Van Alstyne, 2008; Oldroyd, 2007). Oldroyd (2007) found that individuals connected to fewer others have superior performance. Carefully managing the number of ties may have the cumulative effect of reducing cognitive constraint *and* reducing structural constraint. Moreover, some individuals may be unable to reduce their networks due to their position in the organizational hierarchy. For instance, a CEO's administrator may be required to interact with many individuals and may receive a high volume of information, but he or she is likely to lack the autonomy to reduce the number of contacts and the concomitant volume of information.

The argument above presupposes that volume is directly correlated with the number of network ties. The work of Aral, Brynjolfsson, and Van Alstyne (2006), however, demonstrates that this may not be the case. Individuals may receive differential communication flows independent of their network size. Some ties may introduce vast amounts of information while other ties introduce very little. It may be easier for brokers to directly handle the volume of information rather than seek to make changes to their network structure. Network structures can also be designed to reduce the burden of information processing by generating filtering systems.

Increasing Information Processing Capabilities

Stars can increase their information processing capability and decrease the effect of information processing constraint. They do this primarily by increasing their information utilization skills (Oldroyd & Morris, 2012). Scholars often refer to this organizational capability as absorptive capacity. Individuals can also possess absorptive capacity that is based on their past experience and human capital investments. When stars make firm-specific human capital investments around getting to know the individuals and jobs within a firm, they increase their potential ability to process internal information that comes from multiple sources within the firm (Ployhardt, Call, & McFarland, 2017).

Another way to improve individual's information processing capabilities is to focus on information filtering mechanisms and information technologies. For instance, to process information for application requires organizational processes and information systems that enable an individual to actually use the information coming to them (Grant, 1996). The information system allows information from others to be: 1) codified and made simpler to understand, and 2) captured in a storage system that allows for longevity of the information.

One example is seen in organizations where valuable information is captured in short lessons-learned or templates that allow users to apply information coming to them from others in a more comprehensive and understandable format. They are also able to apply this information more quickly, allowing them to deal with larger amounts of information flow. In addition, networks can work to eliminate fluctuations in the flow of information. Oldroyd (2007) found that individuals who experience more variation in the flow of information they receive are likely to have poorer performance. Thus, the standardization of information needs to be of both content and volume.[1]

Increasing an individual's information processing capability enables them to process more information in the same amount of time or reduce the volume of information processes. Figure 31.1 below is a graphical representation of these phenomena. The goal is to shift the curve upward and simultaneously to the right. The shift to the right is the result of processing more information at comparable costs. The shift upward is the result of extracting more value from the same volume of information. This is accomplished by more effectively utilizing information.

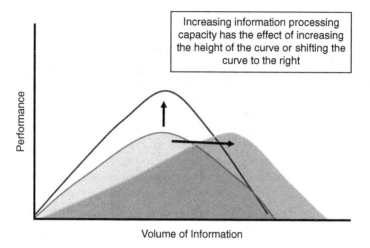

Figure 31.1 The performance effects of increasing information processing capacity

The Movement of Stars

Research has proven that stars are more highly sought after and that possessing star status does lead to increased movement between organizations (Kang et al., 2018). The movement of stars is not always positive, however. Scholars have found that stars see drops in productivity when they move to another organization (Groysberg & Lee, 2009). Groysberg et al. (2008) also mention how star employees are often unable to replicate their exceptional performance. This could be due to the fact that sometimes the value of a star is tied only to the value of an organization and cannot be transferred. Therefore, hiring stars can be a risky decision for firms, so the firms must understand what makes stars likely to move and what source the stars' value comes from.

Star Employees and Tenure

One thing that will affect the movement and the value of a star is their tenure. Kang et al. (2018) found that although stars are more likely to move than non-star employees, a star gradually becomes less likely to move as their tenure increases. The same result is also seen as the success and status of the firm increases.

A young, successful employee sends signals to the market that their human capital is transferable and valuable to other organizations. If an employee is a star employee at an early stage in their career, they send signals of strong potential. Their value comes not from years of networking and developing human capital, but from their won investments and skills. Young stars have human capital that is transferrable to other firms and that holds the potential to grow into more value.

An employee with more human capital, or in this case, experience with the specific firm, is seen to have made more firm-specific investments, and their human capital is believed to be less transferable. Older employees, those with more tenure, are often less motivated and willing to learn, but the younger employees, in contrast, will bring in up-to-date knowledge and the desire to learn (Kang et al., 2018).

To gain the most out of hiring a star, firms should look for stars that are younger and have less tenure. These are the stars who are not only more likely to move, but also who can provide more value through their transferrable human capital.

Organizations' Value Versus Stars' Value

The value of the star employee needs to be considered in relation to the incumbent firm; incumbent firms, especially those of high status, can often distort the value. For example, a high-status firm would likely have more resources and programs that might allow the employee to become a star (Kang et al., 2018).

Stars in low-status firms have an advantage here, because their human capital is entirely their own and they can send clear signals of their value.

The contextual factors that stars are embedded in can also add to their value. This embedded perspective attributes much of a star's performance to the social and organizational factors in which they are working (Morris & Snell, 2011). For example, Oldroyd and Morris (2012) point out that much of a star's value is attributable to their non-redundant social ties within an organization. A star's social connections might be part of their value, and movement away from their social connections can decrease their value and their performance at the new hiring firm.

Not every star employee can and will provide equal value to the hiring firm. Firms need to be able to disentangle the performance and value of the star from the status and value of the incumbent firm to be able to understand if the star had portable human capital and value.

Human Capital and Star Employees

A star employee can create more value for their organization and themselves as they develop firm-specific human capital. This development of firm-specific human capital can also simultaneously develop general human capital. As these employees develop their human capital, managers need to deal correctly with their star employees so that both the star and the firm can optimize their value capture.

The Advantage of Human Capital

Human capital has a large advantage for star employees. Stars do not only gain their value based on their performance, but also from their collaboration and human capital (Kehoe & Tzabbar, 2014). A star's human capital investments and their creation of economic value for the organization affect the bargaining power of the said star employee (Ganco, Franco, & Agarwal, 2012; Ployhart & Moliteron, 2011). This can be attributed to the fact that human capital investments result in high-performance of tasks and high status among peers and competitors (Kehoe et al., 2016).

It has been determined that there are two types of human capital: general and specific (Becker, 1964). General human capital has value in a wide variety of settings. It can be simple, like the ability to read and write, or more abstract, like the ability to communicate or the ability to lead. When people invest in general human capital, it is in anticipation of a reward, often related to earning (Wright & McMahan, 1992). Such investments in general human capital also give the employee bargaining power with the employer.

While general skills allow employees to show their value, these skills are often less valuable to a firm than specific human capital is (Barney, 1991). Specific human capital is narrower, such as working with a specific team of people or a specialized skill set. One reason firm-specific human capital is so valuable is that it is not as easily imitated as general human capital (Barney, 1991; Wright & MacMahan, 1992). On a downside, because firm-specific human capital is specific only to that firm, employees may not be compensated for making such investments unless external competitors are willing to pay for the investments (Becker, 1964; Williamson, 1975)

General and specific knowledge and human capital are not separable like some people view them to be. When an employee makes firm-specific investments, they not only develop skills valuable to their company (Park, Howard, & Gomulaya, 2018), but these skills can also be valuable to competitors and can be transferred to other firms (Greenwood, Hinings, & Brown, 1990). Firm-specific investments should be a sign of general human capital and should increase employee mobility (Morris et al., 2017). The skills gained by firm-specific investments are within the individual, who has the liberty to create new knowledge or use their skills in new ways (Chadwick & Dabu, 2009; Felin & Hesterly, 2007). All of this shows that firm-specific human capital investments may create both firm-specific and general human capital. As a star develops their firm-specific human capital, they are developing general human capital at the same time.

Managing Stars with Renegotiation

As star employees make specific investments, it makes them more sought after, and it is believed that they are more likely to leave a firm. In fact, literature has proved that stars possess more loyalty to the profession than to the company (Gardner, 2005; Greenwood et al., 2008). Managers need to work differently with their star employees if they desire to keep their star employees at their firm. The traditional ideas and approaches of human capital and stars are not realistic, and so Morris et al. (2018) propose the idea of renegotiation to help managers and star employees.

Boxall (2013) suggests that an organization must recognize the need for employees' interests to be aligned with those of the organization; not just once, but with constant changes and adjustments over time. A step further, Collings (2014, 2017) suggests that organizations need to also align their vision to the changing skills and preferences of their valuable employees. In addition, Managers need to consider the perspectives of their star employees. Trevor et al. (2007) give the example that stars will most likely expect higher employment outcomes, and, for this reason, stars should be involved in pay and business decisions.

Decision rights, or internal organizational agreements about who has power for specific parts of a firm's operation (Jensen & Meckling, 1995), can be used to help stars feel like part of the firm and can help the managers meet the expectations of their star employees. Morris et al. (2018) point out that while knowledge and guidance regarding the initiation of decision rights exist, there is a need for understanding the renegotiation of said decision rights as a star progresses within the firm.

The process of negotiation starts when the employee is hired. With each negotiation, the one who expects to gain the most will retain the decision rights (Grossman & Hart, 1986). Because of this, it is likely that at the beginning, the firm will retain most of the rights. As the employee reaches stardom, there should be a renegotiation and they should be given more rights (Morris, Alvarez, & Barney, 2018). Eventually, management will need to move aside and let the star lead themselves, or else it is likely the star will feel undervalued and leave the firm.

It is important for managers to recognize that renegotiation more than a zero-sum game; rather, it is the opportunity to allow the star to understand their value and to have the independence to create more value of their own. This will help the firm earn more instead of losing the employee to a competitor (Morris et al., 2018).

This renegotiation and shift of decision rights is a gradual process, one that fully allows the firm and star to benefit. As the star works their way up in the firm, the firm gradually forfeits the decision rights until the star is independent and able to create and grow their own value. The purpose of renegotiation is to not only help the firm capture the full value of the employee but also to help the employee capture the full value of the firm (see Morris et al., 2018 for details). Stars are important employees, who contribute to much of the success of a firm, and it is important for managers to effectively deal with stars and create maximum value for both the firm and the star.

Future Research

This research on star employees suggests several avenues of future research. For example, future research could examine how specific talent management practices might actually help stars stay committed to the organization and at the same time increase organizational performance. Researchers could also examine practices involving training employees to deal more effectively with work overload, and to structure work practices to reduce work burdens for star employees. Such research might help to retain star employees within the firm.

We also suggest that some stars may be better suited than others to deal with exponentially high levels of increased workloads and requests for help. For example, Grigoriou and Rothaermel (2014) found that relational stars (stars who were more open to sharing information and helping others) create more value for the organization than their less helpful peers. Future research could explore how relational stars are rewarded and their turnover levels to try to understand how organizations might more effectively reward and retain relational stars.

Next, it would be interesting to explore how the incessant overload of stars impacts various aspects of their performance. Does overload cause a decrease generally across all aspects of performance, or does it limit only certain kinds of performance? We posit that status will likely be unaffected by overload, but these differences could be fruitfully examined in future empirical research. As a result, future research could examine other factors that may help to separate the star's more generally applicable human capital from their other sources of value that are likely linked to the organization itself, and not the star.

The research we review is primarily limited to performance, firm status, and industry tenure. There are, however, more areas that could be considered, such as social network, trust, or intellectual capacity. Future research could examine the other factors that may help to separate the star's human capital from the sources that are linked to the organization. Moreover, future research could examine specific economic and emotional reasons that affect the star employee's decision to move to another organization that are above and beyond how much value they are capturing and their decision-making rights.

Conclusion

In sum, this chapter explores how to effectively manage star employees. Proposed management ideas explore how to ensure that the stars' work performance does not decrease or that their turnover does not increase. We also propose a framework to help managers know how to work with their emerging star employees so that they stay within the firm. In essence, we explore how key talent management strategies targeted at the individual competencies, organizational processes, and network-wide conditions may help to mitigate the detrimental effects of star overload, along with how the tenure and human capital status of a star and the incumbent firm can affect the value and movement of the star.

Note

1 These strategies at the individual level mirror the efforts of firms. Typically, organizations engage in two strategies to cope with uncertainty and increased information needs. First, they implement structural mechanisms and information processing capability to limit the information flow and thereby reduce uncertainty, and second, they develop buffers to reduce the effect of uncertainty (Daft and Lengel, 1986). A classic example of the first strategy is the redesign of business processes in organizations and implementation of integrated IS that improve information flow and reduce uncertainty within organizational subunits. A similar strategy is creating better information flow between organizations to address the uncertainties in the supply chain. An example of the second strategy is building inventory buffers to reduce the effect of uncertainty in demand or supply; another example is adding extra safety buffers in product design due to in product working conditions.

References

Aguinis, H., & O'Boyle, E., 2014. Star performers in twenty-first century organizations. *Personnel Psychology,* 67(2), 313–350.

Aguinis, H., O'Boyle Jr, E., Gonzalez-Mulé, E., & Joo, H., 2016. Cumulative advantage: Conductors and insulators of heavy-tailed productivity distributions and productivity stars. *Personnel Psychology,* 69(1): 3–66.

Barney, J. B. 1991. Firm resources and sustained competitive advantage. *Journal of Management,* 17: 99–120.

Becker, B. E., & Huselid, M. A. 2006. Strategic human resource management: Where do we go from here? *Journal of Management,* 32(6): 898–925.

Becker, G. S. 1964. *Human capital: A theoretical and empirical analysis, with special reference to education.* Chicago: University of Chicago Press.

Berg, J. M., Grant, A. M., & Johnson, V. 2010. When callings are calling: Crafting work and leisure in pursuit of unanswered occupational callings. *Organization Science,* 21(5): 973–994.

Berman, S. L., Down, J., & Hill, C. W. L. 2002. Tacit knowledge as a source of competitive advantage in the national basketball association. *Academy of Management Journal,* 45(1): 13–31.

Boxall, P. 2013. Mutuality in the management of human resources: Assessing the quality of alignment in employment relationships. *Human Resource Management Journal,* 23(1), 3–17.

Brockbank, W., & Ulrich, D. 2005. Higher knowledge for higher aspirations. **Human Resource Management,** 44: 489–504. doi: 10.1002/hrm.20086

Call, M. L., Nyberg, A. J., & Thatcher, S., 2015. Stargazing: An integrative conceptual review, theoretical reconciliation, and extension for star employee research. *Journal of Applied Psychology,* 100(3), p.623.

Campbell, B. A., Ganco, M., Franco, A. M., & Agarwal, R. 2012. Who leaves, where to, and why worry? Employee mobility, entrepreneurship and effects on source firm performance. **Strategic Management Journal,** 33(1), 65–87.

Carpenter, M. A., & Fredrickson, J. W. 2001. Top management teams, global strategic posture, and the moderating role of uncertainty. *Academy of Management Journal,* 44(3): 533–545.

Chadwick, C. A., & Dabu, A. 2009. Human resources, human resource management, and the competitive advantage of firms: Toward a more comprehensive model of causal linkages. **Organization Science** 20(1), 253–272.

Chen, J. S., & Garg, P., 2018. Dancing with the stars: Benefits of a star employee's temporary absence for organizational performance. **Strategic Management Journal,** 39(5): 1239–1267.

Collings, D. G. (2014). Toward mature talent management: Beyond shareholder value. **Human Resource Development Quarterly,** 25(3): 301–319.

Collings, D. G. (2017). Workforce differentiation. In D. Collings, Mellahi & Cascio (Eds.), **The Oxford handbook of talent management.** Oxford, UK: Oxford University Press.

Cummings, J. N., & Cross, R. 2003. Structural properties of work groups and their consequences for performance. **Social Networks,** 25(3): 197–210.

Cutrell, E., Czerwinski, M., & Horvitz, E. 2001. **Notification, disruption, and memory: Effects of messaging interruptions on memory and performance.** Proceedings of Interact 2001: IFIP Conference on Human-Computer Interaction, Tokyo, Japan.

Daft, R. L., & Huber, G. P. 1987. How organizations learn: A communication framework, **Research in the Sociology of Organizations,** 5: 1–36.

Eccles, R. F., & Crane, D. B. 1988. **Doing deals.** Boston, MA: Harvard Business School Press.

Emerson, R. M. 1962. Power-dependence relations. **American Sociological Review,** 27(1): 31–41.

Eppler, M. J., & Mengis, J. 2004. The concept of information overload: A review of literature from organization science, accounting, marketing, MIS, and related disciplines. **The Information Society,** 20(5): 325–344.

Ernst, H., Leptein, C., & Vitt, J. 2000. Inventors are not alike: The distribution of patenting output among industrial R&D personnel. **IEEE Transactions on Engineering Management,** 47(2): 184–199.

Felin, T., W. S. Hesterly. 2007. The knowledge-based view, nested heterogeneity, and new value creation: Philosophical considerations on the locus of knowledge. **Academy of Management Review,** 32(1) 195–218.

Ganco, M., Ziedonis, R. H., & Agarwal, R., 2015. More stars stay, but the brightest ones still leave: Job hopping in the shadow of patent enforcement. **Strategic Management Journal,** 36(5): 659–685.

Gardner, T. M. 2005. Interfirm competition for human resources: Evidence from the software industry. *Academy of Management Journal,* 48(2): 237–256.

Greenwood, R., Hinings, C. R., & Brown, J. 1990. P²-form strategic management: Corporate practices in professional partnerships. *Academy of Management Journal,* 33(4): 722–755.

Greenwood, R., Li, S. X., Prakash, R., Deephouse, D. L. 2005. Reputation, diversification, and organizational explanations of performance in professional service firms. **Organization Science,** 16: 661–673.

Greenwood, R., Oliver, C., Sahlin, K., & Suddaby, R. 2008. **Sage handbook of organizational institutionalism.** London, UK: Sage.

Grigoriou, K., & Rothaermel, F. T., 2017. Organizing for knowledge generation: Internal knowledge networks and the contingent effect of external knowledge sourcing. **Strategic Management Journal,** 38(2): 395–414.

Grossman, S. J., & Hart. O. D. 1986. The costs and benefits of ownership: A theory of vertical and lateral integration. *Journal of Political Economy,* 96(4) 691–719.

Groysberg, B. 2010. **Chasing stars: The myth of talent and the portability of performance.** Princeton, NJ: Princeton University Press.

Groysberg, B., & Lee, L. E. 2008. The effect of colleague quality on top performance: The case of security analysts. *Journal of Organizational Behavior,* 29(8): 1123–1144.

Groysberg, B., Lee, L. E., & Nanda, A. 2008. Can they take it with them? The portability of star knowledge workers' performance. **Management Science,** 54(7): 1213–1230.

Hall, S. 1992. How technique is changing science. **Science,** 257: 344–349.

Hallowell, E. M. 2005. Overloaded circuits: Why smart people underperform. **Harvard Business Review,** 83(1): 1–9.

Hallowell, E. M. 2011. **Shine: Using brain science to get the best from your people.** Boston: Harvard Business Review Press.

Hausknecht, J. P., Rodda, J., & Howard, M. J. 2009. Targeted employee retention: Performance-based and job-related differences in reported reasons for staying. **Human Resource Management,** 48: 269–288.

Hwang, Y., Kettinger, W. J., & Yi, M. Y. 2010. Understanding information behavior and the relationship to job performance. *Communications of the Association for Information Systems,* 27(8).

Insead, L. C., & Chatain, O., 2008. Competitors' resource-oriented strategies: Acting on competitors' resources through interventions in factor markets and political markets. *Academy of Management Review,* 33(1): 97–121.

Itami, H. 1987. *Mobilizing invisible assets.* Cambridge, MA: Harvard University Press.

Jacoby, J. 1977. Information load and decision quality: Some contested issues. *Journal of Marketing Research,* 14(4): 569–573.

Jensen, M. C., & Heckling, W. H. 1995. Specific and general knowledge, and organizational structure. *Journal of Applied Corporate Finance,* 8(2): 4–18.

Jeong, H., Tombor, B., Albert, R., Oltvai, Z. N., & Barabasi, A.L., 2000. The large scale organization of metabolic networks. *Nature,* 47: 651–654.

Jett, Q. R., & George, J.M. 2003. Work interrupted: A closer look at the role of interruptions in organizational life. *Academy of Management Review,* 28(3): 494–507.

Kalyuga, S., Ayres, P., Chandler, P., & Sweller, J. 2003. The expertise reversal effect. *Educational Psychologist,* 38(1): 23–31.

Kanfer, R., & Ackerman, P. L. 1989. Motivation and cognitive abilities: An integrative/aptitude-treatment interaction approach to skill acquisition. *Journal of Applied Psychology,* 74(4): 657–690.

Kang, S. C., Morris, S. S., & Snell S. A. 2007. Relational archetypes, organizational learning, and value creation: Extending the human resource architecture. *Academy of Management Review,* 32(1): 236–256.

Kang, S. C., Oldroyd, J. B., Morris, S.S., & Kim, J. 2017. Reading the stars: Determining human capital's value in the hiring process. *Human Resource Management,* 57(1): 55–64.

Kehoe, R. R., Lepak, D. P., & Bentley, F. S. 2016. Let's call a star a star. *Journal of Management,* 2. doi: doi. org/10.1177/0149206316628644

Kelley, R., & Caplan, J. 1993. How Bell Labs creates star performers. *Harvard Business Review,* 71(4): 128–139.

Kirmeyer, S. L.1998. Coping with competing demands: Interruption with the type-A pattern. *Journal of Applied Psychology,* 73(4): 621–629.

Kostova, T., & Roth, K. 2003. Social capital in multinational corporations and a micro-macro model of its formation. *Academy of Management Review,* 28: 297–317.

Lakoff, G. 1987. *Fire, women, and dangerous things.* Chicago, IL: University of Chicago Press.

Lazear, E. P. 1986. Raids and offer matching. *Research in Labor Economics,* 8: 141–165.

Lechner, C., Frankenberger, K., & Floyd, S.W. 2010. Task contingencies in the curvilinear relationships between intergroup networks and initiative performance. *Academy of Management Journal,* 53(4): 865–889.

LePine, J. A., Colquitt, J. A., & Erez, A. 2000. Adaptability to changing task contexts: Effects of general cognitive ability, conscientiousness, and openness to experience. *Personnel Psychology,* 53(3): 563–593.

Locke, E. A. 1965. The relationship of task success to task liking and satisfaction. *Journal of Applied Psychology,* 49: 379–385.

Marx, M., Strumsky, D., & Fleming, L. 2009. Mobility, skills, and the Michigan non-compete experiment. *Management Science,* 55(6): 875–889.

McGregor, J. 2010. How to keep your star employees. *Fortune,* October 27.

Miller, G. A. 1956. The magical number seven, plus or minus two: Some limits on our capacity for processing information. *Psychological Review,* 63:81–91.

Minsky, M. A. 1975. *A framework for the representation of knowledge. The psychology of computer vision.* New York: McGraw-Hill.

Morris, S., Alvarez, S. A., & Barney, J. 2018. Dancing with the stars: The practical value of theory in managing star employees. *Academy of Management Perspectives,* 11. doi: doi.org/10.5465/amp.2017.0223

Morris, S., Alvarez, S., Barney, J., & Molloy, J. 2010. *Employee investments in firm-specific human capital and firm level competitive advantage.* Working manuscript.

Morris, S. S., Alvarez, S. A., Barney, J. B., & Molloy, J. C. 2017. Firm-specific human capital investments as a signal of general value: Revisiting assumptions about human capital and how it is managed. *Strategic Management Journal,* 38(4): 912–919.

Morris, S. & Oldroyd, J. 2009. To boost knowledge transfer, tell me a story. *Harvard Business Review,* 5: 23.

Morris, S., & Snell, S. 2011. Intellectual capital configurations and organizational capability: An empirical examination of human resource subunits in the multinational enterprise. *Journal of International Business Studies,* 42: 805–827.

Morris, S., Wright, P., Trevor, J., Stiles, P., Stahl, G., Snell, S., Paauwe, J., & Farndale, E. 2009. Global challenges to replicating HR: The role of people, processes, and systems. *Human Resource Management,* 48(6): 973–995.

Nahapiet, J., & Ghoshal, S. 1998. Social capital, intellectual capital, and the organizational advantage. *Academy of Management Review,* 23(2): 242–266.

Narin, F., & Breitzman, A. 1995. Inventive productivity. *Research Policy,* 24: 507–519.

Newman, M. E. J. 2002. Assortative mixing in networks. *Physical Review Letters,* 89(20): art no. 208701.

Newman, M. E. J., & Park, J. 2003. Why social networks are different from other types of networks. *Physical Review Letters,* 68, art no. 036122.

Noe, R. A. 1988. An investigation of the determinants of successful assigned mentoring relationships. *Personnel Psychology,* 41(3): 457–479.

O'Boyle, E. (2017). Star employees. In D. G. Collings, K. Mellahi, & W. F. Cascio (Eds.), *Oxford handbook of talent management.* Oxford, UK: Oxford University Press.

Oldham, G. T., Kulik, C. T., & Stepina, L. P. 1991. Physical environments and employee reactions: Effects of stimulus-screening skills and job complexity. *Academy of Management Journal,* 34(4): 929–938.

Oldroyd, J. B., & Morris, S.S., 2012. Catching falling stars: A human resource response to social capital's detrimental effect of information overload on star employees. *Academy of Management Review,* 37(3): 396–418.

Oskamp, S. 1965.Overconfidence in case-study judgments. *Journal of Consulting Psychology,* 29(3): 261–265.

Park, H. D., Howard, M.D., & Gomulya, D. M., 2018. The impact of knowledge worker mobility through an acquisition on breakthrough knowledge. *Journal of Management Studies,* 55(1): 86–107.

Perlow, L. A. 1999. The time famine: Toward a sociology of work time. *Administrative Science Quarterly,* 44(1): 57–81.

Perrow, C. 1999. Organizing to reduce the vulnerabilities of complexity. *Journal of Contingencies and Crisis Management,* 7(3): 150–155.

Phillips-Jones, L. 1983. Establishing a formalized mentoring program. *Training & Development Journal,* 37(2): 38–42.

Ployhart, R. E., Call, M. L., & McFarland, L. A., 2017. Autonomous learning, human capital resources, and value capture. *Autonomous Learning in the Workplace:* 287–304.

Ployhart, R. E., & Moliterno, T. P. 2011. Emergence of the human capital resource: A multilevel model. *Academy of Management Review,* 36(1): 127–150.

Podolny, J. M., & Baron, J. N. 1997. Resources and relationships: Social networks and mobility in the workplace. *American Sociological Review,* 62(5): 673–693.

Rasiel, E. M., & Friga, P. N. 2002. *The McKinsey mind: Understanding and implementing the problem-solving tools and management techniques of the world's top strategic consulting firm.* New York: McGraw-Hill.

Ready, D., Conger, J., Hill, L., & Stecker, E., 2010. The anatomy of a high potential. *Business Strategy Review,* 21(3): 52–55.

Rudolph, J. W., & Repenning, N. P. 2002. Disaster dynamics: Understanding the role of quantity in organizational collapse. *Administrative Science Quarterly,* 47(1): 1–30.

Rumelhart, D. E. 1975. Notes on a schema for stories. In D. G. Bobrow & A. Collins (Eds.), *Representation and understanding: Studies in cognitive science.* New York: Academic Press.

Sackett, P. R., Gruys, M. L., & Ellingson, J. E. 1998. Ability-personality interactions when predicting job performance. *Journal of Applied Psychology,* 83(4): 545–556.

Schank, R. C., & Abelson, R. P. 1977 *Scripts, plans, goals, and understanding.* Hillsdale, NJ: Lawrence Erlbaum Associates.

Schick, A. G., Gorden, L. A., & Haka, S. 1990. Information overload: A temporal approach. *Accounting, Organizations, and Society,* 15: 199–220.

Schwab, D. P. 1991. Contextual variables in employee performance-turnover relationships. *Academy of Management Journal,* 34(4): 966–975.

Seibert, S. E., Kraimer, M. L., & Liden, R.C. 2001. A social capital theory of career success. *Academy of Management Journal,* 44(2): 219–237.

Shaw, J. D., Duffy, M. K., Johnson, J. L., & Lockhart, D. E. 2005. Turnover, social capital losses, and performance. *Academy of Management Journal,* 48(4): 594–606.

Shumsky, R. A., & Pinker, E. J. 2003. Gatekeepers and referrals in services. *Management Science,* 49(7): 839–856.

Smith, P. K., Jostmann, N. B., Galinsky, A. D., & Van Dijk, W. W. 2008. Lacking power impairs executive functions. *Psychological Science,* 19: 351–398.

Snell, S. A., Youndt, M. A., & Wright, P. M. 1996. Establishing a framework for research in strategic human resource management: Merging resource theory and organizational learning. *Human Resource Management,* 14: 61–90.

Spence, M. 1973. Job market signaling. *Quarterly Journal of Economics,* 87(3): 355–374.

Sproull, L., & Kiesler, S. 1991.Computers, networks, and work. *Scientific American,* 265: 116–123.

Sternberg, R. J. 1977. Component processes in analogical reasoning. *Psychological Review,* 84(4): 353–378.

Streufert, S. C. 1973. Effects of information relevance on decision making in complex environments. *Memory and Cognition,* 1(3): 224–228.

Subramaniam, M., & Youndt, M. A. 2005. The influence of intellectual capital on the types of innovative capabilities. *Academy of Management Journal,* 48(3): 450–463.

Sweller, J., van Merrienboer, J. J. G., & Paas, F. G. 1998. Cognitive architecture and instructional design. *Educational Psychology Review,* 10(3): 251–296.

Szulanski, G. 1996. Exploring internal stickiness: Impediments to the transfer of best practice within the firm. *Strategic Management Journal,* Winter Special Issue 17: 27–43.

Szulanksi, G. 2000. Appropriability and the challenge of scope. In G. Dosi, R. R. Nelson, S. G. Winter (Eds.). *The nature and dynamics of organizational capabilities:* 69–98. Oxford, UK: Oxford University Press.

Tang, F., Xi, Y., & Ma, J. 2006. Estimating the effect of organizational structural on knowledge transfer: A neural network approach. *Expert Systems with Applications,* 30: 796–800.

Thompson, J.D. 1967. *Organizations in action: Social science bases of administrative theory.* New York: McGraw-Hill.

Trevor, C. O., Hausknecht, J. P. & Howard. M. J. 2007. Why high and low performers leave and what they find elsewhere: Job performance effects on employment transitions. *CAHRS Working Paper Series,* WP07-11.

Tushman, M. L., & Scanlan, T. J. 1981. Boundary spanning individuals: Their role in information transfer and their antecedents. *Academy of Management Journal,* 24(2): 289–305.

Tzabbar, D., & Kehoe, R. R. 2014. Can opportunity emerge from disarray? An examination of exploration and exploitation following star scientist turnover. *Journal of Management,* 40(2): 449–482.

Walsh, J. P., & Ellwood, J. W. (1991). Mergers, acquisitions, and the pruning of managerial deadwood. *Strategic Management Journal,* 12: 201–217.

Walsh, J. P., & Ungson, G. R. 1991. Organizational memory. *Academy of Management Review,* 16(1): 57–91.

Wegner, D. M. 1986. Transactive memory: A contemporary analysis of the group mind. In B. Mullen & G. R. Goethals (Eds.), *Theories of group behavior:* 185–205. New York: Springer–Verlag.

Williamson, O. E. 1975. *Markets and hierarchies: Analysis and antitrust implications.* New York: Free Press.

Witt, L. A., & Burke, L. A. 2002. Moderators of the openness to experience-performance relationship. *Journal of Managerial Psychology,* 17(8): 712–721.

Wright, P. M., & McMahan, G. C. 1992. Theoretical perspectives for strategic human resource management. *Journal of Management,* 18(2): 295–320.

Zucker, L. G., Darby, M. R., & Armstrong, J. 1998. Geographically localized knowledge: Spillovers or markets? *Economic Inquiry,* 26: 65–86.

32

WHEN RISING STARS FALTER

High Potential Status as an Impediment to Learning from Failure

Len Karakowsky

Igor Kotlyar

Introduction

Madsen and Desai (2010) defined organizational learning as any modification to an organization's knowledge and performance that occurs as a consequence of experience. Learning from experience is critical since changes in an organization's knowledge drive observable changes in performance (Argote & Miron-Spektor, 2011; Madsen & Desai, 2010; Musaji, Schulze, & De Castro, 2020; Richter & Semrau, 2019). The extant literature has identified three criteria that must be fulfilled for organizational experience to enhance observed organizational performance: 1) such experience must motivate organization members to modify the organization's knowledge; 2) members need to derive meaningful new knowledge from experience; and 3) changes made to organizational knowledge must change the subsequent behavior of members.

This chapter focuses largely on the second condition. That is, we are interested in understanding factors that can influence an organization member's ability to derive new knowledge from experience. Specifically, we consider how the receipt of status-based labels can influence the recipient's capacity to learn from a failure experience.

What constitutes a failure experience? For decision makers to consider any performance to be a success, it must exceed a target aspiration level (i.e., the lowest level of performance that the decision maker deems acceptable) (Greve, 2003). Performance that falls below the target level is deemed a failure (Cyert & March, 1963; March & Simon, 1958). Given that organization members do not always attain target aspiration levels, learning from a failure experience is critically important for the organization's long-term well-being (Morris & Moore, 2000). While failure is naturally considered to be risky and potentially detrimental, it has also been recognized that failure brings with it an opportunity to learn by adapting based on past errors of self or others (e.g., Bolinger & Brown, 2015; Simpson & Maltese, 2017). In fact, many scholars as well as practitioners have drawn attention to the need to accommodate failure as a means for promoting creativity and innovation (Maltese, Simpson, & Anderson, 2018; Wagner, 2012).

To learn from failure, decision makers must engage in *mindful reflection* involving complex thought processes (Langer, 1989; Morris & Moore, 2000; Weick & Roberts, 1993). It is through such processes that failure can motivate organization members to rectify mistakes, challenge inaccurate assumptions, and innovate (Sitkin, 1992). However, recent observations have questioned that capacity of organization members to adeptly learn from failure. In her article for *Harvard Business Review*, management scholar Amy Edmondson astutely observed that, "The wisdom of learning from failure is incontrovertible. Yet organizations that do it well are extraordinarily rare" (2011: 49). Consistent with Madsen and Desai's (2010) assertion, to assist organizations in benefitting from a failure experience, there is a need for greater research inquiry into factors that can influence the process of learning from such experiences.

DOI: 10.4324/9781315474687-32

The focus of this chapter is on how organizationally-assigned status labels, such as the *high-potential* label, can impede the capacity to learn from failure.

Status-based labels are ubiquitous in organizations. *Status characteristics theory* (or *expectation states theory*) (Berger et al., 1972) asserts that status is accorded to an individual based on others' assessments of the individual's expected performance on the task at hand. Status differences may also be accentuated via the tendency to categorize individuals based on membership in salient social categories (Tajfel, 1981; Turner et al., 1987) and consequently arises in such contexts as *high-potential employee* practices.

High-potential employee practices have arisen via strategic talent management efforts to identify, develop, and retain the best employees (Silzer & Dowell, 2009). Specifically, the label of *high-potential* refers to those employees who are seen as possessing the talents and abilities necessary for advancement in the organization (Cappelli, 2008a, 2008b; Collings & Mellahi, 2009; Slan-Jerusalim & Hausdorf, 2007). In other words, such individuals are perceived to possess the capacity to rise to leadership positions in the organization given their demonstrated potential to lead (e.g., Wade et al., 2006).

The practice of labeling employees as high status/high-potential creates differentiated expectations of capability and future performance. A central element of high-potential practices is the designation of and subsequent focus on those employees who demonstrate the highest potential to succeed in leadership/strategic positions in the organization in the future (Finkelstein, Costanza, & Goodwin, 2018). Therefore, while the term *high-potential employee* is derived form a formal organizational practice, it is connected in meaning to the term *star* or *rising star,* given that scholars such as Long, Baer, Colquitt, Outlaw, & Dhensa-Kahlon have defined a *star* as a "a top performer who seems to be on *the fast track* in the organization and is expected to make a clear contribution to the firm" (2015: 465).

Given the above observations, high-potential employees can be viewed as *rising stars*. That is, such individuals have attained a label based on expectations of future performance and capability. Of course, such individuals have yet to entirely *prove themselves* and thereby attain tangible *stardom*. These rising stars/high-potentials are afforded such status labels given perceptions that they are "able and willing, and likely to ascend the corporate ladder" (Iles, 1997: 347). Consequently, the high-potential designation can impact recipients' attitudes and behaviors (e.g., Mueller & Dweck, 1998).

The literature has found intuitive appeal in the assertion that high status labels, together with the opportunities they afford, can act as cues to boost the recipient's self-efficacy and thereby boost performance (e.g., Tierney & Farmer, 2003). The literature has typically underscored the benefits that high-potential labels garner for the recipients (e.g., Graffin et al., 2008; Magee & Galinsky, 2008; Malmendier & Tate, 2009). For example, according to the research, individuals who are conferred with a high-potential label receive greater social support, such as the allocation of a mentor and the opportunity to acquire more enriching or challenging work assignments compared to their counterparts who have not received such labels (Magee & Galinsky, 2008; Podolny & Phillips, 1996; Van Der Vegt, Bunderson, & Oosterhof, 2006).

While the research cited above lauds high-potential labels as a boost to the recipients' efficacy and performance, the research has not fully explored the impact of high-potential labels in the context of failure experiences. That is, while we know that high-potential status affords opportunities for advancement along with elevated expectations for success, we don't fully understand what happens when recipients of such labels fail to meet expectations associated with those labels.

In their report for *Harvard Business Review*, Martin and Schmidt noted that "nearly 40% of internal job moves made by people identified by their companies as '*high potential*' end in failure" (2010: 56). Similarly, Ready, Conger, and Hill observed that, while the conferral of high potential presents opportunities for advancement, it can also generate challenges for the recipient:

> It's great to be recognized for what you can do and how you might contribute to your company's future, but *high-potential* status comes at a price. For starters, there's no tenure. People can – and do – fall off the list, and some remove themselves voluntarily or by default... [R]emaining a *high potential* is not guaranteed, and we found that anywhere from 5% to 20% drop off the rolls each year, whether by choice or not. Among the reasons for losing a spot on

the *high-potential* list are making a poor transition into a new role, diminished performance two years in a row, behavior that's out of line with the company's culture and values, and a significant visible failure. (2010: 84)

Dries and deGrieter (2014) suggested that the literature needs to more fully address the psychological dynamics of high-potential programs to better assess their utility. There is little doubt that a better understanding of the experiences of high-potential employees is required if improvements are to be made. Unfortunately, there have been no systematic efforts to examine the experiences of high-potential employees, and little is known regarding the psychological impact of receiving high-potential status (Björkman, Ehrnrooth, Mäkelä, Smale, & Sumelius, 2013; Dries, Forrier, De Vos, & Pepermans, 2014; Dries & Pepermans, 2008).

The broad aim of this chapter is to offer conceptual insight into important implications of the use of such high-status labels in the workplace. Specifically, we draw upon extant theory and research to reflect upon the double-edged sword of high employee status in the realm of learning from an experience of failure. Our paper addresses the question: How might the receipt of a high-status label impact the recipients who subsequently fail to achieve levels of performance congruent with such high-status labels?

Consider the following example. Imagine a new sales associate who has been viewed as a high potential. That individual is perceived as someone who will likely generate high-performance and demonstrate leadership potential. However, if that individual's performance does not meet initial expectations, we can consider this to be a failure experience. Failure to "live up" to expectations can be viewed as a form of negative feedback regarding an organization member's efforts (Shepherd, Patzelt, & Wolfe, 2011).

According to the extant research, individuals who respond constructively to failure are encouraged to search for solutions or improvements (Lench & Levine, 2008; McGrath, 2001). That is, when individuals are confronted by unexpected or repeated negative feedback that current behaviors are not successful, strategies are changed to adapt performance to the feedback (Lench & Levine, 2008; Petrovski, 1985). In this regard, failure feedback can offer an important learning experience for the individual (Shepherd, Patzelt, Holger, & Wolfe, 2011; Sitkin, 1992) because the acquisition of knowledge and skills from the failure experience can be applied in future efforts (Shepherd et al., 2011; Spreitzer, Sutcliffe, Dutton, Sonenshein, & Grant, 2005). However, for an individual's failure experience to transfer to actionable knowledge, the information must be effectively processed (Weick, 1990; Sutcliffe & Weick, 2007).

In the sections that follow, we explore how the receipt of a high-status label (i.e., the high-potential label) can undermine the capacity to learn from a failure experience. It is our view that the possession of such high-status labels can impede the recipient's ability to effectively cope with and respond to experiences of performance failure in the workplace. Below, we present a conceptual framework that identifies the challenges a high-potential label can present to those recipients who have failed to meet expectations associated with such labels. After briefly introducing our framework, the remainder of this chapter will discuss the elements of the framework in detail and their relationships.

High Status and the Challenge of Learning from Failure: A Conceptual Framework

Our conceptual framework (Figure 32.1) draws attention to the challenges faced by high-potential employees who are confronted with a failure experience at work. The model illustrates how such high-status labels can generate impediments to productive coping with a failure experience and hence impede learning from failure. As we will explain in detail below, our model possesses two central elements: 1) the cognitive implications of receiving a high-potential label; and 2) the cognitive implications of failure for a high-potential individual.

The capacity of a high-potential label to interfere with a constructive response to failure stems from the influence of such a label on the cognitions of the recipient. Perceptions of *visibility* or *scrutiny* combined with *status-loss apprehension* contribute to a dysfunctional strategy for coping with failure. We will explain how the choice of coping strategy, together with a pattern of ego-defensiveness,

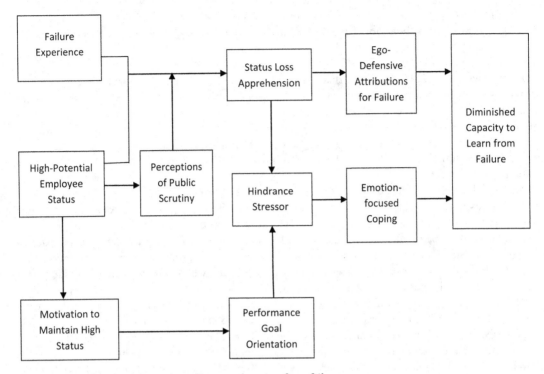

Figure 32.1   High potential as an impediment to learning from failure

will undermine the high-potential employee's capacity to learn from failure. All these elements are examined in detail in the sections that follow.

The High Potential Label and Status Loss Apprehension

The notion that high status affords individuals the capacity to freely confront the risk involved in work endeavors is premised on the assumption that such individuals will not jeopardize their status in the event that such efforts fail. That is, much of the extent research has assumed that high status is irrevocable or immutable. Based on that assumption, individuals possessing high status harbor no fear of status loss as a result of failed efforts. Consistent with this rationale, conferring high status on a business executive will allegedly attenuate the negative effects of any public scrutiny or criticism. Such individuals, free of external evaluation concerns, will largely be driven by the intrinsic rewards associated with creative efforts (c.f., Phillips & Zuckerman, 2001). However, all these benefits of high status exist only under conditions of status stability (i.e., when the individual's high status is immutable). This begs the question: How stable are status hierarchies?

Status hierarchies are stable when perceptions of high–status individuals are enduring (Humphrey, 1985), and low status individuals internalize their positions and believe them to be appropriate (Jost & Banaji, 1994). However, not all status hierarchies are stable. Status loss is a common experience in organizations (Neeley, 2013) and is reflected in such activities as being demoted or being denied an expected promotion or salary increase (Marr & Thau, 2014). Marr and Thau asserted that, "Status loss is not restricted to those struggling at the bottom of a hierarchy. People at the top (e.g., a highly ranked fund manager, a star analyst, or an award-winning director) can also experience status loss" (2014: 223). That is, even those labeled as high status, are not immune from status loss should they fail to meet expectations (Groysberg, Polzer, & Elfenbein, 2011; Willer, 2009). Given this risk of status loss, individuals are willing to expend considerable effort to maintain their status (Auriol & Renault, 2008; Bendersky & Hays, 2012; Bendersky & Shah, 2012; Pettit, Yong, & Spataro, 2010).

The critical importance of protecting one's status is due to the close connection between an individual's status and their social identity. Social identity theory posits that an individual makes sense of who they are based on where they see themselves within a social hierarchy (Tajfel, 1979). For example, the high-potential designation can be considered as a status cue, an individuating attribute that sets an individual apart in terms of levels of social esteem and valuation (Deephouse & Suchman, 2008). An individual will be assigned high status only to the extent that others are willing to confer it (Blader & Chen, 2011; Fragale, Overbeck, & Neale, 2011). Consequently, whether status is gained or lost depends on how well one manages others' perceptions of one's competence (Anderson, Brion, Moore, & Kennedy, 2012; Bendersky & Shah, 2012; Cheng, Tracy, Foulsham, Kingstone, & Henrich, 2013).

According to Hogg, the motivation to maintain a positive social identity may reflect one of the "most basic human motives" (2006: 120). The notion of self-enhancement, according to Pfeffer and Fong, reflects the tendency of an individual to "selectively perceive or construe ambiguous information in a manner that makes the individual appear more accomplished, successful, and capable" (2005: 374). According to self-enhancement theory (Swann, Griffin, Predmore, & Gaines, 1987; Swann, Pelham, & Krull, 1989), individuals will react most favorably to performance feedback that enhances their self-image. Discrepancies between expectations and outcomes create psychological discomfort that individuals seek to reduce (Swann et al., 1987; Swann, Pelham et al., 1989). These patterns should particularly apply to high-potential individuals whose status has been made salient.

As indicated above, those identified as high-potential employees are aware of the status label that has been conferred upon them. Moreover, this status cue is integrated into the implicit assumptions high-potential employees harbor regarding their relationship with their employer (Suazo et al., 2009). Because high-potential individuals are viewed as competent performers, they are expected to demonstrate strong levels of performance (e.g., Haines & Jost, 2000; Sande, Ellard, & Ross, 1986; Sutton & Hargadon, 1996). High-status individuals are more dependent on their status to maintain a positive self-view, compared to lower-status individuals who do not place as much emphasis on their status label (Marr & Thau, 2014). Similarly, Tajfel and Turner (1986) asserted that individuals are more likely to incorporate their higher-status memberships into their self-concept rather than their lower-status memberships.

As Marr and Thau (2014) posited, high-status individuals, by perceiving their high status as a central component of their self, will boost their self-worth. Given that high-status individuals are more concerned with maintaining their status in their group (Blader & Chen, 2011), such individuals can experience self-threat when a central aspect of their self-identity is challenged (Baumeister, Smart, & Boden, 1996; Campbell & Sedikides, 1999). The possibility of losing status presents a greater self-threat to high status as opposed to low status individuals (Marr & Thau, 2014). Added to the elevated status loss concerns is the salience of public visibility associated with the high-potential label. This is consistent with the observation of Call, Nyberg, & Thatcher that, "Organizations often highlight top performers, but some top performers may prefer to avoid the scrutiny and expectations that accompany public attention" (2015: 629).

Given the research cited above, there are two fundamental challenges that arise as a consequence of being labeled a *high-potential*. First, the high-potential label can serve as a status cue that primes the recipient to expect performance feedback that enhances their self-image. Because status loss presents a greater self-threat to high-status individuals (Blader & Chen, 2011; Marr & Thau, 2014), a failure experience can be extremely unsettling for a high-potential employee who must confront an event that is starkly incongruent with their enhanced self-image. This is reflected in the following proposition.

Proposition 1: *Failure experienced by high-potential employees will trigger higher levels of status loss apprehension compared to a failure experienced by those not labeled as high-potential.*

The High-Potential Label and Public Scrutiny

As suggested above, the public nature of a high-potential label can thrust the recipient into the spotlight, making their presence, behavior, and performance much more visible, compared to life before this status conferral. Consequently, high-potential labels can represent a double-edged sword to the recipients. The

Tall Poppy Syndrome (Feather, 1998) asserts that individuals who achieve *conspicuous success* become highly visible to others because of their social status (referred to as *Tall Poppies*). This is consistent with research that has suggested that perceptions of public visibility or scrutiny are higher for individuals who possess some kind of distinction in the workplace (Fragale et al., 2009; Giordano, 1983; Graffin et al., 2013; Rhee & Haunschild, 2006). For example, Wade et al. (2006) found that high-status CEOs were subject to higher pay-performance sensitivities. That is, in comparison to lower status CEOs, star CEOs were paid more when their firms performed well but were paid less when their firm's performance was poor (Wade et al., 2006).

Consistent with the notion of the *Tall Poppy*, the high-potential label can arouse perceptions of public visibility or scrutiny. Organizations can formally communicate to those who have been identified as high-potential to encourage those individuals to take advantage of the special opportunities for advancement (Ready, Conger, Hill & Stecker, 2010). Such information can also be provided in an informal, discrete manner (Bournois & Roussillon, 1992; Dries & Pepermans, 2008; Silzer & Church, 2010). Even when communication isn't direct, employees are typically aware of the high-potential employee practice (Bournois & Roussillon, 1992), and identification of high-potential employees is often communicated (intentionally or unintentionally) through such channels as performance reviews, compensation and benefits decisions, and procedural changes (Dries & De Gieter, 2014). In addition, individuals can usually surmise who is included in the list of high-potentials based on "the type of assignments people receive, who they have lunch with, who sponsors or mentors them, and their visibility in the organization" (Derr, Jones & Toomey, 1988: 276).

Given the observations above, it is quite common for the entire organization to be aware of who has been conferred with the high-potential label. A number of research scholars have observed that employees who become *rising stars* (i.e., are afforded a high-status label) in their workplace tend to garner increased visibility, which is accompanied by further scrutiny as well as potential envy (Call et al., 2015; Lam et al., 2011; Fragale, Rosen, Xu, & Merideth, 2009). Therefore, it can be asserted that the high-potential label has the capacity to increase the visibility under which a high-potential employee performs. Such visibility can serve to make failure more salient.

On the other hand, individuals whose status is less conspicuous (i.e., those who do not possess the high-potential label) do not face this same degree of public scrutiny. Failing is much more threatening when it is experienced *in front of a crowd* rather as *part of the crowd*. Consequently, the high potential-label brings with it a higher level of perceived visibility that will accentuate any feelings of status loss threat that can arise following a failure experience. Taken together, high-potential employees can suffer from a greater concern for status loss which is made more salient by the sense of public scrutiny associated with the high-potential or high-status label. This is reflected in the following proposition.

Proposition 2: *Perceived visibility associated with the high-potential label will accentuate the impact of a failure experience on status loss apprehension.*

The High-Potential Label, Goal Orientation, and Strategies for Coping with Failure

Individuals' goal orientation reflects their approach to regulating attention and effort when undertaking, interpreting, and responding to achievement situations (DeShon & Gillespie, 2005). One such orientation is referred to as a *learning goal orientation*, which emphasizes the development of competence and task mastery, and nurtures intrinsic motivation in a task (Dweck, 1999). That is, an individual with a learning orientation will be more focused on the learning process rather than on the outcome (Dweck, 1986; Dweck & Elliott, 1983; VandeWalle, 1997). Such motivation prompts individuals to confront challenges and obstacles experienced in performance situations (Gong, Huang, & Farh, 2009; Hirst et al., 2009) and to persevere toward accomplishment (Amabile, 1996). Given that this orientation facilitates persistence in the face of obstacles (e.g., Cron, Slocum, VandeWalle, & Fu, 2005), it will motivate individuals to respond constructively to a failure experience. For individuals with a learning goal orientation, failing is not a threatening experience and is considered as an opportunity to learn and improve (Cron et al., 2005).

A second, type of orientation is referred to as *performance goal orientation*, which emphasizes the demonstration of competence to others (Elliot & McGregor, 2001). Under this orientation, individuals are typically motivated by extrinsic factors including rewards, acknowledgement, or avoiding criticism (VandeWalle, 1997). Such an orientation exists where individuals are motivated to pursue favorable competence evaluations (VandeWalle, Brown, Cron, & Slocum, 2001). Given that individuals with a high-performance goal orientation are preoccupied with demonstrating competence, they have less tolerance or interest in learning from failure (Janssen & Van Yperen, 2004). Moreover, such individuals consider failure as threatening since it can damage their reputation. Therefore, in contrast to a learning goal orientation, individuals who possess a performance goal orientation are not as equipped to deal constructively with failure.

According to the research, goal orientation can be triggered by the situation (Bouffard, Boisvert, Vezeau, & Larouche, 1995; Bunderson & Sutcliffe, 2003; Dweck & Leggett, 1988; Elliot & Church, 1997; Payne, Youngcourt, & Beaubien, 2007). Based on that view, arguably, the conferral of high-potential status can influence the type of goal orientation adopted by individuals. Those selected as high-potential employees clearly have a motivation to *prove* themselves in order to maintain their high status. Given that status loss presents a greater self-threat to high-status individuals (Blader & Chen, 2011), such individuals will be more concerned with *looking good* compared to their lower-status counterparts (Marr & Thau, 2014). This is consistent with the findings of Tzabbar (2009) and Kehoe and Tzabbar (2015) who observed that high-status individuals (referred to as *stars* in their research) often act in ways that seek to preserve their status or power.

When an individual's concern for *looking good* is made salient, they will more likely adopt a performance goal orientation rather than a learning goal orientation (Brett & VandeWalle, 1999; Vande-Walle, Brown, Cron, & Slocum, 1999; Seijts, Latham, Tasa, & Latham, 2004). Moreover, the type of goal-orientation adopted has consequences for how individuals perceive a failure experience – as a *threat to status* or as *an opportunity to learn*.

An individual's choice of coping strategy is dependent on factors that are unique to that person, such as their beliefs, values, and goals (Stein, Trabasso, Folkman, & Richards, 1997). When an individual appraises a situation to be threatening or challenging, the consequent stress requires a coping response (Folkman, Lazarus, Dunkel-Schetter, DeLongis, & Gruen, 1986; Latack, 1986; Lazarus & Folkman, 1984). The appraisal is based on individual perception of the stressful situation and the attribution of meaning accorded to it (Fugate, Kinicki, & Prussia, 2008; Lazarus & Folkman, 1984). Therefore an individual's beliefs, values, goals, and emotions can shape how the situation is perceived and thereby influence the coping strategy ultimately employed (Stein et al., 1997). The strategies employed can be *problem-focused* coping or *emotion-focused* coping (Lazarus & Folkman, 1984); both are based on perceptions of the type of stressor being faced.

Individuals engaging in problem-focused coping strategies perceive they have the capacity to alter their current situation and therefore adopt behaviors to deal with any threats (Boyd et al., 2009). Individuals who are able to adopt a constructive, *problem-focused* coping strategy typically view those threats as *challenge stressors*. Stressors are likely to be perceived as challenge stressors when the individual believes they possesses the necessary resources to positively respond to the stressor and thereby promote self-growth and achievement (Boyd et al., 2009).

On the other hand, *hindrance stressors* are perceived as less welcoming due to their threatening-nature and which result in constraints on personal growth and achievement (Binnewies & Wörnlein, 2011; LePine, Podsakoff, & LePine, 2005). When a threat is perceived as a hindrance stressor, an *emotion-focused* strategy is employed given the need to regulate emotional distress (Lazarus & Folkman, 1984). Such responses are characterized by escapist or avoidance-type behaviors (Lazarus & Folkman, 1984).

Empirical research has offered evidence that problem-focused coping strategies are much more productive than emotion-focused coping strategies for a range of consequences including job performance (Wright, 1990), psychological adjustment (Love & Irani, 2007), avoidance of burnout (Leiter, 1991; Semmer, 2003), and adjustment to new work environments (Feldman & Thomas, 1992; Stahl &

Caligiuri, 2005; Vanderwielen, 2001). Given the dysfunctional nature of emotion-focused coping strategies in comparison to problem-focused strategies, the question is: How might high-potential labels influence whether the recipient views failure as a hindrance stressor (emotion-focused coping) or a challenge stressor (problem-focused coping)?

As indicated above, individuals focused on a performance-goal orientation are more concerned with maintaining their *high status*. For those individuals, failure is viewed as a hindrance stressor rather than a challenge stressor. The consequent emotional coping mechanism interferes with the capacity to objectively assess how the failure occurred and how to productively respond. This suggests that salient, high-status labels can unwittingly encourage the recipients of those labels to fear failure as a threat rather than as an opportunity to learn and thereby to improve performance in the future. Such individuals are less likely to focus on learning from their mistakes since they are overly concerned with status loss. All these assertions are expressed in the following series of propositions.

Proposition 3. *High potential employees' concern for status maintenance encourages a performance goal orientation rather than a learning goal orientation.*

Proposition 4. *Given their focus on performance goal orientation, high-potential employees who experience failure will more likely perceive such failure as a hindrance stressor and therefore adopt an emotion-focused coping strategy.*

Proposition 5. *The adoption of an emotion-focused coping strategy impedes the capacity (of high-potential employees) to learn from their failure experience.*

The High-Potential Label and Ego-Based Attributions of Failure

As indicated above, the research has often pointed to the range of benefits associated with communicating high expectations to subordinates (e.g., Tierney & Farmer, 2003). The conferral of high status can positively influence self-expectations of success, self-efficacy, and performance (DeWall, Baumeister, Mead, & Vohs, 2011). All this suggests that the high-potential status label can prime recipients to expect success rather than failure following performance efforts. However, much less is known about the role that these expectations play following performance that does not "live up to" the expectations associated with the high-potential designation. That is: What impact does failure have on high-status individuals given their prior expectations of success?

Attribution theory and research (Kelley, 1967; Schroth & Shah, 2000; Weiner, 1972) suggest that when performance outcomes conflict with expected performance levels, individuals will generate a spontaneous causal analysis. According to attribution theory, individuals are motivated to evaluate a situation in order to understand why an outcome/event occurred (Kelley, 1967; Weiner, 1985). This practice stems from the need to maintain a sense of "cognitive mastery" over the environment (Kelley, 1967).

In addition, the tendency for individuals to attribute success to internal factors and failure to external factors has been explained through the concept of ego defensive or self-serving biases (e.g., Webster & Beehr, 2013). Egocentric attributions provide a means to increase or maintain self-esteem of the actor by permitting a person to take credit for success and avoid blame for failure (Heider, 1958). The ego-based origin of internal attributions of success and external attributions of failure has been supported in a number of research efforts that identified the protection of self-esteem as the source of such attributions (Blader & Bobocel, 2005; Frieze & Weiner, 1971; Webster & Beehr, 2013). This self-serving bias permits individuals to buffer themselves from the negative psychological impact that an unfavorable outcome may have on self-esteem (Blader & Bobocel, 2005; Schroth & Shah, 2000).

Bem (1972) and Miller and Ross (1975) argued that alternate explanations to egocentric attribution may also explain the differential attributions of success and failure. One major alternative discussed in the literature is based on the notion of expectations, that is, expectations regarding task performance, as the primary source for causal attributions. Research has found support for the view that behavior/

performance that is expected (i.e., consistent with beliefs about the individual) will be attributed to stable internal factors (i.e., ability), while unexpected behavior/performance is attributed to unstable or external factors (e.g., Deaux, 1976; Feather, 1969; Frieze & Weiner, 1971).

Interestingly, Norvell and Forsyth (1984) found that, following failure feedback, subjects that perceived themselves as highly expert (high status) tended to generate more ego-based or self-serving attributions (Weiner, 1972). Consistent with this line of reasoning, for *high-potential* employees, their high-status label can trigger high ego-involvement in tasks that test their abilities to advance in the organization. This salient cue will trigger ego-based attributions for the cause of the failure. Such individuals will more likely attribute the source of failure to factors external to themselves.

As explained above, high-potential employees are more sensitive to the threat of status loss compared to their lower status counterparts. Threatened by the risk of failure, high-status individuals are motivated to reduce the cognitive strain caused by the failure experience. Consistent with the research cited earlier, a high-status individual will more likely deflect the source of failure to external sources in order to defend their esteem or ego. In other words, a failure experience will tend to trigger external causal attributions for high-potential individuals since they view themselves as highly expert. This external attribution allows such individuals to feel less responsible for the unsuccessful outcome.

What are the ramifications of high-status individuals deferring responsibility for failure to external causes? External attributions for failure suggest that the outcome was beyond the individual's control and consequently those attributions discourage the high-potential individual to learn from this failure (Shepherd, Patzelt, & Wolfe, 2011). Consequently, such thinking encourages a dysfunctional approach to coping with failure, deflecting it and shifting responsibility outside one's self.

Sometimes a failure experience may be the result of inexperience or the lack of requisite skills. If the individual attributes failure to external causes, then they overlook this deficiency and therefore avoid taking personal responsibility for the failure. The pattern of assigning personal failure to external (situational) causes (Wagner & Gooding, 1997) therefore can impede the capacity to learn from a failure experience. In line with these assertions, the following propositions can be generated.

Proposition 6: *Compared to their non-labeled counterparts, individuals labeled as high-potential will more likely engage in defensive attributions (external attribution; e.g., bad luck) following a failure experience.*

Proposition 7: *External attributions for failure reduce the capacity to learn from a failure experience.*

Directions for Future Research

The popularity of high-potential practices reflects the increasing pressure for organizations to build long-term competitive advantage (Cappelli, 2008; Ready, Conger, Hill, & Stecker, 2010). Unfortunately, though much investment is directed toward the development of high-potential employees, there is no firm evidence that high-potential employees consistently advance successfully through this program. Consequently, recent research has endeavored to examine factors influencing the success or failure of high-potential employee practices. For example, research has been focused on the accuracy of high-potential labels as predictors of real status (Dries, 2009; Ready et al., 2010). Research elsewhere has assessed the impact of high-potential practices on B players, those not selected for the high-potential program (e.g., Gelens, Hofmans, Dries, & Pepermans, 2014). Ironically, minimal attention has been directed at exploring the psychological impact on the individuals selected as participants in high-potential practices (Dries et al., 2014), nor has sufficient research attention focused on the experiences of high-potentials (Dries & Pepermans, 2008).

This chapter presented a conceptual framework to guide future research in exploring the manner in which high-potential status can impact recipient responses to a failure experience. Drawing from a range of literatures, we proposed that individuals labeled as high-potential may be less equipped to respond productively to experiences of failure. Among our central assertions was the notion that a high-potential label reflects high-performance expectations, which, if not reached, can result in status loss. Consequently, the receipt of a high-potential designation can trigger a performance goal orientation and elevate perceptions of visibility or scrutiny.

Taken together, these factors increase the salience of any potential threats to status, including the possibility of failure. The cognitive implications include the tendency of high-status individuals, who are fearful of status loss, to defer responsibility for any failure to external sources. For such individuals, failure is seen not as an opportunity to learn (a challenge stressor) but rather as a threat to their elevated status (a hindrance stressor). The resultant coping strategy (emotion-focused coping) can further undermine the capacity to learn from a failure experience.

The conceptual model presented in this chapter is intended to draw attention to the double-edged sword of high-potential labeling for the recipients. While such status can offer opportunities for advancement, it can also prime individuals to be more acutely sensitive to the threat of status loss, thereby creating impediments to learning from failure. Our focus on the downside of the high-potential label is not intended to deny its positive influence or to exclude the impact of other contextual elements on an individual's capacity to learn from failure. However, acknowledging the challenges arising from high-potential labeling can expand our understanding of the consequences of these labels for the cognitions and behaviors of the recipients. Further exploring the context of high-potential behavior and responses to feedback can shed greater light on sources of influence on such behavior.

A number of research scholars have cautiously pointed out that high-potential practices essentially generate a workforce differentiation approach to talent management, which includes the allocation of a disproportionate amount of resources and opportunities provided to those employees designated as high-potentials (Aguinis et al., 2011; Cappelli & Keller, 2014; Finkelstein et al., 2018; Prato & Ferraro, 2018). While high-potential employee practices are aimed at developing employees who demonstrate leadership potential (Collings & Mellahi, 2009), uncertainty remains as to whether such practices effectively nurture the commitment, engagement, and loyalty of those valued employees in order to retain them (Vloeberghs et al., 2005).

We hope this chapter encourages much needed empirical exploration of the cognitive impact of *high-status* or *high-potential* conferral on the recipients. Many organizations regard the practice of identifying high-potentials as an important component of building a long-term competitive advantage. However, labeling individuals as high-potential can present a double-edged sword for the recipients. On the one hand, high-potential labeling can boost self-efficacy and provide needed opportunities for development. On the other hand, such labeling can also ignite vulnerabilities stemming from this high-status cue and thus can undermine the capacity to learn from a failure experience.

References

Adler, F. 1956. The value concept in sociology. *American Journal of Sociology,* 62(3): 272–279.

Aguinis, H., Boyd, B. K., Pierce, C. A., Short, J. C., Huselid, M. A., & Becker, B. E. 2011. Bridging micro and macro domains: Workforce differentiation and strategic human resource management. *Journal of Management,* 37(2): 421–428.

Allport, G. W. 1937. *Personality.* New York: Holt.

Anderson, C. Brion, S., Moore, D. A., & Kennedy, J. A., 2012. A status enhancement account of overconfidence. *Journal of Personality and Social Psychology,* 103(4): 718.

Argote, L., & Miron-Spektor, E. 2011. Organizational learning: From experience to knowledge. *Organization Science,* 22(5): 1123–1137.

Auriol, E., & Renault, R. 2008. Status and incentives. *The Rand Journal of Economics,* 39(1): 305–326.

Bandura, A. 1989. Self-regulation of motivation and action through internal standards and goal systems. In L. A. Pervin (Eds.), *Goals concepts in personality and social psychology.* Hillsdale, NJ: Erlbaum.

Barney, J. B. 1991. Firm resources and sustained competitive advantage. *Journal of Management,* 17(1): 99–120.

Baumeister, R. F., Smart, L., & Boden, J. M. 1996. Relation of threatened egotism to violence and aggression: The dark side of high self- esteem. *Psychological Review,* 103(1): 5–14.

Becker, B. E., & Huselid, M. A. 1998. High performance work systems and firm performance: A synthesis of research and managerial implications. In G. R. Ferris (Ed.), *Research in personnel and human resource management* (Vol. 16): 53–101. Greenwich, CT: JAI Press.

Becker, G. S. 2009. *Human capital: A theoretical and empirical analysis, with special reference to education.* Chicago: University of Chicago Press.

Bem, D. J. 1972. Constructing cross-situational consistencies in behaviour: Some thoughts on Alker's critique of Mischel. *Journal of Personality,* 40(1): 17–26.

Bendersky, C., & Hays, N. A. 2012. Status conflict in groups. *Organization Science,* 23(2): 323–340.

Bendersky, C., & Shah, N. P. 2012. The cost of status enhancement: Performance effects of individuals' status mobility in task groups. *Organization Science,* 23(2): 308–322.

Berger, J., Cohen, B. P., & Zelditch Jr, M. 1972. Status characteristics and social interaction. *American Sociological Review,* 37(3): 241–255.

Binnewies, C., & Wornlein. S. C. 2011. What makes a creative day? A diary study on the interplay between affect, job stressors, and job control. *Journal of Organizational Behavior,* 32(4): 589–607.

Björkman, I., Ehrnrooth, M., Mäkelä, K., Smale, A., & Sumelius, J. 2013. Talent or not? Employee reactions to talent identification. *Human Resource Management,* 52(2): 195–214.

Blader, S. L., & Bobocel, R. 2005. Wanting is believing: Understanding psychological processes in organizational justice by examining subjectivity in justice judgments. In S. Gilliland, D. Steiner, D. Skarlicki, & K. Van den Bos (Eds.), *Research in social issues in management: What motivates fairness in organizations?:* 3–29. Greenwich, CT: Information Age Publishing.

Blader, S. L., & Chen, Y. R. 2011. What influences how high-status people respond to lower-status others? Effects of procedural fairness, outcome favorability, and concerns about status. *Organization Science,* 22(4): 1040–1060.

Blau, P. 1955. *The dynamics of bureaucracy.* Chicago: Chicago University Press.

Bolinger, A., & Brown, K. 2015. Entrepreneurial failure as a threshold concept: The effects of student experiences. *Journal of Management Education,* 39(4): 452–475.

Bouffard, T., Boisvert, J., Vezeau, C., & LaRouche, C. 1995. The impact of goal orientation on self-regulation and performance among college students. *British Journal of Educational Psychology,* 65(3): 317–329.

Bournois, F., & Roussillon, S. 1992. The management of 'highflier' executives in France: The weight of the national culture. *Human Resource Management Journal,* 3(1): 37–56.

Boyd, N. G., Lewin, J. E., & Sager, J. K. 2009. A model of stress and coping and their influence on individual and organizational outcomes. *Journal of Vocational Behavior,* 75(2): 197–211.

Brett, J. F., & Atwater, L. E. 2001. 360 degree feedback: Accuracy, reactions, and perceptions of usefulness. *Journal of Applied Psychology,* 86(5): 930–942.

Brett, J. F., & VandeWalle, D. 1999. Goal orientation and goal content as predictors of performance in a training program. *Journal of Applied Psychology,* 84(6): 863–873.

Bunderson, J. S., & Sutcliffe, K. M. 2003. Management team learning orientation and business unit performance. *Journal of Applied Psychology,* 88(3): 552–560.

Call, M. L., Nyberg, A. J., & Thatcher, S. 2015. Stargazing: An integrative conceptual review, theoretical reconciliation, and extension for star employee research. *Journal of Applied Psychology,* 100(3): 623–640.

Campbell, W. K., & Sedikides, C. 1999. Self-threat magnifies the self-serving bias: A meta-analytic integration. *Review of General Psychology,* 3(1): 23.

Campion, M. A., & Lord, R. G. 1982. A control-system conceptualization of the goal setting and changing process. *Organizational Behavior and Human Performance,* 30(2): 265–287.

Cappelli, P. 2008a. Talent management for the twenty-first century. *Harvard Business Review,* 86(3): 74–81.

Cappelli, P. 2008b. *Talent on demand: Managing talent in an uncertain age.* Boston, MA: Harvard Business School Press.

Cappelli, P., & Keller, J. R. 2014. Talent management: Conceptual approaches and practical challenges. *Annual Review of Organizational Psychology and Organizational Behavior,* 1(1): 305–331.

Chacko, T. I., & McElroy, J. C. 1983. The cognitive component in Locke's theory of goal setting: Suggestive evidence for a causal attribution interpretation. *Academy of Management Journal,* 26(1): 104–118.

Cheng, J. T., Tracy, J. L., Foulsham, T., Kingstone, A., & Henrich, J. 2013. Two ways to the top: Evidence that dominance and prestige are distinct yet viable avenues to social rank and influence. *Journal of Personality and Social Psychology,* 104(1): 103.

Clapham, S. E., & Schwenk, C. R. 1991. Self-serving attributions, managerial cognition, and company performance. *Strategic Management Journal,* 12(3): 219–229.

Collings, D., & Mellahi, K. 2009. Strategic talent management: A review and research agenda. *Human Resource Management Review,* 19(4): 304–313.

Cron, W. L., Slocum, J. W., VandeWalle, D., & Fu, Q. 2005. The role of goal orientation on negative emotions and goal setting when initial performance falls short of one's performance goal. *Human Performance,* 18(1): 55–80.

Cyert, R. M., & March, J. G. 1963. *A behavioral theory of the firm:* 169–187. Englewood Cliffs, NJ: Prentice-Hall

Darley, J. M., & Gross, P. H. 1983. A hypothesis-confirming bias in labelling effects. *Journal of Personality and Social Psychology,* 44(1): 20.

Deaux, K. 1976. Sex: A perspective on the attribution process. In J. H. Harvey, W. J. Ickes, & R. F. Kidd (Eds.), *New Directions in Attribution Research:* 335–352. Hillsdale, N.J.: Erlbaum.

Deephouse, D. L., & Suchman, M. 2008. Legitimacy in organizational institutionalism. In R. Greenwood, C. Oliver, & R. Suddaby (Eds.), *The Sage handbook of organizational institutionalism:* 49–77. London: Sage Publications.

Derr, C. B., Jones, C., & Toomey, E. L. 1988. Managing high-status employees: Current practices in thirty-three U.S. corporations. *Human Resource Management,* 27(3): 273–290.

DeShon, R. P., & Gillespie, J. Z. 2005. A motivated action theory account of goal orientation. *Journal of Applied Psychology,* 90(6): 1096–1127.

DeWall, C. N., Baumeister, R. F., Mead, N. L., & Vohs, K. D. 2011. How leaders self- regulate their task performance: Evidence that power promotes diligence, depletion and disdain. *Journal of Personality and Social Psychology,* 100(1): 47.

Dittes, J. E., & Kelley, H. H. 1956. Effects of different conditions of acceptance upon conformity to group norms. *Journal of Abnormal and Social Psychology,* 53(1): 100.

Dries, N. 2009. Antecedents and outcomes in careers of high status, key experts and average performance. *Academy of Management Annual Meeting Proceedings,* 2009(1): 1–6.

Dries, N. 2013. The psychology of talent management: A review and research agenda. *Human Resource Management Review,* 23(4): 272–285.

Dries, N., & De Gieter, S. 2014. Information asymmetry in high status programs: A status risk for psychological contract breach. *Personnel Review,* 43(1): 136–162

Dries, N., Forrier, A., De Vos, A., & Pepermans, R. 2014. Self-perceived employability, organization-rated status and the psychological contract. *Journal of Managerial Psychology,* 29(5): 565–581.

Dries, N., Pepermans, R. 2008. "Real" high-potential careers: An empirical study into the perspectives of organisations and high potentials. *Personnel Review,* 37(1): 85–108.

Dries, N., Van Acker, F., & Verbruggen, M. 2012. How 'boundaryless' are the careers of *high status,* key experts and average performers? *Journal of Vocational Behavior,* 81(2): 271–279.

Dries, N., Vantilborgh, T., & Pepermans, R. 2012. The role of learning agility and career variety in the identification and development of high status employees. *Personnel Review,* 41(3): 340–358.

Duboulo, M. 2004. The transitional space and self-recovery: A psychoanalytical approach to high-status managers' training. *Human Relations,* 57(4): 467–496.

Dustin, D. S. 1966. Member reactions to team performance. *Journal of Social Psychology,* 69(2): 237–243.

Dweck, C. S. 1986. Motivational processes affecting learning. *American Psychologist,* 41(10): 1040–1048.

Dweck, C. S. 1999. Caution–praise can be dangerous. *American Educator,* 23(1): 4–9.

Dweck, C. S., & Elliott, E. S. 1983. Achievement motivation. In E. M. Hetherington (Eds.), *Handbook of child psychology: Socialization, personality, and social development:* 643–691. New York: Wiley.

Dweck, C. S., & Leggett, E. 1988. A social-cognitive approach to motivation and personality. *Psychological Review,* 95(2): 256–273

Eden, D. 1984. Self-fulfilling prophecy as a management tool: Harnessing Pygmalion. *Academy of Management Review,* 9(1): 64–73.

Edmondson, A. C. 2011. Strategies for learning from failure. *Harvard Business Review,* 89(4): 48–55.

Elliot, A. J., & McGregor, H. A. 2001. A 2 x 2 achievement goal framework. *Journal of Personality and Social Psychology,* 80(3): 501–519.

Elliot, E., & Church, M. 1997. A hierarchical model of approach and avoidance achievement motivation. *Journal of Personality and Social Psychology,* 72(1): 218–232.

Feather, N. T. 1969. Attribution of responsibility and valence of success and failure in relation to initial confidence and task performance. *Journal of Personality and Social Psychology,* 13(2): 129.

Feather, N. T. 1998. Attitudes toward high achievers, self-esteem, and value priorities for Australian, American, and Canadian students. *Journal of Cross-Cultural Psychology,* 29(6): 749–759.

Feather, N. T., & Simon, J. G. 1971. Attribution of responsibility and valence of outcome in relation to initial confidence and success and failure of self and other. *Journal of Personality and Social Psychology,* 18(2): 173–188.

Feldman, D. C., and Thomas, D. C. 1992. Career management issues facing expatriates. *Journal of International Business Studies,* 23(2): 271–294.

Finkelstein, L. M., Costanza, D. P., & Goodwin, G. F. 2018. Do your high potentials have potential? The impact of individual differences and designation on leader success. *Personnel Psychology,* 71(1): 3–22.

Folkman, S., Lazarus, R. S., Dunkel-Schetter, C., Delongis, A., & Gruen, R. J. 1986. Dynamics of a stressful encounter: Cognitive appraisal, coping, and encounter outcomes. *Journal of Personality and Social Psychology,* 50(5): 992–1003.

Forsyth, D., & Schlenker, B. 1977. Attributing the causes of performance: Effects of performance quality, task importance, and future testing. *Journal of Personality,* 45(2): 220–236.

Fragale, A. R., Overbeck, J. R., & Neale, M. A. 2011. Resources versus respect: Social judgments based on targets' power and status positions. *Journal of Experimental Social Psychology,* 47(4): 767–775.

Fragale, A. R., Rosen, B., Xu, C., & Merideth, I. 2009. The higher they are, the harder they fall: The effects of wrongdoer status on observer punishment recommendations and intentionality attributions. *Organizational Behavior and Human Decision Processes,* 108(1): 53–65.

Frieze, I., & Weiner, B. 1971. Cue utilization and attributional judgments for success and failure. *Journal of Personality,* 39(4): 591–605.

Fugate, M., Kinicki, A. J., & Prussia, G. P. 2008. Employee coping with organizational change: An examination of alternative theoretical perspectives and models. *Personnel Psychology,* 61(1): 1–36.

Gecas, V., & Seff, M. A. 1990. Social class and self-esteem: Psychological centrality, compensation, and the relative effects of work and home. *Social Psychology Quarterly,* 53(2): 165–173.

Gelens, J., Hofmans, J., Dries, N., & Pepermans, R. 2014. Talent management and organizational justice: Employee reactions to *high status* identification. *Human Resource Management Journal,* 24(2): 159–175.

Giordano, P. C. 1983. Sanctioning the high-status deviant: An attributional analysis. *Social Psychology Quarterly,* 46(4): 329–342.

Gong, Y., Huang, J.-C., & Farh, J. L. 2009. Employee learning orientation, transformational leadership, and employee creativity: The mediating role of employee creative self-efficacy. *Academy of Management Journal,* 52(4): 765–778.

Graffin, S. D., Bundy, J., Porac, J. F., Wade, J. B., & Quinn, D. P. 2013. Falls from grace and the hazards of high status: The 2009 British MP expense scandal and its impact on parliamentary elites. *Administrative Science Quarterly,* 58(3): 313–345.

Graffin, S. D., Wade, J. B., Porac, J. F., & McNamee, R. C. 2008. The impact of CEO status diffusion on the economic outcomes of other senior managers. *Organization Science,* 19(3): 457–474.

Greve, H. R. 2003. *Organizational learning from performance feedback: A behavioral perspective on innovation and change.* New York: Cambridge University Press.

Groysberg, B., Polzer, J. T., & Elfenbein, H. A. 2011. Too many cooks spoil the broth: How high-status individuals decrease group effectiveness. *Organization Science,* 22(3): 722–737.

Haines, E. L., & Jost, J. T. 2000. Placating the powerless: Effects of legitimate and illegitimate explanation on affect, memory, and stereotyping. *Social Justice Research,* 13(3): 219–236.

Heider, F. 1958. *The psychology of interpersonal relations.* New York: Wiley

Higgins, E. T. 1987. Self-discrepancy: A theory relating self and affect. *Psychological Review,* 94(3): 319–340.

Hirst G., Knippenberg D. V., & Zhou J. 2009. A cross-level perspective on employee creativity: Goal orientation, team learning behavior, and individual creativity. *Academy of Management Journal,* 52(2): 280–293.

Hogg, M. A. 2006. Social identity theory. In P. J. Burke (Eds.), *Contemporary social psychological theories:* 111–136. Palo Alto, CA: Stanford University Press.

Humphrey, R. 1985. How work roles influence perception: Structural-cognitive processes and organizational behavior. *American Sociological Review,* 50(2): 242–252.

Iles, P. 1997. Sustainable high-potential career development: A resource-based view. *Career Development International,* 2(7): 347–353.

Janssen, O., & Van Yperen, N. W. 2004. Employees' goal orientations, the quality of leader-member exchange, and the outcomes of job performance and job satisfaction. *Academy of Management Journal,* 47(3): 368–384.

Jones, E. E., & Davis, K. E. 1965. From acts to dispositions the attribution process in person perception. *Advances in Experimental Social Psychology,* 2: 219–266.

Jost, J. T., & Banaji, M. R. 1994. The role of stereotyping in system-justification and the production of false consciousness. *British Journal of Social Psychology,* 33(1): 1–27.

Jussim, L., Yen, H., & Aiello, J. R. 1995. Self-consistency, self-enhancement, and accuracy in reactions to feedback. *Journal of Experimental Social Psychology,* 31(4): 322–356.

Kehoe, R. R., & Tzabbar, D. 2015. Lighting the way or stealing the shine? An examination of the duality in star scientists' effects on firm innovative performance. *Strategic Management Journal,* 36(5): 709–727.

Kelley, H. 1967. Attribution theory in social psychology. In D. Levine (Eds.), *Nebraska Symposium on Motivation:* 192–238. Lincoln: University of Nebraska.

Kelley, H. H., & Michela, J. L. 1980. Attribution theory and research. *Annual Review of Psychology,* 31(1): 457–501.

Kluger A. N., Lewinsohn S., & Aiello J. R. 1994. The influence of feedback on mood: Linear effects on pleasantness and curvilinear effects on arousal. *Organizational Behaviour and Human Decision Processes,* 60(2): 276–299

Korman, A. K. 1970. Toward a hypothesis of work behavior. *Journal of Applied Psychology,* 54(1): 31–41.

Kotlyar, I., & Karakowsky, L. 2012. *Rising stars and falling commitment: Self-perceived status and responses to performance feedback.* Presented at the Academy of Management Meetings, Boston, MA.

Langer, E. J. 1989. Minding matters: The consequences of mindlessness–mindfulness. In L. Berkowitz (Ed.), *Advances in experimental social psychology:* 137–173. San Diego, CA: Academic Press.

Latack, J. G. 1986. Coping with job stress: Measures and future directions for scale development. *Journal of Applied Psychology,* 71(3): 377–385.

Lawler, E. L. 1971. *Pay and organization effectiveness: A psychological view.* New York: McGraw Hill.

Lazarus, R. S., & Folkman, S. 1984. *Stress, appraisal, and coping.* New York: Springer

Ledford, G., & Kochanski, J. 2004. Allocation training and development resources based on organizational excellence by identifying, developing a contribution. In L. Berger & D. Berger (Eds.), *The talent management handbook: Creating and promoting your best people:* 199–217. New York: McGraw-Hill.

Leiter, M. P. 1991. Coping patterns as predictors of burnout: The function of control and escapist coping patterns. *Journal of Organizational Behavior,* 12(2): 123–144.

Lench, H. C., & Levine, L. J. 2008. Goals and responses to failure: Knowing when to hold them and when to fold them. *Motivation and Emotion,* 32(2): 127–140

Lepak, D. P., & Snell, S. A. 1999. The human resource architecture: toward a theory of human capital allocation and development. *Academy of Management Review,* 24(1): 31–48.

LePine, J. A., Podsakoff, N. P., & LePine, M. A. 2005. A meta-analytic test of the challenge stressor–hindrance stressor framework: An explanation for inconsistent relationships among stressors and performance. *Academy of Management Journal,* 48(5): 764–775.

Long, D. M., Baer, M. D., Colquitt, J. A., Outlaw, R., & Dhensa-Kahlon, R. K. 2015. What will the boss think? The impression management implications of supportive relationships with star and project peers. *Personnel Psychology,* 68(3): 463–498.

Love, P. E. D., & Irani, Z. 2007. Coping and psychological adjustment among information technology personnel. *Industrial Management and Data Systems,* 107(6): 824–844.

Luginbuhl, J. E., Crowe, D. H., & Kahan, J. P. 1975. Causal attributions for success and failure. *Journal of Personality and Social Psychology,* 31(1): 86.

Madsen, P. M., & Desai, V. 2010. Failing to learn? The effects of failure and success on organizational learning in the global orbital launch vehicle industry. *Academy of Management Journal,* 53(3): 451.

Magee, J. C., & Galinksy, A. D. 2008. Eight social hierarchies: The self- reinforcing nature of power and status. *Academy of Management Annals,* 2(1): 351–398.

Maltesea, A., Simpson, A., & Anderson, A. 2018. Failing to learn: The impact of failures during making activities. *Thinking Skills and Creativity,* 30: 116–124.

March, J. G., & Simon, H. A. 1958. *Organizations.* Oxford, England: Wiley.

Marr, J. C., & Thau, S. 2014. Falling from great (and not-so-great) heights: How initial status position influences performance after status loss. *Academy of Management Journal,* 57(1): 223–248.

Martin, J., & Schmidt, C. 2010. How to keep your top talent. *Harvard Business Review,* 88(5): 54–61.

McGrath, R. G. 2001. Exploratory learning, innovative capacity and managerial oversight. *Academy of Management Journal,* 44(1): 118–131.

McMahan, I. D. 1973. Relationships between causal attributions and expectancy of success. *Journal of Personality and Social Psychology,* 28(1): 108.

Meyer, W., Bachmann, M., Biermann, U., Hempelmann, M., Ploger, F., & Spiller, H. 1979. The informational value of evaluative behavior: Influences of praise and blame on perceptions of ability. *Journal of Educational Psychology,* 71(2): 259–268.

Miller, D. T. 1976. Ego involvement and attributions for success and failure. *Journal of Personality and Social Psychology,* 34(5), 901.

Miller, D. T., & Ross, M. 1975. Self-serving biases in the attribution of causality: Fact or fiction? *Psychological Bulletin,* 82(2): 213.

Mitchell, T., Green, S., & Wood, R. 1981. An attributional model of leadership and the poor performing subordinate: Development and validation. In B. M. Staw & L. L. Cummings (Eds.), *Research in Organizational Behavior.* Greenwich, CT: JAI Press.

Morris, M. W., & Moore, P. C. 2000. The lessons we (don't) learn: Counterfactual thinking and organizational accountability after a close call. *Administrative Science Quarterly,* 45(4): 737–765.

Mueller, C. M., & Dweck, C. S. 1998. Praise for intelligence can undermine children's motivation and performance. *Journal of Personality and Social Psychology,* 75(1): 33.

Musaji, S., Schulze, W., & De Castro, J. 2020. How long does it take to get to the learning curve? *Academy of Management Journal,* 63(1): 205–227.

Neeley, T. B. 2013. Language matters: Status loss and achieved status distinctions in global organizations. *Organization Science,* 24(2): 476–497.

Norvell, N., & Forsyth, D. R. 1984. The impact of inhibiting of facilitating causal factors on group members' reactions after success and failure. *Social Psychology Quarterly,* 47(3), 293–297.

Payne, S. C., Youngcourt, S. S., & Beaubien, J. M. 2007. A meta- analytic examination of the goal orientation nomological net. *Journal of Applied Psychology,* 92(1): 128–150.

Pearce, J. L., & Porter, L. W. 1986. Employee responses to formal appraisal feedback. *Journal of Applied Psychology,* 71(2): 211–218.

Pepermans, R., Vloeberghs, D., & Perkisas, B. 2003. *High status* identification policies: An empirical study among Belgian companies. *Journal of Management Development,* 22(8): 660–678.

Perrewé, P., & Zellars, K. 1999. An examination of attributions and emotions in the transactional approach to the organizational stress process. *Journal of Organizational Behavior,* 20(5): 739–752.

Petrovski, H. 1985. *To engineer is human: The role of failure in successful design.* New York: St. Martin's Press.

Pettit, N. C., Yong, K., & Spataro, S. E. 2010. Holding your place: Reactions to the prospect of status gains and losses. *Journal of Experimental Social Psychology,* 46: 396–401.

Pfeffer, J., & Fong, C. T. 2005. Building organization theory from first principles: The self-enhancement motive and understanding power and influence. *Organization Science,* 16(4): 372–388.

Phillips, D. J., & Zuckerman, E. W. 2001. Middle-status conformity: Theoretical restatement and empirical demonstration in two markets. *American Journal of Sociology,* 107(2): 379–429.

Podolny, J. M., & Phillips, D. J. 1996. The dynamics of organizational status. *Industrial and Corporate Change,* 5(2): 453–471.

Prato, M., & Ferraro, F. 2018. Starstruck: How hiring high-status employees affects incumbents' performance. *Organization Science,* 29(5): 755–774.

Ready, D. A., Conger, J. A., & Hill, L. A. 2010. Are you a high status? *Harvard Business Review,* 88(6): 78–84.

Ready, D., Conger, J., Hill, L., & Stecker, E. 2010. The anatomy of a high status. *Business Strategy Review,* 21(3), 52–55.

Regan, D. T., Straus, E., & Fazio, R. 1974. Liking and the attribution process. *Journal of Experimental Social Psychology,* 10(4): 385–397.

Rhee, M., & Haunschild, P. R. 2006. The liability of good reputation: A study of product recalls in the U.S. automobile industry. *Organizational Science,* 17(1): 101–117.

Richter, W., & Semrau, T. 2019. Employee learning from failure: A team-as-resource perspective. *Organization Science,* 30(4): 694–714.

Rosenfield, D., & Stephan, W. G. 1978. Sex differences in attributions for sex-typed tasks. *Journal of Personality,* 46(2), 244–259.

Sande, G. N., Ellard, J. H., & Ross, M. 1986. Effect of arbitrarily assigned status labels on self-perceptions and social perceptions: The mere position effect. *Journal of Personality and Social Psychology,* 50(4): 684.

Sapolsky, R. M. 2004. *Why zebras don't get ulcers: The acclaimed guide to stress, stress- related diseases and coping.* New York: Macmillan.

Schroth, H. A., & Shah, P. P. 2000. Procedures: Do we really want to know them? An examination of the effects of procedural justice on self-esteem. *Journal of Applied Psychology,* 85(3): 462.

Seijts, G. H., Latham, G. P., Tasa, K., & Latham, B. W. 2004. Goal setting and goal orientation: An integration of two different yet related literatures. *Academy of Management Journal,* 47(2): 227–239.

Semmer, N. 2003. Job stress interventions and organization of work. In J. Campbell Quick & L. E. Tetrick (Eds.), *Handbook of occupational health psychology.* Washington, DC: American Psychological Association.

Shepherd, D., Patzelt, H., & Wolfe, M. 2011. Moving forward from project failure: Negative emotions, affective commitment, and learning from the experience. *Academy of Management Journal,* 54(6): 361–380.

Shrauger, S. 1975. Responses to evaluation as a function of initial self-perceptions. *Psychological Bulletin,* 82(4), 581–596.

Silzer, R. F., & Church, A.H. 2010. Identifying and assessing high status talent: Current organizational practices. In R. F. Silzer & B. E. Dowell (Eds.), *Strategy driven talent management: A leadership imperative.* San Francisco, CA: Jossey-Bass

Simpson, A., & Maltese, A. 2017. Failure is a major component of learning anything: The role of failure in the development of STEM professionals. *Journal of Science Education and Technology,* 2(2): 223–237.

Sitkin, S. 1992. Learning through failure: The strategy of small losses. In B. M. Staw & L. L. Cummings (Eds.), *Research in organizational behaviour.* Greenwich, CT: JAI Press.

Slan, R., & Hausdorf, P. 2004. *Leadership succession: High status identification and development.* Toronto: University of Guelph/MICA Management Resources.

Slan-Jerusalim, R., & Hausdorf, P. A. 2007. Managers' justice perceptions of *high status* identification practices. *Journal of Management Development,* 26(10): 933–950.

Spreitzer, G., Sutcliffe, K., Dutton, J., Sonenshein, S., & Grant, A. M. 2005. A socially embedded model of thriving at work. *Organization Science,* 16(5): 537–549.

Stahl, G. K., & Caligiuri, P. 2005. The effectiveness of expatriate coping strategies: The moderating role of cultural distance, position level, and time on the international assignment. *Journal of Applied Psychology,* 90(4): 603–615.

Stajkovic, A. D., & Luthans, F. 1998. Self-efficacy and work-related performance: A meta-analysis. *Psychological Bulletin,* 124(2): 240.

Steele, C. M. 1988. The psychology of self-affirmation: Sustaining the integrity of the self. In L. Berkowitz (Ed.), *Advances in experimental social psychology:* 261–302. San Diego, CA: Academic Press.

Steele, C. M., Spencer, S. J., & Lynch, M. 1993. Self-image resilience and dissonance: The role of affirmational resources. *Journal of Personality and Social Psychology,* 64(6): 885–896.

Stein, N., Trabasso, T., Folkman, S., & Richards, R. A. 1997. Appraisal and goal processes as predictors of psychological well-being in bereaved caregivers. *Journal of Personality and Social Psychology,* 72(4): 872–884.

Suazo, M. M., Martinez, P. G., & Sandoval, R. 2009. Creating psychological and legal contracts through human resource practices: A signaling theory perspective. *Human Resource Management Review,* 19(2): 154–166.

Sutcliffe, K. M., & Weick, K. E. 2007. *Managing the unexpected: Resilient performance in an age of uncertainty.* San Francisco, CA: Jossey-Bass.

Sutton, R. I., & Hargardon, A. 1996. Brainstorming groups in context: Effectiveness in a product design firm. *Administrative Science Quarterly,* 41(4): 685–718.

Swann, W. 1990. To be adored or to be known: The interplay of self-enhancement and self-verification. In R. M. Sorrentino & E. T. Higgins (Eds.), *Foundations of social behavior:* 408–448. New York: Guilford.

Swann, W. B., Griffin, J. J., Predmore, S. C., & Gaines, B. 1987. The cognitive–affective crossfire: When self-consistency confronts self-enhancement. *Journal of Personality and Social Psychology,* 52(5): 881.

Swann Jr, W. B., Pelham, B. W., & Krull, D. S. 1989. Agreeable fancy or disagreeable truth? Reconciling self-enhancement and self-verification. *Journal of Personality and Social Psychology,* 57(5): 782.

Swann, W. B., Polzer, J. T., Seyle, D. C., & Ko, S. J. 2004. Finding value in diversity: Verification of personal and social self-views in diverse groups. *Academy of Management Review,* 29(1): 9–27.

Tajfel, H. 1979. Individuals and groups in social psychology. *British Journal of Social and Clinical Psychology,* 18(2): 183–190.

Tajfel, H. 1981. *Human groups and social categories: Studies in social psychology.* Cambridge, UK: Cambridge University Press Archive.

Tajfel, H., & Turner, J. 1986. The social identity theory of intergroup behavior. In S. Worchel & W. Austin (Eds.), *Psychology of intergroup relations.* Chicago: Nelson-Hall

Taylor, M. S., Fisher, C. D., & Ilgen, D. R. 1984. Individuals' reactions to performance feedback in organizations. In K. Rowland & G. R. Ferris (Eds.), *Research in personnel and human resources management:* 231–272. Greenwich, CT: JAI Press.

Taylor, S. E., & Brown, J. D. 1988. Illusion and well-being: A social psychological perspective on mental health. *Psychological Bulletin,* 103(2): 193–210

Taylor, S. E., & Fiske, S. T. 1975. Point of view and perceptions of causality. *Journal of Personality and Social Psychology,* 32(3): 439–445.

Tienery, P., & Farmer, S. 2004. The Pygmalion process and employee creativity. *Journal of Management,* 30(3): 413–432.

Turner, J. C., Hogg, M. A., Oakes, P. J., Reicher, S. D., & Wetherell, M. S. 1987. *Rediscovering the social group: A self-categorization theory.* Oxford, England: Basil Blackwell.

Tzabbar, D. 2009. When does scientist recruitment affect technological repositioning? *Academy of Management Journal,* 52(5): 873–896.

Van Der Vegt, G. S., Bunderson, J. S., & Oosterhof, A. 2006. Expertness diversity and interpersonal helping in teams: Why those who need the most help end up getting the least. *Academy of Management Journal,* 49(5): 877–893.

Vanderwielen, J. J. 2001. Cognitive appraisal, coping, and the psychological and sociocultural adjustment of expatriates. *Dissertation Abstracts International: The Physical Sciences and Engineering,* 62(3-B): 1630.

VandeWalle, D. 1997. Development and validation of a work domain goal orientation instrument. *Educational and Psychological Measurement,* 57(6): 995–1015.

VandeWalle, D., Brown, S., Cron, W., & Slocum, J. 1999. The influence of goal orientation and self-regulation tactics on sales performance. *Journal of Applied Psychology,* 84(2): 249–259.

VandeWalle, D., Cron, W., & Slocum, J. 2001. The role of goal orientation following performance feedback. *Journal of Applied Psychology,* 86(4): 629.

Van Yperen, N. W. 2003. The perceived profile of goal orientation within firms: Differences between employees working for successful and unsuccessful firms employing either performance-based pay or job-based pay. *European Journal of Work and Organizational Psychology,* 12(3): 229–243.

Vloeberghs, D., Pepermans, R., & Thielemans, K. 2005. High- status development policies: An empirical study among Belgian companies. *Journal of Management Development,* 24(6): 546–558.

Wade, J. B., Porac, J. F., Pollock, T. G., & Graffin, S. D. 2006. The burden of celebrity: The impact of CEO certification contests on CEO pay and performance. *Academy of Management Journal,* 49(4), 643–660.

Wagner, J. A., & Gooding, R. Z. 1997. Equivocal information and attribution: An investigation of patterns of managerial sense making. *Strategic Management Journal,* 18(4): 275–286.

Wagner, T. 2012. *Creating innovators: The making of young people who will change the world.* New York: Scribner.

Webster, J. R., & Beehr, T. A. 2013. Antecedents and outcomes of employee perceptions of intra-organizational mobility channels. *Journal of Organizational Behavior,* 34(7): 919–941.

Weick, K.E. 1990. The vulnerable system: An analysis of the Tenerife air disaster. *Journal of Management,* 16(3): 571–593.

Weick, K. E., & Roberts, K. H. 1993. Collective mind in organizations: Heedful interrelating on flight decks. *Administrative Science Quarterly,* 38(3): 357–381.

Weiner, B. 1972. *Theories of motivation: From mechanism to cognition.* Chicago: Markham.

Wiener, B. 1985. An attributional theory of achievement motivation and emotion. *Psychological Review,* 92(4): 548.

Weiner, B., & Kukla, A. 1970. An attributional analysis of achievement motivation. *Journal of Personality and Social Psychology,* 15(1): 1.

Willer, R. 2009. Groups reward individual sacrifice: The status solution to the collective action problem. *American Sociological Review.* 74(1): 23–43.

Wright, T. A. 1990. Coping and job performance. *Perceptual and Motor Skills,* 71(2): 403–408.

Wright, P., Kroll., M., Pray, B., & Lado, A. 1995. Strategic orientations, competitive advantage, and business performance. *Journal of Business Research,* 33(2): 143–151.

33

TALENT MANAGEMENT, STARS, AND GEOGRAPHICALLY DISTRIBUTED TEAMS

Julia Eisenberg

Introduction

Greater reliance on teams to structure and coordinate work in modern organizations highlights the need to better understand how to manage talent in the context of teamwork. Advances in technology, opportunities to decrease costs, and ability to access expertise regardless of employee's location have led to increasing prevalence of geographically distributed teams (Eisenberg & DiTomaso, 2019; Gilson, Maynard, Jones Young, Vartiainen, & Hakonen, 2015; Powell, Piccoli, & Ives, 2004). Geographically distributed teams, or virtual teams, are defined as groups of colleagues who collaborate using a variety of information technology communication tools to accomplish common goals (Cummings & Dennis, 2018; Maes & Weldy, 2018; Magni, Ahuja, & Maruping, 2018).

On the one hand, geographically dispersed teams offer a number of benefits ranging from economic benefits to accessing the most qualified talent without having to deal with logistics or regulations (Maes & Weldy, 2018). On the other hand, these types of teams face additional challenges related to geographical dispersion among individuals, which exacerbates teamwork due to reduced face-to-face interactions, hindering their relationship bonds (Cummings & Dennis, 2018).

Increasing numbers of organizations are relying on virtual teams, with about 30–45% of employees working remotely in formal and ad hoc teams (Cummings & Dennis, 2018). Some estimate that around 80% of employees are in some ways involved in virtual teams (Magni et al., 2018), while others suggest that practically all teams in the corporate environment are now virtual (Maes & Weldy, 2018). The prevalence of virtual teams seems to be increasing since a recent survey of 1,620 respondents from 90 countries suggests that 88% of respondents believe that virtual teams are crucial (2018 Trends in High-Performing Global Virtual Teams, 2018). Further, a review of the virtual teams research also highlighted that many believe the number of dispersed teams will continue to grow (Gilson et al., 2015). These trends highlight the relevance of virtual teams to the discussion of modern organizational team structures for academia as well as practice.

Trends in teamwork have been shifting towards more virtual collaboration even among the so-called "traditional" collocated teams due to employees working from home, as part of an ongoing flexible work arrangement or on an ad hoc basis, while traveling, or for other reasons, highlighting the need to examine the influence of this context on employee collaboration (Dixon & Panteli, 2010; Eisenberg & DiTomaso, 2019). Reliance on the electronic communication medium exacerbates teamwork among employees, even for those employees who collaborate virtually at least part of the time. Reduced face-to-face interactions diminish the strength of dispersed team member relationships and make talent management (TM) within geographically dispersed teams more complex. Lack of geographical proximity and the reduced interactions will likely make it harder for human resource managers to understand the

DOI: 10.4324/9781315474687-33

needs, aspirations, and concerns of team members across a multitude of contexts. This is likely to complicate TM in terms of how talent is assigned and utilized.

Star employees or "stars" are associated with a range of benefits in the context of traditional teams (Call, Nyberg, & Thatcher, 2015). While there are multiple approaches to defining the so-called stars, I extend earlier definitions and define them here as those workers who have disproportionally high visibility, access to social capital, and ability to add unique and prolonged organizational value through their performance (Call et al., 2015). Despite the multiple benefits associated with stars, many concur that managing stars is difficult in organizational setting (e.g., Morris, Alvarez, & Barney, 2017). Managing stars in the context of geographical dispersion is even more challenging due to the added level of complexity associated with lack of face-to-face interactions and reduced utilization of star's power.

The aim of this chapter is to provide a summary of selected research related to the intersection of virtual teams and TM of stars and to facilitate future research in this area. By examining the influence of stars and high-potential individuals on teams characterized by challenges associated with geographical dispersion, I contribute to the literature by extending existing research related to TM to the increasingly prevalent context of geographically distributed teams. A comprehensive review of the virtual teams literature is beyond the scope of this chapter but as listed in Table 33.1 (end of the chapter), selected studies provide an overview of the virtual teams literature over the last ten years to guide future research in this domain.

This chapter will first outline the challenges of geographically dispersed team collaboration, then discuss issues of utilizing stars and high-performers more generally as well as in the context of geographical dispersion, and finally conclude by outlining opportunities for future research.

Complexity of Geographically Dispersed Teamwork Collaboration

Geographical dispersion necessitates reliance on computer-mediated communication, which is associated with greater complexity in team member collaborations. Teams characterized by dispersion are frequently associated with dysfunctions, such as communication and collaboration challenges,

Table 33.1 References to summary research in the area of virtual teams over the last 10 years

Dulebohn, J. H., & Hoch, J. E. 2017. Virtual teams in organizations. **Human Resource Management Review**, 27(4): 569–574.

Ebrahim, A., Ahmed, S., & Taha, Z. 2009. Virtual teams: A literature review. **Australian Journal of Basic and Applied Sciences**, 3(3): 1–9.

Foster, M. K., Abbey, A., Callow, M. A., Zu, X., & Wilbon, A. D. 2015. Rethinking virtuality and its impact on teams. **Small Group Research**, 46(3): 267–299.

Gibson, C., Huang, L., Kirkman, B. L., & Shapiro, D. L. 2014. Where global and virtual meet: The value of examining the intersection of these elements in twenty-first-century teams. **Annual Review of Organizational Psychology and Organizational Behavior**, 1(1): 217–244.

Gilson, L. L., Maynard, M. T., & Bergiel, E. B. 2013. Virtual team effectiveness: An experiential activity. **Small Group Research**, 44(4): 412–427.

Gilson, L., Maynard, M. T., Jones Young, N. C., Vartiainen, M., & Hakonen, M. 2015. Virtual teams research: 10 years, 10 themes, and 10 opportunities. **Journal of Management**, 41(5): 1313–1337.

Maes, J. D., & Weldy, T. G. 2018. Building effective virtual teams : Expanding OD research and practice. **Organization Development Journal,** Fall: 83–90.

Mesmer-Magnus, J. R., DeChurch, L. A., Jimenez-Rodriguez, M., Wildman, J., & Shuffler, M. 2011. A meta-analytic investigation of virtuality and information sharing in teams. **Organizational Behavior and Human Decision Processes**, 115(2): 214–225.

Ortiz de Guinea, A., Webster, J., & Staples, D. S. 2012. A meta-analysis of the consequences of virtualness on team functioning. **Information & Management**, 49(6): 301–308.

Seshadri, V., & Elangovan, N. 2019. Role of manager in geographically distributed team: A review. **Journal of Management**, 6(1): 122–129.

reduced team member engagement, more time to build trust, perceptions of isolation, among others (Dulebohn & Hoch, 2017; Seshadri & Elangovan, 2019).

There are a number of reasons for problematic team dynamics when team members are not collocated in the same office. First, geographically dispersed team members are more likely to experience fragile and temporal trust (Bierly, Stark, & Kessler, 2009; Jarvenpaa & Leidner, 1999), which may be influenced by diminished interpersonal relationships and the limited information available about others on a virtual team (Cummings & Dennis, 2018). Some have suggested that "trust needs touch" (Handy, 1995: 46), which makes it harder for geographically distributed team members to establish trusting relationships, despite multiple technological advancements (Cummings & Dennis, 2018).

Second, increased electronic dependence reduces social cues that help establish relationships as well as interpret interactions and feedback (Gibson, Gibbs, Stanko, Tesluk, & Cohen, 2011). Lack of social cues makes it more difficult for team members to be aware of each other to benefit from team members' capabilities.

Third, boundaries in virtual environments are less defined than in traditional forms leading to more flexibility in roles and responsibilities but also highlighting the crucial role of effective communication that enables boundary-spanning across various points (Dibble & Gibson, 2018).

Fourth, geographical distance is also frequently associated with additional boundaries to collaboration stemming from work in global teams, such as cultural differences, coordination across multiple time zones, potential language differences, and variations in local norms.

These factors associated with global work contribute to greater levels of misunderstandings, hindering team members' ability to relate to each other and collaborate. Finally, work across multiple offices may also highlight status differences between team members based on their office location, influencing identification related processes and potentially creating location based subgroups (O'Leary & Mortensen, 2010). Creation of subgroups hinders teamwork because it may create tensions in the team among the different subgroups (Antino, Rico, & Thatcher, 2018; Carton & Cummings, 2012; Polzer, Crisp, Jarvenpaa, & Kim, 2006).

In sum, teamwork characterized by geographical dispersion is associated with a number of factors that may hinder members' ability to create strong relationship bonds, which in turn affects awareness dispersed teammates have of each other's knowledge, connections, and abilities. Further, even when team members are aware of what others can bring to the team, they may hesitate to trust that connection, negatively influencing an individual's potential contribution and necessitating a more involved TM approach.

Talent Management of Star Employees

While there are a multitude of ways to define *talent* in the context of organizational work, I follow earlier widespread conceptualizations that focus on star performers, "whose personification of exceptional talent is evidenced in their disproportionately high productivity and significant external visibility relative to their industry peers" in terms of knowledge, abilities and skills they contribute (Kehoe, Rosikiewicz, & Tzabbar, 2017: 153). Stars demonstrate excessively high and sustained performance, exhibit high levels of internal and external visibility that accents their performance and gives them access to greater resources (Call et al., 2015). In their integrative conceptual review of star employee research, Call et al. (2015) suggested that stars possess relevant social capital through their central network position with access to knowledge, control, and camaraderie.

Stars also act as role models for their team members, reducing uncertainty associated with adopting a new approach or utilizing a new practice, providing an opportunity to learn by observing to their colleagues (Kehoe et al., 2017). Kehoe et al. (2017) suggest that stars contribute to the team not only directly through their exceptional performance, but even more importantly, they utilize their capabilities to positively influence their teams' outcomes such as knowledge sharing and overall performance. Further, stars' mentoring style behavior helps advance colleagues' career success due to feedback and support they provide related to important career related decisions as well as sponsorship of mentees that provides access to a broader network of connections (Kehoe et al., 2017).

Stars frequently act as boundary spanners, utilizing their positions as network hubs to collect and disseminate key information, combining it with their own expertise to access crucial external resources to facilitate success of their teams, spanning both formal and informal boundaries (Kehoe et al., 2017). Stars' status facilitates the respect of stakeholders across different levels and helps them attract additional resources, further reinforcing their position, in line with the age-old adage "success breeds success." Stars have the ability to integrate information and expertise of various team members to facilitate accomplishing team tasks (Tzabbar & Vestal, 2015).

For example, in the pharmaceutical industry, star scientists play a crucial boundary spanning role connecting industry and academia, decoding the jargon and facilitating communication as well as knowledge flow, in many cases possessing the key knowledge themselves (Hess & Rothaermel, 2011). While stars generally benefit combined levels of team productivity, there are significant variations in how stars collaborate with colleagues, and their influence is not always positive (Kehoe & Tzabbar, 2015).

Challenges of Utilizing Stars In The Context of Geographical Dispersion: The Boundaries of Stars' Effectiveness

Stars bring many benefits to their teams and organizations, as is reviewed in detail above. More recently, TM literature has also focused on examining boundary conditions to stars' effectiveness (e.g., Kehoe & Tzabbar, 2015). While many emphasize the importance of stars to facilitate team performance, others question it, particularly across different contexts, because focusing on one individual may be counterproductive to team cohesion due to increased internal competition, threatening team performance (Oltra & Vivas-López, 2013). Oltra and Vivas-López (2017) further suggest that rather than focusing on the stars, developing collective team talent and focusing on its performance is more effective.

Kehoe and Tzabbar (2015) found that stars sometimes had a negative influence on contributions from other team members due to concerns about their own relevance and position, fighting for their spot as a thought leader. This might be particularly problematic in an environment where stars may feel threatened in their positions due to lack of sufficient knowledge about other contexts relevant to their team members. While stars get disproportionate attention, credit, and access to opportunities, their performance depends on their ability to collaborate with others to increase both quality and quantity of their output (Call et al., 2015), which may be hindered in some contexts where team members do not have opportunities to consistently work closely together.

Star employees bring many benefits to organizations, such as bringing in a new set of ideas and unique skills (Chen & Garg, 2018), which can be tremendously helpful across a variety of contexts, including geographically dispersed teams. However, stars' unique skill may not always fit across different environments, such as those associated with multiple office locations, due to routines that are aligned to utilize conventional skills (Chen & Garg, 2018).

Additionally, the benefits of star employees may not extend to geographically dispersed teams in the same way as when stars and their team members are collocated and have greater number of opportunities to collaborate in close proximity to each other. In the context of geographical dispersion of team members, such benefits may be limited due to reduced levels of knowledge spillover, frequently attributed to stars (Kehoe & Tzabbar, 2015).

Research suggests that cohesion among team members who are not stars may be more likely to lead to greater team performance than an overemphasis on individual stars contributing to a team (Oltra & Vivas-López, 2013). When stars have limited familiarity with various needs and context associated with office locations of their team members, they may be less likely to facilitate cohesive productive relationships with these geographically dispersed members, hindering team processes. In general, being new to a problem is detrimental to one's performance and overall efficiency, when compared to someone with long-term experience (Collings & Isichei, 2018), which may reflect the limitations on stars' performance in a new to them environment associated with multiple dispersed offices that each may have a different set of norms. When stars collaborate with geographically distributed colleagues, whose environment may be new and unfamiliar to the star due to their distance, it may limit the extent to which stars could be influential in helping their team members be more productive.

Stars' roles within their teams, associated with facilitating knowledge exchange due to their network centrality and access to information, should enable them to integrate resources for increased team success (Kehoe et al., 2017). However, it may have variability in its effects depending on contextual factors associated with differences in organizational environment, resource availability, reporting structure, among others, across geographically dispersed office locations of team members. There are a number of factors that may limit stars' effectiveness in positively influencing their team members and in turn team outcomes, which are outlined next.

Boundary Spanning

Stars integrate knowledge of everyone on the team to facilitate teamwork (Tzabbar & Vestal, 2015). Integrating resources requires that stars have a keen awareness of what goes on around them, acting as a boundary spanner. However, in a geographically dispersed environment, it is likely that stars will have diminished opportunities for interaction with fellow team mates to be well versed in both team members' abilities as well as needs to be able to provide more targeted assistance. Thus, due to these reduced opportunities to know about each other's needs, stars' efficiency as a boundary spanner may be reduced because they are less likely to identify an area of need and even if they do, they may find it harder to influence a teammate from a distance.

Some have suggested that globally dispersed work necessitates the involvement of a broker who facilitates interactions and knowledge sharing among team members (Eisenberg & Mattarelli, 2017). A broker need not be a star but should have skills related to helping colleagues overcome boundaries associated with working across multiple contexts and set of norms. While the stars may be well positioned to facilitate the work of their collocated team members, they may not be as effective in taking on such brokerage roles to facilitate the work of team members who operate in a different office.

Status differences associated with work across multiple offices may exacerbate relationships among team members due to different identification targets. Identification is associated with self-enhancement through favoring in-group members at the expense of negative beliefs about out-group members to increase self-esteem (Tajfel & Turner, 1986). Some office locations are perceived as lower status, leading to stereotypes and perceptions of status differences (Leonardi & Rodriguez-Lluesma, 2013), particularly in global settings, which may negatively influence relationships among geographically dispersed workers, hindering their team collaboration (Levina & Vaast, 2008).

Status differences may also limit boundary spanning behavior of a star, depending on how fellow team members perceive the star's status. A star from a lower status location may be less likely to influence team members in higher status locations because they are less likely to assign as much value to the star's expertise as if this individual was from their higher status office.

Conversely, if a star is from a higher status location, they may have less interest or incentive to get involved with team members from a lower status location and using their expertise to work closely together to find a better solution. When star's performance is not clearly notable and when higher resource allocation received by the star is not perceived as fair by fellow team members from other locations, they may feel resentful (Call et al., 2015), hindering teamwork.

Relationship Bonds, Social Capital, and Mentoring

Lack of close relationship bonds, associated with geographically dispersed work, may also diminish the effect of having a star act in their mentoring role. The feedback and support stars are able to provide in their mentoring capacity to facilitate colleague's career success (Kehoe et al., 2017) may be limited in an environment characterized by lack of close face-to-face interactions and relationships.

First, colleagues may be less likely to ask for a star's advice and mentorship when they work in a different office since they may be uncomfortable asking someone they do not know well. Second, stars may be less effective in providing advice in an environment where they are unfamiliar with the local norms and may have fewer connections. Their network centrality is evaluated based on how well they are connected from the point of view of their primary office, rather than across the whole company and all of its potentially numerous locations, which may result in misleading inflation of stars' effectiveness.

Ability to gather social capital and thus gain goodwill support and build relationships with fellow employees is crucial for star's ability to influence others (Call et al., 2015). However, building relationships in a geographically distributed environment is significantly more difficult due to lack of face-to-face interactions and absence of opportunities for informal contact, which can negatively influence star's ability to gather social capital as effectively as in traditional teams. Lack of strong relationship bonds may also influence stars' ability to utilize their social capital. Having relevant social capital helps stars access unique opportunities to apply their expertise to different areas, relying on their ability to work with others to increase performance outcomes (Call et al., 2015).

However, if the social capital stars have is only relevant in the office where they primarily work, it may not be as influential in other offices where their geographically dispersed team members are located. Social capital may also be harder to develop and maintain in a geographically dispersed organization. Further, it may be weaker within a dispersed network where colleagues have diminished opportunities to interact and foster the strength of their connections. Therefore, stars may find it harder to utilize their social capital.

Trust

Social capital is in part based on trusting relationships among people. Further, boundary spanning relationships characterized by exchanges of novel and valuable knowledge rely on and have more value when colleagues trust each other (Call et al., 2015; Levin & Cross, 2004). However, trust is more difficult to establish in an environment characterized by geographical dispersion and particularly in globally dispersed teams (Jarvenpaa & Leidner, 1999). While computer mediated communication facilitates collaboration among geographically dispersed team members, lack of high levels of mutual trust and ability to attain shared understanding are more difficult in the dispersed environment (Maynard, Mathieu, Rapp, & Gilson, 2012).

A star leader who feels trusted by those whose interest they represent, may be more motivated to achieve set goals due to opportunities related to star's self-enhancement (Call et al., 2015). However, this motivation may be hindered if a star does not believe they can foster sufficient trust to enable them to step into a more leadership type role to represent fellow team members. In a geographically dispersed environment, where trust levels among team members are expected to be lower due to lack of strong bonds, stars may not be as motivated to be engaged with their team members to first learn what they need and to then facilitate their work utilizing all available resources.

Diminished levels of trust may also reduce the extent to which a star can utilize their human capital, which is one of their strengths. Human capital stems from employee's ability to accomplish complex tasks, trusting relationships with team members, but it is usually valuable in a specific and limited context within an organization (Morris et al., 2017). Morris et al. (2017) suggest that stars frequently underestimate the importance of trusting relationships as a contributing factor to a star's productivity. When that is the case, stars may be less likely to make an effort to consciously foster trust with fellow teammates from geographically distributed offices, which may exasperate the extent to which they collaborate with each other and in turn their overall team dynamics.

Transaction Memory Systems and Shared Mindset

Geographical dispersion of team members is also detrimental to transaction memory systems (TMS), characterized by knowledge specialization, task credibility, and task coordination, due to reduced trust and awareness of each other's expertise and talents (Maynard et al., 2012). TMS highlights the importance for team members to develop an understanding of where and how to leverage relevant knowledge (Maynard & Gilson, 2013). In their review, Maynard et al. (2012) suggest that the concept of TMS is an important theme to be studied in the context of geographical dispersion. It is also relevant to the discussion of the limitations of stars' effectiveness in the context of dispersion for a number of reasons.

First, knowledge specialization focuses on differentiating expertise across team members that could be utilized for team tasks. Part of stars' influence is to apply expertise to facilitate the work of other team members. However, if stars are not aware of what is required as well as team members' capabilities, their likelihood of making a substantial difference in applying their own expertise to facilitate team members' effectiveness may be reduced. Second, task credibility is the degree to which team members believe in each other's abilities. If team members are less aware of a star team member's expertise and ability, they are less likely to be positively influenced by presence of such a star member. Third, task coordination utilizes team members' awareness of each other's expertise and enables information flow in the needed direction.

However, due to geographical boundaries, team members may find it harder to be aware and easily access each other's expertise to apply it to their work. Stars may be less visible to team members in other offices and stars are also less likely to be aware of opportunities for them to apply their expertise and connections, reducing the likelihood of seamless task coordination. In sum, while multiple studies of transactive memory systems have demonstrated positive influence TMS has on team performance in traditional collocated teams, a recent review suggests the need to reevaluate the effects of TMS in the context of complexity associated with today's teams that are frequently dispersed across multiple boundaries (Maynard et al., 2012).

When team members are collocated, their frequent face-to-face interactions foster better TMS, in part due to greater understanding of norms as well as the development of shared mental models. This may facilitate communication and the development of collaboration that integrates star's knowledge with other team members, which in turn leads to more effective knowledge sharing, including applying stars' tacit knowledge (Kehoe et al., 2017). These types of collaborative exchanges are crucial for successful team outcomes. However, geographical dispersion will make communication and collaboration among team members who are not collocated and thus rely on the electronic medium of communication, more complex (DeSanctis & Monge, 1999; Marlow, Lacerenza, & Salas, 2017). The geographically dispersed environment will likely make it harder for stars to convey their expertise and share relevant tacit knowledge where needed. It may also make it harder to develop a shared mental model.

Shared mental models represent a convergence of team members' perceptions and mental representations of their team work and common knowledge about their team's internal and external environment, which is especially relevant for geographically dispersed teams' performance (Maynard & Gilson, 2013). Yet, being on the same page and sharing mental models may be more difficult in the context of dispersion. Therefore, a star may find it harder to influence geographically dispersed team members, who may have a different mental model and be less likely to follow their star team member's guidance and leadership.

Global Geographical Dispersion

As the environment characterizing today's teams is evolving and unlike what it was in the past, it is important to take into consideration the new challenges that add complexity to how talent is managed in teams frequently characterized not just by geographical but also by global dispersion (Maynard, Vartiainen, Sanchez, & Sanchez, 2017). Thus, when geographically dispersed teams are characterized by global dispersion, it further complicates team dynamics associated with managing star performers. For example, the extent to which expatiates adjust to their role is affected by their expectations and could be helped by various training, including cross-cultural training (Caligiuri, Phillips, Lazarova, Tarique, & Peter, 2001). It may be expected that star power of these talented individuals is so great that it does not necessitate additional help to adjust nor does it require training, which may hinder their chances of succeeding in exerting their influence across global office locations.

A recent review of global TM literature suggests that many challenges associated with global work environment are specific to a particular region (Tarique & Schuler, 2010). More generally, challenges of managing talent in the context of global dispersion are more complex. It is unproductive to assume that talented experts could make a crucial difference to their organization's performance or that greater numbers of star employees will lead to greater success due to variability in the surrounding organizational environment (Minbaeva & Collings, 2013). Minbaeva and Collings (2013) suggest that when a star is moved to another location, their star power may be reduced and that a local alternative may be a better fit than relocating talent, whose influence maybe bounded. This highlights the importance of taking context into consideration when evaluating the benefits of a star employee.

Global dispersion literature has highlighted the importance of selecting diverse employees with broad expertise ranging from local to global, rather than selecting them based on a set of possibly biased assumptions (Bruning & Cadigan, 2012). Among various biased assumptions is likely the overly optimistic belief about the positive influence of star performers on a team. Following Bruning and Cadigan (2012), it is more important to focus on utilizing the expertise of employees who have broad knowledge and represent diverse backgrounds rather than that they are stars in one particular location. Being a star in one office does not translate to an individual being successful in contributing to the team across various offices, particularly when team members are globally distributed.

Not only may star's influence be limited but identifying and evaluating stars may be more complex across a geographically and globally distributed team environment due to lack of standardized human resource practices when it comes to TM across culturally distinct environments. The greater the distance between decision makers and talent, the less likely an employee would be recognized as talent (Schuler, Mellahi, McDonnell, & Collings, 2017). In their review of TM, Schuler et al. (2017) suggested that subsidiaries may purposefully avoid identifying their star employees to the parent company as there is nothing in it for them, and the larger multinational corporation would not be able to manage talent from dispersed locations at the level of the headquarters. This may further complicate the role of a star in a dispersed team environment.

In summary, as outlined in Table 33.1, global teams add a level of complexity to TM. While presence of a star may bring benefits, it is also likely to make team interactions more complex to manage due to additional boundaries separating team members associated with differences in cultural norms and time zone, among many others. Additional number of stars may further complicate team dynamics due to factors such as increased chance of competition among the stars, intra-team politics, and subgroup formation around each star, reducing cohesion and negatively influencing team outcomes. The most complex case is one where multiple stars are part of a global team, where factors that exacerbate teamwork across global boundaries are compounded by dynamics that negatively influence multiple stars potentially competing within a team.

Opportunities for Future Research

TM and stars research is increasingly relevant as companies search for "unicorns" to quickly and efficiently solve problems in an environment characterized by fast paced changes. Given teamwork related trends related to accessing expertise at multiple locations, leading to increasing prevalence of geographically dispersed teams, it is important to understand the effects of stars in the context of dispersion. Research related to these industry trends is still in a nascent stage and offers multiple opportunities for future research to contribute to disciplines ranging from human resource management to teamwork.

As employees move from one office location to another, it is important for them to build social capital and attain status at their new location to enable them to act in their boundary-spanning role across locations (Eisenberg & Mattarelli, 2017), which requires significant efforts on the part of the individual and the organization (Moeller, Maley, Harvey, & Kiessling, 2016).

Future research should examine the effects of stars' transfers across offices and the influence such shifts have on team members at the old and the new location. How team members perceive stars based on their location, may be important to stars' ability to influence them. For example, some team members may rely on identification with the team or patterns of interactions to determine whether an individual is a member of their team or not, regardless of formal team designations (Mortensen, 2014). Further, as stars shift from higher to lower status team office locations or from lower to higher status locations, it is important to gain an understand how such transfers affect star's ability to influence team members across various offices and utilize their network centrality to act in boundary spanning roles.

In teams that are fluid and dynamic, identifying talent due to advancements in technology may be more streamlined, resulting in greater access to resources and capabilities across team and geographical boundaries (Dibble & Gibson, 2018). However, an environment characterized by fluid and dynamic teams expects individuals to be flexible about their team membership and adapt to work across team boundaries that is associated with greater complexity (Dibble & Gibson, 2018). As traditional conceptualizations of teams are constantly evolving (Gilson et al., 2015), with many modern teams having fluid and multiple team membership patterns (Mortensen & Haas, 2018), there is a need to examine the effects of such context on traditional approaches to TM.

Future studies should examine how stars can influence team members who may only participate in a team part time, prioritizing their commitment to multiple teams. Further, a star who is a member of multiple teams could be an expert in one team but may not have adequate qualifications to be considered a star in another team, where their influence is only tangential. Future studies should examine how reduced time commitment of stars due to their team structure affects their effectiveness. First, what is the effect of a star's multiple team membership commitments on their influence across these different teams. Second, how does the fluid team structure and cross boundary work relate to fellow team members' perceptions of a star as a member of their team and the resulting perceptions of a star's effectiveness.

Given globalization trends, rather than just examining stars in the context of geographically dispersed team environments, future studies should evaluate the influence of stars on team members across culturally different contexts and in collaboration with team members across cultural boundaries. A star may have to take on the role of a cultural broker role to increase their effectiveness as a boundary spanner and maintain their network centrality (Eisenberg & Mattarelli, 2017), which may require specialized training. Thus, organizations should consider adding specialized training for their top talent to help these experts be more effective at collaborating across geographical but especially global boundaries since such context may completely change the appropriate approach to teamwork.

Not only do cultural values and norms vary across locations, but so do human resource policies related to compensation practices and the value assigned to them by local employees (Schuler et al., 2017). Lack of perceptions of equity in how stars are treated across office locations may influence how stars are perceived and valued, influencing stars' effectiveness. Further, human resource managers may also need to consider how to best recruit, manage, and motivate stars in the context of geographical dispersion. While such capable individuals have a lot of potential, their influence may be limited in an environment where their relationship bonds with team members are diminished due to fewer opportunities for interactions across geographical distance.

Since geographically dispersed team research suggests that even occasional face-to-face interactions significantly facilitate relationships and trust among team members, future research may want to examine the effects of offsite events or special opportunities for interactions to help stars establish the types of ties and relationships that may facilitate their effectiveness in positively influencing fellow team members and in turn their team success.

Conclusion

Talent management research related to stars has highlighted many benefits associated with having such an individual and what a star could bring to their team and the larger organization. Recent integrative conceptual review highlighted the need to examine the boundaries of stars' effectiveness (Call et al., 2015). Our aim was to outline the complexity of a geographically dispersed environment as a way to better understand the limitation of the influence exerted by a star and to summarize future research opportunities in this area. Stars have a lot of potential to positively influence geographically dispersed teams, but first they have to be able to address the added complexity associated with technology mediated communication and reduced strength of relationship bonds, among other factors. While stars may have numerous ways to enhance team dynamics and outcomes in traditional teams, their influence may be limited by complex factors associated with geographic and especially global dispersion of team members.

References

Antino, M., Rico, R., & Thatcher, S. 2019. Structuring reality through the faultlines lens: The effects of structure, fairness, and status conflict on the activated faultlines-performance relationship. *Academy of Management Journal,* 62(5): 1444–1470.

Bierly, P. E., Stark, E. M., & Kessler, E. H. 2009. The moderating effects of virtuality on the antecedents and outcome of NPD team trust. *Journal of Product Innovation Management,* 26: 551–565.

Bruning, N. S., & Cadigan, F. 2014. Diversity and global talent management: Are there cracks in the glass ceiling and glass border? *People & Strategy,* 37(3): 18–22.

Caligiuri, P., Phillips, J., Lazarova, M., Tarique, I., & Peter, B. 2001. The theory of met expectations applied to expatriate adjustment: The role of cross-cultural training. *The International Journal of Human Resource Management,* 12(3): 357–372.

Call, M. L., Nyberg, A. J., & Thatcher, S. M. B. 2015. Stargazing: An integrative conceptual review, theoretical reconciliation, and extension for star employee research. *Journal of Applied Psychology,* 100(3): 623–640.

Carton, A. M., & Cummings, J. N. 2012. A theory of subgroups in work teams. *Academy of Management Review,* 37(3): 441–470.

Chen, J. S., & Garg, P. 2018. Dancing with the stars: Benefits of a star employee's temporary absence for organizational performance. *Strategic Management Journal,* 39(5): 1239–1267.

Collings, D. G., & Isichei, M. 2018. The shifting boundaries of global staffing: integrating global talent management, alternative forms of international assignments and non-employees into the discussion. *International Journal of Human Resource Management,* 29(1): 165–187.

Cummings, J., & Dennis, A. R. 2018. Virtual first impressions matter: The effect of enterprise social networking sites on impression formation in virtual teams. *MIS Quarterly,* 42(3): 697–717.

DeSanctis, G., & Monge, P. 1999. Introduction to the special issue: Communication processes for virtual organizations. *Organization Science,* 10(6): 693–703.

Dibble, R., & Gibson, C. B. 2018. Crossing team boundaries: A theoretical model of team boundary permeability and a discussion of why it matters. *Human Relations,* 71(7): 925–950.

Dixon, K. R., & Panteli, N. 2010. From virtual teams to virtuality in teams. *Human Relations,* 63(8): 1177–1197.

Dulebohn, J. H., & Hoch, J. E. 2017. Virtual teams in organizations. *Human Resource Management Review,* 27(4): 569–574.

Eisenberg, J., & DiTomaso, N. 2019. Structural decisions about configuration, assignments, and geographical distribution in teams: Influences on team communications and trust. *Human Resource Management Review,* online.

Eisenberg, J., & Mattarelli, E. 2017. Building bridges in global virtual teams: The role of multicultural brokers in overcoming the negative effects of identity threats on knowledge sharing across subgroups. *Journal of International Management,* 23: 399–411.

Gibson, C., Gibbs, J., Stanko, T., Tesluk, P., & Cohen, S. G. (2011). Including the "I" in virtuality and modern job design: Extending the job characteristics model to include the moderating effect of individual experiences of electronic dependence and copresence. *Organization Science,* 22: 1–19.

Gilson, L., Maynard, M. T., Jones Young, N. C., Vartiainen, M., & Hakonen, M. 2015. Virtual teams research: 10 years, 10 themes, and 10 opportunities. *Journal of Management,* 41(5): 1313–1337.

Handy, C. 1995. Trust and the virtual organization. *Harvard Business Review,* 28(4): 126.

Hess, A., & Rothaermel, F. 2011. When are assets complementary? Star scientists, strategic alliances, and innovation in the pharmaceutical industry. *Strategic Management Journal,* 32: 895–909.

Jarvenpaa, S., & Leidner, D. E. 1999. Communication and trust in global virtual teams. *Organization Science,* 10(6): 791–815.

Kehoe, R., Rosikiewicz, B., & Tzabbar, D. 2017. Talent and teams. In D. G. Collings, K. Mellahi, & W. F. Cascio (Eds.), *The Oxford handbook of talent management:* 153–168. New York, NY: Oxford University Press.

Kehoe, R., & Tzabbar, D. 2015. Lighting the way or stealing the shine? An examination of the duality in star scientists' effects on firm innovative performance. *Strategic Management Journal,* 20(1): 397–403.

Leonardi, P. M., & Rodriguez-Lluesma, C. 2013. Occupational stereotypes, perceived status differences, and intercultural communication in global organizations. *Communication Monographs,* 80: 478–502.

Levin, D. Z., & Cross, R. 2004. The strength of weak ties you can trust: The mediating role of trust in effective knowledge transfer. *Management Science,* 50(11): 1477–1490.

Levina, N., & Vaast, E. 2008. Innovating or doing as told? Status differences and overlapping boundaries in off-shore collaboration. *MIS Quarterly,* 32(2): 307–332.

Maes, J. D., & Weldy, T. G. 2018. Building effective virtual teams: Expanding OD research and practice. *Organization Development Journal,* Fall: 83–90.

Magni, M., Ahuja, M. K., & Maruping, L. M. 2018. Distant but fair: Intra-team justice climate and performance in dispersed teams. *Journal of Management Information Systems,* 35(4): 1031–1059.

Marlow, S. L., Lacerenza, C. N., & Salas, E. 2017. Communication in virtual teams: A conceptual framework and research agenda. *Human Resource Management Review,* (4): 575–584.

Maynard, M. T., & Gilson, L. 2013. The role of shared mental model development in understanding virtual team effectiveness. *Group & Organization Management,* 39(1): 3–32.

Maynard, M. T., Mathieu, J. E., Rapp, T. L., & Gilson, L. 2012. Something(s) old and something(s) new: Modeling drivers of global virtual team effectiveness. *Journal of Organizational Behavior,* 33: 342–365.

Maynard, M. T., Vartiainen, M., Sanchez, A., & Sanchez, D. 2017. Virtual teams: Utilizing talent-management thinking to assess what we currently know about making virtual teams successful. In D. Collings, K. Mellahi, & W. Cascio (Eds.), *The Oxford handbook of talent management:* 193–214. New York, NY: Oxford University Press.

Minbaeva, D., & Collings, D. G. 2013. Seven myths of global talent management. *International Journal of Human Resource Management,* 24(9): 1762–1776.

Moeller, M., Maley, J., Harvey, M., & Kiessling, T. 2016. Global talent management and inpatriate social capital building: A status inconsistency perspective. *International Journal of Human Resource Management,* 27(9): 991–1012.

Morris, S., Alvarez, S., & Barney, J. B. 2018. Dancing with the stars: The practical value of theory in managing star employees. *Academy of Management Perspectives,* online.

Mortensen, M. 2014. Constructing the team: The antecedents and effects of membership model divergence. *Organization Science,* 25(3): 909–931.

Mortensen, M., & Haas, M. R. 2018. Perspective—rethinking teams: From bounded membership to dynamic participation. *Organization Science,* 29(2): 191–355.

O'Leary, M. B., & Mortensen, M. 2010. Go (con)figure: Subgroups, imbalance, and isolates in geographically dispersed teams. *Organization Science,* 21(1): 115–131.

Oltra, V., & Vivas-López, S. 2013. Boosting organizational learning through team-based talent management: What is the evidence from large Spanish firms? *The International Journal of Human Resource Management,* 24(9): 1853–1871.

Polzer, J. T., Crisp, C. B., Jarvenpaa, S., & Kim, J. W. 2006. Extending the faultline model to geographically dispersed teams: How colocated subgroups can impair group functioning. *Academy of Management Journal,* 49(4): 679–692.

Powell, A., Piccoli, G., & Ives, B. 2004. Virtual teams: A review of current literature and directions for future research. *ACM SIGMIS Database,* 35(1): 6–36.

RW3 CultureWizard. 2018. *Trends in high-performing global virtual teams.* https://content.ebulletins.com/hubfs/C1/Culture%20Wizard/LL-2018%20Trends%20in%20Global%20VTs%20Draft%2012%20and%20a%20half.pdf.

Schuler, R., Mellahi, K., McDonnell, A., & Collings, D. G. (2017). Talent management: A systematic review and future prospects. *European Journal of International Management,* 11(1): 86.

Seshadri, V., & Elangovan, N. 2019. Role of manager in geographically distributed team: A review. *Journal of Management,* 6(1): 122–129.

Tajfel, H., & Turner, J. C. 1986. The social identity theory of intergroup behaviour. In S. Worchel & W. G. Austin (Eds.), *Psychology of Intergroup Relations* (2nd ed.): 276–293.

Tarique, I., & Schuler, R. S. 2010. Global talent management: Literature review, integrative framework, and suggestions for further research. *Journal of World Business,* 45(2): 122–133.

Tzabbar, D., & Vestal, A. 2015. Bridging the social chasm in geographically distributed R&D teams: The moderating effects of relational strength and status asymmetry on the novelty of team innovation. *Organization Science,* 26(3): 811–829.

34

TALENT SPOTTING

A Review of Meanings and Identification Tools

Anthony McDonnell

Agnieszka Skuza

Introduction

In recent decades "talent" has become a commonly used, everyday term. Much of this has been due to the success of the entertainment industry with productions such as *X-Factor* and *America's Got Talent* that have been replicated across multiple countries worldwide. These television programs seek to identify individuals who are viewed as possessing abilities beyond the norm in terms of their voice or act and who may go on to be successful acts in the entertainment industry. While there is a strong consistency in format of these shows from country to country the same cannot be said over what is viewed as talent. What one "judge" sees as talented can often differ to other "judges".

This situation appears somewhat similar in the practitioner and academic management literature where talent appears to be increasingly talked about. Talent management (TM) research has escalated considerably over the past decade as evidenced by several review papers (e.g., Collings & Mellahi, 2009; Lewis & Heckman, 2006; McDonnell, 2011; McDonnell, Collings, Mellahi, & Schuler, 2017; Thunnissen, Boselie & Fruytier, 2016) and special issues (e.g., Gallardo-Gallardo, Thunnissen, & Scullion, 2020; McDonnell, Collings, & Burgess, 2013; Scullion, Collings, & Caligiuri, 2010). Of particular note in the context of this chapter is that TM research continues to typically fail to indicate how talent is defined or conceptualized. In line with this, Gallardo-Gallardo, Dries, & Gonzalez-Cruz suggest that "talent as an underlying construct is taken for granted and thus not defined explicitly. A continued lack of clarity may continue to hold the field back with accusations of TM merely being a case of "old wine in new bottles" (2013: 290) likely to remain common.

Concerns about the extent to which organizations manage their talent effectively are evident with the following quote from an article in *The Economist* endemic of this: "companies do not even know how to define 'talent', let alone how to manage it" (*The Economist*, 2006: 4). Overall, it appears that organizations struggle to articulate their meaning of talent (Strack et al., 2013). To what extent does a lack of clarity on what talent means matter? We contend that it is incredibly important as misidentification of talent will be more common and the likelihood of individuals being placed in roles for which they are ill-equipped will also be increased. This can potentially lead to disastrous consequences as illustrated in the fall of energy company Enron (see Michaels et al., 2001). However, effectively and objectively identifying talent is an incredibly challenging task that is likely to never result in perfect solutions, yet we argue there is a need to critically examine how to improve how we undertake the process.

This chapter reviews the extant literature on the definition or meaning of talent. We then proceed to illustrate the variety of tools organizations tend to use in identifying talent. Finally, we articulate several research avenues that scholars may wish to pursue to aid understanding of the talent concept.

DOI: 10.4324/9781315474687-34

Defining Talent

We argue that for organizations to engage in effective TM then the starting point must be seeking clarity on what is meant by "talent" within their own context. If the aim is to identify and manage talent then presumably you need to first understand what is meant by talent. While there is a need for processes around the identification process, prior to this requires clarity on what it is that the organization is looking for when it talks about talent. Too often there is an assumption that this is clear to all (Wiblen & McDonnell, 2019). A failure in having clarity of understanding among key stakeholders increases the likelihood of negative workplace and motivational impacts. These can arise when people are unclear on how individual employees are classified as talent while other employees do not receive such a designation (Gelens, Hofmans, Dries, & Petermans, 2014). It also increases the probability of individuals being placed in roles they are unsuitable for. According to Wiblen & McDonnell (2019: 1), "Much scholarship appears to make significant assumptions that everyone knows (and agrees) what we are talking about when we talk about talent."

In developing clarity on what talent means within context, we suggest that understanding the strategic position of the organization is critical. TM should be strongly centered on understanding and satisfying the organizational needs and requirements to achieve competitive advantage and growth. Therefore, in defining talent, this should be in line with the organization's strategic intent (Joyce & Slocum, 2012). "Put Strategy, Not People, First" (Becker, Huselid, & Beatty, 2009: 1). The pursuit of a universal definition of talent is neither desired nor feasible, but there needs to be an organizational specific and appropriate meaning behind talent. What may be talent in one organization may not be in another given the different corporate strategies. In addition, talent within an organization can take multiple forms. In other words, it may not merely refer to one particular group or pool of people.

The problem of there being limited clarity on what talent means is not merely relevant to practice but also endemic in published research. In looking to the TM literature for guidance, it becomes evident that few papers consider the definition of talent explicitly. For example, in a review of TM empirical papers, Gallardo-Gallardo and Thunnissen (2016) report that 28 articles presented no definition of talent, a further 36 were classified as having some indirect consideration of it, while an additional 17 discussed different definitions but never made clear what definition was being adopted. Therefore, a mere 15 papers provided an explicit definition of talent.

Where there is some consideration of what talent means, it appears to often refer in some guise to high-performers and high-potentials. It is argued here that this may be insufficient in that an organizational view of talent should take organizational context (i.e., corporate strategy, availability) into account, and more than high-potentials and performers may be viewed as pivotal. In addition, there is likely to be considerable variation in how stakeholders give meaning to high-performers, and in particular, high-potentials.

Recent review papers provide some assistance on the different guises talent may take (see Table 34.1). The literature points to talent being defined in the context of an object or subject approach (Gallardo-Gallardo et al., 2013). The subject approach being very much centered on the person as talent, which can then be divided into an inclusive or exclusive view. The inclusive approach views every individual as talent, and the focus is on facilitating everybody to achieve their potential and make a maximum contribution to the organization. Hence, talent is a "euphemism for people" (Lewis & Heckman, 2016: 141).

On the other hand, the exclusive perspective views talent as not centered on every employee but rather, focused on a subset(s) of the workforce that is perceived as adding greater value to the achievement of organizational objectives than others. An exclusive perspective can be linked to the somewhat sinister mantra expressed in the political satire novel *Animal Farm* (Orwell, 1944), whereby all employees are equal but some are more equal than others. Although on the one level, every employee contributes to the achievement of an organization's strategic objectives, it is argued that some employees can have a more telling and important impact (Boudreau & Ramstad, 2007). This is in part due to the person's

Table 34.1 Key papers on clarifying the meaning of/defining talent

Authors (Year of Publication)	Key Objective/Findings of Paper
Gallardo-Gallardo, Dries, & Gonzalez-Cruz (2013)	*Conceptual paper* Proposes two approaches taken to talent in the literature: the subject and object approach.
Meyers & van Woerkom (2014)	*Conceptual paper* Examines philosophies of talent that underpin talent management through proposing four different talent philosophies that vary in their perceptions of talent: rare, universal, stable, developable.
Nijs, Gallardo-Gallardo, Dries, & Sels (2014)	*Review/Conceptual paper* Proposes 11 propositions in their conceptual framework of the definition, operationalization, and measurement of talent.
Tansley (2011)	*Review paper* Charts how the term "talent" has evolved over several centuries from a denomination of weight and a monetary unit to a treasure to a special natural ability.
Wiblen & McDonnell (2019)	*Empirical paper* Illuminates the meaning of "talent" according to multi-level and business unit stakeholders. Demonstrates that while stakeholders may talk about talent in the same way, they may mean different things.

capacity and abilities but also to having the right people in the right roles where better performance can lead to increased value for the organization. Key to this is the idea that differential performance in roles does not always lead to improvements in value for the organization (Collings & Mellahi, 2009). However, there is little research that critically examines and provides support on whether some individuals provide substantially enhanced value as purported.

The subject approach requires greater clarity in that whether an organization adopts an inclusive or exclusive approach, there remains a need to understand the abilities, qualities, traits, and skills of its employees to assist the achievement of each individual's potential and maximize the contribution to the organization. This is important in terms of setting an overall talent agenda and culture in the organization. We suggest that there are degrees of inclusivity and exclusivity that may exist in how organizations define talent as opposed to it being a simple dichotomy – exclusive versus inclusive.

Hybridization is possible within organizations (Stahl et al., 2012) with Sharna and Wiblen (2019) demonstrating the diversity of talent meanings across business units of a financial services firm. Where an exclusive approach is more evident, this should not mean those outside of these talent pools are bereft of investment and developmental opportunities. There should be differentiated investment based on strategic value but the rest of the workforce should not be ignored. It is important that all employees are provided with opportunities for training and development, and that talent identification needs to be an ongoing, dynamic, and fluid.

The object perspective is focused on the characteristics individuals possess. This may refer to the individual's capacity, capabilities, abilities, competences, knowledge, experience, skills, levels of commitment and performance, and potential to add value in different and/or higher level positions. Essentially, talent is then conceptualized, implicitly or explicitly, around some or all of these characteristics. Within this perspective, several sub-approaches are evident (Gallardo-Gallardo et al., 2013; Meyers et al., 2013).

First, talent may be viewed as innate, the possession of natural ability, or a person who is naturally gifted. "The notion that some people are born with more than others is firmly ingrained in everyday psychology (Simonton, 1999: 435). Second, talent can be about the possession of competencies that are viewed as fundamental to the achievement of high-performance levels. Third, talent can be viewed as mastery of specified practices. Fourth, the demonstration of high-performance may be another means to which one labels an individual as talent. Fifth, talent can be viewed as possession of strengths or "potentials for excellence" (Biswas-Diener, Kashdan, & Minhas, 2011, 106). This is akin to high-potential as opposed to being distinct (Meyers et al., 2013).

A more supplementary view of talent resides in the need to demonstrate high levels of commitment. It is viewed as supplementary in the context of high commitment being insufficient on its own to be a determinant of talent status. Ulrich (2006) suggest that talent may be best viewed as encompassing three elements: 1) competence signifies an individual's skills, knowledge, and values; 2) contribution denotes an individual's output and role in organizational performance; and 3) commitment relates to the level of employee engagement with their work and actions in terms of how they apply their competences in the organization.

Gallardo-Gallardo et al. (2013) propose a final means of how talent is conceptualized as being about fit to the context of work. However, we view this as an overarching element of how talent should be defined rather than a specific and distinct conceptualization. In other words, the perspective taken is that context is central but rather than this being a specific talent as object approach, it should be considered as integral to all conceptualizations in that an individual may not perform in the same manner in every situation (Coulson-Thomas, 2012). There is great importance behind being in the right place with the right supports, in the right position and it being the right time for high-performance to be achieved. This also raises the issue of the TM being overly individualist and neglecting that people do not operate in isolation to their colleagues.

Potential

The concept of "potential" appears especially critical in views around what or whom is talent. It appears that recognizing talent requires a shift from solely concentrating on the input's an individual possesses but heavily considering the likely outputs (Huselid, Beatty, & Becker, 2005). The conceptualizations of talent as being about high potential fails to address the challenge of how you identify potential in an objective manner. Potential can be viewed as a latent factor (i.e., not readily observable) that is the precondition of future success. Given it is the possibility or a promise (i.e., something not yet realized), it may be viewed in more innate terms (Altman, 1997; Yost & Chang, 2009).

The measurement of potential therefore takes on great importance. Potential can be considered in wider terms than solely about leadership talent but also incorporate technical experts. At a basic level, high-potentials refer to individuals with a large capacity for future growth. This is often discussed in terms of an individuals' capacity and ability to be promoted at least two levels above their current position. This may be a more problematic view in the organization of today given the flatter structures in place.

The extent to which potential can validly be recognized is open to question. Cappelli and Keller (2014) note that there appears to be a strong reliance on potential being identified through line managers asked evaluations, which is built into the 9-box grid, long associated with GE. This approach is fraught with problems, and there is little confidence that it will lead to valid results.

Silzer and Church (2009) offer a three-dimension model of how potential can be evaluated. First, there are the foundation dimensions that are those viewed as stable characteristics related to one's personality and cognition. Second, they refer to the growth dimension. This is related to the ability and motivation of an individual to learn and improve. These foundational dimensions are therefore pressed on the idea that people can develop their capabilities, which may be applied to a variety of different positions. Finally, they refer to career dimensions which incorporate leadership ability, performance rewards, and knowledge and value. The ability and capacity for learning and continuous improvement appears especially important, with Karaevli and Hall (2003) suggesting this to be far more important than seeking to identify the future competences required of roles and individuals. This is, however, a significant challenge if you are seeking to make fair, objective, reliable, and valid decisions. Given this is an exercise in forecasting, there is a danger that considerations of potential may amount to little more than crystal ball gazing.

Moving Forward

Wiblen (2016) suggests that viewing talent as a socially constructed concept, that is provided meaning within organizational contexts, may be a useful way in moving understanding forward. Here, clarity on whether talent entails individuals, the possession of valuable capabilities or skills, pivotal roles, or is all inclusive can be determined through a process of negotiation within each organizational context. It is not necessarily about whether one of the specified perspectives of talent is better than another, but what is more important is thinking through how it relates to the organization's mission and strategic objectives (Wiblen & McDonnell, 2019).

As noted, this may range from a highly exclusive or elitist view to something more inclusive, one that focuses on stable characteristics of individuals or where potential is identified that then needs to be developed. The failure to provide clarity on what talent means is going to continue hindering not only the development of stronger TM but also the effectiveness of organizational practice (Gallardo-Gallardo et al., 2013).

In line with the above recommendation on ensuring clarity of meaning of the specific purpose of each organization stems a word of caution that organizations do not solely view talent and TM about being solely focused on leaders or those with the potential to move into the C-suite. While clearly pivotal for all organizations, it is important for organizations to consider what the strategic roles are along with its pivotal people. These are the roles whereby the performance of different incumbents can have a significantly positive or negative role on the organization. For example, there may be functional and technical roles whereby different performance levels by the incumbent substantially alter organizational success (Cappelli, 2009). These types of roles may require talent considerably different to what may be viewed as talent in the context of future senior leaders. As a result, different definitions of talent may exist within the organization, but it is argued here that there should be clarity as to what these are and why they exist.

In sum, talent appears to mean whatever a person, whether that is a manager or researcher, wants it to be. Obtaining consensus on a definition of talent in the field is neither desirable or feasible, but it is important for both researchers and organizations alike to have clarity on what the construct means within their context.

Identifying Talent

In discussing the need to have clarity of what talent means in specific organizational context, there is an implication that talent is discernible. Being able to spot or identify talent is therefore a vital activity. Of note is that talent identification appears to be an activity that organizations do rather poorly. For example, CEB, a member-based U.S. advisory organization, indicated that more than 65% of firms stated an issue with misidentifying their talent, which was leading to performance challenges (HR Review, 2014). In many cases, it appears that identifying talent is based more on "gut" and subjectivity with limited use of scientific or systematic type evaluations. Such approaches are fraught with danger, arguably more so in exclusive systems of TM, where identification may be strongly biased by those within the assessor's network or who are deemed to be like them (Dries, 2013).

Apposite to the gut instinct approach we have witnessed an explosion of interest in HR or talent analytics (Boudreau, 2014). Increasingly the arguments are made for organizations to engage with the possibilities offered by data analytics to make better informed decisions on who is talent and how TM impacts organizational performance. Underpinning arguments for organizations to take more of an analytical approach to talent decisions is that improved decision making is likely vis-à-vis the use of gut instinct (Davenport, Harris, & Shapiro, 2010; Lawler, Levenson, & Boudreau, 2004). There also exists potential for some negative impacts from a strong reliance on analytics whereby talent clones are created, leading us closer to homophily rather than diversity (Makela, Bjorkman, & Ehrnrooth, 2010; McDonnell, 2011). Consequently, caution needs to be exercised in basing decision purely on data.

Overall, much of the research advocates the use of transparent and systematic processes for identification, which theoretically allows all employees to be considered as to their talent status (Collings & Mellahi, 2009). The development of shared meaning among stakeholders is important and to then utilize appropriate tools to evaluate and identify individuals.

Talent Identification Tools

There appears to be a key role for data and analytics that can assist the movement of talent identification to a decision science approach as long advocated by Bourdreau and Ramstad (2002). However, we know little on how organizations go about identifying their talent (Church & Rotolo, 2013). Wiblen (2016) found evidence of a stakeholder discourse around the usefulness of metrics and eHRM in identifying talent. However, there was also a strong discourse around the negative impact of systematic processes reliant on data and analytics. Specifically, she found evidence of organizational leaders talking up the use of observation as a mechanism to identifying talent. In effect, observational and subjective forms of evaluation were held as offering much positivity in terms of identifying a strong and diverse talent pool and providing flexibility. Even where more objective data could be used, it tended not to be drawn on with a preference for being able to call it as you see it.

To consider the tools that may be used to evaluate and identify talent we draw on recent empirical work by Skuza (2017)[1] that consisted of 32 case studies incorporating 196 interviews and multi-level respondents (HR director, middle/line managers, and individual talents) from multinational corporations (MNCs) operating in Poland. Results indicated that 100% of interviewers used evaluation forms (performance, competencies, behavior, and attitudes) and senior manager reviews, 88.8% used interviews with the potential talent, 63.8% used 360-degree feedback instruments, 52% used personality tests or cognitive ability tests, 38.3% used assessment centers, 37.8% used review meetings, and 20.9% used observation during strategic workshops.

Unsurprisingly, Skuza (2017) found that a significant variety of assessment techniques and tools were in place to identify talent. The key focus of the talent identification tools were on the evaluation of behaviors, competencies, and commitment. Each of the 32 firms in the sample reported the use of performance evaluation forms conducted by direct managers, and the use of senior managerial reviews. The performance evaluations were viewed as a central starting point for being designated as a talent, in that achieving a particular level of performance was pivotal. Consequently, past performance was vital, and it appeared was often conflated with views of potential. The evaluation forms were long exercises amounting to 40–50 pages, in each case encompassing detailed descriptions of behavioral and attitudinal justification for nomination as talent. Evidence-based assessment with examples supporting managers' opinions and descriptions was suggested as standard. The senior managerial reviews were primarily focused on making the final decision for individual's nomination and drew heavily from the evaluation forms provided by direct managers. There was a strong perception that these reviews contributed the most to the strategic importance of talent identification process.

Almost 90% of organizations utilized interviews with potential talents and 64% utilized 360-degree feedback instruments. Interviews were mainly used to understand candidate's career preferences, past experiences, and lessons learned from those experiences. In other words, there was a strong emphasis on establishing an individual's growth and learning journey. In some companies, these interviews could last several hours. However, their effectiveness as a talent predictor was perceived as low when compared to the other tools. This view emerged due to the concern that they could be distorted by the tendency of the interviewee to excessively foster positive self-image and to try to fulfill the interviewer expectations.

Another tool used in the talent identification process was personality and cognitive ability tests, which were used by about half of the case organizations. Those tests were used primarily for predicting the future potential of individuals. Assessment centers included behavioral exercises and different psychometric tests that played an important role in assessing future potential. Although they were used by just over two-thirds of the MNCs, their effectiveness in talent identification was perceived to be one of the highest. Review meetings, which are also highly evaluated as the identification tool, are usually held on the business unit level and include all managers that report to the head of the business unit. During those meetings managers discuss talent issues at a business-unit level, review managers' assessment ratings, and development plans for talents. These were evident in 38% of the organizations, but where used were viewed as the most effective tool. Only 12% of studied organizations applied calibration discussions on an organizational level. This we argue may increase the likelihood of inconsistency in identifying talent, but might also influence the level of managers' commitment to TM, which indeed was considered as a key challenge and tension by the HR directors.

In sum, Skuza's (2017) data displayed a range of tools for identifying talent. It was apparent that the identification process incorporated much more than an annual performance appraisal but was technically informed by a multitude of data. While subjectivity was involved in decision making, this was not with the aid as opposed to in isolation to a series of data.

Challenges and A Future Research Agenda

Taking TM as incorporating some degree of exclusivity, a significant issue raises its head in terms of the extent to which identification decisions are viewed as fair and transparent. Minbaeva and Collings (2013) suggest that the idea that talent decisions are fair to be a myth, arguing that identification decisions are often based on incomplete information. While there is little argument with the idea that talent identification decisions are bounded, this does not dispel the need for developing more objective means to base judgements on the potential of individuals.

Where there is a lack of understanding of what it takes to be labeled a talent in an organization and/ or decisions on the process of identifying is unclear and inconsistent, there are likely to be a range of negative impacts, particularly where exclusive type approaches are adopted. In Skuza's (2017) research on MNCs in Poland, individual talents had a relatively good general grasp that evaluations of talent status were based around performance levels, potential, and commitment. However, almost half of these talents were unclear how these were measured. The lack of transparency in talent decisions may lead to problems around views of distributive justice among those employees who were not identified as talents (Dries, 2013; Gelens et al., 2013).

An aspect in the TM literature that has received minimal to no attention is with respect to the impact of how organizations define and identify talent on diversity. The criteria and processes used are likely to have a significant impact. Consequently, this is an area that organizations should consider when establishing talent identification criteria and processes, as well as having diversity of the talent pool(s) as a measure that is monitored.

The female glass ceiling is now well acknowledged and led to significant changes by many governments and organizations aimed at addressing the problem (though positive change remains relatively slow). Meanwhile, it can be argued that people with disabilities and ethnic minorities are faced with a starker situation. The impact of talent identification processes on the diversity of talent pools merits consideration.

The use of data analytics offers organizational leaders and HR practitioners alike the opportunity to make better decisions around identifying talent and understanding the current internal talent stocks. However, while the use of analytics can aid a more objective and transparent approach to talent decisions and better understanding how TM impacts organizational performance, there is a need for caution. There is a danger that organizations place too much reliance on a small number of metrics when attempting to evaluate performance and/or potential, which may seek individuals' focus on playing the system rather than on continual learning and improvement (Davenport et al., 2010).

There is the danger whereby the metrics that organizations use are less about how they are intrinsically linked to organizational objectives but end up being about more straightforward, quantifiable elements. Hence, the metrics collected are chosen not because they are the most relevant to organizational performance but because they are the easiest to measure (Fowler, 1990). For such reasons, arguments have been made and which some MNCs appear to incorporate around the idea of measures that not only establish the results achieved by employees but also "how they reflect or exemplify shared values" (Stahl et al., 2012).

In discussing the definition and process of identifying talent, the focus is heavily centered on the individual. This is problematic in that individuals do not work in isolation, and performance may be strongly linked to their surrounding context and the inherent support network. Employees that may not be identified as talent, high-potentials, or A players often may play critical roles in the effective performance of teams and departments, and by logical association on other individual's performance. Such staff may not necessarily possess the same level of potential as other colleagues but they may be the glue that binds things together.

Consequently, there is a need to consider in depth the behaviors and values that are critical to individual, team, and organizational performance and how that should be tied into evaluation criteria. There is also a challenge around the extent to which star employees can move to other firms and easily achieve the same performance levels. The argument is that there are firm specific idiosyncrasies that will impact the portability of talent in other firms. According to Groysberg, Lee, and Nanda (2008: 1226): "The performance of an outstanding worker is not owned by the worker alone; it is a property of the worker/firm combination, and encompasses firm-specific human capital embedded in colleague relationships and firm capabilities."

Adopting very narrow conceptualizations based on inputs (e.g., qualifications) may be harmful to organizational health. There is a danger by organizations adopting very individualist cultures and approaches to TM that it could lead to unhealthy internal competition among employees (Pfeffer, 2001). This may lead to the destruction of a team-oriented focus. Research that considers how to provide adequate consideration to the context in which a person is performing would be especially welcome.

Another key issue that, has received little to no attention in the extant literature, is the role that timing plays on identification decisions. To what extent is talent identification a point in time or dynamic process? How do organizations take account of the potential "late-bloomer"? On the other side, if you are designated as a talent, is that a designation for life or is it more fluid, whereby individuals may move in and out of talent pools? A follow-on question would be: What impact does it have on an individual if having been in the talent pool they subsequently lose that status? These are important questions that merit critical enquiry to help inform better practice.

Although there has been significant inroads in terms of research from the emerging world, the TM literature has a decidedly Anglo-Saxon feel to its origin and development. This is potentially problematic in that there is a lack of consideration in how contextual factors impact TM. For example, the individualist nature of much of the Western world sees a greater attribution of success to levels of innateness, such as intelligence and creativity (Kitayama, Markus, Matsumoto, & Norasakkunkit, 1997). However, this appears at odds with more collectivist countries where attributing performance almost entirely to one's own individual talent is problematic.

The final challenge we reflect upon is with respect to the communication of talent identification decisions. What impact does not being classified as talent have on employees? While it is very difficult to arrive at positive effects for these individuals, the extent of the negativity will be strongly related to feelings as to how transparent and fair were the identification process and decisions taken. Cappelli and Keller (2014: 316) make an interesting observation when they noted that if identification decisions are "based on performance, it could motivate LoPo [employees not categorized as high-potentials/talent] to perform better; if it is based on attributes they cannot control, such as personality and IQ, it will quite likely have a demotivating effect". Little research has focused on the effects of the communication of talent status on those not selected, thus, this is a pressing area for future investigation.

Conclusion

There is a notional meaning of the term talent whereby it means employees who perceptibly add to the organization's net value. To undertake effective TM must mean that being able to spot or identify talent takes on a critical meaning. This chapter has explored two critical, interrelated aspects of effective TM: the definition and identification of talent. We argue that talent has to be viewed as a dynamic, evolving construct because with business model change, there is likely to be significant implications for the type of executives required, the way that employees are managed, and the contribution that different people can make. In effect, the talent requirements of an organization will differ throughout its history.

We also urge caution in failing to adequately contextualize the performance of individuals. There is some research that demonstrates star performers find it difficult to replicate their performance levels when they move to a new firm (Groysberg et al., 2008; Huckman & Pisano, 2006), which is ascribed to the importance of intra-firm social networks and the need to develop these from the start in a new organization. While the field of TM research moves from infancy to adolescence, there remain very substantial gaps in our knowledge and understanding on the concept that underpins the entire field: what talent means.

Note

1 Please note that parts of this section and greater detail can be found in Skuza (2017) which is in the Polish language.

References

Altman, Y. 1997. The high-potential fast-flying achiever: themes from the English language literature 1976-1995. *Career Development International,* 2(7): 324-330.

Asplund, K. 2020. When profession trumps potential: The moderating role of professional identification in employees' reactions to talent management. *The International Journal of Human Resource Management,* 31(4): 539-561.

Becker, B. E., Huselid, M. A., & Beatty, R. W. 2009. *The differentiated workforce: Transforming talent into strategic impact.* Boston, MA: Harvard Business School Press.

Biswas-Diener, R., Kashdan, T. B., & Minhas, G. 2011. A dynamic approach to psychological strength development and intervention. *Journal of Positive Psychology,* 6: 106-118.

Boudreau, J. W. 2014. Workforce analytics of the future: Using predictive analytics to forecast talent needs. *Harvard Business Review,* Webinar 11 November 2014.

Boudreau, J. W., & Ramstad, P. M. 2005. Talentship, talent segmentation, and sustainability: A new HR decision science paradigm for a new strategy definition. *Human Resource Management,* 42: 129-36.

Cappelli, P. 2009. A supply chain model for talent management. *People & Strategy,* 32: 4-7.

Cappelli, P., & Keller, J.R. 2014. Talent management: Conceptual approaches and practical challenges. *Annual Review of Organizational Psychology and Organizational Behaviour,* 1: 305-331.

Church, A. H., & Rotolo, C. T. 2013. How are top companies assessing their high-potentials and senior executives? A talent management benchmark study. *Consulting Psychology Journal: Practice and Research,* 65: 199-223.

CIPD. 2012. *Learning and development 2012.* London: CIPD.

Collings, D. G., & Mellahi, K. 2009. Strategic talent management: A review and research agenda. *Human Resource Management Review,* 19: 304-313.

Coulson-Thomas, C. 2012. Talent management and building high performance organisations. *Industrial and Commercial Training,* 44: 429-438.

Davenport, T., Harris, J., & Shapiro, J. 2010. Competing on talent analytics. *Harvard Business Review,* 10: 52-58.

Dries, N. 2013. The psychology of talent management: A review and research agenda. *Human Resource Management Review,* 23: 272-285.

Fowler, A. 1990. Performance management: The MBO of the 90s. *Personnel Management,* 22(7): 47-51.

Gallardo-Gallardo, E., Dries, N., & González-Cruz, T. F. 2013. What is the meaning of 'talent' in the world of work? *Human Resource Management Review,* 23: 290-300.

Galladro-Gallardo, E., & Thunnissen, M. 2016. Standing on the shoulders of giants? A critical review of empirical talent management research. *Employee Relations,* 38(1): 31-56.

Gallardo-Gallardo, E., Thunnissen, M., & Scullion, H. 2020. Talent management: Context matters. *The International Journal of Human Resource Management,* 31(4): 457-473.

Gelens, J., Hofmans, J., Dries, N., & Pepermans, R. 2014. Talent management and organisational justice: Employee reactions to high potential identification. *Human Resource Management Journal,* 24: 159-175.

Groysberg, B., Lee, L. E., & Nanda, A. 2008. Can they take it with them? The portability of star knowledge workers' performance. *Management Science,* 54(7): 1213-1230.

Huckman, R. S., & Pisano, G. P. 2006. The firm specificity of individual performance: Evidence from cardiac surgery. *Management Science,* 52(4): 473-488.

Huselid, M. A., Beatty, R. W., & Becker, B. E. 2005. A players or A positions? The strategic logic of workforce management. *Harvard Business Review,* 83(12): 110-117.

HR Review 2014. Two-thirds of companies are identifying their true high potential candidates. *HR Review,* March 26. http://www.hrreview.co.uk/hr-news

Joyce, W. F, & Slocum, J. W. 2012. Top management talent, strategic capabilities, and firm performance. *Organizational Dynamics,* 41(3): 183-193.

Karaevli, A., & Hall, D. T. 2003. Growing leaders for turbulent times: Is succession planning up to the challenge? *Organizational Dynamics,* 32, 62-79.

Kitayama, S., Markus, H. R., Matsumoto, H., & Norasakkunkit, V. 1997. Individual and collective processes in the construction of the self: Self-enhancement in the United States and self-criticism in Japan. *Journal of Personality and Social Psychology,* 72(6): 1245-1267.

Lawler, E., Levenson, A., & Boureau, J. 2004. HR metrics and analytics: Use and impact. *Human Resource Planning,* 27(4): 27-35.

Lewis, R. E., & Heckman, R. J. 2006. Talent management: A critical review. *Human Resource Management Review,* 16: 139-154.

Makela, K., Bjorkmann, I., & Ehrnrooth, M. 2010. How do MNCs establish their talent pools? Influences on individuals' likelihood of being labelled a talent. *Journal of World Business,* 45: 134-142.

McDonnell, A. 2011. Still fighting the war for talent? Bridging the science versus practice gap. *Journal of Business and Psychology,* 26: 169-173.

McDonnell, A., Collings, D. G., & Burgess, J. 2012. Talent management in the Asia-Pacific. *Asia Pacific Journal of Human Resources,* 50(4): 391-398.

McDonnell, A., Collings, D. G., Mellahi, K., & Schuler, R. 2017. Talent management: A systematic review and future prospects. *European Journal of International Management,* 11: 86-128.

Meyers, M. C., van Woerkom, M., & Dries, N. 2013. Talent—innate or acquired? Theoretical considerations and their implications for talent management. *Human Resource Management Review,* 24: 305-321.

Minbaeva, D., & Collings, D. G. 2013. Seven myths of global talent management. *International Journal of Human Resource Management,* 24: 1762-1776.

Pfeffer, J. 2001. Fighting the war for talent is hazardous to your organization's health. *Organizational Dynamics,* 29: 248-259.

Scullion, H., Collings, D. G., & Caligiuri, P. 2010. Global talent management. *Journal of World Business,* 45: 105-108.

Skuza A. 2017. Zarzadzanie talentami a orientacja na uczenie sie przedsiebiorstw - uwarunkowania, procesy, modelowanie. *Poznan University of Economics and Business.*

Silzer, R., & Church, A. H. 2009. The pearls and perils of identifying potential. *Industrial and Organizational Psychology,* 2: 377-412.

Simonton, D. K. 1999. Talent and its development: An emergenic and epigenetic model. *Psychology Review,* 106(3): 435-457.

Stahl, G., Bjorkmann, I., Farndale, E., Morris, S., Paauwe, J., Stiles, P., Trevor, J., & Wright, P. 2012. Six principles of effective global talent management. *MIT Sloan Management Review,* 53: 25-32.

Strack, R., Caye, J., Leicht, M., Villis, U., Böhm, H., & McDonnell, M. 2013. *The future of HR in Europe: Key challenges through 2015.* Boston, MA: The Boston Consulting Group (BCG).

The Economist. 2006. Survey: Talent. *The Economist* (October 5).

Thunnissen, M., Boselie, P., & Fruytier, B. 2013. A review of talent management: 'Infancy or adolescence?'. *International Journal of Human Resource Management,* 24: 1744-1761.

Ulrich, D. 2006. The talent trifecta. *Workforce Management:* 32-33.

Wiblen, S. 2016. Framing the usefulness of eHRM in talent management: A case study of talent identification in a professional services firm. *Canadian Journal of Administrative Sciences,* 33: 95-107.

Wiblen, S., & McDonnell, A. 2019. Connecting 'talent' meanings and multi-level context: A discursive approach. *The International Journal of Human Resource Management.*

Yost, P. R., & Chang, G. 2009. Everyone is equal, but some are more equal than others. *Industrial and Organizational Psychology,* 2: 442-445.

35

TALENT ACQUISITION

A Critical First Step for Effective Talent Management

James A. Breaugh

Introduction

An organization's success regardless of how defined (e.g., profitability, growth) is tied to the type of individuals it employs (Cappelli, 2019; Cappelli & Keller, 2014). Because the talent acquisition process influences the type of persons who apply for job openings and thus are hired, it plays a critical role in an employer's success. This chapter reviews research on talent acquisition and highlights issues meriting future investigation. The coverage in this chapter is selective. Readers interested in a more extensive treatment of research concerning talent acquisition should refer to sources cited in this chapter.

In recent years, the use of the term *talent acquisition* has frequently replaced the use of the term *employee recruitment* (Breaugh, 2016). As used in this chapter, talent acquisition refers to a process that encompasses strategic actions by an employer that are intended to (a) bring a job opening to the attention of potential job candidates, (b) influence whether these individuals apply for the opening, (c) affect whether they maintain interest in the open position until a job offer is extended, and (d) influence whether a job offer is accepted. From this definition, it should be apparent that I do not address employee selection, which is sometimes treated as part of the talent acquisition process.

As discussed by Cappelli and Keller (2014), some researchers view the talent acquisition process as involving pivotal jobs that have a large impact on an employer's performance. Studies of pivotal jobs (e.g., Brands & Fernandez-Mateo, 2017) have focused on such positions as investment banker, senior executive, and research scientist. Organizations that emphasize that certain jobs are of greater value often adopt a workforce differentiation strategy (Becker, Huselid, & Beatty, 2009) in which more resources are allocated to these jobs. In terms of talent acquisition, a workforce differentiation strategy can involve spending more money and more time on acquiring high-impact talent. Other researchers (e.g., O'Boyle & Aguinis, 2014) have taken a more inclusive approach to talent acquisition. This perspective recognizes that employees in what may appear to be relatively inconsequential positions can have a sizable impact on an employer's success. I adopt the more inclusive view in discussing talent acquisition. However, when research is available to draw upon, I address filling high-impact positions.

The Job Applicant's Perspective

A brief treatment of the job applicant's perspective is needed to provide a context for my coverage of talent acquisition issues. An important factor that researchers have largely ignored is how to get the attention of the individuals an employer is trying to attract (Breaugh, 2013). This can be a particular challenge if the individuals targeted are not actively looking for a job. In terms of motivating individuals to apply for a position and remain interested in it until it is filled, research has shown that job

DOI: 10.4324/9781315474687-35

(e.g., compensation, advancement potential) and organizational (e.g., location, reputation) characteristics are key factors (Furnham & Palaiou, 2017). Research (e.g., Giumetti & Raymark, 2017) also has shown that individuals are more attracted to a job opening if they believe their abilities match job requirements and if they perceive they are likely to receive a job offer. In addition to these factors, applicants' perceptions of their interactions with recruiters (e.g., respectful treatment) and aspects of the site visit (e.g., flexibility in scheduling a trip) have been shown to impact whether individuals apply for a job and remain interested in it (Harold, Holtz, Greipentrog, Brewer, & Marsch, 2016). Although I could only provide a cursory treatment of variables that influence a job applicant, the importance of the variables covered will become apparent in the remainder of this chapter.

Targeting Specific Types of Employees for Talent Acquisition

Arguably, the most important talent acquisition decision an employer makes involves the type of person (e.g., a competitor's workers) to target for recruitment. Focusing on the wrong type of individual can result in job applicants who lack the knowledge, skills, abilities, and other characteristics (KSAOs) needed to perform a job, applicants who are unlikely to accept a job offer because they do not view the organization as an attractive place to work, and/or applicants who may leave a job soon after hiring due to unmet expectations (Breaugh, 2016).

Targeting External versus Internal Talent

Recently, organizations have increased the frequency with which they fill non-entry level job openings externally (Cappelli & Keller, 2014). Doing so has potential advantages such as bringing in new knowledge, but also disadvantages. For example, hiring an outsider can result in resentment on the part of current employees who were interested in the position that was filled. In a study that involved how an investment bank filled high-level positions, Bidwell (2011) compared the effects of promoting or transferring current employees versus filling job openings externally. He found that external hires had more education, more experience, and were paid more than internal candidates. Importantly, Bidwell also found that external hires performed at a lower level than internal candidates for their first two years and had a higher turnover rate. In a study involving star security analysts (as rated by *Institutional Investor*), Groysberg and Lee (2009) found that the performance of external hires declined upon joining a new firm in comparison to analysts who did not change firms.

Targeting Former Employees

A limitation of recruiting external job candidates is that, compared to its employees, an employer lacks information on external candidates and they lack information concerning what working for the employer is like (Shipp, Furst-Holloway, Harris, & Rosen, 2014). This lack of information can result in both parties making uninformed decisions that can lead to negative outcomes (e.g., an employer being disappointed with the performance of a new hire; a new hire quitting because a job did not meet expectations). One way to avoid such problems is for an employer to target former employees. Doing so should result in the employer and the recruit being more fully informed.

Although little research has been conducted on so-called boomerang employees, a study by Swider, Liu, Harris, and Gardner (2017) showed the value of targeting certain types of former employees. They examined the performance (indexed by a player efficiency rating) of players in the National Basketball Association who returned to their former teams. Swider et al. found the performance of boomerang employees during their initial tenure was positively related to their performance upon returning to their original team. Thus, an employer may want to consider a person's prior performance in making a rehiring decision. However, the results of additional analyses by Swider et al. are particularly noteworthy. Having controlled for potential confounding variables, they found that, in comparison to boomerang employees, players who remained with their original team performed at a higher level. Williams, Labig, and Stone (1993) also examined the value of targeting former employees. They reported that rehired nurses were more knowledgeable about the hospital they were rejoining than other nurses and that pre-hire knowledge was negatively related to turnover.

Targeting Local Applicants

A factor an employer should consider in deciding on the type of individuals to target is whether relocation will be necessary. For example, Becker, Connolly, and Slaughter (2010) found that having to relocate made it more likely that applicants would reject job offers. They also reported that this relationship was weaker for experienced employees,] which suggests that having to move may be less of a detriment in filling higher-level positions. For jobs that are suitable for telecommuting, the location of a job opening may not be important. However, this is only speculation due to a lack of research addressing the issue.

Summary and Future Research

By targeting the right type of individuals, an employer is more likely to develop an applicant pool with the needed KSAOs and with accurate job expectations, which in turn should result in better performance and a higher retention rate. In completing this overview of targeting issues, I would emphasize the need for additional research. For example, Breaugh (2012) presented a theoretical case for an employer targeting individuals who have worked in similar jobs and/or for similar organizations due to their having more information on what working for the employer would be like, but he did not present empirical findings supporting such targeting. Research is also lacking on the effects of targeting part-time workers, virtual employees, and contingent workers

Talent Acquisition Messages

Having decided on the type of individuals it wishes to attract, an employer needs to craft recruitment messages (e.g., a message shared by executive recruiters) suitable for this audience. In planning a talent acquisition process, an employer should make sure that its communications convey a consistent message. Sending inconsistent messages (this is more likely to occur if there are different information sources) has been shown to result in communications being viewed as lacking credibility (Windscheid, Bowes-Sperry, Kidder, Cheung, Morner, & Lievens, 2016).

The Amount of Information Conveyed, Its Specificity, and Its Realism

Research (e.g., Frasca & Edwards, 2017) suggests that providing more information concerning a job opening results in a position being viewed as more attractive and there being a higher probability of a job offer being accepted. However, providing a lot of general information concerning a job opening is not sufficient. It is important that the information shared is specific in nature (e.g., stating the salary range for a position rather than stating that salaries are competitive). For example, a study by *Bäker (2015) showed that* sharing specific information about the KSAOs an employer sought facilitated applicant self-selection resulting in a more qualified applicant pool. A study by Schmidt, Chapman, and Jones (2014) demonstrated that providing specific information about job rewards resulted in higher quality applicants.

The realism of the information presented about a position during the talent acquisition process has received considerable attention. Providing realistic information to applicants (e.g., by means of a realistic job preview) has been found to: (a) reduce the inflated job expectations that many applicants possess, (b) result in applicant withdrawal if a job is not perceived as a good fit, (c) cause individuals to view an employer as trustworthy, and (d) lessen the turnover rate of new hires (Baur, Buckley,

Bagdasarov, & Dharmasiri, 2014). Although conveying realistic information about a job can result in applicants withdrawing as job candidates (Bretz & Judge, 1998), this is not always the case (Van Hoye & Lievens, 2009). Furthermore, it is generally better for an organization to lose individuals who do not perceive a good fit during the talent acquisition process than after hiring.

Conveying Information about an Organization's Employment Brand

As commonly defined, an employment brand refers to how individuals (e.g., current employees, persons external to an organization) perceive what working for an organization is like (Lievens & Slaughter, 2016). An employment brand does not typically refer to attributes of a position. Rather, it refers to the larger employment experience as affected by an organization's culture (e.g., concern for work-life balance). Some employers convey a holistic employment brand (e.g., a Catholic hospital communicating that it practices Christian values). Others present different employment brands to different groups it is trying to attract talent. A good employment brand is important because it affects the attractiveness of job openings.

Although many organizations put considerable effort into communicating an appealing employment brand (Lievens & Slaughter, 2016), the effect of such branding is influenced by whether prospective job applicants perceive it as credible. In some cases the credibility of an employment brand is easily evaluated (e.g., when an applicant has previously worked for an employer). Other ways an individual may try to assess the veracity of the employment brand an organization has shared is through a third party. For example, Van Hoye (2013) discussed the influence on brand credibility of the use of Word-of-Mouth sources (e.g., comments appearing on websites such as Glassdoor). A study by Dineen and Allen (2016) presents intriguing results concerning employment branding. They examined the effect of organizations being rated as one of the "Best Places to Work" by an independent company. This designation was found to improve applicant pool quality and lower turnover rates in subsequent years, especially for smaller employers.

Message Content in Relation to Recruiting Minorities and Women

Research on message content in relation to attracting minorities and women merits special attention given some employers are particularly interested in hiring them. In terms of minorities, McKay and Avery (2006) showed the inclusion of text supporting affirmative action was viewed positively, and Avery (2003) documented the benefits of including pictures of minorities in supervisory positions in recruitment literature. More recently, Linos, Reinhardt, and Ruda (2017) showed that, by changing the wording of a job advertisement in a way that lessened applicant anxiety about the selection system for becoming a police officer, test scores of minority applicants increased by 12% (non-minority scores increased 2%).

In terms of the recruitment of women, Gaucher, Friesen, and Kay (2011) showed that male-gendered wording in job advertisements is common across a range of jobs and that such wording discourages women from applying for jobs even when they possess the necessary skills. Similarly, Brands and Fernandez-Mateo (2017) found that executive positions are often described in masculine terms, which may explain why women were less likely to apply for jobs in male-dominated fields such as finance and consulting (Barbulescu & Bidwell, 2013).

The Recruitment Message: Additional Considerations

Research (e.g., Walker, Helmuth, Feild, & Bauer, 2015) has shown that certain types of information may be more appropriate to share at different stages of the talent acquisition process. For example, information about a job opening's location might be shared in a job advertisement. Information about the work group one would be joining might be more appropriate to convey during a site visit. As shown by

Swider, Zimmerman, and Barrick (2015), in planning a strategic communication process, an employer should take steps to differentiate itself over time from other organizations with which it may be competing for high-potential employees.

To this point, I have discussed the messages sent during the talent acquisition process in terms of their direct effects on job applicants. However, variables related to a message's intended recipients also are important. For example, Walker Feild, Giles, and Bernerth (2008) showed that, compared to less experienced persons, persons with more work experience were more affected by the content of a job advertisement and less influenced by peripheral aspects of it (e.g., an attractive layout). Kanar, Collins, and Bell (2015) examined whether a person's familiarity with an employer moderated the degree to which a recruitment message could change how a person viewed the employer. They found that being more familiar with an employer diminished the effect of a recruitment message.

Summary and Future Research

Although research has increased our understanding of the effects of message characteristics, future research is needed. For example, Kanar et al.'s (2015) results suggest it is hard to change initial attitudes about working for an employer, especially if it is perceived negatively. Breaugh (2013) discussed several factors (e.g., selective attention, confirmation bias) that may explain Kanar et al.'s findings. Future research that tests whether such psychological factors apply to the talent acquisition process (how can an employer change the attitude of a high-potential employee who is not predisposed to working there?) should be informative. Additional research on the wording of recruitment messages is also needed. For example, research by Gaucher et al. (2011) suggests that employers may be discouraging women from pursuing jobs. It would be interesting to know if the wording of ads might be affecting other groups (e.g., are youth-oriented messages discouraging older employees from applying?).

Methods to Use for Attracting Talent

Having decided on the type of individuals to target and the type of messages to send, an organization needs to determine how to bring a job opening to the attention of the individuals it seeks to attract. In this section, I focus on four methods (i.e., employee referrals, an employer's website, social media, and executive search firms). Readers interested in a more extensive treatment than I am able to provide are referred to several chapters in Yu and Cable (2013).

Employee Referrals

An employee referral program involves employees of an organization actively seeking out potential candidates to fill job openings. Based upon the findings of past studies, a case can be made for referral programs being the most effective approach for filling jobs (Pieper, 2015). Several benefits of using employee referrals have been noted (Breaugh, 2012). Among these are: (a) current employees are an excellent way to bring a job opening to the attention of desirable prospective candidates who are not looking for a position, (b) current employees are a good source for providing realistic job information to applicants, and (c) referrers often are able to provide information on prospective candidates that may not be easily discovered by commonly used selection devices.

Studies have presented mixed results concerning the outcomes of using employee referrals. For example, in some studies (e.g., Pallais & Sands, 2017), referred employees performed at a higher level and were less prone to turnover than employees recruited via other methods. In other studies (e.g., Pieper, Trevor, Weller, & Duchon, 2019), no performance or turnover differences were found. Some moderating conditions may explain these inconsistent results. For example, Pallais and Sands (2017) reported that the performance level of referred employees was greater if they worked closely with those who referred them, and Peiper et al. (2017) discovered that the presence of the referrer (i.e., the person continued to work for the organization during the period of the study) was linked to referrals performing at a higher level and being less likely to leave.

Given that many employers are positively disposed to using employee referrals to acquire talent, a key question is: "How do you motivate employees to make referrals?" A study by Pieper, Greenwald, and Schlachter (2017) addressed this question. Their results showed three variables motivated referrals: the offering a referral bonus, the size of the bonus, and the commitment of the employee to the employer. In contrast, the perceived risk of making a referral (i.e., fear of referring someone who does not perform well) was negatively related to the likelihood of a referral being made.

In concluding this section on the use of employee referrals, two final points are noted. First, it has been suggested (Antoninis, 2006) that the use of employee referrals is likely to have stronger effects when used to recruit individuals for higher-level and/or more complex positions because the referring employee may be able provide insight into personal attributes of an applicant (e.g., work ethic) that are hard to uncover using traditional selection devices. Second, more research is needed on the factors (e.g., providing realism) that have been hypothesized to explain why the use of referrals has positive outcomes.

Employer Websites

A number of employers rely on their websites for generating job applicants (Landers & Schmidt, 2016). Doing so can have advantages (e.g., low cost per applicant generated), especially if an employer is well-known by the type of individuals it has targeted and has a positive reputation (Breaugh, 2013). However, the use of an employer's website has limitations. For example, open positions may not be brought to the attention of potential job candidates if they are not looking for a new job.

Studies of employer websites (e. g., Allen, Biggane, Pitts, Otondo, & Van Scotter, 2013) have consistently shown the importance of ease of navigation, site aesthetics, and, most importantly, the positivity of the information provided (Landers & Schmidt, 2016). However, an organization needs to be wary of its website being unrealistically positive in tone. Job seekers have reported website information as lacking credibility (Cable & Yu, 2006), and information of lower credibility can detract from organizational attractiveness (Frasca & Edwards, 2017).

In terms of enhancing the credibility of website information, research (e.g., Walker, Bauer, Cole, Bernerth, Feild, & Short, 2013) has shown that an employer publicizing awards it has won from independent organizations can be effective as can presenting employee testimonials. Including such information is likely to have a greater effect on individuals who are unfamiliar with an organization due to their making inferences from it about unknown aspects of an organization (Walker, Feild, Giles, Bernerth, & Short, 2011).

A potential drawback of an employer using its website to attract job applicants is it may be overwhelmed with applications. As a method to address this possibility, an organization might consider providing information that helps a site visitor evaluate person-organization fit. In this regard, Hinojosa, Walker, and Payne (2015) found perceived person-organization fit was related to job pursuit intentions. Dineen, Ling, Ash, and Del Vecchio (2007) found that an employer providing information about person-organization fit (i.e., website visitors received a score that indicated the degree of similarity between what a person sought in an employer and what the employer offered) predicted organization attractiveness. A final study of relevance for reducing the number of applicants was conducted by Selden and Orenstein (2011).They found that websites that provided more specific information about a job opening generated fewer applications, which they interpreted as a reflection of individuals withdrawing from job consideration if they did not perceive a good fit with the job or the organization.

Social Media

Although commonly used by employers to acquire talent, the use of social media (e.g., texting, job boards, Twitter) has received little attention from researchers (Landers & Schmidt, 2016). As defined by

Wikipedia, social media refers to computer-mediated technology that facilitates the sharing of information. From this definition, the breadth of the term should be apparent. For example, an employer could place an advertisement on a job board such as Indeed.com or it could contract with LinkedIn so that an announcement of a job opening is sent to individuals who meet certain criteria (e.g., nurses with home health care experience). The latter approach would bring a job opening to the attention of individuals who are not actively looking for a job; the former approach is unlikely to.

It is also important to note the speed with which innovation is changing social media. As an example, just a few years ago, LinkedIn only allowed an employer to have a site in which it could post job openings and provide information, (e.g., publicize awards it had won). Today, subscribers to a premium service can search LinkedIn's database using whatever criteria they choose (e.g., years of experience in the airline industry). Based upon the results of such a search, an employer can reach out to individuals who possess the desired characteristics but who may not be looking for a position. In considering the use of social media for talent acquisition, it suffices to say that different approaches that fall under this label can vary in important ways (e.g., attracting the attention of passive job seekers, facilitating one-way versus two-way interchanges), which may limit or enhance their effectiveness.

Van Hoye and Lievens (2007) conducted one of the first studies of social media. They examined whether information supplied on a company-independent website (a site similar to a job board) had greater credibility and therefore a greater effect on employer attractiveness than information supplied on a company website. The results of their simulation study were consistent with their expectations. Carpentier, Van Hoye, Stockman, Schollaert, Van Theemsche, and Jacobs (2017) had nursing students visit the Facebook and LinkedIn websites of a hospital. In comparison to simply reading textual information taking from the hospital's website, visiting the Facebook and LinkedIn sites positively influenced students' views of the hospital's brand and attractiveness. In a similar study, Francesca and Edwards (2017) compared a standardized recruitment message conveyed via Facebook, a YouTube video, or an employer's website. Across a number of criteria (e.g., organizational attractiveness), a Facebook message was most effective, possibly due to its being seen as the most credible information source.

Executive Search Firms

Executive search firms are a primary mechanism for filling high-level or high-leverage positions (Brands & Fernandez-Mateo, 2017). They are an excellent approach for bringing an open position to the attention of highly sought after individuals (e.g., executives, Wall Street analysts) who are employed. To date, little research has examined variables (e.g., types of screening used to make decisions about whom to target, whether payment is based on successfully filling positions) that may affect the relative effectiveness of executive search firms. However, a number of studies have addressed the success of the individuals placed and factors that may moderate this success. I review of few of these studies to provide a sense of the type of studies conducted and future research needed.

Groysberg (2010) conducted a study of star Wall Street investment analysts who changed firms. Having reviewed the careers of more than 1,000 analysts, he concluded that star analysts who changed employers did not perform as well as they did at their previous firms. Based on over 200 interviews, Groysberg (2010) concluded that a star analyst's prior excellence was closely tied to the context in which the person worked (e.g., organization culture, proprietary resources, and colleagues). An exception to the reported decline in performance was found for analysts who moved with their "team" to a new employer. Groysberg (2010) also provided evidence his results for investment analysts generalized to other professions (e.g., general managers). The studies previously discussed by Bidwell (2011) and Groysberg and Lee (2009) are consistent with those reported by Groysberg (2010), which suggests that firms should think carefully about poaching star employees from other employers.

Recently, two sets of researchers (Call, Nyberg, & Thatcher, 2015; Kehoe, Lepak, & Bentley, 2017) have presented detailed conceptual analyses of star employees based upon their reviews of existing research. Among the interesting issues they addressed are: (a) there are different types of star employees (e.g., a star label based on current performance versus status), (b) there are certain situations that are most beneficial for hiring stars (e.g., when a star brings new knowledge and is willing to share it), and (c) how stars are formed (e.g., they have social capital and worked in visible positions). Although both of these papers contribute to the research literature on star employees, as stressed by their authors, research supporting many of their contentions is needed.

Summary and Future Research

From the research reviewed, it should be evident that it can make a difference what method(s) an employer uses to acquire talent. For example, some methods are better than others for reaching individuals who are not actively looking for a job, and some methods are perceived by applicants as presenting more credible information. Given the attention being paid to the potential of social media, rigorous research on this topic is particularly needed, especially more fine-grained research (e.g., receiving a text may be viewed differently from an online verbal chat). As demonstrated by a study by Cromheeke, Van Hoye, and Lievens (2013), a more modern approach is not automatically better. They found that in recruiting engineers receiving a postcard advertising a job opening generated more resumes and higher quality candidates than receiving an email. Although why this occurred is not clear, it may be that, given the number of emails that many individuals receive, a postcard was more likely to attract attention.

The Timing of Talent Acquisition Activities

Representative Studies

Research has established the importance of the timeliness of talent acquisition activities. For example, in a study involving college students, Turban and Cable (2003) reported that employers that began interviewing later in the academic year received fewer applications and applications of lower quality. Schreurs, Derous, Van Hooft, Proost, and De Witte (2009) found that the more time that elapsed between when an application was submitted and when a person was scheduled for initial screening, the less likely an applicant was to appear for screening. Becker et al. (2010) investigated the effect of a delay between an applicant's final interview and receiving a job offer. For samples of college graduates and more experienced workers, the longer the delay, the less likely a job offer was accepted.

Carless and Hetherington (2011) examined the issue of timeliness in terms of an objective and a subjective measure. They reported no association between rated employer attractiveness and the time that elapsed between the submission of a job application and being invited for an interview. However, a recruit's perception of the timeliness of the interview offer was related to employer attractiveness. Finally, Ryan, Ali, Hauer, and French-Vitet (2017) examined the impact of individuals' satisfaction with the timeliness of an employer's communications concerning the status of their job application. Timeliness satisfaction was positively related to perceptions of applicant treatment and organizational attractiveness.

Summary and Future Research

There is considerable evidence that delays during the talent acquisition process can adversely affect the number of applications received, the quality of the applicants, and whether a job offer was accepted. With regard to future research, investigations of the reasons that have been offered for the effect of delays during the talent acquisition process are needed. For example, researchers (e.g., Becker et al., 2010) have suggested that applicants make attributions about what a delay signals (e.g., I was not the employer's first choice for the position). Yet, to date, empirical studies have not shown a connection between these explanations and actual delays.

The Job Applicant Site Visit to an Organization

Representative Research

Rynes, Bretz, and Gerhart (1991) conducted one of the first studies that focused on a site visit. They reported that 30% of their sample rejected job offers from employers they had initially been attracted to after a site visit. A key factor that caused applicants to lose interest in employers was unprofessional treatment. Boswell, Roehling, LePine, and Moynihan (2003) documented the importance of site visit arrangements (e.g., a well-organized schedule) and site visit interactions (e.g., an applicant met with people from their department and higher-level managers).

McKay and Avery (2006) focused on the reactions of minority candidates. They found three aspects of a site visit were important: the number of minorities working at the site, the level of the jobs minorities held, and interactions observed between minorities and non-minorities. Slaughter, Cable, and Turban (2014) focused on how a site visit could affect the confidence an applicant had concerning his or her beliefs about an employer. They found that, for applicants who lacked confidence in their beliefs, a positive site experience (e.g., interacting with a knowledgeable recruiter) had a beneficial and linear effect on beliefs about the employer. For applicants who had confidence in their pre-visit beliefs about an employer, the site visit had a beneficial effect, but less so than for low-confidence applicants.

Summary and Future Research

Although the site visit has received relatively little attention from researchers, the research that has been conducted shows a site visit can have a substantial impact on job applicants. This is not surprising. A site visit provides an employer with an extended period of time to share more information about a position, more specific information, and more realistic information. Because much of the information acquired during a site visit involves direct experience (e.g., a site visitor sees prospective coworkers interacting), this information should be perceived as being highly credible.

In terms of future research, I would note two issues. First, greater attention should be paid to exactly what occurs during the site visit and the impact it has. Second, data needs to be gathered from organizational representatives in addition to site visitors. Past research makes it impossible to know whether what a site visitor's reports reflect an idiosyncratic view or a shared perspective.

Loose Ends

Legal Issues and Employee Poaching

Space does not allow for an in-depth treatment of legal issues that are relevant to the talent acquisition process (e.g., Angwin, Scheiber, & Tobin, 2017, described how using Facebook to target younger age groups can result in an age discrimination claim). However, to provide a sense of the relevance of legal issues, the issue of poaching is instructive. I have already addressed research on hiring individuals who worked for competitors. It suffices to say that the success of this strategy is at best mixed (Groysberg, 2010). Nevertheless, poaching continues to be a common practice (Sheldon & Li, 2013). If an employer decides to target a competitor's employees, it needs to be certain it is not using proprietary information (e.g., an executive hired away from a competitor provides a list of their former firm's employees). Doing so is illegal (Korosec, 2017). Given a concern about their own talent being poached, some companies have entered into anti-poaching agreements. Such agreements are legally dangerous. For example, in a case involving an anti-poaching agreement among Silicon Valley companies (e.g., Apple, Intel), the companies agreed to a settlement of $415 million to be paid to over 64,000 engineers affected by their "anti-poach" list (Roberts, 2015).

Recruiters

Given the various roles that recruiters play in the talent acquisition process, it is not surprising that their behavior has been shown to influence important outcomes (e.g., applications received, job offer acceptance rate) of the talent acquisition process (Connerley, 2013). Research (e.g., Uggerslev et al., 2012) has shown that applicants respond more favorably to recruiters who are perceived as informative, personable, trustworthy, and competent. In recent years, research on recruiters has diminished. Given that research (e.g., Rynes, Bretz, & Gerhart, 1991) has shown that recruiter behavior, especially unprofessional conduct, can have important effects (e.g., high quality candidates losing interest in an employer), this is unfortunate.

Conclusion

In this chapter, I have provided a selective review of the current state of research on a variety of topics relevant to the acquisition of talent and have suggested future areas for research. My hope is that readers of this chapter will appreciate the significance of various aspects of the talent acquisition process. The major take-away of this chapter should be: done well, the talent acquisition process should result in a pool of applicants who possess important attributes (e.g., knowledge, experience, work ethic, interest) for successfully filling a job opening.

References

Allen, D. G., Biggane, J. E., Pitts, M., Otondo, R., & Van Scotter, J. 2013. Reactions to recruitment web sites: Visual and verbal attention, attraction, and intentions to pursue employment. *Journal of Business and Psychology,* 28: 263-285.

Angwin, J., Scheiber, N., & Tobin, A. (December 20, 2017). Facebook job ads raise concerns about age discrimination. *New York Times.*

Antoninis, M. 2006. The wage effects from the use of personal contacts as hiring channels. *Journal of Economic Behavior & Organization,* 59: 133-146.

Avery, D. R. 2003. Reactions to diversity in recruitment advertising – Are differences black and white? *Journal of Applied Psychology,* 88: 672-679.

Baker, A. 2015. The downside of looking for team players in job advertisements. *Journal of Business Economics,* 85: 157-179.

Barbulescu, R., & Bidwell, M. 2013. Do women choose different jobs from men? Mechanisms of application segregation in the market for managerial workers. *Organization Science,* 24: 737-756

Baur, J. E., Buckley, M. R., Bagdasarov, Z., & Dharmasiri, A. S. 2014. A historical approach to realistic job previews: An exploration into their origins, evolution, and recommendations for the future. *Journal of Management History,* 20: 200-223.

Becker, B. B., Huselid, M. A., & Beatty, R. W. 2009. *The differentiated workforce: Transforming talent into strategic impact.* Boston, MA: Harvard Business Press.

Becker, W. J., Connolly, T., & Slaughter, J. E. 2010. The effect of job offer timing on offer acceptance, performance, and turnover. *Personnel Psychology,* 63: 223-241.

Bidwell, M. 2011. Paying more to get less: Specific skills, matching, and the effects of external hiring versus internal promotion. *Administrative Science Quarterly,* 56: 369-407.

Boswell, W. R., Roehling, M. V., LePine, M. A., & Moynihan, L. M. 2003. Individual job choice decisions and the impact of job attributes and recruitment practices: A longitudinal field study. *Human Resource Management,* 42: 23-37.

Brands, R. A., & Fernandez-Mateo, I. 2017. Learning out: How negative recruitment experiences shape women's decisions to compete for executive roles. *Administrative Science Quarterly,* 62: 405-442.

Breaugh, J. A. 2012. Employee recruitment: Current knowledge and suggestions for future research. In N. Schmitt (Ed.), *The Oxford handbook of personnel assessment and selection:* 68-87. New York: Oxford University Press.

Breaugh, J. A. 2013. Employee recruitment. *Annual Review of Psychology,* 64: 389-416.

Breaugh, J. A. 2016. *Talent acquisition.* SHRM Foundation's Effective Practice Guidelines Series.

Bretz, R. D., & Judge, T. A. 1998. Realistic job previews: A test of the adverse self-selection hypothesis. *Journal of Applied Psychology,* 83: 330-337.

Cable, D., & Yu, K. Y. 2006. Managing job seekers' organizational image beliefs: The role of media richness and media credibility. *Journal of Applied Psychology,* 91: 828-840.

Call, M. L., Nyberg, A. J., & Thatcher, S. M. 2015. Stargazing: An integrative conceptual review, theoretical reconciliation, and extension of star employee research. *Journal of Applied Psychology,* 100: 623-640.

Cappelli, P. 2019. Your approach to hiring is all wrong. *Harvard Business Review,* 97(3): 48-58.

Cappelli, P., & Keller, J. R. 2014. Talent management: Conceptual approaches and practical challenges. *Annual Review of Organizational Psychology and Organizational Behavior* 1: 305-331.

Carless, S. A., & Hetherington, K. 2011. Understanding the applicant recruitment experience: Does timeliness matter? *International Journal of Selection and Assessment,* 19: 105-108.

Carpentier, M., Van Hoye, G., Stockman, S., Schollaert, E., Van Theemsche, B., & Jacobs, G. 2017. Recruiting nurses through social media: Effects on employer brand and attractiveness. *Journal of Advanced Nursing,* 73: 2696-2708.

Connerley, M. L. 2013. Recruiter effects and recruitment outcomes. In K. Y. Yu, & D. M. Cable, (Eds.), *The Oxford handbook of employee recruitment:* 21-35. New York: Oxford University Press.

Cromheecke, S., Van Hoye, G., & Lievens, F. 2013, Changing things up in recruitment: Effects of a 'strange' recruitment medium on applicant pool quantity and quality. *Journal of Occupational and Organizational Psychology:* 86, 410-416.

Dineen, B. R., & Allen, D. G. 2016. Third party employment branding: Human capital inflows and outflows following 'Best Places to Work' certifications. *Academy of Management Journal,* 59: 90-112.

Dineen, B. R., Ling, J., Ash, S. R., & Del Vecchio, D. 2007. Aesthetic properties and message customization: Navigating the dark side of web recruitment. *Journal of Applied Psychology,* 92: 356-372.

Frasca, K. J., & Edwards, M. R. 2017. Web-based corporate, social, and video recruitment media: Effects of media richness and source credibility on organizational attraction. *International Journal of Selection and Assessment,* 25: 125-137.

Furnham, A., & Palaiou, K. 2017. Applicant attraction to organizations and job choice. In H. W. Goldstein, E. D. Pulakos, J. Passmore, & C. Semedo (Eds.), *The Wiley handbook of the psychology of recruitment, selection, and employee retention:* 71-90. New York: Wiley-Blackwell.

Gaucher, D., Friesen J., & Kay, A. C. 2011. Evidence that gendered wording in job advertisements exists and sustains gender inequality. *Journal of Personality and Social Psychology,* 101: 109-128.

Giumetti, G. W., & Raymark, P. H. 2017. Engagement, procedural fairness, and perceived fit as predictors of applicant withdrawal intentions: A longitudinal field study. *International Journal of Selection and Assessment,* 25: 161-170.

Groysberg, B. 2010. *Chasing stars: The myth of talent and the portability of performance.* Princeton, NJ: Princeton University Press.

Groysberg, B., & Lee, L. 2009. Hiring stars and their colleagues: Exploration and exploitation in professional service firms. *Organization Science,* 20: 740-758.

Harold, C. M., Holtz, B. C., Griepentrog, B. K., Brewer, L. M., & Marsh, S. M. 2016. Investigating the effects of applicant perceptions on job offer acceptance. *Personnel Psychology,* 69: 199-227.

Kanar, A. M., Collins, C. J., & Bell, B. S. 2015. Changing an unfavorable employer reputation: the roles of recruitment message-type and familiarity with employer. *Journal of Applied Social Psychology,* 45: 509-521.

Korosec, K. 2017. Tesla sues former employee and ex-director of Google self-driving project. *Fortune.* January 26.

Landers, R. N., & Schmidt, G. B. 2016. *Social media in employee selection and recruitment: theory, practice, and current challenges.* New York: Springer.

Lievens, F., & Slaughter, J. E. 2016. Employer image and employer branding: What we know and what we need to know. In F. Morgeson (Ed.), *Annual review of organizational psychology and organizational behavior.* Palo Alto, CA: Annual Reviews.

Linos, E., Reinhard, J., & Ruda, S. 2017. Levelling the playing field in police recruitment: Evidence from a field experiment on test performance. *Public Administration,* 95: 943-956.

McKay, P. F., & Avery, D. R. 2006. What has race got to do with it? Unraveling the role of racioethnicity in job seekers' reactions to site visits. *Personnel Psychology,* 59: 395-429.

O'Boyle, E. H., & Aguinis, H. 2014. Superstar performers in twenty-first-century organizations. *Personnel Psychology,* 67: 313-350.

Pallais, A., & Sands, E. G. 2016. Why the referential treatment? Evidence from field experiments on referrals. *Journal of Political Economy,* 124: 1793-1828.

Pieper, J. 2015. Uncovering the nuances of referral hiring: How referrer characteristics affect referral hires' performance and likelihood of voluntary turnover. *Personnel Psychology,* 68: 811-858.

Pieper, J. Greenwald, J. M., & Schachter, S. D. 2017. Motivating employee referrals: The interactive effects of referral bonus, perceived risk in referring, and affective commitment. *Human Resource Management,* 16: 1-16.

Pieper, J. R., Trevor, C.O., Weller, I., & Duchon, D. (2019,). Referral hire presence implications for referrer turnover and job performance. *Journal of Management,* 45(5): 1858-1888.

Roberts, J. J. 2015. *Tech workers get average of $5,770 under final anti-poaching settlement. Fortune. September 3.*

Ryan, A. M., Ali, A. A., Hauer, T., & French-Vitet, J. 2017. Timeliness is key to the candidate experience. *Personnel Assessment and Decisions,* 3: 38-50.

Rynes, S. L., Bretz, R. D., Jr., & Gerhart, B. 1991. The importance of recruitment in job choice: A different way of looking. *Personnel Psychology,* 44: 487-521.

Schmidt, J. A., Chapman, D. S., & Jones, D. A. 2014. Does emphasizing different types of person–environment fit in online job ads influence application behavior and applicant quality? Evidence from a field experiment. *Journal of Business and Psychology, 30:* 267-282.

Schreurs, B., Derous, E., Van Hooft, E, A., Proost, K., & De Witte, K. 2009. Predicting applicants' job pursuit behavior from their selection expectations: The mediating role of the theory of planned behavior. *Journal of Organizational Behavior,* 30: 761-83.

Selden, S., & Orenstein, J. 2011. Government e-recruiting web sites: The influence of e-recruitment content and usability on recruiting and hiring outcomes in US state governments. *International Journal of Selection and Assessment,* 19: 31-40.

Sheldon, P., & Li, Y. 2013. Localized poaching and skills shortages of manufacturing employees among MNEs in china. *Journal of World Business,* 48: 186.

Shipp, A. J., Furst-Holloway, S., Harris, T. B., & Rosen, B. 2014. Gone today but here tomorrow: Extending the unfolding model of turnover to consider boomerang employees. *Personnel Psychology,* 67: 421-462.

Slaughter, J. E., Cable, D. M., & Turban, D. T. 2014. Changing job seekers' image perceptions during recruitment visits: The moderating role of belief confidence. *Journal of Applied Psychology,* 99: 1146-1158.

Swider, B. W., Liu, J. T., Harris, T. B., & Gardner, R. G. 2017. Employees on the rebound: Toward a framework for boomerang employee performance. *Journal of Applied Psychology,* 102: 890-909.

Swider, B. W., Zimmerman, R. D., & Barrick, M. R. 2015. Searching for the right fit: Applicant person-organization fit development during the recruitment process. *Journal of Applied Psychology,* 100: 880-893.

Uggerslev, K. L., Fassina, N. E., & Kraichy, D. 2012. Recruiting through the stages: A meta-analytic test of predictors of applicant attraction at different stages of the recruiting process. *Personnel Psychology,* 65: 597-660.

Van Hoye, G. 2013. Word of mouth as a recruitment source: An integrative model. In K. Y. Yu & D. M. Cable (Eds.), *The Oxford handbook of recruitment:* 251-268. New York: Oxford University Press.

Van Hoye, G., & Lievens, F. 2009. Tapping the grapevine: A closer look at word-of-mouth as a recruiting source. *Journal of Applied Psychology,* 94: 341-352.

Walker, H. J., Field, H. S., Giles, W. F., & Bernerth, J. B. 2008. The interactive effects of job advertisement characteristics and applicant experience on reactions to recruitment messages. *Journal of Occupational and Organizational Psychology,* 81: 619-638.

Walker, H. J., Feild, H. S., Giles, W. F., Bernerth, J. B., & Short, J. C. 2011. So what do you think of the organization? A contextual priming explanation for recruitment web site characteristics as antecedents of job seekers' organizational image perceptions. *Organizational Behavior and Human Decision Process,* 114: 165-178.

Walker, H. J., Helmuth, C. A., Feild, H. S., & Bauer, T. N. 2015. Watch what you say: Job applicants' justice perceptions from initial organizational correspondence. *Human Resource Management,* 54: 999-1011

Windscheid, L., Bowes-Sperry, L., Kidder, D., Cheung, H., Morner, M., & Lievens, F. 2016. *Journal of Applied Psychology,* 101: 1329-1341.

Williams, C. R., Labig, C. E., & Stone, T. H. 1993. Recruitment sources and posthire outcomes for job applicants and new hires: A test of two hypotheses. *Journal of Applied Psychology,* 42: 163-172.

Yu, K. Y., & Cable, D. M. 2013. *The Oxford handbook of employee recruitment.* New York: Oxford University Press.

36

APPROACHES TO DEVELOPING HIGH-POTENTIAL TALENT

Intended and Unintended Consequences

Miriam Lacey

Kevin Groves

Introduction

Organizations across the globe invest substantial resources in the training and development of leadership talent. Leadership training is a US$366 billion global industry, and the U.S.A. alone spends $166 billion annually on leadership development (Training Industry, 2020; Westfall, 2019). One important recipient of these resources are high-potential (hipo) employees and the processes and programs that support their identification and development as leaders. Defined as employees who are identified as having advancement potential at least two levels above their current role (Church & Silzer, 2014), hipo employees receive targeted leadership development opportunities and resources with the aim of deepening bench strength in critical leadership roles.

In addition to attracting the attention of leadership scholars, the global leadership development industry is shaped by numerous consulting and professional services firms. The Association for Talent Development (ATD), Center for Creative Leadership (CCL), Korn Ferry, Human Capital Institute (HCI), and Development Dimensions International (DDI) represent a sample of the major consulting organizations that specialize in leadership development, including the identification and development of hipo talent.

The major leadership development consulting firms report that investments in hipo talent development practices realize a range of performance benefits for organizations across industries. For example, CCL (2020) reports that leadership development programs effectively drive an organization's new strategic initiatives, including acceleration of the digital transformation and the development of new business partnerships that are requisite for executing new strategies. The Ken Blanchard Companies reports that human resource and learning/development professionals are increasingly focusing their talent development efforts on mid-level and frontline leaders, and specifically targeting the development of change readiness and increased access to training as program priorities (Witt, 2020).

Summarizing the overall state of hipo programs across industries, Korn Ferry (2020) reports that only 29% of human resource professionals are confident that their respective organizations have the future leaders needed to drive the business, while just 14% are confident in their ability to select the best talent for their hipo programs. With only 13% of HR professionals reporting the use of a validated hipo assessment for identifying talent for participation in leadership development programs, Korn Ferry concludes that organizations would greatly benefit from the use of such tools for their hipo programs.

Harvard Business Publishing Corporate Learning (HBPCL) (2018), the leadership development organization affiliated with Harvard Business School, concluded in its semi-annual report on the state of leadership development that three powerful forces are redefining the nature of work, the workplace, and talent development initiatives: 1) the rapid pace of globalization (leading across cultural and physical boundaries); 2) the rise of free agents (rapidly increasing the portion of the workforce

DOI: 10.4324/9781315474687-36

that are contractors and freelancers); and 3) the leader emergence of Generation Y and Generation Z (shifting expectations regarding work, learning, and leadership). Overall, HBPCL concludes that revenue growth, market positions, and future growth potential are all associated with organizations where leadership development initiatives are strongly aligned with the business and valued by executive teams.

Initial research on the efficacy of hipo programs provides encouraging evidence of their impact across a range of performance outcomes, including financial metrics (Bernthal & Wellins, 2005; Bush, Skiba, Liu, & Li, 2016; Crowe, Garman, Li, Helton, Anderson, & Butler, 2017; Favaro, Karlsson, & Neilson, 2010), adaptation to strategic shifts (Harris, 2020), leadership stability and bench strength in critical roles (Groves, 2017, 2019), reducing bias in identifying leadership talent and increasing diversity in leadership roles (Pinsight, 2020), leadership competency development (Martorano, 2020), and a range of workforce performance indicators, such as employee engagement, turnover intent, turnover, and organizational citizenship behaviors (Malik, Singh, & Chan, 2017; Patidar, Gupta, Azbik, & Weech-Maldanado, 2016).

The argument for developing internal hipo leadership programs is underscored by research indicating the many benefits of developing and promoting internal talent for senior leadership roles (Deortentiis, Ployhart, Van Iddekinge, & Heetderks, 2018; Berns & Klarner, 2017; Harrell, 2016; Schepker, Nyberg, Ulrich, & Wright, 2018). As a bridge field that has only recently entered the lexicon of academia across various professional organizations (Association for Talent Development, Human Resource Planning Society, Society for Industrial-Organizational Psychology, Academy of Management, etc.), talent management and specifically the field of hipo leadership is drawing increasing attention from scholars, consulting firms, and corporations.

Notwithstanding the surge in growth and prominence of hipo programs (Buckner & Marberry, 2018; Church, Rotolo, Ginther, & Levine 2015), numerous challenges lurk beneath the surface that demand further scrutiny. With the average pool of hipo employees comprising just 10% of the workforce (Church & Silzer, 2014; Silzer & Dowell, 2010), organizations with hipo programs risk leaving potentially talented individuals behind, inadvertently creating a second-class citizenry. The barriers to inclusion result in the loss of strategically-aligned development opportunities for the vast majority of employees.

Regrettably, the excluded workforce is often composed of a higher concentration of women and individuals from diverse socio-economic and ethnic backgrounds than the hipo population, which is often reflective of the nominators (Greer & Virick, 2008). Overall, many organizations have developed hipo programs without proper attention to a range of unintended side effects resultant of managerial cognitive errors. Common managerial thinking errors sub-optimize approaches to identifying hipo talent, allow rater bias to influence selection, and promote self-serving behaviors, while simultaneously violating tenets of organizational justice (Lacey & Groves, 2014). Indeed, a careful examination of the current state of hipo approaches reveals a disconnect between hipo assessment and development processes, and existing theory and research.

This chapter discusses the complexity and interaction of the factors driving the unintended consequences of hipo programs and processes, including a review of adult learning theories underpinning hipo programs, hipo leadership frameworks, the performance outcomes of hipo programs, and two categories of management thinking errors. The chapter also presents theory from which hipo stakeholders can draw a set of guiding principles or "success factors" that ameliorate unintended negative consequences via greater attention to organizational justice –distributive, procedural, and interactional-relationship. Finally, the chapter concludes with a discussion of directions for future research.

Adult Learning in a Vuca Environment

Popularized by the U.S. military in the 1990s as a way to describe the increasingly convoluted and complex geopolitical landscape in which it operated, VUCA (volatile, uncertain, chaotic, and ambiguous) is also an apt description of the current business environment. Enormous pressure is placed on organizations to prepare a new generation of leaders who possess a different set of skills, competencies, and experiences (Chatman & Cha, 2003) needed to address the uncertain future landscape of business. Intent to upgrade participant competence and leverage their connections within the organization, hipo processes strive to reflect the best thinking of educators, through careful selection of design, content, and delivery methods that capitalize on the foundation of adult learning theory.

Four adult learning theories operate prevalently in companies with mature learning and leadership development offerings: 1) adult learning principles based on andragogy (Knowles, 1973) promote the high involvement of the learner; 2) self-directed learning (Brouse, 2007; Tough, 1971) opportunities abound from online lessons to self-help books; 3) experiential learning (Kolb & Frye, 1974; Kolb, 1983; Kolb & Kolb, 2005) is heavily utilized in workshops and job rotations that provide real world compe-tency building heuristic approaches and concrete experience with opportunities for reflection; and 4) transformative learning (Mezirow, 1978, 2009), focused on shifting the learner's viewpoint through critical reflection on one's underlying assumptions and beliefs with an eye to consciously innovate. These adult learning theories are now foundational to most leadership programs, with the latter playing the most dominant part in hipo processes.

The chief criticisms of andragogy, self-directed learning (SDL), and experiential learning are that each of them is too rational, autonomous, and linear; and for experiential learning specifically, learners do not necessarily move around the cycle systematically (Merriam, 2001). Further, many scholars argue these theories are not uniquely adult but actually describe all learners.

VUCA environments demand leaders who are more flexible and able to engage in multidimensional thinking and decision-making that mirrors the complexity of the business. Research on managerial cog-nition and thinking theory has advanced by developing more complex approaches that integrate both linear decision-making and information-processing styles, with nonlinear thinking, which includes intuition, insight, creativity, and other forms of subconscious or unconscious information (Dane & Pratt, 2007; Vance, Groves, Paik, & Kindler, 2007). These push leaders to utilize multiple forms of information-processing and decision-making.

hipo programs benefit from identifying talent who possess these attributes while also providing shared learning experiences for participants that reinforce both linear and nonlinear information-processing and decision-making. Favored above other adult learning theories, transformative learning theory (Mezirow & Taylor, 2009) incorporates aspects of each of the major learning theories (andragogy, self-directed learning, and experiential learning), and offers talent management professionals and adult educators proven teaching strategies based on substantive research framed within sound theoretical assumptions (Taylor, 2007).

Transformative Learning Theory

To address the limitations summarized above and specifically rising to the challenge of whether either andragogy, SDL, or experiential learning describe a learning theory that is uniquely adult, Mezirow (1978, 2000) proposed an alternative called transformative learning theory. Transformative learning, with its focus on shifting the learner's viewpoints through critical reflection (reflection on one's under-lying assumptions and beliefs with an eye to consciously innovate) is now foundational to most lead-ership offerings (Church et al., 2015). The following discussion presents a case for the critical role of transformative learning across multiple elements of today's hipo efforts.

For hipo processes seeking to raise their participants to the next level, transformative learning engenders sense-making in adult learners, particularly the learning process of paradigmatic shifts (Taylor & Cranton, 2012). Such shifts are necessary for organizations to implement change exponen-tially rather than the small steps inherent in continuous improvement of common business processes.

This was originally described by Argyris' seminal work on (1971) double-loop learning – learning that goes beyond simple cause and effect and questions the system itself through reflection, and then later popularized by Senge (2007). Experience, awareness, and reflection are constants in learning that are embedded in complexity of relationships – with ourselves, others, and socio-economic contexts (Bryan, Kreuter, & Brownson, 2009). Transformative learning attributes can be seen in various elements of hipo development approaches (Yost & Plunkett, 2010), such as paradigm shifting, authenticity, peer learning relationships, sense of community, dialogue, and action learning experiences.

High-Potential Talent Frameworks

Of the many salient topics and components that comprise the field of talent management, the challenge of clearly defining and identifying hipo talent remains one of the most intense and ongoing debates (Church, 2014). In part due to the efforts of consultants and executive search firms to meet the strong demand for effective hipo talent frameworks, there are many different models of hipo leadership utilized in industry (Church et al., 2015; Church & Rotolo, 2013). After decades of experimentation, there remains limited conceptual agreement regarding the design of hipo programs.

Despite the lack of a consensus definition and model of hipo talent, there are two complementary hipo talent frameworks that are comprehensive, grounded in theory and research, and prescriptive for senior executives, board members, human resource professionals, and other key stakeholders. Summarized below, these models include the Dries and Pepermans (2012) integrated model of leadership potential, and Church and Silzer's (2014) Leadership Potential BluePrint ("BluePrint"). While the Dries and Pepermans' model offers strong empirical grounding and academic rigor, the Church and Silzer model enjoys greater utilization in industry. While they use different labels, both frameworks share a similar view regarding the interplay of individual differences, behavioral competencies, and knowledge bases (functional and technical skills) for determining one's leadership potential. The following discussion briefly describes the primary hipo leadership dimensions that comprise these models, followed by discussion of the highly practical applications of the Church and Silzer model for organizations across industries.

Among the many hipo models, we selected the Dries and Pepermans (2012) and Church and Silzer (2014) models for the following reasons. First, both models have been published in highly respected, peer-reviewed journals and validated via empirical studies. Second, the models are integrative such that they incorporate and build upon existing theory and research findings on hipo assessment. For example, these models further develop and integrate prior hipo leadership theory and research on learning agility (Lombardo & Eichinger, 2000), end-state and learning-oriented competencies (Spritzer, McCall, & Mahoney 1997), and core personality variables associated with leadership potential (Hogan, Curphy, & Hogan, 1997). Given our goal of identifying both the intended and unintended outcomes associated with hipo models and associated industry practices, such as succession planning and talent review processes (Zhang & Rajagopalan, 2010), we selected the Dries and Pepermans and Church and Silzer models due to their relevance and increasing applications across industries.

Based on an extensive literature review of the existing leadership potential research from 1986 to 2010, as well as a series of qualitative and quantitative data analytic approaches, Dries and Pepermans (2012) developed a multi-dimensional model consisting of four quadrants or sets of factors that identify hipo leadership talent. In addition to rigorous grounding in theory and research, this model has received strong support from executives, line managers, and HR professionals concerning practical relevance and utility in organizations.

This model was not developed for commercial purposes, a specific consulting project or corporate need, or to align with a predetermined theoretical perspective or *a priori* theory (e.g., Big Five personality). Rather, this model was developed to integrate and improve upon existing models of hipo leadership, including Hezlett, Ronnkvist, Holt, and Hazucha (1997); Hogan, Curphy, and Hogan (1994); Lombardo and Eichinger (2000), Silzer and Church (2010); and Spreitzer, McCall, and Mahoney (1997). The four quadrants and their associated hipo leadership criteria or factors include the following: analytical skills (e.g., intellectual curiosity, strategic insight); learning agility (willingness to learn, emotional intelligence; drive (results orientation, perseverance), and emergent leadership (motivation to lead, self-promotion).

Similar to the Dries and Pepermans' (2012) integrated model, Church and Silzer's (2014) BluePrint offers a comprehensive framework that also provides a prescriptive approach to assessing leadership potential. The ability for practitioners to readily apply the model to their organizations' talent challenges represents an important and distinguishing feature of the BluePrint framework and explains its popularity. Specifically, this model offers organizations multiple applications across HR processes and employee career stages. The BluePrint is a multidimensional framework that includes three levels or types of dimensions and six building blocks that reflect the skills and abilities comprising leadership potential. Supported by rigorous research and validated in numerous industry contexts (Silzer & Church, 2009, 2010), the framework outlines the practical implications for assessment, training, and leadership development practices across each building block or element of the model. An overview of the BluePrint model and its hipo dimensions is provided in Table 36.1.

The Silzer and Church BluePrint model (Church & Silzer, 2014; Silzer & Church, 2009) offers several important insights for academia and industry alike. First, the career dimensions (leadership skills and functional/technical skills) represent the most malleable building blocks and the most direct means to enhance an individual's or group's leadership potential. Indeed, at \$25 billion, leadership training and development programs represent the single largest investment of all employee development initiatives by organizations across industries (O'Leonard, 2014). Conversely, the personality characteristics and cognitive capabilities (foundational dimensions) represent the facets of hipo

Table 36.1 Church & Silzer (2014) BluePrint high-potential leadership model

	Foundational	*Growth*	*Career*
Dimensions	• Personality Characteristics: individual differences in psychology and behavior; social and interpersonal skills; assertiveness and dominance; and maturity, emotional self-control, and resilience • Cognitive Capabilities: General intelligence, strategic and conceptual thinking, and the ability to deal with complexity and ambiguity.	• Learning Skills: adaptability, learning interest, orientation, and openness to feedback; ability to effectively learn from experiences and adopt a learning mindset or learning agility (Lombardo & Eichinger, 2000). • Motivational Skills: drive, energy, and initiative; career ambition and organizational commitment; results and achievement orientation.	• Leadership Skills: managing people; motivating, influencing, and inspiring others; and developing others. • Functional Capabilities: technical capabilities in a given area of expertise and business knowledge or acumen of the organization and industry.
Summary	• Identifies a pair of core building blocks of high-potential talent: cognitive capabilities and personality characteristics • Consistent with aptitude-treatment-interaction (ATI) theory as foundational cognitive capabilities and personality characteristics are likely to moderate the efficacy of assessment, training, leadership development, and other hipo practices (Goska & Ackerman, 1996).	• Intervening or moderating variables that facilitate an individual's leadership growth and learning of new skills and behaviors • Growth dimensions are primarily aligned with the learning agility and emergent leadership categories of the Dries and Pepermen's (2012) model.	• Career dimensions are primarily aligned with the emergent leadership element of the Dries and Pepermans (2012) model. • Functional/technical skills and business knowledge represent distinguishing dimensions of the BluePrint model for identifying high-potential talent.

talent that are the most difficult (if not impossible) to change or further develop in an individual. Furthermore, the BluePrint framework specifies the "contextual factors" that play an integral role in contributing to how organizations and executive teams conceptualize and formally assess leadership potential.

Although not included as elements of the hipo model, these contextual factors represent critical issues that influence the effectiveness of an organization's talent review process. These factors include performance history, mobility, background demographics, cultural fit, and readiness. Overall, Silzer and Church state that "the ideal high-potential assessment and development talent management process would incorporate a fully validated multi-trait, multi-method approach based on all of the dimensions outlined in the *Leadership Potential BluePrint* (Church & Silzer, 2014: 57).

Intended and Unintended Outcomes of High-Potential Approaches

The research indicates that organizations willing to invest in robust hipo programs realize impressive financial and workforce performance outcomes. For example, the intended outcomes are demonstrated by studies that show several key financial metrics, including total shareholder return, mean net revenue per employee, and return on equity are associated with strong talent management practices (Bernthal & Wellins, 2005; Guthridge & Komm, 2008; Pfeffer, 1994). Along a similar vein, numerous studies have demonstrated that exemplary talent management practices are associated with greater depth of succession plans across critical executive roles, substantially higher placement of internal candidates for open executive roles, and lower rates of executive derailment and turnover (Fegley, 2006; Groves, 2017; Nadler, 2007).

Notwithstanding these promising research results illustrating the positive effects mentioned supra, organizations that develop strong hipo approaches also experience unintended outcomes by often failing to cultivate the full range of leadership talent that exists across management levels and throughout the line staff. In short, hipo approaches designed according to the best practices presented in this chapter – relevant adult learning theoretical foundations, hipo leadership competency models, etc. – are still very much at risk for creating unintended negative consequences associated with organizational justice and managerial cognitive errors.

Consider the following inadvertent outcomes of a hallmark framework of hipo identification optimally developed with the best intentions: the assessment and placement of talent into a nine-box grid or equivalent tool. These assessment tools are commonly used as part of annual talent review processes and designate a subset of employees as demonstrating "high potential" for leadership roles. Employees assessed as both strong performers (via direct manager assessment during the performance appraisal process) and hipo (via direct manager assessment of hipo leadership competencies) are provided highly differentiated and advanced development opportunities: exposure to executives for mentoring, critical job assignments, job rotations, targeted courses and education, and other learning experiences. The development plans for employees who are not assessed as both high-performers and hipo are most often limited to plans that focus on their current position, and are excluded from advanced and highly targeted development opportunities, including exposure to senior organizational leaders. Moreover, many organizations struggle with creating succession plans for senior executive roles that are diverse with respect to gender and ethnicity, which suggests that the hipo assessment process may unintentionally "weed out" such candidates due to rater bias, managerial thinking or cognitive errors, and/or broader organizational culture factors.

National surveys indicate that the average size of the hipo pool across industries is approximately 10% (Silzer & Dowell, 2010). As such, any critical analysis of the state of hipo approaches must scrutinize the unintended consequences for the remaining 90% of the workforce. Inadvertently, organizations that diligently address the 10% identified as hipo may simultaneously create a 90% majority of second-class citizens who perceive numerous violations of organizational justice – distributive, procedural, and interactional-relationship (Lacey & Groves, 2014).

Extensive research on organizational justice indicates that employee perceptions of justice violations, particularly for hipo employees, are incredibly costly for organizations, including adverse impact on productivity, engagement, retention, cohesion, and many other attitudinal and performance outcomes. Fortunately, there are several talent management "success factors" that facilitate an organization's capability to overcome these unintentional consequences of hipo programs. The following section provides a discussion of the two primary categories of management cognition errors that cause organizational malfunctions and violate employee perceptions of organizational justice.

Management Thinking Errors Reinforce Second Class Citizenry and Cause Organizational Justice Violations

Savvy managers take advantage of evidence-based counsel offered by scholars and other subject matter experts regarding the assessment and development of employees, particularly those identified as demonstrating hipo for future leadership roles. Less progressive organizations can inadvertently thwart careers by tolerating common thinking errors about employee assessment in general, and hipo in particular. Importantly, these common thinking errors often disproportionately impact women, ethnic minorities, and employees who represent lower-status business divisions and functions.

Widespread notions of justice insist on fair distribution of resources and opportunities (Cropanzano, Bowen, & Gilliland, 2007), issues that are strongly challenged by management thinking errors resident in common hipo approaches. These errors result in the creation of second-class citizens of 90% of the workforce. For the purposes of this chapter, two broad categories of management thinking errors that tend to disregard organizational justice are identified that directly impact hipo eligibility and selection: rater bias and self-serving management behaviors.

Rater Bias

Possibly the most pernicious challenge to hipo approaches is implicit person bias (Wattles, 2017). Behavioral scientists advise that everyone has bias and research has identified as many as twenty-one biases (Revelian, 2017), all operating underneath conscious awareness. Forward thinking companies seeking to upgrade organization justice devote resources to increase inclusion and diversity. They attempt to reduce unconscious bias and raise managerial consciousness through organizational supports such as goal setting, training, and discussion. This popular avenue, however, after spending multi-millions, has shown little promise in our world-class organizations. Rater bias is unyielding as only slight gains in diverse hiring, promotion, and inclusion in hipo have been witnessed by Google (Winegarner, 2017), Facebook (2017), and Microsoft (2016). Even managers who have studied rater bias and value fair evaluation are subject to their own unconscious preference for that which is similar and familiar.

After employees are sorted into hipo versus non-hipo populations, the former receives specialized developmental attention while the latter is given little attention. Commonly run as a highly exclusive in-group, hipo processes are often reflective of the race, gender, and socio-economic class of the individuals steering them – usually white males (Fiegerman, 2017). Similar to the common rater errors associated with performance appraisal and other employee evaluation processes (Latham, Almost, Mann, & Moore, 2005), the sociodemographic characteristics of the appraiser can have a significant impact on the talent pools being evaluated as part of hipo programs. The similar-to-me bias in which "like picks like" is an ever-present challenge for management teams evaluating employee talent for hipo programs.

For example, the C-suite executive teams in U.S. healthcare are disproportionately comprised of white males (Institute for Diversity in Health Management, 2013) and are generally not reflective of the communities that they serve (Helfat, Harris, & Wolfson, 2006). A recent American College of Healthcare Executives (ACHE) survey illustrated that women achieve CEO positions at approximately 50% of the rate at which their equally credentialed male counterparts achieve such positions (ACHE, 2012).

These results and other industry-specific findings suggest that busy managers predictably adopt their company's existing hipo processes without much thought as to the unintended side effects. Unless stewarded by well-informed human resource partners, typical hipo processes have an unintended consequence: they coincidentally make it possible for managers to avoid difficult issues such as rater bias and self-serving behaviors. Both of which in turn impact employee perceptions of organization justice resulting in employee disengagement or decisions not to stay.

New avenues need to be created to find stronger, more potent methods for addressing rater-bias to upgrade procedural, distributive, and relational justice in organizations (Fujimoto, Hartel, & Azmat, 2013; Lind, E. 2001). One promising new theory is joint evaluation (Bohnet, van Geen, & Bazerman, 2016). Using discrete indicators, two or more potential candidates are evaluated side by side, simultaneously, not separately. This new method of evaluation may offer an efficacious alternative as one method that may prove reliable toward the amelioration of unconscious bias. Findings clearly show that when candidates were evaluated at the same time, people who did not resemble the rater were more likely to be represented.

Self-serving Behaviors

Ambitious managers, complying with traditional company norms and bonus structures that reward individual performance, can become myopically focused on their respective unit's performance, and lose sight of organization-wide decisions and priorities for the general good of the company. They engage in self-serving behaviors (Cohn, Khurana, & Reeves, 2005) that directly benefit themselves: talent hoarding – safeguarding the current talent so they stay rather than go to another business unit for development or advancement; political gamesmanship – avoiding the topic of hipo and not broadcasting the merits of your unit's workers; and unilateral career decision making – not putting high-performers' names forward for hipo consideration for fear of losing them to job rotation or promotion.

These sub-optimized paths create feelings of resource scarcity and replace organizational benefits with personal rewards and diminish organization-wide performance. New avenues need to be created to find stronger, more potent methods for addressing self-serving behaviors to upgrade distributive, procedural, and relational justice in organizations.

In efforts to ameliorate self-serving behaviors, theory sheds some light. Super-ordinate goal theory for organizational performance, in which all managers commit to shared goals instead of individual performance, can help managers pull together in their efforts to steward the organization (Hochli, Brugger, & Messner, 2018). Also promising, is the theory on mindsets (Scheier, Carver, & Bridges 2001) reflecting a manager's possible orientation to scarcity – which contributes to self-serving behaviors, versus abundance – which contributes to collaboration on super-ordinate goals where distributive, procedural, and relationship justices are widely served.

Executive team sponsorship of the hipo system simultaneously ensures strategic alignment and viability, and underscores a culture of collaboration among business units and personalities. Executive interest, mentorship, and nurturing of future leaders instill greater commitment from young careerists, and reduces opportunities for nepotism and manager self-serving decisions, while promoting perceptions of organization justice. Their stewardship helps managers find the right balance between hipo placement in the organization and keeping high-performing people delivering results in their respective units.

Mindset Shifts can Ameliorate Management Thinking Errors and Upgrade Organizational Justice

Accepted social norms of fair treatment, as promoted through corporate social responsibility initiatives, currently challenge several common hipo practices and also reveal uneven *distribution* of opportunity, limited participation without transparent *procedures*, and meager chances of *interacting* with mentor relationships (Cropanzano, Bowen, & Gilliland, 2007). These injustices can permeate hipo programs and processes, and create a second-class citizenry. Fortunately, talent management research has developed theory and uncovered a range of principles that effectively mitigate the unintended consequences of managerial thinking errors (Silzer & Dowell, 2010). These key considerations can dilute the primary unwanted side-effects resultant from elitism, rater bias, and self-serving "political" behaviors, and they also limit the challenges experienced by the inadvertent creation of second-class citizenry.

Two Fundamental Mindset Shifts

It is understandable that not all employees are hipo and not all can be accommodated by the hipo system. There are talented individuals, however, whose talents and energies remain unknown and untapped. It is estimated that over 70% of organizations risk not identifying the correct people for their hipo programs (Hudson, 2007). Bars to entry for those who may be thought of as second-class citizens can be reduced while simultaneously upgrading procedural, distributive and interactional justice by increasing hipo transparency and providing multiple paths to participate in hipo.

From Secrecy to Transparency

Having a closed, and/or secret approach to developing tomorrow's leaders sets up hipos as an elite class. When excluded from special treatment, those non-hipos who would like to participate can experience feelings of marginality, isolation, and stress (Lacey & Groves, 2014). Making the hipo system transparent helps ameliorate the discouragement and under-valued feelings of the second-class citizenry (Groves, 2017). This dilutes the stark contrast of the non-hipo world of work, and upgrades earmarks of distributive justice and procedural justice that are important for employee perceptions of fair treatment. Transparency can also positively impact intention to stay, and act to bolster career aspirations, and encourage pro-active management of one's career.

From One Person's Opinion to Multiple Paths

When only the direct supervisor can identify participants for hipo, they act as the "lion at the gate," where one person determines another's potential career. Expanding the avenues to include self-nomination and/or other-nomination reduces the impact of the rater's underlying perceptual biases. This has been successful as evidenced by one mid-sized private equity firm that increased transparency by installing a process in 2011 whereby any employee can initiate conversations about hipo eligibility with a manager at any time. It also provides the "rank and file" with access to management. Multiple paths to obtain a hipo nomination diminishes employee perceptions of organizational justice violations.

Directions for Further Research

One disruptive challenge to the development of hipo processes and programs based on adult learning theory comes from Siemens (2004, 2005) and Downes (2005). Both authors promote connectivism as a needed alternative to previous conceptions of learning, and dismiss traditional education principles that rest by in large on information and knowledge acquisition wherein subject matter is distributed in units to learners as pre-determined by teachers. They argue that in a VUCA world, where the amount of available information is overwhelming and growing exponentially, learners are spontaneously taking the helm to engage in offerings provided by the World Wide Web and virtual networks. Social networks, via nodes of learning, are now performing the job of providing information that is selected by the learner according to an individual's interest, preference, and network affiliations.

Connectivism views learning as messy, chaotic, and serendipitous. It complies with all four requirements of all four adult learning theories that underscore all hipo development: andragogy, self-directed, experiential, and transformative. It does not, however, follow the usual rules about subject matter selection, instructional design, method, pace, etc., commonly shaped by previous conceptions of learning that shape most management and hipo development programs.

Due to rapid growth and availability of data, the act of learning has shifted from acquisition to assimilation, from understanding individual elements to comprehending an entire space and, thereby, understanding how elements connect (Hug, 2007). Indeed, the identification and development of business leaders capable of identifying and synthesizing increasing volumes of data across multiple categories of types (linear, nonlinear, tacit, explicit) remain a central challenge for HR managers and business schools charged with developing business leaders. Siemens and Downes argue that educational opportunities that rely on old theories that ignore the networked nature of society, life, and learning, largely miss the point of how fundamentally our world has changed.

Scholars (Kerr, 2007; Kop & Hill, 2008) are in the midst of debating whether connectivism should be taken seriously, as it has not yet established the criteria of a true theory. Since connectivism, however, disregards the tried and true it may be erroneous to apply traditional standards to a conceptual paradigm that defies those standards. The proverbial jury is still out on connectivism, but we believe the changing nature of how information is offered and assimilated will likely be embraced in some fashion by innovative hipo programs. It may even be essential to allow connectivism theory to influence the design and delivery of hipo programs, as it currently impacts learners regardless of whether it is embedded in hipo approaches or not. It may be as simple as accelerating SDL options or making them integral to the education process. Connectivism as a theory may also assert itself into the establishment of sense-making communities of learners that assemble and disband with membership constantly changing. It may bring about an instability to hipo programs that should be anticipated by HR professionals, so they are ready to adapt with diverse learning agility agendas.

According to Mezirow, "Fostering these liberating conditions for making more autonomous and informed choices and developing a sense of self-empowerment is the cardinal goal of adult education" (2000: 26). This captures the essence of connectivism's allure since learners are self-directed, concretely choosing learning experiences at will, finding like-minded learners to interact with, and shifting paradigms as a result. The overarching challenge for HR leaders tasked with hipo development is to ensure alignment between adult learning offerings –and the range of self-directed learning options therein – and the organization's strategic goals. Future research should examine the factors or policies that allow HR professionals to successfully manage the tension or balance between self-directed learning and shorter-term business objectives.

Whether these things happen sooner or later, the implications for hipo programs and their cohorts are profound. Commonly, hipo systems include employees who are global in orientation and who operate virtually across multiple locations. Adding complexity to work life, COVID-19 has further necessitated operating remotely. Work place systems, including leadership development approaches, have all become essentially virtual. Hipo programs now find the Internet is foundational to their work of communicating with and guiding hipo participants in their development. Also observed is the ease of just-in-time, learning-on-demand; hipo can reach out any time of day or night to find answers to developmental questions they have, and are no longer limited to the pre-selected offerings by talent management professionals. Such spontaneous learning is student driven-rather than teacher/expert-driven and as such is readily customizable to student interests and needs. As such, we offer the following questions for future research:

- How best to create developmental environments where all employees see themselves as being treated fairly despite the exclusionary aspects of hipo programs? Put differently, how can organizations that are committed to both corporate social responsibility and justice provide these simultaneously alongside the specialized development inherent in hipo approaches?
- How can hipo talent effectively and sustainably establish trusting and effective relationships if most everything – hipo status, preferential treatment, exclusive development opportunities, etc. – is

temporary and in flux? As illustrated in the best practice recommendations, organizations with exemplary hipo policies adopt a fluid, flexible approach to assessing talent, such that environmental changes, create shifting talent needs and reevaluation of leadership talent.

- How can organizations leverage theory and research on teams and how to assemble hipo talent with ever-changing skill sets and learning interests? Future research should examine how hipo development programs, which often include action learning teams comprised of multiple hipo leaders who are tasked with an enterprise-wide challenge or opportunity, can effectively meet a dynamic and evolving set of learning and development needs.
- What will these newer learning opportunities do to the human need for stability and predictability? Future studies of hipo programs and processes should identify the hipo talent that is excluded from accelerated development opportunities due to a personal preference for the stability and predictability of their current roles. For many hipo programs, an employee's desire to advance to more senior positions and willingness to accept new and emerging roles is an eligibility requirement for inclusion in the program. For many industries, such as technology and health care, organizations struggle to attract hipo talent into many people management positions and the leadership track. The hipo field would benefit from a better understanding of the talent that is essentially "left behind" due to the inability to craft career tracks for highly talented individuals who prefer to remain in current positions.
- Will the dynamism and fluidity of connectivism among hipo workers weaken or support standardized protocols viewed as imperative for dependable quality and delivery of services and products? What about the long-term impacts of connectivism on standardized routines and business process controls as hipos take the reins of company leadership?
- How best to establish learning protocols that support hipos rather than interfere with learning?

References

American College of Healthcare Executives. 2012. *A comparison of the career attainments of men and women healthcare executives.* ACHE: Division of Member Services, Research. http://www.ache.org/pubs/research/2012-Gender-Report-FINAL.pdf, first accessed January 1, 2017.

Argyris, C. 1971. Double-loop learning. *Harvard Business Report,* 9-10: 115-125.

Bass, B. M. 1985. *Leadership and performance beyond expectations.* New York. Free Press.

Berns, K., & Klarner, P. 2017. A review of the CEO succession literature and a future research program. *Academy of Management Perspectives,* 31(2): 83-108.

Bernthal, P., & Wellins, S. 2005. *Leadership forecast 2005-2006: Best practices for tomorrow's global leaders.* Pittsburgh, PA: Development Dimensions International.

Bohnet, I., van Geen, A., & Bazerman, M. 2016. When performance trumps gender bias: Joint versus separate evaluation. *Management Science,* 62(5): 1225-1234.

Brouse, C. 2007. Promoting self-directed learning in three online health promotion and wellness courses. *Journal of Authentic Learning,* 4(1): 25-33.

Bryan, R., Kreuter, M., & Brownson, R. 2009. Integrating adult learning principles into training for public health practice. *Health Promotion Practice,* 10(4): 557-563.

Buckner, M., & Marberry, M. 2018. How to identify and grow high potentials: A CEO's perspective with proven results. *People & Strategy,* 41(1): 22-27.

Bush, J., Skiba, T., Liu, W., & Li, A. 2016. The financial impact of strategic development and high potential programs. *Journal of Organizational Psychology,* 16(2): 99-112.

Center for Creative Leadership. 2020. *Leadership development accelerates digital transformation.* https://www.ccl.org/articles/client-successes/leadership-development-accelerates-digital-transformation/.

Chapman, J., & Cha, S. E. 2003. Leading by leveraging culture, *California Management Review,* 45(4): 20-34.

Church, A. 2014. What do we know about developing leadership potential? The role of OD in strategic talent management. *OD Practitioner,* 46(3): 52-61.

Church, A., & Rotolo, C. 2013. How are top companies assessing their high-potentials and senior executives? A talent management benchmark study. *Consulting Psychology Journal: Practice and Research,* 65(3): 199-223.

Church, A., & Rotolo, C., Ginther, N., & Levine, R. 2015. How are top companies designing and managing their high-potential programs? A follow-up talent management benchmarks study. *Consulting Psychology Journal: Practice and Research,* 67(1): 17-47.

Church, A., & Silzer, R. 2014. Going behind the corporate curtain with a BluePrint for leadership potential: An integrated framework for identifying high-potential talent. *People & Strategy,* 36(4): 50-58.

Cohn, J., Khurana, R., & L. Reeves. 2005. Growing talent as if your business depended on it. *Harvard Business Review,* 10: 1-6.

Cropanzano, R., Bowen, D., & Gilliland, S. 2007. The management of organization justice. *Academy of Management Perspectives,* 21(4): 34-48.

Crowe, D., Garman, A., Li, C., Helton, J., Anderson, M., & Butler, P. 2017. Leadership development practices and hospital performance outcomes. *Health Services Management Research,* 30(3): 140-147.

Dane, E., & Pratt, M. 2008. Exploring intuition and its role in managerial decision-making. *Academy of Management Review,* 32(1): 33-54.

Delizonna, L. 2017. High performing teams need psychological safety. *Harvard Business Review,* 8(24).

DeOrtentiis, P., Ployhart, R., Van Iddekinge, C., & Heetderks, T. 2018. Build or buy? The individual and unit-level performance of internally versus externally selected managers over time. *Journal of Applied Psychology,* 103(8): 916-928.

Downes, S. 2005. *An introduction to connective knowledge.* http://www.downes.ca/cgi-bin/page.cgi?post=33034, first accessed November 12, 2006.

Dries, N., & Pepermans, R. 2012. How to identify leadership potential: Development testing of a consensus model. *Human Resource Management,* 51(3): 361-385.

Eisen, M. 2001. Peer-based professional development viewed through the lens of transformative learning. *Holistic Nursing Practice,* 16(1): 30-42.

Facebook. 2017. *Managing unconscious bias.* https://managingbias.fb.com/, first accessed April 2017.

Favaro, K., Karlsson, P., & Neilson, G. 2010. CEO Succession 2000-2009: A decade of convergence and compression. *Strategy & Business,* Summer: 59. https://www.strategy-business.com/article/10208?gko=9345d.

Fegley, S. 2006. *Succession planning: A survey report.* Alexandria, VA: Society for Human Resource Management.

Fiegerman, S. 2017. *Google's search for non-white male employees shows few results.* http://money.cnn.com/2016/07/01/technology/google-diversity-stalls/index.html?iid=EL.

Fujimoto, Y., Hartel, C., & Azmat, F. 2013. Towards a diversity justice management model: Integrating organizational justice and diversity management. *Social Responsibility Journal,* 9(1): 148-166.

Goska, R., & Ackerman, P. 1996. An aptitude-treatment interaction approach to transfer within training. *Journal of Educational Psychology,* 88(2): 249-259.

Greer, C., & Virick, M. 2008. Diverse succession planning: Lessons from the industry leaders. *Human Resource Management,* 47(2): 351-367.

Groves, K. 2017. *Winning strategies: Building a sustainable leadership pipeline through talent management & succession planning.* Bozeman, MT: Second River Healthcare.

Groves, K. 2019. Confronting an inconvenient truth: Developing succession management capabilities for the inevitable loss of executive talent. *Organizational Dynamics,* 48(4): 1-12.

Guthridge, M. & Komm, A. 2017. Why multinationals struggle to manage talent, *The McKinsey Quarterly.* https://www.slideshare.net/KamelionWorld/why-multinationals-struggle-to-manage-talent, first accessed January 1, 2017.

Harvard Business Publishing Corporate Learning. 2018. *The 2018 state of leadership development: Meeting the transformation imperative.* https://www.harvardbusiness.org/insight/the-state-of-leadership-development-meeting-the-transformation-imperative/.

Harrell, E. 2016. Succession planning: What the research says. *Harvard Business Review,* 12: 71-74.

Harris, P. 2020. Start with people, end with solutions. *Talent Development: 2020 Best Practices,* 74: 58-75.

Helfat, C., Harris, D., & Wolfson, P. 2006. The pipeline to the top: Women and men in the top executive ranks of U. S. corporations. *Academy of Management Perspectives,* 20(4).

Hezlett, S., Ronnkvist, A., Holt, K., & Hazucha, J. 1997. *The PROFILOR technical summary.* Minneapolis, MN: Personnel Decisions International.

Hochli, B., Brugger, A., & Messner, C. 2018. How focusing on superordinate goals motivates broad, long-term goal pursuit: A theoretical perspective. *Frontiers in Psychology.* doi: https://doi.org/10.3389/fpsyg.2018.01879.

Hogan, R., Curphy, G., & Hogan, J. 1994. What we know about leadership: Effectiveness and personality. *American Psychologist,* 49: 493-504.

Hudson. 2007. HR insights – high potential programs: Investing in long-term business leadership. *The Hudson Report.* April-June.

Hug, T. 2007. *Didactics of microlearning: Concepts, discourses and examples.* Münster: Waxmann Verlag.

Imel, S. 1998. *Transformative learning in adulthood.* Washington, DC: Office of Educational Research and Improvement. (ERIC Document Reproduction Service No. ED42326). http://www.cete.org/acve/docgen.asp?tbl=digest&ID=53, first accessed April 29, 2004.

Institute for Diversity in Health Management. 2013. *Diversity and disparities: Benchmark study of U.S. hospitals in 2013.* http://www.hpoe.org/Reports-HPOE/Diversity_Disparities_14_Web.pdf, first accessed January 1, 2017.

Kerr, B. 2007. *A challenge to connectivism.* Transcript of Keynote Speech, Online Connectivism Conference. University of Manitoba. http://ltc.umanitoba.ca/wiki/index.php?title=Kerr_Presentation.

Knowles, M. 1973. *The adult learner: A neglected species.* Houston, TX: Gulf Publishing Co.

Kolb, D. A. 1983. *Experiential learning: Experience as the source of learning and development* (Vol. 1). Englewood Cliffs, NJ: Prentice-Hall.

Kolb, D. A., & Fry, R. E. 1974. *Toward an applied theory of experiential learning.* MIT Alfred P. Sloan School of Management.

Kolb, A., & Kolb, D. 2005. Learning styles and learning spaces: Enhancing experiential learning in higher education. *Academy of Management Learning & Education,* 4(2): 193-212.

Kop, R., & Hill, A. 2008. Connectivism: Learning theory of the future or vestige of the past? *International Review of Research in Open and Distributed Learning,* 9(3).

Korn Ferry. 2020. *Leadership development: CEOs' strategic powerhouse.* Korn Ferry Institute. https://www.kornferry.com/content/dam/kornferry/docs/article-migration/Leadership-development-CEOs-strategic-powerhouse.pdf.

Lacey, M., & Groves, K. 2014. Talent management collides with corporate social responsibility: Creation of inadvertent hypocrisy. *Journal of Management Development,* 33(4): 399-409.

Latham, G., Almost, J., Mann, S., & Moore, C. 2005. New developments in performance management. *Organizational Dynamics,* 34(1): 77-87.

Lind, E. A. 2001. Fairness heuristic theory: Justice judgments as pivotal cognitions in organizational relations. In J. Greenberg & R. Cropanzano (Eds.), *Advances in Organizational Justice:* 56-88. Stanford, CA: Stanford University Press.

Lombardo, M., & Eichinger, R. 2000. High potentials as high learners. *Human Resource Management,* 39: 321-330.

Luthans, F., & Avolio, B. J. 2003. Authentic leadership: A positive developmental approach. In K. S. Cameron, J. E. Dutton, & R. E. Quinn (Eds.), *Positive Organizational Scholarship:* 241-261. San Francisco, CA: Barrett-Koehler.

Luthans, F., & Youssef, C. M. 2004. Human, social, and now positive psychological capital management: Investing in people for competitive advantage. *Organizational Dynamics,* 33(2), 143-160.

Malik, A., Singh, P., & Chan, C. 2017. High potential programs and employee outcomes: The roles of organizational trust and employee attributions. *Career Development International,* 22(7): 772-796.

Martorano, M. 2020. Upskilling the next generation of leaders. *Talent Development,* 74(1): 62-63.

McCall, M., Lombardo, M., & Morrison, A. 1988. *The lessons of experience: How successful executives develop on the job.* New York: Free Press.

Merriam, S. B. 2001. Andragogy and self-directed learning: Pillars of adult learning theory. *New Directions for Adult and Continuing Education,* 89: 3-14.

Mezirow, J. 1978. Perspective transformation. *Adult Education,* 28(2): 100-109.

Mezirow, J. 2000. *Learning as transformation.* San Francisco, CA: Jossey-Bass.

Mezirow, J., & Taylor, E. 2009. *Learning as transformation.* San Francisco, CA: Jossey-Bass.

Microsoft. 2016. https://blogs.microsoft.com/blog/2016/11/17/global-diversity-inclusion-update-microsoft-deepening-commitment/.

Nadler, D. 2007. The CEO's second act. *Harvard Business Review,* 85(1): 66-72.

Nebus, J. 2006. Building collegial information networks: A theory of advice network generation. *Academy of Management Review,* 31(3): 615-637.

O'Leonard, K. 2014. *The corporate learning factbook 2014: Benchmarks, trends and analysis of US training market.* Bersin by Deloitte.

O'Leonard, K., & Krider, J. 2014. *Leadership development factbook 2014: Benchmarks and trends in U.S. leadership development,* Bersin by Deloitte. http://www.bersin.com/Practice/Detail.aspx?docid=17478&mode=search&p=Leadership-Development, first accessed June 1, 2015.

Patidar, N., Gupta, S., Azbik, G., & Weech-Maldanado, R. 2016. Succession planning and financial performance: Does competition matter? *Journal of Healthcare Management,* 61(3): 215-227.

Pfeffer, J. 1994. Competitive advantage through people: Unleashing the power of the workforce. *California Management Review,* 36(2): 9-28.

Pinsight 2020. *Repairing the broken rung: Overcoming bias in the leadership pipeline.* https://www.pinsight.com/publication/white-paper/repairing-the-broken-rung-overcoming-bias-in-the-leadership-pipeline/.

Pohland, P., & B. Bova, 2000. Professional development for transformational learning. *International Journal on Leadership in Education,* 3(2): 15-29.

Revelian. 2017. *Improving diversity – How to reduce unconscious bias when hiring.* White paper. http://www.revelian.com/wp-content/uploads/2017/03/revelian_unconscious_bias_whitepaper.pdf, first accessed April 15, 2017.

Senge, P. 2006. *The fifth discipline.* New York: Doubleday Publishers.

Scheier, M. F., Carver, C. S., & Bridges, M. W. 2001. Optimism, pessimism, and psychological well-being. In E. C. Chang (Ed.), *Optimism and pessimism: Implications for theory, research, and practice:* 189-216. Washington, DC: American Psychological Association.

Schein, E. 1993. One dialogue, culture and learning organizations. *Organizational Dynamics,* 22, Summer.

Schepker, D., Nyberg, A., Ulrich, M., & Wright, P. 2018. Planning for future leadership: Procedural rationality, formalized succession processes, and CEO influence in CEO succession planning. *Academy of Management Journal,* 61(2): 523-552.

Siemens, G. 2004. Connectivism: A learning theory for the digital age. *International Journal of Instructional Technology and Distance Learning.* http://www.itdl.org/Journal/Jan_05/article01.htm, first accessed November 12, 2006.

Siemens, G. 2005. *Meaning making, learning, subjectivity.* http://connectivism.ca/blog/2005/12/meaning_making_learning_subjec.html, first accessed November 12, 2006.

Silzer, R., & Church, A. 2009. The pearls and perils of identifying potential. *Industrial and Organizational Psychology,* 2: 377-412.

Silzer, R., & Church, A. 2010. Identifying and assessing high-potential talent: Current organizational practices. In R. Silzer & B. E. Dowell (Eds.), *Strategy-driven talent management: A leadership imperative:* 213-280. San Francisco, CA: Jossey-Bass.

Silzer, R., & Dowell, B. 2010. Strategic talent management matters. In R. Silzer & B. Dowell (Eds.), *Strategy-driven talent management: A leadership imperative:* 3-72. San Francisco, CA: Jossey-Bass.

Spreitzer, G., McCall, M., & Mahoney, J. 1997. Early identification of international executive potential. *Journal of Applied Psychology,* 82: 6-29.

Taylor, E. W. 2007. An update of transformative learning theory: A critical review of the empirical research (1999-2005). *International Journal of Lifelong Education,* 26(2), 173-191.

Taylor, E. W., & Cranton, P. 2012. *The handbook of transformative learning: Theory, research, and practice.* San Francisco, CA: Jossey-Bass.

Tough, A. (1971). *The adult's learning projects: A fresh approach to theory and practice in adult learning.* Toronto: Ontario Institute for Studies in Education.

Training Industry. 2020. *Size of the training industry.* https://trainingindustry.com/wiki/outsourcing/size-of-training-industry/.

Vance, C., Groves, K., Paik, Y., & Kindler, H. 2007. Understanding and measuring linear-nonlinear thinking style for enhanced management education and professional practice. *Academy of Management Learning & Education,* 6(2): 167-185.

Wattles, J. 2017. *Storm at Google over engineer's anti-diversity manifesto.* http://money.cnn.com/2017/08/06/technology/culture/google-diversity/index.html, first accessed August 7, 2017.

Westfall, C. 2019. Leadership development is a $366 billion industry: Here's why most programs don't work. *Forbes,* June 20, 2019. https://www.forbes.com/sites/chriswestfall/2019/06/20/leadership-development-why-most-programs-dont-work/#240ababa61de.

Winegarner, B. 2017. Google's hardest moonshot: De-bugging its race problem. *Fast Company.* https://www.fastcompany.com/3066914/google-and-tech-struggle-to-hack-bias-and-diversity; https://rework.withgoogle.com/subjects/unbiasing.

Witt, D. 2020. *2020 leadership development trends, challenges and opportunities. The Ken Blanchard companies.* https://resources.kenblanchard.com/blanchard-leaderchat/2020-leadership-development-trends-challenges-and-opportunities.

Yost, Y., & Plunkett, M. 2010. Developing leadership talent through experiences. In R. Silzer & B. Dowell (Eds.), *Strategy-driven talent management:* 313-348. San Francisco, CA: Jossey-Bass.

Zhang, Y., & Rajagopalan, N. 2010. CEO succession planning: Finally at the center stage of the boardroom. *Business Horizons,* 1: 455-462.

37

EFFECTIVE COACHING FOR HIGH-POTENTIALS

A Talent Management Approach

Margarita Nyfoudi

Konstantinos Tasoulis

Introduction

Workplace coaching, one of the most well-regarded training and development (T&D) practices, is increasingly utilized for the development of high-potential talent (e.g., Cooke, Saini, & Wang, 2014; Sonnenberg, van Zijderveld, & Brinks, 2014). This increase corresponds to a proliferation of organizational talent management (TM) initiatives aimed at developing broad-based collective capabilities to achieve strategic organizational objectives (Day & O'Connor, 2017). For instance, coaching has been identified as an integral part of 95% of the most learning-driven companies (Daly & Overton, 2017) and a fundamental leader behavior (Lee, Idris, & Tuckey, 2019).

In this chapter, we define coaching as the interaction between a coach and one or more job incumbents, during which the coach uses a specific process to guide the coachee(s) towards the identification and achievement of work-related goals (Nyfoudi, 2016). Coaching differs from other dyadic workplace interventions, such as mentoring and counseling, in that it focuses on specific and work-related goals rather than on generic and/or personal goals and in that the coach may not necessarily be senior to the coachee. Recent studies highlight the importance of coaching on triggering a variety of work-related outcomes at the individual, team, and organizational levels, such as employee well-being, performance, satisfaction, and the development of skills and competencies (see Jones, Woods, & Guillaume, 2016 for a meta-analysis).

Nevertheless, we still have little understanding of the way in which coaching is conducted effectively in the workplace (Athanasopoulou & Dopson, 2018). Coaching talented employees may take a plethora of different forms. For example, coaching could be formal or informal, developmental or remedial, interim or continuous. Blind adoption without adequate deliberation of the types of and the processes that comprise coaching may lead not only to a less effective utilization of business resources for TM purposes but also to a false appreciation of the potential of coaching to contribute to the strategic objectives of the organization. Furthermore, a need exists to pay more attention to the context within which coaching takes place (Ye, Wang, Wendt, Wu, & Euwema, 2016). For instance, given that talented employees represent a specific segment within the organization with particular abilities, attitudes, and characteristics (Ulrich & Smallwood, 2012), customized coaching initiatives are more likely to be successful in achieving TM objectives than are organization-wide coaching initiatives.

The aim of this chapter is to offer more clarity about the practice of coaching high-potential talent by situating coaching within the field of TM and identifying ways in which coaching may be conducted more effectively for high-potential employees. In this respect, we first review selected studies on coaching and identify its constituent parts. Then, we examine the different types of coaching and identify those types that are more conducive to high-potential employees. This section is followed by a discussion of factors influencing the effectiveness of coaching, and we conclude the chapter with suggestions for further research.

471

DOI: 10.4324/9781315474687-37

A Brief Examination of the Coaching Literature

The word coaching originates from the Hungarian word "kocsi", which means wagon (Oxford Dictionaries, 2019), and it was introduced into the management literature by Mace (1950). However, it was not until the work of Fournies (1978) and Evered and Selman (1989) that coaching started gaining momentum in the workplace, thus triggering the ever-increasing practitioners' and academics' interest in the practice. Indeed, ever since these two publications, a plethora of articles have been published on workplace coaching ranging from conceptual papers to systematic reviews and meta-analyses.

Overall, the coaching literature may be divided into three phases (Nyfoudi, 2018). Table 37.1 enlists a selection of studies from each phase. In the first phase, which incorporates publications up until the beginning of the 21st century, scholars were concerned with identifying and defining coaching as a workplace practice. The majority of this body of work was conceptual or adopted a qualitative research design with the aim of explicating the process of coaching, i.e., describing the construct and its constituent parts (e.g., Evered & Selman, 1989; Olivero, Bane, & Kopelman, 1997; Tobias, 1996).

During this phase, several well-known coaching models were outlined (e.g., Allebaugh, 1983; Whitmore, 1992). Based on this early work, contemporary scholars seem to concur that the process of coaching consists of three main processes: goal setting, feedback/evaluation, and plan implementation (Ellinger, 2013; Latham, Ford, & Tzabbar, 2012). Goal setting relates to the objectives set by the coachee with the help of the coach; feedback/evaluation refers to the continuous and constructive assessment of the coachee's progress carried out by the coach; and finally, plan implementation pertains to the process of the coachee actuating what has been discussed and agreed upon during the coaching conversations.

The second phase of the coaching literature comprises work mainly published within the first decade of the 21st century. This phase includes two literature streams (Nyfoudi, 2018). The first stream examined the main principles of coaching that included the importance of the chemistry and power dynamics between the coach and coachee, the readiness of the coachee for development, and the coach's need to have good listening skills and respect for ethics (e.g., De Haan & Burger, 2005, Hooijberg & Lane, 2009; Jarvis, Lane, & Fillery-Travis, 2006; Reissner & Toit, 2011; Shannahan, Bush, & Shannahan, 2013; Shaw & Linnecar, 2007).

The second stream explored the different types of workplace coaching, including scale development studies that aimed to construct measures to assess coaching quantitatively and taxonomy studies that endeavored to categorize the different types of coaching. In doing so, scholars differentiated coaching in terms of the status of the coach, the purpose of coaching, and the methodological approach adopted during coaching (Fillery-Travis & Lane, 2006; Grant & Zackon, 2004; Segers et al., 2011). These studies offered clarifications and highlighted the possible added value of coaching. However, there is still ambiguity in terms of the way in which the three main processes of coaching (goal setting, feedback/evaluation, and plan implementation) are combined and exhibited in the workplace in relation to specific types of coaching, such as coaching high-potential talent. This ambiguity hinders our further understanding of the construct, as well as its effectiveness in the workplace.

The last phase entails a wealth of research that is mainly quantitative in nature and adopts multisource, multilevel, and/or longitudinal research designs (Nyfoudi, 2018). This body of work has been published in high impact journals, such as *The Leadership Quarterly, Academy of Management Learning and Education, Human Resource Management, Journal of Work and Organizational Psychology,* and *Personnel Psychology* (e.g., Dahling et al., 2016; de Haan, Bertie, Day, & Sills, 2010; Dello Russo, Miraglia, & Borgogni, 2017; Jones, et al., 2016; Ladegar & Gjerder, 2014; Latham et al., 2012; Segers et al., 2011; Segers & Inceoglu, 2012). The majority of these studies identify the antecedents and consequences of the construct and acknowledge that there is a different nomological network for different types of coaching. Although all types of coaching comprise the three main processes (goal setting, feedback/evaluation, and plan implementation), each type is related to a diverse number of antecedents and consequences. Hence, prior to any adoption of coaching for T&D purposes, it is important to examine high-potential talent and identify the type of coaching that is more likely to trigger positive T&D outcomes.

Table 37.1 Representative literature on the three phases of coaching

Authors	Main points / Conclusions
1st Phase	
Evered & Selman (1989)	• Coaching as a conversation and a committed partnership.
	• Coaching represents a paradigm shift enabling a new management culture based on the intention to empower others, in contrast to the old culture based on the intention to control.
	• Coaching being at the "heart" of management.
Olivero, Bane, & Kopelman (1997)	• Executive coaching impacts on training transferability.
	• Training coupled with coaching yielded productivity increases almost four times higher than those of training alone.
	• Goal setting and public presentation as the most critical aspects of the coaching process.
Allebaugh (1983)	• Coaching as a better alternative to performance appraisal.
	• Coaching as a positive and collaborative process.
	• FARE model (coachee's functions, authority, responsibilities, and expectations).
	• Two-way feedback.
2nd Phase	
Hooijberg & Lane (2009)	• Coaches' skills, coachee responsibility, and coach-coachee chemistry as antecedents of effective coaching sessions.
	• Coaches who interpret results from multisource feedback, inspire action, and conduct themselves professionally, enable coachee commitment and stronger emphasis on action plans.
Shannahan, Bush, & Shannahan (2013)	• Salespeople coachability, salesperson trait competitiveness, and sales manager leadership style.
	• Sales performance is highest when all three factors are in place.
	• Coachability mediates the relationship between transformational leadership and sales performance.
Segers, Vloeberghs, Henderickx, & Inceoglu, (2011)	• The Coaching Cube typology: (a) coaching agenda (e.g., skills coaching, performance coaching); (b) type of coach (e.g., internal/external coaches, self-coaching); (c) coaching methodology (e.g., emotionality or rationality).
3rd Phase	
Dahling, Taylor, Chau, & Dwight (2016)	• The managers' coaching skills are related to team-level role clarity and coachees' sales goal attainment.
Dello Russo, Miraglia, & Borgogni (2017)	• Findings indicate that coaching managers are perceived as being less manipulative in their performance appraisal ratings, by older employees in particular.
Jones, Woods, & Guillaume (2016)	• Coaching is positively related to overall organizational outcomes as well as specific outcome criteria (e.g., individual results, skills, and affective criteria).
	• Coaching is more effective when internal rather than external coaches are used.
Ladegard & Gjerde (2014)	• Coaching is related to leader role efficacy and leaders' trust in employees.
	• Such changes were positively affected by the coach's extent of facilitative behavior.
	• Increased trust in subordinates was in turn related to reduced turnover intentions.
Latham, Ford, & Tzabbar (2012)	• Feedback obtained by third parties (e.g., mystery shoppers) and used for employee coaching improves individual and organizational outcomes.
Segers & Inceoglu (2012)	• Coaching was more likely to be present in organizations following a prospector business strategy and was least present in those adopting a defender strategy.
	• In prospector organizations, coaching was integrated with other management practices in configurations (e.g., continuous training and succession planning).

Sources: Allebaugh, 1983; Dahling et al., 20016; Dello Russo et al., 2017; Evered & Selman, 1989; Jones et al., 2016; Hooijberg & Lane, 2009; Ladegard & Gjerde, 2014; Latham et al., 2012; Olivero et al., 1997; Segers et al., 2011; Segers & Inceoglu, 2012; Shannahan et al., 2013.

High-Potential Talent and the Need for Coaching

Among the various definitions of talent (Thunissen, Boselie, & Fruytier, 2013), we adopt the perspective that organizational talent encompasses employees who have high potential and who are high-performers (Gallardo-Gallardo, Dries, & Gonzalez-Cruz, 2013). High-potential employees, who represent the focus of this chapter, are typically seen as those individuals who possess the qualities (e.g., character, motivation, skills) to perform successfully in wider and/or alternating roles within the organization (Silzer & Church, 2009). High-performing employees are a small group of employees who are exceptional in terms of skills and abilities or output (Silzer & Dowell, 2010). These employees have been extensively examined within the executive development literature and, in particular, within executive coaching literature (see Athanasopoulou & Dopson, 2018 for a review).

For example, the extant literature has investigated the way in which executive coaching contributes to leader outcomes (Jones et al., 2016) and organizational learning (Swart & Harcup, 2013), the influence of gender on the relationship between the executive coach and the coachee (Gray & Goregaokar, 2010), and the characteristics that play an important role in the development of high-performing employees, such as self-regulation (Yeow & Martin, 2013) and self-acceptance (Athanasopoulou, Moss-Cowan, Smets, & Morris, 2018). However, there is a lack of studies that explore coaching for high-potential employees.

High-potential employees are part of a TM approach that emphasizes positioning, i.e., the identification of strategic positions in the organization and allocation of talented individuals to these positions (e.g., Al Ariss et al., 2014; Collings & Mellahi, 2009; McDonnell, Collings, Mellahi, & Schuler, 2017). This approach turns the attention away from talent per se and towards positions that are strategic for the sustainability and enhancement of the competitive advantage of the organization, as well as the development of talent to fill these positions.

In other words, high-potentials form a pool of employees who are developed specifically for the strategic needs of the organization and to occupy strategic organizational positions. This type of employee usually represents 10–15% of the workforce of an organization (Ulrich & Smallwood, 2012) and experiences a dedicated human resources (HR) architecture for TM purposes (Collings & Mellahi, 2009). For example, as soon as an employee is identified as being high potential, they tend to undertake specialized assignments and to undergo exclusive training and development initiatives (Meyers & van Woerkom, 2014).

Coaching, as a dialogic and personalized intervention, fits well with the selective nature of TM programs designed exclusively for high-potential and high-performing employees. In fact, Anderson, Frankovelgia, and Hernez-Broome (2009) found that among all senior leaders who participated in their study, those who received coaching were mostly high-potential employees. While attending to the needs of each participant is less of a priority in other developmental practices, such as training workshops, the practice of coaching not only necessitates the active engagement of the coachee but also adapts to the coachee's profile.

Furthermore, coaching high-potential employees seems to correspond to the function for which the verb *coach* was initially used, i.e., to "convey a valued person from where one was to where one wants to be" (Whitherspoon & White, 1996: 124). The coach sets specific goals for development together with the high-potential coachee and provides feedback to facilitate the latter's transition from the talent pool to a strategic position. In this respect, coaching contributes to the effective deployment of talent within the organization; hence, it is also conducive to talent positioning.

Overall, coaching high-potential employees is part of a TM approach (Collings & Mellahi, 2009), which has been devised for the development and deployment of the talent pool of the organization. It is a specialized resource that is offered to a restricted number of job incumbents, who differ from the rest of the employees in that they possess qualities that allow them to successfully operate in strategic organizational positions. Coaching high-potential employees is formed by the three main processes of coaching: goal setting, feedback/evaluation, and plan implementation, which vary in purpose, formality, and frequency, respectively. However, not all variations are conducive to talent development and positioning. The following section examines in detail the way in which these three processes may be configured to effectively coach high-potential employees.

Coaching Conducive to Talent Development and Positioning

The adoption of coaching for talent development and positioning warrants substantial deliberation over the way in which the processes of goal setting, feedback and plan implementation take place. The aim of this part of the chapter is to examine each of these processes in relation to high-potential talent. We do so by adopting Nyfoudi's (2018) framework, which consists of a spherical three-dimensional axis to represent each process within coaching. These processes include *goal setting* that takes place during coaching, the type of *feedback* the coachee receives, and the frequency in which the coachee *implements* the agreed plan.

In terms of goal setting, studies have identified two different types of coaching: corrective and developmental (Morgeson, 2005; Wageman, 2001). Corrective coaching focuses on correcting past defective behavior or performance. In contrast, developmental coaching focuses less on weaknesses and underperformance and more on helping the coachee enhance already existing competencies and behavior. Considering that high-potential talent is likely to already possess the required skills, knowledge, and abilities (Collings & Mellahi, 2009), goal setting during coaching needs to be rather developmental.

In other words, coaching high-potential employees needs to aim at future possibilities and how to further enhance already existing competencies. Moreover, given the importance in TM initiatives of developing capacity to fill in strategic positions within the organization (Collings & Mellahi, 2009), coaching high-potential employees entails goal setting that focuses more on enabling the talent to be successfully appointed within the organization than on developing skills and competencies that are not relevant or applicable to the organization.

In regard to the formality of feedback, the coach may choose to follow a formal or an informal type of approach. Formal coaching entails setting up specific coaching meetings to evaluate progress and help the coachee interpret the feedback received. Informal coaching refers to a more naturally occurring approach, whereby the coach offers their constructive input to the coachee while on the job and without the need for a planned session. Executive coaching is when feedback is formally offered during prearranged coaching sessions run by a coach who is often external to the organization (Baron & Morin, 2010). In contract, coaching high-potential employees is when feedback differs depending on the stage of talent positioning. In particular, while a high-potential employee is in the talent pool, feedback is usually delivered through formal coaching sessions.

Once individual talent has been placed into a strategic position, feedback offered through coaching takes place on a more informal basis; for example, by the manager of the high-potential employee on the job or during a social event. In this respect, informing individuals that they belong to the talent pool of the organization has been found to be more beneficial in terms of their commitment to higher performance and strategic objectives, as well as to decrease the likelihood of turnover (Bjorkman et al., 2013).

Plan implementation (i.e., the way in which the coachee actualizes what is discussed during coaching) may take place either for a limited amount of time or continuously. In the first case, coaching would focus on implementing a set plan (i.e., the development of a competency or a particular attitude); in the second case, the focus would continuously shift to a different or revised plan. In both cases, the coachee has a key role in taking responsibility for plan implementation (DeRue, Barnes, & Morgeson, 2010); hence, their attitude towards coaching is rather significant in the success of the intervention. As with feedback, plan implementation in relation to coaching for high-potential employees depends on the stage of positioning. When a high-potential employee is identified and forms part of the talent pool of the organization, the plan implementation is interim and terminates with the allocation of the high-potential employee to a strategic position. Thereupon, if coaching continues, the implementation becomes an ongoing process that adjusts to the priorities of the strategic position to which the high-potential employee has been deployed.

Overall, our discussion has established that coaching is conducive to talent development and positioning when it has a developmental focus and is either interim and formal or continuous and informal. Beyond the focus, degree of formality, and frequency of coaching for high-potential employees, there are other factors that may influence the effectiveness of talent development coaching. The following section examines these factors in more detail.

Factors Influencing Coaching for Talent Development

In this section, we draw on the extant literature to examine factors that may enable or hinder the effective implementation of coaching. We differentiate between factors related to the coach, the coachee, their relationship, and the organization and summarize them in Table 37.2.

The Coach

The role of the coach is pivotal in developing and retaining talent. A growing number of studies have identified several skills, knowledge, attitudes, and other attributes (SKAOs) required by effective coaches (e.g., Jones et al., 2016; Kombakaran, Yang, Baker, & Fernandes, 2008; Stern, 2008). These SKAOs could be either generic to any type of coach or specific to coaching for talent development. An effective coach needs to be business savvy to be able to understand the unique context and objectives of the organization and thus gain credibility with coachees (Stern, 2008). In addition, competent coaches tend to be both self-aware and self-restrained, as well as handle the coaching relationship with confidentiality and discretion (Kombakaran, et al., 2008).

Related to this point, a debate exists regarding the extent to which coaches need a background in psychology. While some researchers argue that coaches need to be fully qualified psychologists to avoid unintentionally harming their coachees (Berglas, 2002), others recommend that coachees possess

Table 37.2 Factors influencing coaching for talent development

Coach Attributes	Coachee Attributes	Nature of Coach-Coachee Relationship	Organizational-level Factors
Personal skills and characteristics:	Motivation to develop	Quality of relationship/ chemistry	Organizational culture
Business savvy	Attitude towards feedback		Strategic integration
Self-awareness		Trust	
Integrity	Attitude towards coaching	Confidentiality, provision of a safe environment	Role modeling
Commitment to helping others			Supportive competency frameworks
Compassion, sensitivity approachability	Availability/Time		
Rapport-building communication	Own initiative		Aligned HR practices
Diagnostic skills			
Multicultural skills			Underlying HR philosophy
Knowledge of:			
Coaching models, activities and tools			
Psychology			
Type of coach (internal/external)			

Sources: Alvey & Barcley, 2007; Anderson et al., 2009; Berglas, 2002; Blucket, 2005; Bono et al., 2009; Clutterback & Megginson, 205; Gavett, 2013; Gregory et al., 2008; Hooijberg & Lane, 2009; Hutchinson & Purcell, 2010; Ianiro et al., 2012; Ianiro et al., 2015; Jones & Spooner, 2006; Jones et al., 2016; Kombakaran et al., 2008; Larcker et al., 2013; Lindbom, 2007; Natale & Diamante, 2005; Stern, 2008.

"psychological mindedness" (Blucket, 2005). The latter refers to the capacity of the coach to reflect on themselves, their coachees, and their relationship with each other, as well as to have a thorough insight of diverse coaching activities and tools (Stern, 2008).

Furthermore, since coaching is a dyadic intervention necessitating trust and open communication, effective coaches possess strong interpersonal skills, such as rapport-building, approachability, communication, and diagnostic skills (e.g., detecting hidden agendas), as well as compassion and sensitivity (Bono, Purvanova, Towler, & Peterson, 2009). Assigned with the responsibility of facilitating learning, coaches need to have a passion for developing others, to focus on the needs of the coachees, and to prioritize the latter's professional development (Bono et al., 2009).

Moreover, given the increasing importance of global talent management (Tarique & Schuler, 2010), it is important that coaching is contextualized and that the coach prioritizes those practices that are most relevant to the local culture. A qualitative, cross-cultural study in Asia and Europe revealed that a focus on performance objectives and results was seen as a best practice for coaching in Asia, while a focus on the coach's own personal development was seen as a key theme in Europe. However, some best practices were common in both continents, such as the use of instruments and assessments, as well as cultural awareness (Gentry, Manning, Wolf, & Hernez-Broone, 2013).

Beyond the SKAOs required by coaches, the appointment of an internal or external coach is also relevant to coaching effectiveness. The meta-analytic study of Jones et al. (2016) yielded that the type of coach indeed moderates the effectiveness of coaching in the workplace. In this study, coaching was found to be more effective when it was conducted by internal rather than external coaches (the study excluded direct managers and supervisors). The researchers attributed the higher success rate of internal coaches to their familiarity with the organization, which could enable them to coach the employees more effectively in comparison to external coaches. This finding is aligned with CIPD's (2015) survey findings, indicating that internal coaching is expected to grow at a much higher rate compared to that of external coaching (62% versus 1%, respectively).

The Coachee

The coachee's motivation to learn and develop is critical for the effectiveness of coaching for *talent development*. Coaching for talent development purposes, rather than being a remedial intervention that is imposed on an individual, relies on the assumption that the talented coachee embraces personal development practices and is eager to learn. In this respect, a survey conducted on over 200 CEOs, board directors, and senior executives by Stanford University and the Miles Group found that respondents, almost in their entirety, enjoyed coaching and that 78% of the CEOs claimed that it was their own idea, rather than the board's, to receive coaching (Larcker et al., 2013).

Larcker et al. (2013) supports the idea that willingness to develop oneself, indicated by self-initiated coaching, is an important coachee attribute, which helps ensure that a positive experience is obtained from the practice. If the coachee is pressured to receive coaching, then resistance is a problem that the coach is likely to face (Natale & Diamante, 2005). In addition to a talent's motivation to learn and develop, readiness to accept feedback and act upon it is another quality that influences coaching effectiveness, since coachees need to reflect and learn from their mistakes (Gregory, Levy, & Jeffers, 2008)

Attitudes towards coaching (as opposed to other development practices) are also likely to influence the effectiveness of coaching, as well as the actual willingness to be coached (Gavett, 2013). Larcker et al. (2013) revealed that only a third of the CEOs and approximately half of senior executives actually received coaching. This sizeable proportion of respondents who are not being coached could be attributed to lack of time, little genuine interest in being coached, or the stigma attached to coaching as a corrective intervention for those who "need improvement" (Gavett, 2013). Receiving coaching and "needing support" can be interpreted as a sign of weakness, especially when there is a need to embrace "masculine" norms and traits such as self-reliance (Levant & Kopecky, 1995). This stigma might still dissuade senior executives from being coached.

The Coach-Coachee Relationship

Scholars accentuate the importance of the coach-coachee relationship as a major driver of coaching effectiveness (Alvey & Barclay, 2007; Hooijberg & Lane, 2009; Ianiro, Lehmann-Willenbrock, & Kauffeld, 2015). The quality of this relationship is largely determined by the degree of trust between the two parties (Hodgetts, 2002), which in turn depends mostly on the degree of confidentiality (Alvey & Barclay, 2007). To maintain confidentiality and build a trustworthy relationship, a coach needs to ensure that the talent feels safe to show vulnerability and share sensitive information (Lindbom, 2007). Managing confidentiality is a pressing concern when the coaches are internal members of the organization (Lindbom, 2007), since they may be familiar with people or events discussed in coaching and use information for personal gain.

In addition, to improve coaching chemistry, talent managers who employ coaching for talent development need to engage in skillful and considerate matching of the parties (Hooijberg & Lane, 2009) to ensure that they are compatible. Compatibility goes beyond a consideration of matching criteria, such as gender and experience, and refers to the fit of personality traits and styles (Ianiro, Schermuly, & Kauffeld, 2012). In a study of 33 coach-coachee dyads, the degree of similarity between the coach's and the coachee's traits of dominance and affiliation was positively related to the quality of the relationship as well as goal attainment. In other words, interpersonal similarity seems beneficial for coaching, suggesting that coachees need a "companion" who is similar to them, rather than a "rescuer" (2012: 13).

Another study examining the dynamics of the interpersonal behaviors of 30 coach-coachee dyads found that the coaches' dominant and friendly approach triggered coachees to demonstrate similar dominance in the coaching process. As a result of coachees' higher dominance in the process, overall goals were more likely to be attained (Ianiro et al., 2015). While such studies on the interpersonal dynamics between the coach and the coachee are scarce, there is little doubt that the matching process and coach-coachee compatibility is an important determinant of the coaching relationship and its effectiveness.

The Organization

At the organizational level, an important factor that facilitates effective coaching for talent development is an organizational culture in which leaders, managers, and employees employ a coaching approach in their interactions with others to create shared value for all stakeholders (Clutterbuck & Megginson, 2005). Such a culture necessitates leadership dedication and coaching to become a strategic priority for the organization (Lindbom, 2007). Whether the organization adopts such a culture is likely to relate to the underlying HR philosophy of the key organizational decision-makers (board, senior and middle management, and HR) (Paauwe, 2004), including the perception of talent as a fixed or evolving capacity (Meyers et al., 2013).

According to a survey of 347 business leaders by the Center for Creative Leadership (Anderson et al., 2009), a coaching culture is linked to several positive organizational outcomes, such as higher utilization and sharing of knowledge, transparent and participative decision-making, and prioritization of development. However, while 29% of the survey respondents indicated that it was extremely important to make coaching part of the culture, only 6% believed that their organization was very effective in doing so (Anderson et al., 2009). The difficulty of imbuing an organization with the features of a coaching culture is in line with arguments that such a culture may not be a priority for firms, since it requires considerable investment of time and effort, while the benefits are difficult to measure (Clutterbuck & Megginson, 2005).

If such a culture is deemed appropriate, it needs to be aligned with the firm's business strategy, linked to its organizational development plan, and clearly embedded in practices such as leadership and management development, performance management, and rewards. More specifically, developing a coaching culture involves the following five-step approach: (a) seeding the organization with leaders who are role models in terms of their coaching SKAOs and behaviors; (b) developing a competency framework that encompasses coaching goals, tactics, and measures; (c) coaching senior leadership teams in creating cultural change; (d) recognizing and rewarding coaching behaviors; and (e) integrating coaching with other HR processes, including selection, training and succession (Anderson et al., 2009).

It is thus important to align the coaching culture to various practices within the organization, otherwise the organization might jeopardize coaching effectiveness. Indeed, the importance of firm-level alignment to coaching is illustrated in the study of Hutchinson and Purcell (2010), who found that many healthcare professionals were unsatisfied with coaching, as it was offered within a context of low recognition by senior management, resource constraints (e.g., heavy workload), and lack of role clarity (i.e., ambiguity between the role of a clinician and a manager).

Future Research

The field of coaching talent seems ripe for more theoretical frameworks and empirical evidence. Research endeavors can be informed by the main theories used in the fields of TM and coaching, such as the resource-based view, social exchange, institutional and signaling theory (McDonnell et al., 2017), and adult learning theories and positive psychology (Cox, 2015). A comprehensive review of 111 empirical studies on coaching denoted convergence among the factors that contribute to coaching effectiveness, yet research gaps remain in terms of determining the primary beneficiaries of coaching, the factors that contribute to coach credibility, and the influence of the organizational and social context (Blackman, Moscardo, & Gray, 2016). Evidently, future research may be enriched by a cross-utilization of these two different literature streams.

In terms of research topics, there is a need to evaluate how different types of coaching are conducive to talent development. Scholars can also examine the idiosyncrasies of coaching different types of talent (e.g., high-potential and high-performing employees), as well as talent at different hierarchical levels. Given that only a few scientific studies have incorporated a stakeholders' perspective (Thunissen et al., 2013), researchers may examine outcomes related to multiple stakeholders and consider the views of coaches as well as talented coaches. It is likely that each stakeholder is related to a different set of outcomes, since their goals, role, and experience with coaching are likely to differ.

Further research is also needed in terms of understanding the meaning, processes, and effectiveness of coaching talent in a global, multicultural context. Studies with this purpose may draw from the literature on global talent management (e.g., Farndale, Pai, Sparrow, & Scullion. 2014; Tarique & Schuler, 2010), and the body of work on the psychology of coaching that examines coaching effectiveness in different economic, cultural, and regulatory contexts (Odendaal & le Roux, 2016).

Last but not least, research efforts may concentrate on establishing the return on investment in terms of employing coaching, not only in general for talent development purposes but also in particular for talent positioning. For example, future studies may adopt an experimental research design to compare the effectiveness of coaching-facilitated talent positioning with other talent allocation programs, such as mentoring or placements.

Conclusion

Talent development is a powerful lever, creating value for individuals and organizations, not least because it is less challenging to inculcate organizational values into employees who are growing within the organization while also institutionalizing their talent (Brady, Bolchover, & Sturgess, 2008). In this chapter, we examined coaching as an effective talent development practice that may successfully facilitate the deployment of talent to strategic organizational positions. In doing so, we defined coaching and briefly examined the academic literature on the practice.

We identified two coaching configurations that are more conducive to talent development depending on the phase of talent positioning. In the first phase, prior to deployment, coaching is usually developmental, formal, and for an interim period of time. In the second phase, following deployment, coaching takes the form of a developmental, informal, and continuous workplace practice. We also examined several coach-, coachee-, and organizational-related factors that may influence the effectiveness of the practice and identified avenues for future research. All in all, we hope that this chapter not only offers clarification in terms of the effective implementation of coaching as talent development practice but also promotes further research interest on the topic.

References

Al Ariss, A., Cascio, W. F., & Paauwe, J. 2014. Talent management: Current theories and future research directions. *Journal of World Business,* 49: 173–179.

Allenbaugh, G. E. 1983. Coaching: A management tool for a more effective work performance. *Management Review,* 72(5): 21–26.

Alvey, S., & Barclay, K. 2007. The characteristics of dyadic trust in executive coaching. *Journal of Leadership Studies,* 1: 18–27

Anderson, M. C., Frankovelgia, C., & Hernez-Broome, G. 2009. Creating coaching cultures: What business leaders expect and strategies to get there. *Center for Creative Leadership.* https://www.ccl.org/wp-content/uploads/2016/07/CreatingCoachingCultures.pdf

Athanasopoulou, A., & Dopson, S. (2018). A systematic review of executive coaching outcomes: Is it the journey or the destination that matters the most? *The Leadership Quarterly,* 29(1): 70–88.

Athanasopoulou, A., Moss-Cowan, A., Smets, M., & Morris, T. (2018). Claiming the corner office: Female CEO careers and implications for leadership development. *Human Resource Management,* 57: 617–639.

Baron, L., & Morin, L. 2010. The impact of executive coaching on self-efficacy related to management soft-skills. *Leadership & Organization Development Journal,* 31: 18–38.

Bjorkman, I., Ehrnrooth, M., Makela, K., Smale, A. & Sumelius, J. 2013. Talent or not? Employee reactions to talent identification. *Human Resource Management,* 52: 195–214.

Blackman, A., Moscardo, G., & Gray, D.E. 2016. Challenges for the theory and practice of business coaching. A systematic review of empirical evidence. *Human Resource Development Review,* 15(4): 459–486.

Bono, J. E., Purvanova, R. K., Towler, A. J., & Peterson, D. B. 2009. A survey of executive coaching practices. *Personnel Psychology,* 62: 361–404

Brady, C., Bolchover, D., & Sturgess, B. 2008. Managing in the talent economy: The football model for business. *California Management Review,* 50(4): 54–73.

CIPD. 2015. *Learning & Development 2015.* London: CIPD. https://www.cipd.co.uk/knowledge/strategy/development/surveys

Clutterbuck, D., & Megginson, D. 2005. *Making coaching work: Creating a coaching culture.* London, CIPD.

Collings, D. G., & Mellahi, K. 2009. Strategic talent management: A review and research agenda. *Human Resource Management Review,* 19: 304–313.

Cooke, F. L., Saini, D. S., & Wang, J. 2014. Talent management in China and India: A comparison of management perceptions and human resource practices. *Journal of World Business,* 49: 225–235.

Cox, E. 2015. Coaching and adult learning: Theory and practice. *New Directions for Adult and Continuing Education,* 148: 27–38.

Dahling, J. J., Taylor, S. R., Chau, S. L., & Dwight, S. A. 2016. Does coaching matter? A multilevel model linking managerial coaching skill and frequency to sales goal attainment. *Personnel Psychology,* 69: 863–894.

Daly, J. & Overton, L. 2017. *Driving the new learning organization: How to unlock the potential of L&D.* London: Towards Maturity. https://www.cipd.co.uk/Images/driving-the-new-learning-organisation_2017-how-to-unlock-the-potential-of-Land-d_tcm18-21557.pdf

Day, D. V., & O'Connor, P. M. G. 2017. Talent development: Building organisational capability. In D. G. Collings, K. Mellahi, & W. F. Cascio (Eds.), *The Oxford handbook of talent management.* Oxford, UK: Oxford University Press.

De Haan, E., Bertie, C., Day, A., & Sills, C. 2010. Clients' critical moments of coaching: Toward a "client model" of executive coaching. *Academy of Management Learning & Education,* 9: 607–621.

De Haan, E., & Burger, Y. 2013. Coaching methodologies. *Coaching with Colleagues* (2nd ed.). Basingstoke: Palgrave Macmillan.

Dello Russo, S., Miraglia, M., & Borgogni, L. 2017. Reducing organizational politics in performance appraisal: The role of coaching leaders for age-diverse employees. *Human Resource Management,* 56: 769–783.

DeRue, D. S., Barnes, C. M., & Morgeson, F. P. 2010. Understanding the motivational contingencies of team leadership. *Small Group Research,* 41: 621–651.

Ellinger, A. D. 2013. Supportive supervisors and managerial coaching: Exploring their intersections. *Journal of Occupational and Organizational Psychology,* 86: 310–316.

Evered, R. D., & Selman, J. C. 1989. Coaching and the art of management. *Organizational Dynamics,* 18(2): 16–32.

Farndale, E., Pai, A., Sparrow, P., & Scullion, H. 2014. Balancing individual and organizational needs in global talent management: A mutual-benefits perspective. *Journal of World Business,* 49(2): 204–214.

Fillery-Travis, A., & Lane, D. (2006). Does coaching work or are we asking the wrong question? *International Coaching Psychology Review,* 1: 24–36.

Fournies, F. F. 1978. *Coaching for improved work performance.* Bridgewater, NJ: Van Nostrand Reinhold Co.

Gallardo-Gallardo, E., Dries, N., & Gonzalez-Cruz, T. F. 2013. What is the meaning of talent in the world of work? *Human Resource Management Review,* 23: 290–300.

Gavett, G. 2013. Research: What CEOs really want from coaching. *Harvard Business Review.* https://hbr.org/2013/08/research-ceos-and-the-coaching

Gentry, W. A., Manning, L., Wolf, A. K., Hernez-Broome, G., & Allen, L. W. 2013. What coaches believe are best practices for coaching: A qualitative study of interviews from coaches residing in Asia and Europe. *Journal of Leadership Studies,* 7: 18–31.

Grant, A. M., & Zackon, R. 2004. Executive, workplace and life coaching: Findings from a largescale survey of international coach federation members. *International Journal of Evidence-Based Coaching and Mentoring,* 2(2): 1–15.

Gray, D. E., & Goregaokar, H. 2010. Choosing an executive coach: The influence of gender on the coach-coachee matching process. *Management Learning,* 41: 525–544.

Gregory, J. B., Levy, P. E., & Jeffers, M. 2008. Development of a model of the feedback process within executive coaching. *Consulting Psychology Journal: Practice and Research,* 60(1): 42–56.

Hooijberg, R., & Lane, N. 2009. Using multisource feedback coaching effectively in executive education. *Academy of Management Learning & Education,* 8: 483–493.

Hutchinson, S., & Purcell, J. 2010. Managing ward managers for roles in HRM in the NHS: overworked and under-resourced. *Human Resource Management Journal,* 20(4): 357–374.

Ianiro, P. M, Lehmann-Willenbrock, N., & Kauffeld, S. 2015. Coaches and clients in action: A sequential analysis of interpersonal coach and client behavior. *Journal of Business Psychology,* 30: 435–456.

Ianiro, P. M., Schermuly, C. C., & Kauffeld, S. 2012. Why interpersonal dominance and affiliation matter: An interaction analysis of the coach-client relationship. *Coaching: An International Journal of Theory, Research and Practice,* 6: 1, 25–46.

Jarvis, J., Lane, D., & Fillery-Travis, A. 2006. *The case for coaching: Making evidence-based decisions.* London: CIPD.

Jones, R. J., Woods, S. A., & Guillaume, Y. R. F. 2016. The effectiveness of workplace coaching: A meta-analysis of learning and performance outcomes from coaching. *Journal of Occupational and Organizational Psychology,* 89: 249–277.

Kombakaran, F. A., Yang, J. A., Baker, M. N., & Fernandes, P. B. 2008. Executive coaching: It works! *Consulting Psychology Journal: Practice and Research,* 60: 78–90.

Ladegard, G., & Gjerde, S. 2014. Leadership coaching, leader role-efficacy, and trust in subordinates: A mixed methods study assessing leadership coaching as a leadership development tool. *The Leadership Quarterly,* 25: 631–646.

Larcker, D. F., Miles, S., Tayan, B., & Gutman, M. E. 2013. *Executive coaching survey.* Stanford, CA: Miles Group and Stanford University. https://www.gsb.stanford.edu/sites/gsb/files/publication-pdf/cgri-survey-2013-executive-coaching.pdf

Latham, G. P., Ford, R. C., & Tzabbar, D. 2012. Enhancing employee and organizational performance through coaching based on mystery shopper feedback: A quasi-experimental study. *Human Resource Management,* 51: 213–229.

Lee, M. C. C., Idris, M. A., & Tuckey, M. 2019. Supervisory coaching and performance feedback as mediators of the relationships between leadership styles, work engagement, and turnover intention. *Human Resource Development International,* 22: 257–282.

Levant, R. F., & Kopecky, G. 1995. *Masculinity reconstructed: Changing the rules of manhood – at work, in relationships, and family life.* New York: Dutton.

Lindbom, D. 2007. A culture of coaching: The challenge of managing performance for long-term results. *Organization Development Journal,* 25(1): 101–106.

McDonnell, A., Collings, D. G., Mellahi, K., & Schuler, R. 2017. Talent management: A systematic review and future prospects. *European Journal of International Management,* 11: 86–128.

C., & van Woerkom, M. (2014). The influence of underlying philosophies on talent management: Theory, implications for practice, and research agenda. *Journal of World Business,* 49(2): 192–203.

Meyers, M. C., van Woerkom, M., & Dries, N. 2013. Talent - Innate or acquired? Theoretical considerations and their implications for talent management. *Human Resource Management Review,* 23: 305–321.

Morgeson, F. P. 2005. The external leadership of self-managing teams: Intervening in the context of novel and disruptive events. *Journal of Applied Psychology,* 90: 497–508.

Natale, S. M., & Diamante, T. (2005). The five stages of executive coaching: Better process makes better practice. *Journal of Business Ethics,* 59(4): 361–74.

Nyfoudi, M. 2016. Coaching. In A. Wilkinson, & S. Johnstone (Eds.), *Encyclopedia of human resource management.* London: Edward Elgar Publishing.

Nyfoudi, M. 2018. *Workplace coaching: Types and processes.* Working Paper. Birmingham, UK: University of Birmingham.

Odendaal A., & Le Roux, A. R. 2016. Contextualising coaching psychology within multi-cultural contexts. In L. van Zyl, M. Stander, & A. Odendaal (Eds.), *Coaching psychology: Meta-theoretical perspectives and applications in multicultural contexts.* Cham: Springer.

Olivero, G., Bane, K. D., & Kopelman, R. E. 1997. Executive coaching as a transfer of training tool: Effects on productivity in a public agency. *Public Personnel Management,* 26: 461–469.

Oxford Dictionaries. 2019. Oxford University Press. http://www.oxforddictionaries.com

Reissner, S. C., & Toit, A. Du. 2011. Power and the tale: coaching as storyselling. *Journal of Management Development,* 30: 247–259.

Segers, J., & Inceoglu, I. 2012. Exploring supportive and developmental career management through business strategies and coaching. *Human Resource Management,* 51: 99–120.

Segers, J., Vloeberghs, D., Henderickx, E., & Inceoglu, I. 2011. Structuring and understanding the coaching Industry: The coaching cube. *Academy of Management Learning & Education,* 10: 204–221.

Shannahan, K. J., Bush, A., & Shannahan, R. 2013. Are your salespeople coachable? How salesperson coachability, trait competitiveness, and transformational leadership enhance sales performance. *Journal of the Academy of Marketing Science,* 41: 40–54.

Shaw, P. J. A., & Linnecar, R. 2007. *Business coaching: Achieving practical results through effective engagement.* Chichester: Capstone Publishing LT&D.

Silzer, R., & Church, A. H. 2009. The pearls and perils of identifying potential. *Industrial and Organizational Psychology,* 2: 377–412.

Silzer, R., & Dowell, B. E. (Eds.). 2010. *Strategy-driven talent management: A leadership imperative.* San Francisco, CA: John Wiley & Sons.

Sonnenberg, M., van Zijderveld, V., & Brinks, M. 2014. The role of talent-perception incongruence in effective talent management. *Journal of World Business,* 49(2): 272–280.

Stern, L. R. 2008. *Executive coaching: Building and managing your professional practice.* Hoboken, NJ: John Wiley.

Swart, J., & Harcup, J. 2013. "If I learn do we learn?": The link between executive coaching and organizational learning. *Management Learning,* 44: 337–354.

Tarique, I., & Schuler, R. S. 2010. Global talent management: Literature review, integrative framework, and suggestions for further research. *Journal of World Business,* 45: 122–133.

Thunnisen, M., Boselie, P., & Fruytier, B. G. M. 2013. A review of talent management: "Infancy or adolescence"?. *International Journal of Human Resource Management,* 24(9): 1744–1761.

Ulrich, D., & Smallwood, N. (2012). What is talent? *Leader to Leader,* 63: 55–61.

Wageman, R. 2001. How leaders foster self-managing team effectiveness: Design choices versus hands-on coaching. *Organization Science,* 12: 559–577.

Witherspoon, R., & White, R. P. 1996. Executive coaching: A continuum of roles. *Consulting Psychology Journal: Practice and Research,* 48: 124–133.

Ye, R., Wang, X.-H., Wendt, J. H., Wu, J., & Euwema, M. C. 2016. Gender and managerial coaching across cultures: Female managers are coaching more. *The International Journal of Human Resource Management,* 27: 1791–1812.

Yeow, J., & Martin, R. (2013). The role of self-regulation in developing leaders: A longitudinal field experiment. *The Leadership Quarterly,* 24: 625–637.

38

TALENT MANAGEMENT AND DEVELOPING LEADERSHIP TALENT

Chandana Sanyal

Julie Haddock-Millar

Introduction

An important aspect of talent management in the contemporary organization is the investment and development of leaders including leadership development. Developing leadership talent is viewed as a key lever in delivering competitive advantage in business today. This has led to considerable rise in the investment in leadership development programs including executive programs, coaching, mentoring, and other related interventions. It is estimated that organizations spend billions of dollars on developing the leadership skills of their people (Riggio, 2008). Leadership development as a concept has become more significant and strategic for all organizations (Leskiw & Singh, 2007). There exists an array of differing approaches and practices in the pursuit of securing effective leadership talent (Van Velsor, McCauley, & Ruderman, 2010) but researchers are still struggling to understand the leadership development phenomenon. This is not surprising as the concept of leadership itself is still continuously evolving.

Against this backdrop, the aim of this chapter is four-fold. First, we provide an overview summary of the literature on leadership theories and how they have developed over the last fifty years. We provide an analysis of different theories and approaches, including the concept and definition. We illustrate the degree of divergence and wide-ranging constructs that have developed in the field. Second, we consider the development of theory and empirical research on leadership development and the practice of leadership development. Next, we explore the extent to which approaches and models to evaluating leadership development interventions have been considered both in research and practice at the individual, organizational, and community level. Finally, we conclude and identify a number of topics and research streams warranting further attention.

Leadership Theories

There are "almost as many different definitions of leadership as there are people who have tried to define it" (Stogdill, 1974: 7). While most of us have a general grasp of what leadership is, defining the term is challenging for both practitioners and scholars. With more than a century of academic work on this topic, many definitions, approaches, and dimensions of leadership have emerged and evolved during this period. This is because leadership can take on multiple meanings and appearances rather than mean just one thing (Day & Harrison, 2007).

Leadership can be viewed from multiple perspectives: as a personality with special traits or characteristics; an act or behavior shown by the leader; the capability, knowledge, and skills demonstrated by the leader; the process used by the leader to bring groups together; or transformative change and the power relationship that exists between leaders and followers. Table 38.1 provides a brief overview of the

DOI: 10.4324/9781315474687-38

Table 38.1 Overview of leadership theories or approaches

Theory & Approach	Author's Definition & Concept
The trait or great man theory (Bass, 1990; Bryman, 1992; Carlyle, 1993; Kreitner & Kinicki, 2001)	This approach is essentially the "great person" theory of leadership that focuses on identifying the innate *qualities and characteristics* of acknowledged leaders (e.g., Catherine the Great, Mohandas Gandhi, Abraham Lincoln, Napoleon Bonaparte).
The functional or skills approach (Adair, 1983; Katz, 1955; Mumford et al., 2000; Yammarino, 2000)	This is a leader-centered perspective on leadership, with emphasis on *skills and ability* that can be learned to develop individuals in the team, build the team, and achieve required tasks or goals.
The behavioral approach/ leadership style (Blake & McCanse, 1991; Blake & Mouton, 1985; Mullins, 2007; Tannenbaum & Schhmidt, 1973)	This approach extends *beyond* the leader himself/herself, and considers the effects that leaders have on the actual performance of groups by examining *leader behaviors* and relating them to outcomes. The leader's attitude and behaviors they exhibit in their day-to-day dealings result in a range of leadership styles.
Path-goal theory (Evans, 1996; House, 1971; House & Dessler, 1974)	The path-goal theory is about how leaders motivate followers to accomplish designated goals. For the leader, the imperative is to use a style of leadership that best meets followers' motivational needs.
Situational and contingency models of leadership (Hersey & Blanchard, 2001)	The contingency approach suggests a wide range of different but equally valid way of leading and managing people. Situational leadership focuses on appropriate leadership styles for groups or individual followers who are at different stages of "readiness" or "maturity" to achieve a task.
Transactional leadership (French & Raven, 1968)	Transactional leadership relies on the leader's capacity to negotiate appropriate follower behaviors based on legitimate rewards or punishments, although there is an inherent assumption that the leader has the appropriate authority to offer such rewards or administer punishments.
Transformational leadership (Alimo-Metcalfe, 1995; Burns, 1978; Lowe & Gardner, 2000)	Transformational leadership is a process by which leaders create high levels of motivation and commitment by generating and communicating a clear vision and often, appealing to higher ideas and values among followers.
Inspirational leadership (Adair, 2003)	The inspirational leader creates and communicates a vision, has a passion and a dynamism that drives both the leader, and engages the enthusiasm and efforts of the led, even exhibiting unconventional behavior and performing heroic deeds.
Spiritual leadership (Sanders, 1967)	Spiritual leadership is developed within an intrinsic motivation model that incorporates vision, hope/faith, and altruistic love, theories of workplace spirituality, and spiritual survival. The purpose of spiritual leadership is to create vision and value congruence across the strategic, empowered team, and individual levels and, ultimately, to foster higher levels of organizational commitment and productivity.
Servant leadership (Greenleaf, 1970)	Servant leadership emphasizes that leaders be attentive to the concerns of their followers, empathize with them, and nurture them. Servant leaders put their followers first, empower them, and help them develop their full personal capabilities.
Distributed leadership (Gronn, 2000)	Distributed leadership is a group activities that works through and within relationships rather than individual action. This dimension of leadership uses three forms of engagement: spontaneous collaboration, intuitive working relationships, and institutionalized practices.

Table 38.1 Overview of leadership theories or approaches (*Continued*)

Theory & Approach	Author's Definition & Concept
Leader-Member Exchange (LMX) Theory (Dansereau, Graen, & Haga, 1975; Graen & Uhl-Bien, 1995; Uhl-Bien, 2006)	The LMX theory conceptualizes leadership as a process that is centred on the interactions between leaders and followers. Rather than leaders treating followers in a collective way, the focus is on the differences that might exist between the leader and each of the leader's followers and the need for effective leader-member exchange to achieve effective leadership.
Ethical leadership (Northouse, 2007)	Ethical leadership is directed by respect for ethical beliefs and values and for the dignity and rights of others. It is thus related to concepts such as trust, honesty, consideration, justice, and fairness.
Authentic leadership (Avolio, Luthans, & Walumbwa, 2004; George et al., 2007)	Authentic leaders are deeply aware of how they think and behave and are perceived by others as being aware of their own and others' values and moral perspectives, knowledge, and strengths; aware of the context in which they operate; and who are confident, hopeful, optimistic, resilient, and of high moral character
Eco-leadership (Western, 2007)	Eco-leadership recognizes that within an organization there are interdependent parts that make up a whole; the leader must value all stakeholder relationships, create connectivity and sustainability, underpinned by an ethical and socially responsible stance.

leadership theories and approaches included in this chapter, with brief definitions showing the range and evolvement of thinking around leadership.

As can be seen from this list, views of leadership have evolved from role-based authority, to interpersonal influence, to an emergent property of dyads, collective or larger social systems (Day & Harrison, 2007; Yammarino, 2013). Traditionally, leadership theories have mainly focused on the individual, determining the specific traits, personality, behaviors, and competencies leaders need to be effective (Day et al., 2013; Hanson, 2013; Yukl, 2013), i.e., the focus is on who the leaders are, what the leaders do, and the effect of their behavior on teams or groups.

However, there has been a gradual shift to more collective and social aspects of leadership as highlighted in the Leader-Member Exchange Theory, eco-leadership, and distributed leadership. Another dimension of leadership is the circumstances in which the leadership activity occurs; the situational and contingency models of leadership focus of this aspect, highlighting the need to consider the organizational and environmental context of the leader.

As theories of leadership have evolved, the learning and development interventions to support individuals and organizations have also been emerged in the quest to build leadership capability (Hanson, 2013; Day et al., 2013). Most types of leadership development have used one or more leadership theories, models, or approaches as an educational focus (Day & O'Connor, 2003; Schriesheim & Neider, 1989). From our experience as practitioner academics, we think that holistic leadership development should encompass understanding and practice of appropriate leadership behaviors, the significance of the context in which the leader operates, and the social and relational aspect of leadership. Thus, familiarity of the relevant leadership theories can contribute significantly to developing and designing leadership development programs and interventions. For example, the leader's behavioral approach has been the focus of a number of studies (Tannenbaum, Weschler, & Massarik, 2013), and although it can be argued that behaviors can be learned, short-term training interventions may not always be effective (Day et al., 2013).

Challenges facing contemporary leaders are ill-defined and leadership work is reliably subject to unpredictable and unforeseen outcomes, especially in environments characterized as "volatile, uncertain, complex and ambiguous" (VUCA) (Johnson, 2012). Therefore, training interventions will need to present leadership in such messy realities rather than as a set of straight-forward positive, individual skills and competencies. Here, the contingency and situational leadership theories can be integrated to emphasize that the organizational context will impact leadership activities – it is not just about who the leader is, or what the leader does but the context in which the leader works.

The Leader-Member Exchange Theory (Dansereau, Graen, & Haga, 1975; Graen & Uhl-Bien, 1995; Uhl-Bien, 2006) and the theory of distributed/shared leadership (Gronn, 2000; Hillier, Day, & Vance, 2006) can be applied to shift the emphasis from traditional individualistic focus to collective and social aspects of leadership, focusing on relational aspects of leadership development.

Thus, the development of leadership talent must be iterative, multi-relational, and contextual (Osborn, Hunt, & Jaunch, 2002). Vince and Pedler (2018) strongly argue against leadership development that only emphasizes the positive and draws attention to the contradictions inherent in leadership work. To be able to address such challenges, more recent research and practice of leadership has shifted the lens to understanding and enhancing the developmental processes required to support and guidance leaders and organizations to navigate leadership development as a connected and multifaceted frame and not simply as linear processes (Day et al., 2013; Lowe & Gardner, 2001).

Construct of Leadership Development

Although there are extensive theoretical and empirical studies on leadership theories, in comparison, there is relatively limited scholarly theory of, empirical research on, and practice of leadership development (Day et al., 2014). It is difficult to generalize about how leadership talent should be developed because of variation in situations and organizational context. Just identifying a suitable leadership theory may not be sufficient to motivate effective leadership as human development involves a complex set of processes that need to be understood and addressed (Day et al., 2013; Day et al., 2014; Day, Harrison, & Halpin, 2009).

Also, some organizational context and nature of work has moved away from relying on a single leader to provide leadership of a team, to collaborative and shared processes within an effective team to constitute its collective leadership (Day, Gronn, & Salas, 2004; Kozlowski & Bell, 2003; Pearce & Conger, 2003). The approaches to leadership development has to encompass this aspect of distributed or shared leadership (Gronn, 2000; Hillier, Day, & Vance, 2006).

Generally, leadership development can be constructed as a process of learning for leaders through both planned and deliberate interventions as well as recognized opportunities that may be unplanned and undeliberate experiences to build and enhance their leadership capabilities. For example, planned interventions may involve attending training days and workshops aimed at developing "the collective capacity of organizational members to engage effectively in leadership roles and processes" (Day, 2000: 582). However, it is also recognized that effective leadership development occur through experiences outside of formal training (McCall, Lombardo, & Morrison, 1988; McCauley, Ruderman, Ohlott, & Morrow, 1994; Ohlott, 2004). For example, unplanned learning can take place through contributing to a senior management meeting that one may not have previously attended or by observing and reflecting on a specific event or situation related to managing and/or leading people and/or projects. Thus, leadership talent development can be planned and deliberate as well as an emergent process (Gold, Thorpe, & Mumford, 2010).

Over the years, researchers have also sought to distinguish between the concepts of leader development (the leader within at the individual level) and leadership development (leadership in action in the organization) (Clarke, 2013; Day, 2000; McCauley & van Velsor, 2004). McCauley and van Velsor (2004: 2) define leader development as being about "the expansion of a person's capacity to be effective in leadership roles and processes" and is therefore concerned with the development of an individual's skills, knowledge, and competencies associated with formal leader roles (Clarke, 2013). Day (2000) makes a clear distinction between leader development and leadership development and suggests that leader development focus on developing individual leaders, whereas leadership development focuses on a process of development that inherently involves multiple individuals (e.g., leaders and followers or among peers in a self-managed work team).

Hanson (2013: 108) suggests that this distinction is important "because leading is both an internal process of personal discovery of values and beliefs and an external action of influencing, directing, and building teams and organizations". He argues that in the plural nature of developing leaders, the leader development and leadership development is also an important construct as both are interconnected and essential aspects of building leadership talent (Hernez–Broome & Hughes, 2004).

Thus, leadership development activities cannot continue to be offered without first understanding and evaluating the interfacing relationship with the individual, their needs, as well as the organizational context in which they operate. A more pluralist understanding is required to appreciate the political dynamics, the cultural, and symbolic context in which leadership development occurs (Burgiyn & Jackson, 1977). Mabey (2013) through a comprehensive research of leadership development literature categorized leadership development under four headings or discourses: *functional discourse* where the emphasis is on building and retaining leadership capabilities for optimum performance; *interpretive discourse* to assist leaders to make sense of what is happening at work, enabling social construction, and understanding of lived experiences within the context of work: the *dialogic discourse* through activities to explore identity and relational aspects of leadership, which can be liberating and challenging at the same time; and the *critical discourse* that emphasizes value of the "whole experience" engaging with the emotional and moral issues inherent is leadership practice.

In essence, developing leadership talent is a multi-layered process, ideally involving a blended learning approach that incorporates formal, informal, and experiential learning. Hanson suggests that we need to consider:

> the whole leadership development system before we "do" leadership development, so both leaders and organizations can map their development effort in an aligned and supported way… and move away from isolated methods toward an interconnected process of personal and organizational discovery and learning. (2013: 107)

Through his research, Hanson (2013) has developed the Leadership Development Interface Model that offers an interconnected perspective of leadership development and explores a "whole system" view so both leaders and organizations can engage, plan, and evaluate their development effort in an aligned and supported way. We will discuss this further in a later section.

Consequently, to address leader development with the individual level focus, a set of intra-personal competencies and skills, such as self-awareness, self-regulation, and self-motivation (Day, 2000), have to be addressed through the development process. More recently, it has been recognized that with increasing unpredictability and contradictions in leadership work (Vince & Pedler, 2018), a deeper-level of personal transformation and self –awareness associated with leader identity (Nicholson & Carroll, 2013) may also need to be considered in developing today's leaders.

Research into leader development has therefore focused on understanding and evaluating formal and informal learning and development processes that can contribute to this, and how organizations can engage in a collaborative way to support this process (Clarke, 2013; Day, Gronn, & Salas, 2004; Dragoni et al., 2009; Orvis & Ratwani, 2010; Reichard & Johnson, 2011). Similarly, to address leadership development, which is seen as a dynamic process, the focus of leadership development shifts towards building social capital, with emphasis on inter-personal skills development for both the leader and the follower focusing on relational, collective, and social concepts to build trust and respect (Day, 2000; McCallum & O'Connell 2009). Thus, the construct of leadership development requires a broader perspective, taking into consideration the development of the leader as an individual and the leadership in action in the organizational context.

We next explore these two aspects of developing leadership talent as an individual (leader development) and in action within the organization (leadership development).

Developing the Leader at the Individual Level – Leader Development

The development of the leader as an individual focuses on building and enhancing the individual's capability to undertake the role of a leader. This involves improving an individual's mastery of cognitive, socio-emotional, and behavioral skills associated with leadership (Day, 2011). These skills are linked to individuals developing intra-personal perspective in building self-awareness around values, beliefs, character, spirit, and personality (Tichy, 1997). They also help to develop key leader attributes of openness, trust, creativity, along with practical, social, and general intelligence (Iszatt-White & Saunders, 2017). By developing these skills, a leader will gain the capacity and capability to adapt when dealing with complex situations and problems that confront managerial leaders in business today.

In exploring these intra-personal aspects of developing a leader, researchers have examined cognitive and meta-cognitive skills to assessed leadership potential (Marshall-Miles et al., 2007); the role of personality (Day et al., 2009; deVries, 2012); when leaders performance at their best (Strang & Kuhnert, 2009); experience and learning from experience (Day et al., 2009; Lord & Hill, 2005); and leader identity (Ibarra et al., 2010; Lord & Hill, 2005; Vince & Pedlar, 2018).

Mumford et al. (2007) presented four leadership skills – cognitive, interpersonal, business, and strategic – as a conceptualized strataplex (layered) across the organization and show that specific skills requirements vary by organizational level. Strenberg (2008) suggests developing and integrating skills of wisdom, intelligence, and creativity that are essential for effective decision making in a leader. These related intra-personal skills of complex problem solving, creative thinking, social judgement skills, and solution construction skills (Mumford et al., 2000; Mumford, Zaccaro et al., 2000) can be acquired through learning and development processes both planned and structured such as training days and workshops as well as emergent such as experiential learning.

A key aspect of leader development is that "it is ultimately about facilitating an identity transition" to create new leadership options (Ibarra et al., 2010: 673). Research suggests that seeing oneself as a leader or having "leader" as a core part of one's identity is an important precursor to taking on leadership roles and engaging in actions to further develop one's capacity for effective leadership (Ashford & DeRue, 2012). Therefore, in developing the individual leader, focus has to be placed on their life experience – the conscious or unconscious philosophy of life that impact values, beliefs, and living authentically (Avolio & Luthans, 2006; Hanson, 2013).

Bennis (1995) suggests that if the leader is to be effective, attention must be given to the leader within. Leaders that are able to see their whole life as a part of the leadership journey is crucial as building relationships and trust comes from a leader's self-orientation (Green & Howe, 2012; Hanson, 2013). This enables leaders to fully understand their own mind-set and attitude in relation to why and how they lead (Ready & Conger, 2007). Nicholson and Carroll (2013) establish that "identity undoing" (addressed through moments of being destabilized, unraveled, and deconstructed in leadership development) through exploration of the role of power in identity construction using planned and initiated interactions can enable leadership learning through critical reflection. Thus, leaders who are able to learn from their experience, particularly using reflective practice (Avolio, 2005; DeRue et al., 2012), are able to enhance their leadership facilitative skills.

Leader development also requires the input from others through feedback and observation (Hanson, 2013). Introspections of self and others can help to make personal shifts leading to change in behavior (Kegan & Lahey, 2009; McCauley & Van Velsor, 2005). A range of psychometric assessments and diagnostics, including 360 degree feedback, are often used in leadership programs. Leader development will occur when an individual is receptive and fully engages with the organizational feedback loops and are committed to acting on them to improve and enhance the way they lead (Alldredge & Nilan, 2000, Hanson, 2013). However, facilitation and support is required of the organization in this process to ensure that the feedback is appropriately interpreted and acted on (Goldsmith, Lyons, & Freas, 2000; Rosti & Shipper, 1998). Individuals need to be supported through the 360 degree process to ensure that "self-and other agreement" (i.e., how leaders rate themselves and how others rate them) is interpreted appropriately to maximize learning and development of the leader. Leaders also require guidance and coaching to consider multi-perspectives and understand internal motivation (London & Smither, 2002). Thus, coaching and mentoring are also used as one-to-one learning interventions in leadership programs.

In fact, Day (2011) emphasizes that for a leader development experience to be most effective, it needs to be embedded in the organizational context. So development program for leaders will need to consider the organizational culture that can either embed and support or stifle leader development. An appropriate power and decision making structure and strong learning culture will sustain the development process. It is also essential to ensure that the training activities are tailored to development needs of the individuals to be most effective (Mumford et al., 2000). At the same time, participants have to be willing to learn, fully engage in the learning interventions, identify with the leader within them, and critically reflect on their experiences as a part of their on-going leadership development.

Developing the Leader within the Organization – Leadership Development

In developing the leader within the organization, the emphasis moves from building human capital, which focus primarily on individual leader attributes (i.e., knowledge, skills, attitude) as discussed above to social capital, which is about making connections and interactions within a social context (Day et al., 2013). Thus, to develop leaders in organizations, it is important to understand the development of social interactions that occur within the leadership process and build those interactive, technical and connective skills required in the process of leading organizational strategy, and operations, as well as leading people and teams (Hanon, 2013; Kaplan & Kaiser, 2006).

As leadership is both dependent on and the product of a social context (Day, Zaccaro, & Halpin, 2004), leadership development can occur only within this context. Research on leadership development has established that certain psychological processes (such as self-knowledge, interpersonal skills, communication competence, and cultural competence) and contextual influences (such as organizational climate, group/organization composition, economic environment, and organizational support for diversity) moderate the development of high quality relationships in diverse leader-member dyads (Boyd & Taylor, 1998; Scandura & Lankau, 1996). Therefore, for effective leadership development, these aspects have to be considered while planning and designing learning interventions.

It has been argued that aspects of leadership development can be built into formal and informal learning interventions (Hernez-Broome & Hughes, 2004). A range of interventions can be developed and initiated to support leaders within this process: strengthen contact within the workplace through building networks, off-site activities, mentoring; assimilate learning and insight through leadership training and 360-degree feedback; and improve identification through job assignments and action learning (Day et al., 2013).

Hanson (2013) observes that such leadership development initiatives can either be stand alone or a menu of connected interventions. His overview of the mainstream thinking and literature on how leadership development is approached in organizations includes development of leadership through leadership competencies or capability indictors, traditional classroom-based leadership training, action learning that involves working on real organization issues, 360- degree feedback, and executive coaching. It must be noted that some of these interventions are relevant for developing the individual leader as discussed previously.

For example, feedback as a process of development has been particularly identified as a way of ensuring longitudinal evaluation at multilevel focusing on intrapersonal and interpersonal changes to facilitate leadership development. This includes self-assessment not only of how a leader may view themselves and how others view them, but also how individuals think others view them (Day et al., 2013; Taylor & Hood, 2011). This helps a leader gain understanding of expectations at various levels within the organization. This useful insight can be applied effectively within leadership development to support an individual to enhance their areas of strength and build on areas of lesser strength at the individual level, leading to enhancing and improving relational and social aspects of leaderships that are crucial to creating connectivity and sustainability in business today.

There also appears to be shift or at least blending of non-cognitive learning with cognitive learning methods in leadership development to access intuition, feelings, emotions, stories, active listening, empathy, and awareness in the moment (Taylor & Ladkin, 2009). These authors identified four processes that are particular to the way in which arts-based methods contribute to the development of individual managers and leaders: through the transference of artistic skills, through projective techniques, through the evocation of "essence," and through creating, which they refer to as "making" of artifacts such as masks, collages, or sculpture.

Other art-based methods and creative techniques introduce leaders to forms of art such as literature, drama, music, and drawing (Springborg, 2012; Sutherland, 2013) to provide an experiential learning opportunity through that leaders can learn by "transforming aesthetic experiences to develop non-rational, non-logical capabilities and self–knowledge" (Sutherland, 2013: 25). These experiences have the potential to connect cognitive and emotional processes that challenges underpinning assumptions, and highlight the relational and subjective aspect of human experience (Taylor & Ladkin, 2010).

The importance of learning through experience is also highlighted by several authors in developing globally savvy leaders with strategic thinking and cultural competence (DeRue & Wellman, 2009; Dragoni et al., 2014). Global work experience that involves going on international assignments, managing multinational business operations, and building working relationships with those from different countries can significantly improve leadership capabilities, particularly for those working in international global contexts. Didactic learning opportunities related to global leadership tasks can also include cross-cultural training, diversity training, and language training (Caligiuri & Tarique, 2006), however, the greatest development occurs when individuals have significant interpersonal contact with different countries (Caligiuri, 2006).

Some researchers have specifically highlighted the importance of values and emotions in developing leadership, particularly to develop authentic leadership (Avolio & Gardner, 2005). The literature also suggests that self-narrative as a method in which leaders' self-stories also contribute to their on-going development (Shamir & Eilam, 2005). There are more recent examples of leadership development that look beyond building capabilities, knowledge, behavior, and performance to focusing on coping with resilience (Romanoska et al., 2013) and improving health and well-being (Holmberg, Larson, & Backstrom, 2016) that has relevance for leadership roles in turbulent organizations and fluid work situation in current times.

Use of mindfulness practice in leadership development is another method to enhance managerial leaders' capacity for self-care and resilience (Sanyal & Rigg, 2017) and builds capabilities of collaboration and leading in complexity (Olivier et al., 2016). There are a number of studies that have adopted a complexity perspective that requires leaders to develop skills in building and managing networks effectively, engage in sense making with teams to promote shared understanding, counteract barriers to knowledge exchange, and foster the positive value of tension to build social capital (Bovaired, 2008; Clarke, 2013; Umble et al., 2005).

Consequently, leadership development is more dynamic than liner, and the leader can be supported through more than one interrelated learning interventions to build knowledge, engage in sense making, and create shared meaning within their context to lead effectively. The development of the leader as an individual is equally important as developing the leader in the context of the organization; one is aligned to the other, and integration of both is required for developing effective leadership talent to address complex and adaptive leadership challenges in business today. Thus, an ideal leadership development program will align these two dimensions of developing leadership talent by taking into account significance of the organizational context, its purpose for leader and leadership development, and the interfacing relationships between the organization and the leader (Olivares, Peterson, & Hess, 2007).

Aligning Leader and Leadership Development – An Holistic Approach

Although developing the leader as an individual and in the context of the organization is essential, traditionally most leadership programs tend to have a functionalist approach, focusing on the improving performance by developing individual skills and attributes of the leader (Day, 2000; Day, Zaccaro, & Halpin, 2004; Mabey, 2013). Drawing on the work of the Center for Creative Leadership, McCauley and van Velsor (2004) suggest that a systemic approach needs to be taken to develop leadership talent. Several authors have developed frameworks that go beyond a static list of leadership development interventions to a more holistic approach that address the needs and context of individuals and the organizations. We have identified three leadership development frameworks that offer this inclusive approach.

First, Quatro, Waldman, and Galvin (2007) propose that for leadership development programs and initiatives to be holistic in their scope, they explicitly need to address the analytical, conceptual, emotional, and spiritual (ACES) domains of leadership practice development. This involves developing leaders that are adept at understanding and managing discrete complexity (analytical), as well as interrelated complexity and fostering creativity (conceptual). At the same time, it encompasses developing leaders who are attuned to emotional issues (emotional) and are able to recognize the value of spirituality (spiritual) to connect followers not only to their individual tasks but also organizational mission linked to mora and ethical values. The authors highlight that these four domains are interrelated and posit that the development efforts will need to take into account the inter-connection between the domains.

The author also offer a classification for leadership development interventions for the ACES model. The leadership development mechanisms are classified into the "classroom context" (formal learning that take in either an indoor or outdoor classroom setting), "job context" (activities that are experiential, have a less formal structure, and are tied to the actual job performance of the individual), and "organizational context" (mechanisms and activities that exit or take place at the organizational level, such as culture, core values, mission/vision, and HR strategies). The organizational context offers an overarching role in the development process across all four domains of the ACES model of leadership development.

The second leadership development framework that represents alignment of leader and leadership development is the Leadership Development Interface Model (Hanson, 2013). The author has developed a four-quadrant leadership development interface model that connects leaders and leadership development with individuals and organizations for which they work. Through his empirical research, he presents "an aligned systemic view of the leadership development interface [which] will lead to more effective and measurable leadership development outcomes" (2007: 108).

His model consists of the leader development at individual level through the *leader reflection and discovery,* i.e., the leader's own understanding of how they view themselves and the world around them and how this impacts the way they lead. Self-assessment, personality diagnostics, personal narrative, and mind mapping can be used as development tools for leaders to ascertain and challenge their values, personality, personal well-being, authenticity, character/qualities, and personal goals/vision. The development of the leader at organizational level can be best achieved through *leader multi-level feedback,* i.e., formal assessment, 360-degree feedback, uncovering multi-stakeholder perspectives, measuring ability/potential, and coaching to ascertain how they are doing and to highlight areas of development as mentioned earlier.

Next, leadership development needs a learning place that is real and supported, and has a *context and purpose and is fit* both for the individual and organizational performance. This can be addressed through performance expectations, providing an appropriate learning space, succession planning, action learning, and ability to work within the organizational leadership culture. This can add a critical aspect to leadership development.

Finally, leadership development can build skills and behavior that lead to effective leadership learning as an outcome and action. This can be achieved through competence and skills training, building networks and connections within the organization, formal and informal life-ling education, and team and hierarchical interactions. Here, appropriate interventions and processes can be mapped and implemented. These four aspects within Hanson's (2013) model offer classification of development activities and processes whereby leaders may spend some of their leadership journey in each of the quadrants. It is the alignment and interconnectedness of these four aspects that provide a holistic framework for both leader and leadership development "offering opportunity towards more meaningful, measures and successful leadership improvement for both individuals and organizations" (2013: 113).

Finally, another simplified framework for development of both intrapersonal and interpersonal leadership capacities across the individual's career and life span is offered by O'Connell (2014), which incorporates key capabilities required for 21st century leaders. He offers five "webs of belief" synthesized from established and emerging leadership scholarship as constructs for a guide for leaders to adapt to new information, new experiences, new levels of complexities, and new context over the course of the life the career:

1. *learning*: creativity/expertise – development of the leader's cognitive organizing principles and belief in the capacity to continuously gain and integrate knowledge and practice;
2. *reverence*: rational collective – ongoing development of capacity to accept, understand, and respect differences;
3. *purpose*: self-regulation – development of the leader's personal intentions, mission, passion, and contribution to self and others' welfare;
4. *authenticity*: self-awareness/positive moral perspective – knowing one's self and beliefs, and enacting and behaving according to these convictions; and
5. *flaneur*: balance/reflexivity – the capacity to adopt a philosophical and spirit-led approach through reflective practice).

Although, this may appear to be a simple framework, these "webs of beliefs" create a doctrine for holism for leadership development (Drath et al., 2008; O'Connell, 2014), which addresses the need to look beyond the notion that leadership development occurs only through specially designed programs. Rather they present leadership development as an on-going continuous process that can take place anywhere (Day, 2000).

The key aspects of these frameworks offer a guide for an integrated approach to developing leadership talent. The features and approaches within these models can be used by individual leaders, their direct manages, and human resource development practitioners. The models can also be used to build a common understanding of leadership development among wider stakeholders of leadership development. The shift from micro elements of leadership development interventions to a macro interfacing endeavor of developing the leader at individual level and in the organizational context will help both leaders and organizations to achieve more meaningful and cost effective leadership development (Hanson, 2013).

Leadership Development Effectiveness

As leadership development continues to be redefined in the changing context of the organization and work, new approaches and models of evaluating leadership development interventions have been considered both in research and practice. Taking into account content, process, and outcome, few studies examine the behavioral, psychological, and financial impact of leadership development. Traditionally, evaluation approaches tend to focus primarily on the individual leader (Belling, James, & Ladkin, 2004; Holton & Baldwin, 2003; Kirkpatrick, 1998). However, in light of recent trends in relation to leadership development investment, there is an increased emphasis on the return on investment and impact evaluation.

Identifying appropriate markets and proxies to track over time has received increased attention. Consequently, the long-term impact of leadership development at the organizational level has become an important consideration (Collins, 2001). It is also suggested that leadership development can achieve community-wide goals such as improvements in health and public welfare (Martineau & Patterson, 2010), extending the evaluation of leadership development beyond the organizational level to encompass and community and social perspective.

Day's (2000) review of effectiveness of popular leadership development practices makes a distinction between leader development (human capital) and leadership development (social capital). Gardner et al. (2005) have offered a model of authentic leadership evaluation that includes cognitive elements focusing on leader and follower self-awareness, individual leader-follow behavior, and the historical and proximal contexts, taking into account previous experiences of individuals as well as the organizational climate. Here, the primary evaluation criteria was at the individual level.

Ely et al.'s (2010) evaluation model is an integrative framework for evaluating leadership coaching based on Kirkpatrick's four-level taxonomy, which takes into account the factors that bring about positive coaching outcomes such as rapport, trust, and collaboration in the relationship, as well as the challenges and support as a part of the process. Orvis and Langkamer (2010) also focus on both the process and the outcomes in their model for evaluating leader self-development with specific emphasis on content relevancy, learner engagement, challenge, structure, and experiential variety. Hoppe and Reinelt (2010) shifted the focus of leadership evaluation to impact on leadership networks, highlighting the need for evaluation at community level.

Several authors advocate a layered approach to evaluation of leadership development. For example, the EvaluLead Framework (Grove, Kibel, & Hass, 2007) offers a comprehensive methodology that advocates evaluating four parameters of leadership training and development: the context (purpose), results types (forms and depth of change required), domains of evaluation (personal growth, job or career performance, social systems change, organizational outputs and values, community norms), and forms of inquiry (approaches to collecting data).

Similarly, Clarke (2012) put forward a multilevel evaluation model following calls from the practitioner and academic community for more integrated approaches to theory building in leadership. His model consists of five levels of analysis – individual (leader and follower), dyad (leader and follower), team, organization, and community. Here, at the individual level, the leader's knowledge, skills, behaviors, identity, and self-awareness are assessed alongside the follower motivation, trust, organizational commitment, and performance. The relational quality and building of social capital are analyzed at the dyad level. The leadership impact at the team and organizational level are evaluated through its effectiveness and performance at these levels. This model recognizes the need to shift the emphasis of evaluating leadership development from individual level to analysing patterns of relationships and overall impact at team and organizational levels.

This is taken a step further by Edwards and Turnbull (2013), who advocate that the cultural context in which leaders are developed must be integrated within the evaluation process. They suggest a cultural approach to evaluating leadership development involving multiple stakeholders with multiple perspectives across the organization and community.

Overall, the impact of leadership development in today's organizations needs to be considered at individual, organizational, and community levels (Clarke, 2012; Clarke & Higgs, 2010) and take into account content, process, and outcomes.

Conclusions and Future Research Directions

Throughout this chapter, we have explored the extent to which leadership theory research and approaches have developed over the last fifty years and the degree to which thinking and practice have evolved. Over this time, numerous topics and strands have emerged including transactional leadership, spiritual leadership, servant leadership, distributed leadership, and ethical leadership. The views of leadership have evolved from role-based authority to interpersonal influence, to an emergent property of dyads, collection, or larger social systems. This represents a shift towards collection and social aspects of leadership.

Alongside the evolving nature of leadership theory is the approach adopted by organizations to create learning and development interventions to support individuals, teams, and the wider organization to build leadership capability and positively impact performance. Relative to leadership theory, there is limited scholarly theory and empirical research on leadership development and the practice of leadership development. Academics and practitioners have attempted to distinguish the concepts of leader development and leadership development. In developing the leaders within organizations, the emphasis shifts from building human capital to social capital. This is an important distinction as the practice of leadership development transitions from the development of individual attributes to connections and interactions within the social context.

In terms of future research directions, there are a number of topics and research streams that require further attention. We need to further understand the interfacing relationship with the individual, their needs, as well as the organizational context in which they operate in order to address the multifarious leadership development requirements. A more pluralist understanding is required to appreciate the political dynamics and the cultural and symbolic context in which leadership development occurs. Second, we need a more comprehensive understanding on the specific methods and interventions to support the development of leadership development. Finally, an integrated framework of leadership development evaluation is needed to consider the extent to which processes and outcomes positively or negatively impact on behavioral, psychological, and financial aspects of different approaches and models.

In conclusion, leadership development is a vitally important area of study and practice because as society, communities, and organizations change, so do the needs of individuals and teams. Understanding the interplay between society, communities, organizations, teams, and individuals is a necessity if we are to further develop leadership theory and practice.

References

Adair, J. 1983. *Effective leadership.* London. Pan Books.

Alimo-Metcalfe, B. 2010. An investigation of female and male constructs of leadership and empowerment. *Gender in Management: An International Journal,* 25(8): 640-648.

Alldredge, M. E., & Nilan, K. J. 2000. 3M's leadership competency model: An internally developed solution. *Human resource management,* 39(2-3): 133-145.

Ashford, S. J., & DeRue, D. S. 2012. Developing as a leader: The power of mindful engagement. *Organizational Dynamics,* 41(2): 146-154.

Avolio, B. J. 2005. *Leadership development in balance: Made/born.* Psychology Press.

Avolio, B. J., Luthans, F., & Ryan, C. 2006. *The high impact leader.* New York: McGraw Hill.

Bass, B. M., & Stogdill, R. M. 1990. *Handbook of leadership* (3rd ed.). New York, NY: The Free Press

Belling, R., James, K., & Ladkin, D. 2004. Back to the workplace: How organisations can improve their support for management learning and development. *Journal of Management Development,* 23(3): 234-255.

Bennis, W. 1995. Creating leaders: Leaders are created by experience, and they coach others from experience. *Executive excellence,* 12: 5-5.

Blake, R. R., & McCanse, A. A. 1991. *Leadership dilemmas–grid solutions.* Gulf Professional Publishing.

Blake, R. R., & Mouton, J. S. 1985. *The managerial grid III: A new look at the classic that has boosted productivity and profits for thousands of corporations worldwide.* Butterworth-Heinemann.

Bovaird, T. 2008. Emergent strategic management and planning mechanisms in complex adaptive systems: The case of the UK Best Value initiative. *Public Management Review,* 10(3), 319-340.

Boyd, N. G., & Taylor, R. R. 1998. A developmental approach to the examination of friendship in leader-follower relationships. *The Leadership Quarterly,* 9(1): 1-25.

Bryman, A. 1992. *Charisma and leadership in organizations.* Sage Publications.

Burns, J. M. 1978. *Leadership, 1978.* New Yorker: Harper & Row.

Caligiuri, P. 2006. Developing global leaders. *Human Resource Management Review,* 16(2): 219-228.

Caligiuri, P., & Tarique, I. 2006. International assignee selection and cross-cultural training and development. In I. Bjorkman & G. Stahi (Eds.), *Handbook of research in international human resource management,* London: Edward Elgar Publishing.

Carlyle, T. 1993. *On heroes, hero-worship, and the heroic in history* (Vol. 1). University of California Press.

Clarke, N. 2012. Evaluating leadership training and development: A levels-of-analysis perspective. *Human Resource Development Quarterly,* 23(4): 441-460.

Clarke, N., & Higgs, M. 2010. Leadership training across business sectors: Report to the university forum for human resource development, (UFHRD). *University of Southampton School of Management.*

Clarke, N., & Higgs, M. 2016. How strategic focus relates to the delivery of leadership training and development. *Human Resource Management, 55*(4): 541-565.

Collins, D. B. 2001. Organizational performance: The future focus of leadership development programs. *Journal of Leadership Studies,* 7(4): 43-54.

Day, D. V. 2000. Leadership development: A review in context. *The Leadership Quarterly,* 11(4): 581-613.

Day, D. V. 2011. Leadership development. In A. Bryman, D. Collinson, K. Grint, B. Jackson, & M. Uhl-Bein (Eds.), *The Sage handbook of leadership:* 37-50.

Day, D. V., Fleenor, J. W., Atwater, L. E., Sturm, R. E., & McKee, R. A. 2014. Advances in leader and leadership development: A review of 25 years of research and theory. *The Leadership Quarterly,* 25(1): 63-82.81-613.

Day, D. V., Gronn, P., & Salas, E. 2004. Leadership capacity in teams. *The Leadership Quarterly,* 15(6): 857-880.

Day, D. V., & Harrison, M. M. 2007. A multilevel, identity-based approach to leadership development. *Human Resource Management Review,* 17(4): 360-373.

Day, D. V., Harrison, M. M., & Halpin, S. M. 2009. *An integrative approach to leader development.* New York, NY: Psychology Press.

Day, D. V. & O'Connor, P. M. 2003. *Leadership development: Understanding the process. The future of leadership development:* 11-28. Mahwah, NJ: Lawrence Elbaum Associates Inc.

Day, D. V., Zaccaro, S. J., & Halpin, S. M. 2004. *Leader development for transforming organizations: Growing leaders for tomorrow.* Psychology Press.

Demmy, T. L., Kivlahan, C., Stone, T. T., Teague, L., & Sapienza, P. 2002. Physicians' perceptions of institutional and leadership factors influencing their job satisfaction at one academic medical center. *Academic Medicine,* 77(12): 1235-1240.

DeRue, D. S., Nahrgang, J. D., Hollenbeck, J. R., & Workman, K. 2012. A quasi-experimental study of after-event reviews and leadership development. *Journal of Applied Psychology,* 97(5): 997.

DeRue, D. S., & Wellman, N. 2009. Developing leaders via experience: The role of developmental challenge, learning orientation, and feedback availability. *Journal of Applied Psychology,* 94(4): 859.

De Vries, R. E. 2012. Personality predictors of leadership styles and the self–other agreement problem. *The Leadership Quarterly,* 23(5): 809-821.

Dragoni, L., Oh, I. S., Tesluk, P. E., Moore, O. A., VanKatwyk, P., & Hazucha, J. 2014. Developing leaders' strategic thinking through global work experience: The moderating role of cultural distance. *Journal of Applied Psychology,* 99(5): 867.

Dragoni, L., Tesluk, P. E., Russell, J. E., & Oh, I. S. 2009. Understanding managerial development: Integrating developmental assignments, learning orientation, and access to developmental opportunities in predicting managerial competencies. *Academy of Management Journal,* 52(4): 731-743.

Drath, W. H., McCauley, C. D., Palus, C. J., Van Velsor, E., O'Connor, P. M., & McGuire, J. B. (2008). Direction, alignment, commitment: Toward a more integrative ontology of leadership. *The Leadership Quarterly,* 19(6): 635-653.

Edwards, G., & Turnbull, S. 2013. A cultural approach to evaluating leadership development. *Advances in Developing Human Resources,* 15(1): 46-60.

Ely, K., Boyce, L. A., Nelson, J. K., Zaccaro, S. J., Hernez-Broome, G., & Whyman, W. 2010. Evaluating leadership coaching: A review and integrated framework. *The Leadership Quarterly,* 21(4): 585-599.

Evans, M. G. 1996. R J House's "A path-goal theory of leader effectiveness". *The Leadership Quarterly,* 7(3): 305-309.

French, J. R., Raven, B., & Cartwright, D. 1968. The bases of social power. In D. Cartwright, & A. Zander (Eds.), *Group dynamics: Research and theory.* London: Harper & Row.

Gardner, W. L., Avolio, B. J., Luthans, F., May, D. R., & Walumbwa, F. 2005. "Can you see the real me?" A self-based model of authentic leader and follower development. *The Leadership Quarterly,* 16(3): 343-372.

Gold, J., Thorpe, R., & Mumford, A. 2010. *Leadership and management development.* Kogan Page Publishers.

Goldsmith, M., Lyons, L., & Freas, A. 2000. *Coaching for leadership.* San Francisco, CA: Jossey-Bass.

Green, C. H., & Howe, A. P. 2011. *The trusted advisor field book: A comprehensive toolkit for leading with trust.* John Wiley & Sons.

Grove, J., Kibel, B., & Haas, T. 2007. EvaluLEAD: An open-systems perspective on evaluating leadership development In K. M. Hannum, J. W. Martineau, & C. Reinelt. (Eds.), *The handbook of leadership development evaluation:* 71-110, San Francisco, CA: Jossey-Bass.

Hanson, B. 2013. The leadership development interface: Aligning leaders and organizations toward more effective leadership learning. *Advances in Developing Human Resources,* 15(1): 106-120.

Hernez-Broome, G., & Hughes, R. J. 2004. Leadership development: Past, present, and future. *Human Resource Planning,* 27(1).

Hersey, P., & Blanchard, K. H., 2001. *Management of organizational behaviour. leading human resources* (8th ed.) London: Prentice Hall.

Hiller, N. J., Day, D. V., & Vance, R. J. 2006. Collective enactment of leadership roles and team effectiveness: A field study. *The Leadership Quarterly,* 17(4): 387-397.

Holmberg, R., Larsson, M., & Bäckström, M. 2016. Developing leadership skills and resilience in turbulent times: A quasi-experimental evaluation study. *Journal of Management Development,* 35(2): 154-169.

Holton III, E. F., & Baldwin, T. T. 2003. *Improving learning transfer in organizations.* John Wiley & Sons.

Hoppe, B., & Reinelt, C. 2010. Social network analysis and the evaluation of leadership networks. *The Leadership Quarterly,* 21(4): 600-619.

House, R. J. 1971. A path goal theory of leader effectiveness. *Administrative Science Quarterly,* 16(3): 321-339.

House, R. J., & Dessler, G. 1974. The path-goal theory of leadership: Some post hoc and a priori tests. In J. G. Hunt & L. L. Larson (Eds.), *Contingency approaches to leadership:* 29-55. Carbondale, IL: Southern Illinois University.

Ibarra, H., Snook, S., & Guillen Ramo, L. 2010. Identity-based leader development. In N. Nohria & R. Khurana (Eds.), *Handbook of leadership theory and practice:* 657-678. Harvard Business Press.

Iszatt-White, M., & Saunders, C. 2017. *Leadership* (2nd.). Oxford University Press.

Johansen, R. 2012. *Leaders make the future: Ten new leadership skills for an uncertain world.* Berrett-Koehler Publishers.

Katz, R. L. 1955. Skills of an effective administrator. *Harvard Business Review,* 33(1): 33-42.

Kegan, R., & Lahey, L. L. 2009. *Immunity to change: How to overcome it and unlock potential in yourself and your organization.* Harvard Business Press.

Kirkpatrick, D. I. 1998. *Evaluating training programs: The four levels.* San Francisco, CA: Berrett-Koehler.

Kozlowski, S. W., & Bell, B. S. 2003. Work groups and teams in organizations. In W. C. Borman, D. R. Ilgen, & R. J. Klimoski (Eds.), *Handbook of psychology* (Vol. 12): Industrial and Organizational Psychology: 333-375. New York: Wiley-Blackwell.

Kreitner, R. and Kinicki, A. 2001. *Organizational Behaviour* (5th ed.). New York: McGraw-Hill.

Leskiw, S. L., & Singh, P. 2007. Leadership development: Learning from best practices. *Leadership & Organization Development Journal,* 28(5): 444-464.

London, M., & Smither, J. W. 2002. Feedback orientation, feedback culture, and the longitudinal performance management process. *Human Resource Management Review,* 12(1): 81-100.

Lord, R. G., & Hall, R. J. 2005. Identity, deep structure and the development of leadership skill. *The Leadership Quarterly,* 16(4): 591-615.

Lowe, K. B., & Gardner, W. L. 2000. Ten years of the leadership quarterly: Contributions and challenges for the future. *The Leadership Quarterly,* 11(4): 459-514.

Mabey, C. 2013. Leadership development in organizations: Multiple discourses and diverse practice. *International Journal of Management Reviews,* 15(4): 359-380.

Marshall-Mies, J. C., Fleishman, E. A., Martin, J. A., Zaccaro, S. J., Baughman, W. A., & McGee, M. L. 2000. Development and evaluation of cognitive and metacognitive measures for predicting leadership potential. *The Leadership Quarterly,* 11(1):135-153.

Martineau, J., & Patterson, T. 2010. Evaluating leader development. In E. Van Velsor, C. D. McCauley, & M. N. Ruderman (Eds.), *Handbook of leadership development:* 251-281 (3rd ed.). San Francisco, CA: Jossey-Bass.

McCall, L., Lombardo, M. & Morrison, M. 1988. *The lessons of experience: How successful executives develop on the job.* Lexington, MA: Lexington Books.

McCallum, S., & O'Connell, D. 2009. Social capital and leadership development: Building stronger leadership through enhanced relational skills. *Leadership & Organization Development Journal,* 30(2): 152-166.

McCauley, C. D., Ruderman, M. N., Ohlott, P. J., & Morrow, J. E. 1994. Assessing the developmental components of managerial jobs. *Journal of Applied Psychology,* 79(4): 544-560.

McCauley, C. D., & Van Velsor, E. (Eds.). 2004. *The center for creative leadership handbook of leadership development.* San Francisco, CA: Jossey-Bass.

Mullins, L. J. (2007). *Management and organisational behaviour.* Pearson Education.

Mumford, M. D., Marks, M. A., Connelly, M. S., Zaccaro, S. J., & Reiter-Palmon, R. 2000. Development of leadership skills: Experience and timing. *The Leadership Quarterly,* 11(1): 87-114.

Mumford, M. D., Zaccaro, S. J., Connelly, M. S., & Marks, M. A. 2000a. Leadership skills: Conclusions and future directions. *The Leadership Quarterly,* 11(1): 155-170.

Mumford, M. D., Zaccaro, S. J., Johnson, J. F., Diana, M., Gilbert, J. A., & Threlfall, K. V. 2000b. Patterns of leader characteristics: Implications for performance and development. *The Leadership Quarterly,* 11(1):115-133.

Mumford, T. V., Campion, M. A., & Morgeson, F. P. 2007. The leadership skills strataplex: Leadership skill requirements across organizational levels. *The Leadership Quarterly*, 18(2): 154-166.

Nicholson, H., & Carroll, B. 2013. Identity undoing and power relations in leadership development. *Human Relations*, 66(9):1225-1248.

Northouse, G. 2007. *Leadership theory and practice* (3rd ed.). Thousand Oak: Sage.

O'Connell, P. K. 2014. A simplified framework for 21st century leader development. *The Leadership Quarterly*, 25(2): 183-203.

Ohlott, P. J. 2004. Job assignments. In C. McCauley & E. V. Velsor (Eds.), *The Center for Creative Leadership handbook of leadership development:* 151-182. San Francisco, CA: Jossey-Bass.

Olivares, O. J., Peterson, G., & Hess, K. P. 2007. An existential-phenomenological framework for understanding leadership development experiences. *Leadership & Organization Development Journal*, 28(1): 76-91.

Orvis, K. A., & Ratwani, K. L. 2010. Leader self-development: A contemporary context for leader development evaluation. *The Leadership Quarterly*, 21(4): 657-674.

Osborn, R. N., Hunt, J. G., & Jauch, L. R. 2002. Toward a contextual theory of leadership. *The Leadership Quarterly*, 13(6): 797-837.

Pearce, C., & Conger, J. (2003). All those years ago: the historical underpinnings of shared leadership. In C. L. Pearce & J. A. Conger (Eds.), *Shared leadership: Reframing the hows and whys of leadership:* 1-18. SAGE.

Quatro, S. A., Waldman, D. A., & Galvin, B. M. 2007. Developing holistic leaders: Four domains for leadership development and practice. *Human Resource Management Review*, 17(4): 427-441.

Ready, D. A., & Conger, J. A. 2007. Make your company a talent factory. *Harvard Business Review*, 85(6): 68-77.

Reitz, M., Chaskalson, M., Olivier, S., & Waller, L. 2016. *The mindful leader: Developing the capacity for resilience and collaboration in complex times through mindfulness practice.* Ashridge House, UK: Ashridge Management College.

Riggio, R. E. (2008). Leadership development: The current state and future expectations. *Consulting Psychology Journal: Practice and Research*, 60(4): 383.

Romanowska, J., Larsson, G., & Theorell, T. 2013. Effects on leaders of an art-based leadership intervention. *Journal of Management Development*, 32(9): 1004-1022.

Rosti Jr, R. T., & Shipper, F. 1998. A study of the impact of training in a management development program based on 360 feedback. *Journal of Managerial Psychology*, 13(1/2): 77-89.

Sanyal, C. & Rigg, C. 2017). *In what ways does the introduction of 'mindfulness' in a leadership and management programme help managers to learn about self-care and resilience: A pilot case study within a public sector leadership and management post-graduate programme.* UFHRD Annual Conference 2017: Indigenous Research and Identity in HRD in a Globalized World. Lisbon, Portugal.

Scandura, T. A., & Lankau, M. J. (1996). Developing diverse leaders: A leader-member exchange approach. *The Leadership Quarterly*, 7(2): 243-263.

Schriesheim, C. A., & Neider, L. L. (1989). Leadership theory and development: The coming "new phase". *Leadership & Organization Development Journal*, 10(6): 17-26.

Shamir, B., & Eilam-Shamir, G. 2018. "What's your story?" A life-stories approach to authentic leadership development. In *Leadership now: Reflections on the legacy of Boas Shamir:* 51-76. Emerald Publishing Limited.

Springborg, C. 2012. Perceptual refinement: Art-based methods in managerial education. *Organizational Aesthetics*, 1(1): 116-137.

Sternberg, R. J. 2008. The WICS approach to leadership: Stories of leadership and the structures and processes that support them. *The Leadership Quarterly*, 19(3): 360-371.

Stogdill, R. M. 1974. *Handbook of leadership: A survey of theory and research.* New York: Free Press.

Strang, S. E., & Kuhnert, K. W. 2009. Personality and leadership developmental levels as predictors of leader performance. *The Leadership Quarterly*, 20(3): 421-433.

Sutherland, I. 2013. Arts-based methods in leadership development: Affording aesthetic workspaces, reflexivity and memories with momentum. *Management Learning*, 44(1): 25-43.

Tannenbaum, R., & Schmidt, W. H. (1973). How to choose a leadership pattern. *Harvard Business Review*, 51(3): 162-180.

Tannenbaum, R., Weschler, I., & Massarik, F. 2013. *Leadership and organization (RLE: organizations): A behavioural science approach.* Routledge.

Taylor, S. N., & Hood, J. N. 2011. It may not be what you think: Gender differences in predicting emotional and social competence. *Human Relations*, 64(5): 627-652.

Taylor, S. S., & Ladkin, D (2009. Understanding arts-based methods in managerial development. *Academy of Management Learning & Education*, 8(1): 55-69.

Tichy, N. M., & Cohen, E. 1997. *The leadership engine.* New York, NY: HarperCollins.

Uhl-Bien, M. 2006. Relational leadership theory: Exploring the social processes of leadership and organizing. *The Leadership Quarterly*, 17(6): 654-676. doi: https://doi-org.rlib.pace.edu/10.1016/j.leaqua.2006.10.007

Umble, K., Steffen, D., Porter, J., Miller, D., Hummer-McLaughlin, K., Lowman, A., & Zelt, S. 2005. The National Public Health Leadership Institute: Evaluation of a team-based approach to developing collaborative public health leaders. *American Journal of Public Health,* 95(4): 641-644.

Van Velsor, E., McCauley, C. D., & Ruderman, M. N. (Eds.). 2010. *The center for creative leadership handbook of leadership development:* 251-284 (3rd ed.). San Francisco, CA: Jossey-Bass.

Vince, R., & Pedler, M. 2018. Putting the contradictions back into leadership development. *Leadership & Organization Development Journal,* 39(7): 859-872.

Yammarino, F. J. 2000. Leadership skills: Introduction and overview. *Leadership Quarterly,* 11(1): 5-9.

Yammarino, F. 2013. Leadership: Past, present, and future. *Journal of Leadership & Organizational Studies,* 20(2): 149-155.

Yukl, G. A. 2013. *Leadership in organizations.* Pearson Education India.

SECTION V

Outcomes of Talent Management

39

TALENT ANALYTICS

Alec Levenson

Introduction

Talent analytics is in high demand and shows no sign of abating (Angrave et al., 2016; CIPD, 2013; Levenson, 2011; Levenson, 2018; Marler & Boudreau, 2017; Mercer 2020). The fact that handbook chapters are now being written about it is one indication of its importance (Fink & Sturman, 2017; this chapter). Yet that also begs the question of what is talent analytics, how durable is the current phenomenon, and what has to happen to increase both relevance and longevity?

If I take a cynical view, I could say that the "new" field of talent analytics is just old wine in new bottles (Levenson, 2014). And there is some truth to that. Social scientists have been using scientific methods and advanced analytics to examine organizational phenomena for over a century, dating back to the work of Frederick Taylor (1923) and the launch of the field of scientific management. Over that time, there has been a wide array of advancements in our understanding of how to measure and manage people and processes in organizations, coming from the fields of organization behavior and industrial-organizational psychology.

Yet even viewed in that skeptical light, there is a lot that is new about how talent analytics is led within organizations today. Up until recently, talent analytics was conducted largely outside of organizations. Researchers would often partner closely with organizations to get access to data, share insights, and sometimes even help drive change using collaborative and action research methods (Cummings & Worley, 2009; Krout, 1996; Lewin, 1946; Nadler, 1977; Noffke & Somekh, 2009; Reason & Bradbury, 2006; Shani et al., 2008; Zhang et al., 2015). Yet the overwhelming majority of the analytical work was defined and conducted by people working outside the organization. As recently as the early 2000s, among very large companies, the type that are most likely to have the resources and desire to conduct advanced talent analytics internally, less than one-fifth reported providing HR analytic support for business decisions or having a data-based talent strategy (Lawler et al., 2004).

Today, in contrast, the activities more and more are internally led. In fact, when people say "talent analytics" or "HR analytics" today, the default assumption is that the analysis is conducted internally (Baesons et al., 2017; CIPD, 2013; Fink, 2017; Rasmussen & Ulrich, 2015; Welbourne, 2015). This paradigm shift in less than two decades has major implications for how insights are derived, and how decision making and organizational effectiveness are impacted.

In this chapter, I highlight some key aspects of the current state of talent analytics and how it is applied in organizations. I do not provide a comprehensive review of current techniques. Instead, I focus on strengths and weaknesses of how talent analytics is being applied, with recommendations on areas for improvement.

DOI: 10.4324/9781315474687-39

I address three aspects of the state of talent analytics in organizations today. The first is where talent analytics has been historically and how it is currently evolving in most forward-looking organizations: finding better analysis and measurement for common HR issues such as turnover, recruiting, competencies, and identifying candidates for promotion. In each case, talent analytics is helping move the focus from efficiency to effectiveness of the processes. Yet despite that progress, significant gaps are still not being addressed.

The other two perspectives are my take on where talent analytics needs to evolve to address those gaps: more longitudinal data construction and analysis, and more systems analysis, including treating talent as more of a group and organizational phenomenon and not just individual phenomenon. And, in case that isn't enough, I end the chapter with a brief critique of general challenges of applying common statistical approaches that are perceived as cutting edge and best practice in organizational settings today.

A Brief History of Human Resources Analytics

HR analytics as a field started to emerge in the early 2000s (Lawler et al., 2004; Marler & Boudreau, 2017). Its beginnings cannot be traced to a specific article or study. Rather, it was around this time when a number of phenomena came together to coalesce around the concept of HR analytics as an important focus for organizations to pursue.

One trend was a longstanding call for HR to be more strategic and take more of an "outside/in" approach (Rasmussen & Ulrich, 2015), along with a continuing frustration that HR has had difficulty figuring out precisely how to do that (Levenson, 2018, summarizes the evidence gathered by Lawler et al., 2006, and by Lawler & Boudreau, 2009, 2012, 2015). At the same time, the continual digitization of information on people and HR processes that used to be stored in analog form has enabled greater measurement and availability of data for analysis. Simultaneously, the universal adoption of balanced scorecards as business management tools (Kaplan & Norton, 1996) has put pressure on HR leaders to produce metrics to populate the people quadrant of the scorecards, which has pushed them to seek the best metrics possible.

Today, the popularity of HR analytics is inescapable. Aside from the explosion in Internet searches on the topic (Levenson, 2011), another sure sign is the growing number of articles, including special issues of practitioner-oriented journals (Fink & Vickers, 2011; Huselid, 2018; Minbaeva, 2017; Workforce Solutions Review, 2014, 2015) and books (Bassi et al., 2010; Bhattacharyya, 2017; Fitz-enz, 2010; Guenole et al., 2017; Isson & Harriott, 2016; Levenson, 2015; Marr, 2018; Pease et al., 2013; Phillips & Phillips, 2015; Sesil, 2013; Smith, 2013; Soundararajan & Singh, 2017; Sundmark, 2018).

Talent analytics is a true bridge field, a partnership between scholars and practitioners, most clearly reflected in the techniques and frameworks that are derived from traditional social science (Levenson, 2018), by the contributions of researchers and scholars (Guenole et al., 2017), by the growth in companies building internal HR analytics capability including centers of expertise (Lawler et al., 2004; Levenson, 2011), and most recently by the arrival of the discipline's own "For Dummies" book (West, 2019).

Talent Analytics Defined

Today there are many terms used to describe analytics applied to people in organizations, including HR analytics, talent analytics, people analytics, and workforce analytics. For the most part, they all refer to the same thing. The original name – HR analytics – was first adopted because it described where the analytics was conducted, from within the HR function. More recently, talent analytics, people analytics, and workforce analytics have all been used, largely interchangeably, and have supplanted calling the discipline HR analytics.

My sense is that the original term has been largely cast aside for two interconnected reasons related to branding. First, calling something "HR" emphasizes the work of the function, which often has negative connotations about non-value-adding HR process. And calling it "talent," "people", or "workforce" emphasizes the human elements of the business, not the HR supporting function. Here I use the term talent analytics.

Talent analytics typically includes analyses of HR processes. The word "talent" when used in an organizational context often includes aspects of both headcount and skills. All three of those form separate but related parts of what talent analytics focuses on: HR processes, headcount (roles, people), and skills.

Consider the following, all of which are in the domain of talent analytics:

- When McKinsey talked about the "War for Talent" in the late 1990s, he was referring to having enough of the right people to manage the business effectively (Michaels et al., 2001).
- Competencies were developed to capture the importance of knowledge, skills, and abilities for job performance (Spencer & Spencer, 1993).
- HR processes focus on making sure there are enough people with the right profiles to fill the roles needed to get the work done, and making sure they are managed appropriately.

The distinction between skills, which are a characteristic of people, versus tasks, which are part of the work, is an important one. There is a long history in HR analytics of focusing on both jobs and people without a clear differentiation, so the vast majority of talent analytics today does not distinguish between skills versus tasks. Yet that difference is very important for two reasons.

First, someone may have a particular skill set, yet that does not ensure that the skills are applied on the job in the right place and the right time, that is, in the exact way needed to properly execute the job tasks. That distinction is important when the question asked is, "How can people's productivity be enhanced?" Talent analytics traditionally would ask if the right people are in the job, and look for fit or misfit between the individuals' competencies and the jobs' requirements. Yet having the required knowledge, skills, and ability does not ensure they are applied in the right place, at the right time, and in the right way. Broadening the inquiry to include application of the competencies in the job context is important: Do we see the skills being applied such that the job tasks are performed properly? Posed this way, the question of skill possession versus application is similar to Kirkpatrick's approach to evaluating the impacts of training, which differentiated between acquiring the skills versus successfully applying them on the job (Kirkpatrick, 1959).

Second, focusing only on people when thinking about job tasks can lead to too-narrow analysis that ignores the importance of job design in driving productivity (Parker & Wall, 1998). Traditional talent analytics takes the job as given. A more strategic reinterpretation of talent analytics broadens the scope to include how the work is designed, including which tasks are assigned to which jobs or roles (Levenson & Fink, 2017). This enables answering questions such as: Can organizational productivity and profitability be enhanced by reconfiguring which roles are responsible for which tasks?

A related point is the difference between talent versus talent management (TM). A large and growing field within HR in recent years is TM (Cascio & Boudreau, 2016; Collings et al., 2017; Collings & Mellahi, 2009; Lewis & Heckman, 2006; McDonnell et al., 2017; Schuler et al., 2011; Sparrow et al., 2014; Tarique & Schuler, 2010; Thunnisseen et al., 2013). TM as a discipline within companies is relatively new but also a bit of a catch-all for activities that used to be organized and managed separately within the HR function. It includes elements focused on headcount and the HR processes used to manage headcount, including workforce planning, recruiting, and succession planning. It can include performance management and rewards because of their importance for attracting and retaining talent. But it largely takes the job as given and doesn't address the competencies needed (Spencer & Spencer, 1993), including how they could be tweaked to improve the job design, matching of people to roles, the role of compensation in driving motivation and productivity, and how all these elements together contribute to organizational effectiveness.

The word "talent" universally is used to refer to *individual* level aspects of people and jobs. It is not used to talk about group (team) or organization level aspects. Yet, as I argue in the final part of this chapter, it should be expanded to include that broader focus. When people talk about the war for talent, TM, and so on, the ultimate objective is improved organizational performance. A more comprehensive systems view of talent, encompassing what the organization needs for strategic success, requires a broader view of talent that includes group and organization level capabilities (Levenson, 2016, 2018).

When people talk about talent or capability, it's typically framed as "what the person can do," meaning what they are capable of. Described that way, talent is different from performance. Yet competency models, which are a modern development designed to measure talent (Spencer & Spencer, 1993), embody elements of both skills and performance. The idea is that it is not sufficient to have knowledge, skills, and ability *in theory*; rather, someone should only be considered competent if they both have those and demonstrate them effectively on the job. The notion of talent combines both the ability to perform with the motivation and follow-through to perform (Lawler, 1973; Vroom, 1964).

All this means that elements of performance have to be included in any discussion about talent analytics, even though the focus on the discussion here is squarely on talent and not performance. This is especially the case for the discussion of team and organizational talent in the final section. We can talk about motivation to perform for the individuals on a team or in an organization, but there is no group-level analog to individual motivation at either the team or organizational levels. So talent at the team and organizations levels even more so includes demonstrated capability, which is a type of performance.

Analytics, Not Metrics

When the topic of analytics is raised in both academic and practitioner circles, the issue of metrics is never far behind. Practitioners often think that the objective of analytics is to come up with "the best metrics" that can be used to manage the workforce. Academics and researchers do not do enough to dispel that myth and educate practitioners on what really matters. As a consequence, there remains today too much of an obsession with HR and talent metrics instead of analytics (Levenson, 2015).

My assertion at first may seem odd, especially since the almost obsessive focus in business on strategic, operational, and financial metrics is not misguided. For the sake of brevity, let's call these three metrics "business" metrics. The reality is that business metrics are the foundation of how business is managed, not just as common practice but a true "best practice", which actually improves firm performance. Business metrics give leaders the clarity of knowing how the firm performs on key criteria such as quality, uptime, waste, customer service, cost-effectiveness, cash flow, return on equity, and so much more. The critical importance of these metrics underpins the almost universal popularity of Kaplan and Norton's (1996) balanced scorecard approach, which helps leaders narrow down which business metrics are most important.

Paradoxically, the success of the balanced scorecard in promoting a sharp focus on a limited set of business metrics has had an unintended consequence of promoting the use of HR and talent metrics without ensuring the metrics chosen are best suited for improving business performance (Levenson, 2015). The problem is that in order for a metric to be included in a scorecard and/or used for constant monitoring and management of people-related processes, it has to be measured consistently, accurately, reliably, and efficiently (i.e., with *care*) even while very few people-related metrics satisfy those criteria (Levenson, 2015). As a consequence, the quadrant of the balanced scorecard is typically populated with the most readily available people metrics, such as turnover and safety, even though they typically are marginally relevant for linking people processes to the needed improvements in strategy execution and organizational effectiveness (Boudreau & Ramstad, 2007; Levenson, 2015).

This challenge has been known and acknowledged for over two decades, starting with Kaplan and Norton's (1996) admission that the people-related quadrant failed to live up to its potential at the same time that the three business-metric-focused quadrants had been (and continue to be) widely used to improve managerial decision making:

> [W]hen it comes to specific measures concerning employee skills, strategic information availability, and organizational alignment, companies have devoted virtually no effort for measuring either the outcomes or the drivers of these capabilities. This gap is disappointing since one the most important goals for adopting the scorecard measurement and management framework is to promote the growth of individual and organizational capabilities... Frequently, the advocates for employee training and reskilling, for employee empowerment, for information systems, and for motivating the work force take these programs as ends in themselves. The programs are justified as being inherently virtuous, but not as means to help the organization accomplish specific long-run economic and customer objectives .... This gap leads to frustration: senior executives wonder how long they are expected to continue to make heavy investments in employees and systems without measurable outcomes, while human resource and information system advocates wonder why their efforts are not considered more central and more strategic to the organization. (1996: 144)

The fact that the issue has persisted and been called out by other authors both one decade (Boudreau & Ramstad, 2007) and two decades (Levenson, 2015) after Kaplan and Norton's admission is evidence that focusing on metrics first is not the right approach. The challenge is not that people metrics are irrelevant, because they absolutely are relevant. However, the problem lies in focusing on metrics first, before analytics. The solution is to do the right analysis first because the purpose of talent analytics is to yield better decisions (Fink & Sturman, 2017), after which certain metrics may emerge as both strategic and actionable (Levenson, 2015).

Current Practice and Contemporaneous Changes in How Talent Analytics Is Being Applied in Organizations

Fink and Sturman's (2017) chapter on HR metrics and talent analytics provides an excellent overview of the current state of talent analytics. I draw heavily from their discussion and provide some highlights here, and encourage you to read their contribution for greater details.

As noted by Fink and Sturman (2017), there has been over a century of work done in the social sciences, especially within the field of industrial-organizational psychology, developing and evaluating theories that can explain why people behave the way they do in organizations. A comprehensive review of that history would require an entire volume of books (at minimum), and attempting to provide even a cursory review is beyond the scope of this chapter. Instead, what follows is a sample of some of the more relevant theoretical perspectives that any talent analytics practitioner should be aware of as they apply analytics to reveal insights to improve managerial decision making. The list is far from exhaustive and should serve only as a suggested starting point.

Analysis of recruiting efficacy and turnover should incorporate guidance from the literatures on turnover (Hom & Kinicki, 2001; McClean et al., 2013; Steel, 2002; Trevor, 2001; Vandenberg & Nelson, 1999), employee fit and embeddedness (Cable & DeRue, 2002; Crossley et al., 2007; Major et al., 1995), and career success (Eby et al., 2003; Forret & Dougherty, 2004; Gunz & Heslin, 2005; Judge et al., 1999; Ng et al., 2005), among others. Assessments of performance management effectiveness at minimum need to acknowledge the challenges of measuring and managing performance (Campbell et al., 1970; Feldman, 1981; Kerr, 1975; Lawler, 2003, 2011; Lawler et al., 2012; Smith, 1976), the importance of goal setting in driving motivation and performance (Latham & Kinne, 1974; Latham & Yukl, 1975; Locke, 1968, 1978; Tolchinsky & King, 1980), and the critical role of job design (Blumberg & Pringle, 1982; Hackman & Lawler, 1971; Levenson, 2015; Parker & Wall, 1998) and compensation design (Bloom & Milkovich, 1998; Cadsby et al., 2007; Kahn & Sherer, 1990; Lawler, 1971; Lawler & Hackman, 1969) in driving engagement and performance. The literature on career development and internal labor markets (Arthur & Rousseau, 1996; Doeringer & Piore, 1971; Foulkes, 1980; Granrose & Portwood, 1987; Hall, 1976; Osterman, 1984) offer important guidance for analyses of feeder roles and succession planning in organizations.

Even more important is the guidance provided by the teams literature, which is one of the least appreciated by analytics professionals because most of the HR function and business leaders focus too much at the individual when trying to measure and diagnose the sources of organizational challenges (Levenson, 2014, 2015, 2018). The literature on teams is incredibly wide and deep, with innumerable insights that can and should be applied within talent analytics, of which very few are known within organizations.

Central topics include how well-functioning teams are more productive than collections of individuals; how to build and manage a true team where the members are interdependent with each other; the measures that predict team success, such as shared understanding, integration, trust, bounded membership, and stability; and the role of teams in high-performance work systems (Appelbaum & Batt, 1994; Balkundi & Harrison, 2006; Blasi & Kruse, 2006; Cappelli & Neumark, 2001; Cohen & Bailey, 1997; Cooke, 1994; DeRue et al., 2008; Gibson, 2001; Gilson et al., 2005; Hackman, 1987; Hackman, 1998; Hackman & Oldham, 1980; Hackman & Wageman, 2005; Ichniowski, Shaw, & Prennushi, 1997; Joshi & Knight, 2015; Kirkman et al., 2004; Maznevski & Chudoba, 2000; Millhiser et al., 2011; Ohland et al., 2012; Wageman, 2001; Wageman et al., 2005).

A third category of literature is a cautionary one: the link between HR practices and firm performance. The true insights from this literature are essential for talent analytics practitioners to understand because they are not widely promoted or understood; and because there are many sophisticated, statistically savvy consultants who do not know the science – or purposefully ignore it – and use it to sell dubious advice. The debate in the academic literature is whether specific HR and work practices "cause" firm performance, which is what the early contributions in the literature appeared to show (Arthur, 1994; Delaney & Huselid, 1996; Huselid, 1995), though later contributions called into question whether the evidence showed true causality (Huselid & Becker, 1996; Wall & Wood, 2005; Wright et al., 2005).

The most reasonable conclusion seems to be that HR practices can help contribute to improved performance, but that they don't necessarily exert a direct and independent impact on business results; rather, they are best used in combination with ways of organizing and managing the work that are mutually reinforcing (Combs et al., 2006; Gibson et al., 2007; Ichniowski et al., 1997; MacDuffie, 1995). This "it depends" type of conclusion highlights the importance of applying talent analytics with great attention paid to the context and complexity of determining what precisely "causes" the desired business outcomes.

Fink and Sturman (2017) draw a distinction between HR reporting and HR metrics on the one hand, and talent analytics on the other. HR reporting focuses on "counting" within HR (Cascio & Boudreau, 2011) and covers standard data, such as headcount, spans of control, compensation amounts, cost per hire, numbers of attendees in training programs, time to fill open positions, and HR expenses as a proportion of total company spending. HR metrics, in contrast, help evaluate how HR is performing relative to its objectives and can include benchmarking, balanced scorecards (Kaplan & Norton, 1996), the Kirkpatrick approach for training evaluation (Kirkpatrick, 1959), human resource accounting (Flamholtz, 1999), and utility analysis (Boudreau, 1983; Sturman, 2000).

According to Fink and Sturman (2017), talent analytics' main purpose is to enable better decision making. It often uses the measures that come from HR reporting and metrics, but does not stop there. A step of deeper analysis is needed to inform better decisions (Levenson, 2015). For example, analyzing the quality of hire from different sources can lead the HR recruiting team to shift resources and focus from certain universities and types of employee referral to others. Different vendors of executive education could have varied impacts in terms of leadership competency development and behaviors exhibited on the job. There always are multiple potential drivers of employee turnover; talent analytics uses multivariate statistics to evaluate the relative importance of the potential drivers against each other to determine which levers will best reduce turnover. And so on.

Fink and Sturman (2017) provide a very nice review of the kinds of issues addressed by a century of research and practice in industrial-organizational (IO) psychology. They note that talent analytics draws heavily from IO psychology when it comes to optimizing existing processes such as recruiting, performance management, leadership development, and training. At the same time, talent analytics, when it's done well, can effectively address big "what if" questions, such as "Where can we find the talent that we need to succeed?", "How can we reduce turnover of key personnel?", and "How can we enable teams to more effectively accomplish their goals?"

A very large segment of talent analytics both historically and in recent years has focused heavily on tactical analyses that are needed for the business to maintain operations. This includes a lot of basics such as workforce planning (Levenson & Fink, 2017), training evaluation (Kirkpatrick, 1959), comparing the usefulness of different performance rating systems (Ledford et al., 2016), measuring the usefulness of leadership development programs (Russon & Reinelt, 2004), examining ways to reduce time to fill and increase candidate quality for open positions (Boudreau & Ramstad, 2007), and more. These types of analyses are focused squarely on improving the efficiency and effectiveness of current HR systems and processes (Boudreau & Ramstad, 2007), with a lot of emphasis on HR program cost and ability to reach operational goals, such as the number of people participating in a program, completion of a process, and minimizing the time to fill an open position.

One step up in sophistication from those types of analyses are ones that address issues of employee behavior and managerial performance, including motivation/engagement, retention and productivity (Bloom & Milkovich, 1998; Blumberg & Pringle, 1982; Campbell et al., 1970; Casdby et al., 2007; Crossley et al., 2007; Hom & Kinicki, 2001; Lawler et al., 2012; Vandenbeg & Nelson, 1999). These analyses go beyond evaluating HR efficiency and instead focus primarily on HR effectiveness, with a potential to show a link to business impact (Boudreau & Ramstad, 2007). Examples of program and evaluation objectives include reducing turnover, increasing engagement, improving communication between supervisors and subordinates, and increasing teamwork and cross-functional collaboration.

Improving HR efficiency and effectiveness is very important to provide cost-effective HR and enable continuous improvement in HR operations in service of the business. Those activities all contribute to what I call keeping the lights on, even though they may not be essential for improving strategy execution and overall organizational effectiveness (Levenson, 2015, 2018). The challenge facing HR and talent professionals is how to prioritize what to evaluate and where change efforts should be concentrated. There are too many areas where some kind of improvement is possible, and usually desired, yet there is not enough time and organizational energy to tackle them all.

The problem is that most HR metrics evolved from accounting systems and weren't developed as part of a decision science (Boudreau & Ramstad, 2007). The data on employees that are collected in the normal course of doing business are designed to keep track of how many people work for the organization and how much they cost. Such data are very important starting points for understanding what happens with talent in the organization. However, way too often the analysis starts and ends with only those data, and doesn't consider questions that need other data for answers. This puts the data cart before the analytics horse, and removes the very critical step of first defining the strategic or operational issues to be addressed before launching the analytics (Levenson, 2015, 2018).

The rest of this section reviews specific examples of how talent analytics today is being commonly applied in organizations to improve insights.

Turnover Analytics

Headcount and turnover reports are fairly easy to produce, and many organizations devote a lot of time, energy, and organizational resources into creating them. They then convene meetings with managers across the organization to discuss the trends and determine what should happen. Unless turnover is extremely low, the usual assumption is that the people receiving the report should use it to work on lowering turnover, or at least ensuring it doesn't increase. A moderate increase in turnover can launch initiatives to reduce it.

Time and again when I talk to HR leaders and managers about the value of these reports, the typical response is indifference. In some cases they are viewed as helpful because they provide a platform for HR to have a meaningful conversation with the business. In other cases, the reports are produced because the business leaders want some kind of regular HR report and there isn't an alternative that would be easy to produce. In certain cases the reports help identify areas of potential concern about employee engagement that warrant addressing. Yet almost never are they capable of addressing any core questions about the barriers to improved business performance, and are therefore treated as more of a marginally useful exercise rather than a source of deep insights.

A more useful alternative to the typical turnover and headcount reports for talent analytics would focus on the drivers of attraction and retention for key employee groups. This requires going beyond headcount and using survey-based measures of intention to turnover to model the drivers of turnover, as is commonly done in the research literature (Hom & Kinicki, 2001; McClean et al., 2013; Steel, 2002; Trevor, 2001; Vandenberg & Nelson, 1999). Moving from turnover reports to turnover modeling is becoming more common in organizations but still has a long way to go before becoming standard practice.

Recruiting Analytics

Similarly, a lot of attention is paid to the efficiency and effectiveness of the recruiting function. Traditionally, evaluating recruiting amounted to evaluating the cost per hire and time to fill open positions, both efficiency measures (Boudreau & Ramstad, 2007). Talent analytics as commonly applied in organizations has broadened the focus to effectiveness by examining the quality of talent sourced by different recruiters and sources of applicants (social media advertising, employee referrals, college recruiting, and so on). Innovations include tracking people hired to see how they perform in terms of retention, performance ratings, and promotions.

Despite these gains, there is still additional room for improvement in recruiting analytics, especially around the issue of person-job fit, meaning how well the person is matched to the job and the organization (Cable & DeRue, 2002; Crossley et al., 2007; Major et al., 1995). The research literature is clear that matches are improved when realistic job previews are used so that candidates truly understand the work (McEvoy & Cascio, 1985; Premack & Wanous, 1985; Reilly et al., 1981). Full-fledged realistic job previews – trying out the job on a trial basis or experiencing parts of the job in a pre-hire simulation – are not economically feasible in most cases, but understanding the research can lead to a sharper focus on how accurately relevant experience is measured among job applicants.

Another area for improvement is greater integration with TM decisions that are made post-hire. Given the likelihood of a bad match – turnover in almost all roles is highest for new hires because of bad initial matches – one way to reduce organizational turnover that arises from the recruiting process is to do better mitigation once it is clear there is poor person-job fit. The vast majority of organizations treat hiring decisions as local problems: if someone is hired into a role that is a poor fit, it is viewed as the problem of the department that owns the budget for the role. Some organizations look more holistically at their talent across departments and actively work to find a different role if new hires appear to be good potential employees for other roles, even if they aren't for the role they were hired to do. If talent analytics is applied to measure the extent of post-hire assessment and mitigation of poor person-job fit, that in turn could help reduce new hire turnover.

A third area where talent analytics can help improve recruiting effectiveness is evaluating the validity of competency models, the topic of the next section.

Competency Analytics

Competency profiles identify the knowledge, skills, and ability needed to perform a role effectively, and can be constructed for any job. In the case of frontline (independent contributor) roles, the profiles are both helpful and usually accurate at identifying the skills needed for effective performance. Perhaps because of their accuracy and usefulness for non-managerial roles (Hollenbeck & McCall, 2003; Spreitzer et al., 1993), and the common practice of tying compensation to skills (Ledford et al., 2008; Ledford & Heneman, 2011), competency models for frontline roles do not appear to garner a lot of attention by people doing talent analytics in organizations. The lack of analysis may imply general satisfaction with their performance.

In the case of managerial roles, in contrast, competency models both get a lot more attention and are much less accurate and useful (Levenson et al., 2006), which may be why they get so much attention. There is an entire industry of pundits and leadership experts who have no shortage of the latest ideas on how to be a great (or at least effective) leader. Understanding why managerial competency models are so prominent, and the attention of so much analysis, requires some discussion of how they are constructed, what they measure, and what they fail to measure.

Competency models are constructed using a measurable and intuitively appealing way. For the role under consideration, two groups are constructed: high-performers and average to low performers. The observable behaviors of both groups are measured and compared. Behaviors exhibited more often by the higher performing group are classified as targets (components) of the competency model. The skills needed to exhibit those behaviors are then included in the model (Spencer & Spencer, 1983).

For frontline roles, this process leads to clear and identifiable tasks that typically are directly linked to better job performance. For example, a more competent machine operator will do certain tasks better or more often than one who is less competent, and the classification process identifies those tasks. Measuring whether the machine is being operated effectively is typically straightforward. Combining the two sets of measurements together yields the competency model with behaviors that are directly tied to better performance.

For managerial jobs, in contrast, there are two fundamental problem: defining good performance and measuring the behaviors that matter. Identifying good performance is inherently difficult because there is very little that managers do themselves to directly impact their group's objectives. That is why there is such strong appeal of measuring observed managerial behaviors, such as how they communicate, set direction, provide feedback, coach, and so on – the typical domains of most managerial competency models. We all know that such behaviors *should* help their teams to be effective, so the benefits of measuring differences in exhibited behaviors seems intuitively obvious.

Yet there is a large domain of managerial behaviors that are important for performance and which are excluded from managerial competency models (Hollenbeck & McCall, 2003). For example, decision making quality, or judgement, is essential for good performance, but also is not measurable by observing how the managers act – the basis for standard competency model creation and measurement.

Similarly, competency model measurement typically focuses on how often or consistently managers exhibit the behaviors. However, effective performance often requires applying specific behaviors in the right place at the right time. This means that a manager who, for example, is rated as an effective communicator nonetheless could fail in their duties if they don't choose the right way to communicate in one specific instance. Thus, the failure to do a particular behavior for one day throughout the entire year could hurt their performance even while they receive high marks in the annual competency evaluation by demonstrating good communication the other 364 days of the year.

When it comes to analysis of managerial competency models, talent analytics professionals spend a lot of time trying to validate their usefulness. Yet they are severely handicapped by both the measurement issues discussed above and by cultural bias. It is common to test the validity of a model by looking to see whether people identified as highly competent succeed, either via performance ratings or getting promoted to higher level roles. Yet because the models focus on observed behaviors and not actual performance, they can reinforce biases that push people to make sure someone fits the culture.

For example, many organizations can be characterized as having very distinct cultures, with descriptors such as hard driving, analytical, inclusive, and so on. Managerial competency models typically will include behaviors consistent with those cultural attributes. When early-career managers are selected and promoted on the basis of those attributes, they succeed in part because their behaviors reinforce the prevailing culture, which in turn appears to validate the competency models' focus on those attributes. This is a validation of sorts, but quite limited in terms of value to the organization.

The fundamental question in this case is whether the organization needs to reinforce its strengths or shore up its weaknesses. If the most pressing business issue is doing the same thing in the same ways, only better, then reinforcing dominant cultural norms and behaviors is the right focus of the managerial competency model. In contrast, if there are significant concerns about institutional weaknesses arising from the dominant culture – group think, lack of diversity of thought and managerial approaches – then focusing the managerial competency model on prevailing cultural norms and behaviors could under-mine strategy execution and organizational effectiveness.

Talent Potential Analytics

Another TM area that receives a lot of attention in organizations is the evaluation of potential, espe-cially for promotion to higher level roles.

The challenge for organizations is accuracy of the evaluation. Similar to the challenges of successful recruiting, the ability to predict how well someone will perform in a new role depends to a great extent on how similar the tasks of the new role are to the previous role: the more similar, the greater the prediction accuracy (McCauley et al., 1994; Spreitzer et al., 1997). This means that there should be relatively straight-forward measurements applied to evaluating the accuracy of potential ratings. Yet, as far as I can tell, very little analytics are applied to address potential rating accuracy in the vast majority of cases.

The reasons for the lack of attention I believe are twofold. First, formal succession management in many companies is a relatively new process, so typically there is not a long track record of predicting potential and seeing how those predictions pan out. Having people go through the process of system-atically reviewing all managers at each level of the hierarchy and assign potential ratings is more than many organizations are willing to sign up for. So in those cases where there is a consistent succession management process, people in talent analytics roles may shy away from doing systematic evaluation for fear of calling attention to deficiencies in the process and undermining support for an HR process that is being followed systematically.

Second, discussions about who will take on future leadership roles are heavily influenced by organ-izational politics. When considering the range of various HR programs and processes that could be addressed by talent analytics, addressing the problems with potential ratings focuses attention on the people doing the ratings: leaders evaluating others who are beneath them in the hierarchy. Calling attention to the biases and mistakes made during a rating process always has the potential for creating conflict in the organization, including challenges to the legitimacy of the analytics conducted to iden-tify those mistakes. When the people being challenged are leaders up and down the hierarchy, the polit-ical risk is even greater. Consequently, talent analytics professionals may choose to focus their attention elsewhere. So while the potential for improving ratings processes exists, strong cultural forces both within the HR function and among the organizational leadership often lead to talent analytics being focused elsewhere.

Future Evolution #1: The Missing Temporal and Team Dimensions
of Talent Analytics and Data Construction

HR data systems are built around the need to count and keep track of people working for the organ-ization (Boudreau & Ramstad, 2007). They are designed to provide a current snapshot of the organiza-tion that focuses on individuals and roles. Historical data is not preserved in an easy to access format. And the data that is collected systematically focuses on counting measures and jobs in isolation: how many people there are in a role; role titles without detailed job descriptions; spans of control; etc. Consequently, it is usually difficult at best to do detailed longitudinal analysis of people's careers, their performance, and the teams they worked in (Fink & Sturman, 2017).

Yet the longitudinal and team views are precisely what is needed for accurate analysis of many important organizational issues. Consider the question of careers (Arthur & Rousseau, 1996; Eby et al., 2003; Forret & Dougherty, 2004). Being able to accurately describe and promote careers is essential for an organization to clearly articulate the employee value proposition of joining and staying. Yet it is very difficult to construct accurate descriptions of career progression from standard enterprise data warehouses. The focus of such systems is real time reporting of current information. Where historical information is preserved, it's usually only kept active for one or two years prior; anything older is purged from the system either entirely (destroyed) or stored in backup media that are not easily accessible (tapes, disks, drives). The consequence in either case is that is it not possible to call up the entire work history for anyone with tenure longer than a year or two.

In some rare cases, I have come across HR analytics groups that recognize the value of preserving the historical information and have found solutions that work. The most reliable and accessible way for them to do so is to create their own year-by-year "snapshots" of the historical data for the entire organization and store them in separate computer systems from the original data warehouse, where they can be accessed on demand easily by the HR analytics group. This requires setting up an entirely different data warehouse structure than the corporate default, along with the personnel capable of preserving and working with it. To do this means investing a great deal of money, people and time to build and maintain the bespoke system.

A very recent development in the world of IT and data warehousing is the notion of a "data lake" which removes the barriers towards accessing historical data that otherwise would sit in hard-to-access archival systems and data siloes (Stein & Morrison, 2014). HR analytics groups fortunate enough to have access to such data lakes should face fewer barriers to conducting true longitudinal analysis. However, access to the data alone is only one part of the challenge.

Even in cases where the historical HR data is preserved, constructing accurate pictures of careers is a nontrivial task. Job titles often do not accurately or fully reflect the true roles and responsibilities. A truly accurate, task-based, and company-wide description of careers is possible only in cases where there are meticulously constructed job family taxonomies that have been in place for a decade or longer. The overwhelming majority of companies do not have such taxonomies at all, while the ones that do typically implemented them only recently. Despite these challenges, it is not impossible to construct reasonably accurate pictures of how careers have evolved in the past at a company; however, doing so requires a great deal of time and effort.

An entirely different problem is the challenge of constructing accurate descriptions of teams: who was on them, who they reported to, how long they existed, what they did, and what was their performance (Cohen & Bailey, 1997). Performance management systems are built on the premise that individual performance is what needs to be measured, monitored, and rewarded. This is the case because conceptually, we want to hold people accountable for their contributions to the organization. Moreover, logistically, we can only reward someone for their contribution if we can tie their compensation to some kind of performance rating. These two reasons are why it is only individual performance that is systematically evaluated and recorded in HR information systems (HRIS).

Yet performance is not an individual level phenomenon. Team performance depends on the contributions of each person, and, except in very rare circumstances, can only be evaluated in aggregate (Cohen & Bailey 1997). It's impossible to determine if a team was successful based on the individual performance ratings because team members often get individual ratings that are substantially different than the team's actual performance. Sometimes that is because they did what they could and yet the team still did not succeed. Since the true causes of team success are often hard to pin down, there is a reluctance to hold individual team members accountable unless there is clear evidence linking their contribution – or lack thereof – directly to the team's performance.

Another reason why individual performance ratings deviate from team performance is because of multiple team membership (Cohen & Bailey, 1997). People often are on many different teams, so their contribution to any one team has only a small impact on their individual performance rating. And people who are on only one team typically have individual job duties unrelated to the team's perform-ance; if they perform those duties effectively that helps improve their individual performance rating even if the team falls far short of meeting its performance objectives.

Team performance usually is the ultimate objective for organizations to succeed in executing the strategy and achieving operational goals. In order for talent analytics to best contribute to organiza-tional success, the focus ultimately needs to be on team performance, not individual performance because tracking individual performance and performance ratings is never sufficient to determine a team's success (Levenson, 2015). That kind of analysis requires detailed information on not just the team's performance but also its composition: who was on the team at different points in time, and who was responsible for which aspects of the team's processes.

In an ideal world, we would have detailed information on all teams: their goals, composition, per-formance against the goals, how effectively they were led, the actions of individual team members, and much more. Collecting all of that data consistently for all teams is cost prohibitive, and of necessity has to be limited to deep-dive, one-off analyses focused on diagnosing the performance of specific teams or groups of teams doing similar work (like sales teams, R&D teams, customer service teams). Certain information can and should be collected systematically, such as which teams exist, who is on them, when members join and leave, who the members report to (both the team leader(s) and their individual managers) and similar team demographics, which can be gathered and stored more cost effectively. Yet even this basic information is typically not collected systematically and certainly not historically.

The lack of basic historical team demographic information makes the construction of accurate career paths and models of individual and team performance very difficult. Just because someone might have been in certain roles over time, knowing the job title does not provide enough infor-mation to determine what they did: which teams they were on, how they contributed, and how the teams performed. So whatever conclusions can be reached based on the data that can be constructed on past work experience within the organization, it is spotty at best and usually has major holes that need to be shored up. More systematic collection of team participation data would go a long ways toward plugging those holes.

Those holes can create challenges when attempting to evaluate leader or manager effectiveness. Evaluations of managerial effectiveness often focus on information such as 360 evaluations of behaviors against a managerial competency model, even though those evaluations typically fall short of deter-mining how a leader actually performs (Levenson et al., 2006). Their performance will be judged on the basis of how their teams performed, but not necessarily on their ability to make a difference in improving the performance of the team. So a manager who is put in charge of turning around a team or site with bad performance can suffer less-than-top ratings even if they do a great job of closing the per-formance gap, until the team's performance recovers to the point where it meets or exceeds its goals, the manager can suffer a negative halo effect. Conversely, an adequate manager who is fortunate to be trans-ferred into a new role, taking over from an excellent manager who left behind a well-developed team, can be the beneficiary of a positive halo effect, getting undeserved credit for the team's performance.

The challenge is that team performance is never achieved through managerial behaviors alone, even when the measured behaviors are important inputs into team success: communication, goal setting, coaching, etc. (Cohen & Bailey, 1997). In the same way that accurate accounting of team member-ship and team performance is essential for understanding individual careers and a team member's contributions to organizational success, that same information is needed for accurate modeling and measuring of managerial effectiveness and performance. In the absence of such data it is very hard to know whether the organization's talent is contributing in meaningful ways. Who someone "is" as an employee or leader today can only really be effectively described by knowing their detailed history, which is a longitudinal description.

From a practical standpoint, there are many more ways in which longitudinal data are essential for talent analytics to take the next step in its evolution. Anytime a reorganization changes reporting lines, historical data are needed to understand team membership, who reported to whom, and the names used for specific roles, teams, and business units. Changes in job design can make job and career histories difficult to analyze unless historical job descriptions and other key information is preserved. Evaluating the impact of training programs or leadership development programs is much more effective when done over time.

Fink and Sturman (2017) address a number of reasons why longitudinal data can be challenging to collect and preserve, including privacy concerns and the challenges of constructing and storing longitudinal data. Their observations are on target, but that does not lessen the importance of trying to do so. Historical data can greatly increase the depth of understanding around people's careers, and both team and organizational performance.

Future Evolution #2: Talent as Group and Organizational Capability

Measuring and improving team and group performance is not possible by focusing only on individual performance of the team or group members, which was discussed in detail in the previous section. There is a similar problem when it comes to the entire way we think about talent – if what you care about ultimately is team or organizational performance. Everyone conceives of talent as an individual-level phenomenon, synonymous with the competencies (knowledge, skills, and ability) needed to perform the work. Yet in the same way that group-level performance is not equal to the sum of individual performance, the same holds for group-level talent: we need a different way of thinking about talent as both a group-level and organization-level capability, in addition to the traditional individual-level capability (Levenson, 2016, 2018).

To understand what "talent" really means, a systems lens is needed. The systems approach directly addresses the complexity of how business results are actually achieved. In the systems view, talent is much more than individual competencies or skills. I think that "capability" is a better label because it applies equally well at the individual, team, and organizational levels; here I will use talent and capability interchangeably.

Individual capability is a stand-in for what someone brings to the table to get the job done: the competencies (knowledge, skills, and abilities) that enable them to do the work they are responsible for. Team capability is similar but also quite distinct. Team capabilities include individual competencies plus team-level phenomena such as having a shared understanding of the team's goals and how to accomplish them; trust among the team members that they can rely on each other; integration of the team member's planning and tasks; and more. In this view, a team's capability is more than the stock of technical knowledge about how to do each job on the team; it also includes the collective knowledge and alignment among the team members about how to work effectively as a team (Levenson, 2015).

Organizational capability is how the work of the enterprise is executed, across all roles and processes, and is much more than just the sum of individual capabilities of the people, and even all the teams. It includes issues around silo decision making, cross-functional collaboration, and alignment of structures, processes and people from beginning to end of the production cycle. For example, innovation is one type of organizational capability. In order to have innovation, you need the building blocks provided by the role competencies of engineers, software programmers, and/or scientific researchers. You also need the teams of engineers, software programmers, and researchers to do their collective jobs and integrate appropriately with all other parts of the organization. Organizational innovation is never accomplished solely through the individual contributions of people in those roles. We also need the right mix and alignment of organization design, culture, and processes.

The glue that holds organizational performance together is interdependencies among roles (Cohen & Bailey, 1997). Talent is not just what people do on their own, in total isolation from everyone else in the organization; it's also how they interface and integrate their work as needed to accomplish the organizational objectives. The interdependencies among roles are created by those integration points.

Because integration is a two-way street, requiring coordinated effort with other people, someone who shirks their responsibilities can put in a minimal effort to make it appear they are trying to effectively integrate when the reality couldn't be more different. No matter what a job description says, people can only focus on accomplishing so many objectives. So they prioritize and do not always view integrating their work with other people and teams as a top priority. Consequently, organizational performance suffers from not enough coordination and collaboration. Yet because they usually accomplish the majority of the other objectives on their plates, they nonetheless can receive satisfactory or even high-performance ratings. The organizational (talent) challenge is how to get them to do every single part of their job effectively, not just most of their responsibilities.

To evaluate and improve organizational capability, the first step for talent analytics is to assess the organization's strategy and competitive advantage. Competitive advantage comes first because it's easy to lose sight of the ultimate business objectives (Levenson, 2015, 2018), many of which often are at odds with each other (cost versus quality, cost versus customer service). The competitive advantage challenge is identifying which business processes and parts of the organization are more deserving of attention and additional resources. Every leader's job would be easier if they were given more resources, so they all can legitimately stake a claim for greater spending on their people. Yet only certain business processes, roles, and parts of the organization contribute more directly to competitive advantage, strategically speaking, those parts that have priority for incremental investment.

For example, large consumer products companies (food, beauty products, toiletries, household cleaning items, etc.) derive their competitive advantage from branding and distribution. They make their money through economies of scale in creating national brands and having very large distribution systems that can efficiently move extremely high volumes of products to all corners of an economy. They have R&D and customer service functions, yet those functions are not a primary source of competitive advantage. They need efficient manufacturing, but world class manufacturing is not central to their strategic success. In contrast, pharmaceuticals or microprocessors companies require greater care and quality control (than consumer products) to ensure their products are not contaminated by the manufacturing processes. World class manufacturing processes are a source of competitive advantage in pharmaceuticals and microprocessors, but not in consumer goods.

Once you know the details of the organizational capability you're trying to build and maintain, and where improvements are most needed, the next step for talent analytics is to analyze the source of the gaps (Levenson, 2015, 2018). Where is the organization design supportive of the organization capability? Where is there silo behavior that undermines strategy execution? What role does culture play in enabling behaviors that support the strategic objectives, and where does it work at cross purposes? Prioritizing business needs based on competitive advantage needs provides guidance on where talent development efforts should be concentrated at both the organizational and individual levels. The objective of talent analytics should be to come up with that guidance.

The first two steps that should be deployed when doing talent analytics are identifying competitive advantage challenges first and then the organizational factors that underlie them (Levenson, 2015, 2018). Those two steps should be taken before looking at issues within specific teams or jobs because many employee behavior and motivation challenges arise at least partly from imperfections in the organization or team design.

A Closing Caution on Talent Analytics

In addition to the challenges facing the successful application of talent analytics outlined in this chapter, there are additional risks that arise from nuances of accurately measuring and evaluating social and psychological phenomena in organizations.

One category of risks comes from not understanding issues such as effect sizes, how much variance is explained by an analysis, and the importance of looking for unexplained factors that weren't part of an analysis. A second issue is ignoring the criticality of qualitative analysis, and the proper approaches needed to assess phenomena that occur at the organizational, business unit, or function levels, where the sample size is generated by only one or a handful of unique observations.

In the same way that published scientific research suffers from a bias towards publishing statistically significant results, and de-emphasizes the practical significance of the findings, that same phenomenon exists for analyses done by talent analytics professionals. The presence of large numbers of industrial-organizational psychologists and the growing number of data scientists, both within organizations and in consulting, helps to mitigate that bias, because such professionals can help with proper structuring and interpretation of statistical analyses. Yet the temptation is always there to cut corners and highlight statistically significant results that can help show that HR is helping to promote better data-based decision making, even though the quality of decision making may not be improved. And only the largest companies can afford to employ full-time the services of such highly trained professionals, leaving large capability gaps among the vast majority of organizations.

The problem of variance explained is a bigger issue because even among the statistically well-trained there is a tendency to forget that the objective in business is not just to understand how results are produced on average, but how to improve results across the board. This requires the ability to look for evidence that can be both contradictory yet correct at the same time. For example, consider an analysis that "proves" that hiring new college graduates has a greater success rate at producing senior executives 10–20 years later. Such an analysis would support ensuring that at least some portion of early-career management roles are staffed by new college graduates.

Taken to the (wrong) logical conclusion, one might conclude that therefore *only* new college graduates should be hired. Yet the vast majority of companies I've worked with over the past two decades would immediately reject such a conclusion because it has no face validity. The reason is because there are many more considerations at stake than just the production of future senior executives. Lower-level managerial roles serve many additional purposes, and the first and most important priority is managing the day-to-day processes of the organization. Producing future senior executives is also important, but cannot be used to overrule meeting the immediate business process management objectives.

Consequently, almost all organizations employ a mix of people with very different profiles, including new college graduates working alongside experienced managers who either are promoted from the ranks of the frontline workers (and thus may have no college education at all) or who are career middle managers, meaning they lack either the aptitude or desire to advance to upper level management. The most "plain vanilla" statistical models would reject employing all three types of managers both side-by-side. Yet that mix nonetheless is precisely what the organization needs to meet the competing, and often contradictory objectives, of maximizing current performance while providing the space for future managers to develop on the job – and make mistakes that everyone knows will hurt current performance.

An even bigger risk comes from a lack of sophistication in doing qualitative analysis (Levenson, 2015) and understanding the limitations of standard statistical analysis such as regression and anova. These are issues that help separate the IO psychologists and similar classically trained social scientists from the rapidly growing ranks of data scientists.

Regarding qualitative analysis, data scientists and those not trained in the techniques of organizational development usually do not understand its centrality for addressing most important organizational issues. Stakeholder interviews and qualitative assessments of organizational alignment, culture, cross-functional collaboration, and more, are essential tools for organizational diagnosis, yet are de-emphasized, if mentioned at all, in most approaches that embrace an "analytics" title (Levenson, 2015). It often seems that an entire class of extremely well trained statisticians and data analysis experts has no real understanding that interviews can produce more reliable information (data) than any poorly-crafted survey that is mistakenly given credit for producing "objective" data.

The other blind spot exhibited by most statistically oriented people working in talent analytics is a lack of understanding about levels of analysis issues, especially when the focus is the entire organization or a business unit or function. Because there is only one "observation" (unique entity generating the observed outcomes and data), it is impossible to apply classical statistics because of the small sample problem: when the sample size is one, there is no mean to be calculated, no standard deviation, and certainly no multivariate techniques (regression, anova, etc.) to be applied. Yet rather than embrace the techniques needed in such situations – qualitative and case study analysis – the overwhelming majority of talent analytics practitioners are much more likely to walk away from the problem and look for simpler problems where data is already available to which they can apply their toolkit of stats techniques.

In truth there are many more cautionary notes to be made about the blind application of data science and analytics in organizational settings, and the blind spots these create among people who have decided to work within the field of talent analytics. Broadly speaking, the problem lies in a reluctance or inability to take a step back from the data and analysis and ask, "what else could be going on here?... what else could be driving the behaviors we're seeing?... what other ways of looking at the situation can help provide the business leaders the insights they need for better decision making?"

The last example of this I want to call out is an overreliance on the insights that come from applying classical statistical analysis in the interest of identifying which differences matter in organizational settings. In particular, the importance of paying attention to outliers – rather than ignoring them or trying to explain them away because they don't fit the neat story the analyst wants to tell based on their carefully constructed statistical model.

This problem can be called the risks of ignoring the tails of the distribution. In the context of applying regression, anova, and other multivariate models, this means acknowledging that, in essence, such models compare mean differences in subgroups, and ignore dispersion around the mean. In doing so, very incorrect conclusions can be reached, such as "people with blue hair are more productive working in this job than are people with orange hair." Such a statement virtually always comes from an analysis of mean differences between the two groups; so long as there is a large enough difference in the means, the conclusion is reached that makes it appear that *all* members of the more-productive group (blue hair) have superior performance compared to *all* members of the other group (orange hair).

Yet in all virtually cases known to social science, the distributions of performance – or whatever the outcome measure in question is – across the two groups are overlapping; meaning that there are many orange haired people who are more productive than most blue haired people, and many blue haired people are less productive than most orange haired people. Thus it is simultaneously true that *on average* one group is more productive than the other, yet biasing hiring and promotion policies towards the apparently more productive group would set the organization up for rejecting superstar orange haired employees who could make all the difference in meeting strategic, operational, and financial goals that enable winning in the marketplace; and such policies would be biased towards hiring and retaining lower-productivity blue haired employees.

The bottom line is that no analytical technique should be taken at face value without questioning the value of the insights provided, and whether the real needs of the business are being served by the analysis. If you take anything away from this discussion of talent analytics, that is the most crucial point. Sometimes the challenges arise from focusing too much on the individual level, and not enough on the team and organizational levels. Sometimes the stumbling block is not doing longitudinal analysis. And sometimes the problem lies in being too much of a statistician, and not using one's other observational senses: talking to stakeholders, getting a "feel" for what is driving behavior even if it can't be proven with "objective" data, and looking at how everything comes together at a systems level. In all cases, the solution requires being critical and questioning the analysis to ensure the insights are how they seem, and that they address the fundamental challenges that the business needs solved.

References

Angrave, D., Charlwood, A., Kirkpatrick, I., Lawrence, M., & Stuart, M. 2016. HR and analytics: Why HR is set to fail the big data challenge. *Human Resource Management Journal*, 26(1): 1-11.

Applebaum, E., & Batt, R. 1994. *The new American workplace: Transforming work systems in the United States.* Ithaca, NY: ILR Press.

Arthur, J. B. 1994. Effects of human resource systems on manufacturing performance and turnover. *Academy of Management Journal*, 37(3): 670-687.

Arthur, M. B., & Rousseau, D. M. 1996. *The boundaryless career,* New York: Oxford University Press.

Baesons, B., De Winne, S., & Sels, L. 2017. Is your company ready for HR analytics? *Sloan Management Review,* 58(2): 20-21.

Balkundi, P. & Harrison, D. A. 2006. Ties, leaders, and time in teams: Strong inference about network structure's effects on team viability and performance. *Academy of Management Journal,* 49(1): 49-68.

Bassi, L., Carpenter, R., & McMurrer, D. 2010. *HR analytics handbook: Report of the state of knowledge,* Amsterdam: Reed Business.

Bhattacharyya, D. K. 2017. *HR analytics: Understanding theories and applications,* New Delhi: Sage Publications India Pvt. Ltd.

Blasi, J., & Kruse, D. 2006. U.S. high-performance work practices at century's end. *Industrial Relations,* 45: 4, 547-578.

Bloom, M., & Milkovich, G. T. 1998. Relationships among risk, incentive pay, and organizational performance. *Academy of Management Journal,* 41(3): 283-297.

Blumberg, M., & Pringle, C. D. 1982. The missing opportunity in organizational research: some implications for a theory of work performance. *Academy of Management Review,* 7(4): 560-569.

Boudreau, J. W. 1983. Economic considerations in estimating the utility of human resource productivity improvements. *Personnel Psychology,* 36: 551-557.

Boudreau, J. W., & Ramstad, P. M. 2007. *Beyond HR: The new science of human capital.* Boston, MA: Harvard Business School Press.

Cable, D. M., & DeRue, D. S. 2002. The convergent and discriminant validity of subjective fit perceptions. *Journal of Applied Psychology,* 87(5): 875-884.

Cadsby, C. B., Song, F., & Tapon, F. 2007. Sorting and incentive effects of pay for performance: An experimental investigation. *Academy of Management Journal,* 50(2): 387-405.

Campbell, J. P., Dunnette, M. D., Lawler, E. E., & Weick, K. 1970. *Managerial behavior, performance, and effectiveness,* New York: McGraw-Hill.

Cappelli, P., & Neumark, D. 2001. Do "high-performance" work practices improve establishment-level outcomes? *Industrial and Labor Relations Review,* 54(4): 737-775.

Cascio, W. & Boudreau, J. 2011. *Investing in People: Financial Impact of Human Resource Initiatives* (2nd ed.). Pearson Education Inc.

Cascio, W. F. & Boudreau, J. W. 2016. The search for global competence: From international HR to talent management. *Journal of World Business,* 51(1): 103-114.

CIPD. 2013. *Talent analytics and big data – The challenge for HR.* London: Chartered Institute for Personnel and Development.

Cohen, S., & Bailey, D. E. 1997. What makes teams work: Group effectiveness research from the shop floor to the executive suite. *Journal of Management,* 23(3): 239-290.

Collings, D. G., & Mellahi, K. 2009. Strategic talent management: A review and research agenda. *Human Resource Management Review,* 19: 304-313.

Collings, D. G., Mellahi, K., & Cascio, W. F. 2017. *The Oxford handbook of talent management.* Oxford, UK: Oxford University Press.

Combs, J., Liu, Y., Hall, A., & Ketchen, D. 2006. How much do high-performance work practices matter? A meta-analysis of their effects on organizational performance. *Personnel Psychology,* 59: 501-528.

Cooke, W. 1994. Employee participation programs, group-based incentives, and company performance. *Industrial and Labor Relations Review,* 47: 4, 594-609.

Crossley, C. D., Bennett, R. J., Jex, S. M., & Burnfield, J. L. 2007. Development of a global measure of job embeddedness and integration into a traditional model of voluntary turnover. *Journal of Applied Psychology,* 92(4): 1031-1042.

Cummings, T. G., & Worley, C. G. 2009. *Organization development and change.* Independence, KY: Cengage Learning.

Delaney, J. T., & Huselid, M. A. 1996. The impact of human resource management practices on perceptions of organizational performance. *Academy of Management Journal,* 39(4): 949-969.

DeRue, D. S., Hollenbeck, J. R., Johnson, M. D., Ilgen, D. R., & Jundt, D. K. 2008. How different team downsizing approaches influence team-level adaptation and performance. *Academy of Management Journal,* 51(1): 182-196.

Doeringer, P. B., & Piore, M. J. 1971. *Internal labor markets and manpower analysis.* Lexington, MA: Heath.

Eby, L. T., Butts, M., & Lockwood, A. 2003. Predictors of success in the era of the boundaryless career. *Journal of Organizational Behavior,* 24(6): 689-708.

Feldman, J. M. 1981. Beyond attribution theory: cognitive processes in performance appraisal, *Journal of Applied Psychology,* 66(2): 127-148.

Fink, A. A. 2017. Getting results with talent analytics. *People & Strategy,* 40(3): 36-40.

Fink, A. A., & Sturman, M. C. 2017. HR Metrics. In D. Collings, K. Mellahi, & W. Cascio (Eds.), *The Oxford handbook of talent management:* 375-396. New York: Oxford University Press.

Fink, A. A., & Vickers, M. 2011. Fresh approaches to HR analytics. *People & Strategy,* 34(2): 3.

Fitz-enz, J. 2010. *The new HR analytics: Predicting the economic value of your company's human capital investments.* New York: American Management Association.

Flamholtz, E. G. 1999. *Human resource accounting: advances in methods and applications* (3rd ed.). New York: Spring Science+Business Media.

Forret, M. L., & Dougherty, T. W. 2004. Networking behaviors and career outcomes: differences for men and women? *Journal of Organizational Behavior,* 25(3): 419-437.

Foulkes, F. K. 1980. *Personnel policies in large nonunion companies,* Englewood Cliffs, NJ: Prentice-Hall.

Gibson, C. B. 2001. Me and us: Differential relationships among goal-setting training, efficacy and effectiveness at the individual and team level. *Journal of Organizational Behavior,* 22(7): 789-808.

Gilson, L. L., Mathieu, J. E., Shalley, C. E., & Ruddy, T. M. 2005. Creativity and standardization: Complementary or conflicting drivers of team effectiveness? *Academy of Management Journal,* 48(3): 521-531.

Granrose, C. S., & Portwood, J. D. 1987. Matching individual career plans and organizational career management. *Academy of Management Journal,* 30(4): 699-720.

Guenole, N., Ferrar, J., & Feinzig, S. 2017. *The power of people: How successful organizations use workforce analytics to improve business performance.* New York: Pearson FT Press.

Gunz, H. P., & Heslin, P. A. 2005. Reconceptualizing career success. *Journal of Organizational Behavior,* 26: 105-111.

Hackman, J. R. 1987. The design of work teams. In J. Lorsch (Ed.), *Handbook of organizational behavior:* 315-342. Englewood Cliffs, NJ: Prentice-Hall.

Hackman, J. R. 1998. Why teams don't work. In R. S. Tindale (Ed.), *Theory and research on small groups:* 245-267. New York: Plenum.

Hackman, J. R., & Lawler, E. E. 1971. Employee reactions to job characteristics. *Journal of Applied Psychology,* 56: 259-286.

Hackman, J. R., & Oldham, G. R. 1980. *Work redesign.* Reading, MA: Addison-Wesley.

Hackman, J. R., & Wageman, R. 2005. A theory of team coaching. *Academy of Management Review,* 30(2): 269-287.

Hall, D. T. 1976. *Careers in organizations,* Pacific Palisades, CA: Goodyear.

Hollenbeck, G. P., & McCall, Jr., M. W. 2003. Competence, not competencies: making global executive development work. In W. H. Mobley & P. W. Dorfman (Eds.), *Advances in global leadership:* 101-119. Oxford: Elsevier Science Ltd.

Hom, P. W., & Kinicki, A. J. 2001. Toward a greater understanding of how dissatisfaction drives employee turnover. *Academy of Management Journal,* 44(5): 975-987.

Huselid, M. A. 1995. The impact of human resource management practices on turnover, productivity, and corporate financial performance. *Academy of Management Journal,* 38(3): 635-672.

Huselid, M. A. 2018. The science and practice of workforce analytics: Introduction to the HRM special issue. *Human Resource Management,* 57: 679-684.

Huselid, M., & Becker, B. 1996. Methodological issues in cross-sectional and panel estimates of the human resource-firm performance link. *Industrial Relations,* 35: 400-422.

Ichniowski, C., Shaw, K., & Prennushi, G. 1997. The effects of human resource management practices on productivity. *American Economic Review,* 87: 291-313.

Isson, J. P., & Harriott, J. S. 2016. *People analytics in the era of big data: Changing the way you attract, acquire, develop, and retain talent.* Hoboken, NJ: John Wiley & Sons.

Joshi, A. & Knight, A. P. 2015. Who defers to whom and why? Dual pathways linking demographic differences and dyadic deference to team effectiveness. *Academy of Management Journal,* 58(1): 59-84.

Judge, T. A., Higgins, C. A., Thoresen, C. J., & Barrick, M. R. 1999. The big five personality traits, general mental ability, and career success. *Personnel Psychology,* 52(3): 621-652.

Kahn, L. M., & Sherer, P. D. 1990. Contingent pay and managerial performance. *Industrial and Labor Relations Review,* 43(3): Special issue: Do compensation policies matter?: 107S-120S.

Kaplan, R. S., & Norton, D. P. 1996. *The balanced scorecard: Translating strategy into action.* Boston, MA: Harvard Business Review Press.

Kerr, S. 1975. On the folly of rewarding A, while hoping for B. *Academy of Management Journal,* 18: 769-783.

Kirkman, B. L., Rosen, B., Tesluk, P. E., & Gibson, C. B. 2004. The impact of team empowerment on virtual team performance: The moderating role of face-to-face interaction. *Academy of Management Journal,* 47(2): 187-208.

Kirkpatrick, D. L. 1959. Techniques for evaluating training programs. *Journal of American Society for Training and Development,* 13(11-12).

Kraut, A. I. 2006. *Getting action from organizational surveys: New concepts, technologies, and applications.* San Francisco, CA: Jossey-Bass.

Latham, G. P., & Kinne, S. B. 1974. Improve job performance through training and goal setting. *Journal of Applied Psychology,* 59: 187-191.

Latham, G. P., & Yukl, G. A. 1975. A review of research on the application of goal setting in organizations. *Academy of Management Journal,* 18: 824-845.

Lawler, E. E. 1971. *Pay and organizational effectiveness: A psychological view.* New York: McGraw-Hill.

Lawler, E. E. 1973. *Motivation in work organizations.* Monterey, CA: Brooks/Cole.

Lawler, E. E. 2003. Reward practices and performance management system effectiveness. *Organizational Dynamics,* 32(4): 396-404.

Lawler, E. E. 2011. Creating an effective appraisal system. In K. Oaks & P. Galagan (Eds.), *The executive guide to integrated talent management.* Alexandra, VA: American Society for Training & Development.

Lawler, E. E., Benson, G., & McDermott, M. 2012. What makes performance appraisals effective. *Compensation & Benefits Review,* 44(4): 191-200.

Lawler, III, E. E. & Boudreau, J. W. 2009. *Achieving excellence in human resources management: An assessment of human resources functions.* Stanford, CA: Stanford Business Books.

Lawler, III, E. E. & Boudreau, J. W. 2012. *Effective human resource management: A global analysis.* Stanford, CA: Stanford Business Books.

Lawler, III, E. E., & Boudreau, J. W. 2015. *Global trends in human resource management: A twenty-year analysis.* Stanford, CA: Stanford Business Books.

Lawler, III, E. E., Boudreau, J. W., & Mohrman, S. A. 2006. *Achieving strategic excellence: An assessment of human resource organizations.* Stanford, CA: Stanford Business Books.

Lawler, E. E., & Hackman, J. R. 1969. Impact of employee participation in the development of pay incentive plans: a field experiment. *Journal of Applied Psychology,* 53: 467-471.

Lawler, E. E., Levenson, A. R., & Boudreau, J. W. 2004. HR metrics and analytics: Use and impact. *Human Resource Planning,* 27(4): 27-35.

Ledford, G. E., Benson, G., & Lawler, E. E. 2016. Aligning research and the current practice of performance management. *Industrial and Organizational Psychology,* 9(2): 253-377.

Ledford, G. E., & Heneman, III, H. G. (2011). Skill-based pay. *Society for Industrial & Organizational Psychology "SIOP Science" Series.*

Ledford, G., Heneman, R. L., & Salimaki, A. 2008. Skill, knowledge, and competency pay. In L. A. Berger & D. R. Berger (Eds.), *The compensation handbook* (5th ed.). New York: McGraw-Hill.

Levenson, A. 2011. Using targeted analytics to improve talent decisions, *People & Strategy,* 34(2): 34-43.

Levenson, A. 2014. *Employee surveys that work: Improving design, use, and organizational impact.* San Francisco, CA: Berrett-Koehler.

Levenson, A. 2014. The promise of big data for HR. *People & Strategy,* 36(4): 22-26.

Levenson, A. 2015. *Strategic analytics: Advancing strategy execution and organizational effectiveness.* San Francisco, CA: Berrett-Koehler Publishers.

Levenson, A. 2016. Measuring and maximizing the impact of talent development. *TD at Work,* 33(1615).

Levenson, A. 2018. Using workforce analytics to improve strategy execution. *Human Resource Management,* 57: 685-700.

Levenson, A., & Fink, A. 2017. Workforce planning that really is strategic. *Talent Analytics Quarterly,* 3: 24-31.

Levenson, A., Van der Stede, W. A., & Cohen, S. G. 2006. Measuring the relationship between managerial competencies and performance. *Journal of Management,* 32(3): 360-380.

Lewis, R. E., & Heckman, R. J. 2006. Talent management: A critical review. *Human Resource Management Review,* 16: 139-154.

Lewin, K. 1946. Action research and minority problems. *Journal of Social Issues,* 2: 34-46.

Locke, E. A. 1968. Toward a theory of task performance and incentives. *Organizational Behavior and Human Performance,* 3: 157-189.

Locke, E. A. 1978. The ubiquity of the technique of goal setting in theories of and approaches to employee motivation. *Academy of Management Review,* 3: 594-601.

MacDuffie, J. P. 1995. Human resource bundles and manufacturing performance. *Industrial and Labor Relations Review,* 48(2): 197-221.

Major, D. A., Kozlowski, S. W. J., Chao, G. T., & Gardner, P. D. 1995. A longitudinal investigation of newcomer expectations, early socialization outcomes, and the moderating effects of role development factors. *Journal of Applied Psychology,* 80(3): 418-431.

Marler, J. H., & Boudreau, J. W. 2017. An evidence-based review of HR analytics. *The International Journal of Human Resource Management,* 28(1): 3-26.

Marr, B. 2018. *Data-driven HR: How to use analytics and metrics to drive performance.* London: Kogan Page.

Maznevski, M. L. & Chudoba, K. M. 2000. Bridging space over time: Global virtual team dynamics and effectiveness. *Organization Science,* 11(5): 473-492.

McCauley, C. R., Ruderman, M. N., Ohlott, P. J., & Morrow, J. E. 1994. Assessing the developmental components of managerial jobs. *Journal of Applied Psychology,* 79(4): 544-560.

McClean, E. J., Burris, E. R., & Detert, J. R. 2013. When does voice lead to exit? It depends on leadership. *Academy of Management Journal,* 56(2): 525-548.

McDonnell, A., Collings, D. G., Mellahi, K., & Schuler, R. S. 2017. Talent management: An integrative review and research agenda. *European Journal of International Management,* 11(1): 86-128.

McEvoy, G. M., & Cascio, W. F. 1985. Strategies for reducing employee turnover: a meta-analysis. *Journal of Applied Psychology,* 70(2): 342-353.

Mercer. 2020. *Win with empathy. Global talent trend 2020 report.* Mercer. https://www.mercer.com/our-thinking/career/global-talent-hr-trends.html

Michaels, E., Handfield-Jones, H., & Axelrod, B. 2001. *The war for talent.* Boston, MA: Harvard University Press.

Millhiser, W. P., Coen, C. A., & Solow, D. 2011. Understanding the role of worker interdependence in team selection. *Organization Science,* 22(3): 772-787.

Minbaeva, D. 2017. Human capital analytics: Why aren't we there? Introduction to the special issue. *Journal of Organizational Effectiveness: People and Performance,* 4(2): 110-118.

Nadler, D. A. 1977. *Feedback and organization development: Using data-based methods.* Prentice Hall Organization Development Series. Upper Saddle River, NJ: FT Press.

Ng, T. W. H., Eby, L. T., Sorensen, K. L., & Feldman, D. C. 2005. Predictors of objective and subjective career success: a meta-analysis. *Personnel Psychology,* 58: 367-408.

Noffke, S., & Somekh, B. 2009. *The SAGE handbook of action research.* Los Angeles: Sage Publications Ltd.

Ohland, M. W., Loughry, M. L., Woehr, D. J., Bullard, L. G., Felder, R. M., Finelli, C. J., Layton, R. A., Pomeranz, H. R., & Schmucker, D. G. 2012. The comprehensive assessment of team member effectiveness: Development of a behaviorally anchored rating scale for self- and peer evaluation. *Academy of Management Learning & Education,* 11(4): 609-630.

Osterman, P. 1984. *Internal labor markets,* Cambridge, MA: MIT Press.

Parker, S., & Wall, T. D. 1998. *Job and work design: Organizing work to promote well-being and effectiveness.* Los Angeles: Sage Publications.

Pease, G., Byerly, B., & Fitz-enz, J. 2013. *Human capital analytics: How to harness the potential of your organization's greatest asset.* Hoboken, NJ: John Wiley & Sons.

Phillips, P. P., & Phillips, J. J. 2015. *Making human capital analytics work: Measuring the ROI of human capital processes and outcomes.* New York: McGraw-Hill Education.

Premack, S. L., & Wanous, J. P. 1985. A meta-analysis of realistic job preview experiments. *Journal of Applied Psychology,* 70(4): 706-719.

Rasmussen, T., & Ulrich, D. 2015. Learning from practice: How HR analytics avoids being a management fad. *Organizational Dynamics,* 44: 236-242.

Reason, P., & Bradbury, H. 2006. *The handbook of action research.* Los Angeles: Sage.

Reilly, R. R., Brown, B., Blood, M. R., & Malatesta, C. Z. 1981. The effects of realistic previews: a study and discussion of the literature. *Personnel Psychology,* 34: 823-834.

Russon, C., & Reinelt, C. 2004. The results of an evaluation scan of 55 leadership development programs. *Journal of Leadership and Organizational Studies,* 10(3): 104-107.

Schuler, R. S., Jackson, S. E., & Tarique, I. 2011. Global talent management and global talent challenges: Strategic opportunities for IHRM. *Journal of World Business,* 46: 506-516.

Sesil, J. C. 2013. *Applying advanced analytics to HR management decisions: methods for selection, developing incentives, and improving collaboration.* New York: Pearson FT Press.

Shani, A. B., Mohrman, S. A., Pasmore, W. A., Stymme, B., & Adler, N. 2008. *Handbook of collaborative research.* Los Angeles, CA: Sage Publications.

Smith, P. C. 1976. Behavior, results, and organizational effectiveness: The problem of criteria. In M. D. Dunette (Ed.), *Handbook of industrial and organizational psychology.* Chicago: Rand McNally.

Smith, T. 2013. *HR analytics: The what, why and how.* CreateSpace Independent Publishing Platform.

Soundararajan, R. & Singh, K. 2017. *Winning on HR analytics: Leveraging data for competitive advantage.* New Delhi: Sage Publications India Pvt Ltd.

Sparrow, P. R., Scullion, H., & Tarique, I. 2014. *Strategic talent management: Contemporary issues in international context.* Cambridge, MA: Cambridge University Press.

Spencer, L. M., Jr., & Spencer, S. M. 1993. *Competence at work: Models for superior performance.* New York: John Wiley.

Spreitzer, G. M., McCall, Jr., M. W., & Mahoney, J. D. 1997. Early identification of international executive potential. *Journal of Applied Psychology,* 82: 6-29.

Steel, R. P. 2002. Turnover theory at the empirical interface: problems of fit and function. *Academy of Management Review,* 27(3): 346-360.

Stein, B., & Morrison, A. 2014. The enterprise data lake: better integration and deeper analytics, *Technology forecast: Rethinking integration,* Issue 1, PriceWaterhouse Coopers. http://www.pwc.com/en_US/us/technology-forecast/2014/cloud-computing/assets/pdf/pwc-technology-forecast-data-lakes.pdf

Sturman, M. C. 2000. Implications of utility analysis adjustments for estimates of human resource intervention value. *Journal of Management,* 26: 281-299.

Sundmark, L. 2017. *Doing HR analytics: A practitioner's handbook with R examples,* CreateSpace Independent Publishing Platform.

Tarique, I., & Schuler, R. S. 2010. Global talent management: Literature review, integrative framework, and suggestions for future research. *Journal of World Business,* 45: 122-133.

Taylor, F. 1923. *The principles of scientific management,* New York: Harper and Row.

Thunnissen, M., Boselie, P., & Fruytier, B. 2013. A review of talent management: 'Infancy or adolescence?' *International Journal of Human Resources Management,* 24(9): 1744-1761.

Tolchinsky, P. D., & King, D.C. (1980). Do goals mediate the effects of incentives on performance? *Academy of Management Review,* 5(3): 455-467.

Trevor, C. O. 2001. Interactions among actual ease-of-movement determinants and job satisfaction in the prediction of voluntary turnover. *Academy of Management Journal,* 44(4): 621-638.

Vandenberg, R. J., & Nelson, J. B. 1999. Disaggregating the motives underlying turnover intentions: when do intentions predict turnover behavior? *Human Relations,* 52(10): 1313-1336.

Vroom, V. H. 1964. *Work and motivation.* Hoboken, NJ: John Wiley & Sons.

Wageman, R. 2001. How leaders foster self-managing team effectiveness: Design choices versus hands-on coaching. *Organization Science,* 12(5): 559-577.

Wageman, R., Hackman, J. R., & Lehman, E. 2005. Team diagnostic survey: Development of an instrument. *Journal of Applied Behavioral Science,* 41(4): 373-398.

Wall, T. D., & Wood, S. J. 2005. The romance of human resource management and business performance, and the case for big science. *Human Relations,* 58(4): 429-462.

Welbourne, T. M. 2015. Data-driven storytelling: The missing link in HR data analytics. *Employment Relations Today,* 41(4): 27-33.

Workforce Solutions Review. 2014. *Big data: What could it mean for HR and the enterprise?* Special issue, 5(2): May.

Workforce Solutions Review. 2015. *Big data. Special issue,* 6(6): November.

Wright, P. M., Gardner, T. M., Moynihan, L. M., & Allen, M. R. 2005. The relationship between HR practices and firm performance: examining causal order. *Personnel Psychology,* 58: 409-446.

Zhang, W., Levenson, A., & Crossley, C. 2015. Move your research from the ivory tower to the board room: A primer on action research for academics, consultants, and business executives. *Human Resource Management,* 54(1): 151-174.

40

INTEGRATING TALENT MANAGEMENT AND PERFORMANCE MANAGEMENT

A Workforce Differentiation Perspective

Brian Burgess

Shaun Pichler

Introduction

The discussion of talent management (TM) has been burgeoning over the last decade with CEOs such as GE's Jack Welch acknowledging that "Having the most talented people in each of our businesses is the most important thing. If we don't, we lose" (Michaels et al., 2001). Indeed, it seems that businesses are crying for improved strategies for the identification, acquisition, placement, and development of highly "talented" individuals.

However, the TM literature has left scholars and practitioners with much to be desired as far as useful frameworks integrating the TM literature with the performance management literature. This is because definitions of TM and talent are not offered in much of the literature or, when offered, differ across sources (Ashton & Morton, 2005; Gallardo-Gallardo et al., 2020; Huang & Tansley, 2012; King & Vaiman, 2019; Lewis & Heckman, 2006; Sparrow 2019). In fact, scholars have identified a research-practice gap in the sense that there is more interest in TM among practitioners than academics (Lewis & Heckman, 2006). Conversely, the performance management (PM) literature is clearer in terms of definitions and processes and provides immense opportunity for integrating PM with TM.

The main goal of this chapter, therefore, is to integrate the TM and PM literatures. We hope to identify opportunities for utilizing TM and PM strategies to bolster human resources management (HRM), as well as to delineate directions for future research in this area. In the next two sections of the chapter, we provide reviews of the TM and PM literatures, respectively. We then explain how TM and PM are connected in relation to workforce differentiation (Aguinis et al., 2011; Becker et al., 2009; Collings, 2017). Additionally, we will offer a definition of talent based on the concept of workforce differentiation. We then explain why TM and PM practices should be designed in consideration of each other, but also in consideration of key contextual factors, such as firm strategy, culture, and human capital. Lastly, we suggest that the PM of stars and other top performers are of upmost importance due to their differential contribution to firm performance.

The over-arching proposition guiding our review is that when TM and PM practices are designed strategically (i.e., in an integrated way based on workforce differentiation), firms should gain a source of competitive advantage. We conclude our chapter with directions for future research and implications for management and organization.

DOI: 10.4324/9781315474687-40

Talent Management

Lewis and Heckman (2006) argue that there is no clear meaning of the term "talent management" in that it is simply used to refer to the strategic importance of a particular HR function, and that the term "talent" is simply a paraphrase for people. We agree with these authors that simply defining TM as bundles of HR practices, or the strategic implementation of specific HR practices, is simply "old wine in new bottles" and offers very little in the way of theory, research, and practice. This is because TM has generally been associated with practices such as recruitment, selection, and succession planning. However, TM has begun to differentiate itself by placing an increased emphasis on the role of high-performing individuals, such as A players and stars as strategic resources. From this, it provides opportunity to integrate TM and PM by way of providing a full view of how to manage and source top performers.

Based upon our analysis, we will center our analysis on A players and stars, and build on the definition of TM provided by Collings and Mellahi (2009) that suggests that TM encompasses:

> activities and processes that involve the systematic identification of key positions that differentially contribute to the organization's sustainable competitive advantage, the development of a talent pool of high-potential and high performing incumbents to fill these roles, and the development of a differentiated HR architecture to facilitate filling these positions with competent incumbents, and to ensure their continued commitment to the organization.

From this, we argue that the TM literature provides guidance for allocating resources to those roles and people that will elicit the highest return on investment, while also directing decisions about how A-players and stars should be developed, in what roles, and from what source – internal versus external to the firm. For the purposes of this chapter, we define A players as those individuals who are highest-performing and in positions of strategic importance (Huselid et al., 2005). We define stars as "those with disproportionately high and prolonged (a) performance, (b) visibility, and (c) relevant social capital" (Call et al., 2015).

TM Discussions Around A Players and Stars Affecting Training, Development, and Succession Planning

The precise definition of "talent" in the TM paradigm has vacillated among practitioners and academics: from defining it as human capital, high-performance, high-potential, or even as an individual's personal strengths (Cascio & Luthans, 2014; Luthans, 2002). However, in our view, it is imperative that the definition be clear enough to provide guidance for the distribution of scarce organizational resources. While skills take deliberate and guided practice to develop (Ericsson et al., 1993; Gangné, 2004), practitioners generally lack the resources to develop skills from infancy to mastery. Therefore, they often seek to promote and develop those individuals who are high-performing because these characteristics are most apparent and do not necessarily require psychometric measures of potential. Accordingly, the TM literature provides insight into how resources can best be allocated to training, development, and, we argue, PM efforts. Here, we define talent in terms of its more colloquial usage: talented individuals are those who are very high-performing.

To guide resource distribution, TM proponents suggest differentiating and stratifying the workforce by identifying highly talented individuals as well as strategic positions – those who differentially contribute to the enactment of strategic objectives – and allocating disproportional resources to them (Becker, Huselid, & Beatty, 2009). Some suggest stratifying the workforce into those A, B, and C players in order to more discriminately allocate resources and to create pools of skilled incumbents (Huselid et al., 2005). Because of this, scholars have characterized TM as relatively elitist compared to other HR paradigms in that it focuses on workforce differentiation (Collings & Mellahi, 2009).

Elitist or not, we argue that workforce differentiation provides a useful framework for integrating the talent and PM literatures.

Indeed, it seems to be the case that some individuals contribute far more than the average employee, which may justify differentiation on an economic basis. Hunter, Schmidt, and Judiesch (1990) found that, in complex jobs, the top 1% of employees tend to outperform average workers by 127%. For computer programmers, top performers tend to out produce the average performer by a factor of eight, and top inventors tend to outproduce the average by a factor of ten (Groysberg, Sant, & Abrahams, 2008; Narin & Breitzman, 1995). Aguinis and O'Boyle (2014) argue that the distribution of performance across individuals is not always normally distributed, but often follows a power-law distribution wherein talent and performance are exponentially related with a "quasi-infinite" variance, and small increases in performance lead to extreme increases in productivity (O'Boyle & Kroska, 2017).

In this case, it is possible to have individuals who produce at a degree that is theoretically nearly impossible under a normal performance distribution schema. While it is not prudent to assume that all positions will have a power-law distribution, TM's focus on those positions that have large variances in performance means that strategic roles may be more likely to fit this distribution. Aguinis and O'Boyle (2014) argue that more jobs in the 21st century are likely to meet this distribution as white-collar jobs, which are not limited by as many physical constraints, become the norm. O'Boyle and Aguinis (2012) found that 94% of the jobs they studied fit a power-law distribution, including fields such as academics, athletes, entertainers, and politicians. This provides ample evidence for focusing development efforts on high-performers as they have the potential to contribute disproportionately to the bottom line of a company.

Yet, practitioners feel that there is a dearth of such highly talented individuals. In fact, Ready and Conger (2007) found that of the 40 companies around the world that they surveyed in 2005, nearly all of them expressed a scarcity of high-potential employees to fill their strategic roles. They also note that they "have attended multiple executive committee meetings where companies have been forced to pass on hundreds of millions of dollars of new business because they didn't have the talent to see their growth strategies through to fruition" (2007: 2).

However, those on the farthest end of an exponential distribution, often fitting into the definition of stars, are by definition rare and may not be realistic for most firms to attain due to their high cost and scarcity. What a firm identifies as talent depends not only on individual-level factors, such as motivation and performance, but also the strategic value of positions within which these individuals are embedded. Markedly, some positions contribute more to the execution of a firm's strategic objectives than others and, therefore, managers should be more judicious in recruiting, selecting, and monitoring for these positions (Huselid, Beatty, & Becker, 2005). This is unique in that it is "position" rather than "people" focused.

The extent to which certain positions are more valuable than others should be determined by firm characteristics, such as strategy and culture. For instance, customer service positions are valuable to Nordstrom given its differentiation business strategy based on exceptional customer service (MacMillan & McGrath, 1997), while Walmart's purchasers drive their price leadership strategy. Due to their high value, a disproportionate amount of resources should be allocated to these roles that (a) have an disproportionate contribution to the achievement of its strategic imperatives, (b) have large variations in the quality of work among employees in the position, and (c) its ability to substantially increase revenue and decrease cost (Bordreau & Ramstad, 2005; Huselid, Beatty, & Becker, 2005).

In the same regard, strategic positions with high-performance and/or low variability in performance require less investment but disproportionate attention to ongoing success (Huselid, Beatty, & Becker, 2005). This enables an organization to direct their resources toward those positions that will lead to the highest marginal return on investment rather than investing in lower-return positions.

Notably, this is not possible unless well-defined strategic objectives have been established and the organization has delineated the means by which it intends to compete in the marketplace: cost leadership, product differentiation, or otherwise. Thus, it is advisable to utilize resources to develop those skills that will aid in the accomplishment of strategic objectives as they relate to customer care, company culture, cost cutting, and revenue growth.

Those positions or skills that are strategy-, cost-, or revenue-driving are those that should be the focus of recruitment, selection, training, and development efforts. Additionally, we argue that these positions, and the A players that occupy them, should be the focus of PM efforts and be provided with greater emphasis on the proper execution of performance measurement, appraisal, compensation, and goal setting.

TM Discussions Around A Players and Stars Affecting Recruitment, Selection, and Retention

TM also seeks to improve recruitment and selection practices by providing strategies for creating and sourcing "talent pools". Stewart (1997) differentiated human resources along two dimensions: difficulty to replace and value-added. Human resources that are difficult to replace and high-value are those that HR practitioners and line managers should be most interested in since they are more valuable not only to the business, but also in terms of replacement costs. Due to the scarcity, value, and inimitability of firm-specific skills and knowledge, such as internal policies and culture, Lepak and Snell (1999) suggest that business should "make" and develop firm specific skills, as well as other rare and valuable skills, and ensure their retention. In contrast, they argue that employers should contract for skills that are not valuable and not unique, as well as purchase skills that are of high value but not unique. This is of immense strategic value because the business gains more agility in reacting to changing environments by pushing recruitment and selection costs off to a third party.

The emerging research on talent pools and skill portability can guide recruitment and selection in a TM framework. TM suggests developing talent pools of high-performing individuals who can fill openings in pivotal positions (Collings & Mellahi, 2009; Smilansky, 2006; Sparrow, 2007). The creation of talent pools can be done by having groups of high-potential individuals at one or many levels of an organization who are engaging in training and development programs that will prepare them to be success at higher levels of the organization. This requires recruiting "ahead of the curve" and, in high-performing organizations, often times recruiting talented individuals prior to creating roles for them (Stahl et al., 2007, Sparrow 2007).

Cappelli (2008), however, argues that organizations are withdrawing from training efforts, and argues that this may be beneficial as it pushes skill development costs off to other organizations or even employees by encouraging further education and external training. Many organizations are reaping the benefit of people who are pre-trained in another organization by sourcing pools of these skills from the open market (Defillippi & Arthur, 1994; Spender, 1989), and this is becoming ever-more facile in job-hopping culture.

However, external sourcing of talent pools may not always be prudent. As Groysberg, Sant, and Abrahams (2008) argue, an individual's high performance may not always be transferable to another organization or position. They posit that non-transferable skills rely heavily on collaborative performance and/or firm-specific knowledge such as firm processes, procedures, culture, and implicit social knowledge—whereas transferable skills are those that are generalizable, such as motivating employees, organizing, and budgeting. This is exemplified by Groysberg et al. (2008) who found that security analysts, frequently cited as highly portable due to their ownership of their skills and client relationships, still experienced a decline in performance of up to five years when moving to a new firm and that their success was dependent on the HR practices of the acquiring firm.

Bidwell (2011) showed that external hires at an investment bank performed worse than lesser paid internal hires from comparable jobs, showing that internal hires may be both more effective as well as cost efficient. Additionally, the transitional performance of GE executives who moved to different firms also experienced a decline in performance, which was predicted by the congruence of their experience with the strategies of the new firm. That is, experience in cost cutting did not help in organizations focused on differentiation, as well as if they were able to bring other team members with them (Groysberg, Mclean, & Nohria, 2006). Therefore, "poaching" these skills may not be advisable in all cases but, if done, should be done with consideration of firm strategy and culture.

Dokko and Jiang (2017) argue that performance can change across organizations depending on the transferability of human and social capital, as well as effects on employees' identity. They further argue that human and social capital can have differing organizational outcomes depending on whether the employee is leaving or entering an organization. For example, much of human capital can be related to firm-specific norms, behavioral habits, and processes that allow an individual to efficiently interface with their nested organization. While some skills, such as those related to computer programs used or general industry knowledge, may be transferable, these skills are imbedded in institutional knowledge that may not be appropriate to a new organization. Additionally, some of the mental modes that are brought from a source organization may amount to poor behaviors and work norms in their new organization (Dokko & Jiang, 2017).

The value of one's integration into behavioral, cognitive, and procedural norms is often underestimated by both firms and the individuals who work in them as these implicit skills take time and develop and are important for performance. Therefore, it is beneficial (in most cases) to focus on the retention and succession planning in order to save these firm-specific skills.

Social capital, being "the resources available to individuals as a result of their positions in the social structures or the quality and quantity of their social relationships" (Adler & Kwon, 2002), also has wide influence on those entering and leaving an organization. For example, someone with significant social capital within their firm can continue to benefit their original firm after they leave, because they share new processes and market knowledge with their friends from their old organization (Dokko & Jiang, 2017). These kinds of benefits can only be derived when the employee moves to a comparable firm such as a client or supplier (Carnahan & Somaya, 2013), but can be harmful if they move to a competitor (Somaya, Williamson, & Lorinkova, 2008).

However, this is also dependent on the relationships that that individual can maintain after leaving. These benefits provide incentives for organizations to maintain relationships with former employees through alumni networks or other means. Nonetheless, if the individual moves to an unrelated firm, the loss of social capital utilization amounts to a detriment for both the employee and the firm that they choose to leave. Therefore, the loss of an A player or star may not always result in a loss, but does come at the grave risk of losing important human and social capital to competitors.

All in all, practitioners can gain higher a return on investment by centering training and development efforts, as well as PM efforts, on those pivotal positions that abnormally drive revenue growth, cost reduction, and strategy implementation with an additional emphasis on positions with large variability in performance. Additionally, unique, valuable, and firm-specific skills should be the highlight of development for those positions. Increased effort should be afforded to the recruitment, selection, and retention of positions requiring rare and valuable skills as these skills come at a high replacement and recruitment cost.

Lastly, when sourcing pools of A players, businesses need to be deliberate in the types of skills they keep internally or contract for, as well as be aware of what types of positions can best be filled from internal development or from the market. They can then apply PM efforts to maintaining consistent performance, encourage measurable growth, and increase retention and commitment of incumbents fitting these criteria.

Performance Management

Whereas TM is more about sourcing, identifying, and supporting high-performers, performance management (PM) is generally focused on improving the performance of all workers through various policies and practices. Nonetheless, these practices may be of particular importance to the identification and management of A players and stars and, when resources are scarce, these would be the main targets of PM efforts. Performance management is defined as "a continuous process of identifying, measuring, and developing the performance of individuals and teams and aligning performance with strategic goals of the organization" (Aguinis, 2013: 2). A number of processes and practices are involved in PM including performance planning and evaluation, coaching, performance appraisal and feedback, and compensation and reward systems (e.g., Aguinus, 2013).

PM is typically characterized as a cyclical process of identifying, measuring, and developing the performance of individuals and teams (Aguinis, 2013). It begins with performance planning, when the manager ensures that the ratee has a clear understanding or knowledge of performance standards and expectations, and it ends with a formal performance review, often simply called *the appraisal*. This is a formal meeting between a manager and a subordinate employee to evaluate and discuss the extent to which performance standards and expectations were met in the prior review cycle. In between these two interactions, performance planning and the appraisal review, managers should be providing frequent feedback, which may be informal and/or built into the appraisal process. This is an ideal model that organizations may or may not follow. In the extreme opposite case, the whole process is truncated into the formal appraisal (typically once a year) in which the planning is conducted and no feedback is provided between the appraisals (Steelman, Levy, & Snell, 2004).

In terms of performance planning, most of the PM literature has focused on goal-setting. The goal setting literature is one of the largest within the broader management and organization literature, and concepts from goal setting have been applied across many contexts from work performance to weight loss. There a two key propositions of goal setting theory that have been supported across numerous studies (e.g., Mento et al., 1987): First, performance is higher when goals are set as compared to when there is a lack of a clear goal. Second, performance is higher when goals are specific and difficult, commonly known as stretch goals. Goal setting increases performance due to several mechanisms: goals direct attention, increase effort and persistence, and indirectly affect performance through increased discovery and knowledge acquisition (Locke & Latham, 2002).

Goal setting is an essential element of the PM process. It is important to note that goal-setting in the context of performance planning should occur early in the PM process. In other words, goal-setting during performance planning is different from participation in the actual performance appraisal review itself, which can include goal-setting (Cawley, Keeping, & Levy, 1998). Goal-setting during performance planning is also tied to the concept of adequate notice in performance appraisal –it is important that employees clearly understand the goals to which they will be held accountable at the end of the review cycle for the process to be perceived as fair (Folger et al., 1992).

After the performance planning stage, it is important that managers provide employees with regular and ongoing feedback (Aguinis, 2013). In other words, it is important for managers to regularly monitor employee performance, and provide clear, contingent feedback especially for critical performance incidents (London, 2003). Without ongoing feedback, employees will develop a lack of understanding about how their behaviors and results are tied to the goals set during the performance planning process. In this sense, ongoing performance feedback is also an aspect of adequate notice in due process performance appraisal.

With more frequent feedback, employees will more clearly understand the performance levels to which they will be held accountable in the review period (Folger et al., 1992). Recent research has shown that both knowledge of performance standards, which can be achieved in part through goal setting, and frequent feedback are both essential to employee reactions to performance appraisal, and that frequent feedback strengthens the positive relationship between knowledge of performance standards and reactions (Pichler, Beenen, & Wood, 2017).

After goals have been set and managers and employees have had ongoing discussions about performance, it is important for managers to evaluate performance and provide formal feedback during an appraisal review session. Much of the PM literature has focused on performance feedback, including the evaluation of performance and the appraisal review session. In fact, when it comes to improving PM, many look to improving the delivery of performance feedback (DeNisi & Pritchard, 2006). This is perhaps largely because the key purpose of performance feedback, including performance appraisal, is to improve individual and team performance, thus increasing the productivity of an overall business unit. If performance feedback is ineffective, then this over-arching purpose is defeated.

The focus on performance feedback is also due to a science-practice gap in the literature (Balzer & Sulsky, 1992). That is, there has been a significant scholarly focus on performance feedback since the 1920s (DeNisi & Pritchard, 2006), but practitioners have asserted that they find little value in this research. This is perhaps largely because this literature had, for many years, focused on a so-called psychometric approach, i.e., on mitigating rater errors in performance ratings and improve rating accuracy (see Pichler, 2012). Although important in its own right, this has little connection to how to effectively deliver performance feedback in organizations. Practitioners have every right to be concerned. A meta-analysis by Kluger and DeNisi (1996) showed that feedback sessions often lead to negative effects on performance. Of course, this is opposite of the intended consequence of PM and feedback.

In recent years, and partly in response to the science-practice gap, scholars have focused on aspects of PM and feedback that have not only important theoretical but practical implications as well. Scholars have focused on contextual aspects of the performance feedback process, including the feedback environment (Steelman, Levy, & Snell, 2004), the social context of performance feedback (Judge & Ferris, 1993; Levy & Williams, 2004; Pichler, 2012), and due process performance appraisal (Cawley, Keeping, & Levy, 1998; Folger et al., 1992; Pichler et al., 2016). This research has also focused on reactions to performance feedback itself (e.g., Keeping & Levy, 2000) and to contextual aspects of performance feedback (e.g., Pichler, 2012).

The focus on reactions to performance feedback is critical since employees are unlikely to attend to feedback if they react negatively, e.g., feel that their feedback was unfair or inaccurate. Negative reactions may lead to reduced motivation and ultimately to *lower* performance (Levy & Williams, 2004; Pichler, 2012). This is perhaps why many performance feedback sessions result in negative performance, i.e., negative reactions to performance feedback.

This body of work has shown that when employees feel that their organization is open to and supportive of performance feedback, when they have a high-quality relationship with their manager, and when feedback systems are implemented in a way that is procedurally fair, reactions are more positive as is subsequent performance (see Jawahar, 2010; Pichler, 2012; Pichler et al., 2017).

Compensation is an important part of the PM process for a number of reasons, perhaps especially because it is used to direct attention to goals and to sustain employee motivation. When it comes to total compensation, there are a variety of pay forms including base wages, benefits, pay for performance, and services (Milkovich & Newman, 2002). The efficiency wage theory (e.g., Katz, 1986) has provided an important framework for understanding the importance of base wages. The basic idea here is that higher wages will make firms more attractive in labor markets, and thus firms will benefit economically from more qualified employees, as well as from higher levels of effort and thus productivity.

An issue here is that higher wages make firms more attractive to qualified and unqualified employees. For higher wages to benefit firms economically, they must have other HRM systems in place, such as rigorous employee selection processes. In fact, higher wages are part of a high-performance work system or a mutually reinforcing set of HR policies and practices (see Ramsey et al., 2000).

Pay for performance, or contingent pay, comes in a variety of forms and can vary in terms of timeframe, i.e., short- versus long-term, as well as level of analysis, i.e., the individual, group, business unit, or firm level (Milkovich & Newman, 2002). Some examples include individual incentives, team bonuses, gainsharing, and profit sharing plans. There is an extensive literature on pay for performance. The key principle here is to provide monetary rewards that are tied to measured performance that are within the control of employees (Durham & Bartol, 2000). This is because, when designed properly, pay for performance can increase organizational attractiveness and retention, as well as improve employee motivation. For instance, research has shown that incentives have statistically and practically significant effects on performance (e.g., Jenkins et al., 1998).

Other types of pay for performance, such as merit pay, are more questionable in terms of their effectiveness, but this is largely due to how such plans are implemented. That is, although merit pay is designed to be a significant reward for high performance, it is often implemented as a sort of cost of living adjustment, and is thus not motivating, especially to high-performers (see Heneman, 1992). In general, when pay for performance is tied closely to performance measurement and evaluation, and when it is designed and implemented effectively, it can increase employee performance and productivity (Rynes et al., 2005).

Integrating Talent Management and Performance Management for A Players and Stars

The integration of PM practices into the TM framework is imperative to protect the investments that businesses place in their talent and critical roles by providing outcomes such as heightened performance, job commitment, persistent work effort, guided competency development, and reduced turnover. Indeed, the large variations in performance and the immense recruitment costs associated with these roles bear risks and opportunities that should be managed with the upmost assiduity. We agree with Heckman and Lewis (2006) that for TM to be strategic, it should be part of strategy formulation and not just strategy implementation. Thus, the design of talent and PM systems should be influenced by and supportive of a firm's strategy, but this should be a two-way conversation between line executives and HR managers. In other words, if HR managers are left out of the discussion about which positions are most valuable and what types of practices should be used to increase performance in those positions, important information may be overlooked, such as about realities around the supply and demand of labor for those positions.

Choices about which TM and PM practices should be implemented, and how they should be implemented, will depend upon firm characteristics. For instance, group-based contingent pay will be more appropriate for firms with group-based work designs and egalitarian cultures, whereas individual-based contingent pay is more appropriate for firms with relatively inegalitarian cultures and individual-based work designs. Group-based contingent pay can enhance collaboration, thus ultimately increasing the retention of workers who fit with a more egalitarian, team-based culture (Milkovich & Newman, 2002). Assuming the most appropriate talent and PM systems have been chosen, and that they have been implemented effectively, the attitudes, behaviors, and performance of individuals in strategically valuable positions should be higher all else equal and should contribute to the competitive advantage of the firm.

Furthermore, it is important to identify high-performers in strategically valuable positions: being those that drive revenue, cut costs, are difficult to replace, and/or are necessary for the implementation of the organization's strategy. Given that TM requires focusing on high-performing individuals, a firm must utilize performance measures in order to identify those who are high-performing. This is particularly important in roles with more qualitative outcomes, such as a customer service representative at Nordstrom, rather than those with easily quantifiable jobs, such as a purchaser at Walmart.

This can and perhaps should be done by line managers working collaboratively with HR professionals. Line managers have unique knowledge and information about individuals' performance, whereas HR practitioners can work to develop the most effective ways to measure and evaluate relative performance within positions. To measure performance and variations in performance, it is important to compare performance between individuals working in the same highly valuable position. Without accurate performance measurement, it would not be possible to appropriately identify those positions meeting the TM criterion of large variations in performance, nor those individuals who perform well within them. From this, HR and line managers should collaborate to appropriately delineate the standards by which and how performance should be measured.

Next, there are many outcomes of PM practices, such as heightened performance and reduced turnover, that are very important to success in highly valuable positions and the management of the talented individuals in these roles. When done effectively, PM can increase employee job satisfaction and commitment (Fletcher & Williams, 1996), employee motivation and performance (e.g., Dieleman et al., 2006), and the retention of high-performers (e.g., Aguinis, 2013: 8).

Research also shows that PM is tied to firm performance (Gerhart & Milkovich, 1992). For instance, firms with effective PM systems are 51% more likely to perform better in terms of financial outcomes (Aguinis, 2013: 4). Nonetheless, the PM and TM strategies that organizations use as a means to this end should be done with acute focus on firm characteristics. To provide guidance to their integration, we provide a generalized framework here.

A Players

First, these practices and their related outcomes are of paramount importance for aiding A players in consistently performing at their best due to the fact that intra-person variability accounts for more of the variability in performance than that of variations in between-person performance (Binnewies, Sonnentag, & Mojza, 2009; Deadrick, Bennett, & Russell, 1997, Fisher & Noble, 2004; Minbashian, Earl, & Bright, 2013; Steward & Nandkeolyar, 2006, 2007; Thoresen, Bradley, Bliese, & Thoresen, 2004). A meta-analysis by Dalal, Bhave, and Fiset (2014) found that within-person variability accounted for approximately 63% of job and task performance over time, as well as 49% of counterproductive work behavior, 39% of proactive behavior, and 43% of organizational citizenship behavior. PM systems that effectively motivate high-performers will lead to more consistent performance through persistent effort.

Minbashian (2017) argues that variability in performance can be described by short-term and long-term variations in performance, as well as individual differences. Whereas individual differences such as intelligence and personality characteristics are states that cannot be managed (they must be selected for), short- and long-term variations in performance can be influenced using PM strategies. For example, Minbashian (2017) argues that short-term variability in performance is a function of self-regulatory capacity, cognitive processes, affective reactions, and situational and task characterizes, all of which are positively related to PM practices.

Because performance appraisal and feedback should be a two-way process in which the employees discuss their challenges, these can be used to ascertain situation- and task-related problems that denigrate performance. Additionally, given that individuals are more likely to allocate psychological resources to a task when they feel they will be rewarded with financial or social incentives (Kanfer, 1987), immediate feedback may be used to reward performance at a micro level and to direct cognitive processes and increase regulatory capacity.

Goal setting also increases performance through goal directed attention and increased effort and persistence (Locke & Latham, 2002), and therefore is positively related to regulatory capacity as long-term variations are accumulations of short-term performance. Minbashian (2017) also posits that long-term variations in performance are a function of changes in job-relevant knowledge and skills, work attitudes, and changes in job and organizational characteristics. Goal setting, partnered with training and development efforts, can be utilized to direct discovery and knowledge acquisition (Locke & Latham 2002), whereas multi-directional feedback can be utilized to identify challenges associated with job and organizational characteristics.

PM practices, such as goal setting, can be utilized to maintain the engagement of highly skilled individuals. Because challenging but achievable tasks tend to activate increased effort, satisfaction, and productivity (Minibashian, Wood, & Beckerman, 2010), we suggest that high-potential individuals may tend to be less motivated and place less effort into performing menial tasks. In fact, the research by Minbashian and Luppino (2014) suggests that task complexity for an individual decreases over time as they require less cognitive effort when their skills develop. This may be especially tenuous due to their status as highly talented individuals.

Consequently, stretch goals should be developed and monitored (Mento et al., 1987) to challenge high-performers to continually improve performance and work toward new goals. Indeed, this requires increased effort on the part of managers to identify high-potentials, monitor their engagement, and continually provide new challenges if needed. Organizations that fail to adequately meet an A player's potential with equivalent complexity may lose out on performance and may even fail to recognize the full potential of that individual. This means that PM strategies are necessary to identify and challenge these individuals so that they maintain peak performance.

Star Performers

The management of star performers, being those who enjoy extremely high-performance relative to their peers as well as high visibility both inside and outside their organization, also bring special challenges and opportunities for the uses of PM practices. It is important to note up front that little to no research has been conducted on PM practices in star contexts, leaving this area rather obfuscated. Nonetheless, star performers, as follows from our previous discussion on power-distributions, contribute substantially more to firm value than the average person, and marginal increases in their performance can lead to a similar exponential increase in value (Aguinus & O'Boyle 2014; O'Boyle & Kroska, 2017). Individuals such as Michael Jordon, Steve Jobs, Shigeru Miyamoto, among others have had tremendous influence on both their firms and their entire industries, enticing large profits for their organizations and those that partner with them.

According to the resource-based view, competitive advantage is acquired through the acquisition of skills that are rare, valuable, inimitable, and non-substitutable (Barney, 2001). Therefore, average performers or even high-performing individuals cannot provide competitive advantage, whereas stars meet these criteria by definition (O'Boyle & Kroska, 2017). Their performance, therefore, must be carefully managed to both increase their performance and ensure that there are no adverse effects on their performance.

Stars pose very unique challenges due to their immense value, influence on organizational resources, and extreme desirability to other businesses. Given that stars are so valuable, they present a great risk with regards to them leaving. Stars therefore are capable of leveraging their value to negotiate desirable and idiosyncratic work arrangements that are not awarded to others (see Rousseau, 2001). Stars may be more or less receptive to PM strategies and have asymmetrical power. Ultimately, however, these individuals are more likely to leave (Maltarich et al., 2010; Nyberg, 2010; Trevor et al., 1997) due to their ease of movement (Nyberg, 2010; Trevor, 2001).

The retention and the management of stars' performance is critical. Thus, PM practices may be very beneficial with the management of stars. For example, star performers are likely to prefer contingent pay where they can be rewarded proportionally for performance. While this is likely to lead to large differences in pay between stars and non-stars, pay dispersion as a result of rewarding these high-performers is associated with greater performance and retention (Reilly & Gerhart, 2012). Team-based contingent pay may also be a way to decrease star portability by making them more reliant on their team, as well as more accountable to the performance of their team members.

Firms would also be well served to ensure that the star is aware of the personal risks associated with their performance portability (Groysberg, Sant, & Abrahams, 2008). It is also important to note that some practices implemented to retain high-performers may lead to higher turnover in lower level positions due to injustice perceptions caused by differentiation (Rousseau et al., 2006; Shaw & Gupta, 2007) of pay distribution (Lazear, 1999) and other idiosyncratic arrangements (see Aguinus & O'Boyle, 2014; Rousseau, 2001). The loss of a star may not have only negative consequences however (see Chen & Garg 2018; Dokko & Jiang, 2017).

It is also important to ensure that the work of a star in not impeded by the work of others and, in turn, that the star does not hurt the work of others and lead to opportunity costs. For example, having members on a team who are not complimentary to the star's skills or are redundant may lead to decreased performance (Polyhart & Cragun, 2017). Additionally, managers should ensure that the star is not limited by time constraints, ensuring time is strategy-directed (research, sales calls, analysis, etc.) while non-value-added work (administrative tasks) should be done by others (Polyhart & Cragun, 2017).

Conversely, Kehoe and Tzabbar (2015) showed that the presence of a star can decrease innovative leadership due to the star monopolizing resources, potentially leading to forgoing profitable ideas from teammates. However, they also found that stars with a large breadth of knowledge and better collaborative strength lead to more emergent leadership, and that teams often benefited from the star being second on a project. This may be promising as PM practices such as team-based pay and coaching may help a star collaborate with others or diversify skills and assuage this challenge.

Next, following the value of the position, commensurate effort should be placed in ensuring that the appraisal process is received positively by providing proper adequate notice of performance standards, having sufficient evidence to support performance based claims, and allowing the employee to participate in the review process (Cawley, Keeping, & Levy, 1998; Folger et al., 1992; Pichler et al., 2016). The consequential upturn in fairness perceptions as well and increased effort mitigate negative reactions that reduce motivation and decrease performance (Jawahar, 2010; Levy & Williams, 2004; Pichler, 2012) that could lead to dire costs in critical roles and top performers. Supervisors of these critical roles should also place more effort into their relationship with these talented employees. This is because quality relationships with the performance appraisal rater is strongly correlated with positive reactions to the appraisal process (Pichler, 2012). Ultimately, this will aid in the retention and engagement of highly talented employees and may reduce significant vacillations in performance and obviate replacement costs.

PM strategies such as goal setting, coaching, performance improvement plans and appraisals, and continent pay can be utilized to encourage skill development and ensure continuing commitment to high-performance. This can aid in the development to talent pools that can fill openings in important roles.

From High-Potential to Star Performer

To build talent pools that can be directed into strategic positions, practitioners must be able to identify talent at all levels, being those who are high-potential prior to hiring, those who are currently high-performing, and those who are stars, and be able to direct that talent from one level to the next. Prior to organization entry, high-potential individuals can be identified utilizing psychometric measures such as IQ (being a strong predictor of performance) as well as the Big 5 personality tests (where conscientiousness is most predictive of performance) (Barrick & Mount, 1991). They can then be trained in firm-specific skills and then measured on their performance to see if their performance meets or exceeds that of comparable others.

High-performers must be identified through supervisor rating, 360-degree feedback mechanisms, objective measures, or other performance measures that are often part of a PM system. While performance is easy to identify in roles with objective performance measures (e.g., sales revenue), it is not as easy in roles that have fewer concrete outcomes (e.g., customer satisfaction or expediency in processing reports). Therefore, supervisors and managers must play careful attention to those qualitative roles to identify high-performers and reward them appropriately. Without such measures, a non-high-performer could be promoted due to poor rater reliability or high-performing talent could be missed.

Moving someone along the spectrum from high-performer to star, however, is a much different challenge due to the psychological prerequisites for being a star. High IQ would be an obvious prerequisite, but one longitudinal study of 12 children with IQs in excess of 180 found that almost all had reached star status in their professions by age 22 (Hollingworth, 1942). That is, to suggest that those who will rise to stardom will likely do so quickly or at a minimum be identifiable. O'Boyle and Kroska (2017) also posit that stars may demonstrate higher levels of narcissism and psychopathy compared to

Table 40.1 Developing talent from high-potential to stardom

Type of Employee	Unique Challenges	PM and HR Strategies
High potential	• Lack of firm specific skills • Social integration • Realization of potential	• Coaching • Measurement • Appraisal/feedback • Onboarding & ongoing training • External recruitment
High performing	• Within-person variability • Retention • Development & succession planning	• Coaching • Measurement • Appraisal/feedback • Cross-training & development • Internally developed
Stars★	• Retention • Knowledge transfer • Power-sharing	• Contingent team-based pay • Informal feedback • Provides coaching and feedback • Early recruitment

★May differ on type of star (see Kehoe, Lepak, & Bentley, 2018)

average, as CEOs tend to exhibit these traits (Babiak, Neumann, & Hare, 2010; Resick, Whitman, Weingarden, & Hiller, 2009). True stars may sometimes be difficult to even develop.

Stars are also in the best position facilitate PM practices given that they have immense social influence (Pfeffer, 1981) and would be most capable of bringing someone else to stardom. However, any time spent aiding other colleagues may detract from other value-added activities. More research should be done to elucidate these challenges. Nonetheless, it may be prudent to apply these star management styles to any of a firm's top performers given that the power law distribution of performance seems to behave with scale invariance (Aguinis & O'Boyle, 2014). In and where a star has been removed from a system, a firm would still see value from their top performers where small increases in performance leads to large returns. The total value created, however, would still be less than that of a star.

Based on the theories, concepts, and arguments presented in this chapter, we offer the following table (see Table 40.1) as a framework to guide the PM of individuals from high-potential to star.

Discussion

There is little doubt that many firms today are looking to human resources (HR) as a source of sustained competitive advantage. This is increasingly important given challenges of globalization, shortages of highly-skilled labor, and increased competitive pressures. HR are a source of competitive advantage in that effective HRM is related positively to firm performance (e.g., Huselid, 1995). That said, exactly how firms can most effectively leverage HR is a matter of extensive debate and is dependent upon firm strategy, structure, and culture. The over-arching proposition of this chapter is that when TM and PM practices are integrated in a way so as to reinforce workforce differentiation, firms will gain a source of sustained competitive advantage.

Implicit in our analysis is that organizations may also seek to utilize PM discriminately based upon different types of employees (high-potential, high-performing, and stars) and positions (strategic and non-strategic), and that people at various levels may have different psychological needs and appraisals. This differentiation is important for directing resources toward those individuals who are likely to add the largest value to a firm since PM strategies require time and money to implement. However, these strategies may have implications for justice perceptions in the workplace. Therefore, more research is needed as how the integration of TM and PM is related to employee reactions and attitudes, and how these reactions can be managed.

Implications for Theory and Future Research

Our over-arching position is consistent with the resource-based view of the firm (Barney, 1991). Individuals in positions that are difficult to replace (e.g., due to labor force shortages) are likely to be rarer than other individuals and their importance warrants additional attention. When individuals in these positions gain more firm-specific knowledge through various TM practices, such as employee development, and when their performance is managed effectively, their performance should increase and so too will their inimitability. Employee knowledge and skills will be more closely tied to a particular firm's production methods, culture, work design, etc., and these ties will be difficult for other firms to quickly or easily imitate. If these links are supported empirically, this provides further evidence for the resource-based view of the firm as an important theoretical lens by which to understand the value of HR and effective HRM.

This provides some important directions for future research. At a high level, we suggest that future research on TM should simultaneously consider PM practices and vice versa. There is very little if any research, to our knowledge, that has investigated both TM and PM in the same study. For instance, do firms that design TM and PM systems so as to support high-performers in strategically valuable positions outperform firms that do not? Do firms that tailor their TM and PM based on competitive strategy and organizational culture outperform firms that do not? These, we believe, are important empirical questions worthy of research attention.

Additional attention should be placed on PM in the context of stars as not all PM practices may make sense for star employees. Stars may perceive formal appraisals, training efforts, coaching, or other PM practices as a waste of time or otherwise unbeneficial due to their top performance. Indeed, in some instances, they may not be the target of many PM efforts but rather the enactor of PM as they would be in the best position to provide coaching, feedback, and appraisals to others, and their insights might be perceived as more valuable to their co-workers. However, engaging in either receiving or providing PM practices may take away from star productivity. Lastly, these practices may vary based on whether the star is a performance star, social star, or universal star (see Kehoe, Lepak, & Bentley, 2018). While many of these PM practices are very likely to lead to positive outcomes, more research is needed to delineate when this is the case.

The more specific links we identified through our integration of TM and PM should also be investigated empirically. For instance, if careful attention is paid to perceptions of performance appraisal fairness among employees in strategically valuable positions, will this in fact lead to higher performance and increased retention? This, we argue, is one of several key TM questions raised by our review. If high-performing individuals in strategically valuable positions do not feel their appraisal process was fair, this could lead to a host of negative outcomes not only for employees, such as reduced motivation (see Pichler, 2012), but also for the firm, especially since these are precisely the employees our review would suggest are most valuable and thus should be supported and retained.

Implications for Practice

The TM literature relies on several assumptions, for example, that attracting and retaining human capital is both increasingly difficult and increasingly important, given growing competitive pressures from globalization and international demographic trends. These trends include the increasingly tight labor markets for highly skilled workers in the northern hemisphere, and the increasingly short tenure of employment relationships for knowledge workers (e.g., Tucker, Kao, & Verma, 2005). We argue that these assumptions are increasingly true, and that these trends will increase the importance of TM and the integration of TM and PM into the future. Our review offers some specific recommendations for managers and organizations so as to help firms address these challenges.

For TM or PM to be optimally effective, these should be designed in consideration of each other and implemented in a differentiated architecture. While this is perhaps straightforward, it is rarely put into practice (Cappelli, 2008). PM systems should be designed not only to identify and effectively reward high-performers, but also to identify high-potential individuals that would be a good fit with strategically valuable positions.

For this to happen, it is important that TM and PM processes be tied to a workforce differentiation HR strategy, and that C-suite executives are bought into this strategy. Put differently, it is important that TM and PM be part of strategy formulation and implementation, that HR challenges are discussed among top management teams, and that there are ongoing discussions between line managers and HR managers about top talent. In this way, TM and PM practices can be integrated with each other and designed in such a way so as to support a firm's characteristics, such as competitive strategy, environmental and competitive challenges, culture, and so on.

With that said, an important consideration here is that, in modern job-hopping culture where people sell their skills on the open market, there is significant risk associated with investing in employees. As above, we have witnessed a war for talent for some time and, in our view, talent has won. Highly-skilled, high-performing individuals, especially those in tight labor markets, have leverage over employers and are often so-called free agents, i.e., not contractually bound in terms of their employment relationship and therefore able to move freely between firms.

This suggests that there is a high potential for individuals to take their newly developed skills to another organization to receive a higher wage. This necessitates an increased emphasis on strategies that retain those individuals with unique, often company specific and valuable skills, as well as those talented individuals that inhabit roles of strategic importance. Nonetheless, developing employees and creating succession plans come at a high risk of losing that employee to a competitor (Cappelli, 2008).

Notwithstanding, it remains a strategic imperative that businesses be diligent in their TM as a business is merely an amalgamation of teams of people. The introductory quote from Peter Druker that "developing talent is a business' most important task—the sine qua non of competition in a knowledge economy" still reigns true. Excellent businesses do have strategic processes in place for the development and management of their talent (Ready & Conger, 2007) and that is why they thrive.

References

Adler, P. S., & Kwon, S. W. 2002. Social capital: Prospects for a new concept. *Academy of Management Review,* 27(1): 17-40.

Aguinis, H. 2013. *Performance management.* Saddle River, NJ: Pearson.

Aguinis, H., Boyd, B. K., Pierce, C. A., Short, J. C., Huselid, M. A., & Becker, B. E. 2011. Bridging micro and macro domains: Workforce differentiation and strategic human resource management. *Journal of Management,* 37(2): 421-428. doi: https://doi.org/10.1177/0149206310373400

Aguinis, H., & O'Boyle Jr, E. 2014. Star performers in twenty-first century organizations. *Personnel Psychology,* 67(2): 313-350.

Ashton, C., & Morton, L. 2005. Managing talent for competitive advantage: Taking a systemic approach to talent management. *Strategic HR Review,* 4(5): 28-31.

Babiak, P., Neumann, C. S., & Hare, R. D. 2010. Corporate psychopathy: Talking the walk. *Behavioral Sciences & the Law,* 28(2): 174-193.

Balzer, W. K., & Sulsky, L. M. 1992. Halo and performance appraisal research: A critical examination. *Journal of Applied Psychology,* 77(6): 975.

Barney, J. B. 2001. Resource-based theories of competitive advantage: A ten-year retrospective on the resource-based view. *Journal of Management,* 27(6): 643-650.

Barrick, M. R., & Mount, M. K. 1991. The big five personality dimensions and job performance: a meta-analysis. *Personnel Psychology,* 44(1): 1-26.

Becker, B. E., Huselid, M. A., & Beatty, R. W. 2009. *The differentiated workforce: Transforming talent into strategic impact.* Cambridge, MA: Harvard Business Press.

Benson, G. S. 2006. Employee development, commitment and intention to turnover: A test of 'employability' policies in action. *Human Resource Management Journal,* 16(2): 173-192.

Bidwell, M. 2011. Paying more to get less: The effects of external hiring versus internal mobility. *Administrative Science Quarterly,* 56(3): 369-407.

Binnewies, C., Sonnentag, S., & Mojza, E. J. 2009. Daily performance at work: Feeling recovered in the morning as a predictor of day-level job performance. *Journal of Organizational Behavior,* 30(1): 67-93.

Boudreau, J. W., & Ramstad, P. M. 2005. Talentship, talent segmentation, and sustainability: A new HR decision science paradigm for a new strategy definition. *Human Resource Management,* 44(2): 129-136.

Buckingham, M., & Clifton, D. O. 2001. *Now, discover your strengths.* Simon and Schuster.

Call, M. L., Nyberg, A. J., & Thatcher, S. 2015. Stargazing: An integrative conceptual review, theoretical reconciliation, and extension for star employee research. *Journal of Applied Psychology,* 100(3): 623.

Cappelli, P. 2008. Talent management for the twenty-first century. *Harvard Business Review,* 86(3): 74.

Carnahan, S., & Somaya, D. 2013. Alumni effects and relational advantage: The impact on outsourcing when a buyer hires employees from a supplier's competitors. *Academy of Management Journal,* 56(6): 1578-1600.

Cascio, W. F., & Luthans, F. 2014. Reflections on the metamorphosis at Robben Island: The role of institutional work and positive psychological capital. *Journal of Management Inquiry,* 23(1): 51-67.

Cawley, B. D., Keeping, L. M., & Levy, P. E. 1998. Participation in the performance appraisal process and employee reactions: A meta-analytic review of field investigations. *Journal of Applied Psychology,* 83(4): 615.

Chen, J. S., & Garg, P. 2018. Dancing with the stars: Benefits of a star employee's temporary absence for organizational performance. *Strategic Management Journal,* 39(5): 1239-1267.

Collings, D. G. 2017. Workforce differentiation. *Oxford handbook of talent management:* 301-317.

Collings, D. G., & Mellahi, K. 2009. Strategic talent management: A review and research agenda. *Human Resource Management Review,* 19(4): 304-313.

Dalal, R. S., Bhave, D. P., & Fiset, J. 2014. Within-person variability in job performance: A theoretical review and research agenda. *Journal of Management,* 40(5): 1396-1436.

Deadrick, D. L., Bennett, N., & Russell, C. J. 1997. Using hierarchical linear modeling to examine dynamic performance criteria over time. *Journal of Management,* 23(6): 745-757.

DeFillippi, R. J., & Arthur, M. B. 1994. The boundaryless career: A competency-based perspective. *Journal of Organizational Behavior,* 15(4): 307-324.

DeNisi, A. S., & Pritchard, R. D. 2006. Performance appraisal, performance management and improving individual performance: A motivational framework. *Management and Organization Review,* 2(2): 253-277.

Dieleman, M., Toonen, J., Touré, H., & Martineau, T. 2006. The match between motivation and performance management of health sector workers in Mali. *Human Resources for Health,* 4(1): 2.

Dokko, G., & Jiang, W. 2017. Managing talent across organizations: The portability of individual performance. *Oxford handbook of talent management:* 115-133.

Durham, C. C., & Bartol, K. M. 2000. Pay for performance. *Handbook of principles of organizational behavior:* 150-165.

Ericsson, K. A., Krampe, R. T., & Tesch-Römer, C. 1993. The role of deliberate practice in the acquisition of expert performance. *Psychological Review,* 100(3): 363.

Fisher, C. D., & Noble, C. S. 2004. A within-person examination of correlates of performance and emotions while working. *Human Performance,* 17(2): 145-168.

Fletcher, C., & Williams, R. 1996. Performance management, job satisfaction and organizational commitment. *British Journal of Management,* 7(2): 169-179.

Folger, R., Konovsky, M. A., & Cropanzano, R. 1992. A due process metaphor for performance appraisal. *Research in Organizational Behavior,* 14: 129-129.

Gallardo-Gallardo, E., Thunnissen, M., & Scullion, H. 2020. Talent management: context matters. *International Journal of Human Resource Management,* 31(4): 457-473.

Gagné, F. 2004. Transforming gifts into talents: The DMGT as a developmental theory. *High Ability Studies,* 15(2): 119-147.

Gerhart, B., & Milkovich, G. T. 1992. Employee compensation: Research and practice. Inn M. D. Dunnette & L. M. Hough (Eds.), *Handbook of industrial and organizational psychology,* Vol. 3: 481-569. Palo Alto.

Groysberg, B., McLean, A. N., & Nohria, N. 2006. Are leaders portable?. *Harvard Business Review,* 84(5): 92.

Groysberg, B., & Nanda, A. 2004. Can they take it with them? The portability of star knowledge workers' performance: Myth or reality?. In *Econometric Society 2004 North American Winter Meetings* (No. 465). Econometric Society.

Groysberg, B., Sant, L., & Abrahams, R. 2008. When 'stars' migrate, do they still perform like stars?. *MIT Sloan Management Review,* 50(1): 41.

Heneman, R. L. 1992. *Merit pay: Linking pay increases to performance ratings.* Addison-Wesley/Addison Wesley Longman.

Hollingworth, L. S. 1942. *Children above IQ 180: Origin and development.* World Book.

Huang, J., & Tansley, C. 2012. Sneaking through the minefield of talent management: The notion of rhetorical obfuscation. *The International Journal of Human Resource Management,* 23(17): 3673-3691.

Hunter, J. E., Schmidt, F. L., & Judiesch, M. K. 1990. Individual differences in output variability as a function of job complexity. *Journal of Applied Psychology,* 75(1): 28.

Huselid, M. A. 1995. The impact of human resource management practices on turnover, productivity, and corporate financial performance. *Academy of Management Journal,* 38(3): 635-672.

Huselid, M. A., Becker, B. E., & Beatty, R. W. 2005. The workforce scorecard: Managing human capital to execute strategy. *Harvard Business Review Press,* 8.

Huselid, M. A., Beatty, R. W., & Becker, B. E. 2005. 'A players' or 'A positions'?. *Harvard Business Review,* 83(12): 110-117.

Jawahar, I. M. 2010. The mediating role of appraisal feedback reactions on the relationship between rater feedback-related behaviors and ratee performance. *Group & Organization Management,* 35(4): 494-526.

Jenkins Jr, G. D., Mitra, A., Gupta, N., & Shaw, J. D. 1998. Are financial incentives related to performance? A meta-analytic review of empirical research. *Journal of Applied Psychology,* 83(5), 777-787.

Judge, T. A., & Ferris, G. R. 1993. Social context of performance evaluation decisions. *Academy of Management Journal,* 36(1): 80-105.

Kanfer, R. 1987. Task-specific motivation: An integrative approach to issues of measurement, mechanisms, processes, and determinants. *Journal of Social and Clinical Psychology,* 5(2): 237-264.

Katz, L. F. 1986. Efficiency wage theories: A partial evaluation. *NBER Macroeconomics Annual,* 1: 235-276.

Keeping, L. M., & Levy, P. E. 2000. Performance appraisal reactions: Measurement, modeling, and method bias. *Journal of Applied Psychology,* 85(5): 708.

Kehoe, R. R., Lepak, D. P., & Bentley, F. S. 2018. Let's call a star a star: Task performance, external status, and exceptional contributors in organizations. *Journal of Management,* 44(5): 1848-1872.

Kehoe, R. R., & Tzabbar, D. 2015. Lighting the way or stealing the shine? An examination of the duality in star scientists' effects on firm innovative performance. *Strategic Management Journal,* 36(5): 709-727.

King, K. A., & Vaiman, V. 2019. Enabling effective talent management through a macro-contingent approach: A framework for research and practice. *Business Research Quarterly,* 22(3): 194-206.

Kluger, A. N., & DeNisi, A. 1996. The effects of feedback interventions on performance: A historical review, a meta-analysis, and a preliminary feedback intervention theory. *Psychological Bulletin,* 119(2): 254.

Lazear, E. P. 1999. *Output-based pay: incentives or sorting?* (No. w7419). National Bureau of Economic Research.

Lepak, D. P., & Snell, S. A. 1999. The human resource architecture: Toward a theory of human capital allocation and development. *Academy of Management Review,* 24(1): 31-48.

Levy, P. E., & Williams, J. R. 2004. The social context of performance appraisal: A review and framework for the future. *Journal of Management,* 30(6): 881-905.

Lewis, R. E., & Heckman, R. J. 2006. Talent management: A critical review. *Human Resource Management Review,* 16(2): 139-154.

Locke, E. A., & Latham, G. P. 2002. Building a practically useful theory of goal setting and task motivation: A 35-year odyssey. *American Psychologist,* 57(9): 705.

London, M. 2003. *Job feedback: Giving, seeking, and using feedback for performance improvement.* Psychology Press.

Luthans, F. 2002. Positive organizational behavior: Developing and managing psychological strengths. *The Academy of Management Executive,* 16(1): 57-72.

MacMillan, I. C., & McGrath, R. G. 1997. Discovering new points of differentiation. *Harvard Business Review,* 75: 133-145.

Maltarich, M. A., Nyberg, A. J., & Reilly, G. 2010. A conceptual and empirical analysis of the cognitive ability–voluntary turnover relationship. *Journal of Applied Psychology,* 95(6): 1058.

Marescaux, E., De Winne, S., & Sels, L. 2013. HR practices and affective organisational commitment:(when) does HR differentiation pay off?. *Human Resource Management Journal,* 23(4): 329-345.

Mento, A. J., Steel, R. P., & Karren, R. J. 1987. A meta-analytic study of the effects of goal setting on task performance: 1966-1984. *Organizational Behavior and Human Decision Processes,* 39(1): 52-83.

Milkovich, G. T., Newman, J. M., & Milkovich, C. 2002. *Compensation* (Vol. 8). New York: McGraw-Hill.

Minbashian, A. 2017. Within-person variability in performance. *The Oxford handbook of talent management:* 66.

Minbashian, A., Earl, J., & Bright, J. E. 2013. Openness to experience as a predictor of job performance trajectories. *Applied Psychology,* 62(1): 1-12.

Minbashian, A., & Luppino, D. 2014. Short-term and long-term within-person variability in performance: An integrative model. *Journal of Applied Psychology,* 99(5): 898.

Minbashian, A., Wood, R. E., & Beckmann, N. 2010. Task-contingent conscientiousness as a unit of personality at work. *Journal of Applied Psychology,* 95(5): 793.

Narin, F., & Breitzman, A. 1995. Inventive productivity. *Research policy,* 24(4): 507-519.

Nyberg, A. 2010. Retaining your high performers: Moderators of the performance–job satisfaction–voluntary turnover relationship. *Journal of Applied Psychology,* 95(3): 440.

O'Boyle Jr, E., & Aguinis, H. 2012. The best and the rest: Revisiting the norm of normality of individual performance. *Personnel Psychology,* 65(1): 79-119.

O'Boyle, E., & Kroska, S. 2017. Star performers. *Oxford handbook of talent management:* 43-65.

Peterson, C., & Seligman, M. E. 2006. The Values in Action (VIA) classification of strengths. *A Life Worth Living: Contributions to Positive Psychology:* 29-48.

Pfeffer, J. 1981. Understanding the role of power in decision making. *Power in Organizations:* 404-423.

Pichler, S. 2012. The social context of performance appraisal and appraisal reactions: A meta-analysis. *Human Resource Management,* 51(5): 709-732.

Pichler, S., Beenen, G., & Wood, S. 2017. *Feedback frequency and appraisal reactions: A meta-analytic test of moderators.* Academy of Management Best Paper Proceedings.

Pichler, S., Varma, A., Michel, J. S., Levy, P. E., Budhwar, P. S., & Sharma, A. 2016. Leader-member exchange, group-and individual-level procedural justice and reactions to performance appraisals. *Human Resource Management,* 55(5): 871-883.

Polyhart, E. P. & Cragun, O. R. 2017 Human capital resource complementarities. *Oxford Handbook of Talent Management:* 134-149.

Ramsay, H., Scholarios, D., & Harley, B. 2000. Employees and high-performance work systems: testing inside the black box. *British Journal of industrial relations,* 38(4): 501-531.

Ready, D. A., & Conger, J. A. 2007. Make your company a talent factory. *Harvard Business Review,* 85(6): 68.

Renzulli, J. S. 2005. Applying gifted education pedagogy to total talent development for all students. *Theory into Practice,* 44(2): 80-89.

Resick, C. J., Whitman, D. S., Weingarden, S. M., & Hiller, N. J. 2009. The bright-side and the dark-side of CEO personality: examining core self-evaluations, narcissism, transformational leadership, and strategic influence. *Journal of Applied Psychology,* 94(6): 1365.

Robinson, C., Fetters, R., Riester, D., & Bracco, A. 2009. The paradox of potential: A suggestion for guiding talent management discussions in organizations. *Industrial and Organizational Psychology,* 2(4): 413.

Rousseau, D. M., Ho, V. T., & Greenberg, J. 2006. I-deals: Idiosyncratic terms in employment relationships. *Academy of Management Review,* 31(4): 977-994.

Rynes, S. L., Gerhart, B., & Parks, L. 2005. Personnel psychology: Performance evaluation and pay for performance. *Annual Review of Psychology,* 56: 571-600.

Shaw, J. D., & Gupta, N. 2007. Pay system characteristics and quit patterns of good, average, and poor performers. *Personnel Psychology,* 60(4): 903-928.

Smilansky, J. 2006. *Developing executive talent: Best practices from global leaders.* Chichester: John Wiley.

Sparrow, P. 2007. Globalization of HR at function level: four UK-based case studies of the international recruitment and selection process. *International Journal of Human Resource Management,* 18: 845-867.

Sparrow, P. 2019. A historical analysis of critiques in the talent management debate. *Business Research Quarterly,* 22(3): 160-170.

Stahl, G. K., Björkman, I., Farndale, E., Morris, S. S., Paauwe, J., Stiles, P., & Wright, P. M. 2007. *Global talent management: How leading multinationals build and sustain their talent pipeline:* 24. INSEAD faculty and research working papers.

Steelman, L. A., Levy, P. E., & Snell, A. F. 2004. The feedback environment scale: Construct definition, measurement, and validation. *Educational and Psychological Measurement,* 64(1): 165-184.

Stewart, G. L., & Nandkeolyar, A. K. 2006. Adaptation and intraindividual variation in sales outcomes: Exploring the interactive effects of personality and environmental opportunity. *Personnel Psychology,* 59(2): 307-332.

Stewart, G. L., & Nandkeolyar, A. K. 2007. Exploring how constraints created by other people influence intraindividual variation in objective performance measures. *Journal of Applied Psychology,* 92(4): 1149.

Stewart, T. 1997. A. 1997. *Intellectual capital: The new wealth of organizations.* New York: Doubleday Dell Publishing Group.

Somaya, D., Williamson, I. O., & Lorinkova, N. 2008. Gone but not lost: The different performance impacts of employee mobility between cooperators versus competitors. *Academy of Management Journal,* 51(5): 936-953.

Spender, J. C. 1989. *Industry recipes.* Oxford: Basil Blackwell.

Thoresen, C. J., Bradley, J. C., Bliese, P. D., & Thoresen, J. D. 2004. The big five personality traits and individual job performance growth trajectories in maintenance and transitional job stages. *Journal of Applied Psychology,* 89(5): 835.

Tims, M., & Bakker, A. B. 2010. Job crafting: Towards a new model of individual job redesign. *SA Journal of Industrial Psychology,* 36(2): 1-9.

Trevor, C. O. 2001. Interactions among actual ease-of-movement determinants and job satisfaction in the prediction of voluntary turnover. *Academy of Management Journal,* 44(4): 621-638.

Trevor, C. O., Gerhart, B., & Boudreau, J. W. 1997. Voluntary turnover and job performance: Curvilinearity and the moderating influences of salary growth and promotions. *Journal of Applied Psychology,* 82(1): 44.

Trevor, C. O., Reilly, G., & Gerhart, B. 2012. Reconsidering pay dispersion's effect on the performance of interdependent work: Reconciling sorting and pay inequality. *Academy of Management Journal,* 55(3): 585-610.

Tucker, E., Kao, T., & Verma, N. 2005. Next-generation talent management. *Business Credit,* 107: 20-27.

Wood, A. M., Linley, P. A., Maltby, J., Kashdan, T. B., & Hurling, R. 2011. Using personal and psychological strengths leads to increases in well-being over time: A longitudinal study and the development of the strengths use questionnaire. *Personality and Individual Differences,* 50(1): 15-19.

41

THE RELATIONSHIP BETWEEN TALENT MANAGEMENT AND INDIVIDUAL AND ORGANIZATIONAL PERFORMANCE

Benjamin Krebs
Marius Wehner

Introduction

Recent survey-based studies across the U.S.A. and Canada document that talent development is the number one priority in majority of organizations (LinkedIn, 2017, 2018, 2019), and most research on talent management (TM) presumes a positive relationship between TM and organizational performance. However, despite the growing interest in TM (McDonnell, Collings, Mellahi, & Schuler, 2017), literature reviews have repeatedly documented weak evidence base on the relationship between TM and organizational performance (Collings, 2014, 2015, 2017; Gallardo-Gallardo & Thunnissen, 2016; McDonnell et al., 2017). Moreover, research on individual outcomes of TM practices and talent designation suggests there are positive and negative effects on "talents" and "non-talents", but the evidence is inconclusive (De Boeck, Meyers, & Dries, 2018). Therefore, how the individual-level effects of TM affect organizational outcomes remains uncertain.

In this chapter, we synthesize theoretical perspectives and empirical accounts on the relationship between TM and individual and organizational performance. For this purpose, our review bridges several fields of research, examining the academic and practitioner literature on individual and organizational outcomes of TM and related studies on status in organizations and leadership development. In doing so, we seek to extend the perspective on TM and outline the ways in which future research could overcome the shortcomings of previous research and connect with the literature on strategic human resource management (HRM) and human capital to help develop the field.

Observers have repeatedly noted that the progress of the field has been hampered by a lack of agreement as to what constitutes talent and TM (Cappelli & Keller, 2014; Lewis & Heckman, 2006; McDonnell et al., 2017). Relatedly, reviews have documented that a high number of studies on TM lack an explicit theoretical foundation or make use of theoretical frameworks only superficially to accentuate the authors' line of reasoning (Gallardo-Gallardo & Thunnissen, 2016; McDonnell et al., 2017). For these reasons, we decided to opt for a selective review of theoretical and empirical work, speaking to the relationship between TM and organizational performance.

In particular, we focused our review on studies that (explicitly or implicitly, based on our reading) conform to TM defined as the practice of disproportionately investing resources in an exclusive subset of employees with the requisite cognitive abilities and social-, growth-, and learning-competencies to succeed in strategically valuable positions in the future (cf. Finkelstein et al., 2018: 4; Latukha & Veselova, 2018: 4). This workforce differentiation approach to TM (Collings & Mellahi, 2009; Collings, Mellahi, & Cascio, 2018) is typically reflected in talent searches within specific employee groups (e.g., professionals and managers) and highly selective talent identification (Swailes, Downs, & Orr, 2014).

DOI: 10.4324/9781315474687-41

Outcomes of Talent Management: The Individual Level

Theoretical Perspectives

Effects of Talent Status

The majority of studies focusing on individual-level outcomes of TM are concerned with *positive* employee reactions to talent designation. From a social exchange (Blau, 1964) or psychological contract perspective (Rousseau, 1995), talent designation entails a (promise of) preferential treatment, which talents reciprocate with discretionary effort and commitment (De Boeck et al., 2018). Relatedly, talent designation reflects the assignment of status to employees and as such is associated with superior resources that talent can exploit to achieve higher levels of performance (Bothner, Kim, & Smith, 2012). From a motivational perspective, talent status triggers a Pygmalion effect (Eden, 1984) by signaling appreciation of past contributions and a belief in employees' potential to succeed in more senior roles, thereby increasing employees' self-efficacy and, in turn, performance.

From a status perspective, talent designation may also entail *negative* reactions. Status can be detrimental to performance when status is seen as an end in itself, resulting in self-satisfaction and complacency (Ehrnrooth et al., 2018; Pfeffer, 2001), and when status distracts individuals from their actual duties (Bothner et al., 2012). The literature on high-performers suggests that employees who excel in their work environment display behavioral tendencies that provoke harmful coworker behaviors as a means of counterbalancing threats to status, identity, or resources (e.g., Jensen, Patel, & Raver, 2014). Moreover, Park, Chae, and Kim (2017) argued that supervisors' overreliance on high-performers puts them at risk of role overload.

Effects of Non-talent Status

It is difficult to imagine any positive effects of TM on non-talent (Cappelli & Keller, 2014). From an ethical perspective, the preferential treatment of an exclusive group of employees equates to withholding opportunities from excluded employees (Swailes, 2013). From a social exchange and equity perspective, these ethical concerns translate into tangible threats to the identity of non-talent and to the exchange relationship with their employer, resulting in retaliation against talented coworkers (e.g., through victimization; Jensen et al., 2014) or their employer (e.g., through withdrawal behaviors; Hanisch & Hulin, 1990) to restore equity.

From a motivational perspective, non-talent status triggers a Golem effect (Eden, 1984) by signaling incommensurate contributions and a disbelief in employees' potential to succeed in more senior roles, thereby lowering employees' self-efficacy and, in turn, performance. From an organizational justice perspective, organizations may buffer the negative consequences of low perceived distributive justice pertaining to non-talent status when TM is perceived as procedurally, informationally, and interpersonally fair (Gelens, Dries, Hofmans, & Pepermans, 2013).

From a social comparison perspective, in contrast, comparisons of non-talent with talent could result in either negative *or* positive effects on work attitudes and behaviors of non-talent, but we currently lack knowledge about the conditions under which non-talent engages in (favorable or unfavorable) comparisons with talent (cf. De Boeck, Dries, & Meyers, 2017).

Empirical Evidence

Positive Effects of Talent Status

Talent has been shown to surpass non-talent on a wide range of work attitudes and behaviors (cf. De Boeck et al., 2018).[1] Positive differences between talent and non-talent have been found with respect to:

- in-role behaviors, including work effort (see Table 41.1, study 1) and job performance (10)
- extra-role behaviors, including competency development (2, 9) and organizational citizenship behaviors (5, 6)

Table 41.1 Quantitative individual-level studies on talent status and TM practices conforming to WD-type TM definition

Study	Reference	Theory	Outcomes	Predictors	Mediators	Moderators	Method and Sample
1	Gelens et al. (2014)	RBV, OJT	Job satisfaction, work effort	Talent status	Perceived distributive justice	Perceived procedural justice	Survey; N=203 senior hipos, junior hipos non-hipos from one firm
2	Swailes & Blackburn (2016)	RBV, ET, SET, PT	Covered domains: competency development, organizational justice, supervisory/organizational support, career development motivation	Talent status	–	–	Mixed; N=34 employees from 3 talent pools (emerging talent, scientists, leadership group) and control group from one firm
3	Dries et al. (2012)	WD, new careers theory	Career satisfaction	Supervisor-rated performance, career orientation	Serial multiple mediation: Talent status; employer inducements; employee attitudes	–	Survey; N=941 hipos, key experts, and average performers from 12 firms
4	Gelens et al. (2015)	WD, ST	Affective commitment	Study 1: Talent status; Study 2: Management trainee status	Perceived organizational support	–	Survey study 1: N=203 hipos and non-hipos from one firm Survey study 2: N=202 management trainees and non-trainees from another firm
5	Seopa et al. (2015)	PCT	Transactional/relational PC, organizational commitment, affective trust, OCB, turnover intention	Talent status	–	–	Survey; N=195 talent pool- and non-talent-pool employees from 3 firms
6	Malik et al. (2017)	SET, HR attribution theory	Affective commitment, job satisfaction, turnover intent, OCB	Talent status	hipo attributions (commitment-focused, control-focused)	Organizational trust	Survey; N=242 employees from general working population (talent and non-talent), screened for existence of hipo program in their firm
7	Dries et al. (2014)	RBV/WD, SET, PCT, ST	Perceived employer/employee PC obligations w.r.t. time frame and performance requirements	Talent status, self-perceived employability	–	–	Survey; N=103 hipos and non-hipo from 5 firms

(*Continued*)

Table 41.1 Quantitative individual-level studies on talent status and TM practices conforming to WD-type TM definition (*Continued*)

Study	Reference	Theory	Outcomes	Predictors	Mediators	Moderators	Method and Sample
8	Björkman, Ehrnrooth, Mäkelä, Smale, & Sumelius (2013)	SET	Accepting increasing performance demands, commitment to building competencies, support of strategic priorities, identification with unit and MNC, turnover intentions	Talent status (awareness)	-	-	Survey; N=769 professionals/managers who believe they have been designated as talent/who do not know/who believe they have not been designated as talent from 9 firms
9	Khoreva & Vaiman (2015)	SET, EXT	Actual participation in leadership development activities	Talent status, perceived effectiveness of leadership development	Willingness to participate in leadership development activities	-	Survey; N=330 employees from 8 firms believed to be potential top managers 8 years ahead
10	Dries & Pepermans (2007)	Personal factors model	Job performance, career commitment, emotional intelligence	Talent status	-	-	Survey; N=102 hipo managers and non-hipo managers from 3 firms
11	Kotlyar (2013)	PT, SDT	Performance expectations, task commitment, performance satisfaction	Publicly communicated hipo status based on prediction of "outstanding performance"	-	Privately communicated performance feedback	Laboratory experiment; N=277 undergraduate students in 2 (hipo status) x 2 (performance feedback) experimental design with multiple rounds of a real-effort task
12	Kotlyar et al. (2014)	SDT	Perceived public scrutiny, motivation for status change, risk tolerance in decision-making	Experimentally manipulated talent status: studies 1-2: talent vs. non-talent; study 3: talent vs. non-talent vs. no info	-	-	Vignette experiments; study 1/2/3: N=45/159/245 undergraduate HR and business students
13	Chami-Malaeb and Garavan (2013)	RBV, SET	Intention to stay	Talent development practices, leadership development practices	Affective commitment	-	Survey; N=238 hipos from 9 firms

14	Khoreva et al. (2017)	SET, PCT	Commitment to competence development	Perceived TM practice effectiveness (w.r.t. a variety of temporary assignments); gender	PC fulfillment	Gender	Survey; N=439 employees from 11 firms believed to be potential top managers 7–8 years ahead
15	Mensah and Bawole (2018)	AMO theory, P-O fit theory	Job satisfaction, OCB	Number of perceived TM practices	P-O fit	–	Survey; N=232 employees designated as talent from 33 firms
16	Ehrnrooth et al. (2018)	PCT	Talent obligations (i.e., commitment of employees to serve their employers' interests)	Employer inducements: PC fulfillment; performance management (PA-rewards link, target setting and feedback in PA); leadership development practices	–	Talent status awareness	Survey; N=321 employees designated as talent from 8 companies
17	Höglund (2012)	RBV/WD, PCT	(Perceived) Organi-zational human capital	Skill-enhancing HRM	Serial mediation: talent inducements; obligations to develop skills	–	Qualitative prestudy: 17 face-to-face interviews with heads of HR in MNCs. Quantitative survey: N=126 professionals/ managers (business school alumni)
18	Sonnenberg et al. (2014)	PCT	PC fulfillment	Perceived number of TM practices, perceived talent-differentiation strategy (inclusive vs. exclusive)	Incongruence in talent status perception	–	Mixed; Survey with N=2660 talent and non-talent employees from 21 firms, interviews with firms' TM executives

Note: hipo =High-potential employees (used interchangeably with "talent" in the TM literature); RBV=Resource-based view; OJT=Organizational justice theory; ET=Equity theory; SET=Social exchange theory; PT=Pygmalion theory; WD=Workforce differentiation; ST=Signaling theory; PC(T)=Psychological contract (theory); OCB=Organizational citizen-ship behaviors; EXT=Expectancy theory; EI=Emotional Intelligence; SDT=Self-discrepancy theory; AMO=Ability-motivation-opportunity; P–O fit=Person–organization fit; PA=Performance appraisal.

- job (1, 6) and career satisfaction (3)
- perceptions concerning the exchange relationship between employee and employer, including distributive (1, 2) and procedural justice (2), supervisory, (2) and organizational support (2-4); and perceptions of a relational psychological contract (5)
- various forms of commitment, including overall organizational commitment (3, 5, 8); affective commitment (4, 6); intention to stay (or, inversely related, turnover intentions) (6, 8); commitment towards career (2) and competency development (8, 9); and commitment towards supporting strategic priorities (8) and satisfying heightened performance demands (8).

The reported findings include moderated (1, 6, 11) and mediated effects (1, 3, 4, 6, 9), such that some relationships are more complex than suggested by this synthesis. For example, Gelens et al. (2014) found the association of talent status with work effort to be fully mediated by distributive justice (i.e., talent status did not directly affect work effort) and to reverse depending on the level of procedural justice (i.e., was positive (negative) when procedural justice was high (low)).

Negative Effects of Talent Status

A key theme of qualitative studies on responses to talent status is a mismatch in the perceived mutual obligations between employers and talent. These studies document a mismatch in expectations with respect to the responsibility for career development (Dries & De Gieter, 2014; Dries & Pepermans, 2008), the provision of and demand for clear career perspectives (Dries & Pepermans, 2008; Thunnissen, 2016), and what talents believe they owe their employer and what they believe their employer owes them (Dries & De Gieter, 2014).

This last mentioned mismatch is also supported by evidence from a quantitative study (Table 41.1, study 7). Another mismatch concerns conflicting behavioral demands – talents are expected to conform to corporate culture and existing power structures while challenging the status quo and demonstrating their uniqueness at the same time (Daubner-Siva, Ybema, Vinkenburg, & Beech, 2018; Dubouloy, 2004).

Evidence from quantitative studies suggests that talent or high-performer status instills self-satisfaction and complacency (Table 41.1, studies 11, 16), provokes undesirable status-maintaining behaviors to the detriment of task performance (12), and provokes envy and harming behaviors by non-talent coworkers who perceive their own status, identity, or resources to be threatened (e.g., Campbell, Liao, Chuang, Zhou, & Dong, 2017; Jensen et al., 2014; Reh, Tröster, & Van Quaquebeke, 2018).

Effects of Non-talent Status

Apart from the studies evidencing that talent scores higher on many work attitudes and behaviors than non-talent, evidence on the effects of non-talent status is limited to one exploratory qualitative study that provides evidence in the expected direction (Table 41.1, study 2). However, for detrimental effects of non-talent status to occur, employees must be aware of their exclusion from the talent pool, which might not be very common. Considering employees' tendency to overestimate their abilities and performance (Dunning, Heath, & Suls, 2004) and that few companies communicate their TM programs to all employees (Church & Rotolo, 2013), many non-talents will believe they have been designated as talent. In support of this argument, Sonnenberg, van Zijderveld, and Brinks (2014) found that 84% of actual non-talents in a large sample of employees from 21 multinational companies believe they have been designated as talent.

Effects of TM Practices

A small number of studies have investigated the relationship between (organization-level) TM practices as perceived by talent (Table 41.1, studies 13–16), or talent and non-talent (17, 18), on individual (13–18) and organizational outcomes (17). These studies report positive relationships between TM practices and outcomes such as affective commitment (13), intention to stay (13), perceived obligations or commitment to develop competencies (14, 17), psychological contract fulfillment (14, 18), organizational citizenship behaviors (15), job satisfaction (15), person–organization fit (15), and organization-level human capital (17). In contrast, Ehrnrooth et al. (2018; study 16) find self-aware talent to show higher commitment to serve their employer's interests only with respect to some talent inducements they examined.

Effects of Leadership Development Practices

In a recent meta-analysis, Lacerenza, Reyes, Marlow, Joseph, and Salas (2017) demonstrated that leadership development practices are more effective than previously thought. For the development of (global) leadership talent, (international) developmental work experiences are considered to be the most important and most commonly used growth opportunities (DeRue & Wellman, 2009; King et al., 2012; Tarique & Schuler, 2018). The accumulation of international work experience and the resulting dynamic cross-cultural competencies are positively related to a number of favorable individual outcomes, including strategic thinking competency (Dragoni et al., 2014), cross-cultural adjustment and performance (Shaffer, Harrison, Gregersen, Black, & Ferzandi, 2006), and global leadership effectiveness (Caligiuri & Tarique, 2012).

Shortcomings and Future Research Avenues

Endogeneity Concerns in Studies on Talent Status

Owing to the cross-sectional nature of the survey studies on individual outcomes of talent status, the observed differences in work attitudes and behaviors between talent and non-talent could have existed prior to talent designation and caused talent designation in the first place, such that the effects of talent status are likely overestimated. With regard to endogeneity concerns, three avenues might be fruitful for future research. First, researchers may exploit insider information to conduct research in organizational settings, which helps to eliminate specific endogeneity concerns (Shaw, 2009), for example, by measuring work attitudes and behaviors prior to and following the implementation of a TM program or by examining programs that closely resemble TM, but provide a more controlled setting (see, e.g., Gelens et al., 2015; study 2).

Second, identifying instrumental variables that strongly correlate with talent status and only correlate with the outcome variable through talent status (cf. Bascle, 2008) would allow for a more accurate estimation of the effect of talent status and help eliminate reverse causality as an alternative explanation. Third, laboratory or vignette experiments (cf. Aguinis & Bradley, 2014) in which talent status is manipulated allow for drawing causal inferences when carefully designed (see, e.g., Kotlyar, 2013; Kotlyar et al., 2014).

The Role of Social Comparison Processes for the Effects of Non-talent Status

From a social comparison perspective, whether and with which consequences non-talent engages in social comparisons with talent has not yet been investigated (cf. De Boeck et al., 2017). Studies on high-performer victimization commonly draw on social comparison theory, but offer limited insights into comparisons of non-talents with talents since they focus on work group contexts (see, e.g., Jensen et al., 2014) in which employees directly compete for work-related resources. In contrast, because talents are few in number and scattered across the workforce, talents and non-talents primarily compete for developmental (rather than work-related) resources and hence at a much more abstract level.

Evidence on the complexity of social comparison processes suggests that non-talents may not necessarily engage in (unfavorable) comparisons with talents. Social comparison research has evidenced that individuals selectively choose comparison referents based on factors such as similarity in performance-related attributes (e.g., education, work experience) and physical proximity (e.g., coworkers in a subsidiary versus headquarters employees), and engage in either upward or downward comparisons depending on the motivation of comparison, which can result in both positive and negative affective reactions (Suls, Martin, & Wheeler, 2002).

Hence, even if non-talent engages in upward comparisons with talent, this does not necessarily cause negative reactions. Social comparison research has evidenced that individuals who are motivated by self-improvement prefer comparisons with others who are (thought to be) *slightly* better off (Buunk & Gibbons, 2007), which can have positive effects on subsequent performance (e.g., Blanton, Buunk, Gibbons, & Kuyper, 1999). Hence, upward comparisons with talents as superior role models may provide inspiration and hope to be designated as talent in the future, increase self-efficacy and motivation, and, in turn, performance.

If non-talents, in contrast, believe that talents *substantially* outperform them, they will not choose talents as career referents. Moreover, even if non-talents recognize talents as salient career referents, they might engage in self-protection strategies to counteract identity threats in anticipation of (unfavorable) upward comparisons (Alicke, LoSchiavo, Zerbst, & Zhang, 1997; Mussweiler, Gabriel, & Bodenhausen, 2000; Shepperd & Taylor, 1999). Future research should empirically test these possibilities in light of the potentially adverse effects of social comparisons of non-talent with talent.

The Analytical Primacy of Organizational Outcomes

Considering that exclusion from the talent pool could potentially harm the morale of a large fraction of employees and that even talents show favorable (e.g., higher commitment) *and* unfavorable reactions (e.g., exaggerated expectations of employers' obligations), how these individual-level effects aggregate to impact organization-level outcomes is open to speculation, especially when seen from a long-term perspective. Therefore, studies on individual outcomes of TM necessarily draw an incomplete picture. As management scholars and scholar-practitioners, we are ultimately interested in whether management practices offer returns to *organizational* outcomes (Schneider, 2018). Therefore, we need multilevel studies examining both distal (e.g., financial performance) and proximal outcomes that ideally reflect common causes of positive *and* negative effects of TM (e.g., turnover among talent and non-talent).

Outcomes of Talent Management: The Organizational Level

Theoretical Perspectives

The workforce differentiation (WD) approach to TM (Collings, 2017; Collings et al., 2018; Collings & Mellahi, 2009) currently offers the most complete and compelling framework to substantiate the TM-performance hypothesis from an organization-level perspective. Its logic of disproportionate allocation of resources to strategic positions and those employees who have the most potential to succeed in these positions (in the future) (Finkelstein, Costanza, & Goodwin, 2018) is supported by evidence that top performers contribute disproportionately to firm performance (Aguinis & O'Boyle Jr., 2014).

Strategic positions are those which translate and enact an organization's strategy and provoke high variation in individual performance, thus providing upside potential from a managerial perspective (Huselid, Beatty, & Becker, 2005). Collings and Mellahi (2009) argue that effective TM in the tradition of WD builds on the identification of strategic positions, the development of talent pools to fill these positions, and a differentiated HR architecture that serves the needs of talent and supports the development of talent pools (see also Collings et al., 2018).

Empirical Evidence

As reviews have repeatedly documented, evidence on the link between TM and organizational performance is weak (Collings, 2014, 2015, 2017; Gallardo-Gallardo & Thunnissen, 2016; McDonnell et al., 2017). This includes evidence from research on leadership development, which almost exclusively focuses on individual outcomes (cf. Avolio, Avey, & Quisenberry, 2010). We only found two organization-level studies investigating leadership development practices that partially overlap with practices used to operationalize TM (e.g., coaching and mentoring), but these studies did not focus on differentiation between talent and non-talent (Table 41.2, studies 1, 2).

Table 41.2 Quantitative organization–level studies on TM systems and practices

Study	Reference	Definition of TM	Theory	Outcomes	Predictors	Mediators	Moderators	Method and Sample
1	Mabey & Ramirez (2005)	Management development	RBV	Productivity	MD (e.g., fast-track programs), MD ethos (e.g., emphasis on developing potential), MD provision (e.g., mentoring/ coaching); perceived importance of MD	–	–	Survey; N=179 firms
2	Subramony et al. (2018)	Leadership development	RBV	Sales growth	Differentiation (e.g., mentoring/ coaching) and integration leadership development practices (e.g., stretch assignments)	Multiple mediation: Organizational human capital; organizational social capital	–	Survey; N=223 firms
3	Ernst & Young (2010)	TM effectiveness (internal and external alignment of TM programs)	A theoretical, exploratory approach	ROE (average ROE per annum over 5-year period)	"TM effectiveness": Internal (growth strategy) and external (from global to unit scale) alignment of TM programs	–	–	Survey; N=43 firms
4	Ringo et al. (2008)	Develop strategy, attract, retain, motivate, develop, deploy, manage, connect, enable, transform and sustain	A theoretical, exploratory approach	Change in operating profit from 2003–2006	6 clusters based on number of TM practices and rated effectiveness were regrouped to 2 clusters based on firm size	–	–	Survey; N=289 firms
5	Guthridge & Komm (2008)	Global TM, comprising inclusive and exclusive elements (e.g., achieving cultural diversity vs. internal talent pools)	A theoretical, exploratory approach	Profit per employee, benchmarked against industry (no further information provided)	Self-assessed effectiveness of firm's global TM practices	–	–	Survey; N > 450 CEOs/directors/ senior (HR) managers from 22 firms

(Continued)

Table 41.2 Quantitative organization-level studies on TM systems and practices (*Continued*)

Study	Reference	Definition of TM	Theory	Outcomes	Predictors	Mediators	Moderators	Method and Sample
6	Lehmberg et al. (2009)	GE's TM system, focused on managerial talent and developing experience in diverse industries	RBV, but phenomenon-based approach	Standardized cumulative abnormal returns, return on assets	Firms announcing the appointment of ex-GE executives as their CEOs	–	–	Event study; N=78 firms that had and had not appointed ex-GE executives as CEO (matched samples)
7	Latukha & Veselova (2018)	WD	Absorptive capacity theory	Perceived financial performance (5 indicators) relative to industry average or main competitor over the past 3 years	TM: ability to predict talent demand, learning and development programs, employees' motivation, monetary and nonmonetary rewards, diversity in the work place	Absorptive capacity	Country (China, Russia)	Survey; N=120 firms
8	Glaister et al. (2018)	WD	RBV	Perceived financial performance (profit growth, profit margin) relative to other firms in the industry over the past 3 years	HRM practices (e.g., career planning, job analysis, personality/attitudes tests)	Extent of use of 15 TM practices (targeted at managerial population)	HRM-strategy alignment	Survey; N=198 firms
9	Son et al. (2020)	WD	RBV, SCT, human capital theory	Perceived innovation (technological/organizational/process innovation); voluntary turnover	Practices specifically targeting talent (e.g., providing talent with preferential benefits, mentoring schemes, challenging tasks)	–	HRM investments (selection ratio, extensive training, pay and benefit level)	Survey; N=1,126 observations from multiple sources (HR managers, general managers) from 444 firms (2007–2013)

Note: RBV=Resource-based view; MD=Management development; WD=Workforce differentiation; SCT=Social comparison theory.

Empirical knowledge about the effect of TM practices on organizational outcomes has long been limited to anecdotal evidence (e.g., Ashton & Morton, 2005), studies focusing on respondents' beliefs about the effectiveness of TM (e.g., Bethke-Langenegger, Mahler, & Staffelbach, 2011; CIPD, 2014; Ringo, Schweyer, DeMarco, Jones, & Lesser, 2008), studies based on small (convenience) samples (Ernst & Young, 2010; Guthridge & Komm, 2008), studies that re-labeled HRM to TM (e.g., Barkhuizen et al., 2014; Mahfoozi, Salajegheh, Ghorbani, & Sheikhi, 2018) and, more generally, (academic and practitioner) studies that do not conform to conventional academic standards with respect to (reporting on) methodology (e.g., Andrianova, Maor, & Schaninger, 2018; Devi, 2017). For example, a common methodological flaw of practitioner studies is to test the association between performance and a measure reflecting respondents' belief on how effective TM is for improving performance rather than an objective measure of TM (Table 41.2, studies 3–5).

However, what we can learn from practitioner studies is that while organizational representatives perceive TM as important to organizational success and rate TM among their top priorities (Chartered Institute of Personnel and Development [CIPD], 2017; PricewaterhouseCoopers, 2012; Strack et al., 2014), few perceive their TM activities to be very effective (Andrianova et al., 2018; CIPD, 2014; 2015). This suggests, but does not conclusively demonstrate, that organizations struggle to achieve a significant return on investment in TM activities. In addition, internal moves of employees identified as talent often fail (Martin & Schmidt, 2010).

In contrast, the four scholarly studies that emerged from our literature review are largely supportive of a positive relationship between TM and organizational performance (Table 41.2, studies 6–9). First, Lehmberg et al. (2009) evaluated the value added by TM at General Electrics (GE), which is renowned for its extensive efforts in developing leadership talent. For this purpose, the authors examined whether firms that appointed ex-GE executives to be their CEOs benefited from larger increases in share price – reflecting the market's evaluation of future discounted cash flows – compared to a matched sample of firms that appointed non-GE outsiders (39 announcements each).

The authors reasoned that if ex-GE executives appointed as CEOs built up managerial capabilities during their time at GE that are superior to those in the general labor market for CEOs, then firms (and investors) should expect superior organizational performance. The analyses confirmed that investors expected ex-GE CEOs to lead their firms to outperform firms with non-GE CEOs, but no differences were found with respect to return on assets two to three years after the appointments, possibly due to low statistical power. Moreover, Lehmberg et al. (2009) acknowledge that while GE's TM system might be generalizable to other firms on a theoretical level, actual implementation might nevertheless prove difficult for most firms (e.g., because not all elements are well known and understood).

Second, using a sample of 120 large Chinese and Russian firms, Latukha and Veselova (2018) found a positive effect of TM on firm performance, mediated through a firm's absorptive capacity, which is defined as the ability to evaluate and utilize newly acquired external knowledge (Cohen & Levinthal, 1990). The operationalization of TM indirectly covered the identification of strategic positions through respondents' perceptions of their firms' ability to predict talent demand and practices that may support the development of talent pools (see Table 41.2, study 7).

Third, using a sample of 198 Turkish firms of different sizes and industries, Glaister et al. (2018) found that the effect of basic HRM practices on firm performance was fully mediated by the extent to which TM practices were used for the career development of managers. The operationalization of TM covered career development practices that may support the development of talent pools.

Fourth, using a sample of 444 South Korean firms of different sizes and industries, Son et al. (2020) found that TM practices (unconditionally) increased innovation and, in addition, increased turnover rates when levels of HRM investments were high. Hence, while preferential practices for an elitist group of employees leveraged the effectiveness of these employees' human capital in generating innovation, the same practices were also associated with higher levels of turnover, which the authors attributed to a competitive, uncooperative, unfair, and disharmonious organizational climate created by TM practices (Son et al., 2020). Unfortunately, the data did not allow the authors to distinguish between talent and non-talent turnover rates such that it remains open to speculation on which employee group has been affected by TM and in which direction. A noteworthy feature of this study concerns the longitudinal data that allowed the authors to include lagged outcome variables as predictors, thus providing evidence that TM does not merely pick up the effect of slack resources on future innovation output.

Shortcomings and Future Research Avenues

Catching Up with Research on Strategic HRM

To legitimize the study of TM within the wider field of strategic HRM and to move towards making causal claims, empirical research on the link between TM and organizational performance must connect with the level of methodological rigor that has evolved in studies on the HRM-performance link (cf. Saridakis, Lai, & Cooper, 2017). First, TM scholars could gather objective organizational perform-ance measures from independent sources for comparability of point estimates and to prevent common method bias (Podsakoff, MacKenzie, Lee, & Podsakoff, 2003). Second, we encourage efforts to collect panel data (see, e.g., Son et al., 2020) to account for unobserved heterogeneity between organizations, thus counteracting omitted variable bias (Baltagi, 2008, p. 6f.). Third, future studies could control for the influence of "good management" (Bloom, Genakos, Sadun, & Van Reenen, 2012) to rule out one of the most plausible alternative explanations for positive relationships between HR practices and organ-izational performance (Guest, 2011, p. 7).

Considering the important role of senior executives in TM (Silzer & Dowell, 2010) and that their ability to manage talent is likely correlated with their more general qualities as executives, the effect of TM could merely reflect the "quality" of general management rather than the TM practices per se.

Value Creation Versus Value Appropriation

To connect with recent discussions in the strategic human capital literature (e.g., Boon, Eckardt, Lepak, & Boselie, 2017; Chadwick, 2017; Molloy & Barney, 2015), TM research could incorporate the dis-tinction between value creation and value appropriation in the development of theory (cf. Sparrow & Makram, 2015). More precisely, TM entails both direct (e.g., talents demand higher wages) and indirect human capital costs (e.g., senior managers' time spent on TM activities) that must be weighed against the value created by the investment in human capital (cf. Barney & Wright, 1998). Hence, firms ought to be favored idiosyncratically to garner human capital rents (Chadwick, 2017). As an example, we suggest the capability to identify and match strategic positions with suitable talent pool members as an idiosyncratic firm capability.

Practices to Support the Development of Talent Pools

There is a need to examine which individual HR practices are needed to support the development of talent pools. Although we observe some convergence in operationalizing TM based on practices reported in the yearly surveys by the CIPD (e.g., CIPD, 2014; for examples, see Glaister et al., 2018; Mensah & Bawole, 2018; Sonnenberg et al., 2014), the selection of these practices is not informed by theory and narrowly confined to talent development. Neither does the dominant theoretical account on TM, WD (Collings & Mellahi, 2009), suggest specific practices, but – owing to its contingency perspective – "[...] argues[s] that the key is to deploy HR practices that are appropriate to the context of the organisation" (Collings & Mellahi, 2009: 309). Therefore, we call for the integration of findings from related streams of research such as leadership development to theoretically derive a bundle of TM practices covering the full TM cycle: talent attraction, identification, development, and retention (Meyers & van Woerkom, 2014: 192).

Operationalizing the Strategic Positions Construct

While the WD approach towards TM offers intriguing theoretical insights, its emphasis on the identification of strategic positions poses a challenge to empirical researchers seeking to operationalize the strategic positions construct (Aguinis et al., 2011: 425). More specifically, whether and how organizations use the criteria of strategic impact and performance variability to identify strategic positions and in how far they focus on positions rather than individuals (McDonnell et al., 2017: 104) remains an empirical question that has yet to be answered. Therefore, we support the call by Cappelli and Keller (2014: 324) for exploratory research on the strategic positions construct.

We also see promise in field experiments in collaboration with companies that have been advised on TM by McKinsey, which, according to a recent *McKinsey Quarterly* article (Barriere, Owens, & Pobereskin, 2018), has adopted a strategic positions perspective consistent with the WD approach to TM (Collings & Mellahi, 2009). Barriere et al. (2018) provide a case study on how to identify "critical roles" based on a projected five-year operating margin (or estimates of value creation for support functions) to arrive at a list of 50 positions a CEO can directly oversee. Based on the authors' experience, 60 (30)% of these roles are two (three) layers below the CEO and sometimes in counterintuitive places, suggesting that most critical roles are not necessarily predefined by hierarchical level. However, consistent with findings by McDonnell, Gunnigle, Lavelle, and Lamare (2016), most of these roles coincide with executive leader positions, which are commonly assumed to be the main focus of TM (cf. Finkelstein et al., 2018).

Conclusion

In this chapter, we attempted to integrate theoretical insights and empirical evidence on the link between TM and both individual and organizational performance with the idea of informing readers about the basic theoretical and empirical knowledge and possible avenues for future research. In conclusion, the literature on individual outcomes of TM serves as evidence that talent scores higher than non-talent on diverse work attitudes and behaviors, but the cross-sectional nature of these studies leaves open whether these differences existed prior to talent designation (for an exception, see Gelens et al., 2015). Moreover, except for two experimental studies (Kotlyar, 2013; Kotlyar et al., 2014), research on individual outcomes does not differentiate between the effects of talent status per se and the TM practices associated with talent status (cf. De Boeck et al., 2018), although this is a minor concern from a practical point of view.

More importantly, there remains limited evidence on the reactions to non-talent status and long-term outcomes of talent status, while (largely supportive) evidence on a positive association between TM practices and organizational outcomes is just beginning to accumulate. The study by Son et al. (2020) illustrates best the current knowledge on the performance implications of TM, indicating that TM might be a "double-edged sword" with both beneficial and detrimental effects on organizational outcomes. Therefore, more research is necessary to investigate under which conditions TM translates into superior organizational performance.

Note

1 We based our review of quantitative individual-level studies on talent status and TM practices on the articles identified by De Boeck et al. (2018) for their review, but added two experimental studies (Kotlyar, 2013; Kotlyar, Karakowsky, Jo Ducharme, & A. Boekhorst, 2014) as well as four studies that were published later (Ehrnrooth et al., 2018; Khoreva, Vaiman, & Van Zalk, 2017; Malik, Singh, & Chan, 2017; Mensah & Bawole, 2018); we excluded three studies that did not conform to our definition of TM (Barkhuizen, Mogwere, & Schutte, 2014; Du Plessis, Barkhuizen, Stanz, & Schutte, 2015; Luna-Arocas & Morley, 2015).

References

Aguinis, H., Boyd, B. K., Pierce, C. A., Short, J. C., Huselid, M. A., & Becker, B. E. 2011. Bridging micro and macro domains: Workforce differentiation and strategic human resource management. *Journal of Management,* 37(2): 421-428.

Aguinis, H., & Bradley, K. J. 2014. Best practice recommendations for designing and implementing experimental vignette methodology studies. *Organizational Research Methods,* 17(4): 351-371.

Aguinis, H., & O'Boyle Jr., E. 2014. Star performers in twenty-first century organizations. *Personnel Psychology,* 67(2): 313-350.

Alicke, M. D., LoSchiavo, F. M., Zerbst, J., & Zhang, S. 1997. The person who out performs me is a genius: Maintaining perceived competence in upward social comparison. *Journal of Personality and Social Psychology,* 73(4): 781-789.

Andrianova, S., Maor, D., & Schaninger, B. (2018). Winning with your talent-management strategy. https://www. mckinsey.com/business-functions/organization/our-insights/winning-with-your-talent-management -strategy

Ashton, C., & Morton, L. 2005. Managing talent for competitive advantage: Taking a systemic approach to talent management. *Strategic HR Review,* 4(5): 28-31.

Avolio, B. J., Avey, J. B., & Quisenberry, D. 2010. Estimating return on leadership development investment. *The Leadership Quarterly,* 21(4): 633-644.

Baltagi, B. 2008. *Econometric analysis of panel data.* Chichester, UK: John Wiley & Sons.

Barkhuizen, N., Mogwere, P., & Schutte, N. 2014. Talent management, work engagement and service quality orientation of support staff in a higher education institution. *Mediterranean Journal of Social Sciences,* 5(4): 69.

Barney, J. B., & Wright, P. M. 1998. On becoming a strategic partner: The role of human resources in gaining competitive advantage. *Human Resource Management,* 37(1): 31-46.

Barriere, M., Owens, M., & Pobereskin, S. 2018. Linking talent to value. *McKinsey Quarterly* (4): 1-9.

Bascle, G. 2008. Controlling for endogeneity with instrumental variables in strategic management research. *Strategic Organization,* 6(3): 285-327.

Bethke-Langenegger, P., Mahler, P., & Staffelbach, B. 2011. Effectiveness of talent management strategies. *European Journal of International Management,* 5(5): 524-539.

Björkman, I., Ehrnrooth, M., Mäkelä, K., Smale, A., & Sumelius, J. 2013. Talent or not? Employee reactions to talent identification. *Human Resource Management,* 52(2): 195-214.

Blanton, H., Buunk, B. P., Gibbons, F. X., & Kuyper, H. 1999. When better-than-others compare upward: Choice of comparison and comparative evaluation as independent predictors of academic performance. *Journal of Personality & Social Psychology,* 76(3): 420-430.

Blau, P. M. 1964. *Exchange and power in social life.* New Brunswick, NJ: Transaction Publishers.

Bloom, N., Genakos, C., Sadun, R., & Van Reenen, J. 2012. Management practices across firms and countries. *Academy of Management Perspectives,* 26(1): 12-33.

Boon, C., Eckardt, R., Lepak, D. P., & Boselie, P. 2017. Integrating strategic human capital and strategic human resource management. *The International Journal of Human Resource Management:* 1-34.

Bothner, M. S., Kim, Y.-K., & Smith, E. B. 2012. How does status affect performance? Status as an asset vs. status as a liability in the PGA and NASCAR. *Organization Science,* 23(2): 416-433.

Buunk, A. P., & Gibbons, F. X. 2007. Social comparison: The end of a theory and the emergence of a field. *Organizational Behavior and Human Decision Processes,* 102(1): 3-21.

Caligiuri, P., & Tarique, I. 2012. Dynamic cross-cultural competencies and global leadership effectiveness. *Journal of World Business,* 47(4): 612-622.

Campbell, E., Liao, H., Chuang, A., Zhou, J., & Dong, Y. 2017. Hot shots and cool reception? An expanded view of social consequences for high performers. *Journal of Applied Psychology,* 102(5): 845-866.

Cappelli, P., & Keller, J. R. 2014. Talent management: Conceptual approaches and practical challenges. *Annual Review of Organizational Psychology and Organizational Behavior,* 1(1): 305-331.

Chadwick, C. 2017. Toward a more comprehensive model of firms' human capital rents. *Academy of Management Review,* 42(3): 499-519.

Chami-Malaeb, R., & Garavan, T. 2013. Talent and leadership development practices as drivers of intention to stay in Lebanese organisations: The mediating role of affective commitment. *International Journal of Human Resource Management,* 24(21): 4046-4062.

Chartered Institute of Personnel and Development. 2014. *Learning and development: Annual survey report 2014.* London, UK: Chartered Institute of Personnel and Development; https://www.cipd.co.uk/Images/ learning-and-development_2014_tcm18-11296.pdf

Chartered Institute of Personnel and Development. 2015. *Learning and development: Annual survey report 2015.* London, UK: Chartered Institute of Personnel and Development. https://www.cipd.co.uk/Images/ learning-and-development_2014_tcm18-11296.pdf

Chartered Institute of Personnel and Development. 2017. *Resourcing and talent planning: Survey report 2017.* London: Chartered Institute of Personnel and Development; Hays.

Church, A. H., & Rotolo, C. T. 2013. How are top companies assessing their high-potentials and senior executives? A talent management benchmark study. *Consulting Psychology Journal: Practice and Research,* 65(3): 199-223.

Cohen, W. M., & Levinthal, D. A. 1990. Absorptive capacity: A new perspective on learning and innovation. *Administrative Science Quarterly,* 35(1): 128-152.

Collings, D. G. 2014. Toward mature talent management: Beyond shareholder value. *Human Resource Development Quarterly,* 25(3): 301-319.

Collings, D. G. 2015. The contribution of talent management to organization success. In K. Kraiger, J. Passmore, N. R. d. Santos, & S. Malvezzi (Eds.), *The Wiley Blackwell handbook of the psychology of training, development, and performance improvement:* 247-260. Chichester, UK: John Wiley & Sons, Ltd.

Collings, D. G. 2017. Workforce differentiation. In D. G. Collings, K. Mellahi, & W. F. Cascio (Eds.), *The Oxford handbook of talent management:* 299-317. Oxford, UK: Oxford University Press.

Collings, D. G., & Mellahi, K. 2009. Strategic talent management: A review and research agenda. *Human Resource Management Review,* 19(4): 304-313.

Collings, D. G., Mellahi, K., & Cascio, W. 2018. Global talent management and performance in multinational enterprises: A multilevel perspective. *Journal of Management:* 8.

Daubner-Siva, D., Ybema, S., Vinkenburg, C. J., & Beech, N. 2018. The talent paradox: Talent management as a mixed blessing. *Journal of Organizational Ethnography,* 7(1): 74-86.

De Boeck, G., Dries, N., & Meyers, M. C. 2017. Individual-level outcomes of talent management: Assumptions versus evidence. *Academy of Management Paper Proceedings 2017,* (1).

De Boeck, G., Meyers, M. C., & Dries, N. 2018. Employee reactions to talent management: Assumptions versus evidence. *Journal of Organizational Behavior,* 39(2): 199-213.

DeRue, D. S., & Wellman, N. 2009. Developing leaders via experience: The role of developmental challenge, learning orientation, and feedback availability. *Journal of Applied Psychology,* 94(4): 859-875.

Devi, S. 2017. Impact of talent management on organizational performance: Role of employee engagement. *International Journal of Management Studies,* 4(1): 17-27.

Dragoni, L., Oh, I.-S., Tesluk, P. E., Moore, O. A., VanKatwyk, P., & Hazucha, J. 2014. Developing leaders' strategic thinking through global work experience: The moderating role of cultural distance. *Journal of Applied Psychology,* 99(5): 867-882.

Dries, N., & De Gieter, S. 2014. Information asymmetry in high potential programs. *Personnel Review,* 43(1): 136-162.

Dries, N., Forrier, A., De Vos, A., & Pepermans, R. 2014. Self-perceived employability, organization-rated potential, and the psychological contract. *Journal of Managerial Psychology,* 29(5): 565-581.

Dries, N., & Pepermans, R. 2007. Using emotional intelligence to identify high potential: a metacompetency perspective. *Leadership & Organization Development Journal,* 28(8): 749-770.

Dries, N., & Pepermans, R. 2008. "Real" high-potential careers: An empirical study into the perspectives of organisations and high potentials. *Personnel Review,* 37(1): 85-108.

Dries, N., Van Acker, F., & Verbruggen, M. 2012. How 'boundaryless' are the careers of high potentials, key experts and average performers? *Journal of Vocational Behavior,* 81(2): 271-279.

Dubouloy, M. 2004. The transitional space and self-recovery: A psychoanalytical approach to high-potential managers' training. *Human Relations,* 57(4): 467-496.

Dunning, D., Heath, C., & Suls, J. M. 2004. Flawed self-assessment: Implications for health, education, and the workplace. *Psychological Science in the Public Interest,* 5(3): 69-106.

Du Plessis, L., Barkhuizen, N., Stanz, K., & Schutte, N. 2015. The management side of talent: Causal implications for the retention of Generation Y employees. *Journal of Applied Business Research,* 31(5): 1767-1780.

Eden, D. 1984. Self-fulfilling prophecy as a management tool: Harnessing Pygmalion. *Academy of Management Review,* 9(1): 64-73.

Ehrnrooth, M., Bjorkman, I., Makela, K., Smale, A., Sumelius, J., & Taimitarha, S. 2018. Talent responses to talent status awareness: Not a question of simple reciprocation. *Human Resource Management Journal,* 28(3): 443-461.

Ernst & Young. 2010. *Managing today's global workforce: Elevating talent management to improve business.* London: Ernst & Young Global Limited. http://www.globalbusinessnews.net/b4/vsites/22/storydoc/Mana gingTodaysGlobalWorkforce_100524.pdf

Finkelstein, L., Costanza, D., & Goodwin, G. 2018. Do your high potentials have potential? The impact of individual differences and designation on leader success. *Personnel Psychology,* 71(1): 3-22.

Gallardo-Gallardo, E., & Thunnissen, M. 2016. Standing on the shoulders of giants? A critical review of empirical talent management research. *Employee Relations,* 38(1): 31-56.

Gelens, J., Dries, N., Hofmans, J., & Pepermans, R. 2013. The role of perceived organizational justice in shaping the outcomes of talent management: A research agenda. *Human Resource Management Review,* 23(4): 341-353.

Gelens, J., Dries, N., Hofmans, J., & Pepermans, R. 2015. Affective commitment of employees designated as talent: Signalling perceived organisational support. *European Journal of International Management,* 9(1): 9-27.

Gelens, J., Hofmans, J., Dries, N., & Pepermans, R. 2014. Talent management and organisational justice: Employee reactions to high potential identification. *Human Resource Management Journal,* 24(2): 159-175.

Glaister, A. J., Karacay, G., Demirbag, M., & Tatoglu, E. 2018. HRM and performance: The role of talent management as a transmission mechanism in an emerging market context. *Human Resource Management Journal,* 28(1): 148-166.

Guest, D. E. 2011. Human resource management and performance: Still searching for some answers. *Human Resource Management Journal,* 21(1): 3-13.

Guthridge, M., & Komm, A. B. 2008. Why multinationals struggle to manage talent. *The McKinsey Quarterly,* 5: 1-5.

Hanisch, K., & Hulin, C. 1990. Job attitudes and organizational withdrawal: An examination of retirement and other voluntary withdrawal behaviors. *Journal of Vocational Behavior,* 37(1): 60-78.

Höglund, M. 2012. Quid pro quo? Examining talent management through the lens of psychological contracts. *Personnel Review,* 41(2): 126-142.

Huselid, M. A., Beatty, R. W., & Becker, B. E. 2005. 'A players' or 'A positions'? *Harvard Business Review,* 83(12): 110-117.

Jensen, J. M., Patel, P. C., & Raver, J. L. 2014. Is it better to be average? High and low performance as predictors of employee victimization. *Journal of Applied Psychology,* 99(2): 296-309.

Khoreva, V., & Vaiman, V. 2015. Intent vs. action: Talented employees and leadership development. *Personnel Review,* 44(2): 200-216.

Khoreva, V., Vaiman, V., & Van Zalk, M. 2017. Talent management practice effectiveness: investigating employee perspective. *Employee Relations,* 39(1): 19-33.

King, E. B., Botsford, W., Hebl, M. R., Kazama, S., Dawson, J. F., & Perkins, A. 2012. Benevolent sexism at work: Gender differences in the distribution of challenging developmental experiences. *Journal of Management,* 38(6): 1835-1866.

Kotlyar, I. 2013. The double edge sword of "high potential" expectations. *Europe's Journal of Psychology,* 9(3): 581-596.

Kotlyar, I., Karakowsky, L., Jo Ducharme, M., & A. Boekhorst, J. 2014. Do "rising stars" avoid risk?: Status-based labels and decision making. *Leadership & Organization Development Journal,* 35(2): 121-136.

Lacerenza, C. N., Reyes, D. L., Marlow, S. L., Joseph, D. L., & Salas, E. 2017. Leadership training design, delivery, and implementation: A meta-analysis. *Journal of Applied Psychology,* 102(12): 1686.

Latukha, M., & Veselova, A. 2018. Talent management, absorptive capacity, and firm performance: Does it work in China and Russia? *Human Resource Management:* 1-17.

Lehmberg, D., Rowe, W. G., White, R. E., & Phillips, J. R. 2009. The GE paradox: Competitive advantage through fungible non-firm-specific investment. *Journal of Management,* 35(5): 1129-1153.

Lewis, R. E., & Heckman, R. J. 2006. Talent management: A critical review. *Human Resource Management Review,* 16(2): 139-154.

LinkedIn. 2017. *2017 workplace learning report - How modern L&D pros are tackling top challenges.* https://learning.linkedin.com/elearning-solutions-guides/2017-workplace-learning-report?trk=lilblog_02-07-17_WLR-announcement_tl&cid=70132000001AyziAAC

LinkedIn. 2018. *The rise and responsibility of talent development in the new labor market.* https://learning.linkedin.com/content/dam/me/learning/en-us/pdfs/linkedin-learning-workplace-learning-report-2018.pdf

LinkedIn. 2019. *2019 Workplace learning report. Why 2019 is the breakout year for the talent developer.* https://learning.linkedin.com/content/dam/me/business/en-us/amp/learning-solutions/images/workplace-learning-report-2019/pdf/workplace-learning-report-2019.pdf

Luna-Arocas, R., & Morley, M. J. 2015. Talent management, talent mindset competency and job performance: The mediating role of job satisfaction. *European Journal of International Management,* 9(1): 28-51.

Mabey, C., & Ramirez, M. 2005. Does management development improve organizational productivity? A six-country analysis of European firms. *The International Journal of Human Resource Management,* 16(7): 1067-1082.

Mahfoozi, A., Salajegheh, S., Ghorbani, M., & Sheikhi, A. 2018. Developing a talent management model using government evidence from a large-sized city, Iran. *Cogent Business & Management,* 5(1).

Malik, A. R., Singh, P., & Chan, C. 2017. High potential programs and employee outcomes The roles of organizational trust and employee attributions. *Career Development International,* 22(7): 772-796.

Martin, J., & Schmidt, C. 2010. How to keep your top talent. *Harvard Business Review,* 88(5): 54-61.

McDonnell, A., Collings, D. G., Mellahi, K., & Schuler, R. 2017. Talent management: a systematic review and future prospects. *European Journal of International Management,* 11(1): 86-128.

McDonnell, A., Gunnigle, P., Lavelle, J., & Lamare, R. 2016. Beyond managerial talent: 'Key group' identification and differential compensation practices in multinational companies. *The International Journal of Human Resource Management,* 27(12): 1299-1318.

Mensah, J. K., & Bawole, J. N. 2018. Testing the mediation effect of person-organisation fit on the relationship between talent management and talented employees' attitudes. *International Journal of Manpower,* 39(2): 319-333.

Meyers, M. C., & van Woerkom, M. 2014. The influence of underlying philosophies on talent management: Theory, implications for practice, and research agenda. *Journal of World Business,* 49(2): 192-203.

Molloy, J., & Barney, J. 2015. Who captures the value created with human capital? A market-based view. *Academy of Management Perspectives,* 29(3): 309-325.

Mussweiler, T., Gabriel, S., & Bodenhausen, G. V. 2000. Shifting social identities as a strategy for deflecting threatening social comparisons. *Journal of Personality and Social Psychology,* 79(3): 398.

Park, J., Chae, H., & Kim, H. 2017. When and why high performers feel job dissatisfaction: A resource flow approach. *Social Behavior and Personality: An International Journal,* 45(4): 617-627.

Pfeffer, J. 2001. Fighting the war for talent is hazardous to your organization's health. *Organizational Dynamics,* 29(4): 248-259.

Podsakoff, P. M., MacKenzie, S. B., Lee, J. Y., & Podsakoff, N. P. 2003. Common method biases in behavioral research: a critical review of the literature and recommended remedies. *Journal of Applied Psychology,* 88(5): 879-903.

PricewaterhouseCoopers. 2012. *15th annual global CEO survey 2012 - Delivering results, growth, and value in a volatile world.*

Reh, S., Tröster, C., & Van Quaquebeke, N. 2018. Keeping (future) rivals down: Temporal social comparison predicts coworker social undermining via future status threat and envy. *Journal of Applied Psychology,* 103(4): 399-415.

Ringo, T., Schweyer, A., DeMarco, M., Jones, R., & Lesser, E. 2008. *Part 1 - Understanding the opportunities for success.* Somers, NY: IBM Global Business Services. https://public.dhe.ibm.com/common/ssi/ecm/gb/en/gbe03071usen/GBE03071USEN.PDF

Rousseau, D. M. 1995. *Psychological contracts in organizations: Understanding written and unwritten agreements.* Thousand Oaks, CA: Sage Publications.

Saridakis, G., Lai, Y., & Cooper, C. 2017. Exploring the relationship between HRM and firm performance: A meta-analysis of longitudinal studies. *Human Resource Management Review,* 27(1): 87-96.

Schneider, B. 2018. Being competitive in the talent management space. *Industrial and Organizational Psychology-Perspectives on Science and Practice,* 11(2): 231-236.

Seopa, N., Wöcke, A., & Leeds, C. 2015. The impact on the psychological contract of differentiating employees into talent pools. *Career Development International,* 20(7): 717-732.

Shaffer, M. A., Harrison, D. A., Gregersen, H., Black, J. S., & Ferzandi, L. A. 2006. You can take it with you: Individual differences and expatriate effectiveness. *Journal of Applied Psychology,* 91(1): 109.

Shaw, K. 2009. Insider econometrics: A roadmap with stops along the way. *Labour Economics,* 16(6): 607-617.

Shepperd, J. A., & Taylor, K. M. 1999. Ascribing advantages to social comparison targets. *Basic and Applied Social Psychology,* 21(2): 103-117.

Silzer, R., & Dowell, B. E. 2010. Strategic talent management matters *Strategy-driven talent management: A leadership imperative:* 3-72. San Francisco, CA: Jossey-Bass.

Son, J., Park, O., Bae, J., & Ok, C. 2020. Double-edged effect of talent management on organizational performance: The moderating role of HRM investments. *The International Journal of Human Resource Management:* 31 (17) 2188-2216.

Sonnenberg, M., van Zijderveld, V., & Brinks, M. 2014. The role of talent-perception incongruence in effective talent management. *Journal of World Business,* 49(2): 272-280.

Sparrow, P. R., & Makram, H. 2015. What is the value of talent management? Building value-driven processes within a talent management architecture. *Human Resource Management Review,* 25(3): 249-263.

Strack, R., Caye, J.-M., Gaissmaier, T., Orglmeister, C., Tamboto, E., Von der Linden, C., ... Jauregui, J. 2014. *Creating people advantage 2014-2015. How to set up great HR functions: Connect, prioritize, impact.* Boston, MA: The Boston Consulting Group, Inc.; World Federation of People Management Associations. https://www.bcgperspectives.com/Images/Creating_People_Advantage_2014_2015_Dec_2014_tcm80-177846.pdf

Subramony, M., Segers, J., Chadwick, C., & Shyamsunder, A. 2018. Leadership development practice bundles and organizational performance: The mediating role of human capital and social capital. *Journal of Business Research,* 83: 120-129.

Suls, J., Martin, R., & Wheeler, L. 2002. Social comparison: Why, with whom, and with what effect? *Current Directions in Psychological Science,* 11(5): 159-163.

Swailes, S. 2013. The ethics of talent management. *Business Ethics: A European Review,* 22(1): 32-46.

Swailes, S., & Blackburn, M. 2016. Employee reactions to talent pool membership. *Employee Relations,* 38(1): 112-128.

Swailes, S., Downs, Y., & Orr, K. 2014. Conceptualising inclusive talent management: potential, possibilities and practicalities. *Human Resource Development International,* 17(5): 529-544.

Tarique, I., & Schuler, R. 2018. A multi-level framework for understanding global talent management systems for high talent expatriates within and across subsidiaries of MNEs: Propositions for further research. *Journal of Global Mobility-the Home of Expatriate Management Research,* 6(1): 79-101.

Thunnissen, M. 2016. Talent management: For what, how and how well? An empirical exploration of talent management in practice. *Employee Relations,* 38(1): 57-72.

INDEX

Printed in the United States
by Baker & Taylor Publisher Services